A DICTIONARY
OF THE BIBLE

By William Smith, L.L.D.

Revised and Edited by

F. N. and M. A. Peloubet

THOMAS NELSON PUBLISHERS
Nashville • Atlanta • London • Vancouver

Library of Congress Cataloging-in-Publication Data

Smith, William, Sir, 1813–1893.
  A dictionary of the Bible.

    Cover title: Smith's Bible dictionary.
    Includes index.
    1. Bible--Dictionaries. I. Peloubet, F. N.
(Francis Nathan), 1831–1920. II. Peloubet, M. A. T.
(Mary Abby Thaxter) III. Title. IV. Title: Smith's
Bible dictionary. V. Title: Bible dictionary.
[BS440.S6   1986]   220.3   86–5281
ISBN 0–8407–5542–2
ISBN 0–8407–3085–3 (pbk.)

Printed in the United States of America
21 22 23 24 25 26 27 28 29 30 31 32 33 34 35 36 37 38 39 40 — 02 01 00 99

PREFACE.

EVERY one acknowledges the great value of Dr. William Smith's Bible Dictionary, as containing "the fruit of the ripest biblical scholarship of England," and that much of this value remains in his own condensation of his larger work into one smaller volume, which is the basis of the present volume.

At the request of the publishers of this volume to make an abridgment of this work, and adapt it to the present wants of Sunday-school teachers, we have faithfully endeavored to embody the following results:

1. The main body of the work is precisely as Dr. Smith himself made it.

2. We have made some abridgments, but almost entirely of matter not specially helpful or interesting to teachers, or to any who would not be likely to have the large four-volume edition.

3. We have added all the *proper names* used in the *New Revision*, where they have differed from those in the Authorized Version.

4. The signification of all the proper names has been inserted from the best authorities, in addition to the few which are found in the former editions.

5. The results of the latest research, especially in regard to the topography of Palestine, are embodied in various articles.

6. Some subjects have been rearranged, to make them clearer, and sometimes fuller and more definite information has been given.

7. The dates at which persons lived and events took place have been inserted, not because absolute reliance can be placed on their accuracy, but in order to show the relative positions of each, and hence to give a clearer idea of the history and progress of events. The dates are in accordance with Archbishop Ussher's system as printed in our common Bibles. Those after the reign of David, from which time a good degree of accuracy is obtainable, are from M'Clintock and Strong's large Cyclopedia.

8. All important changes are marked with the signature "ED.," so that Dr. Smith may not be regarded as responsible for them.

9. Special thanks are due to the American Sunday-School Union for the use of some of the very excellent illustrations from Schaff's *Bible Dictionary*.

F. N. AND M. A. PELOUBET.

v

LIST OF WRITERS.

ALFORD, REV. HENRY, D.D.,
Dean of Canterbury.
BAILEY, REV. HENRY, B.D.,
Warden of St. Augustine's College, Canterbury.
BARRY, REV. ALFRED, B.D.,
Principal of Cheltenham College.
BEVAN, REV. WILLIAM L., M.A.,
Vicar of Hay, Brecknockshire.
BLAKESLEY, REV. JOSEPH W., B.D.,
Canon of Canterbury.
BONAR, REV. HORATIUS, D.D.,
Kelso, N. B., author of "The Land of Promise," etc.
BROWN, REV. THOMAS E., M.A.,
Vice-Principal of King William's College, Isle of Man.
BROWNE, REV. E. HAROLD, D.D.,
Lord Bishop of Ely.
BROWNE, REV. ROBERT W., M.A.,
Archdeacon of Bath.
BULLOCK, REV. WILLIAM T., M.A.,
Sec. of the Society for the Propagation of the Gospel.
CLARK, REV. SAMUEL, M.A.,
Vicar of Bredwardine with Brobury, Herefordshire.
COOK, REV. F. C., M.A.,
Canon of Exeter.
COTTON, REV. GEORGE E. L., D.D.,
Lord Bishop of Calcutta.
DAVIES, REV. J. LLEWELYN, M.A.,
Rector of Christ Church, Marylebone.
DAY, REV. GEORGE E., D.D.,
Prof. of Biblical Theology, Yale College, New Haven.
DEUTSCH, EMANUEL, M.R.A.S.,
University of Berlin and British Museum.
DRAKE, REV. WILLIAM, M.A.,
Hon. Canon of Worcester.
EDDRUP, REV. EDWARD P., M.A.,
Principal of the Theological College, Salisbury.
ELLICOTT, REV. CHARLES J., D.D.,
Lord Bishop of Gloucester and Bristol.
ELWIN, REV. WHITWELL, B.A.,
Rector of Booton, Norfolk.
ENCYCLOPÆDIA BRITANNICA.
FARRAR, REV. FREDERICK W., M.A.,
Assistant Master of Harrow School.
FELTON, C. C., LL.D.,
Prof. of Greek Lit., Harv. Univ., Cambridge, Mass.
FERGUSSON, JAMES, F.R.S., F.R.A.S.,
Royal Institution of British Architects.
FFOULKES, EDMUND S., M.A.,
Late Fellow of Jesus College, Oxford.
FITZGERALD, REV. WILLIAM, D.D.,
Lord Bishop of Killaloe.
GARDEN, REV. FRANCIS, M.A.,
Subdean of the Chapel Royal.
GOTCH, F. W., LL.D.,
Hebrew Examiner, University of London.
GROVE, GEORGE,
Crystal Palace, Sydenham.
HACKETT, REV. HORATIO B., D.D.,
Prof. of Bib. Literature, Theological Sem., Newton, Ms.
HAWKINS, REV. ERNEST, B.D.,
Canon of Westminster.
HAYMAN, REV. HENRY, M.A.,
Head Master of Grammar School, Cheltenham.
HERVEY, LORD ARTHUR C., M.A.,
Author of "Genealogies of our Lord Jesus Christ."
HESSEY, REV. JAMES A., D.C.L.,
Head Master of Merchant Tailors' School.
HOOKER, JOSEPH D., M.D., F.R.S.,
Royal Botanic Gardens, Kew.
HORNBY, REV. J. J., M.A.,
Principal of Bishop Cosin's Hall.
HOUGHTON, REV. WILLIAM, M.A.,
Rector of Preston, Salop.

HOWSON, REV. JOHN S., D.D.,
Joint-author of "Life and Epistles of St. Paul."
HUXTABLE, REV. EDGAR, M.A.,
Subdean of Wells.
JONES, REV. W. BASIL, M.A.,
Prebendary of York and St. David's.
LAYARD, AUSTEN H., D.C.L., M.P.,
Author of "Nineveh and its Remains," etc.
LEATHES, REV. STANLEY, M.A., M.R.S.L.,
Professor of Hebrew, King's College, London.
LIGHTFOOT, REV. JOSEPH B., D.D.,
Hulsean Professor of Divinity, Cambridge, England.
MARKS, REV. D. W.,
Professor of Hebrew, University College, London.
MEYRICK, REV. FREDERICK, M.A.,
Her Majesty's Inspector of Schools.
OPPERT, PROF. JULES,
Author of "Chronology of Babylon," Paris.
ORGER, REV. EDWARD R., M.A.,
Fellow of St. Augustine's College, Canterbury.
ORMEROD, REV. THOMAS J., M.A.,
Archdeacon of Suffolk.
PELOUBET, F. N. and M. A.
PEROWNE, REV. JOHN J. S., B.D.,
Vice Principal of St. David's College, Lampeter.
PEROWNE, REV. THOS. T., B.D.,
Fellow and Tutor, Corpus Christi College, Cambridge.
PHILLOTT, REV. H. W., M.A.,
Rector of Staunton-on-Wye.
PLUMPTRE, REV. EDWARD H., M.A.,
Professor of Divinity, King's College, London.
POOLE, E. STANLEY, M.R.A.S.,
South Kensington Museum.
POOLE, R. STUART, M.R.S.L.,
Author of "Horæ Ægyptiacæ," etc.
PORTER, REV. J. LESLIE, M.A.,
Author of "Handbook of Syria and Palestine."
PRITCHARD, REV. CHAS., M.A., F.R.S.,
Late Fellow of St. John's College, Cambridge, England
RAWLINSON, REV. GEORGE, M.A.,
Author of "Great Monarchies of the Ancient World."
ROSE, REV. HENRY J., B.D.,
Rector of Houghton Conquest, Bedfordshire.
SELWYN, REV. WILLIAM W., B.D.,
Margaret Professor of Divinity, Cambridge, England.
SMITH, REV. D. T., D.D.,
Prof. of Sacred Lit., Theological Sem., Bangor, Me.
SMITH, WILLIAM, LL.D. (Editor),
Classical Examiner, University of London.
STANLEY, REV. ARTHUR P., D.D.,
Dean of Westminster.
STOWE, REV. CALVIN E., D.D.,
Late Prof. of Sacred Lit., Theo. Sem., Andover, Mass.
THOMPSON, REV. JOSEPH P., D.D.,
Author of "Egypt, Past and Present," N. Y. city.
THOMSON, REV. WILLIAM, D.D.,
Lord Archbishop of York.
THRUPP, REV. JOSEPH F., M.A.,
Vicar of Barrington.
TREGELLES, SAMUEL P., LL.D.,
Author "Acc. of the Printed Text of the Gr. N. T."
TRISTRAM, REV. H. B., M.A., F.L.S.,
Author of "The Land of Israel."
TWISLETON, HON. EDW., M.A.,
Late Fellow of Baliol College, Oxford.
VENABLES, REV. EDMUND, M.A.,
Bonchurch, Isle of Wight.
WESTCOTT, REV. BROOKE F., M.A.,
Author of "Introduction to the Study of the Gospels"
WORDSWORTH, REV. CHRISTOPHER, D.D
Archdeacon of Westminster.
WRIGHT, WILLIAM ALDIS, M.A.,
Librarian of Trinity College, Cambridge, England.

vi

ABBREVIATIONS

A.D.............*Anno Domini* (Latin) = in the year of our Lord.
anc...............ancient.
Ann..............*Annals* of Tacitus, a Roman historian.
Ant..............Antiquities.
A.U.C............*anno urbis conditæ*=in the year of the building of the city, Rome.
B. & D...........Hist. of Bel and the Dragon (Apoc.).
Bar...............Baruch (Apoc.).
B.C...............Before Christ.
B. R..............*Biblical Researches*, by Dr. Robinson.
Cant.............Canticles or Song of Solomon (O. T.).
cf..................*conferer* (French) = compare.
ch. and chs...chapter and chapters, respectively.
1 Chron.........1st Book of Chronicles (O. T.).
2 Chron.........2d Book of Chronicles (O. T.).
Cic. in Verr...Cicero's oration against Verres.
cir................*circa* (Latin) = about.
Col...............Ep. to the Colossians (N. T.).
Comm...........Commentary.
comp............compare.
1 Cor.............1st Ep. to the Corinthians (N. T.).
2 Cor.............2d Ep. to the Corinthians (N. T.).
Cyc..............Cyclopedia.
Dan..............Daniel (O. T.).
Deut.............Deuteronomy (O. T.).
Dict.............Dictionary.
Eccles...........Ecclesiastes (O. T.).
Ecclus..........Ecclesiasticus (Apoc.).
ed................edition.
e. g..............*exempli gratia* (Latin) = for example.
Eph.............Ep. to the Ephesians (N. T.).
1 Esd...........1st Book of Esdras (Apoc.).
2 Esd...........2d Book of Esdras (Apoc.).
Euseb...........Eusebius, a Greek historian, who died A.D. 340.
Ex...............Exodus (O. T.).
Ezek...........Ezekiel (O. T.).
f.................following (verse or page).

fem..............feminine.
ff................following (verses or pages).
Gal..............Ep. to the Galatians (N. T.).
Gen.............Genesis (O. T.).
Gr...............Greek.
Hab..........Habakkuk (O. T.).
Hag.............Haggai (O. T.).
Handb..........Handbook.
Heb.............Hebrews or Ep. to the Hebrews (N. T.).
Herod...........Herodotus, a Greek historian, B.C. 484.
Hist............History.
Hor. Sat........*Satires* of Horace, a Roman poet, B.C. 65-8.
Hos............Hosea (O. T.).
ib. or ibid......*ibidem* (Latin) = in the same place.
i. e............*id est* (Latin) = that is.
in loc.............*in loco* (Latin) = in the place or on the passage cited.
Isa..............Isaiah (O. T.).
Jud..............Judith (Apoc.).
Jer............Jeremiah (O. T.).
Jon.............Jonah (O. T.).
Jos..............Josephus, *Antiquities of the Jews.*
Jos. B. J........Josephus, *Bellum Judaicum* = Jewish War.
Josh............Joshua (O. T.).
Juven. Sat.....*Satires* of Juvenal, a Roman poet.
Lam.............Lamentations of Jeremiah (O.T.).
l. c..............*loco citato* (Latin) = at the place cited.
ll. cc.............*locis citatis* (Latin) = at the places cited.
Lev.............Leviticus (O. T.).
lib..............*liber* (Latin) = book.
Linn...........Linnæus, the Swedish naturalist.
lit..............literal, or literally.
Liv..............Livy, a Roman historian.
LXX..........The Seventy, *i. e.* the Septuagint.
1 Macc..........1st Book of Maccabees (Apoc.).
2 Macc..........2d Book of Maccabees (Apoc.).
3 Macc..........3d Book of Maccabees (Apoc.).

4 Macc............4th Book of Maccabees (Apoc.).	Rom...............Ep. to the Romans (N. T.).
Mal................Malachi (O. T.).	1 Sam.............1st Book of Samuel (O. T.).
marg..............margin or marginal.	2 Sam.............2d Book of Samuel (O. T.).
Mart..............Martial, a Roman poet, A.D. 40–	S. and P........*Sinai and Palestine*, by Stanley.
100.	sc.....................*scilicet* (Latin) = that is to say.
Matt.......... ....Gospel according to Matthew.	sq. or seq......*sequens*(Latin)=following(verse).
Mic................Micah (O. T.).	seqq ....*sequentia* (Latin) = following
Mod. Eg.........*Modern Egyptians*, by Lane.	(verses).
MS........ ......Manuscript.	Suet............Suetonius, a historian, A.D. 100.
MSS.......... .....Manuscripts.	Sus... ....History of Susanna (Apoc.).
Nah.......... .....Nahum (O. T.).	Syr..............Syria or Syriac.
Neh..............Nehemiah (O. T.).	Tac..............Tacitus, a Roman historian, A.D.
Nin. and Bab..*Nineveh and Babylon*, by Layard.	56–135.
Num..............Numbers (O. T.).	1 Thess... ....1st Ep. to the Thessalonians
Obad.............Obadiah (O. T.).	(N. T.).
p., pp.............page and pages, respectively.	2 Thess... ....2d Ep. to the Thessalonians
Pers..............Persian.	(N. T.).
1 Pet.............1st Ep. of Peter (N. T.).	1 Tim............1st Ep. to Timothy (N. T.).
2 Pet.............2d Ep. of Peter (N. T.).	2 Tim............2d Ep. to Timothy (N. T.).
Philip..... ....Ep. to the Philippians (N. T.).	Tit................Ep. to Titus (N. T.).
Phil.......... .....Ep. to Philemon (N. T.).	Tob.......... ....Tobit (Apoc.).
Polyb............Polybius, a Greek historian, B.C.	ver., vs..........verse, verses.
205–123.	viz................*videlicet* (Latin) = namely.
Prov.......... ...Proverbs (O. T.).	vol................volume.
Ps., Pss.........Psalm or Psalms (O. T.), respec-	Wisd.............Wisdom (Apoc.).
tively.	Zech............Zechariah (O. T.).
Ptol..............Ptolemy.	Zeph............Zephaniah (O. T.).
R.................Rabbi (before a Jewish name).	?....... ....denotes *section* or subdivision of
Rawl......... ...Rawlinson.	chapter.
Rev,.............Revelation, or Apocalypse (N.T.).	=.................denotes *equivalent to*.

Words in brackets and printed in small capitals, thus [TALMUD], refer the reader, for further information, to those articles in the Dictionary.

A DICTIONARY OF THE BIBLE.

A. See ALPHA.

Aa'ron (*a teacher*, or *lofty*), the son of Amram and Jochebed, and the elder brother of Moses and Miriam. Num. 26 : 59; 33 : 3). (B.C. 1573.) He was a Levite, and is first mentioned in Ex. 4 : 14. He was appointed by Jehovah to be the interpreter, Ex. 4 : 16, of his brother Moses, who was "slow of speech;" and accordingly he was not only the organ of communication with the Israelites and with Pharaoh, Ex. 4 : 30; 7 : 2, but also the actual instrument of working most of the miracles of the Exodus. Ex. 7 : 19, etc. On the way to Mount Sinai, during the battle with Amalek, Aaron with Hur stayed up the weary hands of Moses, when they were lifted up for the victory of Israel. Ex. 17 : 9. He is mentioned as dependent upon his brother and deriving all his authority from him. Left, on Moses' departure into Sinai, to guide the people, Aaron is tried for a moment on his own responsibility, and he fails from a weak inability to withstand the demand of the people for visible "gods to go before them," by making an image of Jehovah, in the well-known form of Egyptian idolatry (Apis or Mnevis). He repented of his sin, and Moses gained forgiveness for him. Deut. 9 : 20. Aaron was now consecrated by Moses to the new office of the high priesthood. Ex. 29 : 9. From this time the history of Aaron is almost entirely that of the priesthood, and its chief feature is the great rebellion of Korah and the Levites. Leaning, as he seems to have done, wholly on Moses, it is not strange that he should have shared his sin at Meribah and its punishment. See MOSES. Num. 20 : 10–12. Aaron's death seems to have followed very speedily. It took place on Mount Hor, after the transference of his robes and office to Eleazar. Num. 20:28. This mount is still called the "Mountain of Aaron." See HOR. The wife of Aaron was Elisheba, Ex. 6 : 23; and the two sons who survived him, Eleazar and Ithamar. The high priesthood descended to the former, and to his descendants until the time of Eli, who, although of the house of Ithamar, received the high priesthood and transmitted it to his children; with them it continued till the accession of Solomon, who took it from Abiathar and restored it to Zadok (of the house of Eleazar). See ABIATHAR.

Aar'onites, 1 Chron. 12 : 27, priests of the family of Aaron.

Ab (*father*), an element in the composition of many proper names, of which Abba is a Chaldaic form, having the sense of " endowed with," " possessed of."

Ab. See MONTH.

Abad'don. See APOLLYON.

Abag'tha (*God-given*), one of the seven eunuchs in the Persian court of Ahasuerus. Esther 1 : 10.

Ab'ana (*perennial, stony*), one of the " rivers of Damascus." 2 Kings 5 : 12. The *Barada* and the *Awaj* are now the chief streams of Damascus, the former representing the Abana and the latter the Pharpar of the text. The *Barada* (Abana) rises in the Antilibanus, at about 23 miles from the city, after flowing through which it runs across the plain, of whose fertility it is the chief source, till it loses itself in the lake or marsh *Bahret-el-Kibliyeh.*

Ab'arim (*regions beyond*), a mountain or range of highlands on the east of the Jordan, in the land of Moab, facing Jericho, and forming the eastern wall of the Jordan valley at that part. Its most elevated spot was " the Mount Nebo, ' head' of ' the' Pisgah," from which Moses viewed the Promised Land before his death. These mountains are mentioned in Num. 27 : 12; 33 : 47, 48, and Deut. 32 : 49.

Ab'ba. See AB.

Ab'da. 1. Father of Adoniram. 1 Kings 4 : 6.

2. Son of Shammua, Neh. 11 : 17; called Obadiah in 1 Chron. 9 : 16.

Ab'de-el, father of Shelemiah. Jer. 36 : 26.

Ab'di (*my servant*). 1. A Merarite, and ancestor of Ethan the singer. 1 Chron. 6 : 44. (B.C. before 1015.)

2. The father of Kish, a Merarite, in the reign of Hezekiah. 2 Chron. 29 : 12. (B.C. befôre 736.)

3. One of the Bene-Elam in the time of Ezra, who had married a foreign wife. Ezra 10 : 26. (B.C. 659.)

Ab'di-el (*the servant of God*), son of Guni and father of Ahi, one of the Gadites who were settled in the land of Bashan, 1 Chron. 5 : 15, in the days of Jotham king of Judah. (B.C. 758.)

Ab'don (*servile*). 1. A judge of Israel, Judges 12 : 13, 15 ; perhaps the same

murdered by his brother Cain, Gen. 4 : 1-16 ; he was a keeper or feeder of sheep. Our Lord spoke of Abel as the first martyr, Matt. 23 : 35 ; so did the early Church subsequently. The traditional site of his murder and his grave are pointed out near Damascus.

A'bel, the name of several places in Palestine, probably signifies a *meadow.*

A'bel-beth-ma'achah (*meadow of the house of oppression*), a town of some importance, 2 Sam. 20 : 15, in the extreme north of Palestine, which fell an early prey to the invading kings of Syria, 1 Kings 15 : 20, and Assyria. 2 Kings 15 : 29.

A'bel-ma'im (*Abel on the waters*), also called simply Abel, 2 Sam. 20 : 14, 18, another name for Abel-bethmaachah. 2 Chron. 16 : 4.

A'bel-meho'lah (*meadow of the dance*), in the northern part of the Jordan valley, 1 Kings 4 : 12, to which the routed Bedouin host fled from Gideon. Judges 7 : 22. Here Elisha was found at his plough by Elijah returning up the valley from Horeb. 1 Kings 19 : 16–19.

A'bel-mizra'im (*meadow of Egypt*), the

River Abana (now Barada) and Damascus.

name given by the Canaanites to the floor of Atad, at which Joseph, his brothers and the Egyptians made their mourning for Jacob. Gen. 50 : 11. It was beyond (on the east of) Jordan. See ATAD. (Schaff and others say it was on the *west* bank, for the writer was on the east of Jordan. It was near Jericho, or perhaps Hebron.)

person as Bedan, in 1 Sam. 12 : 11. (B.C. 1233–1225.)

2. Son of Shashak. 1 Chron. 8 : 23.

3. First-born son of Jehiel, son of Gideon. 1 Chron. 8 : 30 ; 9 : 35, 36.

4. Son of Micah, a contemporary of Josiah, 2 Chron. 34 : 20, called Achbor in 2 Kings 22 : 12. (B.C. 628.)

5. A city in the tribe of Asher, given to the Gershonites, Josh. 21 : 30 ; 1 Chron. 6 : 74 ; the modern Abdeh, 10 miles northeast of Accho.

Abed'nego (i. e. *servant of Nego,* perhaps the same as *Nebo*), the Chaldæan name given to Azariah, one of the three friends of Daniel, miraculously saved from the fiery furnace. Dan. 3. (B.C. about 600.)

A'bel (i. e. *breath, vapor, transitoriness,* probably so called from the shortness of his life), the second son of Adam,

A'bel-shit'tim (*the meadow of the acacias*), in the "plains" of Moab, on the low level of the Jordan valley, opposite Jericho. The last resting-place of Israel before crossing the Jordan. Num. 33 : 49. The place is most frequently mentioned by its shorter name of Shittim. See SHITTIM.

A'bel, Stone of ("the great abel"), the place where the ark rested in the field of Joshua at Beth-shemesh. 1 Sam. 6 : 18.

A'bez (*lofty*), a town in the possession of Issachar, named between Kishion and Remeth in Josh. 19 : 20 only.

A'bi, mother of King Hezekiah, 2 Kings 18 : 2; written ABIJAH in 2 Chron. 29 : 1.

Abi'a, Abi'ah, or Abi'jah. 1. Son of Becher, the son of Benjamin. 1 Chron. 7:8.
2. Wife of Hezron. 1 Chron. 2 : 24.
3. Second son of Samuel. 1 Sam. 8 : 2; 1 Chron. 7 : 28.
4. The son of Rehoboam. 1 Chron. 3 : 10; Matt. 1 : 7. See ABIJAH, 1.
5. Mother of King Hezekiah. [ABI.]
6. Same as ABIJAH, 4.

Abi'a, Course of, the eighth of the 24 courses or classes into which the priests were divided for serving at the altar. 1 Chron. 24; Luke 1 : 5. See ABIJAH, 4.

A'bi-al'bon (*father of strength*). See ABIEL.

Abi'asaph (*father of gathering*, i. e. *gathered*), Ex. 6 : 24, otherwise written **Ebi'asaph.** 1 Chron. 6 : 23, 37; 9 : 19. One of the descendants of Korah, and head of the Korhites. Among the remarkable descendants of Abiasaph were Samuel the prophet, 1 Sam. 1 : 11, and Heman the singer.

Abi'athar (*father of abundance*, i. e. *liberal*), high priest and fourth in descent from Eli. (B.C. 1060–1012.) Abiathar was the only one of all the sons of Ahimelech the high priest who escaped the slaughter inflicted upon his father's house by Saul, in revenge for his having inquired of the Lord for David and given him the shew-bread to eat. 1 Sam. 22. Abiathar having become high priest fled to David, and was thus enabled to inquire of the Lord for him. 1 Sam. 23 : 9; 30 : 7; 2 Sam. 2 : 1; 5 : 19, etc. He adhered to David in his wanderings while pursued by Saul; he was with him while he reigned in Hebron, and afterwards in Jerusalem. 2 Sam. 2 : 1–3. He continued faithful to him in Absalom's rebellion. 2 Sam. 15 : 24, 29, 35, 36; 17 : 15–17; 19 : 11. When, however, Adonijah set himself up for David's successor on the throne, in opposition to Solomon, Abiathar sided with him, while Zadok was on Solomon's side. For this Abiathar was deprived of the high priesthood. Zadok had joined David at Hebron, 1 Chron. 12 : 28, so that there were henceforth two high priests in the reign of David, and till the deposition of Abiathar by Solomon, when Zadok became the sole high priest.

Abib (*green fruits*). [MONTH.]

Abi'da, or Abi'dah (*father of knowledge*), a son of Midian. Gen. 25 : 4; 1 Chron. 1 : 33.

Abi'dan (*father of the judge*), chief of the tribe of Benjamin at the time of the Exodus. (B.C. 1491.) Num. 1 : 11; 2 : 22; 7 : 60, 65; 10 : 24.

A'bi-el or Ab'i-el (*father of strength*, i. e. *strong*). 1. Father of Kish, and consequently grandfather of Saul, 1 Sam. 9 : 1, as well as of Abner, Saul's commander-in-chief. 1 Sam. 14 : 51. (B.C. 1093-1055.)
2. One of David's mighty men. 1 Chron. 11 : 32. In 2 Sam. 23 : 31 he is called ABI-ALBON. (B.C. 1053.)

Abi-e'zer (*father of help, helpful*). 1. Eldest son of Gilead, and descendant of Manasseh. Josh. 17 : 2; 1 Chron. 7 : 18. (B.C. 1450.) He was the ancestor of the great judge Gideon. [GIDEON.]
2. One of David's mighty men. 2 Sam. 23 : 27; 1 Chron. 11 : 28; 27 : 12. (B.C. 1014.)

Ab'igail (*father*, i. e. *source, of joy*). 1. The beautiful wife of Nabal, a wealthy owner of goats and sheep in Carmel. (B.C. 1060.) When David's messengers were slighted by Nabal, Abigail supplied David and his followers with provisions, and succeeded in appeasing his anger. Ten days after this Nabal died, and David sent for Abigail and made her his wife. 1 Sam. 25 : 14, etc. By her he had a son, called Chileab in 2 Sam. 3 : 3, but Daniel in 1 Chron. 3 : 1.
2. A sister of David, married to Jether the *Ishmaelite*, and mother, by him, of Amasa. 1 Chron. 2 : 17. In 2 Sam. 17 : 25, for *Israelite* read *Ishmaelite*. (B.C. 1068.)

Abiha'il (*father of*, i. e. *possessing, strength*). 1. Father of Zuriel, chief of the Levitical family of Merari, a contemporary of Moses. Num. 3 : 35. (B.C. 1490.)
2. Wife of Abishur. 1 Chron. 2 : 29.
3. Son of Huri, of the tribe of Gad. 1 Chron. 5 : 14.
4. Wife of Rehoboam. She is called the daughter, *i. e.* descendant, of Eliab, the elder brother of David. 2 Chron. 11 : 18. (B.C. 972.)
5. Father of Esther and uncle of Mordecai. Esther 2 : 15; 9 : 29.

Abi'hu (*he (God) is my father*), the second son, Num. 3 : 2, of Aaron by Elisheba. Ex. 6 : 23. Being, together with his elder brother Nadab, guilty of offering strange fire to the Lord, he was consumed by fire from heaven. Lev. 10 : 1, 2. (B.C. 1490.)

Abi'hud (*father of renown, famous*), son of Bela and grandson of Benjamin. 1 Chron. 8 : 3.

Abi'jah or **Abi'jam** (*my father is Jehovah*). 1. Son and successor of Rehoboam on the throne of Judah. 1 Kings 14 : 21; 2 Chron. 12 : 16. He is called ABIJAH in Chronicles, ABIJAM in Kings. He began to reign B.C. 959, and reigned three years. He endeavored to recover the kingdom of the Ten Tribes, and made war on Jeroboam. He was successful in battle, and took several of the cities of Israel. We are told that he walked in all the sins of Rehoboam. 1 Kings 14 : 23, 24.

2. The second son of Samuel, called ABIAH in our version. [ABIA, ABIAH, No. 3.]

3. Son of Jeroboam I., king of Israel; died in his childhood. 1 Kings 14.

4. A descendant of Eleazar, who gave his name to the eighth of the 24 courses into which the priests were divided by David. 1 Chron. 24 : 10; 2 Chron. 8 : 14; Neh. 12 : 4, 17.

5. One of the priests who entered into a covenant with Nehemiah to walk in God's law, Neh. 10 : 7; unless the name is rather that of a family, and the same with the preceding.

Abi'jam. [ABIJAH, 1.]

Ab'ila. [ABILENE.]

Abile'ne (*land of meadows*), Luke 3 : 1, a city situated on the eastern slope of Antilibanus, in a district fertilized by the river Barada (Abana). The city was 18 miles from Damascus, and stood in a remarkable gorge called *Sûk Wady Barada*.

Abim'a-el (*father of Mael*), a descendant of Joktan, Gen. 10 : 28; 1 Chron. 1 : 22, and probably the progenitor of an Arab tribe (Mali).

Abim'elech (*father of the king*), the name of several Philistine kings, was probably a common title of these kings, like that of Pharaoh among the Egyptians and that of. Cæsar and Augustus among the Romans. Hence in the title of Ps. 34 the name of Abimelech is given to the king, who is called Achish in 1 Sam. 21 : 11. 1. A Philistine, king of Gerar, Gen. 20, 21, who, exercising the right claimed by Eastern princes of collecting all the beautiful women of their dominions into their harem, Gen. 12 : 15;

Esther 2 : 3, sent for and took Sarah. A similar account is given of Abraham's conduct on this occasion to that of his behavior towards Pharaoh. [ABRAHAM.] (B.C. 1920.)

2. Another king of Gerar in the time of Isaac, of whom a similar narrative is recorded in relation to Rebekah. Gen. 26 : 1, etc. (B.C. 1817.)

3. Son of the judge Gideon by his Shechemite concubine. Judg. 8 : 31. (B.C. 1322–1319.) After his father's death he murdered all his brethren, 70 in number, with the exception of Jotham, the youngest, who concealed himself; and he then persuaded the Shechemites to elect him king. Shechem now became an independent state. After Abimelech had reigned three years, the citizens of Shechem rebelled. He was absent at the time, but he returned and quelled the insurrection. Shortly after he stormed and took Thebez, but was struck on the head by a woman with the fragment of a millstone, comp. 2 Sam. 11 : 21; and lest he should be said to have died by a woman, he bade his armor-bearer slay him.

4. A son of Abiathar. 1 Chron. 18 : 16.

Abin'adab. 1. A Levite, a native of Kirjath-jearim, in whose house the ark remained 20 years. 1 Sam. 7 : 1, 2; 1 Chron. 13 : 7. (B.C. 1124.)

2. Second son of Jesse, who followed Saul to his war against the Philistines. 1 Sam. 16 : 8; 17 : 13. (B.C. 1063.)

3. A son of Saul, who was slain with his brothers at the fatal battle on Mount Gilboa. 1 Sam. 31 : 2. (B.C. 1053.)

4. Father of one of the twelve chief officers of Solomon. 1 Kings 4 : 11. (B.C. before 1014.)

Ab'iner (*father of light*). Same as ABNER. 1 Sam. 14 : 50, margin.

Abin'o-am, the father of Barak. Judges 4 : 6, 12; 5 : 1, 12. (B.C. 1300.)

Abi'ram. 1. A Reubenite, son of Eliab, who with Korah, a Levite, organized a conspiracy against Moses and Aaron. Num. 16. [For details, see KORAH.] (B.C. 1490.)

2. Eldest son of Hiel the Bethelite, who died when his father laid the foundations of Jericho, 1 Kings 16 : 34, and thus accomplished the first part of the curse of Joshua. Josh. 6 : 26. (B.C. after 905.)

Ab'ishag, a beautiful Shunammite (from Shunem, in the tribe of Issachar), taken into David's harem to comfort him in his extreme old age. 1 Kings 1 : 1–4.

Abisha'i, or **Abish'a-i** (*father of a gift*), the eldest of the three sons of Zeruiah, David's sister, and brother to Joab and Asahel. 1 Chron. 2 : 16. Like his two brothers he was the devoted follower of David. He was his companion in the desperate night expedition to the camp of Saul. 1 Sam. 26 : 6–9. (B.C. 1055.) On the outbreak of Absalom's rebellion he remained true to the king, and commanded a third part of the army in the decisive battle against Absalom. He rescued David from the hands of a gigantic Philistine, Ishbi-benob. 2 Sam. 21 : 17. His personal prowess on this, as on another occasion, when he fought single-handed against three hundred, won for him a place as captain of the second three of David's mighty men. 2 Sam. 23 : 18; 1 Chron. 11 : 20.

Abish'alom (*father of peace*), father or grandfather of Maachah, who was the wife of Rehoboam and mother of Abijah. 1 Kings 15 : 2, 10. He is called Absalom in 2 Chron. 11 : 20, 21. This person must be David's son. See LXX.; 2 Sam. 14 : 27.

Abishu'a, or **Abish'u-a** (*father of deliverance*). 1. Son of Bela, of the tribe of Benjamin. 1 Chron. 8 : 4.

2. Son of Phinehas, the son of Eleazar, and father of Bukki, in the genealogy of the high priests. 1 Chron. 6 : 4, 5, 50, 51; Ezra 7 : 4, 5.

Ab'ishur (*father of the wall*), son of Shammai. 1 Chron. 2 : 28.

Ab'ital (*father of the dew*), one of David's wives. 2 Sam. 3 : 4; 1 Chron. 3 : 3.

Ab'itub (*father of goodness*), son of Shaharaim by Hushim. 1 Chron. 8 : 11.

Abi'ud (*father of praise*), descendant of Zorobabel in the genealogy of Jesus Christ. Matt. 1 : 13.

Ablution. [PURIFICATION.]

Ab'ner (*father of light*). 1. Son of Ner, who was the brother of Kish, 1 Chron. 9 : 36, the father of Saul. (B.C. 1063.) Abner, therefore, was Saul's first cousin, and was made by him commander-in-chief of his army. 1 Sam. 14 : 51; 17 : 57; 26 : 5–14. After the death of Saul David was proclaimed king of Judah; and some time subsequently Abner proclaimed Ish-bosheth, Saul's son, king of Israel. War soon broke out between the two rival kings, and a " very sore battle " was fought at Gibeon between the men of Israel under Abner and the men of Judah under Joab. 1 Chron. 2 : 16.

Abner had married Rizpah, Saul's concubine, and this, according to the views of Oriental courts, might be so interpreted as to imply a design upon the throne. Rightly or wrongly, Ish-bosheth so understood it, and he even ventured to reproach Abner with it. Abner, incensed at his ingratitude, opened negotiations with David, by whom he was most favorably received at Hebron. He then undertook to procure his recognition throughout Israel; but after leaving his presence for the purpose was enticed back by Joab, and treacherously murdered by him and his brother Abishai, at the gate of the city, partly, no doubt, from fear lest so distinguished a convert to their cause should gain too high a place in David's favor, but ostensibly in retaliation for the death of Asahel. David, in sorrow and indignation, poured forth a simple dirge over the slain hero. 2 Sam. 3 : 33, 34.

2. The father of Jaasiel, chief of the Benjamites in David's reign, 1 Chron. 27 : 21; probably the same as the preceding.

Abomination of Desolation, mentioned by our Saviour, Matt. 24 : 15, as a sign of the approaching destruction of Jerusalem, with reference to Dan. 9 : 27; 11 : 31; 12 : 11. The prophecy referred ultimately to the destruction of Jerusalem by the Romans, and consequently the " abomination " must describe some occurrence connected with that event. It appears most probable that the profanities of the Zealots constituted the abomination, which was the sign of impending ruin; but most people refer it to the standards or banners of the Roman army. They were abomination because there were idolatrous images upon them.

A'braham (*father of a multitude*) was the son of Terah, and founder of the great Hebrew nation. (B.C. 1996–1822.) His family, a branch of the descendants of Shem, was settled in Ur of the Chaldees, beyond the Euphrates, where Abraham was born. Terah had two other sons, Nahor and Haran. Haran died before his father in Ur of the Chaldees, leaving a son, Lot; and Terah, taking with him Abram, with Sarai his wife and his grandson Lot, emigrated to Haran in Mesopotamia, where he died. On the death of his father, Abram, then in the 75th year of his age, with Sarai and Lot, pursued his course to the land of Canaan, whither he was directed by divine command, Gen. 12 : 5, when he received the general promise that he should become the founder of a great nation, and that all the families of the earth should be blessed in him. He passed through the heart of the country by the great highway to Shechem, and pitched his tent beneath the terebinth of Moreh. Gen. 12 : 6. Here he received in vision from Jehovah the further revelation that this was the land which his descendants should inherit. Gen. 12 : 7. The next halting-place of the wanderer was on a mountain between Bethel and Ai, Gen. 12 : 8; but the country was suffering from famine, and Abram journeyed still southward to the rich cornlands of Egypt. There, fearing that the great beauty of Sarai might tempt the powerful monarch of Egypt and expose his own life to peril, he arranged that Sarai should represent herself as his sister, which her actual relationship to him, as probably the daughter of his brother Haran, allowed her to do with some semblance of truth. But her beauty was reported to the king, and she was taken into the royal harem. The deception was discovered, and Pharaoh with some indignation dismissed Abram from the country. Gen. 12 : 10-20. He left Egypt with great possessions, and, accompanied by Lot, returned by the south of Palestine to his former encampment between Bethel and Ai. The increased wealth of the two kinsmen was the ultimate cause of their separation. Lot chose the fertile plain of the Jordan near Sodom, while **Abram pitched his** tent among the oak groves of Mamre, close to Hebron. Gen. 13. Lot with his family and possessions having been carried away captive by Chedorlaomer king of Elam, who had invaded Sodom, Abram pursued the conquerors and utterly routed them not far from Damascus. The captives and plunder were all recovered, and Abram was greeted on his return by the king of Sodom, and by Melchizedek king of Salem, priest of the most high God, who mysteriously appears upon the scene to bless the patriarch and receive from him a tenth of the spoil. Gen. 14. After this the thrice-repeated promise that his descendants should become a mighty nation and possess the land in which he was a stranger was confirmed with all the solemnity of a religious ceremony. Gen. 15. Ten years had passed since he had left his father's house, and the fulfillment

of the promise was apparently more distant than at first. At the suggestion of Sarai, who despaired of having children of her own, he took as his concubine Hagar, her Egyptian maid, who bore him Ishmael in the 86th year of his age. Gen. 16. [HAGAR; ISHMAEL.] But this was not the accomplishment of the promise. Thirteen years elapsed, during which Abram still dwelt in Hebron, when the covenant was renewed, and the rite of circumcision established as its sign. This most important crisis in Abram's life, when he was 99 years old, is marked by the significant change of his name to Abraham, "father of a multitude;" while his wife's from Sarai became Sarah. The promise that Sarah should have a son was repeated in the remarkable scene described in ch. 18. Three men stood before Abraham as he sat in his tent door in the heat of the day. The patriarch, with true Eastern hospitality, welcomed the strangers, and bade them rest and refresh themselves. The meal ended, they foretold the birth of Isaac, and went on their way to Sodom. Abraham accompanied them, and is represented as an interlocutor in a dialogue with Jehovah, in which he pleaded in vain to avert the vengeance threatened to the devoted cities of the plain. Gen. 18 : 17-33. In remarkable contrast with Abraham's firm faith with regard to the magnificent fortunes of his posterity stands the incident which occurred during his temporary residence among the Philistines in Gerar, whither he had for some cause removed after the destruction of Sodom. It was almost a repetition of what took place in Egypt a few years before. At length Isaac, the long-looked-for child, was born. Sarah's jealousy, aroused by the mockery of Ishmael at the "great banquet" which Abraham made to celebrate the weaning of her son, Gen. 21 : 9, demanded that, with his mother Hagar, he should be driven out. Gen. 21 : 10. But the severest trial of his faith was yet to come. For a long period the history is almost silent. At length he receives the strange command to take Isaac, his only son, and offer him for a burnt offering at an appointed place. Abraham hesitated not to obey. His faith, hitherto unshaken, supported him in this final trial, "accounting that God was able to raise up his son, even from the dead, from whence also he received him in a figure." Heb. 11 : 19. The sacrifice was stayed by the angel of Jehovah, the promise of spiritual blessing made for the first time, and Abraham with his son returned to Beersheba, and for a time dwelt there. Gen. 22. But we find him after a few years in his original residence at Hebron, for there Sarah died, Gen. 23 : 2, and was buried in the cave of Machpelah. The remaining years of Abraham's life are marked by but few incidents. After Isaac's marriage with Rebekah and his removal to Lahai-roi, Abraham took to wife Keturah, by whom he had six children, Zimran, Jokshan, Medan, Midian, Ishbok and Shuah, who became the ancestors of nomadic tribes inhabiting the countries south and southeast of Palestine. Abraham lived to see the gradual accomplishment of the promise in the birth of his grandchildren Jacob and Esau, and witnessed their growth to manhood. Gen. 25 : 26. At the goodly age of 175 he was "gathered to his people," and laid beside Sarah in the tomb of Machpelah by his sons Isaac and Ishmael. Gen. 25 : 7–10.

A'bram (*a high father*), the earlier name of Abraham.

Ab'salom (*father of peace*), third son of David by Maachah, daughter of Talmai king of Geshur, a Syrian district adjoining the northeast frontier of the Holy Land. (Born B.C. 1050.) Absalom had a sister, Tamar, who was violated by her half-brother Amnon. The natural avenger of such an outrage would be Tamar's full brother Absalom. He brooded over the wrong for two years, and then invited all the princes to a sheep-shearing feast at his estate in Baal-hazor, on the borders of Ephraim and Benjamin. Here he ordered his servants to murder Amnon, and then fled for safety to his grandfather's court at Geshur, where he remained for three years. At the end of that time he was brought back by an artifice of Joab. David, however, would not see Absalom for two more years; but at length Joab brought about a reconciliation. Absalom now began at once to prepare for rebellion. He tried to supplant his father by courting popularity, standing in the gate, conversing with every suitor, and lamenting the difficulty which he would find in getting a hearing. He also maintained a splendid retinue, 2 Sam. 15 : 1, and was admired for his personal beauty. It is probable too that the great tribe of Judah had taken some offence at David's

government. Absalom raised the standard of revolt at Hebron, the old capital of Judah, now supplanted by Jerusalem. The revolt was at first completely successful; David fled from his capital over the Jordan to Mahanaim in Gilead, and Absalom occupied Jerusalem. At last, after being solemnly anointed king at Jerusalem, 2 Sam. 19 : 10, Absalom crossed the Jordan to attack his father, who by this time had rallied round him a considerable force. A decisive battle was fought in Gilead, in the wood of Ephraim. Here Absalom's forces were totally defeated, and as he himself was escaping his long hair was entangled in the branches of a terebinth, where he was left hanging while the mule on which he was riding ran away from under him. He was dispatched by Joab in spite of the prohibition of David, who, loving him to the last, had desired that his life might be spared. He was buried in a great pit in the forest, and the conquerors threw stones over his grave, an old proof of bitter hostility. Josh. 7 : 26.

Absalom's Pillar.

Absalom's Pillar, or **Place,** a monument or tomb which Absalom had built during his lifetime in the king's dale, *i. e.* the valley of the Kedron, at the foot of Mount Olivet, near Jerusalem, 2 Sam. 18 : 18, comp. with 14 : 27, for his three sons, and where he probably expected to be buried. The tomb there now, and called by Absalom's name, was probably built at a later date.

Ac'cad, one of the cities in the land of Shinar. Gen. 10 : 10. Its position is quite uncertain.

Ac'caron. [EKRON.]

Ac'cho (the PTOLEMAIS of the Maccabees and New Testament), now called *Acca,* or more usually by Europeans *St. Jean d'Acre,* the most important seaport town on the Syrian coast, about 30 miles south of Tyre. It was situated on a slightly projecting headland, at the northern extremity of that spacious bay which is formed by the bold promontory of Carmel on the opposite side. Later it was named Ptolemais, after one one of the Ptolemies, probably Soter. The only notice of it in the New Testament is in Acts 21 : 7, where it is called *Ptolemais.*

Acel'dama (*the field of blood*) (*Akeldama* in the Revised Version), the name given by the Jews of Jerusalem to a

Aceldama. (*From an original Photograph.*)

field near Jerusalem purchased by Judas with the money which he received for the betrayal of Christ, and so called from his violent death therein. Acts 1 : 19. The "field of blood" is now shown on the steep southern face of the valley or ravine of Hinnom, "southwest of the supposed pool of Siloam."

Acha'ia (*trouble*) signifies in the New Testament a Roman province which included the whole of the Peloponnesus and the greater part of Hellas proper, with the adjacent islands. This province, with that of Macedonia, comprehended the whole of Greece; hence Achaia and Macedonia are frequently mentioned together in the New Testament to indicate all Greece. Acts 18 : 12 ; 19 : 21 ; Rom. 15 : 26 ; 16 : 5 ; 1 Cor. 16 : 15 ; 2 Cor. 7 : 5 ; 9 : 2 ; 11 : 10 ; 1 Thess. 1 : 7, 8. In the time of the emperor Claudius it was governed by a proconsul, translated in the Authorized Version "deputy," of Achaia. Acts 18 : 12.

Acha'icus (*belonging to Achaia*), a name of a Christian. 1 Cor. 16 : 17.

A'chan (*troubler*), an Israelite of the tribe of Judah, who, when Jericho and all that it contained were accursed and devoted to destruction, secreted a portion of the spoil in his tent. For this sin he was stoned to death with his whole family by the people, in a valley situated between Ai and Jericho, and their remains, together with his property, were burnt. Josh. 7 : 19–26. From this event the valley received the name of Achor (i. e. *trouble*). [ACHOR.] (B.C. 1450.)

A'char = A'chan. 1 Chron. 2 : 7.

A'chaz = A'haz, king of Judah. Matt. 1 : 9.

Ach'bor (*mouse*). 1. Father of Baal-hanan king of Edom. Gen. 36 : 38, 39 ; 1 Chron. 1 : 49.

2. Son of Michaiah, a contemporary of Josiah, 2 Kings 22 : 12, 14; Jer. 26 : 22; 36 : 12, called ABDON in 2 Chron. 34 : 20. (B.C. 623.)

A'chim, son of Sadoc and father of Eliud in our Lord's genealogy. Matt. 1 : 14. The Hebrew form of the name would be *Jachin*, which is a short form of Jehoiachin, *the Lord will establish.*

A'chish (*angry*), a Philistine king of Gath, who in the title to the 34th Psalm is called Abimelech. David twice found a refuge with him when he fled from Saul. (B.C. 1061.) On the first occasion he was alarmed for his safety, feigned madness, and was sent away.

Ach'metha. [ECBATANA.]

A'chor, Valley of (*valley of trouble*), the spot at which Achan was stoned. Josh. 7 : 24, 26. On the northern boundary of Judah, Josh. 15 : 7, near Jericho.

Ach'sa. 1 Chron. 2 : 49. [ACHSAH]

Ach'sah (*ankle-chain, anklet*), daughter of Caleb. Her father promised her in marriage to whoever should take Debir. Othniel, her father's younger brother, took that city, and accordingly received the hand of Achsah as his reward. Caleb added to her dowry the upper and lower springs. (B.C. 1450–1426.) Josh. 15 : 15–19; Judges 1 : 11–15.

Ach'shaph (*fascination*), a city within the territory of Asher, named between Beten and Alammelech, Josh. 19 : 25; originally the seat of a Canaanite king. Josh. 11 : 1 ; 12 : 20.

Ach'zib (*lying, false*). 1. A city in the lowlands of Judah, named with Keilah and Mareshah. Josh. 15 : 44; Micah 1 : 14. It is probably the same with CHEZIB and CHOZEBA, which see.

2. A town belonging to Asher, Josh. 19 : 29, from which the Canaanites were not expelled, Judges 1 : 31; afterwards Ecdippa. It is now *es-Zib*, on the seashore, 2 h. 20 m. north of Acre.

Acrab'bim. See MAALEH-ACRAB-BIM, Josh. 15 : 3, in the margin.

Acts of the Apostles, the fifth book in the New Testament and the second treatise by the author of the third Gospel, traditionally known as Luke. The book commences with an inscription to one Theophilus, who was probably a man of birth and station. The readers were evidently intended to be the members of the Christian Church, whether Jews or Gentiles; for its contents are such as are of the utmost consequence to the whole Church. They are *the fulfillment of the promise of the Father by the descent of the Holy Spirit,* and *the results of that outpouring by the dispersion of the gospel among Jews and Gentiles.* Under these leading heads all the personal and subordinate details may be arranged. First St. Peter becomes the prime actor under God in the founding of the Church. He is the centre of the first group of sayings and doings. The opening of the door to Jews, ch. 2, and Gentiles, ch. 10, is his office, and by him, in good time, is accomplished. Then the preparation of Saul of Tarsus for the work to be done, the progress, in his hand, of that work, his journeyings, preachings and perils, his stripes and imprisonments, his testifying in Jerusalem and being brought to testify in Rome,—these are the subjects of the latter half of the book, of which the great central figure is the apostle Paul. The history given in the Acts occupies about 33 years, and the reigns of the Roman emperors Tiberius, Caligula, Claudius and Nero. It seems most probable that the place of writing was Rome, and the time about two years from the date of St. Paul's arrival there, as related in ch. 28 : 30. This would give us for the publication about 63 A.D.

Ad'adah (*festival* or *boundary*), one of the cities in the extreme south of Judah, named with Dimonah and Kedesh. Josh. 15 : 22.

A'dah (*ornament, beauty*). 1. The first of the two wives of Lamech, by whom were borne to him Jabal and Jubal. Gen. 4 : 19. (B.C. 3600.)

2. A Hittitess, one of the three wives of Esau, mother of Eliphaz. Gen. 36 : 2, 10, 12, 16. In Gen. 26 : 34 she is called BASHEMATH. (B.C. 1797.)

Ada'iah (*adorned by Jehovah*). 1. Maternal grandfather of King Josiah, and native of Boscath in the lowlands of Judah. 2 Kings 22 : 1. (B.C. 648.)

2. A Levite of the Gershonite branch, and ancestor of Asaph. 1 Chron. 6 : 41. In v. 21 he is called IDDO.

3. A Benjamite, son of Shimhi, 1 Chron. 8 : 21, who is apparently the same as Shema in v. 13.

4. A priest, son of Jehoram. 1 Chron. 9 : 12; Neh. 11 : 12.

5. Ancestor of Maaseiah, one of the captains who supported Jehoiada. 2 Chron. 23 : 1.

6. One of the descendants of Bani,

who had married a foreign wife after the return from Babylon. Ezra 10 : 29. (B.C. 459.)

7. The descendant of another Bani, who had also taken a foreign wife. Ezra 10 : 39.

8. A man of Judah, of the line of Pharez. Neh. 11 : 5.

Adali'a (*a fire-god*), the fifth son of Haman. Esther 9 : 8.

Ad'am (*red earth*), the name given in Scripture to the first man. It apparently has reference to the ground from which he was formed, which is called in Hebrew *Adamah*. The idea of *redness of color* seems to be inherent in either word. The creation of man was the work of the sixth day—the last and crowning act of creation. Adam was created (not born) a perfect man in body and spirit, but as innocent and completely inexperienced as a child. The man Adam was placed in a garden which the Lord God had planted " eastward in Eden," for the purpose of dressing it and keeping it. [EDEN.] Adam was permitted to eat of the fruit of every tree in the garden but one, which was called ("the tree of the knowledge of good and evil," because it was the test of Adam's obedience. By it Adam could know good and evil in the divine way, through obedience ; thus knowing good by experience in resisting temptation and forming a strong and holy character, while he knew evil only by observation and inference. Or he could " know good and evil," in Satan's way, by experiencing the evil and knowing good only by contrast.—ED.) The prohibition to taste the fruit of this tree was enforced by the menace of death. There was also another tree which was called " the tree of life." While Adam was in the garden of Eden, the beasts of the field and the fowls of the air were brought to him to be named. After this the Lord God caused a deep sleep to fall upon him, and took one of his ribs from him, which he fashioned into a woman and brought her to the man. At this time they are both described as being naked without the consciousness of shame. By the subtlety of the serpent the woman who was given to be with Adam was beguiled into a violation of the one command which had been imposed upon them. She took of the fruit of the forbidden tree and gave it to her husband. The propriety of its name was immediately shown in the results which followed : self-con-

sciousness was the first-fruits of sin ; their eyes were opened and they knew that they were naked. Though the curse of Adam's rebellion of necessity fell upon him, yet the very prohibition to eat of the tree of life after his transgression was probably a manifestation of divine mercy, because the greatest malediction of all would have been to have the gift of indestructible life superadded to a state of wretchedness and sin. The divine mercy was also shown in the promise of a deliverer given at the very time the curse was imposed, Gen. 3 : 15, and opening a door of hope to Paradise regained for him and his descendants. Adam is stated to have lived 930 years. His sons mentioned in Scripture are Cain, Abel and Seth ; it is implied, however, that he had others.

Ad'am. *Man*, generically, for the name Adam was not confined to the father of the human race, but like *homo* was applicable to *woman* as well as to *man*. Gen. 5 : 2.

Ad'am, a city on the Jordan, " beside Zaretan," in the time of Joshua. Josh. 3 : 16.

Ad'amah (*red earth*), one of the " fenced cities " of Naphtali, named between Chinnereth and Ramah. Josh. 19 : 36.

Adamant, the translation of the Hebrew word *Shamir* in Ezek. 3 : 9 and Zech. 7 : 12. In Jer. 17 : 1 it is translated " diamond." In these three passages the word is the representative of some stone of excessive hardness, and is used metaphorically. It is very probable that by *Shamir* is intended *emery*, a variety of *corundum*, a mineral inferior only to the diamond in hardness.

Ad'ami (*my man, earth*), a place on the border of Naphtali. Josh. 19 : 33.

A'dar (*high*), a place on the south boundary of Judah. Josh. 15 : 3.

A'dar. [MONTH.]

Ad'asa (*new*), a place in Judea, about four miles from Beth-horon. 1 Macc. 7 : 40, 45. [HADASHAH.]

Ad'be-el (*offspring of God*), a son of Ishmael, Gen. 25 : 13 ; 1 Chron. 1 : 29, and probably the progenitor of an Arab tribe. (B.C. about 1850.)

Ad'dan (*strong* or *stony*), one of the places from which some of the captivity returned with Zerubbabel to Judea who could not show their pedigree as Israelites. Ezra 2 : 59. Called ADDON Neh. 7 : 61.

Ad'dar (*mighty one*), son of Bela, 1 Chron. 8 : 3; called ARD in Num. 26 : 40.

Ad'der. This word is used for any poisonous snake, and is applied in this general sense by the translators of the Authorized Version. The word adder occurs five times in the text of the Authorized Version (see below), and three times in the margin as synonymous with *cockatrice*, viz., Isa. 11 : 8; 14 : 29; 59 : 5. It represents four Hebrew words:

1. *Acshub* is found only in Ps. 140 : 3, and may be represented by the *Toxicoa* of Egypt and North-Africa.

2. *Pethen.* [ASP.]

3. *Tsepha*, or *Tsiphoni*, occurs five times in the Hebrew Bible. In Prov. 23 : 32 it is translated *adder*, and in Isa. 11 : 8, 14 : 29, 59 : 5, Jer. 8 : 17, it is rendered *cockatrice.* From Jeremiah we learn that it was of a hostile nature,

Horned Cerastes (*Adder*).

and from the parallelism of Isa. 11 : 8 it appears that the *Tsiphoni* was considered even more dreadful than the *Pethen.*

4. *Shephiphon* occurs only in Gen. 49 : 17, where it is used to characterize the tribe of Dan. The habit of lurking in the sand and biting at the horse's heels here alluded to suits the character of a well-known species of venomous snake, and helps to identify it with the celebrated horned viper, the asp of Cleopatra (*Cerastes*), which is found abundantly in the dry sandy deserts of Egypt, Syria and Arabia. The cerastes is extremely venomous. Bruce compelled a specimen to scratch eighteen pigeons upon the thigh as quickly as possible, and they all died in nearly the same interval of time.

Ad'di (*ornament*). Luke 3 : 28. Son of Cosam, and father of Melchi in our Lord's genealogy; the third above Salathiel.

Ad'don (*lord*). [ADDAN.]

A'der (*flock*), a Benjamite, son of Beriah, chief of the inhabitants of Aijalon. 1 Chron. 8 : 15. The name is more correctly Eder.

Ad'ida, a fortified town near Jerusalem, probably the HADID of Ezra 2 : 33, and referred to in Macc. 12 : 38.

A'di-el (*ornament of God*). 1. A prince of the tribe of Simeon, descended from the prosperous family of Shimei. 1 Chron. 4 : 36. He took part in the murderous raid made by his tribe upon the peaceable Hamite shepherds of the valley of Gedor in the reign of Hezekiah. (B.C. about 711.)

2. A priest, ancestor of Maasiai. 1 Chron. 9 : 12.

3. Ancestor of Azmaveth, David's treasurer. 1 Chron. 27 : 25. (B.C. 1050.)

A'din (*dainty, delicate*), ancestor of a family who returned from Babylon with Zerubbabel, to the number of 454, Ezra 2 : 15, or 655 according to the parallel list in Neh. 7 : 20. (B.C. 536.) They joined with Nehemiah in a covenant to separate themselves from the heathen. Neh. 10 : 16. (B.C. 410.)

Ad'ina (*slender*), one of David's captains beyond the Jordan, and a chief of the Reubenites. 1 Chron. 11 : 42.

Adi'no, or Ad'ino, the Eznite. 2 Sam. 23 : 8. See JASHOBEAM.

Aditha'im (*double ornament*), a town belonging to Judah, lying in the low country, and named, between Sharaim and hag-Gederah, in Josh. 15 : 36 only.

Adla'i, or **Ad'la-i** (*justice of Jehovah*), ancestor of Shaphat, the overseer of David's herds that fed in the broad valleys. 1 Chron. 27 : 29. (B.C. before 1050.)

Ad'mah (*earthy, fortress*), one of the "cities of the plain," always coupled with Zeboim. Gen. 10 : 19; 14 : 2, 8; Deut. 29 : 23; Hos. 11 : 8.

Ad'matha (*given by the highest*), one of the seven princes of Persia. Esther 1 : 14.

Ad'na (*rest, pleasure*). 1. One of the family of Pahath-moab, who returned with Ezra and married a foreign wife. Ezra 10 : 30. (B.C. 459.)

2. A priest, descendant of Harim in the days of Joiakim, the son of Jeshua. Neh. 12 : 15. (B.C. 500.)

Ad'nah (*pleasure*). 1. A Manassite who deserted from Saul and joined the fortunes of David on his road to Ziklag from the camp of the Philistines. He was captain of a thousand of his tribe, and fought at David's side in the pursuit of the Amalekites. 1 Chron. 12 : 20. (B.C. 1054.)

2. The captain of over 300,000 men of Judah who were in Jehoshaphat's army. 2 Chron. 17 : 14. (B.C. 908.)

Adon'i-Be'zek (*lord of Bezek*), king of Bezek, a city of the Canaanites. [BE-ZEK.] This chieftain was vanquished by the tribe of Judah, Judges 1 : 3-7, who cut off his thumbs and great toes, and brought him prisoner to Jerusalem, where he died. He confessed that he had inflicted the same cruelty upon 70 petty kings whom he had conquered. (B.C. 1425.)

Adoni'jah (*my Lord is Jehovah*). 1. The fourth son of David by Haggith, born at Hebron while his father was king of Judah. 2 Sam. 3 : 4. (B.C. about 1050.) After the death of his three brothers, Amnon, Chileab and Absalom, he became eldest son; and when his father's strength was visibly declining, put forward his pretensions to the crown. Adonijah's cause was espoused by Abiathar and by Joab the famous commander of David's army. [JOAB.] His name and influence secured a large number of followers among the captains of the royal army belonging to the tribe of Judah, comp. 1 Kings 1 : 5; and these, together with all the princes except Solomon, were entertained by Adonijah at a great sacrificial feast held "by the stone Zoheleth, which is by En-rogel." [EN-ROGEL.] Apprised of these proceedings, David immediately caused Solomon to be proclaimed king, 1 Kings 1 : 33, 34, at Gihon. [GIHON.] This decisive measure struck terror into the opposite party, and Adonijah fled to the sanctuary, but was pardoned by Solomon on condition that he should "show himself a worthy man." 1 Kings 1 : 52. The death of David quickly followed on these events; and Adonijah begged Bath-sheba to procure Solomon's consent to his marriage with Abishag, who had been the wife of David in his old age. 1 Kings 1 : 3. This was regarded as equivalent to a fresh attempt on the throne [ABSALOM; ABNER]; and therefore Solomon ordered him to be put to death by Benaiah. 1 Kings 2 : 25.

2. A Levite in the reign of Jehoshaphat. 2 Chron. 17 : 8.

3. The same as Adonikam. Neh. 10 : 16. [ADONIKAM.]

Adoni'kam, or **Adon'ikam.** The sons of Adonikam, 666 in number, were among those who returned from Babylon with Zerubbabel. Ezra 2 : 13; Neh. 7 : 18; 1 Esd. 5 : 14. (B.C. 506-410.) The name is given as ADONIJAH in Neh. 10 : 16.

Adoni'ram (*lord of heights*), 1 Kings 4 : 6. By an unusual contraction ADORAM, 2 Sam. 20 : 24 and 1 Kings 12 : 18; also HADORAM, 2 Chron. 10 : 18, chief receiver of the tribute during the reigns of David, 2 Sam. 20 : 24, Solomon, 1 Kings 4 : 6, and Rehoboam. 1 Kings 12 : 18. This last monarch sent him to collect the tribute from the rebellious Israelites, by whom he was stoned to death. (B.C. 1014-973.)

Adonize'dek (*lord of justice*), the Amorite king of Jerusalem who organized a league with four other Amorite princes against Joshua. The confederate kings having laid siege to Gibeon, Joshua marched to the relief of his new allies and put the besiegers to flight. The five kings took refuge in a cave at Makkedah, whence they were taken and slain, their bodies hung on trees, and then buried in the place of their concealment. Josh. 10 : 1-27. (B.C. 1450.)

Adoption, an expression used by St. Paul in reference to the present and prospective privileges of Christians. Rom. 8 : 15, 23; Gal. 4 : 5; Eph. 1 : 5. He probably alludes to the Roman custom by which a person not having children of his own might adopt as his son one born of other parents. The relationship was to all intents and purposes the same as existed between a natural father and son. The term is used figuratively to show the close relationship to God of the Christian. Gal. 4 : 4, 5; Rom. 8 : 14-17. He is received into God's family from the world, and becomes a child and heir of God.

A'dor, or **Ado'ra.** [ADORAIM.]

Adora'im (*double mound*), a fortified city built by Rehoboam, 2 Chron. 11 : 9, in Judah. Adoraim is probably the same place with Adora, 1 Macc. 13 : 20, unless that be Dor, on the seacoast below Carmel. Robinson identifies it with *Dura*, a "large village" on a rising ground west of Hebron.

Ado'ram. [ADONIRAM; HADORAM.]

Adoration. The acts and postures by which the Hebrews expressed adoration bear a great similarity to those still in use among Oriental nations. To rise up and suddenly prostrate the body was the most simple method; but, generally speaking, the prostration was conducted in a more formal manner, the person falling upon the knee and then gradually inclining the body until the forehead touched the ground. Such prostration was usual in the worship of Jehovah, Gen. 17 : 3; Ps. 95 : 6; it was the formal mode of receiving visitors, Gen. 18 : 2, of doing obeisance to one of superior station, 2 Sam. 14 : 4, and of showing respect to equals. 1 Kings 2 : 19. It was accompanied by such acts as a kiss, Ex. 18 : 7, laying hold of the knees or feet of the person to whom the adoration was paid, Matt. 28 : 9, and kissing the ground on which he stood. Ps. 72 : 9; Micah 7 : 17. Similar adoration was paid to idols, 1 Kings 19 : 18; sometimes, however, the act consisted simply in kissing the hand to the object of reverence, Job 31 : 27, and in kissing the statue itself. Hos. 13 : 2.

Adram′melech (*splendor of the king*). 1. The name of an idol introduced into

Adrammelech.

Samaria by the colonists from Sepharvaim. 2 Kings 17 : 31. He was worshipped with rites resembling those of Molech, children being burnt in his honor. Adrammelech was probably the male power of the sun, and ANAMMELECH, who is mentioned with Adram-

melech as a companion god, the female power of the sun.

2. Son of the Assyrian king Sennacherib, who, with his brother Sharezer, murdered their father in the temple of Nisroch at Nineveh, after the failure of the Assyrian attack on Jerusalem. The parricides escaped into Armenia. 2 Kings 19 : 37; 2 Chron. 32 : 21; Isa. 37 : 38.

Adramyt′tium, named from *Adramys,* brother of Crœsus king of Lydia, a seaport in the province of Asia [ASIA], situated on a bay of the Ægean Sea, about 70 miles north of Smyrna, in the district anciently called Æolis, and also Mysia. See Acts 16 : 7. [MITYLENE.] Acts 27 : 2. The modern *Adramyti* is a poor village.

A′dria, more properly **A′drias,** the Adriatic Sea. Acts 27 : 27. The word seems to have been derived from the town of Adria, near the Po. In Paul's time it included the whole sea between Greece and Italy, reaching south from Crete to Sicily. [MELITA.]

A′dri-el (*flock of God*), son of Barzillai, to whom Saul gave his daughter Merab, although he had previously promised her to David. 1 Sam. 18 : 19. (B.C. about 1062.) His five sons were amongst the seven descendants of Saul whom David surrendered to the Gibeonites. 2 Sam. 21 : 8.

Adul′lam (*justice of the people*), Apocr. ODOLLAM, a city of Judah in the lowland of the Shefelah, Josh. 15 : 35; the seat of a Canaanite king, Josh. 12 : 15, and evidently a place of great antiquity. Gen. 38 : 1, 12, 20. Fortified by Rehoboam, 2 Chron. 11 : 7, it was one of the towns reoccupied by the Jews after their return from Babylon, Neh. 11 : 30, and still a city in the time of the Maccabees. 2 Macc. 12 : 38. Adullam was probably near *Deir Dubban,* five or six miles north of Eleutheropolis. The limestone cliffs of the whole of that locality are pierced with extensive excavations, some one of which is doubtless the "cave of Adullam," the refuge of David. 1 Sam. 22 : 1; 2 Sam. 23 : 13; 1 Chron. 11 : 15.

Adultery. Ex. 20 : 14. The parties to this crime, according to Jewish law, were a married woman and a man who was not her husband. The Mosaic penalty was that both the guilty parties should be stoned, and it applied as well to the betrothed as to the married woman, provided she were free. Deut. 22 : 22-24. A bondwoman so offending was to be scourged, and the man was to make a trespass offering. Lev. 19 : 20–22. At a later time, and when, owing to Gentile example, the marriage tie became a looser bond of union, public feeling in regard to adultery changed, and the penalty of death was seldom or never inflicted. The famous trial by the waters of jealousy, Num. 5 : 11–29, was probably an ancient custom, which Moses found deeply seated. (But this ordeal was wholly in favor of the innocent, and exactly opposite to most ordeals. For the water which the accused drank was perfectly harmless, and only by a miracle could it produce a bad effect; while in most ordeals the accused must suffer what naturally produces death, and be proved innocent only by a miracle. Symbolically adultery is used to express unfaithfulness to covenant vows to God, who is represented as the husband of his people.)

Adum′mim (*the going up to*), a rising ground or pass "over against Gilgal," and "on the south side of the 'torrent,'" Josh. 15 : 7 ; 18 : 17, which is the position still occupied by the road leading up from Jericho and the Jordan valley to Jerusalem, on the south face of the gorge of the *Wady Kelt*. Luke 10 : 30–36.

Advocate, or *Paraclete,* one that pleads the cause of another. 1 John 2 : 1. Used by Christ, John 14 : 16 ; 15 : 26 ; 16 : 7, to describe the office and work of the Holy Spirit, and translated *Comforter,* i. e. (see margin of Revised Version) Advocate, Helper, Intercessor. This use of the word is derived from the fact that the Jews, being largely ignorant of the Roman law and the Roman language, had to employ Roman *advocates* in their trials before Roman courts. Applied to Christ, 1 John 2 : 1.

Æ′gypt. [EGYPT.]

Æne′as (*laudable*), a paralytic at Lydda healed by St. Peter. Acts 9 : 33, 34.

Æ′non (*springs*), a place "near to Salim," at which John baptized. John 3 : 23. It was evidently west of the Jordan, comp. 3 : 22 with 26, and with 1 : 28, and abounded in water. It is given in the *Onomasticon* as eight miles south of Scythopolis, "near Salem and the Jordan."

Æra. [CHRONOLOGY.]

Æthio′pi-a. [ETHIOPIA.]

Affinity. [MARRIAGE.]

Ag′abus (*a locust*), a Christian prophet in the apostolic age, mentioned in Acts 11 : 28 and 21 : 10. He predicted, Acts 11 : 28, that a famine would take place in the reign of Claudius. Josephus mentions a famine which prevailed in Judea in the reign of Claudius, and swept away many of the inhabitants. (In Acts 21 : 10 we learn that Agabus and Paul met at Cæsarea some time after this.)

A′gag (*flame*), possibly the title of the kings of Amalek, like Pharaoh of Egypt. One king of this name is mentioned in Num. 24 : 7, and another in 1 Sam. 15 : 8, 9, 20, 32. The latter was the king of the Amalekites, whom Saul spared contrary to Jehovah's well-known will. Ex. 17 : 14 ; Deut. 25 : 17. For this act of disobedience Samuel was commissioned to declare to Saul his rejection, and he himself sent for Agag and cut him in pieces. (B.C. about 1070.) [SAMUEL.] Haman is called the AGAGITE in Esther 3 : 1, 10 ; 8 : 3, 5. The Jews consider him a descendant of Agag the Amalekite.

A′gagite. [AGAG.]

A′gar. [HAGAR.]

Agate, a beautifully-veined semi-transparent precious stone, a variety of quartz. Its colors are delicately arranged in stripes or bands or blended in clouds. It is mentioned four times in the text of the Authorized Version, viz., in Ex. 28 : 19 ; 39 : 12 ; Isa. 54 : 12 ; Ezek. 27 : 16. In the two former passages, where it is represented by the Hebrew word *shebo,* it is spoken of as forming the second stone in the third row of the high priest's breastplate ; in each of the two latter places the original word is *cadced,* by which, no doubt, is intended a different stone. [RUBY.] Our English *agate* derives its name from the Achates, on the banks of which it was first found.

Age, Old. The aged occupied a prominent place in the social and political system of the Jews. In *private* life they were looked up to as the depositaries of knowledge, Job 15 : 10 ; the young were ordered to rise up in their presence, Lev. 19 : 32 ; they allowed them to give their opinion first, Job 32 : 4 ; they were taught to regard gray hairs as a "crown of glory," Prov. 16 : 31 ; 20 : 29. The attainment of old age was regarded as a special blessing. Job 5 : 26. In *public* affairs age formed under Moses the main qualification of those who acted as the representatives of the people in all matters of difficulty and deliberation. [ELDERS.]

Ag'ee, or **A'gee** (*fugitive*), a Hararite, father of Shammah, one of David's three mightiest heroes. 2 Sam. 23 : 11. (B.C. 1050.)

Agriculture. This was little cared for by the patriarchs. The pastoral life, however, was the means of keeping the sacred race, whilst yet a family, distinct from mixture and locally unattached, especially whilst in Egypt. When grown into a nation it supplied a similar check on the foreign intercourse, and became the basis of the Mosaic commonwealth. "The land is mine," Lev. 25 : 23, was a dictum which made agriculture likewise the basis of the theocratic relation. Thus every family felt its own life with intense keenness, and had its divine tenure which it was to guard from alienation. The prohibition of culture in the sabbatical year formed a kind of rent reserved by the divine Owner. Landmarks were deemed sacred, Deut. 19 : 14, and the inalienability of the heritage was insured by its reversion to the owner in the year of jubilee; so that only so many years of occupancy could be sold. Lev. 25 : 8–16, 23–35.

Rain.—Water was abundant in Palestine from natural sources. Deut. 8 : 7; 11 : 8–12. Rain was commonly expected soon after the autumnal equinox. The period denoted by the common scriptural expressions of the "early" and the "latter rain," Deut. 11: 14; Jer. 5 : 24; Hos. 6 : 3; Zech. 10 : 1; James 5 : 7, generally reaching from November to April, constituted the "rainy season," and the remainder of the year the "dry season."

Crops.—The cereal crops of constant mention are wheat and barley, and more rarely rye and millet(?). Of the two former, together with the vine, olive and fig, the use of irrigation, the plough and the harrow, mention is made in the book of Job, 31 : 40; 15 : 33; 24 : 6; 29 : 19; 39 : 10. Two kinds of cumin (the black variety called "fitches," Isa. 28 : 27), and such podded plants as beans and lentils, may be named among the staple produce.

Ploughing and Sowing.—The plough was probably very light, one yoke of oxen usually sufficing to draw it. Mountains and steep places were hoed. Isa. 7 : 25. New ground and fallows, Jer. 4 : 3; Hos. 10 : 12, were cleared of stones and of thorns, Isa. 5 : 2, early in the year,

sowing or gathering from "among thorns" being a proverb for slovenly husbandry. Job 5 : 5; Prov. 24 : 30, 31. Sowing also took place without previous ploughing, the seed being scattered broadcast and ploughed in afterwards. The soil was then brushed over with a light harrow, often of thorn bushes. In highly-irrigated spots the seed was trampled in by cattle. Isa. 32 : 20. Seventy days before the passover was the time prescribed for sowing. The oxen were urged on by a goad like a spear. Judges 3 : 31. The proportion of harvest gathered to seed sown was often vast; a hun-

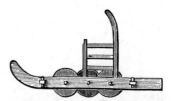

Threshing Instrument (side view).

Threshing Instrument (upper view).

dred fold is mentioned, but in such a way as to signify that it was a limit rarely attained. Gen. 26 : 12; Matt. 13 : 8. Sowing a field with divers seed was forbidden. Deut. 22 : 9.

Reaping and Threshing.—The wheat, etc., was reaped by the sickle or pulled up by the roots. It was bound in sheaves. The sheaves or heaps were carted, Amos 2 : 13, to the floor—a circular spot of hard ground, probably, as now, from 50 to 80 or 100 feet in diameter. Gen. 1 : 10, 11; 2 Sam. 24 : 16, 18. On these the oxen, etc., forbidden to be muzzled, Deut. 25 : 4, trampled out the grain. At a later time the Jews used a threshing sledge called *morag*, Isa. 41 : 15; 2 Sam. 24 : 22; 1 Chron. 21 : 23, probably resembling the *noreg*, still employed in Egypt —a stage with three rollers ridged with iron, which, aided by the driver's weight, crushed out, often injuring, the grain, as well as cut or tore the straw, which thus became fit for fodder. Lighter grains were beaten out with a stick. Isa. 28 : 27. The use of animal manure was frequent. Ps. 83 : 10; 2 Kings 9 : 37; Jer. 8 : 2, etc.

Threshing Floor (Eastern).

Winnowing.—The shovel and fan, Isa. 30 : 24, indicate the process of winnowing—a conspicuous part of ancient husbandry. Ps. 35 : 5; Job 21 : 18; Isa. 17 : 13. Evening was the favorite time, Ruth 3 : 2, when there was mostly a breeze. The fan, Matt. 3 : 12, was perhaps a broad shovel which threw the grain up against the wind. The last process was the shaking in a sieve to separate dirt and refuse. Amos 9 : 9. Fields and floors were not commonly enclosed; vineyards mostly were, with a tower and other buildings. Num. 22 : 24; Ps. 80 : 13; Isa. 5 : 5; Matt. 21 : 33; comp. Judges 6 : 11. The gardens also and orchards were enclosed, frequently by banks of mud from ditches.

With regard to occupancy, a tenant might pay a fixed money rent, Cant. 8 : 11, or a stipulated share of the fruits. 2 Sam. 9 : 10; Matt. 21 : 34. A passer by might eat any quantity of corn or grapes, but not reap or carry off fruit. Deut. 23 : 24, 25; Matt. 12 : 1. The rights of the corner to be left, and of gleaning [CORNER; GLEANING], formed the poor man's claim on the soil for support. For his benefit, too, a sheaf forgotten in carrying to the floor was to be left; so also with regard to the vineyard and the olive grove. Lev. 19 : 9, 10; Deut. 24 : 19.

Agrip'pa. [HEROD.]

A'gur (*a gatherer*, i. e. *together of wise men*), the son of Jakeh, an unknown Hebrew sage, who uttered or collected the sayings of wisdom recorded in Prov. 30.

A'hab (*uncle*). 1. Son of Omri, seventh king of Israel, reigned B.C. 919–896. He married Jezebel, daughter of Ethbaal king of Tyre; and in obedience to her wishes, caused a temple to be built to Baal in Samaria itself, and an oracular grove to be consecrated to Astarte. See 1 Kings 18 : 19. One of Ahab's chief tastes was for splendid architecture, which he showed by building an ivory house and several cities. Desiring to add to his pleasure-grounds at Jezreel the vineyard of his neighbor Naboth, he proposed to buy it or give land in exchange for it; and when this was refused by Naboth in accordance with the Levitical law, Lev. 25 : 23, a false accusation of blasphemy was brought against him, and he was murdered, and Ahab took possession of the coveted fields. 2 Kings 9 : 26. Thereupon Elijah declared that the entire extirpation of Ahab's house was the penalty appointed for his long course of wickedness. [ELIJAH.] The execution, however, of the sentence was delayed in consequence of Ahab's deep repentance. 1 Kings 21.

Ahab undertook three campaigns against Ben-hadad II. king of Damascus, two defensive and one offensive. In the first Ben-hadad laid siege to Samaria, but was repulsed with great loss. 1 Kings 20 : 1–21. Next year Ben-hadad again invaded Israel by way of Aphek, on the east of Jordan; yet Ahab's vict ry was so complete that Ben-hadad himself fell into his hands, but was released contrary to God's will, 1 Kings 20 : 22–34, on condition of restoring the cities of Israel, and admitting Hebrew commissioners into Damascus. After this great success Ahab enjoyed peace for three years, when he attacked Ramoth in Gilead, on the east of Jordan, in conjunction with Jehoshaphat king of Judah, which town he claimed as belonging to Israel. Being told by the prophet Micaiah that he would fall, he disguised himself, but was slain by "a certain man who drew a bow at a venture." When buried in Samaria, the dogs licked up his blood as a servant was washing his chariot; a partial fulfillment of Elijah's prediction, 1 Kings 21 : 19, which was more literally accomplished in the case of his son. 2 Kings 9 : 26.

2. A lying prophet, who deceived the captive Israelites in Babylon, and was burnt to death by Nebuchadnezzar. Jer. 29 : 21.

Ahar'ah (*after the brother*), third son of Benjamin. 1 Chron. 8 : 1. [AHER; AHIRAM.]

Ahar'hel (*behind the breastwork*), a name occurring in an obscure fragment of the genealogies of Judah. 1 Chron. 4 : 8.

Ahas'a-i (*whom Jehovah holds*), a priest, ancestor of Maasiai, Neh. 11 : 13; ralled JAHZERAH in 1 Chron. 9 : 12.

Ahas'ba-i (*blooming*), father of Eliphelet, one of David's thirty-seven captains. 2 Sam. 23 : 34. In the corrupt list in 1 Chron. 11 : 35, Eliphelet appears as "Eliphal the son of Ur." (B.C. about 1050.)

Ahashve'rosh. Another (the Hebrew) form of AHASUERUS. Ezra 4 : 6, in margin.

Ahasue'rus (*lion-king*), the name of one Median and two Persian kings mentioned in the Old Testament.

1. In Dan. 9 : 1 Ahasuerus is said to be the father of Darius the Mede. [DARIUS.] This first Ahasuerus is Cyaxares, the conqueror of Nineveh. (Began to reign B.C. 634.)

2. The Ahasuerus king of Persia, referred to in Ezra 4 : 6, must be Cambyses, thought to be Cyrus' successor, and perhaps his son. (B.C. 529.)

3. The third is the Ahasuerus of the book of Esther. This Ahasuerus is probably Xerxes of history, Esther 1 : 1 (B.C. 485), and this conclusion is fortified by the resemblance of character and by certain chronological indications, the accounts of his life and character agreeing with the book of Esther. In the third year of Ahasuerus was held a great feast and assembly in Shushan the palace, Esther 1 : 3, following a council held to consider the invasion of Greece. He divorced his queen Vashti for refusing to appear in public at this banquet, and married, four years afterwards, the Jewess Esther, cousin and ward of Mor-

decai. Five years after this, Haman, one of his counsellors, having been slighted by Mordecai, prevailed upon the king to order the destruction of all the Jews in the empire. But before the day appointed for the massacre, Esther and Mordecai induced the king to put Haman to death, and to give the Jews the right of self-defence.

Aha'va (*water*), a place, Ezra 8 : 15, or a river, 8 : 21, on the banks of which Ezra collected the second expedition which returned with him from Babylon to Jerusalem. Perhaps it is the modern *Hit*, on the Euphrates due east of Damascus.

A'haz (*possessor*), eleventh king of Judah, son of Jotham, reigned 741–726, about sixteen years. At the time of his accession, Rezin king of Damascus and Pekah king of Israel had recently formed a league against Judah, and they proceeded to lay siege to Jerusalem. Upon this Isaiah hastened to give advice and encouragement to Ahaz, and the allies failed in their attack on Jerusalem. Isa. 7, 8, 9. But the allies inflicted a most severe injury on Judah by the capture of Elath, a flourishing port on the Red Sea, while the Philistines invaded the west and south. 2 Kings 16; 2 Chron. 28. Ahaz, having forfeited God's favor by his wickedness, sought deliverance from these numerous troubles by appealing to Tiglath-pileser king of Assyria, who freed him from his most formidable enemies. But Ahaz had to purchase this help at a costly price; he became tributary to Tiglath-pileser. He was weak, a gross idolater, and sought safety in heathen ceremonies, making his son pass through the fire to Molech, consulting wizards and necromancers, Isa. 8 : 19, and other idolatrous practices. 2 Kings 23 : 12. His only service of permanent value was the introduction of the sun-dial. He died at the age of 36, but was refused a burial with the kings his ancestors. 2 Chron. 28 : 27.

2. Son of Micah. 1 Chron. 8 : 35, 36; 9 : 42.

Ahazi'ah (*sustained by the Lord*). 1. Son of Ahab and Jezebel, eighth king of Israel, reigned B.C. 896–895. After the battle of Ramoth in Gilead, in which Ahab perished [AHAB], the vassal king of Moab refused his yearly tribute; comp. Isa. 16 : 1. Before Ahaziah could take measures for enforcing his claim, he was seriously injured by a fall through a lattice in his palace at Samaria. Being an idolater, he sent to inquire of the oracle of Baalzebub in the Philistine city of Ekron whether he should recover his health. But Elijah, who now for the last time exercised the prophetic office, rebuked him for this impiety, and announced to him his approaching death. The only other recorded transaction of his reign, his endeavor to join the king of Judah in trading to Ophir, is related under JEHOSHAPHAT. 1 Kings 22 : 49-53; 2 Kings 1; 2 Chron. 20 : 35-37.

2. Fifth king of Judah, son of Jehoram and Athaliah (daughter of Ahab), and therefore nephew of the preceding Ahaziah, reigned one year, B.C. 884. He is called AZARIAH, 2 Chron. 22 : 6, probably by a copyist's error, and JEHOAHAZ. 2 Chron. 21 : 17. He was 22 years old at his accession. 2 Kings 8 : 26 (his age 42, in 2 Chron. 22 : 2, is a copyist's error). Ahaziah was an idolater, and he allied himself with his uncle Jehoram king of Israel against Hazael, the new king of Syria. The two kings were, however, defeated at Ramoth, where Jehoram was severely wounded. The revolution carried out in Israel by Jehu under the guidance of Elisha broke out while Ahaziah was visiting his uncle at Jezreel. As Jehu approached the town, Jehoram and Ahaziah went out to meet him; the former was shot through the heart by Jehu, and Ahaziah was pursued and mortally wounded. He died when he reached Megiddo.

Ah'ban (*brother of the wise; discreet*), son of Abishur by his wife Abihail. 1 Chron. 2 : 29. He was of the tribe of Judah.

A'her (*following*), ancestor of Hushim, a Benjamite. The name occurs in the genealogy of Benjamin. 1 Chron. 7 : 12. It is not improbable that Aher and Ahiram, Num. 26 : 38, are the same.

A'hi (*a brother*). 1. A Gadite, chief of a family who lived in Gilead in Bashan, 1 Chron. 5 : 15, in the days of Jotham king of Judah. (B.C. 758.)

2. A descendant of Shamer, of the tribe of Asher. 1 Chron. 7 : 34.

Ahi'ah, or **Ahi'jah** (*friend of Jehovah*). 1. Son of Ahitub, grandson of Phinehas and great-grandson of Eli, succeeded his father as high priest in the reign of Saul. 1 Sam. 14 : 3, 18. Ahiah is probably the same person as Ahimelech the son of Ahitub. (B.C. 980.)

2. One of Solomon's princes. 1 Kings 4 : 3.

3. A prophet of Shiloh, 1 Kings 14 : 2, hence called the Shilonite, 11 : 29, of whom we have two remarkable prophecies extant, the one in 1 Kings 11 : 30-39, addressed to Jeroboam, announcing the rending of the ten tribes from Solomon; the other in 1 Kings 14 : 6-16, in which he foretold the death of Abijah, the king's son, who was sick, and the destruction of Jeroboam's house on account of the images which he had set up. 1 Kings 14 : 2, 3. (B.C. about 956.)

4. Father of Baasha king of Israel. 1 Kings 15 : 27, 33.

5. Son of Jerahmeel. 1 Chron. 2 : 25.

6. Son of Bela. 1 Chron. 8 : 7.

7. One of David's mighty men. 1 Chron. 11 : 36.

8. A Levite in David's reign. 1 Chron. 26 : 20.

9. One of the "heads of the people" who joined in the covenant with Nehemiah. Neh. 10 : 26.

Ahi'am, son of Sharar the Hararite (or of Sacar, 1 Chron. 11 : 35), one of David's thirty mighty men. 2 Sam. 23 : 33. (B.C. 1050.)

Ahi'an, a Manassite of the family of Shemidah. 1 Chron. 7 : 19.

Ahi-e'zer (*brother of help*). 1. Son of Ammishaddai, hereditary chieftain of the tribe of Dan. Num. 1 : 12; 2 : 25; 7 : 66. (B.C. 1490.)

2. The Benjamite chief of a body of archers in the time of David. 1 Chron. 12 : 3. (B.C. 1050.)

Ahi'hud (*brother of renown*). 1. The son of Shelomi and prince of the tribe of Asher. Num. 34 : 27.

2. Chieftain of the tribe of Benjamin. 1 Chron. 8 : 7.

Ahi'jah. [AHIAH.]

Ahi'kam (*a brother who raises up*), son of Shaphan the scribe, an influential officer at the court of Josiah, was one of the delegates sent by Hilkiah to consult Huldah. 2 Kings 22 : 12-14. In the reign of Jehoiakim he successfully used his influence to protect the prophet Jeremiah. Jer. 26 : 24. He was the father of Gedaliah. [GEDALIAH.] (B.C. 641.)

Ahi'lud (*a brother of one born*, i. e. before him). 1. Father of Jehoshaphat, the recorder or chronicler of the kingdom in the reigns of David and Solomon. 2 Sam. 8 : 16; 20 : 24; 1 Kings 4 : 3; 1 Chron. 18 : 15. (B.C. before 1015.)

2. The father of Baana, one of Solomon's twelve commissariat officers. 1 Kings 4 : 12. It is uncertain whether he is the same with the foregoing.

Ahim'a-az (*brother of anger*). 1. Son of Zadok, the high priest in David's reign, and celebrated for his swiftness of foot. During Absalom's rebellion he carried to David the important intelligence that Ahithophel had counselled an immediate attack upon David and his followers. 2 Sam. 15 : 24–37 ; 17 : 15–22. Shortly afterwards he was the first to bring to the king the good news of Absalom's defeat. 2 Sam. 18 : 19–33. (B.C. 972–956.)
2. Saul's wife's father. 1 Sam. 14 : 50. (B.C. before 1093.)
3. Solomon's son-in-law. 1 Kings 4 : 15. (B.C. after 1014.)

Ahi'man (*brother of the right hand*). 1. One of the three giant Anakim who inhabited Mount Hebron, Num. 13 : 22, 23, seen by Caleb and the spies. (B.C. 1490.) The whole race was cut off by Joshua, Josh. 11 : 21, and the three brothers were slain by the tribe of Judah. Judges 1 : 10.
2. A Levite porter. 1 Chron. 9 : 17.

Ahim'elech (*brother of the king*). 1. Son of Ahitub, 1 Sam. 22 : 11, 12, and high priest at Nob in the days of Saul. He gave David the shew-bread to eat, and the sword of Goliath ; and for so doing was put to death, with his whole house, by Saul's order. Abiathar alone escaped. [ABIATHAR.] (B.C. 1085–1060.)
2. A Hittite. 1 Sam. 26 : 6.

Ahi'moth (*brother of death*), a Levite apparently in the time of David. 1 Chron. 6 : 25. In v. 35, for *Ahimoth* we find MAHATH, as in Luke 3 : 26.

Ahin'adab (*brother the noble*, i. e. *a noble brother*), son of Iddo, one of Solomon's twelve commissaries who supplied provisions for the royal household. 1 Kings 4 : 14. (B.C. 1014–975.)

Ahin'o-am (*brother of grace*, i. e. *gracious*). 1. The daughter of Ahimaaz and wife of Saul. 1 Sam. 14 : 50. (B.C. about 1090.)
2. A native of Jezreel who was married to David during his wandering life. 1 Sam. 25 : 43. (B.C. 1060.) She lived with him and his other wife Abigail at the court of Achish, 27 : 3 ; was taken prisoner with her by the Amalekites when they plundered Ziklag, 30 : 5, but was rescued by David. 30 : 18.

Ahi'o (*brotherly*). 1. Son of Abinadab, who accompanied the ark when it was brought out of his father's house. 2 Sam. 6 : 3, 4 ; 1 Chron. 13 : 7. (B.C. 1043.)
2. A Benjamite, one of the sons of Beriah. 1 Chron. 8 : 14.
3. A Benjamite, son of Jehiel. 1 Chron. 8 : 31 ; 9 : 37.

Ahi'ra (*brother of evil*, i. e. *unlucky*), chief of the tribe of Naphtali. Num. 1 : 15 ; 2 : 29 ; 7 : 78, 83 ; 10 : 27.

Ahi'ram (*brother of height, lofty*), one of the sons of Benjamin, and ancestor of the AHIRAMITES. Num. 26 : 38. In Gen. 46 : 21 the name appears as "Ehi and Rosh." It is uncertain whether Ahiram is the same as AHER, 1 Chron. 7 : 12, or AHARAH, 1 Chron. 8 : 1.

Ahis'amach (*brother of help*), a Danite, father of Aholiab, one of the architects of the tabernacle. Ex. 31 : 6 ; 35 : 34 ; 38 : 23. (B.C. 1490.)

Ahish'ahar (*brother of the dawn*), one of the sons of Bilhan, the grandson of Benjamin. 1 Chron. 7 : 10.

Ahi'shar, the controller of Solomon's household. 1 Kings 4 : 6.

Ahith'ophel (*brother of foolishness*), a native of Giloh, was a privy councillor of David, whose wisdom was highly esteemed, though his name had an exactly opposite signification. 2 Sam. 16 : 23. (B.C. 1055–1023.) He was the grandfather of Bath-sheba. Comp. 2 Sam. 11 : 3 with 23 : 34. Ahithophel joined the conspiracy of Absalom against David, and persuaded him to take possession of the royal harem, 2 Sam. 16 : 21, and recommended an immediate pursuit of David. His advice was wise ; but Hushai advised otherwise. When Ahithophel saw that Hushai's advice prevailed, he despaired of success, and returning to his own home "put his household in order and hanged himself." 2 Sam. 17 : 1–23.

Ahi'tub (*brother of goodness*). 1. The son of Phinehas and grandson of Eli, and therefore of the family of Ithamar. 1 Sam. 14 : 3 ; 22 : 9, 11. (B.C. 1125.) He was succeeded by his son Ahijah (AHIMELECH). (B.C. 1085.)
2. Son of Amariah, and father of Zadok the high priest, 1 Chron. 6 : 7, 8 ; 2 Sam. 8 : 17, of the house of Eleazar. (B.C. before 1045.)

Ah'lab (*fertile*), a city of Asher from which the Canaanites were not driven out. Judges 1 : 31.

Ahla'i, or **Ah'la-i** (*ornamental*), daughter of Sheshan, whom, having no issue, he gave in marriage to his Egyptian slave Jarha. 1 Chron. 2 : 31, 35. From her were descended Zabad, one of David's mighty men, 1 Chron. 11 : 41, and Azariah, one of the captains of hundreds in the reign of Joash. 2 Chron. 23 : 1.

Aho'ah (*brotherly*), son of Bela, the son of Benjamin. 1 Chron. 8 : 4. In 1 Chron. 8 : 7 he is called AHIAH. The patronymic, AHOHITE, is found in 2 Sam. 23 : 9, 28 ; 1 Chron. 11 : 12, 29 ; 27 : 4.

Aho'hite. [AHOAH.]

Aho'lah and **Aho'libah** (*my tabernacle*), two symbolical names, are described as harlots, the former representing Samaria and the latter Judah. Ezek. 23.

Aho'li-ab, a Danite of great skill as a weaver and embroiderer, whom Moses appointed with Bezaleel to erect the tabernacle. Ex. 35 : 30–35. (B.C. 1490.)

Aholiba'mah, or **Aholib'amah** (*my tabernacle is exalted*), one of the three wives of Esau. (B.C. 1797.) She was the daughter of Anah. Gen. 36 : 2, 25. In the earlier narrative, Gen. 26 : 34 Aholibamah is called Judith, which may have been her original name.

Ahuma'i (*brother of water,* i. e. *cowardly*), son of Jahath, a descendant of Judah, and head of one of the families of the Zorathites. 1 Chron. 4 : 2.

Ahu'zam (*possession*), properly Ahuzzam, son of Ashur, the father or founder of Tekoa, by his wife Naarah. 1 Chron. 4 : 6.

Ahuz'zath (*possessions*), one of the friends of the Philistine king Abimelech, who accompanied him at his interview with Isaac. Gen. 26 : 26. (B.C. about 1877.)

A'i (*heap of ruins*). 1. A city lying east of Bethel and "beside Bethaven." Josh. 7 : 2 ; 8 : 9. It was the second city taken by Israel after the passage of the Jordan, and was "utterly destroyed." Josh. 7 : 3–5 ; 8 ; 9 : 3 ; 10 : 1, 2 ; 12 : 9.

2. A city of the Ammonites, apparently attached to Heshbon. Jer. 49 : 3.

A-i'ah (*clamor*). 1. Son of Zibeon, a descendant of Seir and ancestor of one of the wives of Esau, 1 Chron. 1 : 40, called in Gen. 36 : 24 AJAH. He probably died before his father, as the succession fell to his brother Anah.

2. Father of Rizpah, the concubine of Saul. 2 Sam. 3 : 7 ; 21 : 8, 10, 11. (B.C. before 1040.)

A-i'ath (feminine of *Ai*), a place named by Isaiah, Isa. 10 : 28, in connection with Migron and Michmash, probably the same as Ai.

A-i'ja, like Aiath probably a variation of the name Ai, mentioned with Michmash and Bethel. Neh. 11 : 31.

Aij'alon, or **Aj'alon** (*place of gazelles*). 1. A city of the Kohathites. Josh. 21 : 24 ; 1 Chron. 6 : 69. It was a Levitical city and a city of refuge. It was originally allotted to the tribe of Dan, Josh. 19 : 42 ; Authorized Version, AJALON, which tribe, however, was unable to dispossess the Amorites of the place. Judges 1 : 35. Aijalon was one of the towns fortified by Rehoboam, 2 Chron. 11 : 10, and the last we hear of it is as being in the hands of the Philistines. 2 Chron. 28 : 18. Being on the very frontier of the two kingdoms, we can understand how Aijalon should be spoken of sometimes, 1 Chron. 6 : 69, comp. with 66, as in Ephraim, and sometimes, 2 Chron. 11 : 10 ; 1 Sam. 14 : 31, as in Judah and Benjamin. It is represented by the modern *Yalo*, a little to the north of the Jaffa road, about 14 miles out of Jerusalem.

2. A broad and beautiful valley near the city of Aijalon over which Joshua commanded the moon to stand still during the pursuit after the battle of Gibeon. Josh. 10 : 12.

3. A place in Zebulon, mentioned as the burial-place of Elon, one of the Judges. Judges 12 : 12.

Aij'eleth Sha'har (*the hind of the morning dawn*), found once only in the Bible, in the title of Ps. 22. It probably describes to the musician the melody to which the psalm was to be played.

A'in (*spring, well*). 1. One of the landmarks on the eastern boundary of Palestine. Num. 34 : 11. It is probably *'Ain el-'Azy*, the main source of the Orontes.

2. One of the southernmost cities of Judah, Josh. 15 : 32 ; afterwards allotted to Simeon, Josh. 19 : 7 ; 1 Chron. 4 : 32, and given to the priests. Josh. 21 : 16.

A'jah = **A-i'ah,** 1. Gen. 36 : 24.

Aj'alon. [AIJALON.]

A'kan (*sharp-sighted*), son of Ezer, one of the "dukes" or chieftains of the Horites, and descendant of Seir. Gen. 36 : 27. He is called JAKAN in 1 Chron. 1 : 42.

Akel'dama. Revised Version of Acts 1 : 19 for ACELDAMA.

Ak'kub (*insidious*). 1. A descendant of Zerubbabel and son of Elioenai. 1 Chron. 3 : 24.

2. One of the porters or doorkeepers

at the east gate of the temple. (B.C. 536–440.)

3. One of the Nethinim, whose family returned with Zerubbabel. Ezra 2 : 45. (B.C. 536.)

4. A Levite who assisted Ezra in expounding the law to the people. Neh. 8 : 7.

Akrab'bim (*the ascent of*, or *the going up to*); also MAALEH-ACRABBIM (*the scorpion pass*), a pass between the south end of the Dead Sea and Zin, forming one of the landmarks on the south boundary at once of Judah, Josh. 15 : 3, and of the Holy Land. Num. 34 : 4. Also the boundary of the Amorites. Judges 1 : 36. As to the name, scorpions abound in the whole of this district.

Alabaster, from the Arabic *al bastraton*, a whitish stone, or from *Albastron*,

Alabaster Vases.
Inscription on the centre vessel denotes the quantity it holds.

the place in Egypt where it is found. It occurs only in Matt. 26 : 7; Mark 14 : 3; Luke 7 : 37. The ancients considered alabaster to be the best material in which to preserve their ointments. The Oriental alabaster (referred to in the Bible) is a translucent carbonate of lime, formed on the floors of limestone caves by the percolation of water. It is of the same material as our marbles, but differently formed. It is usually clouded or banded like agate, hence sometimes called onyx marble.

Our common alabaster is different from this, being a variety of gypsum or sulphate of lime, used in its finer forms for vases, etc.; in the coarser it is ground up for plaster of Paris. The noted sculptured slabs from Nineveh are made of this material.

Al'ameth, properly **Al'emeth** (*covering*), one of the sons of Becher, the son of Benjamin. 1 Chron. 7 : 8.

Alam'melech (*king's oak*), a place within the limits of Asher, named between Achshaph and Amad. Josh. 19 : 26 only.

Al'amoth (*virgins*). Ps. 46, title; 1 Chron. 15 : 20. Some interpret it to mean a musical instrument, and others a melody.

Al'emeth (*covering*), a Benjamite, son of Jehoadah or Jarah, 1 Chron. 8 : 36; 9 : 42, and descended from Jonathan the son of Saul. (B.C. after 1077.)

Alexan'der III. (*helper of men—brave*), king of Macedon, surnamed the Great, the son of Philip and Olympias, was born at Pella B.C. 356, and succeeded his father B.C. 336. Two years afterwards he crossed the Hellespont (B.C. 334) to carry out the plans of his father, and execute the mission of Greece to the civilized world. He subjugated Syria and Palestine B.C. 334–332. Egypt next submitted to him B.C. 332, and in this year he founded Alexandria. In the same year he finally defeated Darius at Gaugamela, who in B.C. 330 was murdered. The next two years were occupied by Alexander in the consolidation of his Persian conquests and the reduction of Bactria. In B.C. 327 he crossed the Indus; turning westward he reached Susa B.C. 325, and proceeded to Babylon B.C. 324, which he chose as the capital of his empire. In the next year (B.C. 323) he died there of intemperance, at the early age of 32, in the midst of his gigantic plans; and those who inherited his conquests left his designs unachieved and unattempted. cf. Dan. 7 : 6; 8 : 5; 11 : 3. Alexander is intended in Dan. 2 : 39 and also Dan. 7 : 6; 8 : 5–7; 11 : 3, 4, the latter indicating the rapidity of his conquests and his power. He ruled with great dominion, and did according to his will, Dan. 11 : 3; "and there was none that could deliver . . . . out of his hand." Dan. 8 : 7.

Alexan'der. 1. Son of Simon the Cyrenian, who was compelled to bear the cross for our Lord. Mark 15 : 21.

2. One of the kindred of Annas the high priest. Acts 4 : 6.

3. A Jew at Ephesus whom his countrymen put forward during the tumult raised by Demetrius the silversmith, Acts 19 : 33, to plead their cause with the mob.

4. An Ephesian Christian reprobated by St. Paul in 1 Tim. 1 : 20 as having, together with one Hymenæus, put from him faith and a good conscience, and so made shipwreck concerning the faith. This may be the same with

5. Alexander the coppersmith, mentioned by the same apostle, 2 Tim. 4 : 14, as having done him many mischiefs.

Alexan′dri-a, or **Alexandri′a** (from *Alexander*), 3 Macc. 3 : 1; Acts 18 : 24; 6 : 9, the Hellenic, Roman and Christian capital of Egypt.

Situation.—(Alexandria was situated on the Mediterranean Sea, directly opposite the island of Pharos, 12 miles west of the Canopic branch of the Nile and 120 miles from the present city of Cairo.) It was founded by Alexander the Great, B.C. 332, who himself traced the ground plan of the city. The work thus begun was continued after the death of Alexander by the Ptolemies.

Description.—Under the despotism of the later Ptolemies the trade of Alexandria declined, but its population and wealth were enormous. Its importance as one of the chief corn-ports of Rome secured for it the general favor of the first emperors. Its population was mixed from the first. According to Josephus, Alexander himself assigned to the Jews a place in his new city. Philo estimates the number of the Alexandrine Jews in his time at a little less than 1,000,000; and adds that two of the five districts of Alexandria were called "Jewish districts," and that many Jews lived scattered in the remaining three. "For a long period Alexandria was the greatest of known cities." After Rome became the chief city of the world, Alexandria ranked second to Rome in wealth and importance, and second to Athens only in literature and science. Its collection of books grew to be the greatest library of ancient times, and contained at one time 700,000 rolls or volumes. Here was made the Septuagint translation of the Old Testament into Greek, begun about B.C. 285. The commerce of Alexandria, especially in grain, was very great. According to the common legend, St. Mark first "preached the gospel in Egypt, and founded the first church in Alexandria." At the beginning of the second century the number of Christians at Alexandria must have been very large, and the great leaders of Gnosticism who arose there (Basilides, Valentinus) exhibit an exaggeration of the tendency of the Church.

Present Condition.—The city is now called *Scanderia.* Its population in 1871 was 219,000 (*Encyc. Brit.*), and is increasing. "Cleopatra's Needle," lately set up in New York, was taken from this city.

Alexan′drians, the Jewish colonists of Alexandria, who were admitted to the

The Almug.

privileges of citizenship and had had a synagogue at Jerusalem. Acts 6 : 9.

Algum or **Almug Trees,** the former occurring in 2 Chron. 2 : 8; 9 : 10, 11, the latter in 1 Kings 10 : 11, 12. These words are identical. From 1 Kings 10 : 11, 12; 2 Chron. 9 : 10, 11, we learn that the almug was brought in great plenty from Ophir for Solomon's temple and house, and for the construction of musical instruments. It is probable that this tree is the red sandal wood, which is a native of India and Ceylon. The wood is very heavy, hard and fine grained, and of a beautiful garnet color.

Ali′ah. [ALVAH.]

Ali′an. [ALVAN.]

Allegory, a figure of speech, which has been defined by Bishop Marsh, in accordance with its etymology, as "a representation of one thing which is intended to excite the representation of another thing." ("A figurative representation containing a meaning other than and in addition to the literal." "A fable or parable is a short allegory with one definite moral."—*Encyc. Brit.*) In every allegory there is a twofold sense—the immediate or historic, which is understood from the words, and the ultimate, which is concerned with the things signified by the words. The allegorical interpretation is not of the words, but of the things signified by them, and not only may, but actually does, coexist with the literal interpretation in every allegory, whether the narrative in which it is conveyed be of things possible or real. An illustration of this may be seen in Gal. 4 : 24, where the apostle gives an allegorical interpretation to the historical narrative of Hagar and Sarah, not treating that narrative as an allegory in itself, as our Authorized Version would lead us to suppose, but drawing from it a deeper sense than is conveyed by the immediate representation. (Addison's *Vision of Mirza* and Bunyan's *Pilgrim's Progress* are among the best allegories in all literature.)

Alleluia, so written in Rev. 19 : 6, foll., or more properly HALLELUJAH, *praise ye Jehovah*, as it is found in the margin of Ps. 104 : 35; 105 : 45; 106; 111 : 1; 112 : 1; 113 : 1; comp. Ps. 113 : 9; 115 : 18; 116 : 19; 117 : 2. The literal meaning of "hallelujah" sufficiently indicates the character of the Psalms in which it occurs as hymns of praise and thanksgiving.

Alliances. On the first establishment of the Hebrews in Palestine no connections were formed between them and the surrounding nations. But with the extension of their power under the kings alliances became essential to the security of their commerce. Solomon concluded two important treaties exclusively for commercial purposes; the first with Hiram king of Tyre, 1 Kings 5 : 2–12; 9 : 27, the second with a Pharaoh, king of Egypt. 1 Kings 10 : 28, 29. When war broke out between Amaziah and Jeroboam II. a coalition was formed between Rezin, king of Syria, and Pekah on the one side, and Ahaz and Tiglath-pileser, king of Assyria, on the other. 2 Kings 16 : 5–9.

The formation of an alliance was attended with various religious rites. A victim was slain and divided into two parts, between which the contracting parties passed. Gen. 15 : 10. Generally speaking, the oath alone is mentioned in the contracting of alliances, either between nations, Josh. 9 : 15, or individuals. Gen. 25 : 28; 31 : 53; 1 Sam. 20 : 17; 2 Kings 11 : 4. The event was celebrated by a feast. Gen. *l. c.*; Ex. 24 : 11; 2 Sam. 3 : 12, 20. Salt, as symbolical of fidelity, was used on these occasions. Occasionally a pillar or a heap of stones was set up as a memorial of the alliance. Gen. 31 : 52. Presents were also sent by the parties soliciting the alliance. 1 Kings 15 : 18; Isa. 30 : 6; 1 Macc. 15 : 18. The fidelity of the Jews to their engagements was conspicuous at all periods of their history, Josh. 9 : 18, and any breach of covenant was visited with very severe punishment. 2 Sam. 21 : 1; Ezek. 17 : 16.

Al′lon (*an oak*), a Simeonite, ancestor of Ziza, a prince of his tribe in the reign of Hezekiah. 1 Chron. 4 : 37. (B.C. 727.)

Allon, a large strong tree of some description, probably an oak.

1. ALLON, more accurately ELON, a place named among the cities of Naphtali. Josh. 19 : 33. Probably the more correct construction is to take it with the following word, *i. e.*, "the oak by Zaanannim." [ELON.]

2. ALLON-BACHUTH (*oak of weeping*), the tree under which Rebekah's nurse, Deborah, was buried. Gen. 35 : 8.

Almo′dad (*measure*), the first in order of the descendants of Joktan. Gen. 10 : 26; 1 Chron. 1 : 20.

Al′mon (*concealed*), a city within the tribe of Benjamin, with "suburbs" given to the priests. Josh. 21 : 18. [ALEMETH.]

Al′mon-diblatha′im (*concealing the two cakes*), one of the latest stations of the Israelites, between Dibon-gad and the mountains of Abarim. Num. 33 : 46, 47. It is probably identical with Beth-diblathaim.

Almond Tree; Almond. This word is found in Gen. 43 : 11; Ex. 25 : 33, 34; 37 : 19, 20; Num. 17 : 8; Eccles. 12 : 5; Jer. 1 : 11, in the text f the Authorized Version. It is invariably represented by the same Hebrew word, *shaked*, meaning *hasten*. Jer. 1 : 11, 12. The almond tree is a native of Asia and North Africa, but it is cultivated in the milder parts of Europe. " It resembles the peach tree in form, blossom and fruit. It is in fact only another species of the same genus." The height of the tree is about 12 or 14 feet; the flowers are pink, and arranged for the most part in pairs; the leaves are long, ovate, with a serrated margin and

Almond.

an acute point. The covering of the fruit is downy and succulent, enclosing the hard shell which contains the kernel. It is this nut for which the tree is chiefly valued. It is curious to observe, in connection with the almond-bowls of the golden candlestick, that, in the language of lapidaries, almonds are pieces of rock crystal, even now used in adorning branch candlesticks.

Alms. The duty of alms-giving, especially in kind, consisting chiefly in portions to be left designedly from produce of the field, the vineyard and the oliveyard, Lev. 19 : 9, 10 ; 23 : 22 ; Deut. 15 : 11 ; 24 : 19 ; 26 : 2–13 ; Ruth 2 : 2, is strictly enjoined by the law. Every third year also, Deut. 14 : 28, each proprietor was directed to share the tithe of his produce with "the Levite, the stranger, the fatherless and the widow." The theological estimate of alms-giving among the Jews is indicated in the following passages : Job 31 : 17 ; Prov. 10 : 2 ; 11 : 4 ; Esther 9 : 22 ; Ps. 112 : 9 ; Acts 9 : 36, the case of Dorcas ; 10 : 2, of Cornelius ; to which may be added Tobit 4 : 10, 11 ; 14 : 10, 11, and Ecclus. 3 : 30 ; 40 : 24. The Pharisees were zealous in alms-giving, but too ostentatious in their mode

of performance, for which our Lord finds fault with them. Matt. 6 : 2. The duty of relieving the poor was not neglected by the Christians. Matt. 6 : 1–4 ; Luke 14 : 13 ; Acts 20 : 35 ; Gal. 2 : 10. Regular proportionate giving was expected. Acts 11 : 30 ; Rom. 15 : 25–27 ; 1 Cor. 16 : 1–4.

Almug Trees. [ALGUM TREES.]

Aloes, Lign Aloes (in Heb. *Ahalim*, *Ahaloth*), the name of a costly and sweet-smelling wood which is mentioned in Num. 24 : 6 ; Ps. 45 : 8 ; Prov. 7 : 17 ; Cant. 4 : 14 ; John 19 : 39. It is usually

Lign Aloes.

identified with the *Aquilaria agallochum*, an aromatic wood much valued in India. This tree sometimes grows to the height of 120 feet, being 12 feet in girth.

A'loth, a place or district, forming with Asher the jurisdiction of the ninth of Solomon's commissariat officers. 1 Kings 4 : 16.

Alpha (A), the first letter of the Greek alphabet. With *Omega* (Ω), the last letter, it is used in the Old Testament and in the New to express the eternity of God, as including both the beginning and the end. Rev. 1 : 8, 11 ; 21 : 6 ; 22 : 13 ; Isa. 41 : 4 ; 44 : 6 ; hence these letters became a favorite symbol of the eternal divinity of our Lord, and were used for this purpose in connection with the

cross, or the monogram of Christ (*i. e.* the first two letters, *ch* and *r*, of Christ's name in Greek). Both Greeks and Hebrews employed the letters of the alphabet as numerals.

Alphabet. [WRITING.]

Alphæ'us (*changing*), the father of the apostle James the Less, Matt. 10 : 3; Mark 3 : 18; Luke 6 : 15; Acts 1 : 13, and husband of Mary. John 19 : 25. [MARY.] In this latter place he is called Clopas (not, as in the Authorized Version, Cleophas).

Altar. The first altar of which we have any account is that built by Noah when he left the ark. Gen. 8 : 20. In the early times altars were usually built in certain spots hallowed by religious associations, *e.g.*, where God appeared. Gen. 12 : 7; 13 : 18; 26 : 25; 35 : 1. Though generally erected for the offering of sacrifice, in some instances they appear to have been only memorials. Gen. 12 : 7; Ex. 17 : 15, 16. Altars were most probably originally made of earth. The law of Moses allowed them to be made of either earth or unhewn stones. Ex. 20 : 24, 25.

I. *The Altar of Burnt Offering.* It differed in construction at different times. (1) In the tabernacle, Ex. 27 : 1 ff.; 38 : 1 ff., it was comparatively small and portable. In shape it was square. It was five cubits in length, the same in breadth, and three cubits high. It was made of planks of shittim (or acacia) wood overlaid with brass. The interior was hollow. Ex. 27 : 8. At the four corners were four projections called horns, made, like the altar itself, of shittim wood overlaid with brass, Ex. 27 : 2, and to them the victim was bound when about to be sacrificed. Ps. 118 : 27. Round the altar, midway between the top and bottom, ran a projecting ledge, on which perhaps the priest stood when officiating. To the outer edge of this, again, a grating or network of brass was affixed, and reached to the bottom of the altar. At the four corners of the network were four brazen rings, into which were inserted the staves by which the altar was carried. These staves were of the same materials as the altar itself. As the priests were forbidden to ascend the altar by steps, Ex. 20 : 26, it has been conjectured that a slope of earth led gradually up to the ledge from which they officiated. The place of the altar was at "the door of the tabernacle of the congregation." Ex. 40 : 29. (2) In Solomon's temple the altar was considerably larger in its dimensions. It differed too in the material of which it was made, being entirely of brass. 1 Kings 8 : 64; 2 Chron. 7 : 7. It had no grating, and instead of a single gradual slope, the ascent to it was probably made by three successive platforms, to each of which it has been supposed that steps led. The

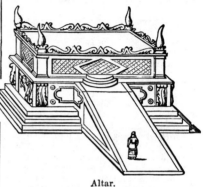

Altar.

altar erected by Herod in front of the temple was 15 cubits in height and 50 cubits in length and breadth. According to Lev. 6 : 12, 13, a perpetual fire was to be kept burning on the altar.

II. *The Altar of Incense*, called also the *golden* altar to distinguish it from the altar of burnt offering, which was called the *brazen* altar. Ex. 38 : 30. (*a*) That in the tabernacle was made of acacia wood, overlaid with pure gold. In shape it was square, being a cubit in length and breadth and two cubits in height. Like the altar of burnt offering it had horns at the four corners, which were of one piece with the rest of the altar. This altar stood in the holy place, "before the vail that is by the ark of the testimony." Ex. 30 : 6; 40 : 5. (*b*) The altar of Solomon's temple was similar, 1 Kings 7 : 48; 1 Chron. 28 : 18, but was made of cedar overlaid with gold.

III. *Other Altars.* In Acts 17 : 23 reference is made to an altar to an unknown god. There were several altars in Athens with this inscription, erected during the time of a plague, since they knew not what god was offended and required to be propitiated.

Al-taschith (*destroy not*), found in the introductory verse to Psalms 57, 58, 59, 75. It was probably the beginning of some song or poem to the tune of which those psalms were to be chanted.

A'lush (*a crowd of men*), one of the stations of the Israelites on their journey to Sinai, the last before Rephidim. Num. 33 : 13, 14.

Al'vah (*evil*), a duke of Edom, Gen. 36 : 40; written ALIAH in 1 Chron. 1 : 51.

Al'van (*tall*), a Horite, son of Shobal, Gen. 36 : 23; written ALIAN in 1 Chron. 1 : 40.

A'mad (*enduring*), an unknown place in Asher, between Alammelech and Misheal. Josh. 19 : 26 only.

Amad'atha, Esther 16 : 10, 17, and **Amad'athus**. Esther 12 : 6. [HAMMEDATHA.]

A'mal (*labor*), an Asherite, son of Helem. 1 Chron. 7 : 35.

Am'alek (*dweller in a valley*), a son of Eliphaz by his concubine Timnah, grandson of Esau, and chieftain ("duke," Authorized Version) of Edom. Gen. 36 : 12, 16; 1 Chron. 1 : 36. (B.C. about 1700.)

Am'alekites, a nomadic tribe of uncertain origin, which occupied the peninsula of Sinai and the wilderness intervening between the southern hill-ranges of Palestine and the border of Egypt. Num. 13 : 29; 1 Sam. 15 : 7; 27 : 8. Their wealth consisted in flocks and herds. Mention is made of a "town," 1 Sam. 15 : 5, but their towns could have been little more than stations or nomadic enclosures. The Amalekites first came in contact with the Israelites at Rephidim, but were signally defeated. Ex. 17 : 8-16. In union with the Canaanites they again attacked the Israelites on the borders of Palestine, and defeated them near Hormah. Num. 14 : 45. Saul undertook an expedition against them. 1 Sam. 14 : 48. Their power was thenceforth broken, and they degenerated into a horde of banditti. Their destruction was completed by David. 1 Sam. 30 : 1–17.

Am'alekites, Mount of, a mountain in Ephraim, Judges 12 : 15, probably so named because the Amalekites once held possession of it.

A'mam (*gathering place*), a city in the south of Judah, named with Shema and Moladah in Josh. 15 : 26 only.

A'man. [HAMAN.] Esther 10 : 7; 12 : 6; 13 : 3, 12; 14 : 17; 16 : 10, 17.

Am'ana (*a covenant*), apparently a mountain in or near Lebanon. Cant. 4 : 8. It is commonly assumed that this is the mountain in which the river Abana, 2 Kings 5 : 12, has its source.

Amari'ah (*the Lord says*, i. e. *promises*). 1. Father of Ahitub, according to

1 Chron. 6 : 7, 52, and son of Meraioth, in the line of the high priests.

2. The high priest in the reign of Jehoshaphat. 2 Chron. 19 : 11. He was the son of Azariah.

3. The head of a Levitical house of the Kohathites. 1 Chron. 23 : 19; 24 : 23.

4. The head of one of the twenty-four courses of priests. 2 Chron. 31 : 15; Neh. 10 : 3; 12 : 2, 13.

5. One of the sons of Bani in the time of Ezra. Ezra 10 : 42.

6. A priest who returned with Zerubbabel. Neh. 10 : 3; 12 : 2, 13.

7. A descendant of Pharez. Neh. 11 : 4.

8. An ancestor of Zephaniah the prophet. Zeph. 1 : 1.

Am'asa (*a burden*). 1. Son of Ithra or Jether, by Abigail, David's sister. 2 Sam. 17 : 25. He joined in Absalom's rebellion, B.C. 1023, was appointed commander-in-chief, and suffered defeat by Joab. 2 Sam. 18 : 6. David, incensed against Joab for killing Absalom, forgave Amasa and appointed him Joab's successor. 2 Sam. 19 : 13. Joab afterwards, when they were both in pursuit of the rebel Sheba, pretending to salute Amasa, stabbed him with his sword. 2 Sam. 20 : 10.

2. A prince of Ephraim, son of Hadlai, in the reign of Ahaz. 2 Chron. 28 : 12.

Amasa'i, or **Amas'a-i** (*burdensome*). 1. A Kohathite, father of Mahath and ancestor of Samuel. 1 Chron. 6 : 25, 35.

2. Chief of the captains of Judah and Benjamin, who deserted to David while an outlaw at Ziklag. 1 Chron. 12 : 18. (B.C. 1060.)

3. One of the priests who blew trumpets before the ark. 1 Chron. 15 : 24.

4. Another Kohathite, in the reign of Hezekiah. 2 Chron. 29 : 12.

Amasha'i, or **Amash'a-i** (*burdensome*), son of Azareel, a priest in the time of Nehemiah, Neh. 11 : 13; apparently the same as MAASIAI. 1 Chron. 9 : 12. (B.C. 440.)

Amasi'ah (*whom Jehovah bears*), son of Zichri and captain of 200,000 warriors of Judah in the reign of Jehoshaphat. 2 Chron. 17 : 16. (B.C. 910.)

A'math. [HAMATH.]

Amazi'ah (*the strength of the Lord*). 1. Son of Joash, and eighth king of Judah, reigned B.C. 837–809. He succeeded to the throne at the age of 25, on the murder of his father, and punished the murderers. In order to restore his kingdom to the greatness of Jehoshaphat's days, he made war on the Edomites, defeated them in the Valley of Salt, south of the Dead Sea, and took their capital, Selah or Petra, to which he gave the name of Jokteel, *i. e.* " God-subdued." Flushed with his success, he challenged Joash king of Israel to battle, but was completely defeated, and himself was taken prisoner and conveyed by Joash to Jerusalem, which opened its gates to the conqueror. Amaziah lived 15 years after the death of Joash; and in the 29th year of his reign was murdered by conspirators at Lachish, whither he had retired from Jerusalem for safety. 2 Chron. 25 : 27.

2. A descendant of Simeon. 1 Chron. 4 : 34.

3. A Levite. 1 Chron. 6 : 45.

4. Priest of the golden calf at Bethel, who endeavored to drive the prophet Amos from Israel into Judah. Amos 7 : 10, 12, 14.

Ambassador, a person of high rank employed by a government to represent it and transact its business at the seat of government of some other power. The earliest examples of ambassadors employed occur in Num. 20 : 14; 21 : 21; Judges 11 : 7–19; afterwards in that of the fraudulent Gibeonites, Josh. 9 : 4, etc., and in the instances of civic strife mentioned Judges 11 : 12 and 20 : 12. Ambassadors are found to have been employed not only on occasions of hostile challenge or insolent menace, 1 Kings 20 : 2, 6; 2 Kings 14 : 8, but of friendly compliment, of request for alliance or other aid, of submissive deprecation and of curious inquiry. 2 Kings 14 : 8; 16 : 7; 18 : 14; 2 Chron. 32 : 31. Ministers are called ambassadors of Christ.

Ambassage, embassy, a message of a public nature brought by ambassadors. The word also sometimes includes the ambassadors themselves. Luke 14 : 32.

Amber (Heb. *chasmal*) occurs only in Ezek.1 : 4, 27; 8 : 2. It is usually supposed that the Hebrew word *chasmal* denotes a metal, and not the fossil resin called *amber*.

Amen, literally " true;" and, used as a substantive, "that which is true," " truth," Isa. 65 : 16; a word used in strong asseverations, fixing, as it were, the stamp of truth upon the assertion which it accompanied, and making it binding as an oath. Comp. Num. 5 : 22.

In the synagogues and private houses it was customary for the people or members of the family who were present to say " amen " to the prayers which were offered. Matt. 6 : 13; 1 Cor. 14 : 16. And not only public prayers, but those offered in private, and doxologies, were appropriately concluded with "amen." Rom. 9 : 5; 11 : 36; 15 : 33; 16 : 27; 2 Cor. 13 : 14, etc.

Amethyst (Heb. *achlamah*), a subspecies of quartz of a bluish-violet color. Mention is made of this precious stone, which formed the third in the third row of the high priest's breastplate, in Ex. 28 : 19; 39 : 12. It occurs also in Rev. 21 : 20.

A'mi (*builder*), one of Solomon's servants, Ezra 2 : 57; called AMON in Neh. 7 : 59.

Amin'adab. Matt. 1 : 4; Luke 3 : 33. [AMMINADAB, 1.]

Amit'ta-i (*true*), father of the prophet Jonah. 2 Kings 14 : 25 ; Jonah 1 : 1.

Am'mah (*head*), **The hill of,** a hill facing Giah by the way of the wilderness of Gibeon, named as the point to which Joab pursued Abner. 2 Sam. 2 : 24.

Am'mi, *i. e.*, as explained in the margin of the Authorized Version, *my people.* Hos. 2 : 1.

Am'mi-el (*people of God*). 1. The spy from the tribe of Dan. Num. 13 : 12. (B.C. 1490.) He perished by the plague for his evil report.

2. Father of Machir of Lo-debar. 2 Sam. 9 : 4, 5; 17 : 27.

3. Father of Bath-sheba, 1 Chron. 3 : 5, called ELIAM in 2 Sam. 11 : 3.

4. The sixth son of Obed-edom, 1 Chron. 26 : 5, and one of the doorkeepers of the temple. (B.C. 1014.)

Am'mihud (*people of praise*). 1. An Ephraimite, father of Elishama, the chief of the tribe at the time of the Exodus. Num. 1 : 10; 2 : 18; 7 : 48, 53; 10 : 22; 1 Chron. 7 : 26, and, through him, ancestor of Joshua. (B.C. 1491.)

2. A Simeonite, father of Shemuel. Num. 34 : 20.

3. The father of Pedahel, prince of the tribe of Naphtali. Num. 34 : 28.

4. The father of Talmai king of Geshur. 2 Sam. 13 : 37.

5. A descendant of Pharez, son of Judah. 1 Chron. 9 : 4.

Ammin'adab (*one of the prince's people*). 1. Son of Ram or Aram, and father of Nahshon, or NAASSON (as it is

written Matt. 1 : 4; Luke 3 : 32); Num.
1 : 7; 2 : 3; Ruth 4 : 19, 20; 1 Chron. 2 :
10. One of the ancestors of Jesus
Christ.

2. The chief of the 112 sons of Uzziel,
a junior Levitical house of the family
of the Kohathites. Ex. 6 : 23; 1 Chron.
15 : 10, 11.

3. In 1 Chron. 6 : 22, Izhar, the son of
Kohath, is called AMMINADIB; probably
a clerical error.

Ammin'adib. Probably another
form of Amminadab. He was noted
for the swiftness of his chariots. Cant. 6 :
12. It is uncertain whether we ought to
read here AMMINADIB, with the Authorized Version, or *my willing people*, as
in the margin.

Ammishad'da-i (*people of the Almighty*), the father of Ahiezer, prince
of the tribe of Dan at the time of the
Exodus. Num. 1 : 12; 2 : 25; 7 : 66, 71;
10 : 25. (B.C. 1491.)

Ammiz'abad (*people of the Giver*, i.e.
God), the son of Benaiah, who commanded the third division of David's
army. 1 Chron. 27 : 6. (B.C. 1050.)

Am'mon (*sons of renown, mountaineers*), **Am'monites, Children of Ammon,** a people descended from Ben-ammi, the son of Lot by his younger
daughter. Gen. 19 : 38; comp. Ps. 83 : 7,
8. The Ammonites are frequently mentioned with the Moabites (descendants
of Ben-ammi's half-brother), and sometimes under the same name. Comp.
Judges 10 : 6; 2 Chron. 20 : 1; Zeph. 2 :
8, etc. The precise position of the territory of the Ammonites is not ascertain-
able. In the earliest mention of them,
Deut. 2 : 20, they are said to have dwelt
in their place, Jabbok being their border.
Num. 21 : 24; Deut. 2 : 37; 3 : 16. Land
or country is, however, but rarely ascribed to them. Their capital city was
Rabbath, called also Rabbath Ammon,

Rabbath Ammon, Capital of the Ammonites. (*From a Photograph.*)

on the Jabbok. We find everywhere
traces of the fierce habits of marauders
in their incursions, 1 Sam. 11 : 2; Amos
1 : 13, and a very high degree of crafty
cruelty to their foes. Jer. 41:6, 7; Judges
7 : 11, 12. Moab was the settled and
civilized half of the nation of Lot, and
Ammon formed its predatory and Bedouin section. On the west of Jordan
they never obtained a footing. The

hatred in which the Ammonites were held by Israel is stated to have arisen partly from their denial of assistance, Deut. 23 : 4, to the Israelites on their approach to Canaan. But whatever its origin the animosity continued in force to the latest date. The tribe was governed by a king, Judges 11 : 12, etc.; 1 Sam. 12 : 12; 2 Sam. 10 : 1; Jer. 40 : 14, and by "princes." 2 Sam. 10 : 3 ; 1 Chron. 19 : 3. The divinity of the tribe was Molech [MOLECH], and they were gross idolaters.

Ammoni′tess, a woman of Ammonite race. 1 Kings 14 : 21, 31; 2 Chron. 12 : 13.

Am′mon-no. See NO-AMON.

Am′non (*faithful*). 1. Eldest son of David. (B.C. 1052.) He dishonored his half-sister Tamar, and was in consequence murdered by her brother. 2 Sam. 13 : 1–29.

2. Son of Shimon. 1 Chron. 4 : 20.

A′mok, a priest who returned with Zerubbabel. Neh. 12 : 7, 20. (B.C. 536.)

A′mon, or **A′men** (*the mysterious*), an Egyptian divinity, whose name oc-

Amon.

curs in that of No-amon. Nah. 3 : 8. Amen was one of the eight gods of the first order, and chief of the triad of Thebes. He was worshipped at that city as Amen-Ra, or " Amen the Sun."

A′mon (*builder*). 1. One of Ahab's governors. 1 Kings 22 : 26; 2 Chron. 18 : 25.

2. King of Judah, son and successor of Manasseh, reigned two years, from B.C. 642 to 640. Amon devoted himself wholly to the service of false gods, but was killed in a conspiracy, and was succeeded by his son Josiah.

Am′orite, the Am′orites (*dwellers on the summits, mountaineers*), one of the chief nations who possessed the land of Canaan before its conquest by the Israelites. As dwelling on the elevated portions of the country, they are contrasted with the Canaanites, who were the dwellers in the lowlands; and the two thus formed the main broad divisions of the Holy Land, Num. 13 : 29; and see Gen. 14 : 7; Deut. 1 : 7, 20, "mountain of the Amorites;" 44; Josh. 5 : 1; 10 : 6; 11 : 3. They first occupied the barren heights west of the Dead Sea, at the place called afterwards Engedi. From this point they stretched west to Hebron. At the date of the invasion of the country, Sihon, their then king, had taken the rich pasture land south of the Jabbok. This rich tract, bounded by the Jabbok on the north, the Arnon on the south, the Jordan on the west and "the wilderness" on the east, Judges 11 : 21, 22, was, perhaps, in the most special sense the "land of the Amorites," Num. 21 : 31; Josh. 12 : 2, 3; 13 : 10; Judges 11 : 21, 22; but their possessions are distinctly stated to have extended to the very foot of Hermon, Deut. 3 : 8; 4 : 48, embracing "Gilead and all Bashan," 3 : 10, with the Jordan valley on the east of the river. 4 : 49. After the conquest of Canaan nothing of importance is heard of the Amorites in the Bible.

A′mos (*burden*), native of Tekoa in Judah, about six miles south of Bethlehem, originally a shepherd and dresser of sycamore trees, who was called by God's Spirit to be a prophet, although not trained in any of the regular prophetic schools. Amos 1 : 1; 7 : 14, 15. He travelled from Judah into the northern kingdom of Israel or Ephraim, and there exercised his ministry, apparently not for any long time. (His date cannot be later than B.C. 808, for he lived in the reigns of Uzziah king of Judah and Jeroboam king of Israel; but his ministry probably took place at an earlier date, perhaps about the middle of Jeroboam's reign. Nothing is known of the time or manner of his death.—ED.)

A'mos, Book of. The book of the prophecies of Amos seems to be divided into four principal portions closely connected together. (1) From 1 : 1 to 2 : 3 he denounces the sins of the nations bordering on Israel and Judah. (2) From 2 : 4 to 6 : 14 he describes the state of those two kingdoms, especially the former. (3) From 7 : 1 to 9 : 10 he relates his visit to Bethel, and sketches the impending punishment of Israel. At last he promises blessings. The chief peculiarity of the style consists in the number of allusions to natural objects and agricultural occupations, as might be expected from the early life of the author.

A'moz (*strong*), father of the prophet Isaiah, and, according to rabbinical tradition, brother of Amaziah king of Judah. 2 Kings 19 : 2, 20 ; 20 : 1 ; Isa. 1 : 1. (B.C. before 756.)

Amphip'olis (*a city surrounded by the sea*), a city of Macedonia, through

View of Amphipolis.

which Paul and Silas passed on their way from Philippi to Thessalonica. Acts 17 : 1. It was distant 33 Roman miles from Philippi, to the southwest, and about three miles from the sea. Its site is now occupied by a village called *Neokhorio;* in Turkish *Jeni-Keni*, or "New Town."

Am'plias (*large*), a Christian at Rome. Rom. 16 : 8. (A.D. 55.)

Amplia'tus (Revised Version, Rom. 16 : 8) (the full name of which AMPLIAS,

above, is the contraction. The name in this form is "common in the sepulchral inscriptions of persons connected with Cæsar's household." (A.D. 55.)—ED.)

Am'ram (*an exalted people*). 1. A Levite of the family of the Kohathites, and father of Moses. Ex. 6 : 18, 20. (B.C. 1571.)

2. A son of Dishon and descendant of Seir, 1 Chron. 1 : 41 ; properly "Hamram" = HEMDAN in Gen. 36 : 26.

3. One of the sons of Bani in the time of Ezra, who had married a foreign wife. Ezra 10 : 34. (B.C. 459.)

Am'ramites. A branch of the great Kohathite family of the tribe of Levi, Num. 3 : 27 ; 1 Chron. 26 : 23 ; descended from Amram, the father of Moses.

Am'raphel (*keeper of the gods*), perhaps a Hamite king of Shinar or Babylonia, who joined the victorious incursion of the Elamite Chedorlaomer against the kings of Sodom and Gomorrah and the cities of the plain. Gen. 14. (B.C. 1898.)

Amulets were ornaments, gems, scrolls, etc., worn as preservatives against the power of enchantments, and generally inscribed with mystic forms or characters. The "earrings" in Gen. 35 : 4 were obviously connected with idolatrous worship, and were probably amulets taken from the bodies of the slain Shechemites. They are subsequently mentioned among the spoils of Midian. Judges 8 : 24. In Hos. 2 : 13 is another like reference. The "earrings" in Isa. 3 : 20 were also amulets.

Am'zi (*strong*). 1. A Levite of the family of Merari. 1 Chron. 6 : 46.

2. A priest. Neh. 11 : 12.

A'nab (*grape-town*), a town in the mountains of Judah, Josh. 15 : 50, named with Debir and Hebron as once belonging to the Anakim. Josh. 11 : 21.

A'nah (*one who answers*), the son of Zibeon and father of Aholibamah, one of Esau's wives. Gen. 36 : 2, 14, 25. He is supposed to have discovered the "hot springs" (not "mules," as in the Authorized Version) in the desert as he fed the asses of Zibeon his father. (B.C. 1797.)

Anah'arath (*gorge* or *pass*), a place within the border of Issachar, named with Shihon and Rabbith. Josh. 19 : 19.

Anai'ah (*whom Jehovah answers*). 1. Probably a priest. Neh. 8 : 4.

2. One of the "heads of the people" who signed the covenant with Nehemiah. Neh. 10 : 22.

An'akim (*long-necked*), a race of giants, descendants of Arba, Josh. 15 : 13 ; 21 : 11, dwelling in the southern part of Canaan, and particularly at Hebron, which from their progenitor received the name of "city of Arba." Anak was the name of the race rather than that of an individual. Josh. 14 : 15. The race appears to have been divided into three tribes or families, bearing the names Sheshai, Ahiman and Talmai. Though the warlike appearance of the Anakim had struck the Israelites with terror in the time of Moses, Num. 13 : 28; Deut. 9 : 2, they were nevertheless dispossessed by Joshua, Josh. 11 : 21, 22, and their chief city, Hebron, became the possession of Caleb. Josh. 15 : 14; Judges 1 : 20. After this time they vanish from history.

An'amim, a Mizraite people or tribe. Gen. 10 : 13 ; 1 Chron. 1 : 11.

Anam'melech (*image of the king*), one of the idols worshipped by the colonists introduced into Samaria from Sepharvaim. 2 Kings 17 : 31. He was worshipped with rites resembling those of Molech, and is the companion-god to Adrammelech.

A'nan (*a cloud*), one of the "heads of the people" who signed the covenant with Nehemiah. Neh. 10 : 26. (B.C. 410.)

Ana'ni (*protected by Jehovah*), the seventh son of Elioenai, descended from the royal line of Judah. 1 Chron. 3 : 24.

Anani'ah (*protected by Jehovah*), probably a priest, and ancestor of Azariah, who assisted in rebuilding the city wall in the days of Nehemiah. Neh. 3 : 23. (B.C. before 446.)

Anani'ah, a place, named between Nob and Hazor, in which the Benjamites lived after their return from captivity. Neh. 11 : 32.

Anani'as (*whom Jehovah has graciously given*). 1. A high priest in Acts 23 : 2–5 ; 24 : 1. He was the son of Nebedæus. He was nominated to the office by Herod king of Chalcis, in A.D. 48; was deposed shortly before Felix left the province, and assassinated by the Sicarii at the beginning of the last Jewish war.

2. A disciple at Jerusalem, husband of Sapphira. Acts 5 : 1–11. Having sold his goods for the benefit of the church, he kept back a part of the price, bringing to the apostles the remainder as if it was the whole, his wife being privy to the scheme. St. Peter denounced the fraud, and Ananias fell down and expired.

3. A Jewish disciple at Damascus, Acts 9 : 10–17, of high repute, Acts 22 : 12, who sought out Saul during the period of blindness which followed his conversion, and announced to him his future commission as a preacher of the gospel. Tradition makes him to have been afterwards bishop of Damascus, and to have died by martyrdom.

A'nath (*answer*), father of Shamgar. Judges 3 : 31; 5 : 6.

Anathema, which literally means a thing suspended, is the equivalent of the Hebrew word signifying a thing or person *devoted*. Any object so devoted to Jehovah was irredeemable. If an inanimate object, it was to be given to the priests, Num. 18 : 14; if a living creature or even a man, it was to be slain. Lev. 27 : 28, 29. The word anathema frequently occurs in St. Paul's writings, and is generally translated *accursed*. An examination of the passages in which it occurs shows that it had acquired a more general sense as expressive either of strong feeling, Rom. 9 : 3, or of dislike and condemnation. 1 Cor. 12 : 3; 16 : 22; Gal. 1 : 9.

An'athoth (*answers to prayer*). 1. Son of Becher, a son of Benjamin. 1 Chron. 7 : 8.

2. One of the "heads of the people" who signed the covenant in the time of Nehemiah. Neh. 10 : 19. (B.C. 410.)

An'athoth, a priests' city belonging to the tribe of Benjamin, with "suburbs." Josh. 21 : 18; 1 Chron. 6 : 60. Anathoth lay about three miles from Jerusalem. Isa. 10 : 30. The cultivation of the priests survives in tilled fields of grain, with figs and olives. There are the remains of walls and strong foundations, and the quarries still supply Jerusalem with building stones.

Anchor. Acts 27 : 29.

An'drew (*manly*), one of the apostles of our Lord, John 1 : 40; Matt. 4 : 18, brother of Simon Peter. He was of Bethsaida, and had been a disciple of John the Baptist, leaving him to follow our Lord. By his means his brother Simon was brought to Jesus. John 1 : 41. His place among the apostles seems to have been fourth, next after the three Peter, James and John, and in company with Philip. Mark 3 : 18; Acts 1 : 13.

The traditions about him are various. He is said to have preached in Scythia, in Greece, in Asia Minor and Thrace, and to have been crucified at Patræ in Achaia.

Androni'cus (*man-conqueror*). 1: An officer left as viceroy, 2 Macc. 4 : 31, in Antioch by Antiochus Epiphanes during his absence. 2 Macc. 4 : 31–38. (B.C. 171.)

2. Another officer of Antiochus Epiphanes who was left by him on Garizem. 2 Macc. 5 : 23.

3. A Christian at Rome, saluted by St. Paul, Rom. 16 : 7, together with Junia.

A'nem (*two springs*), a city of Issachar, with "suburbs," belonging to the Gershonites. 1 Chron. 6 : 73.

A'ner (*boy*), a city of Manasseh, west of Jordan, with "suburbs," given to the Kohathites. 1 Chron. 6 : 70.

A'ner, one of the three Amorite chiefs of Hebron who aided Abraham in the pursuit after the four invading kings. Gen. 14 : 13, 24.

Aneth'othite, 2 Sam. 23 : 27, **Anet'-othite,** 1 Chron. 27 : 12, and **An'toth-ite,** 1 Chron. 11 : 28 ; 12 : 3, an inhabitant of Anathoth, of the tribe of Benjamin.

Angel of the Lord. Gen. 16 : 7, etc. (The special form in which God manifested himself to man, and hence Christ's visible form before the incarnation. Compare Acts 7 : 30–38 with the corresponding Old-Testament history ; and Gen. 18 : 1, 13, 14, 33 and 19 : 1.)

Angels. By the word "angels" (*i. e.* "messengers" of God) we ordinarily understand a race of spiritual beings of a nature exalted far above that of man, although infinitely removed from that of God—whose office is "to do him service in heaven, and by his appointment to succor and defend men on earth." I. *Scriptural use of the word.*—There are many passages in which the expression "angel of God" is certainly used for a manifestation of God himself. Gen. 22 : 11 with 12, and Ex. 3 : 2 with 6 and 14. It is to be observed, also, that side by side with these expressions we read of God's being manifested in the form of *man*—as to Abraham at Mamre, Gen. 18 : 2, 22, comp. 19 : 1 ; to Jacob at Penuel, Gen. 32 : 24, 30 ; to Joshua at Gilgal, Josh. 5 : 13, 15, etc. Besides this, which is the highest application of the word angel, we find the phrase used of any messengers of God, such as the prophets,

Isa. 42 : 19 ; Hag. 1 : 13 ; Mal. 3 : 1, the priests, Mal. 2 : 7, and the rulers of the Christian churches. Rev. 1 : 20.

II. *Nature of angels.*—Angels are termed "spirits," as in Heb. 1 : 14 ; but it is not asserted that the angelic nature is incorporeal. The contrary seems expressly implied 'in Luke 20 : 36 ; Philip. 3 : 21. The angels are revealed to us as beings such as man might be, and will be when the power of sin and death is removed, because always beholding his face, Matt. 18 : 10, and therefore being "made like him." 1 John 3 : 2. Their *number* must be very large, 1 Kings 22 : 19 ; Matt. 26 : 53 ; Heb. 12 : 22 ; their *strength* is great, Ps. 103 : 20 ; Rev. 5 : 2 ; 18 : 21 ; their *activity* marvellous, Isa. 6 : 2–6 ; Matt. 26 : 53 ; Rev. 8 : 13 ; their *appearance* varied according to circumstances, but was often brilliant and dazzling. Matt. 28 : 2–7 ; Rev. 10 : 1, 2. Of the nature of "fallen angels," the circumstances and nature of the temptation by which they fell, we know absolutely nothing. All that is certain is that they "left their first estate," and that they are now "angels of the devil." Matt. 25 : 41 ; Rev. 12 : 7, 9. On the other hand, the title specially assigned to the angels of God—that of the "holy ones," see Dan. 4 : 13, 23 ; 8 : 13 ; Matt. 25 : 31—is precisely the one which is given to those men who are renewed in Christ's image. Comp. Heb. 2 : 10 ; 5 : 9 ; 12 : 23.

III. *Office of the angels.*—Of their office in heaven we have only vague prophetic glimpses, as in 1 Kings 22 : 19 ; Isa. 6 : 1–3 ; Dan. 7 : 9, 10 ; Rev. 6 : 11, etc., which show us nothing but a neverceasing adoration. They are represented as being, in the widest sense, agents of God's providence, *natural* and *supernatural*, to the body and to the soul. In one word, they are Christ's ministers of grace now, as they shall be of judgment hereafter. Matt. 13 : 39, 41, 49 ; 16 : 27 ; 24 : 31, etc. That there are degrees of the angelic nature, both fallen and unfallen, and special titles and agencies belonging to each, is clearly declared by St. Paul, Eph. 1 : 21 ; Rom. 8 : 38 ; but what their general nature is it is useless to speculate.

A'niam (*sighing of the people*), a Manassite, son of Shemidah. 1 Chron. 7 : 19.

A'nim (*fountains*), a city in the mountains of Judah, named with Eshtemoh and Goshen. Josh. 15 : 50.

Anise. This word occurs only in Matt. 23 : 23. It is by no means a matter of certainty whether the anise (*Pimpinella anisum*, Lin.) or the dill (*Anethum graveolens*) is here intended, though the probability is more in favor of the latter plant. "Anise is an annual plant growing to the height of one foot, carries a white flower, and blooms from

Anise.

June till August. The seeds are imported and used in large quantities on account of their aromatic and carminative properties. It grows wild in Egypt, in Syria, Palestine and all parts of the Levant. Among the ancients anise seems to have been a common pot-herb in every garden. Although it is less used in medicine by the moderns than by the ancients, it still retains its former reputation as an excellent stomachic, particularly for delicate women and young children. The Romans chewed it in order to keep up an agreeable moisture in the mouth and to sweeten the breath, while some Orientals still do the same." Dill, a somewhat similar plant, is an annual, bearing small aromatic seeds, used also for cookery and medicine.

Anklet. This word does not occur in the Authorized Version; but anklets are referred to in Isa. 3 : 16, 18, 20. They were fastened to the ankle band of each

leg; were as common as bracelets and armlets, and made of much the same materials. The pleasant jingling and tinkling which they made as they knocked against each other was no doubt one of the reasons why they were admired. They are still worn in the East.

An'na (*grace*), a "prophetess" in Jerusalem at the time of our Lord's presentation in the temple. Luke 2 : 36. She was of the tribe of Asher.

An'nas (*humble*), the son of one Seth, was appointed high priest A.D. 7 by Quirinus, the imperial governor of Syria, but was obliged by Valerius Gratus, procurator of Judea, to give way to Ismael, son of Phabi, at the beginning of the reign of Tiberius, A.D. 14. About A.D. 25 Joseph Caiaphas, son-in-law of Annas, became high priest, John 18 : 13; but in Luke 3 : 2 Annas and Caiaphas are both called high priests. Our Lord's first hearing, John 18 : 13, was before Annas, who then sent him bound to Caiaphas. Some maintain that the two, Annas and Caiaphas, were together at the head of the Jewish people,—Caiaphas as actual high priest, Annas as president of the Sanhedrin. Acts 4 : 6. Others again suppose that Annas held the office of *sagan*, or substitute of the high priest; others still that Annas held the title and was really the ruling power. He lived to old age, having had five sons high priests.

Anointing, in Holy Scripture, is either, I. Material—with oil—or II. Spiritual—with the Holy Ghost. I. MATERIAL.—1. *Ordinary.* Anointing the body or head with oil was a common practice with the Jews, as with other Oriental nations. Deut. 28 : 40; Ruth 3 : 3; Micah 6 : 15. Anointing the head with oil or ointment seems also to have been a mark of respect sometimes paid by a host to his guests. Luke 7 : 46 and Ps. 23 : 5. 2. *Official.* It was a rite of inauguration into each of the three typical offices of the Jewish commonwealth. *a.* Prophets were occasionally anointed to their office, 1 Kings 19 : 16, and were called messiahs, or anointed. 1 Chron. 16 : 22; Ps. 105 : 15. *b.* Priests, at the first institution of the Levitical priesthood, were all anointed to their offices, Ex. 40 : 15; Num. 3 : 3; but afterwards anointing seems to have been specially reserved for the high priest, Ex. 29 : 29; Lev. 16 : 32; so that "the priest that is anointed," Lev. 4 : 3, is generally thought to mean the high priest. *c.* Kings. Anointing was the principal and divinely-appointed ceremony in the inauguration of the Jewish kings. 1 Sam. 9 : 16; 10 : 1; 1 Kings 1 : 34, 39. The rite was sometimes performed more than once. David was thrice anointed. *d.* Inanimate objects also were anointed with oil, in token of their being set apart for religious service. Thus Jacob anointed a pillar at Bethel. Gen. 31 : 13; Ex. 30 : 26–28. 3. *Ecclesiastical.* Anointing with oil is prescribed by St. James to be used for the recovery of the sick. James 5 : 14. Analogous to this is the anointing with oil practiced by the twelve. Mark 6 : 13. II. SPIRITUAL.—1. In the Old Testament a Deliverer is promised under the title of Messiah, or Anointed, Ps. 2 : 2; Dan. 9 : 25, 26; and the nature of his anointing is described to be spiritual, with the Holy Ghost. Isa. 61 : 1; see Luke 4 : 18. In the New Testament Jesus of Nazareth is shown to be the Messiah, or Christ, or Anointed, of the Old Testament, John 1 : 41; Acts 9 : 22; 17 : 2, 3; 18 : 4, 28; and the historical fact of his being anointed with the Holy Ghost is asserted and recorded. John 1 : 32, 33; Acts 4 : 27; 10 : 38. Christ was anointed as prophet, priest and king. 2. Spiritual anointing with the Holy Ghost is conferred also upon Christians by God. 2 Cor. 1 : 21. "Anointing" expresses the sanctifying influences of the Holy Spirit upon Christians, who are priests and kings unto God.

Ant (Heb. *nemâlâh*). This insect is mentioned twice in the Old Testament: in Prov. 6 : 6; 30 : 25. In the former of these passages the diligence of this insect is instanced by the wise man as an example worthy of imitation; in the second passage the ant's wisdom is especially alluded to; for these insects, "though they be little on the earth, are exceeding wise." (For a long time European commentators and naturalists denied that ants stored up grain for future use, as was asserted in Proverbs; but while this is true of most of the 104 European species, two of those species do lay up food, and are called *harvesting ants.* Like species have been found in Texas and South America, and are known to exist in Palestine. They show many other proofs of their skill. Some of them build wonderful houses; these

are often several stories high, sometimes five hundred times the height of the builders, with rooms, corridors, and vaulted roofs supported by pillars. Some species keep a kind of cows; others have a regular army of soldiers; some keep slaves. "No closer imitation of the ways of man could be found in the entire animal economy." (See *Encyc. Brit.*) McCook's "The Honey Ants" gives many curious facts about the habits of this peculiar kind of ant, and of the harvesting ants of the American plains.—ED.)

An'tichrist. This term is employed by the apostle John alone, and is defined by him in a manner which leaves no doubt as to its intrinsic meaning. With regard to its application there is less certainty. In the first passage—1 John 2 : 18—in which it occurs, the apostle makes direct reference to the false Christs whose coming, it had been foretold, should mark the last days. In v. 22 we find, "he is antichrist, that denieth the Father and the Son;" and still more positively, "every spirit that confesseth not that Jesus Christ is come in the flesh is of antichrist." Comp. 2 John 7. From these emphatic and repeated definitions it has been supposed that the object of the apostle in his first epistle was to combat the errors of Cerinthus, the Docetæ and the Gnostics on the subject of the Incarnation. (They denied the union of the divine and human in Christ.)

The coming of Antichrist was believed to be foretold in the "vile person" of Daniel's prophecy, Dan. 11 : 21, which received its first accomplishment in Antiochus Epiphanes, but of which the complete fulfillment was reserved for the last times. He is identified with "the man of sin, the son of perdition." 2 Thess. 2 : 3. This interpretation brings Antichrist into close connection with the gigantic power of evil, symbolized by the "beast," Rev. 13, who received his power from the dragon (*i. e.* the devil, the serpent of Genesis), continued for forty and two months, and was invested with the kingdom of the ten kings who destroyed the harlot Babylon, Rev. 17 : 12, 17, the city of seven hills. The destruction of Babylon is to be followed by the rule of Antichrist for a short period, Rev. 17 : 10, to be in his turn overthrown in "the battle of that great day of God Almighty," Rev. 16 : 14, with the false prophet and all his followers. Rev. 19. The personality of Antichrist is to be inferred as well from the personality of his historical precursor as from that of him to whom he stands opposed. Such an interpretation is to be preferred to that which regards Antichrist as the embodiment and personification of all powers and agencies inimical to Christ, or of the Antichristian might of the world.

An'tioch (from *Antiochus*). 1. In Syria. The capital of the Greek kings of Syria, and afterwards the residence of the Roman governors of the province which bore the same name.

Situation.—This metropolis was situated where the chain of Lebanon, running northward, and the chain of Taurus, running eastward, are brought to an abrupt meeting. Here the Orontes

Antioch in Syria.

breaks through the mountains; and Antioch was placed at a bend of the river, 16½ miles from the Mediterranean, partly on an island, partly on the levee which forms the left bank, and partly on the steep and craggy ascent of Mount Silpius, which rose abruptly on the south. It is about 300 miles north of Jerusalem. In the immediate neighborhood was Daphne, the celebrated sanctuary of Apollo, 2 Macc. 4 : 33 ; whence the city was sometimes called *Antioch by Daphne*, to distinguish it from other cities of the same name.

Description.—The city was founded in the year 300 B.C., by Seleucus Nicator. It grew under the successive Seleucid kings till it became a city of great extent and of remarkable beauty. One feature, which seems to have been characteristic of the great Syrian cities,—

a vast street with colonnades, intersecting the whole from end to end,—was added by Antiochus Epiphanes. By Pompey it was made a free city, and such it continued till the time of Antoninus Pius.

Tetradrachm of Antioch.

The early emperors raised there some large and important structures, such as aqueducts, amphitheatres and baths. (Antioch, in Paul's time, was the third city of the Roman empire, and contained over 200,000 inhabitants. Now it is a small, mean place of about 6000.—ED.)

Bible History.—No city, after Jerusalem, is so intimately connected with the history of the apostolic church. Jews were settled there from the first in large numbers, were governed by their own ethnarch, and allowed to have the

Fortress of Antonia; called Pilate's House.

same political privileges with the Greeks. The chief interest of Antioch, however, is connected with the progress of Christianity among the heathen. Here the first Gentile church was founded, Acts 11 : 20, 21; here the disciples of Jesus Christ were first called Christians. 11 : 26. It was from Antioch that St. Paul started on his three missionary journeys.

2. IN PISIDIA, Acts 13 : 14; 14 : 19, 21; 2 Tim. 3 : 11, on the borders of Phrygia, corresponds to *Yalobatch*, which is distant from *Ak-sher* six hours over the mountains. This city, like the Syrian Antioch, was founded by Seleucus Nicator. Under the Romans it became a *colonia*, and was also called Cæsarea.

Anti'ochus (*an opponent*), the name of a number of kings of Syria who lived during the interval between the Old and New Testaments, and had frequent connection with the Jews during that period. They are referred to in the Apocrypha, especially in the books of the Maccabees.

An'tipas (*like the father*), martyr at Pergamos, Rev. 2 : 13, and according to tradition the bishop of that place. (A.D. before 100.)

An'tipas. [HEROD.]

Antipa'tris, or **Antip'atris** (*for his father*), a town to which the soldiers conveyed St. Paul by night on their march. Acts 23 : 31. Its ancient name was Capharsaba; and Herod, when he rebuilt the city, changed it to Antipatris, in honor of his father, Antipater. The village *Kefr-Saba* still retains the ancient name of Antipatris.

Anto'nia (from *Marc Antony*) (a square stone fortress or castle adjoining the northwest corner of the temple area at Jerusalem. There was a tower at each corner. It was rebuilt by Herod the Great, and named by him from Marc Antony. From the stairs of this castle Paul addressed the multitude who had assaulted him. Acts 21 : 31–40.—ED.)

Antothi'jah (*answers of Jehovah*), a Benjamite, one of the sons of Jeroham. 1 Chron. 8 : 24.

An'tothite, a dweller at Anathoth. 1 Chron. 11 : 28; 12 : 3. [ANATHOTH.]

A'nub (*confederate*), son of Coz and descendant of Judah, through Ashur the father of Tekoa. 1 Chron. 4 : 8.

Apel'les (*called*), a Christian saluted by St. Paul in Rom. 16 : 10. Tradition makes him bishop of Smyrna or Heraclea. (A.D. 55.)

Apes (Heb. *kôphim*) are mentioned in 1 Kings 10 : 22 and 2 Chron. 9 : 21. There can be little doubt that the apes were brought from the same country which supplied ivory and peacocks, both of which are common in Ceylon; and Sir E. Tennent has drawn attention to the fact that the Tamil names for apes, ivory and peacocks are identical with the Hebrew.

Aphar'sathchites,   Aphar'sites, Aphar'sacites, the names of certain tribes, colonies from which had been planted in Samaria by the Assyrian leader Asnapper. Ezra 4 : 9; 5 : 6. The first and last are regarded as the same. Whence these tribes came is entirely a matter of conjecture.

A'phek (*strength*), the name of several places in Palestine. 1. A royal city of the Canaanites, the king of which was killed by Joshua, Josh. 12 : 18; probably the same as APHEKAH in Josh. 15 : 53.

2. A city, apparently in the extreme north of Asher, Josh. 19 : 30, from which the Canaanites were not ejected, Judges

1 : 31; though here it is APHIK. This is probably the same place as APHEK, Josh. 13 : 4, on the extreme north "border of the Amorites," identified with the Aphaca of classical times, the modern *Afka*.

3. A place at which the Philistines encamped while the Israelites pitched in Eben-ezer, before the fatal battle in which the sons of Eli were killed and the ark was taken. 1 Sam. 4 : 1. This would be somewhere to the northwest of and at no great distance from Jerusalem.

4. The scene of another encampment of the Philistines, before an encounter not less disastrous than that just named, —the defeat and death of Saul. 1 Sam. 29 : 1. It is possible that it may be the same place as the preceding.

5. A city on the military road from Syria to Israel. 1 Kings 20 : 26. It is now found in *Fik*, at the head of the *Wady Fik*, six miles east of the Sea of Galilee.

Aphe'kah (*strong place*), a city of Judah, in the mountains, Josh. 15 : 53; probably the same as APHEK, 1.

Aphi'ah (*refreshed*), one of the forefathers of King Saul. 1 Sam. 9 : 1.

A'phik (*strong*), a city of Asher from which the Canaanites were not driven out. Judges 1 : 31. Probably the same place as APHEK, 2.

Aph'rah (*dust*), **The house of,** a place mentioned in Micah 1 : 10. Its site is uncertain.

Aph'ses (*the dispersion*), chief of the 18th of the 24 courses in the service of the temple. 1 Chron. 24 : 15.

Apoc'alypse. A Greek word meaning *revelation*, applied chiefly to the book of Revelation by John. [REVELATION.]

Apoc'rypha (*concealed, hidden*). 1. *Old Testament Apocrypha.*—The collection of books to which this term is popularly applied includes the following (the order given is that in which they stand in the English version): I. 1 Esdras; II. 2 Esdras; III. Tobit; IV. Judith; V. The rest of the chapters of the book of Esther, which are found neither in the Hebrew nor in the Chaldee; VI. The Wisdom of Solomon; VII. The Wisdom of Jesus the Son of Sirach, or Ecclesiasticus; VIII. Baruch; IX. The Song of the Three Holy Children; X. The History of Susanna; XI. The History of the destruction of Bel and the Dragon; XII. The Prayer of Manasses king of Judah; XIII. 1 Maccabees; XIV. 2 Maccabees. The primary meaning of *apocrypha*, "hidden, secret," seems, toward the close of the second century, to have been associated with the signification "spurious," and ultimately to have settled down into the latter. The separate books of this collection are treated of in distinct articles. Their relation to the canonical books of the Old Testament is discussed under CANON.

2. *New Testament Apocrypha.*—(A collection of legendary and spurious Gospels, Acts of the Apostles, and Epistles. They are so entirely inferior to the genuine books, so full of nonsensical and unworthy stories of Christ and the apostles, that they have never been regarded as divine, or bound up in our Bibles. It is said that Mohammed obtained his ideas of Christ entirely from these spurious gospels.—ED.)

Apollo'nia (*belonging to Apollo*), a city of Macedonia, through which Paul and Silas passed in their way from Philippi and Amphipolis to Thessalonica. Acts 17 : 1. According to the *Antonine Itinerary* it was distant 30 Roman miles from Amphipolis and 37 Roman miles from Thessalonica.

Apol'los (*given by Apollo*), a Jew from Alexandria, eloquent (which may also mean *learned*) and mighty in the Scriptures; one instructed in the way of the Lord, according to the imperfect view of the disciples of John the Baptist, Acts 18 : 24, but on his coming to Ephesus during a temporary absence of St. Paul, A.D. 54, more perfectly taught by Aquila and Priscilla. After this he became a preacher of the gospel, first in Achaia and then in Corinth. Acts 18 : 27; 19 : 1. When the apostle wrote his First Epistle to the Corinthians, Apollos was with or near him, 1 Cor. 16 : 12; probably at Ephesus in A.D. 57. He is mentioned but once more in the New Testament, in Titus 3 : 13. After this nothing is known of him. Tradition makes him bishop of Cæsarea.

Apol'lyon, or, as it is literally in the margin of the Authorized Version of Rev. 9 : 11, "*a destroyer*," is the rendering of the Hebrew word ABADDON, "the angel of the bottomless pit." From the occurrence of the word in Ps. 88 : 11, the rabbins have made Abaddon the nethermost of the two regions into which they divide the lower world; but that in Rev. 9 : 11

Abaddon is the angel and not the abyss is perfectly evident in the Greek.

Apostle (*one sent forth*), in the New Testament originally the official name of those twelve of the disciples whom Jesus chose to send forth first to preach the gospel and to be with him during the course of his ministry on earth. The word also appears to have been used in a non-official sense to designate a much wider circle of Christian messengers and teachers. See 2 Cor. 8 : 23; Philip. 2 : 25. It is only of those who were officially designated apostles that we treat in this article. Their names are given in Matt. 10 : 2-4, and Christ's charge to them in the rest of the chapter.

Their office.—(1) The original qualification of an apostle, as stated by St. Peter on the occasion of electing a successor to the traitor Judas, was that he should have been personally acquainted with the whole ministerial course of our Lord, from his baptism by John till the day when he was taken up into heaven. (2) They were chosen by Christ himself. (3) They had the power of working miracles. (4) They were inspired. John 16 : 13. (5) Their work seems to have been pre-eminently that of founding the churches and upholding them by supernatural power specially bestowed for that purpose. (6) The office ceased, as a matter of course, with its first holders; all continuation of it, from the very conditions of its existence (cf. 1 Cor. 9 : 1), being impossible.

Early history and training. — The apostles were from the lower ranks of life, simple and uneducated; some of them were related to Jesus according to the flesh; some had previously been disciples of John the Baptist. Our Lord chose them early in his public career. They seem to have been all on an equality, both during and after the ministry of Christ on earth. Early in our Lord's ministry he sent them out two and two to preach repentance and to perform miracles in his name. Matt. 10; Luke 9. They accompanied him in his journeys, saw his wonderful works, heard his discourses addressed to the people, and made inquiries of him on religious matters. They recognized him as the Christ of God, Matt. 16 : 16; Luke 9 : 20, and ascribed to him supernatural power, Luke 9 : 54; but in the recognition of the spiritual teaching and mission of Christ they made very slow progress, held back

as they were by weakness of apprehension and by national prejudices. Even at the removal of our Lord from the earth they were yet weak in their knowledge, Luke 24 : 21; John 16 : 12, though he had for so long been carefully preparing and instructing them. On the feast of Pentecost, ten days after our Lord's ascension, the Holy Spirit came down on the assembled church, Acts 2; and from that time the apostles became altogether different men, giving witness with power of the life and death and resurrection of Jesus, as he had declared they should. Luke 24 : 48; Acts 1 : 8, 22; 2 : 32; 3 : 15; 5 : 32; 13 : 31.

Later labors and history.—First of all the mother-church at Jerusalem grew up under their hands, Acts 3-7, and their superior dignity and power were universally acknowledged by the rulers and the people. Acts 5 : 12 ff. Their first mission out of Jerusalem was to Samaria, Acts 8 : 5-25, where the Lord himself had, during his ministry, sown the seed of the gospel. Here ends the first period of the apostles' agency, during which its centre is Jerusalem and the prominent figure is that of St. Peter. The centre of the second period of the apostolic agency is Antioch, where a church soon was built up, consisting of Jews and Gentiles; and the central figure of this and of the subsequent period is St. Paul. The third apostolic period is marked by the almost entire disappearance of the twelve from the sacred narrative, and the exclusive agency of St. Paul, the great apostle of the Gentiles. Of the missionary work of the rest of the twelve we know absolutely nothing from the sacred narrative.

Appa'im, or **Ap'paim** (*the nostrils*), son of Nadab, and descended from Jerahmeel, the founder of an important family of the tribe of Judah. 1 Chron. 2 : 30, 31.

Appeal. The principle of appeal was recognized by the Mosaic law in the establishment of a central court under the presidency of the judge or ruler for the time being, before which all cases too difficult for the local courts were to be tried. Deut. 17 : 8, 9. According to the above regulation, the appeal lay in the time of the Judges to the judge, Judges 4 : 5, and under the monarchy to the king. Jehoshaphat delegated his judicial authority to a court permanently established for the purpose. 2 Chron. 19 : 8. These courts were re-established by

Ezra. Ezra 7 : 25. After the institution of the Sanhedrin the final appeal lay to them. St. Paul, as a Roman citizen, exercised a right of appeal from the jurisdiction of the local court at Jerusalem to the emperor. Acts 25 : 11.

Ap'phia (*fruitful*), a Christian woman addressed jointly with Philemon and Archippus in Phil. 2; apparently a member of Philemon's household, and not improbably his wife. (A.D. 57.)

Ap'pii Fo'rum (*market-place of Appius*), a well-known station on the Appian Way, the great road which led from Rome to the neighborhood of the Bay of Naples. Acts 28 : 15. There is no difficulty in identifying the site with some ruins near *Treponti*. [THREE TAVERNS.]

Ap'pius, Market of. Revised Version for Appii Forum. Acts 28 : 15.

Apple Tree, Apple (Heb. *tappûach*). Mention of the apple tree occurs in the Authorized Version in Cant. 2 : 3; 8 : 5, and Joel 1 : 12. The fruit of this tree is alluded to in Prov. 25 : 11 and Cant. 2 : 5; 7 : 8. It is a difficult matter to say what is the specific tree denoted by the Hebrew word *tappûach*. ("The apple proper is rare in Syria, and its fruit inferior.") Most modern writers maintain that it is either the quince or the citron; (others speak of the apricot, which is abundant and deliciously perfumed.) The quince has some plausible arguments in its favor. Its fragrance was held in high esteem by the ancients. The quince was sacred to Venus. On the other hand, Dr. Royle says, "The rich color, fragrant odor and handsome appearance of the citron, whether in flower or in fruit, are particularly suited to the passages of Scripture mentioned above." But neither the quince nor the citron nor the apple appears fully to answer to all the scriptural allusions. The *orange* would answer all the demands of the scriptural passages, and orange trees are found in Palestine; but there does not appear sufficient evidence that this tree was known in the earlier times to the inhabitants of Palestine. The question of identification, therefore, must still be left an open one.

Aq'uila (*an eagle*), a Jew whom St. Paul found at Corinth on his arrival from Athens. Acts 18 : 2. (A.D. 52.) He was a native of Pontus, but had fled, with his wife Priscilla, from Rome, in consequence of an order of Claudius commanding all Jews to leave the city. He became acquainted with St. Paul, and they abode together, and wrought at their common trade of making the Cilician tent or hair-cloth. On the departure of the apostle from Corinth, a year and six months after, Priscilla and Aquila accompanied him to Ephesus. There they remained, and there they taught Apollos. At what time they became Christians is uncertain.

Ar (*a city*), or **Ar of Moab,** one of the chief places of Moab. Num. 21 : 28; Isa. 15 : 1. In later times the place was known as Areopolis and Rabbath-Moab. The site is still called *Rabba*. It lies about halfway between *Kerak* and the *Wady Mojeb*, 10 or 11 miles from each, the Roman road passing through it.

A'ra (*lion*), one of the sons of Jether, the head of a family of Asherites. 1 Chron. 7 : 38.

A'rab (*ambush*), a city of Judah in the mountainous district, probably in the neighborhood of Hebron; mentioned only in Josh. 15 : 52.

Ar'abah (*burnt up*). Although this word appears in the Authorized Version in its original shape only in Josh. 18 : 18, yet in the Hebrew text it is of frequent occurrence. It indicates more particularly the deep-sunken valley or trench which forms the most striking among the many striking natural features of Palestine, and which extends with great uniformity of formation from the slopes of Hermon to the Elanitic Gulf (*Gulf of Akabah*) of the Red Sea; the most remarkable depression known to exist on the surface of the globe. Through the northern portion of this extraordinary fissure the Jordan rushes through the lakes of Huleh and Gennesaret down its tortuous course to the deep chasm of the Dead Sea. This portion, about 150 miles in length, is known amongst the Arabs by the name of *el-Ghor*. The southern boundary of the Ghor is the wall of cliffs which crosses the valley about 10 miles south of the Dead Sea. From their summits, southward to the Gulf of Akabah, the valley changes its name, or, it would be more accurate to say, retains its old name of *Wady el-Arabah*.

Ara'bia (*desert, barren*), a country known in the Old Testament under two designations:—1. *The East Country*, Gen. 25 : 6, or perhaps the *East*, Gen. 10 : 30; Num. 23 : 7; Isa. 2 : 6; and *Land of the Sons of the East*, Gen. 29 : 1; Gentile name, *Sons of the East*. Judges 6 : 3; 7 : 12;

1 Kings 4 : 30; Job 1 : 3; Isa. 11 : 14; Jer. 49 : 28; Ezek. 25 : 4. From these passages it appears that *Land of the East* and *Sons of the East* indicate, primarily, the country east of Palestine, and the tribes descended from Ishmael and from Keturah; and that this original signification may have become gradually extended to Arabia and its inhabitants generally, though without any strict limitation. 2. *'Aráb* and *'Arab,* whence Arabia. 2 Chron. 9 : 14; Isa. 21 : 13; Jer. 25 : 24; Ezek. 27 : 21. (Arabia is a triangular peninsula, included between the Mediterranean and Red seas, the Indian Ocean and the Persian Gulf. Its extreme length, north and south, is about 1300 miles, and its greatest breadth 1500 miles.—*Encyc. Brit.*)

Arab Chieftain.

Divisions.—Arabia may be divided into *Arabia Proper,* containing the whole peninsula as far as the limits of the northern deserts; *Northern Arabia (Arabia Deserta),* constituting the great desert of Arabia; and *Western Arabia,* the desert of Petra and the peninsula of Sinai, or the country that has been called *Arabia Petræa.* I. *Arabia Proper,* or the *Arabian peninsula,* consists of high table-land, declining towards the north. Most of it is well peopled, watered by wells and streams, and enjoys periodical rains. The most fertile tracts are those on the southwest and south. II. *Northern Arabia,* or the Arabian Desert, is a high, undulating, parched plain, of which the Euphrates forms the natural boundary from the Persian Gulf to the frontier of Syria, whence it is bounded by the latter country and the desert of Petra on the northwest and west, the peninsula of Arabia forming its southern limit. It has few oases, the water of the wells is generally either brackish or unpotable, and it is visited by the sand-wind called *Samoom.* The inhabitants, principally descended from Ishmael and from Keturah, have always led a wandering and pastoral life. They conducted a considerable trade of merchandise of Arabia and India from the shores of the Persian Gulf. Ezek. 27 : 20–24. III. *Western Arabia* includes the peninsula of Sinai [SINAI] and the desert of Petra, corresponding generally with the limits of Arabia Petræa. The latter name is probably derived from that of its chief city, not from its stony character. It was mostly peopled by descendants of Esau, and was generally known as the land of Edom or Idumæa [EDOM], as well as by its older appellation, the desert of Seir or Mount Seir. [SEIR.]

Inhabitants. — (Arabia, which once ruled from India to the Atlantic, now has eight or nine millions of inhabitants, about one-fifth of whom are Bedouin or wandering tribes, and the other four-fifths settled Arabs.—*Encyc. Brit.*) 1. The descendants of JOKTAN occupied the principal portions of the south and southwest of the peninsula, with colonies in the interior. The principal Joktanite kingdom, and the chief state of ancient Arabia, was that of the Yemen. 2. The ISHMAELITES appear to have entered the peninsula from the northwest. That they have spread over the whole of it (with the exception of one or two districts on the south coast), and that the modern nation is predominantly Ishmaelite, is asserted by the Arabs. 3. Of the descendants of KETURAH the Arabs say little. They appear to have settled chiefly north of the peninsula in Desert Arabia, from Palestine to the Persian Gulf. 4. In northern and western Arabia are other peoples, which, from their geographical position and mode of life, are sometimes classed with the Arabs. Of these are AMALEK, the descendants of ESAU, etc.

(*Productions.* — The productions are varied. The most noted animal is the horse. Camels, sheep, cattle, asses, mules and cats are common. Agricultural products are coffee, wheat, barley, millet, beans, pulse, dates and the common garden plants. In pasture lands Arabia is peculiarly fortunate. In mineral products it is singularly poor, lead being most abundant.—*Encyc. Brit.*)

Religion.—The most ancient idolatry of the Arabs we must conclude to have been fetishism. Magianism, an importation from Chaldæa and Persia, must be reckoned among the religions of the pagan Arabs; but it never had very numerous followers. Christianity was introduced into southern Arabia toward the close of the second century, and about a century later it had made great progress. It flourished chiefly in the Yemen, where many churches were built. Judaism was propagated in Arabia, principally by Karaites, at the captivity. They are now nominally Mohammedans.

Language.—Arabic, the language of Arabia, is the most developed and the richest of Shemitic languages, and the only one of which we have an extensive literature; it is, therefore, of great importance to the study of Hebrew.

Government.—Arabia is now under the government of the Ottoman empire.

Ara'bians, the nomadic tribes inhabiting the country to the east and south of Palestine, who in the early times of Hebrew history were known as Ishmaelites and descendants of Keturah.

A'rad (*a wild ass*), a Benjamite, son of Beriah, who drove out the inhabitants of Gath. 1 Chron. 8 : 15. (B.C. 536.)

A'rad, a royal city of the Canaanites, named with Hormah and Libnah. Josh. 12 : 14. The wilderness of Judah was to "the south of Arad." Judges 1 : 16. It may be identified with a hill, *Tel 'Arâd*, an hour and a half northeast by east from *Milh* (Moladah), and eight hours from Hebron.

A'rah (*wayfaring*). 1. An Asherite, of the sons of Ulla. 1 Chron. 7 : 39.

2. The sons of Arah returned with Zerubbabel in number 775 according to Ezra 2 : 5, but 652 according to Neh. 7 : 10. (B.C. 536.) One of his descendants, Shechaniah, was the father-in-law of Tobiah the Ammonite. Neh. 6 : 18.

A'ram (*high*). 1. The name by which the Hebrews designated, generally, the country lying to the northeast of Palestine; the great mass of that high tableland which, rising with sudden abruptness from the Jordan and the very margin

of the Lake of Gennesaret, stretches, at an elevation of no less than 2000 feet above the level of the sea, to the banks of the Euphrates itself. Throughout the Authorized Version the word is, with only a very few exceptions, rendered, as in the Vulgate and LXX., SYRIA. Its earliest occurrence in the book of Genesis is in the form of *Aram-naharaim, i. e.* the "highland of or between the two rivers." Gen. 24 : 10, Authorized Version "Mesopotamia." In the later history we meet with a number of small nations or kingdoms forming parts of the general land of Aram; but as Damascus increased in importance it gradually absorbed the smaller powers, 1 Kings 20 : 1, and the name of Aram was at last applied to it alone. Isa. 7 : 8; also 1 Kings 11 : 24, 25; 15 : 18, etc.

2. Another Aram is named in Gen. 22 : 21, as a son of Kemuel and descendant of Nahor.

3. An Asherite, one of the sons of Shamer. 1 Chron. 7 : 34.

4. Son of Esrom or Hezron, and the Greek form of the Hebrew RAM. Matt. 1 : 3, 4; Luke 3 : 33.

A'ram-nahara'im (*highlands of two rivers*). Ps. 60, title. [ARAM.]

A'ram-zo'bah. Ps. 60, title. [ARAM, 1.]

Arami'tess, a female inhabitant of Aram. 1 Chron. 7 : 14.

A'ran (*wild goat*), a Horite, son of Dishan and brother of Uz. Gen. 36 : 28; 1 Chron. 1 : 42.

Ar'arat (*high* or *holy ground*), a mountainous district of Asia mentioned in the Bible in connection with the following events:—(1) As the resting-place of the ark after the deluge. Gen. 8 : 4. (2) As the asylum of the sons of Sennacherib. 2 Kings 19 : 37; Isa. 37 : 38; Authorized Version has "the land of Armenia." (3) As the ally, and probably the neighbor, of Minni and Ashchenaz. Jer. 51 : 27. [ARMENIA.] The name Ararat was unknown to the geographers of Greece and Rome, as it still is to the Armenians of the present day; but it was an ancient name for a portion of Armenia. In its biblical sense it is descriptive generally of the Armenian highlands—the lofty plateau which overlooks the plain of the Araxes on the north and of Mesopotamia on the south. Various opinions have been put forth as to the spot where the ark rested, as described in Gen. 8 : 4; (but it is probable that it rested on some of the lower portions of the range than on the lofty peak to which exclusively) Europeans have given the name Ararat, the mountain which is called *Massis* by the Armenians, *Agri-Dagh*, i. e. *Steep Mountain*, by the Turks, and *Kuh-i-Nuh*, i. e. *Noah's Mountain*, by the Persians. It rises immediately out of the plain of the Araxes, and terminates in two conical peaks, named the Great and Less Ararat, about seven miles distant from each other; the former of which attains an elevation of 17,260 feet above the level of the sea and about 14,000 above the plain of the Araxes, while the latter is lower by 4000 feet. The summit of the higher is covered with eternal snow for about 3000 feet. *Arguri*, the only village known to have been built on its slopes, was the spot where, according to tradition, Noah planted his vineyard. "The mountains of Ararat," as co-extensive with the Armenian plateau from the base of *Ararat*

Mount Ararat. (*From a Photograph.*)

in the north to the range of *Kurdistán* in the south, we notice the following characteristics of that region as illustrating the Bible narrative: (1) Its *elevation*. It rises to a height of from 6000 to 7000 feet above the level of the sea. (2) Its *geographical position*. Viewed with reference to the dispersion of the nations, Armenia is the true centre of the world; and at the present day Ararat is the great boundary-stone between the empires of Russia, Turkey and Persia. (3) Its *physical character*. The plains as well as the mountains supply evidence of volcanic agency. (4) The *climate*. Winter lasts from October to May, and is succeeded by a brief spring and a summer of intense heat. (5) The *vegetation*. Grass grows luxuriantly on the plateau, and furnishes abundant pasture during the summer months to the flocks of the nomad Kurds. Wheat, barley and vines ripen at far higher altitudes than on the Alps and the Pyrenees.

Arau'nah (*ark*), a Jebusite who sold his threshing-floor on Mount Moriah to David as a site for an altar to Jehovah, together with his oxen. 2 Sam. 24 : 18–24; 1 Chron. 21 : 25.

Ar'ba (*city of the four*), the progenitor of the Anakim, or sons of Anak, from whom their chief city, HEBRON, received its name of Kirjath-Arba. Josh. 14 : 15; 15 : 13; 21 : 11.

Ar'bah. Hebron, or Kirjath-Arba, as

"the city of Arbah" is always rendered elsewhere. Gen. 35 : 27.

Ar'bathite, a native of the Arabah or *Ghor.* [ARABAH.] Abi-albon the Arbathite was one of David's mighty men. 2 Sam. 23 : 31; 1 Chron. 11 : 32.

Ar'bite, a native of Arab. Paarai the Arbite was one of David's guard. 2 Sam. 23 : 35.

Arch of Titus. A triumphal arch erected at Rome, and still remaining

Arch of Titus at Rome.

there, to commemorate the conquest of Judea and the destruction of Jerusalem by the emperor Titus. It was erected after his death, A.D. 91, by the senate and people of Rome. It was a magnificent structure, decorated with bas-reliefs and inscriptions, and is of especial interest because its historic bas-reliefs represent the captors carrying in triumph to Rome the golden candlestick and sacred utensils from the Jewish temple at Jerusalem. From these we obtain our best idea of their shape.—ED.

Archela'us (*prince of the people*), son of Herod the Great by a Samaritan woman, Malthaké, and, with his brother Antipas, brought up at Rome. At the death of Herod (B.C. 4) his kingdom was divided between his three sons, Herod Antipas, Archelaus and Philip. Archelaus never properly bore the title of king, Matt. 2 : 22, but only that of ethnarch. In the tenth year of his reign, or the ninth according to Dion Cassius, *i.e.* A.D. 6, a complaint was preferred against him by his brothers and his subjects on the ground of his tyranny, in consequence of which he was banished to Vienne in Gaul, where he is generally said to have died.

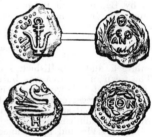

Coins of Archelaus.

Archery. [ARMS.]

Ar'chevites, perhaps the inhabitants of Erech, some of whom had been placed as colonists in Samaria. Ezra 4 : 9.

Ar'chi. Josh. 16 : 2. A place in the neighborhood of Bethel, on the boundary between Ephraim and Benjamin. It designates a clan perhaps originally from Erech in Babylonia, of which Hushai was one. [ARCHITE.]

Archip'pus (*master of the horse*), a Christian teacher in Colossæ, Col. 4 : 17, called by St. Paul his "fellow soldier," Phil. 2. He was probably a member of Philemon's family. (A.D. 62.)

Ar'chite, The (as if from a place named Erech, on the frontiers of Ephraim), the usual designation of David's friend Hushai. 2 Sam. 15 : 32; 17 : 5, 14; 1 Chron. 27 : 33.

Architecture. The book of Genesis, 4 : 17, 20, 22, appears to divide mankind into two great characteristic sections,

viz., the "dwellers in tents" and the "dwellers in cities." To the race of Shem is attributed, Gen. 10 : 11, 12, 22 ; 11 : 2–9, the foundation of those cities in the plain of Shinar, Babylon, Nineveh and others. The Israelites were by occupation shepherds, and by habit dwellers in tents. Gen. 47 : 3. They had therefore originally, speaking properly, no architecture. From the time of the occupation of Canaan they became dwellers in towns and in houses of stone. Lev. 14 : 34, 45 ; 1 Kings 7 : 10. The peaceful reign and vast wealth of Solomon gave great impulse to architecture ; for besides the temple and his other great works, he built fortresses and cities in various places, among which Baalath and Tadmor are in all probability represented by Baalbec and Palmyra. But the reigns of Herod and his successors were especially remarkable for their great architectural works. Not only was the temple restored, but the fortifications and other public buildings of Jerusalem were enlarged and embellished. Luke 21 : 5. The town of Cæsarea was built on the site of Strato's Tower ; Samaria was enlarged, and received the name of Sebaste. Of the original splendor of these great works no doubt can be entertained ; but of their style and appearance we can only conjecture that they were formed on Greek and Roman models. The enormous stones employed in the Assyrian, Persepolitan and Egyptian buildings find a parallel in the substructions of Baalbec and in the huge blocks which still remain at Jerusalem, relics of the buildings either of Solomon or of Herod.

Arctu'rus (*bear-keeper*). The Hebrew words *'Ash* and *'Aish*, rendered "Arcturus" in the Authorized Version of Job 9 : 9 ; 38 : 32, in conformity with the Vulgate of the former passage, are now generally believed to be identical, and to represent the constellation Ursa Major, known commonly as the Great Bear or Charles' Wain.

Ard (*one that descends*), the son of Bela and grandson of Benjamin. Gen. 46 : 21 ; Num. 26 : 40. In 1 Chron. 8 : 3 he is called ADDAR.

Ard'ites, the descendants of Ard or Addar, the grandson of Benjamin. Num. 26 : 40.

Ar'don (*fugitive*), a son of Caleb, the son of Hezron, by his wife Azubah. 1 Chron. 2 : 18.

Are'li (*heroic*), a son of Gad. Gen.

46 : 16 ; Num. 26 : 17. His descendants are called Arelites. Num. 26 : 17.

Areop'agite, a member of the court of Areopagus. Acts 17 : 34. [MARS' HILL.]

Areop'agus. [MARS' HILL.]

Are'tas, or **Ar'etas** (*graver*). 1. A contemporary of Antiochus Epiphanes, B.C. 170, and Jason. 2 Macc. 5 : 8.

2. The Aretas alluded to by St. Paul, 2 Cor. 11 : 32, was father-in-law of Herod Antipas.

Ar'gob (*stony*), a tract of country on the east of the Jordan, in Bashan, the kingdom of Og, containing 60 great and fortified cities. In later times it was called Trachonitis, and it is now apparently identified with the *Lejah*, a very remarkable district south of Damascus and east of the Sea of Galilee. Deut. 3 : 4, 13, 14.

Ar'gob, perhaps a Gileadite officer who was governor of Argob. He was either an accomplice of Pekah in the murder of Pekahiah or was slain by Pekah. 2 Kings 15 : 25.

Arid'a-i (*the strong*), ninth son of Haman. Esther 9 : 9.

Arid'atha, sixth son of Haman. Esther 9 : 8.

Ari'eh (*lion*). Either one of the accomplices of Pekah in his conspiracy against Pekahiah, or one of the princes of Pekahiah who was put to death with him. 2 Kings 15 : 25. (B.C. 757.)

A'riel (*lion of God*). 1. One of the "chief men" who under Ezra directed the caravan which he led back from Babylon to Jerusalem. Ezra 8 : 16. (B.C. 459.) The word occurs also in reference to two Moabites slain by Benaiah. 2 Sam. 23 : 20 ; 1 Chron. 11 : 22. Many regard the word as an epithet, "lion-like ;" but it seems better to look upon it as a proper name, and translate "two [sons] of Ariel."

2. A designation given by Isaiah to the city of Jerusalem. Isa. 29 : 1, 2, 7. We must understand by it either "lion of God," as the chief city, or "hearth of God," a synonym for the altar of burnt offering. On the whole it seems most probable that, as a name given to Jerusalem, Ariel means "lion of God," whilst the word used by Ezekiel, Ezek. 43 : 15, 16, means "hearth of God."

Arimathæ'a (*heights*). Matt. 27 : 57 ; Luke 23 : 51 ; John 19 : 38. St. Luke calls it "a city of Judea." It is identified by many with the modern *Ramleh*.

A'rioch (*venerable*). 1. The king of

Ellasar, one of the allies of Chedorlaomer in his expedition against his rebellious tributaries. Gen. 14 : 1. (B.C. 1921–1912.)

2. The captain of Nebuchadnezzar's body-guard. Dan. 2 : 14, etc.

3. Properly *Eirioch*, or *Erioch*, mentioned in Judith 1 : 6 as king of the Elymæans.

Aris'a-i (*lion-like*), eighth son of Haman. Esther 9 : 9.

Aristar'chus (*the best ruler*), a Thessalonian, Acts 20 : 4; 27 : 2, who accompanied St. Paul on his third missionary journey. Acts 19 : 29. He was with the apostle on his return to Asia, Acts 20 : 4; and again, 27 : 2, on his voyage to Rome. We trace him afterwards as St. Paul's fellow prisoner in Col. 4 : 10 and Phil. 24. Tradition makes him bishop of Apamea.

Aristobu'lus (*the best counsellor*), a resident at Rome, some of whose household are greeted in Rom. 16 : 10. Tradition makes him one of the 70 disciples, and reports that he preached the gospel in Britain.

Ark, Noah's. [NOAH.]

Ark of the Covenant.

Ark of the Covenant. The first piece of the tabernacle's furniture, for which precise directions were delivered. Ex. 25. I. *Description.*—It appears to have been an oblong chest of shittim (acacia) wood, 2½ cubits long by 1½ broad and deep. Within and without gold was overlaid on the wood, and on the upper side or lid, which was edged round about with gold, the mercy-seat was placed. The ark was fitted with rings, one at each of the four corners, and through these were passed staves of the same wood similarly overlaid, by which it was carried by the Kohathites. Num. 7 : 9; 10 : 21. The ends of the staves were visible without the veil in the holy place of the temple of Solomon. 1 Kings 8 : 8. The ark, when transported, was enveloped in the "veil" of the dismantled tabernacle, in the curtain of badgers' skins, and in a blue cloth over all, and was therefore not seen. Num. 4 : 5, 20.

II. Its purpose was to contain inviolate the divine autograph of the two tables, that "covenant" from which it derived its title. It was also probably a reliquary for the pot of manna and the rod of Aaron.

III. *History.*—Before David's time its abode was frequently shifted. It sojourned among several, probably Levitical, families, 1 Sam. 7 : 1; 2 Sam. 6 : 3, 11; 1 Chron. 13 : 13; 15 : 24, 25, in the border villages of eastern Judah, and did not take its place in the tabernacle, but dwelt in curtains, *i. e.* in a separate tent pitched for it in Jerusalem by David. Subsequently the temple, when completed, received, in the installation of the ark in its shrine, the signal of its inauguration by the effulgence of divine glory instantly manifested. It was probably taken captive or destroyed by Nebuchadnezzar, 2 Esdr. 10 : 22, so that there was no ark in the second temple.

Ark of Moses. A small boat or basket made of the papyrus, a reed which grows in the marshes of Egypt. It was covered with bitumen to make it water-tight.

Ar'kite, The, from *Arka*, one of the families of the Canaanites, Gen. 10 : 17; 1 Chron. 1 : 15, and from the context evidently located in the north of Phœnicia. The site which now bears the name of '*Arka* lies on the coast, 2 to 2½ hours from the shore, about 12 miles north of

Tripoli and 5 south of the *Nahr el-Kebir*.

Armaged'don (*the hill* or *city of Megiddo*). Rev. 16 : 16. The scene of the struggle of good and evil is suggested by that battle-field, the plain of Esdraelon, which was famous for two great victories, of Barak over the Canaanites and of Gideon over the Midianites; and for two great disasters, the deaths of Saul and Josiah. Hence it signifies in Revelation a place of great slaughter, the scene of a terrible retribution upon the wicked. The Revised Version gives the name as *Har-Magedon, i. e.* the *hill* (as *Ar* is the *city*) of *Megiddo.*—ED.)

Arme'nia (*land of Aram*) is nowhere mentioned under that name in the original Hebrew, though it occurs in the English version, 2 Kings 19 : 37, for Ararat. *Description.*—Armenia is that lofty plateau whence the rivers Euphrates, Tigris, Araxes and Acampsis pour down their waters in different directions; the first two to the Persian Gulf, the last two respectively to the Caspian and Euxine seas. It may be termed the *nucleus* of the mountain system of western Asia. From the centre of the plateau rise two lofty chains of mountains, which run from east to west. *Divisions.*—Three districts are mentioned in the Bible. (1) ARARAT is mentioned as the place whither the sons of Sennacherib fled. Isa. 37 : 38. It was the central district, surrounding the mountain of that name. (2) MINNI only occurs in Jer. 51 : 27. It is probably identical with the district Minyas, in the upper valley of the *Murad-su* branch of the Euphrates. (3) TOGARMAH is noticed in two passages of Ezekiel, 27 : 14; 38 : 6, both of which are in favor of its identity with Armenia. *Present condition.*—The Armenians, numbering about two millions, are nominally Christians. About half of them live in Armenia. Their favorite pursuit is commerce. The country is divided, as to government, between Russia, Turkey and Persia.—ED.

Armlet, an ornament universal in the East, especially among women; used by princes as one of the insignia of royalty, and by distinguished persons in general. The word is not used in the Authorized Version, as even in 2 Sam. 1 : 10 it is rendered by " the bracelet on his arm."

Armo'ni, son of Saul by Rizpah. 2 Sam. 21 : 8.

Arms, Armor. The subject naturally divides itself into—1. Offensive weapons : Arms. II. Defensive weapons : Armor.

I. *Offensive weapons.*—1. Apparently the earliest known and most widely used was the *Chereb* or SWORD. Very little can be gathered as to its shape, size, ma-

Soldier in full Armor.

terial or mode of use. Perhaps if anything is to be inferred it is that the *Chereb* is both a lighter and a shorter weapon than the modern sword. It was carried in a sheath, 1 Sam. 17 : 51; 2 Sam. 20 : 8; 1 Chron. 21 : 27, slung by a girdle, 1 Sam. 25 : 13, and resting upon the thigh, Ps. 45 : 3; Judges 3 : 16, or upon the hips. 2 Sam. 20 : 8. 2. Next we have the SPEAR; and of this weapon we meet with at least three distinct kinds. *a.* The *Chanith,* a "spear," and that of the largest kind. It was the weapon of Goliath, 1 Sam. 17 : 7, 45; 2 Sam. 21 : 19; 1 Chron. 20 : 5, and also of other giants, 2 Sam. 23 : 21; 1 Chron. 11 : 23, and mighty warriors. 2 Sam. 2 : 23; 23 : 18; 1 Chron. 11 : 11, 20. *b.* Apparently lighter than the preceding was the *Cidón* or "javelin." When not in action the

Cîdôn was carried on the back of the warrior, 1 Sam. 17:6, Authorized Version "target." *c.* Another kind of spear was the *Rômach.* In the historical books it occurs in Num. 25:7 and 1 Kings 18:28, and frequently in the later books, as in

Egyptian Archer.

1 Chron. 12:8 ("buckler"); 2 Chron. 11:12. (It varied much in length, weight and size.) *d.* The *Shelach* was probably a lighter missile or "dart." See 2 Chron. 23:10; 32:5 ("darts"); Neh. 4:17, 23 (see margin); Job 33:18; 36:12; Joel 2:8. *e. Shebet,* a rod or staff, is used once only to denote a weapon. 2 Sam.

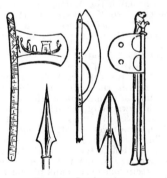

Egyptian Battle-axes.

18:14. 3. Of missile weapons of offence the chief was undoubtedly the BOW, *Kesheth.* The ARROWS were carried in a quiver. Gen. 27:3; Isa. 22:6; 49:2; Ps. 127:5. From an allusion in Job 6:4 they would seem to have been some-

times poisoned; and Ps. 120:4 may point to a practice of using arrows with some burning material attached to them. 4. The SLING is first mentioned in Judges 20:16. This simple weapon, with which David killed the giant Philistine, was the natural attendant of a shepherd. Later in the monarchy, slingers formed part of the regular army. 2 Kings 3:25. 5. The BATTLE-AXE, Jer. 51:20, a powerful weapon, of whose exact form we have no knowledge.

II. *Armor.* — 1. The BREASTPLATE, enumerated in the description of the arms of Goliath, a "*coat* of mail," literally a "*breastplate* of scales." 1 Sam. 17:5. This word has furnished one of the names of Mount Hermon. See Deut. 3:9. 2. The HABERGEON is mentioned but twice—in reference to the gown of the high priest. Ex. 28:32; 39:23. It was probably a quilted shirt or doublet. 3. The HELMET is referred to in 1 Sam.

Assyrian Helmets.

17:5; 2 Chron. 26:14; Ezek. 27:10. 4. GREAVES or defences for the feet, made of brass, are named in 1 Sam. 17:6 only. 5. Two kinds of SHIELD are distinguishable. *a.* The large shield, encompassing, Ps. 5:12, the whole person. When not in actual conflict it was carried before the warrior. 1 Sam. 17:7, 41. *b.* Of smaller dimensions was the *buckler* or *target,* probably for use in hand-to-hand fight. 1 Kings 10:16; 2 Chron. 9:15, 16.

Army. I. JEWISH ARMY. — Every man above 20 years of age was a soldier, Num. 1:3: each tribe formed a regiment, with its own banner and its own leader, Num. 2:2; 10:14: their positions in the camp or on the march were accurately fixed, Num. 2: the whole army started and stopped at a given signal, Num. 10:5, 6: thus they came up out of Egypt ready for the fight. Ex. 13:18. On the approach of an enemy a conscription was made from the general body, under the direction of a muster-master, Deut. 20 : 5 ; 2 Kings 25 : 19, by whom also the officers were appointed. Deut. 20 : 9. The army was then divided into thousands and hundreds under their respective captains, Num. 31 : 14, and still further into families. Num. 2 : 34 ; 2 Chron. 25 : 5 ; 26 : 12. With the kings arose the custom of maintaining a body-guard, which formed the nucleus of a standing army, and David's band of 600, 1 Sam. 23 : 13 ; 25 : 13, he retained after he became king, and added the CHERETHITES and PELETHITES. 2 Sam. 15 : 18 ; 20 : 7. David further organized a national militia, divided into twelve regiments under their respective officers, each of which was called out for one month in the year. 1 Chron. 27. It does not appear that the system established by David was maintained by the kings of Judah ; but in Israel the proximity of the hostile kingdom of Syria necessitated the maintenance of a standing army. The maintenance and equipment of the soldiers at the public expense dates from the establishment of a standing army. It is doubtful whether the soldier ever received pay even under the kings.

II. ROMAN ARMY.—The Roman army

Roman Captain or Centurion.

was divided into legions, the number of which varied considerably (from 3000 to 6000), each under six tribuni ("chief captains," Acts 21 : 31), who commanded by turns. The legion was subdivided into ten cohorts (" band," Acts 10 : 1), the cohort into three maniples, and the maniple into two centuries, containing originally 100 men, as the name implies, but subsequently from 50 to 100 men, according to the strength of the legion. There were thus 60 centuries in a legion, each under the command of a centurion. Acts 10 : 1, 22 ; Matt. 8 : 5 ; 27 : 54. In addition to the legionary cohorts, independent cohorts of volunteers served under the Roman standards. One of these cohorts was named the Italian, Acts 10 : 1, as consisting of volunteers from Italy. The head-quarters of the Roman forces in Judea were at Cæsarea.

Ar'nan. In the received Hebrew text " the sons of Arnan " are mentioned in the genealogy of Zerubbabel. 1 Chron. 3 : 21.

Ar'ni. (Used in the Revised Version for Aram in Luke 3 : 33, and is probably another name or form of the name of Aram. [ARAM, 4.])

Ar'non (*roaring*), the river or torrent which formed the boundary between Moab and the Amorites, on the north of Moab, Num. 21 : 13, 14, 24, 26 ; Judges 11 : 22, and afterwards between Moab and Israel (Reuben). Deut. 2 : 24, 36 ; 3 : 8, 12, 16 ; 4 : 48 ; Josh. 12 : 1, 2 ; 13 : 9, 16 ; Judges 11 : 13, 26. There can be no doubt that the *Wady el-Mojeb* of the present day is the Arnon. Its principal source is near *Katrane*, on the Haj route.

A'rod (*a wild ass*), a son of Gad, Num. 26 : 17, called ARODI in Gen. 46 : 16.

Ar'odi. [AROD.]

Ar'odites. [AROD.]

Ar'oer (*ruins*). 1. A city on the torrent Arnon, the southern point of the territory of Sihon king of the Amorites, and afterwards of the tribe of Reuben, Deut. 2 : 36 ; 3 : 12 ; 4 : 48 ; Josh. 12 : 2 ; 13 : 9, 16 ; Judges 11 : 26 ; 2 Kings 10 : 33 ; 1 Chron. 5 : 8, but later again in possession of Moab. Jer. 48 : 19. It is the modern *Arâ'ir*, upon the very edge of the precipitous north bank of the *Wady Mojeb.*

2. Aroer, " that is ' facing ' Rabbah " (Rabbah of Ammon), a town built by and belonging to Gad. Num. 32 : 34 ; Josh. 13 : 25 ; 2 Sam. 24 : 5. This is probably the place mentioned in Judges 11 : 33, which was shown in Jerome's time.

3. Aroer, in Isa. 17 : 2, if a place at all, must be still farther north than either of the two already named.

4. A town in Judah, named only in 1 Sam. 30 : 28, perhaps *Wady Ar'árah*, on the road from Petra to Gaza.

Aro'erite. Hothan the Aroerite was the father of two of David's captains. 1 Chron. 11 : 44.

Ar'pad, or **Ar'phad** (*strong city*), Isa. 36 : 19 ; 37 : 13, a city or district in Syria, apparently dependent on Damascus. Jer. 49 : 23. No trace of its existence has yet been discovered. 2 Kings 18 : 34 ; 19 : 13 ; Isa. 10 : 9.

Arphax'ad (*stronghold of the Chaldees*). 1. The son of Shem and ancestor of Eber. Gen. 10 : 22, 24 ; 11 : 10.

2. Arphaxad, a king "who reigned over the Medes in Ecbatana," Judith 1 : 1–4 ; perhaps the same as Phraortes, who fell in a battle with the Assyrians, 633 B.C.

Arrows. [ARMS.]

Artaxerx'es (*the great warrior*). 1. The first Artaxerxes is mentioned in Ezra 4 : 7, and appears identical with Smerdis, the Magian impostor and pretended brother of Cambyses, who usurped the throne B.C. 522, and reigned eight months.

2. In Neh. 2 : 1 we have another Artaxerxes. We may safely identify him with Artaxerxes Macrocheir or Longimanus, the son of Xerxes, who reigned B.C. 464–425.

Ar'temas (*gift of Artemis*), a companion of St. Paul. Titus 3 : 12. According to tradition he was bishop of Lystra.

Ar'uboth (*windows*), the third of Solomon's commissariat districts. 1 Kings 4 : 10. It included Sochoh, and was therefore probably a name for the rich corn-growing lowland country.

Aru'mah (*height*), a place apparently in the neighborhood of Shechem, at which Abimelech resided. Judges 9 : 41.

Ar'vad (*wandering*). Ezek. 27 : 8, 11. The island of *Ruad*, which lies off Tortosa (*Tartus*), two or three miles from the Phoenician coast. In agreement with this is the mention of "the Arvadite," in Gen. 10 : 18 and 1 Chron. 1 : 16, as a son of Canaan, with Zidon, Hamath and other northern localities.

Ar'vadite. [ARVAD.]

Ar'za, prefect of the palace at Tirzah to Elah king of Israel, who was assassinated at a banquet in his house by Zimri. 1 Kings 16 : 9.

A'sa (*physician*, or *cure*). 1. Son of Abijah and third king of Judah (B.C. 956–916.) (His long reign of 41 years was peaceful in its earlier portion, and he undertook the reformation of all abuses, especially of idolatry. He burnt the symbol of his grandmother Maachah's religion and deposed her from the dignity of "king's mother,") and renewed the great altar which the idolatrous priests apparently had desecrated. 2 Chron. 15 : 8. Besides this he fortified cities on his frontiers, and raised an army, amounting, according to 2 Chron. 14 : 8, to 580,000 men, a number probably exaggerated by an error of the copyist. During Asa's reign, Zerah, at the head of an enormous host, 2 Chron. 14 : 9, attacked Mareshah. There he was utterly defeated, and driven back with immense loss to Gerar. The peace which followed this victory was broken by the attempt of Baasha of Israel to fortify Ramah. To stop this Asa purchased the help of Ben-hadad I. king of Damascus, by a large payment of treasure, forced Baasha to abandon his purpose, and destroyed the works which he had begun at Ramah. In his old age Asa suffered from gout. He died, greatly loved and honored, in the 41st year of his reign.

2. Ancestor of Berechiah, a Levite who resided in one of the villages of the Netophathites after the return from Babylon. 1 Chron. 9 : 16.

As'ahel (*made by God*). 1. Nephew of David, being the youngest son of his sister Zeruiah. He was celebrated for his swiftness of foot. When fighting under his brother Joab at Gibeon, he pursued Abner, who was obliged to kill him in self-defence. 2 Sam. 2 : 18 ff. [ABNER.] (B.C. 1050.)

2. One of the Levites in the reign of Jehoshaphat, who went throughout the cities of Judah to instruct the people in the knowledge of the law. 2 Chron. 17 : 8. (B.C. 910.)

3. A Levite in the reign of Hezekiah, who had charge of the tithes and dedicated things in the temple. 2 Chron. 31 : 13. (B.C. 927.)

4. A priest, father of Jonathan, in the time of Ezra. Ezra 10 : 15. He is called AZAEL in 1 Esd. 9 : 14. (B.C. before 459.)

Asahi'ah (*the Lord hath made*), a servant of King Josiah, sent by him to seek information of Jehovah respecting the book of the law which Hilkiah found in the temple, 2 Kings 22 : 12, 14 ; also called ASAIAH. 2 Chron. 34 : 20. (B.C. 641.)

Asai'ah (*the Lord hath made*). 1. A prince of one of the families of the Simeonites in the reign of Hezekiah. 1 Chron. 4 : 36. (B.C. 910.)

2. A Levite in the reign of David, chief of the family of Merari. 1 Chron. 6 : 30. With 120 of his brethren he took part in bringing the ark from the house of Obed-edom to the city of David. 1 Chron. 15 : 6, 11.

3. The first-born of "the Shilonite," from Shiloni, 1 Chron. 9 : 5, who with his family dwelt in Jerusalem after the return from Babylon. (B.C. 536.) In Neh. 11 : 5 he is called MAASEIAH.

4. 2 Chron. 34 : 20. [ASAHIAH.]

A'saph (*collector of the people*). 1. A Levite, son of Berechiah, one of the leaders of David's choir. 1 Chron. 6 : 39. Psalms 50 and 73–83 are attributed to him; and he was in after times celebrated as a seer as well as a musical composer. 2 Chron. 29 : 30; Neh. 12 : 46. (B.C. 1050.)

2. The father or ancestor of Joah, the chronicler to the kingdom of Judah in the reign of Hezekiah, 2 Kings 18 : 18, 37; Isa. 36 : 3, 22; probably the same as the preceding.

3. The keeper of the royal forest or "paradise" of Artaxerxes, Neh. 2 : 8; a Jew, in high office at the court of Persia. (B.C. 536.)

4. Ancestor of Mattaniah, the conductor of the temple-choir after the return from Babylon. 1 Chron. 9 : 15; Neh. 11 : 17. Most probably the same as 1 and 2.

A'saph, Sons of. (A school of poets and musical composers founded by Asaph.)

Asar'e-el (*whom God hath bound* (by an oath)), a son of Jehaleleel, in the genealogies of Judah. 1 Chron. 4 : 16.

Asare'lah (*upright toward God*), one of the sons of Asaph, a musician, 1 Chron. 25 : 2; called JESHARELAH in ver. 14.

As'calon. [ASHKELON.]

As'enath (*worshipper of Neith*), daughter of Potipherah, priest, or possibly prince, of On [POTIPHERAH], wife of Joseph, Gen. 41 : 45, and mother of Manasseh and Ephraim. Gen. 41 : 50; 46 : 20. (B.C. 1715.)

A'ser. Luke 2 : 36; Rev. 7 : 6. [ASHER.]

Ash (Heb. *óren*), only in Isa. 44 : 14. As the true ash is not a native of Pales-

tine, some understand this to be a species of pine tree. Perhaps the larch (*Laryx europæa*) may be intended.

A'shan (*smoke*), a city in the low country of Judah. Josh. 15 : 42. In Josh. 19 : 7 and 1 Chron. 4 : 32 it is mentioned again as belonging to Simeon. It has not yet been identified.

Ash'bea (*I adjure*), a proper name, but whether of a person or place is uncertain. 1 Chron. 4 : 21.

Ash'bel (*reproof of God*), second son of Benjamin and ancestor of the Ashbelites. Gen. 46 : 21; Num. 26 : 38; 1 Chron. 8 : 1.

Ash'chenaz. 1 Chron. 1 : 6; Jer. 51 : 27. [ASHKENAZ.]

Ash'dod, or **Azo'tus** (*a stronghold*), Acts 8 : 40; one of the five confederate cities of the Philistines, situated about 30 miles from the southern frontier of Palestine, three from the Mediterranean Sea, and nearly midway between Gaza and Joppa. It was assigned to the tribe of Judah, Josh. 15 : 47, but was never subdued by the Israelites. Its chief importance arose from its position on the high road from Palestine to Egypt. It is now an insignificant village, with no memorials of its ancient importance, but is still called *Esdud*.

Ash'dodites, the inhabitants of Ashdod, Neh. 4 : 7; called Ashdothites in Josh. 13 : 3.

Ash'doth-pis'gah, Deut. 3 : 17; Josh. 12 : 3; 13 : 20; and in Deut. 4 : 49, Authorized Version, translated *springs of Pisgah, i. e.* a valley or fountain near Mount Pisgah.

Ash'er, Apocrypha and New Testament, **A'ser** (*blessed*), the eighth son of Jacob, by Zilpah, Leah's handmaid. Gen. 30 : 13. (B.C. 1753.) The general position of his tribe was on the seashore from Carmel northward, with Manasseh on the south, Zebulun and Issachar on the southeast, and Naphtali on the northeast. Josh. 19 : 24–31; 17 : 10, 11 and Judges 1 : 31, ·32. They possessed the maritime portion of the rich plain of Esdraelon, probably for a distance of 8 or 10 miles from the shore. This territory contained some of the richest soil in all Palestine.

Ash'er, a place which formed one boundary of the tribe of Manasseh on the south. Josh. 17 : 7. Mr. Porter suggests that *Teyâsir* may be the Asher of Manasseh. *Handbook*, p. 348.

Ash'erah (*straight*), the name of a

Ashdod.

Phœnician goddess, or rather of the idol itself (Authorized Version "grove"). Asherah is closely connected with ASH-TORETH and her worship, Judges 3 : 7, comp. 2 : 3 ; Judges 6 : 25 ; 1 Kings 18 : 19 ; Ashtoreth being, perhaps, the proper name of the goddess, whilst Asherah is the name of her image or symbol, which was of wood. See Judges 6 : 25-30 ; 2 Kings 23 : 14.

Ash'erites, descendants of Asher, and members of his tribe. Judges 1 : 32.

Ashes. The ashes on the altar of burnt offering were gathered into a cavity in its surface. The ashes of a red heifer burnt entire, according to regulations prescribed in Num. 19, had the ceremonial efficacy of purifying the unclean, Heb. 9 : 13, but of polluting the clean. [SACRIFICE.] Ashes about the person, especially on the head, were used as a sign of sorrow. [MOURNING.]

Ash'ima, a god of the Hamathite colonists in Samaria. 2 Kings 17 : 30. It has been regarded as identical with the Pan of the Greeks.

Ash'kelon, As'kelon, Apocrypha **As'calon** (*migration*), one of the five cities of the Philistines, Josh. 13 : 3 ; 1 Sam. 6 : 17 ; a seaport on the Mediterranean, 10 miles north of Gaza. Samson went down from Timnath to Ashkelon. Judges 14 : 19. In the post-biblical times Ashkelon rose to considerable importance. Near the town were the temple and sacred lake of Derceto, the Syrian Venus. The soil around was remarkable for its fertility. Ashkelon played a memorable part in the struggles of the Crusades.

Ash'kenaz (*spreading fire*), one of the three sons of Gomer, son of Japhet. Gen. 10 : 3. We may probably recognize the tribe of Ashkenaz on the northern shore of Asia Minor in the name of Lake Ascanius, and in Europe in the name *Scand*-ia, *Scand*-inavia. Knobel considers that Ashkenaz is to be identified with the German race.

Ash'nah, the name of two cities, both in the lowlands of Judah : (1) named between Zoreah and Zanoah, and therefore probably northwest of Jerusalem, Josh. 15 : 33 ; and (2) between Jiptah and Nezib, and therefore to the southwest of Jerusalem. Josh. 15 : 43. Each, according to Robinson's map (1857), would be about 16 miles from Jerusalem.

Ash'penaz (*horse-nose*), the master of the eunuchs of Nebuchadnezzar. Dan. 1 : 3.

Ash'riel, properly **As'riel** (*vow of God*). 1 Chron. 7 : 14.

Ash'taroth, and once **As'taroth** (*a star*), a city on the east of Jordan, in Bashan, in the kingdom of Og, doubtless so called from being a seat of the worship of the goddess of the same name. Deut. 1 : 4; Josh. 9 : 10; 12 : 4; 13 : 12.

Ashte'rathite, a native or inhabitant of Ashtaroth, 1 Chron. 11 : 44, beyond Jordan.

Ash'teroth Karna'im (*Ashteroth of the two horns* or *peaks*), a place of very great antiquity, the abode of the Rephaim. Gen. 14 : 5. The name reappears but once, as Carnaim or Carnion, 1 Macc. 5 : 26, 43, 44; 2 Macc. 12 : 21, 26, in "the land of Galaad." It is probably the modern *Es-Sanamein*, on the Haj route, about 25 miles south of Damascus.

Ash'toreth (*a star*), the principal female divinity of the Phœnicians, called Ishtar by the Assyrians and Astarte by the Greeks and Romans. She was by

Figure of Ashtoreth.

some ancient writers identified with the moon. But on the other hand the Assyrian Ishtar was not the moon-goddess, but the planet Venus; and Astarte was by many identified with the goddess Venus (or Aphrodite), as well as with the plant of that name. It is certain that the worship of Astarte became identified with that of Venus, and that this worship was connected with the most impure rites is apparent from the close connection of this goddess with ASHERAH. 1 Kings 11 : 5, 33; 2 Kings 23 : 13.

Ash'ur (*black*), the posthumous son of Hezron by his wife Abiah. 1 Chron. 2 : 24; 4 : 5. He became "father" or founder of the town of Tekoa. (B.C. 1658.)

Ash'urites, The. Only in 2 Sam. 2 : 9. By some of the old interpreters the name is taken as meaning the Geshurites; but if we follow the Targum of Jonathan, "the Asherites" will denote the inhabitants of the whole of the country west of the Jordan above Jézreel.

Ash'vath, one of the sons of Japhlet, of the tribe of Asher. 1 Chron. 7 : 33.

A'sia (*orient*). The passages in the New Testament where this word occurs are the following: Acts 2 : 9; 6 : 9; 16 : 6; 19 : 10, 22, 26, 27; 20 : 4, 16, 18; 21 : 27; 27 : 2; Rom. 16 : 5; 1 Cor. 16 : 19; 2 Cor. 1 : 8; 2 Tim. 1 : 15; 1 Pet. 1 : 1; Rev. 1 : 4, 11. In all these it may be confidently stated that the word is used for a Roman province which embraced the western part of the peninsula of Asia Minor, and of which Ephesus was the capital.

Asiar'chæ (*chief of Asia*) (Authorized Version; Acts 19 : 31), officers chosen annually by the cities of that part of the province of Asia of which Ephesus was, under Roman government, the metropolis. They had charge of the public games and religious theatrical spectacles, the expenses of which they bore.

A'siel (*created by God*). 1. A Simeonite whose descendant Jehu lived in the reign of Hezekiah. 1 Chron. 4 : 35.

2. One of the five swift writers whom Esdras was commanded to take to write the law and the history of the world. 2 Esd. 14 : 24.

As'nah (*thorn-bush*). The children of Asnah were among the Nethinim who returned with Zerubbabel. Ezra 2 : 50.

Asnap'per (*swift*), mentioned in Ezra 4 : 10 as the person who settled the Cuthæans in the cities of Samaria. He was probably a general of Esarhaddon. (B.C. 712.)

Asp (Heb. *pethen*), translated *adder* in Ps. 58 : 4; 91 : 13. Probably the Egyptian cobra, a small and very poisonous serpent, a dweller in the holes of walls, Isa. 11 : 8, and a snake upon which the serpent-charmers practiced their art.

Aspal'athus, the name of some sweet perfume mentioned in Ecclus. 24 : 15. The *Lignum rhodianum* is by some supposed to be the substance indicated by the *aspalathus;* the plant which yields it is the *Convolvulus scoparius* of Linnæus.

As′patha, third son of Haman. Esth. 9 : 7.

As′phar, the pool in the "wilderness of Thecoe." 1 Macc. 9 : 33. Is it possible that the name is a corruption of *lacus Asphaltites?*

As′riel, the son of Gilead and great-grandson of Manasseh. Num. 26 : 31; Josh. 17 : 2. He was the founder of the family of the Asrielites. (B.C. 1444.)

Eastern Ass.

Ass. Five Hebrew names of the genus *Asinus* occur in the Old Testament. 1. *Chamôr* denotes the male domestic ass. 2. *Athôn,* the common domestic she-ass. 3. *Aïr,* the name of a wild ass, which occurs Gen. 32 : 15 ; 49 : 11. 4. *Pere,* a species of wild ass mentioned Gen. 12 : 16. 5. *Arôd* occurs only in Job 39 : 5 ; but in what respect it differs from the *Pere* is uncertain. The ass in eastern countries is a very different animal from what he is in western Europe. The most noble and honorable amongst the Jews were wont to be mounted on asses. (With us the ass is a symbol of stubbornness and stupidity, while in the East it is especially remarkable for its patience, gentleness, intelligence, meek submission and great power of endurance."—*L. Abbott.* The color is usually a reddish brown, but there are white asses, which are much prized. The ass was the animal of peace, as the horse was the animal of war; hence the appropriateness of Christ in his triumphal entry riding on an ass. The wild ass is a beautiful animal.—ED.) Mr. Layard remarks that in fleetness the wild ass (*Asinus hemippus*) equals the gazelle, and to overtake it is a feat which only one or two of the most celebrated mares have been known to accomplish.

As′shur, second son of Shem, Gen. 10 : 22; also the Hebrew form for Assyria. [ASSYRIA.]

Asshu′rim (*steps*), a tribe descended from Dedan, the grandson of Abraham. Gen. 25 : 3. Knobel considers them the same with the Asshur of Ezek. 27 : 23, and connected with southern Arabia.

As′sir (*captive*). 1. Son of Korah. Ex. 6 : 24; 1 Chron. 6 : 22.

2. Son of Ebiasaph, and a forefather of Samuel. 1 Chron. 6 : 23, 37.

3. Son of Jeconiah, 1 Chron. 3 : 17, unless "Jeconiah the captive" be the true rendering.

As′sos, or **As′sus** (*approaching*), a seaport of the Roman province of Asia, in the district anciently called Mysia, on the northern shore of the Gulf of Adramyttium, and about seven miles from Lesbos. Acts 20 : 13, 14.

As′sur. Ezra 4 : 2; Ps. 83 : 8. [ASSHUR; ASSYRIA.]

Assyr′ia, As′shur, was a great and powerful country lying on the Tigris, Gen. 2 : 14, the capital of which was Nineveh. Gen. 10 : 11, etc. It derived its name apparently from Asshur, the son of Shem, Gen. 10 : 22, who in later times was worshipped by the Assyrians as their chief god.

1. *Extent.*—The boundaries of Assyria differed greatly at different periods. Probably in the earliest times it was confined to a small tract of low country lying chiefly on the left bank of the Tigris. Gradually its limits were extended, until it came to be regarded as comprising the whole region between the Armenian mountains (lat. 37° 30′) upon the north, and upon the south the country about Baghdad (lat. 33° 30′). Eastward its boundary was the high range of Zagros, or mountains of *Kurdistán;* westward it was, according to the views of some, bounded by the Mesopotamian desert, while according to others it reached the Euphrates.

2. *General character of the country.*— On the north and east the high mountain-chains of Armenia and Kurdistán are succeeded by low ranges of limestone hills of a somewhat arid aspect. To these ridges there succeeds at first an undulating zone of country, well watered and fairly productive, which extends in length for 250 miles, and is interrupted only by a single limestone range. Above

and below this barrier is an immense level tract, now for the most part a wilderness, which bears marks of having been in early times well cultivated and thickly peopled throughout.

3. *Original peopling.* — Scripture informs us that Assyria was peopled from Babylon, Gen. 10 : 11, and both classical tradition and the monuments of the country agree in this representation.

4. *Date of the foundation of the kingdom.*—As a country, Assyria was evidently known to Moses. Gen. 2 : 14; 25 : 18; Num. 24 : 22, 24. The foundation of the Assyrian empire was probably not very greatly anterior to B.C. 1228.

5. *History.* — The Mesopotamian researches have rendered it apparent that the original seat of government was not at Nineveh, but at *Kileh-Sherghat*, on the right bank of the Tigris. The most remarkable monarch of the earlier kings was called Tiglath-pileser. He appears to have been king towards the close of the twelfth century, and thus to have been contemporary with Samuel. Afterwards followed Pul, who invaded Israel in the reign of Menahem, 2 Kings 15 : 29, about B.C. 770, and Shalmaneser, who besieged Samaria three years, and destroyed the kingdom of Israel B.C. 721, himself or by his successor Sargon, who usurped the throne at that time. Under Sargon the empire was as great as at any former era, and Nineveh became a most beautiful city. Sargon's son Sennacherib became the most famous of the Assyrian kings. He began to reign 704 B.C. He invaded the kingdom of Judea in the reign of Hezekiah. He was followed by Esarhaddon, and he by a noted warrior and builder, Sardanapalus. In Scripture it is remarkable that we hear nothing of Assyria after the reign of Esarhaddon, and profane history is equally silent until the attacks began which brought about her downfall. The fall of Assyria, long previously prophesied by Isaiah, Isa. 10 : 5-19, was effected by the growing strength and boldness of the Medes, about 625 B.C. The prophecies of Nahum and Zephaniah (2 : 13-15) against Assyria were probably delivered shortly before the catastrophe.

6. *General character of the empire.*— The Assyrian monarchs bore sway over a number of petty kings through the entire extent of their dominions. These native princes were feudatories of the great monarch, of whom they held their crown by the double tenure of homage and tribute. It is not quite certain how far Assyria required a religious conformity from the subject people. Her religion was a gross and complex polytheism, comprising the worship of thirteen principal and numerous minor divinities, at the head of all of whom stood the chief god, Asshur, who seems to be the deified patriarch of the nation. Gen. 10 : 22.

7. *Civilization of the Assyrians.*—The civilization of the Assyrians was derived originally from the Babylonians. They were a Shemitic race, originally resident in Babylonia (which at that time was Cushite), and thus acquainted with the Babylonian inventions and discoveries, who ascended the valley of the Tigris and established in the tract immediately below the Armenian mountains a separate and distinct nationality. Still, as their civilization developed it became in many respects peculiar. Their art is of home growth. But they were still in the most important points barbarians. Their government was rude and inartificial, their religion coarse and sensual, and their conduct of war cruel.

8. *Modern discoveries in Assyria.*— (Much interest has been excited in reference to Assyria by the discoveries lately made there, which confirm and illustrate the Bible. The most important of them is the finding of the stone tablets or books which formed the great library at Nineveh, founded by Shalmaneser B.C. 860, but embodying tablets written 2000 years B.C. This library was more than doubled by Sardanapalus. These tablets were broken into fragments, but many of them have been put together and deciphered by the late Mr. George Smith, of the British Museum. All these discoveries of things hidden for ages, but now come to light, confirm the Bible.—ED.)

As'taroth. Deut. 1 : 4. [ASHTAROTH.]

Astar'te. [ASHTORETH.]

Asup'pim, and **House of,** 1 Chron. 26 : 15, 17, literally *house of the gatherings.* Some understand it as the proper name of chambers on the south of the temple; others of certain store-rooms, or of the council chambers in the outer court of the temple in which the elders held their deliberations.

Asyn'critus (*incomparable*), a Christian at Rome, saluted by St. Paul. Rom. 16 : 14.

A'tad (*thorn*), **The threshing-floor of,** called also Abel-mizraim, Gen. 50 : 10, 11, afterwards called Beth-hogla, and known to have lain between the Jordan and Jericho, therefore on the west side of Jordan.

At'arah (*a crown*), a wife of Jerahmeel, and mother of Onam. 1 Chron. 2 : 26.

At'aroth (*crowns*). 1. One of the towns in the "land of Jazer and land of Gilead," Num. 32 : 3, east of the Jordan, taken and built by the tribe of Gad. Num. 32 : 34.

2. A place on the (south ?) boundary of Ephraim and Manasseh. Josh. 16 : 2, 7. It is impossible to say whether Ataroth is or is not the same place as

3. ATAROTH-ADAR, or -ADDAR, on the west border of Benjamin, "near the 'mountain' that is on the south side of the nether Beth-horon." Josh. 16 : 5 ; 18 : 13. Perhaps the modern *Atâra*, six miles northeast of Bethel.

4. "ATAROTH, THE HOUSE OF JOAB," a place(?) occurring in the list of the descendants of Judah. 1 Chron. 2 : 54.

A'ter (*shut up*). 1. The children of Ater were among the porters or gatekeepers of the temple who returned with Zerubbabel. Ezra 2 : 42 ; Neh. 7 : 45.

2. The children of ATER OF HEZEKIAH to the number of 98 returned with Zerubbabel, Ezra 2 : 16 ; Neh. 7 : 21, and were among the heads of the people who signed the covenant with Nehemiah. Neh. 10 : 17.

A'thach (*lodging place*). 1 Sam. 30 : 30. As the name does not occur elsewhere, it has been suggested that it is an error of the transcriber for Ether, a town in the low country of Judah. Josh. 15 : 42.

Athai'ah (*whom Jehovah made*), a descendant of Pharez, the son of Judah, who dwelt at Jerusalem after the return from Babylon, Neh. 11 : 4 ; called UTHAI in 1 Chron. 9 : 4.

Athali'ah (*afflicted of the Lord*), daughter of Ahab and Jezebel, married Jehoram, the son of Jehoshaphat king of Judah, and introduced into that kingdom the worship of Baal. (B.C. 891.) After the great revolution by which Jehu seated himself on the throne of Samaria, she killed all the members of the royal family of Judah who had escaped his sword. 2 Kings 11 : 1. From the slaughter one infant, named Joash, the youngest son of Ahaziah, was rescued by his aunt Jehosheba, wife of Jehoiada, 2 Chron. 23 : 11, the high priest. 2 Chron. 24 : 6. The child was brought up under Jehoiada's care, and concealed in the temple for six years, during which period Athaliah reigned over Judah. At length Jehoiada thought it time to produce the lawful king to the people, trusting to their zeal for the worship of God and their loyalty to the house of David. His plan was successful, and Athaliah was put to death.

Athe'nians, natives of Athens. Acts 17 : 21.

Ath'ens (*city of Athene*), the capital of Attica, and the chief seat of Grecian learning and civilization during the golden period of the history of Greece.

Description.—Athens is situated about three miles from the seacoast, in the central plain of Attica. In this plain rise several eminences. Of these the most prominent is a lofty insulated mountain, with a conical peaked summit, now called the Hill of St. George, and which bore in ancient times the name of *Lycabettus.* This mountain, which was not included within the ancient walls, lies to the northeast of Athens, and forms the most striking feature in the environs of the city. It is to Athens what Vesuvius is to Naples, or Arthur's Seat to Edinburgh. Southwest of Lycabettus there are four hills of moderate height, all of which formed part of the city. Of these the nearest to Lycabettus, and at the distance of a mile from the latter, was the *Acropolis,* or citadel of Athens, a square craggy rock rising abruptly about 150 feet, with a flat summit of about 1000 feet long from east to west, by 500 feet broad from north to south. Immediately west of the Acropolis is a second hill of irregular form, the *Areopagus* (Mars' Hill). To the southwest there rises a third hill, the *Pnyx,* on which the assemblies of the citizens were held. South of the city was seen the Saronic Gulf, with the harbors of Athens.

History.—Athens is said to have derived its name from the prominence given to the worship of the goddess Athena (Minerva) by its king, Erechtheus. The inhabitants were previously called Cecropidæ, from Cecrops, who, according to tradition, was the original founder of the city. This at first occupied only the hill or rock which afterwards became the Acropolis ; but gradually the buildings spread over the ground at the southern foot of this hill. It was not till the time of Pisistratus and his sons (B.C. 560-514) that the city began to assume any degree of splendor. The most remarkable building of these despots was the gigantic temple of the Olympian Zeus or Jupiter. Under Themistocles the Acropolis began to form the centre of the city, round which the new walls described an irregular circle of about 60 stadia or 7½ miles in circumference. Themistocles transferred the naval station of the Athenians to the peninsula of Pi-

ræus, which is distant about 4½ miles from Athens, and contains three natural harbors. It was not till the administration of Pericles that the walls were built which connected Athens with her ports.

Buildings.—Under the administration of Pericles, Athens was adorned with numerous public buildings, which existed in all their glory when St. Paul visited the city. The Acropolis was the centre of the architectural splendor of Athens. It was covered with the temples of gods and heroes; and thus its platform pre-

Erechtheum.   Parthenon.   Turkish Tower.

Modern City.   Temple of Theseus.   Southwestern part of Modern City.

Athens.

sented not only a sanctuary, but a museum containing the finest productions of the architect and the sculptor, in which the whiteness of the marble was relieved by brilliant colors, and rendered still more dazzling by the transparent clearness of the Athenian atmosphere. The chief building was the *Parthenon* (*i. e.* House of the Virgin), the most perfect production of Grecian architecture. It derived its name from its being the temple of Athena Parthenos, or Athena the Virgin, the invincible goddess of war. It stood on the highest part of the Acropolis, near its centre. It was entirely of Pentelic marble, on a rustic basement of ordinary limestone, and its architecture, which was of the Doric order, was of the purest kind. It was adorned with

the most exquisite sculptures, executed by various artists under the direction of Phidias. But the chief wonder of the Parthenon was the colossal statue of the virgin goddess executed by Phidias himself. The Acropolis was adorned with another colossal figure of Athena, in bronze, also the work of Phidias. It stood in the open air, nearly opposite the Propylæa. With its pedestal it must have been about 70 feet high, and consequently towered above the roof of the Parthenon, so that the point of its spear and the crest of its helmet were visible off the promontory of Sunium to ships approaching Athens. The *Areopagus*, or Hill of Ares (Mars), is described elsewhere. [MARS' HILL.] The Pnyx, or place for holding the public assemblies of the Athenians, stood on the side of a low rocky hill, at the distance of about a quarter of a mile from the Areopagus. Between the Pnyx on the west, the Areopagus on the north and the Acropolis on the east, and closely adjoining the base of these hills, stood the *Agora* or "*Market*," where St. Paul disputed

Temple ot Victory at Athens.

daily. Through it ran the road to the gymnasium and gardens of the *Academy*, which were situated about a mile from the walls. The Academy was the place where Plato and his disciples taught. East of the city, and outside the walls, was the *Lyceum*, a gymnasium dedicated to Apollo Lyceus, and celebrated as the place in which Aristotle taught.

Character.—The remark of the sacred historian respecting the inquisitive character of the Athenians, Acts 17 : 21, is attested by the unanimous voice of antiquity. Their natural liveliness was partly owing to the purity and clearness of the atmosphere of Attica, which also allowed them to pass much of their time in the open air. The Athenian carefulness in religion is confirmed by the ancient writers. Of the Christian church, founded by St. Paul at Athens, according to ecclesiastical tradition, Dionysius the Areopagite was the first bishop. [DIONYSIUS.]

Present condition.—(The population of Athens in 1871 was 48,000. Its university has 52 professors and 1200 students.

Educational institutions are very numerous. A railway connects the Piræus or port with the city, and its terminus stands in the midst of what was once the Agora.—ED.)

Ath'la-i (*whom Jehovah afflicts*), one of the sons of Bebai, who put away his foreign wife at the exhortation of Ezra. Ezra 10 : 28.

Atonement, The day of. I. The great day of national humiliation, and the only one commanded in the Mosaic law. [FASTS.] The mode of its observance is described in Lev. 16, and the conduct of the people is emphatically enjoined in Lev. 23 : 26-32.

II. *Time.*—It was kept on the tenth day of Tisri, that is, from the evening of the ninth to the evening of the tenth of that month, five days before the feast of tabernacles. Tisri corresponds to our September–October, so that the 10th of Tisri would be about the first of October. [FESTIVALS.]

III. *How observed.*—It was kept by the people as a high solemn sabbath. On this occasion only the high priest was permitted to enter into the holy of holies. Having bathed his person and dressed himself entirely in the holy white linen garments, he brought forward a young bullock for a sin offering, purchased at his own cost, on account of himself and his family, and two young goats for a sin offering, with a ram for a burnt offering, which were paid for out of the public treasury, on account of the people. He then presented the two goats before the Lord at the door of the tabernacle and cast lots upon them. On one lot "*For Jehovah*" was inscribed, and on the other "*For Azazel*." A phrase of unusual difficulty. The best modern scholars agree that it designates the *personal being* to whom the goat was sent, probably Satan. This goat was called the *scapegoat*. After various sacrifices and ceremonies the goat upon which the lot "*For Jehovah*" had fallen was slain and the high priest sprinkled its blood before the mercy-seat in the same manner as he had done that of the bullock. Going out from the holy of holies he purified the holy place, sprinkling some of the blood of both the victims on the altar of incense. At this time no one besides the high priest was suffered to be present in the holy place. The purification of the holy of holies and of the holy place being thus completed, the high priest laid his hands upon the head of the goat on which the lot "*For Azazel*" had fallen, and confessed over it all the sins of the people. The goat was then led, by a man chosen for the purpose, into the wilderness, into "a land not inhabited," and was there let loose. The high priest after this returned into the holy place, bathed himself again, put on his usual garments of office, and offered the two rams as burnt offerings, one for himself and one for the people.

IV. *Significance.*—In considering the meaning of the particular rites of the day, three points appear to be of a very distinctive character. 1. The white garments of the high priest. 2. His entrance into the holy of holies. 3. The scapegoat. The writer of the Epistle to the Hebrews, Heb. 9 : 7–25, teaches us to apply the first two particulars. The high priest himself, with his person cleansed and dressed in white garments, was the best outward type which a living man could present in his own person of that pure and holy One who was to purify his people and to cleanse them from their sins. But respecting the meaning of the scapegoat we have no such light to guide us, and the subject is one of great doubt and difficulty. It has been generally considered that it was dismissed to signify the carrying away of the sins of the people, as it were, out of the sight of Jehovah. If we keep in view that the two goats are spoken of as parts of one and the same sin offering, we shall not have much difficulty in seeing that they form together but one symbolical expression; the slain goat setting forth the act of sacrifice, in giving up its own life for others "to Jehovah;" and the goat which carried off its load of sin "for complete removal" signifying the cleansing influence of faith in that sacrifice.

At'roth (*crowns*), a city of Gad. Num. 32: 35.

At'ta-i (*opportune*). 1. Grandson of Sheshan the Jerahmeelite through his daughter Ahlai, whom he gave in marriage to Jarha, his Egyptian slave. 1 Chron. 2 : 35, 36. His grandson Zabad was one of David's mighty men. 1 Chron. 11 : 41.

2. One of the lion-faced warriors of Gad, captains of the host, who forded the Jordan at the time of its overflow, and joined David in the wilderness. 1 Chron. 12 : 11. (B.C. 1060.)

3. Second son of King Rehoboam by Maachah the daughter of Absalom. 2 Chron. 11 : 20. (B.C. 975.)

Attali'a (from *Attalus*), a coast-town of Pamphylia, mentioned Acts 14 : 25. It was built by Attalus Philadelphus, king of Pergamos, and named after the monarch. All its remains are characteristic of the date of its foundation. Leake fixes Attalia at *Adalia*, on the south coast of Asia Minor, north of the *Duden Su*, the ancient Catarrhactes.

Augus'tus (*venerable*) **Cæ'sar**, the first Roman emperor. He was born A.U.C. 691, B.C. 63. His father was Caius Octavius; his mother was Atia, daughter of Julia the sister of C. Julius Cæsar. He was principally educated by his great-uncle Julius Cæsar, and was made his heir. After his murder, the young Octavius, then Caius Julius Cæsar Octavianus, was taken into the triumvirate with Antony and Lepidus, and, after the removal of the latter, divided the empire with Antony. The struggle for the supreme power was terminated in favor of Octavianus by the battle of Actium, B.C. 31. On this victory he was saluted imperator by the senate, who conferred on him the title Augustus, B.C. 27. The first link binding him to New Testament history is his treatment of Herod after the battle of Actium. That prince, who had espoused Antony's side, found himself pardoned, taken into favor and confirmed, nay even increased, in his power. After Herod's death, in A.D. 4, Augustus divided his dominions, almost exactly according to his dying directions, among his sons. Augustus died in Nola in Campania, Aug. 19, A.U.C. 767, A.D. 14, in his 76th year; but long before his death he had associated Tiberius with him in the empire.

Augus'tus' Band. Acts 27 : 1. [ARMY.]

A'va (*ruin*), a place in the empire of Assyria, apparently the same as Ivan. 2 Kings 17 : 24.

A'ven (*nothingness*). 1. The "plain of Aven" is mentioned by Amos (1 : 5) in his denunciation of Syria and the country to the north of Palestine. This Aven is by some supposed to be the once magnificent Heliopolis, "city of the sun," now Baalbek (Bäl'bĕk) of Cœle-Syria, whose ruins are one of the wonders of the ages. It was situated in a plain near the foot of the Anti-Libanus range of mountains, 42 miles northwest of Damascus. It is famous for the colossal ruins of its temples, one of which, with its courts and porticos, extended over 1000 feet in length. The temples were built of marble or limestone and granite. Some of the columns were 7 feet in diameter and 62 feet high, or, including capital and pedestal, 89 feet. Some of the building-stones were 64 feet long and 12 feet thick. The temples are of Roman origin.

2. In Hos. 10 : 8 the word is clearly an abbreviation of Bethaven, that is, Bethel. Comp. 4 : 15, etc.

3. The sacred city of Heliopolis or On, in Egypt. Ezek. 30 : 17.

A′vim (*ruins*), **A′vims** or **A′vites.** 1. A people among the early inhabitants of Palestine, whom we meet with in the southwest corner of the seacoast, whither they may have made their way northward from the desert, Deut. 2 : 23 ; probably the same as the Hivites.

2. The people of Avva, among the colonists who were sent by the king of Assyria to reinhabit the depopulated cities of Israel. 2 Kings 17 : 31.

Ruins of Baalbek (now called Aven).

A′vith (*ruins*), the city of Hadad ben-Bedad, one of the kings of Edom before there were kings in Israel. Gen. 36 : 35 ; 1 Chron. 1 : 46.

Awl, a tool of which we do not know the ancient form. The only notice of it is in connection with the custom of boring the ear of the slave. Ex. 21 : 6 ; Deut. 15 : 17.

A′zal, a name only occurring in Zech. 14 : 5. It is mentioned as the limit to which the ravine of the Mount of Olives will extend when "Jehovah shall go forth to fight."

Azali′ah (*whom the Lord reserved*), the father of Shaphan the scribe in the

reign of Josiah. 2 Kings 22 : 3 ; 2 Chron. 34 : 8. (B.C. before 641.)

Azani′ah (*whom the Lord hears*), the father or immediate ancestor of Jeshua the Levite, in the time of Nehemiah. Neh. 10 : 9.

Azar′a-el, a Levite musician. Neh. 12 : 36.

Aza′re-el, or **Azar′e-el** (*whom the Lord helps*). 1. A Korhite who joined David in his retreat at Ziklag. 1 Chron. 12 : 6. (B.C. 1060.)

2. A Levite musician of the family of Heman in the time of David, 1 Chron. 25 : 18 ; called UZZIEL in 25 : 4. (B.C. 1050.)

3. Son of Jeroham, and prince of the tribe of Dan when David numbered the people. 1 Chron. 27 : 22.

4. One of the sons of Bani, who put away his foreign wife on the remonstrance of Ezra. Ezra 10 : 41. (B.C. 459.)

5. Father or ancestor of Maasiai, or Amashai, a priest who dwelt in Jerusalem after the return from Babylon. Neh. 11 : 13; comp. 1 Chron. 9 : 12. (B.C. about 440.)

Azari'ah (*whom the Lord helps*), a common name in Hebrew, and especially in the families of the priests of the line of Eleazar, whose name has precisely the same meaning as Azariah. It is nearly identical, and is often confounded, with Ezra as well as with Zerahiah and Seraiah. The principal persons who bore this name were—

1. Son of Ahimaaz. 1 Chron. 6 : 9. He appears from 1 Kings 4 : 2 to have succeeded Zadok, his grandfather, in the high priesthood, in the reign of Solomon, Ahimaaz having died before Zadok. (B.C. about 1000.) [AHIMAAZ.]

2. A chief officer of Solomon's, the son of Nathan, perhaps David's grandson. 1 Kings 4 : 5.

3. Tenth king of Judah, more frequently called Uzziah. 2 Kings 14 : 21; 15 : 1, 6, 7, 8, 17, 23, 27; 1 Chron. 3 : 12. (B.C. 810.)

4. Son of Ethan, of the sons of Zerah, where, perhaps, Zerahiah is the more probable reading. 1 Chron. 2 : 8.

5. Son of Jehu of the family of the Jerahmeelites, and descended from Jarha the Egyptian slave of Sheshan. 1 Chron. 2 : 38, 39. He was probably one of the captains of hundreds in the time of Athaliah mentioned in 2 Chron. 23 : 1. (B.C. 886.)

6. The son of Johanan. 1 Chron. 6 : 10. He must have been high priest in the reigns of Abijah and Asa. (B.C. 939.)

7. Another Azariah is inserted between Hilkiah, in Josiah's reign, and Seraiah, who was put to death by Nebuchadnezzar, in 1 Chron. 6 : 13, 14.

8. Son of Zephaniah, a Kohathite, and ancestor of Samuel the prophet. 1 Chron. 6 : 36. Apparently the same as Uzziah in ver. 24.

9. Azariah, the son of Oded, 2 Chron. 15 : 1, called simply Oded in ver. 8, was a remarkable prophet in the days of King Asa, and a contemporary of Azariah the son of Johanan the high priest, and of Hanani the seer. (B.C. 939.)

10. Son of Jehoshaphat king of Judah. 2 Chron. 21 : 2. (B.C. 910.)

11. Another son of Jehoshaphat, and brother of the preceding. 2 Chron. 21 : 2.

12. In 2 Chron. 22 : 6 Azariah is a clerical error for Ahaziah.

13. Son of Jeroham, one of the captains of Judah in the time of Athaliah. 2 Chron. 23 : 1.

14. The high priest in the reign of Uzziah king of Judah. The most memorable event of his life is that which is recorded in 2 Chron. 26 : 17–20. (B.C. 810.) Azariah was contemporary with Isaiah the prophet and with Amos and Joel.

15. Son of Johanan, one of the captains of Ephraim in the reign of Ahaz. 2 Chron. 28 : 12.

16. A Kohathite, father of Joel, in the reign of Hezekiah. 2 Chron. 29 : 12. (B.C. 726.)

17. A Merarite, son of Jehalelel, in the time of Hezekiah. 2 Chron. 29 : 12.

18. The high priest in the days of Hezekiah. 2 Chron. 31 : 10, 13. He appears to have co-operated zealously with the king in that thorough purification of the temple and restoration of the temple services which was so conspicuous a feature in his reign. He succeeded Urijah, who was high priest in the reign of Ahaz.

19. Son of Maaseiah, who repaired part of the wall of Jerusalem in the time of Nehemiah. Neh. 3 : 23, 24. (B.C. 446–410.)

20. One of the leaders of the children of the province who went up from Babylon with Zerubbabel. Neh. 7 : 7.

21. One of the Levites who assisted Ezra in instructing the people in the knowledge of the law. Neh. 8 : 7.

22. One of the priests who sealed the covenant with Nehemiah, Neh. 10 : 2, and probably the same with the Azariah who assisted in the dedication of the city wall. Neh. 12 : 33.

23. Jer. 43 : 2 (Jezaniah).

24. The original name of Abed-nego. Dan. 1 : 6, 7, 11, 19. He appears to have been of the seed-royal of Judah. (B.C. 603.)

A'zaz (*strong*), a Reubenite, father of Bela. 1 Chron. 5 : 8.

Azazi'ah (*whom the Lord strengthens*).
1. A Levite musician in the reign of David, appointed to play the harp in the service which attended the procession by which the ark was brought up from the house of Obed-edom. 1 Chron. 15 : 21. (B.C. 1043.)

2. The father of Hoshea, prince of the tribe of Ephraim when David numbered the people. 1 Chron. 27 : 20.

3. One of the Levites in the reign of Hezekiah, who had charge of the tithes and dedicated things in the temple. 2 Chron. 31 : 13.

Az'buk (*strong devastation*), father or ancestor of Nehemiah, the prince of part of Bethzur. Neh. 3 : 16.

Aze'kah (*dug over*), a town of Judah, with dependent villages, lying in the Shefelah or rich agricultural plain. It is most clearly defined as being near Shochoh, 1 Sam. 17 : 1 ; but its position has not yet been recognized.

A'zel (*noble*), a descendant of Saul. 1 Chron. 8 : 37, 38 ; 9 : 43, 44.

A'zem (*bone*), a city in the extreme south of Judah, Josh. 15 : 29, afterwards allotted to Simeon. Josh. 19 : 3. Elsewhere it is EZEM.

Az'gad (*strength of fortune*). The children of Azgad, to the number of 1222 (2322 according to Neh. 7 : 17), were among the laymen who returned with Zerubbabel. Ezra 2 : 12 ; 8 : 12. With the other heads of the people they joined in the covenant with Nehemiah. Neh. 10 : 15. (B.C. 536.)

A'ziel (*whom God comforts*), a Levite. 1 Chron. 15 : 20. The name is a shortened form of Jaaziel in ver. 18.

Azi'za (*strong*), a layman of the family of Zattu, who had married a foreign wife after the return from Babylon. Ezra 10 : 27.

Az'maveth (*strong unto death*). 1. One of David's mighty men, a native of Bahurim, 2 Sam. 23 : 31 ; 1 Chron. 11 : 33, and therefore probably a Benjamite. (B.C. 1060.)

2. A descendant of Mephibosheth, or Merib-baal. 1 Chron. 8 : 36 ; 9 : 42.

3. The father of Jeziel and Pelet, two of the skilled Benjamite slingers and archers who joined David at Ziklag, 1 Chron. 12 : 3 ; perhaps identical with No. 1.

4. Overseer of the royal treasures in the reign of David. 1 Chron. 27 : 25.

Az'maveth, a place to all appearance in Benjamin, being named with other towns belonging to that tribe. Ezra 2 : 24. The name elsewhere occurs as BETH-AZMAVETH.

Az'mon (*strong*), a place named as being on the southern boundary of the Holy Land, apparently near the torrent of Egypt (*Wadi el-Arish*). Num. 34 : 4, 5 ; Josh. 15 : 4. It has not yet been identified.

Az'noth-ta'bor (*the ears* (*i. e.* possibly the summits) *of Tabor*), one of the landmarks of the boundary of Naphtali. Josh. 19 : 34. The town, if town it be, has hitherto escaped recognition.

A'zor (*a helper*), son of Eliakim, in the line of our Lord. Matt. 1 : 13, 14.

Azo'tus. [ASHDOD.]

Az'riel (*whom God helps*). 1. The head of a house of the half-tribe of Manasseh beyond Jordan, a man of renown 1 Chron. 5 : 24. (B.C. 741.)

2. A Naphtalite, ancestor of Jerimoth, the head of the tribe at the time of David's census. 1 Chron. 27 : 19. (B.C. 1015.)

3. The father of Seraiah, an officer of Jehoiakim. Jer. 36 : 26. (B.C. 605.)

Az'rikam (*help against the enemy*). 1. A descendant of Zerubbabel, and son of Neariah of the royal line of Judah. 1 Chron. 3 : 23.

2. Eldest son of Azel, and descendant of Saul. 1 Chron. 8 : 38 ; 9 : 44. (B.C. after 1037.)

3. A Levite, ancestor of Shemaiah, who lived in the time of Nehemiah. 1 Chron. 9 : 14 ; Neh. 11 : 15. (B.C. before 536.)

4. Governor of the house, or prefect of the palace, to King Ahaz, who was slain by Zichri, an Ephraimite hero, in the successful invasion of the southern kingdom by Pekah king of Israel. 2 Chron. 28 : 7. (B.C. 738.)

Azu'bah (*forsaken*). 1. Wife of Caleb, son of Hezron. 1 Chron. 2 : 18, 19.

2. Mother of King Jehoshaphat. 1 Kings 22 : 42 ; 2 Chron. 20 : 31. (B.C. 950.)

A'zur, properly **Az'zur** (*he that assists*). 1. A Benjamite of Gibeon, and father of Hananiah the false prophet. Jer. 28 : 1.

2. Father of Jaazaniah, one of the princes of the people against whom Ezekiel was commanded to prophesy. Ezek. 11 : 1.

Az'zah (*the strong*). The more accurate rendering of the name of the well-known Philistine city Gaza. Deut. 2 : 23 ; 1 Kings 4 : 24 ; Jer. 25 : 20.

Az'zan (*very strong*), the father of Paltiel prince of the tribe of Issachar, who represented his tribe in the division of the promised land. Num. 34 : 26.

Az'zur (*one who helps*), one of the heads of the people who signed the covenant with Nehemiah. Neh. 10 : 17. (B.C. 410.) The name is probably that of a family, and in Hebrew is the same as is elsewhere represented by AZUR.

B.

Ba′al (*lord*). 1. A Reubenite. 1 Chron. 5 : 5.

2. The son of Jehiel, and grandfather of Saul. 1 Chron. 8 : 30; 9 : 36.

Ba′al, the supreme male divinity of the Phœnician and Canaanitish nations, as Ashtoreth was their supreme female divinity. Some suppose Baal to correspond to the sun and Ashtoreth to the moon; others that Baal was Jupiter and Ashtoreth Venus. There can be no doubt of the very high antiquity of the worship of Baal. It prevailed in the time of Moses among the Moabites and Midianites, Num. 22 : 41, and through them spread to the Israelites. Num. 25 : 3–18; Deut. 4 : 3. In the times of the kings it became the religion of the court and people of the ten tribes, 1 Kings 16 : 31–33; 18 : 19, 22, and appears never to have been permanently abolished among them. 2 Kings 17 : 16. Temples were erected to Baal in Judah, 1 Kings 16 : 32, and he was worshipped with much ceremony. 1 Kings 18 : 19, 26–28; 2 Kings 10 : 22. The attractiveness of this worship to the Jews undoubtedly grew out of its licentious character. We find this worship also in Phœnician colonies. The religion of the ancient British islands much resembled this ancient worship of Baal, and may have been derived from it. Nor need we hesitate to regard the Babylonian Bel, Isa. 46 : 1, or Belus, as essentially identical with Baal, though perhaps under some modified form. The plural, BAALIM, is found frequently, showing that he was probably worshipped under different compounds, among which appear—

1. BAAL-BERITH (*the covenant Baal*), Judges 8 : 33; 9 : 4; the god who comes into covenant with the worshippers.

2. BAAL-ZEBUB (*lord of the fly*), and worshipped at Ekron. 2 Kings 1 : 2, 3, 16.

3. BAAL-HANAN. *a.* The name of one of the early kings of Edom. Gen. 36 : 38, 39; 1 Chron. 1 : 49, 50. *b.* The name of one of David's officers, who had the superintendence of his olive and sycamore plantations. 1 Chron. 27 : 28.

4. BAAL-PEOR (*lord of the opening, i. e.* for others to join in the worship). We have already referred to the worship of this god. The narrative (Num. 25) seems clearly to show that this form of Baal-worship was connected with licentious rites.

Ba′al, *geographical.* This word occurs the prefix or suffix to the names of several places in Palestine, some of which are as follows:

1. BAAL, a town of Simeon, named only in 1 Chron. 4 : 33, which from the parallel list in Josh. 19 : 8 seems to have been identical with BAALATH-BEER.

2. BAALAH (*mistress*). *a.* Another name for KIRJATH-JEARIM, or KIRJATH-BAAL, the well-known town, now *Kuriet el Enab.* Josh. 15 : 9, 10; 1 Chron. 13 : 6. *b.* A town in the south of Judah, Josh. 15 : 29, which in 19 : 3 is called BALAH, and in the parallel list, 1 Chron. 4 : 29, BILHAH.

3. BAALATH (*mistress*), a town of Dan named with Gibbethon, Gath-rimmon and other Philistine places. Josh. 19 : 44.

4. BAALATH-BEER (*lord of the well*). BAAL 1, a town among those in the south part of Judah, given to Simeon, which also bore the name of RAMATH-NEGEB, or "the height of the south." Josh. 19 : 8.

5. BAAL-GAD (*lord of fortune*), used to denote the most northern, Josh. 11 : 17; 12 : 7, or perhaps northwestern, 13 : 5, point to which Joshua's victories extended. It was in all probability a Phœnician or Canaanite sanctuary of Baal under the aspect of Gad or Fortune.

6. BAAL-HAMON (*lord of a multitude*), a place at which Solomon had a vineyard, evidently of great extent. Cant. 8 : 11.

7. BAAL-HAZOR (*village of Baal*), a place where Absalom appears to have had a sheep-farm, and where Amnon was murdered. 2 Sam. 13 : 23.

8. MOUNT BAAL-HERMON (*lord of Hermon*), Judges 3 : 3, and simply Baal-hermon. 1 Chron. 5 : 23. This is usually considered as a distinct place from Mount Hermon; but we know that this mountain had at least three names (Deut. 3 : 9), and Baal-hermon may have been a fourth in use among the Phœnician worshippers of Baal.

9. BAAL-MEON (*lord of the house*), one of the towns which were built by the Reubenites. Num. 32:38. It also occurs in 1 Chron. 5:8, and on each occasion with Nebo. In the time of Ezekiel it was Moabite, one of the cities which were the "glory of the country." Ezek. 25:9.

10. BAAL-PERAZIM (*lord of divisions*), the scene of a victory of David over the Philistines, and of a great destruction of their images. 2 Sam. 5:20; 1 Chron. 14:11. See Isa. 28:21, where it is called MOUNT PERAZIM.

11. BAAL-SHALISHA (*lord of Shalisha*), a place named only in 2 Kings 4:42; apparently not far from Gilgal; comp. 4:38.

12. BAAL-TAMAR (*lord of the palm tree*), a place named only in Judges 20:33, as near Gibeah of Benjamin. The palm tree (*tâmâr*) of Deborah, Judges 4:5, was situated somewhere in the locality, and is possibly alluded to.

13. BAAL-ZEPHON (*lord of the north*), a place in Egypt near where the Israelites crossed the Red Sea. Num. 33:7; Ezek. 14:2, 9. We place Baal-zephon on the western shore of the Gulf of Suez, a little below its head, which at that time was about 30 or 40 miles northward of the present head.

Ba'alah. [BAAL, No. 2.]

Ba'alath. [BAAL, Nos. 3, 4.]

Ba'ale of Judah. [BAAL, No. 2, *a*.]

Ba'ali. Hos. 2:16. [BAAL.]

Ba'alim. [BAAL.]

Ba'alis, king of the Ammonites at the time of the destruction of Jerusalem by Nebuchadnezzar. Jer. 40:14. (B.C. 588.)

Ba'ana. 1. The son of Ahilud, Solomon's commissariat officer in Jezreel and the north of the Jordan valley. 1 Kings 4:12. (B.C. 1000.)

2. Father of Zadok, who assisted in rebuilding the wall of Jerusalem under Nehemiah. Neh. 3:4. (B.C. 446.)

Ba'anah. 1. Son of Rimmon, a Benjamite, who with his brother Rechab murdered Ish-bosheth. For this they were killed by David, and their mutilated bodies hung up over the pool at Hebron. 2 Sam. 4:2, 5, 6, 9. (B.C. 1046.)

2. A Netophathite, father of Heleb or Heled, one of David's mighty men. 2 Sam. 23:29; 1 Chron. 11:30. (B.C. before 1066.)

3. Accurately Baana, son of Hushai, Solomon's commissariat officer in Asher. 1 Kings 4:16. (B.C. 1012.)

4. A man who accompanied Zerubbabel on his return from the captivity. Ezra 2:2; Neh. 7:7. Possibly the same person is intended in Neh. 10:27. (B.C. 536.)

Ba'ara (*brutish*), one of the wives of Shaharaim, a descendant of Benjamin. 1 Chron. 8:8.

Ba-asei'ah, or **Basse'iah** (*work of Jehovah*), a Gershonite Levite, one of the forefathers of Asaph the singer. 1 Chron. 6:40 [25]. (B.C. 1310.)

Ba'asha (*wicked*), B.C. 953–931, third sovereign of the separate kingdom of Israel, and the founder of its second dynasty. He was son of Ahijah of the tribe of Issachar, and conspired against King Nadab, 1 Kings 15:27, and killed him with his whole family. He appears to have been of humble origin. 1 Kings 16:2. It was probably in the 13th year of his reign that he made war on Asa, and began to fortify Ramah. He was defeated by the unexpected alliance of Asa with Ben-hadad I. of Damascus. Baasha died in the 24th year of his reign, and was buried in Tirzah, Cant. 6:4, which he had made his capital. 1 Kings 16:6; 2 Chron. 16:1–6.

Ba'bel (*confusion*), **Bab'ylon** (Greek form of *Babel*), is properly the capital city of the country which is called in Genesis *Shinar*, and in the later books *Chaldea*, or the land of the Chaldeans. The first rise of the Chaldean power was in the region close upon the Persian Gulf; thence the nation spread northward up the course of the rivers, and the seat of government moved in the same direction, being finally fixed at Babylon, perhaps not earlier than B.C. 1700.

I. *Topography of Babylon—Ancient descriptions of the city.*—All the ancient writers appear to agree in the fact of a district of vast size, more or less inhabited, having been enclosed within lofty walls, and included under the name of Babylon. With respect to the exact extent of the circuit they differ. The estimate of Herodotus and of Pliny is 480 stades (60 Roman miles, 53 of our miles), of Strabo 385, of Q. Curtius 368, of Clitarchus 365 and of Ctesias 360 stades (40 miles). (George Smith, in his "Assyrian Discoveries," differs entirely from all these estimates, making the circuit of the city but *eight* miles.) Perhaps Herodotus spoke of the *outer* wall, which could be traced in his time. Taking the lowest estimate of the extent of the circuit, we shall have for the space within the rampart an area of above 100 square miles— nearly five times the size of London! It is evident that this vast space cannot have been entirely covered with houses. The city was situated on both sides of the river Euphrates, and the two parts were connected together by a stone bridge five stades (above 1000 yards) long and 30 feet broad. At either extremity of the bridge was a royal palace, that in the eastern city being the more magnificent of the two. The two palaces were joined not only by the bridge, but by a tunnel under the river. The houses, which were frequently three or four stories high, were laid out in straight streets crossing each other at right angles.

II. *Present state of the ruins.*—A portion of the ruins is occupied by the modern town of *Hillah.* About five miles above Hillah, on the opposite or left bank of the Euphrates, occurs a series of artificial mounds of enormous size. They consist chiefly of three great masses of building,—the high pile of unbaked brickwork which is known to the Arabs as *Babil,* 600 feet square and 140 feet high; the building denominated the *Kasr* or palace, nearly 2000 feet square and 70 feet high; and a lofty mound, upon which stands the modern tomb of *Amrám-ibn-'Alb.* Scattered over the country on both sides of the Euphrates are a number of remarkable mounds, usually standing single, which are plainly of the same date with the great mass of ruins upon the river bank. Of these by far the most striking is the vast ruin called the *Birs-Nimrûd,* which many regard as the tower of Babel, situated about six miles to the southwest of Hillah. [BABEL, TOWER OF.]

III. *Identification of sites.*—The great mound of *Babil* is probably the ancient temple of Belus. The mound of the *Kasr* marks the site of the great palace of Nebuchadnezzar. The mound of *Amrám* is thought to represent the "hanging gardens" of Nebuchadnezzar; but most probably it represents the ancient palace, coeval with Babylon itself, of which Nebuchadnezzar speaks in his inscriptions as adjoining his own more magnificent residence.

IV. *History of Babylon.*—Scripture represents the "beginning of the kingdom" as belonging to the time of Nimrod. Gen. 10 : 6–10. The early annals of Babylon are filled by Berosus, the native historian, with three dynasties: one of 49 Chaldean kings, who reigned 458 years; another of 9 Arab kings, who reigned 245 years; and a third of 49 Assyrian monarchs, who held dominion for 526 years. The line of Babylonian kings becomes exactly known to us from B.C. 747. The "Canon of Ptolemy" gives us the succession of Babylonian monarchs from B.C. 747 to B.C. 331, when the last Persian king was dethroned by Alexander. On the fall of Nineveh, B.C. 625, Babylon became not only an independent kingdom, but an empire. The city was taken by surprise B.C. 539, as Jeremiah had prophesied, Jer. 51 : 31, by Cyrus, under Darius, Dan. 5, as intimated 170 years earlier by Isaiah, Isa. 21 : 1–9, and, as Jeremiah had also foreshown, Jer. 51 : 39, during a festival. With the conquest of Cyrus commenced the decay of Babylon, which has since been a quarry from which all the tribes in the vicinity have derived the bricks with which they have built their cities. The "great city" has thus emphatically "become heaps." Jer. 51 : 37.

Birs-Nimrûd.

Ba'bel, Tower of. The "tower of Babel" is only mentioned once in Scripture, Gen. 11 : 4, 5, and then as incomplete. It was built of bricks, and the "slime" used for mortar was probably bitumen. Such authorities as we possess represent the building as destroyed soon after its erection. When the Jews, however, were carried captive into Babylonia, they thought they recognized it in the famous temple of Belus, the modern *Birs-Nimrûd*. But the *Birs-Nimrûd*, though it cannot be the tower of Babel itself, may well be taken to show the probable shape and character of the edifice. This building appears to have been a sort of oblique pyramid built in seven receding stages, each successive one being nearer to the southwestern end, which constituted the back of the building. The first, second and third stories were each 26 feet high, the remaining four being 15 feet high. On the seventh stage there was probably placed the ark or tabernacle, which seems to have been again 15 feet high, and must have nearly, if not entirely, covered the top of the seventh story. The entire original height, allowing three feet for the platform, would thus have been 156 feet, or, without the platform, 153 feet.

Bab'ylon, in the Apocalypse, is the symbolical name by which Rome is denoted. Rev. 14 : 8 ; 17 : 18. The power of Rome was regarded by the later Jews as was that of Babylon by their forefathers. Comp. Jer. 51 : 7 with Rev. 14 : 8. The occurrence of this name in 1 Pet. 5 : 13 has given rise to a variety of conjectures, many giving it the same meaning as in the Apocalypse ; others refer it to Babylon in Asia, and others still to Babylon in Egypt. The most natural supposition of all is that by Babylon is intended the old Babylon of Assyria, which was largely inhabited by Jews at the time in question.

Babylo'nians, the inhabitants of Babylon, a race of Shemitic origin, who were among the colonists planted in the cities of Samaria by the conquering Assyrians. Ezra 4 : 9.

Babylonish garment, literally "robe of Shinar," Josh. 7 : 21 ; an ample robe, probably made of the skin or fur of an animal, comp. Gen. 25 : 25, and ornamented with embroidery, or perhaps a variegated garment with figures inwoven in the fashion for which the Babylonians were celebrated.

Ba'ca (*weeping*), **The Valley of,** a valley in Palestine, through which the exiled Psalmist sees in vision the pilgrims passing in their march towards the sanctuary of Jehovah at Zion. Ps. 84 : 6. That it was a real locality is most probable from the use of the definite article before the name. The rendering of the Targum is Gehenna, *i. e.* the Ge-Hinnom or ravine below Mount Zion. This locality agrees well with the mention of becaim (Authorized Version "mulberry") trees in 2 Sam. 5 : 23.

Bach'rites, The, the family of BECHER, son of Ephraim. Num. 26 : 35.

Badger Skins. There is much obscurity as to the meaning of the word *tachash*, rendered "badger" in the Authorized Version, Ex. 25 : 5 ; 35 : 7, etc. The ancient versions seem nearly all agreed that it denotes not an animal but a color, either black or sky-blue. The badger is not found in the Bible lands. The Arabic *duchash* or *tuchash* denotes a dolphin, including seals and cetaceans. The skins referred to are probably those of these marine animals, some of which are found in the Red Sea. The skin of the *Halicore*, one of these, from its hardness would be well suited for making soles for shoes. Ezek. 16 : 10.

Bag is the rendering of several words in the Old and New Testaments. 1. *Chârítîm*, the "bags" in which Naaman bound up the two talents of silver for Gehazi. 2 Kings 5 : 23. They were long cone-like bags of the size to hold a precise amount of money, and tied or sealed for that amount, as we stamp the value on a coin. 2. *Cîs*, a bag for carrying weights, Deut. 25 : 13; also used as a purse. Prov. 1 : 14. 3. *Cêlî*, in Gen. 42 : 25, is the "sack" in which Jacob's sons carried the corn which they brought from Egypt. 4. The shepherd's "bag" used by David was for the purpose of carrying the lambs unable to walk. Zech. 11 : 15, 16. 5. *Tschar*, properly a "bundle," Gen. 42 : 35, appears to have been used by travellers for carrying money during a long journey. Prov. 7 : 20. 6. The "bag" which Judas carried was probably a small box or chest. John 12 : 6 ; 13 : 29.

Baha'rumite, The. [BAHURIM.]

Bahu'rim (*low grounds*), a village, 2 Sam. 16 : 5, apparently on or close to the road leading up from the Jordan valley to Jerusalem, and near the south boundary of Benjamin.

Ba'jith (*the house*), referring to the "temple" of the false gods of Moab, as opposed to the "high places" in the same sentence. Isa. 15 : 2, and comp. 16 : 12.

Bakbak'kar (*admirable*), a Levite, apparently a descendant of Asaph. 1 Chron. 9 : 15. (B.C. 588.)

Bak'buk (*bottle*). "Children of Bakbuk" were among the Nethinim who returned from captivity with Zerubbabel. Ezra 2 : 51; Neh. 7 : 53. (B.C. before 536.)

Bakbuki'ah (*wasting of Jehovah*), a Levite in the time of Nehemiah. Neh. 11 : 17; 12 : 9. (B.C. after 536.)

Bake. Reference to baking is found in Lev. 26 : 26; 1 Sam. 8 : 13; 2 Sam. 13 : 8; Jer. 7 : 18; 37 : 21; Hos. 7 : 4-7.

Ba'laam (B.C. 1451), the son of Beor, a man endowed with the gift of prophecy. Num. 22 : 5. He is mentioned in conjunction with the five kings of Midian, apparently as a person of the same rank. Num. 31 : 8; cf. 31 : 16. He seems to have lived at Pethor, Deut. 23 : 4; Num. 22 : 5, on the river Euphrates, in Mesopotamia. Such was his reputation that when the Israelites were encamped in the plains of Moab, Balak, the king of Moab, sent for Balaam to curse them. Balaam at first was prohibited by God from going. He was again sent for by the king and again refused, but was at length allowed to go. He yielded to the temptations of riches and honor which Balak set before him; but God's anger was kindled at this manifestation of determined self-will, and the angel of the Lord stood in the way for an adversary against him. See 2 Pet. 2 : 16. Balaam predicted a magnificent career for the people whom he was called to curse, but he nevertheless suggested to the Moabites the expedient of seducing them to commit fornication. The effect of this is recorded in Num. 25. A battle was afterwards fought against the Midianites, in which Balaam sided with them, and was slain by the sword of the people whom he had endeavored to curse. Num. 31 : 8.

Ba'lac. Rev. 2 : 14. [BALAK.]

Bal'adan. [MERODACH-BALADAN.]

Ba'lah. Josh. 19 : 3. [BAAL, *Geogr.* No. 2, *b.*]

Ba'lak (*spoiler*), son of Zippor, king of the Moabites, who hired Balaam to curse the Israelites; but his designs were frustrated in the manner recorded in Num. 22 : 24. (B.C. 1451.)

Balances. Reference to balances is found in Lev. 19 : 36. They were in

common use, gold and silver being paid out and received by weight. Reference

Egyptian Balancer weighing Rings of Gold.

is also made in Micah 6 : 11; Hosea 12 : 7, to the dishonest practice of buying by heavier and selling by lighter weights.

Bal'amo. [BAAL, *Geogr.* No. 6.]

Baldness. Natural baldness seems to have been uncommon, since it exposed people to public derision. Lev. 13 : 29; 2 Kings 2 : 23; Isa. 3 : 24; 15 : 2; Jer. 47 : 5; Ezek. 7 : 18. Artificial baldness marked the conclusion of a Nazarite's vow, Num. 6 : 9; Acts 18 : 18, and was a sign of mourning.

Balm (from *balsam*, Heb. *tzŏrí, tĕzrí*) occurs in Gen. 37 : 25; 43 : 11; Jer. 8 : 22;

Balm of Gilead.

46 : 11; 51 : 8; Ezek. 27 : 17. (It is an aromatic plant, or the resinous odorifer

ous sap or gum which exudes from such plants.) It is impossible to identify it with any certainty. It may represent the gum of the *Pistacia lentiscus*, or more probably that of the *Balsamodendron opobalsamum*, allied to the *balm of Gilead*, which abounded in Gilead east of the Jordan. The trees resembled fig trees (or grape vines), but were lower, being but 12 to 15 feet high. It is now called the BALM OF GILEAD, or *Meccabalsam*, the tree or shrub being indigenous in the mountains around Mecca. [INCENSE; SPICES.] Hasselquist says that the exudation from the plant "is of a yellow color, and pellucid. It has a most fragrant smell, which is resinous, balsamic and very agreeable. It is very tenacious or glutinous, sticking to the fingers, and may be drawn into long threads." It was supposed to have healing as well as aromatic qualities.

Ba'mah (*high place*). Found only in Ezek. 20 : 29, applied to places of idolatrous worship.

Ba'moth-ba'al (*heights of Baal*), a sanctuary of Baal in the country of Moab, Josh. 13 : 17,which is probably mentioned in Num. 21 : 19 under the shorter form of Bamoth, or Bamoth-in-the-ravine (20), and again in Isa. 15 : 2.

Band. The "band of Roman soldiers" referred to in Matt. 27 : 27 and elsewhere was the tenth part of a legion. It was called a "cohort," and numbered 400 to 600 men. [See ARMY.]

Ba'ni (*built*). 1. A Gadite, one of David's mighty men. 2 Sam. 23 : 36. (B.C. 1046.)

2. A Levite of the line of Merari, and forefather to Ethan. 1 Chron. 6 : 46.

3. A man of Judah of the line of Pharez. 1 Chron. 9 : 4.

4. "Children of Bani" returned from captivity with Zerubbabel. Ezra 2 : 10; 10 : 29, 34; Neh. 10 : 14; 1 Esd. 5 : 12. [BINNUI; MANI.]

5. An Israelite "of the sons of Bani." Ezra 10 : 38.

6. A Levite. Neh. 3 : 17.

7. A Levite. Neh. 8 : 7 ; 9 : 4, 5 ; 10 : 13.

8. Another Levite, of the sons of Asaph. Neh. 11 : 22.

Banner. [See ENSIGN.]

Banquets, among the Hebrews, were not only a means of social enjoyment, but were a part of the observance of religious festivity. At the three solemn festivals the family also had its domestic feast. Deut. 16 : 11. Sacrifices, both or-

dinary and extraordinary, Ex. 34 : 15; Judges 16 : 23, included a banquet. Birthday banquets are only mentioned Gen. 40 : 20; Matt. 14 : 6. The usual time of the banquet was the evening, and to begin early was a mark of excess. Eccles. 10 : 16; Isa. 5 : 11. The most essential materials of the banqueting-room, next to the viands and wine, which last was often drugged with spices, Prov. 9 : 2, were perfumed unguents, garlands or loose flowers, white or brilliant robes; after these, exhibitions of music, singers and dancers, riddles, jesting and merriment. Judges 14 : 12; 2 Sam. 19 : 35; Neh. 8 : 10; Eccles. 10 : 19; Isa. 5 : 12; 25 : 6; 28 : 1; Matt. 22 : 11; Luke 15 : 25. The posture at table in early times was sitting, 1 Sam. 16 : 11; 20 : 5, 18, and the guests were ranged in order of dignity. Gen. 43 : 33 ; 1 Sam. 9 : 22. Words which imply the recumbent posture belong to the New Testament.

Baptism. It is well known that ablution or bathing was common in most ancient nations as a preparation for prayers and sacrifice or as expiatory of sin. In warm countries this connection is probably even closer than in colder climates; and hence the frequency of ablution in the religious rites throughout the East. Baptism in the name of the Father, Son and Holy Ghost is the rite or ordinance by which persons are admitted into the Church of Christ. It is the public profession of faith and discipleship. Baptism signifies—1. A confession of faith in Christ; 2. A cleansing or washing of the soul from sin; 3. A death to sin and a new life in righteousness. The *mode* and *subjects* of baptism being much-controverted subjects, each one can best study them in the works devoted to those questions. The command to baptize was co-extensive with the command to preach the gospel. All nations were to be evangelized; and they were to be made disciples, admitted into the fellowship of Christ's religion, by baptism. Matt. 28 : 19. It appears to have been a kind of transition from the Jewish baptism to the Christian. The distinction between John's baptism and Christian baptism appears in the case of Apollos, Acts 18 : 26, 27, and of the disciples at Ephesus mentioned Acts 19 : 1–6. We cannot but draw from this history the inference that in Christian baptism there was a deeper spiritual significance.

Barab'bas (*son of Abba*), a robber,

John 18 : 40, who had committed murder in an insurrection, Mark 15 : 7; Luke 23 : 18, in Jerusalem, and was lying in prison at the time of the trial of Jesus before Pilate.

Bar'achel (*God has blessed*), father of Elihu. Job 32 : 2, 6. [Buz.]

Barachi'as. Matt. 23 : 35. [Zacharias.]

Ba'rak (*lightning*), son of Abinoam of Kedesh, a refuge city in Mount Naphtali, was incited by Deborah, a prophetess of Ephraim, to deliver Israel from the yoke of Jabin. Judges 4. He utterly routed the Canaanites in the plain of Jezreel (Esdraelon). (B.C. 1291–1251.)

Barbarian. "Every one not a Greek is a barbarian" is the common Greek definition, and in this strict sense the word is used in Rom. 1 : 14. It often retains this primitive meaning, as in 1 Cor. 14 : 11; Acts 28 : 24.

Barhu'mite, The. [Bahurim.]

Bari'ah (*fugitive*), a descendant of the royal family of Judah. 1 Chron. 3 : 22. (B.C. before 410.)

Bar-je'sus (*son of Jesus*). [Elymas.]

Bar-jo'na (*son of Jonah*). [Peter.]

Bar'kos (*painted*). "Children of Barkos" were among the Nethinim who returned from the captivity with Zerubbabel. Ezra 2 : 53; Neh. 7 : 55. (B.C. 536.)

Barley is one of the most important of the cereal grains, and the most hardy of them all. It was grown by the Hebrews, Lev. 27 : 16; Deut. 8 : 8; Ruth 2 : 17, etc., who used it for baking into bread, chiefly among the poor, Judges 7 : 13; 2 Kings 4 : 42; John 6 : 9, 13, and as fodder for horses. 1 Kings 4 : 28. The barley harvest, Ruth 1 : 22; 2 : 23; 2 Sam. 21 : 9, 10, takes place in Palestine in March and April, and in the hilly districts as late as May. It always precedes the wheat harvest, in some places by a week, in others by fully three weeks. In Egypt the barley is about a month earlier than the wheat; whence its total destruction by the hail storm. Ex. 9 : 31.

Bar'nabas (*son of consolation* or *comfort*), a name given by the apostles, Acts 4 : 36, to Joseph (or Jose), a Levite of the island of Cyprus, who was early a disciple of Christ. In Acts 9 : 27 we find him introducing the newly-converted Saul to the apostles at Jerusalem. Barnabas was sent to Jerusalem, Acts 11 : 19–26, and went to Tarsus to seek Saul, as one specially raised up to preach to the Gentiles. Acts 26 : 17. He brought him to Antioch, and was sent with him to Jerusalem. Acts 11 : 30. On their return, they were ordained by the church for the missionary work, Acts 13 : 2, and sent forth (A.D. 45). From this time Barnabas and Paul enjoy the title and dignity of apostles. Their first missionary journey is related in Acts 13 : 14. Returning to Antioch (A.D. 47 or 48), they were sent (A.D. 50), with some others, to Jerusalem. Acts 15 : 1, 36. Afterwards they parted, and Barnabas took Mark and sailed to Cyprus, his native island. Here the Scripture notices of him cease. The epistle attributed to Barnabas is believed to have been written early in the second century.

Bar'sabas (*son of Sabas* or *rest*). [Joseph Barsabas; Judas Barsabas.]

Barsab'bas. Revised Version of Acts 1 : 23 for Bar'sabas.

Barthol'omew (*son of Tolmai*), one of the twelve apostles of Christ. Matt. 10 : 3; Mark 3 : 18; Luke 6 : 14; Acts 1 : 13. It has been not improperly conjectured that he is identical with Nathanael. John 1 : 45 ff. He is said to have preached the gospel in India, that is, probably, Arabia Felix, and according to some in Armenia.

Bartimæ'us (*son of Timeus*), a blind beggar of Jericho who, Mark 10 : 46 ff., sat by the wayside begging as our Lord passed out of Jericho on his last journey to Jerusalem.

Ba'ruch (*blessed*). 1. Son of Neriah, the friend, Jer. 32 : 12, amanuensis, Jer. 26 : 4–32, and faithful attendant of Jeremiah. Jer. 36 : 10 ff. (B.C. 603.) He was of a noble family, comp. Jer. 51 : 59; Bar. 1 : 1, and of distinguished acquirements. His enemies accused him of influencing Jeremiah in favor of the Chaldæans, Jer. 43 : 3; cf. 27 : 13, and he was imprisoned until the capture of Jerusalem, B.C. 586. By the permission of Nebuchadnezzar he remained with Jeremiah at Mizpeh, Jos. Ant. x. 9, § 1, but was afterwards forced to go down to Egypt. Jer. 43 : 6. Nothing is known certainly of the close of his life.

2. The son of Zabbai, who assisted Nehemiah in rebuilding the walls of Jerusalem. Neh. 3 : 20. (B.C. 446.)

3. A priest, or family of priests, who signed the covenant with Nehemiah. Neh. 10 : 6. (B.C. 410.)

4. The son of Col-bozeh, a descendant of Perez or Pharez, the son of Judah. Neh. 11 : 5. (B.C. 536.)

Ba'ruch, Book of. One of the apocryphal books of the Old Testament. The book was held in little esteem by the Jews, and both its date and authorship are very uncertain.

Barzil'la-i (*iron*, i. e. *strong*). 1. A wealthy Gileadite who showed hospitality to David when he fled from Absalom. 2 Sam. 17 : 27. (B.C. 1023.) He declined the king's offer of ending his days at court. 2 Sam. 19 : 32–39.

2. A Meholathite, whose son Adriel married Michal, Saul's daughter. 2 Sam. 21 : 8. (B.C. before 1062.)

3. Son-in-law to Barzillai the Gileadite. Ezra 2 : 61; Neh. 7 : 63, 64. (B.C. before 536.)

View of Bashan.

Ba'shan (*fruitful*), a district on the east of Jordan. It is sometimes spoken of as the "land of Bashan," 1 Chron. 5 : 11, and comp. Num. 21 : 33; 32 : 33, and sometimes as "all Bashan." Deut. 3 : 10, 13; Josh. 12 : 5; 13 : 12, 30. It was taken by the children of Israel after their conquest of the land of Sihon from Arnon to Jabbok. The limits of Bashan are very strictly defined. It extended from the "border of Gilead" on the south to Mount Hermon on the north, Deut. 3 : 3, 10, 14; Josh. 12 : 5; 1 Chron. 5 : 23, and from the Arabah or Jordan valley on the

west to Salchah (*Sulkhad*) and the border of the Geshurites and the Maachathites on the east. Josh. 12 : 3–5; Deut. 3 : 10. This important district was bestowed on the half-tribe of Manasseh, Josh. 13 : 29–31, together with "half Gilead." This country is now full of interesting ruins, which have lately been explored and from which much light has been thrown upon Bible times. See Porter's "Giant Cities of Bashan."

Ba'shan-ha'voth-ja'ir (*Bashan of the villages of Jair*), a name given to Argob after its conquest by Jair. Deut. 3 : 14.

Bash'emath (*fragrant, pleasing*), daughter of Ishmael, the last married of the three wives of Esau. Gen. 26 : 34; 36 : 3, 4, 13. (B.C. after 1797.) In Gen. 28 : 9 she is called Mahalath.

Basin. Among the smaller vessels for the tabernacle or temple service, many must have been required to receive from the sacrificial victims the blood to be sprinkled for purification. The "basin" from which our Lord washed the disciples' feet was probably deeper and larger than the hand-basin for sprinkling.

Basket. The Hebrew terms used in the description of this article are as follows: (1) *Sal*, so called from the *twigs* of which it was originally made, specially used for holding bread. Gen. 40 : 16 ff.; Ex. 29 : 3, 23; Lev. 8 : 2, 26, 31; Num. 6 : 15, 17, 19. (2) *Salsillôth*, a word of kindred origin, applied to the basket used in gathering grapes. Jer. 6 : 9. (3) *Tene*, in which the first-fruits of the harvest were presented. Deut. 26 : 2, 4. (4) *Celub*, so called from its similarity to a bird-cage. (5) *Dûd*, used for carrying fruit, Jer. 24 : 1, 2, as well as on a larger scale for carrying clay to the brick-yard, Ps. 81 : 6 (*pots*, Authorized Version), or for holding bulky articles. 2

Egyptian Baskets.

Kings 10 : 7. In the New Testament baskets are described under three different terms.

Bas'math (*fragrant, pleasing*), a daughter of Solomon, married to Ahimaaz, one of his commissariat officers. 1 Kings 4 : 15. (B.C. after 1014.)

Bastard. Among those who were excluded from entering the congregation, even to the tenth generation, was the bastard. Deut. 23 : 2. The term is not, however, applied to any illegitimate offspring, born out of wedlock, but is restricted by the rabbins to the issue of any connection within the degrees prohibited by the law.

Bat. Lev. 11 : 19; Deut. 14 : 18. Many travellers have noticed the immense numbers of bats that are found in caverns in the East, and Mr. Layard says that on the occasion of a visit to a cavern these noisome beasts compelled him to retreat.

Bath, Bathing. This was a prescribed part of the Jewish ritual of purification in cases of accident, or of leprous or ordinary uncleanness, Lev. 15 ; 16 : 28 ; 22 : 6 ; Num. 19 : 7, 19 ; 2 Sam. 11 : 2, 4; 2 Kings 5 : 10 ; as also after mourning, which always implied defilement. Ruth 3 : 3 ; 2 Sam. 12 : 20. The eastern climate made bathing essential alike to health and pleasure, to which luxury added the use of perfumes. Esther 2 : 12 ; Judith 10 : 3 ; Susan. 17. The "pools," such as that of Siloam and Hezekiah, 2 Kings 20 : 20 ; Neh. 3 : 15, 16 ; Isa. 22 : 11 ; John 9 : 7, often sheltered by porticos, John 5 : 2, are the first indications we have of public bathing accommodation.

Bath. [MEASURES.]

Bath-rab'bim (*daughter of many*), The gate of, one of the gates of the ancient city of Heshbon. Cant. 7 : 4 (5).

Bath'-sheba, or **Bath-she'ba** (*daughter of the oath*), 2 Sam. 11 : 3, etc., also called Bath-shua in 1 Chron. 3 : 5, the daughter of Eliam, 2 Sam. 11 : 3, or Ammiel, 1 Chron. 3 : 5, the son of Ahithophel, 2 Sam. 23 : 34, and wife of Uriah the Hittite. (B.C. 1035.) The child which was the fruit of her adulterous intercourse with David died; but after marriage she became the mother of four sons, Solomon, Matt. 1 : 6, Shimea, Shobab and Nathan. When Adonijah attempted to set aside the succession promised to Solomon, Bath-sheba informed the king of the conspiracy. 1 Kings 1 : 11, 15, 23. After the accession of Solomon, she, as queen-mother, requested permission of her son for Adonijah to take in marriage Abishag the Shunammite. 1 Kings 2 : 21–25.

Bath-shu'a. [BATH-SHEBA.]

Battering-ram, Ezek. 4 : 2 ; 21 : 22, a large beam with a head of iron which was sometimes made to resemble the head of a ram. It was suspended by ropes to a beam supported by posts, and balanced so as to swing backward and forward, and was impelled by men against the wall. In attacking the walls of a fort or city, the first step appears to have been to form an inclined plane or bank of earth, comp. Ezek. 4 : 2, "cast a mount against it," by which the besiegers could bring their battering-rams and other engines to the foot of the walls. "The battering-rams," says Mr. Layard, "were of several kinds. Some were joined to movable towers which held warriors and armed men. The whole then formed one great temporary building, the top of which is represented in sculptures as on a level with the walls, and even turrets, of the besieged city. In some bas-reliefs the battering-ram is without wheels : it was then perhaps constructed upon the spot and was not intended to be moved."

Battle-axe. Jer. 51 : 20. [MAUL.]

Battlement. Among the Jews a battlement was required by law to be built upon every house. It consisted of a low wall built around the roofs of the houses to prevent persons from falling off, and sometimes serving as a partition from another building. Deut. 22 : 8 ; Jer. 5 : 10.

Bav'a-i, son of Henadad, ruler of the district of Keilah in the time of Nehemiah. Neh. 3 : 18. (B.C. 446.)

Bay tree. A species of laurel, *Laurus nobilis.* An evergreen, with leaves like our mountain laurel. Ps. 37 : 35.

Baz'lith (*asking*). "Children of Bazlith" were among the Nethinim who returned with Zerubbabel. Neh. 7 : 54. In Ezra 2 : 52 the name is given as BAZLUTH. (B.C. 536.)

Baz'luth. [BAZLITH.]

Bdellium (*bedôlach*). Gen. 2 : 12 ; Num. 11 : 7. It is quite impossible to say whether *bedôlach* denotes a mineral or an animal production or a vegetable exudation. Bdellium is an odoriferous exudation from a tree which is perhaps the *Borassus flabelliformis,* Lin., of Arabia Felix.

Beacon. A signal or conspicuous mark erected on an eminence for direction. Isa. 30 : 17.

Beali'ah (*Jehovah is lord*), a Benjamite who went over to David at Ziklag. 1 Chron. 12 : 5. (B.C. 1062.)

Be'aloth (*ladies*), a town in the extreme south of Judah. Josh. 15 : 24.

Beans. 2 Sam. 17 : 28 ; Ezek. 4 : 9. Beans are cultivated in Palestine, which produces many of the leguminous order of plants, such as lentils, kidney-beans, vetches, etc.

Bear. 1 Sam. 17 : 34 ; 2 Sam. 17 : 8. The Syrian bear, *Ursus syriacus*, which is without doubt the animal mentioned in the Bible, is still found on the higher mountains of Palestine. During the

Syrian Bear.

summer months these bears keep to the snowy parts of Lebanon, but descend in winter to the villages and gardens. It is probable also that at this period in former days they extended their visits to other parts of Palestine.

Beard. Western Asiatics have always cherished the beard as the badge of the dignity of manhood, and attached to it the importance of a feature. The Egyptians, on the contrary, for the most part shaved the hair of the face and head, though we find some instances to the contrary. The beard is the object of an oath, and that on which blessing or shame is spoken of as resting. The custom was and is to shave or pluck it and the hair out in mourning, Ezra 9 : 3 ; Isa. 15 : 2 ; 50 : 6 ; Jer. 41 : 5 ; 48 : 37 ; Bar. 6 : 31 ; to neglect it in seasons of permanent affliction, 2 Sam. 19 : 24, and to regard any insult to it as the last outrage which enmity can inflict. 2 Sam. 10 : 4. The beard was the object of salutation. 2 Sam.

20 : 9. The dressing, trimming, anointing, etc., of the beard was performed with much ceremony by persons of wealth and rank. Ps. 133 : 2. The removal of the beard was a part of the ceremonial treatment proper to a leper. Lev. 14 : 9.

Beb'a-i (*fatherly*). 1. "Sons of Bebai," 623 (Neh. 628) in number, returned from Babylon with Zerubbabel, Ezra 2 : 11 ; Neh. 7 : 16 (B.C. 536), and at a later period twenty-eight more under Zechariah, son of Bebai, returned with Ezra. Ezra 8 : 11. Four of this family had taken foreign wives. Ezra 10 : 28. The name occurs also among those who sealed the covenant. Neh. 10 : 15.

2. Father of Zechariah, who was the leader of the twenty-eight men of his tribe mentioned above.

Be'cher (*young* or *first-born*). 1. The second son of Benjamin, according to the list in both Gen. 46 : 21 and 1 Chron. 7 : 6, but omitted in 1 Chron. 8 : 1. (B.C. about 1690.)

2. Son of Ephraim, Num. 26 : 35, called BERED in 1 Chron. 7 : 20. Same as the preceding.

Becho'rath (*first-born*), son of Aphiah or Abiah, and grandson of Becher according to 1 Sam. 9 : 1 ; 1 Chron. 7 : 8. (B.C. before 1093.)

Bed. The Jewish bed consisted of the mattress, a mere mat, or one or more quilts ; the covering, a finer quilt, or sometimes the outer garment worn by day, 1 Sam. 19 : 13, which the law provided should not be kept in pledge after sunset, that the poor man might not lack his needful covering, Deut. 24 : 13 ; the pillow, 1 Sam. 19 : 13, probably formed of sheep's fleece or goat's skin, with a stuffing of cotton, etc. ; the bedstead, a divan or bench along the side or end of the room, sufficing as a support for the bedding. Besides we have bedsteads made of ivory, wood, etc., referred to in Deut. 3 : 11 ; Amos 6 : 4. The ornamental portions were pillars and a canopy, Judith 13 : 9, ivory carvings, gold and silver, and probably mosaic work, purple and fine linen. Esth. 1 : 6 ; Cant. 3 : 9, 10. The ordinary furniture of a bed-chamber in private life is given in 2 Kings 4 : 10.

Be'dad (*solitary*), the father of Hadad king of Edom. Gen. 36 : 35 ; 1 Chron. 1 : 46. (B.C. before 1093.)

Be'dan (*son of judgment*). 1. Mentioned in 1 Sam. 12 : 11 as a judge of

Israel between Jerubbaal (Gideon) and Jephthah. The Chaldee Paraphrast reads Samson for Bedan; the LXX., Syriac and Arabic all have Barak. Ewald suggests that it may be a false reading for Abdon. (B.C. about 1150.)

2. The son of Gilead. 1 Chron. 7 : 17.

Bede-i'ah, one of the sons of Bani, in the time of Ezra, who had taken a foreign wife. Ezra 10 : 35. (B.C. 458.)

Bee (*debôrâh*). Deut. 1 : 44; Judges 14 : 8; Ps. 118 : 12; Isa. 7 : 18. Bees abounded in Palestine, honey being a common article of food, Ps. 81 : 16, and was often found in the clefts of rocks and in hollow trees. 1 Sam. 14 : 25, 27. English naturalists know little of the species of bees that are found in Palestine, but are inclined to believe that the honey-bee of Palestine is distinct from the honey-bee (*Apis mellifica*) of this country. The passage in Isa. 7 : 18 refers "to the custom of the people in the East of calling attention to any one by a significant *hiss* or rather *hist*."

We read, Judges 14 : 8, that "after a time," probably many days, Samson returned to the carcass of the lion he had slain, and saw bees and honey therein. "If any one here represents to himself a corrupt and putrid carcass, the occurrence ceases to have any true similitude, for it is well known that in these countries, at certain seasons of the year, the heat will in the course of twenty-four hours completely dry up the moisture of dead camels, and that, without their undergoing decomposition, their bodies long remain like mummies, unaltered and entirely free from offensive odor."— *Œdmann.*

Be-eli'ada (*the Lord knows*), one of David's sons, born in Jerusalem. 1 Chron. 14 : 7. In the lists in Samuel the name is ELIADA. (B.C. after 1045.)

Be-el'zebub. [See BEELZEBUL.]

Be-el'zebul (*lord of the house*), the title of a heathen deity, to whom the Jews ascribed the sovereignty of the evil spirits; Satan, the prince of the devils. Matt. 10 : 25; 12 : 24; Mark 3 : 22; Luke 11 : 15 ff. The correct reading is without doubt *Beelzebul*, and not *Beelzebub*.

Be'er (*a well*). 1. One of the latest halting-places of the Israelites, lying beyond the Arnon. Num. 21 : 16–18. This is possibly the BEER-ELIM of Isa. 15 : 8.

2. A place to which Jotham, the son of Gideon, fled for fear of his brother Abimelech. Judges 9 : 21.

Be-e'ra (*a well*), son of Zophah, of the tribe of Asher. 1 Chron. 7 : 37. (B.C. after 1450.)

Be-e'rah, prince of the Reubenites, carried away by Tiglath-pileser. 1 Chron. 5 : 6. (B.C. 738.)

Be-er-e'lim (*well of heroes*), a spot named in Isa. 15 : 8 as on the "border of Moab." Num. 21 : 16; comp. 13.

Be-e'ri. 1. The father of Judith, one of the wives of Esau. Gen. 26 : 34. [ANAH.] (B.C. 1797.)

2. Father of the prophet Hosea. Hos. 1 : 1. (B.C. before 725.)

Be-er-laha'i-roi (*a well of the living*), a living spring, Authorized Version, *fountain*, comp. Jer. 6 : 7, between Kadesh and Bered, in the wilderness. Gen. 24 : 62.

Be-e'roth (*wells*), one of the four cities of the Hivites who deluded Joshua into a treaty of peace with them. Josh. 9 : 17. It is now *el-Bireh*, which stands about 10 miles north of Jerusalem.

Be-e'roth of the children of Jaakan, the wells in the region of the tribe of Bene-Jaakan, which formed one of the halting-places of the Israelites in the desert. Deut. 10 : 6. In Num. 33 : 31 the name is given as BENE-JAAKAN only.

Be-er'-sheba, or **Be-er-she'ba** (*well of the oath*), the name of one of the old places in Palestine which formed the southern limit of the country. There are two accounts of the origin of the name. According to the first, the well was dug by Abraham, and the name given, Gen. 21 : 31; the other narrative ascribes the origin of the name to Isaac instead of Abraham. Gen. 26 : 31–33. Beersheba was given to Judah, Josh. 15 : 28, and then to Simeon. Josh. 19 : 2; 1 Chron. 4 : 28. In the often-quoted "from Dan even unto Beersheba," Judges 20 : 1, it represents the southern boundary of Canaan, as Dan the northern. In the time of Jerome it was still a considerable place, and still retains its ancient name —*Bir es-Sebâ*. There are at present on the spot two principal wells and five smaller ones. The two principal wells are on or close to the northern bank of the *Wady es-Sebâ*. The larger of the two, which lies to the east, is, according to Dr. Robinson, 12½ feet in diameter, and at the time of his visit (April 12) was 44½ feet to the surface of the water. The masonry which encloses the well extends downward 28½ feet. The other well is 5 feet in diameter, and was 42 feet to the water. The curb-stones around the mouth of both wells are worn into deep grooves by the action of the ropes of so many centuries. These wells are in constant use to-day. The five lesser wells are in a group in the bed of the wady. On some low hills north of the large wells are scattered the foundations and ruins of a town of moderate size.

Be-esh'terah (*house of Ashterah*).

Beersheba. (*From an original Photograph.*)

one of the two cities allotted to the sons of Gershon out of the tribe of Manasseh beyond Jordan. Josh. 21 : 27. Probably identical with Ashtaroth. 1 Chron. 6 : 71.

Beetle. [LOCUST.]

Beeves. Same as cattle. Lev. 22 : 19. [See BULL.]

Beggar, Begging. The poor among the Hebrews were much favored. They were allowed to glean in the fields, and to gather whatever the land produced in the year in which it was not tilled. Lev. 19 : 10 ; 25 : 5, 6 ; Deut. 24 : 19. They were also invited to feasts. Deut. 14 : 29 and 26 : 12. The Israelite could not be an absolute pauper. His land was inalienable, except for a certain term, when it reverted to him or his posterity. And if this resource were insufficient, he could pledge the services of himself and family for a valuable sum. Those who were indigent through bodily infirmities were usually taken care of by their kindred. A beggar was sometimes seen, however, and was regarded and abhorred as a vagabond. Ps. 109 : 10. In later times beggars were accustomed, it would seem, to have a fixed place at the corners of the streets, Mark 10 : 46, or at the gates of the temple, Acts 3 : 2, or of private houses. Luke 16 : 20.

Be'hemoth (*great beasts*). There can be little or no doubt that by this word, Job 40 : 15-24, the hippopotamus is intended, since all the details descriptive of the *behemoth* accord entirely with the ascertained habits of that animal. The hippopotamus is an immense creature having a thick and square head, a large mouth often two feet broad, small eyes and ears, thick and heavy body, short legs terminated by four toes, a short tail, skin without hair except at the extremity of the tail. It inhabits nearly the whole of Africa, and has been found of the length of 17 feet. It delights in the water, but feeds on herbage on land. It is not found in Palestine, but may at one time have been a native of western Asia.

Be'kah. [WEIGHTS AND MEASURES.]

Bel. [BAAL.]

Be'la (*destruction*). 1. One of the five cities of the plain which was spared

Hippopotamus.

at the intercession of Lot, and received the name of Zoar. Gen. 14 : 2; 19 : 22. [ZOAR.]

2. Son of Beor, who reigned over Edom in the city of Dinhabah, eight generations before Saul. Gen. 36 : 31–33; 1 Chron. 1 : 43, 44.

3. Eldest son of Benjamin, according to Gen. 46 : 21 (Authorized Version "Belah"); Num. 26 : 38, 40; 1 Chron. 7 : 6; 8 : 1, and head of the family of the Belaites.

4. Son of Ahaz, a Reubenite. 1 Chron. 5 : 8.

Be'lah. [BELA, 3.]

Be'la-ites, The. Num. 26 : 38. [BELA, 3.]

Be'lial. The meaning of this word as found in the Scriptures is *worthlessness,* and hence *recklessness, lawlessness.* The expression *son* or *man of Belial* must be understood as meaning simply a worthless, lawless fellow. The term as used in 2 Cor. 6 : 15 is generally understood as an appellative of Satan, as the personification of all that was bad.

Bellows. The word occurs only in Jer. 6 : 29, where it denotes an instrument to heat a smelting furnace. Wilkinson in "Ancient Egypt," iii. 338, says, "They consisted of a leather, secured and fitted into a frame, from which a long pipe extended for carrying the wind to the fire. They were worked by the feet, the operator standing upon them, with one

under each foot, and pressing them alternately, while he pulled up each exhausted skin with a string he held in his hand."

Bells. In Ex. 28 : 33 the bells alluded to were the golden ones, 72 in number, round the hem of the high priest's ephod. The object of them was "that his sound might be heard." Ex. 28 : 34; Ecclus. 45 : 9. To this day bells are frequently attached, for the sake of their pleasant sound, to the anklets of women. The little girls of Cairo wear strings of them around their feet. In Zech. 14 : 20 "bells of the horses" were concave or flat pieces of brass, which were sometimes attached to horses for the sake of ornament.

Belshaz'zar (*prince of Bel*), the last king of Babylon. In Dan. 5 : 2 Nebuchadnezzar is called the father of Belshazzar. This, of course, need only mean grandfather or ancestor. According to the well-known narrative, Belshazzar gave a splendid feast in his palace during the siege of Babylon (B.C. 538), using the sacred vessels of the temple, which Nebuchadnezzar had brought from Jerusalem. The miraculous appearance of the handwriting on the wall, the calling in of Daniel to interpret its meaning, the prophecy of the overthrow of the kingdom, and Belshazzar's death, are recorded in Dan. 5.

Belteshaz'zar (*favored by Bel*). [DANIEL.]

Ben (*son*), a Levite, one of the porters appointed by David for the ark. 1 Chron. 15 : 18.

Bena'iah (*made by the Lord*). 1. The son of Jehoiada the chief priest, 1 Chron. 27 : 5, of the tribe of Levi, though a native of Kabzeel, 2 Sam. 23 : 20; set by David, 1 Chron. 11 : 25, over his body-guard. 2 Sam. 8 : 18; 20 : 23; 1 Kings 1 : 38; 1 Chron. 18 : 17. One of the mighty men. 2 Sam. 23 : 22, 23; 1 Chron. 11 : 25; 27 : 6. The exploits which gave him this rank are narrated in 2 Sam. 23 : 20, 21; 1 Chron. 11 : 22. He was captain of the host for the third month. 1 Chron. 27 : 5. Benaiah remained faithful to Solomon during Adonijah's attempt on the crown, 1 Kings 1 : 8, 10, 32, 38, 44, and was raised into the place of Joab as commander-in-chief of the whole army. 1 Kings 2 : 35; 4 : 4. (B.C. 1005.)

2. Benaiah the Pirathonite, an Ephraimite, one of David's thirty mighty men, 2 Sam. 23 : 30; 1 Chron. 11 : 31, and the captain of the eleventh monthly course. 1 Chron. 27 : 14.

3. A Levite in the time of David, who "played with a psaltery on Alamoth." 1 Chron. 15 : 18, 20; 16 : 5.

4. A priest in the time of David, appointed to blow the trumpet before the ark. 1 Chron. 15 : 24; 16 : 6.

5. A Levite of the sons of Asaph. 2 Chron. 20 : 14.

6. A Levite in the time of Hezekiah. 2 Chron. 31 : 13.

7. One of the "princes" of the families of Simeon. 1 Chron. 4 : 36.

8. Four laymen in the time of Ezra who had taken strange wives. Ezra 10 : 25, 30, 35, 43.

9. The father of Pelatiah. Ezek. 11 : 1, 13.

Ben-am'mi (*son of my people*), the son of the younger daughter of Lot, and progenitor of the Ammonites. Gen. 19 : 38. (B.C. 1897.)

Ben-eb'erak (*son of lightning*), one of the cities of the tribe of Dan, mentioned only in Josh. 19 : 45.

Bene-ja'akan (*sons of Jaakan*), a tribe who gave their name to certain wells in the desert which formed one of the halting-places of the Israelites on their journey to Canaan. [BEEROTH BENE-JAAKAN.] Also given in Gen. 36 : 27 as AKAN.

Bene-ke'dem (*the children of the East*), an appellation given to a people or to peoples dwelling to the east of Palestine. It occurs in Gen. 29 : 1; Judges 6 : 3, 33; 7 : 12; 8 : 10; Job 1 : 3.

Ben-ha'dad (*son of Hadad*), the name of three kings of Damascus. BEN-HADAD I., king of Damascus, which in his time was supreme in Syria. He made an alliance with Asa, and conquered a great part of the north of Israel. 1 Kings 15 : 18. His date is B.C. 950.

BEN-HADAD II., son of the preceding, and also king of Damascus. Long wars with Israel characterized his reign. Some time after the death of Ahab, Ben-hadad renewed the war with Israel, attacked Samaria a second time, and pressed the siege so closely that there was a terrible famine in the city. But the Syrians broke up in the night in consequence of a sudden panic. Soon after Ben-hadad fell sick, and sent Hazael to consult Elisha as to the issue of his malady. On the day after Hazael's return Ben-hadad was murdered, probably by some of his own servants. 2 Kings 8 : 7-15. Ben-hadad's death was about B.C. 890, and he must have reigned some 30 years.

BEN-HADAD III., son of Hazael, and his successor on the throne of Syria. When he succeeded to the throne, Jehoash recovered the cities which Jehoahaz had lost to the Syrians, and beat him in Aphek. 2 Kings 13 : 17, 25. The date of Ben-hadad III. is B.C. 840.

Ben-ha'il (*son of the host, strong*), one of the princes whom King Jehoshaphat sent to teach in the cities of Judah. 2 Chron. 17 : 7.

Ben-ha'nan (*son of the gracious*), son of Shimon, in the line of Judah. 1 Chron. 4 : 20.

Beni'nu (*our son*), a Levite; one of those who sealed the covenant with Nehemiah. Neh. 10 : 13 (14).

Ben'jamin (*son of the right hand, fortunate*). 1. The youngest of the children of Jacob. His birth took place on the road between Bethel and Bethlehem, near the latter, B.C. 1729. His mother, Rachel, died in the act of giving him birth, naming him with her last breath Ben-oni (*son of my sorrow*). This was by Jacob changed into Benjamin. Gen. 35 : 16, 18. Until the journeys of Jacob's sons and of Jacob himself into Egypt we hear nothing of Benjamin. Nothing personal is known of him. Henceforward the history of Benjamin is the history of the tribe.

2. A man of the tribe of Benjamin, son of Bilhan, and the head of a family of warriors. 1 Chron. 7 : 10.

3. One of the "sons of Harim," an Israelite in the time of Ezra who had married a foreign wife. Ezra 10 : 32.

Ben'jamin, The tribe of. The contrast between the warlike character of the tribe and the peaceful image of its progenitor comes out in many scattered notices. Benjamin was the only tribe which seems to have pursued archery to any purpose, and their skill in the bow, 1 Sam. 20 : 20, 36; 2 Sam. 1 : 22; 1 Chron. 8 : 40; 12 : 2; 2 Chron. 17 : 17, and the sling, Judges 20 : 16, is celebrated. The dreadful deed recorded in Judges 19 was defended by Benjamin. Later the tribe seems, however, to assume another position, as Ramah, 1 Sam. 9 : 12, etc., Mizpeh, 1 Sam. 7 : 5, Bethel and Gibeon, 1 Kings 3 : 4, were all in the land of

Benjamin. After the struggles and contests which followed the death of Saul, the history of Benjamin becomes merged in that of the southern kingdom.

Ben'jamin, The land of. The proximity of Benjamin to Ephraim during the march to the promised land was maintained in the territory allotted to each. That given to Benjamin formed almost a parallelogram, of about 26 miles in length by 12 in breadth, lying between Ephraim, the Jordan, Judah and Dan. The general level of this part of Palestine is not less than 2000 feet above the Mediterranean or than 3000 feet above the valley of the Jordan, the surrounding country including a large number of eminences—almost every one of which has borne some part in the history of the tribe—and many torrent beds and deep ravines.

Ben'jamin, High gate or **gate of.** Jer. 20 : 2 ; 37 : 13 ; 38 : 7 ; Zech. 14 : 10. [JERUSALEM.]

Be'no (*his son*), a Levite of the sons of Merari. 1 Chron. 24 : 26, 27.

Ben-o'ni (*son of my sorrow*). Gen. 35 : 18. [BENJAMIN.]

Ben-zo'heth (*son of Zoheth*), a descendant of Judah. 1 Chron. 4 : 20.

Be'on. Num. 32 : 3. [BETH-BAAL-MEON.] Comp. ver. 38.

Be'or (*burning* or *torch*). 1. The father of Bela, one of the early Edomite kings. Gen. 36 : 32 ; 1 Chron. 1 : 43. 2. Father of Balaam. Num. 22 : 5 ; 24 : 3, 15 ; 31 : 8 ; Deut. 23 : 4 ; Josh. 13 : 22 ; 24 : 9 ; Micah 6 : 5. He is called BOSOR in the New Testament. (B.C. before 1450.)

Be'ra (*son of evil*), king of Sodom. Gen. 14 : 2 ; also 17, 21.

Ber'achah (*blessing*), a Benjamite who attached himself to David at Ziklag. 1 Chron. 12 : 3. (B.C. 1054.)

Ber'achah, Valley of, a valley in which Jehoshaphat and his people assembled to "bless" Jehovah after the overthrow of the hosts of Moabites. 2 Chron. 20:26. It is now called *Bereikût*, and lies between Tekua and the main road from Bethlehem to Hebron.

Berachi'ah (*blessed of Jehovah*), a Gershonite Levite, father of Asaph. 1 Chron. 6 : 39. [BERECHIAH.]

Berai'ah (*created by Jehovah*), son of Shimhi, a chief man of Benjamin. 1 Chron. 8 : 21.

Bere'a (*well watered*). 1. A city of Macedonia, mentioned in Acts 17 : 10, 13.

It is now called *Verria* or *Kara-Verria*, and is situated on the eastern slope of the Olympian mountain range, and has 15,000 or 20,000 inhabitants. 2. The modern *Aleppo*, mentioned in 2 Macc. 13 : 4. 3. A place in Judea, apparently not very far from Jerusalem. 1 Macc. 9 : 4.

Berechi'ah (*blessed of Jehovah*). 1. A descendant of the royal family of Judah. 1 Chron. 3 : 20. 2. A man mentioned as the father of Meshullam, who assisted in rebuilding the walls of Jerusalem. Neh. 3 : 4, 30 ; 6 : 18. 3. A Levite. 1 Chron. 9 : 16. 4. A doorkeeper for the ark. 1 Chron. 15 : 23. 5. One of the tribe of Ephraim in the time of Ahaz. 2 Chron. 28 : 12. 6. Father of Asaph the singer. 1 Chron. 15 : 17. [BERACHIAH.] 7. Father of Zechariah. Zech. 1 : 1, 7.

Be'red (*hail*). 1. A place in the south of Palestine, near the well Lahai-roi. Gen. 16 : 14. 2. A son or descendant of Ephraim, 1 Chron. 7 : 20, possibly identical with Becher in Num. 26 : 35.

Bereni'ce. [BERNICE.]

Be'ri (*a well*), son of Zophah, of the tribe of Asher. 1 Chron. 7 : 36.

Beri'ah (*in evil,* or *a gift*). 1. A son of Asher. Gen. 46 : 17 ; Num. 26 : 44, 45. 2. A son of Ephraim. 1 Chron. 7 : 20 23. 3. A Benjamite. 1 Chron. 8 : 13, 16. 4. A Levite. 1 Chron. 23 : 10, 11.

Beri'ites. [BERIAH, 1.]

Be'rites, The, a tribe of people who are named with Abel and Beth-maachah, and who were therefore doubtless situated in the north of Palestine. 2 Sam. 20 : 14.

Be'rith. Judges 9 : 46. [BAAL-BERITH.]

Berni'ce, or **Bereni'ce** (*bringing victory*), the eldest daughter of Herod Agrippa I. Acts 12 : 1, etc. She was first married to her uncle Herod, king of Chalcis, and after his death (A.D. 48) she lived under circumstances of great suspicion with her own brother, Agrippa II., in connection with whom she is mentioned, Acts 25 : 13, 23 ; 26 : 30, as having visited Festus on his appointment as procurator of Judea.

Ber'odach-bal'adan. 2 Kings 20 : 12. [MERODACH-BALADAN.]

Bero'thah (*toward the wells*), **Bero'-**

tha-i (*my wells*). The first of these two names is given by Ezekiel, 47 : 16, in connection with Hamath and Damascus as forming part of the northern boundary of the promised land. The second is mentioned, 2 Sam. 8 : 8, in the same connection. The well-known city *Beirût* (Berytus) naturally suggests itself as identical with one at least of the names; but in each instance the circumstances of the case seem to require a position farther east. They were probably in the vicinity of the springs near the present Hasbeya.

Bero'thite, The. 1 Chron. 11 : 39. [BEEROTH.]

Beryl (*tarshish*) occurs in Ex. 28 : 20. It is generally supposed that the *tarshish* derives its name from the place so called, in Spain. Beryl is a mineral of great hardness, and, when transparent, of much beauty. By *tarshish* the modern yellow topaz is probably intended, while in Rev. 21 : 20 a different stone is perhaps referred to, probably the mineral now called beryl, which is identical with the emerald except in color, being a light green or bluish-green.

Be'sa-i (*sword*). "Children of Besai" were among the Nethinim who returned to Judea with Zerubbabel. Ezra 2 : 49; Neh. 7 : 52.

Besode'iah (*in the secret of the Lord*), father of one of the repairers of the wall of Jerusalem. Neh. 3 : 6.

Be'som, a brush or broom of twigs for sweeping. Isa. 14 : 23.

Be'sor, The brook (*cool*), a torrent-bed or wady in the extreme south of Judah. 1 Sam. 30 : 9, 10, 21.

Be'tah (*confidence*), a city belonging to Hadadezer king of Zobah, mentioned with Berothai. 2 Sam. 8 : 8. In the parallel account, 1 Chron. 18 : 8, the name is called Tibhath.

Be'ten (*height*), one of the cities on the border of the tribe of Asher. Josh. 19 : 25.

Beth, the most general word for a house or habitation. It has the special meaning of a temple or house of worship. Beth is more frequently employed in compound names of places than any other word.

Bethab'ara (*house of the ford*), a place beyond Jordan, in which, according to the Received Text of the New Testament, John was baptizing. John 1 : 28. If this reading be correct, Bethabara may be identical with Beth-barah (*fords of Abârah*), the ancient ford of Jordan on the road to Gilead; or, which seems more likely, with Beth-nimrah, on the east of the river, nearly opposite Jericho. The Revised Version reads BETHANY, which see below.

Beth'-anath (*house of echo* or *reply*), one of the "fenced cities" of Naphtali, named with Beth-shemesh, Josh. 19 : 38; from neither of them were the Canaanites expelled. Judges 1 : 33.

Beth'-anoth (*house of echo*), a town in the mountainous district of Judah, named with Halhul, Beth-zur and others in Josh. 15 : 58 only.

Beth'any (*house of dates*, or *house of misery*), a village which, scanty as are the notices of it contained in Scripture, is more intimately associated in our minds than perhaps any other place with the most familiar acts and scenes of the last days of the life of Christ. It was situated "at" the Mount of Olives, Mark 11 : 1; Luke 19 : 29, about fifteen stadia (furlongs, *i. e.* 1½ or 2 miles) from Jerusalem, John 11 : 18, on or near the usual road from Jericho to the city, Luke 19 : 29, comp. 1; Mark 11 : 1, comp. 10 : 46, and close by the west(?) of another village called *Bethphage*, the two being several times mentioned together. Bethany was the home of Mary and Martha and Lazarus, and is now known by a name derived from Lazarus — *el-'Azarîyeh* or *Lazarieh*. It lies on the eastern slope of the Mount of Olives, fully a mile beyond the summit, and not very far from the point at which the road to Jericho begins its more sudden descent towards the Jordan valley. *El-'Azarîyeh* is a ruinous and wretched village, a wild mountain hamlet of some twenty families. Bethany has been commonly explained "house of dates," but it more probably signifies "house of misery." H. Dixon, "Holy Land," ii. 214, foll.

Beth'any. In the Revised Version for BETHABARA, John 1 : 28, where Jesus was baptized by John. It was probably an obscure village near Bethabara, and in time its name faded out and was replaced by the larger and more important Bethabara.

Beth-ar'abah (*house of the desert*), one of the six cities of Judah which were situated down in the Arabah, the sunk valley of the Jordan and Dead Sea, Josh. 15 : 61, on the north border of the tribe. It is also included in the list of the towns of Benjamin. Josh. 18 : 22.

Bethany. (*From an original Photograph.*)

Beth'-aram (*house of the height*), accurately BETH-HARAM, one of the towns of Gad on the east of Jordan, described as in "the valley," Josh. 13 : 27, and no doubt the same place as that named BETH-HARAN in Num. 32 : 36.

Beth-ar'bel (*house of God's court*), named only in Hosea 10 : 14, as the scene of a sack and massacre by Shalman.

Beth-a'ven (*house of nothingness,* i. e. *of idols*), a place on the mountains of Benjamin, east of Bethel, Josh. 7 : 2; 18 : 12, and lying between that place and Michmash. 1 Sam. 13 : 5; 14 : 23. In Hosea 4 : 15; 5 : 8; 10 : 5, the name is transferred to the neighboring Bethel,— once the "house of God," but then the house of idols, of "naught."

Beth-az'maveth (*house of Azmaveth*). Under this name is mentioned, in Neh. 7 : 28 only, the town of Benjamin which is elsewhere called AZMAVETH and BETH-SAMOS.

Beth-baal-me'on (*house of Baalmeon*), a place in the possessions of Reuben, on the downs (Authorized Version "plain") east of Jordan. Josh. 13 : 17. At the Israelites' first approach its name was BAAL-MEON, Num. 32 : 38, or, in its contracted form, BEON, 32 : 3, to which the Beth was possibly a Hebrew addition. Later it would seem to have come into possession of Moab, and to be known either as Beth-meon, Jer. 48 : 23, or Baal-meon. Ezek. 25 : 9. The name is still attached to a ruined place of considerable size a short distance to the southwest of *Hesbân*, and bearing the name of "the fortress of *Mi'ûn*," or *Maéin.*

Beth-ba'rah (*house of the ford*), named only in Judges 7 : 24. It derives its chief interest from the possibility that its more modern representative may have been Beth-abara, where John baptized. It was probably the chief ford of the district.

Beth-bir'e-i (*house of my creation*), a town of Simeon, 1 Chron. 4 : 31, which by comparison with the parallel list in Josh. 19 : 6 appears to have had also the name of BETH-LEBAOTH. It lay to the extreme south.

Beth'-car (*house of the lamb*), a place named as the point to which the Israelites pursued the Philistines, 1 Sam. 7 : 11, and therefore west of Mizpeh.

Beth-da'gon (*house of Dagon*). 1. A city in the low country of Judah, Josh. 15 : 41, and therefore not far from the Philistine territory.

2. A town apparently near the coast, named as one of the landmarks of the boundary of Asher. Josh. 19 : 27.

Beth-diblatha'im (*house of fig-cakes*), a town of Moab, Jer. 48 : 22, apparently the place elsewhere called AL-MON-DIBLATHAIM.

Beth'el (*the house of God*). 1. A well-known city and holy place of central Palestine, about 12 miles north of Jerusalem. If we are to accept the precise definition of Gen. 12 : 8, the name of Bethel would appear to have existed at this spot even before the arrival of Abram in Canaan. Gen. 12 : 8; 13 : 3, 4. Bethel was the scene of Jacob's vision. Gen. 28 : 11–19; 31 : 13. Jacob lived there. Gen. 35 : 1–8. The original name was Luz. Judges 1 : 22, 23. After the conquest Bethel is frequently heard of. In the troubled times when there was no king in Israel, it was to Bethel that the people went up in their distress to ask counsel of God. Judges 20 : 18, 26, 31 ; 21 : 2; Authorized Version, "house of God." Here was the ark of the covenant. Judges 20 : 26–28 ; 21 : 4. Later it is named as one of the holy cities to which Samuel went in circuit. 1 Sam. 7 : 16. Here Jeroboam placed one of the two calves of gold. Toward the end of Jeroboam's life Bethel fell into the hands of Judah. 2 Chron. 13 : 19. Elijah visited Bethel, and we hear of "sons of the prophets" as resident there. 2 Kings 2 : 2, 3. But after the destruction of the Baal worship by Jehu, Bethel comes once more into view. 2 Kings 10 : 29. After the desolation of the northern kingdom by the king of Assyria, Bethel still remained an abode of priests. 2 Kings 17 : 27, 28. In later times Bethel is named only once under the scarcely-altered name of *Beitin*. Its ruins still lie on the right-hand side of the road from Jerusalem to Nablûs.

2. A town in the south part of Judah, named in Josh. 12 : 16 and 1 Sam. 30 : 27. In Josh. 15 : 30 ; 19 : 4 ; 1 Chron. 4 : 29, 30, the place appears under the names of CHESIL, BETHUL and BETHUEL; Hiel the Bethelite is recorded as the rebuilder of Jericho. 1 Kings 16 : 34.

3. In Josh. 16 : 1 and 1 Sam. 13 : 2 Mount Bethel, a hilly section near Bethel, is referred to.

Beth-e'mek (*house of the valley*), a place on or near the border of Asher, on the north side of which was the ravine of Jiphthah-el. Josh. 19 : 27.

Be'ther (*depth*), **The mountains of.** Cant. 2 : 17. There is no clue to guide us as to what mountains are intended here.

Bethes'da (*house of mercy*, or *the flow-*

ing *water*), the Hebrew name of a reservoir or tank, with five "porches," close upon the sheep-gate or "market" in Jerusalem. John 5 : 2. The largest reservoir—*Birket Israil*—360 feet long, 120 feet wide and 80 feet deep, within the walls of the city, close by St. Stephen's Gate, and under the northeast wall of the Haram area, is generally considered to

Traditional Pool of Bethesda.

be the modern representative of Bethesda. Robinson, however, suggests that the ancient Bethesda is identical with what is now called the *Pool of the Virgin*, an intermittent pool, south of *Birket Israil* and north of the pool of Siloam.

Bethe'zel (*neighbor's house*), a place named only in Micah 1 : 11. From the context it was doubtless situated in the plain of Philistia.

Beth-ga'der (*house of the wall*), doubtless a place, though it occurs in the genealogies of Judah as if a person. 1 Chron. 2 : 51.

Beth-ga'mul (*camel-house*), a town of Moab, in the downs east of Jordan. Jer. 48 : 23; comp. 21.

Beth-gil'gal. Same as Gilgal. Neh. 12 : 29.

Beth-hac'cerem (*house of the vine*). Neh. 3 : 14; Jer. 6 : 1. A beacon station near Tekoa, supposed to be the *Frank Mountain*, a few miles southeast of Bethlehem.

Beth-ha'ran. Num. 32 : 36. It is no doubt the same place as BETH-ARAM. Josh. 13 : 27.

Beth-hog'la (*partridge-house*), and **Hog'lah,** a place on the border of Judah, Josh. 15 : 6, and of Benjamin. Josh. 18 :

19, 21. A magnificent spring and a ruin between Jericho and the Jordan still bear the names of *Ainhajala*.

Beth-ho′ron (*house of caverns*), the name of two towns or villages, an "upper" and a "nether," Josh. 16 : 3, 5; 1 Chron. 7 : 24, on the road from Gibeon to Azekah, Josh. 10 : 10, 11, and the Philistine plain. 1 Macc. 3 : 24. Beth-horon lay on the boundary line between Benjamin and Ephraim, Josh. 16 : 3, 5, and, Josh. 18 : 13, 14, was counted to Ephraim, Josh. 21 : 22; 1 Chron. 7 : 24, and given to the Kohathites. Josh. 21 : 22; 1 Chron. 6 : 68 (53). The two Beth-horons still survive in the modern villages of *Beit-'ûr, et-tahta* and *el-foka*.

Beth-jesh′imoth (*house of deserts*), or **Jes′imoth,** a town or place east of Jordan, on the lower level at the south end of the Jordan valley, Num. 33 : 49, and named with Ashdod-pisgah and Beth-peor. It was one of the limits of the encampment of Israel before crossing the Jordan. Later it was allotted to Reuben, Josh. 12 : 3; 13 : 20, but came at last into

Bethlehem from the Chapel of the Nativity.

the hands of Moab, and formed one of the cities which were "the glory of the country." Ezek. 25 : 9.

Beth-leb′aoth (*house of lionesses*), a town in the lot of Simeon, Josh. 19 : 6, in the extreme south of Judah. [Josh. 15 : 32, LEBAOTH.] In 1 Chron. 4 : 31 the name is given BETH-BIREI.

Beth′lehem (*house of bread*). 1. One of the oldest towns in Palestine, already in existence at the time of Jacob's return to the country. Its earliest name was EPHRATH or EPHRATAH. See Gen. 35 : 16, 19; 48 : 7. After the conquest Bethlehem appears under its own name, BETHLEHEM-JUDAH. Judges 17 : 7; 1 Sam. 17 : 12; Ruth 1 : 1, 2. The book of Ruth is a page from the domestic history of Bethlehem. It was the home of

Ruth, Ruth 1 : 19, and of David. 1 Sam. 17 : 12. It was fortified by Rehoboam. 2 Chron. 11 : 6. It was here that our Lord was born, Matt. 2 : 1, and here that he was visited by the shepherds, Luke 2 : 15–17, and the Magi. Matt. 2. The modern town of *Beit-lahm* lies to the east of the main road from Jerusalem to Hebron, six miles from the former. It covers the east and northeast parts of the ridge of a long gray hill of Jura limestone, which stands nearly due east and west, and is about a mile in length. The hill has a deep valley on the north and another on the south. On the top lies the village in a kind of irregular triangle The population is about 3000 souls, entirely Christians. The Church of the Nativity, built by the empress Helena

A.D. 330, is the oldest Christian church in existence. It is built over the grotto where Christ is supposed to have been born.

2. A town in the portion of Zebulun, named nowhere but in Josh. 19 : 15. Now known as *Beit-lahm.*

Bethlo'mon. 1 Esd. 5 : 17. [BETH-LEHEM, 1.]

Beth-ma'achah (*house of oppression*), a place named only in 2 Sam. 20 : 14, 15. In the absence of more information we can only conclude that it is iden-tical with Maachah or Aram-maachah, one of the petty Syrian kingdoms in the north of Palestine. Comp. 2 Kings 15 : 29.

Beth-mar'caboth (*house of the chariots*), one of the towns of Simeon, situated to the extreme south of Ju-dah. Josh. 19 : 5; 1 Chron. 4 : 31. In the parallel list, Josh. 15 : 31, MADMAN-NAH occurs in place of Beth-marca-both.

Beth-me'on. Jer. 48 : 23. A con-tracted form of Beth-baal-meon.

Chapel of the Nativity, Bethlehem.

Beth-nim'rah (*house of leopards*), one of the fenced cities on the east of Jordan, taken and built by the tribe of Gad, Num. 32 : 36, and described as lying in the valley beside Beth-haran. Josh. 13 : 27. In Num. 32 : 3 it is called sim-ply NIMRAH. The name still survives in the modern *Nahr Nimrim*, above Jer-icho on the Jordan.

Beth-pa'let (*house of flight*), a town among those in the extreme south of Judah, named in Josh. 15 : 27.

Beth-paz'zez (*house of the disper-sion*), a town of Issachar named with En-haddah, Josh. 19 : 21, and of which nothing is known.

Beth-pe'or (*house of Peor*), a place on the east of Jordan, opposite Jericho, and six miles above Libias or Beth-haran. Josh. 13 : 20; Deut. 3 : 29; 4 : 46.

Beth'-pha-ge (g hard) (*house of figs*), the name of a place on the Mount of Olives, on the road between Jericho and Jerusalem. It was apparently close to Bethany. Matt. 21 : 1; Mark 11 : 1; Luke 19 : 29.

Beth-phe'let. Neh. 11 : 26. [BETH-PALET.]

Beth'-rapha, a name which occurs in the genealogy of Judah as the son of Eshton. 1 Chron. 4 : 12.

Beth-re'hob (*house of Rehob*), a place mentioned as having near it the valley in which lay the town of Laish or

Dan. Judges 18 : 28. It was one of the little kingdoms of Aram or Syria. 2 Sam. 10 : 6. Robinson conjectures that this ancient place is represented by the modern *Hûnin*.

Bethsa'ida (*house of fish*) **of Galilee,** John 12 : 21, a city which was the native place of Andrew, Peter and Philip, John 1 : 44; 12 : 21, in the land of Gennesareth, Mark 6 : 45, comp. 53, and therefore on the west side of the lake. By comparing the narratives in Mark 6 : 31–53 and Luke 9 : 10–17 it appears certain that the Bethsaida at which the five thousand were fed must have been a second place of the same name on the

Site of Bethsaida. (*From an original Photograph.*)

east of the lake. (But in reality "there is but one Bethsaida, that known on our maps as Bethsaida Julias."—L. Abbot in *Biblical and Oriental Journal*. The fact is that Bethsaida was a village on both sides of the Jordan as it enters the Sea of Galilee on the north, so that the western part of the village was in Galilee and the eastern portion in Gaulonitis, part of the tetrarchy of Philip. This eastern portion was built up into a beautiful city by Herod Philip, and named by him *Bethsaida Julias*, after Julia the daughter of the Roman emperor Tiberius Cæsar. On the plain of Butaiha, a mile or two to the east, the five thousand were fed. The western part of the town remained a small village.—ED.)

Beth-she'an (*house of rest*), or in Samuel, BETHSHAN, a city which belonged to Manasseh, 1 Chron. 7 : 29, though within the limits of Issachar, Josh. 17 : 11, and therefore on the west

of Jordan. Comp. 1 Macc. 5 : 52. In later times it was called Scythopolis. 2 Macc. 12 : 29. The place is still known as *Beisân*. It lies in the Ghôr or Jordan valley, about twelve miles south of the Sea of Galilee and four miles west of the Jordan.

Beth-she'mesh (*house of the sun*). 1. One of the towns which marked the north boundary of Judah. Josh. 15 : 10. It is now *'Ainshems*, about two miles from the great Philistine plain, and sev' from Ekron.

2. A city on the border of Issacha. Josh. 19 : 22.

3. One of the "fenced cities" of Naphtali. Josh. 19 : 38 ; Judges 1 : 33.

4. An idolatrous temple or place in Egypt. Jer. 43 : 13. In the middle ages Heliopolis was still called by the Arabs *Ain Shems*.

Beth-shit'tah (*home of the acacia*), one of the spots to which the flight of the host of the Midianites extended after their discomfiture by Gideon. Judges 7 : 22.

Beth-tap'puah (*home of apples*), one of the towns of Judah, in the mountainous district, and near Hebron. Josh. 15 : 53 ; comp. 1 Chron. 2 : 43. Here it has actually been discovered by Robinson under the modern name of *Teffûh*, five miles west of Hebron, on a ridge of high table-land.

Be'thuel (*dweller in God*), the son of Nahor by Milcah ; nephew of Abraham, and father of Rebekah, Gen. 22 : 22, 23 ; 24 : 15, 24, 47 ; 28 : 2. In Gen. 25 : 20 and 28 : 5 he is called "Bethuel the Syrian."

Be'thul (*dweller in God*), a town of Simeon in the south, named with Eltolad and Hormah, Josh. 19 : 4 ; called also Chesil and Bethuel. Josh. 15 : 30 ; 1 Chron. 4 : 30.

Beth'-zur (*house of rock*), a town in the mountains of Judah, built by Jeroboam, Josh. 15 : 58 ; 2 Chron. 11 : 7, now *Beit-zûr*. It commands the road from Beersheba and Hebron, which has always been the main approach to Jerusalem from the south.

Bet'onim, a town of Gad, apparently on the northern boundary. Josh. 13 : 26.

Betrothing. [MARRIAGE.]

Beu'lah (*married*), the name which the land of Israel is to bear when "the land shall be married." Isa. 62 : 4.

Be′za-i (Be′za) (*conqueror*). "Children of Bezai," to the number of 323, returned from captivity with Zerubbabel. Ezra 2 : 17 ; Neh. 7 : 23 ; 10 : 18.

Bezal′e-el (*in the shadow of God*). 1. The son of Uri, the son of Hur, of the tribe of Judah, and one of the architects of the tabernacle. Ex. 31 : 1–6. His charge was chiefly in all works of metal, wood and stone. (B.C. 1490.)

2. One of the sons of Pahath-moab who had taken a foreign wife. Ezra 10 : 30. (B.C. 458.)

Be′zek (*lightning*). 1. The residence of Adonibezek, Judges 1 : 5, in the lot of Judah. ver. 3.

2. Where Saul numbered the forces of Israel and Judah before going to the relief of Jabesh-gilead. 1 Sam. 11 : 8. This was doubtless somewhere in the centre of the country, near the Jordan valley. No identification of either place has been made in modern times.

Be′zer (*gold ore*), son of Zophah, one of the heads of the houses of Asher. 1 Chron. 7 : 37.

Be′zer in the wilderness, a city of refuge in the downs on the east of the Jordan. Deut. 4 : 43 ; Josh. 20 : 8 ; 21 : 36 ; 1 Chron. 6 : 78.

Bi′ble. The Bible is the name given to the revelation of God to man contained in sixty-six books or pamphlets, bound together and forming one book and only one, for it has in reality one author and one purpose and plan, and is the development of one scheme of the redemption of man.

I. Its Names.—(1) *The Bible,* i. e. *The Book,* from the Greek "ta biblia," the books. The word is derived from a root designating the inner bark of the linden tree, on which the ancients wrote their books. It is *the* book, as being superior to all other books. But the application of the word BIBLE to the collected books of the Old and New Testaments is not to be traced farther back than the fifth century of our era. (2) *The Scriptures, i. e.* the writings, as recording what was spoken by God. (3) *The Oracles, i. e.* the things spoken, because the Bible is what God spoke to man, and hence also called (4) *The Word.* (5) *The Testaments* or *Covenants,* because it is the testimony of God to man, the truths to which God bears witness ; and is also the *covenant* or agreement of God with man for his salvation. (6) *The Law,* to express that it contains God's commands to men.

II. Composition.—The Bible consists of two great parts, called the Old and New Testaments, separated by an interval of nearly four hundred years. These Testaments are further divided into sixty-six books, thirty-nine in the Old Testament and twenty-seven in the New. These books are a library in themselves, being written in every known form of literature. Twenty-two of them are historical, five are poetical, eighteen are prophetical, twenty-one are epistolary. They contain logical arguments, poetry, songs and hymns, history, biography, stories, parables, fables, eloquence, law, letters and philosophy.

There are at least thirty-six different authors, who wrote in three continents, in many countries, in three languages, and from every possible human standpoint. Among these authors were kings, farmers, mechanics, scientific men, lawyers, generals, fishermen, ministers and priests, a tax-collector, a doctor, some rich, some poor, some city bred, some country born—thus touching all the experiences of men—extending over 1500 years.

III. Unity.—And yet the Bible is but *one* book, because God was its real author, and therefore, though he added new revelations as men could receive them, he never had to change what was once revealed. The Bible is a unit, because (1) It has but one purpose, the salvation of men. (2) The character of God is the same. (3) The moral law is the same. (4) It contains the development of one great scheme of salvation.

IV. Original Languages. — The Old Testament was written in Hebrew, a Shemitic language, except that parts of the books of Ezra (5 : 8 ; 6 : 12 ; 7 : 12–26) and of Daniel (2 : 4–7 : 28), and one verse in Jeremiah (Jer. 10 : 11), were written in the Chaldee language. The New Testament is written wholly in Greek.

V. Ancient Manuscripts of the Original.—There are no ancient Hebrew manuscripts older than the tenth century, but we know that these are in the main correct, because we have a translation of the Hebrew into Greek, called the Septuagint, made nearly three hundred years before Christ. Our Hebrew Bibles are a reprint from what is called the Masoretic text. The ancient Hebrew had only the consonants printed, and the vowels were vocalized in pronunciation, but were not written. Some Jewish scholars living at Tiberias, and at Sora by the Euphrates, from the sixth to the twelfth century, punctuated the Hebrew text, and wrote in the vowel points and other tone-marks to aid in the reading of the Hebrew; and these, together with notes of various kinds, they called *Masora* (tradition), hence the name Masoretic text.

Of the Greek of the New Testament there are a number of ancient manuscripts. They are divided into two kinds, the *Uncials*, written wholly in *capitals*, and the *Cursives*, written in a *running hand*. The chief of these are—(1) *the Alexandrian* (*codex Alexandrinus*, marked A), so named because it was found in Alexandria in Egypt, in 1628. It dates back to A.D. 350, and is now in the British Museum. (2) The *Vatican* (*codex Vaticanus*, B), named from the Vatican library at Rome, where it is kept. Its date is A.D. 300 to 325. (3) The *Sinaitic* (*codex Sinaiticus*), so called from the convent of St. Catherine on Mount Sinai, where it was discovered by Dr. Tischendorf in 1844. It is now at St. Petersburg, Russia. This is one of the earliest and best of all the manuscripts.

VI. TRANSLATIONS.—The Old Testament was translated into Greek by a company of learned Jews at Alexandria, who began their labor about the year B.C. 286. It is called the *Septuagint*, *i. e.* the Seventy, from the tradition that it was translated by seventy (more exactly seventy-two) translators. The *Vulgate*, or translation of the Bible into Latin by Jerome, A.D. 385-405, is the authorized version of the Roman Catholic Church. The first English translation of the whole Bible was by John de Wickliffe (1324-1384). Then followed that of William Tyndale (1525) and several others.

As the sum and fruit of all these appeared our present *Authorized Version*, or *King James Version*, in 1611. It was made by forty-seven learned men, in two years and nine months, with a second revision which took nine months longer. These forty-seven formed themselves into six companies, two of whom met at Westminster, two at Oxford and two at Cambridge. The present English edition is an improvement, in typographical and grammatical correctness, upon this revision, and in these respects is nearly perfect. [See VERSIONS.]

A REVISED VERSION of this authorized edition has been in process of preparation by eighty American and English scholars, of various denominations, the English committee having been appointed in 1870 and the American in 1871. This revision was necessary because of the changes in the English language during the last 270 years, and because much light has been thrown upon the original Scriptures, and upon all matters pertaining to biblical studies. The *Revised New Testament* was published simultaneously in this country and in England in May, 1881, and in less than six months more than four million copies had been issued.

VII. DIVISIONS INTO CHAPTERS AND VERSES.—The present division of the whole Bible into chapters was made by Cardinal Hugo de St. Cher about 1250. The present division into verses was introduced by Robert Stephens in his Greek Testament, published in 1551, in his edition of the Vulgate, in 1555. The first English Bible printed with these chapters and verses was the Geneva Bible, in 1560.

VIII. CIRCULATION OF THE BIBLE.— The first book ever printed was the Bible; and more Bibles have been printed than any other book. It has been translated into 226 different languages. The British and Foreign Bible Society (founded in 1804) has issued (1881) 91,014,448 Bibles and portions of the Bible; and the American Bible Society (founded in 1816) has issued (1881) 38,882,814 copies. In all, so far as known, there have been issued by all the Bible societies since 1804 one hundred and sixty-five million copies; but it is said that probably as many more copies have been issued by private publishers.—ED.

Bich'ri (*first-born*), 2 Sam. 20 : 1, an ancestor of Sheba.

Bid'kar (*son of stabbing*, i. e. *one who stabs*), Jehu's "captain," originally his fellow officer, 2 Kings 9 : 25, who completed the sentence on Jehoram, son of Ahab.

Bier. [BURIAL.]

Big'tha (*gift of God*), one of the seven chamberlains or eunuchs of the harem of King Ahasuerus. Esther 1 : 10. (B.C. 483.)

Big'than, or **Big'thana** (*gift of God*), a eunuch (chamberlain, Authorized Version) in the court of Ahasuerus, one of those "who kept the door," and conspired with Teresh against the king's life. Esther 2 : 21. (B.C. 479.)

Big'va-i (*happy*). 1. "Children of Bigvai," 2056 (Neh. 2067) in number, returned from the captivity with Zerubbabel, Ezra 2 : 14; Neh. 7 : 19, and 72 of them at a later date with Ezra. Ezra 8 : 14. (B.C. 536.)

2. Apparently one of the chiefs of Zerubbabel's expedition, Ezra 2 : 2; Neh. 7 : 7, whose family afterwards signed the covenant. Neh. 10 : 16. (B.C. 410.)

Bil'dad (*son of contention*), the second of Job's three friends. He is called "the Shuhite," which implies both his family and nation. Job 2 : 11. (B.C. about 2000.)

Bil'eam (*foreigners*), a town in the western half of the tribe of Manasseh, named only in 1 Chron. 6 : 70; same as Ibleam and Gath-rimmon. Josh. 17 : 11 and 21 : 24.

Bil'gah (*first-born*). 1. A priest in the time of David; the head of the fifteenth course for the temple service. 1 Chron. 24 : 14. (B.C. 1015.)

2. A priest or priestly family who returned from Babylon with Zerubbabel and Jeshua. Neh. 12 : 5, 18. (B.C. 536.)

Bil'ga-i. Neh. 10 : 8. [BILGAH, 2.]

Bil'hah (*timid, bashful*), handmaid of Rachel, Gen. 29 : 29, and concubine of Jacob, to whom she bore Dan and Naphtali. Gen. 30 : 3–8; 35 : 25; 46 : 25; 1 Chron. 7 : 13. (B.C. 1753.)

Bil'han (*modest*). 1. A Horite chief dwelling in Mount Seir. Gen. 36 : 27; 1 Chron. 1 : 42.

2. A Benjamite, son of Jediael. 1 Chron. 7 : 10.

Bil'shan (*eloquent*), one of Zerubbabel's companions on his expedition from Babylon. Ezra 2 : 2; Neh. 7 : 7. (B.C. 536.)

Bim'hal (*circumcised*), one of the sons of Japhlet in the line of Asher. 1 Chron. 7 : 33.

Bin'ea (*fountain*), one of the descendants of Saul. 1 Chron. 8 : 37; 9 : 43. (B.C. 850.)

Bin'nu-i (*familyship*). 1. A Levite, father of Noadiah. Ezra 8 : 33.

2. One who had taken a foreign wife. Ezra 10 : 30.

3. Another Israelite who had also taken a foreign wife. Ezra 10 : 38.

4. Altered from BANI in the corresponding list in Ezra. Neh. 7 : 15.

5. A Levite, son of Henadad, who assisted at the reparation of the wall of

Jerusalem, under Nehemiah. Neh. 3 : 24; 10 : 9.

Birds. [SPARROW.]

Bir'sha (*son of godlessness*), a king of Gomorrah. Gen. 14 : 2.

Birthdays. The custom of observing birthdays is very ancient, Gen. 40 : 20; Jer. 20 : 15; and in Job 1 : 4, etc., we read that Job's sons "feasted every one his day." In Persia birthdays were celebrated with peculiar honors and banquets, and in Egypt those of the king were kept with great pomp. It is very probable that in Matt. 14 : 6 the feast to commemorate Herod's accession is intended, for we know that such feasts were common, and were called "the day of the king." Hos. 7 : 5.

Birthright, the advantages accruing to the *eldest son*. These were not definitely fixed in patriarchal times. Great respect was paid to him in the household, and, as the family widened into a tribe, this grew into a sustained authority, undefined save by custom, in all matters of common interest. Thus the "princes" of the congregation had probably rights of primogeniture. Num. 7 : 2; 21 : 18; 25 : 14. Gradually the rights of the eldest son came to be more definite: (1) The functions of the priesthood in the family, with the paternal blessing. (2) A "double portion" of the paternal property was allotted by the Mosaic law. Deut. 21 : 15–17. (3) The eldest son succeeded to the official authority of the father. The first-born of the king was his successor by law. 2 Chron. 21 : 3. In all these Jesus was the *first-born* of the Father.

Bir'zavith, a name occurring in the genealogies of Asher. 1 Chron. 7 : 31.

Bishop. The word originally signified an "overseer" or spiritual superintendent. The titles bishop and elder, or presbyter, were essentially equivalent. Bishop is from the Greek, and denotes one who exercises the *function* of overseeing. Presbyter was derived from the *office* in the synagogue. Of the order in which the first elders or bishops were appointed, as of the occasion which led to the institution of the office, we have no record. The duties of the bishop-elders appear to have been as follows : 1. General superintendence over the spiritual well-being of the flock. 1 Pet. 5 : 2. 2. The work of teaching, both publicly and privately. 1 Thess. 5 : 12; Titus 1 : 9; 1 Tim. 5 : 17. 3. The work of visiting the sick. James 5 : 14. 4. Among other acts of charity, that of receiving strangers occupied a conspicuous place. 1 Tim. 3 : 2; Titus 1 : 8. Peter calls Christ "the shepherd and bishop of your souls." 1 Pet. 2 : 25.

Bishopric, the district over which the jurisdiction of a bishop extended. Acts 1 : 20; 1 Tim. 3 : 1.

Bithi'ah (*daughter of the Lord*), daughter of a Pharaoh, and wife of Mered. 1 Chron. 4 : 18. (B.C. about 1491.)

Bith'ron, more accurately **the Bithron** (*a craggy gorge or ravine*), a place, doubtless a district, in the Jordan valley on the east side of the river. 2 Sam. 2 : 29.

Bithyn'ia, a Roman province of Asia Minor. Mentioned only in Acts 16 : 7 and in 1 Pet. 1 : 1. The chief town of Bithynia was Nicæa, celebrated for the general Council of the Church held there in A.D. 325 against the Arian heresy.

Bitter herbs. The Israelites were commanded to eat the paschal lamb "with unleavened bread and with bitter herbs." Ex. 12 : 8. These "bitter herbs" consisted of such plants as chiccory, bitter cresses, hawkweeds, sow-thistles and wild lettuces, which grow abundantly in the peninsula of Sinai, in Palestine and in Egypt. The purpose of this observance was to recall to the minds of the Israelites their deliverance from the bitter bondage of the Egyptians.

Bittern. The word occurs in Isa. 14 : 23; 34 : 11; Zeph. 2 : 14, and we are inclined to believe that the Authorized Version is correct. The bittern (*Botaurus stellaris*) belongs to the *Ardeidæ*, the heron family of birds, and is famous for the peculiar nocturnal booming sound which it emits.

Bizjoth'jah (*contempt of Jehovah*), a town in the south of Judah. Josh. 15 : 28.

Biz'tha (*eunuch*), the second of the seven eunuchs of King Ahasuerus' harem. Esther 1 : 10. (B.C. 483.)

Blains, violent ulcerous inflammations, the sixth plague of Egypt, Ex. 9 : 9, 10, and hence called in Deut. 28 : 27, 35 "the botch of Egypt." It seems to have been the black leprosy, a fearful kind of elephantiasis.

Blasphemy, in its technical English sense, signifies the speaking evil of God, and in this sense it is found Ps. 74 : 18; Isa. 52 : 5; Rom. 2 : 24, etc. But according to its derivation it may mean any species of calumny and abuse : see 1 Kings 21 : 10; Acts 18 : 6; Jude 9, etc. Blasphemy was punished by stoning, which was inflicted on the son of Shelomith. Lev. 24 : 11. On this charge both our Lord and St. Stephen were condemned to death by the Jews.

The blasphemy against the Holy Ghost, Matt. 12 : 32; Mark 3 : 28, consisted in attributing to the power of Satan those unquestionable miracles which Jesus performed by "the finger of God" and the power of the Holy Spirit. It is plainly such a state of willful, determined opposition to God and the Holy Spirit that no efforts will avail to lead to repentance. Among the Jews it was a sin against God answering to treason in our times.

Blas'tus (*sprout*), the chamberlain of Herod Agrippa I. Acts 12 : 20.

Blindness is extremely common in the East from many causes. Blind beggars figure repeatedly in the New Testament (Matt. 12 : 22), and "opening the eyes of the blind" is mentioned in prophecy as a peculiar attribute of the Messiah. Isa. 29 : 18; 42 : 7, etc. The Jews were specially charged to treat the blind with compassion and care. Lev. 19 : 14; Deut. 27 : 18. Blindness willfully inflicted for political or other purposes is alluded to in Scripture. 1 Sam. 11 : 2; Jer. 39 : 7.

Blood. To blood is ascribed in Scripture the mysterious sacredness which belongs to life, and God reserves it to himself when allowing man the dominion over and the use of the lower animals for food. Thus reserved, it acquires a double power : (1) that of sacrificial atonement; and (2) that of becoming a curse when wantonly shed, unless duly expiated. Gen. 9 : 4; Lev. 7 : 26; 17 : 11–13.

Blood, Revenger of. He who avenged the blood of one who had been killed. The nearest relative of the deceased became the authorized avenger of blood. Num. 35 : 19. The law of retaliation was not to extend beyond the immediate offender. Deut. 24 : 16; 2 Kings 14 : 6; 2 Chron. 25 : 4; Jer. 31 : 29, 30; Ezek. 18 : 20.

Boaner'ges, a name signifying *sons of thunder*, given by our Lord to the two sons of Zebedee, James and John, probably on account of their fiery earnestness. Mark 3 : 17. See Luke 9 : 54; Mark 9 : 38; comp. Matt. 20 : 20, etc.

Boar. [SWINE.]

Bo'az (*fleetness*). 1. A wealthy Bethlehemite, kinsman to Elimelech the husband of Naomi. He married Ruth, and redeemed the estates of her deceased husband Mahlon. Ruth 4 : 1 ff. Boaz is mentioned in the genealogy of Christ, Matt. 1 : 5. (B.C. 1250, but there is great difficulty in assigning his date.)

2. The name of one of Solomon's brazen pillars erected in the temple porch. [JACHIN.] It stood on the left, and was eighteen cubits high. 1 Kings 7 : 15, 21 ; 2 Chron. 3 : 15 ; Jer. 52 : 21.

Boch'eru (*youth*), son of Azel, according to the present Hebrew text of 1 Chron. 8 : 38.

Bo'chim (*the weepers*), a place on the west of Jordan, above Gilgal ; so named from the weeping of Israel. Judg. 2 : 1, 5.

Bo'han (*thumb*), a Reubenite. Josh. 15 : 6 ; 18 : 17.

Bo'han, Stone of, a stone erected in honor of Bohan, on the boundary between Judah and Benjamin, in the valley of Achor, along the eastern side of the present *Wady Dahr,* running into the Dead Sea.

Boil. [MEDICINE.]

Bondage. [SLAVE.]

Book. [WRITING.]

Booths. [SUCCOTH ; TABERNACLES, FEAST OF.]

Booty consisted of captives of both sexes, cattle, and whatever a captured city might contain, especially metallic treasures. Within the limits of Canaan no captives were to be made, Deut. 20 : 14, 16 ; beyond these limits, in case of warlike resistance, all the women and children were to be made captives, and the men put to death. The law of booty is given in Num. 31 : 26-47. As regarded the army, David added a regulation that the baggage guard should share equally with the troops engaged. 1 Sam. 30 : 24, 25.

Bo'oz. Matt. 1 : 5 ; Luke 3 : 32. [BOAZ.]

Bos'cath. 2 Kings 22 : 1. [BOZKATH.]

Bo'sor, same as BEOR. 2 Pet. 2 : 15.

Bottle. The Arabs keep their water, milk and other liquids in leathern bottles. These are made of goatskins. When the animal is killed they cut off its feet and its head, and draw it in this manner out of the skin without opening its belly. The great leathern bottles are made of the skin of a he-goat, and the small ones, that serve instead of a bottle of water on

Skin Bottles.

Arab Water-carrier.

Eastern Tear-bottles.

the road, are made of a kid's skin. The effect of external heat upon a skin bottle is indicated in Ps. 119 : 83, "a bottle in the smoke," and of expansion produced by fermentation in Matt. 9 : 17, "new wine in old bottles." Vessels of metal, earthen or glassware for liquids were in use among the Greeks, Egyptians, Etruscans and Assyrians, and also no doubt among the Jews, especially in later times. Thus Jer. 19 : 1, "a potter's earthen bottle." (Bottles were made by the ancient Egyptians of alabaster, gold, ivory and stone. They were of most exquisite workmanship and elegant forms. Tear-bottles were small urns of glass or pottery, made to contain the tears of mourners at funerals, and placed in the sepulchres at Rome and in Palestine. In some ancient tombs they are found in great numbers. Ps. 56 : 8 refers to this custom.—ED.)

Bow. Gen. 37 : 10. The eastern mode of salutation, by kneeling upon one knee and bending the head forward till it touched the ground.

Box tree. Isa. 41 : 19; 60 : 13. A beau-

Ruins of Bozrah. (*From an original Photograph.*)

tiful evergreen growing in many parts of Europe and Asia. Its hard wood is much prized by engravers. The reference in Isa. 60 : 13 is supposed by some to mean a species of cedar.

Bo'zez (*the height*), one of the two sharp rocks between the passages by which Jonathan entered the Philistine garrison. It seems to have been that on the north. 1 Sam. 14 : 4, 5.

Boz'kath (*rocky height*), a city of Judah in the lowlands. Josh. 15 : 39; 2 Kings 22 : 1.

Boz'rah (*fortress*). 1. In Edom, the city of Jobab the son of Zerah, one of the early kings of that nation. Gen. 36 : 33; 1 Chron. 1 : 44. Mentioned by Isaiah, 34 : 6; 63 : 1, in connection with Edom, and by Jeremiah, 49 : 13, 22; Amos, 1 : 12, and Micah, 2 : 12. Its modern representative is *el-Busaireh*, which lies on the mountain district to the southeast of the Dead Sea.

2. In his catalogue of the cities of the land of Moab, Jeremiah, 48 : 24, mentions a Bozrah as in "the plain country" (ver. 21), *i. e.* the high level downs on the east of the Dead Sea.

Bracelet. [See ARMLET.] Bracelets of fine twisted Venetian gold are still common in Egypt. In Gen. 38 : 18, 25 the word rendered "bracelet" means probably a string by which a seal-ring was suspended. Men as well as women wore bracelets, as we see from Cant. 5 : 14. Layard says of the Assyrian kings, "The arms were encircled by armlets, and the wrists by bracelets."

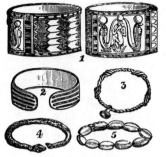

Bracelets.

1. Gold Egyptian Bracelets. 2. Silver Bracelet. 3. Bronze, with Bell attached, from Mummy of a Girl. 4. Iron, with Cornelian Setting. 5. Bracelet of Cowries.

Bramble. [THORNS.]

Brass. The word *nechôsheth* is improperly translated by "brass." In most places of the Old Testament the correct translation would be copper, although it may sometimes possibly mean bronze, a compound of copper and tin. Indeed a simple metal was obviously intended, as we see from Deut. 8 : 9; 33 : 25; Job 28 : 2. Copper was known at a very early period. Gen. 4 : 22.

Brazen serpent. [SERPENT.]

Egyptian Loaves and Seed Bread.

Bread. The preparation of bread as an article of food dates from a very early period. Gen. 18 : 6. The corn or grain employed was of various sorts. The best bread was made of wheat, but "barley" and spelt were also used. John 6 : 9, 13; Isa. 28 : 25. The process of making bread was as follows: the flour was first mixed with water or milk; it was then kneaded with the hands (in Egypt with the feet also) in a small wooden bowl or "kneading-trough" until it became dough. Ex. 12 : 34, 39; 2 Sam. 13 : 3; Jer. 7 : 18. When the kneading was completed, leaven was generally added [LEAVEN]; but when the time for preparation was short, it was omitted, and unleavened cakes, hastily baked, were eaten, as is still the prevalent custom among the Bedouins. Gen. 18 : 6; 19 : 3; Ex. 12 : 39; Judges 6: 19; 1 Sam. 28 : 24. The leavened mass was allowed to stand for some time, Matt. 13 : 33; Luke 13 : 21; the dough was then divided into round cakes, Ex. 29 : 23; Judges 7 : 13; 8 : 5; 1 Sam. 10 : 3; Prov. 6 : 26, not unlike flat stones in shape and appearance, Matt. 7 : 9, comp. 4 : 3, about a span in diameter and a finger's breadth in thickness. In the towns where professional bakers resided, there were no doubt fixed ovens, in shape and size resembling those in use among ourselves; but more usually each household possessed a portable oven, consisting of a stone or metal jar, about three feet high, which was heated inwardly with wood, 1 Kings 17 : 12; Isa. 44 : 15; Jer. 7 : 18, or dried grass and flower-stalks. Matt. 6 : 30.

Breastplate. [ARMS.]

Brethren of Jesus. [JAMES.]

Brick. Gen. 11 : 3. The bricks in use among the Jews were much larger than with us, being usually from 12 to 13 inches square and 3½ inches thick; they thus possess more of the character of tiles. Ezek. 4 : 1. The Israelites, in common with other captives, employed by the Egyptian monarchs in making bricks and in

Assyrian Brick from Nimroud, inscribed with Shalmaneser's Name and Title.

building. Ex. 1 : 14; 5 : 7. Egyptian bricks were not generally dried in kilns, but in the sun. That brick-kilns were

Jews and Captives making Bricks in Egypt.

known is evident from 2 Sam. 12 : 31; Jer. 43 : 9. When made of the Nile mud they required straw to prevent cracking. [See STRAW.]

Bride, Bridegroom. [MARRIAGE.]

Brigandine. Jer. 46 : 4; elsewhere "habergeon," or "coat of mail."

Brimstone. Brimstone, or sulphur, is found in considerable quantities on the shores of the Dead Sea. Gen. 19 : 24. It is a well-known simple mineral substance, crystalline, easily melted, very inflammable, and when burning emits a peculiar suffocating odor. It is found in great abundance near volcanoes. The soil around Sodom and Gomorrah abounded in sulphur and bitumen.

Brother. The Hebrew word is used in various senses in the Old Testament, as, 1. Any kinsman, and not a mere brother; e. g. nephew, Gen. 13 : 8; 14 : 16; husband, Cant. 4 : 9. 2. One of the same tribe. 2 Sam. 19 : 13. 3. Of the same people, Ex. 2 : 11, or even of a cognate people. Num. 20 : 14. 4. An ally. Amos 1 : 9. 5. Any friend. Job 5 : 15. 6. One of the same office. 1 Kings 9 : 13. 7. A fellow man. Lev. 19 : 17. 8. Metaphorically of any similarity, as in Job 30 : 19. The word ἀδελφός has a similar range of meanings in the New Testament.

Buk'ki (*wasting*). 1. Son of Abishua and father of Uzzi, fifth from Aaron in the line of the high priests in 1 Chron. 6 : 5 (6 : 5, 51, Authorized Version), and in the genealogy of Ezra. Ezra 7 : 4.

2. Son of Jogli, prince of the tribe of Dan, one of the ten men chosen to apportion the land of Canaan between the tribes. Num. 34 : 22.

Bukki'ah (*wasting from Jehovah*), a Kohathite Levite, of the sons of Heman, one of the musicians in the temple. 1 Chron. 25 : 4, 13.

Bul (*rain*). [MONTH.]

Bull, Bullock, terms used synonymously with ox, oxen, and properly a generic name for horned cattle when of full age and fit for the plough. It is variously rendered "bullock," Isa. 65 : 25, "cow," Ezek. 4 : 15, "oxen," Gen. 12 : 16. *Kine* is used in the Bible as the plural of cow. In Isaiah 51 : 20, the "wild bull" ("wild ox" in Deut. 14 : 5) was possibly one of the larger species of antelope, and took its name from its swiftness. Dr. Robinson mentions large herds of black and almost hairless buffaloes as still existing in Palestine, and these may be the animal indicated.

Bulrush (or papyrus), a reed growing in the shallow water on the banks of the Nile. It grows to the height of 12 or 15 feet, with a stalk two or three inches in diameter. The stalks are very pliable and can be very closely interwoven, as is evident from their having been used in the construction of arks. Ex. 2 : 3, 5. Paper was made from this plant, from which it derives its name.

Bulrush.

Bu'nah (*understanding*), a son of Jerahmeel, of the family of Pharez in Judah. 1 Chron. 2 : 25.

Bun'ni (*my understanding*). 1. One of the Levites in the time of Nehemiah. Neh. 9 : 4.

2. Another Levite, but of earlier date than the preceding. Neh. 11 : 15.

Burial, Sepulchres. [TOMBS.] On this subject we have to notice—1. The place of burial, its site and shape; 2. The mode of burial; 3. The prevalent notions regarding this duty.

1. A natural cave enlarged and adapted by excavation, or an artificial imitation of one, was the standard type of sepulchre. Sepulchres, when the owner's means permitted it, were commonly prepared beforehand, and stood often in gardens, by roadsides, or even adjoining houses. Kings and prophets alone were probably buried within towns. 1 Kings 2 : 10; 16 : 6, 28. Cities soon became populous and demanded cemeteries, Ezek. 39 : 15, which were placed without the walls. Sepulchres were marked sometimes by pillars or by pyramids. Such as were not otherwise noticeable were scrupulously "whited," Matt. 23 : 27, once a year, after the rains before the passover, to warn passers-by of defilement.

2. "The manner of the Jews" included the use of spices, where they could command the means. 2 Chron. 16 : 10. A portion of these was burnt in honor of the deceased, and to this use was probably destined part of the one hundred pounds weight of "myrrh and aloes" in our Lord's case. In no instance, save that of Saul and his sons, were the bodies burned; and even then the bones were interred, and re-exhumed for solemn entombment. It was the office of the next of kin to perform and preside over the whole funeral office; though public buriers were not unknown in New Testament times. Acts 5 : 6, 10. The body was borne by the nearest relatives. The grave-clothes were probably of the fashion worn in life, but swathed and fastened with bandages, and the head covered separately.

3. The precedent of Jacob's and Joseph's remains being returned to the land of Canaan was followed, in wish at least, by every pious Jew.

Burnt offering. The word is applied to the offering which was wholly consumed by fire on the altar, and the whole of which, except the refuse ashes, "ascended" in the smoke to God. The meaning of the whole burnt offering was that which is the original idea of all sacrifice, the offering by the sacrificer of himself, soul and body, to God—the submission of his will to the will of the Lord. The ceremonies of the burnt offering are given in detail in the book of Leviticus. [SACRIFICE.]

Bush. The Hebrew word *sĕneh* occurs only in those passages which refer to Jehovah's appearance to Moses "in the flame of fire in the bush." Ex. 3 : 2, 3, 4; Deut. 33 : 16. It is quite impossible to say what kind of thorn bush is intended; but it was probably the acacia, a small variety of the shittim tree found in the Sinai region.

Bushel. [WEIGHTS AND MEASURES.]

Butler. One of the officers of the king's household, Neh. 1 : 11, who had charge of the wine and poured it out for the king. The chief butler, as the title signifies, was in charge of the butlers. Gen. 40 : 1–13.

Butter. Curdled milk. Gen. 18 : 8; Deut. 32 : 14; Judges 5 : 25; Job 20 : 17. Milk is generally offered to travellers in Palestine in a curdled or sour state, *lebben*, thick, almost like butter. Hasselquist describes the method of making butter employed by the Arab women: "they made butter in a leather bag, hung on three poles erected for the purpose, in the form of a cone, and drawn to and fro by two women."

Buz (*contempt*). 1. The second son of Milcah and Nahor. Gen. 22 : 21. Elihu "the Buzite" was probably a descendant of Buz.

2. A name occurring in the genealogies of the tribe of Gad. 1 Chron. 5 : 14.

Bu'zi (*contempt*), father of Ezekiel the prophet. Ezek. 1 : 3.

C.

Cab. [MEASURES.]

Cab'bon, a town in the low country of Judah. Josh. 15 : 40.

Ca'bul. 1. One of the landmarks on the boundary of Asher, Josh. 19 : 27 ; now *Kabûl*, 9 or 10 miles east of *Accho*.

2. Name of the land given to Hiram by Solomon. 1 Kings 9 : 10–13.

Cæ'sar, always in thé New Testament the Roman emperor, the sovereign of Judea. John 19 : 12, 15 ; Acts 17 : 7.

Cæsare'a (Acts 8 : 40 ; 9 : 30 ; 10 : 1, 24 ; 11 : 11 ; 12 : 19 ; 18 : 22 ; 21 : 8, 16 ; 23 : 23, 33 ; 25 : 1, 4, 6, 13) was situated on the coast of Palestine, on the line of the great road from Tyre to Egypt, and about halfway between Joppa and Dora. The distance from Jerusalem was about 70 miles ; Josephus states it in round numbers as 600 stadia. In Strabo's time there was on this point of the coast merely a town called "Strato's Tower," with a landing-place, whereas in the time of Tacitus Cæsarea is spoken of as being the head of Judea. It was in this interval that the city was built by Herod the Great. It was the official residence of the Herodian kings, and of Festus, Felix and the other Roman procurators of Judea. Here also lived Philip the deacon and his four prophesying daughters. Cæsarea continued to be a city of some importance even in the time of the Crusades, and the name still lingers on the site (*Kaisariyeh*), which is a complete desolation, many of the building-stones having been carried to other towns.

Cæsare'a Philip'pi is mentioned only in the first two Gospels, Matt. 16 : 13 ; Mark 8 : 27, and in accounts of the same transactions. It was at the easternmost and most important of the two recognized sources of the Jordan, the other being at *Tel-el-Kadi*. The spring rises from and the city was built on a limestone terrace in a valley at the base of Mount Hermon, 20 miles north of the Sea of Galilee. It was enlarged by Herod Philip, and named after Cæsar, with his own name added to distinguish it from Cæsarea. Its present name is *Banias*, a village of some 50 houses, with many interesting ruins. Cæsarea Philippi has no Old Testament history, though it has been not unreason-

ably identified with *Baal-gad*. It was visited by Christ shortly before his transfiguration, Matt. 16 : 13–28, and was the northern limit of his journeys. Mark 8 : 27.

Cage. The term so rendered in Jer. 5 : 27 is more properly a *trap*, in which decoy birds were placed. In Rev. 18 : 2 the Greek term means a prison.

Ca'iaphas, or **Ca-i'aphas** (*depression*), in full JOSEPH CAIAPHAS, high priest of the Jews under Tiberius. Matt. 26 : 3, 57 ; John 11 : 49 ; 18 : 13, 14, 24, 28 ; Acts 4 : 6. The procurator Valerius Gratus appointed him to the dignity. He was son-in-law of Annas. [ANNAS.]

Cain (*possession*). Gen. 4. He was the eldest son of Adam and Eve ; he followed the business of agriculture. In a fit of jealousy, roused by the rejection of his own sacrifice and the acceptance of Abel's, he committed the crime of murder, for which he was expelled from Eden, and led the life of an exile. He settled in the land of Nod, and built a city, which he named after his son Enoch. His descendants are enumerated, together with the inventions for which they were remarkable. (B.C. 4000.)

Cain, one of the cities in the low country of Judah, named with Zanoah and Gibeah. Josh. 15 : 57.

Cain'an (*possessor*). 1. Son of Enos, aged 70 years when he begat Mahalaleel his son. He lived 840 years afterwards, and died aged 910. Gen. 5 : 9–14.

2. Son of Arphaxad, and father of Sala, according to Luke 3 : 36, 37, and usually called the second Cainan. He is nowhere named in the Hebrew MSS. It seems certain that his name was introduced into the genealogies of the Greek Old Testament in order to bring them into harmony with the genealogy of Christ in St. Luke's Gospel.

Ca'lah (*completion, old age*), one of the most ancient cities of Assyria. Gen. 10 : 11. The site of Calah is probably marked by the *Nimrûd* ruins. If this be regarded as ascertained, Calah must be considered to have been at one time (about B.C. 930–720) the capital of the empire.

Calamus. [REED.]

Ruins at Cæsarea.

View of the Valley of Cæsarea Philippi.

Cal'col (*sustenance*), a man of Judah, son or descendant of Zerah. 1 Chron. 2 : 6. Probably identical with CHALCOL.

Caldron, a vessel for boiling flesh, for either ceremonial or domestic use. 1 Sam. 2 : 14; 2 Chron. 35 : 13; Job 41 : 20; Micah 3 : 3.

Ca'leb (*capable*). 1. According to 1 Chron. 2 : 9, 18, 19, 42, 50, the son of Hezron the son of Pharez the son of Judah, and the father of Hur, and consequently grandfather of Caleb the spy. (B.C. about 1600.)

2. Son of Jephunneh, one of the twelve spies sent by Moses to Canaan. Num. 13 : 6. (B.C. 1490.) He and Oshea or Joshua the son of Nun were the only two of the whole number who encouraged the people to enter in boldly to the land and take possession of it. Forty-five years afterwards Caleb came to Joshua and claimed possession of the land of the Anakim, Kirjath-arba or Hebron, and the neighboring hill country. Josh. 14. This was immediately granted to him, and the following chapter relates how he took possession of Hebron, driving out the three sons of Anak ; and how he offered Achsah his daughter in marriage to whoever would take Kirjath-sepher, *i. e.* Debir; and how when Othniel, his younger brother, had performed the feat, he not only gave him his daughter to wife, but with her the upper and nether springs of water which she asked for. It is probable that Caleb was a foreigner by birth, —a proselyte, incorporated into the tribe of Judah.

Calf. The calf was held in high esteem by the Jews as food. 1 Sam. 28 : 24; Luke 15 : 23. The molten calf prepared by Aaron for the people to worship, Ex. 32 : 4, was probably a wooden figure laminated with gold, a process which is known to have existed in Egypt. [AARON.]

Cal'neh, or **Cal'no** (*fortress of Anu*), appears in Gen. 10 : 10 among the cities of Nimrod. Probably the site is the modern *Niffer*. In the eighth century B.C. Calneh was taken by one of the Assyrian kings, and never recovered its prosperity. Isa. 10 : 9; Amos 6 : 2.

Cal'vary. [See GOLGATHA.]

Camel. The species of camel which was in common use among the Jews and the heathen nations of Palestine was the Arabian or one-humped camel, *Camelus arabicus.* The dromedary is a swifter animal than the baggage-camel, and is used chiefly for riding purposes; it is merely a finer breed than the other. The Arabs call it the *heirie.* The speed of the dromedary has been greatly exaggerated, the Arabs asserting that it is swifter than the horse. Eight or nine miles an hour is the utmost it is able to perform; this pace, however, it is able to keep up

Camels.

for hours together. The Arabian camel carries about 500 pounds. "The hump on the camel's back is chiefly a store of fat, from which the animal draws as the wants of his system require; and the Arab is careful to see that the hump is in good condition before a long journey. Another interesting adaptation is the thick sole which protects the foot of the camel from the burning sand. The nostrils may be closed by valves against blasts of sand. Most interesting is the provision for drought made by providing the second stomach with great cells in which water is long retained. Sight and smell is exceedingly acute in the camel." —*Johnson's Encyc.* It is clear from Gen. 12 : 16 that camels were early known to the Egyptians. The importance of the camel is shown by Gen. 24 : 64; 37 : 25; Judges 7 : 12; 1 Sam. 27 : 9; 1 Kings 10 : 2; 2 Chron. 14 : 15; Job 1 : 3; Jer. 49 : 29, 32, and many other texts. John the Baptist wore a garment made of camel's hair, Matt. 3 : 4; Mark 1 : 6, the coarser hairs of the camel; and some have supposed that Elijah was clad in a dress of the same stuff.

Ca'mon (*full of grain*), the place in which Jair the judge was buried. Judges 10 : 5.

Camp. [ENCAMPMENT.]

Camphire. There can be no doubt that " camphire " is the *Lawsonia alba*

Camphire.

of botanists, the *henna* of Arabian naturalists. The henna plant grows in Egypt, Syria, Arabia and northern India. The flowers are white and grow in clusters, and are very fragrant. The whole shrub is from four to six feet high. S. of Sol. 4 : 13.

Ca'na (*place of reeds*) **of Galilee,** once **Cana in Galilee,** a village or town not far from Capernaum, memorable as the scene of Christ's first miracle, John 2 : 1, 11; 4 : 46, as well as of a subsequent one, John 4 : 46, 54, and also as the native place of the apostle Nathanael. John 21 : 2. The traditional site is at *Kefr-Kenna*, a small village about 4½ miles northwest of Nazareth. The rival site is a village situated farther north, about five miles north of *Seffurieh* (Sepphoris) and nine north of Nazareth.

Ca'naan (Ca'nan) (*low, flat*). 1. The fourth son of Ham, Gen. 10 : 6; 1 Chron. 1 : 8, the progenitor of the Phœnicians [ZIDON], and of the various nations who before the Israelite conquest peopled the seacoast of Palestine, and generally the whole of the country westward of the Jordan. Gen. 10 : 13; 1 Chron. 1 : 13. (B.C. 2347.)

2. The name "Canaan" is sometimes employed for the country itself.

Ca'naan, The land of (lit. *lowland*), a name denoting the country west of the Jordan and the Dead Sea, and between those waters and the Mediterranean; given by God to Abraham's posterity, the children of Israel. Ex. 6 : 4; Lev. 25 : 38. [PALESTINE.]

Cananæ'an. Matt. 10 : 4. Used in the Revised Version in place of "Canaanite." [See CANAANITE.]

Ca'naanite, The, the designation of the apostle Simon, otherwise known as "Simon Zelotes." It occurs in Matt. 10 : 4; Mark 3 : 18, and is derived from a Chaldee or Syriac word by which the Jewish sect or faction of the "Zealots" was designated—a turbulent and seditious sect, especially conspicuous at the siege of Jerusalem. They taught that all foreign rule over Jews was unscriptural, and opposed that rule in every way.

Ca'naanites, The, a word used in two senses : 1. A tribe which inhabited a particular locality of the land west of the Jordan before the conquest; and 2. The people who inhabited generally the whole of that country. 1. In Gen. 10 : 18–20 the seats of the Canaanite tribe are given as on the seashore and in the Jordan valley; comp. Josh. 11 : 3. 2. Applied as a general name to the non-Israelite inhabitants of the land, as we have already seen was the case with "Canaan." Instances of this are, Gen. 12 : 6; Num. 21 : 3. The Canaanites were descendants of Canaan. Their language was very similar to the Hebrew. The Canaanites were probably given to commerce; and thus the name became probably in later times an occasional synonym for a merchant.

Canda'ce, or **Can'da-ce** (*prince of servants*), a queen of Ethiopia (Meroë), mentioned Acts 8 : 27. (A.D. 38.) The name was not a proper name of an individual, but that of a dynasty of Ethiopian queens.

Candlestick, which Moses was commanded to make for the tabernacle, is described Ex. 25 : 31–37; 37 : 17–24. It was not strictly a "candlestick," as it held seven richly-adorned lamps. With

Kefr-Kenna—Cana in Galilee. (*From an original Photograph.*)

its various appurtenances it required a talent of "pure gold;" and it was not moulded, but "of beaten work," and has been estimated to have been worth in our money over $25,000. From the Arch of Titus, where are sculptured the spoils taken from Jerusalem, we learn that it consisted of a central stem, with six branches, three on each side. It was about five feet high. [See ARCH OF TITUS.] The candlestick was placed on the south side of the first apartment of the tabernacle, opposite the table of shew-bread, Ex. 25 : 37, and was lighted every evening and dressed every morning. Ex.

Golden Candlestick. (*From the Arch of Titus.*)

27 : 20, 21; 30 : 8; comp. 1 Sam. 3 : 2. Each lamp was supplied with cotton and about two wineglasses of the purest olive oil, which was sufficient to keep it burning during a long night. In Solomon's temple, instead of or in addition to this candlestick there were ten golden candle-sticks similarly embossed, five on the right and five on the left. 1 Kings 7 : 49; 2 Chron. 4 : 7. They were taken to Babylon. Jer. 52 : 19. In the temple of Zerubbabel there was again a single candlestick. 1 Macc. 1 : 21; 4 : 49.

Candlestick, in Matt. 5 : 15; Mark 4 : 21, is merely a lamp-stand, made in various forms, to hold up the simple Oriental hand-lamps.

Cane. [REED.]

Cankerworm. [LOCUST.]

Can'neh. Ezek. 27 : 23. [See CAL-NEH.]

Canon of Scripture, The, may be generally described as the " collection of books which form the original and authoritative written rule of the faith and practice of the Christian Church," *i. e.* the Old and New Testaments. The word

canon, in classical Greek, is properly a *straight rod*, "a rule" in the widest sense, and especially in the phrases "the rule of the Church," "the rule of faith," "the rule of truth." The first direct application of the term *canon* to the Scriptures seems to be in the verses of Amphilochius (cir. 380 A.D.), where the word indicates the rule by which the contents of the Bible must be determined, and thus secondarily an index of the constituent books. The uncanonical books were described simply as "those without" or "those uncanonized." The canonical books were also called "books of the testament," and Jerome styled the whole collection by the striking name of "the holy library," which happily expresses the unity and variety of the Bible. After the Maccabean persecution the history of the formation of the Canon is merged in the history of its contents. The Old Testament appears from that time as a whole. The complete Canon of the New Testament, as commonly received at present, was ratified at the third Council of Carthage (A.D. 397), and from that time was accepted throughout the Latin Church. Respecting the books of which the Canon is composed, see the article BIBLE. (The books of Scripture were not *made* canonical by act of any council, but the council gave its sanction to the results of long and careful investigations as to what books were really of divine authority and expressed the universally-accepted decisions of the church. The Old Testament Canon is ratified by the fact that the present Old Testament books were those accepted in the time of Christ and endorsed by him, and that of the 275 quotations of the Old Testament in the New, no book out of the Canon is quoted from except perhaps the words of Enoch in Jude.—ED.)

Canopy. Judith 10 : 21; 13 : 9; 16 : 19. The canopy of Holofernes is the only one mentioned.

Canticles (*Song of Songs*), entitled in the Authorized Version THE SONG OF SOLOMON. It was probably written by Solomon about B.C. 1012. It may be called a drama, as it contains the dramatic evolution of a simple love-story. *Meaning.*—The schools of interpretation may be divided into three: *the mystical* or *typical, the allegorical*, and *the literal*. 1. The *mystical* interpretation owes its origin to the desire to find a literal basis of fact for the allegorical. This basis is either the marriage of Solomon with Pharaoh's daughter or his marriage with an Israelitish woman, the Shulamite. 2. The *allegorical*. According to the Talmud the *beloved* is taken to be God; the *loved one*, or bride, is *the congregation of Israel*. In the Christian Church the Talmudical interpretation, imported by Origen, was all but universally received. 3. The *literal* interpretation. According to the most generally-received interpretation of the modern literalists, the Song is intended to display *the victory of humble and constant love over the temptations of wealth and royalty. Canonicity.*—The book has been rejected from the Canon by some critics; but in no case has its rejection been defended on *external* grounds. It is found in the LXX. and in the translations of Aquila, Symmachus and Theodotion. It is contained in the catalogue given in the Talmud, and in the catalogue of Melito; and in short we have the same evidence for its canonicity as that which is commonly adduced for the canonicity of any book of the Old Testament.

Caper′naum (*village of Nahum*) was

Site of Tell Hûm (Capernaum).

on the western shore of the Sea of Galilee. Matt. 4 : 13; comp. John 6 : 24. It was in the "land of Gennesaret," Matt. 14 : 34; comp. John 6 : 17, 21, 24. It was of sufficient size to be always called a "city," Matt. 9 : 1; Mark 1 : 33; had its own synagogue, in which our Lord frequently taught, Mark 1 : 21; Luke 4 : 33, 38; John 6 : 59; and there was also a customs station, where the dues were gathered both by stationary and by itinerant officers. Matt. 9 : 9; 17 : 24; Mark 2 : 14; Luke 5 : 27. The only interest attaching to Capernaum is as the residence of our Lord and his apostles, the scene of so many miracles and "gracious words." It was when he returned thither that he is said to have been "in the house." Mark 2 : 1. The spots which lay claim to its site are, 1. *Khan Minyeh*, a mound of ruins which takes its name from an old khan hard by. This mound is situated close upon the seashore at the northwestern extremity of the plain (now *El Ghuweir*). 2. Three miles north of *Khan Minyeh* is the other claimant, *Tell Hûm*, —ruins of walls and foundations covering a space of half a mile long by a quarter wide, on a point of the shore projecting into the lake and backed by a very gently-rising ground. It is impossible to locate it with certainty, but the probability is in favor of *Tell Hûm*.

Caphar, one of the numerous words employed in the Bible to denote a village or collection of dwellings smaller than a city (*Ir*). Mr. Stanley proposes to render it by "hamlet." In names of places it occurs in Chephar-ha-Ammonai, Chephirah, Caphar-salama. To us its chief interest arises from its forming a part of the name of Capernaum, *i. e.* Caphar-nahum.

Caph'tor, Caph'torim (*a crown*), thrice mentioned as the primitive seat of the Philistines, Deut. 2 : 23 ; Jer. 47 : 4 ; Amos 9 : 7, who are once called **Caphtorim.** Deut. 2 : 23. Supposed to be in Egypt, or near to it in Africa.

Cappado'cia, Cappado'cians (*province of good horses*), Acts 2 : 9 ; 1 Pet. 1 : 1, the largest province in ancient Asia Minor. Cappadocia is an elevated table-land intersected by mountain chains. It seems always to have been deficient in wood ; but it was a good grain country, and particularly famous for grazing. Its Roman metropolis was Cæsarea. The native Cappadocians seem to have originally belonged to the Syrian stock.

Captain. 1. As a purely military title, "captain" answers to *sar* in the Hebrew army and *tribune* in the Roman. The "captain of the guard" in Acts 28 : 16 was probably the *præfectus prætorio.* 2. *Kâtsin*, occasionally rendered captain, applies sometimes to a military, Josh. 10 : 24 ; Judges 11 : 6, 11 ; Isa. 22 : 3 ; Dan. 11 : 18, sometimes to a civil command, *e. g.* Isa. 1 : 10 ; 3 : 6. 3. The "captain of the temple," mentioned Luke 22 : 4 ; Acts 4 : 1 ; 5 : 24, superintended the guard of priests and Levites who kept watch by night in the temple.

Captive. A prisoner of war. Such were usually treated with great cruelty by the heathen nations. They were kept for slaves, and often sold ; but this was a modification of the ancient cruelty, and a substitute for putting them to death. Although the treatment of captives by the Jews seems sometimes to be cruel, it was very much milder than that of the heathen, and was mitigated, as far as possible in the circumstances, by their civil code.

Captivities of the Jews. The present article is confined to the forcible deportation of the Jews from their native land, and their forcible detention, under the Assyrian or Babylonian kings.

Captivities of Israel.—The kingdom of Israel was invaded by three or four successive kings of Assyria. Pul or Sardanapalus, according to Rawlinson, imposed a tribute (B.C. 771 or 762, Rawl.) upon Menahem. 2 Kings 15 : 19 and 1

Chron. 5 : 26. Tiglath-pileser carried away (B.C. 740) the trans-Jordanic tribes, 1 Chron. 5 : 26, and the inhabitants of Galilee, 2 Kings 15 : 29, comp. Isa. 9 : 1, to Assyria. Shalmaneser twice invaded, 2 Kings 17 : 3, 5, the kingdom which remained to Hoshea, took Samaria (B.C. 721) after a siege of three years, and carried Israel away into Assyria. This was the end of the kingdom of the ten tribes of Israel.

Captivities of Judah.—Sennacherib (B.C. 713) is stated to have carried into Assyria 200,000 captives from the Jewish cities which he took. 2 Kings 18 : 13. Nebuchadnezzar, in the first half of his reign (B.C. 606–562), repeatedly invaded Judea, besieged Jerusalem, carried away the inhabitants to Babylon, and destroyed the temple. The 70 years of captivity predicted by Jeremiah, Jer. 25 : 12, are dated by Prideaux from B.C. 606. The captivity of Ezekiel dates from B.C. 598, when that prophet, like Mordecai the uncle of Esther, Esther 2 : 6, accompanied Jehoiachin. The captives were treated not as slaves but as colonists. The Babylonian captivity was brought to a close by the decree, Ezra 1 : 2, of Cyrus (B.C. 536), and the return of a portion of the nation under Sheshbazzar or Zerubbabel (B.C. 535), Ezra (B.C. 458) and Nehemiah (B.C. 445). Those who were left in Assyria, Esther 8 : 9, 11, and kept up their national distinctions, were known as The Dispersion. John 7 : 35 ; 1 Pet. 1 : 1 ; James 1 : 1.

The lost tribes.—Many attempts have been made to discover the ten tribes existing as a distinct community ; but though history bears no witness of their present distinct existence, it enables us to track the footsteps of the departing race in four directions after the time of the Captivity. 1. Some returned and mixed with the Jews. Luke 2 : 36 ; Philip. 3 : 5, etc. 2. Some were left in Samaria, mingled with the Samaritans, Ezra 6 : 21 ; John 4 : 12, and became bitter enemies of the Jews. 3. Many remained in Assyria, and were recognized as an integral part of the Dispersion ; see Acts 2 : 9 ; 26 : 7. 4. Most, probably, apostatized in Assyria, adopted the usages and idolatry of the nations among whom they were planted, and became wholly swallowed up in them.

Carbuncle. This word represents two Hebrew words. The first may be a general term to denote any *bright, spark-*

ling gem, Isa. 54 : 12 ; the second, Ex. 28 : 17 ; 39 : 10 ; Ezek. 28 : 13, is supposed to be the smaragdus or emerald.

Car'cas (*severe*), the seventh of the seven "chamberlains," *i. e.* eunuchs, of King Ahasuerus. Esther 1 : 10. (B.C. 483.)

Car'chemish (*fortress of Chemosh*) occupied nearly the site of the later *Mabug* or Hierapolis. It seems to have commanded the ordinary passage of the Euphrates at *Bir* or *Birekjik.* Carchemish appears to have been taken by Pharaoh Necho shortly after the battle of Megiddo (cir. B.C. 608), and retaken by Nebuchadnezzar after a battle three years later, B.C. 605. Jer. 46 : 2.

Care'ah (*bald head*), father of Johanan, 2 Kings 25 : 23 ; elsewhere spelt KAREAH.

Ca'ria, the southern part of the region which in the New Testament is called ASIA, and the southwestern part of the peninsula of Asia Minor. Acts 20 : 15 ; 27 : 7.

Mount Carmel and Haifa. (*From a Photograph.*)

Car'mel (*fruitful place* or *park*). 1. A mountain which forms one of the most striking and characteristic features of the country of Palestine. It is a noble ridge, the only headland of lower and central Palestine, and forms its southern boundary, running out with a bold bluff promontory, nearly 600 feet high, almost into the very waves of the Mediterranean, then extending southeast for a little more than twelve miles, when it terminates suddenly in a bluff somewhat corresponding to its western end. In form Carmel

is a tolerably continuous ridge, its highest point, about four miles from the eastern end, being 1740 feet above the sea. That which has made the name of Carmel most familiar to the modern world is its intimate connection with the history of the two great prophets of Israel, Elijah and Elisha. 2 Kings 2 : 25 ; 4 : 25 ; 1 Kings 18 : 20–42. It is now commonly called *Mar Elyas; Kūrmel* being occasionally, but only seldom, heard.

2. A town in the mountainous country of Judah, Josh. 15 : 55, familiar to us as the residence of Nabal. 1 Sam. 25 : 2, 5, 7, 40.

Car'mi (*vine dresser*). 1. The fourth son of Reuben, the progenitor of the family of the Carmites. Gen. 46 : 9 ; Ex. 6 : 14 ; Num. 26 : 6 ; 1 Chron. 5 : 3.

2. A man of the tribe of Judah, father of Achan, the "troubler of Israel." Josh. 7 : 1, 18 ; 1 Chron. 2 : 7 ; 4 : 1.

Carpenter. [HANDICRAFT.]

Car'pus, a Christian at Troas. 2 Tim. 4 : 13.

Carriage. This word signifies what we now call "baggage." In the margin of 1 Sam. 17 : 20 and 26 :5-7, and there only, "carriage" is employed in the sense of a wagon or cart.

Carshe'na (*illustrious*), one of the seven princes of Persia and Media. Esther 1 : 14.

Cart, Gen. 45 : 19, 27 ; Num. 7 : 3, 7, 8, a vehicle drawn by cattle, 2 Sam. 6 : 6 ; to be distinguished from the chariot drawn by horses. Carts and wagons were either open or covered, Num. 7 : 3, and were used for conveyance of persons, Gen. 45 : 19, burdens, 1 Sam. 6 : 7, 8, or produce. Amos 2 : 13. The only cart used in western Asia has two wheels of solid wood.

Carving. The arts of carving and engraving were much in request in the construction of both the tabernacle and the temple, Ex. 31 : 5 ; 35 :33 ; 1 Kings 6 : 18, 35 ; Ps. 74 : 6, as well as in the ornamentation of the priestly dresses. Ex. 28 : 9-36 ; 2 Chron. 2 : 7, 14 ; Zech. 3 : 9.

Casiph'ia (*silvery, white*), a place of uncertain site on the road between Babylon and Jerusalem. Ezra 8 : 17.

Cas'luhim (*fortified*), a Mizraite people or tribe. Gen. 10 : 14 ; 1 Chron. 1 : 12.

Cassia. Ex. 30 : 24 ; Ezek. 27 : 19.

The cassia bark of commerce is yielded by various kinds of *Cinnamomum*, which grow in different parts of India. The Hebrew word in Ps. 45 : 8 is generally supposed to be another term for cassia.

Castle. [FENCED CITIES.]

Cas'tor and Pol'lux, Acts 28 : 11, the twin sons of Jupiter and Leda, were regarded as the tutelary divinities of sailors; hence their image was often used as a figure-head for ships. They appeared in heaven as the constellation *Gemini*. In art they were sometimes represented simply as stars hovering over a ship.

Caterpillar. The representative in the Authorized Version of the Hebrew word *châsil* and *yelek*. 1. *Châsil* occurs in 1 Kings 8 : 37; 2 Chron. 6 : 28; Ps. 78 : 46; Isa. 33 : 4; Joel 1 : 4, and seems to be applied to a locust, perhaps in its larva state. 2. *Yelek*. [LOCUST.]

Cattle. [BULL.]

Cau'da. Acts 27 : 16. The form given in the Revised Version to *Clauda*, an island south of Crete. It bears a closer relation to the modern name *Gaudonesi* of the Greek, the *Gauda* of P. Mela. (*Clauda.*—ED.)

Caul, a sort of ornamental head-dress, Isa. 3 : 18, with a net for its base. The name is derived from the caul, the membranous bag which encloses the heart—the pericardium.—ED.

Cave. The most remarkable caves noticed in Scripture are, that in which Lot dwelt after the destruction of Sodom, Gen. 19 : 30; the cave of Machpelah, Gen. 23 : 17; cave of Makkedah, Josh. 10 : 10; cave of Adullam, 1 Sam. 22 : 1; cave of Engedi, 1 Sam. 24 : 3; Obadiah's cave, 1 Kings 18 : 4; Elijah's cave in Horeb, 1 Kings 19 : 9; the rock sepulchres of Lazarus and of our Lord. Matt. 27 : 60; John 11 : 38. Caves were used for temporary dwelling-places and for tombs.

Cedar. The Hebrew word *erez*, invariably rendered "cedar" by the Authorized Version, stands for that tree in most of the passages where the word occurs. While the word is sometimes used in a wider sense, Lev. 14 : 6, for evergreen cone-bearing trees, generally the cedar of Lebanon (*Cedrus libani*) is intended. 1 Kings 7 : 2; 10 : 27; Ps. 92 : 12; S. Sol. 5 : 15; Isa. 2 : 13; Ezek. 31 : 3–6. The wood is of a reddish color, of bitter taste and aromatic odor, offensive to insects, and very durable. The cedar is a type of the Christian, being ever-

green, beautiful, aromatic, wide spreading, slow growing, long lived, and having many uses. As far as is at present known, the cedar of Lebanon is confined in Syria to one valley of the Lebanon range, viz., that of the Kedisha river, which flows

The Cedar.

from near the highest point of the range westward to the Mediterranean, and enters the sea at the port of Tripoli. The grove is at the very upper part of the valley, about 15 miles from the sea, 6500 feet above that level, and its position is moreover above that of all other arboreous vegetation. ("Of the celebrated cedars on Mount Lebanon, eleven groves still remain. The famous B'Sherreh grove is three-quarters of a mile in circumference, and contains about 400 trees, young and old. Perhaps a dozen of these are very old; the largest, 63 feet in girth and 70 feet high, is thought by some to have attained the age of 2000 years."—*Johnson's Encyc.*)

Ce'dron. John 18 : 1. [See KIDRON.]

Ceiling. The descriptions of Scripture, 1 Kings 6 : 9, 15; 7 : 3; 2 Chron. 3 : 5, 9; Jer. 22 : 14; Hag. 1 : 4, and of Josephus, show that the ceilings of the temple and the palaces of the Jewish kings were formed of cedar planks applied to the beams or joists crossing from wall to wall. "Oriental houses seem to have been the reverse of ours, the ceiling being of wood, richly ornamented, and the floor of plaster or tiles."

Celosyria. [CŒLESYRIA.]

Cen'chrea, or **Cenchre'a** (accurately **Cenchre'æ**) (*millet*), the eastern harbor of Corinth (*i. e.* its harbor on the Saronic Gulf) and the emporium of its trade with the Asiatic shores of the Mediterranean, as Lechæum on the Corinthian Gulf connected it with Italy and the west. St. Paul sailed from Cenchreæ, Acts 18 : 18, on his return to Syria from his second missionary journey. An organized church seems to have been formed here. Rom. 16 : 1.

Censer.

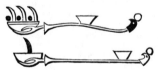

Egyptian Censers.

Censer, a small portable vessel of metal fitted to receive burning coals from the altar, and on which the incense for burning was sprinkled. 2 Chron. 26 : 19;

Luke 1 : 9. The only distinct precepts regarding the use of the censer are found in Lev. 16 : 12 and in Num. 4 : 14. Solomon prepared "censers of pure gold" as part of the temple furniture. 1 Kings 7 : 50; 2 Chron. 4 : 22. The word rendered "censer" in Heb. 9 : 4 probably means the "altar of incense."

Census. [TAXING.]

Centurion. [ARMY.]

Ce'phas. [PETER.]

Chaff, the husk of corn or wheat which was separated from the grain by being thrown into the air, the wind blowing away the chaff, while the grain was saved. The carrying away of chaff by the wind is an ordinary scriptural image of the destruction of the wicked and of their powerlessness to resist God's judgments. Ps. 1 : 4; Isa. 17 : 13; Hos. 13 : 3; Zeph. 2 : 2.

Chain. Chains were used, 1. As badges of office; 2. For ornament; 3. For confining prisoners. 1. The gold chain placed about Joseph's neck, Gen. 41 : 42, and that promised to Daniel, Dan. 5 : 7, are instances of the first use. In Ezek. 16 : 11 the chain is mentioned as the symbol of sovereignty. 2. Chains for ornamental purposes were worn by men as well as women. Prov. 1 : 9; Judith 10 : 4. The Midianites adorned the necks of their camels with chains. Judges 8 : 21, 26. Step-chains were attached to the ankle-rings. Isa. 3 : 16, 18. 3. The means adopted for confining prisoners among the Jews were fetters similar to our handcuffs. Judges 16 : 21; 2 Sam. 3 : 34; 2 Kings 25 : 7; Jer. 39 : 7. Among the Romans the prisoner was handcuffed to his guard, and occasionally to two guards. Acts 12 : 6, 7; 21 : 33.

Chalcedony, only in Rev. 21 : 19. The name is applied in modern mineralogy to one of the varieties of agate. It is generally translucent and exhibits a great variety of colors. So named because it was found near the ancient Chalcedon, near Constantinople.

Chal'col. 1 Kings 4 : 31. [CALCOL.]

Chalde'a, more correctly **Chaldæ'a,** the ancient name of a country of Asia bordering on the Persian Gulf. Chaldea proper was the southern part of Babylonia, and is used in Scripture to signify that vast alluvial plain which has been formed by the deposits of the Euphrates and the Tigris. This extraordinary flat, unbroken except by the works of man, extends a distance of 400 miles along the course of the rivers, and is on an average about 100 miles in width. In addition to natural advantages these plains were nourished by a complicated system of canals, and vegetation flourished bountifully. It is said to be the only country in the world where wheat grows wild.

Herodotus declared (i. 193) that grain commonly returned two hundred fold to the sower, and occasionally three hundred fold.

Cities.—Babylonia has long been celebrated for the number and antiquity of its cities. The most important of

Ruins of Mugheir (probable site of Ur of the Chaldees).

those which have been identified are Borsippa (*Birs-Nimrûd*), Sippara or Sepharvaim (*Mosaib*), Cutha (*Ibrahim*), Calneh (*Niffer*), Erech (*Warka*), Ur (*Mugheir*), Chilmad (*Kalwadha*), Larancha (*Senkereh*), Is (*Hit*), Duraba (*Akkerkuf*); but besides these there were a multitude of others, the sites of which have not been determined.

Present condition.—This land, once so rich in corn and wine, is to-day but a mass of mounds, "an arid waste; the dense population of former times is vanished, and no man dwells there." The Hebrew prophets applied the term "land of the Chaldeans" to all Babylonia and "Chaldeans" to all the subjects of the Babylonian empire.

Chalde'ans, or **Chaldees'.** It appears that the Chaldeans (*Kaldai* or *Kaldi*) were in the earliest times merely one out of the many Cushite tribes inhabiting the great alluvial plain known afterwards as Chaldea or Babylonia. Their special seat was probably that southern portion of the country which is found to have so late retained the name

of Chaldea. In process of time, as the *Kaldi* grew in power, their name gradually prevailed over those of the other tribes inhabiting the country; and by the era of the Jewish captivity it had begun to be used generally for all the inhabitants of Babylonia. It appears that while, both in Assyria and in later Babylonia, the Shemitic type of speech prevailed for civil purposes, the ancient Cushite dialect was retained, as a learned language for scientific and religious literature. This is no doubt the "learning" and the "tongue" to which reference is made in the book of Daniel, 1 : 4. The Chaldeans were really the learned class; they were priests, magicians or astronomers, and in the last of the three capacities they probably effected discoveries of great importance. In later times they seem to have degenerated into mere fortune-tellers.

Chaldees', or **Chal'dees.** [CHALDEANS.]

Chalk stones. [LIME.]

Chamber. Gen. 43 : 30 ; 2 Sam. 18 : 33 ; Ps. 19 : 5 ; Dan. 6 : 10. The word chamber in these passages has much the same significance as with us, meaning the private rooms of the house—the guest chamber, as with us, meaning a room set apart for the accommodation of the visiting friend. Mark 14 : 14, 15; Luke 22 : 12. The upper chamber was used more particularly for the lodgment of strangers. Acts 9 : 37.

Chamberlain, an officer attached to the court of a king, who formerly had charge of the private apartments or chambers of the palace. He kept the accounts of the public revenues. The office held by Blastus, "the king's chamberlain," was entirely different from this. Acts 12 : 20. It was a post of honor which involved great intimacy and influence with the king. For chamberlain as used in the Old Testament, see EUNUCH.

Chameleon, a species of lizard. The reference in Lev. 11 : 30 is to some kind of an unclean animal, supposed to be the lizard, known by the name of the "monitor of the Nile," a large, strong

The Charger.

Chameleon.

reptile common in Egypt and other parts of Africa.

Chamois (pronounced often shăm'ĕ), the translation of the Hebrew *zemer* in Deut. 14 : 5. But the translation is incorrect; for there is no evidence that the chamois has ever been seen in Palestine or the Lebanon. It is probable that some mountain sheep is intended.

Cha'naan. [CANAAN.]

Chapiter, the capital of a pillar; *i. e.* the upper part, as the term is used in modern architecture.

Chapman (*i.e.* cheap man), merchant.

Char'ashim, The valley of (*ravine of craftsmen*), a place near Lydda, a few miles east of Joppa. 1 Chron. 4 : 14.

Char'chemish. 2 Chron. 35 : 20. [CARCHEMISH.]

Charger, a shallow vessel for receiving water or blood, also for presenting offerings of fine flour with oil. Num. 7 : 79. The daughter of Herodias brought the head of St. John the Baptist in a charger, Matt. 14 : 8; probably a trencher or platter. [BASIN.]

Chariot, a vehicle used either for warlike or peaceful purposes, but most commonly the former. The Jewish chariots were patterned after the Egyptian, and consisted of a single pair of wheels on an axle, upon which was a car with high front and sides, but open at the back. The earliest mention of chariots in Scripture is in Egypt, where Joseph, as a mark of distinction, was placed in Pharaoh's second chariot. Gen. 41 : 43. Later on we find mention of Egyptian char-

Egyptian Chariot.

iots for a warlike purpose. Ex. 14 : 7. In this point of view chariots among some nations of antiquity, as elephants among others, may be regarded as filling the place of heavy artillery in modern times, so that the military power of a nation might be estimated by the number of its chariots. Thus Pharaoh in pursuing Israel took with him 600 chariots. The Philistines in Saul's time had 30,000. 1 Sam. 13 : 5. David took from Hadadezer, king of Zobah, 1000 chariots, 2 Sam. 8 : 4, and from the Syrians a little later 700, 2 Sam. 10 : 18, who, in order to recover their ground, collected 32,000 chariots. 1 Chron. 19 : 7. Up to this time the Israelites possessed few or no chariots. They were first introduced by David, 2 Sam. 8 : 4, who raised and maintained a force of 1400 chariots, 1 Kings 10 : 25, by taxation on certain cities agreeably to eastern custom in such matters. 1 Kings 9 : 19; 10 : 25. From this time chariots were regarded as among the most important arms of war. 1 Kings 22 : 34; 2 Kings 9 : 16, 21; 13 : 7, 14; 18 : 24; 23 : 30; Isa. 31 : 1. Most commonly two persons, and sometimes three, rode in the chariot, of whom the third was employed to carry the state umbrella. 1 Kings 22 : 34; 2 Kings 9 : 20, 24; Acts 8 : 38. The prophets allude frequently to chariots as typical of power. Ps. 20 : 7; 104 : 3; Jer. 51 : 21; Zech. 6 : 1.

Char'ran. Acts 7 : 2, 4. [HARAN.]

Chase. [HUNTING.]

Che'bar (*length*), a river in the "land of the Chaldeans." Ezek. 1 : 3; 3 : 15, 23, etc. It is commonly regarded as identical with the Habor, 2 Kings 17 : 6, and perhaps the Royal Canal of Nebuchadnezzar,—the greatest of all the cuttings in Mesopotamia.

Che'bel (*cord*), one of the singular topographical terms in which the ancient Hebrew language abounded. We find it always attached to the region of Argob. Deut. 3 : 4, 13, 14; 1 Kings 4 : 13.

Chedorlao'mer, or **Chedorla'omer** (*servant of Laomer*), a king of Elam, in the time of Abraham, who with three other chiefs made war upon the kings of Sodom, Gomorrah, Admah, Zeboim and Zoar, and reduced them to servitude. Gen. 14 : 17.

Cheese is mentioned only three times in the Bible, and on each occasion under a different name in the Hebrew. 1 Sam. 17 : 18; 2 Sam. 17 : 29; Job 10 : 10. It is difficult to decide how far these terms correspond with our notion of cheese, for they simply express various degrees of coagulation. Cheese is not at the pres-

ent day common among the Bedouin Arabs, butter being decidedly preferred; but there is a substance closely corresponding to those mentioned in 1 Sam. 17, 2 Sam. 17, consisting of coagulated buttermilk, which is dried until it becomes quite hard, and is then ground; the Arabs eat it mixed with butter.

Che'lal (*perfection*), Ezra 10 : 30, one who had a strange wife.

Chel'luh (*completed*), Ezra 10 : 35, another like the above.

Che'lub. 1. A man among the descendants of Judah.

2. Ezri the son of Chelub, one of David's officers. 1 Chron. 27 : 26.

Chelu'bai (*capable*), the son of Hezron. Same as Caleb. 1 Chron. 2 : 9, 18, 42.

Chem'arim, The (*those who go about in black,* i. e. *ascetics*). In the Hebrew applied to the priests of the worship of false gods. 2 Kings 23 : 5; Hos. 10 : 5, in margin; Zeph. 1 : 4.

Che'mosh (*subduer*), the national deity of the Moabites. Num. 21 : 29; Jer. 48 : 7, 13, 46. In Judges 11 : 24 he also appears as the god of the Ammonites. Solomon introduced, and Josiah abolished, the worship of Chemosh at Jerusalem. 1 Kings 11 : 7; 2 Kings 23 : 13. Also identified with Baal-peor, Baalzebub, Mars and Saturn.

Chena'anah (*merchant*). 1. Son of Bilhan, son of Jediael, son of Benjamin, head of a Benjamite house, 1 Chron. 7 : 10, probably of the family of the Belaites. [BELA.]

2. Father or ancestor of Zedekiah the false prophet. 1 Kings 22 : 11, 24; 2 Chron. 18 : 10, 23.

Chen'ani (a contraction of Chenaniah), one of the Levites who assisted at the solemn purification of the people under Ezra. Neh. 9 : 4.

Chenani'ah (*established by the Lord*), chief of the Levites when David carried the ark to Jerusalem. 1 Chron. 15 : 22; 26 : 29.

Che'phar - Haam'monai (*hamlet of the Ammonites*), a place mentioned among the towns of Benjamin. Josh. 18 : 24.

Chephi'rah (*the hamlet*), one of the four cities of the Gibeonites, Josh. 9 : 17, named afterwards among the towns of Benjamin. Ezra 2 : 25; Neh. 7 : 29.

Che'ran (*lyre*), one of the sons of Dishon the Horite "duke." Gen. 36 : 26; 1 Chron. 1 : 41.

Cher′ethim (*axe-men*), Ezek. 25 : 16, same as CHERETHITES.

Cher′ethites (*executioners*) and **Pel′ethites** (*couriers*), the life-guards of King David. 2 Sam. 8 : 18; 15 : 18; 20 : 7, 23; 1 Kings 1 : 38, 44; 1 Chron. 18 : 17. It is plain that these royal guards were employed as executioners, 2 Kings 11 : 4, and as couriers, 1 Kings 14 : 27. But it has been conjectured that they may have been foreign mercenaries, and therefore probably Philistines, of which name Pelethites may be only another form.

Che′rith, The brook (*cutting, ravine*), the torrent-bed or *wady* in which Elijah hid himself during the early part of the three-years drought. 1 Kings 17 : 3, 5. The position of the Cherith has been much disputed. The argument from probability is in favor of the Cherith being on the east of Jordan, and the name may possibly be discovered there.

Cher′ub, apparently a place in Babylonia from which some persons of doubtful extraction returned to Judea with Zerubbabel. Ezra 2 : 59; Neh. 7 : 61.

Cherub, Cherubim. The symbolical figure so called was a composite creature-form which finds a parallel in the religious insignia of Assyria, Egypt and Persia, *e. g.* the sphinx, the winged bulls and lions of Nineveh, etc. A cherub guarded paradise. Gen. 3 : 24. Figures of cherubim were placed on the mercy-seat of the ark. Ex. 25 : 18. A pair of colossal size overshadowed it in Solomon's temple with the canopy of their contiguously extended wings. 1 Kings 6 : 27. Those on the ark were to be placed with wings stretched forth, one at each end of the mercy-seat, and to be made "of the mercy-seat." Their wings were to be stretched upwards, and their faces "towards each other and towards the mercy-seat." It is remarkable that with such precise directions as to their position, attitude and material, nothing, save that they were winged, is said concerning their shape. On the whole it seems likely that the word "cherub" meant not only the composite creature-form, of which the man, lion, ox and eagle were the elements, but, further, some peculiar and mystical form. (Some suppose that the cherubim represented *God's providence* among men, the four faces expressing the characters of that providence : its wisdom and intelligence (man), its strength (ox), its kingly authority (lion), its swiftness, far-sighted (eagle). Others, combining all the other references with the description of the living creatures in Revelation, make the cherubim to represent *God's redeemed people.* The qualities of the four faces are those which belong to God's people. Their facing four ways, towards all quarters of the globe, represents their duty of extending the truth. The wings show swiftness of obedience; and only the redeemed can sing the song put in their mouths in Rev. 5 : 8–14.—ED.)

Ches′alon (*hopes*), a place named as one of the landmarks on the west part of the north boundary of Judah, Josh. 15 : 10, probably *Kesla*, about six miles to the northeast of *Ainshems*, on the western mountains of Judah.

Che′sed (*increase*), fourth son of Nahor. Gen. 22 : 22.

Che′sil (*idolatrous*), a town in the extreme south of Palestine, Josh. 15 : 30, 15 miles southwest of Beersheba. In Josh. 19 : 4 the name is BETHUL.

Chest. By this word are translated in the Authorized Version two distinct Hebrew terms : 1. *Arôn ;* this is invariably used for the ark of the covenant, and, with two exceptions, for that only. The two exceptions alluded to are (*a*) the "coffin" in which the bones of Joseph were carried from Egypt, Gen. 50 : 26, and (*b*) the "chest" in which Jehoiada the priest collected the alms for the repairs of the temple. 2 Kings 12 : 9, 10 ; 2 Chron. 24 : 8–11. 2. *Gĕnăzim,* "chests." Ezek. 27 : 24 only.

Chestnut tree (Heb. *'armôn.* Gen. 30 : 37; Ezek. 31 : 8). Probably the "palm tree" (*Platanus orientalis*) is intended. This tree thrives best in low and rather moist situations in the north of Palestine, and resembles our sycamore or buttonwood (*Platanus occidentalis*).

Chesul′loth (*the loins*), one of the towns of Issachar. Josh. 19 : 18. From its position in the lists it appears to be between Jezreel and Shunem (*Salam*).

Che′zib (*lying*), a name which occurs but once, Gen. 38 : 5; probably the same as ACHZIB.

Chi′don (*a javelin*), the name which in 1 Chron. 13 : 9 is given to the threshing-floor at which the accident to the ark took place. In the parallel account in 2 Sam. 6 the name is given as NACHON.

Children. The blessing of offspring, but especially of the male sex, is highly valued among all eastern nations, while the absence is regarded as one of the severest punishments. Gen. 16 : 2; Deut. 7 : 14; 1 Sam. 1 : 6; 2 Sam. 6 : 23; 2 Kings 4 : 14; Isa. 47 : 9; Jer. 20 : 15; Ps. 127 : 3, 5. As soon as the child was born it was washed in a bath, rubbed with salt and wrapped in swaddling clothes. Ezek. 16 : 4; Job 38 : 9; Luke 2 : 7. On the 8th day the rite of circumcision, in the case of a boy, was performed and a name given. At the end of a certain time (forty days if a son and twice as long if a daughter) the mother offered sacrifice for her cleansing. Lev. 12 : 1-8; Luke 2 : 22. The period of nursing appears to have been sometimes prolonged to three years. Isa. 49 : 15; 2 Macc. 7 : 27. The time of weaning was an occasion of rejoicing. Gen. 21 : 8. Both boys and girls in their early years were under the care of the women. Prov. 31 : 1. Afterwards the boys were taken by the father under his charge. Daughters usually remained in the women's apartments till marriage. Lev. 21 : 9; Num. 12 : 14; 1 Sam. 9 : 11. The authority of parents, especially of the father, over children was very great, as was also the reverence enjoined by the law to be paid to parents. The inheritance was divided equally between all the sons except the eldest, who received a double portion. Gen. 25 : 31; 49 : 3; Deut. 21 : 17; Judges 11 : 2, 7; 1 Chron. 5 : 1, 2. Daughters had by right no portion in the inheritance; but if a man had no son, his inheritance passed to his daughters, who were forbidden to marry out of the father's tribe. Num. 27 : 1, 8; 36 : 2, 8.

Chil'eab (*like his father*), a son of David by Abigail. [ABIGAIL.]

Chil'ion (*pining, sickly*), the son of Naomi and husband of Ruth. Ruth 1 : 2-5; 4 : 9. (B.C. 1250.)

Chil'mad (*enclosure*), a place or country mentioned in conjunction with Sheba and Asshur. Ezek. 27 : 23.

Chim'ham (*longing*), a follower, and probably a son, of Barzillai the Gileadite, who returned from beyond Jordan with David. 2 Sam. 19 : 37, 38, 40. (B.C. 1023.) David appears to have bestowed on him a possession at Bethlehem, on which, in later times, an inn or *khan* was standing. Jer. 41 : 17.

Chim'han. [CHIMHAM.]

Chin'nereth (*circuit*), accurately Cinnareth, a fortified city in the tribe of Naphtali, Josh. 19 : 35 only, of which no trace is found in later writers, and no remains by travellers.

Chin'nereth, Sea of. Num. 34 : 11; Josh. 13 : 27, the inland sea, which is most familiarly known to us as the "Lake of Gennesareth" or "Sea of Galilee."

Chin'neroth. [CHINNERETH.]

Chi'os (*snowy*), an island of the Ægean Sea, 12 miles from Smyrna. It is separated from the mainland by a strait of only 5 miles. Its length is about 32 miles, and in breadth it varies from 8 to 18. Paul passed it on his return voyage from Troas to Cæsarea. Acts 20 : 15. It is now called Scio.

Chis'leu. [MONTH.]

Chis'lon (*confidence*), father of Elidad, the prince of the tribe of Benjamin, chosen to assist in the division of the land of Canaan among the tribes. Num. 34 : 21. (B.C. 1450.)

Chis'loth-ta'bor (*loins of Tabor*), a place to the border of which reached the border of Zebulun. Josh. 19 : 12. It may be the village *Iksâl*, which is now standing about 2½ miles to the west of Mount Tabor.

Chit'tim, Kit'tim (*bruisers*), a family or race descended from Javan. Gen. 10 : 4; 1 Chron. 1 : 7. Authorized Version KITTIM. Chittim is frequently noticed in Scripture. Num. 24 : 24; Isa. 23 : 1, 12; Jer. 2 : 10; Ezek. 27 : 6; Dan. 11 : 30. In the above passages, the "isles of Chittim," the "ships of Chittim, the "coasts of Chittim," are supposed to refer to the island of Cyprus. Josephus considered Cyprus the original seat of the Chittim. The name Chittim, which in the first instance had applied to Phœnicians only, passed over to the islands which they had occupied, and thence to the people who succeeded the Phœnicians in the occupation of them.

Chi'un (*a statue*, perhaps of Saturn), an idol made by the Israelites in the wilderness. [REMPHAN.]

Chlo'e (*green herb*), a woman mentioned in 1 Cor. 1 : 11.

Chora'shan. 1 Sam. 30 : 30. It may, perhaps, be identified with ASHAN of Simeon.

Chora'zin, one of the cities in which our Lord's mighty works were done, but named only in his denunciation. Matt. 11 : 21; Luke 10 : 13. St. Jerome describes it as on the shore of the lake, two miles from Capernaum, but its modern site is uncertain.

Choze'ba. 1 Chron. 4 : 22. Perhaps the same as ACHZIB.

Christ. [JESUS.]

Chris'tian. The disciples, we are told, Acts 11 : 26, were first called Christians at Antioch on the Orontes, somewhere about A.D. 43. They were known to each other as, and were among themselves called, *brethren,* Acts 15 : 1, 23; 1 Cor. 7 : 12; *disciples,* Acts 9 : 26; 11 : 29; *believers,* Acts 5 : 14; *saints,* Rom. 8 : 27; 15 : 25. The name " Christian," which, in the only other cases where it appears in the New Testament, Acts 26 : 28, 1 Pet. 4 : 16, is used contemptuously, could not have been applied by the early disciples to themselves, but was imposed upon them by the Gentile world. There is no reason to suppose that the name

Ruins of Kerazeh (Chorazin).

" Christian" of itself was intended as a term of scurrility or abuse, though it would naturally be used with contempt.

Chron'icles, First and Second Books of, the name originally given to the record made by the appointed historiographers in the kingdoms of Israel and Judah. In the LXX. these books are called *Paralipomena* (*i. e.* things omitted), which is understood as meaning that they are supplementary to the books of Kings. The constant tradition of the Jews is that these books were for the most part compiled by Ezra. One of the greatest difficulties connected with the captivity and return must have been the maintenance of that genealogical distribution of the lands which yet was a vital point of the Jewish economy. To supply this want and that each tribe might secure the inheritance of its fathers on its return was one object of the author of these books. Another difficulty intimately connected with the former was the maintenance of the temple services at Jerusalem. Zerubbabel, and after him Ezra and Nehemiah, labored most earnestly to restore the worship of God among the people, and to reinfuse something of national life and spirit into their hearts. Nothing could more effectually aid these designs than setting before the people a compendious history of the kingdom of David, its prosperity under God; the sins that led to its overthrow; the captivity and return. These considerations explain the plan and scope of that historical work which consists of the two books of Chronicles. The first book contains the sacred history by genealogies from the Creation to David, including an account of David's reign. In the second book he continues the story, giving the history of the kings of Judah, without those of Israel, down to the return from the captivity. As regards the *materials* used by Ezra, they are not difficult to discover. The genealogies are obviously transcribed from some register, in which were preserved the genealogies of the tribes and families drawn up at different times; while the history is mainly drawn from the same documents as those used in the books of Kings. [KINGS, BOOKS OF.]

Chronology. By this term we understand the technical and historical chronology of the Jews and their ancestors from the earliest time to the close of the New Testament Canon. 1. TECHNICAL CHRONOLOGY.—The technical part of Hebrew chronology presents great difficulties. 2. HISTORICAL CHRONOLOGY.—The historical part of Hebrew chronology is not less difficult than the technical. The information in the Bible is indeed direct rather than inferential, although there is very important evidence of the latter kind, but the present state of the numbers makes absolute certainty in many cases impossible. Three principal systems of biblical chronology have been founded, which may be termed the Long System, the Short, and the Rabbinical. There is a fourth, which, although an offshoot in part of the last, can scarcely be termed biblical, inasmuch as it depends for the most part upon theories, not only independent of but repugnant to the Bible: this last is at present peculiar to Baron Bunsen. The principal advocates of the Long chronology are Jackson, Hales and Des-Vignoles. Of the Short chronology Ussher may be considered as the most able advocate. The Rabbinical chronology accepts the biblical numbers, but makes the most arbitrary corrections. For the date of the Exodus it has been virtually accepted by Bunsen, Lepsius and Lord A. Hervey.

	Hales.	Jackson.	Ussher.	Petavius.	Bunsen.
	B.C.	B.C.	B.C.	B.C.	B.C.
Creation	5411	5426	4004	3983	(Adam) cir. 20,000
Flood	3155	3170	2348	2327	(Noah) cir. 10,000
Abram leaves Haran	2078	2023	1921	1961	
Exodus	1648	1593	1491	1531	1320
Found'n of Solomon's Temple	1027	1014	1012	1012	1004
Destr'n of Solomon's Temple	586	586	588	589	586

The numbers given by the LXX. for the antediluvian patriarchs would place the creation of Adam 2262 years before the end of the flood, or B.C. cir. 5361 or 5421.

Chrysolite, one of the precious stones in the foundation of the heavenly Jerusalem. Rev. 21 : 20. It has been already stated [BERYL] that the chrysolite of the ancients is identical with the modern Oriental topaz, the *tarshish* of the Hebrew Bible.

Chrysoprase occurs only in Rev. 21 : 20. The true chrysoprase is sometimes found in antique Egyptian jewelry set alternately with bits of lapis-lazuli. It is probable, therefore, that this is the stone named as the tenth in the walls of the heavenly Jerusalem.

Chrysoprasus, Latin form of CHRYSOPRASE.

Chub, the name of a people in alliance with Egypt in the time of Nebuchadnezzar, Ezek. 30 : 5, and probably of northern Africa.

Chun, 1 Chron. 18 : 8, called Berothai in 2 Sam. 8 : 8.

Church. 1. The derivation of the word is generally said to be from the Greek *kuriakon* (κυριακόν), "belonging to the Lord." But the derivation has been too hastily assumed. It is probably connected with *kirk*, the Latin *circus, circulus*, the Greek *kuklos* (κύκλος), because the congregations were gathered in circles. 2. *Ecclesia* (ἐκκλησία), the Greek word for church, originally meant an assembly called out by the magistrate, or by legitimate authority. It was in this last sense that the word was adopted and applied by the writers of the New Testament to the Christian congregation. In the one Gospel of St. Matthew the church is spoken of no less than thirty-six times as "the kingdom." Other descriptions or titles are hardly found in the evangelists. It is Christ's household, Matt. 10 : 25; the salt and light of the world, Matt. 5 : 13, 15; Christ's flock, Matt. 26 : 31; John 10 : 1; its members are the branches growing on Christ the Vine, John 15; but the general description of it, not metaphorical but direct, is that it is a kingdom. Matt. 16 : 19. From the Gospel then we learn that Christ was about to establish his heavenly kingdom on earth, which was to be the substitute for the Jewish Church and kingdom, now doomed to destruction. Matt. 21 : 43.

The day of Pentecost is the birthday of the Christian Church. Before they had been individual followers of Jesus; now they became his mystical body, animated by his spirit. On the evening of the day of Pentecost, the 3140 members of which the Church consisted were—(1) Apostles; (2) previous Disciples; (3) Converts. In Acts 2 : 41 we have indirectly exhibited the essential conditions of church communion. They are (1) Baptism, baptism implying on the part of the recipient repentance and faith ; (2) Apostolic Doctrine ; (3) Fellowship with the Apostles; (4) the Lord's Supper; (5) Public Worship. The *real* Church consists of all who belong to the Lord Jesus Christ as his disciples, and are one in love, in character, in hope, in Christ as the head of all, though as the body of Christ it consists of many parts.

Chu'shan-rishatha'im (*chief of two governments*), the king of Mesopotamia who oppressed Israel during eight years in the generation immediately following Joshua. Judges 3 : 8. (B.C. after 1420.) His yoke was broken from the neck of the people of Israel by Othniel, Caleb's nephew. Judges 3 : 10.

Chu'za, properly **Chu'zas** (*the seer*), the house-steward of Herod Antipas. Luke 8 : 3.

Cic'car. [JORDAN.]

Cilic'ia (*the land of Celix*), a maritime province in the southeast of Asia Minor, bordering on Pamphylia in the west, Lycaonia and Cappadocia in the north, and Syria in the east. Acts 6 : 9. Cilicia was from its geographical position the high road between Syria and the west; it was also the native country of St. Paul, hence it was visited by him, firstly, soon after his conversion, Acts 9 : 30; Gal. 1 : 21, and again in his second apostolical journey. Acts 15 : 41.

Cinnamon, a well-known aromatic substance, the rind of the *Laurus cinnamomum*, called *Korunda-gauhah* in Ceylon. It is mentioned in Ex. 30 : 23 as one of the component parts of the holy anointing oil. In Rev. 18 : 13 it is enumerated among the merchandise of the great Babylon.

Cin'neroth. 1 Kings 15 : 20. This was possibly the small enclosed district north of Tiberias, and by the side of the lake, afterwards known as "the plain of Gennesareth."

Circumcision was peculiarly, though not exclusively, a *Jewish* rite. It was enjoined upon Abraham, the father of the nation, by God, at the institution and as the token of the covenant, which assured to him and his descendants the promise of the Messiah. Gen. 17. It was thus made a necessary condition of Jewish nationality. Every male child was to be circumcised when eight days old, Lev. 12 : 3, on pain of death. The biblical notice of the rite describes it as distinctively Jewish ; so that in the New Testament "the circumcision" and "the uncircumcision" are frequently used as synonyms for the Jews and the Gentiles. The rite has been found to prevail extensively in both ancient and modern times. Though Mohammed did not enjoin circumcision in the Koran, he was circumcised himself, according to the custom of his country ; and circumcision is now as common among the Mohammedans as among the Jews. The process of restoring a circumcised person to his natural condition by a surgical operation was sometimes undergone. Some of the Jews in the time of Antiochus Epiphanes, wishing to assimilate themselves to the heathen around them, "made themselves uncircumcised." Against having recourse to this practice, from an excessive anti-Judaistic tendency, St. Paul cautions the Corinthians. 1 Chron. 7 : 18.

Cis, the father of Saul, Acts 13 : 21, usually called KISH.

Cistern, a receptacle for water, either conducted from an external spring or proceeding from rain-fall. The dryness of the summer months and the scarcity of springs in Judea made cisterns a necessity, and they are frequent throughout the whole of Syria and Palestine. On the long-forgotten way from Jericho to Bethel, "broken cisterns" of high antiquity are found at regular intervals. Jerusalem depends mainly for water upon its cisterns, of which almost every private house possesses one or more, excavated in the rock on which the city is built. The cisterns have usually a round opening at the top, sometimes built up with stonework above and furnished with a curb and a wheel for the bucket. Eccles. 12 : 6. Empty cisterns were sometimes used as prisons and places of confinement. Joseph was cast into a "pit," Gen. 37 : 22, as was Jeremiah. Jer. 38 : 6.

Cities. The earliest notice in Scripture of city-building is of Enoch by Cain, in the land of his exile. Gen. 4 : 17. After the confusion of tongues the descendants of Nimrod founded Babel, Erech, Accad and Calneh, in the land of Shinar, and Asshur, a branch from the same stock, built Nineveh, Rehoboth-by-the-river, Calah and Resen, the last being "a great city." The earliest description of a city, properly so called, is that of Sodom. Gen. 19 : 1–22. Even before the time of Abraham there were cities in Egypt, Gen. 12 : 14, 15 ; Num. 13 : 22, and the Israelites, during their sojourn there, were employed in building or fortifying the " treasure cities " of Pithom and Raamses. Ex. 1 : 11.

Fenced cities, fortified with high walls, Deut. 3 : 5, were occupied and perhaps partly rebuilt after the conquest, by the settled inhabitants of Syria on both sides of the Jordan.

Cities of refuge, six Levitical cities specially chosen for refuge to the involuntary homicide until released from banishment by the death of the high priest. Num. 35 : 6, 13, 15 ; Josh. 20 : 2, 7, 9. There were three on each side of Jordan. 1. KEDESH, in Naphtali. 1 Chron. 6 : 76. 2. SHECHEM, in Mount Ephraim. Josh. 21 : 21 ; 1 Chron. 6 : 67 ; 2 Chron. 10 : 1. 3. HEBRON, in Judah. Josh. 21 : 13 ; 2 Sam. 5 : 5 ; 1 Chron. 6 : 55 ; 29 : 27 ; 2 Chron. 11 : 10. 4. On the east side of Jordan—BEZER, in the tribe of Reuben, in the plains of Moab. Deut. 4 : 43 ; Josh. 20 : 8 ; 21 : 36 ; 1 Macc. 5 : 26. 5. RAMOTH-GILEAD, in the tribe of Gad. Deut. 4 : 43 ; Josh. 21 : 38 ; 1 Kings 22 : 3. 6. GOLAN, in Bashan, in the half-tribe of Manasseh. Deut. 4 : 43 ; Josh. 21 : 27 ; 1 Chron. 6 : 71.

Cit'ims. 1 Macc. 8 : 5. [CHITTIM.]

Citizenship. The use of this term in Scripture has exclusive reference to the usages of the Roman empire. The privilege of Roman citizenship was originally acquired in various ways, as by purchase, Acts 22 : 28, by military services, by favor or by manumission. The right once obtained descended to a man's children. Acts 22 : 28. Among the privileges attached to citizenship we may note that a man could not be bound or imprisoned without a formal trial, Acts 22 : 29, still less be scourged. Acts 16 : 37 ; Cic. *in Verr.* v. 63, 66. Another privilege attaching to citizenship was the appeal from a provincial tribunal to the emperor at Rome. Acts 25 : 11.

Citron. [APPLE TREE.]

Clau'da (*lame*), Acts 27 : 16, a small island nearly due west of Cape Matala on the south coast of Crete, and nearly due south of Phœnice ; now *Gozzo*.

Clau'dia (*lame*), a Christian woman mentioned in 2 Tim. 4 : 21, as saluting Timotheus.

Clau'dius (*lame*), fourth Roman emperor, reigned from 41 to 54 A.D. He was nominated to the supreme power mainly through the influence of Herod Agrippa the First. In the reign of Claudius there were several famines, arising from unfavorable harvests, and one such occurred in Palestine and Syria. Acts 11 : 28–30. Claudius was induced by a tumult of the

Coin of Claudius.

Jews in Rome to expel them from the city. · cf. Acts 18 : 2. The date of this event is uncertain. After a weak and foolish reign he was poisoned by his fourth wife, Agrippina, the mother of Nero, October 13, A.D. 54.

Clau'dius Lys'ias. [LYSIAS.]

Clay. As the sediment of water remaining in pits or in streets, the word is used frequently in the Old Testament, Ps. 18 : 42 ; Isa. 57 : 20 ; Jer. 38 : 6, and in the New Testament, John 9 : 6, a mixture of sand or dust with spittle. It is also found in the sense of potter's clay. Isa. 41 : 25. The great seat of the pottery of the present day in Palestine is Gaza, where are made the vessels in dark-blue clay so frequently met with. Another use of clay was for sealing. Job 38 : 14. Our Lord's tomb may have been thus sealed, Matt. 27 : 66, as also the earthen vessel containing the evidences of Jeremiah's purchase. Jer. 32 : 14. The seal used for public documents was rolled on the moist clay, and the tablet was then placed in the fire and baked.

Clem'ent (*mild, merciful*), Philip. 4 : 3, a fellow laborer of St. Paul when he was at Philippi. (A.D. 57.) It was generally believed in the ancient Church that this Clement was identical with the bishop of Rome who afterwards became so celebrated.

Cle'opas (*of a renowned father*), one of the two disciples who were going to Emmaus on the day of the resurrection. Luke 24 : 18. Some think the same as Cleophas in John 19 : 25. But they are probably two different persons. Cleopas is a Greek name, contracted from Cleopater, while Cleophas, or Clopas as in the Revised Version, is an Aramaic name, the same as Alphæus.

Cle′ophas, Revised Version **Clo′-pas,** the husband of Mary the sister of the Virgin Mary. John 19 : 25. He was probably dead before Jesus' ministry began, for his wife and children constantly appear with Joseph's family in the time of our Lord's ministry.—*Englishman's Cyc.* [CLEOPAS; ALPHÆUS.]

Clothing. [DRESS.]

Cloud. The shelter given, and refreshment of rain promised, by clouds give them their peculiar prominence in Oriental imagery. When a cloud appears rain is ordinarily apprehended, and thus the "cloud without rain" becomes a proverb for the man of promise without performance. Prov. 16 : 15; Isa. 18 : 4; 25 : 5; Jude 12; comp. Prov. 25 : 14. The cloud is a figure of transitoriness, Job 30 : 15; Hos. 6 : 4, and of whatever intercepts divine favor or human supplication. Lam. 2 : 1; 3 : 44. A bright cloud at times visited and rested on the mercy-seat. Ex. 29 : 42, 43; 1 Kings 8 : 10, 11; 2 Chron. 5 : 14; Ezek. 43 : 4, and was by later writers named Shechinah.

Cloud, Pillar of. The pillar of cloud by day and of fire by night that God caused to pass before the camp of the children of Israel when in the wilderness. The cloud, which became a pillar when the host moved, seems to have rested at other times on the tabernacle, whence God is said to have "come down *in* the pillar." Num. 12 : 5; so Ex. 33 : 9, 10. It preceded the host, apparently resting on the ark which led the way. Ex. 13 : 21; 40 : 36, etc.; Num. 9 : 15–23; 10 : 34.

Clouted, patched. Josh. 9 : 5.

Cni′dus (nidus), a city of great consequence, situated at the extreme southwest of the peninsula of Asia Minor, on a promontory now called *Cape Crio,* which projects between the islands of Cos and Rhodes. See Acts 21 : 1. It is now in ruins.

Coal. The first and most frequent use of the word rendered coal is a live ember, burning fuel. Prov. 26 : 21. In 2 Sam. 22 : 9, 13, "coals of fire" are put metaphorically for the lightnings proceeding from God. Ps. 18 : 8, 12, 13; 140 : 10. In Prov. 26 : 21, fuel not yet lighted is clearly signified. The fuel meant in the above passage is probably charcoal, and not coal in our sense of the word.

Coast, border, with no more refer-

ence to lands bordering on the sea than to any other bordering lands.

Coat. [DRESS.]

Cock. Matt. 26 : 34; Mark 13 : 35; 14 : 30, etc. The domestic cock and hen were early known to the ancient Greeks and Romans, and as no mention is made in the Old Testament of these birds, and no figures of them occur on the Egyptian monuments, they probably came into Judea with the Romans, who, as is well known, prized these birds both as articles of food and for cock-fighting.

Cockatrice. [ADDER.]

Cockle probably signifies bad weeds or fruit. Job 31 : 40.

Cœle-Syr′ia (sĕl′ĕ) (*hollow Syria*), the remarkable valley or hollow which intervenes between Libanus and Anti-Libanus, stretching a distance of nearly a hundred miles. The only mention of the region as a separate tract of country which the Jewish Scriptures contain is probably that in Amos 1 : 5, where "the inhabitants of the plain of Aven" are threatened in conjunction with those of Damascus. The word is given in the Authorized Version as CELO-SYRIA.

Coffer (*argaz*), a movable box hanging from the side of a cart. 1 Sam. 6 : 8, 11, 15. The word is found nowhere else.

Coffin. [BURIAL.]

Col-ho′zeh (*all-seeing*), a man of the tribe of Judah in the time of Nehemiah. Neh. 3 : 15; 11 : 5. (B.C. 536.)

Collar. For the proper sense of this term, as it occurs in Judges 8 : 26, see EARRINGS.

College, The. In 2 Kings 22 : 14, it is probable that the word translated "college" represents here not an institution of learning, but that part of Jerusalem known as the "lower city" or suburb, built on the hill Akra, including the Bezetha or new city.

Colony, a designation of Philippi, in Acts 16 : 12. After the battle of Actium, Augustus assigned to his veterans those parts of Italy which had espoused the cause of Antony, and transported many of the expelled inhabitants to Philippi, Dyrrhachium and other cities. In this way Philippi was made a Roman colony with the "Jus Italicum." At first the colonists were all Roman citizens, and entitled to vote at Rome.

Colors. The terms relative to color, occurring in the Bible, may be arranged in two classes, the first including those applied to the description of natural objects, the second those artificial mixtures which were employed in dyeing or painting. The *purple* and the *blue* were derived from a small shellfish found in the Mediterranean, and were very costly, and hence they were the royal colors. *Red*, both scarlet and crimson, was derived from an insect resembling the cochineal. The natural colors noticed in the Bible are white, black, red, yellow and green. The only fundamental color of which the Hebrews appear to have had a clear conception was *red;* and even this is not very often noticed.

Colos'se, more properly **Colos'sæ,** was a city of Phrygia in Asia Minor, in the upper part of the basin of the Mæander, on the Lycus. Hierapolis and Laodicea were in its immediate neighborhood. Col. 1:2; 4:13, 15, 16; see Rev. 1:11; 3:14. St. Paul is supposed by some to have visited Colosse and

Colosse.

founded or confirmed the Colossian church on his third missionary journey. Acts 18:23; 19:1.

Colos'sians, The Epistle to the, was written by the apostle St. Paul during his first captivity at Rome. Acts 28:16. (A.D. 62.) The epistle was addressed to the Christians of the city of Colosse, and was delivered to them by Tychicus, whom the apostle had sent both to them, Col. 4:7, 8, and to the church of Ephesus, Eph. 6:21, to inquire into their state and to administer exhortation and comfort. The main object of the epistle is to warn the Colossians against a spirit of semi-Judaistic and semi-Oriental philosophy which was corrupting the simplicity of their belief, and was noticeably tending to obscure the eternal glory and dignity of Christ. The similarity between this epistle and that to the Ephesians is striking. The latter was probably written at a later date.

Comforter. John 14:16. The name given by Christ to the Holy Spirit. The original word is *Paraclete,* and means first *Advocate,* a defender, helper, strengthener, as well as comforter.

Commerce. From the time that men began to live in cities, trade, in some shape, must have been carried on to supply the town-dwellers with necessaries from foreign as well as native sources, for we find that Abraham was rich, not only in cattle, but in silver, gold and gold and silver plate and ornaments. Gen. 13:2; 24:22, 53. Among trading nations mentioned in Scripture, Egypt holds in very early times a prominent position. The internal trade of the Jews, as well as the external, was much promoted by the festivals, which brought large numbers of persons to Jerusalem. 1 Kings 8 : 63. The places of public market were chiefly the open spaces near the gates, to which goods were brought for sale by those who came from the outside. Neh. 13 : 15, 16; Zeph. 1 : 10. The traders in later times were allowed to intrude into the temple, in the outer courts of which victims were publicly sold for the sacrifice. Zech. 14 : 21; Matt. 21 : 12; John 2 : 14.

Conani'ah (*made by Jehovah*), one of the chiefs of the Levites in the time of Josiah. 2 Chron. 35 : 9. (B.C. 628.)

Concubine. The difference between wife and concubine was less marked among the Hebrews than among us, owing to the absence of moral stigma. The difference probably lay in the absence of the right of the bill of divorce, without which the wife could not be repudiated. With regard to the children of wife and of concubine, there was no such difference as our illegitimacy implies. The latter were a supplementary family to the former; their names occur in the patriarchal genealogies, Gen. 22 : 24; 1 Chron. 1 : 22, and their position and provision would depend on the father's will. Gen. 25 : 6. The state of concubinage is assumed and provided for by the law of Moses. A concubine would generally be either (1) a Hebrew girl bought of her father; (2) a Gentile captive taken in war; (3) a foreign slave bought; or (4) a Canaanitish woman, bond or free. The rights of the first two were protected by the law, Ex. 21 : 7; Deut. 21 : 10–14; but the third was unrecognized and the fourth prohibited. Free Hebrew women also might become concubines. To seize on royal concubines for his use was often a usurper's first act. Such was probably the intent of Abner's act, 2 Sam. 3 : 7, and similarly the request on behalf of Adonijah was construed. 1 Kings 2 : 21–24.

Conduit, meaning an aqueduct or trench through which water was carried. Tradition, both oral and as represented by Talmudical writers, ascribes to Solomon the formation of the original aqueduct by which water was brought to Jerusalem.

Coney (*shâphân*), a gregarious animal of the class Pachydermata, which is found in Palestine, living in the caves and clefts of the rocks, and has been erroneously identified with the rabbit or coney. Its scientific name is *Hyrax syriacus*. The hyrax satisfies exactly the

expressions in Ps. 104 : 18; Prov. 30 : 26. Its color is gray or brown on the back, white on the belly; it is like the alpine marmot, scarcely of the size of the do-

The Coney.

mestic cat, having long hair, a very short tail and round ears. It is found on Lebanon and in the Jordan and Dead Sea valleys.

Congregation. This describes the Hebrew people in its collective capacity under its peculiar aspect as a holy community, held together by religious rather than political bonds. Sometimes it is used in a broad sense as inclusive of foreign settlers, Ex. 12 : 19, but more properly as exclusively appropriate to the Hebrew element of the population. Num. 15 : 15. The congregation was governed by the father or head of each family and tribe. The number of these representatives being inconveniently large for ordinary business, a further selection was made by Moses of 70, who formed a species of standing committee. Num. 11 : 16. Occasionally indeed the whole body of the people was assembled at the door of the tabernacle, hence usually called the tabernacle of the congregation. Num. 10 : 3. The people were strictly bound by the acts of their representatives, even in cases where they disapproved of them. Josh. 9 : 18.

Coni'ah. [JECONIAH.]

Cononi'ah (*appointed by the Lord*), a Levite, ruler of the offerings and tithes in the time of Hezekiah. 2 Chron. 31 : 12, 13. (B.C. 726.)

Consecration. [PRIEST.]

Convocation. This term (with one exception—Isa. 1 : 13) is applied invariably to meetings of a *religious* character, in contradistinction to *congregation*.

Cooking. As meat did not form an article of ordinary diet among the Jews, the art of cooking was not carried to any perfection. Few animals were slaughtered except for purposes of hospitality or festivity. The proceedings on such occasions appear to have been as follows:—On the arrival of a guest, the animal, either a kid, lamb or calf, was killed, Gen. 18 : 7 ; Luke 15 : 23, its throat being cut so that the blood might be poured out, Lev. 7 : 26 ; it was then flayed, and was ready for either roasting or boiling. In the former case the animal was preserved entire, Ex. 12 : 46, and roasted either over a fire, Ex. 12 : 8, of wood, Isa. 44 : 16, or perhaps in an oven, consisting simply of a hole dug in the earth, well heated, and covered up. Boiling, however, was the more usual method of cooking.

Co'os. Acts 21 : 1. [Cos.]

Copper, Heb. *nĕchôsheth*, in the Authorized Version always rendered "brass," except in Ezra 8 : 27 and Jer. 15 : 12. It was almost exclusively used by the ancients for common purposes, and for every kind of instrument, as chains, pillars, lavers and the other temple vessels. We read also of copper mirrors, Ex. 38 : 8, and even of copper arms, as helmets, spears, etc. 1 Sam. 17 : 5, 6, 38 ; 2 Sam. 21 : 16.

Coral. Ezek. 27 : 16. A production of the sea, formed by minute animals called zoophites. It is their shell or house. It takes various forms, as of trees, shrubs, hemispheres. The principal colors are red and white. It was used for beads and ornaments. With regard to the estimation in which coral was held by the Jews and other Orientals, it must be remembered that coral varies in price with us. Pliny says that the Indians valued coral as the Romans valued pearls. Job 28 : 18.

Corban, an offering to God of any sort, bloody or bloodless, but particularly in fulfillment of a vow. The law laid down rules for vows, (1) affirmative ; (2) negative. Lev. 27 ; Num. 30. Upon these rules the traditionists enlarged, and laid down that a man might interdict himself by vow, not only from using for himself, but from giving to another or receiving from him, some particular object, whether of food or any other kind whatsoever. The thing thus interdicted was considered as *corban*. A person might thus exempt himself from any inconvenient obligation under plea of corban. It was practices of this sort that our Lord reprehended, Matt. 15 : 5 ; Mark 7 : 11, as annulling the spirit of the law.

Cord. The materials of which cord was made varied according to the strength required ; the strongest rope was probably made of strips of camel hide, as still used by the Bedouins. The finer sorts were made of flax, Isa. 19 : 9, and probably of reeds and rushes. In the New Testament the term is applied to the whip which our Saviour made, John 2 : 15, and to the ropes of a ship. Acts 27 : 32.

Co're. Jude 11. [KORAH, 1.]

The Coriander.

Coriander. The plant called *Coriandrum sativum* is found in Egypt, Persia and India, and has a round tall stalk ; it bears umbelliferous white or reddish flowers, from which arise globular, grayish, spicy seed-corns, marked with fine striæ. It is mentioned twice in the Bible. Ex. 16 : 31 ; Num. 11 : 7.

Cor'inth, an ancient and celebrated city of Greece, on the Isthmus of Corinth, and about 40 miles west of Athens. In consequence of its geographical position it formed the most direct communication between the Ionian and Ægean seas. A remarkable feature was the *Acrocorinthus*, a vast citadel of rock, which rises abruptly to the height of 2000 feet above the level of the sea, and the summit of which is so extensive that it once contained a whole town. The situation of Corinth, and the possession of its eastern and western harbors, Cenchreæ and Lechæum, are the secrets of its history. Corinth was a place of great mental activity, as well as of commercial and

Acrocorinthus, Corinth.

manufacturing enterprise. Its wealth was so celebrated as to be proverbial; so were the vice and profligacy of its inhabitants. The worship of Venus here was attended with shameful licentiousness. Corinth is still an episcopal see.

Coin of Corinth.

The city has now shrunk to a wretched village, on the old site and bearing the old name, which, however, is corrupted into *Gortho*. St. Paul preached here, Acts 18 : 11, and founded a church, to which his Epistles to the Corinthians are addressed. [EPISTLES TO THE CORINTHIANS.]

Corinth'ians, First Epistle to the, was written by the apostle St. Paul toward the close of his nearly three-years stay at Ephesus, Acts 19 : 10; 20 : 31, which, we learn from 1 Cor. 16 : 8, probably terminated with the Pentecost of A.D. 57 or 58. The bearers were probably (according to the common subscription) Stephanas, Fortunatus and Acha-

icus. It appears to have been called forth by the information the apostles had received of dissension in the Corinthian church, which may be thus explained : — The Corinthian church was planted by the apostle himself, 1 Cor. 3 : 6, in his second missionary journey. Acts 18 : 1, *seq.* He abode in the city a year and a half. Acts 18 : 11. A short time after the apostle had left the city the eloquent Jew of Alexandria, Apollos, went to Corinth, Acts 19 : 1, and gained many followers, dividing the church into two parties, the followers of Paul and the followers of Apollos. Later on Judaizing teachers from Jerusalem preached the gospel in a spirit of direct antagonism to St. Paul *personally*. To this third party we may perhaps add a fourth, that, under the name of " the followers of Christ," 1 Cor. 2 : 12, sought at first to separate themselves from the factious adherence to particular teachers, but eventually were driven by antagonism into positions equally sectarian and inimical to the unity of the church. At this momentous period, before parties had become consolidated and had distinctly withdrawn from communion with one another, the apostle writes; and in the outset of the epistle, 1 Cor. 1–4 : 21, we have his noble and impassioned protest against this fourfold rending of the robe of Christ.

Corinth'ians, Second Epistle to the, was written a few months subsequent to the first, in the same year— about the autumn of A.D. 57 or 58—at Macedonia. The epistle was occasioned by the information which the apostle had received from Titus, and also, as it would certainly seem probable, from Timothy, of the reception of the first epistle. This information, as it would seem from our present epistle, was mainly favorable; the better part of the church were returning to their spiritual allegiance to their founder, 2 Cor. 1 : 13, 14; 7 : 9, 15, 16; but there was still a faction who strenuously denied Paul's claim to apostleship. The contents of this epistle comprise, (1) the apostle's account of the character of his spiritual labors, chs. 1–7; (2) directions about the collections, chs. 8, 9; (3) defence of his own apostolical character, chs. 10–13 : 10. The words in 1 Cor. 5 : 9 seem to point to further epistles to this church

Corinth.

Remains of Ruined Temple at Corinth.

by Paul, but we have no positive evidence of any.

Cormorant, the representative in the Authorized Version of the Hebrew words *kâath* and *shâlâc*. As to the former, see PELICAN. *Shâlâc* occurs only as the name of an unclean bird in Lev. 11 : 17 ; Deut. 14 : 17. The word has been variously rendered. The etymology points to some plunging bird. The common cormorant (*Phalacrocorax carbo*), which some writers have identified with the *shâlâc*, is unknown in the eastern Mediterranean ; another species is found south of the Red Sea, but none on the west coast of Palestine.

The Cormorant.

Corn. The most common kinds were wheat, barley, spelt, Authorized Version, Ex. 9 : 32 and Isa. 28 : 25, "rye ;" Ezek. 4 : 9 "fitches" and millet ; oats are mentioned only by rabbinical writers. Our Indian corn was unknown in Bible times. Corn-crops are still reckoned at twentyfold what was sown, and were anciently much more. Gen. 41 : 22. The Jewish law permitted any one in passing through a field of standing corn to pluck and eat. Deut. 23 : 25 ; see also Matt. 12 : 1. From Solomon's time, 2 Chron. 2 : 10, 15, as agriculture became developed under a settled government, Palestine was a corn-exporting country, and her grain was largely taken by her commercial neighbor Tyre. Ezek. 27 : 17 ; comp. Amos 8 : 5.

Corne'lius (*of a horn*), a Roman centurion of the Italian cohort stationed in Cæsarea, Acts 10 : 1, etc., a man full of good works and alms-deeds. With his household he was baptized by St. Peter, and thus Cornelius became the first-fruits of the Gentile world to Christ.

Corner. The "corner" of the field was not allowed, Lev. 19 : 9, to be wholly reaped. It formed a right of the poor to carry off what was so left, and this was a part of the maintenance from the soil to which that class were entitled. Under the scribes, minute legislation fixed one-sixtieth as the portion of a field which was to be left for the legal "corner." The proportion being thus fixed, all the grain might be reaped, and enough to satisfy the regulation subsequently separated from the whole crop. This "corner" was, like the gleaning, tithe-free.

Corner-stone, a quoin or corner-stone, of great importance in binding together the sides of a building. The phrase "corner-stone" is sometimes used to denote any principal person, as the princes of Egypt, Isa. 19 : 13, and is thus applied to our Lord. Isa. 28 : 16 ; Matt. 21 : 42 ; 1 Pet. 2 : 6, 7.

Cornet (Heb. *shôphâr*), a loud-sounding instrument, made of the horn of a ram or of a chamois (sometimes of an ox), and used by the ancient Hebrews for signals, Lev. 25 : 9, and much used by the priests. 1 Chron. 15 : 28.

Cos, or **Co'os** (now *Stanchio* or *Stanko*). This small island of the Grecian Archipelago has several interesting points of connection with the Jews. Herod the Great conferred many favors on the island. St. Paul, on the return from his third missionary journey, passed the night here, after sailing from Miletus. Probably referred to in Acts 21 : 1.

Co'sam (*a diviner*), son of Elmodam, in the line of Joseph the husband of Mary. Luke 3 : 28.

Cotton. Cotton is now both grown and manufactured in various parts of Syria and Palestine ; but there is no proof that, till they came in contact with Persia, the Hebrews generally knew of it as a distinct fabric from linen. [LINEN.]

Couch. [BED.]

Council. 1. The great council of the Sanhedrin, which sat at Jerusalem. [SANHEDRIN.]

2. The lesser courts, Matt. 10 : 17 ; Mark 13 : 9, of which there were two at Jerusalem and one in each town of Pal-

estine. The constitution of these courts is a doubtful point. The existence of local courts, however constituted, is clearly implied in the passages quoted from the New Testament; and perhaps the "judgment," Matt. 5 : 21, applies to them.

3. A kind of jury or privy council, Acts 25 : 12, consisting of a certain number of assessors, who assisted Roman governors in the administration of justice and in other public matters.

Court (Heb. *châtsêr*), an open enclosure surrounded by buildings, applied in the Authorized Version most commonly to the enclosures of the tabernacle and the temple. Ex. 27 : 9 ; 40 : 33 ; Lev. 6 : 16 ; 1 Kings 6 : 36 ; 7 : 8 ; 2 Kings 23 : 12 ; 2 Chron. 33 : 5, etc.

Covenant. The Heb. *bĕrith* means primarily "a cutting," with reference to the custom of cutting or dividing animals in two and passing between the parts in ratifying a covenant. Gen. 15 ; Jer. 34 : 18, 19. In the New Testament the corresponding word is *diathêcē* (διαθήκη), which is frequently translated *testament* in the Authorized Version. In its biblical meaning of a compact or agreement between two parties the word is used—1. Of a covenant between God and man ; *e. g.* God covenanted with Noah, after the flood, that a like judgment should not be repeated. It is not precisely like a covenant between men, but was a promise or agreement by God. The principal covenants are the *covenant of works*—God promising to save and bless men on condition of perfect obedience—and the *covenant of grace*, or God's promise to save men on condition of their believing in Christ and receiving him as their Master and Saviour. The first is called the Old Covenant, from which we name the first part of the Bible the Old Testament, the Latin rendering of the word covenant. The second is called the New Covenant, or New Testament. 2. Covenant between man and man, *i. e.* a solemn compact or agreement, either between tribes or nations, Josh. 9 : 6, 15 ; 1 Sam. 11 : 1, or between individuals, Gen. 31 : 44, by which each party bound himself to fulfill certain conditions and was assured of receiving certain advantages. In making such a covenant God was solemnly invoked as witness, Gen. 31 : 50, and an oath was sworn. Gen. 21 : 31. A sign or witness of the covenant was sometimes framed, such as a gift,

Gen. 21 : 30, or a pillar or heap of stones erected. Gen. 31 : 52.

Cow. [BULL.]

Coz (*thorn*), a man among the descendants of Judah. 1 Chron. 4 : 8.

Coz'bi (*deceitful*), daughter of Zur, a chief of the Midianites. Num. 25 : 15, 18.

Crane. The crane (*Grus cinerea*) is a native of Europe and Asia. It stands about four feet high. Its color is ashen

The Crane.

gray, with face and neck nearly black. It feeds on seeds, roots, insects and small quadrupeds. It retires in winter to the warmer climates. Jer. 8 : 7.

Create. To create is to cause something to exist which did not exist before, as distinguished from *make*, to re-form something already in existence.

Creation. (The creation of all things is ascribed in the Bible to God, and is the only reasonable account of the origin of the world. The *method* of creation is not stated in Genesis, and as far as the account there is concerned, each part of it may be, after the first acts of creation, by evolution, or by direct act of God's will. The word *create* (bârà) is used but three times in the first chapter of Genesis —(1) as to the origin of matter; (2) as to the origin of life; (3) as to the origin of man's soul; and science has always failed to do any of these acts thus ascribed to

God. All other things are said to be *made*. The *order of creation* as given in Genesis is in close harmony with the order as revealed by geology, and the account there given, so long before the records of the rocks were read or the truth discoverable by man, is one of the strongest proofs that the Bible was inspired by God.—ED.)

Creditor. [LOAN.]

Cres'cens (*growing*), 2 Tim. 4 : 10, an assistant of St. Paul, said to have been one of the seventy disciples.

Crete, the modern *Candia*. This large island, which closes in the Greek Archipelago on the south, extends through a distance of 140 miles between its extreme points. Though exceedingly

View of Crete. Mount Ida in the distance.

bold and mountainous, this island has very fruitful valleys, and in early times it was celebrated for its hundred cities. It seems likely that a very early acquaintance existed between the Cretans and the Jews. Cretans, Acts 2 : 11, were among those who were at Jerusalem at the great Pentecost. In Acts 27 : 7-12

Coin of Crete.

we have an account of Paul's shipwreck near this island ; and it is evident from Titus 1 : 5 that the apostle himself was here at no long interval of time before he wrote the letter. The Cretans were proverbial liars. Titus 1 : 12.

Cretes. Acts 2 : 11. Cretans, inhabitants of Crete.

Crisping pins. Isa. 3 : 22. The original word means some kind of female ornament, probably a reticule or richly-ornamented purse, often made of silk inwrought with gold or silver.

Cris'pus (*curled*), ruler of the Jewish synagogue at Corinth, Acts 18 : 8 ; baptized with his family by St. Paul. 1 Cor. 1 : 14. (A.D. 50.)

Cross. As the emblem of a slave's death and a murderer's punishment, the cross was naturally looked upon with the profoundest horror. But after the celebrated vision of Constantine, he ordered his friends to make a cross of gold and gems, such as he had seen, and "the towering eagles resigned the flags unto the cross," and "the tree of cursing and shame" "sat upon the sceptres and was engraved and signed on the foreheads of kings." (Jer. Taylor, "Life of Christ," iii., xv. 1.) The new standards were called by the name Labarum, and may be seen on the coins of Constantine the

Great and his nearer successors. The Latin cross, on which our Lord suffered, was in the form of the letter T, and had an upright above the cross-bar, on which the "title" was placed. There was a projection from the central stem, on which the body of the sufferer rested.

Three Forms of the Cross.

This was to prevent the weight of the body from tearing away the hands. Whether there was also a support to the feet (as we see in pictures) is doubtful. An inscription was generally placed above the criminal's head, briefly expressing his guilt, and generally was carried before him. It was covered with white gypsum, and the letters were black.

Crown. This ornament, which is both ancient and universal, probably

Crowns.

1. Crown of Upper Egypt. **2.** Crown of Upper and Lower Egypt united. **3.** Assyrian Crown, from Nineveh Marbles. **4.** Laurel Crown. **5.** Crown of Herod the Great. **6.** Crown of Aretas, King of Arabia.

originated from the fillets used to prevent the hair from being dishevelled by the wind. Such fillets are still common;

they gradually developed into turbans, which by the addition of ornamental or precious materials assumed the dignity of mitres or crowns. Both the ordinary priests and the high priest wore them. The crown was a symbol of royalty, and was worn by kings, 2 Chron. 23 : 11, and also by queens. Esther 2 : 17. The head-dress of bridegrooms, Ezek. 24 : 17 ; Isa. 61 : 10 ; Bar. 5 : 2, and of women, Isa. 3: 20 ; a head-dress of great splendor, Isa. 28 : 5 ; a wreath of flowers, Prov. 1 : 9 ; 4 : 9, denote crowns. In general we must attach to it the notion of a costly *turban* irradiated with pearls and gems of priceless value, which often form aigrettes for feathers, as in the crowns of modern Asiatic sovereigns. Such was probably the crown which weighed (or rather "was worth") a talent, mentioned in 2 Sam. 12 : 30, taken by David from the king of Ammon at Rabbah, and used as the state crown of Judah. 2 Sam. 12 : 30. In Rev. 12 : 3 ; 19 : 12, allusion is made to "*many* crowns" worn in token of extended dominion. The laurel, pine or parsley crowns given to victors in the great games of Greece are finely alluded to by St. Paul. 1 Cor. 9 : 25 ; 2 Tim. 2 : 5, etc.

Crown of thorns, Matt. 27 : 29. Our Lord was crowned with thorns in mockery by the Roman soldiers. Obviously some small flexile thorny shrub is meant; perhaps *Capparis spinosa.* "Hasselquist, a Swedish naturalist, supposes a very common plant, *naba* or *nubka* of the Arabs, with many small and sharp spines; soft, round and pliant branches; leaves much resembling ivy, of a very deep green, as if in designed mockery of a victor's wreath."—*Alford.*

Crucifixion was in use among the Egyptians, Gen. 40 : 19, the Carthaginians, the Persians, Esther 7 : 10, the Assyrians, Scythians, Indians, Germans, and from the earliest times among the Greeks and Romans. Whether this mode of execution was known to the ancient Jews is a matter of dispute. Probably the Jews borrowed it from the Romans. It was unanimously considered the most horrible form of death. Among the Romans the degradation was also a part of the infliction, and the punishment if applied to freemen was only used in the case of the vilest criminals. The one to be crucified was stripped naked of all his clothes, and then followed the most awful moment of all. He was laid down upon the implement of torture. His arms were stretched along the cross-beams, and at the centre of the open palms the point of a huge iron nail was placed, which, by the blow of a mallet, was driven home into the wood. Then through either foot separately, or possibly through both together, as they were placed one over the other, another huge nail tore its way through the quivering flesh. Whether the sufferer was also bound to the cross we do not know; but, to prevent the hands and feet being torn away by the weight of the body, which could not " rest upon nothing but four great wounds," there was, about the centre of the cross, a wooden projection strong enough to support, at least in part, a human body, which soon became a weight of agony. Then the " accursed tree " with its living human burden was slowly heaved up and the end fixed firmly in a hole in the ground. The feet were but a little raised above the earth. The victim was in full reach of every hand that might choose to strike. A death by crucifixion seems to include all that pain and death can have of the horrible and ghastly,—dizziness, cramp, thirst, starvation, sleeplessness, traumatic fever, tetanus, publicity of shame, long continuance of torment, horror of anticipation, mortification of untended wounds, all intensified just up to the point at which they can be endured at all, but all stopping just short of the point which would give to the sufferer the relief of unconsciousness. The unnatural position made every movement painful; the lacerated veins and crushed tendons throbbed with incessant anguish; the wounds, inflamed by exposure, gradually gangrened ; the arteries, especially of the head and stomach, became swollen and oppressed with surcharged blood ; and, while each variety of misery went on gradually increasing, there was added to them the intolerable pang of a burning and raging thirst. Such was the death to which Christ was doomed.—*Farrar's* "*Life of Christ.*" The crucified was watched, according to custom, by a party of four soldiers, John 19 : 23, with their centurion, Matt. 27 : 66, whose express office was to prevent the stealing of the body. This was necessary from the lingering character of the death, which sometimes did not supervene even for three days, and was at last the result of gradual benumbing and starvation. But for this guard, the persons might have been taken down and recovered, as was

actually done in the case of a friend of Josephus. Fracture of the legs was especially adopted by the Jews to hasten death. John 19 : 31. In most cases the body was suffered to rot on the cross by the action of sun and rain, or to be devoured by birds and beasts. Sepulture was generally therefore forbidden ; but in consequence of Deut. 21 : 22, 23, an express national exception was made in favor of the Jews. Matt. 27 : 58. This accursed and awful mode of punishment was happily abolished by Constantine.

Cruse, a small vessel for holding water, such as was carried by Saul when on his night expedition after David, 1 Sam. 26 : 11, 12, 16, and by Elijah. 1 Kings 19 : 6.

Crystal, the representative in the Authorized Version of two Hebrew words. 1. *Zecûcith* occurs only in Job 28 : 17, where "glass" probably is intended. 2. *Kerach* occurs in numerous passages in the Old Testament to denote " ice," " frost," etc. ; but once only, Ezek. 1 : 22, as is generally understood, to signify " crystal." The ancients supposed rock-crystal to be merely ice congealed by intense cold. The similarity of appearance between ice and crystal caused no doubt the identity of the terms to express these substances. The Greek word occurs in Rev. 4 : 6 ; 21 : 1. It may mean either " ice " or " crystal."

Cubit. [WEIGHTS AND MEASURES.]

Cuckoo, Lev. 11 : 16 ; Deut. 14 : 15, the name of some unclean bird, and probably of some of the larger petrels which abound in the east of the Mediterranean.

Cucumbers (Heb. *kishshuim*). This word occurs in Num. 11 : 5 as one of the good things of Egypt for which the Israelites longed. Egypt produces excellent cucumbers, melons, etc., the *Cucumis chate* being the best of its tribe yet known. Besides the *Cucumis chate*, the common cucumber (*C. sativus*), of which the Arabs distinguish a number of varieties, is common in Egypt. " Both *Cucumis chate* and *C. sativus*," says Mr. Tristram, " are now grown in great quantities in Palestine. On visiting the Arab school in Jerusalem (1858) I observed that the dinner which the children brought with them to school consisted, without exception, of a piece of barley-cake and a raw cucumber, which they ate rind and all." The " lodge in a garden of cucumbers," Isa. 1 : 8, is a rude temporary shelter erected in the open grounds where vines, cucumbers, gourds, etc., are grown, in which some lonely man or boy is set to watch, either to guard the plants from robbers or to scare away the foxes and jackals from the vines.

Cummin, one of the cultivated plants of Palestine. Isa. 28 : 25, 27 ; Matt. 23 : 23. It is an umbelliferous plant something like fennel. The seeds have a bitterish warm taste and an aromatic flavor. The Maltese are said to grow it at the present day, and to thresh it in the manner described by Isaiah.

Cup. The cups of the Jews, whether of metal or earthenware, were possibly borrowed, in point of shape and design, from Egypt and from the Phœnicians, who were celebrated in that branch of workmanship. Egyptian cups were of various shapes, either with handles or without them. In Solomon's time all his drinking vessels were of gold, none of silver. 1 Kings 10 : 21. Babylon is compared to a golden cup. Jer. 51 : 7. The great laver, or "sea," was made with a rim like the rim of a cup (côs), "with flowers of lilies," 1 Kings 7 : 26, a form which the Persepolitan cups resemble. The cups of the New Testament were often no doubt formed on Greek and Roman models. They were sometimes of gold. Rev. 17 : 4.

Cupbearer, an officer of high rank with Egyptian, Persian and Assyrian as well as Jewish monarchs. 1 Kings 10 : 5. It was his duty to fill the king's cup and present it to him personally. Neh. 1 : 11. The chief cupbearer, or butler, to the king of Egypt was the means of raising Joseph to his high position. Gen. 40 : 1, 21 ; 41 : 9.

Cush (*black*), a Benjamite mentioned only in the title to Ps. 7. He was probably a follower of Saul, the head of his tribe. (B.C. 1061.)

Cush, the name of a son of Ham, apparently the eldest, and of a territory or territories occupied by his descendants. The Cushites appear to have spread along tracts extending from the higher Nile to the Euphrates and Tigris. History affords many traces of this relation of Babylonia, Arabia and Ethiopia.

Cu'shan (*blackness*), Hab. 3 : 7, possibly the same as Cushan-rishathaim (Authorized Version Chushan-) king of Mesopotamia. Judges 3 : 8, 10.

Cu'shi. Properly "the Cushite," "the Ethiopian," a man apparently attached to Joab's person. 2 Sam. 18 : 21–25, 31, 32.

Cuth, or **Cu'thah,** one of the countries whence Shalmaneser introduced colonists into Samaria. 2 Kings 17 : 24, 30. Its position is undecided.

Cuttings [in the flesh]. Cuttings in the flesh, or the laceration of one's body for the "propitiation of their gods," 1 Kings 18 : 28, constituted a prominent feature of idolatrous worship, especially among the Syrians. The Israelites were prohibited from indulging in such practices. Lev. 19 : 28 ; 21 : 5 ; Deut. 14 : 1 ; Jer. 16 : 6.

Cymbal, Cymbals, a percussive musical instrument. Two kinds of cymbals are mentioned in Ps. 150 : 5, "loud cymbals" or *castagnettes,* and "high-sounding cymbals." The former consisted of four small plates of brass or of some other hard metal ; two plates were attached to each hand of the performer, and were struck together to produce a great noise. The latter consisted of two larger plates, one held in each hand and struck together as an accompaniment to other instruments. Cymbals were used not only in the temple but for military purposes, and also by Hebrew women as a musical accompaniment to their national dances. Both kinds of cymbals are still common in the East.

Cypress (Heb. *tirzâh*). The Hebrew word is found only in Isa. 44 : 14. We are quite unable to assign any definite rendering to it. The true cypress is a native of the Taurus. The Hebrew word points to some tree with a hard grain, and this is all that can be positively said of it.

Cy'prus, an island of Asia in the Mediterranean. It is about 140 miles long and 50 miles wide at the widest part. Its two chief cities were Salamis, at the east end of the island, and Paphos, at the west end. "Cyprus occupies a distinguished place in both sacred and profane history. It early belonged to the Phœnicians of the neighboring coast ; was afterwards colonized by Greeks ; passed successively under the power of the Pharaohs, Persians, Ptolemies and Romans, excepting a short period of independence in the fourth century B.C. It was one of the chief seats of the worship of Venus, hence called Cypria. Recently the discoveries in Cyprus by Cesnola have excited new interest.—*Ap-*

Cyprus.

pendency of Egypt, and a Roman province B.C. 75. Simon, who bore our Saviour's cross, Matt. 27 : 32, was a native
of Cyrene. Jewish dwellers in Cyrenaica were in Jerusalem at Pentecost,
Acts 2 : 10, and gave their name to one
of the synagogues in Jerusalem. Acts 6 :
9. Christian converts from Cyrene were
among those who contributed actively to
the formation of the first Gentile church
at Antioch. Acts 11 : 20.

Cyre'nius (*warrior*), the Greek form
of the Roman name of Quirinus. The
full name is Publius Sulpicius Quirinus.
He was consul B.C. 12, and was made
governor of Syria after the banishment
of Archelaus in A.D. 6. He probably
was twice governor of Syria; his first
governorship extended from B.C. 4 (the
year of Christ's birth) to B.C. 1. It was
during this time that he was sent to make
the enrollment which caused Joseph and
Mary to visit Bethlehem. Luke 2 : 2. The
second enrollment is mentioned in Acts
5 : 37.

Cy'rus (*the sun*), the founder of the
Persian empire—see 2 Chron. 36 : 22, 23;
Dan. 6 : 28; 10 : 1, 13—was, according
to the common legend, the son of Cambyses, a Persian of the royal family of
the Achæmenidæ. When he grew up to
manhood his courage and genius placed
him at the head of the Persians. His
conquests were numerous and brilliant.
He defeated and captured the Median
king B.C. 559. In B.C. 546(?) he defeated
Crœsus, and the kingdom of Lydia was
the prize of his success. Babylon fell
before his army, and the ancient dominions of Assyria were added to his empire
B.C. 538. The prophet Daniel's home for
a time was at his court. Dan. 6 : 28. The
edict of Cyrus for the rebuilding of the
temple, 2 Chron. 36 : 22, 23; Ezra 1 : 1-4;
3 : 7; 4 : 3; 5 : 13, 17; 6 : 3, was in fact
the beginning of Judaism; and the great
changes by which the nation was trans
formed into a church are clearly marked
His tomb is still shown at Pasargadæ, the
scene of his first decisive victory.

pleton's Am. Encyc. It was the native
place of Barnabas, Acts 4 : 36, and was
visited by Paul. Acts 13 : 4-13; 15 : 39;
21 : 3. See also Acts 27 : 4.

Cyre'ne, the principal city of that
part of northern Africa which was anciently called Cyrenaica, lying between
Carthage and Egypt, and corresponding
with the modern Tripoli. Though on
the African coast, it was a Greek city,
and the Jews were settled there in large
numbers. The Greek colonization of this

Coin of Cyrene.

part of Africa under Battus began as
early as B.C. 631. After the death of
Alexander the Great it became a de-

D.

Dab'areh (*pasture*), Josh. 21 : 28, or DABERATH, a town on the boundary of Zebulun. Josh. 19 : 12. Under the name of *Debarieh* it still lies at the western foot of Tabor.

Dab'basheth (*a hill-place*), a town on the boundary of Zebulun. Josh. 19 : 11.

Dab'erath. [See DABAREH.]

Da'gon (*a fish*), apparently the masculine, 1 Sam. 5 : 3, 4, correlative of Atargatis, was the national god of the Philistines. The most famous temples of Dagon were at Gaza, Judges 16 : 21–30, and Ashdod. 1 Sam. 5 : 5, 6; 1 Chron. 10 : 10. The latter temple was destroyed by Jonathan in the Maccabæan wars. Traces of the worship of Dagon likewise appear in the names Caphar-dagon (near Jamnia) and Beth-dagon in Judah, Josh.

The Fish-God. (*From a bas-relief from Khorsabad.*)

15 : 41, and Asher. Josh. 19 : 27. Dagon was represented with the face and hands of a man and the tail of a fish. 1 Sam. 5 : 5. The fish-like form was a natural emblem of fruitfulness, and as such was likely to be adopted by seafaring tribes in the representation of their gods.

Dala-i'ah (*freed by Jehovah*), a descendant of the royal family of Judah. 1 Chron. 3 : 24.

Dalmanu'tha, a town on the west side of the Sea of Galilee, near Magdala. Matt. 15 : 39 and Mark 8 : 10. [MAGDALA.] Dalmanutha probably stood at the place called *'Ain-el-Bárideh*, "the cold fountain."

Dalma'tia, a mountainous district on the eastern coast of the Adriatic Sea. St. Paul sent Titus there. 2 Tim. 4 : 10.

Dal'phon (*swift*), the second of the ten sons of Haman. Esther 9 : 7. (B.C. 510.)

Dam'aris (*a heifer*), an Athenian woman converted to Christianity by St. Paul's preaching. Acts 17 : 34. (A.D. 48.) Chrysostom and others held her to have been the wife of Dionysius the Areopagite.

Damas'cus, one of the most ancient and most important of the cities of Syria. It is situated 130 miles northeast of Jerusalem, in a plain of vast size and of extreme fertility, which lies east of the great chain of Anti-Libanus, on the

The East Gate of Damascus.

edge of the desert. This fertile plain, which is nearly circular and about 30 miles in diameter, is due to the river *Barada*, which is probably the "Abana" of Scripture. Two other streams, the *Wady Helbon* upon the north and the *Awaj*, which flows direct from Hermon, upon the south, increase the fertility of the Damascene plain, and contend for the honor of representing the "Pharpar" of Scripture. According to Josephus, Damascus was founded by Uz, grandson of Shem. It is first mentioned in Scripture in connection with Abraham, Gen. 14 : 15, whose steward was a native of the place. Gen. 15 : 2. At one

The Great Mosque at Damascus.

time David became complete master of the whole territory, which he garrisoned with Israelites. 2 Sam. 8 : 5, 6. It was in league with Baasha, king of Israel, against Asa, 1 Kings 15 : 19 ; 2 Chron. 16 : 3, and afterwards in league with Asa against Baasha. 1 Kings 15 : 20. Under Ahaz it was taken by Tiglath-pileser, 2 Kings 16 : 7, 8, 9, the kingdom of Damascus brought to an end, and the city itself destroyed, the inhabitants being carried captive into Assyria. 2 Kings 16 : 9 ; comp. Isa. 7 : 8 and Amos 1 : 5. Afterwards it passed successively under the dominion of the Assyrians, Babylonians, Persians, Macedonians, Romans and Saracens, and was at last captured by the Turks in 1516 A.D. Here the apostle Paul was converted and preached the gospel. Acts 9 : 1–25.

Damascus has always been a great centre for trade. Its present population is from 100,000 to 150,000. It has a delightful climate. Certain localities are shown as the site of those scriptural events which specially interest us in its history. Queen's Street, which runs straight through the city from east to west, may be the street called Straight. Acts 9 : 11. The house of Judas and that of Ananias are shown, but little confidence can be placed in any of these traditions.

Dan (*a judge*). 1. The fifth son of Jacob, and the first of Bilhah, Rachel's maid. Gen. 30 : 6. (B.C. after 1753.) The origin of the name is given in the exclamation of Rachel. The records of Dan are unusually meagre. Only one son is attributed to him, Gen. 46 : 23 ; but his tribe was, with the exception of Judah, the most numerous of all. In the division of the promised land Dan was the last of the tribes to receive his portion, which was the smallest of the twelve. Josh. 19 : 48. But notwithstanding its smallness it had eminent natural advantages. On the north and east it was completely embraced by its two brother tribes Ephraim and Benjamin, while on the southeast and south it joined Judah, and was thus surrounded by the three most powerful states of the whole confederacy. It was a rich and fertile district ; but the Amorites soon "forced them into the mountain," Judges 1 : 34, and they had another portion granted them. Judges 18. In the "security" and "quiet," Judges 18 : 7, 10, of their

Wall of Damascus.

rich northern possession the Danites enjoyed the leisure and repose which had been denied them in their original seat. In the time of David Dan still kept its place among the tribes. 1 Chron. 12 : 35.

The Street called Straight. (Damascus.)

Asher is omitted, but the "prince of the tribe of Dan" is mentioned in the list of 1 Chron. 27 : 22. But from this time forward the name as applied to the tribe vanishes; it is kept alive only by the northern city. In the genealogies of 1 Chron. 2–12, Dan is omitted entirely. Lastly, Dan is omitted from the list of those who were sealed by the angel in the vision of St. John. Rev. 7 : 5–7.

2. The well-known city, so familiar as the most northern landmark of Palestine, in the common expression "from Dan even to Beersheba." The name of the place was originally LAISH or LE-SHEM. Josh. 19 : 47. After the establishment of the Danites at Dan it became the acknowledged extremity of the country. It is now *Tell el-Kadi*, a mound, three miles from Banias, from the foot of which gushes out one of the largest fountains in the world, the main source of the Jordan.

Dan'ites, The. The descendants of Dan and the members of his tribe. Judges 13 : 2 ; 18 : 1, 11 ; 1 Chron. 12 : 35.

Dan-ja'an (*Danian*, i. e. belonging to Dan). 2 Sam. 24 : 6. Probably the same as DAN.

Dance. The dance is spoken of in Holy Scripture universally as symbolical of some rejoicing, and is often coupled for the sake of contrast with mourning, as in Eccles. 3 : 4 ; comp. Ps. 30 : 11 ; Matt. 11 : 17. In the earlier period it is found combined with some song or refrain, Ex. 15 : 20 ; 32 : 18, 19 ; 1 Sam. 21 : 11, and with the tambourine (Authorized Version "timbrel"), more especially in those impulsive outbursts of popular feeling which cannot find sufficient vent in voice or in gesture singly. Dancing formed a part of the religious ceremonies of the Egyptians, and was also common in private entertainments. For the most part dancing was carried on by the women, the two sexes seldom and not customarily intermingling. The one who happened to be near of kin to the champion of the hour led the dance. In the earlier period of the Judges the dances of the virgins of Shiloh, Judges 21 : 19–23, were certainly part of a religious festivity. Dancing also had its place among merely festive amusements, apart from any religious character. Jer. 31 : 4, 13 ; Mark 6 : 22.

Dance, a musical instrument of percussion, supposed to have been used by the Hebrews at an early period of their history.

Dan'iel (*judgment of God*). 1. The second son of David, by Abigail the Carmelitess. 1 Chron. 3 : 1. In 2 Sam. 3 : 3 he is called Chileab. (B.C. about 1051.)

2. The fourth of "the greater prophets." Nothing is known of his parentage or family. He appears, however, to have been of royal or noble descent, Dan. 1 : 3, and to have possessed considerable personal endowments. Dan. 1 : 4. He was taken to Babylon in "the third year of Jehoiakim" (B.C. 604), and trained for the king's service. He was divinely supported in his resolve to abstain from the "king's meat" for fear of defilement. Dan. 1 : 8–16. At the close of his three-years discipline, Dan. 1 : 5, 18, Daniel had an opportunity of exercising his peculiar gift, Dan. 1 : 17, of interpreting

dreams, on the occasion of Nebuchadnezzar's decree against the Magi. Dan. 2 : 14 ff. In consequence of his success he was made "ruler of the whole province of Babylon." Dan. 2 : 48. He afterwards interpreted the second dream of Nebuchadnezzar, Dan. 4 : 8–27, and the handwriting on the wall which disturbed the feast of Belshazzar. Dan. 5 : 10–28. At the accession of Darius he was made first of the "three presidents" of the empire, Dan. 6 : 2, and was delivered from the lions' den, into which he had been cast for his faithfulness to the rites of his faith. Dan. 6 : 10–23; cf. Bel and Dr. 29–42. At the accession of Cyrus he still retained his prosperity, Dan. 6 : 28, cf. 1 : 21, though he does not appear to have remained at Babylon, cf. Dan. 1 : 21; and in "the third year of Cyrus" (B.C. 534) he saw his last recorded vision, on the banks of the Tigris. Dan. 10 : 1, 4. In the prophecies of Ezekiel mention is made of Daniel as a pattern of righteousness, Ezek. 14 : 14, 20, and wisdom. Ezek. 28 : 3. The narrative in Dan. 1 : 11 implies that Daniel was conspicuously distinguished for purity and knowledge at a very early age.

3. A descendant of Ithamar, who returned with Ezra. Ezra 8 : 2.

4. A priest who sealed the covenant drawn up by Nehemiah, B.C. 445. Neh. 10 : 6. He is perhaps the same as No. 3.

Dan′iel, The book of, stands at the head of a series of writings in which the deepest thoughts of the Jewish people found expression after the close of the prophetic era. Daniel is composed partly in the vernacular Aramaic (Chaldee) and partly in the sacred Hebrew. The introduction, Dan. 1–2 : 4 a, is written in Hebrew. On the occasion of the "Syriac" (i. e. Aramaic) answer of the Chaldeans, the language changes to Aramaic, and this is retained till the close of the seventh chapter (2 : 4 b–7). The personal introduction of Daniel as the writer of the text, 8 : 1, is marked by the resumption of the Hebrew, which continues to the close of the book. ch. 8–12.

The book may be divided into three parts. The first chapter forms an introduction. The next six chapters, 2–7, give a general view of the progressive history of the powers of the world, and of the principles of the divine government as seen in the events of the life of Daniel. The remainder of the book, chs. 8–12, traces in minuter detail the

fortunes of the people of God, as typical of the fortunes of the Church in all ages. In the first seven chapters Daniel is spoken of *historically*; in the last five he appears *personally* as the writer. The cause of the difference of person is commonly supposed to lie in the nature of the case. It is, however, more probable that the peculiarity arose from the manner in which the book assumed its final shape. The book exercised a great influence upon the Christian Church. The New Testament incidentally acknowledges each of the characteristic elements of the book, its miracles, Heb. 11 : 33, 34, its predictions, Matt. 24 : 15, and its doctrine of angels. Luke 1 : 19, 26.

The authenticity of the book has been attacked in modern times. (But the evidence, both external and internal, is conclusive as to its genuineness. Rawlinson, in his "Historical Evidences," shows how some historical difficulties that had been brought against the book are solved by the inscription on a cylinder lately found among the ruins of Ur in Chaldea.—ED.)

Dan′iel, Apocryphal additions to. The Greek translations of Daniel contain several pieces which are not found in the original text. The most important are contained in the Apocrypha of the English Bible under the titles of *The Song of the Three Holy Children*, *The History of Susannah*, and *The History of . . . Bel and the Dragon*. The first of these is supposed to be the triumphal song of the three confessors in the furnace, Dan. 3 : 23, praising God for their deliverance, of which a chief part (35–66) has been used as a hymn in the Christian Church since the fourth century. The second, called also *The Judgment of Daniel*, relates the story of the clearing of Susannah from a charge of adultery; and the third gives an exaggerated account of Daniel's deliverance.

Dan′nah, a city in the mountains of Judah, Josh. 15 : 49, and probably south or southwest of Hebron. No trace of its name has been discovered.

Da′ra. 1 Chron. 2 : 6. [DARDA.]

Dar′da (*pearl of wisdom*), a son of Mahol, one of four men of great fame for their wisdom, but surpassed by Solomon. 1 Kings 4 : 31. (B.C. before 1010.)

Daric (from *dara*, a *king*), Authorized Version "dram," 1 Chron. 29 : 7; Ezra 2 : 69; 8 : 27; Neh. 7 : 70, 71, 72, a gold coin current in Palestine in the period after the return from Babylon. It weighed 128 grains, and was worth about five dollars. At these times there was no large issue of gold money except by the Persian kings. The darics which have been discovered are thick pieces of pure gold, of archaic style, bearing on the obverse the figure of a king with bow and javelin or bow and dagger, and on the reverse an irregular incuse square. The silver daric was worth about fifty cents.

Dari'us (*lord*), the name of several kings of Media and Persia. 1. DARIUS THE MEDE, Dan. 6 : 1; 11 : 1, "the son of Ahasuerus," Dan. 9 : 1, who succeeded to the Babylonian kingdom on the death of Belshazzar, being then sixty-two years old. Dan. 5 : 31; 9 : 1. (B.C. 538.) Only one year of his reign is mentioned, Dan. 9 : 1; 11 : 1, but that was of great importance for the Jews. Daniel was advanced by the king to the highest dignity, Dan. 6 : 1 ff., and in his reign was cast into the lions' den, Dan. 6. This Darius is probably the same as "Astyages," the last king of the Medes.

2. DARIUS, the son of Hystaspes the founder of the Perso-Arian dynasty. Upon the usurpation of the magian Smerdis, he conspired with six other Persian chiefs to overthrow the impostor, and on the success of the plot was placed upon the throne, B.C. 521. With regard to the Jews, Darius Hystaspes pursued the same policy as Cyrus, and restored to them the privileges which they had lost. Ezra 5 : 1, etc.; 6 : 1, etc.

3. DARIUS THE PERSIAN, Neh. 12 : 22, may be identified with Darius II. Nothus (Ochus), king of Persia B.C. 424–3 to 405–4; but it is not improbable that it points to Darius III. Codomannus, the antagonist of Alexander and the last king of Persia, B.C. 336–330.

Darkness is spoken of as encompassing the actual presence of God, as that out of which he speaks,—the envelope, as it were, of divine glory. Ex. 20 : 21; 1 Kings 8 : 12. The plague of darkness in Egypt was miraculous. The darkness "over all the land," Matt. 27 : 45, attending the crucifixion has been attributed to an eclipse, but was undoubtedly miraculous, as no eclipse of the sun could have taken place at that time, the moon being at the full at the time of the passover. Darkness is also, as in the expression "land of darkness," used for the state of the dead, Job 10 : 21, 22; and frequently, figuratively, for ignorance and

unbelief, as the privation of spiritual light. John 1 : 5; 3 : 19.

Dar'kon (*scatterer*). Children of Darkon were among the "servants of Solomon" who returned from Babylon with Zerubbabel. Ezra 2 : 56; Neh. 7 : 58. (B.C. before 536.)

Dates. 2 Chron. 31 : 5, marg. [PALM TREE.]

Da'than (*belonging to a fountain*), a Reubenite chieftain, son of Eliab, who joined the conspiracy of Korah the Levite. Num. 16 : 1; 26 : 9; Deut. 11 : 6; Ps. 106 : 17. (B.C. 1490–1452.)

Daughter. The word is used in Scripture not only for daughter, but for granddaughter or other female descendant. Gen. 24 : 48. It is used of the female inhabitants of a place or country, Gen. 6 : 2; Luke 23 : 28, and of cities in general, Isa. 10 : 32; 23 : 12, but more specifically of dependent towns or hamlets, while to the principal city the correlative "mother" is applied. Num. 21 : 25. "Daughters of music," *i. e.* singing birds, Eccles. 12 : 4, refers to the power of making and enjoying music.

Da'vid (*well-beloved*), the son of Jesse. His life may be divided into three portions: 1. His youth before his introduction to the court of Saul; 2. His relations with Saul; 3. His reign.

1. *The early life of David* contains in many important respects the antecedents of his future career. It appears that David was the youngest son, probably the youngest child, of a family of ten, and was born in Bethlehem B.C. 1085. The first time that David appears in history at once admits us to the whole family circle. The annual sacrificial feast is being held when Samuel appears, sent by God to anoint one of Jesse's sons as king of Israel in place of Saul. 1 Sam. 16 : 1. Rejecting the elder sons as they pass before him, 16 : 6–10, Samuel sends for the youngest, David, who was "keeping the sheep," and anoints him. 1 Sam. 16 : 11–13. As David stood before Samuel we are enabled to fix his appearance at once in our minds. He was of short stature, with red or auburn hair, such as is not unfrequently seen in his countrymen of the East at the present day. In later life he wore a beard. His bright eyes are specially mentioned, 1 Sam. 16 : 12, and generally he was remarkable for the grace of his figure and countenance ("fair of eyes," "comely," "goodly,"

1 Sam. 16 : 12, 18; 17 : 42), well made, and of immense strength and agility. His swiftness and activity made him like a wild gazelle, his feet like hart's feet, and his arms strong enough to break a bow of steel. Ps. 18 : 33, 34. After the anointing David resumes his accustomed duties, and the next we know of him he is summoned to the court to chase away the king's madness by music, 1 Sam. 16 : 14-19, and in the successful effort of David's harp we have the first glimpse into that genius for music and poetry which was afterwards consecrated in the Psalms. After this he returned to the old shepherd life again. One incident alone of his solitary shepherd life has come down to us—his conflict with the lion and the bear in defence of his father's flocks. 1 Sam. 17 : 34, 35. It was some years after this that David suddenly appears before his brothers in the camp of the army, and hears the defiant challenge of the Philistine giant Goliath. With his shepherd's sling and five small pebbles he goes forth and defeats the giant. 1 Sam. 17 : 40-51.

2. *Relations with Saul.*—We now enter on a new aspect of David's life. The victory over Goliath had been a turning-point of his career. Saul inquired his parentage, and took him finally to his court. Jonathan was inspired by the romantic friendship which bound the two youths together to the end of their lives. Unfortunately David's fame proved the foundation of that unhappy jealousy of Saul towards him which, mingling with the king's constitutional malady, poisoned his whole future relations to David. His position in Saul's court seems to have been first armor-bearer, 1 Sam. 16 : 21; 18 : 2, then captain over a thousand, 18 : 13, and finally, on his marriage with Michal, the king's second daughter, he was raised to the high office of captain of the king's body-guard, second only, if not equal, to Abner, the captain of the host, and Jonathan, the heir apparent. David was now chiefly known for his successful exploits against the Philistines, by one of which he won his wife, and drove back the Philistine power with a blow from which it only rallied at the disastrous close of Saul's reign. He also still performed from time to time the office of minstrel; but the successive attempts of Saul upon his life convinced him that he was in constant danger. He had two faithful allies, however, in the court—the son of Saul, his friend Jonathan, and the daughter of Saul, his wife Michal. Warned by the one and assisted by the other, he escaped by night, and was from thenceforward a fugitive. He at first found a home at the court of Achish, among the Philistines; but his stay was short. Discovered possibly by "the sword of Goliath," his presence revived the national enmity of the Philistines against their former conqueror, and he only escaped by feigning madness. 1 Sam. 21 : 13. His first retreat was the cave of Adullam. In this vicinity he was joined by his whole family, 1 Sam. 22 : 1, and by a motley crowd of debtors and discontented men, 22 : 2, which formed the nucleus of his army. David's life for the next few years was made up of a succession of startling incidents. He secures an important ally in Abiathar, 1 Sam. 23 : 6; his band of 400 at Adullam soon increased to 600, 23 : 13; he is hunted by Saul from place to place like a partridge. 1 Sam. 23 : 14, 22, 25-29; 24 : 1-22; 26. He marries Abigail and Ahinoam. 1 Sam. 25 : 42, 43. Finally comes the news of the battle of Gilboa and the death of Saul and Jonathan. 1 Sam. 31. The reception of the tidings of the death of his rival and of his friend, the solemn mourning, the vent of his indignation against the bearer of the message, the pathetic lamentation that followed, will close the second period of David's life. 2 Sam. 1 : 1-27.

3. *David's reign.*—1. As king of Judah at Hebron, 7½ years. 2 Sam. 2 : 1-5 : 5. Here David was first formally anointed king. 2 Sam. 2 : 4. To Judah his dominion was nominally confined. Gradually his power increased, and during the two years which followed the elevation of Ish-bosheth a series of skirmishes took place between the two kingdoms. Then rapidly followed the successive murders of Abner and of Ish-bosheth. 2 Sam. 3 : 30; 4 : 5. The throne, so long waiting for him, was now vacant, and the united voice of the whole people at once called him to occupy it. For the third time David was anointed king, and a festival of three days celebrated the joyful event. 1 Chron. 12 : 39. One of David's first acts after becoming king was to secure Jerusalem, which he seized from the Jebusites and fixed the royal residence there. Fortifications were added by the king and by Joab, and it was known by the special name of the " city

of David." 2 Sam. 5 : 9 ; 1 Chron. 11 : 7. The ark was now removed from its obscurity at Kirjath-jearim with marked solemnity, and conveyed to Jerusalem.

The erection of the new capital at Jerusalem introduces us to a new era in David's life and in the history of the monarchy. He became a king on the scale of the great Oriental sovereigns of Egypt and Persia, with a regular administration and organization of court and camp ; and he also founded an imperial dominion which for the first time realized the prophetic description of the bounds of the chosen people. Gen. 15 : 18-21. During the succeeding ten years the nations bordering on his kingdom caused David more or less trouble, but during this time he reduced to a state of permanent subjection the Philistines on the west, 2 Sam. 8 : 1 ; the Moabites on the east, 2 Sam. 8 : 2, by the exploits of Benaiah, 2 Sam. 23 : 20 ; the Syrians on the northeast as far as the Euphrates, 2 Sam. 8 : 3 ; the Edomites, 2 Sam. 8 : 14, on the south ; and finally the Ammonites, who had broken their ancient alliance, and made one grand resistance to the advance of his empire. 2 Sam. 10 : 1-19 ; 12 : 26-31.

Three great calamities may be selected as marking the beginning, middle and close of David's otherwise prosperous reign, which appear to be intimated in the question of Gad, 2 Sam. 24 : 13, " a three-years famine, a three-months flight or a three-days pestilence." *a.* Of these the first (the three-years famine) introduces us to the last notices of David's relations with the house of Saul, already referred to. *b.* The second group of incidents contains the tragedy of David's life, which grew in all its parts out of the polygamy, with its evil consequences, into which he had plunged on becoming king. Underneath the splendor of his last glorious campaign against the Ammonites was a dark story, known probably at that time only to a very few—the double crime of adultery with Bath-sheba and the virtual murder of Uriah. The

clouds from this time gathered over David's fortunes, and henceforward "the sword never departed from his house." 2 Sam. 12 : 10. The outrage on his daughter Tamar, the murder of his eldest son Amnon, and then the revolt of his best-beloved, Absalom, brought on the crisis which once more sent him forth a wanderer, as in the days when he fled from Saul. 2 Sam. 15 : 18. The final battle of Absalom's rebellion was fought in the " forest of Ephraim," and terminated in the accident which led to the young man's death ; and, though nearly heart-broken at the loss of his son, David again reigned in undisturbed peace at

The Tomb of David. (*From an original Photograph.*)

Jerusalem. 2 Sam. 20 : 1-22. *c.* The closing period of David's life, with the exception of one great calamity, may be considered as a gradual preparation for the reign of his successor. This calamity was the three-days pestilence which visited Jerusalem at the warning of the prophet Gad. The occasion which led to this warning was the census of the people taken by Joab at the king's orders, 2 Sam. 24 : 1-9 ; 1 Chron. 21 : 1-7 ; 27 : 23, 24, which was for some reason sinful in God's sight. 2 Sam. 24. A formidable conspiracy to interrupt the succession broke out in the last days of David's reign ; but the plot was stifled, and Solomon's inauguration took place under his father's auspices. 1 Kings 1 : 1-53. By this time David's infirmities had grown upon him. His last song is preserved—a striking union of the ideal of a just ruler which he had placed before him and of the difficulties which he had felt in realizing it. 2 Sam. 23 : 1–7. His last words to his successor are general exhortations to his duty. 1 Kings 2 : 1–9. He died, according to Josephus, at the age of 70, and "was buried in the city of David." After the return from the captivity, "the sepulchres of David" were still pointed out "between Siloah and the house of the mighty men," or "the guard-house." Neh. 3 : 16. His tomb, which became the general sepulchre of the kings of Judah, was pointed out in the latest times of the Jewish people. The edifice shown as such from the Crusades to the present day is on the southern hill of modern Jerusalem, commonly called Mount Zion, under the so-called "Cœnaculum;" but it cannot be identified with the tomb of David, which was emphatically *within* the walls.

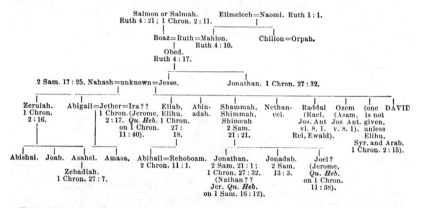

Salmon or Salmah. Ruth 4 : 21; 1 Chron. 2 : 11.

Elimelech=Naomi. Ruth 1 : 1.

Boaz=Ruth=Mahlon. Ruth 4 : 10.

Chilion=Orpah.

Obed. Ruth 4 : 17.

2 Sam. 17 : 25, Nahash=unknown=Jesse.

Jonathan. 1 Chron. 27 : 32.

Zeruiah. 1 Chron. 2 : 16.

Abigail=Jether=Ira ? ? 1 Chron. (Jerome, Elihu. 2 : 17. *Qu. Heb.* on 1 Chron. 11 : 40).

Eliab, Elihu. 1 Chron. 27 : 18.

Abinadab.

Shammah, Shimmah, Shimeah 2 Sam. 21 : 21.

Nethaneel.

Raddai (Rael, Jos. Ant vi. 8. 1. Rei, Ewald).

Ozem (Asam, Jos. Ant. v. 8. 1).

(one DAVID is not given, unless Elihu, Syr. and Arab. 1 Chron. 2 : 15).

Abishai.

Joab.

Asahel. Zebadiah. 1 Chron. 27 : 7.

Amasa.

Abihail=Rehoboam. 2 Chron. 11 : 1.

Jonathan. 2 Sam. 21 : 1; 1 Chron. 27 : 32. (Nathan ? ? Jer. *Qu. Heb.* on 1 Sam. 16 : 12).

Jonadab. 2 Sam. 13 : 3.

Joel? (Jerome, *Qu. Heb.* on 1 Chron. 11 : 38).

Da'vid, City of. [JERUSALEM.]

Day. The variable length of the natural day at different seasons led in the very earliest times to the adoption of the civil day (or one revolution of the sun) as a standard of time. The Hebrews reckoned the day from evening to evening, Lev. 23 : 32, deriving it from Gen. 1 : 5, " the *evening* and the *morning* were the first day." The Jews are supposed, like the modern Arabs, to have adopted from an early period minute specifications of the parts of the natural day. Roughly, indeed, they were content to divide it into "morning, evening and noonday," Ps. 55 : 17; but when they wished for greater accuracy they pointed to six unequal parts, each of which was again subdivided. These are held to have been—1. "The dawn." 2. "Sunrise." 3. "Heat of the day," about 9 o'clock. 4. "The two noons," Gen. 43 : 16; Deut. 28 : 29. 5. "The cool (lit. *wind*) of the day," before sunset, Gen. 3 : 8,—so called by the Persians to this day. 6. "Evening." Before the captivity the Jews divided the night into three watches, Ps. 63 : 6; 90 : 4, viz. the first watch, lasting till midnight, Lam. 2 : 19; the "middle watch," lasting till cockcrow, Judges 7 : 19; and the "morning watch," lasting till sunrise. Ex. 14 : 24. In the New Testament we have allusions to four watches, a division borrowed from the Greeks and Romans. These were—1. From twilight till 9 o'clock, Mark 11 : 11; John 20 : 19. 2. Midnight, from 9 till 12 o'clock, Mark 13 : 35. 3. Till 3 in the morning, Mark 13 : 35; 3 Macc. 5 : 23. 4. Till daybreak. John 18 : 28. The word held to mean "hour" is first found in Dan. 3 : 6, 15; 5 : 5. Perhaps the Jews, like the Greeks, learned from the Babylonians the division of the day into twelve parts. In our Lord's time the division was common. John 11 : 9.

Daysman, an old English term, meaning *umpire* or *arbitrator.* Job 9 : 33.

Deacon. The office described by this title appears in the New Testament as the correlative of bishop. [BISHOP.] The two are mentioned together in Philip. 1 : 1; 1 Tim. 3 : 2, 8. Its original meaning implied a helper, an assistant. The bishops were the " elders," the deacons the young active men, of the church. The narrative of Acts 6 is commonly referred to as giving an account of the institution of this office. The apostles, in order to meet the complaints of the Hellenistic Jews that their widows were neglected in the daily ministration, call on the body of believers to choose seven men " full of the Holy Ghost and of wisdom," whom they " may appoint over this business." It may be questioned, however, whether the seven were not appointed to higher functions than those of the deacons of the New Testament. *Qualifications and duties.*—Special directions as to the qualifications for and the duties of deacons will be found in Acts 6 : 1–6 and 1 Tim. 3 : 8–12. From the analogy of the synagogue, and from the scanty notices in the New Testament, we may think of the deacons or " young men" at Jerusalem as preparing the rooms for meetings, distributing alms, maintaining order at the meetings, baptizing new converts, distributing the elements at the Lord's Supper.

Deaconess. The word διάκονος is found in Rom. 16 : 1 (Authorized Version " servant ") associated with a female name, and this has led to the conclusion that there existed in the apostolic age, as there undoubtedly did a little later, an order of women bearing that title, and exercising in relation to their own sex functions which were analogous to those of the deacons. On this hypothesis it has been inferred that the women mentioned in Rom. 16 : 6, 12 belonged to such an order. The rules given as to the conduct of women in 1 Tim. 3 : 11, Titus 2 : 3, have in like manner been referred to them, and they have been identified even with the " widows" of 1 Tim. 5 : 3–10.

Dead Sea. This name nowhere occurs in the Bible, and appears not to have existed until the second century after Christ. [See SEA, THE SALT.]

Dearth. [FAMINE.]

De'bir (*a sanctuary*), the name of three places of Palestine. 1. A town in the mountains of Judah, Josh. 15 : 49, one of a group of eleven cities to the west of Hebron. The earlier name of Debir was Kirjath-sepher, " city of book," Josh. 15 : 15; Judges 1 : 11, and Kirjath-sannah, " city of palm." Josh. 15 : 49. It was one of the cities given with their " suburbs" to the priests. Josh. 21 : 15; 1 Chron. 6 : 58. Debir has not been dis-

covered with certainty in modern times; but about three miles to the west of Hebron is a deep and secluded valley called the *Wady Nunkûr*, enclosed on the north by hills, of which one bears a name certainly suggestive of Debir—*Dewir-ban*. 2. A place on the north boundary of Judah, near the " valley of Achor." Josh. 15 : 7. A *Wady Dabor* is marked in Van de Velde's map as close to the south of *Neby Mûsa*, at the northwest corner of the Dead Sea. 3. The "border of Debir" is named as forming part of the boundary of Gad, Josh. 13 : 26, and as apparently not far from Mahanaim.

De'bir, king of Eglon; one of the five kings hanged by Joshua. Josh. 10 : 3, 23. (B.C. 1445.)

Deb'orah (*a bee*). (B.C. 1857.) 1. The nurse of Rebekah. Gen. 35 : 8. Deborah accompanied Rebekah from the house of Bethuel, Gen. 24 : 59, and is only mentioned by name on the occasion of her burial under the oak tree of Bethel, which was called in her honor Allon-bachuth.

2. A prophetess who judged Israel. Judges 4, 5. (B.C. 1316.) She lived under the palm tree of Deborah, between Ramah and Bethel in Mount Ephraim, Judges 4 : 5, which, as palm trees were rare in Palestine, " is mentioned as a well-known and solitary landmark." She was probably a woman of Ephraim. Lapidoth was probably her husband, and not Barak, as some say. She was not so much a judge as one gifted with prophetic command, Judges 4 : 6, 14; 5 : 7, and by virtue of her inspiration " a mother in Israel." The tyranny of Jabin, a Canaanitish king, was peculiarly felt in the northern tribes, who were near his capital and under her jurisdiction. Under her direction Barak encamped on the broad summit of Tabor. Deborah's prophecy was fulfilled, Judges 4 : 9, and the enemy's general perished among the " oaks of the wanderers " (Zaanaim), in the tent of the Bedouin Kenite's wife, Judges 4 : 21, in the northern mountains. Deborah's title of " prophetess " includes the notion of inspired poetry, as in Ex. 15 : 20; and in this sense the glorious triumphal ode, Judges 5, well vindicates her claim to the office.

Debtor. [LOAN.]

De'dan (*low country*). 1. The name of a son of Raamah, son of Cush. Gen 10 : 7; 1 Chron. 1 : 9.

2. **A son of** Jokshan, son of Keturah. Gen. 25 : 3; 1 Chron. 1 : 32. (B.C. after 1988.)

Ded'anim, descendants of Dedan I. Isa. 21 : 13. [DEDAN.]

Dedication, Feast of the, the festival instituted to commemorate the purging of the temple and the rebuilding of the altar after Judas Maccabæus had driven out the Syrians, B.C. 164. 1 Macc. 4 : 52–59. It is named only once in the canonical Scriptures. John 10 : 22. It commenced on the 25th of Chisleu (early in December), the anniversary of the pollution of the temple by Antiochus Epiphanes, B.C. 167. Like the great Mosaic feasts, it lasted eight days, but it did not require attendance at Jerusalem. It was an occasion of much festivity, and was celebrated in nearly the same manner as the feast of tabernacles, with the carrying of branches of trees and with much singing. In the temple at Jerusalem the "Hallel" was sung every day of the feast.

Deer. [FALLOW-DEER.]

Degrees, Songs of, a title given to fifteen Psalms, from 120 to 134 inclusive. Four of them are attributed to David, one is ascribed to the pen of Solomon, and the other ten give no indication of their author. With respect to the term rendered in the Authorized Version "degrees" a great diversity of views prevails, but the most probable opinion is that they were pilgrim songs, sung by the people as they went up to Jerusalem.

De'havites, mentioned only once in Scripture, Ezra 4 : 9, among the colonists planted in Samaria after the completion of the captivity of Israel. They are probably the Daï or Dahi, mentioned by Herodotus (i. 125) among the nomadic tribes of Persia.

De'kar (*a lancer*). The son of Dekar, *i. e.* Ben Dekar, was Solomon's commissariat officer in the western part of the hill-country of Judah and Benjamin, Shaalbim and Bethshemesh. 1 Kings 4 : 9. (B.C. before 1014.)

Dela-i'ah (*freed by Jehovah*). 1. A priest in the time of David, leader of the twenty-third course of priests. 1 Chron. 24 : 18. (B.C. 1014.)

2. "Children of Delaiah" were among the people of uncertain pedigree who returned from Babylon with Zerubbabel. Ezra 2 : 60; Neh. 7 : 62. (B.C. 536.)

3. Son of Mehetabeel and father of Shemaiah. Neh. 6 : 10. (B.C. before 410.)

4. Son of Shemaiah, one of the "princes" about the court of Jehoiakim. Jer. 36 : 12, 25. (B.C. 604.)

Del'ilah, or **Deli'lah** (*languishing*), a woman who dwelt in the valley of Sorek, beloved by Samson. Judges 16 : 4–18. There seems to be little doubt that she was a Philistine courtesan. [SAMSON.] (B.C. 1141.)

Deluge. [NOAH.]

De'mas (*governor of the people*), most probably a contraction from Demetrius, or perhaps from Demarchus, a companion of St. Paul, Phil. 24; Col. 4 : 14, during his first imprisonment at Rome. (B.C. 57.) At a later period, 2 Tim. 4 : 10, we find him mentioned as having deserted the apostle through love of this present world, and gone to Thessalonica.

Deme'trius (*belonging to Ceres*). 1. A maker of silver shrines of Artemis at Ephesus. Acts 19 : 24 (about A.D. 52). These were small models of the great temple of the Ephesian Artemis, with her statue, which it was customary to carry on journeys, and place on houses as charms.

2. A disciple, 3 John 12, mentioned with commendation (about A.D. 90). Possibly the first Demetrius, converted; but this is very doubtful.

Demon. In the Gospels generally, in James 2 : 19 and in Rev. 16 : 14 the demons are spoken of as spiritual beings, at enmity with God, and having power to afflict man not only with disease, but, as is marked by the frequent epithet "unclean," with spiritual pollution also. They "believe" the power of God "and tremble," James 2 : 19; they recognized the Lord as the Son of God, Matt. 8 : 29; Luke 4 : 41, and acknowledged the power of his name, used in exorcism, in the place of the name of Jehovah, by his appointed messengers, Acts 19 : 15; and looked forward in terror to the judgment to come. Matt. 8 : 29. The description is precisely that of a nature akin to the angelic in knowledge and powers, but with the emphatic addition of the idea of positive and active wickedness.

Demoniacs. This word is frequently used in the New Testament, and applied to persons suffering under the possession of a demon or evil spirit, such possession generally showing itself visibly in bodily disease or mental derangement. It has been maintained by many persons that our Lord and the evangelists, in referring to demonical possession, spoke only in accommodation to the general belief of the Jews, without any assertion as to its truth or its falsity. It is concluded that, since the symptoms of the affliction were frequently those of bodily disease (as dumbness, Matt. 9 : 32; blindness, Matt. 12 : 22; epilepsy, Mark 9 : 17–27), or those seen in cases of ordinary insanity (as in Matt. 8 : 28; Mark 5 : 1–5), the demoniacs were merely persons suffering under unusual diseases of body and mind. But demoniacs are frequently distinguished from those afflicted with bodily sickness, see Mark 1 : 32; 16 : 17, 18; Luke 6 : 17, 18; the same outward signs are sometimes referred to possession, sometimes merely to disease, comp. Matt. 4 : 24 with 17 : 15; Matt. 12 : 22 with Mark 7 : 32, etc.; the demons are represented as speaking in their own persons with superhuman knowledge. Matt. 8 : 29; Mark 1 : 24; 5 : 7; Luke 4 : 41, etc. All these things speak of a personal power of evil. Twice our Lord distinctly connects demoniacal possession with the power of the evil one. Luke 10 : 18. Lastly, the single fact recorded of the entrance of the demons at Gadara, Mark 5 : 10–14, into the herd of swine, and the effect which that entrance caused, is sufficient to overthrow the notion that our Lord and the evangelists do not assert or imply any objective reality of possession. We are led, therefore, to the ordinary and literal interpretation of these passages, that there are evil spirits, subjects of the evil one, who, in the days of the Lord himself and his apostles especially, were permitted by God to exercise a direct influence over the souls and bodies of certain men.

Denarius (*containing ten*), Authorized Version "penny," Matt. 18 : 28; 20 : 2, 9, 13, a Roman silver coin in the time of our Saviour and the apostles, worth about 15 cents. It took its name from its being first equal to ten "asses," a number afterwards increased to sixteen. It was the principal silver **coin of** the Roman commonwealth. From the parable of the laborers in the vineyard it would seem that a denarius was then the ordinary pay for a day's labor. Matt. 20 : 2, 4, 7, 9, 10, 13.

Deputy. Acts 13 : 7, 8, 12; 19 : 38. The Greek word signifies proconsul, the title of the Roman governors who were appointed by the senate.

Der'be. Acts 14 : 20, 21; 16 : 1; 20 : 4. The exact position of this town has not yet been ascertained, but its general situation is undoubted. It was in the eastern part of the great upland plain of Lycaonia, which stretches from Iconium eastward along the north side of the chain of Taurus. (Rev. L. H. Adams, a missionary, identifies it with the modern *Divlé*, a town of about 4500 inhabitants, on the ancient road between Tarsus and Lystra.—ED.)

Desert. Not a stretch of sand, an utterly barren waste, but a wild, uninhabited region. The words rendered in the Authorized Version by "desert," when used in the historical books denote definite localities.

1. ARABAH. This word means that very depressed and enclosed region—the deepest and the hottest chasm in the world—the sunken valley north and south of the Dead Sea, but more particularly the former. [ARABAH.] Arabah in the sense of the Jordan valley is translated by the word "desert" only in Ezek. 47 : 8.

2. MIDBAR. This word, which our translators have most frequently rendered by "desert," is accurately "the pasture ground." It is most frequently used for those tracts of waste land which lie beyond the cultivated ground in the immediate neighborhood of the towns and villages of Palestine, and which are a very familiar feature to the traveller in that country. Ex. 3 : 1; 5 : 3; 19 : 2.

3. CHARBAH appears to have the force of dryness, and thence of desolation. It is rendered "desert" in Ps. 102 : 6; Isa. 48 : 21; Ezek. 13 : 4. The term commonly employed for it in the Authorized Version is "waste places" or "desolation."

4. JESHIMON, with the definite article, apparently denotes the waste tracts on both sides of the Dead Sea. In all these cases it is treated as a proper name in the Authorized Version. Without the article it occurs in a few passages of poetry, in the following of which it is rendered "desert:" Ps. 78 : 40; 106 : 14; Isa. 43 : 19, 20.

De'uel, or **De-u'el** (*invocation of God*), father of Eliasaph, the "captain" of the tribe of Gad at the time of the numbering of the people at Sinai. Num. 1 : 14; 7 : 42, 47; 10 : 20. (B.C. 1491.) The same man is mentioned again in Num. 2 : 14, but here the name appears as Reuel.

Deuteron'omy—which means "the

repetition of the law"—consists chiefly of three discourses delivered by Moses shortly before his death. Subjoined to these discourses are the Song of Moses, the Blessing of Moses, and the story of his death. 1. The first discourse. Deut. 1 : 1–4 : 40. After a brief historical introduction the speaker recapitulates the chief events of the last forty years in the wilderness. To this discourse is appended a brief notice of the severing of the three cities of refuge on the east side of the Jordan. Deut. 4 : 41–43. 2. The second discourse is introduced like the first by an explanation of the circumstances under which it was delivered. Deut. 4 : 44–49. It extends from chap. 5 : 1–26 : 19, and contains a recapitulation, with some modifications and additions, of the law already given on Mount Sinai. 3. In the third discourse, Deut. 27 : 1–30 : 20, the elders of Israel are associated with Moses. The people are commanded to set up stones upon Mount Ebal, and on them to write "all the words of this law." Then follow the several curses to be pronounced by the Levites on Ebal, Deut. 27 : 14–26, and the blessings on Gerizim. Deut. 28 : 1–14. 4. The delivery of the law as written by Moses (for its still further preservation) to the custody of the Levites, and a charge to the people to hear it read once every seven years, Deut. 31 ; the Song of Moses spoken in the ears of the people, Deut. 31 : 30–32 : 44; and the blessing of the twelve tribes. Deut. 33. 5. The book closes, Deut. 34, with an account of the death of Moses, which is first announced to him ch. 32 : 48–52. The book bears witness to its own authorship, Deut. 31 : 19, and is expressly cited in the New Testament as the work of Moses. Matt. 19 : 7, 8; Mark 10 : 3; Acts 3 : 22; 7 : 37. The last chapter, containing an account of the death of Moses, was of course added by a later hand, and probably formed originally the beginning of the book of Joshua. [PENTATEUCH.]

Devil (*slanderer*). The name describes Satan as slandering God to man and man to God. The former work is, of course, a part of his great work of temptation to evil; and is not only exemplified but illustrated as to its general nature and tendency by the narrative of Gen. 3. The other work, the slandering or accusing man before God, is the imputation of selfish motives, Job 1 : 9, 10, and its refutation is placed in the self-sacrifice of those "who loved not their own lives unto death." [SATAN; DEMON.]

Dew. This in the summer is so copious in Palestine that it supplies to some extent the absence of rain and becomes important to the agriculturist. Thus it is coupled in the divine blessing with rain, or mentioned as a prime source of fertility, Gen. 27 : 28; Deut. 33 : 13; Zech. 8 : 12, and its withdrawal is attributed to a curse. 2 Sam. 1 : 21; 1 Kings 17 : 1; Hag. 1 : 10. It becomes a leading object in prophetic imagery by reason of its penetrating moisture without the apparent effort of rain, Deut. 32 : 2; Job 29 : 19; Ps. 133 : 3; Hos. 14 : 5; while its speedy evanescence typifies the transient goodness of the hypocrite. Hos. 6 : 4; 13 : 3.

Diadem. What the "diadem" of the Jews was we know not. That of other nations of antiquity was a fillet of silk, two inches broad, bound round the head and tied behind. Its invention is attributed to Liber. Its color was generally white; sometimes, however, it was of blue, like that of Darius; and it was sown with pearls or other gems, Zech. 9 : 16, and enriched with gold. Rev. 9 : 7. It was peculiarly the mark of Oriental sovereigns. In Esther 1 : 11; 2 : 17, we have *cether* for the turban worn by the Persian king, queen or other eminent persons to whom it was conceded as a

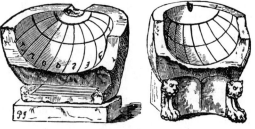

Ancient Dials.

special favor. The diadem of the king differed from that of others in having an *erect* triangular peak. The words in Ezek. 23 : 15 mean long and flowing turbans of gorgeous colors. [CROWN.]

Dial. "An instrument for showing the time of day from the shadow of a style or gnomon on a graduated arc or surface;" rendered "steps" in Authorized Version, Ex. 20 : 26; 1 Kings 10 : 19, and "degrees," 2 Kings 20 : 9, 10, 11; Isa. 38 : 8, where to give a consistent rendering we should read with the margin the "degrees" rather than the "dial" of Ahaz. It is probable that the dial of Ahaz was really a series of steps or stairs, and that the shadow (perhaps of some column or obelisk on the top) fell on a

Diana of the Ephesians.

greater or smaller number of them according as the sun was low or high. The terrace of a palace might easily be thus ornamented.

Diamond (Heb. *yahălóm*), a gem, crystallized carbon, the most valued and brilliant of precious stones, remarkable for its hardness, the third precious stone in the second row on the breastplate of the high priest, Ex. 28 : 18; 39 : 11, and mentioned by Ezekiel, 28 : 13, among the precious stones of the king of Tyre.

Some suppose *yahălóm* to be the "emerald." Respecting *shâmîr*, which is translated "diamond" in Jer. 17 : 1, see under ADAMANT.

Dia'na. This Latin word, properly denoting a Roman divinity, is the representative of the Greek *Artemis*, the tutelary goddess of the Ephesians, who plays so important a part in the narrative of Acts 19. The Ephesian Diana was, however, regarded as invested with very different attributes, and is rather to be identified with Astarte and other female divinities of the East. The head wore a mural crown, each hand held a bar of metal, and the lower part ended in a

Temple of Diana of the Ephesians.

rude block covered with figures of animals and mystic inscriptions. This idol was regarded as an object of peculiar sanctity, and was believed to have fallen down from heaven. Acts 19 : 35.

Dibla'im (*double cake*), mother of Hosea's wife Gomer. Hos. 1 : 3. (B.C. before 725.)

Dib'lath (accurately DIBLAH), a place named only in Ezek. 6 : 14. Probably only another form of RIBLAH.

Di'bon (*wasting*). 1. A town on the east side of Jordan, in the rich pastoral country, which was taken possession of and rebuilt by the children of Gad. Num. 32 : 3, 34. From this circumstance it possibly received the name of DIBON-GAD. Num. 33 : 45, 46. Its first mention is in Num. 21 : 30, and from this it appears to have belonged originally to the Moabites. We find Dibon counted to Reuben in the lists of Joshua. Josh. 13 : 9, 17. In the time of Isaiah and Jeremiah, however, it was again in possession of Moab. Isa. 15 : 2; Jer. 48 : 18, 22, comp. 24. In modern times the name *Dhiban* has been discovered as attached to extensive ruins on the Roman road, about three miles north of the Arnon (*Wady Modjeb*).

2. One of the towns which were re-

inhabited by the men of Judah after the return from captivity, Neh. 11 : 25 ; identical with DIMONAH.

Di'bon-gad. [DIBON.]

Dib'ri, a Danite, father of Shelomith. Lev. 24 : 11.

Didrachmon. [MONEY ; SHEKEL.]

Did'ymus (*the twin*), a surname of the apostle Thomas. John 11 : 16 ; 20 : 24 ; 21 : 2. [THOMAS.]

Dik'lah (*palm grove*). Gen. 10 : 27 ; 1 Chron. 1 : 21, a son of Joktan, whose settlements, in common with those of the other sons of Joktan, must be looked for in Arabia. It is thought that Diklah is a part of Arabia containing many palm trees.

Dil'ean (*gourd*), one of the cities in the lowlands of Judah. Josh. 15 : 38. It has not been identified with certainty.

Dim'nah (*dung*), a city in the tribe of Zebulun, given to the Merarite Levites. Josh. 21 : 35.

Di'mon (*river bed*), **The waters of,** some streams on the east of the Dead Sea, in the land of Moab, against which Isaiah uttered denunciation. Isa. 15 : 9. Gesenius conjectures that the two names Dimon and Dibon are the same.

Dimo'nah, a city in the south of Judah, Josh. 15 : 22, perhaps the same as DIBON in Neh. 11 : 25.

Di'nah (*judged, acquitted*), the daughter of Jacob by Leah. Gen. 30 : 21. (B.C. about 1751.) She accompanied her father from Mesopotamia to Canaan, and, having ventured among the inhabitants, was violated by Shechem the son of Hamor, the chieftain of the territory in which her father had settled. Gen. 34. Shechem proposed to make the usual reparation by paying a sum to the father and marrying her. Gen. 34 : 12. This proposal was accepted, the sons of Jacob demanding, as a condition of the proposed union, the circumcision of the Shechemites. They therefore assented ; and on the third day, when the pain and fever resulting from the operation were at the highest, Simeon and Levi, own brothers of Dinah, attacked them unexpectedly, slew all the males, and plundered their city.

Di'naites, Ezra 4 : 9, the name of some of the Cuthæan colonists who were placed in the cities of Samaria after the captivity of the ten tribes.

Din'habah, Gen. 36 : 32 ; 1 Chron. 1 : 43, the capital city, and probably the birthplace, of Bela, son of Beor king of Edom.

Dionys'ius (*devoted to Dionysus*, i. *Bacchus*) **the Areop'agite,** Acts 17 . 34, an eminent Athenian, converted tr Christianity by the preaching of St. Paul. (A.D. 52.) He is said to have been first bishop of Athens. The writings which were once attributed to him are now confessed to be the production of some neo-Platonists of the sixth century.

Diot'rephes (*nourished by Jove*), a Christian mentioned in 3 John 9, but of whom nothing is known.

Disciple. [APOSTLES.]

Diseases. [MEDICINE.]

Di'shan (*antelope*), the youngest son of Seir the Horite. Gen. 36 : 21, 28, 30 ; 1 Chron. 1 : 38, 42.

Di'shon (*antelope*). 1. The fifth son of Seir. Gen. 36 : 21, 26, 30 ; 1 Chron. 1 : 38.

2. The son of Anah, and grandson of Seir. Gen. 36 : 25 ; 1 Chron. 1 : 38.

Dispersion, The Jews of the, or simply THE DISPERSION, was the general title applied to those Jews who remained settled in foreign countries after the return from the Babylonian exile, and during the period of the second temple. At the beginning of the Christian era the Dispersion was divided into three great sections, the Babylonian, the Syrian, the Egyptian. From Babylon the Jews spread throughout Persia, Media and Parthia. Large settlements of Jews were established in Cyprus, in the islands of the Ægean, and on the western coast of Asia Minor. Jewish settlements were also established at Alexandria by Alexander and Ptolemy I. The Jewish settlements in Rome were consequent upon the occupation of Jerusalem by Pompey, B.C. 63. The influence of the Dispersion on the rapid promulgation of Christianity can scarcely be overrated. The course of the apostolic preaching followed in a regular progress the line of Jewish settlements. The mixed assembly from which the first converts were gathered on the day of Pentecost represented each division of the Dispersion. Acts 2 : 9-11. (1) Parthians . . . Mesopotamia ; (2) Judea (*i. e. Syria*) . . . Pamphylia ; (3) Egypt . . . Greece ; (4) Romans . . . , and these converts naturally prepared the way for the apostles in the interval which preceded the beginning of the separate apostolic missions. St. James and St. Peter wrote to the Jews of the Dispersion. James 1 : 1 ; 1 Pet. 1 : 1.

Divination is a "foretelling future events, or discovering things secret by the aid of superior beings, or other than human means." It is used in Scripture of *false* systems of ascertaining the divine will. It has been universal in all ages, and all nations alike civilized and savage. Numerous forms of divination are mentioned, such as divination by rods, Hos. 4 : 12; divination by arrows, Ezek. 21 : 21; divination by cups, Gen. 44 : 5; consultation of teraphim, 1 Sam. 15 : 23; Ezek. 21 : 21; Zech. 10 : 2 [TERAPHIM]; divination by the liver, Ezek. 21 : 21; divination by dreams, Deut. 13 : 2, 3; Judges 7 : 13; Jer. 23 : 32; consultation of oracles. Isa. 41 : 21–24; 44 : 7. Moses forbade every species of divination, because a prying into the future clouds the mind with superstition, and because it would have been an incentive to idolatry. But God supplied his people with substitutes for divination which would have rendered it superfluous, and left them in no doubt as to his will in circumstances of danger, had they continued faithful. It was only when they were unfaithful that the revelation was withdrawn. 1 Sam. 28 : 6; 2 Sam. 2 : 1; 5 : 23, etc. Superstition not unfrequently goes hand in hand with skepticism, and hence, amid the general infidelity prevalent throughout the Roman empire at our Lord's coming, imposture was rampant. Hence the lucrative trade of such men as Simon Magus, Acts 8 : 9, Bar-jesus, Acts 13 : 6, the slave with the spirit of Python, Acts 16 : 16, the vagabond Jews, exorcists, Luke 11 : 19; Acts 19 : 13, and others, 2 Tim. 3 : 13; Rev. 19 : 20, etc., as well as the notorious dealers in magical books at Ephesus. Acts 19 : 19.

Divorce, "a legal dissolution of the marriage relation." The law regulating this subject is found Deut. 24 : 1–4, and the cases in which the right of a husband to divorce his wife was lost are stated *ibid.*, 22 : 19, 29. The ground of divorce is a point on which the Jewish doctors of the period of the New Testament differed widely; the school of Shammai seeming to limit it to a moral delinquency in the woman, whilst that of Hillel extended it to trifling causes, *e. g.*, if the wife burnt the food she was cooking for her husband. The Pharisees wished perhaps to embroil our Saviour with these rival schools by their question, Matt. 19 : 3; by his answer to which, as well as by his previous maxim, Matt. 5 : 31, he declares that he regarded all the lesser causes than "fornication" as standing on too weak ground, and declined the question of how to interpret the words of Moses.

Diz'ahab (*region of gold*), a place in the Arabian desert, mentioned Deut. 1 : 1, is identified with *Dahab*, a cape on the western shore of the Gulf of Akabah.

Dod'a-i (*loving, amorous*), an Ahohite who commanded the course of the second month. 1 Chron. 27 : 4. It is probable that he is the same as DODO, 2.

Dod'anim (*leaders*), Gen. 10 : 4; 1 Chron. 1 : 7, a family or race descended from Javan, the son of Japhet. Gen. 10 : 4; 1 Chron. 1 : 7. Dodanim is regarded as identical with the Dardani, who were found in historical times in Illyricum and Troy.

Dod'avah (*love of the Lord*), a man of Maresha in Judah, father of Eliezer, who denounced Jehoshaphat's alliance with Ahaziah. 2 Chron. 20 : 37.

Do'do (*loving*). 1. A man of Bethlehem, father of Elhanan, who was one of David's thirty captains. 2 Sam. 23 : 24; 1 Chron. 11 : 26. He is a different person from

2. DODO THE AHOHITE, father of Eleazar, the second of the three mighty men who were over the thirty. 2 Sam. 23 : 9; 1 Chron. 11 : 12. (B.C. before 1046.)

Do'eg (*fearful*), an Idumean, chief of Saul's herdmen. (B.C. 1062.) He was at Nob when Ahimelech gave David the sword of Goliath, and not only gave information to Saul, but when others declined the office, himself executed the king's order to destroy the priests of Nob, with their families, to the number of 85 persons, together with all their property. 1 Sam. 21 : 7; 22 : 9, 18, 22; Ps. 52.

Dog, an animal frequently mentioned in Scripture. It was used by the Hebrews as a watch for their houses, Isa. 56 : 10, and for guarding their flocks. Job 30 : 1. Then also, as now. troops of hungry and semi-wild dogs used to wander about the fields and the streets of the cities, devouring dead bodies and other offal, 1 Kings 14 : 11; 21 : 19, 23; 22 : 38; Ps. 59 : 6, and thus became so savage and fierce and such objects of dislike that fierce and cruel enemies are poetically styled dogs in Ps. 22 : 16, 20. Moreover the dog being an unclean animal, Isa. 66 : 3, the epithets dog, dead dog, dog's head, were used as terms of reproach or of humility in speaking of one's self. 1

Syrian Dog.

Sam. 24 : 14; 2 Sam. 3 : 8; 9 : 8; 16 : 9; 2 Kings 8 : 13.

Doors. [GATE.]

Doph'kah (*cattle-driving*), a place mentioned Num. 33 : 12 as a station in the desert where the Israelites encamped. [WILDERNESS OF THE WANDERING.]

Dor (*dwelling*), Josh. 17 : 11; 1 Kings 4 : 11, an ancient royal city of the Canaanites, Josh. 12 : 23, whose ruler was an ally of Jabin king of Hazor against Joshua. Josh. 11 : 1, 2. It appears to have been within the territory of the tribe of Asher, though allotted to Manasseh. Josh. 17 : 11; Judges 1 : 27. Solomon stationed at Dor one of his twelve purveyors. 1 Kings 4 : 11. Jerome places it on the coast, " in the ninth mile from Cæsarea, on the way to Ptolemais." Just at the point indicated is the small village of *Tantûra*, probably an Arab corruption of *Dora*, consisting of about thirty houses, wholly constructed of ancient materials.

Dor'cas (*gazelle*). [TABITHA.]

Dosith'eus, a " priest and Levite" who carried the translation of Esther to Egypt. Esther 11 : 1, 2.

Do'tha-im. [DOTHAN.]

Do'than (*two wells*), a place first mentioned Gen. 37 : 17 in connection with the history of Joseph, and apparently as in the neighborhood of Shechem. It next appears as the residence of Elisha. 2 Kings 6 : 13. It was known to Eusebius, who places it 12 miles to the north of Sebaste (Samaria); and here it has been discovered in our own times, still bearing its ancient name unimpaired.

Dove. The first mention of this bird occurs in Gen. 8. The dove's rapidity of flight is alluded to in Ps. 55 : 6; the beauty of its plumage in Ps. 68 : 13; its dwelling in the rocks and valleys in Jer. 48 : 28 and Ezek. 7 : 16; its mournful voice in Isa. 38 : 14; 59 : 11; Nah. 2 : 7; its harmlessness in Matt. 10 : 16; its simplicity in Hos. 7 : 11, and its amativeness in Cant. 1 : 15; 2 : 14. Doves are kept in a domesticated state in many parts of the East. In Persia pigeon-houses are erected at a distance from the dwellings, for the purpose of collecting the dung as manure. There is probably an allusion to such a custom in Isa. 60 : 8.

Dove's dung. Various explanations have been given of the passage in 2 Kings 6 : 25. Bochart has labored to show that it denotes a species of *cicer*, " chick-pea," which he says the Arabs call *usnân*, and sometimes improperly " dove's " or " sparrow's dung." Great quantities of these are sold in Cairo to the pilgrims going to Mecca. Later authorities incline to think it the bulbous

Dove.

root of the *Star of Bethlehem* (*ornithogalum, i. e.* bird-milk), a common root in Palestine, and sometimes eaten.—ED. can scarcely be believed that even in the worst horrors of a siege a substance so vile as is implied by the literal rendering should have been used for food.

Dowry. [MARRIAGE.]

Drachm, Luke 15 : 8, 9; 2 Macc. 4 : 19; 10 : 20; 12 : 43, a Greek silver coin, varying in weight on account of the use of different talents. In Luke denarii (Authorized Version "piece of silver") seem to be intended. [MONEY; SILVER.]

Dragon. The translators of the Authorized Version, apparently following

Star of Bethlehem (Dove's Dung).

the Vulgate, have rendered by the same word "dragon" the two Hebrew words *tan* and *tannin*, which appear to be quite distinct in meaning. 1. The former is used, always in the plural, in Job 30 : 29; Ps. 44 : 19; Isa. 34 : 13; 43 : 20; Jer. 9 : 11. It is always applied to some creatures inhabiting the desert, and we should conclude from this that it refers rather to some wild beast than to a serpent. The Syriac renders it by a word which, according to Pococke, means a "jackal." 2. The word *tannin* seems to refer to any great monster, whether of the land or the sea, being indeed more usually applied to some kind of serpent or reptile, but not exclusively restricted to that sense. Ex. 7 : 9, 10, 12; Deut. 32 : 33; Ps. 91 : 13. In the New Testament it is found only in the Apocalypse, Rev. 12 : 3, 4, 7, 9, 16, 17, etc., as applied metaphorically to "the old serpent, called the devil, and Satan."

Dram. [DARIC.]

Dreams. The Scripture declares that the influence of the Spirit of God upon the soul extends to its sleeping as well as its waking thoughts. But, in accordance with the principle enunciated by St. Paul in 1 Cor. 14 : 15, dreams, in which the understanding is asleep, are placed below the visions of prophecy, in which the understanding plays its part. Under the Christian dispensation, while we read frequently of trances and visions, dreams are never referred to as vehicles of divine revelation. In exact accordance with this principle are the actual records of the dreams sent by God. The greater number of such dreams were granted, for prediction or for warning, to those who were aliens to the Jewish covenant. And where dreams are recorded as means of God's revelation to his chosen servants, they are almost always referred to the periods of their earliest and most imperfect knowledge of him. Among the Jews, "if any person dreamed a dream which was peculiarly striking and significant, he was permitted to go to the high priest in a peculiar way, and see if it had any special import. But the observance of ordinary dreams and the consulting of those who pretend to skill in their interpretation are repeatedly forbidden. Deut. 13 : 1–5; 18 : 9–14."—*Schaff.*

Dress. This subject includes the following particulars: 1. Materials; 2. Color and decoration; 3. Name, form, and mode of wearing the various articles; 4. Special usages relating thereto.

1. *Materials.*—After the first "apron" of fig leaves, Gen. 3 : 7, the skins of animals were used for clothing. Gen. 3 : 21. Such was the "mantle" worn by Elijah. Pelisses of sheepskin still form an ordinary article of dress in the East. The art of weaving hair was known to the Hebrews at an early period, Ex. 25 : 4; 26 : 7; and wool was known earlier still. Gen. 38 : 12. Their acquaintance with linen and perhaps cotton dates from the captivity in Egypt, 1 Chron. 4 : 21; silk was introduced much later. Rev. 18 : 12. The use of mixed material, such as wool and flax, was forbidden. Lev. 19 : 19; Deut. 22 : 11.

2. *Color and decoration.*—The prevailing color of the Hebrew dress was the natural white of the materials employed, which might be brought to a high state of brilliancy by the art of the fuller. Mark 9 : 3. The notice of scarlet thread, Gen. 38 : 28, implies some acquaintance with dyeing. The elements of ornament-

ation were — (1) weaving with threads previously dyed, Ex. 35 : 25; (2) the introduction of gold thread or wire, Ex. 27 : 6 ff.; (3) the addition of figures. Robes decorated with gold, Ps. 45 : 13, and with silver thread, cf. Acts 12 : 21, were worn by royal personages; other kinds of embroidered robes were worn by the wealthy, Judges 5 : 30; Ps. 45 : 14; Ezek. 16 : 13; as well as purple, Prov. 31 : 22; Luke 16 : 19, and scarlet. 2 Sam. 1 : 24.

3. *The names, forms, and modes of wearing the robes.*—The general characteristics of Oriental dress have preserved a remarkable uniformity in all ages: the modern Arab dresses much as the ancient Hebrew did. The costume of the men and women was very similar; there was sufficient difference, however, to mark the sex, and it was strictly forbidden to a woman to wear the appendages, such as the staff, signet-ring, and other ornaments, of a man; as well as to a man to wear the outer robe of a woman. Deut. 22 : 5. We shall first describe the robes which were common to the two sexes, and then those which were peculiar to women. (1) *The inner garment* was the most essential article of dress. It was a closely-fitting garment, resembling in form and use our shirt, though unfortunately translated "coat" in the Authorized Version. The material of which it was made was either wool, cotton or linen. It was without sleeves, and reached only to the knee. Another kind reached to the wrists and ankles. It was in either case kept close to the body by a girdle, and the fold formed by the overlapping of the robe served as an inner pocket. A person wearing the inner garment alone was described as *naked*. (2) There was an *upper* or *second* tunic, the difference being that it was longer than the first. (3) The *linen cloth* appears to have been a wrapper of fine linen, which might be used in various ways, but especially as a night-shirt. Mark 14 : 51. (4) *The outer garment* consisted of a quadrangular piece of woollen cloth, probably resembling in shape a Scotch plaid. The size and texture would vary with the means of the wearer. It might be worn in various ways, either wrapped round the body or thrown over the shoulders like a shawl, with the ends or "skirts" hanging down in front; or it might be thrown over the head, so as to conceal the face. 2 Sam. 15 : 30; Esther 6 : 12.

The ends were skirted with a fringe and bound with a dark purple ribbon, Num. 15 : 38; it was confined at the waist by a girdle. The outer garment was the poor man's bed clothing. Ex. 22 : 26, 27. The dress of the women differed from that of the men in regard to the outer garment, the inner garment being worn equally

Fringed Garment.

by both sexes. Cant. 5 : 3. Among their distinctive robes we find a kind of shawl, Ruth 3 : 15; Isa. 3 : 22, light summer dresses of handsome appearance and ample dimensions, and gay holiday dresses. Isa. 3 : 24. The garments of females were terminated by an ample border of fringe (*skirts*, Authorized Version), which concealed the feet. Isa. 47 : 2; Jer. 13 : 22. The travelling *cloak* referred to by St. Paul, 2 Tim. 4 : 13, is generally identified with the Roman *pœnula*. It is, however, otherwise explained as a travelling-case for carrying clothes or books. The *coat of many colors* worn by Joseph, Gen. 37 : 3, 23, is variously taken to be either a "coat of divers colors" or a tunic furnished with sleeves and reaching down to the ankles. The latter is probably the correct sense.

4. Special usages relating to dress.— The length of the dress rendered it inconvenient for active exercise; hence the outer garments were either left in the house by a person working close by, Matt. 24 : 18, or were thrown off when the occasion arose, Mark 10 : 50; or, if this were not possible, as in the case of a person travelling, they were girded up. 1 Kings 18 : 46; 1 Pet. 1 : 13. On entering a house the upper garment was probably laid aside, and resumed on going out. Acts 12 : 8. In a sitting posture, the garments concealed the feet; this was held to be an act of reverence. Isa. 6 : 2. The number of suits possessed by the Hebrews was considerable : a single suit consisted of an under and an upper garment. The presentation of a robe in many instances amounted to installation or investiture, Gen. 41 : 42; Esther 8 : 15; Isa. 22 : 21; on the other hand, taking it away amounted to dismissal from office. 2 Macc. 4 : 38. The production of the best robe was a mark of special honor in a household. Luke 15 : 22. The number of robes thus received or kept in store for presents was very large, and formed one of the main elements of wealth in the East, Job 22 : 6; Matt. 6 : 19; James 5 : 2, so that *to have clothing* implied the possession of wealth and power. Isa. 3 : 6, 7. On grand occasions the entertainer offered becoming robes to his guests. The business of making clothes devolved upon women in a family. Prov. 31 : 22; Acts 9 : 39. Little art was required in what we may term the tailoring department; the garments came forth for the most part ready made from the loom, so that the weaver supplanted the tailor.

Drink, Strong. The Hebrew term *shêcar*, in its etymological sense, applies to any beverage that had *intoxicating* qualities. With regard to the application of the term in later times we have the explicit statement of Jerome, as well as other sources of information, from which we may state that the following beverages were known to the Jews:—1. *Beer*, which was largely consumed in Egypt under the name of *zythus*, and was thence introduced into Palestine. It was made of barley; certain herbs, such as lupine and skirret, were used as substitutes for hops. 2. *Cider*, which is noticed in the Mishna as *apple wine*. 3. *Honey wine*, of which there were two sorts, one consisting of a mixture of wine, honey and pepper; the other a decoction of the juice

of the grape, termed *dĕbash* (honey) by the Hebrews, and *dibs* by the modern Syrians. 4. *Date wine*, which was also manufactured in Egypt. It was made by mashing the fruit in water in certain proportions. 5. Various other fruits and vegetables are enumerated by Pliny as supplying materials for *factitious* or home-made wine, such as figs, millet, the carob fruit, etc. It is not improbable that the Hebrews applied *raisins* to this purpose in the simple manner followed by the Arabians, viz., by putting them in jars of water and burying them in the ground until fermentation took place.

Dromedary. [CAMEL.]

Drusil'la (*watered by the dew*), daughter of Herod Agrippa I., Acts 24 : 24 ff., and Cypros. Born A.D. 38. She was at first betrothed to Antiochus Epiphanes, prince of Commagene, but was married to Azizus, king of Emesa. Soon after, Felix, procurator of Judea, brought about her seduction by means of the Cyprian sorcerer Simon, and took her as his wife. In Acts 24 : 24 we find her in company with Felix at Cæsarea. Felix had by Drusilla a son named Agrippa, who, together with his mother, perished in the eruption of Vesuvius under Titus.

Dulcimer (Heb. *sumphoniah*), a musical instrument, mentioned in Dan. 3 : 5, 15, probably the bagpipe. The same instrument is still in use amongst peasants in the northwest of Asia and in southern Europe, where it is known by the similar name *sampogna* or *zampogna*.

Du'mah (*silence*). 1. A son of Ishmael, most probably the founder of the Ishmaelite tribe of Arabia, and thence the name of the principal place or district inhabited by that tribe. Gen. 25 : 14; 1 Chron. 1 : 30; Isa. 21 : 11.

2. A city in the mountainous district of Judah, near Hebron, Josh. 15 : 52, represented by the ruins of a village called *ed-Daumeh*, six miles southwest of Hebron.

Dung. The uses of dung were twofold—as manure and as fuel. The manure consisted either of straw steeped in liquid manure, Isa. 25 : 10, or the sweepings, Isa. 5 : 25, of the streets and roads, which were carefully removed from about the houses, and collected in heaps outside the walls of the towns at fixed spots—hence the dung-gate at Jerusalem—and thence removed in due course to the fields. The difficulty of procuring fuel in Syria, Arabia and Egypt has made dung in all ages valuable as a substitute. It was probably used for heating ovens and for baking cakes, Ezra 4 : 12, 15, the equable heat which it produced adapting it peculiarly for the latter operation. Cow's and camel's dung is still used for a similar purpose by the Bedouins.

Dungeon. [PRISON.]

Du'ra (*a circle*), the plain where Nebuchadnezzar set up the golden image, Dan. 3 : 1, has been sometimes identified with a tract a little below *Tekrit*, on the left bank of the Tigris, where the name *Dur* is still found. M. Oppert places the plain (or, as he calls it, the " valley ") of Dura to the southeast of Babylon, in the vicinity of the mound of *Dowair* or *Dùair*, where was found the pedestal of a huge statue.

Dust. [MOURNING.]

E.

Eagle (Heb. *nesher*, i. e. *a tearer with the beak*). At least four distinct kinds of eagles have been observed in Palestine, viz., the golden eagle, *Aquila chrysaëtos*, the spotted eagle, *Aquila nœvia*, the imperial eagle, *Aquila heliaca*, and the very common *Circaëtos gallicus*. The Hebrew *nesher* may stand for any of these different species, though perhaps more particular reference to the golden and imperial eagles and the *griffon vulture* may be intended. The passage in Micah, 1 : 16, "enlarge thy baldness as the eagle," may refer to the griffon vulture, *Vultur fulvus*, in which case the simile is peculiarly appropriate, for the whole head and neck of this bird are destitute of true feathers. The "eagles" of Matt. 24 : 28, Luke 17 : 37, may include the *Vultur fulvus* and *Neophron percnopterus;* though, as eagles frequently prey upon dead bodies, there is no necessity to restrict the Greek word to the *Vulturidæ.* The figure of an eagle is now and has long been a favorite military ensign. The Persians so employed it; a fact which illustrates the passage in Isa. 46 : 11. The same bird was similarly employed by the Assyrians and the Romans.

Earing. Gen. 45 : 6; Ex. 34 : 21. Derived from the Latin *arare*, to plough; hence it means ploughing.

Earnest. 2 Cor. 1 : 22; 5 : 5; Eph. 1 : 14. The Hebrew word was used generally for *pledge*, Gen. 38 : 17, and in its cognate forms for *surety*, Prov. 17 : 18, and *hostage*. 2 Kings 14 : 14. The Greek derivative, however, acquired a more technical sense as signifying the *deposit* paid by the purchaser on entering into an agreement for the purchase of anything. In the New Testament the word is used to signify the pledge or earnest of the superior blessings of the future life.

Earrings. The material of which earrings were made was generally gold, Ex. 32 : 2, and their form circular. They were worn by women and by youth of both sexes. These ornaments appear to have been regarded with superstitious reverence as an amulet. On this account they were surrendered along with the idols by Jacob's household. Gen. 35 :

4. Chardin describes earrings with talismanic figures and characters on them as still existing in the East. Jewels were sometimes attached to the rings. The size of the earrings still worn in eastern countries far exceeds what is usual among ourselves; hence they formed a handsome present, Job 42 : 11, or offering to the service of God. Num. 31 : 50.

Earth. The term is used in two widely-different senses: (1) for the material of which the earth's surface is composed; (2) as the name of the planet on which man dwells. The Hebrew language discriminates between these two by the use of separate terms, *adamah* for the former, *erets* for the latter. 1. *Adamah* is the *earth* in the sense of soil or ground, particularly as being susceptible of cultivation. Gen. 2 : 7. 2. *Erets* is applied in a more or less extended sense—(1) to the whole world, Gen. 1 : 1; (2) to land as opposed to sea, Gen. 1 : 10; (3) to a country, Gen. 21 : 32; (4) to a plot of ground, Gen. 23 : 15; and (5) to the ground on which a man stands. Gen. 33 : 3. The two former senses alone concern us, the first involving an inquiry into the opinions of the Hebrews on cosmogony, the second on geography. 1. *Cosmogony.*—(1) The Hebrew cosmogony is based upon the leading principle that the universe exists, not independently of God, nor yet co-existent with God, nor yet in opposition to him as a hostile element, but dependently upon him, subsequently to him and in subjection to him. (2) Creation was regarded as a progressive work—a gradual development from the inferior to the superior orders of things. 2. *Geography.*—There seem to be traces of the same ideas as prevailed among the Greeks, that the world was a disk, Isa. 40 : 22, bordered by the ocean, with Jerusalem as its centre, like Delphi as the navel, or, according to another view, the highest point of the world. As to the size of the earth, the Hebrews had but a very indefinite notion.

Earthenware. [POTTERY.]

Earthquake. Earthquakes, more or less violent, are of frequent occurrence in Palestine. The most remarkable occurred in the reign of Uzziah. Zech. 14 : 5. From Zech. 14 : 4 we are led to infer that a great convulsion took place at this time in the Mount of Olives, the mountain being split so as to leave a valley between its summit. An earthquake occurred at the time of our Saviour's crucifixion. Matt. 27 : 51–54. Earthquakes are not unfrequently accompanied by fissures of the earth's surface; instances of this are recorded in connection with the destruction of Korah and his company, Num. 16 : 32, and at the time of our Lord's death, Matt. 27 : 51; the former may be paralleled by a similar occurrence at Oppido in Calabria A.D. 1783, where the earth opened to the extent of five hundred and a depth of more than two hundred feet.

East. The Hebrew term *kedem* properly means that which is *before* or *in front of* a person, and was applied to the east from the custom of turning in that direction when describing the points of the compass, *before*, *behind*, the *right* and the *left* representing respectively east, west, south and north. Job 23 : 8, 9. The term as generally used refers to the lands lying immediately eastward of Palestine, viz., Arabia, Mesopotamia and Babylonia; on the other hand *mizrach* is used of the *far* east with a less definite signification. Isa. 42 : 2, 25; 43 : 5; 46 : 11.

Easter. Acts 12 : 4. In the earlier English versions Easter has been frequently used as the translation of *pascha* (*passover*). In the Authorized Version Passover was substituted in all passages but this; and in the new Revision Passover is used here. [PASSOVER.]

E'bal (*stone, bare mountain*). 1. One of the sons of Shobal the son of Seir. Gen. 36 : 23; 1 Chron. 1 : 40.

2. Obal the son of Joktan. 1 Chron. 1 : 22; comp. Gen. 10 : 28.

E'bal, Mount, a mount in the promised land, on which the Israelites were to "put" the curse which should fall upon them if they disobeyed the commandments of Jehovah. The blessing consequent on obedience was to be similarly localized on Mount Gerizim. Deut. 11 : 26–29. Ebal and Gerizim are the mounts which form the sides of the fertile valley in which lies *Nablûs*, the ancient Shechem—Ebal on the north and Gerizim on the south. (They are nearly in the centre of the country of Samaria, about eight hundred feet above Nablûs in the valley; and they are so near that all the vast body of the people could hear the words read from either mountain. The experiment has repeatedly been tried in late years.—ED.) The modern name of Ebal is *Sitti Salamiyah*, from a Mohammedan female saint, whose tomb is standing on the eastern part of the ridge, a little before the highest point is reached.

E'bed (*a servant*). (Many MSS. have EBER.) 1. Father of Gaal, who with his brethren assisted the men of Shechem in their revolt against Abimelech. Judges 9 : 26, 28, 30, 31, 35. (B.C. 1206.)

2. Son of Jonathan; one of the Bene-Adin who returned from Babylon with Ezra. Ezra 8 : 6.

E'bed-me'lech (*a king's servant*), an Ethiopian eunuch in the service of King Zedekiah, through whose interference Jeremiah was released from prison. Jer. 38 : 7 ff.; 39 : 15 ff. (B.C. 1589.)

Eben-e'zer (*stone of help*), a stone set up by Samuel after a signal defeat of the Philistines, as a memorial of the "help" received on the occasion from Jehovah. 1 Sam. 7 : 12. Its position is carefully defined as between Mizpeh and Shen.

E'ber (*the region beyond*). 1. Son of Salah, and great-grandson of Shem. Gen. 10 : 24; 1 Chron. 1 : 19. (B.C. 2277–1813.) [For confusion between Eber and Heber see HEBER.]

2. Son of Elpaal and descendant of Sharahaim of the tribe of Benjamin. 1 Chron. 8 : 12. (B.C. 1400.)

3. A priest in the days of Joiakim the son of Jeshua. Neh. 12 : 20. (B.C. 445.)

Ebi'asaph. 1 Chron. 6 : 23, 37. [See ABIASAPH.]

Ebony, Ezek. 27 : 15, one of the valuable commodities imported into Tyre by the men of Dedan; a hard, heavy and durable wood, which admits of a fine polish or gloss. The most usual color is black, but it also occurs red or green. The black is the heart of a tree called *Diospyros ebenum*. It was imported from India or Ceylon by Phœnician traders.

Ebro'nah (*passage*), one of the halting-places of the Israelites in the desert, immediately preceding Ezion-geber. Num. 33 : 34, 35.

Ecbat'ana. Ezra 6 : 2, margin. In the apocryphal books Ecbatana is frequently mentioned. Two cities named Ecbatana seem to have existed in ancient times, one the capital of northern Media —the Media Atropatênê of Strabo—the other the metropolis of the larger and more important province known as Media Magna. The site of the former appears to be marked by the very curious ruins at *Takht-i-Suleiman* (lat. 36° 28′, long. 47° 9′); while that of the latter is occupied by *Hamadan*, which is one of the most important cities of modern Persia.

Ecclesias'tes (*the preacher*). The title of this book is in Hebrew *Koheleth*, signifying *one who speaks publicly in an assembly*. *Koheleth* is the name by which Solomon, probably the author, speaks of himself throughout the book. The book is that which it professes to be,— the confession of a man of wide experience looking back upon his past life and looking out upon the disorders and calamities which surround him. The writer is a man who has sinned in giving way to selfishness and sensuality, who has paid the penalty of that sin in satiety and weariness of life, but who has through all this been under the discipline of a divine education, and has learned from it the lesson which God meant to teach him.

Ecclesias'ticus, one of the books of the Apocrypha. This title is given in the Latin version to the book which is called in the Septuagint THE WISDOM OF JESUS THE SON OF SIRACH. The word designates the character of the writing, as publicly used in the services of the Church.

Eclipse of the sun. No historical notice of an eclipse occurs in the Bible, but there are passages in the prophets which contain manifest allusion to this phenomenon. Joel 2 : 10, 31; 3 : 15; Amos 8 : 9; Micah 3 : 6; Zech. 14 : 6. Some of these notices probably refer to eclipses that occurred about the time of the respective compositions: thus the date of Amos coincides with a total eclipse which occurred Feb. 9, B.C. 784, and was visible at Jerusalem shortly after noon ; that of Micah with the eclipse of June 5, B.C. 716. A passing notice in Jer. 15 : 9 coincides in date with the eclipse of Sept. 30, B.C. 610, so well known from Herodotus' account (i., 74, 103). The darkness that overspread the world at the crucifixion cannot with reason be attributed to an eclipse, as the moon was at the full at the time of the passover.

Ed (*witness*), a word inserted in the Authorized Version of Josh. 22 : 34, apparently on the authority of a few MSS., and also of the Syriac and Arabic versions, but not existing in the generally-received Hebrew text.

E'dar, Tower of (accur. EDER, *a flock*), a place named only in Gen. 35 : 21. According to Jerome it was one thousand paces from Bethlehem.

E'den (*pleasure*). 1. The first residence of man, called in the Septuagint *Paradise*. The latter is a word of Persian origin, and describes an extensive tract of pleasure land, somewhat like an English park ; and the use of it suggests a wider view of man's first abode than a garden. The description of Eden is found in Gen. 2 : 8-14. In the eastern portion of the region of Eden was the garden planted. The Hiddekel, one of its rivers, is the modern Tigris; the Euphrates is the same as the modern Euphrates. With regard to the Pison and Gihon a great variety of opinion exists, but the best authorities are divided between (1) Eden as in northeast Arabia, at the junction of the Euphrates and Tigris, and their separation again, making the four rivers of the different channels of these two, or (2), and most probably, Eden as situated in Armenia, near the origin of the rivers Tigris and Euphrates, and in which same region rise the Araxes (*Pison* of Genesis) and the Oxus (*Gihon*). 2. One of the marts which supplied the luxury of Tyre with richly-embroidered stuffs. In 2 Kings 19 : 12 and Isa. 37 : 12 "the sons of Eden" are mentioned with Gozan, Haran and Rezeph as victims of the Assyrian greed of conquest. Probability seems to point to the northwest of Mesopotamia as the locality of Eden. 3. BETH-EDEN, "house of pleasure :" probably the name of a country residence of the kings of Damascus. Amos 1 : 5.

E'den. 1. A Gershonite Levite, son of Joah, in the days of Hezekiah. 2 Chron. 29 : 12. (B.C. 727.) 2. Also a Levite, probably identical with the preceding. 2 Chron. 31 : 15.

E'der (*a flock*). 1. One of the towns of Judah, in the extreme south, and on the borders of Edom. Josh. 15 : 21. No trace of it has been discovered in modern times. 2. A Levite of the family of Merari, in the time of David. 1 Chron. 23 : 23 ; 24 : 30.

E'dom, Idumæ'a or Idume'a (*red*). The name Edom was given to Esau, the first-born son of Isaac and twin brother of Jacob, when he sold his birthright to the latter for a meal of lentil pottage. The country which the Lord subsequently gave to Esau was hence called "the country of Edom," Gen. 32 : 3, and his descendants were called Edomites. Edom was called *Mount Seir* and Idumea also. Edom was wholly a mountainous country. It embraced the narrow mountainous tract (about 100 miles long by 20 broad) extending along the eastern side of the Arabah from the northern end of the Gulf of Elath to near the southern end of the Dead Sea. The ancient capital of Edom was Bozrah (*Buseireh*). Sela (Petra) appears to have been the principal stronghold in the days of Amaziah (B.C. 838). 2 Kings 14 : 7. Elath and Ezion-geber were the seaports. 2 Sam. 8 : 14; 1 Kings 9 : 26.

History.—Esau's bitter hatred to his brother Jacob for fraudulently obtaining his blessing appears to have been inherited by his latest posterity. The Edomites peremptorily refused to permit the Israelites to pass through their land. Num. 20 : 18–21. For a period of 400 years we hear no more of the Edomites. They were then attacked and defeated by Saul, 1 Sam. 14 : 47, and some forty years later by David. 2 Sam. 8 : 13, 14. In the reign of Jehoshaphat (B.C. 914) the Edomites attempted to invade Israel, but failed. 2 Chron. 20 : 22. They joined Nebuchadnezzar when that king besieged Jerusalem. For their cruelty at this time they were fearfully denounced by the later prophets. Isa. 34 : 5–8; 63 : 1–4; Jer. 49 : 17. After this they settled in southern Palestine, and for more than four centuries continued to prosper. But during the warlike rule of the Maccabees they were again completely subdued, and even forced to conform to Jewish laws and rites, and submit to the government of Jewish prefects. The Edomites were now incorporated with the Jewish nation. They were idolaters. 2 Chron. 25 : 14, 15, 20. Their habits were singular. The Horites, their predecessors in Mount Seir, were, as their name implies, *troglodytes,* or dwellers in caves; and the Edomites seem to have adopted their dwellings as well as their country. Everywhere we meet with caves and grottos hewn in the soft sandstone strata.

E'domites. [EDOM.]

Ed'rei (*stronghold*). 1. One of the two capital cities of Bashan, in the territory of Manasseh east of the Jordan.

Num. 21 : 33; Deut. 1 : 4; 3 : 10; Josh. 12 : 4. In Scripture it is only mentioned in connection with the victory gained by the Israelites over the Amorites under Og their king, and the territory thus acquired. The ruins of this ancient city, still bearing the name *Edr'a,* stand on a rocky promontory which projects from the southwest corner of the Lejah. The ruins are nearly three miles in circumference, and have a strange, wild look, rising up in dark, shattered masses from the midst of a wilderness of black rocks. 2. A town of northern Palestine, allotted to the tribe of Naphtali, and situated near Kedesh. Josh. 19 : 37. About two miles south of Kedesh is a conical rocky hill called *Tell Khuraibeh,* the "tell of the ruin," which may be the site of Edrei.

Education. There is little trace among the Hebrews in earlier times of education in any other subjects than the law. The wisdom therefore and instruction, of which so much is said in the book of Proverbs, are to be understood chiefly of moral and religious discipline, imparted, according to the direction of the law, by the teaching and under the example of parents. (But Solomon himself wrote treatises on several scientific subjects, which must have been studied in those days.) In later times the prophecies and comments on them, as well as on the earlier Scriptures, together with other subjects, were studied. Parents were required to teach their children some trade. (Girls also went to schools, and women generally among the Jews were treated with greater equality to men than in any other ancient nation.) Previous to the captivity, the chief depositaries of learning were the schools or colleges, from which in most cases proceeded that succession of public teachers who at various times endeavored to reform the moral and religious conduct of both rulers and people. Besides the prophetical schools instruction was given by the priests in the temple and elsewhere. [See SCHOOLS.]

Eg'lah (*a heifer*), one of David's wives during his reign in Hebron. 2 Sam. 3 : 5; 1 Chron. 3 : 3. (B.C. 1055.)

Egla'im (*two ponds*), a place named only in Isa. 15 : 8, probably the same as EN-EGLAIM.

Eg'lon (*calf-like*). 1. A king of the Moabites, Judges 3 : 12 ff., who, aided by the Ammonites and the Amalekites,

Approach to Edom. (*From an original Photograph.*)

Tombs at Petra in Edom. (*From an original Photograph.*)

crossed the Jordan and took " the city of palm trees." (B.C. 1359.) Here, according to Josephus, he built himself a palace, and continued for eighteen years to oppress the children of Israel, who paid him tribute. He was slain by Ehud. [EHUD.]

2. A town of Judah in the low country. Josh. 15 : 39. The name survives in the modern *Ajlan*, a shapeless mass of ruins, about 10 miles from Eleutheropolis and 14 from Gaza, on the south of the great maritime plain.

E'gypt (*land of the Copts*), a country occupying the northeast angle of Africa. Its limits appear always to have been very nearly the same. It is bounded on the north by the Mediterranean Sea, on the east by Palestine, Arabia and the Red Sea, on the south by Nubia, and on the west by the Great Desert. It is divided into upper Egypt—the valley of the Nile—and lower Egypt, the plain of the Delta, from the Greek letter Δ ; it is formed by the branching mouths of the Nile, and the Mediterranean Sea. The portions made fertile by the Nile comprise about 9582 square geographical miles, of which only about 5600 is under cultivation.—*Encyc. Brit.* The Delta extends about 200 miles along the Mediterranean, and Egypt is 520 miles long from north to south from the sea to the First Cataract.

NAMES.—The common name of Egypt in the Bible is " Mizraim." It is in the dual number, which indicates the two natural divisions of the country into an upper and a lower region. The Arabic name of Egypt— *Mizr*— signifies " red mud." Egypt is also called in the Bible " the land of Ham," Ps. 105 : 23, 27, comp. 78 : 51—a name most probably referring to Ham the son of Noah—and " Rahab," the proud or insolent: these appear to be poetical appellations. The common ancient Egyptian name of the country is written in hieroglyphics Kem, which was perhaps pronounced Chem. This name signifies, in the ancient language and in Coptic, " black," on account of the blackness of its alluvial soil. We may reasonably conjecture that Kem is the Egyptian equivalent of Ham.

GENERAL APPEARANCE, CLIMATE, ETC.—The general appearance of the country cannot have greatly changed since the days of Moses. The whole country is remarkable for its extreme fertility, which especially strikes the beholder when the rich green of the fields is contrasted with the utterly bare, yellow mountains or the sand-strewn rocky desert on either side. The climate is equable and healthy. Rain is not very unfrequent on the northern coast, but inland is very rare. Cultivation nowhere depends upon it. The inundation of the Nile fertilizes and sustains the country, and makes the river its chief blessing. The Nile was on this account anciently worshipped. The rise begins in Egypt about the summer solstice, and the inundation commences about two months later. The greatest height is attained about or somewhat after the autumnal equinox. The inundation lasts about three months. The atmosphere, except on the seacoast, is remarkably dry and clear, which accounts for the so perfect preservation of the monuments, with their pictures and inscriptions. The heat is extreme during a large part of the year. The winters are mild,—from 50° to 60° in the afternoon shade, in the coldest season.

CULTIVATION, AGRICULTURE, ETC.— The ancient prosperity of Egypt is attested by the Bible as well as by the numerous monuments of the country. As early as the age of the great pyramid it must have been densely populated. The contrast of the present state of Egypt with its former prosperity is more to be ascribed to political than to physical causes. Egypt is naturally an agricultural country. Vines were extensively cultivated. Of fruit trees, the date palm was the most common and valuable. The gardens resembled the fields, being watered in the same manner by irrigation. Egypt has neither woods nor forests. The commonest large trees are the sycamore fig, the acacia and the mulberry, the date palm and the banana. The best-known fruits are dates, grapes, figs, pomegranates, peaches, oranges, lemons, bananas, melons, olives and mulberries. All kinds of grain are abundant. The gardens produce peas, beans, lentils, celery, radishes, carrots, lettuce, tomatoes, cucumbers, etc. Tobacco, sugar cane, cotton, hemp and flax are raised. The ancient reed, the papyrus, is nearly extinct.—*Encyc. Brit.*

RELIGION.—The basis of the religion was Nigritian fetichism, the lowest kind of nature worship, differing in different parts of the country, and hence obviously indigenous. There were three orders of gods — the eight great gods, the twelve lesser, and the Osirian group. The great doctrines of the immortality of the soul, man's responsibility, and future rewards and punishments, were taught. Among the rites, circumcision is the most remarkable: it is as old as the time of the fourth dynasty.

DOMESTIC LIFE.—The sculptures and paintings of the tombs give us a very full insight into the domestic life of the ancient Egyptians. What most strikes us in their manners is the high position occupied by women, and the entire absence of the harem system of seclusion. Marriage appears to have been universal, at least with the richer class; and if polygamy were tolerated it was rarely practiced. There were no castes, although great classes were very distinct. The funeral ceremonies were far more important than any events of the Egyptian life, as the tomb was regarded as the only true home.

Front of Temple at Aboo Simbel, Nubia.

INDUSTRIAL ARTS.—The industrial arts held an important place in the occupations of the Egyptians. The workers in fine flax and the weavers of white linen are mentioned in a manner that shows they were among the chief contributors to the riches of the country. Isa. 19 : 9. The fine linen of Egypt found its way to Palestine. Prov. 7 : 16. Pottery was a great branch of the native manufactures, and appears to have furnished employment to the Hebrews during the bondage. Ps. 68 : 13; 81 : 6; comp. Ex. 1 : 14.

HISTORY.—The ancient history of Egypt may be divided into three portions: the old monarchy, extending from the foundation of the kingdom to the invasion of the Hyksos; the middle, from the entrance to the expulsion of the Hyksos; and the new, from the re-establishment of the native monarchy by Amasis to the Persian conquest. 1. *The old monarchy.*—Memphis was the most ancient capital, the foundation of which is ascribed to Menes, the first mortal king of Egypt. The names of the kings, divided into thirty dynasties, are handed down in the lists of Manetho,[1] and are

---

[1] Manetho was an Egyptian priest who lived under the Ptolemies in the third century B.C.,

also known from the works which they executed. The most memorable epoch in the history of the old monarchy is that of the Pyramid kings, placed in Manetho's fourth dynasty. Their names are found upon these monuments : the builder of the great pyramid is called Suphis by Manetho, Cheops by Herodotus, and *Khufu* or *Shufu* in an inscrip-

Pyramids of Gizeh, Egypt.

tion upon the pyramid. The erection of the second pyramid is attributed by Herodotus and Diodorus to Chephren; and upon the neighboring tombs has been read the name of *Khafra* or *Shafre*. The builder of the third pyramid is named Mycerinus by Herodotus and Diodorus; and in this very pyramid a coffin has been found bearing the name *Menkura*. The most powerful kings of the old monarchy were those of Manetho's twelfth dynasty : to this period is assigned the construction of the Lake of Moeris and the Labyrinth. 2. *The middle monarchy.* —Of this period we only know that a nomadic horde called *Hyksos*[1] for several centuries occupied and made Egypt tributary; that their capital was Memphis;

and wrote in Greek a history of Egypt, in which he divided the kings into thirty dynasties. The work itself is lost, but the lists of dynasties have been preserved by the Christian writers.
[1] This, their Egyptian name, is derived by Manetho from *hyk*, a king, and *sos*, a shepherd.

that in the Sethroite nome they constructed an immense earth-camp, which they called Abaris; that at a certain period of their occupation two independent kingdoms were formed in Egypt, one in the Thebaid, which held intimate relations with Ethiopia; another at Xois, among the marshes of the Nile; and that, finally, the Egyptians regained their

The Sphinx, Egypt.

independence and expelled the Hyksos, who thereupon retired into Palestine. The Hyksos form the fifteenth, sixteenth and seventeenth dynasties. Manetho says they were Arabs, but he calls the six kings of the fifteenth dynasty Phœnicians. 3. *The new monarchy* extends from the commencement of the eighteenth to the end of the thirtieth dynasty. The kingdom was consolidated by Amasis, who succeeded in expelling the Hyksos, and thus prepared the way for the foreign expeditions which his successors carried on in Asia and Africa, extending from Mesopotamia in the former to Ethiopia in the latter continent. The glorious era of Egyptian history was under the nineteenth dynasty, when Sethi I., B.C. 1322, and his grandson, Rameses the Great, B.C. 1311, both of whom represent the Sesostris of the Greek historians, carried their arms over the whole of western Asia and southward into Soudân, and amassed vast treasures, which were expended on public works. Under the later kings of the nineteenth dynasty the power of Egypt faded: the twentieth and twenty-first dynasties achieved nothing worthy of record; but with the twenty-second we enter upon a period that is interesting from its associations with biblical history, the first of this dynasty, Sheshonk I. (Seconchis), B.C. 990, being the Shishak who invaded Judea in Rehoboam's reign and pillaged the temple. 1 Kings 14 : 25. Probably his successor, Osorkon I., is the Zerah of Scripture, defeated by Asa. Egypt makes no figure in Asiatic history during the twenty-third and twenty-fourth dynasties; under the twenty-fifth it regained, in part at least, its ancient importance. This was an Ethiopian line, the warlike sovereigns of which strove to the utmost to repel the onward stride of Assyria. So, whom we are disposed to identify with Shebek II. or Sebichus, the second Ethiopian, made an alliance with Hoshea, the last king of Israel. Tehrak or Tirhakah, the third of this house, advanced against Sennacherib in support of Hezekiah. After this a native dynasty—the twenty-sixth—of Saite kings again occupied the throne. Psametek I. or Psammetichus I. (B.C. 664), who may be regarded as the head of this dynasty, warred in Palestine, and took Ashdod (Azotus) after a siege of twenty-nine years. Neku or Necho, the son of Psammetichus, continued the war in the east, and marched along the coast of Palestine to attack the king of Assyria. At Megiddo Josiah encountered him (B.C. 608-7), notwithstanding the remonstrance of the Egyptian king, which is very illustrative of the policy of the Pharaohs in the East, 2 Chron. 35 : 21, no less than is his lenient conduct after the defeat and death of the king of Judah. The army of Necho was after a short space routed at Carchemish by Nebuchadnezzar, B.C. 605-4. Jer. 46 : 2. The second successor of Necho, Apries, or Pharaoh-hophra, sent his army into Palestine to the aid of Zedekiah, Jer. 37 : 5, 7, 11—so that the siege of Jerusalem was raised for a time —and kindly received the fugitives from the captured city. He seems to have been afterwards attacked by Nebuchadnezzar in his own country. There is, however, no certain account of a complete subjugation of Egypt by the king of Babylon. Amasis, the successor of Apries, had a long and prosperous reign, and somewhat restored the weight of Egypt in the East. But the new power of Persia was to prove even more terrible to this house than Babylon had been to the house of Psammetichus, and the son of Amasis had reigned but six months when Cambyses reduced the country to the condition of a province of his empire, B.C. 525.

(CHRONOLOGY.—The early history and chronology of Egypt is involved in much uncertainty. Its principal sources are the lists of thirty dynasties of kings given by Manetho, the smaller list of the Turin Papyrus, and the sculptures, paintings and inscriptions on the monuments. There have been lately discovered (1881), in a Coptic convent near Thebes, the ruins of an ancient tomb in which are the mummies of Rameses II. and Thothmes III., and others of the great Pharaohs; but no new light has been thrown on the chronology. Till about the time of Solomon, 1000 B.C., there is much uncertainty as to dates.

EXODUS.—As far back as history records, there were flourishing empires in Egypt. The chief interest to the Bible student, in the early history of Egypt, is whether it agrees with the statements and chronology of the Bible. Egyptian history is so uncertain as to dates that nothing it contains could count against the Bible chronology; but what is known is reconcilable with the usual dates given in our Bibles, and cannot, at the farthest, ask for longer ages than are given in the Septuagint.

PRESENT CONDITION.—Egypt is now, as it has been for many centuries, under the government of the Turks. It contained, in 1874, 5,252,000 inhabitants, seven-eighths of whom are Mohammedans. The ancient Egyptians spoke the Coptic language. The modern Egyptians of the upper and middle classes speak Arabic. The native Christians of Egypt, or Copts, are chiefly descended from the ancient Egyptian race, and they rarely intermarry with other races. These speak the Coptic language, a branch of the ancient Egyptian, but spell their words with the letters of the Greek alphabet.—ED.)

Egyp′tian, Egyp′tians, a native or natives of Egypt.

E′hi (*my brother*), head of one of the Benjamite houses according to the list in Gen. 46 : 21. He seems to be the same as Ahiram in the list in Num. 26 : 38. In 1 Chron. 8 : 1 he is called Aharah, and perhaps also Ahoah in ver. 4, Ahiah, ver. 7, and Aher, ch. 7 : 12.

E'hud (*union*). 1. Ehud son of Bilhan, and great-grandson of Benjamin the patriarch. 1 Chron. 7 : 10 ; 8 : 6.

2. Ehud son of Gera, of the tribe of Benjamin, Judges 3 : 15, the second judge of the Israelites. (B.C. about 1370.) In the Bible he is not called a judge, but a deliverer (*l. c.*): so Othniel, Judges 3 : 9, and all the Judges. Neh. 9 : 27. As a Benjamite he was specially chosen to destroy Eglon, who had established himself in Jericho, which was included in the boundaries of that tribe. He was very strong, and left-handed. [EGLON.]

E'ker (*a rooting up*), a descendant of Judah. 1 Chron. 2 : 27.

Ek'ron (*torn up by the roots; emigration*), one of the five towns belonging to the lords of the Philistines, and the most northerly of the five. Josh. 13 : 3. Like the other Philistine cities its situation was in the lowlands. It fell to the lot of Judah. Josh. 15 : 45, 46 ; Judges 1 : 18. Afterwards we find it mentioned among the cities of Dan. Josh. 19 : 43. Before the monarchy it was again in full possession of the Philistines. 1 Sam. 5 : 10. *Akir*, the modern representative of Ekron, lies about five miles southwest of *Ramleh*. In the Apocrypha it appears as ACCARON. 1 Macc. 10 : 89 only.

El'adah (*whom God has put on*), a descendant of Ephraim through Shuthelah. 1 Chron. 7 : 20.

E'lah (*an oak, strength*). 1. The son and successor of Baasha king of Israel. 1 Kings 16 : 8–10. His reign lasted for little more than a year ; comp. ver. 8 with 10. (B.C. 928–7.) He was killed while drunk, by Zimri, in the house of his steward Arza, who was probably a confederate in the plot.

2. Father of Hoshea, the last king of Israel. 2 Kings 15 : 30 ; 17 : 1. (B.C. 729 or before.)

E'lah. 1. One of the dukes of Edom. Gen. 36 : 41 ; 1 Chron. 1 : 52.

2. Shimei ben-Elah was Solomon's commissariat officer in Benjamin. 1 Kings 4 : 18. (B.C. 1013.)

3. A son of Caleb the son of Jephunneh. 1 Chron. 4 : 15. (B.C. 1450.)

4. Son of Uzzi, a Benjamite, 1 Chron. 9 : 8, and one of the chiefs of the tribe at the settlement of the country. (B.C. 536.)

E'lah, The valley of (*valley of the terebinth*), the valley in which David killed Goliath. 1 Sam. 17 : 2, 19. It lay somewhere near Socoh of Judah and Azekah, and was nearer Ekron than any other Philistine town. 1 Sam. 17.

E'lam (*eternity*). 1. This seems to have been originally the name of a man, the son of Shem. Gen. 10 : 22 ; 1 Chron. 1 : 17. Commonly, however, it is used as the appellation of a country. Gen. 14 : 1, 9 ; Isa. 11 : 11 ; 21 : 2. The Elam of Scripture appears to be the province lying south of Assyria and east of Persia proper, to which Herodotus gives the name of Cissia (iii. 91, v. 49, etc.), and which is termed Susis or Susiana by the geographers. Its capital was Susa. This country was originally peopled by descendants of Shem. By the time of Abraham a very important power had been built up in the same region. It is plain that at this early time the predominant power in lower Mesopotamia was Elam, which for a while held the place possessed earlier by Babylon, Gen. 10 : 10, and later by either Babylon or Assyria.

2. A Korhite Levite in the time of King David. 1 Chron. 26 : 3. (B.C. 1014,)

3. A chief man of the tribe of Benjamin. 1 Chron. 8 : 24.

4. "Children of Elam," to the number of 1254, returned with Zerubbabel from Babylon. Ezra 2 : 7 ; Neh. 7 : 12 ; 1 Esd. 5 : 12. (B.C. 536 or before.) Elam occurs amongst the names of the chief of the people who signed the covenant with Nehemiah. Neh. 10 : 14.

5. In the same lists is a second Elam, whose sons, to the same number as in the former case, returned with Zerubbabel, Ezra 2 : 31 ; Neh. 7 : 34, and which for the sake of distinction is called "the other Elam."

6. One of the priests who accompanied Nehemiah at the dedication of the new wall of Jerusalem. Neh. 12 : 42.

E'lamites. This word is found only in Ezra 4 : 9. The Elamites were the original inhabitants of the country called Elam ; they were descendants of Shem, and perhaps drew their name from an actual man Elam. Gen. 10 : 22.

El'asah (*whom God made*). 1. A priest in the time of Ezra who had married a Gentile wife. Ezra 10 : 22. (B.C. 458.)

2. Son of Shaphan, one of the two men who were sent on a mission by King Zedekiah to Nebuchadnezzar at Babylon. Jer. 29 : 3. (B.C. 594.)

E'lath, E'loth (*a grove*), the name of a town of the land of Edom, commonly mentioned with Ezion-geber, and situate at the head of the Arabian Gulf, which was thence called the Elanitic Gulf. It first occurs in the account of the wanderings, Deut. 2 : 8, and in later times must have come under the rule of David. 2 Sam. 8 : 14. We find the place named again in connection with Solomon's navy. 1 Kings 9 : 26; comp. 2 Chron. 8 : 17. In the Roman period it became a frontier town of the south and the residence of a Christian bishop. The Arabic name is *Eyleh*, and palm groves still exist there, after which it was named.

El-beth'el (*the God of Bethel*), the name which Jacob is said to have bestowed on the place at which God appeared to him when he was flying from Esau. Gen. 35 : 7.

El'daah, Gen. 25 : 4; 1 Chron. 1 : 33, the last in order of the sons of Midian.

El'dad (*favored of God*) and **Me'dad** (*love*), two of the seventy elders to whom was communicated the prophetic power of Moses. Num. 11 : 16, 26. (B.C. 1490.) Although their names were upon the list which Moses had drawn up, Num. 11 : 26, they did not repair with the rest of their brethren to the tabernacle, but continued to prophesy in the camp. Moses, being requested by Joshua to forbid this, refused to do so, and expressed a wish that the gift of prophecy might be diffused throughout the people.

Elder. The term *elder*, or *old man* as the Hebrew literally imports, was one of extensive use, as an official title, among the Hebrews and the surrounding nations, because the heads of tribes and the leading people who had acquired influence were naturally the older people of the nation. It had reference to various offices. Gen. 24 : 2; 50 : 7; 2 Sam. 12 : 17; Ezek. 27 : 9. As betokening a political office, it applied not only to the Hebrews, but also to the Egyptians, Gen. 50 : 7, the Moabites and the Midianites. Num. 22 : 7. The earliest notice of the elders acting in concert as a political body is at the time of the Exodus. They were the representatives of the people, so much so that *elders* and *people* are occasionally used as equivalent terms; comp. Josh. 24 : 1 with 2, 19, 21; 1 Sam. 8 : 4 with 7, 10, 19. Their authority was undefined, and extended to all matters concerning the public weal. Their number and influence may be inferred from 1 Sam. 30 : 26 ff. They retained their position under all the political changes which the Jews underwent. The seventy elders mentioned in Exodus and Num-

bers were a sort of governing body, a parliament, and the origin of the tribunal of seventy elders called the Sanhedrin or Council. In the New Testament Church the elders or presbyters were the same as the bishops. It was an office derived from the Jewish usage of elders or rulers of the synagogues. [BISHOP.]

El'ead (*praised by God*), a descendant of Ephraim. 1 Chron. 7 : 21.

Elea'leh (*the ascending of God*), a place on the east of Jordan, taken possession of and rebuilt by the tribe of Reuben. Num. 32 : 3, 37. By Isaiah and Jeremiah it is mentioned as a Moabite town. Isa. 15 : 4; 16 : 9; Jer. 48 : 34.

Ele'asah (*whom God made*). 1. Son of Helez, one of the descendants of Judah, of the family of Hezron. 1 Chron. 2 : 39. (B.C. after 1046.)

2. Son of Rapha or Rephaiah; a descendant of Saul through Jonathan and Merib-baal or Mephibosheth. 1 Chron. 8 : 37; 9 : 43. (B.C. before 588.)

Elea'zar (*help of God*). 1. Third son of Aaron. After the death of Nadab and Abihu without children, Lev. 10 : 6; Num. 3 : 4, Eleazar was appointed chief over the principal Levites. Num. 3 : 32. With his brother Ithamar he ministered as a priest during their father's lifetime, and immediately before his death was invested on Mount Hor with the sacred garments, as the successor of Aaron in the office of high priest. Num. 20 : 28. (B.C. 1452.) One of his first duties was in conjunction with Moses to superintend the census of the people. Num. 26 : 3. After the conquest of Canaan by Joshua he took part in the distribution of the land. Josh. 14 : 1. The time of his death is not mentioned in Scripture.

2. The son of Abinadab, of the hill of Kirjath-jearim. 1 Sam. 7 : 1. (B.C. 1134.)

3. One of the three principal mighty men of David's army. 2 Sam. 23 : 9; 1 Chron. 11 : 12. (B.C. 1046.)

4. A Merarite Levite, son of Mahli and grandson of Merari. 1 Chron. 23 : 21, 22; 24 : 28.

5. A priest who took part in the feast of dedication under Nehemiah. Neh. 12 : 42. (B.C. 446.)

6. One of the sons of Parosh, an Israelite (*i. e.* a layman) who had married a foreign wife. Ezra 10 : 25.

7. Son of Phinehas, a Levite. Ezra 8 : 33.

8. The son of Eliud, in the genealogy of Jesus Christ. Matt. 1 : 15.

El-Elo'he-Is'rael (*God, the God of Israel*), the name bestowed by Jacob on the altar which he erected facing the city of Shechem. Gen. 33 : 19, 20.

E'leph (*the ox*), one of the towns allotted to Benjamin, and named next to Jerusalem. Josh. 18 : 28.

Elha'nan (*the grace of God*). 1. A distinguished warrior in the time of King David, who performed a memorable exploit against the Philistines. 2 Sam. 21 : 19; 1 Chron. 20 : 5. (B.C. about 1020.) 2. One of "the thirty" of David's guard, and named first on the list. 2 Sam. 23 : 24; 1 Chron. 11 : 26.

E'li (*ascension*), a descendant of Aaron through Ithamar, the youngest of his two surviving sons. Lev. 10 : 1, 2, 12; comp. 1 Kings 2 : 27 with 2 Sam. 8 : 17; 1 Chron. 24 : 3. (B.C. 1214–1116.) He was the first of the line of Ithamar who held the office of high priest. The office remained in his family till Abiathar was thrust out by Solomon, 1 Kings 1 : 7; 2 : 26, 27, when it passed back again to the family of Eleazar in the person of Zadok. 1 Kings 2 : 35. Its return to the elder branch was one part of the punishment which had been denounced against Eli during his lifetime, for his culpable negligence, 1 Sam. 2 : 22–25, when his sons profaned the priesthood; comp. 1 Sam. 2 : 27–36 with 1 Kings 2 : 27. Notwithstanding this one great blemish, the character of Eli is marked by eminent piety, as shown by his meek submission to the divine judgment, 1 Sam. 3 : 18, and his supreme regard for the ark of God. 1 Sam. 4 : 18. In addition to the office of high priest he held that of judge. He died at the advanced age of 98 years, 1 Sam. 4 : 15, overcome by the disastrous intelligence that the ark of God had been taken in battle by the Philistines, who had also slain his sons Hophni and Phinehas.

E'li, E'li, lama sabachthani. The Hebrew form, as Eloi, Eloi, etc., is the Syro-Chaldaic (the common language in use by the Jews in the time of Christ) of the first words of the twenty-second Psalm; they mean "*My God, my God, why hast thou forsaken me?*"

Eli'ab (*God is my father*). 1. Son of Helon and leader of the tribe of Zebulun at the time of the census in the wilderness of Sinai. Num. 1 : 9; 2 : 7; 7 : 24, 29; 10 : 16. (B.C. 1490.) 2. A Reubenite, father of Dathan and Abiram. Num. 16 : 1, 12; 26 : 8, 9; Deut. 11 : 6.

3. One of David's brothers, the eldest of the family. 1 Sam. 16 : 6; 17 : 13, 28; 1 Chron. 2 : 13. (B.C. 1063.) 4. A Levite in the time of David, who was both a "porter" and a musician on the "psaltery." 1 Chron. 15 : 18, 20; 16 : 5. 5. One of the warlike Gadite leaders who came over to David when he was in the wilderness taking refuge from Saul. 1 Chron. 12 : 9. (B.C. 1061.) 6. An ancestor of Samuel the prophet; a Kohathite Levite, son of Nahath. 1 Chron. 6 : 27. (B.C. 1250.) 7. Son of Nathanael, one of the forefathers of Judith, and therefore belonging to the tribe of Simeon. Judith 8 : 1.

Eli'ada (*known by God*). 1. One of David's sons; according to the lists, the youngest but one of the family born to him after his establishment in Jerusalem. 2 Sam. 5 : 16; 1 Chron. 3 : 8. (B.C. after 1033.) 2. A mighty man of war, a Benjamite, who led 200,000 of his tribe to the army of Jehoshaphat. 2 Chron. 17 : 17. (B.C. 945.)

Eli'adah, father of Rezon, the captain of a marauding band that annoyed Solomon. 1 Kings 11 : 23.

Eli'ah (*my God is Jehovah*). 1. A Benjamite, a chief man of the tribe. 1 Chron. 8 : 27. 2. One of the Bene-Elam, an Israelite (*i. e.* a layman) who had married a foreign wife. Ezra 10 : 26.

Eli'ahba (*whom God hides*), one of the thirty of David's guard. 2 Sam. 23 : 32; 1 Chron. 11 : 33. (B.C. 1046.)

Eli'akim (*raised up by God*). 1. Son of Hilkiah, master of Hezekiah's household ("over the house," as Isa. 36 : 3.) 2 Kings 18 : 18, 26, 37. (B.C. 713.) Eliakim was a good man, as appears by the title emphatically applied to him by God, "my servant Eliakim," Isa. 22 : 20, and also in the discharge of the duties of his high station, in which he acted as a "father to the inhabitants of Jerusalem, and to the house of Judah." Isa. 22 : 21. 2. The original name of Jehoiakim king of Judah. 2 Kings 23 : 34; 2 Chron. 36 : 4. 3. A priest in the days of Nehemiah, who assisted at the dedication of the new wall of Jerusalem. Neh. 12 : 41. (B.C. 446.) 4. Eldest son of Abiud or Judah; brother of Joseph, and father of Azor. Matt. 1 : 13.

5. Son of Melea, and father of Jonan. Luke 3 : 30, 31.

Eli'am (*God's people*). 1. Father of Bath-sheba, the wife of David. 2 Sam. 11 : 3.

2. One of David's "thirty" warriors. 2 Sam. 23 : 34.

Eli'as, the Greek form of Elijah.

Eli'asaph. 1. Head of the tribe of Dan at the time of the census in the wilderness of Sinai. Num. 1 : 14; 2 : 14; 7 : 42, 47; 10 : 20. (B.C. 1490.)

2. A Levite, and "chief of the Gershonites" at the same time. Num. 3 : 24.

Eli'ashib (*whom God restores*). 1. A priest in the time of King David, eleventh in the order of the "governors" of the sanctuary. 1 Chron. 24 : 12.

2. One of the latest descendants of the royal family of Judah. 1 Chron. 3 : 24.

3. High priest at Jerusalem at the time of the rebuilding of the walls under Nehemiah. Neh. 3 : 1, 20, 21. (B.C. 446.)

4. A singer in the time of Ezra who had married a foreign wife. Ezra 10 : 24.

5. A son of Zattu, Ezra 10 : 27, and

6. A son of Bani, Ezra 10 : 36, both of whom had transgressed in the same manner. (B.C. 458.)

Eli'athah (*to whom God comes*), a musician in the temple in the time of King David. 1 Chron. 25 : 4, 27.

Eli'dad (*whom God loves*), the man chosen to represent the tribe of Benjamin in the division of the land of Canaan. Num. 34 : 21. (B.C. 1452.)

Eli'el (*to whom God is strength*). 1. One of the heads of the tribe of Manasseh on the east of Jordan. 1 Chron. 5 : 24.

2. A forefather of Samuel the prophet. 1 Chron. 6 : 34.

3. A chief man in the tribe of Benjamin. 1 Chron. 8 : 20.

4. Also a Benjamite chief. 1 Chron. 8 : 22.

5. One of the heroes of David's guard. 1 Chron. 11 : 46.

6. Another of the same guard. 1 Chron. 11 : 47.

7. One of the Gadite heroes who came across Jordan to David when he was in the wilderness of Judah hiding from Saul. 1 Chron. 12 : 11.

8. A Kohathite Levite, at the time of transportation of the ark from the house of Obed-edom to Jerusalem. 1 Chron. 15 : 9, 11. (B.C. 1043.)

9. A Levite in the time of Hezekiah;

one of the overseers of the offerings made in the temple. 2 Chron. 31 : 13. (B.C. 726.)

Elie'na-i (*my eyes are toward God*), a descendant of Benjamin, and a chief man in the tribe. 1 Chron. 8 : 20.

Elie'zer (*God is his help*). 1. Abraham's chief servant, called by him "Eliezer of Damascus." Gen. 15 : 2. (B.C. 1857.)

2. Second son of Moses and Zipporah (B.C. 1523), to whom his father gave this name because "the God of my father was mine help, and delivered me from the sword of Pharaoh." Ex. 18 : 4; 1 Chron. 23 : 15, 17; 26 : 25.

3. One of the sons of Becher, the son of Benjamin. 1 Chron. 7 : 8.

4. A priest in the reign of David. 1 Chron. 15 : 24.

5. Son of Zichri, ruler of the Reubenites in the reign of David. 1 Chron. 27 : 16.

6. Son of Dodavah, of Mareshah in Judah, 2 Chron. 20 : 37, a prophet, who rebuked Jehoshaphat for joining himself with Ahaziah king of Israel. (B.C. 895.)

7. A chief Israelite whom Ezra sent with others from Ahava to Cesiphia, to induce some Levites and Nethinim to accompany him to Jerusalem. Ezra 8 : 16. (B.C. 459.)

8, 9, 10. A priest, a Levite and an Israelite of the sons of Harim, who had married foreign wives. Ezra 10 : 18, 23, 31.

11. Son of Jorim, in the genealogy of Christ. Luke 3 : 29.

Elihoe'na-i (*my eyes are toward Jehovah*), son of Zerahiah, who with 200 men returned from the captivity with Ezra. Ezra 8 : 4. (B.C. 459.)

Eliho'reph (*God is his reward*), one of Solomon's scribes. 1 Kings 4 : 3.

Eli'hu (*whose God is he* (*Jehovah*)). 1. One of the interlocutors in the book of Job. [JOB.] He is described as the "son of Barachel the Buzite."

2. A forefather of Samuel the prophet. 1 Sam. 1 : 1.

3. In 1 Chron. 27 : 18 Elihu "of the brethren of David" is mentioned as the chief of the tribe of Judah.

4. One of the captains of the thousands of Manasseh, 1 Chron. 12 : 20, who followed David to Ziklag after he had left the Philistine army on the eve of the battle of Gilboa.

5. A Korhite Levite in the time of David. 1 Chron. 26 : 7.

Eli'jah (*my God is Jehovah*) has been well entitled " the grandest and the most romantic character that Israel ever produced." " Elijah the Tishbite, . . . of the inhabitants of Gilead " is literally all that is given us to know of his parentage and locality. Of his appearance as he "stood before " Ahab (B.C. 910) with the suddenness of motion to this day characteristic of the Bedouins from his native hills, we can perhaps realize something from the touches, few but strong, of the narrative. His chief characteristic was his hair, long and thick, and hanging down his back. His ordinary clothing consisted of a girdle of skin round his loins, which he tightened when about to move quickly. 1 Kings 18 : 46. But in addition to this he occasionally wore the "mantle " or cape of sheepskin which has supplied us with one of our most familiar figures of speech. His introduction, in what we may call the first act of his life, is of the most startling description. He suddenly appears before Ahab, prophesies a three-years drought in Israel, and proclaims the vengeance of Jehovah for the apostasy of the king. Obliged to flee from the vengeance of the king, or more probably of the queen (comp. 1 Kings 19 : 2), he was directed to the brook Cherith. There in the hollow of the torrent bed he remained, supported in the miraculous manner with which we are all familiar, till the failing of the brook obliged him to forsake it. His next refuge was at Zarephath. Here in the house of the widow woman Elijah performed the miracles of prolonging the oil and the meal, and restored the son of the widow to life after his apparent death. 1 Kings 17. In this or some other retreat an interval of more than two years must have elapsed. The drought continued, and at last the full horrors of famine, caused by the failure of the crops, descended on Samaria. Again Elijah suddenly appears before Ahab. There are few more sublime stories in history than the account of the succeeding events—with the servant of Jehovah and his single attendant on the one hand, and the 850 prophets of Baal on the other; the altars, the descending fire of Jehovah consuming both sacrifice and altar ; the rising storm, and the ride across the plain to Jezreel. 1 Kings 18. Jezebel vows vengeance, and again Elijah takes refuge in flight into the wilderness, where he is again miraculously fed,

and goes forward, in the strength of that food, a journey of forty days to the mount of God, even to Horeb, where he takes refuge in a cave, and witnesses a remarkable vision of Jehovah. 1 Kings 19 : 9– 18. He receives the divine communication, and sets forth in search of Elisha, whom he finds ploughing in the field, and anoints him prophet in his place. ch. 19. For a time little is heard of Elijah, and Ahab and Jezebel probably believed they had seen the last of him. But after the murder of Naboth, Elijah, who had received an intimation from Jehovah of what was taking place, again suddenly appears before the king, and then follows Elijah's fearful denunciation of Ahab and Jezebel, which may possibly be recovered by putting together the words recalled by Jehu, 2 Kings 9 : 26, 36, 37, and those given in 1 Kings 21 : 19–25. A space of three or four years now elapses (comp. 1 Kings 22 : 1, 51 ; 2 Kings 1 : 17) before we again catch a glimpse of Elijah. Ahaziah is on his death-bed, 1 Kings 22 : 51 ; 2 Kings 1 : 1, 2, and sends to an oracle or shrine of Baal to ascertain the issue of his illness ; but Elijah suddenly appears on the path of the messengers, without preface or inquiry utters his message of death, and as rapidly disappears. The wrathful king sends two bands of soldiers to seize Elijah, and they are consumed with fire ; but finally the prophet goes down and delivers to Ahaziah's face the message of death. Not long after Elijah sent a message to Jehoram denouncing his evil doings, and predicting his death. 2 Chron. 21 : 12–15. It was at Gilgal— probably on the western edge of the hills of Ephraim—that the prophet received the divine intimation that his departure was at hand. He was at the time with Elisha, who seems now to have become his constant companion, and who would not consent to leave him. " And it came to pass as they still went on and talked, that, behold, a chariot of fire and horses of fire, and parted them both asunder ; and Elijah went up by a whirl-wind into heaven." (B.C. 896.) Fifty men of the sons of the prophets ascended the abrupt heights behind the town, and witnessed the scene. How deep was the impression which he made on the mind of the nation may be judged of from the fixed belief which many centuries after prevailed that Elijah would again appear for the relief and restoration of his country, as Malachi prophesied. Mal. 4 : 5. He spoke, but left no written words, save the letter to Jehoram king of Judah. 2 Chron. 21 : 12–15.

Eli'ika (*rejected of God*), a Harodite, one of David's guard. 2 Sam. 23 : 25.

E'lim (*strong trees*), Ex. 15 : 27; Num. 33 : 9, the second station where the Israelites encamped after crossing the Red Sea. It is distinguished as having had "twelve wells (rather 'fountains') of water, and three-score and ten palm trees." It is generally identified by the best authorities with *Wady Garundel*, about halfway down the shore of the Gulf of Suez. A few palm trees still remain, and the water is excellent.

Elim'elech (*my God is king*), a man of the tribe of Judah and of the family of the Hezronites, who dwelt in Bethlehem-Ephratah in the days of the Judges. (B.C. 1312.) In consequence of a great dearth in the land he went with his wife, Naomi, and his two sons, Mahlon and Chilion, to dwell in Moab, where he and his sons died without posterity. Ruth 1 : 2, 3, etc.

Elio-e'na-i (*my eyes are toward the Lord*). 1. Eldest son of Neariah, the son of Shemaiah. 1 Chron. 3 : 23, 24.

2. Head of a family of the Simeonites. 1 Chron. 4 : 36. (B.C. after 1451.)

3. Head of one of the families of the sons of Becher, the son of Benjamin. 1 Chron. 7 : 8.

4. A Korhite Levite, and one of the doorkeepers of the "house of Jehovah." 1 Chron. 26 : 3.

5. A priest in the days of Ezra, one of those who had married foreign wives. Ezra 10 : 22. (B.C. 446.) Possibly the same as

6. An Israelite of the sons of Zattu, who had also married a foreign wife. Ezra 10 : 27. (B.C. 458.)

El'iphal (*whom God judges*), son of Ur, one of David's guard. 1 Chron. 11 : 35. [ELIPHELET, 3.]

Eliph'alet (*the God of deliverance*), the last of the thirteen sons born to David after his establishment in Jerusalem. 2 Sam. 5 : 16; 1 Chron. 14 : 7. [ELIPHELET, 2.]

El'iphaz (*God is his strength*). 1. The son of Esau and Adah, and the father of Teman. Gen. 36 : 4; 1 Chron. 1 : 35, 36.

2. The chief of the "three friends" of Job. He is called "the Temanite;" hence it is naturally inferred that he was a descendant of Teman. On him

falls the main burden of the argument, that God's retribution in this world is perfect and certain, and that consequently suffering must be a proof of previous sin. Job 4, 5, 15, 22. The great truth brought out by him is the unapproachable majesty and purity of God. Job 4 : 12–21; 15 : 12–16. [JOB.]

Eliph'eleh (*whom God makes distinguished*), a Merarite Levite, one of the gate-keepers appointed by David to play on the harp "on the Sheminith" on the occasion of bringing up the ark to the city of David. 1 Chron. 15 : 18, 21.

Eliph'elet (*the God of deliverance*). 1. The name of a son of David, one of the children born to him after his establishment in Jerusalem. 1 Chron. 3 : 6. (B.C. after 1044.)

2. Another son of David, belonging also to the Jerusalem family, and apparently the last of his sons. 1 Chron. 3 : 8.

3. One of the thirty warriors of David's guard. 2 Sam. 23 : 34.

4. Son of Eshek, a descendant of King Saul through Jonathan. 1 Chron. 8 : 39. (B.C. before 536.)

5. One of the leaders of the Bene-Adonikam who returned from Babylon with Ezra. Ezra 8 : 13. (B.C. 459.)

6. A man of the Bene-Hashum in the time of Ezra who had married a foreign wife. Ezra 10 : 33. (B.C. 458.)

Elis'abeth (*the oath of God*), the wife of Zacharias and mother of John the Baptist. She was herself of the priestly family, and a relation, Luke 1 : 36, of the mother of our Lord.

Elise'us, the Greek form of the name Elisha.

Eli'sha (*God his salvation*), son of Shaphat of Abel-meholah; the attendant and disciple of Elijah, and subsequently his successor as prophet of the kingdom of Israel. The earliest mention of his name is in the command to Elijah in the cave at Horeb. 1 Kings 19 : 16, 17. (B.C. about 900.) Elijah sets forth to obey the command, and comes upon his successor engaged in ploughing. He crosses to him and throws over his shoulders the rough mantle—a token at once of investiture with the prophet's office and of adoption as a son. Elisha delayed merely to give the farewell kiss to his father and mother and preside at a parting feast with his people, and then followed the great prophet on his northward road. We hear nothing more of Elisha for eight years, until the translation of his master, when he reappears, to become the most prominent figure in the history of his country during the rest of his long life. In almost every respect Elisha presents the most complete contrast to Elijah. Elijah was a true Bedouin child of the desert. If he enters a city it is only to deliver his message of fire and be gone. Elisha, on the other hand, is a civilized man, an inhabitant of cities. His dress was the ordinary garment of an Israelite, the *beged*, probably similar in form to the long *abbeyeh* of the modern Syrians. 2 Kings 2 : 12. His hair was worn trimmed behind, in contrast to the disordered locks of Elijah, and he used a walking-staff, 2 Kings 4 : 29, of the kind ordinarily carried by grave or aged citizens. Zech. 8 : 4. After the departure of his master, Elisha returned to dwell at Jericho, 2 Kings 2 : 18, where he miraculously purified the springs. We next meet with Elisha at Bethel, in the heart of the country, on his way from Jericho to Mount Carmel. 2 Kings 2 : 23. The mocking children, Elisha's curse and the catastrophe which followed are familiar to all. Later he extricates Jehoram king of Israel, and the kings of Judah and Edom, from their difficulty in the campaign against Moab arising from want of water. 2 Kings 3 : 4–27. Then he multiplies the widow's oil. 2 Kings 4 : 5. The next occurrence is at Shunem, where he is hospitably entertained by a woman of substance, whose son dies, and is brought to life again by Elisha. 2 Kings 4 : 8–37. Then at Gilgal he purifies the deadly pottage, 2 Kings 4 : 38–41, and multiplies the loaves. 2 Kings 4 : 42–44. The simple records of these domestic incidents amongst the sons of the prophets are now interrupted by an occurrence of a more important character. 2 Kings 5 : 1–27. The chief captain of the army of Syria, Naaman, is attacked with leprosy, and is sent by an Israelite maid to the prophet Elisha, who directs him to dip seven times in the Jordan, which he does and is healed, 2 Kings 5 : 1–14; while Naaman's servant, Gehazi, he strikes with leprosy for his unfaithfulness. ch. 5 : 20–27. Again the scene changes. It is probably at Jericho that Elisha causes the iron axe to swim. 2 Kings 6 : 1–7. A band of Syrian marauders are sent to seize him, but are struck blind, and he misleads them to Samaria, where they find themselves in the presence of the Israelite king and his troops. 2 Kings 6 : 8–23. During the famine in Samaria, 2 Kings 6 : 24–33, he prophesied incredible plenty, ch. 7 : 1–2, which was soon fulfilled. ch. 7 : 3–20. We next find the prophet at Damascus. Benhadad the king is sick, and sends to Elisha by Hazael to know the result. Elisha prophesies the king's death, and announces to Hazael that he is to succeed to the throne. 2 Kings 8 : 7-15. Finally this prophet of God, after having filled the position for sixty years, is found on his death-bed in his own house. 2 Kings 13 : 14–19. The power of the prophet, however, does not terminate with his death. Even in the tomb he restores the dead to life. ch. 13 : 21.

Eli′shah (*God is salvation*), the eldest son of Javan. Gen. 10 : 4. The residence of his descendants is described in Ezek. 27 : 7 as the isles of Elishah, whence the Phœnicians obtained their purple and blue dyes. Some connect the race of Elishah with the Æolians, others with Elis, and in a more extended sense Peloponnesus, or even Hellas.

Elish′ama (*whom God hears*). 1. The "prince" or "captain" of the tribe of Ephraim in the wilderness of Sinai. Num. 1 : 10; 2 : 18; 7 : 48; 10 : 22. (B.C. 1491.) From 1 Chron. 7 : 26 we find that he was grandfather to the great Joshua.

2. A son of King David. 2 Sam. 5 : 16; 1 Chron. 3 : 8; 14 : 7.

3. Another son of David, 1 Chron. 3 : 6, who in the other lists is called ELISHUA. (B.C. after 1044.)

4. A descendant of Judah. 1 Chron. 2 : 41.

5. The father of Nethaniah and grandfather of Ishmael. 2 Kings 25 : 25; Jer. 41 : 1.

6. Scribe to King Jehoiakim. Jer. 36 : 12, 20, 21. (B.C. 605.)

7. A priest in the time of Jehoshaphat. 2 Chron. 17 : 8. (B.C. 912.)

Elish′aphat (*whom God judges*), son of Zichri; one of the captains of hundreds in the time of Jehoiada. 2 Chron. 23 : 1. (B.C. 877.)

Elish′eba (*God is her oath*), the wife of Aaron. Ex. 6 : 23. She was the daughter of Amminadab, and sister of Nahshon the captain of the host of Judah. Num. 2 : 3. (B.C. 1491.)

Elish′ua (*God is my salvation*), one of David's sons, born after his settlement in Jerusalem. 2 Sam. 5 : 15; 1 Chron. 14 : 5. (B.C. 1044.)

Eli'ud (*God his praise*), son of Achim in the genealogy of Christ. Matt. 1 : 15.

Eliz'aphan (*whom God protects*). 1. A Levite, son of Uzziel, chief of the house of the Kohathites at the time of the census in the wilderness of Sinai. Num. 3 : 30. (B.C. 1491.)

2. Prince of the tribe of Zebulun. Num. 34 : 25.

Eli'zur, prince of the tribe and over the host of Reuben. Num. 1 : 5 ; 2 : 10 ; 7 : 30, 35 ; 10 : 18.

El'kanah, or **El'konah** (*God-provided*). 1. Son, or rather grandson, see 1 Chron. 6 : 22, 23 (7, 8), of Korah, according to Ex. 6 : 24.

2. A descendant of the above in the line of Ahimoth, otherwise Mahath, 1 Chron. 6 : 26, 35 ; Heb. 11 : 20.

3. Another Kohathite Levite, father of Samuel the illustrious judge and prophet. 1 Chron. 6 : 27, 34. (B.C. about 1190.) All that is known of him is contained in the above notices and in 1 Sam. 1 : 1, 4, 8, 19, 21, 23 and 2 : 11, 20.

4. A Levite. 1 Chron. 9 : 16.

5. A Korhite who joined David while he was at Ziklag. 1 Chron. 12 : 6. (B.C. 1054.)

6. An officer in the household of Ahaz king of Judah, who was slain by Zichri the Ephraimite when Pekah invaded Judah. 2 Chron. 28 : 7. (B.C. 739.)

El'kosh (*God my bow*), the birthplace of the prophet Nahum, hence called "the Elkoshite." Nah. 1 : 1. This place is located at the modern *Alkush*, a village on the east bank of the Tigris, about two miles north of Mosul. Some think a small village in Galilee is intended.

El'lasar (*oak*), the city of Arioch, Gen. 14 : 1, seems to be the Hebrew representative of the old Chaldean town called in the native dialect *Larsa* or *Larancha*. *Larsa* was a town of lower Babylonia or Chaldea, situated nearly halfway between Ur (*Mugheir*) and Erech (*Warka*), on the left bank of the Euphrates. It is now *Senkereh*.

Elm. Hos. 4 : 13. [See OAK.]

Elma'dam. In the Revised Version, Luke 3 : 28. Same as ELMODAM.

Elmo'dam (*measure*), son of Er, in the genealogy of Joseph. Luke 3 : 28.

El'naam (*God his delight*), the father of Jeribai and Joshaviah, two of David's guard, according to 1 Chron. 11 : 46.

El'nathan, or **Elna'than** (*God hath given*). 1. The maternal grandfather of Jehoiachin, 2 Kings 24 : 8 ; the same with

Elnathan the son of Achbor. Jer. 26 : 22 ; 36 : 12, 25.

2. The name of three persons, apparently Levites, in the time of Ezra. Ezra 8 : 16.

E'lon (*an oak*). 1. A Hittite, whose daughter was one of Esau's wives. Gen. 26 : 34 ; 36 : 2. (B.C. 1797.)

2. The second of the three sons attributed to Zebulun, Gen. 46 : 14 ; Num. 26 : 26, and the founder of the family of the Elonites. (B.C. 1695.)

3. Elon the Zebulonite, who judged Israel for ten years, and was buried in Aijalon in Zebulun. Judges 12 : 11, 12. (B.C. 1174–1164.)

4. One of the towns in the border of the tribe of Dan. Josh. 19 : 43.

E'lon-beth'-hanan (*oak of the house of grace*) is named with two Danite towns as forming one of Solomon's commissariat districts. 1 Kings 4 : 9.

E'lonites, The. Num. 26 : 26. [ELON, 2.]

El'oth. 1 Kings 9 : 26. [ELATH.]

Elpa'al (*God his wages*), a Benjamite, son of Hushim and brother of Abitub. 1 Chron. 8 : 11. He was the founder of a numerous family.

El'palet (*God his deliverance*), one of David's sons born in Jerusalem. 1 Chron. 14 : 5.

El-pa'ran (*God his deliverance*), literally "the terebinth of Paran." Gen. 14 : 6. [PARAN.]

El'tekeh (*God its fear*), one of the cities in the border of Dan, Josh. 19 : 44, which with its suburbs was allotted to the Kohathite Levites. Josh. 21 : 23.

El'tekon (*God its foundation*), one of the towns of the tribe of Judah in the mountains. Josh. 15 : 59. It has not yet been identified.

El'tolad (*God's kindred*), one of the cities in the south of Judah, Josh. 15 : 30, allotted to Simeon, Josh. 19 : 4, and in possession of that tribe until the time of David. 1 Chron. 4 : 29.

E'lul (*vine; gleaning*). Neh. 6 : 15 ; 1 Macc. 14 : 27. [MONTH.]

Elu'za-i (*God is my praise*), one of the warriors of Benjamin who joined David at Ziklag. 1 Chron. 12 : 5. (B.C. 1054.)

El'ymas (*a wise man*), the Arabic name of the Jewish magus or sorcerer Bar-jesus. Acts 13 : 6 ff. (A.D. 44.)

El'zabad (*whom God hath given*). 1. One of the Gadite heroes who came across the Jordan to David. 1 Chron. 12 : 12.

2. A Korhite Levite. 1 Chron. 26 : 7.

El'zaphan (*whom God protects*), second son of Uzziel, who was the son of Kohath son of Levi. Ex. 6 : 22.

Embalming, the process by which dead bodies are preserved from putrefaction and decay. It was most general among the Egyptians, and it is in connection with this people that the two instances which we meet with in the Old Testament are mentioned. Gen. 50 : 2, 26. The embalmers first removed part of the brain through the nostrils, by means of a crooked iron, and destroyed the rest by injecting caustic drugs. An incision was then made along the flank with a sharp Ethiopian stone, and the whole of the intestines removed. The cavity was rinsed out with palm wine, and afterwards scoured with pounded perfumes. It was then filled with pure myrrh pounded, cassia and other aromatics, except frankincense. This done, the body was sewn up and steeped in natron (saltpetre) for seventy days. When the seventy days were accomplished, the embalmers washed the corpse and swathed it in bandages of linen, cut in strips and smeared

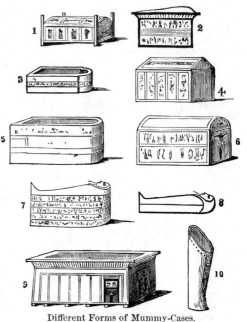

Different Forms of Mummy-Cases.
1, 2, 4, 9. Of wood. 3, 5, 6, 7, 8. Of stone. 10. Of burnt earthenware.

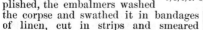

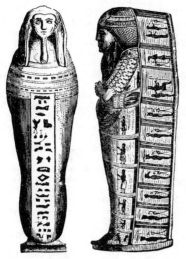

Mummy-Cases.

with gum. They then gave it up to the relatives of the deceased, who provided for it a wooden case, made in the shape of a man, in which the dead was placed, and deposited in an erect position against the wall of the sepulchral chamber. Sometimes no incision was made in the body, nor were the intestines removed, but cedar-oil was injected into the stomach by the rectum. At others the oil was prevented from escaping until the end of the steeping process, when it was withdrawn, and carried off with it the stomach and intestines in a state of solution, while the flesh was consumed by the natron, and nothing was left but the skin and bones. The body in this state was returned to the relatives of the deceased. The third mode, which was adopted by the poorer classes, and cost but little, consisted in rinsing out the intestines with syrmæa, an infusion of senna and cassia, and steeping the body for several days in natron. It does not appear that embalming was practiced by the Hebrews. The cost of embalming was sometimes nearly $2000, varying from this amount down to $200 or $300.

Embroiderer. Various explanations have been offered as to the distinction between "needle-work" and "cunning work." Probably neither term expresses just what is to-day understood by embroidery, though the latter may come nearest to it. The art of embroidery by the loom was extensively practiced among the nations of antiquity. In addition to the Egyptians, the Babylonians were celebrated for it.

Emerald, a precious stone of a rich green color, upon which its value chiefly depends. This gem was the first in the second row on the breastplate of the high priest. Ex. 28 : 18; 39 : 11. It was imported to Tyre from Syria, Ezek. 27 : 16; was used as a seal or signet, Ecclus. 32 : 6, as an ornament of clothing and bedding, Ezek. 28 : 13; Judges 10 : 21, and is spoken of as one of the foundations of Jerusalem. Rev. 21 : 19; Tob. 13 : 16. The rainbow around the throne is compared to emerald in Rev. 4 : 3.

Emerods. Deut. 28 : 27; 1 Sam. 5 : 6, 9, 12; 6 : 4, 5, 11. Probably *hemorrhoidal tumors,* or bleeding piles, are intended. These are very common in Syria at present, Oriental habits of want of exercise and improper food, producing derangement of the liver, constipation, etc., being such as to cause them.

E'mims (*terrors*), a tribe or family of gigantic stature which originally inhabited the region along the eastern side of the Dead Sea. They were related to the Anakim.

Emman'uel. Matt. 1 : 23. [IMMANUEL.]

Em'ma-us, or **Emma'us** (*warm baths*), the village to which the two disciples were going when our Lord appeared to them on the way, on the day of his resurrection. Luke 24 : 13. Luke makes its distance from Jerusalem *sixty stadia* (Authorized Version "threescore furlongs"), or about 7½ miles; and Josephus mentions "a village called Emmaus" at the same distance. The site of Emmaus remains yet to be identified.

Em'mor (*an ass*), the father of Sychem. Acts 7 : 16. [HAMOR.]

En, at the beginning of many Hebrew words, signifies a spring or fountain.

E'nam (*double spring*), one of the cities of Judah in the *Shefelah* or lowland. Josh. 15 : 34.

E'nan (*having eyes*). Ahira ben-Enan was "prince" of the tribe of Naphtali at the time of the numbering of Israel in the wilderness of Sinai. Num. 1 : 15. (B.C. 1491.)

Encampment primarily denoted the resting-place of an army or company of travellers at night, Gen. 32 : 21; Ex. 16 : 13, and was hence applied to the army or caravan when on its march. Gen. 32 : 7, 8; Ex. 14 : 19; Josh. 10 : 5; 11 : 4. The description of the camp of the Israelites, on their march from Egypt, Num. 2, 3, supplies the greatest amount of information on the subject. The tabernacle, corresponding to the chieftain's tent of an ordinary encampment, was placed in the centre, and around and facing it, Num. 2 : 1, arranged in four grand divisions, corresponding to the four points of the compass, lay the host of Israel, according to their standards. Num. 1 : 52; 2 : 2. In the centre, round the tabernacle, and with no standard but the cloudy or fiery pillar which rested over it, were the tents of the priests and Levites. The former, with Moses and Aaron at their head, were encamped on the eastern side. The order of encampment was preserved on the march. Num. 2 : 17.

Enchantments. The words so translated have several significations: the practice of secret arts, Ex. 7 : 11, 22; 8 : 7; "muttered spells," 2 Kings 9 : 22; Micah 5 : 12; the charming of serpents, Eccles. 10 : 11; the enchantments sought by Balaam, Num. 24 : 1; the use of magic, Isa. 47 : 9, 12. Any resort to these methods of imposture was strictly forbidden in Scripture, Lev. 19 : 26; Isa. 47 : 9, etc.; but to eradicate the tendency is almost impossible, 2 Kings 17 : 17, and we find it still flourishing at the Christian era. Acts 13 : 6, 8.

En'-dor (*fountain of Dor*), a place in the territory of Issachar, and yet possessed by Manasseh. Josh. 17 : 11. Endor was the scene of the great victory over Sisera and Jabin. It was here that the witch dwelt whom Saul consulted. 1 Sam. 28 : 7. It was known to Eusebius, who describes it as a large village four miles south of Tabor. Here to the north of *Jebel Duhy* the name still lingers. The distance from the slopes of Gilboa to Endor is seven or eight miles, over difficult ground.

En-egla'im (*fountain of the two calves*), a place named only by Ezekiel, 47 : 10, apparently as on the Dead Sea; but whether near to or far from Engedi, on the east or the west side of the sea, it is impossible to ascertain.

Emmaus.

En-gan'nim (*fountain of the garden*). 1. A city in the low country of Judah, named between Zanoah and Tappuah. Josh. 15 : 34.

2. A city on the border of Issachar, Josh. 19 : 21, allotted with its "suburbs" to the Gershonite Levites, Josh. 21 : 29; probably *Jenin*, the first village encountered on the ascent from the great plain of Esdraelon into the hills of the central country.

En'-gedi or **En-ge'di** (*fount of the kid*), a town in the wilderness of Judah, Josh. 15 : 62, on the western shore of the

Wilderness of Engedi (Dead Sea).

Dead Sea. Ezek. 47 : 10. Its original name was Hazezon-tamar, on account of the palm groves which surrounded it. 2 Chron. 20 : 2. Its site is about the middle of the western shore of the lake, at the fountain of *Ain Jidy*, from which the place gets its name. It was immediately after an assault upon the "Amorites that dwelt in Hazezon-tamar," that the five Mesopotamian kings were attacked by the rulers of the plain of Sodom. Gen. 14 : 7; comp. 2 Chron. 20 : 2. Saul was told that David was in the "wilderness of Engedi;" and he took "three thousand men, and went to seek David and his men upon the rocks of the *wild goats*." 1 Sam. 24 : 1–4. The vineyards of Engedi were celebrated by Solomon. Cant. 1 : 14.

Engine, a term applied exclusively to military affairs in the Bible. The en-

gines to which the term is applied in 2 Chron. 26 : 15 were designed to propel various missiles from the walls of a besieged town. One, with which the Hebrews were acquainted, was the battering-ram, described in Ezek. 26 : 9, and still more precisely in Ezek. 4 : 2; 21 : 22.

Engraver. His chief business was cutting names or devices on rings and seals; the only notices of engraving are in connection with the high priest's dress —the two onyx stones, the twelve jewels and the mitre-plate having inscriptions on them. Ex. 28 : 11, 21, 36.

En-had'dah (*swift fountain*), one of the cities on the border of Issachar named next to Engannim. Josh. 19 : 21.

En-hak'ko-re (*fount of the caller*), the spring which burst out in answer to the cry of Samson after his exploit with the jawbone. Judges 15 : 19.

En-ha'zor (*fount of Hazor*), one of the fenced cities in the inheritance of Naphtali, distinct from Hazor. Josh. 19 : 37. It has not yet been identified.

En-mish'pat (*fount of judgment*). Gen. 14 : 7. [KADESH.]

E'noch (*dedicated*). 1. The eldest son of Cain, Gen. 4 : 17, who called after his name the city which he built. Gen. 4 : 18. (B.C. 3870.)

2. The son of Jared and father of Methuselah. Gen. 5 : 21 ff.; Luke 3 : 37. (B.C. 3378–3013.) In the Epistle of Jude, 14, he is described as "the *seventh* from Adam;" and the number is probably noticed as conveying the idea of divine completion and rest, while Enoch was himself a type of perfected humanity. After the birth of Methuselah it is said, Gen. 5 : 22–24, that Enoch "walked with God three hundred years . . . and he was not; for God took him." The phrase "walked with God" is elsewhere only used of Noah, Gen. 6 : 9; cf. Gen. 17 : 1, etc., and is to be explained of a prophetic life spent in immediate converse with the spiritual world. Like Elijah, he was translated without seeing death. In the Epistle to the Hebrews the spring and issue of Enoch's life are clearly marked.

Both the Latin and Greek fathers commonly coupled Enoch and Elijah as historic witnesses of the possibility of a resurrection of the body and of a true human existence in glory. Rev. 11 : 3.

E'noch, The book of. The first trace of the existence of this work is found in the Epistle of Jude, 14, 15. An apocryphal book called Enoch was known at a very early date, but was lost sight of until 1773, when Bruce brought with him on his return from Egypt three MSS. containing the complete Ethiopic translation. In its present shape the book consists of a series of revelations supposed to have been given to Enoch and Noah, which extend to the most varied aspects of nature and life, and are designed to offer a comprehensive vindication of the action of Providence. Notwithstanding the quotation in Jude, and the wide circulation of the book itself, the apocalypse of Enoch was uniformly and distinctly separated from the canonical Scriptures. Its authorship and date are unknown.

E'non (*springs*), a place "near to Salim," at which John baptized. John 3 : 23. It was evidently west of the Jordan, comp. John 3 : 22 with 26, and with 1 : 28, and abounded in water. This is indicated by the name, which is merely a Greek version of a Chaldee word signifying "springs." Ænon is given in the *Onomasticon* as eight miles south of Scythopolis, "near Salem and the Jordan."

E'nos (*mortal man*), the son of Seth, Gen. 4 : 26; 5 : 6, 7, 9, 10, 11; Luke 3 : 38; properly ENOSH, as in 1 Chron. 1 : 1.

E'nosh. Same as ENOS. 1 Chron. 1 : 1.

En-rim'mon (*fount of the pomegranate*), one of the places which the men of Judah reinhabited after their return from the captivity. Neh. 11 : 29. Perhaps the same as "Ain and Rimmon," Josh. 15 : 32, and "Ain, Remmon," Josh. 19 : 7; and see 1 Chron. 4 : 32.

En-ro'gel (*fount of the fuller*), a spring which formed one of the landmarks on the boundary line between Judah, Josh. 15 : 7, and Benjamin. Josh. 18 : 16. It may be identified with the present "Fountain of the Virgin," '*Ain Umm ed-Daraj*, the perennial source from which the pool of Siloam is supplied.

En-she'mesh (*fountain of the sun*), a spring which formed one of the landmarks on the north boundary of Judah, Josh. 15 : 7, and the south boundary of Benjamin, Josh. 18 : 17; perhaps *Ain-Haud* or *Ain-Chôt*—the "well of the apostles"—about a mile below Bethany.

Ensign (*nês; in the Authorized Version generally "ensign," sometimes*

Roman Standards.

"standard;" *degel*, "standard," with the exception of Cant. 2 : 4, "banner;" *ôth*, "ensign"). The distinction between these three Hebrew terms is sufficiently marked by their respective uses. *Nês* is a *signal*, and not a military standard. It is an occasional signal, which was exhibited on the top of a pole from a bare mountain-top, Isa. 13 : 2; 18 : 3; *degel* a military *standard* for a large division of an army; and *ôth* the same for a small one. Neither of them, however, expresses the idea which "standard" conveys to our minds, viz. a flag. The standards in use among the Hebrews probably resembled those of the Egyptians and Assyrians —a figure or device of some kind elevated on a pole; usually a sacred emblem, such as an animal, a boat, or the king's name.

En-tap'puah. Josh. 17 : 7. [See TAPPUAH.]

Epene'tus (*praiseworthy*), a Christian at Rome, greeted by St. Paul in Rom. 16 : 5, and designated as his beloved and the first-fruit of Asia unto Christ.

Ep'aphras (*lovely*), a fellow laborer with the apostle Paul, mentioned Col. 1 : 7 as having taught the Colossian church the grace of God in truth, and designated a faithful minister of Christ on their behalf. He was at that time with St. Paul at Rome. (A.D. 57.) For Paul's estimate of him see Col. 1 : 7, 8 ; 4 : 12.

Epaphrodi'tus (*lovely*), the full name of which Epaphras is a contraction. Philip. 2 : 25 ; 4 : 18.

E'phah (*gloomy*), the first, in order, of the sons of Midian, Gen. 25 : 4 ; 1 Chron. 1 : 33, afterwards mentioned by Isaiah. Isa. 60 : 6.

E'phah. 1. Concubine of Caleb, in the line of Judah. 1 Chron. 2 : 46.

2. Son of Jahdai ; also in the line of Judah. 1 Chron. 2 : 47.

Ephah. [WEIGHTS AND MEASURES.]

E'pha-i (*gloomy*), a Netophathite, whose sons were among the "captains of the forces" left in Judah after the deportation to Babylon. Jer. 40 : 8 ; 41 : 3, comp. 40 : 13. (B.C. 588.)

E'pher (*a calf*), the second, in order, of the sons of Midian. Gen. 25 : 4 ; 1 Chron. 1 : 33. (B.C. 1820.)

E'pher. 1. A son of Ezra, among the descendants of Judah. 1 Chron. 4 : 17.

2. One of the heads of the families of Manasseh on the east of Jordan. 1 Chron. 5 : 24.

E'phes-dam'mim (*cessation of bloodshed*), a place between Socoh and Arekah, at which the Philistines were encamped before the affray in which Goliath was killed. 1 Sam. 17 : 1. Under the shorter form of PAS-DAMMIM it occurs once again in a similar connection. 1 Chron. 11 : 13.

Ephe'sians, The Epistle to the, was written by the apostle St. Paul during his first captivity at Rome, Acts 28 : 16, apparently immediately after he had written the Epistle to the Colossians [COLOSSIANS, EPISTLE TO], and during that period (perhaps the early part of A. D. 62) when his imprisonment had not assumed the severer character which seems to have marked its close. This epistle was addressed to the Christian church at Ephesus. [EPHESUS.] Its contents may be divided into two portions, the first mainly *doctrinal*, ch. 1–3, the second *hortatory* and *practical*.

Eph'esus (*permitted*), the capital of the Roman province of Asia, and an illustrious city in the district of Ionia, nearly opposite the island of Samos.

Buildings.—Conspicuous at the head of the harbor of Ephesus was the great *temple of Diana* or Artemis, the tutelary divinity of the city. This building was raised on immense substructions, in consequence of the swampy nature of the ground. The earlier temple, which had been begun before the Persian war, was burnt down in the night when Alexander the Great was born ; and another structure, raised by the enthusiastic co-operation of all the inhabitants of "Asia," had taken its place. The magnificence of this sanctuary was a proverb throughout the civilized world. In consequence of this devotion the city of Ephesus was called νεώκορος, Acts 19 : 35, or "warden" of Diana. Another consequence of the celebrity of Diana's worship at Ephesus was that a large manufactory grew up there of portable shrines, which strangers purchased, and devotees carried with them on journeys or set up in their houses. The *theatre*, into which the mob who had seized on Paul, Acts 19 : 29, rushed, was capable of holding 25,000 or 30,000 persons, and was the largest ever built by the Greeks. The *stadium* or circus, 685 feet long by 200 wide, where the Ephesians held their shows, is probably referred to by Paul as the place where he "fought with beasts at Ephesus." 1 Cor. 15 : 32.

Connection with Christianity. — The Jews were established at Ephesus in considerable numbers. Acts 2 : 9 ; 6 : 9. It is here and here only that we find disciples of John the Baptist explicitly mentioned after the ascension of Christ. Acts 18 : 25 ; 19 : 3. The first seeds of Christian truth were possibly sown here immediately after the great Pentecost. Acts 2. St. Paul remained in the place more than two years, Acts 19 : 8, 10 ; 20 : 31, during which he wrote the First Epistle to the Corinthians. At a later period Timothy was set over the disciples, as we learn from the two epistles addressed to him. Among St. Paul's other companions, two, Trophimus and Tychicus, were natives of Asia, Acts 20 : 4, and the latter was probably, 2 Tim. 4 : 12, the former certainly, Acts 21 : 29, a native of Ephesus.

Present condition.—The whole place is now utterly desolate, with the exception of the small Turkish village at *Ayasaluk*. The ruins are of vast extent.

Eph'lal (*judgment*), a descendant of Judah, of the family of Hezron and of Jerahmeel. 1 Chron. 2 : 37.

E'phod (*image*), father of Hanniel of the tribe of Manasseh. Num. 34 : 23.

Ephod, a sacred vestment originally appropriate to the high priest. Ex. 28 : 4.

E'phra-im (*double fruitfulness*), the second son of Joseph by his wife Asenath.

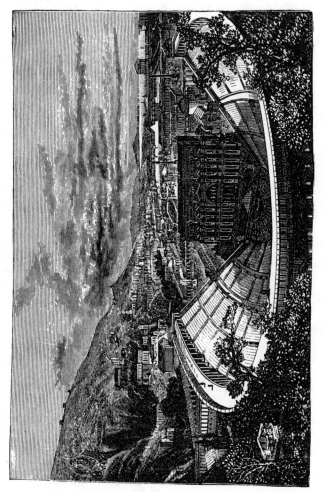

Ancient Ephesus.   Theatre in the foreground.

The Ephesian Temple of Diana (Restored).

(B.C. 1715–1708.) The first indication we have of that ascendency over his elder brother Manasseh which at a later period the tribe of Ephraim so unmistakably possessed is in the blessing of the children by Jacob. Gen. 48.

E'phra-im, that portion of Canaan named after Joseph's second son. Gen. 41 : 50–52. The boundaries of the portion of Ephraim are given in Josh. 16 : 1–10. The south boundary was coincident for part of its length with the north boundary of Benjamin. It extended from the Jordan on the east, at the reach opposite Jericho, to the Mediterranean on the west, probably about Joppa. On the north of Ephraim and Manasseh were the tribes of Asher, Zebulun and Issachar. The territory thus allotted to the "house of Joseph" may be roughly estimated at 55 miles from east to west by 70 from north to south. It was one at once of great richness and great security. Its fertile plains and well-watered valleys could only be reached by a laborious ascent through steep and narrow ravines, all but impassable for an army. Under Joshua the tribe must have taken a high position in the nation, to judge from the tone which the Ephraimites assumed on occasions shortly subsequent to the conquest. After the revolt of Jeroboam the history of Ephraim is the history of the kingdom of Israel, since not only did the tribe become a kingdom, but the kingdom embraced little besides the tribe.

E'phra-im. In "Baal-hazor which is by Ephraim" was Absalom's sheep-farm, at which took place the murder of Amnon, one of the earliest precursors of the great revolt. 2 Sam. 13 : 23. There is no clue to its situation.

E'phra-im, a city "in the district near the wilderness" to which our Lord retired with his disciples when threatened with violence by the priests. John 11 : 54.

E'phra-im, Gate of, one of the gates of the city of Jerusalem, 2 Kings 14 : 13 ; 2 Chron. 25 : 23 ; Neh. 8 : 16 ; 12 : 39, probably at or near the position of the present "Damascus gate."

E'phra-im, Mount, is a district which seems to extend as far south as Ramah and Bethel, 1 Sam. 1 : 1 ; 7 : 17 ; 2 Chron. 13 : 4, 19, compared with 15 : 8, places but a few miles north of Jerusalem, and within the limits of Benjamin.

E'phra-im, The wood of, a wood, or rather a forest, on the east of Jordan,

in which the fatal battle was fought between the armies of David and of Absalom. 2 Sam. 18 : 6.

E'phra-imite. Of the tribe of Ephraim ; elsewhere called "Ephrathite." Judges 12 : 5.

E'phra-in (hamlet), a city of Israel, which Judah captured from Jeroboam. 2 Chron. 13 : 19. It has been conjectured that this Ephrain or Ephron is identical with the Ephraim by which Absalom's sheep-farm of Baal-hazor was situated ; with the city called Ephraim near the wilderness in which our Lord lived for some time ; and with Ophrah, a city of Benjamin, apparently not far from Bethel. But nothing more than conjecture can be arrived at on these points.

Eph'ratah, or **Eph'rath** (fruitful). 1. Second wife of Caleb the son of Hezron, mother of Hur and grandmother of Caleb the spy, according to 1 Chron. 2 : 19, 50, and probably 24, and 4 : 4. (B.C. 1695.)

2. The ancient name of Bethlehem-judah. Gen. 35 : 16, 19 ; 48 : 7.

Eph'rathite. 1. An inhabitant of Bethlehem. Ruth 1 : 2.

2. An Ephraimite. 1 Sam. 1 : 1 ; 1 Kings 11 : 26.

Eph'ron (fawn-like), the son of Zohar, a Hittite, from whom Abraham bought the field and cave of Machpelah. Gen. 23 : 8–17 ; 25 : 9 ; 49 : 29, 30 ; 50 : 13. (B.C. 1860.)

Eph'ron, Mount. The "cities of Mount Ephron" formed one of the landmarks on the northern boundary of the tribe of Judah. Josh. 15 : 9.

Epicure'ans, The, derived their name from Epicurus (342–271 B.C.), a philosopher of Attic descent, whose "Garden" at Athens rivalled in popularity the "Porch" and the "Academy." The doctrines of Epicurus found wide acceptance in Asia Minor and Alexandria. (95–50 B.C.) The object of Epicurus was to find in philosophy a practical guide to happiness. True pleasure and not absolute truth was the end at which he aimed ; experience and not reason the test on which he relied. It is obvious that a system thus framed would degenerate by a natural descent into mere materialism ; and in this form Epicurism was the popular philosophy at the beginning of the Christian era. When St. Paul addressed "Epicureans and Stoics," Acts 17 : 18, at Athens, the philosophy of life was practically reduced to the teaching of these two antagonistic schools.

Epistles, letters; personal correspondence by writing. The twenty-one epistles of the New Testament took the place of tracts among us. In their outward form they are such as might be expected from men who were brought into contact with Greek and Roman customs, themselves belonging to a different race, and so reproducing the imported style with only partial accuracy. They begin (the Epistle to the Hebrews and 1 John excepted) with the names of the writer and of those to whom the epistle is addressed. Then follows the formula of salutation. Then the letter itself commences in the first person, the singular and plural being used indiscriminately. When the substance of the letter has been completed, come the individual messages. The conclusion in this case was probably modified by the fact that the letters were dictated to an amanuensis. When he had done his work, the apostle took up the pen or reed, and added in his own large characters, Gal. 6 : 11, the authenticating autograph. In one instance, Rom. 16 : 22, the amanuensis in his own name adds his salutation. An allusion in 2 Cor. 3 : 1 brings before us another class of letters which must have been in frequent use in the early ages of the Christian Church, by which travellers or teachers were commended by one church to the good offices of others.

Er (*watchful*). 1. First-born of Judah. Er "was wicked in the sight of the Lord; and the Lord slew him." Gen. 38 : 3–7 ; Num. 26 : 19.

2. Descendant of Shelah the son of Judah. 1 Chron. 4 : 21.

3. Son of Jose and father of Elmodam. Luke 3 : 28.

E′ran (*watchful*), the eldest son of Ephraim. Num. 26 : 36.

E′ranites, The. Num. 26 : 36.

E′rech (*length*), one of the cities of Nimrod's kingdom in the land of Shinar, Gen. 10 : 10, doubtless the same as Orchoë, 82 miles south and 43 east of Babylon, the modern designations of the site— *Warka, Irka* and *Irak*—bearing a considerable affinity to the original name.

Eras′tus (*beloved*). 1. One of the attendants of St. Paul at Ephesus, who with Timothy was sent forward into Macedonia. Acts 19 : 22. (A.D. 51.) He is probably the same with Erastus who

is again mentioned in the salutations to Timothy. 2 Tim. 4 : 20.

2. Erastus the chamberlain, or rather the public treasurer, of Corinth, who was one of the early converts to Christianity. Rom. 16 : 23. According to the traditions of the Greek Church, he was first treasurer to the church at Jerusalem, and afterwards bishop of Paneas.

E′ri (*watchful*), son of Gad, Gen. 46 : 16, and ancestor of the Erites. Num. 26 : 16.

Esa′ias, the Greek form of Isaiah. [ISAIAH.]

E′sar-had′don (*victor*), one of the greatest of the kings of Assyria, was the son of Sennacherib, 2 Kings 19 : 37, and the grandson of Sargon, who succeeded Shalmaneser. He appears by his monuments to have been one of the most powerful, if not *the* most powerful, of all the Assyrian monarchs. He is the only one of them whom we find to have actually reigned at Babylon, where he built himself a palace, bricks from which have been recently recovered bearing his name. His Babylonian reign lasted thirteen years, from B.C. 680 to B.C. 667 ; and it was doubtless within this space of time that Manasseh king of Judah, having been seized by his captains at Jerusalem on a charge of rebellion, was brought before him at Babylon, 2 Chron. 33 : 11, and detained for a time as prisoner there. As a builder of great works Esar-haddon is particularly distinguished. Besides his palace at Babylon, he built at least three others in different parts of his dominions, either for himself or his sons, and thirty temples.

E′sau (*hairy*), the eldest son of Isaac, and twin-brother of Jacob. The singular appearance of the child at his birth originated the name. Gen. 25 : 25. Esau's robust frame and "rough" aspect were the types of a wild and daring nature. He was a thorough Bedouin, a "son of the desert." He was much loved by his father, and was of course his heir, but was induced to sell his birthright to Jacob. Mention of his unhappy marriages may be found in Gen. 26 : 34. The next episode in the life of Esau is the loss of his father's covenant blessing, which Jacob secured through the craft of his mother, and the anger of Esau, who vows vengeance. Gen. 27. Later he marries a daughter of Ishmael, Gen. 28 : 8, 9, and soon after establishes himself in Mount Seir, where he was living when Jacob returned from Padan-aram rich and powerful, and the two brothers were reconciled. Gen. 33 : 4. Twenty years thereafter they united in burying Isaac's body in the cave of Machpelah. Of Esau's subsequent history nothing is known; for that of his descendants see EDOM.

Esdra-e′lon. This name is merely the Greek form of the Hebrew word *Jez-* *reel.* "The great plain of Esdraelon" extends across central Palestine from the Mediterranean to the Jordan, separating the mountain ranges of Carmel and Samaria from those of Galilee. The western section of it is properly the plain of Accho or *'Akka.* The main body of the plain is a triangle. Its base on the east extends from *Jenin* (the ancient Engannim) to the foot of the hills below

Plain of Esdraelon. (Jezreel.)

Nazareth, and is about 15 miles long; the north side, formed by the hills of Galilee, is about 12 miles long; and the south side, formed by the Samaria range, is about 18 miles. The apex on the west is a narrow pass opening into the plain of *'Akka.* From the base of this triangular plain three branches stretch out eastward, like fingers from a hand, divided by two bleak, gray ridges—one bearing the familiar name of Mount Gilboa, the other called by Franks Little Hermon, but by natives *Jebel ed-Duhy.* The central branch is the richest as well as the most celebrated. This is the "valley of Jezreel" proper—the battle-field on which Gideon triumphed, and Saul and Jonathan were overthrown. Judges 7 : 1, *seq.*; 1 Sam. 29 and 31. Two things are worthy of special notice in the plain of Esdraelon : 1. Its wonderful richness; 2. Its present desolation. If we except the eastern branches, there is not a single inhabited village on its whole surface, and not more than one-sixth of its soil is cultivated. It is the home of the wild wandering Bedouin.

Es′dras, the form of the name of Ezra the scribe in 1 and 2 Esdras.

Es′dras (*Greek form of Ezra*), **The First Book of,** the first in order of the apocryphal books in the English Bible. The first chapter is a transcript of the last two chapters of 2 Chron., for the most part *verbatim,* and only in one or two parts slightly abridged and paraphrased. Chapters 3, 4, and 5 to the end of ver. 6, are the *original* portions of the book, and the rest is a transcript more or less exact of the book of Ezra, with the chapters transposed and quite otherwise arranged, and a portion of Nehemiah. Hence a twofold design in the compiler is discernible—one to introduce and give scriptural sanction to the legend about Zerubbabel; the other to explain the great obscurities of the book of Ezra, in which, however, he has signally failed. Its author is unknown, and it was probably written in Egypt. It has no historical value.

Es'dras, The Second Book of. This exists in a Latin translation, the Greek being lost. Chapters 3-14 consist of a series of angelic revelations and visions in which Ezra is instructed in some of the great mysteries of the moral world, and assured of the final triumph of the righteous. The date of the book is uncertain. Like the first book, it was probably written in Egypt.

E'sek (*contention*), a well which the herdsmen of Isaac dug in the valley of Gerar. Gen. 26 : 20.

Esh-ba'al (*Baal's man*), 1 Chron. 8 : 33; 9 : 39, the same as Ish-bosheth.

Esh'ban (*wise man*), a Horite; one of the four sons of Dishon. Gen. 36 : 26; 1 Chron. 1 : 41.

Esh'col (*cluster of grapes*), brother of Mamre the Amorite and of Aner, and one of Abraham's companions in his pursuit of the four kings who had carried off Lot. Gen. 14 : 13, 24. (B.C. 1912.)

Esh'col, The valley or **The brook of,** a *wady* in the neighborhood of Hebron (Mamre), explored by the spies who were sent by Moses from Kadesh-barnea. Num. 13 : 23, 24; Deut. 1 : 24. The name is still attached to a spring of fine water called '*Ain Eshkali,* in a valley about two miles north of Hebron.

Esh'e-an (*slope*), one of the cities of Judah. Josh. 15 : 52.

E'shek (*oppression*), one of the late descendants of Saul. 1 Chron. 8 : 39.

Esh'kalonites, The. Josh. 13 : 3. [ASHKELON.]

Esh'taol (*a pass*), a town in the low country—the *Shefelah*—of Judah, afterwards allotted to Dan. Josh. 15 : 33; 19 : 41. Here Samson spent his boyhood, and hither after his last exploit his body was brought. Judges 13 : 25; 16 : 31; 18 : 2, 8, 11, 12.

Esh'taulites, The, with the Zareath-

ites, were among the families of Kirjath-jearim. 1 Chron. 2 : 53.

Eshtem'o-a, and in shorter form **Eshtemoh** (*obedience*), a town of Judah, in the mountains, Josh. 15 : 50, allotted to the priests. Josh. 21 : 14; 1 Chron. 6 : 57. It was one of the places frequented by David and his followers during the long period of their wanderings. 1 Sam. 30 : 28; comp. 31. Its site is at *Semu'a,* a village seven miles south of Hebron.

Esh'ton (*effeminate*), a name which occurs in the genealogies of Judah. 1 Chron. 4 : 11, 12.

Es'li, son of Nagge or Naggai, in the genealogy of Christ. Luke 3 : 25.

Es'ril. 1 Esd. 9 : 34. [AZAREEL, or SHARAI.]

Es'rom (*enclosed*). Matt. 1 : 3; Luke 3 : 33. [HEZRON.]

Essenes', a Jewish sect, who, according to the description of Josephus, combined the ascetic virtues of the Pythagoreans and Stoics with a spiritual knowledge of the divine law. It seems probable that the name signifies *seer,* or *the silent, the mysterious.* As a sect the Essenes were distinguished by an aspiration after ideal purity rather than by any special code of doctrines. There were isolated communities of Essenes, which were regulated by strict rules, analogous to those of the monastic institutions of a later date. All things were held in common, without distinction of property; and special provision was made for the relief of the poor. Self-denial, temperance and labor—especially agriculture—were the marks of the outward life of the Essenes; purity and divine communion the objects of their aspiration. Slavery, war and commerce were alike forbidden. Their best-known settlements were on the northwest shore of the Dead Sea.

Es'ther (*a star*), the Persian name of HADASSAH (*myrtle*), daughter of Abihail, the son of Shimei, the son of Kish, a Benjamite. Esther was a beautiful Jewish maiden. She was an orphan, and had been brought up by her cousin Mordecai, who had an office in the household of Ahasuerus king of Persia—supposed to be the Xerxes of history—and dwelt at "Shushan the palace." When Vashti was dismissed from being queen, the king chose Esther to the place on account of her beauty, not knowing her race or parentage; and on the representation of Haman the Agagite that the Jews scattered through his empire were a pernicious race, he gave him full power and authority to kill them all. The means taken by Esther to avert this great calamity from her people and her kindred are fully related in the book of Esther. The Jews still commemorate this deliverance in the yearly festival Purim, on the 14th and 15th of Adar (February, March). History is wholly silent about both Vashti and Esther.

Es'ther, Book of, one of the latest of the canonical books of Scripture, having been written late in the reign of Xerxes, or early in that of his son Artaxerxes Longimanus (B.C. 444–434). The author is not known. The book of Esther is placed among the hagiographa by the Jews, and in that first portion of them which they call "the five rolls." It is written on a single roll, in a dramatic style, and is read through by the Jews in their synagogues at the feast of Purim, when it is said that the names of Haman's sons are read rapidly all in one breath, to signify that they were all hanged at the same time; while at every mention of Haman the audience stamp and shout and hiss, and the children spring rattles. It has often been remarked as a peculiarity of this book that the name of God does not once occur in it. Schaff gives as the reason for this that it was to permit the reading of the book at the hilarious and noisy festival of Purim, without irreverence. The style of writing is remarkably chaste and simple. It does not in the least savor of romance. The Hebrew is very like that of Ezra and parts of the Chronicles; generally pure, but mixed with some words of Persian origin and some of Chaldaic affinity. In short it is just what one would expect to find in a work of the age to which the book of Esther professes to belong.

E'tam (*lair of wild beasts*). 1. A village of the tribe of Simeon, specified only in the list in 1 Chron. 4 : 32; comp. Josh. 19 : 7.

2. A place in Judah, fortified and garrisoned by Rehoboam. 2 Chron. 11 : 6. Here, according to the statements of Josephus and the Talmudists, were the sources of the water from which Solomon's gardens and pleasure-grounds were fed, and Bethlehem and the temple supplied.

E'tam, The rock, a cliff or lofty rock, into a cleft or chasm of which Samson retired after his slaughter of the Philistines. Judges 15 : 8, 11. This natural stronghold was in the tribe of Judah; and near it, probably at its foot, were Lehi or Ramath-lehi and Enhakkore. Judges 15 : 9, 14, 17, 19. The name Etam was held by a city in the neighborhood of Bethlehem, 2 Chron. 11 : 6, which is known to have been situated in the extremely uneven and broken country round the modern *Urtas*.

E'tham (*bounded by the sea*), one of the early resting-places of the Israelites when they quitted Egypt; described as "in the edge of the wilderness." Ex. 13 : 20; Num. 33 : 6, 7. Etham may be placed where the cultivable land ceases, near the *Seba Biár* or Seven Wells, about three miles from the western side of the ancient head of the gulf.

E'than (*enduring*). 1. Ethan the Ezrahite, one of the four sons of Mahol, whose wisdom was excelled by Solomon. 1 Kings 4 : 31; 1 Chron. 2 : 6. His name is in the title of Ps. 89.

2. Son of Kishi or Kushaiah; a Merarite Levite, head of that family in the time of King David, 1 Chron. 6 : 44, and spoken of as a "singer." With Heman and Asaph, the heads of the other two families of Levites, Ethan was appointed to sound with cymbals. 1 Chron. 15 : 17, 19. (B.C. 1014.)

3. A Gershonite Levite, one of the ancestors of Asaph the singer. 1 Chron. 6 : 42; Heb. 27. (B.C. 1420.)

Eth'anim. [MONTH.]

Ethba'al (*with Baal*), king of Sidon and father of Jezebel. 1 Kings 16 : 31. Josephus represents him as king of the Tyrians as well as of the Sidonians. We may thus identify him with Eithobalus, who, after having assassinated Pheles, usurped the throne of Tyre for thirty-two years. The date of Ethbaal's reign may be given as about B.C. 940–908.

E'ther (*abundance*), one of the cities of Judah in the low country, the *Shefelah*, Josh. 15 : 42, allotted to Simeon. Josh. 19 : 7.

Ethio'pia (*burnt faces*). The country which the Greeks and Romans described as "Æthiopia" and the Hebrews as "Cush" lay to the south of Egypt, and embraced, in its most extended sense, the modern *Nubia, Sennaar, Kordofan* and northern *Abyssinia*, and in its more definite sense the kingdom of Meroë. Ezek. 29 : 10. The Hebrews do not appear to have had much practical acquaintance with Ethiopia itself, though the Ethiopians were well known to them through their intercourse with Egypt. The inhabitants of Ethiopia were a Hamitic race. Gen. 10 : 6. They were divided into various tribes, of which the Sabæans were the most powerful. The history of Ethiopia is closely interwoven with that of Egypt. The two countries were not unfrequently. united under the rule of the same sovereign. Shortly before our Saviour's birth a native dynasty of females, holding the official title of Candace (Plin. vi. 35), held sway in Ethiopia, and even resisted the advance of the Roman arms. One of these is the queen noticed in Acts 8 : 27.

Ethio'pian, properly "Cushite," Jer. 13 : 23; used of Zerah, 2 Chron. 14 : 9 (8), and Ebed-melech. Jer. 38 : 7, 10, 12 ; 39 : 16.

Ethio'pian eunuch, The, a Jewish proselyte, Acts 8 : 26, etc., who was treasurer of Candace queen of Ethiopia, but who was converted to Christianity on a visit to Jerusalem, through Philip the evangelist. Nothing is known of him after his return to Ethiopia.

Ethio'pian woman. The wife of Moses is so described in Num. 12 : 1. She is elsewhere said to have been the daughter of a Midianite, and in consequence of this some have supposed that the allusion is to another wife whom Moses married after the death of Zipporah.

Eth'nan (*hire*), one of the sons of Helah the wife of Ashur. 1 Chron. 4 : 7.

Eth'ni (*munificent*), a Gershonite Levite. 1 Chron. 6 : 41.

Eubu'lus (*prudent*), a Christian at Rome mentioned by St. Paul. 2 Tim. 4 : 21. (A.D. 64.)

Euni'ce (*good victory*), mother of Timotheus. 2 Tim. 1 : 5. (A.D. before 47.)

Eunuch. "The English form of the Greek word which means *bed-keeper*. In the strict and proper sense they were the persons who had charge of the bed-chambers in palaces and larger houses. But as the jealous and dissolute temperament of the East required this charge to be in the hands of persons who had been deprived of their virility, the word eunuch came naturally to denote persons in that condition. But as some of these rose to be confidential advisers of their royal masters or mistresses, the word was occasionally employed to denote persons in such a position, without indicating anything of their proper manhood."—*Abbott.*

Euo'dia. [See EUODIAS.]

Euo'dias (*fragrant*), a Christian woman at Philippi. Philip. 4 : 2. (A.D. 57.) The name is correctly EUODIA, as given in the Revised Version.

Euphra'tes is probably a word of Aryan origin, signifying "*the good and abounding river.*" It is most frequently denoted in the Bible by the term " the river." The Euphrates is the largest, the longest and by far the most important of

Village of Anah on the Euphrates.

the rivers of western Asia. It rises from two chief sources in the Armenian mountains, and flows into the Persian Gulf. The entire course is 1780 miles, and of this distance more than two-thirds (1200 miles) is navigable for boats. The width of the river is greatest at the distance of 700 or 800 miles from its mouth—that is to say, from its junction with the Khabour to the village of *Werai*. It there averages 400 yards. The annual inundation of the Euphrates is caused by the melting of the snows in the Armenian highlands. It occurs in the month of May. The great hydraulic works ascribed to Nebuchadnezzar had for their chief object to control the inundation. The Euphrates is first mentioned in Scripture as one of the four rivers of Eden. Gen. 2 : 14. We next hear of it in the covenant made with Abraham. Gen. 15 : 18. During the reigns of David and Solomon it formed the boundary of the promised land to the northeast. Deut. 11 : 24; Josh. 1 : 4. Prophetical reference to the Euphrates is found in Jer. 13 : 4–7; 46 : 2–10; 51 : 63; Rev. 9 : 14; 16 : 12. "The Euphrates is linked with the most important events in ancient history. On its banks stood the city of Babylon ; the army of Necho was defeated on its banks by Nebuchadnezzar; Cyrus the Younger and Crassus perished after crossing it; Alexander crossed it, and Trajan and Severus descended it."— *Appleton's Cyc.*

Eurac'quila, the word used in the Revised Version instead of euroclydon, in Acts 27 : 14. It is compounded of two words meaning *east* and *north*, and means a northeast gale.

Euroc'lydon (*a violent agitation*), a tempestuous wind or hurricane, cyclone, on the Mediterranean, and very dangerous; now called a "levanter." This wind seized the ship in which St. Paul was ultimately wrecked on the coast of Malta. It came down from the island, and therefore must have blown more or less from the northward. Acts 27 : 14.

Eu'tychus (*fortunate*), a youth at Troas, Acts 20 : 9, who sitting in a window, and having fallen asleep while St. Paul was discoursing, fell from the third story, and being taken up dead, was miraculously restored to life by the apostle.

Evangelist (*publisher of glad tidings*). In the New Testament the "evangelists" appear on the one hand after the "apostles" and "prophets;" on the other before the "pastors" and "teachers." They probably stood between the two. Acts 21 : 8; Eph. 4 : 11. The work of the evangelist is the proclamation of the glad tidings to those who have not known them, rather than the instruction and pastoral care of those who have believed and been baptized. It follows also that the name denotes a *work* rather than an *order.* Its use is nearly like our word *missionary.* The evangelist might or might not be a bishop-elder or a deacon. The apostles, so far as they evangelized, Acts 8 : 25; 14 : 7; 1 Cor. 1 : 17, might claim the title, though there were many evangelists who were not apostles. If the gospel were a written book, and the office of the evangelists was to read or distribute it, then the writers of such books were pre-eminently THE evangelists. In later liturgical language the word was applied ·to the reader of the gospel for the day.

Eve (*life*), the name given in Scripture to the first woman. The account of Eve's creation is found at Gen. 2 : 21, 22. Per-

haps that which we are chiefly intended to learn from the narrative is the foundation upon which the union between man and wife is built, viz., identity of nature and oneness of origin. Through the subtlety of the serpent Eve was beguiled into a violation of the one commandment which had been imposed upon her and Adam. The Scripture account of Eve closes with the birth of Seth.

E'vi (*desire*) one of the five kings or princes of Midian slain by the Israelites. Num. 31 : 8; Josh. 13 : 21.

E'vil-mero'dach (*the fool of Merodach*), 2 Kings 25 : 27, the son and successor of Nebuchadnezzar. He reigned but a short time, having ascended the throne on the death of Nebuchadnezzar in B.C. 561, and being himself succeeded by Neriglissar in B.C. 559. He was murdered by Neriglissar.

Excommunication (*expulsion from communion*). 1. *Jewish excommunication.*—The Jewish system of excommunication was threefold. The twenty-four offences for which it was inflicted are various, and range in heinousness from the offence of keeping a fierce dog to that of taking God's name in vain. The offender was first cited to appear in court; and if he refused to appear or to make amends, his sentence was pronounced. The term of this punishment was thirty days; and it was extended to a second and to a third thirty days when necessary. If at the end of that time the offender was still contumacious, he was subjected to the second excommunication. Severer penalties were now attached. The sentence was delivered by a court of ten, and was accompanied by a solemn malediction. The third excommunication was an entire cutting off from the congregation. The punishment of excommunication is not appointed by the law of Moses; it is founded on the natural right of self-protection which all societies enjoy. In the New Testament, Jewish excommunication is brought prominently before us in the case of the man that was born blind. John 9. In Luke 6 : 22 it has been thought that our Lord referred specifically to the three forms of Jewish excommunication : " Blessed are ye when men shall hate you, and when they shall *sep·arate* you from their company, and shall *reproach* you, and *cast out* your name as evil, for the Son of man's sake."

2. *Christian excommunication.* — Excommunication, as exercised by the

Christian Church, was instituted by our Lord, Matt. 18 : 15, 18, and it was practiced and commanded by St. Paul. 1 Cor. 5 : 11 ; 1 Tim. 1 : 20 ; Titus 3 : 10. In the epistles we find St. Paul frequently claiming the right to exercise discipline over his converts; comp. 2 Cor. 1 : 23; 13 : 10. We find, (1) that it is a spiritual penalty, involving no temporal punishment, except accidentally ; (2) that it consists in separation from the communion of the Church; (3) that its object is the good of the sufferer, 1 Cor. 5 : 5, and the protection of the sound members of the Church, 2 Tim. 3 : 17 ; (4) that its subjects are those who are guilty of heresy, 1 Tim. 1 : 20, or gross immorality, 1 Cor. 5 : 1 ; (5) that it is inflicted by the authority of the Church at large, Matt. 18 : 18, wielded by the highest ecclesiastical officer, 1 Cor. 5 : 3 ; Titus 3 : 10; (6) that this officer's sentence is promulgated by the congregation to which the offender belongs, 1 Cor. 5 : 4, in deference to his superior judgment and command, 2 Cor. 2 : 9, and in spite of any opposition on the part of a minority, 2 Cor. 2 : 6; (7) that the exclusion may be of indefinite duration, or for a period ; (8) that its duration may be abridged at the discretion and by the indulgence of the person who has imposed the penalty, 2 Cor. 2 : 8; (9) that penitence is the condition on which restoration to communion is granted, 2 Cor. 2 : 8 ; (10) that the sentence is to be publicly reversed as it was publicly promulgated. 2 Cor. 2 : 10.

Executioner. The post of executioner was one of high dignity. Potiphar was " captain of the executioners." Gen. 37 : 36 ; see margin. That the " captain of the guard " himself occasionally performed the duty of an executioner appears from 1 Kings 2 : 25, 34.

Ex'odus (that is, *going out* [of Egypt]), the *second book* of the law or Pentateuch. Its author was Moses. It was written probably during the forty-years wanderings in the wilderness, between B.C. 1491 and 1451. It may be divided into two principal parts : 1. Historical, chs. 1 : 1–18 : 27 ; and, 2. Legislative, chs. 19 : 40, 38. 1. The first part contains an account of the following particulars : The great increase of Jacob's posterity in the land of Egypt, and their oppression under a new dynasty, which occupied the throne after the death of Joseph ; the birth, education, flight and return of Moses; the ineffectual attempts to prevail upon Pharaoh to let the Israelites go ; the successive signs and wonders, ending in the death of the first-born, by means of which the deliverance of Israel from the land of bondage is at length accomplished, and the institution of the Passover; finally the departure out of Egypt and the arrival of the Israelites at Mount Sinai. 2. This part gives a sketch of the early history of Israel as a nation ; and the history has three clearly-marked stages. First we see a nation enslaved; next a nation redeemed ; lastly a nation set apart, and through the blending of its religious and political life consecrated to the service of God.

Exodus, The, of the Israelites from Egypt. The common chronology places the date of this event at B.C. 1491, deriving it in this way :—In 1 Kings 6 : 1 it is stated that the building of the temple, in the fourth year of Solomon, was in the 480th year after the exodus. The fourth year of Solomon was about B.C. 1012. Add the 480 years (leaving off one year because neither the fourth nor the 480th was a full year), and we have B.C. 1491 as the date of the exodus. This is probably very nearly correct; but many Egyptologists place it at 215 years later,— about B.C. 1300. Which date is right depends chiefly on the interpretation of the Scripture period of 430 years, as denoting the duration of the bondage of the Israelites. The period of bondage given in Gen. 15 : 13, 14, Ex. 12 : 40, 41 and Gal. 3 : 17 as 430 years has been interpreted to cover different periods. The common chronology makes it extend from the call of Abraham to the exodus, one-half of it, or 215 years, being spent in Egypt. Others make it to cover only the period of bondage spent in Egypt. St. Paul says in Gal. 3 : 17 that from the covenant with (or call of) Abraham to the giving of the law (less than a year after the exodus) was 430 years. But in Gen. 15 : 13, 14 it is said that they should be strangers in a strange land, and be afflicted 400 years, and nearly the same is said in Ex. 12 : 40. But, in very truth, the children of Israel were strangers in a strange land from the time that Abraham left his home for the promised land, and during that whole period of 430 years to the exodus they were nowhere rulers in the land. So in Ex. 12 : 40 it is said that the sojourning of the children of Israel who dwelt in Egypt was 430 years. But it does not say that the sojourning was all in Egypt, but this people who lived in Egypt had been sojourners for 430 years. (*a*) This is the simplest way of making the various statements harmonize. (*b*) The chief difficulty is in the great increase of the children of Israel from 70 to 2,000,000 in so short a period as 215 years, while it is very easy in 430 years. But under the circumstances it is perfectly possible in the shorter period. See on ver. 7. (*c*)

If we make the 430 years to include only the bondage in Egypt, we must place the whole chronology of Abraham and the immigration of Jacob into Egypt some 200 years earlier, or else the exodus 200 years later, or B.C. 1300. In either case special difficulty is brought into the reckoning. (*d*) Therefore, on the whole, it is as well to retain the common chronology, though the later dates may yet prove to be correct.

The Chronology from the Monuments.

AUTHORITIES.	THE PHARAOH AND DATE OF THE EXODUS.		THE PHARAOH OF THE OPPRESSION.	DURATION OF BONDAGE.	THE PHARAOH AND DATE OF THE IMMIGRATION OF JACOB.	
Wilkinson: *Ancient Egyptians.*	Thothmes III.	B.C. 1491	The 18th Dynasty.	215	B.C. 1706	Usirtesen II. 16th Dynasty.
Osburn: *Monumental Egypt.*	Siphtha, the successor of Menephthah.	1314	Rameses II.	430	1706	Aphophis, last king of 15th Dynasty.
S. Birch: *Ancient History from the Monuments—Egypt.*	Menephthah, son of Rameses II.	1300	Rameses II. (Sesostris). B.C. 1355.	430	1730	Seti, or Saites.
Lenormant and Chevallier: *Ancient History of the East.*	Menephthah.	1300	Rameses II.	400	1700	Seti.
Henry Brugsch-Bey: *History of Egypt under the Pharaohs.*	Menephthah.	1300	Rameses II. B.C. 1350.	430	1730	King Nub.
Professor Gustav Seyffarth.	Thothmes III.	1866	The 18th Dynasty.	213	2080	

The history of the exodus itself commences with the close of that of the ten plagues. [PLAGUES, THE TEN.] In the night in which, at midnight, the first-born were slain, Ex. 12 : 29, Pharaoh urged the departure of the Israelites. vs. 31, 32. They at once set forth from Rameses, vs. 37, 39, apparently during the night, v. 42, but towards morning on the 15th day of the first month. Num. 33 : 3. They made three journeys, and encamped by the Red Sea. Here Pharaoh overtook them, and the great miracle occurred by which they were saved, while the pursuer and his army were destroyed. [RED SEA, PASSAGE OF.]

Exorcist, one who pretends to expel evil spirits by conjuration, prayers and ceremonies. Exorcism was frequently practiced among the Jews. Matt. 12 : 27; Acts 19 : 13. David, by playing skillfully on a harp, procured the temporary departure of the evil spirit which troubled Saul. 1 Sam. 16 : 23. The power of casting out devils was bestowed by Christ while on earth upon the apostles,

Matt. 10 : 8, and the seventy disciples, Luke 10 : 17–19, and was, according to his promise, Mark 16 : 17, exercised by believers after his ascension. Acts 16 : 18.

Expiation. [SACRIFICE.]

Eye. (The practice of painting the eyelids to make the eyes look large, lustrous and languishing is often alluded to in the Old Testament, and still extensively prevails among the women of the

Painted Eyes.

East, and especially among the Mohammedans. Jezebel, in 2 Kings 9 : 30, is said to have prepared for her meeting with Jehu by painting her face, or, as it reads in the margin, " put her eyes in paint." See also Ezek. 23 : 40. A small probe of wood, ivory or silver is wet with rose-water and dipped in an impalpable black powder, and is then drawn between the lids of the eye nearly closed, and leaves a narrow black border, which is thought a great ornament.—ED.)

Ez′ba-i (*shining*), father of Naarai, who was one of David's thirty mighty men. 1 Chron. 11 : 37. (B.C. 1046.)

Ez′bon (*working*). 1. Son of Gad, and founder of one of the Gadite families. Gen. 46 : 16; Num. 26 : 16.

2. Son of Bela, the son of Benjamin according to 1 Chron. 7 : 7.

Ezeki′as. Matt. 1 : 9, 10. [HEZEKIAH.]

Eze′ki-el (*the strength of God*), one of the four greater prophets, was the son of a priest named Buzi, and was taken captive in the captivity of Jehoiachin, eleven years before the destruction of Jerusalem. He was a member of a community of Jewish exiles who settled on the banks of the Chebar, a " river " or stream of Babylonia. He began prophesying B.C. 595, and continued until B.C.

573, a period of more than twenty-two years. We learn from an incidental allusion, Ezek. 24 : 18, that he was married, and had a house, Ezek. 8 : 1, in his place of exile, and lost his wife by a sudden and unforeseen stroke. He lived in the highest consideration among his companions in exile, and their elders consulted him on all occasions. He is said to have been murdered in Babylon and to have been buried on the banks of the Euphrates. The tomb, said to have been built by Jehoiachin, is shown, a few days journey from Bagdad.

Ezekiel was distinguished by his stern and inflexible energy of will and character and his devoted adherence to the rites and ceremonies of his national religion. The depth of his *matter* and the marvellous nature of his visions make him occasionally obscure.

Prophecy of Ezekiel.—The book is divided into two great parts, of which the destruction of Jerusalem is the turning-point. Chapters 1–24 contain predictions delivered before that event, and chs. 25–48 after it, as we see from ch. 26 : 2. Again, chs. 1–32 are mainly occupied with correction, denunciation and reproof, while the remainder deal chiefly in consolation and promise. A parenthetical section in the middle of the book, chs. 25–32, contains a group of prophecies against *seven* foreign nations, the septenary arrangement being apparently intentional. There are no direct quotations from Ezekiel in the New Testament, but in the Apocalypse there are many parallels and obvious allusions to the later chapters—40–48.

E′zel (*departure*)**, The stone,** a well-known stone in the neighborhood of Saul's residence, the scene of the parting of David and Jonathan. 1 Sam. 20 : 19.

E′zem (*bone*), one of the towns of Simeon. 1 Chron. 4 : 29.

E′zer (*treasure*). 1. A son of Ephraim, who was slain by the aboriginal inhabitants of Gath while engaged in a foray on their cattle. 1 Chron. 7 : 21. (B.C. before 1491.)

2. A priest who assisted in the dedication of the walls of Jerusalem under Nehemiah. Neh. 12 : 42. (B.C. 446.)

3. Father of Hushah of the sons of Hur. 1 Chron. 4 : 4.

4. One of the Gadite chiefs who fought with David. 1 Chron. 12 : 8, 9. (B.C. 1054.)

5. One who aided in repairing the wall at Jerusalem; a Levite. Neh. 3 : 19.

E'zion-ga'ber, or **E'zion-ge'ber** (*giant's backbone*), Num. 33 : 35; Deut. 2 : 8; 1 Kings 9 : 26; 22 : 48; 2 Chron. 8 : 17, the last station named for the encampment of the Israelites before they came to the wilderness of Zin. It probably stood at *Ain el-Ghudyân*, about ten miles up what is now the dry bed of the Arabah, but which was probably then the northern end of the gulf.

Ez'nite, The. According to the statement of 2 Sam. 23 : 8, Adino the Eznite was another name for Jashobeam, a Tachmonite. 1 Chron. 11 : 11. (Probably the words are a corruption for the Hebrew "he lifted up his spear."—*Fausset.*)

Ez'ra (*help*), called ESDRAS in the Apocrypha, the famous scribe and priest. He was a learned and pious priest residing at Babylon in the time of Artaxerxes Longimanus. The origin of his influence with the king does not appear, but in the seventh year of his reign he obtained leave to go to Jerusalem, and to take with him a company of Israelites. (B.C. 457.) The journey from Babylon to Jerusalem took just four months; and the company brought with them a large freewill offering of gold and silver, and silver vessels. It appears that Ezra's great design was to effect a religious reformation among the Palestine Jews. His first step was to enforce separation upon all who had married foreign wives. Ezra 10. This was effected in little more than six months after his arrival at Jerusalem. With the detailed account of this important transaction Ezra's autobiography ends abruptly, and we hear nothing more of him till, thirteen years afterwards, in the twentieth of Artaxerxes, we find him again at Jerusalem with Nehemiah. It seems probable that after effecting the above reformations he returned to the king of Persia. The functions he executed under Nehemiah's government were purely of a priestly and ecclesiastical character. The date of his death is uncertain. There was a Jewish tradition that he was buried in Persia. The principal works ascribed to him by the Jews are—1. The institution of the great synagogue; 2. The settling the canon of Scripture, and restoring, correcting and editing the whole sacred volume; 3. The introduction of the Chaldee character instead of the old Hebrew or Samaritan; 4. The authorship of the books of Chronicles, Ezra, Nehemiah, and, some add, Esther; and, many of the Jews say, also of the books of Ezekiel, Daniel, and the twelve prophets; 5. The establishment of synagogues.

Ez'ra, Book of, is a continuation of the books of Chronicles. The period covered by the book is eighty years, from the first of Cyrus, B.C. 536, to the beginning of the eighth of Artaxerxes, B.C. 456. It consists of the contemporary historical journals kept from time to time, containing, chs. 1–12, an account of the return of the captives under Zerubbabel, and the rebuilding of the temple in the reign of Cyrus and Cambyses. Most of the book is written in Hebrew, but from chs. 4 : 8 to 6 : 19 it is written in Chaldee. The last four chapters, beginning with ch. 7, continue the history after a gap of fifty-eight years—from the sixth of Darius to the seventh of Artaxerxes—narrating his visit to Jerusalem, and giving an account of the reforms there accomplished, referred to under EZRA. Much of the book was written by Ezra himself, though the first chapter was probably written by Daniel; and other hands are evident.

Ez'rahite, The (*son of Zerah*), a title attached to two persons—Ethan, 1 Kings 4 : 31; Ps. 89, title, and Heman, Ps. 88, title.

Ez'ri (*help of Jehovah*), son of Chelub, superintendent of King David's farm-laborers. 1 Chron. 27 : 26. (B.C. 1014.)

F.

Fable. A fable is a narrative in which beings irrational, and sometimes inanimate, are, for the purpose of moral instruction, feigned to act and speak with human interests and passions.—*Encyc. Brit.* The fable differs from the parable in that—1. The parable always relates what actually takes place, and is true to fact, which the fable is not; and 2. The parable teaches the higher heavenly and spiritual truths, but the fable only earthly moralities. Of the fable, as distinguished from the parable [PARABLE], we have but two examples in the Bible: 1. That of the trees choosing their king, addressed by Jotham to the men of Shechem, Judges 9 : 8–15; 2. That of the cedar of Lebanon and the thistle, as the answer of Jehoash to the challenge of Amaziah. 2 Kings 14 : 9. The fables of false teachers claiming to belong to the Christian Church, alluded to by writers of the New Testament, 1 Tim. 1 : 4; 4 : 7; Titus 1 : 14; 2 Pet. 1 : 16, do not appear to have had the character of fables, properly so called.

Fair Ha'vens, a harbor in the island of Crete, Acts 27 : 8, though not mentioned in any other ancient writing, is still known by its own Greek name, and appears to have been the harbor of Lasæa.

Fairs, a word which occurs only in Ezek. 27, and there no less than seven times, vs. 12, 14, 16, 19, 22, 27, 33; in the last of these verses it is rendered "wares," and this we believe to be the true meaning of the word throughout.

Fallow deer (called fallow from its reddish-brown color) (Heb. *yachmŭr*). The Hebrew word, which is mentioned only in Deut. 14 : 5 and 1 Kings 4 : 23, probably denotes the *Alcelaphus bubalis* (the bubale or wild cow) of Barbary and North Africa. It is about the size of a stag, and lives in herds. It is almost exactly like the European roebuck, and is valued for its venison.

Famine. In the whole of Syria and Arabia, the fruits of the earth must ever be dependent on rain; the watersheds having few large springs, and the small rivers not being sufficient for the irrigation of even the level lands. If therefore the heavy rains of November and December fail, the sustenance of the people is cut off in the parching drought of harvest-time, when the country is almost devoid of moisture. Egypt, again, owes all its fertility to its mighty river, whose annual rise inundates nearly the whole land. The causes of dearth and famine in Egypt are defective inundation, preceded, accompanied and followed by prevalent easterly and southerly winds. Famine is likewise a natural result in the

The Fallow Deer.

East when caterpillars, locusts or other insects destroy the products of the earth. The first famine recorded in the Bible is that of Abraham after he had pitched his tent on the east of Bethel, Gen. 12 : 10; the second in the days of Isaac, Gen. 26 : 1, *seq.* We hear no more of times of scarcity until the great famine of Egypt, which "was over all the face of the earth." Gen. 41 : 53–57. The modern history of Egypt throws some curious light on these ancient records of famines; and instances of their recurrence may be cited to assist us in understanding their course and extent. The most remarkable famine was that of the reign of the Fátimee Khaleefeh, El-Mustansir billáh, which is the only instance on record of one of seven years duration in Egypt since the time of Joseph (A.H. 457–464, A.D. 1064–1071). Vehement drought and pestilence continued for seven consecutive years, so that the people ate corpses, and animals that died of themselves. The famine of Samaria resembled it in many particulars; and that very briefly recorded in 2 Kings 8 : 1, 2 affords another instance of one of seven years. In Arabia famines are of frequent occurrence.

Winnowing-Fans.

Fan, a *winnowing-shovel,* with which grain was thrown up against the wind to be cleansed from the chaff and straw. Isa. 30 : 24; Matt. 3 : 12. A large wooden fork is used at the present day.

Farthing. Two names of coins in the New Testament are rendered in the Authorized Version by this word: 1. *Quadrans,* Matt. 5 : 26; Mark 12 : 42, a

A Farthing.

coin current in the time of our Lord, equivalent to three-eighths of a cent; 2. The *assarion,* equal to one cent and a half. Matt. 10 : 29; Luke 12 : 6.

Fasts. 1. One fast only was appointed by the Mosaic law, that on the day of atonement. There is no mention of any other periodical fast in the Old Testament except in Zech. 7 : 1–7; 8 : 19. From these passages it appears that the Jews, during their captivity, observed four annual fasts,—in the fourth, fifth, seventh and tenth months.

2. Public fasts were occasionally proclaimed to express national humiliation and to supplicate divine favor. In the case of public danger the proclamation appears to have been accompanied with the blowing of trumpets. Joel 2 : 1–15. (See 1 Sam. 7 : 6; 2 Chron. 20 : 3; Jer. 36 : 6–10.) Three days after the feast of tabernacles, when the second temple was completed, "the children of Israel assembled with fasting, and with sackclothes and earth upon them," to hear the law read and to confess their sins. Neh. 9 : 1.

3. Private occasional fasts are recognized in one passage of the law—Num. 30 : 13. The instances given of individuals fasting under the influence of grief, vexation or anxiety are numerous.

4. In the New Testament the only references to the Jewish fasts are the mention of "the fast" in Acts 27 : 9 (generally understood to denote the day of atonement) and the allusions to the weekly fasts. Matt. 9 : 14; Mark 2 : 18; Luke 5 : 33; 18 : 12; Acts 10 : 30. These fasts originated some time after the captivity.

5. The Jewish fasts were observed with various degrees of strictness. Sometimes there was entire abstinence from food. Esther 4 : 16, etc. On other occasions there appears to have been only a restriction to a very plain diet. Dan. 10 : 3. Those who fasted frequently dressed in sackcloth or rent their clothes, put ashes on their head and went barefoot. 1 Kings 21 : 27; Neh. 9 : 1; Ps. 35 : 13.

6. The sacrifice of the personal will, which gives to fasting all its value, is expressed in the old term used in the law, *afflicting the soul.*

Fat. The Hebrews distinguished between the suet or pure fat of an animal and the fat which was intermixed with the lean. Neh. 8 : 10. Certain restrictions were imposed upon them in reference to the former; some parts of the suet, viz., about the stomach, the entrails, the kidneys, and the tail of a sheep, which grows to an excessive size in many eastern countries, and produces a large quantity of rich fat, were forbidden to be eaten in the case of animals offered to Jehovah in sacrifice. Lev. 3 : 3, 9, 17 ; 7 : 3, 23. The ground of the prohibition was that the fat was the richest part of the animal, and therefore belonged to him. Lev. 3 : 16. The burning of the fat of sacrifices was particularly specified in each kind of offering.

Fat, *i. e.* VAT, the word employed in the Authorized Version to translate the Hebrew term *yekeb*, in Joel 2 : 24 ; 3 : 13. The word commonly used for *yekeb* is "winepress" or "winefat," and once "pressfat." Hag. 2 : 16. The "vats" appear to have been excavated out of the native rock of the hills on which the vineyards lay.

Father. The position and authority of the father as the head of the family are expressly assumed and sanctioned in Scripture, as a likeness of that of the Almighty over his creatures. It lies of course at the root of that so-called patriarchal government, Gen. 3 : 16 ; 1 Cor. 11 : 3, which was introductory to the more definite systems which followed, and which in part, but not wholly, superseded it. The father's blessing was regarded as conferring special benefit, but his malediction special injury, on those on whom it fell, Gen. 9 : 25, 27 ; 27 : 27–40 ; 48 : 15, 20 ; 49 ; and so also the sin of a parent was held to affect, in certain cases, the welfare of his descendants. 2 Kings 5 : 27. The command to honor parents is noticed by St. Paul as the only one of the Decalogue which bore a distinct promise, Ex. 20 : 12 ; Eph. 6 : 2 ; and disrespect towards them was condemned by the law as one of the worst of crimes. Ex. 21 : 15, 17 ; 1 Tim. 1 : 9. It is to this well-recognized theory of parental authority and supremacy that the very various uses of the term " father " in Scripture are due. " Fathers " is used in the sense of seniors, Acts 7 : 2 ; 22 : 1, and of parents in general, or ancestors. Dan. 5 : 2 ; Jer. 27 : 7 ; Matt. 23 : 30, 32.

Fathom. [WEIGHTS AND MEASURES.]

Feasts. [FESTIVALS ; MEALS.]

Fe'lix (*happy*), a Roman procurator of Judea appointed by the emperor Claudi-

us in A.D. 53. He ruled the province in a mean, cruel and profligate manner. His period of office was full of troubles and seditions. St. Paul was brought before Felix in Cæsarea. He was remanded to prison, and kept there two years in hopes of extorting money from him. Acts 24 : 26, 27. At the end of that time Porcius Festus [FESTUS] was appointed to supersede Felix, who, on his return to Rome, was accused by the Jews in Cæsarea, and would have suffered the penalty due to his atrocities had not his brother Pallas prevailed with the emperor Nero to spare him. This was probably about A.D. 60. The wife of Felix was Drusilla, daughter of Herod Agrippa I., who was his third wife and whom he persuaded to leave her husband and marry him.

Fenced cities, *i. e.* cities fortified or defended. The fortifications of the cities of Palestine, thus regularly " fenced," consisted of one or more walls (sometimes of thick stones, sometimes of combustible material), crowned with battlemented parapets, having towers at regular intervals, 2 Chron. 32 : 5 ; Jer. 31 : 38, on which in later times engines of war were placed, and watch was kept by day and night in time of war. Judges 9 : 45 ; 2 Kings 9 : 17 ; 2 Chron. 26 : 9, 15.

The Gecko.

Ferret, one of the unclean creeping things mentioned in Lev. 11 : 30. The animal referred to was probably a reptile of the lizard tribe (the *gecko*). The rabbinical writers seem to have identified this animal with the hedgehog.

Festivals. I. The religious times ordained in the law fall under three heads : 1. Those formally connected with the institution of the Sabbath ; 2. The historical or great festivals ; 3. The day of atonement. 1. Immediately connected with the institution of the Sabbath are—

a. The weekly Sabbath itself. *b.* The seventh new moon, or feast of trumpets. *c.* The sabbatical year. *d.* The year of jubilee. 2. The great feasts are—*a.* The passover. *b.* The feast of pentecost, of weeks, of wheat-harvest or of the first-fruits. *c.* The feast of tabernacles or of ingathering. On each of these occasions every male Israelite was commanded to "appear before the Lord," that is, to attend in the court of the tabernacle or the temple, and to make his offering with a joyful heart. Deut. 27 : 7 ; Neh. 8 : 9–12. The attendance of women was voluntary, but the zealous often went up to the passover. On all the days of holy convocation there was to be an entire suspension of ordinary labor of all kinds, Ex. 12 : 16 ; Lev. 16 : 29 ; 23 : 21, 24, 25, 35 ; but on the intervening days of the longer festivals work might be carried on. The agricultural significance of the three great festivals is clearly set forth in the account of the Jewish sacred year contained in Lev. 23. The times of the festivals were evidently ordained in wisdom, so as to interfere as little as possible with the industry of the people. The value of these great religious festivals was threefold. (1) *Religious effects.—* They preserved the religious faith of the nation and religious unity among the people. They constantly reminded the people of the divinely-wrought deliverances of the past ; promoted gratitude and trust ; and testified the reverence of the people for the temple and its sacred contents. Besides this was the influence of well-conducted temple services upon the synagogues through the land. (2) *Political effects.—*The unity of the nation would be insured by this fusion of the tribes ; otherwise they would be likely to constitute separate tribal states. They would carry back to the provinces glowing accounts of the wealth, power and resources of the country. (3) *Social effects.—*They promoted friendly intercourse between travelling companions ; distributed information through the country at a time when the transmission of news was slow and imperfect ; and imported into remote provincial districts a practical knowledge of all improvements in arts and sciences. 3. For the day of atonement see that article. II. After the captivity, the feast of purim, Esther 9 : 20, *seq.*, and that of the dedication, 1 Macc. 4 : 56, were instituted.

Fes′tus, Por′cius (Festus means

festival), successor of Felix as procurator of Judea, Acts 24 : 27, sent by Nero probably in the autumn of A.D. 60. A few weeks after Festus reached his province he heard the cause of St. Paul, who had been left a prisoner by Felix, in the presence of Herod Agrippa II. and Bernice his sister, Acts 25 : 11, 12. Judea was in the same disturbed state during the procuratorship of Festus which had prevailed through that of his predecessor. He died probably in the summer of A.D. 60, having ruled the province less than two years.

Fetters. Fetters were for the feet only, while chains were for any part of the body. They were usually made of brass, and also in pairs, the word being in the dual number. Iron was occasionally employed for the purpose. Ps. 105 : 18 ; 149 : 8.

Field. The Hebrew *sadeh* is applied to any cultivated ground, and in some instances in marked opposition to the neighboring wilderness. On the other hand the *sadeh* is frequently contrasted with what is enclosed, whether a vineyard, a garden or a walled town. In many passages the term implies what is remote from a house, Gen. 4 : 8 ; 24 : 63 ; Deut. 22 : 25, or settled habitation, as in the case of Esau. Gen. 25 : 27. The separate plots of ground were marked off by stones, which might easily be removed, Deut. 19 : 14 ; 27 : 17 ; cf. Job 24 : 2 ; Prov. 22 : 28 ; 23 : 10 ; the absence of fences rendered the fields liable to damage from straying cattle, Ex. 22 : 5, or fire, Ex. 22 : 6 ; 2 Sam. 14 : 30 ; hence the necessity of constantly watching flocks and herds. From the absence of enclosures, cultivated land of any size might be termed a field.

Fig, Fig tree. The fig tree (*Ficus carica*) is very common in Palestine. Deut. 8 : 8. Mount Olivet was famous for its fig trees in ancient times, and they are still found there. To "sit under one's own vine and one's own fig tree" became a proverbial expression among the Jews to denote peace and prosperity. 1 Kings 4 : 25 ; Micah 4 : 4 ; Zech. 3 : 10. The fig is a pear-shaped fruit, and is much used by the Orientals for food. The young figs are especially prized for their sweetness and flavor. The fruit always appears before the leaves ; so that when Christ saw leaves on the fig tree by the wayside, Mark 11 : 13, he had a right to expect fruit. The usual summer crop of fruits

Figs.

is not gathered till May or June; but in the sunny ravines of Olivet fig trees could have ripe fruit some weeks earlier (*Dr. Thomson*), and it was not strange that so early as Easter Christ might find the young eatable figs, although it was not the usual season for gathering the fruit.

Fir. Isaiah 14 : 8; Ezek. 27 : 5, etc. As the term "cedar" is in all probability applicable to more than one tree, so also "fir" in the Authorized Version represents probably one or other of the following trees: 1. *Pinus sylvestris,* or Scotch fir; 2. Larch; 3. *Cupressus sempervirens,* or cypress, all which are at this day found in the Lebanon. The wood of the fir was used for ship-building, Ezek. 27 : 5; for mu-

sical instruments, 2 Sam. 6 : 5; for beams and rafters of houses, 1 Kings 5 : 8, 10; 2 Chron. 2 : 8. It was a tall evergreen tree of vigorous growth.

Fire is represented as the symbol of Jehovah's presence and the instrument of his power, in the way either of approval or of destruction. Ex. 3 : 2; 14 : 19, etc. There could not be a better symbol for Jehovah than this of fire, it being immaterial, mysterious, but visible, warming, cheering, comforting, but also terrible and consuming. Parallel with this application of fire and with its symbolical meaning are to be noted the similar use for sacrificial purposes and the respect paid to it, or to the heavenly bodies as symbols of deity, which prevailed among so many nations of antiquity, and of which the traces are not even now extinct; *e. g.* the Sabean and Magian systems of worship. Isa. 27 : 9. Fire for sacred purposes obtained elsewhere than from the altar was called "strange fire," and for the use of such Nadab and Abihu were punished with death by fire from God. Lev. 10 : 1, 2; Num. 3 : 4; 26 : 61.

Firepan, one of the vessels of the temple service. Ex. 27 : 3; 38 : 3; 2 Kings 25 : 15; Jer. 52 : 19. The same word is elsewhere rendered "snuff-dish," Ex. 25 : 38; 37 : 23; Num. 4 : 9, and "censer."

Fig Tree.

Lev. 10 : 1 ; 16 : 12 ; Num. 16 : 6 ff. There appear, therefore, to have been two articles so called : one, like a chafing-dish, to carry live coals for the purpose of burning incense ; another, like a snuffer-dish, to be used in trimming the lamps, in order to carry the snuffers and convey away the snuff.

Firkin. [WEIGHTS AND MEASURES.]

Firmament. In Scripture the word denotes an expanse, a wide extent; for such is the signification of the Hebrew word. The original, therefore, does not convey the sense of solidity, but of stretching, extension ; the great arch or expanse over our heads, in which are placed the atmosphere and the clouds, and in which the stars *appear* to be placed, and are *really* seen.— *Webster.*

First-born. Under the law, in memory of the exodus (when the first-born of the Egyptians were slain), the eldest son was regarded as devoted to God, and was in every case to be redeemed by an offering not exceeding five shekels, within one month from birth. If he died before the expiration of thirty days, the Jewish doctors held the father excused, but liable to the payment if he outlived that time. Ex. 13 : 12–15 ; 22 : 29 ; Num. 8 : 17 ; 18 : 15, 16 ; Lev. 27 : 6. The eldest son received a double portion of the father's inheritance, Deut. 21 : 17, but not of the mother's. Under the monarchy the eldest son usually, but not always, as appears in the case of Solomon, succeeded his father in the kingdom. 1 Kings 1 : 30 ; 2 : 22. The male first-born of animals was also devoted to God. Ex. 13 : 2, 12, 13 ; 22 : 29 ; 34 : 19, 20. Unclean animals were to be redeemed with the addition of one-fifth of the value, or else put to death ; or, if not redeemed, to be sold, and the price given to the priests. Lev. 27 : 13, 27, 28.

First-fruits. 1. The law ordered in general that the first of all ripe fruits and of liquors, or, as it is twice expressed, the first of first-fruits, should be offered in God's house. Ex. 22 : 29 ; 23 : 19 ; 34 : 27. It was an act of allegiance to God as the giver of all. No exact quantity was

commanded, but it was left to the spiritual and moral sense of each individual. 2. On the morrow after the passover sabbath, *i. e.* on the 16th of Nisan, a sheaf of new corn was to be brought to the priest and waved before the altar, in acknowledgment of the gift of fruitfulness. Lev. 2 : 12 ; 23 : 5, 6, 10, 12. 3. At the expiration of seven weeks from this time, *i. e.* at the feast of pentecost, an oblation was to be made of two loaves of leavened bread made from the new flour, which were to be waved in like manner with the passover sheaf. Ex. 34 : 22 ; Lev. 23 : 15, 17 ; Num. 28 : 26. 4. The feast of ingathering, *i. e.* the feast of tabernacles, in the seventh month, was itself an acknowledgment of the fruits of the harvest. Ex. 23 : 16 ; 34 : 22 ; Lev. 23 : 39. These four sorts of offerings were national. Besides them, the two following were of an individual kind. 5. A cake of the first dough that was baked was to be offered as a heave offering. Num. 15 : 19, 21. 6. The first-fruits of the land were to be brought in a basket to the

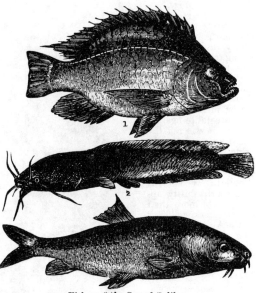

Fishes of the Sea of Galilee.
1. Chromis nilotica. 2. Clarias macracanthus. 3. Labeobarbus canis.

holy place of God's choice, and there presented to the priest, who was to set the basket down before the altar. Deut. 26 : 2–11. The offerings were the per-

Fisherman Casting his Net.

the one used in Egypt, as shown in Wilkinson (iii. 55), or the *draw* or *drag* net, Isa. 19 : 8; Hab. 1 : 15, which was larger, and required the use of a boat. The latter was probably most used on the Sea of Galilee, as the number of boats kept on it was very considerable.

Fitches (*i. e.* VETCHES), without doubt the *Nigella sativa*, an herbaceous annual plant belonging to the natural order *Ranunculaceæ* (the buttercup family), which grows in the south of Europe and in the

quisite of the priests. Num. 18 : 11; Deut. 18 : 4. Nehemiah, at the return from captivity, took pains to reorganize the offerings of first-fruits of both kinds, and to appoint places to receive them. Neh. 10 : 35, 37; 12 : 44. An offering of first-fruits is mentioned as an acceptable one to the prophet Elisha. 2 Kings 4 : 42.

Fish. The Hebrews recognized fish as one of the great divisions of the animal kingdom, and as such gave them a place in the account of the creation, Gen. 1 : 21, 28, as well as in other passages where an exhaustive description of living creatures is intended. Gen. 9 : 2; Ex. 20 : 4; Deut. 4 : 18; 1 Kings 4 : 33. The Mosaic law, Lev. 11 : 9, 10, pronounced unclean such fish as were devoid of fins and scales; these were and are regarded as unwholesome in Egypt. Among the Philistines Dagon was represented by a figure half man and half fish. 1 Sam. 5 : 4. On this account the worship of fish is expressly prohibited. Deut. 4 : 18. In Palestine, the Sea of Galilee was and still is remarkably well stored with fish. (Tristram speaks of fourteen species found there, and thinks the number inhabiting it at least three times as great.) Jerusalem derived its supply chiefly from the Mediterranean. Comp. Ezek. 47 : 10. The existence of a regular fish-market is implied in the notice of the fish-gate, which was probably contiguous to it. 2 Chron. 33 : 14; Neh. 3 : 3; 12 : 39; Zeph. 1 : 10. The Orientals are exceedingly fond of fish as an article of diet. Numerous allusions to the art of fishing occur in the Bible. The most usual method of catching fish was by the use of the net, either the *casting* net, Ezek. 26 : 5, 14; 47 : 10; Hab. 1 : 15, probably resembling

Fennel Flower or Vetches (*Nigella sativa*).

north of Africa. Its black seeds are used like pepper, and have almost as pungent a taste. The Syrians sprinkle these seeds over their flat cakes before they are baked. [See RYE.]

Flag. There are two Hebrew words rendered "flag" in our Bible: 1. A word of Egyptian origin, and denoting "any green and coarse herbage, such as rushes and reeds, which grows in marshy places." Gen. 41 : 2, 18 (here translated meadow). It is perhaps the *Cyperus esculentus.* 2. A word which appears to be used in a very wide sense to denote "weeds of any kind." Ex. 2 : 3, 5; Isa. 19 : 6.

Flagon, a word employed in the Authorized Version to render two distinct Hebrew terms: 1. *Ashishah,* 2 Sam. 6 : 19; 1 Chron. 16 : 3; Cant. 2 : 5; Hos. 3 : 1. It really means a cake of pressed raisins. Such cakes were considered as delicacies; they were also offered to idols. 2. *Nebel,* Isa. 22 : 24, is commonly used for a·bottle or vessel, originally probably a skin, but in later times a piece of pottery. Isa. 30 : 14.

Flax.

Flax, a well-known plant with yellowish stem and bright-blue flowers. Its fibres are employed in the manufacture of linen. The root contains an oil, and after the oil is expressed is used as a food for cattle. Egypt was celebrated for the culture of flax and the manufacture of linen. The spinning was anciently done by women of noble birth. It seems probable that the cultivation of flax for the purpose of the manufacture of linen was by no means confined to Egypt, but that, originating in India, it spread over Asia at a very early period of antiquity. That it was grown in Palestine even before the conquest of that country by the Israelites appears from Josh. 2 : 6. The various processes employed in preparing the flax for manufacture into cloth are indicated : 1. The drying process. 2. The peeling of the stalks and separation of the fibres. 3. The hackling. Isa. 19 : 9. That flax was one of the most important crops in Palestine appears from Hos. 2 : 5, 9.

Flea, an insect but twice mentioned in Scripture, viz., in 1 Sam. 24 : 14; 26 : 20. Fleas are abundant in the East, and afford the subject of many proverbial expressions.

Flesh. [FOOD.]

Flint, a well-known stone, a variety of quartz. It is extremely hard, and strikes fire. It was very abundant in and about Palestine.

Flood. [NOAH.]

Floor. [GABBATHA.]

Flour. [BREAD.]

Flute (1 Kings 1 : 40, marg., PIPE), a musical instrument mentioned amongst others, Dan. 3 : 5, 7, 10, 15, as used at the worship of the golden image which Nebuchadnezzar had set up. It bore a close resemblance to the modern flute, and was made of reeds, of copper, and other material. It was the principal wind-instrument.

Flux, Bloody, Acts 28 : 8, the same as our dysentery, which in the East is, though sometimes sporadic, generally epidemic and infectious, and then assumes its worst form.

Fly, Flies. The two following Hebrew terms denote flies of some kind : 1. *Zĕbúb,* which occurs only in Eccles. 10 : 1 and in Isa. 7 : 18, and is probably a generic name for an insect. 2. *'Arób* ("swarms of *flies,*" "divers sorts of *flies,*" Authorized Version), the name of the insect or insects which God sent to punish Pharaoh; see Ex. 8 : 21–31; Ps. 78 : 45; 105 : 31. The question as to what particular species is denoted, or whether any one species is to be understood, has long been a matter of dispute. As the *árób* are said to have filled the houses of the

Egyptians, it seems not improbable that common flies (*Muscidæ*) are more especially intended. The *árób* may include various species of *Culicidæ* (gnats), such as the mosquito; but the common flies are to this day in Egypt regarded as a "plague," and are the great instrument of spreading the well-known ophthalmia, which is conveyed from one individual to another by these dreadful pests. " It is now generally supposed that the *dog-fly* is meant, which at certain seasons is described as a far worse plague than mosquitos. The bite is exceedingly sharp and painful, causing severe inflammation, especially in the eyelids. Coming in immense swarms, they cover all objects in black and loathsome masses, and attack every exposed part of a traveller's person with incredible pertinacity."— *Cook*.

Food. The diet of eastern nations has been in all ages light and simple. Vegetable food was more used than animal. Bread was the principal food; preparations of corn were, however, common. The Hebrews used a great variety of articles, John 21:5, to give a relish to bread. Milk and its preparations hold a conspicuous place in eastern diet, as affording substantial nourishment; generally in the form of the modern *leben*, *i. e.* sour milk. Authorized Version "butter;" Gen. 18:8; Judges 5:25; 2 Sam. 17:29. Fruit was another source of subsistence: figs stood first in point of importance; they were generally dried and pressed into cakes. Grapes were generally eaten in a dried state as raisins. Of vegetables we have most frequent notice of lentils, beans, leeks, onions and garlic, which were and still are of a superior quality in Egypt. Num. 11:5. Honey is extensively used, as is also olive oil.

The Orientals have been at all times sparing in the use of animal food; not only does the excessive heat of the climate render it both unwholesome to eat much meat and expensive from the necessity of immediately consuming a whole animal, but beyond this the ritual regulations of the Mosaic law in ancient, as of the Koran in modern, times have tended to the same result. The prohibition expressed against consuming the blood of any animal, Gen. 9:4, was more fully developed in the Levitical law, and enforced by the penalty of death. Lev. 3:17; 7:26; 19:26; Deut. 12:16. Certain portions of the fat of sacrifices were also forbidden, Lev. 3:9, 10, as being set apart for the altar. Lev. 3:16; 7:25.

In addition to the above, Christians were forbidden to eat the flesh of animals portions of which had been offered to idols. All beasts and birds classed as unclean, Lev. 11:1 ff.; Deut. 14:4 ff., were also prohibited. Under these restrictions the Hebrews were permitted the free use of animal food: generally speaking they only availed themselves of it in the exercise of hospitality or at festivals of a religious, public or private character. It was only in royal households that there was a daily consumption of meat. The animals killed for meat were — calves, lambs, oxen not above three years of age, harts, roebucks and fallow deer; birds of various kinds; fish, with the exception of such as were without scales and fins. Locusts, of which certain species only were esteemed clean, were occasionally eaten, Matt. 3:4, but were regarded as poor fare.

Footman, a word employed in the English Bible in two senses: 1. Generally, to distinguish those of the fighting men who went on foot from those who were on horseback or in chariots; 2. In a more special sense, in 1 Sam. 22:17 only, and as the translation of a different term from the above—a body of swift runners in attendance on the king. This body appears to have been afterwards kept up, and to have been distinct from the body-guard—the six hundred and the thirty—who were originated by David. See 1 Kings 14:27, 28; 2 Kings 11:4, 6, 11, 13, 19; 2 Chron. 12:10, 11. In each of these cases the word is the same as the above, and is rendered "guard," with "runners" in the margin in two instances—1 Kings 14:27; 2 Kings 11:13.

Forehead. The practice of veiling the face (forehead) in public for women of the higher classes, especially married women, in the East, sufficiently stigmatizes with reproach the unveiled face of women of bad character. Gen. 24:65; Jer. 3:3. The custom among many Oriental nations both of coloring the face and forehead and of impressing on the body marks indicative of devotion to some special deity or religious sect is mentioned elsewhere. The "jewels for the forehead," mentioned by Ezekiel, 16:12, and in margin of Authorized Version, Gen. 24.22, were in all probability nose-rings. Isa. 3:21.

Forest. Although Palestine has

never been in historical times a woodland country, yet there can be no doubt that there was much more wood formerly than there is at present, and that the destruction of the forests was one of the chief causes of the present desolation.

Fortifications. [FENCED CITIES.]

Fortuna'tus (*fortunate*), 1 Cor. 16 : 17, one of three Corinthians, the others being Stephanas and Achaïcus, who were at Ephesus when St. Paul wrote his first epistle. There is a Fortunatus mentioned in the end of Clement's first epistle to the Corinthians, who was possibly the same person.

Fountain (a spring, in distinction from a well). The springs of Palestine, though short-lived, are remarkable for their abundance and beauty, especially those which fall into the Jordan and into its lakes, of which there are hundreds throughout its whole course. The spring or fountain of living water, the "eye" of the landscape, is distinguished in all Oriental languages from the artificially-sunk and enclosed well. Jerusalem appears to have possessed either more than one perennial spring or one issuing by more than one outlet. In Oriental cities generally public fountains are frequent. Traces of such fountains at Jerusalem may perhaps be found in the names of Enrogel, 2 Sam. 17 : 17, the "Dragon well" or fountain, and the "gate of the fountain." Neh. 2 : 13, 14.

Fowl. Several distinct Hebrew and Greek words are thus rendered in the English Bible. Of these the most common is *'óph*, which is usually a collective term for all kinds of birds. In 1 Kings 4 : 23, among the daily provisions for Solomon's table "fatted fowl" are included. In the New Testament the word translated "fowls" is most frequently that which comprehends all kinds of birds (including *ravens*, Luke 12 : 24). [SPARROW.]

Fox (Heb. *shû'ál*). Probably the jackal is the animal signified in almost all the passages in the Old Testament where the Hebrew term occurs. Though both foxes and jackals abound in Palestine, the *shû'álim* (foxes) of Judges 15 : 4 are evidently jackals and not foxes, for the former animal is gregarious, whereas the latter is solitary in its habits; and Samson could not, for that reason,

have easily caught three hundred foxes, but it was easy to catch that number of jackals, which are concealed by hundreds in the caves and ruins of Syria. It is not probable, however, that Samson sent out the whole three hundred at once. With respect to the jackals and foxes of Pales-

Syrian Fox.

tine, there is no doubt that the common jackal of the country is the *Canis aureus*, which may be heard every night in the villages. It is like a medium-sized dog, with a head like a wolf, and is of a bright-yellow color. These beasts devour the bodies of the dead, and even dig them up from their graves.

Frankincense, a vegetable resin, brittle, glittering, and of a bitter taste, used for the purpose of sacrificial fumigation. Ex. 30 : 34–36. It was called *frank* because of the freeness with which, when burned, it gives forth its odor. It burns for a long time, with a steady flame. It is obtained by successive incisions in the bark of a tree called *Arbor thuris*. The first incision yields the purest and whitest resin, while the product of the after incisions is spotted with yellow, and loses its whiteness altogether as it becomes old. The Hebrews imported their frankincense from Arabia, Isa. 60 : 6 ; Jer. 6 : 20, and more particularly from Saba; but it is remarkable that at present the Arabian libanum or olibanum is of a very inferior kind, and that the finest frankincense imported into Turkey comes through Arabia from the islands of the Indian

Archipelago. There can be little doubt that the tree which produces the Indian frankincense is the *Boswellia serrata* of Roxburgh, or *Boswellia thurifera* of

Frankincense.

Colebrooke, and bears some resemblance when young to the mountain ash. It grows to be forty feet high.

Frog, a well-known amphibious animal of the genus *Rana*. The mention of this reptile in the Old Testament is confined to the passage in Ex. 8 : 2–7, etc., in which the plague of frogs is described, and to Ps. 78 : 45 ; 105 : 30. In the New Testament the word occurs once only, in Rev. 16 : 13. There is no question as to the animal meant. The only known species of frog which occurs at present in Egypt is the *Rana esculenta*, the edible frog of the continent.

Arm Phylactery.

Frontlets, or **Phylacteries.** Ex. 13 : 16 ; Deut. 6 : 8 ; 11 : 18 ; Matt. 23 : 5.

These "frontlets" or "phylacteries" were strips of parchment, on which were written four passages of Scripture, Ex. 13 : 2–10, 11–17 ; Deut. 6 : 4–9, 13–23, in an ink prepared for the purpose. They were then rolled up in a case of black calf-skin, which was attached to a stiffer piece of leather, having a thong one finger broad and one and a half cubits long. They were placed at the bend of the left arm. Those worn on the forehead were written on four strips of parchment, and put into four little cells within a square case on which the letter ש was written. The square had two thongs, on which Hebrew letters were inscribed. That phylacteries were used as amulets is certain, and was very natural. The expression "they make broad their phylacteries," Matt. 23 : 5, refers not so much to the phylactery itself, which seems to have been of a prescribed breadth, as to the case in which the parchment was kept, which the Pharisees, among their other pre-

The Phylactery.

tentious customs, Mark 7 : 3, 4 ; Luke 5 : 33, etc., made as conspicuous as they could. It is said that the Pharisees wore them always, whereas the common people only used them at prayers.

Fuller. The trade of the fullers, so far as it is mentioned in Scripture, appears to have consisted chiefly in cleansing garments and whitening them. The process of fulling or cleansing clothes consisted in treading or stamping on the garments with the feet or with bats in tubs of water, in which some alkaline substance answering the purpose of soap had been dissolved. The substances used for this purpose which are mentioned in Scripture are natron, Prov. 25 : 20; Jer. 2 : 22, and soap. Mal. 3 : 2. Other substances also are mentioned as being employed in cleansing, which, together with alkali, seem to identify the Jewish with the Roman process, as urine and chalk. The process of whitening garments was performed by rubbing into them chalk or earth of some kind. *Creta cimolia* (cimolite) was probably the earth most frequently used. The trade of the fullers, as causing offensive smells, and also as requiring space for drying clothes, appears to have been carried on at Jerusalem outside the city.

Fuller's field, The, a spot near Jerusalem, 2 Kings 18 : 17; Isa. 7 : 3; 36 : 2, so close to the walls that a person speaking from there could be heard on them. 2 Kings 18 : 17, 26. One resort of the fullers of Jerusalem would seem to have been below the city on the southeast side.

But Rabshakeh and his "great host' must have come from the north; and the fuller's field was therefore, to judge from this circumstance, on the table-land on the northern side of the city.

Funerals. [BURIAL.]

Furlong. [WEIGHTS AND MEASURES.]

Furnace. Various kinds of furnaces are noticed in the Bible, such as a smelting or calcining furnace, Gen. 19 : 28; Ex. 9 : 8, 10; 19 : 18, especially a lime-kiln, Isa. 33 : 12; Amos 2 : 1; a refining furnace, Prov. 17 : 3; Nebuchadnezzar's furnace, a large furnace built like a brick-kiln, Dan. 3 : 22, 23, with two openings, one at the top for putting in the materials, and another below for removing them; the potter's furnace, Ecclus. 27 : 5; the blacksmith's furnace. Ecclus. 38 : 28. The Persians were in the habit of using the furnace as a means of inflicting punishment. Dan. 3 : 22, 23; Jer. 29 : 22.

G.

Ga'al (*contempt*), son of Ebed, aided the Shechemites in their rebellion against Abimelech. Judges 9. (B.C. 1206.)

Ga'ash (*earthquake*), a hill of Ephraim, where Joshua was buried. The brooks or valley of Gaash, 2 Sam. 23 : 30; 1 Chron. 11 : 32, were probably at the foot of the hill.

Ga'ba. The same name as GEBA, which see.

Gab'atha. Esther 12 : 1. [BIGTHAN.]

Gab'ba-i (*tax-gatherer*), apparently the head of an important family of Benjamin resident at Jerusalem. Neh. 11 : 8. (B.C. before 536.)

Gabbatha (*elevated; a platform*), the Hebrew or Chaldee appellation of a place, also called "Pavement," where the judgment-seat or bema was planted, from his place on which Pilate delivered our Lord to death. John 19 : 13. It was a tessellated platform outside the prætorium, on the western hill of Jerusalem, for Pilate brought Jesus forth from thence to it.

Ga'briel (*man of God*), an angel sent by God to announce to Zacharias the birth of John the Baptist, and to Mary the birth of Christ. He was also sent to Daniel to explain his visions. Dan. 8 : 16; 9 : 21.

Gad (*a troop*). 1. Jacob's seventh son, the first-born of Zilpah, Leah's maid, and whole-brother to Asher. Gen. 30 : 11–13; 46 : 16, 18. (B.C. 1753–1740.)

2. "The seer," or "the king's seer," *i. e.* David's, 1 Chron. 29 : 29; 2 Chron. 29 : 25, was a "prophet" who appears to have joined David when in the hold. 1 Sam. 22 : 5. (B.C. 1061.) He reappears in connection with the punishment inflicted for the numbering of the people. 2 Sam. 24 : 11–19; 1 Chron. 21 : 9–19. He wrote a book of the Acts of David, 1 Chron. 29 : 29, and also assisted in the arrangements for the musical service of the "house of God." 2 Chron. 29 : 25.

Gad, The tribe of. The country allotted to the tribe of Gad appears, speaking roughly, to have lain chiefly about the centre of the land east of Jordan. The south of that district—from the Arnon (*Wady Mojeb*), about halfway down the Dead Sea, to Heshbon, nearly due east of Jerusalem—was occupied by Reuben, and at or about Heshbon the possessions of Gad commenced. They embraced half Gilead, Deut. 3 : 12, or half the land of the children of Ammon, Josh. 13 : 25, probably the mountainous district which is intersected by the torrent Jabbok, including, as its most northern town, the ancient sanctuary of Mahanaim. On the east the furthest landmark given is "Aroer that is before Rabbah," the present *Amman*. Josh. 13 : 25. West was the Jordan. ver. 27. The character of the tribe is throughout strongly marked—fierce and warlike.

Gad'ites, The, the descendants of Gad, and members of his tribe.

Gad'ara, a strong city situated near the river Hieromax, six miles southeast of the Sea of Galilee, over against Scythopolis and Tiberias, and 16 Roman miles distant from each of those places. Josephus calls it the capital of Peræa. The ruins of this city, now called *Um Keis*, are about two miles in circumference. The most interesting remains of Gadara are its tombs, which dot the cliffs for a considerable distance around the city. Godet says there is still a population of 200 souls in these tombs. Gadara was captured by Vespasian on the first outbreak of the war with the Jews, all its inhabitants were massacred, and the town itself, with the surrounding villages, was reduced to ashes.

Gadarenes', Girgesenes', Gerasenes'. (These three names are used indiscriminately to designate the place where Jesus healed two demoniacs. The first two are in the Authorized Version. Matt. 8 : 28; Mark 5 : 1; Luke 8 : 26. In Mark and Luke the Revised Version uses Gerasenes in place of Gadarenes. The miracle referred to took place, without doubt, near the town of Gergesa, the modern *Kersa*, close by the eastern shore of the Sea of Galilee, and hence in the country of the Gergesenes. But as Gergesa was a small village, and little known, the evangelists, who wrote for men more distant readers, spoke of the event as taking place in the country of the Gadarenes, so named from its largest city, Gadara; and this country included the country of the Gergesenes as a state includes a county. The Gerasenes were the people of the district of which Gerasa was the capital. This city was better known than Gadara or Gergesa; indeed in the Roman age no city of Palestine was better known. "It became one of the proudest cities of Syria." It was situated some 30 miles southeast of Gadara, on the borders of Peræa, and a little north of the river Jabbok. It is now called *Jerash*, and is a deserted ruin. The district of the Gerasenes probably included that of the Gadarenes; so that the demoniac of Gergesa belonged to the country of the Gadarenes and also to that of the Gerasenes, as the same person may, with equal truth, be said to live in the city or the state, or in the United States. For those near by the local name would be used; but in writing to a distant people, as the Greeks and Romans, the more comprehensive and general name would be given. —ED.)

Gad'di (*fortunate*), son of Susi; the Manassite spy sent by Moses to explore Canaan. Num. 13 : 11. (B.C. 1490.)

Gad'diel (*fortune of God*), a Zebulunite, one of the twelve spies. Num. 13 : 10. (B.C. 1490.)

Ga'di, a Gadite, father of Menahem, a king of Israel. 2 Kings 15 : 14, 17.

Ga'ham (*sunburnt*), son of Nahor, Abraham's brother, by his concubine Reumah. Gen. 22 : 24. (B.C. about 1900.)

Ga'har (*hiding-place*). The Bene-Gahar were among the families of Nethinim who returned from the captivity with Zerubbabel. Ezra 2 : 47; Neh. 7 : 49. (B.C. before 536.)

Gai'us, or **Cai'us** (*lord*). 1. A Macedonian who accompanied Paul in his travels, and whose life was in danger from the mob at Ephesus. Acts 19 : 29. (A.D. 54.)
2. Of Derbe. He went with Paul from Corinth in his last journey to Jerusalem. Acts 20 : 4. (A.D. 55.)
3. Of Corinth, whom Paul baptized, and who was his host in his second sojourn in that city. 1 Cor. 1 : 14; Rom. 16 : 23. (These are supposed by some to be only one person.)
4. John's third epistle is addressed to a Christian of this name. We may possibly identify him with No. 2.

Gal'a-ad, the Greek form of the word Gilead.

Ga'lal (*influential*). 1. A Levite, one of the sons of Asaph. 1 Chron. 9 : 15. (B.C. 536.)

2. Another Levite, of the family of Elkanah. 1 Chron. 9 : 16.
3. A third Levite, son of Jeduthun. Neh. 11 : 17. (B.C. 536.)

Gala'tia (*land of the Galli, Gauls*). The Roman province of Galatia may be roughly described as the central region of the peninsula of Asia Minor, bounded on the north by Bithynia and Paphlagonia; on the east by Pontus; on the south by Cappadocia and Lycaonia; on the west by Phrygia.—*Encyc. Brit.* It derived its name from the Gallic or Celtic tribes who, about 280 B.C., made an irruption into Macedonia and Thrace. It finally became a Roman province. The Galatia of the New Testament was really the "Gaul" of the East. The people have always been described as "susceptible of quick impressions and sudden changes, with a fickleness equal to their courage and enthusiasm, and a constant liability to that disunion which is the fruit of excessive vanity. The Galatian churches were founded by Paul at his first visit, when he was detained among them by sickness, Gal. 4 : 13, during his second missionary journey, about A.D. 51. He visited them again on his third missionary tour.

Gala'tians, The Epistle to the, was written by the apostle St. Paul not long after his journey through Galatia and Phrygia, Acts 18 : 23, and probably in the early portion of his two-and-a-half-years stay at Ephesus, which terminated with the Pentecost of A.D. 57 or 58. The epistle appears to have been called forth by the machinations of Judaizing teachers, who, shortly before the date of its composition, had endeavored to seduce the churches of this province into a recognition of circumcision, Gal. 5 : 2, 11, 12; 6 : 12, *seq.*, and had openly sought to depreciate the apostolic claims of St. Paul. Comp. 1 : 1, 11. "Since the days of Luther the Epistle to the Galatians has always been held in high esteem as the gospel's banner of freedom. To it and the Epistle to the Romans we owe most directly the springing up and development of the ideas and energies of the Reformation."—*Meyer.*

Galbanum, one of the perfumes employed in the preparation of the sacred incense. Ex. 30 : 34. The galbanum of commerce is brought chiefly from India and the Levant. It is a resinous gum of a brownish-yellow color and strong disagreeable smell, usually met with in masses, but sometimes found in yellowish tear-like drops. But, though galbanum itself is well known, the plant which yields it has not been exactly determined.

Gal'e-ed (*the heap of witness*), the name given by Jacob to the heap which he and Laban made on Mount Gilead in witness of the covenant then entered into between them. Gen. 31 : 47, 48; comp. 23, 25.

Galile'ans, the inhabitants of Galilee, the northern province of Palestine. The apostles were all Galileans by either birth or residence. Acts 1 : 11. It appears also that the pronunciation of those Jews who resided in Galilee had become peculiar, probably from their contact with their Gentile neighbors. Matt. 26 : 73.

Gal'ilee (*circuit*). This name, which in the Roman age was applied to a large province, seems to have been originally confined to a little "circuit" of country round Kedesh-Naphtali, in which were situated the twenty towns given by Solomon to Hiram king of Tyre as payment for his work in conveying timber from Lebanon to Jerusalem. Josh. 20 : 7; 1 Kings 9 : 11. In the time of our Lord all Palestine was divided into three provinces, Judea, Samaria and Galilee. Luke 17 : 11; Acts 9 : 31; Joseph. *B. J.* iii. 3. The latter included the whole northern section of the country, including the ancient territories of Issachar, Zebulun, Asher and Naphtali. On the west it was bounded by the territory of Ptolemais, which probably included the whole plain of Akka to the foot of Carmel. The southern border ran along the base of Carmel and of the hills of Samaria to Mount Gilboa, and then descended the valley of Jezreel by Scythopolis to the Jordan. The river Jordan, the Sea of Galilee, and the upper Jordan to the fountain at Dan, formed the eastern border; and the northern ran from Dan westward across the mountain ridge till it touched the territory of the Phœnicians. Galilee was divided into two sections, "Lower" and "Upper." *Lower Galilee* included the great plain of Esdraelon with its offshoots, which run down to the Jordan and the Lake of Tiberias, and the whole of the hill country adjoining it on the north to the foot of the mountain range. It was thus one of the richest and most beautiful sections of Palestine. *Upper Galilee* embraced the whole mountain range lying between the upper Jordan and Phœnicia. To this region the name "Galilee of the Gentiles" is given in the Old and New Testaments. Isa. 9 : 1; Matt. 4 : 15. Galilee was the scene of the greater part of our Lord's private life and public acts. It is a remarkable fact that the first three Gospels are chiefly taken up with our Lord's ministrations in this province, while the Gospel of John dwells more upon those in Judea.

(*Galilee in the time of Christ.*—From Rev. Selah Merrill's late book (1881) with this title, we glean the following facts:

Size.—It is estimated that of the 6000 square miles in Palestine west of the Jordan, nearly one-third, almost 2000 square miles, belongs to Galilee.

Population.—The population is between 2,000,000 and 3,000,000. Dr. Merrill argues for the general correctness of Josephus' estimates, who says there were 204 cities and villages in Galilee, the smallest of which numbered 15,000 inhabitants.

Character of the country.—Galilee was a region of great natural fertility. Such is the fertility of the soil that it rejects no plant, for the air is so genial that it suits every variety. The walnut, which delights above other trees in a wintry climate, grows here luxuriantly, together with the palm tree, which is nourished by heat. It not only possesses the extraordinary virtue of nourishing fruits of opposite climes, but also maintains a continual supply of them. Here were found all the productions which made Italy rich and beautiful. Forests covered its mountains and hills, while its uplands, gentle slopes and broader valleys were rich in pasture, meadows, cultivated fields, vineyards, olive groves and fruit trees of every kind.

Character of the Galileans.—They were thoroughly a Jewish people. With few exceptions they were wealthy and in general an influential class. If one should say the Jews were bigoted in religion, he should remember at the same time that in regard to social, commercial and political relations none were more cosmopolitan in either sentiment or practice than they. The Galileans had many manufactures, fisheries, some commerce, but were chiefly an agricultural people. They were eminent for patriotism and courage, as were their ancestors, with great respect for law and order.—ED.)

Gal'ilee, Sea of. So called from the province of Galilee, which bordered on its western side. Matt. 4 : 18. It was also called the "Sea of Tiberias," from the celebrated city of that name. John 6 : 1. At its northwestern angle was a beautiful and fertile plain called "Gennesaret," and from that it derived the name of "Lake of Gennesaret." Luke 5 : 1. It was called in the Old Testament "the Sea of Chinnereth" or "Cinneroth," Num. 34 : 11; Josh. 12 : 3, from a town of that name which stood on or near its shore. Josh. 19 : 35. Its modern name is *Bahr Tubariyeh.* Most of our Lord's public life was spent in the environs of this sea. The surrounding region was then the most densely peopled in all Palestine. No less than *nine* very populous cities stood on the very shores of the lake. The Sea of Galilee is of an oval shape, about thirteen geographical miles long and six broad. It is 60 miles northeast of Jerusalem and 27 east of the Mediterranean Sea. The river Jordan enters it at its northern end and passes out at its southern end. In fact the bed of the lake is just a lower section of the great Jordan valley. Its most remarkable feature is its deep depression, being no less than 700 feet below the level of the ocean. The scenery is bleak and monotonous, being surrounded by a high and almost unbroken wall of hills, on account of which it is exposed to frequent sudden and violent storms. The great depression makes the climate of the shores almost tropical. This is very sensibly felt by the traveller in going down from the plains of Galilee. In summer the heat is intense, and even in early spring the air has something of an Egyptian balminess. The water of the lake is sweet, cool and transparent; and as the beach is everywhere pebbly it has a beautiful sparkling look. It abounds in fish now as in ancient times. There were large fisheries on the lake, and much commerce was carried on upon it.

Gall. 1. *Mererah,* denoting "that which is bitter;" hence the term is applied to the "bile" or "gall" (the fluid secreted by the liver), from its intense bitterness, Job 16 : 13; 20 : 25; it is also used of the "poison" of serpents, Job 20 : 14, which the ancients erroneously believed was their gall. 2. *Rôsh,* generally translated "gall" in the English Bible, is in Hos. 10 : 4 rendered "hemlock:" in Deut. 32 : 33 and Job 20 : 16,

rôsh denotes the "poison" or "venom" of serpents. From Deut. 29 : 18 and Lam. 3 : 19, compared with Hos. 10 : 4, it is evident that the Hebrew term denotes some bitter and perhaps poisonous plant. Other writers have supposed, and with some reason, from Deut. 32 : 32, that some berry-bearing plant must be intended. Gesenius understands poppies; in which case the gall mingled with the wine offered to our Lord at his crucifixion, and refused by him, would be an anæsthetic, and tend to diminish the sense of suffering. Dr. Richardson, "Ten Lectures on Alcohol," p. 23, thinks these drinks were given to the crucified to diminish the suffering through their intoxicating effects.

Gallery, an architectural term describing the porticos or verandas which are not uncommon in eastern houses. It is doubtful, however, whether the Hebrew words so translated have any reference to such an object. (According to the latest researches, the colonnade or else wainscoting is meant. S. of Sol. 1 : 17; Ezek. 41 : 15.—*Schaff.*)

Galley. [SHIP.]

Gal'lim (*fountains*). This is given as the native place of the man to whom Michal, David's wife, was given. 1 Sam. 25 : 44. There is no clue to the situation of the place. The name occurs again in the catalogue of places terrified at the approach of Sennacherib. Isa. 10 : 30.

Gal'lio (*one who lives on milk*), Junius Annæus Gallio, the Roman proconsul of Achaia when St. Paul was at Corinth, A.D. 53, under the emperor Claudius. Acts 18 : 12. He was brother to Lucius Annæus Seneca, the philosopher. Jerome in the Chronicle of Eusebius says that he committed suicide in 65 A.D. Winer thinks he was put to death by Nero.

Gallows. [PUNISHMENTS.]

Gama'liel (*recompense of God*). 1. Son of Pedahzur; prince or captain of the tribe of Manasseh at the census at Sinai, Num. 1 : 10; 2 : 20; 7 : 54, 59, and at starting on the march through the wilderness. ch. 10 : 23. (B.C. 1490.)

2. A Pharisee and celebrated doctor of the law, who gave prudent worldly advice in the Sanhedrin respecting the treatment of the followers of Jesus of Nazareth. Acts 5 : 34 ff. (A.D. 29.) We learn from Acts 22 : 3 that he was the preceptor of St. Paul. He is generally identified with the very celebrated Jewish doctor Gamaliel, grandson of Hillel,

Sea of Galilee.

and who is referred to as authority in the Jewish Mishna.

Games. Among the Greeks the rage for theatrical exhibitions was such that every city of any size possessed its theatre and stadium. At Ephesus an annual contest was held in honor of Diana. It is probable that St. Paul was present when these games were proceeding. A direct reference to the exhibitions that took place on such occasions is made in 1 Cor. 15 : 32. St. Paul's epistles abound with allusions to the Greek contests, borrowed probably from the Isthmian games, at which he may well have been present during his first visit to Corinth. These contests, 1 Tim. 6 : 12 ; 2 Tim. 4 : 7, were divided into two classes, the *pancratium*, consisting of boxing and wrestling, and the *pentathlon*, consisting of leaping, running, quoiting, hurling the spear and wrestling. The competitors, 1 Cor. 9 : 25 ; 2 Tim. 2 : 5, required a long and severe course of previous training, 1 Tim. 4, 8, during which a particular diet was enforced. 1 Cor. 9 : 25, 27. In the Olympic contests these preparatory exercises extended over a period of ten months, during the last of which they were conducted under the supervision of appointed officers. The contests took place in the presence of a vast multitude of spectators, Heb. 12 : 1, the competitors being the spectacle. 1 Cor. 4 : 9 ; Heb. 10 : 33. The games were opened by the proclamation of a herald, 1 Cor. 9 : 27, whose office it was to give out the name and country of each candidate, and especially to announce the name of the victor before the assembled multitude. The judge was selected for his spotless integrity, 2 Tim. 4 : 8 ; his office was to decide any disputes, Col. 3 : 15, and to give the prize, 1 Cor. 9 : 24 ; Phil. 3 : 14, consisting of a crown, 2 Tim. 2 : 5 ; 4 : 8, of leaves of wild olive at the Olympic games, and of pine, or at one period ivy, at the Isthmian games. St. Paul alludes to two only out of the five contests, boxing and running, more frequently to the latter. The Jews had no public games, the great feasts of religion supplying them with anniversary occasions of national gatherings.

Gam'madim. This word occurs only in Ezek. 27 : 11. A variety of explanations of the term have been offered. 1. One class renders it "pygmies." 2. A second treats it as a geographical or local term. 3. A third gives a more general sense to the word "brave warriors."

Hitzig suggests "deserters." After all, the rendering in the LXX.—"guards"— furnishes the simplest explanation.

Ga'mul (*weaned*), a priest, the leader of the twenty-second course in the service of the sanctuary. 1 Chron. 24 : 17. (B.C. 535.)

Garden. Gardens in the East, as the Hebrew word indicates, are enclosures on the outskirts of towns, planted with various trees and shrubs. From the allusions in the Bible we learn that they were surrounded by hedges of thorn, Isa. 5 : 5, or walls of stone. Prov. 24 : 31. For further protection lodges, Isa. 1 : 8 ; Lam. 2 : 6, or watchtowers, Mark 12 : 1, were built in them, in which sat the keeper, Job 27 : 18, to drive away the wild beasts and robbers, as is the case to this day. The gardens of the Hebrews were planted with flowers and aromatic shrubs, Cant. 6 : 2 ; 4 : 16, besides olives, fig trees, nuts or walnuts, Cant. 6 : 12, pomegranates, and others for domestic use. Ex. 23 : 11 ; Jer. 29 : 5 ; Amos 9 : 14. Gardens of herbs, or kitchen gardens, are mentioned in Deut. 11 : 10 and 1 Kings 21 : 2. The rose garden in Jerusalem, said to have been situated westward of the temple mount, is remarkable as having been one of the few gardens which, from the time of the prophets, existed within the city walls. The retirement of gardens rendered them favorite places for devotion.

Ga'reb (*scabby*), one of the heroes of David's army. 2 Sam. 23 : 38.

Ga'reb, The hill, in the neighborhood of Jerusalem, named only in Jer. 31 : 39.

Garlic, Num. 11 : 5, is the *Allium sativum* of Linnæus, which abounds in Egypt.

Garment. [DRESS.]

Gar'mite, The. Keilah the Garmite, *i. e. the descendant of Gerem*, is mentioned in the obscure genealogical lists of the families of Judah. 1 Chron. 4 : 19.

Gash'mu, a variation of the name GESHEM. Neh. 6 : 6. (B.C. 446.)

Ga'tam (*a burnt valley*), the fourth son of Eliphaz the son of Esau, Gen. 36 : 11 ; 1 Chron. 1 : 36, and one of the "dukes" of Eliphaz. Gen. 36 : 16. (B.C. after 1760.)

Garrison. The Hebrew words so rendered in the Authorized Version are derivatives from the root *nâtsab*, to "place, erect," which may be applied to a variety of objects. 1. *Mattsab* and *mattsabah* undoubtedly mean a "garrison" or fortified post. 1 Sam. 13 : 23 ; 14 : 1, 4, 12, 15 ; 2 Sam. 23 : 14. 2. *Netsib* is also used for a "garrison" in 1 Chron. 11 : 16, but elsewhere for a "column" erected in an enemy's country as a token of conquest. 1 Sam. 13 : 3. 3. The same word elsewhere means "officers" placed over a vanquished people. 2 Sam. 8 : 6, 14 ; 1 Chron. 18 : 13 ; 2 Chron. 17 : 2. 4. *Mattsebah* in Ezek. 26 : 11 means a "pillar."

Gate. The gates and gateways of eastern cities anciently held and still hold an important part, not only in the defence but in the public economy of the place. They are thus sometimes taken as representing the city itself. Gen. 22 : 17 ; 24 : 60 ; Deut. 12 : 12 ; Judges 5 : 8 ; Ruth 4 : 10 ; Ps. 87 : 2 ; 122 : 2. Among the special purposes for which they were used may be mentioned—1. As places of public resort. Gen. 19 : 1 ; 23 : 10 ; 34 : 20, 24 ; 1 Sam. 4 : 18, etc. 2. Places for public deliberation, administration of justice, or of audience for kings and rulers or ambassadors. Deut. 16 : 18 ; 21 : 19 ; 25 : 7 ; Josh. 20 : 4 ; Judges 9 : 35, etc. 3. Public markets. 2 Kings 7 : 1. In heathen towns the open spaces near the gates appear to have been sometimes used as places for sacrifice. Acts 14 : 13 ; comp. 2 Kings 23 : 8. Regarded therefore as positions of great importance, the gates of cities were carefully guarded, and closed at nightfall. Deut. 3 : 5 ; Josh. 2 : 5, 7 ; Judges 9 : 40, 44. They contained chambers over the gateway. 2 Sam. 18 : 24. The doors themselves of the larger gates mentioned in Scripture were two-leaved, plated with metal, closed with locks and fastened with metal bars. Deut. 3 : 5 ; Ps. 107 : 16 ; Isa. 45 : 1, 2. Gates not defended by iron were of course liable to be set on fire by an enemy. Judges 9 : 52. The gateways of royal palaces and even of private houses were often richly ornamented. Sentences from the law were inscribed on and above the gates. Deut. 6 : 9 ; Isa. 54 : 12 ; Rev. 21 : 21. The gates of Solomon's temple were very massive and costly, being overlaid with gold and carvings. 1 Kings 6 : 34, 35 ; 2 Kings 18 : 16. Those of the holy place were of olive wood, two-leaved and overlaid with gold ; those of the temple of fir. 1 Kings 6 : 31, 32, 34 ; Ezek. 41 : 23, 24.

Gath (*a wine-press*), one of the five royal cities of the Philistines, Josh. 13 : 3 ; 1 Sam. 6 : 17, and the native place of the giant Goliath. 1 Sam. 17 : 4, 23. It probably stood upon the conspicuous hill now called *Tell-es-Sâfieh*, upon the side of the plain of Philistia, at the foot of the mountains of Judah ; 10 miles east of Ashdod, and about the same distance south by east of Ekron. It is irregular in form, and about 200 feet high. Gath occupied a strong position, 2 Chron. 11 : 8, on the border of Judah and Philistia, 1 Sam. 21 : 10 ; 1 Chron. 18 : 1 ; and from its strength and resources forming the key of both countries, it was the scene of frequent struggles, and was often captured and recaptured. 2 Kings 12 : 17 ; 2 Chron. 11 : 8 ; 26 : 6 ; Amos 6 : 2. The ravages of war to which Gath was exposed appear to have destroyed it at a comparatively early period, as it is not mentioned among the other royal cities by the later prophets. Zeph. 2 : 4 ; Zech. 9 : 5, 6. It is familiar to the Bible student as the scene of one of the most romantic incidents in the life of King David. 1 Sam. 21 : 10–15.

Gath-he′pher, or **Git′tah-he′pher** (*wine-press on the hill*), a town on the border of the territory of Zebulun, not far from Japhia, now *Yâfa*, Josh. 19 : 12, 13, celebrated as the native place of the prophet Jonah. 2 Kings 14 : 25. *El-Meshhad,* a village two miles east of *Sefûrieh,* is the ancient Gath-hepher.

Gath-rim′mon (*press of the pomegranate*). 1. A city given out of the tribe of Dan to the Levites. Josh. 21 : 24 ; 1 Chron. 6 : 69, situated on the plain of Philistia, apparently not far from Joppa. Josh. 19 : 45.

2. A town of the half tribe of Manasseh west of the Jordan, assigned to the Levites. Josh. 21 : 25. The reading Gath-rimmon is probably an error of the transcribers.

Ga′za (*the fortified ; the strong*) (properly *Azzah*), one of the five chief cities of the Philistines. It is remarkable for its continuous existence and importance from the very earliest times. The secret of this unbroken history is to be found in the situation of Gaza. It is the last town in the southwest of Palestine, on the frontier towards Egypt. The same peculiarity of situation has made Gaza important in a military sense. Its name means "the strong ;" and this was well elucidated in its siege by Alexander the Great, which lasted five months. In the conquest of Joshua the territory of Gaza is mentioned as one which he was not able to subdue. Josh. 10 : 41; 11 : 22; 13 : 3. It was assigned to the tribe of Judah, Josh. 15 : 47, and that tribe did obtain possession of it, Judges 1 : 18, but did not hold it long, Judges 3 : 3; 13 : 1, and apparently it continued through the times of Samuel, Saul and David to be a Philistine city. 1 Sam. 6 : 17; 14 : 52; 31 : 1; 2 Sam. 21 : 15. Solomon became master of "Azzah," 1 Kings 4 : 24; but in after times the same trouble with the Philistines recurred. 2 Chron. 21 : 16; 26 : 6;

28 : 18. The passage where Gaza is mentioned in the New Testament (Acts 8 . 26) is full of interest. It is the account of the baptism of the Ethiopian eunuch on his return from Jerusalem to Egypt. Gaza is the modern *Ghuzzeh*, a Mohammedan town of about 16,000 inhabitants, situated partly on an oblong hill of moderate height and partly on the lower ground. The climate of the place is almost tropical, but it has deep wells of excellent water. There are a few palm trees in the town, and its fruit orchards

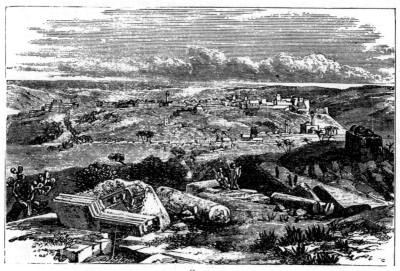

Gaza.

are very productive; but the chief feature of the neighborhood is the wide-spread olive grove to the north and northeast.

Ga′zathites, The, Josh. 13 : 3, the inhabitants of Gaza.

Ga′zer. 2 Sam. 5 : 25; 1 Chron. 14 : 16. [GEZER.]

Ga′zez (*shearer*), a name which occurs twice in 1 Chron. 2 : 46—first as son of Caleb by Ephah his concubine, and second as son of Haran, the son of the same woman. The second is possibly only a repetition of the first. (B.C. after 1688.)

Ga′zites, The, inhabitants of Gaza. Judges 16 : 2.

Gaz′zam (*devouring*). The Bene-Gazzam were among the families of the Nethinim who returned from the cap-

tivity with Zerubbabel. Ezra 2 : 48; Neh. 7 : 51. (B.C. 536.)

Ge′ba (*a hill*), a city of Benjamin, with "suburbs," allotted to the priests. Josh. 21 : 17; 1 Chron. 6 : 60. It is named amongst the first group of the Benjamite towns—apparently those lying near to and along the north boundary. Josh. 18 : 24. Here the name is given as GABA. During the wars of the earlier part of the reign of Saul, Geba was held as a garrison by the Philistines, 1 Sam. 13 : 3, but they were ejected by Jonathan. It is now the modern village of *Jeba*, which stands picturesquely on the top of its steep terraced hill, six miles north of Jerusalem, on the very edge of the great *Wady Suweinit*, looking northward to the opposite village of ancient Michmash, which also retains its old name of *Mŭkhmas.*

Ge′bal (*mountain*), a maritime town of Phœnicia, near Tyre, Ezek. 27 : 9; known by the Greeks as Byblus. It is called *Jebail* by the Arabs, thus reviving the old biblical name.

Ge′ber (*manly*). 1. The son of Geber resided in the fortress of Ramoth-gilead, and had charge of Havoth-jair and the district of Argob. 1 Kings 4 : 13. (B.C. 1013.)

2. Geber the son of Uri had a district south of the former—the "land of Gilead." 1 Kings 4 : 19.

Ge′bim (*grasshoppers*), a village north of Jerusalem, Isa. 10 : 31, apparently between Anathoth (the modern *Anata*) and the ridge on which Nob was situated.

Gedali′ah (*God is my greatness*), son of Ahikam (Jeremiah's protector, Jer. 26 : 24) and grandson of Shaphan the secretary of King Josiah. After the destruction of the temple, B.C. 588, Nebuchadnezzar departed from Judea, leaving Gedaliah with a Chaldean guard, Jer. 40 : 5, at Mizpah to govern the vinedressers and husbandmen, Jer. 52 : 16, who were exempted from captivity. Jeremiah joined Gedaliah; and Mizpah became the resort of Jews from various quarters. Jer. 40 : 6, 11. He was murdered by Ishmael two months after his appointment.

Ged′eon. The Greek form of the Hebrew name GIDEON. Heb. 11 : 32.

Ge′der (*a wall*). The king of Geder was one of the thirty-one kings who were overcome by Joshua on the west of the Jordan. Josh. 12 : 13. (B.C. 1445.) It is possible that it may be the same place as the Geder named in 1 Chron. 4 : 39.

Gede′rah (*a sheepfold*), a town of Judah in the lowland country, Josh. 15 : 36, apparently in its eastern part. No town bearing this name has, however, been yet discovered in this hitherto little-explored district.

Gede′rathite, The, the native of a place called Gederah, apparently in Benjamin. 1 Chron. 12 : 4.

Ged′erite, The, the native of some place named Geder or Gederah. 1 Chron. 27 : 28.

Gede′roth (*sheepfolds*), a town in the low country of Judah. Josh. 15 : 41; 2 Chron. 28 : 18.

Gederotha′im (*two sheepfolds*), a town in the low country of Judah, Josh. 15 : 36, named next in order to Gederah.

Ge′dor (*a wall*), a town in the mountainous part of Judah, Josh. 15 : 58, a few miles north of Hebron. Robinson discovered a *Jedûr* halfway between Bethlehem and Hebron, about two miles west of the road.

Geha′zi (*valley of vision*), the servant or boy of Elisha. He was sent as the prophet's messenger on two occasions to the good Shunammite, 2 Kings 4 (B.C. 889–887); obtained fraudulently money and garments from Naaman, was miraculously smitten with incurable leprosy, and was dismissed from the prophet's service. 2 Kings 5. Later in the history he is mentioned as being engaged in relating to King Joram all the great things which Elisha had done. 2 Kings 8 : 4, 5.

Gehen′na. [HINNOM.]

Gel′iloth (*circuit*), a place named among the marks of the south boundary line of the tribe of Benjamin. Josh. 18 : 17. The name Geliloth never occurs again in this locality, and it therefore seems probable that Gilgal is the right reading.

Gemal′li (*camel-driver*), the father of Ammiel, the Danite spy. Num. 13 : 12. (B.C. 1490.)

Gemari′ah (*perfected by Jehovah*). 1. Son of Shaphan the scribe, and father of Michaiah. He was one of the nobles of Judah, and had a chamber in the house of the Lord, from which Baruch read Jeremiah's alarming prophecy in the ears of all the people, B.C. 606. Jer. 36.

2. Son of Hilkiah, was made the bearer of Jeremiah's letter to the captive Jews. Jer. 29 : 3. (B.C. 594.)

Gems. [STONES, PRECIOUS.]

Genealogy. In Hebrew the term for genealogy or pedigree is "the book of the generations;" and because the oldest histories were usually drawn up on a genealogical basis, the expression often extended to the whole history, as is the case with the Gospel of St. Matthew, where "the book of the generation of Jesus Christ" includes the whole history contained in that Gospel. The promise of the land of Canaan to the seed of Abraham, Isaac and Jacob successively, and the separation of the Israelites from the Gentile world; the expectation of Messiah as to spring from the tribe of Judah; the exclusively hereditary priesthood of Aaron with its dignity and emoluments; the long succession of kings in the line of David; and the whole division and occupation of the land upon genealogical principles by the tribes, families and houses of fathers, gave a deeper importance to the science of genealogy among the Jews than perhaps any other nation. When Zerubbabel brought back the captivity from Babylon, one of his first cares seems to have been to take a census of those that returned, and to settle them according to their genealogies. Passing on to the time of the birth of Christ, we have a striking incidental proof of the continuance of the Jewish genealogical economy in the fact that when Augustus ordered the census of the empire to be taken, the Jews in the province of Syria immediately went each one to his own city. The Jewish genealogical records continued to be kept till near the destruction of Jerusalem. But there can be little doubt that the registers of the Jewish tribes and families perished at the destruction of Jerusalem, and not before. It remains to be said that just notions of the nature of the Jewish genealogical records are of great importance with a view to the right interpretation of Scripture. Let it only be remembered that these records have respect to political and territorial divisions as much as to strictly genealogical descent, and it will at once be seen how erroneous a conclusion it may be that all who are called "sons" of such or such a patriarch or chief father must necessarily be his very children. If any one family or house became extinct, some other would succeed to its place, called after its own chief father. Hence of course a census of any tribe drawn up at a later period would exhibit different divisions from one drawn up at an earlier. The same principle must be borne in mind in interpreting any particular genealogy. Again, when a pedigree was abbreviated, it would naturally specify such generations as would indicate from what chief houses the person descended. Females are named in genealogies when there is anything remarkable about them, or when any right or property is transmitted through them. See Gen. 11 : 29; 22 : 23; 25 : 1–4; 35 : 22–26; Ex. 6 : 23; Num. 26 : 33.

Genealogy of Jesus Christ. The New Testament gives us the genealogy of but one person, that of our Saviour. This is given because it was important to prove that Jesus fulfilled the prophecies spoken of him. Only as the son

and heir of David could he be the Messiah. The following propositions will explain the true construction of these genealogies:—1. They are both the genealogies of Joseph, *i. e.* of Jesus Christ as the reputed and legal son of Joseph and Mary. 2. The genealogy of St. Matthew is Joseph's genealogy as legal successor to the throne of David. St. Luke's is Joseph's private genealogy, exhibiting his real birth as David's son, and thus showing why he was heir to Solomon's crown. The simple principle that one evangelist exhibits that genealogy which contained the successive heirs to David's and Solomon's throne, while the other exhibits the paternal stem of him who was the heir, explains all the anomalies of the two pedigrees, their agreements as well as their discrepancies, and the circumstance of there being two at all. 3. Mary, the mother of Jesus, was in all probability the daughter of Jacob, and first cousin to Joseph her husband. Thus:

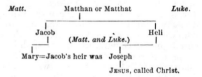

Matt.	Matthan or Matthat	*Luke.*
Jacob	*(Matt. and Luke.)*	Heli
Mary=Jacob's heir was	Joseph	

JESUS, called Christ.

(Godet, Lange and many others take the ground that Luke gives the genealogy of Mary, rendering Luke 3 : 23 thus: Jesus "being (*as was supposed*) the son of Joseph, (*but in reality*) the son of Heli." In this case Mary, as declared in the Targums, was the daughter of Heli, and Heli was the grandfather of Jesus. Mary's name was omitted because "ancient sentiment did not comport with the mention of the mother as the genealogical link." So we often find in the Old Testament the grandson called the son. This view has this greatly in its favor, that it shows that Jesus was not merely the legal but the actual descendant of David; and it would be very strange that in the gospel accounts, where so much is made of Jesus being the son and heir of David and of his kingdom, his *real* descent from David should not be given.—ED.)

Generation. In the long-lived patriarchal age a generation seems to have been computed at 100 years, Gen. 15 : 16, comp. 13, and Ex. 12 : 40; but subsequently the reckoning was the same which has been adopted by modern civilized nations, viz. from thirty to forty years. Job 42 : 16. Generation is also used to signify the men of an age or time, as *contemporaries*, Gen. 6 : 9 ; Isa. 53 : 8 ; *posterity*, especially in legal formulæ, Lev. 3 : 17, etc. ; *fathers*, or *ancestors*. Ps. 49 : 19.

Gen'esis (*origin*), the first book of the law or Pentateuch, so called from its title in the Septuagint, that is, *Creation*. Its *author* was Moses. The *date of writing* was probably during the forty-years wanderings in the wilderness, B.C. 1491–1451.

Time.—The book of Genesis covers 2369 years,—from the creation of Adam, A.M. 1, to the death of Joseph, A.M. 2369, or B.C. 1635.

Character and purpose.—The book of Genesis (with the first chapters of Exodus) describes the steps which led to the establishment of the theocracy. It is a part of the writer's plan to tell us what the divine preparation of the world was, in order to show, first, the significance of the call of Abraham, and next, the true nature of the Jewish theocracy. He begins with the creation of the world, because the God who created the world and the God who revealed himself to the fathers is the same God. The book of Genesis has thus a character at once special and universal.

Construction.—It is clear that Moses must have derived his knowledge of the events which he records in Genesis either from immediate divine revelation or from oral tradition or written documents. The nature of many of the facts related, and the minuteness of the narration, render it extremely improbable that immediate revelation was the source from whence they were drawn. That his knowledge should have been derived from oral tradition appears morally impossible when we consider the great number of names, ages, dates and minute events which are recorded. The conclusion, then, seems fair that he must have obtained his information from written documents coeval, or nearly so, with the events which they recorded, and composed by persons intimately acquainted with the subjects to which they relate. He may have collected these, with additions from authentic tradition or existing monuments, under the guidance of the Holy Spirit, into a single book. Certain it is that several of the first chapters of Genesis

have the air of being made up of selections from very ancient documents, written by different authors at different periods. The variety which is observable in the names and titles of the Supreme Being is appealed to among the most striking proofs of this fact. This is obvious in the English translation, but still more so in the Hebrew original. In Gen. 1 to 2 : 3, which is really one piece of composition, as the title, v. 4, "These are the generations," shows, the name of the Most High is uniformly *Elohim, God*. In ch. 2 : 4 to ch. 3, which may be considered the second document, the title is uniformly *Yehovah Elohim, Lord God ;* and in the third, including ch. 4, it is *Yehovah, Lord*, only ; while in ch. 5 it is *Elohim, God*, only, except in v. 29, where a quotation is made, and *Yehovah* used. It is hardly conceivable that all this should be the result of mere accident. The changes of the name correspond exactly to the changes in the narratives and the titles of the several pieces. "Now, do all these accurate quotations," says Professor Stowe, "impair the credit of the Mosaic books, or increase it ? Is Marshall's Life of Washington to be regarded as unworthy of credit because it contains copious extracts from Washington's correspondence and literal quotations from important public documents ? Is not its value greatly enhanced by this circumstance ? The objection is altogether futile. In the common editions of the Bible the Pentateuch occupies about one hundred and fifty pages, of which perhaps ten may be taken up with quotations. This surely is no very large proportion for an historical work extending through so long a period."—*Bush*. On the supposition that writing was known to Adam, Gen. 1–4, containing the first two of these documents, formed the Bible of Adam's descendants, or the antediluvians. Gen. 1 to 11 : 9, being the sum of these two and the following three, constitutes the Bible of the descendants of Noah. The whole of Genesis may be called the Bible of the posterity of Jacob ; and the five Books of the Law were the first Bible of Israel as a nation.—*Canon Cook.*

Gennes'aret (*garden of the prince*), **Land of.** It is generally believed that this term was applied to the fertile crescent-shaped plain on the western shore of the lake, extending from Khan Minyeh (two or three miles south of Capernaum (*Tel-Hum*)) on the north to the steep hill behind Mejdel (*Magdala*) on the south, and called by the Arabs *el-Ghuweir*, "the little Ghor." Mr. Porter gives the length as three miles, and the greatest breadth as about one mile. Additional interest is given to the land of Gennesaret, or el-Ghuweir, by the probability that its scenery suggested the parable of the sower. It is mentioned only twice in Scripture—Matt. 14 : 34; Mark 6 : 53. Compare Luke 5 : 1.

Gennes'aret, Sea of. [See GALI LEE, SEA OF.]

Gennes'areth. Inaccurately written for GENNESARET.

Gen'tiles (*nations*). All the people who were not Jews were so called by them, being aliens from the worship, rites and privileges of Israel. The word was used contemptuously by them. In the New Testament it is used as equivalent to *Greek*. This use of the word seems to

Gennesaret from Khan Minyeh.

have arisen from the almost universal adoption of the Greek language.

Gen'ubath, the son of Hadad, an Edomite of the royal family, by an Egyptian princess, the sister of Tahpenes, the queen of the Pharaoh who governed Egypt in the latter part of the reign of David. 1 Kings 11 : 20; comp. 16. (B.C. 1015.)

Ge'ra (*a grain*), one of the "sons," *i. e.* descendants, of Benjamin. Gen. 46 : 21. Gera, who is named, Judges 3 : 15, as the ancestor of Ehud, and in 2 Sam. 16 : 5 as the ancestor of Shimei who cursed David, is probably also the same person (though some consider them different persons).

Gerah. [WEIGHTS AND MEASURES.]

Ge'rar (*a lodging-place*), a very ancient city south of Gaza. It occurs chiefly in Genesis, 10 : 19; 20 : 1; 26 : 17; also incidentally in 2 Chron. 14 : 13, 14. It must have trenched on the "south" or "south country" of later Palestine. From a comparison of Gen. 21 : 32 with 26 : 23, 26, Beersheba would seem to be just on the verge of this territory, and perhaps to be its limit towards the northeast.

Gerasenes'. Luke 8 : 26, Revised Version. [See GADARENES.]

Gergesenes'. [See GADARENES.]

Ger'izim (*cutters*), a limestone mountain, 2855 feet high (800 feet above the valley at its foot), in Ephraim, near Shechem (Sychar), from which the blessings were read to the Israelites on entering Canaan. [See EBAL.] According to the traditions of the Samaritans it was here that Abraham sacrificed Isaac, that Melchizedek met the patriarch, that Jacob built an altar, and at its base dug a well, the ruins of which are still seen. Some scholars think there is ground for the first belief (so Smith); but careful observers of the locality discredit it, and believe Moriah to be the spot. [See MO-RIAH.] Gerizim was the site of the Samaritan temple, which was built there after the captivity, in rivalry with the temple at Jerusalem. [See SAMARITANS.] Gerizim is still to the Samaritans what Jerusalem is to the Jews and Mecca to the Mohammedans.

Ger'izites. 1 Sam. 27 : 8. [GERZITES.]

Mount Gerizim and Shechem.

Ger'shom (*a stranger* or *exile*). 1. The first-born son of Moses and Zipporah. Ex. 2 : 22; 18 : 3. (B.C. 1530.)

2. The form under which the name GERSHON—the eldest son of Levi—is given in several passages of Chronicles, viz., 1 Chron. 6 : 16, 17, 20, 43, 62, 71; 15 : 7.

3. The representative of the priestly family of Phinehas, among those who accompanied Ezra from Babylon. Ezra 8 : 2. (B.C. 536.)

Ger'shon (*exile*), the eldest of the three sons of Levi, born before the descent of Jacob's family into Egypt. Gen. 46 : 11; Ex. 6 : 16. (B.C. before 1706.) But, though the eldest born, the families of Gershon were outstripped in fame by their younger brethren of Kohath, from whom sprang Moses and the priestly line of Aaron.

Ger'shonites, The, the family descended from Gershon or Gershom, the son of Levi. "THE GERSHONITE," as applied to individuals, occurs in 1 Chron. 26 : 21. The sons of Gershon (the Gershonites) had charge of the fabrics of the tabernacle—the coverings, curtains, hangings and cords. Num. 3 : 25, 26; 4 : 25, 26.

Ger′zites (*dwellers in the desert*), **The,** a tribe who with the Geshurites and the Amalekites occupied the land between the south of Palestine and Egypt in the time of Saul. 1 Sam. 27 : 8. In the name of Mount Gerizim we have the only remaining trace of the presence of this old tribe of Bedouins in central Palestine.

Ge′sham (*filthy*) (sometimes written GESHAN), one of the sons of Jahdai, in the genealogy of Judah and family of Caleb. 1 Chron. 2 : 47.

Ge′shem and **Gash′mu** (*rain*), an Arabian, mentioned in Neh. 2 : 19 and 6 : 1, 2, 6. (B.C. 446.) We may conclude that he was an inhabitant of Arabia Petræa, or of the Arabian Desert, and probably the chief of a tribe. "Gashum said it" made him a type of those who create a common report.

Ge′shur (*a bridge*), a little principality of Syria, northeast of Bashan. Deut. 3 : 14 ; 2 Sam. 15 : 8. It is highly probable that Geshur was a section of the wild and rugged region now called

The Garden of Gethsemane. (*From an original Photograph.*)

el-Lejah, still a refuge for criminals and outlaws. [ARGOB.]

Gesh′uri and **Gesh′urites.** 1. The inhabitants of Geshur. Deut. 3 : 14 ; Josh. 12 : 5 ; 13 : 11.

2. An ancient tribe which dwelt in the desert between Arabia and Philistia. Josh. 13 : 2 ; 1 Sam. 27 : 8.

Ge′ther (*fear*), the third in order of the sons of Aram. Gen. 10 : 23. No satisfactory trace of the people sprung from this stock has been found.

Gethsem′a-ne (*an oil-press*), a small "farm," Matt. 26 : 36 ; Mark 14 : 32, situated across the brook Kedron, John 18 : 1, probably at the foot of Mount Olivet, Luke 22 : 39, to the northwest and

about one-half or three-quarters of a mile English from the walls of Jerusalem, and 100 yards east of the bridge over the Kedron. There was a "garden," or rather orchard, attached to it, to which the olive, fig and pomegranate doubtless invited resort by their hospitable shade. And we know from the evangelists Luke, 22 : 39, and John, 18 : 2, that our Lord ofttimes resorted thither with his disciples. But Gethsemane has not come down to us as a scene of mirth ; its inexhaustible associations are the offspring of a single event—the agony of the Son of God on the evening preceding his passion. A garden, with eight venerable olive trees, and a grotto to the north, detached from it, and in closer connection with the church of the Sepulchre of the Virgin, are pointed out as *the* Geth-semane. Against the contemporary antiquity of the olive trees it has been urged that Titus cut down all the trees about Jerusalem. The probability would seem to be that they were planted by Christian hands to mark the spot; unless, like the sacred olive of the Acropolis, they may have reproduced themselves.

Geu'el (*majesty of God*), son of Machi the Gadite spy. Num. 13 : 15. (B.C. 1490.)

Ge'zer (*a precipice*), an ancient city of Canaan, whose king, Horam or Elam, coming to the assistance of Lachish, was killed with all his people by Joshua. Josh. 10 : 33; 12 : 12. It formed one of the landmarks on the south boundary of Ephraim, between the lower Beth-horon and the Mediterranean, Josh. 16 : 3, the western limit of the tribe. 1 Chron. 7 : 28. It was allotted with its suburbs to the Kohathite Levites, Josh. 21 : 21; 1 Chron. 6 : 67; but the original inhabitants were not dispossessed, Judges 1 : 29, and even down to the reign of Solomon the Canaanites were still dwelling there, and paying tribute to Israel. 1 Kings 9 : 16. It was burned by Pharaoh in Solomon's time, 1 Kings 9 : 15–17, and given to Solomon's Egyptian wife, and rebuilt by him.

Gez'rites, The. The word which the Jewish critics have substituted in the margin of the Bible for the ancient reading, "the Gerizite." 1 Sam. 27 : 8. [GERZITES, THE.]

Gi'ah (*a waterfall*), a place named only in 2 Sam. 2 : 24 to designate the position of the hill Ammah.

Giants, men of extraordinary size or height. 1. They are first spoken of in Gen. 6 : 4, under the name *Nephilim*. We are told in Gen. 6 : 1–4 that "there *were* Nephilim in the earth," and that afterwards the "sons of God" mingling with the beautiful "daughters of men" produced a race of violent and insolent *Gibborim* (Authorized Version "mighty men").
2. The *Rephaim*, a name which frequently occurs. The earliest mention of them is the record of their defeat by Chedorlaomer and some allied kings at Ashteroth Karnaim. The "valley of Rephaim," 2 Sam. 5 : 18; 1 Chron. 11 : 15; Isa. 17 : 5, a rich valley southwest of Jerusalem, derived its name from them.

They were probably an aboriginal people of which the EMIM, ANAKIM and ZUZIM [which see] were branches. [See also GOLIATH.]

Gib'bar (*gigantic*), the father of some who returned with Zerubbabel from Babylon. Ezra 2 : 20.

Gib'bethon (*a hill*), a town allotted to the tribe of Dan, Josh. 19 : 44, and afterwards given with its "suburbs" to the Kohathite Levites. ch. 21 : 23.

Gib'e-a (*a hill*). Sheva "the father of Macbenah" and "father of Gibea" is mentioned with other names, unmistakably those of places and not persons, among the descendants of Judah. 1 Chron. 2 : 49, comp. 42. This would seem to point out Gibea.

Gib'e-ah, a word employed in the Bible to denote a *hill*. Like most words of this kind it gave its name to several towns and places in Palestine, which would doubtless be generally on or near a hill. They are—1. Gibeah, a city in the mountain district of Judah, named with Maon and the southern Carmel, Josh. 15 : 57; and comp. 1 Chron. 2 : 49, etc.
2. Gibeah of Benjamin first appears in the tragical story of the Levite and his concubine. Judges 19 : 20. It was then a "city," with the usual open street or square, Judges 19 : 15, 17, 20, and containing 700 "chosen men," ch. 20 : 15, probably the same whose skill as slingers is preserved in the next verse. In many particulars Gibeah agrees very closely with *Tuleïl-el-Fûl*, a conspicuous eminence just four miles north of Jerusalem, to the right of the road. We next meet with Gibeah of Benjamin during the Philistine wars of Saul and Jonathan. 1 Sam. 13 : 15, 16. It now bears its full title. As "Gibeah of Benjamin" this place is referred to in 2 Sam. 23 : 29 (comp. 1 Chron. 11 : 31), and as "Gibeah" it is mentioned by Hosea, 5 : 8; 9 : 9; 10 : 9, but it does not again appear in the history. It is, however, almost without doubt identical with
3. Gibeah of Saul. This is not mentioned as Saul's city till after his anointing, 1 Sam. 10 : 26, when he is said to have gone "home" to Gibeah. In the subsequent narrative the town bears its full name. ch. 11 : 4.
4. Gibeah in Kirjath-jearim was no doubt a hill in that city, and the place in which the ark remained from the time of its return by the Philistines till its

removal by David. 2 Sam. 6 : 3, 4; comp. 1 Sam. 7 : 1, 2.

5. Gibeah in the field, named only in Judges 20 : 31 as the place to which one of the "highways" led from Gibeah of Benjamin. It is probably the same as Geba. The "meadows of Gaba" (Authorized Version Gibeah, Judges 20 : 33) have no connection with the "field," the Hebrew word being entirely different.

Gib'e-ath, probably the same as GIBEAH OF BENJAMIN. Josh. 18 : 28.

Gib'eon (*hill city*), one of the four cities of the Hivites, the inhabitants of which made a league with Joshua, Josh. 9 : 3-15, and thus escaped the fate of Jericho and Ai. Comp. ch. 11 : 19. Gibeon lay within the territory of Benjamin, ch. 18 : 25, and with its "suburbs" was allotted to the priests, ch. 21 : 17, of whom it became afterwards a principal station. It retains its ancient name almost intact, *el-Jib.* Its distance from Jerusalem by the main road is about 6½ miles; but there is a more direct road reducing it to five miles.

Gib'eonites, The, the people of Gibeon, and perhaps also of the three cities associated with Gibeon, Josh. 9 : 17—Hivites; and who, on the discovery of the stratagem by which they had obtained the protection of the Israelites, were condemned to be perpetual bondmen, hewers of wood and drawers of water for the congregation, and for the house of God and altar of Jehovah. Josh. 9 : 23, 27. Saul appears to have broken this covenant, and in a fit of enthusiasm or patriotism to have killed some and devised a general massacre of the rest. 2 Sam. 21 : 1, 2, 5. This was expiated many years after by giving up seven men of Saul's descendants to the Gibeonites, who hung them or crucified them "before Jehovah"—as a kind of sacrifice— in Gibeah, Saul s own town. ch. 21 : 4, 6, 9.

Gib'lites, The. [GEBAL.]

Giddal'ti (*I have trained up*), one of the sons of Heman, the king's seer. 1 Chron. 25 : 4.

Gid'del (*very great*). 1. Children of Giddel were among the Nethinim who returned from the captivity with Zerubbabel. Ezra 2 : 47; Neh. 7 : 49.

2. Bene-Giddel were also among the "servants of Solomon" who returned to Judea in the same caravan. Ezra 2 : 56; Neh. 7 : 58. (B.C. 536.)

Gid'eon (*he that cuts down*), youngest son of Joash of the Abiezrites, an undistinguished family who lived at Ophrah, a town probably on the west of Jordan, Judges 6 : 15, in the territory of Manasseh, near Shechem. He was the fifth recorded judge of Israel, and for many reasons the greatest of them all. When we first hear of him he was grown up and had sons, Judges 6 : 11; 8 : 20; and from the apostrophe of the angel, ch. 6 : 12, we may conclude that he had already distinguished himself in war against the roving bands of nomadic robbers who had oppressed Israel for seven years. When the angel appeared, Gideon was threshing wheat with a flail in the wine-press, to conceal it from the predatory tyrants. His call to be a deliverer, and his destruction of Baal's altar, are related in Judges 6. After this begins the second act of Gideon's life. Clothed by the Spirit of God, Judges 6 : 34; comp. 1 Chron. 12 : 18; Luke 24 : 49, he blew a trumpet, and was joined by Zebulun, Naphtali and even the reluctant Asher. Strengthened by a double sign from God, he reduced his army of 32,000 by the usual proclamation. Deut. 20 : 8; comp. 1 Macc. 3 : 56. By a second test at "the spring of trembling" he further reduced the number of his followers to 300. Judges 7 : 5, *seq.* The midnight attack upon the Midianites, their panic, and the rout and slaughter that followed, are told in Judges 7. The memory of this splendid deliverance took deep root in the national traditions. 1 Sam. 12 : 11; Ps. 83 : 11; Isa. 9 : 4; 10 : 26; Heb. 11 : 32. After this there was a peace of forty years, and we see Gideon in peaceful possession of his well-earned honors, and surrounded by the dignity of a numerous household. Judges 8 : 29-31. It is not improbable that, like Saul, he owed a part of his popularity to his princely appearance. Judges 8 : 18. In this third stage of his life occur alike his most noble and his most questionable acts, viz., the refusal of the monarchy on theocratic grounds, and the irregular consecration of a jewelled ephod formed out of the rich spoils of Midian, which proved to the Israelites a temptation to idolatry, although it was doubtless intended for use in the worship of Jehovah.

Gideo'ni (*a cutting down*), a Benjamite, father of Abidan. Num. 1 : 11; 7 : 60, 65; 10 : 24.

Gi'dom (*desolation*), a place named

only in Judges 20 : 45. It would appear to have been situated between Gibeah (*Tuliel-el-Fúl*) and the cliff Rimmon.

Gier-eagle, an unclean bird mentioned in Lev. 11 : 18 and Deut. 14 : 17 ; identical in reality as in name with the *racham* of the Arabs, viz., the Egyptian vulture.

Gift. The giving and receiving of presents has in all ages been not only a more frequent but also a more formal and significant proceeding in the East than among ourselves. We cannot adduce a more remarkable proof of the important part which presents play in the social life of the East than the fact that the Hebrew· language possesses no less than fifteen different expressions for the one idea. The mode of presentation was with as ·much parade as possible. The refusal of a present was regarded as a high indignity. No less an insult was it not to bring a present when the position of the parties demanded it. 1 Sam. 10 : 27.

Gi'hon (*a stream*). 1. The second river of Paradise. Gen. 2 : 13. [EDEN.]

2. A place near Jerusalem, memorable as the scene of the anointing and proclamation of Solomon as king. 1 Kings 1 : 33, 38, 45.

Gil'ala-i (*weighty*), one of the priests' sons at the consecration of the wall of Jerusalem. Neh. 12 : 36. (B.C. 446.)

Mountains of Gilboa.

Gilbo'a (*a bubbling spring*), a mountain range on the eastern side of the plain of Esdraelon, rising over the city of Jezreel. Comp. 1 Sam. 28 : 4 with 29 : 1. It is mentioned in Scripture only in connection with one event in Israelitish his-

tory, the defeat and death of Saul and Jonathan by the Philistines. 1 Sam. 31 : 1; 2 Sam. 1 : 6; 21 : 12 ; 1 Chron. 10 : 1, 8. Of the identity of Gilboa with the ridge which stretches eastward from the ruins of Jezreel no doubt can be entertained. The village is now called *Jelbôu*.

Gil'e-ad (*rocky region*). 1. A mountainous region bounded on the west by the Jordan, on the north by Bashan, on the east by the Arabian plateau, and on the south by Moab and Ammon. Gen. 31 : 21; Deut. 3 : 12–17. It is sometimes called " Mount Gilead," Gen. 31 : 25, sometimes " the land of Gilead," Num. 32 : 1, and sometimes simply " Gilead." Ps. 60 : 7 ; Gen. 37 : 25. The name Gilead, as is usual in Palestine, describes the physical aspect of the country : it signifies " a hard rocky region." The mountains of Gilead, including Pisgah, Abarim and Peor, have a real elevation of from 2000 to 3000 feet ; but their apparent elevation on the western side is much greater, owing to the depression of the Jordan valley, which averages about 1000 feet. Their outline is singularly uniform, resembling a massive wall running along the horizon. Gilead was specially noted for its balm collected from " balm of Gilead " trees, and worth twice its weight in silver.

2. Possibly the name of a mountain west of the Jordan, near Jezreel. Judges 7 : 3. We are inclined, however, to think that the true reading in this place should be GILBOA.

3. Son of Machir, grandson of Manasseh. Num. 26 : 29, 30.

4. The father of Jephthah. Judges 11 : 1, 2.

Gil'e-adites, The, Num. 26 : 29 ; Judges 10 : 3 ; 12 : 4, 5, a branch of the tribe of Manasseh, descended from Gilead.

Gil'gal (*a wheel; rolling*). 1. The site of the first camp of the Israelites on the west of the Jordan, the place at which they passed the first night after crossing the river, and where the twelve stones were set up which had been taken from the bed of the stream, Josh. 4 : 19, 20, comp. 3 ; where also they kept their first passover in the land of Canaan. ch. 5 : 10. It was " in the east border of Jericho," apparently on a hillock or rising ground, Josh. 5 : 3, comp. 9, in the Arboth-Jericho (Authorized Version " the plains"), that is, the hot depressed district of the Ghor which lay between the town and the Jordan. ch. 5 : 10. Here Samuel was judge, and Saul was made king. We again have a glimpse of it, some sixty years later, in the history of David's return to Jerusalem. 2 Sam. 19 : 40. A Gilgal is spoken of in Josh. 15 : 7, in describing the north border of Judah. In Josh. 18 : 17 it is given as Geliloth. Gilgal near Jericho is doubtless intended.

2. In 2 Kings 2 : 1, 2; 4 : 38 is named a Gilgal visited by Elijah and Elisha. This could not be the Gilgal of the low plain of the Jordan, for the prophets are said to have gone *down* to Bethel, which is 3000 feet above the plain. It has been identified with *Jiljilia*, about four miles from Bethel and Shiloh respectively.

3. The "king of the nations of Gilgal," or rather perhaps the "king of Goim at

Gilead.

Gilgal," is mentioned in the catalogue of the chiefs overthrown by Joshua. Josh. 12 : 23. Possibly the site of this place is marked by the modern village *Jiljûlieh*, about four miles south of Antipatris, which lies 16 miles northeast of Joppa. But another Gilgal, under the slightly-different form of *Kilkilieh*, lies about two miles east of Antipatris.

Gi′loh (*exile*), a town in the mountainous part of Judah, named in the first group with Debir and Eshtemoh, Josh. 15 : 51; it was the native place of the famous Ahithophel. 2 Sam. 15 : 12.

Gi′lonite, The, native of Giloh. 2 Sam. 15 : 12; 23 : 34.

Gim′zo (*fertile in sycamores*), a town which with its dependent villages was taken possession of by the Philistines in

the reign of Ahaz. 2 Chron. 28 : 18. The name (*Jimzu*) still remains attached to a large village between two and three miles southwest of Lydda, south of the road between Jerusalem and Jaffa.

Gin, a trap for birds or beasts; it consisted of a net, Isa. 8 : 14, and a stick to act as a spring. Amos 3 : 5.

Gi′nath (*protection*), father of Tibni. 1 Kings 16 : 21, 22.

Gin′netho (*gardener*), one of the chief of the priests and Levites who returned to Judea with Zerubbabel. Neh. 12 : 4. He is doubtless the same person as

Gin′nethon (*gardener*), a priest who sealed the covenant with Nehemiah. Neh. 10 : 6. (B.C. 410.)

Girdle, an essential article of dress in the East, and worn by both men and women. The common girdle was made of leather, 2 Kings 1 : 8; Matt. 3 : 4, like that worn by the Bedouins of the present day. A finer girdle was made of linen, Jer. 13 : 1; Ezek. 16 : 10, embroidered with silk, and sometimes with gold and silver thread, Dan. 10 : 5; Rev. 1 : 13; 15 : 6, and frequently studded with gold and precious stones or pearls. The military girdle was worn about the waist; the sword or dagger was suspended from it. Judges 3 : 16; 2 Sam. 20 : 8; Ps. 45 : 3. Hence girding up the loins denotes preparation for battle or for active exertion. Girdles were used as pockets, as they still are among the Arabs, and as purses, one end of the girdle being folded back for the purpose. Matt. 10 : 9; Mark 6 : 8.

Gir′gasite, The, Gen. 10 : 16, or **Gir′gashites** (*dwelling on a clayey soil*), **The,** one of the nations who were in possession of Canaan east of the Sea of Galilee before the entrance thither of the children of Israel. Gen. 10 : 16; 15 : 21; Deut. 7 : 1.

Gis′pa (*caress*), one of the overseers of the Nethinim, in "the Ophel," after the return from captivity. Neh. 11 : 21.

Git′tah-he′pher. Josh. 19 : 13. [GATH-HEPHER.]

Gitta′im. [GITTITES.]

Git′tites (*belonging to Gath*), the 600 men who followed David from Gath, under Ittai the Gittite, 2 Sam. 15 : 18, 19, and who probably acted as a kind of body-guard. Obed-edom "the Gittite" may have been so named from the town of Gittaim in Benjamin, 2 Sam. 4 : 3; Neh. 11 : 33, or from Gath-rimmon.

Gittith, a musical instrument, by some supposed to have been used by the people of Gath, and by others to have been employed at the festivities of the vintage. Ps. 8, 81, 84.

Gi′zonite, The (*inhabitant of Gizoh*). "The sons of Hashem the Gizonite" are named amongst the warriors of David's guard. 1 Chron. 11 : 34. Kennicott concludes that the name should be Gouni.

Glass. The Hebrew word occurs only in Job 28 : 17, where in the Authorized Version it is rendered "crystal." In spite of the absence of specific allusion to glass in the sacred writings, the Hebrews must have been aware of the invention. From paintings representing the process of glass-blowing which have been discovered at Beni-hassan, and in tombs at other places, we know that the invention was known at least 3500 years ago.

Fragments too of wine-vases as old as the exodus have been discovered in Egypt. The art was also known to the ancient Assyrians. In the New Testament glass is alluded to as an emblem of brightness. Rev. 4 : 6; 15 : 2; 21 : 18.

Gleaning. The gleaning of fruit trees, as well as of corn-fields, was reserved for the poor. [CORNER.]

Glede, the old name for the common kite (*Milvus ater*), occurs only in Deut. 14 : 13, among the unclean birds of prey.

Gnat, a species of mosquito mentioned only in the proverbial expression used by our Saviour in Matt. 23 : 24.

Goad. Judges 3 : 31; 1 Sam. 13 : 21. The Hebrew word in the latter passage probably means the point of the *plough-share*. The former word does probably refer to the goad, the long handle of which might be used as a formidable weapon. The instrument, as still used in countries of southern Europe and western Asia, consists of a rod about eight feet long, brought to a sharp point and sometimes cased with iron at the head.

Syrian Goat.

Goat. There appear to be two or three varieties of the common goat, *Hircus ægagrus*, at present bred in Palestine and Syria, but whether they are identical with those which were reared by the ancient Hebrews it is not possible to say. The most marked varieties are the Syrian goat (*Capra mambrica*, Linn.) and the Angora goat (*Capra angorensis*, Linn.), with fine long hair. As to the "wild goats," 1 Sam. 24 : 2 ; Job 39 : 1 ; Ps. 104 : 18, it is not at all improbable that some species of *ibex* is denoted.

Goat, Scape. [ATONEMENT, DAY OF.]

Go ath (*lowing*), a place apparently in the neighborhood of Jerusalem, and named, in connection with the hill Gareb, only in Jer. 31 : 39.

Gob (*cistern*), a place mentioned only in 2 Sam. 21 : 18, 19, as the scene of two encounters between David's warriors and the Philistines. In the parallel account in 1 Chron. 20 : 4 the name is given as GEZER.

Goblet, a circular vessel for wine or other liquid.

God (*good*). Throughout the Hebrew Scriptures two chief names are used for the one true divine Being — ELOHIM, commonly translated *God* in our version, and JEHOVAH, translated *Lord*. Elohim is the plural of Eloah (in Arabic *Allah*); it is often used in the short form EL (a word signifying *strength*), as in EL-SHAD-DAI, *God Almighty*, the name by which God was specially known to the patriarchs. Gen. 17 : 1 ; 28 : 3 ; Ex. 6 : 3. The etymology is uncertain, but it is generally agreed that the primary idea, is that of *strength, power of effect*, and that it properly describes God in that character in which he is exhibited to all men in his works, as the creator, sustainer and supreme governor of the world. The plural form of Elohim has given rise to much discussion. The fanciful idea that it referred to the *trinity of persons* in the Godhead hardly finds now a supporter among scholars. It is either what grammarians call *the plural of majesty*, or it denotes the *fullness* of divine strength, the *sum of the powers* displayed by God. Jehovah denotes specifically the one true God, whose people the Jews were, and who made them the guardians of his truth. The name is never applied to a false god, nor to any other being except one, the ANGEL-JEHOVAH, who is thereby marked as one with God, and who appears again in the New Covenant as "God manifested in the flesh." Thus much is clear; but all else is beset with difficulties. At a time too early to be traced, the Jews abstained from pronouncing the name, for fear of its irreverent use. The custom is said to have

been founded on a strained interpretation of Lev. 24 : 16 ; and the phrase there used, "THE NAME" (*Shema*), is substituted by the rabbis for the unutterable word. In reading the Scriptures they substituted for it the word ADONAI (*Lord*), from the translation of which by Κύριος in the LXX., followed by the Vulgate, which uses *Dominus*, we have the LORD of our version. The substitution of the word Lord is most unhappy, for it in no way represents the meaning of the sacred name. The key to the *meaning* of the name is unquestionably given in God's revelation of himself to Moses by the phrase "I AM THAT I AM," Ex. 3 : 14 ; 6 : 3. We must connect the name *Jehovah* with the Hebrew substantive verb *to be*, with the inference that it expresses the essential, eternal, unchangeable *being* of Jehovah. But more, it is not the expression only, or chiefly, of an *absolute* truth : it is a *practical revelation* of God, in his essential, unchangeable relation to his chosen people, the basis of his *covenant*.

Gog (*mountain*). 1. A Reubenite, 1 Chron. 5 : 4, son of Shemaiah.

2. Gog and Magog. [See MAGOG.]

Go'lan (*circle*), a city of Bashan, Deut. 4 : 43, allotted out of the half tribe of Manasseh to the Levites, Josh. 21 : 27, and one of the three cities of refuge east of the Jordan. ch. 20 : 8. Its very site is now unknown. It gave its name to the province of Gaulanitis. It lay east of Galilee and north of Gadaritis [GADARA], and corresponds to the modern province of *Jaulân*.

Gold. Gold was known from the very earliest times. Gen. 2 : 11. It was at first used chiefly for ornaments, etc. Gen. 24 : 22. Coined money was not known to the ancients till a comparatively late period ; and on the Egyptian tombs gold is represented as being weighed in rings for commercial purposes. Comp. Gen. 43 : 21. Gold was extremely abundant in ancient times, 1 Chron. 22 : 14 ; 2 Chron. 1 : 15 ; 9 : 9 ; Dan. 3 : 1 ; Nah. 2 : 9 ; but this did not depreciate its value, because of the enormous quantities consumed by the wealthy in furniture, etc. 1 Kings 6 : 22 ; 10 *passim ;* Esther 1 : 6 ; Cant. 3 : 9, 10 ; Jer. 10 : 9. The chief countries mentioned as producing gold are Arabia, Sheba and Ophir. 1 Kings 9 : 28 ; 10 : 1 ; Job 28 : 16.

Gol'gotha (*skull*), the Hebrew name of the spot at which our Lord was crucified. Matt. 27 : 33; Mark 15 : 22; John 19 : 17. By these three evangelists it is interpreted to mean the "place of a skull." Two explanations of the name are given: (1) that it was a spot where executions ordinarily took place, and therefore abounded in skulls; or (2) it may come from the look or form of the spot itself, bald, round and skull-like, and therefore a mound or hillock, in accordance with the common phrase—for which there is no direct authority— "Mount Calvary." Whichever of these is the correct explanation, Golgotha seems to have been a known spot.

Goli'ath (*splendor*), a famous giant of Gath, who "morning and evening for forty days" defied the armies of Israel. 1 Sam. 17. (B.C. 1063.) He was possibly descended from the old Rephaim [GIANTS], of whom a scattered remnant took refuge with the Philistines after their dispersion by the Ammonites. Deut. 2 : 20, 21; 2 Sam. 21 : 22. His height was "six cubits and a span," which, taking the cubit at 21 inches, would make him 10½ feet high. The scene of his combat with David, by whom he was slain, was the "valley of the terebinth," between Shochoh and Arekah, probably among the western passes of Benjamin. In 2 Sam. 21 : 19 we find that another Goliath of Gath was slain by Elhanan, also a Bethlehemite.

Go'mer (*perfect*). 1. The eldest son of Japheth, Gen. 10 : 2, 3, the progenitor of the early Cimmerians, of the later Cimbri and the other branches of the Celtic family, and of the modern Gael and Cymri.

2. The wife of Hosea. Hos. 1 : 3.

Gomor'rah (*submersion*), one of the five "cities of the plain" or "vale of Siddim" that under their respective kings joined battle there with Chedorlaomer, Gen. 14 : 2–8, and his allies, by whom they were discomfited till Abraham came to the rescue. Four out of the five were afterwards destroyed by the Lord with fire from heaven. Gen. 19 : 23–29. One of them only, Zoar (or Bela, which was its original name), was spared at the request of Lot, in order that he might take refuge there. The geographical position of these cities is discussed under SODOM.

Gopher (*pitch*) **wood.** Only once mentioned—Gen. 6 : 14. Two principal conjectures have been proposed:—1. That the ' trees of gopher' are any trees of the resinous kind, such as pine, fir, etc. 2. That gopher is cypress.

Go'shen. 1. The name of a part of Egypt where the Israelites dwelt during the whole period of their sojourn in that country. It was probably situated on the eastern border of the Nile, extending from the Mediterranean to the Red Sea. It contained the treasure-cities of Rameses and Pittim. It was a pasture land, especially suited to a shepherd people, and sufficient for the Israelites, who there prospered, and were separate from the main body of the Egyptians.

2. A district in southern Palestine conquered by Joshua. Josh. 10 : 41. It lay between Gaza and Gibeon.

3. A town in the mountains of Judah, probably in a part of the country of Goshen.

Gos'pels. The name Gospel (from *god* and *spell*, Ang. Sax. *good message* or *news*, which is a translation of the Greek *evaggelion*) is applied to the four inspired histories of the life and teaching of Christ contained in the New Testament, of which separate accounts are given in their place. They were all composed during the latter half of the first century: those of St. Matthew and St. Mark some years before the destruction of Jerusalem; that of St. Luke probably about A.D. 64; and that of St. John towards the close of the century. Before the end of the second century, there is abundant evidence that the four Gospels, as one collection, were generally used and accepted. As a matter of literary history, nothing can be better established than the genuineness of the Gospels. On comparing these four books one with another, a peculiar difficulty claims attention, which has had much to do with the controversy as to their genuineness. In the fourth Gospel the narrative coincides with that of the other three in a few passages only. The received explanation is the only satisfactory one, namely, that John, writing last, at the close of the first century, had seen the other Gospels, and purposely abstained from writing anew what they had sufficiently recorded. In the other three Gospels there is a great amount of agreement. If we suppose the history that they contain to be divided into 89 sections, in 42 of these all the three narratives coincide, 12 more are given by Matthew and Mark only, 5 by Mark and Luke only, and 14 by Matthew and Luke. To these must be added 5 peculiar to Matthew, 2 to Mark and 9 to Luke, and the enumeration is complete. But this applies only to general coincidence as to the facts narrated : the amount of verbal coincidence, that is, the passages either verbally the same or coinciding in the use of many of the same words, is much smaller. It has been ascertained by Stroud that "if the total contents of the several Gospels be represented by 100, the following table is obtained :

Matthew has 42 *peculiarities* and 58 *coincidences.*
Mark   "   7   "   93   "
Luke   " 59   "   41   "
John   " 92   "   8   "

Why four Gospels.—1. To bring four separate independent witnesses to the truth. 2. It is to give the Lord's life from every point of view, four living portraits of one person. There were *four* Gospels because Jesus was to be commended to four races or classes of men, or to four phases of human thought, — the Jewish, Roman, Greek and Christian. Had not these exhausted the classes to be reached, there would doubtless have been more Gospels. In all ages, the Jewish, Roman and Greek natures reappear among men, and, in fact, make up the world of natural men, while the Christian nature and wants likewise remain essentially the same.

The FIRST GOSPEL was prepared by Matthew for the Jew. He gives us the Gospel of Jesus, the Messiah of the Jews, the Messianic royalty of Jesus. He places the life and character of Jesus, as lived on earth, alongside the life and character of the Messiah, as sketched in the prophets, showing Christianity as the fulfillment of Judaism. Mark wrote the SECOND GOSPEL. It was substantially the preaching of Peter to the Romans.

The Gospel for him must represent the character and career of Jesus from the Roman point of view, as answering to the idea of divine power, work, law, conquest and universal sway ; must retain its old significance and ever-potent inspiration as the battle-call of the almighty Conqueror. Luke wrote the THIRD GOSPEL in Greece for the Greek. It has its basis in the gospel which Paul and Luke, by long preaching to the Greeks, had already thrown into the form best suited to commend to their acceptance Jesus as the perfect divine man. It is the gospel of the future, of progressive Christianity, of reason and culture seeking the perfection of manhood. John, "the beloved disciple," wrote the FOURTH GOSPEL

Colocynthus or Wild Gourd.

for the Christian, to cherish and train those who have entered the new kingdom of Christ, into the highest spiritual life. —*Condensed from Prof. Gregory.*

Gourd. 1. *Kikâyôn* only in Jonah 4 : 6–10. The plant which is intended by this word, and which afforded shade to the prophet Jonah before Nineveh, is the *Ricinus communis,* or castor-oil plant, which, a native of Asia, is now naturalized in America, Africa and the south of Europe. This plant varies considerably in size, being in India a tree, but in England seldom attaining a greater height than three or four feet. The leaves are large and palmate, with serrated lobes, and would form an excellent shelter for the sun-stricken prophet. The seeds contain the oil so well known under the name of "castor oil," which has for ages been in high repute as a medicine. It is now thought by many that the plant meant is a vine of the cucumber family, a genuine gourd, which is much used for shade in the East.

2. The wild gourd of 2 Kings 4 : 39, which one of "the sons of the prophets" gathered ignorantly, supposing them to be good for food, is a poisonous gourd, supposed to be the colocynth, which bears a fruit of the color and size of an orange, with a hard, woody shell. As several varieties of the same family, such as melons, pumpkins, etc., are favorite articles of refreshing food amongst the Orientals, we can easily understand the cause of the mistake.

Governor. In the Authorized Version this one English word is the representative of no less than ten Hebrew and four Greek words. 1. The chief of a tribe or family. 2. A ruler in his capacity of *lawgiver* and dispenser of justice. 3. A ruler considered especially as having *power* over the property and persons of his subjects. Gen. 24 : 2 ; Josh. 12 : 2 ; Ps. 105 : 20. The "governors of the people," in 2 Chron. 23 : 20, appear to have been the king's body-guard ; cf. 2 Kings 11 : 19. 4. A *prominent* personage, whatever his capacity. It is applied to a king as the military and civil chief of his people, 2 Sam. 5 : 2 ; 6 : 21 ; 1 Chron. 29 : 22, to the general of an army, 2 Chron. 32 : 21, and to the head of a tribe. 2 Chron. 19 : 11. It denotes an officer of high rank in the palace, the lord high chamberlain. 2 Chron. 28 : 7. It is applied in 1 Kings 10 : 15 to the petty chieftains who were tributary to Solomon, 2 Chron. 9 : 14 ; to the military commander of the Syrians, 1 Kings 20 : 24, the Assyrians, 2 Kings 18 : 24 ; 23 : 8, the Chaldeans, Jer. 51 : 23, and the Medes. Jer. 51 : 38. Under the Persian viceroys, during the Babylonian captivity, the land of the Hebrews appears to have been portioned out among "governors" (*pachôth*) inferior in rank to the satraps, Ezra 8 : 36, like the other provinces which were under the dominion of the Persian king. Neh. 2 : 7, 9. It is impossible to determine the precise limits of their authority or the functions which they had to perform. It appears from Ezra 6 : 8

that these governors were intrusted with the collection of the king's taxes ; and from Neh. 5 : 18 ; 12 : 26 that they were supported by a contribution levied upon the people, which was technically termed "the bread of the governor ;" comp. Ezra 4 : 14. They were probably assisted in discharging their official duties by a council. Ezra 4 : 7 ; 6 : 6. The "governor" beyond the river had a judgment-seat beyond Jerusalem, from which probably he administered justice when making a progress through his province. Neh. 3 : 7. At the time of Christ Judea was a Roman province, governed by a procurator (governor) appointed by Rome.

Go'zan seems in the Authorized Version of 1 Chron. 5 : 26 to be the name of a river ; but in 2 Kings 17 : 6 and 18 : 11 it is evidently applied not to a river but a country. Gozan was the tract to which the Israelites were carried away captive by Pul, Tiglath-pileser and Shalmaneser, or possibly Sargon. It is probably identical with the *Gauzanitis* of Ptolemy, and may be regarded as represented by the Mygdonia of other writers. It was the tract watered by the Habor, the modern *Khabour*, the great Mesopotamian affluent of the Euphrates.

Grape. [VINE.]

Grasshopper. [LOCUST.]

Grave. [BURIAL.]

Greaves, a piece of defensive armor which reached from the foot to the knee, and thus protected the shin of the wearer. It was made of leather or brass.

Greece, Greeks, Gre'cians. The histories of Greece and Palestine are little connected with each other. In Gen. 10 : 2–5 Moses mentions the descendants of Javan as peopling the isles of the Gentiles ; and when the Hebrews came into contact with the Ionians of Asia Minor, and recognized them as the long-lost islanders of the western migration, it was natural that they should mark the similarity of sound between *Javan* and Iones. Accordingly the Old Testament word which is *Grecia*, in Authorized Version *Greece, Greeks*, etc., is in Hebrew *Javan*, Dan. 8 : 21 ; Joel 3 : 6 ; the Hebrew, however, is sometimes retained. Isa. 66 : 19 ; Ezek. 27 : 13. The Greeks and Hebrews met for the first time in the slave-market. The medium of communication seems to have been the Tyrian slave-merchants. About B.C. 800 Joel speaks of the Tyrians as selling the children of Judah to the Grecians, Joel 3 : 6 ; and in Ezek. 27 : 13

the Greeks are mentioned as bartering their brazen vessels for slaves. Prophetical notice of Greece occurs in Dan. 8 : 21, etc., where the history of Alexander and his successors is rapidly sketched. Zechariah, Zech. 9 : 13, foretells the triumphs of the Maccabees against the Græco-Syrian empire, while Isaiah looks forward to the conversion of the Greeks, amongst other Gentiles, through the instrumentality of Jewish missionaries. Isa. 66 : 19. The name of the country, Greece, occurs once in the New Testament, Acts 20 : 2, as opposed to Macedonia. [GENTILES.]

Gre'cian. The term Grecian, or Hellenist, denotes a Jew by birth or religion who spoke Greek. It is used chiefly of foreign Jews and proselytes in contrast with the Hebrews speaking the vernacular Hebrew or Aramæan.—*Bible Dictionary of Tract Society.*

Greyhound, the translation in the text of the Authorized Version, Prov. 30 : 31, of the Hebrew word *zarzir mothnayin, i. e.* "one girt about the loins." Various are the opinions as to what animal "comely in going" is here intended. Some think "a leopard," others "an eagle," or "a man girt with armor," or "a zebra," or "a war-horse girt with trappings." But perhaps the word means "a wrestler," when girt about the loins for a contest.

Grinding. [MILL.]

Grove. 1. A word used in the Authorized Version, with two exceptions, to translate the mysterious Hebrew term *Asherah,* which is not a grove, but probably an idol or image of some kind. [ASHERAH.] It is also probable that there was a connection between this symbol or image, whatever it was, and the sacred symbolic tree, the representation of which occurs so frequently on Assyrian sculptures.

2. The two exceptions noticed above are Gen. 21 : 33 and 1 Sam. 22 : 6 (margin). In the religions of the ancient heathen world groves play a prominent part. In the old times altars only were erected to the gods. It was thought wrong to shut up the gods within walls, and hence trees were the first temples ; and from the earliest times groves are mentioned in connection with religious worship. Gen. 12 : 6, 7 ; Deut. 11 : 30 ; Authorized Version "plain." The groves were generally found connected with temples, and often had the right of affording an asylum.

Gud'godah. Deut. 10 : 7. [See HORHAGIDGAD.]

Guest. [HOSPITALITY.]

Gu'ni (*painted*). 1. A son of Naphtali, Gen. 46 : 24 ; 1 Chron. 7 : 13, the founder of the family of the Gunites. Num. 26 : 48.

2. A descendant of Gad. 1 Chron. 5 : 15.

Gu'nites, The, descendants of Guni, son of Naphtali. Num. 26 : 48.

Gur (*abode*)**, The going up to,** an ascent or rising ground, at which Ahaziah received his death-blow while flying from Jehu after the slaughter of Joram. 2 Kings 9 : 27.

Gur-ba'al (*abode of Baal*)**,** a place or district in which dwelt Arabians, as recorded in 2 Chron. 26 : 7. It appears from the context to have been in the country lying between Palestine and the Arabian peninsula ; but this, although probable cannot be proved.

H.

Ha-ahash'tari (*the courier*), a man or a family immediately descended from Ashur, "father of Tekoa," by his second wife Naarah. 1 Chron. 4 : 6. (B.C. after 1450.)

Habai'ah, or **Haba'jah** (*whom Jehovah hides*). Bene-Habaiah were among the sons of the priests who returned from Babylon with Zerubbabel. Ezra 2 : 61; Neh. 7 : 63. (B.C. before 459.)

Hab'akkuk, or **Habak'kuk** (*embrace*), the eighth in order of the minor prophets. Of the facts of the prophet's life we have no certain information. He probably lived about the twelfth or thirteenth year of Josiah, B.C. 630 or 629.

Hab'akkuk, Prophecy of, consists of three chapters, in the first of which he foreshadows the invasion of Judea by the Chaldeans, and in the second he foretells the doom of the Chaldeans. The whole concludes with the magnificent psalm in ch. 3, a composition unrivalled for boldness of conception, sublimity of thought and majesty of diction.

Habazini'ah (*light of Jehovah*), apparently the head of one of the families of the Rechabites. Jer. 35 : 3. (B.C. before 589.)

Habergeon, a coat of mail covering the neck and breast. [ARMS.]

Ha'bor (*beautiful banks*), the "river of Gozan," 2 Kings 17 : 6 and 18 : 11, is identified beyond all reasonable doubt with the famous affluent of the Euphrates, which is called Aborrhas and Chaboras by ancient writers, and now *Khabour*.

Hachali'ah (*whom Jehovah enlightens*), the father of Nehemiah. Neh. 1 : 1; 10 : 1.

Hach'ilah, The hill, a hill apparently situated in a wood in the wilderness or waste land in the neighborhood of Ziph, in Judah, in the fastnesses or passes of which David and his six hundred followers were lurking when the Ziphites informed Saul of his whereabouts. 1 Sam. 23 : 19; comp. 14, 15, 18.

Hach'moni (*wise*), **Son of,** and **The Hach'monite.** 1 Chron. 11 : 11 ; 27 : 32. Hachmon or Hachmoni was no doubt the founder of a family to which these men belonged : the actual father of Jashobeam was Zabdiel, 1 Chron. 27 : 2, and he is also said to have belonged to the Korhites. 1 Chron. 12 : 6. (B.C. before 1046.)

Ha'dad (*mighty*), originally the indigenous appellation of the sun among the Syrians, and thence transferred to the king as the highest of earthly authorities. The title appears to have been an official one, like Pharaoh. It is found occasionally in the altered form Hadar. Gen. 25 : 15; 36 : 39, compared with 1 Chron. 1 : 30, 50.

1. Son of Ishmael. Gen. 25 : 15; 1 Chron. 1 : 30.

2. A king of Edom who gained an important victory over the Midianites on the field of Moab. Gen. 36 : 35; 1 Chron. 1 : 46.

3. Also a king of Edom, with Pau for his capital. 1 Chron. 1 : 50.

4. A member of the royal house of Edom. 1 Kings 11 : 14 ff. In his childhood he escaped the massacre under Joab, and fled with a band of followers into Egypt. Pharaoh, the predecessor of Solomon's father-in-law, treated him kindly, and gave him his sister-in-law in marriage. After David's death Hadad resolved to attempt the recovery of his dominion. He left Egypt and returned to his own country.

Hadade'zer. 2 Sam. 8 : 3–12; 1 Kings 11 : 23. [HADAREZER.]

Ha'dad-rim'mon is, according to the ordinary interpretation of Zech. 12 : 11, a place in the valley of Megiddo (a part of the plain of Esdraelon, six miles from Mount Carmel and eleven from Nazareth), where a national lamentation was held for the death of King Josiah. It was named after two Syrian idols.

Ha'dar. [HADAD.]

Hadare'zer (*Hadad's help*), son of Rehob, 2 Sam. 8 : 3, the king of the Aramite state of Zobah, who was pursued by David and defeated with great loss. 1 Chron. 18 : 3, 4. (B.C. 1035.) After the first repulse of the Ammonites and their Syrian allies by Joab, Hadarezer sent his army to the assistance of his kindred the people of Maachah, Rehob and Ishtob. 1 Chron. 19 : 16 ; 2 Sam. 10 : 15, comp. 8. Under the command of Shophach or Shobach, the captain of the host, they crossed the Euphrates, joined the other Syrians, and encamped at a place called Helam. David himself came from Jerusalem to take the command of the Israelite army. As on the former occasion, the rout was complete.

Had'ashah (*new*), one of the towns of Judah, in the maritime low country, Josh. 15 : 37 only, probably the ADASA of the Maccabean history.

Hadas'sah (*myrtle*), probably the earlier name of Esther. Esther 2 : 7.

Hadat'tah (*new*). According to the Authorized Version, one of the towns of Judah in the extreme south. Josh. 15 : 25.

Ha'des, in Revised Version. [See HELL.]

Ha'did (*sharp*), a place named, with Lod (Lydda) and Ono, only in the later books of the history. Ezra 2 : 33 ; Neh. 7 : 37 ; 11 : 34. In the time of Eusebius a town called Aditha or Adatha existed to the east of Diospolis (Lydda). This was probably Hadid.

Had'la-i (*rest of God*), a man of Ephraim. 2 Chron. 28 : 12.

Hado'ram (*noble honor*). 1. The fifth son of Joktan. Gen. 10 : 27 ; 1 Chron. 1 : 21. His settlements, unlike those of many of Joktan's sons, have not been identified.

2. Son of Tou or Toi king of Hamath; his father's ambassador to congratulate David on his victory over Hadarezer king of Zobah. 1 Chron. 18 : 10. (B.C. 1035.)

3. The form assumed in Chronicles by the name of the intendant of taxes under David, Solomon and Rehoboam. 2 Chron. 10 : 18. In Kings the name is given in the longer form of ADONIRAM, but in Samuel, 2 Sam. 20 : 24, as ADORAM.

Ha'drach (*dwelling*), a country of Syria, mentioned once only, by the prophet Zechariah. Zech. 9 : 1. The position of the district, with its borders, is here generally stated ; but the name itself seems to have wholly disappeared. It still remains unknown.

Ha'gab (*locust*). Bene-Hagab were among the Nethinim who returned from Babylon with Zerubbabel. Ezra 2 : 46. (B.C. before 536.)

Hag'aba (*locust*). Bene-Hagaba were among the Nethinim who came back from captivity with Zerubbabel. Neh. 7 : 48. The name is slightly different in form from

Hag'abah, under which it is found in the parallel list of Ezra 2 : 45.

Ha'gar (*flight*), an Egyptian woman, the handmaid or slave of Sarah, Gen. 16 : 1, whom the latter gave as a concubine to Abraham, after he had dwelt ten years in the land of Canaan and had no children by Sarah. ch. 16 : 2, 3. (B.C. 1912.) When Hagar saw that she had conceived, " her mistress was despised in her eyes," v. 4, and Sarah, with the anger, we may suppose, of a free woman rather than of a wife, reproached Abraham for the results of her own act. Hagar fled, turning her steps toward her native land through the great wilderness traversed by the Egyptian road. By the fountain in the way to Shur the angel of the Lord found her, charged her to return and submit herself under the hands of her mistress, and delivered the remarkable prophecy respecting her unborn child recorded in vs. 10-12. On her return she gave birth to Ishmael, and Abraham was then eighty-six years old. When Ishmael was about sixteen years old, he was caught by Sarah making sport of her young son Isaac at the festival of his weaning, and Sarah demanded the expulsion of Hagar and her son. She again fled toward Egypt, and when in despair at the want of water, an angel again appeared to her, pointed out a fountain close by, and renewed the former promises to her. Gen. 21 : 9-21. St. Paul, Gal. 4 : 25, refers to her as the type of the old covenant of the law.

Hagarenes', Ha'garites (named after Hagar), a people dwelling to the east of Palestine, with whom the tribes of Reuben made war in the time of Saul. 1 Chron. 5 : 10, 18–20. The same people, as confederate against Israel, are mentioned in Ps. 83 : 6. It is generally believed that they were named after Hagar, and that the important town and district of *Hejer*, on the borders of the Persian Gulf, represent them.

Ha'gerite, The. Jaziz the Hagerite, *i. e.* the descendant of Hagar, had the charge of David's sheep. 1 Chron. 27 : 31.

Hag'ga-i (*festive*), the tenth in order of the minor prophets, and first of those who prophesied after the captivity. With regard to his tribe and parentage history and tradition are alike silent.

Hag'ga-i, Prophecy of. The style of Haggai is generally tame and prosaic, though at times it rises to the dignity of severe invective when the prophet rebukes his countrymen for their selfish indolence and neglect of God's house. **But**

the brevity of the prophecies is so great, and the poverty of expression which characterizes them so striking, as to give rise to a conjecture, not without reason, that in their present form they are but the outline or summary of the original discourses. They were delivered in the second year of Darius Hystaspes (B.C. 520), at intervals from the 1st day of the 6th month to the 24th day of the 9th month in the same year.

Hag'geri (*wanderer*) was one of the mighty men of David's guard, according to 1 Chron. 11 : 38. The parallel passage—2 Sam. 23 : 36—has "Bani the Gadite," which is probably the correct reading. (B.C. 1046.)

Hag'gi (*festive*), second son of Gad. Gen. 46 : 16; Num. 26 : 15.

Haggi'ah (*festival of Jehovah*), a Merarite Levite. 1 Chron. 6 : 30.

Hag'gites, The, a Gadite family sprung from Haggi. Num. 26 : 15.

Hag'gith (*festive; a dancer*), one of David's wives, the mother of Adonijah. 2 Sam. 3 : 4; 1 Kings 1 : 5. (B.C. 1053.)

Ha'i. Same as AI.

Hair. The Hebrews were fully alive to the importance of the hair as an element of personal beauty. Long hair was admired in the case of young men. 2 Sam. 14 : 26. In times of affliction the hair was altogether cut off. Isa. 3 : 17, 24; 15 : 2; Jer. 7 : 29. Tearing the hair, Ezra 9 : 3, and letting it go dishevelled were similar tokens of grief. The usual and favorite color of the hair was black, Cant. 5 : 11, as is indicated in the comparisons in Cant. 1 : 5; 4 : 1; a similar hue is probably intended by the *purple* of Cant. 7 : 5. Pure white hair was deemed characteristic of the divine Majesty. Dan. 7 : 9; Rev. 1 : 14. The chief beauty of the hair consisted in curls, whether of a natural or an artificial character. With regard to the mode of dressing the hair, we have no very precise information; the terms used are of a general character, as of Jezebel, 2 Kings 9 : 30, and of Judith, ch. 10 : 3, and in the New Testament, 1 Tim. 2 : 9; 1 Pet. 3 : 3. The arrangement of Samson's hair into seven locks, or more properly *braids*, Judges 16 : 13, 19, involves the practice of plaiting, which was also familiar to the Egyptians and Greeks. The locks were probably kept in their place by a fillet, as in Egypt. The Hebrews, like other nations of antiquity, anointed the hair profusely with ointments, which

were generally compounded of various aromatic ingredients, Ruth 3 : 3; 2 Sam. 14 : 2; Ps. 23 : 5; 92 : 10; Eccles. 9 : 8, more especially on occasions of festivity or hospitality. Luke 7 : 46. It appears to

Beards. Egyptian, from Wilkinson (top row). Of other nations, from Rosellini and Layard.

have been the custom of the Jews in our Saviour's time to swear by the hair, Matt. 5 : 36, much as the Egyptian women still swear by the side-lock, and the men by their beards.

Hak'katan (*young*). Johanan, son of Hakkatan, was the chief of the Bene-Azgad who returned from Babylon with Ezra. Ezra 8 : 12.

Hak'koz (*thorn*), a priest, the chief of the seventh course in the service of the sanctuary, as appointed by David. 1 Chron. 24 : 10. In Ezra 2 : 61 and Neh. 3 : 4, 21 the name occurs again as KOZ in the Authorized Version.

Haku'pha (*bent*). Bene-Hakupha were among the Nethinim who returned from Babylon with Zerubbabel. Ezra 2 : 51; Neh. 7 : 53.

Ha'lah is probably a different place from the Calah of Gen. 10 : 11. It may be identified with the Chalcitis of Ptolemy.

Ha'lak (*smooth*), **The mount,** a mountain twice, and twice only, named, as the southern limit of Joshua's conquests, Josh. 11 : 17; 12 : 7, but which has not yet been identified.

Hal'hul (*trembling*), a town of Judah in the mountain district. Josh. 15 : 58. The name still remains unaltered, attached to a conspicuous hill a mile to the left of the road from Jerusalem to Hebron, between three and four miles from the latter.

Ha'li (*necklace*), a town on the boundary of Asher, named between Helkath and Beten. Josh. 19 : 25.

Hall, used of the court of the high priest's house. Luke 22 : 55. In Matt. 27 : 27 and Mark 15 : 16 " hall" is synonymous with " prætorium," which in John 18 : 28 is in Authorized Version "judgment hall."

Hallelujah (*praise ye the Lord*). [ALLELUIA.]

Hallo'hesh (*enchanter*), one of the chief of the people who sealed the covenant with Nehemiah. Neh. 10 : 24. (B.C. 410.)

Halo'hesh. Shallum, son of Halohesh, was " ruler of the half part of Jerusalem" at the time of the repair of the wall by Nehemiah. Neh. 3 : 12. (B.C. 446.)

Ham (*hot; sunburnt*). 1. The name of one of the three sons of Noah, apparently the second in age. (B.C. 2448.) Of the history of Ham nothing is related except his irreverence to his father and the curse which that patriarch pronounced. The sons of Ham are stated to have been " Cush and Mizraim and Phut and Canaan." Gen. 10 : 6; comp. 1 Chron. 1 : 8. Egypt is recognized as the "land of Ham" in the Bible. Ps. 78 : 51; 105 : 23; 106 : 22. The other settlements of the sons of Ham are discussed under their respective names. The three most illustrious Hamite nations—the Cushites, the Phœnicians and the Egyptians—were greatly mixed with foreign peoples. Their architecture has a solid grandeur that we look for in vain elsewhere. 2. According to the present text, Gen. 14 : 5, Chedorlaomer and his allies smote the Zuzim in a place called Ham, probably in the territory of the Ammonites (Gilead), east of the Jordan.

Ha'man (*magnificent*), the chief minister or vizier of King Ahasuerus. Esther 3 : 1. (B.C. 473.) After the failure of his attempt to cut off all the Jews in the Persian empire, he was hanged on the gallows which he had erected for Mordecai. The Targum and Josephus interpret the description of him—the Agagite —as signifying that he was of Amalekitish descent. The Jews hiss whenever his name is mentioned on the day of Purim.

Ha'math (*fortress*), the principal city of upper Syria, was situated in the valley of the Orontes, which it commanded from the low screen of hills which forms the water-shed between the source of the Orontes and Antioch. The Hamathites were a Hamitic race, and are included among the descendants of Canaan. Gen. 10 : 18. Nothing appears of the power of Hamath until the time of David. 2 Sam. 8 : 9. Hamath seems clearly to have been included in the dominions of Solomon. 1 Kings 4 : 21–24. The "storecities" which Solomon "built in Hamath," 2 Chron. 8 : 4, were perhaps staples for trade. In the Assyrian inscriptions of the time of Ahab (B.C. 900) Hamath appears as a separate power, in alliance with the Syrians of Damascus, the Hittites and the Phœnicians. About three-quarters of a century later Jeroboam the Second " recovered Hamath." 2 Kings 14 : 28. Soon afterwards the Assyrians took it, 2 Kings 18 : 34; 19 : 13, etc., and from this time it ceased to be a place of much importance. Antiochus Epiphanes changed its name to Epiphaneia. The natives, however, called it Hamath even in St. Jerome's time, and its present name, *Hamah*, is but slightly altered from the ancient form.

Ha'math-zo'bah (*fortress of Zobah*), 2 Chron. 8 : 3, has been conjectured to be the same as Hamath. But the name *Hamath-zobah* would seem rather suited to another Hamath which was distinguished from the " Great Hamath" by the suffix " Zobah."

Ham'athite, The, one of the families descended from Canaan, named last in the list. Gen. 10 : 18; 1 Chron. 1 : 16.

Ham'math (*warm springs*), one of the fortified cities in the territory allotted to Naphtali. Josh. 19 : 35. It was near Tiberias, one mile distant, and had its name Chammath, " hot baths," because it contained those of Tiberias. In the list of Levitical cities given out of Naphtali, Josh. 21 : 32, the name of this place seems to be given as HAMMOTH-DOR.

Hammed'atha (*double*), father of the infamous Haman. Esther 3 : 1, 10; 8 : 5; 9 : 24.

Ham'melech, lit. "*the king*," unnecessarily rendered in the Authorized Version as a proper name. Jer. 36 : 26; 38 : 6.

Hammol'eketh (*the queen*), a daughter of Machir and sister of Gilead. 1 Chron. 7 : 17, 18. (B.C. between 1706 and 1491.)

Ham'mon (*warm springs*). 1. A city in Asher, Josh. 19 : 28, apparently not far from Zidon-rabbah. 2. A city allotted out of the tribe of Naphtali to the Levites, 1 Chron. 6 : 76, and answering to the somewhat similar names HAMMATH and HAMMOTH-DOR in Joshua.

Ham'moth-dor (*dwelling of the warm springs*). [HAMMATH.]

Ham'onah (*multitude*), the name of a city mentioned in Ezekiel. Ezek. 39 : 16.

Ha'mon-gog (*the multitude of Gog*), **The valley of,** the name to be bestowed on a ravine or glen, previously known as "the ravine of the passengers on the east of the sea," after the burial there of "Gog and all his multitude." Ezek. 39 : 11, 15.

Ha'mor (*an ass*), a Hivite who at the time of the entrance of Jacob on Palestine was prince of the land and city of Shechem. Gen. 33 : 19; 34 : 2, 4, 6, 8, 13, 18, 20, 24, 26. (B.C. 1737.) [DINAH.]

Hamu'el (*heat*, i. e. *wrath, of God*), a man of Simeon, of the family of Shaul. 1 Chron. 4 : 26.

Ha'mul (*pitied*), the younger son of Pharez, Judah's son by Tamar. Gen. 46 : 12; 1 Chron. 2 : 5. (B.C. between 1706–1688.)

Ha'mulites, The, the family of the preceding. Num. 26 : 21.

Hamu'tal (*akin to the dew*), daughter of Jeremiah of Libnah; one of the wives of King Josiah. 2 Kings 23 : 31; 24 : 18; Jer. 52 : 1. (B.C. 632–619.)

Hanam'e-el (*whom God graciously gave*), son of Shallum and cousin of Jeremiah. Jer. 32 : 7, 8, 9, 12; and comp. 44. (B.C. 589.)

Ha'nan (*merciful*). 1. One of the chief people of the tribe of Benjamin. 1 Chron. 8 : 23.

2. The last of the six sons of Azel, a descendant of Saul. 1 Chron. 8 : 38; 9 : 44. (B.C. 588.)

3. "Son of Maachah," *i. e.* possibly a Syrian of Aram-maachah, one of the heroes of David's guard. 1 Chron. 11 : 43. (B.C. 1046.)

4. The sons of Hanan were among the Nethinim who returned from Babylon with Zerubbabel. Ezra 2 : 46; Neh. 7 : 49. (B.C. 536.)

5. One of the Levites who assisted Ezra in his public exposition of the law. Neh. 8 : 7. (B.C. 446.) The same person is probably mentioned in ch. 10 : 10.

6. One of the "heads" of "the people," who also sealed the covenant. Neh. 10 : 22. (B.C. 410.)

7. Another of the chief laymen on the same occasion. Neh. 10 : 26.

8. Son of Zaccur, son of Mattaniah,

whom Nehemiah made one of the storekeepers of the provisions collected as tithes. Neh. 13 : 13.

9. Son of Igdaliah. Jer. 35 : 4. (B.C. 410.)

Hanan'e-el (*whom God graciously gave*), **The tower of,** a tower which formed part of the wall of Jerusalem. Neh. 3 : 1; 12 : 39. From these two passages, particularly from the former, it might almost be inferred that Hananeel was but another name for the tower of Meah; at any rate they were close together, and stood between the sheep-gate and the fish-gate. This tower is further mentioned in Jer. 31 : 38. The remaining passage in which it is named, Zech. 14 : 10, also connects this tower with the "corner-gate," which lay on the other side of the sheep-gate.

Hana'ni (*gracious*). 1. One of the sons of Heman, and head of the eighteenth course of the service. 1 Chron. 25 : 4, 25.

2. A seer who rebuked (B.C. 941) Asa king of Judah. 2 Chron. 16 : 7. For this he was imprisoned. ver. 10. He or another Hanani was the father of Jehu the seer, who testified against Baasha, 1 Kings 16 : 1, 7, and Jehoshaphat. 2 Chron. 19 : 2; 20 : 34.

3. One of the priests who in the time of Ezra had taken strange wives. Ezra 10 : 20.

4. A brother of Nehemiah, Neh. 1 : 2, who was made governor of Jerusalem under Nehemiah. ch. 7 : 2.

5. A priest mentioned in Neh. 12 : 36.

Hanani'ah (*gift of God*). 1. One of the fourteen sons of Heman, and chief of the sixteenth course of singers. 1 Chron. 25 : 4, 5, 23. (B.C. 1014.)

2. A general in the army of King Uzziah. 2 Chron. 26 : 11.

3. Father of Zedekiah, in the reign of Jehoiakim. (B.C. before 605.)

4. Son of Azur, a Benjamite of Gibeon and a false prophet in the reign of Zedekiah king of Judah. In the fourth year of his reign, B.C. 595, Hananiah withstood Jeremiah the prophet, and publicly prophesied in the temple that within two years Jeconiah and all his fellow captives, with the vessels of the Lord's house, should be brought back to Jerusalem. Jer. 28. Hananiah corroborated his prophecy by taking from off the neck of Jeremiah the yoke which he wore by divine command, Jer. 27, and breaking it. But Jeremiah was bidden to go and tell Hananiah that for the wooden yoke

which he had broken he should make yokes of iron, so firm was the dominion of Babylon destined to be for seventy years. The prophet Jeremiah added to this rebuke the prediction of Hananiah's death, the fulfillment of which closes the history of this false prophet.

5. Grandfather of Irijah, the captain of the ward at the gate of Benjamin who arrested Jeremiah on the charge of deserting to the Chaldeans. Jer. 37 : 13. (B.C. before 589.)

6. Head of a Benjamite house. 1 Chron. 8 : 24.

7. The Hebrew name of Shadrach. He was of the house of David, according to Jewish tradition. Dan. 1 : 3, 6, 7, 11, 19 ; 2 : 17.

8. Son of Zerubbabel, 1 Chron. 3 : 19, from whom Christ derived his descent. He is the same person who is by St. Luke called Joanna. (B.C. after 536.)

9. One of the sons of Bebai who returned with Ezra from Babylon. Ezra 10 : 28. (B.C. 459.)

10. A priest, one of the makers of the sacred ointments and incense, who built a portion of the wall of Jerusalem in the days of Nehemiah. Neh. 3 : 8.

11. Head of the priestly course of Jeremiah in the days of Joiakim. Neh. 12 : 12. (B.C. 610.)

12. Ruler of the palace at Jerusalem under Nehemiah. The arrangements for guarding the gates of Jerusalem were intrusted to him with Hanani, the Tirshatha's brother. Neh. 7 : 2, 3. (B.C. 446.)

13. An Israelite. Neh. 10 : 23.

Handicraft. Acts 18 : 3 ; 19 : 25 ; Rev. 18 : 22. A trade was taught to all the Jewish boys, as a necessary part of their education. Even the greatest rabbis maintained themselves by trades (*Delitzsch*). Says Rabbi Jehuda, " He who does not teach his son a trade is much the same as if he taught him to be a thief." In the present article brief notices only can be given of such handicraft trades as are mentioned in Scripture.

1. *Smiths or metal-workers.*—The preparation of iron for use either in war, in agriculture or for domestic purposes was doubtless one of the earliest applications of labor ; and together with iron, working in brass, or rather copper alloyed with tin (bronze), is mentioned as practiced in antediluvian times. Gen. 4 : 22.

After the establishment of the Jews in Canaan, the occupation of a smith became recognized as a distinct employment. 1 Sam. 13 : 19. The smith's work and its results are often mentioned in Scripture. 2 Sam. 12 : 31 ; 1 Kings 6 : 7 ; 2 Chron. 26 : 14 ; Isa. 44 : 12 ; 54 : 16. The worker in gold and silver must have found employment among both the Hebrews and the neighboring nations in very early

Carpenter's Shop at Nazareth. (*From an original Photograph.*)

times. Gen. 24 : 22, 53 ; 35 : 4 ; 36 : 18. Various processes of the goldsmith's work are illustrated by Egyptian monuments. After the conquest frequent notices are found of both moulded and wrought metal, including soldering.

2. *Carpenters* are often mentioned in Scripture. Gen. 6 : 14 ; Ex. 37 ; Isa. 44 : 13. In the palace built by David for himself the workmen employed were chiefly foreigners. 2 Sam. 5 : 11. That the Jewish carpenters must have been able to carve with some skill is evident from Isa. 41 : 7 ; 44 : 13. In the New Testament the occupation of a carpenter is mentioned in connection with Joseph the husband of the Virgin Mary, and ascribed to our Lord himself. Matt. 13 : 55 ; Mark 6 : 3. The trade included our cabinet work as well as carpentering.

3. The *masons* employed by David and Solomon, at least the chief of them, were Phœnicians. 1 Kings 5 : 18 ; Ezek. 27 : 9. The large stones used in Solomon's temple are said by Josephus to have been

fitted together exactly without either mortar or clamps, but the foundation stones to have been fastened with lead. For ordinary building mortar was used; sometimes, perhaps, bitumen, as was the case at Babylon. Gen. 11 : 3. The wall "daubed with untempered mortar" of Ezekiel 13 : 10 was perhaps a sort of cob-wall of mud or clay without lime, which would give way under heavy rain. The use of whitewash on tombs is remarked by our Lord. Matt. 23 : 27.

4. *Ship-building* must have been ex-ercised to some extent for the fishing-ves-sels on the Lake of Gennesaret. Matt. 8 : 23; 9 : 1; John 21 : 3, 8. Solomon built ships for his foreign trade. 1 Kings 9 : 26, 27; 22 : 48; 2 Chron. 20 : 36, 37.

5. *Apothecaries* or perfumers appear to have formed a guild or association. Ex. 30 : 25, 35; 2 Chron. 16 : 14; Neh. 3 : 8; Eccles. 7 : 1; 10 : 1; Ecclus. 38 : 8.

6. *Weavers.*—The arts of spinning and weaving both wool and linen were car-ried on in early times, as they usually are still among the Bedouins, by women. Ex. 35 : 25, 26; Lev. 19 : 19; Deut. 22 : 11; 2 Kings 23 : 7; Ezek. 16 : 16; Prov. 31 : 13, 24. The loom with its beam, 1 Sam. 17 : 7, pin, Judges 16 : 14, and shuttle, Job 7 : 6, was perhaps introduced later, but as early as David's time. 1 Sam. 17 : 7.

7. *Dyeing* and *dressing cloth* were prac-ticed in Palestine, as were also *tanning* and *dressing leather.* Josh. 2 : 15–18; 2 Kings 1 : 8; Matt. 3 : 4; Acts 9 : 43.

8. *Barbers.* Num. 6 : 5, 19; Ezek. 5 : 1.

9. *Tent-makers* are noticed in Acts 18 : 3.

10. *Potters* are frequently alluded to. Jer. 18 : 2–6.

11. *Bakers* are noticed in Scripture, Jer. 37 : 21; Hos. 7 : 4; and the well-known valley Tyropœon probably de-rived its name from the occupation of the cheese-makers, its inhabitants.

12. *Butchers*, not Jewish, are spoken of 1 Cor. 10 : 25.

Shoemakers, tailors, glaziers and g ass vessels, *painters* and *gold-workers* are mentioned in the Mishna. *Chel.* viii. 9; xxix. 3, 4; xxx. 1.

Handkerchief, Napkin, Apron. Luke 19 : 20; John 11 : 44; 20 : 7; Acts 19 : 12. These terms were used in much the same manner and having much the same significance as at the present.

Ha'nes, a place in Egypt mentioned only in Isa. 30 : 4. We think that the Chald. Paraphr. is right in identifying it

with Tahpanhes, a fortified town on the eastern frontier.

Hanging, Hangings. 1. The " hanging " was a curtain or " covering " to close an entrance; one was placed be-fore the door of the tabernacle. Ex. 26 : 36, 37; 39 : 38. 2. The " hangings " were used for covering the walls of the court of the tabernacle, just as tapestry is used in modern times. Ex. 27 : 9; 35 : 17; 38 : 9; Num. 3 : 26; 4 : 26.

Han'iel (*grace of God*), one of the sons of Ulla of the tribe of Asher. 1 Chron. 7 : 39.

Han'nah (*grace*), one of the wives of Elkanah, and mother of Samuel. 1 Sam. 1, 2. (B.C. 1141.) A hymn of thanks-giving for the birth of her son is in the highest order of prophetic poetry; its re-semblance to that of the Virgin Mary, comp. 1 Sam. 2 : 1–10 with Luke 1 : 46–55, see also Ps. 113, has been noticed.

Han'nathon (*gracious*), one of the cities of Zebulun. Josh. 19 : 14.

Han'niel (*the favor of God*), son of Ephod and prince of Manasseh. Num. 34 : 23.

Ha'noch (*dedicated*). 1. The third in order of the children of Midian. Gen. 25 : 4.

2. Eldest son of Reuben, Gen. 46 : 9; Ex. 6 : 14; Num. 26 : 5; 1 Chron. 5 : 3, and founder of the family of the Ha-nochites. Num. 26 : 5.

Ha'nun (*favored*). 1. Son of Nahash, 2 Sam. 10 : 1, 2; 1 Chron. 19 : 1, 2, king of Ammon, who dishonored the ambassa-dors of David, 2 Sam. 10 : 4, and involved the Ammonites in a disastrous war. 2 Sam. 12 : 31; 1 Chron. 19 : 6. (B.C. 1035.)

2. A man who, with the people of Za-noah, repaired the ravine gate in the wall of Jerusalem. Neh. 3 : 13. (B.C. 446.)

3. The sixth son of Zalaph, who also as-sisted in the repair of the wall, apparent-ly on the east side. Neh. 3 : 30. (B.C. 446.)

Haphra'im (*two pits*), a city of Issa-char, mentioned next to Shunem. Josh. 19 : 19. About six miles northeast of *Lejjun*, and two miles west of *Solam* (the ancient Shunem), stands the village of *el-'Afûleh*, which may possibly be the representative of Haphraim.

Ha'ra (*mountain land*), 1 Chron. 5 : 26 only, is either a place utterly unknown, or it must be regarded as identical with Haran or Charran.

Har'adah (*fear*), a desert station of the Israelites, Num. 33 : 24, 25; its posi-tion is uncertain.

Ha'ran (*a mountaineer*). 1. The third son of Terah, and therefore youngest brother of Abram. Gen. 11 : 26. (B.C. 1926.) Three children are ascribed to him—Lot, vs. 27, 31, and two daughters, viz., Milcah, who married her uncle Nahor, ver. 29, and Iscah. ver. 29. Haran was born in Ur of the Chaldees, and he died there while his father was still living. ver. 28.

2. A Gershonite Levite in the time of David, one of the family of Shimei. 1 Chron. 23 : 9.

3. A son of the great Caleb by his concubine Ephah. 1 Chron. 2 : 46.

4. HARAN or CHARRAN, Acts 7 : 2, 4, name of the place whither Abraham migrated with his family from Ur of the Chaldees, and where the descendants of his brother Nahor established themselves. Comp. Gen. 24 : 10 with 27 : 43. It is said to be in Mesopotamia, Gen. 24 : 10, or more definitely in Padan-aram, ch. 25 : 20, the cultivated district at the foot of the hills, a name well applying to the beautiful stretch of country which lies below Mount Masius between the Khabour and the Euphrates. Here, about midway in this district, is a small village still called *Harrán*. It was celebrated among the Romans, under the name of Charræ, as the scene of the defeat of Crassus.

Ha'rarite (*the mountaineer*)**, The.** The designation of three of David's guard. 1. Agee, a Hararite. 2 Sam. 23 : 11.

2. Shammah the Hararite. 2 Sam. 23 : 33.

3. Sharar, 2 Sam. 23 : 33, or Sacar, 1 Chron. 11 : 35, the Hararite, was the father of Ahiam, another member of the guard.

Har'bona (*ass-driver*), the third of the seven chamberlains or eunuchs who served King Ahasuerus. Esther 1 : 10. (B.C. 483–475.)

Har'bonah, Esther 7 : 9, the same as the preceding.

Hare (Heb. *arnebeth*) occurs only in Lev. 11 : 6 and Deut. 14 : 7 amongst the animals disallowed as food by the Mosaic law. The hare is at this day called *arnel* by the Arabs in Palestine and Syria. It was erroneously thought by the ancient Jews to have chewed the cud. They were no doubt misled, as in the case of the *shâphân* (*hyrax*), by the habit these animals have of moving the jaw about.

Harem. [HOUSE.]

Ha'reph (*a plucking off*), a name oc-

curring in the genealogies of Judah as a son of Caleb and as "father of Bethgader." 1 Chron. 2 : 51 only.

Ha'reth (*thicket*)**, The forest of,** in which David took refuge, after, at the instigation of the prophet Gad, he had quitted the "hold" or fastness of the cave of Adullam. 1 Sam. 22 : 5.

Harhai'ah (*the Lord is angry*), father of Uzziel. Neh. 3 : 8. (B.C. before 446.)

Har'has (*very poor*), an ancestor of Shallum the husband of Huldah. 2 Kings 22 : 14. (B.C. before 623.)

Har'hur (*inflammation*). The sons of Harhur were among the Nethinim who returned from Babylon with Zerubbabel. Ezra 2 : 51 ; Neh. 7 : 53. (B.C. 536.)

Ha'rim (*flat-nosed*). 1. A priest who had charge of the third division in the house of God. 1 Chron. 24 : 8. (B.C. 1014.)

2. Bene-Harim, probably descendants of the above, to the number of 1017, came from Babylon with Zerubbabel. Ezra 2 : 39 ; Neh. 7 : 42. (B.C. 536.)

3. It further occurs in a list of the families of priests "who went up with Zerubbabel and Jeshua," and of those who were their descendants in the next generation. Neh. 12 : 15.

4. Another family of Bene-Harim, 320 in number, came from the captivity in the same caravan. Ezra 2 : 32 ; Neh. 7 : 35. (B.C. 536.) They also appear among those who had married foreign wives, Ezra 10 : 31, as well as those who sealed the covenant. Neh. 10 : 27. (B.C. 410.)

Hare of Mount Sinai.

Ha'riph (*a plucking off*). A hundred and twelve of the Bene-Hariph returned from the captivity with Zerubbabel

Neh. 7 : 24. The name occurs again among the "heads of the people" who sealed the covenant. ch. 10 : 19.

Harlot. That this class of persons existed in the earliest states of society is clear from Gen. 38 : 15. Rahab, Josh. 2 : 1, is said by the Chald. Paraphr. to have been an innkeeper; but if there were such persons, considering what we know of Canaanitish morals, Lev. 18 : 27, we may conclude that they would, if women, have been of this class. The "harlots" are classed with "publicans," as those who lay under the ban of society, in the New Testament. Matt. 21 : 32.

Har'-magedon (*hill of Megiddo*), Rev. 16 : 16 in the Revised Version for **Armageddon.** The change is chiefly *Har*, hill, in place of *Ar*, city.

Har'nepher (*panting*), one of the sons of Zophah, of the tribe of Asher. 1 Chron. 7 : 36.

Ha'rod (*fear*), **The well of,** a spring by which Gideon and his great army encamped on the morning of the day which ended in the rout of the Midianites, Judges 7 : 1, and where the trial of the people by their mode of drinking apparently took place. The *Ain Jalûd* is very suitable to the circumstances, as being at present the largest spring in the neighborhood.

Ha'rodite, The, the designation of two of the thirty-seven warriors of David's guard, Shammah and Elika, 2 Sam. 23 : 25, doubtless derived from a place named Harod.

Har'oeh, a name occurring in the genealogical lists of Judah. 1 Chron. 2 : 52.

Ha'rorite (the same as Harodite), **The,** the title given to Shammoth, one of the warriors of David's guard. 1 Chron. 11 : 27.

Har'osheth (*workmanship*) **" of the Gentiles "**—so called from the mixed races that inhabited it—a city in the north of the land of Canaan, supposed to have stood on the west coast of the lake Merom, from which the Jordan issues forth in one unbroken stream. It was the residence of Sisera, captain of Jabin king of Canaan, Judges 4 : 2, and it was the point to which the victorious Israelites under Barak pursued the discomfited host and chariots of the second potentate of that name. Judges 4 : 16.

Harp. The harp was the national instrument of the Hebrews, and was well known throughout Asia. Moses assigns

its invention to Jubal during the antediluvian period. Gen. 4 : 21. Josephus records that the harp had ten strings, and

Egyptian Harp.

that it was played on with the plectrum. Sometimes it was smaller, having only eight strings, and was usually played with the fingers.

Harrow. The word so rendered, 2 Sam. 12 : 31; 1 Chron. 20 : 3, is probably a threshing-machine. The verb rendered "to harrow," Job 39 : 10; Isa. 28 : 24; Hos. 10 : 11, expresses apparently the breaking of the clods, and is so far analogous to our harrowing; but whether done by any such machine as we call a "harrow" is very doubtful.

Har'sha (*deaf*). Bene-Harsha were among the families of Nethinim who came back from Babylon with Zerubbabel. Ezra 2 : 52; Neh. 7 : 54.

Hart, the male stag. The word denotes some member of the deer tribe, either the fallow deer or the Barbary deer. The hart is reckoned among the clean animals, Deut. 12 : 15; 14 : 5; 15 : 22, and seems from the passages quoted, as well as from 1 Kings 4 : 23, to have been commonly killed for food.

Ha'rum (*lofty*), father of Aharhel, in one of the most obscure genealogies of Judah. 1 Chron. 4 : 8.

Haru'maph (*slit-nosed*), father or ancestor of Jedaiah. Neh. 3 : 10.

Haru'phite (*native of Hariph*), **The,** the designation of Shephatiah, one of the Korhites who repaired to David at Ziklag. 1 Chron. 12 : 5. (B.C. 1064.)

Ha'ruz (*zealous*), a man of Jotbah,

The Hart.

father of Meshullemeth queen of Manasseh. 2 Kings 21 : 19. (B.C. before 664.)

Harvest. [AGRICULTURE.]

Hasadi′ah (*loved by Jehovah*), one of a group of five persons among the descendants of the royal line of Judah, 1 Chron. 3 : 20, apparently sons of Zerubbabel. (B.C. about 536.)

Hasenu′ah (*the hated*), a Benjamite, of one of the chief families in the tribe. 1 Chron. 9 : 7.

Hashabi′ah (*whom God regards*). 1. A Merarite Levite. 1 Chron. 6 : 45.

2. Another Merarite Levite. 1 Chron. 9 : 14.

3. The fourth of the six sons of Jeduthun, 1 Chron. 25 : 3, who had charge of the twelfth course. ver. 19. (B.C. 1014.)

4. One of the descendants of Hebron the son of Kohath. 1 Chron. 26 : 30.

5. The son of Kemuel, who was prince of the tribe of Levi in the time of David. 1 Chron. 27 : 17. (B.C. 1014.)

6. A Levite, one of the "chiefs" of his tribe, who officiated for King Josiah at his great passover feast. 2 Chron. 35 : 9. (B.C. 623.)

7. A Merarite Levite who accompanied Ezra from Babylon. Ezra 8 : 19.

8. One of the chiefs of the priests who formed part of the same caravan. Ezra 8 : 24. (B.C. 536.)

9. Ruler of half the circuit or environs of Keilah; he repaired a portion of the wall of Jerusalem under Nehemiah. Neh. 3 : 17. (B.C. 446.)

10. One of the Levites who sealed the covenant of reformation after the return from the captivity. Neh. 10 : 11; 12 : 24; comp. 26. (B.C. 446-410.)

11. Another Levite, son of Bunni. Neh. 11 : 15.

12. A Levite, son of Mattaniah. Neh. 11 : 22.

13. A priest of the family of Hilkiah in the days of Joiakim son of Jeshua. Neh. 12 : 21.

Hashab′nah (*whom Jehovah regards*), one of the chief of the "people" who sealed the covenant with Nehemiah. Neh. 10 : 25. (B.C. 410.)

Hashabni′ah (*whom Jehovah regards*). 1. Father of Hattush. Neh. 3 : 10.

2. A Levite who was among those who officiated at the great fast under Ezra and Nehemiah when the covenant was sealed. Neh. 9 : 5. (B.C. 410.)

Hashbad′ana (*considerate judge*), one of the men (probably Levites) who stood on Ezra's left hand while he read the law to the people in Jerusalem. Neh. 8 : 4. (B.C. 410.)

Ha′shem (*fat*). The sons of Hashem the Gizonite are named amongst the members of David's guard in 1 Chron. 11 : 34. (B.C. before 1014.)

Hashmo′nah (*fatness*), a station of the Israelites, mentioned Num. 33 : 29 as next before Moseroth.

Ha′shub (*intelligent*). 1. A son of Pahath-moab, who assisted in the repair of the wall of Jerusalem. Neh. 3 : 11. (B.C. 446.)

2. Another who assisted in the same work. Neh. 3 : 23.

3. One of the heads of the people who sealed the covenant with Nehemiah. Neh. 10 : 23. (B.C. 410.)

4. A Merarite Levite. Neh. 11 : 15.

Hashu′bah (*intelligent*), the first of a group of five men, apparently the latter half of the family of Zerubbabel. 1 Chron. 3 : 20.

Ha′shum (*rich*). 1. Bene-Hashum, 223 in number, came back from Babylon with Zerubbabel. Ezra 2 : 19; 10 : 33; Neh. 7 : 22. (B.C. before 536.) The chief man of the family was among those who sealed the covenant with Nehemiah. Neh. 10 : 18. (B.C. 410.)

2. One of the priests or Levites who stood on Ezra's left hand while he read the law to the congregation. Neh. 8 : 4. (B.C. 410.)

Hashu′pha (*stripped*), one of the families of Nethinim who returned from captivity in the first caravan. Neh. 7 : 46.

Called HASUPHA in Ezra 2 : 43. (B.C. 536.)

Has'rah (*very poor*), the form in which the name Harhas is given in 2 Chron. 34 : 22; comp. 2 Kings 22 : 14.

Hassena'ah. The Bene-Hassenaah rebuilt the fish-gate in the repair of the wall of Jerusalem. Neh. 3 : 3. (B.C. 446.)

Has'shub. [See HASHUB.]

Hasu'pha. [See HASHUPHA.]

Ha'tach (*verily*), one of the eunuchs in the court of Ahasuerus. Esther 4 : 5, 6, 9, 10. (B.C. 474.)

Ha'thath (*fearful*), one of the sons of Othniel the Kenazite. 1 Chron. 4 : 13.

Hat'ipha (*captive*). Bene-Hatipha (*i. e.* sons of Hatipha) were among the Nethinim who returned from Babylon with Zerubbabel. Ezra 2 : 54; Neh. 7 : 56. (B.C. 536.)

Hat'ita (*exploring*). Bene-Hatita (*i. e.* sons of Hatita) were among the "porters" (*i. e.* the gate-keepers) who returned from the captivity with Zerubbabel. Ezra 2 : 42; Neh. 7 : 45. (B.C. 536.)

Hat'til (*doubtful*). Bene-Hattil were among the "children of Solomon's slaves" who came back from captivity with Zerubbabel. Ezra 2 : 57; Neh. 7 : 59. (B.C. 536.)

Hat'tush (*assembled*). 1. A descendant of the kings of Judah, apparently one of the sons of Sheenaniah, 1 Chron. 3 : 22, in the fourth or fifth generation from Zerubbabel. A person of the same name accompanied Ezra from Babylon to Jerusalem. Ezra 8 : 2. In another statement Hattush is said to have returned with Zerubbabel. Neh. 12 : 2.

2. Son of Hashabniah; one of those who assisted Nehemiah in the repair of the wall of Jerusalem. Neh. 3 : 10. (B.C. 446.)

Hau'ran (*caverns*), a province of Palestine twice mentioned by Ezekiel. Ezek. 47 : 16, 18. There can be little doubt that it is identical with the well-known Greek province of Auranitis and the modern *Haurân*, east of the Sea of Galilee, on the borders of the desert, in the tetrarchy of Philip.

Hav'ilah (*circle*). 1. A son of Cush. Gen. 10 : 7.

2. A son of Joktan. Gen. 10 : 29.

Hav'ilah. Gen. 2 : 11. 1. A part of Eden through which flowed the river Pison (Araxes). It was probably the Grecian Colchis, in the northeast corner of Asia Minor, near the Caspian Sea.

2. A district in Arabia Felix, Gen. 10 : 7, named from the second son of Cush; probably the district of Kuâlan, in the northwestern part of Yemen.

Havoth-ja'ir (*villages of Jair*), certain villages on the east of Jordan, in Gilead or Bashan, which were taken by Jair the son of Manasseh, and called after his name. Num. 32 : 41; Deut. 3 : 14. In the records of Manasseh in Josh. 13 : 30 and 1 Chron. 2 : 23, the Havoth-jair are reckoned with other districts as making up sixty "cities." Comp. 1 Kings 4 : 13. There is apparently some confusion in these different statements as to what the sixty cities really consisted of. No less doubtful is the number of the Havoth-jair. In 1 Chron. 2 : 22 they are

Kestrel or Hawk.

specified as twenty-three, but in Judges 10 : 4 as thirty.

Hawk. Lev. 11 : 16; Deut. 14 : 15; Job 39 : 26. The hawk includes various species of the *Falconidæ*. With respect to the passage in Job (*l. c.*) which appears to allude to the migratory habits of hawks, it is curious to observe that of the ten or twelve lesser raptors (hawk tribe) of Palestine, nearly all are summer migrants. The kestrel remains all the year, but the others are all migrants from the south.

Hay (Heb. *châtsir*), the rendering of the Authorized Version in Prov. 27 : 25 and Isa. 15 : 6 of the Hebrew term, which occurs frequently in the Old Testament, and denotes " grass " of any kind. It is quite probable that the modern Orientals do not make hay in our sense of the term; but it is certain that the ancients did mow their grass, and probably made use of the dry material. See Ps. 37 : 2. We may remark that there is an express Hebrew term for " dry grass " or " hay," viz. *chashash*, which, in the only two places where the word occurs, Isa. 5 : 24, 33 : 11, is rendered " chaff " in the Authorized Version.

Haz'a-el (*whom God sees*), a king of Damascus who reigned from about B.C. 886 to B.C. 840. He appears to have been previously a person in a high position at the court of Ben-hadad, and was sent by his master to Elisha to inquire if he would recover from the malady under which he was suffering. Elisha's answer led to the murder of Ben-hadad by his ambitious servant, who forthwith mounted the throne. 2 Kings 8 : 7–15. He was soon engaged in war with the kings of Judah and Israel, for the possession of the city of Ramoth-gilead. *Ibid.* 8 : 28. Towards the close of the reign of Jehu, Hazael led the Syrians against the Israelites (about B.C. 860), whom he " smote in all their coasts," 2 Kings 10 : 32, thus accomplishing the prophecy of Elisha. *Ibid.* 8 : 12. At the close of his life, having taken Gath, *ibid.* 12 : 17 ; comp. Amos 6 : 2, he proceeded to attack Jerusalem, 2 Chron. 24 : 24, and was about to assault the city when Joash bribed him to retire. 2 Kings 12 : 18. Hazael appears to have died about the year B.C. 840, 2 Kings 13 : 24, having reigned forty-six years.

Haza'iah (*whom Jehovah sees*), a man of Judah of the family of the Shilonites, or descendants of Shelah. Neh. 11 : 5.

Ha'zar-ad'ar, etc. [HAZER.]

Hazarma'veth (*court of death*), the third in order of the sons of Joktan. Gen. 10 : 26. The name is preserved in the Arabic *Hadramâwt* and *Hadrumâwt*, the appellation of a province and an ancient people of southern Arabia. Its capital is Satham, a very ancient city, and

its chief ports are Mirbát, Zafári and Kisheem, from whence a great trade was carried on in ancient times with India and Africa.

Hazel. The Hebrew term *lúz* occurs only in Gen. 30 : 37. Authorities are divided between the hazel and the almond tree as representing the *lúz*. The latter is most probably correct.

Hazelelpo'ni (*shade coming upon me*), the sister of the sons of Etam in the genealogies of Judah. 1 Chron. 4 : 3.

Ha'zer, topographically, seems generally employed for the *villages* of people. As a proper name it appears in the Authorized Version—1. In the plural, HAZERIM and HAZEROTH, for which see below. 2. In the slightly different form of HAZOR. 3. In composition with other words :

1. HAZAR-ADDAR (*village of Addar*), a place named as one of the landmarks on the southern boundary of the land promised to Israel. Num. 34 : 4 ; ADAR, Josh. 15 : 3.

2. HAZAR-ENAN (*village of fountains*), the place at which the northern boundary of the land promised to the children of Israel was to terminate. Num. 34 : 9, 10 ; comp. Ezek. 47 : 17 ; 48 : 1.

3. HAZAR-GADDAH (*village of fortune*), one of the towns in the southern district of Judah, Josh. 15 : 27, named between Moladah and Heshmon.

4. HAZAR-SHUAL (*village of jackals*), a town in the southern district of Judah, lying between Hazar-gaddah and Beersheba. Josh. 15 : 28; 19 : 3 ; 1 Chron. 4 : 28.

5. HAZAR-SUSAH (*village of horses*), one of the " cities " allotted to Simeon in the extreme south of the territory of Judah. Josh. 19 : 5.

Haze'rim (*villages*). The Avim, or more accurately the Avvim, are said to have lived " in the villages (Authorized Version ' Hazerim ') as far as Gaza," Deut. 2 : 23, before their expulsion by the Caphtorim.

Haze'roth (*villages*), Num. 11 : 35; 12 : 16; 33 : 17; Deut. 1 : 1, a station of the Israelites in the desert, and perhaps recognizable in the Arabic *Ain Hudhera*, forty miles northeast of Sinai.

Haz'ezon-ta'mar and **Haz'azonta'mar** (*pruning of palm trees*), the ancient name of Engedi. Gen. 14 : 7. The name occurs in the records of the reign of Hezekiah. 2 Chron. 20 : 2.

Ha'zi-el (*vision of God*), a Levite in

the time of David, of the family of Shimei or Shimi, the younger branch of the Gershonites. 1 Chron. 23 : 9. (B.C. 1014.)

Ha'zo (*vision*), a son of Nahor, by Milcah his wife. Gen. 22 : 22. (B.C. about 1900.)

Ha'zor (*castle*). 1. A fortified city, which on the occupation of the country was allotted to Naphtali. Josh. 19 : 36. Its position was apparently between Ramah and Kedesh, *ibid.* 12 : 19, on the high ground overlooking the Lake of Merom. There is no reason for supposing it a different place from that of which Jabin was king. Josh. 11 : 1; Judges 4 : 2, 17; 1 Sam. 12 : 9. It was the principal city of the whole of north Palestine. Josh. 11 : 10. It was fortified by Solomon, 1 Kings 9 : 15, and its inhabitants were carried captive by Tiglath-pileser. 2 Kings 15 : 29. The most probable site of Hazor is *Tell Khuraibeh.*

2. One of the "cities" of Judah in the extreme south, named next in order to Kedesh. Josh. 15 : 23.

3. Hazor-Hadattah = " new Hazor," another of the southern towns of Judah. Josh. 15 : 25.

4. A place in which the Benjamites resided after their return from the captivity. Neh. 11 : 33.

Head-dress. The Hebrews do not appear to have regarded a covering for the head as an essential article of dress. Hats were unknown. The earliest notice we have of such a thing is in connection with the sacerdotal vestments. Ex. 28 : 40. The *tsániph* (something like a turban) is noticed as being worn by nobles, Job 29 : 14, ladies, Isa. 3 : 23, and kings, Isa. 62 : 3; while the *peêr* was an article of holiday dress, Isa. 61 : 3, Authorized Version "beauty;" Ezek. 24 : 17, 23, and was worn at weddings. Isa. 61 : 10. The ordinary head-dress of the Bedouin consists of the *keffieh*, a square handkerchief, generally of red and yellow cotton or cotton and silk, folded so that three of the corners hang down over the back and shoulders, leaving the face exposed, and bound round the head by a cord. It is not improbable that a similar covering was used by the Hebrews on certain occasions. The Assyrian head-dress is described in Ezek. 23 : 15 under the terms "exceeding in dyed attire." The word rendered "hats" in Dan. 3 : 21 properly applies to a *cloak.*

Hearth. One way of baking much practiced in the East is to place the dough

on an iron plate, either laid on or supported on legs above the vessel sunk in the ground, which forms the oven. The cakes baked "on the hearth," Gen. 18 : 6, were probably baked in the existing Bedouin manner, on hot stones covered with ashes. The "hearth" of King Jehoiakim's winter palace, Jer. 36 : 23, was possibly a pan or brazier of charcoal. From this we see that the significance of the Hebrew words translated hearth is not the same as with us.

Heath, Jer. 17 : 6, was some species of juniper, probably the savin, a dwarf, stunted juniper which grows in the most sterile parts of the desert.

Hea'then. [GENTILES.]

Heaven. There are four Hebrew words thus rendered in the Old Testament which we may briefly notice. 1. *Rákí'a*, Authorized Version, firmament. [FIRMAMENT.] 2. *Shámayim.* This is the word used in the expression "the heaven and the earth," or "the upper and lower regions." Gen. 1 : 1. 3. *Máróm*, used for heaven in Ps. 18 : 16; Isa. 24 : 18; Jer. 25 : 30. Properly speaking it means a mountain, as in Ps. 102 : 19; Ezek. 17 : 23. 4. *Shechákím*, "expanses," with reference to the *extent* of heaven. Deut. 33 : 26; Job 35 : 5.. St. Paul's expression "third heaven," 2 Cor. 12 : 2, has led to much conjecture. Grotius said that the Jews divided the heaven into three parts, viz., 1. The air or atmosphere, where clouds gather; 2. The firmament, in which the sun, moon and stars are fixed; 3. The upper heaven, the abode of God and his angels, the invisible realm of holiness and happiness, the home of the children of God.

He'ber (*alliance*). 1. Grandson of the patriarch Asher, Gen. 46 : 17; Num. 26 : 45; 1 Chron. 7 : 31, from whom came the Heberites. Num. 26 : 45.

2. The patriarch Eber. Luke 3 : 35. [EBER.]

3. The father of Socho; a Judite. 1 Chron. 4 : 18.

4. A Benjamite. 1 Chron. 8 : 17.

5. A Benjamite. 1 Chron. 8 : 22.

6. A Gadite. 1 Chron. 5 : 13.

7. The husband of Jael, who slew Sisera by driving a nail into his temple. Judges 4 : 21, 22.

He'brew. This word first occurs as given to Abram by the Canaanites, Gen. 14 : 13, because he had crossed the Euphrates. The name is also derived from *'éber*, "beyond, on the other side," Abraham and his posterity being called Hebrews in order to express a distinction between the races east and west of the Euphrates. It may also be derived from *Heber*, one of the ancestors of Abraham. Gen. 10 : 24. The term Israelite was used by the Jews of themselves among themselves; the term Hebrew was the name by which they were known to foreigners. The latter was accepted by the Jews in their external relations; and after the general substitution of the word *Jew*, it still found a place in that marked and special feature of national contradistinction, the language.

He'brew language. The books of the Old Testament are written almost entirely in the Hebrew language. It is a branch of the Shemitic language, one of the three great divisions into which all languages have been reduced. It is one of the earliest of known languages, and some suppose that it was the original language of man.

He'brews, Epistle to the. 1. *The author.*—There has been a wide difference of opinion respecting the authorship of this epistle. The weight of evidence favors Paul as its author, though some think St. Luke, others Barnabas, and others still Apollos, may have written it. The thoughts are evidently St. Paul's, and he was doubtless the real author, whoever wrote it under him. 2. *To whom written.*—The epistle was probably addressed to the Jews in Jerusalem and Palestine. The argument of the epistle is such as could be used with most effect to a church consisting exclusively of Jews by birth, personally familiar with and attached to the temple service. 3. *Date.*—It was evidently written before the destruction of Jerusalem in A.D. 70, probably about A.D. 62–64. 4. *Place.* —It was probably written in Italy, while Paul was a prisoner at Rome. 5. *Contents.*—With respect to the scope of the epistle, it should be recollected that while the numerous Christian churches scattered throughout Judea, Acts 9 : 31; Gal. 1 : 22, were continually exposed to persecution from the Jews, 1 Thess. 2 : 14, there was in Jerusalem one additional weapon in the hands of the predominant

oppressors of the Christians. The magnificent national temple might be shut against the Hebrew Christian; and even if this affliction were not often laid upon him, yet there was a secret burden which he bore within him, the knowledge that the end of all the beauty and awfulness of Zion was rapidly approaching. The writer of this epistle meets the Hebrew Christians on their own ground, showing that the new faith gave them Christ the Son of God, more prevailing than the high priest as an intercessor; that his

Hebron.

Sabbath awaited them, his covenant, his atonement, his city heavenly not made with hands. Having him, believe in him with all your heart, with a faith in the unseen future strong as that of the saints of old, patient under present and prepared for coming woe, full of energy and hope and holiness and love. Such was the teaching of the Epistle to the Hebrews.

He'bron (*alliance*). 1. The third son of Kohath, who was the second son of Levi. Ex. 6 : 18; Num. 3 : 19; 1 Chron. 6 : 2, 18; 23 : 12. He was the founder of a family of Hebronites, Num. 3 : 27; 26 : 58; 1 Chron. 26 : 23, 30, 31, or Bene-Hebron. 1 Chron. 15 : 9; 23 : 19.

2. A city of Judah, Josh. 15 : 54, situated among the mountains, Josh. 20 : 7,

20 Roman miles south of Jerusalem, and the same distance north of Beersheba. Hebron is one of the most ancient cities in the world still existing; and in this respect it is the rival of Damascus. It was a well-known town when Abraham entered Canaan, 3800 years ago. Gen. 13 : 18. Its original name was Kirjath-arba, Judges 1 : 10, "the city of Arba;" so called from Arba the father of Anak. Josh. 15 : 13, 14; 21 : 13. Sarah died at Hebron; and Abraham then bought from Ephron the Hittite the field and cave of Machpelah, to serve as a family tomb. Gen. 23 : 2–20. The cave is still there; and the massive walls of the *Haram* or mosque, within which it lies, form the most remarkable object in the whole city. Abraham is called by Mohammedans *el-Khulil*, "the Friend," *i. e.* of God, and this is the modern name of Hebron. Hebron now contains about 5000 inhabitants, of whom some fifty families are Jews. It is picturesquely situated in a narrow

Mosque at Hebron covering the Cave of Machpelah.

valley, surrounded by rocky hills. The valley runs from north to south; and the main quarter of the town, surmounted by the lofty walls of the venerable *Haram*, lies partly on the eastern slope. Gen. 37 : 14; comp. 23 : 19. About a mile from the town, up the valley, is one of the largest oak trees in Palestine. This, say some, is the very tree beneath which Abraham pitched his tent, and it still bears the name of the patriarch.

3. One of the towns in the territory of Asher, Josh. 19 : 28; probably Ebdon or Abdom.

He'bronites, The. A family of Kohathite Levites, descendants of Hebron the son of Kohath. Num. 3 : 27; 26 : 58; 1 Chron. 26 : 23.

Hedge. The Hebrew words thus rendered denote simply that which surrounds or encloses, whether it be a stone wall, *geder*, Prov. 24 : 31; Ezek. 42 : 10, or a fence of other materials. The stone walls which surround the sheepfolds of modern Palestine are frequently crowned with sharp thorns.

Hega'i (*eunuch*), one of the eunuchs of the court of Ahasuerus. Esther 2 : 8, 15. (B.C. 474.)

He'ge, another form of the preceding. Esther 2 : 3.

Heifer. 1 Sam. 6 : 7–12; Job 21 : 10; Isa. 7 : 21. The heifer or young cow was not commonly used for ploughing, but only for treading out the corn. Hos. 10 : 11; but see Judges 14 : 18, when it ran about without any headstall, Deut. 25 : 4; hence the expression an "unbroken heifer," Hosea 4 : 16; Authorized Version "backsliding," to which Israel is compared.

Heir. The Hebrew institutions relative to inheritance were of a very simple character. Under the patriarchal system the property was divided among the sons of the legitimate wives, Gen. 21 : 10 ; 24 : 36 ; 25 : 5, a larger portion being assigned to one, generally the eldest, on whom devolved the duty of maintaining the females of the family. The sons of concubines were portioned off with presents. Gen. 25 : 6. At a later period the exclusion of the sons of concubines was rigidly enforced. Judges 11 : 1 ff. Daughters had no share in the patrimony, Gen. 21 : 14, but received a marriage portion. The Mosaic law regulated the succession to real property thus : it was to be divided among the sons, the eldest receiving a double portion, Deut. 21 : 17, the others equal shares ; if there were no sons, it went to the daughters, Num. 27 : 8, on the condition that they did not marry out of their own tribe, Num. 36 : 6 ff. ; otherwise the patrimony was forfeited. If there were no daughters, it went to the brother of the deceased ; if no brother, to the paternal uncle ; and, failing these, to the next of kin. Num. 27 : 9–11.

He′lah (*rust*), one of the two wives of Ashur, father of Tekoa. 1 Chron. 4 : 5.

He′lam (*stronghold*), a place east of the Jordan, but west of the Euphrates, at which the Syrians were collected by Hadarezer, and where David met and defeated them. 2 Sam. 10 : 16, 17.

He:′bah (*fertile*), a town of Asher, probably on the plain of Phœnicia, not far from Sidon. Judges 1 : 31.

Hel′bon (*fertile*), a place mentioned only in Ezek. 27 : 18. Geographers have hitherto represented Helbon as identical with the city of Aleppo, called *Haleb* by the Arabs ; but there are strong reasons against this, and the ancient city must be identified with a village within a few miles of Damascus, still bearing the ancient name *Helbon*, and still celebrated as producing the finest grapes in the country.

Hel′da-i (*worldly*). 1. The twelfth captain of the monthly courses for the temple service. 1 Chron. 27 : 15. (B.C. 1014.)

2. An Israelite who seems to have returned from the captivity. Zech. 6 : 10. (B.C. 520.)

He′leb (*milk*), or **He′led** (*transient*), son of Baanah the Netophathite, one of the heroes of King David's guard. 2 Sam. 23 : 29 ; 1 Chron. 11 : 30.

He′lek (*portion*), one of the descend-

ants of Manasseh, and second son of Gilead, Num. 26 : 30, and founder of the Helekites. (B.C. 1445.)

He′lem (*strength*). 1. A descendant of Asher. 1 Chron. 7 : 35.

2. A man mentioned only in Zech. 6 : 14. Apparently the same as Heldai.

He′leph (*exchange*), the place from which the boundary of the tribe of Naphtali started. Josh. 19 : 33.

He′lez (*strength*). 1. One of "the thirty " of David's guard, 2 Sam. 23 : 26 ; 1 Chron. 11 : 27 ; an Ephraimite, and captain of the seventh monthly course. 1 Chron. 27 : 10. (B.C. 1016.)

2. A man of Judah, son of Azariah. 1 Chron. 2 : 39.

He′li (*ascending*), the father of Joseph the husband of the Virgin Mary, Luke 3 : 23 ; perhaps the grandfather of Mary herself. [See GENEALOGY OF JESUS CHRIST.]

Heliop′olis. [See ON.]

Hel′kath (*portion*), the town named as the starting-point for the boundary of the tribe of Asher, Josh. 19 : 25, and allotted with its "suburbs " to the Gershonite Levites. ch. 21 : 31. Perhaps *Yerka*, seven miles from Acre.

Hel′kath-haz′zurim (*field of rock*), a smooth piece of ground, apparently close to the pool of Gibeon, where the combat took place between the two parties of Joab's men and Abner's men which ended in the death of the whole of the combatants, and brought on a general battle. 2 Sam. 2 : 16.

Hell. In the Old Testament this is the word generally. and unfortunately used by our translators to render the Hebrew *Sheol*. It really means the place of the dead, the unseen world, without deciding whether it be the place of misery or of happiness. It is clear that in many passages of the Old Testament *Sheol* can only mean "the grave," and is so rendered in the Authorized Version ; see, for example, Gen. 37 : 35 ; 42 : 38 ; 1 Sam. 2 : 6 ; Job 14 : 13. In other passages, however, it seems to involve a notion of punishment, and is therefore rendered in the Authorized Version by the word "hell." But in many cases this translation misleads the reader. In the New Testament "hell " is the translation of two words, *Hades* and *Gehenna*. The word *Hades*, like *Sheol*, sometimes means merely "the grave," Acts 2 : 31 ; 1 Cor. 15 : 55 ; Rev. 20 : 13, or in general "the unseen world." It is in this sense that the creeds say of our Lord, "He went down into hell," meaning the state of the dead in general, without any restriction of happiness or misery. Elsewhere in the New Testament Hades is used of a place of torment, Matt. 11 : 23; Luke 16 : 23; 2 Pet. 2 : 4, etc.; consequently it has been the prevalent, almost the universal, notion that Hades is an *intermediate state* between death and resurrection, divided into two parts, one the abode of the blest and the other of the lost. It is used eleven times in the New Testament, and only once translated "grave." 1 Cor. 15 : 55. The word most frequently used (occurring twelve times) in the New Testament for the place of future punishment is *Gehenna* or *Gehenna of fire*. This was originally the valley of Hinnom, south of Jerusalem, where the filth and dead animals of the city were cast out and burned; a fit symbol of the wicked and their destruction. [See HINNOM.]

Hel'lenist (*Grecian*), the term applied in the New Testament to Greek-speaking or "Grecian" Jews. The Hellenists as a body included not only the proselytes of Greek (or foreign) parentage, but also those Jews who, by settling in foreign countries, had adopted the prevalent form of the current Greek civilization, and with it the use of the common Greek dialect. Acts 6 : 1; 9 : 29.

Helmet. [ARMS.]

He'lon (*strong*), father of Eliab, of the tribe of Zebulun. Num. 1 : 9; 2 : 7; 7 : 24, 29; 10 : 16. (B.C. 1491.)

Hem of garment. The importance which the later Jews, especially the Pharisees, Matt. 23 : 5, attached to the hem or fringe of their garments was founded upon the regulation in Num. 15 : 38, 39, which gave a symbolical meaning to it. [See DRESS.]

He'mam (*exterminating*). Hori and Hemam were sons of Lotan, the eldest son of Seir. Gen. 36 : 22.

He'man (*faithful*). 1. Son of Zerah. 1 Chron. 2 : 6; 1 Kings 4 : 31.

2. Son of Joel and grandson of Samuel the prophet, a Kohathite. He is called "the singer," rather the *musician*, 1 Chron. 6 : 33, and was the first of the three Levites to whom was committed the vocal and instrumental music of the temple service in the reign of David. 1 Chron. 15 : 16–22. The 88th Psalm is ascribed to him. (B.C. 1014.)

He'math (*heat*), a person or place named in the genealogical lists of Judah,

as the origin of the Kenites, and the "father" of the house of Rechab. 1 Chron. 2 : 55. (B.C. 1445.)

Hem'dan (*pleasant*), the eldest son of Dishon, son of Anah the Horite. Gen. 36 : 26. [AMRAM, 2.] (B.C. about 1500.)

Hemlock, the common ground or dwarf hemlock, a bitter, poisonous plant. The Hebrew *rôsh* is rendered "hemlock" in two passages, Hos. 10 : 4; Amos 6 : 12, but elsewhere "gall." [GALL.] (It is possible that the plant is rather the poppy than an hemlock.—*Cook*.)

Hen (*rest*), probably a son of Zephaniah, and apparently the same who is called JOSIAH in Zech. 6 : 10.

Hen. The hen is nowhere noticed in the Bible except in Matt. 23 : 37; Luke 13 : 34. That a bird so common in Palestine should receive such slight notice is certainly singular.

He'na (*troubling*), a city the Assyrian kings had reduced shortly before the time of Sennacherib. 2 Kings 19 : 13; Isa. 37 : 13. At no great distance from Sippara (now *Mosaib*) is an ancient town called *Ana* or *Anah*, which may be the same as Hena. It is 20 miles from Babylon, on the Euphrates.

Hen'adad (*grace of Hadad*), the head of a family of the Levites who took a prominent part in the rebuilding of the temple. Ezra 3 : 9.

He'noch. 1. Enoch, 2. 1 Chron. 1 : 3. 2. Hanoch, 1. 1 Chron. 1 : 33.

He'pher (*a well*). 1. The youngest of the sons of Gilead, Num. 26 : 32, and head of the family of the Hepherites. (B.C. before 1450.)

2. Son of Ashur, the "father of Tekoa." 1 Chron. 4 : 6. (B.C. about 1445.)

3. The Mecherathite, one of the heroes of David's guard. 1 Chron. 11 : 36. (B.C. 1046.)

He'pher, a place in ancient Canaan, which occurs in the list of conquered kings. Josh. 12 : 17. It was on the west of Jordan. Comp. 7 and 1 Kings 4 : 10.

He'pherites, The, the family of Hepher the son of Gilead. Num. 26 : 32.

Heph'zi-bah. 1. A name signifying "*my delight in her*," which is to be borne by the restored Jerusalem. Isa. 62 : 4.

2. The queen of King Hezekiah and the mother of Manasseh. 2 Kings 21 : 1. (B.C. 709–696.)

Herald, one who makes public proclamation. The only notice of this officer in the Old Testament occurs in Dan. 3 : 4. The term "herald" might be substituted for "preacher" in 1 Tim. 2 : 7 ; 2 Tim. 1 : 11 ; 2 Pet. 2 : 5.

Herd (a collection of cattle), **Herdsman.** The herd was greatly regarded in both the patriarchal and the Mosaic period. The ox was the most precious stock next to horse and mule. The herd yielded the most esteemed sacrifice, Num. 7 : 3 ; Ps. 69 : 31 ; Isa. 66 : 3 ; also flesh meat, and milk, chiefly converted, probably, into butter and cheese. Deut. 32 : 14 ; 2 Sam. 17 : 29. The agricultural and general usefulness of the ox in ploughing, threshing, and as a beast of burden, 1 Chron. 12 : 40 ; Isa. 46 : 1, made a slaughtering of him seem wasteful. Herdsmen, etc., in Egypt were a low, perhaps the lowest, caste ; but of the abundance of cattle in Egypt, and of the care there bestowed on them, there is no doubt. Gen. 47 : 6, 17 ; Ex. 9 : 4, 20. So the plague of hail was sent to smite especially the cattle, Ps. 78 : 48, the firstborn of which also were smitten. Ex. 12 : 29. The Israelites departing stipulated for, Ex. 10 : 26, and took " much cattle " with them. ch. 12 : 38. Cattle formed thus one of the traditions of the Israelitish nation in its greatest period, and became almost a part of that greatness. The occupation of herdsman was honorable in early times. Gen. 47 : 6 ; 1 Sam. 11 : 5 ; 1 Chron. 27 : 29 ; 28 : 1. Saul himself resumed it in the interval of his cares as king ; also Doeg was certainly high in his confidence. 1 Sam. 21 : 7. Pharaoh made some of Joseph's brethren " rulers over his cattle." David's herdmasters were among his chief officers of state. The prophet Amos at first followed this occupation.

He'res (*the sun*), Judges 1 : 35, a city of Dan, in Mount Ephraim, near Ajalon ; possibly identical with Mount Jearim (Ir-shemesh, city of the sun).

He'resh (*artificer*), a Levite attached to the tabernacle. 1 Chron. 9 : 15. (B.C. 536.)

Her'mas (*Mercury*), the name of a Christian resident at Rome to whom St. Paul sends greetings in his Epistle to the Romans. Rom. 16 : 14. (A.D. 55.) Irenæus, Tertullian and Origen agree in attributing to him the work called *The Shepherd*. It was never received into the canon, but yet was generally cited with respect only second to that which was paid to the authoritative books of the New Testament.

Her'mes (*Mercury*), a Christian men-

tioned in Rom. 16 : 14. According to tradition he was one of the seventy disciples, and afterward bishop of Dalmatia. (A.D. 55.)

Hermog'enes, a person mentioned by St. Paul in the latest of all his epistles, 2 Tim. 1 : 15, when all in Asia had turned away from him. (A.D. 64.)

Her'mon (*a peak, summit*), a mountain on the northeastern border of Palestine, Deut. 3 : 8 ; Josh. 12 : 1, over against Lebanon, Josh. 11 : 17, adjoining the plateau of Bashan. 1 Chron. 5 : 23. It stands at the southern end, and is the culminating point of the anti-Libanus range ; it towers high above the ancient border city of Dan and the fountains of the Jordan, and is the most conspicuous and beautiful mountain in Palestine or Syria. At the present day it is called *Jebel esh-Sheikh,* " the chief mountain," and *Jebel eth-Thelj,* "snowy mountain." When the whole country is parched with the summer sun, white lines of snow streak the head of Hermon. This mountain was the great landmark of the Israelites. It was associated with their northern border almost as intimately as the sea was with the western. Hermon has three summits, situated like the angles of a triangle, and about a quarter of a mile from each other. In two passages of Scripture this mountain is called *Baal-hermon,* Judges 3 : 3 ; 1 Chron. 5 : 23, possibly because Baal was there worshipped. (It is more than probable that some part of Hermon was the scene of the transfiguration, as it stands near Cæsarea Philippi, where we know Christ was just before that event.—ED.) The height of Hermon has never been measured, though it has often been estimated. It may safely be reckoned at 10,000 feet.

Her'monites, The. Properly "*the Hermons,*" with reference to the three summits of Mount Hermon. Ps. 42 : 6 (7).

Her'od (*hero-like*). This family, though of Idumean origin and thus alien by race, was Jewish in faith. I. HEROD THE GREAT was the second son of Antipater, an Idumean, who was appointed procurator of Judea by Julius Cæsar, B.C. 47. Immediately after his father's elevation, when only fifteen years old, he received the government of Galilee, and shortly afterward that of Cœle-Syria. (Though Josephus says he was 15 years old at this time, it is generally conceded that there must be some mistake, as he

Mount Hermon.

lived to be 69 or 70 years old, and died B.C. 4; hence he must have been 25 years old at this time.—ED.) In B.C. 41 he was appointed by Antony tetrarch of Judea. Forced to abandon Judea the following year, he fled to Rome, and received the appointment of king of Judea. In the course of a few years, by the help of the Romans he took Jerusalem (B.C. 37), and completely established his authority throughout his dominions. The terrible acts of bloodshed which Herod perpetrated in his own family were accompanied by others among his subjects equally terrible, from the number who fell victims to them. According to the well-known story, he ordered the nobles whom he had called to him in his last moments to be executed immediately after his decease, that so at least his death might be attended by universal mourning. It was at the time of his fatal illness that he must have caused the slaughter of the infants at Bethlehem. Matt. 2 : 16–18. He adorned Jerusalem with many splendid monuments of his taste and magnificence. The temple, which he built with scrupulous care, was the greatest of these works. The restoration was begun B.C. 20, and the temple itself was completed in a year and a half. But fresh additions were constantly made in succeeding years, so that it was said that the temple was "built in forty and six years," John 2 : 20, the work continuing long after Herod's death. (Herod died of a terrible disease, at Jericho, in April, B.C. 4, at the age of 69, after a long reign of 37 years.—ED.)

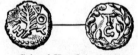

Coin of Herod Antipas.

II. HEROD ANTIPAS was the son of Herod the Great by Malthaké, a Samaritan. He first married a daughter of Aretas, "king of Arabia Petræa," but afterward Herodias, the wife of his half-brother, Herod Philip. Aretas, indignant at the insult offered to his daughter, found a pretext for invading the territory of Herod, and defeated him with great loss. This defeat, according to the famous passage in Josephus, was attributed by many to the murder of John the Baptist, which had been committed by Antipas shortly before, under the influ-

ence of Herodias. Matt. 14 : 4 ff.; Mark 6 : 17 ff.; Luke 3 : 19. At a later time the ambition of Herodias proved the cause of her husband's ruin. She urged him to go to Rome to gain the title of king, cf. Mark 6 : 14; but he was opposed at the court of Caligula by the emissaries of Agrippa, and condemned to perpetual banishment at Lugdunum, A.D. 39. Herodias voluntarily shared his punishment, and he died in exile. Pilate took occasion from our Lord's residence in Galilee to send him for examination, Luke 23 : 6 ff., to Herod Antipas, who came up to Jerusalem to celebrate the Passover. The city of Tiberias, which Antipas founded and named in honor of the emperor, was the most conspicuous monument of his long reign.

III. HEROD PHILIP I. (Philip, Mark 6 : 17) was the son of Herod the Great and Mariamne. He married Herodias, the sister of Agrippa I., by whom he had a daughter, Salome. He was excluded from all share in his father's possessions in consequence of his mother's treachery, and lived afterward in a private station.

Coin of Philip the Tetrarch.

IV. HEROD PHILIP II. was the son of Herod the Great and Cleopatra. He received as his own government Batanea, Trachonitis, Auranitis (Gaulanitis), and some parts about Jamnia, with the title of tetrarch. Luke 3 : 1. He built a new city on the site of Paneas, near the sources of the Jordan, which he called Cæsarea Philippi, Matt. 16 : 13; Mark 8 : 27, and raised Bethsaida to the rank of a city under the title of Julias, and died there A.D. 34. He married Salome, the daughter of Herod Philip I. and Herodias.

V. HEROD AGRIPPA I. was the son of Aristobulus and Berenice, and grandson of Herod the Great. He was brought up at Rome, and was thrown into prison by Tiberius, where he remained till the accession of Caligula, who made him king, first of the tetrarchy of Philip and Lysanias; afterward the dominions of

Antipas were added, and finally Judea and Samaria. Unlike his predecessors, Agrippa was a strict observer of the law,

Coin of Herod Agrippa I.

and he sought with success the favor of the Jews. It is probable that it was with this view he put to death James the son of Zebedee, and further imprisoned Peter. Acts 12 : 1 ff. But his sudden death interrupted his ambitious projects. Acts 12 : 21, 23.

VI. HEROD AGRIPPA II. was the son of Herod Agrippa I. In A.D. 52 the emperor gave him the tetrarchies formerly held by Philip and Lysanias, with the title of king. Acts 25 : 13. The relation in which he stood to his sister Berenice, Acts 25 : 13, was the cause of grave sus-

picion. It was before him that Paul was tried. Acts 26 : 28.

Coin of Titus and Herod Agrippa II.

Hero'dians (from Herod). Matt. 22 : 15 ff.; Mark 12 : 13 ff. Canon Cook describes these persons as "that party among the Jews who were supporters of the Herodian family as the last hope of retaining for the Jews a fragment of national government, as distinguished from absolute dependence upon Rome as a province of the empire. Supporters of the family of Herod, who held their dominions by the grant of the Roman emperor, would be in favor of paying tribute to the supreme power." Matt. 22 : 16.

A Genealogical Table of the Herodian Family, including those members of it who are mentioned in the Gospel according to St. Matthew.

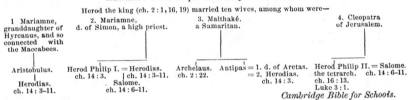

Herod the king (ch. 2 : 1, 16, 19) married ten wives, among whom were—			
1 Mariamne, granddaughter of Hyrcanus, and so connected with the Maccabees.	2. Mariamne, d. of Simon, a high priest.	3. Malthaké. a Samaritan.	4. Cleopatra of Jerusalem.
Aristobulus.	Herod Philip I. = Herodias. ch. 14 : 3.	ch. 14 : 3–11.	Archelaus. ch. 2 : 22.	Antipas = 1. d. of Aretas. = 2. Herodias. ch. 14 : 3.	Herod Philip II. = Salome. the tetrarch. ch. 14 : 6–11. ch. 16 : 13.
Herodias. ch. 14 : 3–11.	. Salome. ch. 14 : 6–11.				Luke 3 : 1.

Cambridge Bible for Schools.

Hero'dias, daughter of Aristobulus, one of the sons of Mariamne and Herod the Great, and consequently sister of Agrippa I. She first married Herod Philip I.; then she eloped from him to marry Herod Antipas, her step-uncle. The head of John the Baptist was granted at the request of Herodias. Matt. 14 : 8–11; Mark 6 : 24–28. (A.D. 29.) She accompanied Antipas into exile to Lugdunum.

Hero'dion, a relative of St. Paul, to whom he sends his salutation amongst the Christians of the Roman church. Rom. 16 : 11. (A.D. 55.)

Heron, Lev. 11 : 19; Deut. 14 : 18, a common large, wading, unclean bird. Nearly all of the species known in English ornithology are found in the vicinity of Palestine. Canon Cook and others think the bird intended is the *plover*

(*Charadrius œdicnemus*), a greedy, thick-kneed, high-flying migratory bird, very common in the East, on the banks of rivers and shores of lakes.—ED.

He'sed (*kindness*), the son of Hesed or Ben-Chesed, was commissary for Solomon. 1 Kings 4 : 10. (B.C. about 995.)

Hesh'bon (*stronghold*), the capital city of Sihon king of the Amorites. Num. 21 : 26. It stood on the western border of the high plain—Mishor, Josh. 13 : 17—and on the boundary line between the tribes of Reuben and Gad. The ruins of *Hesbân*, 20 miles east of the Jordan, on the parallel of the northern end of the Dead Sea, mark the site, as they bear the name, of the ancient Heshbon. There are many cisterns among the ruins. Comp. Cant. 7 : 4.

Hesh'mon (*rich soil*), a place named,

with others, as lying in the extreme south of Judah. Josh. 15 : 27.

Hes'ron, Hez'ron (*enclosed*), the son of Reuben, Num. 26 : 6, and ancestor of the Hezronites. (B.C. about 1700.)

Heth (*terror*), the forefather of the nation of the Hittites. In the genealogical tables of Gen. 10 : 15 and 1 Chron. 1 : 13 Heth is a son of Canaan. Gen. 24 : 3, 4; 28 : 1, 2.

Heth'lon (*hiding-place*), the name of a place on the northern border of Palestine. Ezek. 47 : 15; 48 : 1. In all probability the "way of Hethlon" is the pass at the northern end of Lebanon, and is thus identical with "the entrance of Hamath" in Num. 34 : 8, etc.

Hez'eki (*strong*), a Benjamite, one of the Bene-Elpaal, a descendant of Shaaraim. 1 Chron. 8 : 17. (B.C. 598.)

Hezeki'ah (*the might of Jehovah*). 1. Twelfth king of Judah, son of the apostate Ahaz and Abi or Abijah, ascended the throne at the age of 25, B.C. 726. Hezekiah was one of the three most perfect kings of Judah. 2 Kings 18 : 5; Ecclus. 49 : 4. His first act was to purge and repair and reopen with splendid sacrifices and perfect ceremonial the temple. He also destroyed a brazen serpent, said to have been the one used by Moses in the miraculous healing of the Israelites, Num. 21 : 9, which had become an object of adoration. When the kingdom of Israel had fallen, Hezekiah invited the scattered inhabitants to a peculiar passover, which was continued for the unprecedented period of fourteen days. 2 Chron. 29 : 30, 31. At the head of a repentant and united people, Hezekiah ventured to assume the aggressive against the Philistines; and in a series of victories not only rewon the cities which his father had lost, 2 Chron. 28 : 18, but even dispossessed them of their own cities, except Gaza, 2 Kings 18 : 8, and Gath. He refused to acknowledge the supremacy of Assyria. 2 Kings 18 : 7. Instant war was imminent, and Hezekiah used every available means to strengthen himself. 2 Kings 20 : 20. It was probably at this dangerous crisis in his kingdom that we find him sick and sending for Isaiah, who prophesies death as the result. 2 Kings 20 : 1. Hezekiah's prayer for longer life is heard. The prophet had hardly left the palace when he was ordered to return and promise the king immediate recovery and fifteen years more of life. 2 Kings 20 : 4–6. An embassy coming from Babylon ostensibly to com-

pliment Hezekiah on his convalescence, but really to form an alliance between the two powers, is favorably received by the king, who shows them the treasures which he had accumulated. For this Isaiah foretells the punishment that shall befall his house. 2 Kings 20 : 17. The two invasions of Sennacherib occupy the greater part of the Scripture records concerning the reign of Hezekiah. The first of these took place in the third year of Sennacherib, B.C. 702, and occupies only three verses. 2 Kings 18 : 13–16. Respecting the commencement of the second invasion we have full details in 2 Kings 18 : 17, *seq.*; 2 Chron. 32 : 9, *seq.*; Isa. 36. Sennacherib sent against Jerusalem an army under two officers and his cupbearer, the orator Rabshakeh, with a blasphemous and insulting summons to surrender; but Isaiah assures the king he need not fear, promising to disperse the enemy. 2 Kings 19 : 6, 7. Accordingly that night "the angel of the Lord went out, and smote in the camp of the Assyrians a hundred fourscore and five thousand." Hezekiah only lived to enjoy for about one year more his well-earned peace and glory. He slept with his fathers after a reign of twenty-nine years, in the 56th year of his age, B.C. 697.

2. Son of Neariah, one of the descendants of the royal family of Judah. 1 Chron. 3 : 23.

3. The same name, though rendered in the Authorized Version HIZKIAH, is found in Zeph. 1 : 1.

4. Ater of Hezekiah. [ATER.]

He'zion (*vision*), a king of Aram (Syria), father of Tabrimon and grandfather of Ben-hadad I. 1 Kings 15 : 18. He is probably identical with REZON, the contemporary of Solomon, in 1 Kings 11 : 23. (B.C. before 928.)

He'zir (*swine*). 1. A priest in the time of David, leader of the seventeenth monthly course in the service. 1 Chron. 24 : 15. (B.C. 1014.)

2. One of the heads of the people (laymen) who sealed the solemn covenant with Nehemiah. Neh. 10 : 20. (B.C. 410.)

Hez'ra-i (*enclosed*), one of the thirty heroes of David's guard. 2 Sam. 23 : 35. (B.C. 1046.) In the parallel list, 1 Chron. 11 : 37, the name appears as HEZRO.

Hez'ron (*surrounded by a wall*). 1. A son of Reuben. Gen. 46 : 9; Ex. 6 : 14.

2. A son of Pharez. Gen. 46 : 12; Ruth 4 : 18.

Hez'ronites (*descendants of Hezron*),

The. 1. Descendants of Hezron the son of Reuben. Num. 26 : 6.

2. A branch of the tribe of Judah, descendants of Hezron the son of Pharez. Num. 26 : 21.

Hid'da-i (*for the rejoicing of Jehovah*), one of the thirty-seven heroes of David's guard. 2 Sam. 23 : 30. (B.C. 1046.)

Hid'dekel (*rapid*), one of the rivers of Eden, the river which "goeth eastward to Assyria," Gen. 2 : 14, and which Daniel calls "the great river," Dan. 10 : 4, seems to have been rightly identified by the LXX. with the Tigris. Dekel is clearly an equivalent of Digla or Diglath, a name borne by the Tigris in all ages. The name now in use among the inhabitants of Mesopotamia is *Dijleh*.

Hi'el (*God liveth*), a native of Bethel, who rebuilt Jericho in the reign of Ahab, 1 Kings 16 : 34 (B.C. after 915), and in whom was fulfilled the curse pronounced by Joshua, Josh. 6 : 26, five hundred years before.

Hi-erap'olis (*holy city*), a city of Phrygia, situated above the junction of the rivers Lycus and Mæander, near Colossæ and Laodicea. Mentioned only in Col. 4 : 13 as the seat of a church probably founded by Epaphras.

Higga'ion (*meditation*), a word which occurs three times in the book of Psalms —Ps. 9 : 16; 19 : 14; 92 : 3 (margin). The word has two meanings, one of a general character, implying *thought, reflection,* and another, in Ps. 9 : 16 and Ps. 92 : 3, of a technical nature, the precise meaning of which cannot at this distance of time be determined. (Canon Cook says that it probably means an *interlude,* giving musical expression to the feelings suggested by the preceding words.—ED.)

High places. From the earliest times it was the custom among all nations to erect altars and places of worship on lofty and conspicuous spots. To this general custom we find constant allusion in the Bible, Isa. 65 : 7; Ezek. 6 : 13, and it is especially attributed to the Moabites. Isa. 15 : 2; 16 : 12. Even Abraham built an altar to the Lord on a mountain near Bethel. Gen. 12 : 7, 8; cf. 22 : 2–4; 31 : 54. Notwithstanding this we find that it was implicitly forbidden by the law of Moses, Deut. 12 : 11–14, which also gave the strictest injunction to destroy these monuments of Canaanitish idolatry. Lev. 26. The command was a prospective one, and was not to come into force until such time as the tribes were settled in the promised land. Thus we find that both Gideon and Manoah built altars on high places by divine command. Judges 6 : 25, 26; 13 : 16–23. It is more surprising to find this law absolutely ignored at a much later period, when there was no intelligible reason for its violation—as by Samuel at Mizpeh, 1 Sam. 7 : 10, and at Bethlehem, ch. 16 : 5; by Saul at Gilgal, ch. 13 : 9, and at Ajalon,(?) ch. 14 : 35; by David, 1 Chron. 21 : 26; by Elijah on Mount Carmel, 1 Kings 18 : 30, and by other prophets. 1 Sam. 10 : 5. The explanations which are given are sufficiently unsatisfactory; but it is at any rate certain that the worship in high places was organized and all but universal throughout Judea, not only during, 1 Kings 3 : 2–4, but even after the time of Solomon. At last Hezekiah set himself in good earnest to the suppression of this prevalent corruption, 2 Kings 18 : 4, 22, both in Judah and Israel, 2 Chron. 31 : 1; although so rapid was the growth of the evil that even his sweeping reformation required to be finally consummated by Josiah, 2 Kings 23, and that too in Jerusalem and its immediate neighborhood. 2 Chron. 24 : 3. After the time of Josiah we find no further mention of these Jehovistic high places.

High Priest. Priest.

High priest. The first distinct separation of Aaron to the office of the priesthood, which previously belonged to the first-born, was that recorded Ex. 28. We find from the very first the following characteristic attributes of Aaron and the high priests his successors, as distinguished from the other priests: Aaron alone was anointed, Lev. 8 : 12, whence one of the distinctive epithets of the high priest was "the anointed priest." Lev. 4 : 3, 5, 16 ; 21 : 10 ; see Num. 35 : 25. The anointing of the sons of Aaron, *i. e.* the common priests, seems to have been confined to sprinkling their garments with the anointing oil. Ex. 29 : 21 ; 28 : 41, etc. The high priest had a peculiar dress, which passed to his successor at his death. This dress consisted of eight

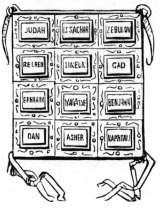

A Breastplate.

parts : (*a*) The *breastplate*, or, as it is further named, vs. 15, 29, 30, the breastplate of judgment. The breastplate was originally two spans long and one span broad, but when doubled it was square, the shape in which it was worn. On it were the twelve precious stones, set in four rows, three in a row, thus corresponding to the twelve tribes — each stone having the name of one of the children of Israel engraved upon it. (*b*) The *ephod*. This consisted of two parts, of which one covered the back and the other the front, *i. e.* the breast and upper part of the body. These parts were clasped together on the shoulder with two large onyx stones, each having engraved on it six of the names of the tribes of Israel. They were further united by a "curious girdle" of gold, blue, purple, scarlet and fine twined linen round the waist. [EPHOD ; GIRDLE.] (*c*) The *robe of the ephod*. This was of inferior material to the ephod itself, being all of blue, ver. 31, which implied its being only of "woven work." ch. 39 :

22. It was worn immediately under the ephod, and was longer than it. The skirt of this robe had a remarkable trimming of pomegranates in blue, red and crimson, with a bell of gold between each pomegranate alternately. The bells were to give a sound when the high priest went in and came out of the holy place. (*d*) The *mitre* or *upper turban*, with its gold plate, engraved with "Holiness to the Lord," fastened to it by a ribbon of blue. (*e*) The broidered *coat* was a tunic or long skirt of linen with a tessellated or diaper pattern, like the setting of a stone. (*f*) The *girdle*, also of linen, was wound round the body several times from the breast downward, and the ends hung down to the ankles. (*g*) The breeches or drawers, of linen, covered the loins and thighs ; and (*h*) The bonnet was a turban of linen, partially covering the head, but not in the form of a cone like that of the high priest when the mitre was added to it. These last four were common to all priests. The high priest alone was permitted to enter the holy of holies, which he did once a year, on the great day of atonement, when he sprinkled the blood of the sin offering on the mercy seat, and burnt incense within the veil. Lev. 16. The manslayer might not leave the city of refuge during the lifetime of the existing high priest. It was also forbidden to the high priest to follow a funeral, or rend his clothes for the dead. It does not appear by whose authority the high priests were appointed to their office before there were kings of Israel. After this the office seems to have been used for political rather than religious purposes. Though at first chosen for life, we find that Solomon deposed Abiathar, 1 Kings 2 : 35, and that Herod appointed a number of high priests, which may account for there being at least two living in Christ's time, Annas and Caiaphas. Luke 3 : 2. The usual age for entering upon the functions of the priesthood, according to 2 Chron. 31 : 17, is considered to have been 20 years, though a priest or high priest was not actually incapacitated if he had attained to puberty. Again, according to Lev. 21 : 17–21, no one that had a blemish could officiate at the altar.

The theological view of the high priesthood does not fall within the scope of this work. It must suffice therefore to indicate that such a view would embrace the consideration of the office, dress, functions and ministrations of the high priest, considered as typical of the priesthood of our Lord Jesus Christ, and as setting forth under shadows the truths which are openly taught under the gospel. This has been done to a great extent in the Epistle to the Hebrews. It would also embrace all the moral and spiritual teaching supposed to be intended by such symbols.

Highways. Though during the sway of the Romans over Palestine they made a few substantial roads for their carts and chariots, yet for the most of the time, as to-day, the Jews had nothing such as we call roads, but only footpaths through which animals walk in single file. These are never cared for; no repairs are made or obstacles removed. This fact brings into striking prominence the figure of preparing a highway for the return of the captives, or the coming of the great King. On special occasions kings had roads prepared for the progress of their armies, or their own going from place to place.—ED.

Hi'len (*place of caves*), the name of a city of Judah allotted with its suburbs to the priests. 1 Chron. 6 : 58.

Hilki'ah (*God is my portion*). 1. Father of Eliakim. 2 Kings 18 : 37 ; Isa. 22 : 20 ; 36 : 22. [ELIAKIM.]

2. High priest in the reign of Josiah. 2 Kings 22 : 4, *seq.* ; 2 Chron. 34 : 9, *seq.* ; 1 Esd. 1 : 8. (B.C. 623.) His high priesthood was rendered particularly illustrious by the great reformation effected under it by King Josiah, by the solemn Passover kept at Jerusalem in the 18th year of that king's reign, and above all by the discovery which he made of the book of the law of Moses in the temple.

3. A Merarite Levite, son of Amzi. 1 Chron. 6 : 45 ; hebr. 30.

4. Another Merarite Levite, second son of Hosah. 1 Chron. 26 : 11.

5. One of those who stood on the right hand of Ezra when he read the law to the people ; doubtless a Levite, and probably a priest. Neh. 8 : 4. (B.C. 410.)

6. A priest of Anathoth, father of the prophet Jeremiah. Jer. 1 : 1. (B.C. before 628.)

7. Father of Gemariah, who was one of Zedekiah's envoys to Babylon. Jer. 29 : 3. (B.C. long before 587.)

Hil'lel (*praise*), a native of Pirathon in Mount Ephraim, father of Abdon, one of the judges of Israel. Judges 12 : 13, 15.

Hills. From the Hebrew *gibeah*, meaning a curved round hill. But our translators have also employed the same English word for the very different term *har*, which has a much more extended sense than *gibeah*, meaning a whole district. For instance, in Ex. 24 : 4 the " hill " is the same which is elsewhere in the same chapter, vs. 12, 13, 18, etc., and book consistently and accurately rendered " mount" and " mountain." The "country of the hills," in Deut. 1 : 7 ; Josh. 9 : 1 ; 10 : 40 ; 11 : 16, is the elevated district of Judah, Benjamin and Ephraim, which is correctly called " the mountain " in the earliest descriptions of Palestine, Num. 13 : 29, and in many subsequent passages.

Hin. [WEIGHTS AND MEASURES.]

Hind, the female of the common stag or *Cervus elaphus.* It is frequently noticed in the poetical parts of Scripture as emblematic of activity, Gen. 49 : 21 ; Ps. 18 : 33, gentleness, Prov. 5 : 19, feminine modesty, Cant. 2 : 7 ; 3 : 5, earnest longing, Ps. 42 : 1, and maternal affection. Jer. 14 : 5. Its shyness and remoteness from the haunts of men are also alluded to, Job 39 : 1, and its timidity, causing it to cast its young at the sound of thunder. Ps. 29 : 9.

Hinge. Both ancient Egyptian and modern Oriental doors were and are hung by means of pivots turning in sockets on both the upper and lower sides. 1 Kings 7 : 50. In Syria, and especially the Haurân, there are many ancient doors consisting of stone slabs with pivots carved out of the same piece, inserted in sockets above and below, and fixed during the building of the house. The allusion in Prov. 26 : 14 is thus clearly explained.

Hin'nom (*lamentation*), **Valley of,** otherwise called " the valley of the son " or " children of Hinnom," a deep and narrow ravine, with steep, rocky sides, to the south and west of Jerusalem, separating Mount Zion to the north from the " hill of evil counsel," and the sloping rocky plateau of the " plain of Rephaim " to the south. The earliest mention of the valley of Hinnom is in Josh. 15 : 8 ; 18 : 16, where the boundary line between the tribes of Judah and Benjamin is described as passing along the bed of the ravine. On the southern brow, overlooking the valley at its eastern extremity, Solomon erected high places for Molech,

1 Kings 11 : 7, whose horrid rites were revived from time to time in the same vicinity by the later idolatrous kings. Ahaz and Manasseh made their children "pass through the fire" in this valley, 2 Kings 16 : 3; 2 Chron. 28 : 3; 33 : 6, and the fiendish custom of infant sacrifice to the fire-gods seems to have been kept up in Tophet, which was another name for this place. To put an end to these abominations the place was polluted by Josiah, who rendered it ceremonially unclean by spreading over it human bones and other corruptions, 2 Kings 23 : 10, 13, 14; 2 Chron. 34 : 4, 5, from which time it appears to have become the common cesspool of the city, into which its sewage was conducted, to be carried off by the waters of the Kidron. From its ceremonial defilement, and from the detested and abominable fire of Molech, if not from the supposed ever-burning funeral piles, the later Jews applied the name of this valley—*Ge Hinnom*, *Gehenna* (land of Hinnom)—to denote the place of eternal torment. In this sense the word is used by our Lord. Matt. 5 : 29; 10 : 28; 23 : 15; Mark 9 : 43; Luke 12 : 5.

Hippopotamus. [BEHEMOTH.]

Hi'rah (*a noble race*), an Adullamite, the friend of Judah. Gen. 38 : 1, 12; and see 20.

Hi'ram, or **Hu'ram** (*noble*). 1. The king of Tyre who sent workmen and materials to Jerusalem, first, 2 Sam. 5 : 11; 1 Chron. 14 : 1, to build a palace for David (B.C. 1064), whom he ever loved, 1 Kings 5 : 1, and again, 1 Kings 5 : 10; 7 : 13; 2 Chron. 2, 16, to build the temple for Solomon, with whom he had a treaty of peace and commerce. 1 Kings 5 : 11, 12. He admitted Solomon's ships, issuing from Joppa, to a share in the profitable trade of the Mediterranean, 1 Kings 10 : 22; and the Jewish sailors, under the guidance of Tyrians, were taught to bring the gold of India, 1 Kings 9 : 26, to Solomon's two harbors on the Red Sea.

2. Hiram was the name of a man of mixed race, 1 Kings 7 : 13, 40, the principal architect and engineer sent by King Hiram to Solomon.

Hit'tites (*descendants of Heth*), **The,** the nation descended from Cheth (Authorized Version HETH), the second son of Canaan. Abraham bought from the "children of Heth" the field and the cave of Machpelah, belonging to Ephron the Hittite. They were then settled at the town which was afterwards, under its new name of Hebron, to become one of the most famous cities of Palestine, and which then bore the name of Kirjath-arba. Gen. 23 : 19; 25 : 9. When the Israelites entered the promised land, we find the Hittites taking part against the invader, in equal alliance with the other Canaanite tribes. Josh. 9 : 1; 11 : 3, etc. Henceforward the notices of the Hittites are very few and faint. We meet with two individuals, both attached to the person of David—1. "Ahimelech the Hittite," 1 Sam. 26 : 6; 2. "Uriah the Hittite," one of "the thirty" of David's body-guard. 2 Sam. 23 : 39; 1 Chron. 11 : 41.

Hi'vites (*villagers*), **The,** descendants—the sixth in order—of Canaan the son of Ham. Gen. 10 : 17; 1 Chron. 1 : 15. We first encounter the actual people of the Hivites at the time of Jacob's return to Canaan. Gen. 34 : 2. We next meet with the Hivites during the conquest of Canaan. Josh. 9 : 7; 11 : 19. The main body of the Hivites were at this time living on the northern confines of western Palestine—"under Hermon, in the land of Mizpeh," Josh. 11 : 3—"in Mount Lebanon, from Mount Baal Hermon to the entering in of Hamath." Judges 3 : 3; comp. 2 Sam. 24 : 7.

Hizki'ah (*might of Jehovah*), an ancestor of Zephaniah the prophet. Zeph. 1 : 1. (B.C. before 635.)

Hizki'jah (*might of Jehovah*), one of those who sealed the covenant with Nehemiah. Neh. 10 : 17. (B.C. 410.)

Ho'bab (*beloved*). This name is found in two places only—Num. 10 : 29; Judges 4 : 11. Hobab was brother-in-law to Moses. (B.C. 1530.)

Ho'bah (*hiding-place*), the place to which Abraham pursued the kings who had pillaged Sodom. Gen. 14 : 15. It was situated "to the north of Damascus."

Hod (*splendor*), one of the sons of Zophah, among the descendants of Asher. 1 Chron. 7 : 37.

Hoda'iah (*praise ye Jehovah*), son of the royal line of Judah. 1 Chron. 3 : 24. (B.C. about 406.)

Hodavi'ah (*praise ye Jehovah*). 1. A man of Manasseh, one of the heads of the half tribe on the east of Jordan. 1 Chron. 5 : 24. (B.C. 720.)

2. A man of Benjamin, son of Hassenuah. 1 Chron. 9 : 7.

3. A Levite, who seems to have given

his name to an important family in the tribe. Ezra 2 : 40. (B.C. before 536.)

Ho'desh (*new moon*), a woman named in the genealogies of Benjamin, 1 Chron. 8 : 9, as the wife of Shaharaim.

Hode'vah (*praise ye Jehovah*). Neh. 7 : 43. [HODAVIAH.]

Hodi'ah (*majesty of Jehovah*), one of the two wives of Ezra, a man of Judah. 1 Chron. 4 : 19. She is doubtless the same person as Jehudijah in ver. 18.

Hodi'jah (*majesty of Jehovah*). 1. A Levite in the time of Ezra and Nehemiah. Neh. 8 : 7; and probably also 9 : 5; 10 : 10. (B.C. 410.)

2. Another Levite at the same time. Neh. 10 : 13.

3. A layman ; one of the "heads" of the people at the same time. Neh. 10 : 18.

Hog'lah (*partridge*), the third of the five daughters of Zelophehad. Num. 26 : 33; 27 : 1; 36 : 11; Josh. 17 : 3. (B.C. 1450.)

Ho'ham (*whom Jehovah impels*), king of Hebron at the time of the conquest of Canaan. Josh. 10 : 3. (B.C. 1450.)

Holofer'nes, or more correctly OLO-FERNES, was, according to the book of Judith, a general of Nebuchadnezzar king of the Assyrians, Judith 2 : 4, who was slain by the Jewish heroine Judith during the siege of Bethulia. (B.C. 350.)

Ho'lon (*sandy*). 1. A town in the mountains of Judah ; one of the first group, of which Debir was apparently the most considerable. Josh. 15 : 51 ; 21 : 15. [HILEN.]

2. A city of Moab. Jer. 48 : 21 only. No identification of it has yet taken place.

Ho'mam (*destruction*), the form under which, in 1 Chron. 1 : 39, an Edomite name appears, which in Gen. 36 : 22 is given HEMAM.

Homer. [WEIGHTS AND MEASURES.]

Honey. The Hebrew *dĕbash* in the first place applies to the product of the bee, to which exclusively we give the name of honey. All travellers agree in describing Palestine as a land "flowing with milk and honey," Ex. 3 : 8; bees being abundant even in the remote parts of the wilderness, where they deposit their honey in the crevices of rocks or in hollow trees. In some parts of northern Arabia the hills are so well stocked with bees that no sooner are hives placed than they are occupied. In the second place

the term *dĕbash* applies to a decoction of the juice of the grape, which is still called *dibs,* and which forms an article of commerce in the East ; it was this, and not ordinary bee-honey, which Jacob sent to Joseph, Gen. 43 : 11, and which the Tyrians purchased from Palestine. Ezek. 27 : 17. A third kind has been described by some writers as "vegetable" honey, by which is meant the exudations of certain trees and shrubs, such as the *Tamarix mannifera,* found in the peninsula of Sinai, or the stunted oaks of Luristan and Mesopotamia. The honey which Jonathan ate in the wood, 1 Sam. 14 : 25, and the "wild honey" which supported John the Baptist, Matt. 3 : 4, have been referred to this species. But it was probably the honey of wild bees.

Hook, Hooks. Various kinds of hooks are noticed in the Bible, of which the following are the most important : 1. Fishing hooks. Job 41 : 2 ; Isa. 19 : 8; Hab. 1 : 15. 2. A *ring,* such as in our country is placed through the nose of a bull, and similarly used in the East for leading about lions—Ezek. 19 : 4, where the Authorized Version has "with chains"—camels and other animals. Called "thorn" in Job 41 : 2. A similar method was adopted for leading prisoners. 2 Chron. 33 : 11. 3. The hooks of the pillars of the tabernacle. Ex. 26 : 32, 37 ; 27 : 10 ff.; 38 : 13 ff. 4. A vine-dresser's pruning-hook. Isa. 2 : 4; 18 :

Flesh-Hooks.

5; Micah 4 : 3; Joel 3 : 10. 5. A flesh-hook for getting up the joints of meat out of the boiling-pot. Ex. 27 : 3; 1 Sam. 2 : 13, 14. 6. Probably "hooks" used for the purpose of hanging up animals to flay them. Ezek. 40 : 43.

Hoph'ni (*pugilist*) and PHINEHAS (*brazen mouth*), the two sons of Eli, who fulfilled their hereditary sacerdotal duties at Shiloh. Their brutal rapacity and lust, 1 Sam. 2 : 12–17, 22, filled the people with disgust and indignation, and provoked the curse which was denounced against their father's house, first by an unknown prophet, 1 Sam. 2 : 27–36, and then by Samuel. ch. 3 : 11–14. They were both cut off in one day in the flower of their age, and the ark which they had accompanied to battle against the Philistines was lost on the same occasion. 1 Sam. 4 : 10, 11. (B.C. 1130.)

Mount Hor.

Hor (*mountain*), **Mount.** 1. The mountain on which Aaron died. Num. 20 : 25, 27. It was "on the boundary line," Num. 20 : 23, or "at the edge," ch. 33 : 37, of the land of Edom. It was the halting-place of the people next after Kadesh, ch. 20 : 22 ; 33 : 37, and they quitted it for Zalmonah, ch. 33 : 41, in the road to the Red Sea. ch. 21 : 4. It was during the encampment at Kadesh that Aaron was gathered to his fathers. Mount Hor is situated on the eastern side of the great valley of the *Arabah*, the highest and most conspicuous of the whole range of the sandstone mountains of Edom, having close beneath it on its eastern side the mysterious city of Petra. It is now the *Jebel Nebi-Harûn*, "the mountain of the prophet Aaron." Its height is 4800 feet above the Mediterranean ; that is to say, about 1700 feet above the town of Petra, 4000 above the level of the Arabah, and more than 6000

above the Dead Sea. The mountain is marked far and near by its double top, which rises like a huge castellated building from a lower base, and is surmounted by a circular dome of the tomb of Aaron, a distinct white spot on the dark red surface of the mountain. The chief interest of Mount Hor consists in the prospect from its summit, the last view of Aaron—that view which was to him what Pisgah was to his brother.

2. A mountain, entirely distinct from the preceding, named in Num. 34 : 7, 8 only, as one of the marks of the northern boundary of the land which the children of Israel were to conquer. This Mount Hor is the great chain of Lebanon itself.

Ho′ram (*mountainous*), king of Gezer at the time of the conquest of the southwestern part of Palestine. Josh. 10 : 33.

Ho′reb (*desert*). [SINAI.]

Ho′rem (*sacred*), one of the fortified places in the territory of Naphtali ; named with Iron and Migdal-el. Josh. 19 : 38. Van de Velde suggests *Hurah* as the site of Horem.

Hor-hagid′gad (*conspicuous mountain*), the name of the desert station where the Israelites encamped, Num. 33 : 32 ; probably the same as Gudgodah. Deut. 10 : 7.

Ho′ri (*cave-dweller*). 1. A Horite, son of Lotan the son of Seir. Gen. 36 : 22 ; 1 Chron. 1 : 39 ; Gen. 36 : 30.

2. A man of Simeon, father of Shaphat. Num. 13 : 5.

Ho′rim and **Ho′rites** (*descendants of Hori*), the aboriginal inhabitants of Mount Seir, Gen. 14 : 6, and probably allied to the Emim and Rephaim. The name *Horite* appears to have been derived from their habits as "cave-dwellers." Their excavated dwellings are still found in hundreds in the sandstone cliffs and mountains of Edom, and especially in Petra.

Hor′mah (*a place laid waste*), or ZEPHATH, Judges 1 : 17, was the chief town of a king of a Canaanitish tribe on the south of Palestine, which was reduced by Joshua, and became a city of the territory of Judah, Josh. 15 : 30 ; 1 Sam. 30 : 30, but apparently belonged to Simeon. 1 Chron. 4 : 30.

Horn. The word "horn" is often used metaphorically to signify strength and honor, because horns are the chief weapons and ornaments of the animals which possess them ; hence they are also used as a type of victory. Of *strength* the horn of the unicorn was the most frequent representative, Deut. 33 : 17, etc., but not always; comp. 1 Kings 22 : 11, where probably horns of iron, worn defiantly and symbolically on the head, are intended. Among the Druses upon

Horns worn as Head-ornaments by modern Orientals.

Mount Lebanon the married women wear silver horns on their heads. In the sense of *honor*, the word horn stands for the *abstract*—" my horn," Job 16 : 15 ; " all the horn of Israel," Lam. 2 : 3—and so for the supreme authority. It also stands for the *concrete*, whence it comes to mean king, kingdom. Dan. 8 : 2, etc.; Zech. 1 : 18. Out of either or both of these last two metaphors sprang the idea of representing gods with horns.

Hornet. The hornet bears a general resemblance to the common wasp, only it is larger. It is exceedingly fierce and voracious, especially in hot climates, and its sting is frequently dangerous. In Scripture the hornet is referred to only as the means which Jehovah employed for the extirpation of the Canaanites. Ex. 23 : 28; Deut. 7 : 20; Josh. 24 : 12; Wisd. 12 : 8. (It is said that the Phaselitæ, a Phœnician people, were driven from their locality by hornets; and other examples are given in Paxton's " Illustrations of Scripture," 1 : 303.—ED.)

Horona'im (*two caverns*), a town of Moab, possibly a sanctuary, named with Zoar and Luhith. Isa. 15 : 5 ; Jer. 48 : 3, 5, 34.

Hor'onite (*native of Horonaim*), **The,** the designation of Sanballat. Neh. 2 : 10, 19 ; 13 : 28. It is derived by Gesenius from Horonaim.

Horse. The most striking feature in the biblical notices of the horse is the exclusive application of it to warlike operations ; in no instance is that useful animal employed for the purposes of ordinary locomotion or agriculture, if we except Isa. 28 : 28. The animated description of the horse in Job 39 : 19-25 applies solely to the war-horse. The Hebrews in the patriarchal age, as a pastoral race, did not stand in need of the services of the horse, and for a long period after their settlement in Canaan they dispensed with it, partly in consequence of the hilly nature of the country, which only admitted of the use of chariots in certain localities, Judges 1 : 19, and partly in consequence of the prohibition in Deut. 17 : 16, which would be held to apply at all periods. David first established a force of cavalry and chariots, 2 Sam. 8 : 4; but the great supply of horses was subsequently effected by Solomon through his connection with Egypt. 1 Kings 4 : 26. Solomon also established a very active trade in horses, which were brought by dealers out of Egypt and resold, at a profit, to the Hittites. With regard to the trappings and management of the horse we have little information. The bridle was placed over the horse's nose, Isa. 30 : 28, and a bit or curb is also mentioned. 2 Kings 19 : 28; Ps. 32 : 9; Prov. 26 : 3 ; Isa. 37 : 29. In the Authorized Version it is incorrectly given " bridle," with the exception of Ps. 32. Saddles were not used until a late period. The horses were not shod, and therefore hoofs as hard " as flint," Isa. 5 : 28, were regarded as a great merit. The chariot-horses were covered with embroidered trappings. Ezek. 27 : 20. Horses and chariots were used also in idolatrous processions, as noticed in regard to the sun. 2 Kings 23 : 11.

Horse-leech, Heb. *'ălûkâh,* occurs once only, viz. Prov. 30 : 15. There is little doubt that *'ălûkâh* denotes some species of leech, or rather is the generic term for any blood-sucking annelid.

Ho'sah (*refuge*), a city of Asher, Josh. 19 : 29, the next landmark on the boundary to Tyre.

Ho'sah, a Merarite Levite, 1 Chron. 26 : 10, chosen by David to be one of the first doorkeepers to the ark after its arrivai in Jerusalem. 1 Chron. 16:38. (B.C. 1014.)

Hosanna (*save now*). "Save, we pray!" the cry of the multitudes as they thronged in our Lord's triumphal procession into Jerusalem. Matt. 21:9, 15; Mark 11:9, 10; John 12:13. The Psalm from which it was taken, the 118th, was one with which they were familiar from being accustomed to recite the 25th and 26th verses at the feast of tabernacles, forming a part of the great hallel. Ps. 113–118.

Hose'a (*salvation*), son of Beeri, and first of the minor prophets. Probably the life, or rather the prophetic career, of Hosea extended from B.C. 784 to 725, a period of fifty-nine years. The prophecies of Hosea were delivered in the kingdom of Israel. Jeroboam II. was on the throne, and Israel was at the height of its earthly splendor. Nothing is known of the prophet's life excepting what may be gained from his book.

Hose'a, Prophecies of. This book consists of fourteen chapters. It is easy to recognize two great divisions in the book: (1) ch. 1 to 3; (2) ch. 4 to end. The subdivision of these several parts is a work of greater difficulty. 1. The first division should probably be subdivided into three separate poems, each originating in a distinct aim, and each after its own fashion attempting to express the idolatry of Israel by imagery borrowed from the matrimonial relation. 2. Attempts have been made to subdivide the second part of the book. These divisions are made either according to reigns of contemporary kings or according to the subject-matter of the poem. The prophecies were probably collected by Hosea himself toward the end of his career. Of his style Eichhorn says, "His discourse is like a garland woven of a multiplicity of flowers; images are woven upon images, metaphor strung upon metaphor. Like a bee he flies from one flower-bed to another, that he may suck his honey from the most varied pieces. . . . Often he is prone to approach to allegory; often he sinks down in obscurity."

Hoshai'ah (*whom Jehovah aids*). 1. A man who assisted in the dedication of the wall of Jerusalem after it had been rebuilt by Nehemiah. Neh. 12:32. (B.C. 446.)

2. The father of a certain Jezaniah or Azariah, who was a man of note after the destruction of Jerusalem by Nebu-

chadnezzar. Jer. 42:1; 43:2. (B.C. after 588.)

Hosh'ama (*whom Jehovah hears*), one of the sons of Jeconiah or Jehoiachin, the last king but one of Judah. 1 Chron. 3:18.

Hoshe'a (*salvation*). 1. The nineteenth, last and best king of Israel. He succeeded Pekah, whom he slew in a successful conspiracy, thereby fulfilling a prophecy of Isaiah. Isa. 7:16. In the third year of his reign (B.C. 726) Shalmaneser cruelly stormed the strong caves of Beth-arbel, Hos. 8:14, and made Israel tributary, 2 Kings 17:3, for three years. At the end of this period Hoshea entered into a secret alliance with So, king of Egypt, to throw off the Assyrian yoke. The alliance did him no good; it was revealed to the court of Nineveh by the Assyrian party in Ephraim, and Hoshea was immediately seized as a rebellious vassal, shut up in prison, and apparently treated with the utmost indignity. Micah 5:1. Of the subsequent fortunes of Hoshea nothing is known.

2. The son of Nun, *i. e.* Joshua, Deut. 32:44; and also in Num. 13:8, though there the Authorized Version has OSHEA.

3. Son of Azaziah, 1 Chron 27:20; like his great namesake, a man of Ephraim, ruler of his tribe in the time of King David. (B.C. 1019.)

4. One of the heads of the people who sealed the covenant with Nehemiah. Neh. 10:23. (B.C. 410.)

Hospitality. Hospitality was regarded by most nations of the ancient world as one of the chief virtues. The Jewish laws respecting strangers, Lev. 19:33, 34, and the poor, Lev. 25:14, *seq.*; Deut. 15:7, and concerning redemption, Lev. 25:23, *seq.*, etc., are framed in accordance with the spirit of hospitality. In the law compassion to strangers is constantly enforced by the words "for ye were strangers in the land of Egypt." Lev. 19:34. And before the law, Abraham's entertainment of the angels, Gen. 18:1, *seq.*, and Lot's, Gen. 19:1, are in exact agreement with its precepts, and with modern usage. Comp. Ex. 2:20; Judges 13:15; 19:17, 20, 21. In the New Testament hospitality is yet more markedly enjoined; and in the more civilized state of society which then prevailed, its exercise became more a social virtue than a necessity of patri-

archal life. The good Samaritan stands
for all ages as an example of Christian
hospitality. The neglect of Christ is
symbolized by inhospitality to our neighbors. Matt. 25 : 43. The apostles urged
the Church to "follow after hospitality,"
Rom. 12 : 13 ; cf. 1 Tim. 5 : 10 ; to remember Abraham's example, Heb. 13 : 2 ; to
"use hospitality one to another without
grudging," 1 Pet. 4 : 9 ; while a bishop
must be a "lover of hospitality." Titus
1 : 8, cf. 1 Tim. 3 : 2. The practice of the
early Christians was in accord with these
precepts. They had all things in common, and their hospitality was a
characteristic of their belief. In
the patriarchal ages we may take
Abraham's example as the most
fitting, as we have of it the fullest
account. "The account," says Mr.
Lane, "of Abraham's entertaining
the three angels, related in the
Bible, presents a perfect picture of
the manner in which a modern Be-
dawee sheikh receives travellers
arriving at his encampment." The
Oriental respect for the covenant
of bread and salt, or salt alone,
certainly sprang from the high
regard in which hospitality was
held.

Ho'tham (*signet ring*), a man of
Asher, son of Heber, of the family of Beriah. 1 Chron. 7 : 32. (B.C. 1490.)

Ho'than (*signet ring*), a man of Aroer,
father of Shama and Jehiel. 1 Chron. 11 :
44. (B.C. 1046.)

Ho'thir (*fullness*), the thirteenth son
of Heman, "the king's seer," 1 Chron.
25 : 4, 28, and therefore a Kohathite Levite. (B.C. 1014.)

Hour. The ancient Hebrews were
probably unacquainted with the division
of the natural day into twenty-four parts ;
but they afterwards parcelled out the
period between sunrise and sunset into a
series of divisions distinguished by the
sun's course. The early Jews appear to
have divided the day into *four* parts,
Neh. 9 : 3, and the night into three
watches, Judges 7 : 19 ; and even in the
New Testament we find a trace of this
division in Matt. 20 : 1–5. At what period
the Jews first became acquainted with
the division of the day into twelve hours
is unknown, but it is generally supposed
they learned it from the Babylonians
during the captivity. It was known to
the Egyptians at a very early period.
They had twelve hours of the day and

of the night. There are two kinds of
hours, viz. (1) the astronomical or equinoctial hour, *i. e.* the 24th part of a civil
day, and (2) the natural hour, *i. e.* the 12th
part of the natural day, or of the time between sunrise and sunset. These are the
hours meant in the New Testament, John
11 : 9, etc., and it must be remembered
that they perpetually vary in length, so
as to be very different at different times of
the year. For the purpose of prayer the
old division of the day into four portions
was continued in the temple service, as
we see from Acts 2 : 15 ; 3 : 1 ; 10 : 9.

Upper Room.

House. The houses of the rural poor
in Egypt, as well as in most parts of
Syria, Arabia and Persia, are generally
mere huts of mud or sunburnt bricks. In
some parts of Palestine and Arabia stone
is used, and in certain districts caves in
the rocks are used as dwellings. Amos 5 :
11. The houses are usually of one story
only, viz., the ground floor, and often
contain only one apartment. Sometimes
a small court for the cattle is attached ;
and in some cases the cattle are housed
in the same building, or the people live
on a raised platform, and the cattle round
them on the ground. 1 Sam. 28 : 24. The
windows are small apertures high up in
the walls, sometimes grated with wood.
The roofs are commonly but not always
flat, and are usually formed of a plaster
of mud and straw laid upon boughs or
rafters ; and upon the flat roofs, tents or
"booths" of boughs or rushes are often
raised to be used as sleeping-places in
summer. The difference between the
poorest houses and those of the class next
above them is greater than between these
and the houses of the first rank. The
prevailing plan of eastern houses of this
class presents, as was the case in ancient

Egypt, a front of wall, whose blank and mean appearance is usually relieved only by the door and a few latticed and projecting windows. Within this is a court or courts with apartments opening

Court of an Eastern House.

into them. Over the door is a projecting window with a lattice more or less elaborately wrought, which, except in times of public celebrations, is usually closed, 2 Kings 9 : 30. An awning is sometimes drawn over the court, and the floor strewed with carpets on festive occasions. The stairs to the upper apartments are in Syria usually in a corner of the court. Around part, if not the whole, of the court is a veranda, often nine or ten feet deep, over which, when there is more than one floor, runs a second gallery of like depth, with a balustrade. When there is no second floor, but more than one court, the women's apartments—*hareem, harem* or *haram*—are usually in the second court; otherwise they form a separate building within the general enclosure, or are above on the first floor. When there is an upper story, the *ka'ah* forms the most important apartment, and thus probably answers to the "upper room," which was often the guest-chamber. Luke 22 : 12; Acts 1 : 13; 9 : 37; 20 : 8. The windows of the upper rooms often project one or two feet, and form a kiosk or latticed chamber. Such may have been "the chamber in the wall." 2 Kings 4 : 10, 11. The "lattice," through which Ahaziah fell, per-

haps belonged to an upper chamber of this kind, 2 Kings 1 : 2, as also the "third loft," from which Eutychus fell. Acts 20 : 9; comp. Jer. 22 : 13. Paul preached in such a room on account of its superior size and retired position. The outer circle in an audience in such a room sat upon a dais, or upon cushions elevated so as to be as high as the window-sill. From such a position Eutychus could easily fall.

There are usually no special bedrooms in eastern houses. The outer doors are closed with a wooden lock, but in some cases the apartments are divided from each other by curtains only. There are no chimneys, but fire is made when required with charcoal in a chafing-dish; or a fire of wood might be kindled in the open court of the house. Luke 22 : 55. Some houses in Cairo have an apartment open in front to the court, with two or more arches and a railing, and a pillar to support the wall above. It was in a chamber of this kind, probably one of the largest size to be found in a palace, that our Lord was being arraigned before the high priest at the time when the denial of him by St. Peter took place. He "turned and looked" on Peter as he stood by the fire in the

Outer Staircase of an Eastern House.

court, Luke 22 : 56, 61; John 18 : 24, whilst he himself was in the "hall of judgment."

In no point do Oriental domestic habits differ more from European than in the use of the roof. Its flat surface is made useful for various household purposes, as drying corn, hanging up linen, and preparing figs and raisins. The roofs are used as places of recreation in the evening, and often as sleeping-places at night. 1 Sam. 9 : 25, 26 ; 2 Sam. 11 : 2 ; 16 : 22 ; Job 27 : 18 ; Prov. 21 : 9 ; Dan. 4 : 29. They were also used as places for devotion and even idolatrous worship. 2 Kings 23 : 12 ; Jer. 19 : 13 ; 32 : 29 ; Zeph. 1 : 5 ; Acts 10 : 9. At the time of the feast of tabernacles booths were erected by the Jews on the tops of their houses. Protection

Eastern Battlemented House.

of the roof by parapets was enjoined by the law. Deut. 22 : 8. Special apartments were devoted in larger houses to winter and summer uses. Jer. 36 : 22 ; Amos 3 : 15. The ivory house of Ahab was probably a palace largely ornamented with inlaid ivory. The circumstance of Samson's pulling down the house by means of the pillars may be explained by the fact of the company being assembled on tiers of balconies above each other, supported by central pillars on the basement ; when these were pulled down the whole of the upper floors would fall also. Judges 16 : 26.

Huk'kok (*incised*), a place on the boundary of Naphtali. Josh. 19 : 34. It has been recovered in *Yakuk*, a village in the mountains of Naphtali, west of the upper end of the Sea of Galilee.

Hu'kok, a name which in 1 Chron. 6 : 75 is erroneously used for HELKATH, which see.

Hul (*circle*), the second son of Aram,

and grandson of Shem. Gen. 10 : 23. The strongest evidence is in favor of the district about the roots of Lebanon.

Hul'dah (*weasel*), a prophetess, whose husband, Shallum, was keeper of the wardrobe in the time of King Josiah. It was to her that Josiah had recourse, when Hilkiah found a book of the law, to procure an authoritative opinion on it. 2 Kings 22 : 14 : 2 Chron. 34 : 22. (B.C. 623.)

Hum'tah (*place of lizards*), a city of Judah, one of those in the mountain district, the next to Hebron. Josh. 15 : 54.

Hunting. Hunting, as a matter of necessity, whether for the extermination of dangerous beasts or for procuring sustenance, betokens a rude and semi-civilized state ; as an amusement, it betokens an advanced state. The Hebrews, as a pastoral and agricultural people, were not given to the sports of the field ; the density of the population, the earnestness of their character, and the tendency of their ritual regulations, particularly those affecting food, all combined to discourage the practice of hunting. The manner of catching animals was, first, either by digging a pitfall, or, secondly, by a trap which was set under ground, Job 18 : 10, in the run of the animal, Prov. 22 : 5, and caught it by the leg, Job 18 : 9 ; or lastly by the use of the net, of which there were various kinds, as for the gazelle, Isa. 51 : 20, Authorized Version, "wild bull," and other animals of that class.

Hu'pham (*coast-man*), a son of Benjamin, founder of the family of the Huphamites. Num. 26 : 39. (B.C. 1688.)

Hu'phamites, The, descendants of Hupham, of the tribe of Benjamin. Num. 26 : 39.

Hup'pah (*protected*), a priest in the time of David. 1 Chron. 24 : 13.

Hup'pim (*protected*), head of a Benjamite family. Gen. 46 : 21 ; 1 Chron. 7 : 12.

Hur (*hole*). 1. A man who is mentioned with Moses and Aaron on the occasion of the battle with Amalek at Rephidim, Ex. 17 : 10, when with Aaron he stayed up the hands of Moses. ver. 12. (B.C. 1491.) He is mentioned again in ch. 24 : 14 as being, with Aaron, left in charge of the people by Moses during his ascent of Sinai. The Jewish tradition is that he was the husband of Miriam, and that he was identical with

2. The grandfather of Bezaleel, the chief artificer of the tabernacle. Ex. 31 : 2 ; 35 : 30 ; 38 : 22.

3. The fourth of the five kings of Midian who were slain with Balaam after the "matter of Peor." Num. 31 : 8. (B.C. 1451.) In a later mention of them, Josh. 13 : 21, they are called princes of Midian and dukes.

4. Father of Rephaiah, who was ruler of half of the environs of Jerusalem, and assisted Nehemiah in the repair of the wall. Neh. 3 : 9. (B.C. before 446.)

5. The "son of Hur"—Ben-Hur —was commissariat officer for Solomon in Mount Ephraim. 1 Kings 4 : 8. (B.C. 995.)

Hu'ra-i, or **Hura'i** (*linen-weaver*), one of David's guard—Hurai of the torrents of Gaash, according to the list of 1 Chron. 11 : 32. [HIDDAI.]

Hu'ram (*noble born*). 1. A Benjamite ; son of Bela, the first-born of the patriarch. 1 Chron. 8 : 5.

2. The form in which the name of the king of Tyre in alliance with David and Solomon—and elsewhere given as HIRAM—appears in Chronicles. 1 Chron. 14 : 1 ; 2 Chron. 2 : 3, 11, 12 ; 8 : 2, 18 ; 9 : 10, 21.

3. The same change occurs in Chronicles in the name of Hiram the artificer, which is given as HURAM in 2 Chron. 2 : 13 ; 4 : 11, 16. [HIRAM.]

Hu'ri (*linen-weaver*), a Gadite ; father of Abihail. 1 Chron. 5 : 14.

Husband. [MARRIAGE.]

Hu'shah (*haste*), a name which occurs in the genealogies of the tribe of Judah. 1 Chron. 4 : 4.

Hu'sha-i, or **Husha'i** (*hasting*), an Archite, *i. e.* possibly an inhabitant of a place called Erec. 2 Sam. 15 : 32 ff. ; 16 : 16 ff. He is called the "friend" of David. 2 Sam. 15 : 37 ; comp. 1 Chron. 27 : 33. To him David confided the delicate and dangerous part of a pretended adherence to the cause of Absalom. (B.C. about 1023.) He was probably the father of Baana. 1 Kgs. 4 : 16.

Hu'sham (*haste*), one of the early kings of Edom. Gen. 36 : 34, 35 ; 1 Chron. 1 : 45, 46.

Hu'shathite (*inhabitant of Hushah*), **The,** the designation of two of the heroes of David's guard. 1. SIBBECHAI. 2 Sam.

21 : 18 ; 1 Chron. 11 : 29 ; 20 : 4 ; 27 : 11. Josephus, however, calls him a Hittite.

2. MEBUNNAI, 2 Sam. 23 : 27, a mere corruption of SIBBECHAI.

Hu'shim (*who makes haste*). 1. In Gen. 46 : 23 "the children of Dan" are said to have been Hushim. The name is plural, as if of a tribe rather than an individual. In Num. 26 : 42 the name is changed to Shuham.

2. A Benjamite, 1 Chron. 7 : 12 ; and here again apparently the plural nature of the name is recognized, and Hushim are stated to be "the sons of Aher."

3. One of the two wives of Shaharaim. 1 Chron. 8 : 8. (B.C. 1450.)

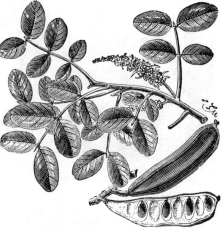

Husks of Swine—Carob Beans.

Husks. This word in Luke 15 : 16 describes really the fruit of a particular kind of tree, viz. the carob or *Ceratonia siliqua* of botanists. It belongs to the locust family. This tree is very commonly met with in Syria and Egypt ; it produces pods, shaped like a horn, varying in length from six to ten inches, and about a finger's breadth, or rather more ; it is dark-brown, glossy, filled with seeds, and has a sweetish taste. It is used much for food by the poor, and for the feeding of swine.

Huz (*light, sandy soil*), the eldest son of Nahor and Milcah. Gen. 22 : 21. (B.C. about 1900.)

Huz'zab (*fixed*), according to the general opinion of the Jews, was the queen of Nineveh at the time when Nahum delivered his prophecy. Nah. 2 : 7. (B.C. about 700.) The moderns follow the rendering in the margin of our English Bible—"that which was established." Still it is not improbable that after all Huzzab may really be a proper name. It may mean "the *Zab* country," or the fertile tract east of the Tigris, watered by the upper and lower *Zab* rivers.

Hyacinth, used in the Revised Version for *jacinth* in Rev. 9 : 17. It is simply another English spelling of the same Greek word.

Hyæna.

Hyæna. Authorities differ as to whether the term *tzábú'a* in Jer. 12 : 9 means a "hyæna" or a "speckled bird." The only other instance in which it occurs is as a proper name, Zeboim, 1 Sam. 13 : 18, "the valley of hyænas," Aquila; Neh. 11 : 34. The striped hyæna (*Hyæna striata*) is found in Africa, Asia Minor, Arabia and Persia, and is more common in Palestine than any other carnivorous animal, except perhaps the jackal. The hyæna is among the mammals what the vulture is among birds,—the scavenger of the wilderness, the woods and the shore. It often attacks animals, and sometimes digs up the dead bodies of men and beasts. From this last habit the hyæna has been regarded as a horrible and mysterious creature. Its teeth are so powerful that they can crack the bones of an ox with ease.—*Appleton's Encyc.* The hyæna was common in ancient as in modern Egypt, and is constantly depicted upon monuments; it must therefore have been well known to the Jews.

Hymenæ'us (*belonging to marriage*), the name of a person occurring twice in the correspondence between St. Paul and Timothy; the first time classed with Alexander, 1 Tim. 1 : 20, and the second time classed with Philetus. 2 Tim. 2 : 17, 18. (A.D. 65–7.) He denied the true doctrine of the resurrection.

Hymn, a religious song or psalm. Eph. 5 : 19; Col. 3 : 16. Our Lord and his apostles sung a hymn after the last supper. In the jail at Philippi, Paul and Silas "sang hymns" (Authorized Version "praises") unto God, and so loud was their song that their fellow prisoners heard them.

Hyssop. (Heb. *ézób*.) The *ézób* was used for sprinkling in some of the sacrifices and purifications of the Jews. In consequence of its detergent qualities, or from its being associated with the purificatory services, the Psalmist makes use of the expression, "Purge me with *ézób*." Ps. 51 : 7. It is described in 1 Kings 4 : 33 as growing on or near walls. (Besides being thus fit for sprinkling, having cleansing properties, and growing on walls, the true hyssop should be a plant common to Egypt, Sinai and Palestine, and capable of producing a stick three or four feet long, since on a stalk of hyssop the sponge of vinegar was held up to Christ on the cross. John 19 : 29. It is impossible to precisely identify the plant, probably because the name was given not to a particular plant but to a *family* of plants associated together by

Hyssop.

qualities easily noticed rather than by close botanical affinities. Different species of the family may have been used at

different times. The hyssop of the Bible is probably one (or all) of three plants:—
1. The common hyssop is "a shrub with low, bushy stalks 1½ feet high, small pear-shaped, close-setting opposite leaves, all the stalks and branches terminated by erect whorled spikes of flowers of different colors in the varieties. It is a hardy plant, with an aromatic smell and a warm, pungent taste; a native of the south of Europe and the East."—ED.)

2. Bochart decides in favor of marjoram, or some plant like it, and to this conclusion, it must be admitted, all ancient tradition points. (This is the *Origanum maru*, the *z'atar* of the Arabs. The French consul at Sidon exhibited to Dr. Thomson ("The Land and the Book," i. 161) a specimen of this "having the fragrance of thyme, with a hot, pungent taste, and long slender stems." Dr. Post of Beirut, in the American edition of Smith's large Dictionary, favors this view.—ED.)

3. But Dr. Royle, after a careful investigation of the subject, arrives at the conclusion that the hyssop is no other than the caper-plant, or *Capparis spinosa* of Linnæus. The Arabic name of this plant, *asuf*, by which it is sometimes, though not commonly, described, bears considerable resemblance to the Hebrew. "It is a bright-green creeper, which climbs from the fissures of the rocks, is supposed to possess cleansing properties, and is capable of yielding a stick to which a sponge might be attached."—*Stanley*, "Sinai and Palestine," 23. It produces a fruit the size of a walnut, called the mountain pepper.

I.

Ib′har (*whom God chooses*), one of the sons of David, 2 Sam. 5 : 15; 1 Chron. 3 : 6; 14 : 5, born in Jerusalem. (B.C. after 1044.)

Ib′le-am (*devouring the people*), a city of Manasseh, with villages or towns dependent on it. Judges 1 : 27. It appears to have been situated in the territory of either Issachar or Asher. Josh. ′7 : 11. The ascent of Gur was "at Ib-′am," 2 Kings 9 : 27, somewhere near the present *Jenin*, probably to the north of it.

Ibne′iah (*whom Jehovah will build up*), son of Jehoram, a Benjamite. 1 Chron. 9 : 8.

Ibni′jah (*whom Jehovah will build up*), a Benjamite. 1 Chron. 9 : 8.

Ib′ri (*Hebrew*), a Merarite Levite of the family of Jaaziah, 1 Chron. 24 : 27, in the time of David. (B.C. 1014.)

Ib′zan (*illustrious*), a native of Bethlehem of Zebulun, who judged Israel for seven years after Jephthah. Judges 12 : 8, 10. (B.C. 1137.)

Ich′abod (*inglorious*), the son of Phinehas and grandson of Eli. 1 Sam. 4 : 21. (B.C. about 1100.)

Iconium.

Ico′nium (*little image*), the modern *Konieh*, was the capital of Lycaonia, in Asia Minor. It was a large and rich city, 120 miles north from the Mediterranean Sea, at the foot of the Taurus mountains, and on the great line of communication between Ephesus and the western coast of the peninsula on one side, and Tarsus, Antioch and the Euphrates on the other. Iconium was a well-chosen place for missionary operations. Acts 14 : 1, 3, 21, 22; 16 : 1, 2; 18 : 23. Paul's first visit here was on his first circuit, in company with Barnabas; and on this occasion he approached it from Antioch in Pisidia, which lay to the west. The modern *Konieh* is between two and three miles in circumference, and contains over 30,000 inhabitants. It contains manufactories of carpets and leather.

Id′alah (*memorial of God*), one of the cities of the tribe of Zebulun, named between Shimron and Bethlehem. Josh. 19 : 15.

Id′bash (*stout*), one of the three sons of Abi-Etam, among the families of Judah. 1 Chron. 4 : 3.

Id′do (*timely* or *lovely*). 1. The father of Abinadab. 1 Kings 4 : 14.

2. A descendant of Gershom, son of Levi. 1 Chron. 6 : 21.

3. Son of Zechariah, ruler of the tribe of Manasseh east of Jordan in the time of David. 1 Chron. 27 : 21.   (B.C. 1014.)

4. A seer whose "visions" against Jeroboam incidentally contained some of the acts of Solomon. 2 Chron. 9 : 29. He appears to have written a chronicle or story relating to the life and reign of Abijah. 2 Chron. 13 : 22.   (B.C. 961.)

5. The grandfather of the prophet Zechariah. Zech. 1 : 1, 7.

6. The chief of those who assembled at Casiphia at the time of the second caravan from Babylon. He was one of the Nethinim. Ezra 8 : 17; comp. 20.   (B.C. 536.)

Idol. An image or anything used as an object of worship in place of the true

Egyptian Idols.

God. Among the earliest objects of worship, regarded as symbols of deity, were the meteoric stones, which the ancients believed to have been images of the gods sent down from heaven. From these they transferred their regard to rough unhewn blocks, to stone columns or pillars of wood, in which the divinity worshipped was supposed to dwell, and which were consecrated, like the sacred stone at Delphi, by being anointed with oil and crowned with wool on solemn days. Of the forms assumed by the idolatrous images we have not many traces in the Bible. Dagon, the fish-god of the Philistines, was a human figure terminating in a fish; and that the Syrian deities were represented in later times in a symbolical human shape we know for certainty. When the process of adorning the image was completed, it was placed in a temple or shrine appointed for it.

Epist. Jer. 12, 19; Wisd. 13 : 15; 1 Cor. 8 : 10.   From these temples the idols were sometimes carried in procession. Epist. Jer. 4, 26, on festival days. Their

The Idol Juggernaut.

priests were maintained from the idol treasury, and feasted upon the meats which were appointed for the idols' use. Bel and the Dragon 3, 13.

Idolatry, strictly speaking, denotes the worship of deity in a visible form, whether the images to which homage is paid are symbolical representations of the true God or of the false divinities which have been made the objects of worship in his stead.

I. *History of idolatry among the Jews.* —The first undoubted allusion to idolatry or idolatrous customs in the Bible is in the account of Rachel's stealing her father's teraphim. Gen. 31 : 19. During their long residence in Egypt the Israelites defiled themselves with the idols of the land, and it was long before the taint was removed. Josh. 24 : 14; Ezek. 20 : 7. In the wilderness they clamored for some visible shape in which they might worship the God who had brought them out of Egypt, Ex. 32, until Aaron made the calf, the embodiment of Apis and emblem of the productive power of nature. During the lives of Joshua and the elders who outlived him they kept true to their allegiance; but the generation following, who knew not Jehovah nor the works he had done for Israel, swerved from the plain path of their fathers, and were caught in the toils of the foreigner. Judges 2. From this time forth their history becomes little more than a chronicle of the inevitable sequence of offence and punishment. Judges 2 : 12, 14. By turns each conquering nation strove to establish the worship of its national god. In later times the practice of secret idolatry was carried to greater lengths. Images were set up on the corn-floors, in the wine-vats, and behind the doors of private houses, Isa. 57 : 8; Hos. 9 : 1, 2; and to check this tendency the statute in Deut. 27 : 15 was originally promulgated. Under Samuel's administration idolatry was publicly renounced, 1 Sam. 7 : 3–6; but in the reign of Solomon all this was forgotten, even Solomon's own heart being turned after other gods. 1 Kings 11 : 14. Rehoboam perpetuated the worst features of Solomon's idolatry, 1 Kings 14 : 22–24, erected golden calves at Bethel and at Dan, and by this crafty state policy severed forever the kingdoms of Judah and Israel. 1 Kings 12 : 26–33. The successors of Jeroboam followed in his steps, till Ahab. The conquest of the ten tribes by Shalmaneser was for them the last scene of the drama of abominations which had been enacted uninterruptedly for upwards of 250 years. Under Hezekiah a great reform was inaugurated, that was not confined to Judah and Benjamin, but spread throughout Ephraim and Manasseh, 2 Chron. 31 : 1, and to all external appearance idolatry was extirpated. But the reform extended little below the surface. Isa. 29 : 13. With the death of Josiah ended the last effort to revive among the people a purer ritual, if not a purer faith. The lamp of David, which had long shed but a struggling ray, flickered for a while and then went out in the darkness of Babylonian captivity. Though the conquests of Alexander caused Greek influence to be felt, yet after the captivity a better condition of things prevailed, and the Jews never again fell into idolatry. The erection of synagogues has been assigned as a reason for the comparative purity of the Jewish worship after the captivity, while another cause has been discovered in the hatred for images acquired by the Jews in their intercourse with the Persians.

II. *Objects of idolatry.*—The sun and moon were early selected as outward symbols of all-pervading power, and the worship of the heavenly bodies was not only the most ancient but the most prevalent system of idolatry. Taking its rise in the plains of Chaldea, it spread through Egypt, Greece, Scythia, and even Mexico and Ceylon. Comp. Deut. 4 · 19; 17 · 3; Job 31 : 20–28. In the later times of the monarchy, the planets or the zodiacal signs received, next to the sun and moon, their share of popular adoration. 2 Kings 23 : 5. Beast-worship, as exemplified in

The Hindoo Idol Pulliar.

the calves of Jeroboam, has already been alluded to. Of pure hero-worship among the Semitic races we find no trace. The singular reverence with which trees have been honored is not without example in the history of the Hebrews. The terebinth (oak) at Mamre, beneath which Abraham built an altar, Gen. 12 : 7; 13 : 18, and the memorial grove planted by him at Beersheba, Gen. 21 : 33, were intimately connected with patriarchal worship. Mountains and high places were chosen spots for offering sacrifice and incense to idols, 1 Kings 11 : 7; 14 : 23; and the retirement of gardens and the thick shade of woods offered great attractions to their worshippers. 2 Kings 16 : 4; Isa. 1 : 29; Hos. 4 : 13. The host of heaven was worshipped on the house-top. 2 Kings 23 : 12; Jer. 19 : 3; 32 : 29; Zeph. 1 : 5. (The modern objects of idolatry are less gross than the ancient, but are none the less idols. Whatever of wealth or honor or pleasure is loved and sought before God and righteousness becomes an object of idolatry.—ED.)

III. *Punishment of idolatry.*—Idolatry to an Israelite was a state offence, 1 Sam. 15 . 23, a political crime of the greatest character, high treason against the majesty of his king. The first and second commandments are directed against idolatry of every form. Individuals and communities were equally amenable to the rigorous code. The individual offender was devoted to destruction, Ex. 22 : 20; his nearest relatives were not only bound to denounce him and deliver him up to punishment, Deut. 13 : 2-10, but their hands were to strike the first blow, when, on the evidence of two witnesses at least, he was stoned. Deut. 17 : 2-5. To attempt to seduce others to false worship was a crime of equal enormity. Deut. 13 : 6-10.

(IV. *Attractions of idolatry.* — Many have wondered why the Israelites were so easily led away from the true God, into the worship of idols. (1) Visible, outward signs, with shows, pageants, parades, have an attraction to the natural heart, which often fails to perceive the unseen spiritual realities. (2) But the greatest attraction seems to have been in licentious revelries and obscene orgies with which the worship of the Oriental idols was observed. This worship, appealing to every sensual passion, joined with the attractions of wealth and fashion and luxury, naturally was a great temptation to a simple, restrained, agricultural people, whose worship and laws demanded the greatest purity of heart and of life.—ED.)

Idume′a (*red*). [EDOM.]

I′gal (*whom God will avenge*). 1. One of the spies, son of Joseph, of the tribe of Issachar. Num. 13 : 7. (B.C. 1490.)

2. One of the heroes of David's guard, son of Nathan of Zobah. 2 Sam. 23 : 36. (B.C. 1046.)

Igdali′ah (*whom Jehovah makes great*), a prophet or holy man—"the man of God"—named once only, Jer. 35 : 4, as the father of Hanan. (B.C. before 406.)

Ig′e-al (*whom God will avenge*), a son of Shemaiah; a descendant of the royal house of Judah. 1 Chron. 3 : 22. (B.C. 406.)

I′im (*ruins*). 1. The partial or contracted form of the name IJE-ABARIM. Num. 33 : 45.

2. A town in the extreme south of Judah. Josh. 15 : 29.

I′je-ab′arim (*ruins of Abarim*), one of the later halting-places of the children of Israel. Num. 21 : 11; 33 . 44. It was on the boundary—the southeast boundary —of the territory of Moab; in the waste uncultivated "wilderness" on its skirts. ch. 21 : 11.

I′jon (*a ruin*), a town in the north of Palestine, belonging to the tribe of Naphtali. It was taken and plundered by the captains of Ben-hadad, 1 Kings 15 · 20; 2 Chron. 16 : 4, and a second time by Tiglath-pileser. 2 Kings 15 : 29. It was situated a few miles northwest of the site of Dan, in a fertile and beautiful little plain called *Merj 'Ayûn.*

Ik′kesh (*perverse*), the father of Ira the Tekoite. 2 Sam. 23 : 26; 1 Chron. 11 : 28; 27 : 9. (B.C. before 1046.)

I′la-i (*exalted*), an Ahohite, one of the heroes of David's guard. 1 Chron. 11 : 29. (B.C. 1046.)

Illyr′icum, an extensive district lying along the eastern coast of the Adriatic, from the boundary of Italy on the north to Epirus on the south, and contiguous to Mœsia and Macedonia on the east. Rom. 15 : 19.

Image. [IDOL.]

Im′la (*whom God will fill up*), father or progenitor of Micaiah the prophet. 2 Chron. 18 : 7, 8. The form IMLAH is employed in the parallel narrative. 1 Kings 22 : 8, 9. (B.C. before 896.)

Imman′uel, that is, *God with us,* the title applied by the apostle Matthew to the Messiah, born of the Virgin, Matt. 1 · 23; Isa. 7 : 14, because Jesus was God united with man, and showed that God was dwelling with men.

Im′mer (*talkative*). 1. The founder of an important family of priests. 1 Chron. 9 : 12; Neh. 11 : 13. This family had charge of, and gave its name to, the sixteenth course of the service. 1 Chron. 24 : 14. (B.C. 1014.)

2. Apparently the name of a place in Babylonia. Ezra 2 : 59; Neh. 7 : 61.

Im′na (*holding back*), a descendant of Asher, son of Helem. 1 Chron. 7 : 35; comp. 40. (B.C. about 1451.)

Im′nah (*holding back*). 1. The firstborn of Asher. 1 Chron. 7 : 30. (B.C. 1706.)

2. Kore ben-Imnah, the Levite, assisted in the reforms of Hezekiah. 2 Chron. 31 : 14. (B.C. 726.)

Im′rah (*stubborn*), a descendant of

Asher, of the family of Zophah 1 Chron. 7 : 36. (B.C. after 1445.)

Im'ri (*eloquent*). 1. A man of Judah, of the great family of Pharez. 1 Chron. 9 · 4. (B.C. much before 536.)

2. Father or progenitor of Zaccur. Neh. 3 : 2. (B.C. before 446.)

Incense, from the Latin "to burn," "a mixture of gums or spices and the like, used for the purpose of producing a perfume when burned;" or the perfume

Altar of Incense.

itself of the spices, etc., burned in worship. The incense employed in the service of the tabernacle was compounded of the perfumes stacte, onycha, galbanum and pure frankincense. All incense which was not made of these ingredients was forbidden to be offered. Ex. 30 : 9. Aaron, as high priest, was originally appointed to offer incense each morning and evening. The times of offering incense were specified in the instructions first given to Moses. Ex. 30 : 7, 8. When the priest entered the holy place with the incense, all the people were removed from the temple, and from between the porch and the altar. Cf. Luke 1 : 10. Profound silence was observed among the congregation who were praying without, cf. Rev. 8 : 1, and at a signal from the prefect the priest cast the incense on the fire, and, bowing reverently toward the holy of holies, retired slowly back-

ward. The offering of incense has formed a part of the religious ceremonies of most ancient nations. It was an element in the idolatrous worship of the Israelites. 2 Chron. 34 : 25 ; Jer. 11 : 12, 17 ; 48 . 35. It would seem to be symbolical, not of prayer itself, but of that which makes prayer acceptable, the intercession of Christ. In Rev. 8 · 3, 4 the incense is spoken of as something distinct from, though offered with the prayers of, all the saints, cf. Luke 1 : 10; and in Rev. 5 : 8 it is the golden vials, and not the odors or incense, which are said to be the prayers of saints.

In'dia. The name of India does not occur in the Bible before the book of Esther, where it is noticed as the limit of the territories of Ahasuerus in the east, as Ethiopia was in the west. Esther 1 : 1 ; 8 : 9. The India of the book of Esther is not the peninsula of Hindostan, but the country surrounding the Indus, the *Punjáb* and perhaps *Scinde*. The people and productions of that country must have been tolerably well known to the Jews. An active trade was carried on between India and western Asia. The trade opened by Solomon with Ophir through the Red Sea consisted chiefly of Indian articles.

Inheritance. [HEIR.]

Ink, Inkhorn. [WRITING.]

Inn. The Hebrew word (*málón*) thus rendered literally signifies "a lodging-place for the night." Inns, in our sense of the term, were, as they still are, unknown in the East, where hospitality is religiously practiced. The khans or caravanserais are the representatives of European inns, and these were established but gradually. The halting-place of a caravan was selected originally on account of its proximity to water or pasture, by which the travellers pitched their tents and passed the night. Such was undoubtedly the "inn" at which occurred the incident in the life of Moses narrated in Ex. 4 : 24 ; comp. Gen. 42 : 27. On the more frequented routes, remote from towns, Jer. 9 : 2, caravanserais were in course of time erected, often at the expense of the wealthy. "A caravanserai is a large and substantial square building. . . . Passing through a strong gateway, the guest enters a large court, in the centre of which is a spacious raised platform, used for sleeping upon at night or for the devotions of the faithful during the day. Around this court are arranged the rooms of the building."

Inspiration. Dr. Knapp gives as the definition of inspiration, " an extraordinary divine agency upon teachers while giving instruction, whether oral or written, by which they were taught what and how they should write or speak." Without deciding on any of the various theories of inspiration, the general doctrine of Christians is that the

Eastern Khan or Inn.

Bible is so inspired by God that it is the infallible guide of men, and is perfectly trustworthy in all its parts, as given by God.

Instant, Instantly, in the Authorized Version, means urgent, urgently or fervently, as will be seen from the following passages : Luke 7 : 4 ; 23 : 23 ; Acts 26 : 7 ; Rom. 12 : 12.

Iphede′iah (*whom Jehovah frees*), a descendant of Benjamin, one of the Bene-Shashak. 1 Chron. 8 : 25.

Ir (*city*). 1 Chron. 7 : 12. [IRI.]

I′ra (*watchful of a city*). 1. " The Jairite," named in the catalogue of David's great officers. 2 Sam. 20 : 26.

2. One of the heroes of David's guard. 2 Sam. 23 : 38 ; 1 Chron. 11 : 40.

3. Another of David's guard, a Tekoite, son of Ikkesh. 2 Sam. 23 : 26 ; 1 Chron. 11 : 28. (B.C. 1046–1014.)

I′rad (*fleet*), son of Enoch ; grandson of Cain, and father of Mehujael. Gen. 4 : 18.

I′ram (*belonging to a city*), a leader of the Edomites, Gen. 36 : 43 ; 1 Chron. 1 : 54, *i. e.* the chief of a family or tribe. No identification of him has been found.

I′ri, or **Ir** (*belonging to a city*), a Benjamite, son of Bela. 1 Chron. 7 : 7, 12.

Iri′jah (*seen by the Lord*), son of Shelemiah, a captain in the ward, who met Jeremiah in the gate of Jerusalem called the " gate of Benjamin," accused him of being about to desert to the Chaldeans, and led him back to the princes. Jer. 37 : 13, 14. (B.C. 589.)

Ir′nahash (*serpent city*), a name which, like many other names of places, occurs in the genealogical lists of Judah. 1 Chron. 4 : 12.

I′ron (*pious*), one of the cities of Naphtali, Josh. 19 : 38, hitherto totally unknown.

Iron is mentioned with brass as the earliest of known metals. Gen. 4 : 22. The natural wealth in iron of the soil of Canaan is indicated by describing it as " a land whose stones are iron." Deut. 8 : 9. (Recent explorations have shown that iron ore is abundant in the northern part of Palestine.—ED.) The book of Job contains passages which indicate that iron was a metal well known. Sheet-iron was used for cooking utensils. Ezek. 4 : 3 ; cf. Lev. 7 : 9. That it was plentiful in the time of David appears from 1 Chron. 22 : 3. The market of Tyre was supplied with bright or polished iron by the merchants of Dan and Javan. Ezek. 27 : 19. The Chalybes of the Pontus were celebrated as workers in iron in very ancient times. The product of their labor is supposed to be alluded to in Jer. 15 : 12 as being of superior quality. Specimens of Assyrian iron-work overlaid with bronze were discovered by Mr. Layard, and are now in the British Museum. Iron weapons of various kinds were found at Nimroud, but fell to pieces on exposure to the air.

Ir'pe-el (*God heals*), one of the cities of Benjamin. Josh. 18 : 27. No trace has yet been discovered of its situation.

Ir-she'mesh (*city of the sun*), a city of the Danites, Josh. 19 : 41, probably identical with Beth-shemesh.

I'ru (*watch*), the eldest son of the great Caleb son of Jephunneh. 1 Chron. 4 : 15. (B.C. 1451.)

I'saac (*laughter*), the son whom Sarah bore to Abraham, in the hundredth year of his age, at Gerar. (B.C. 1897.) In his infancy he became the object of Ishmael's jealousy; and in his youth the victim, in intention, of Abraham's great sacrificial act of faith. When forty years old he married Rebekah his cousin, by whom, when he was sixty, he had two sons, Esau and Jacob. Driven by famine to Gerar, he acquired great wealth by his flocks, but was repeatedly dispossessed by the Philistines of the wells which he sunk at convenient stations. After the deceit by which Jacob acquired his father's blessing, Isaac sent his son to seek a wife in Padan-aram ; and all that we know of him during the last forty-three years of his life is that he saw that son, with a large and prosperous family, return to him at Hebron, Gen. 35 : 27, before he died there, at the age of 180 years. He was buried by his two sons in the cave of Machpelah. In the New Testament reference is made to the offering of Isaac, Heb. 11 : 17 ; James 2 : 21, and to his blessing his sons. Heb. 11 : 20. In Gal. 4 : 28–31 he is contrasted with Ishmael. In reference to the offering up of Isaac by Abraham, the primary doctrines taught are those of sacrifice and substitution, as the means appointed by God for taking away sin; and, as co-ordinate with these, the need of the obedience of faith, on the part of man, to receive the benefit. Heb. 11 : 17. The animal which God provided and Abraham offered was in the whole history of sacrifice the recognized type of " the Lamb of God, that taketh away the sins of the world." Isaac is the type of humanity itself, devoted to death for sin.

Isa'iah, the prophet, son of Amoz. The Hebrew name signifies *Salvation of Jahu* (a shortened form of *Jehovah*). He prophesied concerning Judah and Jerusalem in the days of Uzziah, Jotham, Ahaz and Hezekiah, kings of Judah, Isa. 1 : 1, covering probably 758 to 698 B.C. He was married and had two sons. Rabbinical tradition says that Isaiah, when 90 years old, was sawn asunder in the trunk of a carob tree by order of Manasseh, to which it is supposed that reference is made in Heb. 11 : 37.

Isa'iah, Book of. I. Chapters 1–5 contain Isaiah's prophecies in the reigns of Uzziah and Jotham, foretelling that the present prosperity of Judah should be destroyed, and that Israel should be brought to desolation. In chs. 6, 7 he announces the birth of the child Immanuel, which in ch. 9 is more positively predicted. Chs. 9–12 contain additional prophecies against Israel, chs. 10 : 5–12 : 6 being the most highly-wrought passages in the whole book. Chs. 13–23 contain chiefly a collection of utterances, each of which is styled a " burden," foretelling the doom of Babylon, Philistia, Moab, Ethiopia, Egypt and Tyre. The ode of triumph in ch. 14 : 3–23 is among the most poetical passages in all literature. Chs. 24–27 form one prophecy, essentially connected with the preceding ten " burdens," chs. 13–23, of which it is in effect a general summary. Chs. 23–35 predict the Assyrian invasion, and chs. 36–39 have reference to this invasion; prophecies that were so soon fulfilled. 2 Kings 19 : 35.

II. The last 27 chapters form a separate prophecy, and are supposed by many critics to have been written in the time of the Babylonian captivity, and are therefore ascribed to a "later Isaiah;" but the best reasons are in favor of but one Isaiah. This second part falls into three sections, each consisting of nine chapters:—1. The first section, chs. 40-48, has for its main topic the comforting assurance of the deliverance from Babylon by Koresh (Cyrus), who is even named twice. ch. 41 : 2, 3, 25 ; 44 : 28 ; 45 : 1-4, 13 ; 46 : 11 ; 48 : 14, 15. 2. The second section, chs. 49-56, is distinguished from the first by several features. The person of Cyrus, as well as his name and the specification of Babylon, disappear altogether. Return from exile is indeed spoken of repeatedly and at length, ch. 49 : 9-26 ; 51 : 9-52 : 12 ; 55 : 12, 13 ; 57 : 14, but in such general terms as admit of being applied to the spiritual and Messianic as well as to the literal restoration. 3. This section is mainly occupied with various practical exhortations founded upon the views of the future already set forth. In favor of the authenticity of the last 27 chapters the following reasons may be advanced:—(a) The unanimous testimony of Jewish and Christian tradition, comp. Ecclus. 48 : 24, and the evidence of the New Testament quotations. Matt. 3 : 3 ; Luke 4 : 17 ; Acts 8 : 28 ; Rom. 10 : 16, 20. (b) The unity of design which connects these last 27 chapters with the preceding; the oneness of diction which pervades the whole book ; the peculiar elevation and grandeur of style which characterize the second part as well as the first; the absence of any other name than Isaiah's claiming the authorship; lastly, the Messianic predictions which mark its inspiration, and remove the chief ground of objection against its having been written by Isaiah. In point of style we can find no difficulty in recognizing in the second part the presence of the same plastic genius as we discover in the first.

Is'cah (*one who looks forth*), daughter of Haran the brother of Abram, and sister of Milcah and of Lot. Gen. 11 : 29. In the Jewish traditions she is identified with Sarai. (B.C. about 1920.)

Iscar'iot (*man of Kerioth*). [JUDAS ISCARIOT.]

Ish'bah (*praising*), a man in the line of Judah, commemorated as the "father of Eshtemoa." 1 Chron. 4 : 17.

Ish'bak (*left behind*), a son of Abraham and Keturah, Gen. 25 : 2 ; 1 Chron. 1 : 32, and the progenitor of a tribe of northern Arabia. (B.C. after 1856.)

Ish'bi-be'nob (*he that dwells at Nob*), son of Rapha, one of the race of Philistine giants, who attacked David in battle, but was slain by Abishai. 2 Sam. 21 : 16, 17. (B.C. 1018.)

Ish-bo'sheth (*man of shame*), the youngest of Saul's four sons, and his legitimate successor. (B.C. 1058.) Ish-bosheth was "forty years old when he began to reign over Israel, and reigned two years." 2 Sam. 3 : 10. During these two years he reigned at Mahanaim, though only in name. The wars and negotiations with David were entirely carried on by Abner. 2 Sam. 2 : 12 ; 3 : 6, 12. The death of Abner deprived the house of Saul of its last remaining support. When Ish-bosheth heard of it, "his hands were feeble, and all the Israelites were troubled." He was murdered in his bed.

I'shi (*salutary*). 1. A man of the descendants of Judah, son of Appaim, 1 Chron. 2 : 31 ; one of the great house of Hezron.

2. In a subsequent genealogy of Judah we find another Ishi, with a son Zoheth. 1 Chron. 4 : 20.

3. Head of a family of the tribe of Simeon. 1 Chron. 4 : 42.

4. One of the heads of the tribe of Manasseh on the east of Jordan. 1 Chron. 5 : 24.

I'shi (*my husband*). This word occurs in Hos. 2 : 16. It is the Israelite term, in opposition to Baali, the Canaanite term, with the same meaning, though with a significance of its own.

Ishi'ah (*whom Jehovah lends*), the fifth of the five sons of Izrahiah ; one of the heads of the tribe of Issachar in the time of David. 1 Chron. 7 : 3. (B.C. 1046.)

Ishi'jah (*whom Jehovah lends*), a lay Israelite of the Bene-Harim who had married a foreign wife. Ezra 10 : 31. (B. C. 459.)

Ish'ma (*desolation*), a name in the genealogy of Judah. 1 Chron. 4 : 3.

Ish'mael (*whom God hears*). 1. The son of Abraham by Hagar the Egyptian, his concubine ; born when Abraham was fourscore and six years old. Gen. 16 : 15, 16. (B.C. 1910.) Ishmael was the first-born of his father. He was born in Abraham's house when he dwelt in the plain of Mamre ; and on the institution of the covenant of circumcision, was circumcised, he being then thirteen years old. Gen. 17 : 25. With the institution of the covenant, God renewed his promise respecting Ishmael. He does not again appear in the narrative until the weaning of Isaac. At the great feast made in celebration of the weaning, "Sarah saw the son of Hagar the Egyptian, which she had borne unto Abraham, mocking," and urged Abraham to cast him and his mother out. Comforted by the renewal of God's promise to make of Ishmael a great nation, Abraham sent them away, and they departed and wandered in the wilderness of Beersheba. His mother took Ishmael "a wife out of the land of Egypt." Gen. 21 : 9–21. This wife of Ishmael was the mother of his twelve sons and one daughter. Of the later life of Ishmael we know little. He was present with Isaac at the burial of Abraham. He died at the age of 137 years. Gen. 25 : 17, 18. The sons of Ishmael peopled the north and west of the Arabian peninsula, and eventually formed the chief element of the Arab nation, the wandering Bedouin tribes. They are now mostly Mohammedans, who look to him as their spiritual father, as the Jews look to Abraham. Their language, which is generally acknowledged to have been the Arabic commonly so called, has been adopted with insignificant exceptions throughout Arabia. The term "Ishmaelite" occurs on three occasions: Gen. 37 : 25, 27, 28; 39 : 1; Judges 8 : 24; Ps. 83 : 6.

2. One of the sons of Azel, a descendant of Saul through Meribbaal or Mephibosheth. 1 Chron. 8 : 38; 9 : 44.

3. A man of Judah, father of Zebadiah. 2 Chron. 19 : 11.

4. Another man of Judah, son of Jehohanan; one of the captains of hundreds who assisted Jehoiada in restoring Joash to the throne. 2 Chron. 23 : 1.

5. A priest of the Bene-Pashur, who was forced by Ezra to relinquish his foreign wife. Ezra 10 : 22.

6. The son of Nethaniah; a perfect marvel of craft and villainy, whose treachery forms one of the chief episodes of the history of the period immediately succeeding the first fall of Jerusalem. His exploits are related in Jer. 40 : 7–41 : 15, with a short summary. During the siege of the city he had fled across the Jordan, where he found a refuge at the court of Baalis. After the departure of the Chaldeans, Ishmael made no secret of his intention to kill the superintendent left by the king of Babylon and usurp his position. Of this Gedaliah was warned in express terms by Johanan and his companions, but notwithstanding entertained Ishmael and his followers at a feast, Jer. 41 : 1, during which Ishmael murdered Gedaliah and all his attendants. The same night he killed all Gedaliah's establishment, including some Chaldean soldiers who were there. For two days the massacre remained entirely unknown to the people of the town. On the second day eighty devotees were bringing incense and offerings to the ruins of the temple. At his invitation they turned aside to the residence of the superintendent, and there Ishmael and his band butchered nearly the whole number: ten only escaped by offering a heavy ransom for their lives. This done he descended to the town, surprised and carried off the daughters of King Zedekiah, who had been sent there by Nebuchadnezzar for safety, with their eunuchs and their Chaldean guard, Jer. 41 : 10, 16, and all the people of the town, and made off with his prisoners to the country of the Ammonites. The news of the massacre had by this time got abroad, and Ishmael was quickly pursued by Johanan and his companions. He was attacked, two of his bravos slain, the whole of the prey recovered; and Ishmael himself, with the remaining eight of his people, escaped to the Ammonites.

Ish'maelite (*descendant of Ishmael*). [ISHMAEL.]

Ishma'iah (*Jehovah hears*), son of Obadiah; the ruler of the tribe of Zebulun in the time of King David. 1 Chron. 27 : 19. (B.C. 1046.)

Ish'me-elite, 1 Chron. 2 : 17, and **Ish'me-elites** (*descendants of Ishmael*), Gen. 37 : 25, 27, 28; 39 : 1, the form in which the descendants of Ishmael are given in a few places in the Authorized Version.

Ish'mera-i (*whom Jehovah keeps*), a Benjamite, one of the family of Elpaal. 1 Chron. 8 : 18. (B.C. before 538.)

I'shod (*man of glory*), one of the tribe of Manasseh on the east of Jordan, son of Hammolekcth. 1 Chron. 7 : 18. (B.C.1491.)

Ish'pan (*bald*), a Benjamite, one of the family of Shashak. 1 Chron. 8 : 22. (B.C. before 588.)

Ish'tob (*men of Tob*), apparently one of the small kingdoms or states which formed part of the general country of Aram, named with Zobah, Rehob and Maacah. 2 Sam. 10 : 6, 8.

Ish'uah (*quiet*), the second son of Asher. Gen. 46 : 17. (B.C. 1706.)

Ish'ua-i (*quiet*), the third son of Asher, 1 Chron. 7 : 30, founder of a family bearing his name. Num. 26 : 44; Authorized Version "Jesuites." (B.C. 1706.)

Ish'ui (*quiet*), the second son of Saul by his wife Ahinoam. 1 Sam. 14 : 49, comp. 50. (Died B.C. 1053.)

Isle. The radical sense of the Hebrew word seems to be "habitable places," as opposed to water, and in this sense it occurs in Isa. 42 : 15. Hence it means secondarily any maritime district, whether belonging to a continent or to an island: thus it is used of the shore of the Mediterranean, Isa. 20 : 6; 23 : 2, 6, and of the coasts of Elishah, Ezek. 27 : 7, *i. e.* of Greece and Asia Minor.

Ismachi'ah (*whom Jehovah upholds*), a Levite who was one of the overseers of offerings during the revival under King Hezekiah. 2 Chron. 31 : 13. (B.C. 776.)

Isma'iah (*Jehovah hears*), a Gibeonite, one of the chiefs of those warriors who joined David at Ziklag. 1 Chron. 12 : 4. (B.C. 1064.)

Is'pah (*bald*), a Benjamite of the family of Beriah; one of the heads of his tribe. 1 Chron. 8 : 16. (B.C. before 588.)

Is'rael (*the prince that prevails with God*). 1. The name given, Gen. 32 : 28, to Jacob after his wrestling with the angel, Hos. 12 : 4, at Peniel. Gesenius interprets Israel "soldier of God."

2. It became the national name of the twelve tribes collectively. They are so called in Ex. 3 : 16 and afterward.

3. It is used in a narrower sense, excluding Judah, in 1 Sam. 11 : 8; 2 Sam. 20 : 1; 1 Kings 12 : 16. Thenceforth it was assumed and accepted as the name of the northern kingdom.

4. After the Babylonian captivity, the returned exiles resumed the name Israel as the designation of their nation. The name Israel is also used to denote laymen, as distinguished from priests, Levites and other ministers. Ezra 6 : 16; 9 : 1; 10 : 25; Neh. 11 : 3, etc.

Is'rael, Kingdom of. I. *The kingdom.*—The prophet Ahijah of Shiloh, who was commissioned in the latter days of Solomon to announce the division of the kingdom, left one tribe (Judah) to the house of David, and assigned ten to Jeroboam. 1 Kings 11 : 31, 35. These were probably Joseph (= Ephraim and Manasseh), Issachar, Zebulun, Asher, Naphtali, Benjamin, Dan, Simeon, Gad and Reuben; Levi being intentionally omitted. Eventually the greater part of Benjamin, and probably the whole of Simeon and Dan, were included as if by common consent in the kingdom of Judah. With respect to the conquests of David, Moab appears to have been attached to the kingdom of Israel, 2 Kings 3 : 4; so much of Syria as remained subject to Solomon, see 1 Kings 11 : 24, would probably be claimed by his successor in the northern kingdom; and Ammon was at one time allied, 2 Chron. 20 : 1, we know not how closely or how early, with Moab. The seacoast between Accho and Japho remained in the possession of Israel. The whole population may perhaps have amounted to at least three and a half millions.

II. *The capitals.*—Shechem was the first capital of the new kingdom. 1 Kings 12 : 25. Subsequently Tirzah became the royal residence, if not the capital, of Jer-

oboam, 1 Kings 14 : 17, and of his successors. ch. 15 : 33; 16 : 8, 17, 23. Samaria was chosen by Omri. 1 Kings 16 : 24. Jezreel was probably only a royal residence of some of the Israelitish kings.

III. *History.*—The kingdom of Israel lasted 254 years, from B.C. 975 to B.C. 721. The detailed history of the kingdom will be found under the names of its nineteen kings. See chart of the kings of Judah and Israel, at the end of the work. A summary view may be taken in four periods: (*a*) B.C. 975–929. Jeroboam had not sufficient force of character in himself to make a lasting impression on his people. A king, but not a founder of a dynasty, he aimed at nothing beyond securing his present elevation. Baasha, in the midst of the army at Gibbethon, slew the son and successor of Jeroboam; Zimri, a captain of chariots, slew the son and successor of Baasha; Omri, the captain of the host, was chosen to punish Zimri; and after a civil war of four years he prevailed over Tibni, the choice of half the people. (*b*) B.C. 929–884. For forty-five years Israel was governed by the house of Omri. The princes of his house cultivated an alliance with the kings of Judah, which was cemented by the marriage of Jehoram and Athaliah. The adoption of Baal-worship led to a reaction in the nation, to the moral triumph of the prophets in the person of Elijah, and to the extinction of the house of Ahab in obedience to the bidding of Elisha. (*c*) B.C. 884–772. Unparalleled triumphs, but deeper humiliation, awaited the kingdom of Israel under the dynasty of Jehu. Hazael, the ablest king of Damascus, reduced Jehoahaz to the condition of a vassal, and triumphed for a time over both the disunited Hebrew kingdoms. Almost the first sign of the restoration of their strength was a war between them; and Jehoash, the grandson of Jehu, entered Jerusalem as the conqueror of Amaziah. Jehoash also turned the tide of war against the Syrians; and Jeroboam II., the most powerful of all the kings of Israel, captured Damascus, and recovered the whole ancient frontier from Hamath to the Dead Sea. This short-lived greatness expired with the last king of Jehu's line. (*d*) B.C. 772–721. Military violence, it would seem, broke off the hereditary succession after the obscure and probably convulsed reign of Zachariah. An unsuccessful usurper, Shallum, is followed by the cruel Menahem, who, being unable to make head against the first attack of Assyria under Pul, became the agent of that monarch for the oppressive taxation of his subjects. Yet his power at home was sufficient to insure for his son and successor Pekahiah a ten-years reign, cut short by a bold usurper, Pekah. Abandoning the northern and transjordanic regions to the encroaching power of Assyria under Tiglath-pileser, he was very near subjugating Judah, with the help of Damascus, now the coequal ally of Israel. But Assyria interposing summarily put an end to the independence of Damascus, and perhaps was the indirect cause of the assassination of the baffled Pekah. The irresolute Hoshea, the next and last usurper, became tributary to his invader, Shalmaneser, betrayed the Assyrian to the rival monarchy of Egypt, and was punished by the loss of his liberty, and by the capture, after a three-years siege, of his strong capital, Samaria. Some gleanings of the ten tribes yet remained in the land after so many years of religious decline, moral debasement, national degradation, anarchy, bloodshed and deportation. Even these were gathered up by the conqueror and carried to Assyria, never again, as a distinct people, to occupy their portion of that goodly and pleasant land which their forefathers won under Joshua from the heathen. (Schaff (Bib. Dic.) adds to this summary that " after the destruction of the kingdom of Israel, B.C. 721, the name ' Israel ' began to be applied to the whole surviving people." No doubt many of the kingdom of Israel joined the later kingdom of the Jews after the captivity, and became part of that kingdom.—Ed.)

Is'raelite (*descendant of Israel*). In 2 Sam. 17 : 25, Ithra, the father of Amasa, is called " an Israelite," while in 1 Chron. 2 : 17 he appears as " Jether the Ishmaelite." The latter is undoubtedly the true reading.

Is'sachar (*reward*). 1. The ninth son of Jacob and the fifth of Leah. Gen. 30 : 17, 18. (B.C. 1753-45.) At the descent into Egypt four sons are ascribed to him, who founded the four chief families of the tribe. Gen. 46 : 13; Num. 26 : 23, 25; 1 Chron. 7 : 1. The number of the fighting men of Issachar, when taken in the census at Sinai, was 54,400. During the journey they seem to have steadily increased. The allotment of Issachar lay above that of Manasseh. Josh. 19 :

17-23. In the words of Josephus, " it extended in length from Carmel to the Jordan, in breadth to Mount Tabor." This territory was, as it still is, among the richest land in Palestine. It is this aspect of the territory of Issachar which appears to be alluded to in the blessing of Jacob.

2. A Korhite Levite, one of the doorkeepers of the house of Jehovah, seventh son of Obed-edom. 1 Chron. 26 : 5.

Isshi'ah (*whom Jehovah lends*). 1. A descendant of Moses by his younger son Eliezer. 1 Chron. 24 : 21 ; comp. 23 : 17 ; 26 : 25. (B.C. after 1451.)

2. A Levite of the house of Kohath and family of Uzziel. 1 Chron. 24 : 25. (Uncertain date.)

Issue, Running. Lev. 15 : 2, 3 ; 22 : 4; Num. 5 : 2; 2 Sam. 3 : 29. In Lev. 15 : 3 a distinction is introduced, which merely means that the cessation of the actual flux does not constitute ceremonial cleanness, but that the patient must bide the legal time, seven days, ver. 13, and perform the prescribed purifications and sacrifice. ver. 14.

Is'uah (*quiet*), second son of Asher. 1 Chron. 7 : 30. (B.C. 1706.)

Is'ui (*quiet*), third son of Asher, Gen. 46 : 17, founder of a family called after him, though in the Authorized Version appearing as THE JESUITES. Num. 26 : 44. (B.C. 1706.)

Ital'ian band. [ARMY.]

It'aly. This word is used in the New Testament, Acts 18 : 2 ; 27 : 1 ; Heb. 13 : 24, in the usual sense of the period, *i. e.* in its true geographical sense, as denoting the whole natural peninsula between the Alps and the Straits of Messina.

Ith'a-i (*with the Lord*), a Benjamite, son of Ribai of Gibeah, one of the heroes of David's guard. 1 Chron. 11 : 31. (B.C. 1046.)

Ith'amar (*land of palms*), the youngest son of Aaron. Ex. 6 : 23. (B.C. 1491.) After the death of Nadab and Abihu, Lev. 10 : 1, Eleazar and Ithamar were appointed to succeed to their places in the priestly office. Ex. 28 : 1, 40, 43 ; Num. 3 : 3, 4 ; 1 Chron. 24 : 2. In the distribution of services belonging to the tabernacle, and its transport on the march of the Israelites, the Gershonites and the Merarites were placed under the superintendence of Ithamar. Ex. 38 : 21 ; Num. 4 : 21-33. The high priesthood passed into the family of Ithamar in the person of Eli, but for what reason we are not informed.

Ith'i-el (*God is with me*). 1. A Benjamite, son of Jesaiah. Neh. 11 : 7.

2. One of two persons—Ithiel and Ucal—to whom Agur ben-Jakeh delivered his discourse. Prov. 30 : 1. (B.C. about 900.)

Ith'mah (*bereavedness*), a Moabite, one of the heroes of David's guard. 1 Chron. 11 : 46.

Ith'nan (*given*), one of the towns in the extreme south of Judah. Josh. 15 : 23. No trace of its existence has yet been discovered.

Ith'ra (*excellence*), an Israelite, 2 Sam. 17 : 25, or Ishmaelite, 1 Chron. 2 : 17, the father of Amasa by Abigail, David's sister. (B.C. before 1023.)

Ith'ran (*excellence*). 1. A son of Dishon, a Horite, Gen. 36 : 26; 1 Chron. 1 : 41, and probably a phylarch of a tribe of the Horim. Gen. 36 : 30. (B.C. about 1800.) 2. A descendant of Asher. 1 Chron. 7 : 30-40.

Ith're-am (*abundance of people*), son of David, born to him in Hebron, and distinctly specified as the sixth, and as the child of Eglah, David's wife. 2 Sam. 3 : 5; 1 Chron. 3 : 3.

Ith'rite (*belonging to Jether*)**, The,** the designation of two of the members of David's guard, Ira and Gareb. 2 Sam. 23 : 38; 1 Chron. 11 : 40. They may have come from Jattir, in the mountains of Judah. (B.C. 1046.)

It'tah-ka'zin (*time of the judge*), one of the landmarks of the boundary of Zebulun. Josh. 19 : 13. It has not been identified.

It'ta-i (*with the Lord*). 1. "Ittai the Gittite," *i. e.* the native of Gath, a Philistine in the army of King David. He appears only during the revolution of Absalom. (B.C. 1023.) We first discern him on the morning of David's flight. The king urges him to return. 2 Sam. 15 : 18, 19, comp. 1 Sam. 23 : 13; 27 : 2; 30 : 9, 10, 19, 20. But Ittai is firm; he is the king's slave, and wherever his master goes he will go. Accordingly he is allowed by David to proceed. When the army was numbered and organized by David at Mahanaim, Ittai again appears, now in command of a third part of the force. 2 Sam. 18 : 2, 5, 12.

2. Son of Ribai, from Gibeah of Benjamin; one of the thirty heroes of David's guard. 2 Sam. 23 : 29.

Itur'æ'a (*land of Jether*), a small province on the northwestern border of Palestine, lying along the base of Mount Hermon, only mentioned in Luke 3 : 1. Jetur the son of Ishmael gave his name, like the rest of his brethren, to the little province he colonized. Gen. 25 : 15, 16. It adjoined Trachonitis, and lay along the base of Libanus between Tiberias and Damascus. At the place indicated is situated the modern province of *Jedûr*, which is the Arabic form of the Hebrew Jetur.

I'vah (*ruined*), or **A'va,** which is mentioned in Scripture twice, 2 Kings 18 : 34; 19 : 13; comp. Isa. 37 : 13, in connection with Hena and Sepharvaim, and once, 2 Kings 17 : 24, in connection with Babylon and Cuthah, must be sought in Babylonia, and is probably identical with the modern *Hit*, on the Euphrates.

Ivory. The word translated "ivory" literally signifies the "tooth" of any animal, and hence more especially denotes the substance of the projecting tusks of elephants. The skilled workmen of Hiram, king of Tyre, fashioned the great ivory throne of Solomon, and overlaid it with pure gold. 1 Kings 10 : 18; 2 Chron. 9 : 17. The ivory thus employed was supplied by the caravans of Dedan, Isa. 21 : 13; Ezek. 27 : 15, or was brought, with apes and peacocks, by the navy of Tarshish. 1 Kings 10 : 22. The "ivory house" of Ahab, 1 Kings 22 : 39, was probably a palace, the walls of which were panelled with ivory, like the palace of Menelaus, described by Homer. *Odys.* iv. 73. Beds inlaid or veneered with ivory were in use among the Hebrews. Amos 6 : 4.

Iz'ehar (*oil*), the form in which the name Izhar is given in the Authorized Version of Num. 3 : 19 only.

Iz'eharites (*descendants of Izhar*)**, The.** A family of Kohathite Levites, descended from Izhar the son of Kohath, Num. 3 : 27; called also "Izharites." 1 Chron. 26 : 23, 29.

Iz'har (*oil*), son of Kohath, grandson of Levi, uncle of Aaron and Moses and father of Korah. Ex. 6 : 18, 21; Num. 3 : 19; 16 : 1; 1 Chron. 6 : 2, 18. (B.C. after 1490.) Izhar was the head of the family of the Izharites, 1 Chron. 24 : 22; 26 : 23, or Izeharites. Num. 3 : 27; 1 Chron. 26 : 23, 29.

Iz'rahiah (*whom Jehovah causes to sparkle*), a chieftain of Issachar. 1 Chron. 7 : 3.

Iz'rahite (*descendant of Zerah*)**, The,** the designation of Shamhuth. 1 Chron. 27 : 8. Its real force is probably Zerahite, that is, from the great Judaic family of Zerah.

Iz'ri (*creator*), a Levite leader of the fourth course or ward in the service of the house of God. 1 Chron. 25 : 11. In ver. 3 he is called ZERI. (B.C. 1014.)

J.

Ja'akan (*he shall surround*), the same as Jakan, the forefather of Bene-Jaakan. Deut. 10 : 6.

Ja-ak'obah (*supplanter*), one of the princes of the families of Simeon. 1 Chron. 4 : 36. (B.C. about 710.)

Ja-a'la (*wild she-goat*). Bene-Jaala were among the descendants of "Solomon's slaves" who returned from Babylon with Zerubbabel. Neh. 7 : 58. (B.C. before 536.) The name also occurs as **Ja-a'lah** (*wild goat*). Ezra 2 : 56.

Ja-a'lam (*whom God hides*), a son of Esau, Gen. 36 : 5, 14, 18; comp. 1 Chron. 1 : 35, and a head of a tribe of Edom. (B.C. 1790.)

Ja'ana-i (*whom Jehovah answers*), a chief man in the tribe of Gad. 1 Chron. 5 : 12.

Ja'are-or'egim (*forests of the weavers*), 2 Sam. 21 : 19, a Bethlehemite, and the father of Elhanan who slew Goliath. In the parallel passage, 1 Chron. 20 : 5, Jair is found instead of Jaare, and Oregim is omitted. (B.C. 1063.)

Ja-a'sau (*whom Jehovah made*), one of the Bene-Bani who had married a foreign wife. Ezra 10 : 37. (B.C. 459.)

Ja-a'si-el (*whom God comforts*), son of the great Abner. 1 Chron. 27 : 21. (B.C. 1046–1014.)

Ja-azani'ah (*whom Jehovah hears*). 1. One of the captains of the forces who accompanied Johanan ben-Kareah to pay his respects to Gedaliah at Mizpah, 2 Kings 25 : 23, and who appears afterwards to have assisted in recovering Ishmael's prey from his clutches. Comp. Jer. 41 : 11; 43 : 4, 5. (B.C. 587.)

2. Son of Shaphan. Ezek. 8 : 11. It is possible that he is identical with

3. Son of Azur; one of the princes of the people against whom Ezekiel was directed to prophesy. Ezek. 11 : 1. (B.C. 593.)

4. A Rechabite, son of Jeremiah. Jer. 35 : 3. (B.C. 606.)

Ja-a'zer, or **Ja'zer** (*Jehovah helps*), a town on the east of Jordan, in or near to Gilead. Num. 32 : 1, 3; 1 Chron. 26 : 31. We first hear of it in possession of the Amorites, and as taken by Israel after Heshbon, and on their way from thence to Bashan. Num. 21 : 32. It seems to have given its name to a district of dependent or "daughter" towns, Num. 21 : 32, Authorized Version "villages;" 1 Macc. 5 : 8, the "land of Jazer." Num. 32 : 1.

Ja-azi'ah (*whom Jehovah comforts*), apparently a third son, or a descendant, of Merari the Levite. 1 Chron. 24 : 26, 27. (B.C. before 1014.)

Ja-a'zi-el (*whom Jehovah comforts*), one of the Levites appointed by David to perform the musical service before the ark. 1 Chron. 15 : 18. (B.C. 1014.)

Ja'bal (*stream*), the son of Lamech and Adah, Gen. 4 : 20, and brother of Jubal. He is described as the father of such as dwell in tents and have cattle.

Jabbok (Wady Zurka).

Jab'bok (*emptying*), a stream which intersects the mountain range of Gilead, comp. Josh. 12 : 2, 5, and falls into the Jordan on the east about midway between the Sea of Galilee and the Dead Sea. It was anciently the border of the children of Ammon. Num. 21 : 24; Deut. 2 : 37; 3 : 16. It was on the south bank of the Jabbok that the interview took place between Jacob and Esau, Gen. 32 : 22; and this river afterward became, toward its western part, the boundary between the kingdoms of Sihon and Og. Josh. 12 : 2, 5. Its modern name is *Wady Zurka.*

Ja′besh (*dry*). 1. Father of Shallum, the fifteenth king of Israel. 2 Kings 15 : 10, 13, 14. (B.C. before 770.)

2. Jabesh-gilead, or Jabesh in the territory of Gilead. In its widest sense Gilead included the half tribe of Manasseh, 1 Chron. 27 : 21, as well as the tribes of Gad and Reuben, Num. 32 : 1–42, east of the Jordan; and of the cities of Gilead, Jabesh was the chief. It is first mentioned in Judges 21 : 8–14. Being attacked subsequently by Nahash the Ammonite, it gave Saul an opportunity of displaying his prowess in its defence. 1 Sam. 11 : 1-15. Eusebius places it beyond the Jordan, six miles from Pella on the mountain road to Gerasa; where its name is probably preserved in the *Wady Yabes.*

Ja′bez (*sorrow*). 1. Apparently a place at which the families of the scribes resided who belonged to the families of the Kenites. 1 Chron. 2 : 55.

2. The name occurs again in the genealogies of Judah, 1 Chron. 4 : 9, 10, in a passage of remarkable detail inserted in a genealogy again connected with Bethlehem. ver. 4.

Ja′bin (*whom God observes*). 1. King of Hazor, who organized a confederacy of the northern princes against the Israelites. Josh. 11 : 1-3. Joshua surprised the allied forces by the waters of Merom, ver. 7, and utterly routed them. (B.C. 1448.) During the ensuing wars Joshua again attacked Jabin, and burnt his city. Josh. 11 : 1-14.

2. A king of Hazor, whose general, Sisera, was defeated by Barak. Judges 4 : 2, 13. (B.C. 1316.)

Jab′ne-el (*building of God*). 1. One of the points on the northern boundary of Judah, not quite at the sea, though near it. Josh. 15 : 11. There is no sign, however, of its ever having been occupied by Judah. Josephus attributes it to the Danites. There was a constant struggle going on between that tribe and the Philistines for the possession of all the places in the lowland plains, and it is not surprising that the next time we meet with Jabneel it should be in the hands of the latter. 2 Chron. 26 : 6. Uzziah dispossessed them of it and demolished its fortifications. Called also JABNEH. At the time of the fall of Jerusalem, Jabneh was one of the most popu-

lous places of Judea. The modern village of *Yebna,* more accurately *Ibna,* stands about two miles from the sea, on a slight eminence just south of the *Nahr Rubin.*

2. One of the landmarks on the boundary of Naphtali, Josh. 19 : 33, in upper Galilee.

Jab′neh (*building of God*). 2 Chron. 26 : 6. [JABNEEL.]

Ja′chan (*affliction*), one of seven chief men of the tribe of Gad. 1 Chron. 5 : 13.

Ja′chin (*he shall establish*). 1. One of the two pillars which were set up " in the porch," 1 Kings 7 : 21, or before the temple, 2 Chron. 3 : 17, of Solomon. [BOAZ.]

2. Fourth son of Simeon, Gen. 46 : 10; Ex. 6 : 15; founder of the family of the Jachinites. Num. 26 : 12.

3. Head of the twenty-first course of priests in the time of David. 1 Chron. 9 : 10 ; 24 : 17 ; Neh. 11 : 10.

Jacinth, a precious stone, forming one of the foundations of the walls of the new Jerusalem. Rev. 21 : 20. Called *hyacinth* in the Revised Version. This is simply a different English rendering of the same Greek original. It is probably identical with the *ligure* of Ex. 28 : 19. The jacinth or hyacinth is a red variety of zircon, which is found in square prisms of a white, gray, red, reddish-brown, yellow or pale-green color. The expression in Rev. 9 : 17, " of jacinth," is descriptive simply of a dark-purple color.

Ja′cob (*supplanter*), the second son of Isaac and Rebekah. He was born with Esau, probably at the well of Lahai-roi, about B.C. 1837. His history is related in the latter half of the book of Genesis. He bought the birthright from his brother Esau, and afterward acquired the blessing intended for Esau, by practicing a well-known deceit on Isaac. (Jacob did not obtain the blessing because of his deceit, but in spite of it. That which was promised he would have received in some good way; but Jacob and his mother, distrusting God's promise, sought the promised blessing in a wrong way, and received with it trouble and sorrow.— ED.) Jacob, in his 78th year, was sent from the family home to avoid his brother, and to seek a wife among his kindred in Padan-aram. As he passed through Bethel, God appeared to him. After the lapse of twenty-one years he returned from Padan-aram with two wives, two concubines, eleven sons and a daughter, and large property. He escaped from the angry pursuit of Laban, from a meeting with Esau, and from the vengeance of the Canaanites provoked by the murder of Shechem ; and in each of these three emergencies he was aided and strengthened by the interposition of God, and in sign of the grace won by a night of wrestling with God his name was changed at Jabbok into Israel. Deborah and Rachel died before he reached Hebron ; Joseph, the favorite son of Jacob, was sold into Egypt eleven years before the death of Isaac ; and Jacob had probably exceeded his 130th year when he went thither. He was presented to Pharaoh, and dwelt for seventeen years in Rameses and Goshen, and died in his 147th year. His body was embalmed, carried with great care and pomp into the land of Canaan, and deposited with his fathers, and his wife Leah, in the cave of Machpelah.

The example of Jacob is quoted by the first and the last of the minor prophets. Besides the frequent mention of his name in conjunction with the names of the other two patriarchs, there are distinct references to the events in the life of Jacob in four books of the New Testament —John 1 : 51; 4 : 5, 12; Acts 7 : 12, 16; Rom. 9 : 11–13; Heb. 11 : 21; 12 : 16.

Jacob's Well at Shechem.

Ja'cob's Well, a deep spring in the vicinity of Shechem (called *Sychar* in Christ's time and *Nablûs* at the present day). It was probably dug by Jacob, whose name it bears. On the curb of the well Jesus sat and discoursed with the Samaritan woman. John 4 : 5-26. It is situated about half a mile southeast of Nablûs, at the foot of Mount Gerizim. It is about nine feet in diameter and 75 feet deep. At some seasons it is dry ; at others it contains a few feet of water.

Ja'da (*wise*), son of Onam and brother of Shammai, in the genealogy of the sons of Jerahmeel by his wife Atarah. 1 Chron. 2 : 28, 32. (B.C. after 1445.)

Jada'u (*loving*), one of the Bene-Nebo who had taken a foreign wife. Ezra 10 : 43. (B.C. 459.)

Jaddu'a (*known*). 1. Son and successor in the high priesthood of Jonathan or Johanan. He is the last of the high priests mentioned in the Old Testament, and probably altogether the latest name in the canon. Neh. 12 : 11, 22. (B.C. 406–332.)

2. One of the chief of the people who sealed the covenant with Nehemiah. Neh. 10 : 21. (B.C. 410.)

Ja'don (*judge*), the Meronothite, who assisted to repair the wall of Jerusalem. Neh. 3 : 7. (B.C. 446.)

Ja'el (*mountain goat*), the wife of Heber the Kenite. (B.C. 1316.) In the headlong rout which followed the defeat of the Canaanites by Barak, at Megiddo on the plain of Esdraelon, Sisera, their general, fled to the tent of the Kenite chieftainess, at Kedesh in Naphtali, four miles northwest of Lake Merom. He accepted Jael's invitation to enter, and she flung a mantle over him as he lay wearily on the floor. When thirst prevented sleep, and he asked for water, she brought him buttermilk in her choicest vessel. At last, with a feeling of perfect security, he fell into a deep sleep. Then it was that Jael took one of the great wooden pins which fastened down the cords of the tent, and with one terrible blow with a mallet dashed it through Sisera's temples deep into the earth. Judges 5 : 27. She then waited to meet the pursuing Barak, and led him into her tent that she might in his presence claim the glory of the deed ! Many have supposed that by this act she fulfilled the saying of Deborah, Judges 4 : 9; and hence they have supposed that Jael was actuated by some divine and hidden influence. But the Bible gives no hint of such an inspiration.

Ja'gur (*lodging*), a town of Judah, one of those farthest to the south, on the frontier of Edom. Josh. 15 : 21.

Jah (*Jehovah*), the abbreviated form of Jehovah, used only in poetry. It occurs frequently in the Hebrew, but with a single exception, Ps. 68 : 4, is rendered "Lord" in the Authorized Version. The identity of Jah and Jehovah is strongly marked in two passages of Isaiah—12 : 2 ; 26 : 4. [JEHOVAH.]

Ja'hath (*union*). 1. Son of Libni, the son of Gershom, the son of Levi. 1 Chron. 6 : 20. (B.C. after 1706.)

2. Head of a later house in the family of Gershom, being the eldest son of Shimei, the son of Laadan. 1 Chron. 23 : 10, 11.

3. A man in the genealogy of Judah, 1 Chron. 4 : 2, son of Reaiah ben-Shobal.

4. A Levite, son of Shelomoth. 1 Chron. 24 : 22.

5. A Merarite Levite in the reign of Josiah. 2 Chron. 34 : 12. (B.C. 623.)

Ja'haz, also **Jaha'za, Jaha'zah** and **Jah'zah** (*trodden down*). Under these four forms is given in the Authorized Version the name of a place which in the Hebrew appears as *Yahats* and *Yahtsah*. At Jahaz the decisive battle was fought between the children of Israel and Sihon king of the Amorites. Num. 21 : 23 ; Deut. 2 : 32 ; Judges 11 : 20. It was in the allotment of Reuben. Josh. 13 : 18. Like many others relating to the places east of the Dead Sea, the question of its site must await further research.

Jaha'za (*trodden down*). Josh. 13 : 18. [JAHAZ.]

Jaha'zah (*trodden down*). Josh. 21 : 36 ; Jer. 48 : 21. [JAHAZ.]

Jahazi'ah (*whom Jehovah watches over*), son of Tikvah, apparently a priest. Ezra 10 : 15.

Jaha'zi-el (*whom God watches over*). 1. One of the heroes of Benjamin who joined David at Ziklag. 1 Chron. 12 : 4. (B.C. 1055.)

2. A priest in the reign of David. 1 Chron. 16 : 6.

3. A Kohathite Levite, third son of Hebron. 1 Chron. 23 : 19 ; 24 : 23.

4. Son of Zechariah, a Levite of the Bene-Asaph in the reign of Jehoshaphat. 2 Chron. 20 : 14. (B.C. 896.)

5. The "son of Jahaziel" was the chief of the Bene-Shecaniah who returned from Babylon with Ezra. Ezra 8 : 5. (B.C. before 459.)

Jah'da-i (*whom Jehovah directs*), a man who appears to be thrust abruptly into the genealogy of Caleb, as the father of six sons. 1 Chron. 2 : 47.

Jah'di-el (*whom Jehovah makes joyful*), a chieftain of Manasseh on the east of Jordan. 1 Chron. 5 : 24. (B.C. 320.)

Jah'do (*united*), a Gadite, 1 Chron. 5 : 14, son of Buz and father of Jeshishai.

Jah'le-el (*hoping in Jehovah*), the third of the three sons of Zebulun, Gen. 46 : 14 ; Num. 26 : 26 ; founder of the family of Jahleelites. (B.C. 1706.)

Jah'ma-i (*whom Jehovah guards*), a man of Issachar, one of the heads of the house of Tolah. 1 Chron. 7 : 2. (B.C. 1491.)

Jah'zah (*trodden down*). 1 Chron. 6 : 78. [JAHAZ.]

Jah'ze-el (*whom God allots*), the first of the four sons of Naphtali, Gen. 46 : 24 ; founder of the family of the Jahze-elites. Num. 26 : 48. (B.C. 1306.)

Jahze'rah (*whom God leads back*), a priest of the house of Immer. 1 Chron. 9 : 12.

Jah'zi-el (*whom God allots*), the same as JAHZEEL. 1 Chron. 7 : 13.

Ja'ir (*enlightener*). 1. A man who on his father's side was descended from Judah, and on his mother's from Manasseh. (B.C. 1451.) During the conquest he took the whole of the tract of Argob, Deut. 3 : 14, and in addition possessed himself of some nomad villages in Gilead, which he called after his own name Havoth-jair. Num. 32 : 41 ; 1 Chron. 2 : 23.

2. JAIR THE GILEADITE, who judged Israel for two-and-twenty years. Judges 10 : 3–5. (B.C. 1160.) He had thirty sons, and possessed thirty cities in the land of Gilead, which, like those of their namesake, were called Havoth-jair.

3. A Benjamite, son of Kish and father of Mordecai. Esther 2 : 5. (B.C. before 598.)

4. The father of Elhanan, one of the heroes of David's army. 1 Chron. 20 : 5.

Ja'irite (*descendant of Jair*)**, The.** IRA THE JAIRITE was a priest (Authorized Version "chief ruler") to David. 2 Sam. 20 : 26.

Ja'irus (*whom God enlightens*). 1. A ruler of a synagogue, probably in some town near the western shore of the Sea of Galilee. Matt. 9 : 18 ; Mark 5 : 22 ; Luke 8 : 41. (A.D. 28.)

2. Esther 11 : 2. [JAIR, 3.]

Ja'kan (*sagacious*), son of Ezer the

Horite. 1 Chron. 1 : 42. The same as JAAKAN. [And see AKAN.]

Ja′keh (*pious*). [PROVERBS, BOOK OF.]

Ja′kim (*whom God sets up*). 1. Head of the twelfth course of priests in the reign of David. 1 Chron. 24 : 12. (B.C. 1014.) 2. A Benjamite, one of the Bene-Shimhi. 1 Chron. 8 : 19. (B.C. 588.)

Ja′lon (*abiding*), one of the sons of Ezra. 1 Chron. 4 :17.

Jam′bres. [JANNES AND JAMBRES.]

James (*the Greek form of Jacob, supplanter*). 1. James the son of Zebedee, one of the twelve apostles. He was elder brother of the evangelist John. His mother's name was Salome. We first hear of him in A.D. 27, Mark 1 : 20, when at the call of the Master he left all, and became, once and forever, his disciple, in the spring of 28. Matt. 10 : 2 ; Mark 3 : 14 ; Luke 6 : 13 ; Acts 1 : 13. It would seem to have been at the time of the appointment of the twelve apostles that the name of Boanerges was given to the sons of Zebedee. The " sons of thunder " had a burning and impetuous spirit, which twice exhibits itself. Mark 10 : 37 ; Luke 9 : 54. On the night before the crucifixion James was present at the agony in the garden. On the day of the ascension he is mentioned as persevering, with the rest of the apostles and disciples, in prayer. Acts 1 : 13. Shortly before the day of the passover, in the year 44, he was put to death by Herod Agrippa I. Acts 12 : 1, 2.

2. James the son of Alphæus, one of the twelve apostles. Matt. 10 : 3. Whether or not this James is to be identified with James the Less, the son of Alphæus, the brother of our Lord, is one of the most difficult questions in the gospel history. By comparing Matt. 27 : 56 and Mark 15 : 40 with John 19 : 25, we find that the Virgin Mary had a sister named, like herself, Mary, who was the wife of Clopas or Alphæus (varieties of the same name), and who had two sons, James the Less and Joses. By referring to Matt. 13 : 55 and Mark 6 : 3 we find that a James and a Joses, with two other brethren called Jude and Simon, and at least three sisters, were living with the Virgin Mary at Nazareth. By referring to Luke 6 : 16 and Acts 1 : 13 we find that there were two brethren named James and Jude among the apostles. It would certainly be natural to think that we had here but one family of four brothers and three or more sisters, the children of Clopas and Mary, nephews and nieces of the Virgin Mary. There are difficulties, however, in the way of this conclusion into which we cannot here enter ; but in reply to the objection that the four brethren in Matt. 13 : 55 are described as the brothers of Jesus, not as his cousins, it must be recollected that ἀδελφοί, which is here translated " brethren," may also signify cousins.

James the Less, called the Less because younger or smaller in stature than James the son of Zebedee. He was the son of Alphæus or Clopas and brother of our Lord (see above) ; was called to the apostolate, together with his younger brother Jude, in the spring of the year 28. At some time in the forty days that intervened between the resurrection and the ascension the Lord appeared to him. 1 Cor. 15 : 7. Ten years after we find James on a level with Peter, and with him deciding on the admission of St. Paul into fellowship with the Church at Jerusalem ; and from henceforth we always find him equal, or in his own department superior, to the very chiefest apostles, Peter, John and Paul. Acts 9 : 27 ; Gal. 1 : 18, 19. This pre-eminence is evident throughout the after history of the apostles, whether we read it in the Acts, in the epistles or in ecclesiastical writers. Acts 12 : 17 ; 15 : 13, 19 ; 21 : 18 ; Gal. 2 : 9. According to tradition, James was thrown down from the temple by the scribes and Pharisees ; he was then stoned, and his brains dashed out with a fuller's club.

James, The General Epistle of. The author of this epistle was in all probability James the son of Alphæus, and our Lord's brother. It was written from Jerusalem, which St. James does not seem to have ever left. It was probably written about A.D. 62, during the interval between Paul's two imprisonments. Its main object is not to teach doctrine, but to improve morality. St. James is the moral teacher of the New Testament. He wrote for the Jewish Christians, whether in Jerusalem or abroad, to warn them against the sins to which as Jews they were most liable, and to console and exhort them under the sufferings to which as Christians they were most exposed.

Ja′min (*right hand*). 1. Second son of Simeon, Gen. 46 : 10 ; Ex. 6 : 15 ; 1 Chron. 4 : 24, founder of the family of the Jaminites. Num. 26 : 12. (B.C. 1706.)

2. A man of Judah, second son of Ram the Jerahmeelite. 1 Chron. 2 : 27.

3. One of the Levites who expounded the law to the people. Neh. 8 : 7. (B.C. 410.)

Jam'lech (*whom God makes king*), one of the chief men of the tribe of Simeon. 1 Chron. 4 : 34.

Jam'nia. [JABNEEL.]

Jan'na (*flourishing*), son of Joseph, and father of Melchi, in the genealogy of Christ. Luke 3 : 24. In the Revised Version written JANNAI.

Jan'nes and **Jam'bres,** the names of two Egyptian magicians who opposed Moses. Ex. 7 : 9–13; 2 Tim. 3 : 8, 9. (B.C. 1492.)

Jano'ah (*rest*), a place apparently in the north of Galilee, or the "land of Naphtali,"—one of those taken by Tiglath-pileser in his first incursion into Palestine. 2 Kings 15 : 29. No trace of it appears elsewhere.

Jano'hah (*rest*), a place on the boundary of Ephraim, Josh. 16 : 6, 7, east of Neapolis. A little less than twelve miles from *Nablûs*, and about southeast in direction, two miles from *Akrabeh*, is the village of *Yanûn*, doubtless identical with the ancient Janohah.

Ja'num (*slumber*), a town of Judah in the mountain district, apparently not far from Hebron. Josh. 15 : 53.

Ja'pheth (*enlargement*), one of the three sons of Noah. The descendants of Japheth occupied the "isles of the Gentiles," Gen. 10 : 5—*i. e.* the coast lands of the Mediterranean Sea in Europe and Asia Minor—whence they spread northward over the whole continent of Europe and a considerable portion of Asia.

Japhi'a (*splendid*). The boundary of Zebulun ascended from Daberath to Japhia, and thence passed to Gath-hepher. Josh. 19 : 12. *Yâfa*, two miles south of Nazareth, is not unlikely to be identical with Japhia.

Japhi'a (*splendid*). 1. King of Lachish at the time of the conquest of Canaan by the Israelites. Josh. 10 : 3. (B.C. 1450.)

2. One of the sons of David born to him in Jerusalem. 2 Sam. 5 : 15; 1 Chron. 3 : 7; 14 : 6. (B.C. 1046.)

Japh'let (*whom God delivers*), a descendant of Asher through Beriah. 1 Chron. 7 : 32, 33.

Japh'leti (*the Japhletite*). The boundary of the "Japhletite" is one of the landmarks on the south boundary line of Ephraim. Josh. 16 : 3.

Ja'pho (*beauty*). Josh. 19 : 46. The Hebrew form for the better-known JOPPA. 2 Chron. 2 : 16; Ezra 3 : 7; Jonah 1 : 3. In its modern garb it is *Yâfa*.

Ja'rah (*honey*), a descendant of Saul; son of Micah and great-grandson of Mephibosheth. 1 Chron. 9 : 42, comp. 40.

Ja'reb (*adversary*) is to be explained either as the proper name of a country or person, as a noun in apposition, or as a verb from a root, *râb*, "to contend, plead." All these senses are represented in the Authorized Version and the marginal readings, Hos. 5 : 13; 10 : 6, and the least preferable has been inserted in the text. Jareb is most probably the name of some city of Assyria, or another name of the country itself.

Ja'red (*descent*), one of the antediluvian patriarchs, and father of Enoch. Gen. 5 : 15, 16, 18–20; Luke 3 : 37. In the lists of Chronicles the name is given in the Authorized Version JERED.

Jaresi'ah (*whom Jehovah nourishes*), a Benjamite, one of the Bene-Jehoram. 1 Chron. 8 : 27.

Jar'ha, the Egyptian servant of Sheshan, about the time of Eli, to whom his master gave his daughter and heir in marriage. 1 Chron. 2 : 34, 35. (B.C. before 1491.)

Ja'rib (*adversary*). 1. Named in the list of 1 Chron. 4 : 24 only, as a son of Simeon. Perhaps the same as JACHIN. Gen. 46; Ex. 6; Num. 26.

2. One of the " chief men" who accompanied Ezra on his journey from Babylon to Jerusalem. Ezra 8 : 16. (B.C. 459.)

3. A priest of the house of Jeshua the son of Jozadak, who had married a foreign wife, and was compelled by Ezra to put her away. Ezra 10 : 18. (B.C. 459.)

4. 1 Macc. 14 : 29. A contraction or corruption of the name JOARIB. ch. 2 : 1.

Jar'imoth (*heights*). 1 Esd. 9 : 28. [JEREMOTH.]

Jar'muth (*high*). 1. A town in the low country of Judah. Josh. 15 : 35. Its king, Piram, was one of the five who conspired to punish Gibeon for having made alliance with Israel, Josh. 10 : 3, 5, and who were routed at Beth-horon and put to death by Joshua at Makkedah. ver. 33. Its site is probably the modern *Yarmûk*.

2. A city of Issachar, allotted with its suburbs to the Gershonite Levites. Josh. 21 : 29.

Jaro'ah (*moon*), a chief man of the tribe of Gad. 1 Chron. 5 : 14.

Ja'shen (*sleeping*). Bene-Jashen— "sons of Jashen"—are named in the catalogue of the heroes of David's guard in 2 Sam. 23 : 32. (B.C. 1046.)

Ja'sher (*upright*), **Book of** ("*the book of the upright*"), alluded to in two passages only of the Old Testament. Josh. 10 : 13 and 2 Sam. 1 : 18. It was probably written in verse; and it has been conjectured that it was a collection of ancient records of honored men or noble deeds. It is wholly lost.

Jasho'be-am (*to whom the people turn*), named first among the chief of the mighty men of David. 1 Chron. 11 : 11. (B.C. 1046.) He came to David at Ziklag. His distinguishing exploit was that he slew 300 (or 800, 2 Sam. 23 : 8) men at one time.

Ja'shub (*he turns*). 1. The third son of Issachar, and founder of the family of the Jashubites. Num. 26 : 24; 1 Chron. 7 : 1. (B.C. 1706.)

2. One of the sons of Bani, who had to put away his foreign wife. Ezra 10 : 29. (B.C. 459.)

Jash'ubi-le'hem (*turner back for food*), a person or a place named among the descendants of Shelah, the son of Judah by Bath-shua the Canaanitess. 1 Chron. 4 : 22.

Ja'si-el (*whom God made*), the last named on the list of David's heroes in 1 Chron. 11 : 47.

Ja'son (*one who will heal*), called the Thessalonian, entertained Paul and Silas, and was in consequence attacked by the Jewish mob. Acts 17 : 5, 6, 7, 9. (A.D. 48.) He is probably the same as the Jason mentioned in Rom. 16 : 21. It is conjectured that Jason and Secundus, Acts 20 : 4, were the same.

Jasper, a precious stone frequently noticed in Scripture. It was the last of the twelve inserted in the high priest's breastplate, Ex. 28 : 20; 39 : 13, and the first of the twelve used in the foundations of the new Jerusalem. Rev. 21 : 19. The characteristics of the stone as far as they are specified in Scripture, Rev. 21 : 11, are that it "was most precious," and "like crystal;" we may also infer from Rev. 4 : 3 that it was a stone of brilliant and transparent light. The stone which we name "jasper" does not accord with this description. There can be no doubt that the *diamond* would more adequately answer to the description in the book of Revelation.

Jath'ni-el (*whom God gives*), a Korhite Levite, the fourth of the family of Meshelemiah. 1 Chron. 26 : 2. (B.C. 1014.)

Jat'tir (*pre-eminent*), a town of Judah in the mountain districts, Josh. 15 : 48, one of the group containing Socho, Eshtemoa, etc. See also Josh. 21 : 14; 1 Sam. 30 : 27; 1 Chron. 6 : 57. By Robinson it is identified with *'Attir*, six miles north of Molada and ten miles south of Hebron.

Ja'van (*clay*). 1. A son of Japheth. Gen. 10 : 2, 4. Javan was regarded as the representative of the Greek race. The name was probably introduced into Asia by the Phœnicians, to whom the Ionians were naturally better known than any other of the Hellenic races, on account of their commercial activity and the high prosperity of their towns on the western coast of Asia Minor.

2. A town in the southern part of Arabia (*Yemen*), whither the Phœnicians traded. Ezek. 27 : 19.

Javelin. [ARMS.]

Ja'zer (*Jehovah helps*). [JAAZER.]

Ja'ziz (*whom God moves*), a Hagarite who had charge of the flocks of King David. 1 Chron. 27 : 31. (B.C. 1046.)

Je'arim (*forests*), **Mount,** a place named in specifying the northern boundary of Judah. Josh. 15 : 10. The boundary ran from Mount Seir to "the shoulder of Mount Jearim, which is Cesalon"—that is, Cesalon was the landmark on the mountain. *Kesla*, seven miles due west of Jerusalem, stands on a high point on the north slope of a lofty ridge, which is probably Mount Jearim.

Je-at'era-i (*whom Jehovah leads*), a Gershonite Levite, son of Zerah. 1 Chron. 6 : 21.

Jeberechi'ah (*whom Jehovah blesses*), father of a certain Zechariah, in the reign of Ahaz, mentioned Isa. 8 : 2. (B.C. about 739.)

Je'bus (*threshing-floor*), one of the names of Jerusalem, the city of the Jebusites, also called JEBUSI. Josh. 15 : 8; 18 : 16, 28; Judges 19 : 10, 11; 1 Chron. 11 : 4, 5. [JERUSALEM.]

Jebu'si (*from Jebus*), the name employed for the city of JEBUS. Josh. 15 : 8; 18 : 16, 28.

Jeb'usites (*descendants of Jebus*), **The,** were descended from the third son of Canaan. Gen. 10 : 16; 1 Chron. 1 : 14. The actual people first appear in the invaluable report of the spies. Num. 13 : 29. When Jabin organized his rising against Joshua, the Jebusites joined him. Josh.

11 : 3. "Jebus, which is Jerusalem," lost its king in the slaughter of Beth-horon, Josh. 10 : 1, 5, 26; comp. 12 : 10, was sacked and burned by the men of Judah, Judges 1 : 21, and its citadel final-ly sealed and occupied by David. 2 Sam. 5 : 6. After this they emerge from the darkness but once, in the person of Araunah the Jebusite, "Araunah the king," who appears before us in true kingly dignity in his well-known trans-action with David. 2 Sam. 24 : 23; 1 Chron. 21 : 24, 25.

Jecami′ah (*whom Jehovah gathers*), one of seven who were introduced into the royal line, on the failure of it in the person of Jehoiachin. 1 Chron. 3 : 18.

Jecholi′ah (*strong through Jehovah*), wife of Amaziah king of Judah, and mother of Azariah or Uzziah his succes-sor. 2 Kings 15 : 2. (B.C. 824–807.)

Jeconi′as, the Greek form of Jeconi-ah, an altered form of Jehoiachin. [JE-HOIACHIN.]

Jecoli′ah. The same as JECHOLIAH. 2 Chron. 26 : 3.

Jeconi′ah (*whom Jehovah establishes*). [See JEHOIACHIN.]

Jedai′ah (*praise Jehovah*). 1. Head of the second course of priests, as they were divided in the time of David. 1 Chron. 24 : 7. (B.C. 1014.) Some of them survived to return to Jerusalem after the Babylonish captivity, as appears from Ezra 2 : 36; Neh. 7 : 39.

2. A priest in the time of Jeshua the high priest. Zech. 6 : 10, 14. (B.C. 536.)

Jeda′iah. 1. A Simeonite, forefather of Ziza. 1 Chron. 4 : 37.

2. Son of Harumaph; a man who did his part in the rebuilding of the wall of Jerusalem. Neh. 3 : 10. (B.C. 446.)

Jedi′a-el (*known of God*). 1. A chief patriarch of the tribe of Benjamin. 1 Chron. 7 : 6, 11. It is usually assumed that Jediael is the same as Ashbel, Gen. 46 : 21; Num. 26 : 38; 1 Chron. 8 : 1; but this is not certain.

2. Second son of Meshelemiah, a Le-vite. 1 Chron. 26 : 1, 2.

3. Son of Shimri; one of the heroes of David's guard. 1 Chron. 11 : 45. (B.C. 1046.)

4. One of the chiefs of the thousands of Manasseh who joined David on his march to Ziklag. 1 Chron. 12 : 20; comp. 1 Sam. 30 : 9, 10. (B.C. 1053.)

Jed′idah (*one beloved*), queen of Amon and mother of the good king Jo-siah. 2 Kings 22 : 1. (B.C. 648.)

Jedidi′ah (*beloved of Jehovah*), **Je-did-jah** (*darling of Jehovah*), the name bestowed, through Nathan the prophet, on David's son Solomon. 2 Sam. 12 : 25.

Jed′uthun (*praising*), a Levite of the family of Merari, is probably the same as Ethan. Comp. 1 Chron. 15 : 17, 19 with 1 Chron. 16 : 41, 42; 25 : 1, 3, 6; 2 Chron. 35 : 15. His office was generally to pre-side over the music of the temple service. Jeduthun's name stands at the head of the 39th, 62d and 77th Psalms, indicating probably that they were to be sung by his choir. (B.C. 1014.)

Je-e′zer (*father of help*), Num. 26 : 30, the name of a descendant of Manasseh and founder of the family of the Jeezer-ites. In parallel lists the name is given as ABI-EZER.

Je′gar-sahadu′tha (*heap of testi-mony*), the Aramæan name given by La-ban the Syrian to the heap of stones which he erected as a memorial of the compact between Jacob and himself. Gen. 31 : 47. Galeed, a "witness heap," which is given as the Hebrew equivalent, does not exactly represent Jegar-sahadutha.

Jehal′ele-el (*who praises God*). Four men of the Bene-Jehaleleel are introduced abruptly into the genealogies of Judah. 1 Chron. 4 : 16.

Jehal′elel (*who praises God*), a Merar-ite Levite, father of Azariah. 2 Chron. 29 : 12.

Jehde′iah (*whom Jehovah makes glad*). 1. The representative of the Bene-Shubael, in the time of David. 1 Chron. 24 : 20.

2. A Meronothite who had charge of the she-asses of David. 1 Chron. 27 : 30. (B.C. 1046.)

Jehez′ekel (*whom God makes strong*), a priest to whom was given by David the charge of the twentieth of the twenty-four courses in the service of the house of Je-hovah. 1 Chron. 24 : 16. (B.C. 1014.)

Jehi′ah (*Jehovah lives*), "doorkeeper for the ark" at the time of its establish-ment in Jerusalem. 1 Chron. 15 : 24. (B.C. 1043.)

Jehi′el (*God lives*). 1. One of the Le-vites appointed by David to assist in the service of the house of God. 1 Chron. 15 : 18, 20; 16 : 5.

2. One of the sons of Jehoshaphat king of Judah, put to death by his brother Je-horam. 2 Chron. 21 : 2, 4. (B.C. 887.)

3. One of the rulers of the house of God at the time of the reforms of Josiah. 2 Chron. 35 : 8. (B.C. 623.)

4. A Gershonite Levite. 1 Chron. 23 : 8, who had charge of the treasures. ch. 29 : 8.

5. A son of Hachmoni named in the list of David's officers, 1 Chron. 27 : 32, as "with the king's sons," whatever that may mean.

6. A Levite who took part in the restorations of King Hezekiah. 2 Chron. 29 : 14. (B.C. 726.)

7. Another Levite at the same period. 2 Chron. 31 : 13.

8. Father of Obadiah, of the Bene-Joab. Ezra 8 : 9. (B.C. before 459.)

9. One of the Bene-Elam, father of Shechaniah. Ezra 10 : 2.

10. A member of the same family, who himself had to part with his wife. Ezra 10 : 26.

11. A priest, one of the Bene-Harim, who also had to put away his foreign wife. Ezra 10 : 21. (B.C. 459.)

Jehi'el (*treasured of God*), a perfectly distinct name from the last. 1. A man described as father of Gibeon; a forefather of King Saul. 1 Chron. 9 : 35.

2. One of the sons of Hotham the Aroerite; a member of David's guard. 1 Chron. 11 : 44. (B.C. 1046.)

Jehi'eli (*a Jehielite*), according to the Authorized Version a Gershonite Levite of the family of Laadan. 1 Chron. 26 : 21, 22.

Jehizki'ah (*Jehovah strengthens*), son of Shallum, one of the heads of the tribe of Ephraim in the time of Ahaz. 2 Chron. 28 : 12; comp. 8, 13, 15. (B.C. 738.)

Jeho'adah (*whom Jehovah adorns*), one of the descendants of Saul. 1 Chron. 8 : 36.

Jeho-ad'dan (*whom Jehovah adorns*), queen to King Joash, and mother of Amaziah of Judah. 2 Kings 14 : 2; 2 Chron. 25 : 1. (B.C. 862–837.)

Jeho'ahaz (*whom the Lord sustains*). 1. The son and successor of Jehu, reigned 17 years, B.C. 856–840, over Israel in Samaria. His inglorious history is given in 2 Kings 13 : 1–9. Throughout his reign, ver. 22, he was kept in subjection by Hazael king of Damascus. Jehoahaz maintained the idolatry of Jeroboam; but in the extremity of his humiliation he besought Jehovah, and Jehovah gave Israel a deliverer—probably either Jehoash, vs. 23 and 25, or Jeroboam II., 2 Kings 14 : 24, 25.

2. Jehoahaz, otherwise called Shallum, son of Josiah, whom he succeeded as king of Judah. He was chosen by the people in preference to his elder (comp. 2 Kings 23 : 31 and 36) brother, B C. 610, and he reigned three months in Jerusalem. Pharaoh-necho sent to Jerusalem to depose him and to fetch him to Riblah. There he was cast into chains, and from thence he was taken into Egypt, where he died.

3. The name given, 2 Chron. 21 : 17, to Ahaziah, the youngest son of Jehoram king of Judah.

Jeho'ash (*given by the Lord*), the uncontracted form of Joash. 1. The eighth king of Judah; son of Ahaziah. 2 Kings 11 : 21; 12 : 1, 2, 4, 6, 7, 18; 14 : 13. [JOASH, 1.]

2. The twelfth king of Israel; son of Jehoahaz. 2 Kings 13 : 10, 25; 14 : 8, 9, 11, 13, 15, 16, 17. [JOASH, 2.]

Jeho'hanan (*whom Jehovah gave*), a name of which John is the contraction. 1. A Korhite Levite, one of the doorkeepers to the tabernacle. 1 Chron. 26 : 3; comp. 25 : 1. (B.C. 1014.)

2. One of the principal men of Judah under King Jehoshaphat. 2 Chron. 17 : 15; comp. 13 and 19. (B.C. 910.)

3. Father of Ishmael, one of the "captains of hundreds" whom Jehoiada the priest took into his confidence about the restoration of the line of Judah. 2 Chron. 23 : 1. (B.C. 910.)

4. One of the Bene-Bebai who was forced to put away his foreign wife. Ezra 10 : 28. (B.C. 459.)

5. A priest, Neh. 12 : 13, during the high priesthood of Joiakim. ver. 12. (B. C. 406.)

6. A priest who took part in the dedication of the wall of Jerusalem. Neh. 12 : 42. (B.C. 446.)

Jeho-i'achin (*whom Jehovah has appointed*), son of Jehoiakim, and for three months and ten days king of Judah. (B. C. 597.) At his accession Jerusalem was quite defenceless, and unable to offer any resistance to the army which Nebuchadnezzar sent to besiege it. 2 Kings 24 : 10, 11. In a very short time Jehoiachin surrendered at discretion; and he, and the queen-mother, and all his servants, captains and officers, came out and gave themselves up to Nebuchadnezzar, who carried them, with the harem and the eunuchs, to Babylon. Jer. 29 : 2; Ezek. 17 : 12; 19 : 9. There he remained a prisoner, actually in prison and wearing prison garments, for thirty-six years, viz., till the death of Nebuchadnezzar, when Evilmerodach, succeeding to the throne of

Babylon, brought him out of prison, and made him sit at his own table. The time of his death is uncertain.

Jeho-i′ada (*Jehovah knows*). 1. Father of Benaiah, David's well-known warrior. 2 Sam. 8 : 18; 1 Kings 1 and 2 *passim;* 1 Chron. 18 : 17, etc. (B.C. before 1046.)

2. Leader of the Aaronites, *i. e.* the priests; who joined David at Hebron. 1 Chron. 12 : 27. (B.C. 1053–46.)

3. According to 1 Chron. 27 : 34, son of Benaiah; but in all probability Benaiah the son of Jehoinda is meant. Probably an error in copying. 1 Chron. 18 : 17; 2 Sam. 8 : 18.

4. High priest at the time of Athaliah's usurpation of the throne of Judah, B.C. 884–878, and during the greater portion of the forty-years reign of Joash. He married Jehosheba; and when Athaliah slew all the seed royal of Judah after Ahaziah had been put to death by Jehu, he and his wife stole Joash from among the king's sons and hid him for six years in the temple, and eventually replaced him on the throne of his ancestors. [ATHALIAH.] The destruction of Baal-worship and the restoration of the temple were among the great works effected by Jehoiada. He died B.C. 834.

5. Second priest, or sagan, to Seraiah the high priest. Jer. 29 : 25–29; 2 Kings 25 : 18.

6. Son of Paseach, who assisted to repair the old gate of Jerusalem. Neh. 3 : 6.

Jeho-i′akim (*whom Jehovah sets up*), called Eliakim, son of Josiah and king of Judah. After deposing Jehoahaz, Pharaoh-necho set Eliakim, his elder brother, upon the throne, and changed his name to Jehoiakim, B.C. 608–597. For four years Jehoiakim was subject to Egypt, when Nebuchadnezzar, after a short siege, entered Jerusalem, took the king prisoner, bound him in fetters to carry him to Babylon, and took also some of the precious vessels of the temple and carried them to the land of Shinar. Jehoiakim became tributary to Nebuchadnezzar after his invasion of Judah, and continued so for three years, but at the end of that time broke his oath of allegiance and rebelled against him. 2 Kings 24 : 1. Nebuchadnezzar sent against him numerous bands of Chaldeans, with Syrians, Moabites and Ammonites, 2 Kings 24 : 7, and who cruelly harassed the whole country. Either in an engagement with some of these forces or else by the hand

of his own oppressed subjects Jehoiakim came to a violent end in the eleventh year of his reign. His body was cast out ignominiously on the ground, and then was dragged away and buried "with the burial of an ass," without pomp or lamentation, "beyond the gates of Jerusalem." Jer. 22 : 18, 19; 36 : 30. All the accounts we have of Jehoiakim concur in ascribing to him a vicious and irreligious character. 2 Kings 23 : 37; 24 · 9; 2 Chron. 36 : 5. The reign of Jehoiakim extends from B.C. 609 to B.C. 598, or, as some reckon, 599.

Jeho-i′arib (*whom Jehovah defends*), head of the first of the twenty-four courses of priests. 1 Chron. 24 : 7.

Jehon′adab (*whom Jehovah impels*) and **Jon′adab,** the son of Rechab, founder of the Rechabites, an Arab chief. When Jehu was advancing, after the slaughter of Betheked, on the city of Samaria, he was suddenly met by Jehonadab, who joined him in "slaying all that remained unto Ahab." 2 Kings 10 : 15–17.

Jehon′athan (*whom Jehovah gave*). 1. Son of Uzziah; superintendent of certain of King David's storehouses. 1 Chron. 27 : 25. (B.C. 1014.)

2. One of the Levites who were sent by Jehoshaphat through the cities of Judah, with a book of the law, to teach the people. 2 Chron. 17 : 8. (B.C. 910.)

3. A priest, Neh. 12 : 18, the representative of the family of Shemaiah, ver. 6, when Joiakim was high priest. (B.C. after 536.)

Jeho′ram (*whom Jehovah has exalted*). 1. Son of Ahab king of Israel, who succeeded his brother Ahaziah B.C. 896, and died B.C. 884. The alliance between the kingdoms of Israel and Judah, commenced by his father and Jehoshaphat, was very close throughout his reign. We first find him associated with Jehoshaphat and the king of Edom in a war against the Moabites. The three armies were in the utmost danger of perishing for want of water. The piety of Jehoshaphat suggested an inquiry of Jehovah, through Elisha. After reproving Jehoram, Elisha, for Jehoshaphat's sake, inquired of Jehovah, and received the promise of an abundant supply of water, and of a great victory over the Moabites; a promise which was immediately fulfilled. The allies pursued them with great slaughter into their own land, which they utterly ravaged and destroyed most of its cities. Kirharaseth alone remained, and there the king of Moab made his last stand. An attempt to break through the besieging army having failed, he resorted to the desperate expedient of offering up his eldest son, as a burnt offering, upon the wall of the city, in the sight of the enemy. Upon this the Israelites retired and returned to their own land. 2 Kings 3. A little later, when war broke out between Syria and Israel, we find Elisha befriending Jehoram; but when the terrible famine in Samaria arose, the king immediately attributed the evil to Elisha, and determined to take away his life. The providential interposition by which both Elisha's life was saved and the city delivered is narrated 2 Kings 7, and Jehoram appears to have returned to friendly feeling toward Elisha. 2 Kings 8 : 4. It was soon after these events that the revolution in Syria predicted by Elisha took place, giving Jehoram a good opportunity of recovering Ramoth-gilead from the Syrians. He accordingly made an alliance with his nephew Ahaziah, who had just succeeded Joram on the throne of Judah, and the two kings proceeded to occupy Ramoth-gilead by force. The expedition was an unfortunate one. Jehoram was wounded in battle, and obliged to return to Jezreel to be healed of his wounds. 2 Kings 8 : 29 ; 9 : 14, 15. Jehu and the army under his command revolted from their allegiance to Jehoram, 2 Kings 9, and hastily marching to Jezreel, surprised Jehoram, wounded and defenceless as he was. Jehoram, going out to meet him, fell pierced by an arrow from Jehu's bow on the very plot of ground which Ahab had wrested from Naboth the Jezreelite; thus fulfilling to the letter the prophecy of Elijah. 1 Kings 21 : 29. With the life of Jehoram ended the dynasty of Omri.

2. Eldest son of Jehoshaphat, succeeded his father on the throne of Judah at the age of 32, and reigned eight years, from B.C. 893-2 to 885-4. As soon as he was fixed on the throne, he put his six brothers to death, with many of the chief nobles of the land. He then, probably at the instance of his wife Athaliah the daughter of Ahab, proceeded to establish the worship of Baal. A prophetic writing from the aged prophet Elijah, 2 Chron. 21 : 12, failed to produce any good effect upon him. The remainder of his reign was a series of calamities. First the

Edomites, who had been tributary to Jehoshaphat, revolted from his dominion and established their permanent independence. Next Libnah, 2 Kings 19 : 8, rebelled against him. Then followed invasion by armed bands of Philistines and of Arabians, who stormed the king's palace, put his wives and all his children, except his youngest son Ahaziah, to death, 2 Chron. 22 : 1, or carried them into captivity, and plundered all his treasures. He died of a terrible disease. 2 Chron. 21 : 19, 20.

Jehoshab'e-ath (*whose oath is Jehovah*). 2 Chron. 22 : 11. [See JEHOSHEBA.]

J e h o s h'a p h a t (*whom Jehovah judges*). 1. King of Judah, son of Asa, succeeded to the throne B.C. 914, when he was 35 years old, and reigned 25 years. His history is to be found among the events recorded in 1 Kings 15 : 24; 2 Kings 8 : 16, or in a continuous narrative in 2 Chron. 17 : 1-3. He was contemporary with Ahab, Ahaziah and Jehoram. He was one of the best, most pious and prosperous kings of Judah, the greatest since Solomon. At first he strengthened himself against Israel; but soon afterward the two Hebrew kings formed an alliance. In his own kingdom Jehoshaphat ever showed himself a zealous follower of the commandments of God: he tried to put down the high places and groves in which the people of Judah burnt incense, and sent the wisest Levites through the cities and towns to instruct the people in true morality and religion. Riches and honors increased around him. He received tribute from the Philistines and Arabians, and kept up a large standing army in Jerusalem. It was probably about the 16th year of his reign, B.C. 898, when he became Ahab's ally in the great battle of Ramoth-gilead, for which he was severely reproved by Jehu. 2 Chron. 19 : 2. He built at Ezion-geber, with the help of Ahaziah, a navy designed to go to Tarshish; but it was wrecked at Ezion-geber. Before the close of his reign he was engaged in two additional wars. He was miraculously delivered from a threatened attack of the people of Ammon, Moab and Seir. After this, perhaps, must be dated the war which Jehoshaphat, in conjunction with Jehoram king of Israel and the king of Edom, carried on against the rebellious king of Moab. 2 Kings 3. In his declining years the administration of affairs was placed, probably B.C. 891, in the hands of his son Jehoram.

2. Son of Ahilud, who filled the office of recorder or annalist in the courts of David, 2 Sam. 8 : 16, etc., and Solomon. 1 Kings 4 : 3.

3. One of the priests in David's time. 1 Chron. 15 : 24.

4. Son of Paruah; one of the twelve purveyors of King Solomon. 1 Kings 4 : 17.

5. Son of Nimshi and father of King Jehu. 2 Kings 9 : 2, 14.

Jehosh'aphat, Valley of (*valley of the judgment of Jehovah*), a valley mentioned by Joel only, as the spot in which, after the return of Judah and Jerusalem from captivity, Jehovah would gather all the heathen, Joel 3 : 2, and would there sit to judge them for their misdeeds to Israel. ch. 3 : 12. The scene of "Jehovah's judgment" has been localized, and the name has come down to us attached to that deep ravine which separates Jerusalem from the Mount of Olives, through which at one time the Kedron forced its stream. At what period the name "valley of Jehoshaphat" was first applied to this spot is unknown. It is not mentioned in the Bible or Josephus, but is first encountered in the middle of the fourth century. Both Moslems and Jews believe that the last judgment is to take place there. The steep sides of the ravine, wherever a level strip affords the opportunity, are crowded—in places almost paved—by the sepulchres of the Moslems, or the simpler slabs of the Jewish tombs, alike awaiting the assembly of the last judgment. The name is generally confined by travellers to the upper part of the glen. (Others suppose that the name is only an imaginary one, "the valley of the judgment of Jehovah" referring to some great victories of God's people in which judgment was executed upon the heathen; or perhaps, as Keil, etc., to the end of the world.—ED.)

Jehosh'eba (*Jehovah's oath*), daughter of Joram king of Israel, and wife of Jehoiada the high priest. 2 Kings 11 : 2. Her name in the Chronicles is given JEHOSHABEATH. (B.C. 882.) As she is called, 2 Kings 11 : 2, "the daughter of *Joram*, sister of Ahaziah," it has been conjectured that she was the daughter, not of Athaliah, but of Joram by another wife. She is the only recorded instance of the marriage of a princess of the royal house with a high priest.

Jehosh'ua (*whose help is Jehovah; help of Jehovah* or *saviour*). In this form is given the name of Joshua in Num. 13 : 16. Once more only the name appears,—as

Jehosh'uah, in the genealogy of Ephraim. 1 Chron. 7 : 27.

Jeho'vah (*I am; the eternal living one*). The Scripture appellation of the supreme Being, usually interpreted as signifying self-derived and permanent existence. The Jews scrupulously avoided every mention of this name of God, substituting in its stead one or other of the words with whose proper vowel-points it may happen to be written. This custom, which had its origin in reverence, was founded upon an erroneous rendering of Lev. 24 : 16, from which it was inferred that the mere utterance of the name constituted a capital offence. According to Jewish tradition, it was pronounced but once a year, by the high priest on the day of atonement when he entered the holy of holies; but on this point there is some doubt. When Moses received his commission to be the deliverer of Israel, the Almighty, who appeared in the burning bush, communicated to him the name which he should give as the credentials of his mission : "And God said unto Moses, I AM THAT I AM אֶהְיֶה אֲשֶׁר אֶהְיֶה (*ehyeh ăsher ehyeh*); and he said, Thus shalt thou say unto the children of Israel, I AM hath sent me unto you." That this passage is intended to indicate the etymology of Jehovah, as understood by the Hebrews, no one has ventured to doubt. While Elohim exhibits God displayed in his power as the creator and governor of the physical universe, the name Jehovah designates his nature as he stands in relation to man, as the only almighty, true, personal, holy Being, a spirit and "the father of spirits," Num 16 : 22; comp. John 4 : 24, who revealed himself to his people, made a covenant with them, and became their lawgiver, and to whom all honor and worship are due.

Jeho'vah-ji'reh (*Jehovah will see* or *provide*), the name given by Abraham to the place on which he had been commanded to offer Isaac, to commemorate the interposition of the angel of Jehovah, who appeared to prevent the sacrifice, Gen. 22 : 14, and provided another victim.

Jeho'vah-nis'si (*Jehovah my banner*), the name given by Moses to the

Tomb of St. James (so called), in the Valley of Jehoshaphat.

Tomb of Absalom.   Tomb of St. James.   Tomb of Zechariah

Valley of Jehoshaphat.

altar which he built in commemoration
of the discomfiture of the Amalekites.
Ex. 17 : 15.

Jeho'vah-sha'lom (*Jehovah (is)
peace*), or, with an ellipsis, "Jehovah
the God of peace." The altar erected by
Gideon in Ophrah was so called in memory of the salutation addressed to him by
the angel of Jehovah, "Peace be unto
thee." Judges 6 : 24.

Jehoz'abad (*whom Jehovah gave*). 1.
A Korhite Levite, second son of Obed-
edom, and one of the porters of the south
gate of the temple and of the storehouse
there in the time of David. 1 Chron. 26 :
4, 15, compared with Neh. 12 : 25. (B.C.
1014.)

2. A Benjamite, captain of 180,000
armed men, in the days of King Jehoshaphat. 2 Chron. 17 : 18. (B.C. 910.)

3. Son of Shomer or Shimrith, a Moabitish woman, who with another conspired against King Joash and slew him
in his bed. 2 Kings 12 : 21 ; 2 Chron. 24 :
26. (B.C. 837.)

Jehoz'adak (*Jehovah justifies*), usually called Jozadak or Josedech. He
was the son of the high priest Seraiah. 1
Chron. 6 : 14, 15. When his father was
slain at Riblah by order of Nebuchadnezzar, 2 Kings 25 : 18, 21, Jehozadak
was led away captive to Babylon. 1
Chron. 6 : 15. (B.C. 588.) He himself
never attained the high priesthood, but
he was the father of Jeshua the high
priest, and of all his successors till the
pontificate of Alcimus. Ezra 3 : 2 ; Neh.
12 : 26, etc.

Je'hu (*the living*). 1. The founder of
the fifth dynasty of the kingdom of Israel,
son of Jehoshaphat. 2 Kings 9 : 2. He
reigned over Israel 28 years, B.C. 884–856.
His first appearance in history is when he
heard the warning of Elijah against the
murderer of Naboth. 2 Kings 9 : 25. In
the reigns of Ahaziah and Jehoram,
Jehu rose to importance. He was, under
the last-named king, captain of the host
in the siege of Ramoth-gilead. During
this siege he was anointed by Elisha's
servant, and told that he was appointed
to be king of Israel and destroyer of the
house of Ahab. 2 Kings 9 : 12. The army
at once ordained him king, and he set off
full speed for Jezreel. Jehoram, who
was lying ill in Jezreel, came out to meet
him, as it happened on the fatal field of
Naboth. 2 Kings 9 : 21–24. Jehu seized his
opportunity, and shot him through the
heart. 2 Kings 9 : 24. Jehu himself ad-

vanced to the gates of Jezreel and fulfilled the divine warning on Jezebel as
already on Jehoram. He then entered
on a work of extermination hitherto unparalleled in the history of the Jewish
monarchy. All the descendants of Ahab
that remained in Jezreel, together with
the officers of the court and the hierarchy
of Astarte, were swept away. His next
step was to secure Samaria. For the
pretended purpose of inaugurating anew
the worship of Baal, he called all the
Baalites together at Samaria. The vast
temple raised by Ahab, 1 Kings 16 : 32,
was crowded from end to end. The chief

The Black Obelisk, inscribed with the names
of Jehu and Hazael.

sacrifice was offered, as if in the excess
of his zeal, by Jehu himself. As soon
as it was ascertained that all, and none
but, the idolaters were there, the signal
was given to eighty trusted guards, and a
sweeping massacre removed at one blow
the whole heathen population of the
kingdom of Israel. This is the last public act recorded of Jehu. The remaining
twenty-seven years of his long reign are
passed over in a few words, in which two
points only are material :—He did not
destroy the calf-worship of Jeroboam :—
The transjordanic tribes suffered much
from the ravages of Hazael. 2 Kings 10 :

29–33. He was buried in state in Samaria, and was succeeded by his son Jehoahaz. 2 Kings 10:35. His name is the first of the Israelite kings which appears in the Assyrian monuments.

2. Jehu son of Hanani; a prophet of Judah, but whose ministrations were chiefly directed to Israel. His father was probably the seer who attacked Asa. 2 Chron. 16:7. He must have begun his career as a prophet when very young. He first denounced Baasha, 1 Kings 16:1, 7, and then, after an interval of thirty years, reappeared to denounce Jehoshaphat for his alliance with Ahab. 2 Chron. 19:2, 3. He survived Jehoshaphat and wrote his life. ch. 20:34.

3. A man of Judah of the house of Hezron. 1 Chron. 2:38.

4. A Simeonite, son of Josibiah. 1 Chron. 4:35.

5. Jehu the Antothite was one of the chief of the heroes of Benjamin who joined David at Ziklag. 1 Chron. 12:3.

Jehub'bah (*protected*), a man of Asher, son of Shamer or Shomer, of the house of Beriah. 1 Chron. 7:34. (B.C. perhaps about 1450.)

Je'hucal (*able*), son of Shelemiah; one of two persons sent by King Zedekiah to Jeremiah to entreat his prayers and advice. Jer. 37:3. (B.C. 589.)

Je'hud (*praised*), one of the towns of the tribe of Dan, Josh. 19:45, named between Baalath and Bene-berak.

Jehu'di (*a Jew*), son of Nethaniah, a man employed by the princes of Jehoiakim's court to fetch Baruch to read Jeremiah's denunciation, Jer. 36:14, and then by the king to fetch the volume itself and read it to him. vs. 21, 23. (B.C. 605.)

Jehudi'jah (*the Jewess*). There is really no such name in the Hebrew Bible as that which our Authorized Version exhibits at 1 Chron. 4:18. If it is a proper name at all, it is Ha-jehudijah, like Hammelech, Hak-koz, etc.; and it seems to be rather an appellative, " the Jewess."

Je'hush (*to whom God hastens*), son of Eshek, a remote descendant of Saul. 1 Chron. 8:39.

Je-i'el (*treasured of God*). 1. A Reubenite of the house of Joel. 1 Chron. 5:7.

2. A Merarite Levite, one of the gatekeepers to the sacred tent. 1 Chron. 15:18. His duty was also to play the harp, ver. 21, or the psaltery and harp, 16:5, in the service before the ark. (B.C. 1043.)

3. A Gershonite Levite, one of the Bene-Asaph, forefather of Jahaziel in the time of King Jehoshaphat. 2 Chron. 20:14. (B.C. 910.)

4. The scribe who kept the account of the numbers of King Uzziah's irregular predatory warriors. 2 Chron. 26:11. (B.C. 803.)

5. A Gershonite Levite, one of the Bene-Elizaphan. 2 Chron. 29:13.

6. One of the chiefs of the Levites in the time of Josiah. 2 Chron. 35:9. (B.C. 623.)

7. One of the Bene-Adonikam who formed part of the caravan of Ezra from Babylon to Jerusalem. Ezra 8:13. (B.C. 459.)

8. A layman of the Bene-Nebo, who had taken a foreign wife and had to relinquish her. Ezra 10:43. (B.C. 459.)

Jekab'ze-el (*what God gathers*), a fuller form of the name of KABZEEL, the most remote city of Judah on the southern frontier. Neh. 11:25.

Jekame'am (*who gathers the people together*), a Levite in the time of King David; fourth of the sons of Hebron, the son of Kohath. 1 Chron. 23:19; 24:23. (B.C. 1014.)

Jekami'ah (*whom Jehovah gathers*), son of Shallum, in the line of Ahlai. 1 Chron. 2:41. (B.C. about 588.)

Jeku'thi-el, a man recorded in the genealogies of Judah. 1 Chron. 4:18.

Jemi'ma (*dove*), the eldest of the three daughters born to Job after the restoration of his prosperity. Job 42:14.

Jemu'el (*day of God*), the eldest son of Simeon. Gen. 46:10; Ex. 6:15. (B.C. 1706.)

Jeph'thae (*whom God sets free*), Heb. 11:32, the Greek form of the name JEPHTHAH.

Jeph'thah (*whom God sets free*), a judge about B.C. 1143–1137. His history is contained in Judges 11:1–12:8. He was a Gileadite, the son of Gilead and a concubine. Driven by the legitimate sons from his father's inheritance, he went to Tob and became the head of a company of freebooters in a debatable land probably belonging to Ammon. 2 Sam. 10:6. (This land was east of the Jordan and southeast of Gilead, and bordered on the desert of Arabia.—ED.) His fame as a bold and successful captain was carried back to his native Gilead; and when the time was ripe for throwing off the yoke of Ammon, Jephthah consented to become the captain of the Gileadite bands, on the condition, solemnly ratified before the Lord in Mizpeh, that in the event of his success against Ammon he should still remain as their acknowledged head. Vowing his vow unto God, Judges 11 : 31, that he would offer up as a burnt offering whatsoever should come out to meet him if successful, he went forth to battle. The Ammonites were routed with great slaughter; but as the conqueror returned to Mizpeh there came out to meet him his daughter, his only child, with timbrels and dancing. The father is heart-stricken; but the maiden asks only for a respite of two months in which to prepare for death. When that time was ended she returned to her father, who "did with her according to his vow." The tribe of Ephraim challenged Jephthah's right to go to war as he had done, without their concurrence, against Ammon. He first defeated them, then intercepted the fugitives at the fords of Jordan, and there put forty-two thousand men to the sword. He judged Israel six years, and died. It is generally conjectured that his jurisdiction was limited to the transjordanic region. That the daughter of Jephthah was really offered up to God in sacrifice is a conclusion which it seems impossible to avoid. (But there is no word of approval, as if such a sacrifice was acceptable to God. Josephus well says that "the sacrifice was neither sanctioned by the Mosaic ritual nor acceptable to God." The vow and the fulfillment were the mistaken conceptions of a rude chieftain, not acts pleasing to God. —ED.)

Jephun'neh (*for whom a way is prepared*). 1. Father of Caleb the spy, appears to have belonged to an Edomitish tribe called Kenezites, from Kenaz their founder. See Num. 13 : 6, etc.; 32 : 12, etc.; Josh. 14 : 14, etc.; 1 Chron. 4 : 15. (B.C. 1530.)

2. A descendant of Asher, eldest of the three sons of Jether. 1 Chron. 7 : 38. (B.C. 1017.)

Je'rah (*the moon*), the fourth in order of the sons of Joktan, Gen. 10 : 26; 1 Chron. 1 : 20, and the progenitor of a tribe of southern Arabia.

Jerah'me-el (*mercy of God*). 1. First-born son of Hezron, the son of Pharez, the son of Judah, 1 Chron. 2 : 9, 25–27, 33, 42, and founder of the family of Jerahmeelites. 1 Sam. 27 : 10. (B.C. before 1491.)

2. A Merarite Levite, the representa-

tive of the family of Kish, the son of Mahli. 1 Chron. 24 : 29; comp. 23 : 21. (B.C. 1014.)

3. Son of Hammelech, who was employed by Jehoiakim to make Jeremiah and Baruch prisoners, after he had burnt the roll of Jeremiah's prophecy. Jer. 36 : 26. (B.C. 505.)

Jerah'me-elites (*descendants of Jerahmeel*), **The,** the tribe descended from the first of the foregoing persons. 1 Sam. 27 : 10. They dwelt in the south of Judah.

Je'red (*descent*). 1. Son of Mahalaleel and father of Enoch. 1 Chron. 1 : 2.

2. One of the descendants of Judah signalized as the "father"—*i. e.* the founder—"of Gedor." 1 Chron. 4 : 18.

Jer'ema-i (*dwelling in heights*), a layman, one of the Bene-Hashum, who was compelled by Ezra to put away his foreign wife. Ezra 10 : 33. (B.C. 459.)

Jeremi'ah (*whom Jehovah has appointed*) was "the son of Hilkiah of the priests that were in Anathoth." Jer. 1 : 1.

1. *History.*—He was called very young (B.C. 626) to the prophetic office, and prophesied forty-two years; but we have hardly any mention of him during the eighteen years between his call and Josiah's death, or during the short reign of Jehoahaz. During the reigns of Jehoiakim and Jehoiachin, B.C. 607–598, he opposed the Egyptian party, then dominant in Jerusalem, and maintained that the only way of safety lay in accepting the supremacy of the Chaldeans. He was accordingly accused of treachery, and men claiming to be prophets had their "word of Jehovah" to set against his. Jer. 14 : 13; 23 : 7. As the danger from the Chaldeans became more threatening, the persecution against Jeremiah grew hotter. ch. 18. The people sought his life; then follows the scene in Jer. 19 : 10–13. He was set, however, "as a fenced brazen wall," ch. 15 : 20, and went on with his work, reproving king and nobles and people. The danger which Jeremiah had so long foretold at last came near. First Jehoiakim, and afterwards his successor Jehoiachin, were carried into exile, 2 Kings 24; but Zedekiah, B.C. 597–586, who was appointed by Nebuchadnezzar, was more friendly to the prophet, though powerless to help him. The approach of an Egyptian army, and the consequent departure of the Chaldeans, made the position of Jere-

miah full of danger, and he sought to effect his escape from the city; but he was seized and finally thrown into a prison-pit to die, but was rescued. On the return of the Chaldean army he showed his faith in God's promises, and sought to encourage the people by purchasing the field at Anathoth which his kinsman Hanameel wished to get rid of. Jer. 32 : 6–9. At last the blow came. The city was taken, the temple burnt. The king and his princes shared the fate of Jehoiachin. The prophet gave utterance to his sorrow in the Lamentations. After the capture of Jerusalem, B.C. 586, by the Chaldeans, we find Jeremiah receiving better treatment; but after the death of Gedaliah, the people, disregarding his warnings, took refuge in Egypt, carrying the prophet with them. In captivity his words were sharper and stronger than ever. He did not shrink, even there, from speaking of the Chaldean king once more as "the servant of Jehovah." Jer. 43 : 10. After this all is uncertain, but he probably died in Egypt.

2. *Character.*—Canon Cook says of Jeremiah, "His character is most interesting. We find him sensitive to a most painful degree, timid, shy, hopeless, desponding, constantly complaining and dissatisfied with the course of events, but never flinching from duty. . . . Timid in resolve, he was unflinching in execution; as fearless when he had to face the whole world as he was dispirited and prone to murmuring when alone with God. Judged by his own estimate of himself, he was feeble, and his mission a failure; really, in the hour of action and when duty called him, he was in very truth 'a defenced city, and an iron pillar, and brazen walls against the whole land.' ch. 1 : 18. He was a noble example of the triumph of the moral over the physical nature."

(It is not strange that he was desponding when we consider his circumstances. He saw the nation going straight to irremediable ruin, and turning a deaf ear to all warnings. "A reign of terror had commenced (in the preceding reign), during which not only the prophets but all who were distinguished for religion and virtue were cruelly murdered." "The nation tried to extirpate the religion of Jehovah;" "Idolatry was openly established," "and such was the universal dishonesty that no man trusted another, and society was utterly disorganized." How could one who saw the nation about to reap the awful harvest they had been sowing, and yet had a vision of what they might have been—and might yet be, help indulging in "Lamentations"?—ED.)

Jeremi′ah. Seven other persons bearing the same name as the prophet are mentioned in the Old Testament:—1. Jeremiah of Libnah, father of Hamutal wife of Josiah. 2 Kings 23 : 31. (B.C. before 632.)

2, 3, 4. Three warriors—two of the tribe of Gad—in David's army. 1 Chron. 12 : 4, 10, 13. (B.C. 1061–53.)

5. One of the "mighty men of valor" of the transjordanic half-tribe of Manasseh. 1 Chron. 5 : 24. (B.C. 782.)

6. A priest of high rank, head of the second or third of the twenty-one courses which are apparently enumerated in Neh. 10 : 2–8; 12 : 1, 12. (B.C. 446–410.)

7. The father of Jazaniah the Rechabite. Jer. 35 : 3. (B.C. before 606.)

Jeremi′ah, Book of. "There can be little doubt that the book of Jeremiah grew out of the roll which Baruch wrote down at the prophet's mouth in the fourth year of Jehoiakim. ch. 36 : 2. Apparently the prophets kept written records of their predictions, and collected into larger volumes such of them as were intended for permanent use."—*Canon Cook.*

In the present order we have two great divisions:—I. Chs. 1–45. Prophecies delivered at various times, directed mainly to Judah, or connected with Jeremiah's personal history. II. Chs. 46–51. Prophecies connected with other nations. Looking more closely into each of these divisions, we have the following sections: 1. Chs. 1–21, including prophecies from the thirteenth year of Josiah to the fourth of Jehoiakim; ch. 21 belongs to the later period. 2. Chs. 22–25. Shorter prophecies, delivered at different times, against the kings of Judah and the false prophets. Ch. 25 : 13, 14 evidently marks the conclusion of a series of prophecies; and that which follows, ch. 25 : 15–38, the germ of the fuller predictions in chs. 46–49, has been placed here as a kind of completion to the prophecy of the seventy years and the subsequent fall of Babylon. 3. Chs. 26–28. The two great prophecies of the fall of Jerusalem, and the history connected with them. 4. Chs. 29–31. The message of comfort for the exiles in Babylon. 5. Chs. 32–44. The history of the last two years before the capture of Jerusalem, and of Jeremiah's work in them and in the period that followed. 6. Chs. 46–51. The prophecies against foreign nations, ending with the great prediction against Babylon. 7. The supplementary narrative of ch. 52.

Jeremi′as, the Greek form of the name of Jeremiah the prophet. Matt. 16 : 14.

Jer′emoth (*heights*). 1. A Benjamite chief, a son of the house of Beriah of Elpaal. 1 Chron. 8 : 14; comp. 12 to 18. (B.C. about 588.)

2. A Merarite Levite, son of Mushi. 1 Chron. 23 : 23.

3. Son of Heman; head of the thirteenth course of musicians in the divine service. 1 Chron. 25 : 22. (B.C. 1014.)

4. One of the sons of Elam, and,

5. One of the sons of Zattu, who had taken strange wives. Ezra 10 : 26, 27. (B.C. 459.)

6. The name which appears in the same list as "and RAMOTH," ver. 29.

Jer′emy, the prophet Jeremiah. Matt. 2 : 17; 27 : 9.

Jeri′ah, a Kohathite Levite, chief of the great house of Hebron when David organized the service. 1 Chron. 23 : 19; 24 : 23. B.C. 1014. The same man is mentioned again as JERIJAH. 1 Chron. 26 : 31.

Jer′iba-i (*whom Jehovah defends*), one of the Bene-Elnaan, named among the heroes of David's guard. 1 Chron. 11 : 46.

Jer′icho (*place of fragrance*), a city of high antiquity, situated in a plain traversed by the Jordan, and exactly over against where that river was crossed by the Israelites under Joshua. Josh. 3 : 16. It was five miles of the Jordan and seven miles northwest of the Dead Sea. It had a king. Its walls were so considerable that houses were built upon them. ch. 2 : 15. The spoil that was found in it betokened its affluence. Jericho is first mentioned as the city to which the two spies were sent by Joshua from Shittim. Josh. 2 : 1–21. It was bestowed by him upon the tribe of Benjamin, ch. 18 : 21, and from this time a long interval elapses before Jericho appears again upon the scene. Its second foundation under Hiel the Bethelite is recorded in 1 Kings 16 : 34. Once rebuilt, Jericho rose again slowly into consequence. In its immediate vicinity the sons of the prophets

sought retirement from the world; Elisha "healed the spring of the waters;" and over against it, beyond Jordan, Elijah "went up by a whirlwind into heaven."

Jericho.

2 Kings 2 : 1–22. In its plains Zedekiah fell into the hands of the Chaldeans. 2 Kings 25 : 5; Jer. 39 : 5. In the return under Zerubbabel the "children of Jeri-

Fountain of Elisha at Jericho.

cho," 345 in number, are comprised. Ezra 2 : 34; Neh. 7 : 36. Under Herod the Great it again became an important place. He fortified it and built a number of new palaces, which he named after his friends. If he did not make Jericho his habitual residence, he at last retired thither to die, and it was in the amphitheatre of Jericho that the news of his death was announced to the assembled soldiers and people by Salome. Soon afterward the palace was burnt and the town plundered by one Simon, slave to Herod; but Archelaus rebuilt the former sumptuously, and founded a new town on the plain, that bore his own name; and, most important of all, diverted water from a village called Neæra to irrigate the plain which he had planted with palms. Thus Jericho was once more "a city of palms" when our Lord visited it. Here he restored sight to the blind. Matt. 20:30; Mark 10:46; Luke 18:35. Here the descendant of Rahab did not disdain the hospitality of Zacchæus the publican. Finally, between Jerusalem and Jericho was laid the scene of his story of the good Samaritan. The city was destroyed by Vespasian. The site of ancient (the first) Jericho is placed by Dr. Robinson in the immediate neighborhood of the fountain of Elisha; and that of the second (the city of the New Testament and of Josephus) at the opening of the *Wady Kelt* (Cherith), half an hour from the fountain. (The village identified with Jericho lies a mile and a half from the ancient site, and is called *Riha*. It contains probably 200 inhabitants, indolent and licentious, and about 40 houses. Dr. Olin says it is the " meanest and foulest village of Palestine;" yet the soil of the plain is of unsurpassed fertility.— Ed.)

Je'ri-el (*people of God*), a man of Issachar, one of the six heads of the house of Tola. 1 Chron. 7:2.

Jeri'jah (*people of Jehovah*). [See Jeriah.]

Jer'imoth (*heights*). 1. Son or descendant of Bela. 1 Chron. 7:7. He is perhaps the same as

2, who joined David at Ziklag. 1 Chron. 12:5. (B.C. 1055.)

3. A son of Becher, 1 Chron. 7:8, and head of a Benjamite house.

4. Son of Mushi, the son of Merari. 1 Chron. 24:30.

5. Son of Heman, head of the fifteenth ward of musicians. 1 Chron. 25:4, 22. (B.C. 1014.)

6. Son of Azriel, ruler of the tribe of Naphtali in the reign of David. 1 Chron. 27:19.

7. Son of King David, whose daughter Mahalath was one of the wives of Rehoboam, her cousin Abihail being the other. 2 Chron. 11:18. (B.C. before 1014.)

8. A Levite in the reign of Hezekiah. 2 Chron. 31:13. (B.C. 726.)

Jer'ioth (*curtains*), one of the elder Caleb's wives. 1 Chron. 2:18.

Jerobo'am (*whose people are many*). 1. The first king of the divided kingdom of Israel, B.C. 975–954, was the son of an Ephraimite of the name of Nebat. He was raised by Solomon to the rank of superintendent over the taxes and labors exacted from the tribe of Ephraim. 1 Kings 11:28. He made the most of his position, and at last was perceived by Solomon to be aiming at the monarchy. He was leaving Jerusalem, when he was met by Ahijah the prophet, who gave him the assurance that, on condition of obedience to his laws, God would establish for him a kingdom and dynasty equal to that of David. 1 Kings 11:29–40. The attempts of Solomon to cut short Jeroboam's designs occasioned his flight into Egypt. There he remained until Solomon's death. After a year's longer stay in Egypt, during which Jeroboam married Ano, the elder sister of the Egyptian queen Tahpenes, he returned to Shechem, where took place the conference with Rehoboam [REHOBOAM], and the final revolt which ended in the elevation of Jeroboam to the throne of the northern kingdom. Now occurred the fatal error of his policy. Fearing that the yearly pilgrimages to Jerusalem would undo all the work which he effected, he took the bold step of rending the religious unity of the nation, which was as yet unimpaired, asunder. He caused two golden figures of Mnevis, the sacred calf, to be made and set up at the two extremities of his kingdom, one at Dan and the other at Bethel. It was while dedicating the altar at Bethel that a prophet from Judah suddenly appeared, who denounced the altar, and foretold its desecration by Josiah, and violent overthrow. The king, stretching out his hand to arrest the prophet, felt it withered and paralyzed, and only at the prophet's prayer saw it restored, and acknowledged his divine mission. Jeroboam was at constant war with the house of Judah, but the only act distinctly recorded is a battle with Abijah, son of Rehoboam, in which he was defeated. The calamity was severely felt; he never recovered the blow, and soon after died, in the 22d year of his reign, 2 Chron. 13 : 20, and was buried in his ancestral sepulchre. 1 Kings 14 : 20.

2. Jeroboam II., the son of Joash, the fourth of the dynasty of Jehu. (B.C 825–784.) The most prosperous of the kings of Israel. He repelled the Syrian invaders, took their capital city Damascus, 2 Kings 14 : 28, and recovered the whole of the ancient dominion from Hamah to the Dead Sea. ch. 14 : 25. Ammon and Moab were reconquered, and the transjordanic tribes were restored to their territory, 2 Kings 13 : 5; 1 Chron. 5 : 17–22; but it was merely an outward restoration.

Jer′oham (*cherished*). 1. Father of Elkanah, the father of Samuel, of the house of Kohath. 1 Sam. 1 : 1; 1 Chron. 6 : 27, 34. (B.C. before 1142.)

2. A Benjamite, and the founder of a family of Bene-Jeroham. 1 Chron. 8 : 27. Probably the same as

3. Father (or progenitor) of Ibneiah. 1 Chron. 9 : 8; comp. 3 and 9. (B.C. before 588.)

4. A descendant of Aaron, of the house of Immer, the leader of the sixteenth course of priests; son of Pashur, and father of Adaiah. 1 Chron. 9 : 12. He appears to be mentioned again in Neh. 11 : 12. (B.C. before 586.)

5. Jeroham of Gedor, some of whose sons joined David at Ziklag. 1 Chron. 12 : 7. (B.C. before 1055.)

6. A Danite, whose son or descendant Azareel was head of his tribe in the time of David. 1 Chron. 27 : 22.

7. Father of Azariah, one of the "captains of hundreds" in the time of Athaliah. 2 Chron. 23 : 1. (B.C. before 876.)

Jerubba′ai, or **Jerub′ba-al** (*contender with Baal*), the surname of Gideon, which he acquired in consequence of destroying the altar of Baal, when his father defended him from the vengeance of the Abiezrites. Judges 6 : 32.

Jerub′besheth (*contender with the shame*), a name of Gideon. 2 Sam. 11 : 21.

Jer′uel (*founded by God*), **The wilderness of,** the place in which Jehoshaphat was informed by Jahaziel the Levite that he should encounter the hordes of Ammon, Moab and the Mehunims. 2 Chron. 20 : 16. The name has not been met with.

Jeru′salem (*the habitation of peace*). Jerusalem stands in latitude 31° 46′ 35″

north and longitude 35° 18′ 30′ east of Greenwich. It is 32 miles distant from the sea and 18 from the Jordan, 20 from Hebron and 36 from Samaria. "In several respects," says Dean Stanley, "its situation is singular among the cities of Palestine. Its elevation is remarkable; occasioned not from its being on the summit of one of the numerous hills of Judea, like most of the towns and villages, but because it is on the edge of one of the highest table-lands of the country. Hebron indeed is higher still by some hundred feet, and from the south, accordingly (even from Bethlehem), the approach to Jerusalem is by a slight descent. But from any other side the ascent is perpetual; and to the traveller approaching the city from the east or west it must always have presented the appearance beyond any other capital of the then known world—we may say beyond any important city that has ever existed on the earth—of a mountain city; breathing, as compared with the sultry plains of Jordan, a mountain air; enthroned, as compared with Jericho or Damascus, Gaza or Tyre, on a mountain fastness."—*S. & P.* 170, 1. Jerusalem, if not actually in the centre of Palestine, was yet virtually so. "It was on the ridge, the broadest and most strongly-marked ridge of the backbone of the complicated hills which extend through the whole country from the plain of Esdraelon to the desert."

Roads.—There appear to have been but two main approaches to the city :—1. From the Jordan valley by Jericho and the Mount of Olives. This was the route commonly taken from the north and east of the country. 2. From the great maritime plain of Philistia and Sharon. This road led by the two Beth-horons up to the high ground at Gibeon, whence it turned south, and came to Jerusalem by Ramah and Gibeah, and over the ridge north of the city.

Topography.—To convey an idea of the position of Jerusalem, we may say, roughly, that the city occupies the southern termination of a table-land which is cut off from the country round it on its west, south and east sides by ravines more than usually deep and precipitous. These ravines leave the level of the table-land, the one on the west and the other on the northeast of the city, and fall rapidly until they form a junction below its southeast corner. The eastern one—the valley of the Kedron, commonly called

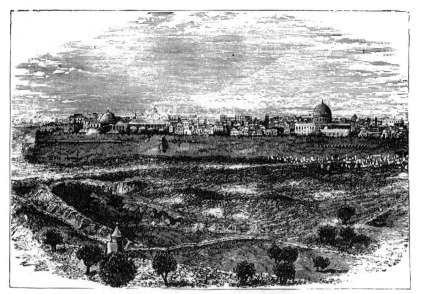

Jerusalem from the Mount of Olives.

General View of Modern Jerusalem. (*From an original Photograph.*)

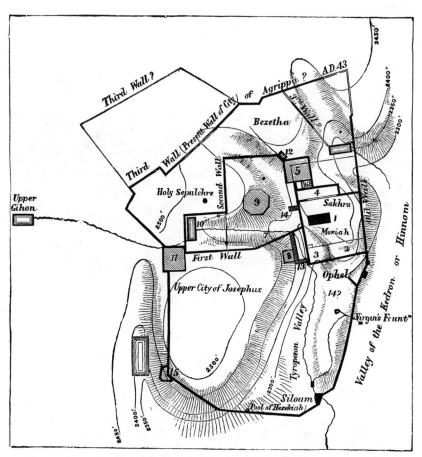

Plan of Jerusalem at the time of King Herod.

1. Temple of Solomon. ⎫	8. Agrippa's Palace.
2. Palace of Solomon. ⎬ Herod's Temple.	9. Zion.
3. Added by Herod. ⎭	10. Lower Pool of Gihon.
4. Exhedra.	11. Herod's Palace.
5. Antonia.	12. Bethesda.
6. Cloisters joining Antonia to Temple.	13. Bridge built by Herod.
7. Xystus.	14. The Lower City.

the valley of Jehoshaphat—runs nearly straight from north to south. But the western one—the valley of Hinnom—runs south for a time, and then takes a sudden bend to the east until it meets the valley of Jehoshaphat, after which the two rush off as one to the Dead Sea. How sudden is their descent may be gathered from the fact that the level at the point of junction—about a mile and a quarter from the starting-point of each—is more than 600 feet below that of the upper plateau from which they began their descent. So steep is the fall of the ravines, so trench-like their character, and so close do they keep to the promontory at whose feet they run, as to leave on the beholder almost the impression of

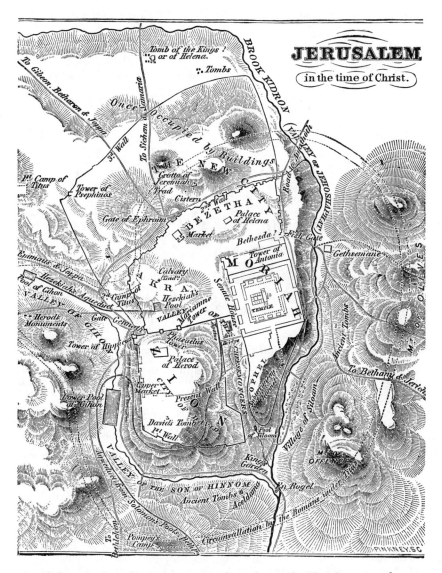

JERUSALEM

in the time of Christ.

the ditch at the foot of a fortress rather than of valleys formed by nature. The promontory thus encircled is itself divided by a longitudinal ravine running up it from south to north, called the valley of the Tyropœon, rising gradually from the south, like the external ones, till at last it arrives at the level of the upper plateau, dividing the central mass into two unequal portions. Of these two, that on the west is the higher and more massive, on which the city of Jeru-

salem now stands, and in fact always
stood. The hill on the east is considerably lower and smaller, so that to a
spectator from the south the city appears
to slope sharply toward the east. Here
was the temple, and here stands now the
great Mohammedan sanctuary with its
mosques and domes. The name of MOUNT
ZION has been applied to the western
hill from the time of Constantine to the

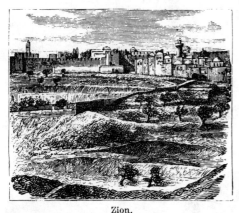

Zion.

present day. The eastern hill, called
MOUNT MORIAH in 2 Chron. 3 : 1, was,
as already remarked, the site of the temple. It was situated in the southwest
angle of the area, now known as the Haram area, and was, as we learn from Josephus, an exact square of a stadium, or
600 Greek feet, on each side. (Conder
(" Bible Handbook," 1879) states that by
the latest surveys the Haram area is a
quadrangle with unequal sides. The
west wall measures 1601 feet, the south
922, the east 1530, the north 1042. It is
thus nearly a mile in circumference, and
contains 35 acres.—ED.) Attached to
the northwest angle of the temple was
the Antonia, a tower or fortress. North of
the side of the temple is the building now
known to Christians as the Mosque of
Omar, but by Moslems called the Dome
of the Rock. The southern continuation
of the eastern hill was named OPHEL,
which gradually came to a point at the
junction of the valleys Tyropœon and
Jehoshaphat; and the northern BEZE-
THA, "the new city," first noticed by Josephus, which was separated from Moriah
by an artificial ditch, and overlooked the

valley of Kedron on the east; this hill
was enclosed within the walls of Herod
Agrippa. Lastly, ACRA lay westward
of Moriah and northward of Zion, and
formed the "lower city" in the time of
Josephus.

Walls.—These are described by Josephus. The *first* or *old wall* was built by
David and Solomon, and enclosed Zion
and part of Mount Moriah. (The second
wall enclosed a portion of the city
called Acra or Millo, on the north
of the city, from the tower of Mariamne to the tower of Antonia. It
was built as the city enlarged in
size; begun by Uzziah 140 years
after the first wall was finished,
continued by Jotham 50 years later,
and by Manasseh 100 years later
still. It was restored by Nehemiah.
Even the latest explorations have
failed to decide exactly what was
its course. (See Conder's Handbook of the Bible, art. *Jerusalem.*)
The *third wall* was built by King
Herod Agrippa, and was intended
to enclose the suburbs which had
grown out on the northern sides of
the city, which before this had been
left exposed. After describing these
walls, Josephus adds that the whole
circumference of the city was 33
stadia, or nearly four English miles,
which is as near as may be the extent indicated by the localities. He then adds
that the number of towers in the old wall
was 60, the middle wall 40, and the new
wall 99.

Water supply.—(Jerusalem had no natural water supply, unless we so consider
the "Fountain of the Virgin," which
wells up with an intermittent action from
under Ophel. The private citizens had
cisterns, which were supplied by the rain
from the roofs; and the city had a water
supply "perhaps the most complete and
extensive ever undertaken by a city," and
which would enable it to endure a long
siege. There were three aqueducts, a
number of pools and fountains, and the
temple area was honeycombed with great
reservoirs, whose total capacity is estimated at 10,000,000 gallons. Thirty of
these reservoirs are described, varying
from 25 to 50 feet in depth; and one, called
the great Sea, would hold 2,000,000 gallons. These reservoirs and the pools
were supplied with water by the rainfall
and by the aqueducts. One of these, constructed by Pilate, has been traced for 40

Eastern Wall and Moslem Tombs.

Walls of Jerusalem.

miles, though in a straight line the distance is but 13 miles. It brought water from the spring Elam, on the south, beyond Bethlehem, into the reservoirs under the temple enclosure.—ED.)

Pools and fountains.—A part of the system of water supply. Outside the walls on the west side were the Upper and Lower Pools of GIHON, the latter close under Zion, the former more to the northwest on the Jaffa road. At the junction of the valleys of Hinnom and Jehoshaphat was ENROGEL, the "Well of Job," in the midst of the king's gardens.

Pool of Hezekiah, inside the Jaffa Gate.

Within the walls, immediately north of Zion, was the "Pool of Hezekiah." A large pool existing beneath the temple (referred to in Ecclus. 1 : 3) was probably supplied by some subterranean aqueduct. The "King's Pool" was probably identical with the "Fountain of the Virgin," at the southern angle of Moriah. It possesses the peculiarity that it rises and falls at irregular periods; it is supposed to be fed from the cistern below the temple. From this a subterranean channel cut through the solid rock leads the water to the pool of SILOAH or SILOAM, which has also acquired the character of being an intermittent fountain. The pool to which tradition has assigned the name of BETHESDA is situated on the north side of Moriah; it is now named *Birket Israil.*

Burial-grounds.—The main cemetery of the city seems from an early date to have been where it is still—on the steep slopes of the valley of the Kedron. The tombs of the kings were in the city of David, that is, Mount Zion. The royal

sepulchres were probably chambers containing separate recesses for the successive kings.

Gardens.—The king's gardens of David and Solomon seem to have been in the bottom formed by the confluence of the Kedron and Hinnom. Neh. 3 : 15. The Mount of Olives, as its name and the names of various places upon it seem to imply, was a fruitful spot. At its foot was situated the garden of Gethsemane. At the time of the final siege the space north of the wall of Agrippa was covered with gardens, groves and plantations of fruit trees, enclosed by hedges and walls; and to level these was one of Titus' first operations. We know that the gate Gennath (*i. e.* "of gardens") opened on this side of the city.

Gates.—The following is a complete list of the gates named in the Bible and by Josephus, with the references to their

The Golden Gate of Jerusalem.

occurrence:—1. Gate of Ephraim. 2 Chron. 25 : 23; Neh. 8 : 16; 12 : 39. This is probably the same as the—2. Gate of Benjamin. Jer. 20 : 2; 37 : 13; Zech. 14 : 10. If so, it was 400 cubits distant from the—3. Corner gate. 2 Chron. 25 : 23; 26 : 9; Jer. 31 : 38; Zech. 14 : 10. 4. Gate of Joshua, governor of the city. 2 Kings 23 : 8. 5. Gate between the two walls. 2 Kings 25 : 4; Jer. 39 : 4. 6. Horse gate. Neh. 3 : 28; 2 Chron. 23 : 15; Jer. 31 : 40. 7. Ravine gate (*i. e.* opening on ravine of Hinnom). 2 Chron. 26 : 9; Neh. 2 : 13, 15;

3 : 13. 8. Fish gate. 2
Chron. 33 : 14; Neh.
3 : 13; Zeph. 1 : 10. 9.
Dung gate. Neh. 2 :
13; 3 : 13. 10. Sheep
gate. Neh. 3 : 1, 32;
12 : 39. 11. East gate.
Neh. 3 : 29. 12. Miph-
kad. Neh. 3 : 31. 13.
Fountain gate (Silo-
am ?). Neh. 12 : 37.
14. Water gate. Neh.
12 : 37. 15. Old gate.
Neh. 12 : 39. 16. Pris-
on gate. Neh. 12 : 39.
17. Gate Harsith (per-
haps the Sun; Au-
thorized Version East
gate). Jer. 19 : 2. 18.
First gate. Zech. 14 :
10. 19. Gate Gennath
(gardens). Jos. *B. J.*
v. 4, ⸹ 4. 20. Essenes'
gate. Jos. *B. J.* 4, ⸹ 2.
To these should be
added the following
gates of the temple :—
Gate Sur, 2 Kings 11 :
6; called also gate of
foundation. 2 Chron.
23 : 5. Gate of the
guard, or behind the

Jaffa Gate and David's Tower, Jerusalem.

St. Stephen's Gate, Jerusalem.

guard, 2 Kings 11 : 6, 19 ; called the high gate. 2 Kings 15 : 35 ; 2 Chron. 23 : 20 ; 27 : 3. Gate Shallecheth. 1 Chron. 26 : 16. At present the chief gates are—1. The Zion's gate and the dung gate, in the south wall ; 2. St. Stephen's gate and the

Street in Jerusalem.

golden gate (now walled up), in the east wall ; 3. The Damascus gate and 4. Herod's gate, in the north wall ; and 5. The Jaffa gate, in the west wall.

Population.—Taking the area of the city enclosed by the two old walls at 750,000 yards, and that enclosed by the wall of Agrippa at 1,500,000 yards, we have 2,250,000 yards for the whole. Taking the population of the old city at the probable number of one person to 50 yards, we have 15,000 and at the extreme limit of 30 yards we should have 25,000 inhabitants for the old city, and at 100 yards to each individual in the

new city about 15,000 more ; so that the population of Jerusalem, in its days of greatest prosperity, may have amounted to from 30,000 to 45,000 souls, but could hardly ever have reached 50,000 ; and assuming that in times of festival one-half was added to this amount, which is an extreme estimate, there may have been 60,000 or 70,000 in the city when Titus came up against it. (Josephus says that at the siege of Jerusalem the population was 3,000,000 ; but Tacitus' statement that it was 600,000 is nearer the truth. This last is certainly within the limits of possibility. —ED.)

Streets, houses, etc. —Of the nature of these in the ancient city we have only the most scattered notices. The " east street," 2 Chron. 29 : 4 ; the " street of the city," *i. e.* the city of David, 2 Chron. 32 : 6 ; the " street facing the water gate," Neh. 8 : 1, 3, or, according to the parallel account in 1 Esdr. 9 : 38, the " broad place of the temple towards the east ;" the " street of the house of God," Ezra 10 : 9 ; the " street of the gate of Ephraim," Neh. 8 : 16 ; and the " open place of the first gate toward the east," must have been not " streets," in our sense of the word, so much as the open spaces found in eastern towns round the inside of the gates. Streets, properly so called, there were, Jer. 5 : 1 ; 11 : 13, etc.; but the name of only one, " the bakers' street," Jer. 37 : 21, is preserved to us. The Via Dolorosa, or street of sorrows, is a part of the street through which Christ is supposed to have been led on his way to his crucifixion. To the houses we have even less clue ; but there is no reason to suppose that in either houses or streets the ancient Jerusalem differed very ma-

Arch of Ecce Homo, Jerusalem.

The Way of the Cross (Via Dolorosa), Jerusalem.

terially from the modern. No doubt the ancient city did not exhibit that air of mouldering dilapidation which is now so prominent there. The whole of the slopes south of the Haram area (the ancient Ophel), and the modern Zion, and the west side of the valley of Jehoshaphat, presents the appearance of gigantic mounds of rubbish. In this point at least the ancient city stood in favorable contrast with the modern, but in many others the resemblance must have been strong.

Annals of the city.—If, as is possible, Salem is the same with Jerusalem, the first mention of Jerusalem is in Gen. 14: 18, about B.C. 2080. It is next mentioned in Josh. 10 : 1, B.C. 1451. The first siege appears to have taken place almost im-mediately after the death of Joshua—*cir.* 1400 B.C. Judah and Simeon "fought against it and took it, and smote it with the edge of the sword, and set the city on fire." Judges 1 : 8. In the fifteen centuries which elapsed between this siege and the siege and destruction of the city by Titus, A.D. 70, the city was besieged no fewer than seventeen times; twice it was razed to the ground, and on two other occasions its walls were levelled. In this respect it stands without a parallel in any city, ancient or modern. David captured the city B.C. 1046, and made it his capital, fortified and enlarged it. Solomon adorned the city with beautiful buildings, including the temple, but made no additions to its walls. The city was taken by the Philistines and Arabians in the reign of Jehoram, B.C. 886, and by the Israelites in the reign of Amaziah, B.C. 826. It was thrice taken by Nebuchadnezzar, in the years B.C. 607, 597 and 586, in the last of which it was ut-

Coin to Commemorate the Capture of Judea, A.D. 70.

terly destroyed. Its restoration commenced under Cyrus, B.C. 538, and was completed under Artaxerxes I., who issued commissions for this purpose to Ezra, B.C. 457, and Nehemiah, B.C. 445. In B.C. 332 it was captured by Alexander the Great. Under the Ptolemies and the Seleucidæ the town was prosperous, until Antiochus Epiphanes sacked it, B.C. 170. In consequence of his tyranny, the Jews rose under the Maccabees, and Jerusalem became again independent, and retained its position until its capture by the Romans under Pompey, B.C. 63. The temple was subsequently plundered by Crassus, B.C. 54, and the city by the Parthians, B.C. 40. Herod took up his residence there as soon as he was appointed sovereign, and restored the temple with great magnificence. On the death of Herod it became the residence of the Roman procurators, who occupied the fortress of Antonia. The greatest siege that it sustained, however, was at the hands of the Romans under Titus, when it held out nearly five months, and when the town vas completely destroyed, A.D. 70. Hadrian restored it as a Roman colony, A.D. 135, and among other buildings erected a temple of Jupiter Capitolinus on the site of the temple. He gave to it the name of Ælia Capitolina, thus combining his own family name with that of the Capitoline Jupiter. The emperor Constantine established the Christian character by the erection of a church on the supposed site of the holy sepulchre, A.D. 336. Justinian added several churches and hospitals about A.D. 532. It was taken by the Persians under Chosroes II. in A.D. 614. The dominion of the Christians in the holy city was now rapidly drawing to a close. In A.D. 637 the patriarch Sophronius surrendered to the khalif Omar in person. With the fall of the Abassides the holy city passed into the hands of the Fatimite dynasty, under whom the sufferings of the Christians in Jerusalem reached their height. About the year 1084 it was bestowed upon Ortok, chief of a Turkman horde. It was taken by the Crusaders in 1099, and for eighty-eight years Jerusalem remained in the hands of the Christians. In 1187 it was retaken by Saladin after a siege of several weeks. In 1277 Jerusalem was nominally annexed to the kingdom of Sicily. In 1517 it passed under the sway of the Ottoman sultan Selim I., whose successor Suliman built the present walls of the city in 1542. Mohammed Aly, the pasha of Egypt, took possession of it in 1832; and in 1840, after the bombardment of Acre, it was again restored to the sultan.

(*Modern Jerusalem*, called by the Arabs *el-Khuds*, is built upon the ruins of ancient Jerusalem. The accumulated rubbish of centuries is very great, being 100 feet deep around the temple walls and 40 feet deep on the hill of Zion. The modern wall, built in 1542, forms an irregular quadrangle about 2½ miles in circuit, with seven gates and 34 towers. It varies in height from 20 to 60 feet. The streets within are narrow, ungraded, crooked, and often filthy. The houses are of hewn stone, with flat roofs and frequent domes. There are few windows toward the street.

The most beautiful part of modern Jerusalem is the former temple area (Mount Moriah), "with its lawns and cypress trees, and its noble dome rising high above the wall." This enclosure, now called *Haram esh-Sherif*, is 35 acres in extent, and is nearly a mile in circuit.

On the site of the ancient temple stands the Mosque of Omar, "perhaps the very noblest specimen of building-art in Asia."

Church of the Holy Sepulchre at Jerusalem.

Interior of the Greek Church of the Holy Sepulchre.

"It is the most prominent as well as the most beautiful building in the whole city." The mosque is an octagonal build-ing, each side measuring 66 feet. It is surmounted by a dome, whose top is 170 feet from the ground.

The Mosque of Omar—Site of Solomon's Temple.

The Church of the Holy Sepulchre, which is claimed, but without sufficient reason, to be upon the site of Calvary, is "a collection of chapels and altars of dif-

View in the Court of the Mosque of Omar

ferent ages and a unique museum of religious curiosities from Adam to Christ."

The present number of inhabitants in Jerusalem is variously estimated. Probably Pierotti's estimate is very near the truth,—20,330; of whom 5068 are Christians, 7556 Mohammedans (Arabs and Turks), and 7706 Jews.—ED.)

Jeru'sha (*possessed*), daughter of Zadok and queen of Uzziah. 2 Kings 15 : 33. (B.C. 806.)

Jeru'shah (*possessed*). 2 Chron. 27 : 1. The same as the preceding.

Jesa'iah (*salvation of Jehovah*). 1. Son of Hananiah, brother of Pelatiah and grandson of Zerubbabel. 1 Chron. 3 : 21 (B.C. after 536.)

2. A Benjamite. Neh. 11 : 7.

Jesha'iah (*salvation of Jehovah*). 1. One of the six sons of Jeduthun. 1 Chron. 25 : 3, 15. (B.C. 1014.)

2. A Levite in the reign of David, eldest son of Rehabiah, a descendant of Amram through Moses. 1 Chron. 26 : 25. [ISSHIAH.] (B.C. before 1014.)

3. The son of Athaliah, and chief of the house of the Bene-Elam who returned with Ezra. Ezra 8 : 7. [JOSIAS.] (B.C. 459.)

4. A Merarite who returned with Ezra. Ezra 8 : 19.

Jesh'anah (*old*), a town which, with its dependent villages, was one of the three taken from Jeroboam by Abijah. 2 Chron. 13 : 19.

Jeshar'elah (*right before God*), son of Asaph, and head of the seventh of the twenty-four wards into which the musicians of the Levites were divided. 1 Chron. 25 : 14. [ASARELAH.] (B.C. 1014.)

Jesheb'e-ab (*father's seat*), head of the fourteenth course of priests. 1 Chron. 24 : 13. [JEHOIARIB.]

Je'sher (*uprightness*), one of the sons of Caleb the son of Hezron by his wife Azubah. 1 Chron. 2 : 18. (B.C. before 1491.)

Jesh'imon (*a wilderness*), a name which occurs in Num. 21 : 20 and 23 : 28, in designating the position of Pisgah and Peor; both described as "facing the Jeshimon." Perhaps the dreary, barren waste of hills lying immediately on the west of the Dead Sea.

Jeshish'a-i (*descended from an old man*), one of the ancestors of the Gadites who dwelt in Gilead. 1 Chron. 5 : 14.

Jeshoha'iah (*whom Jehovah casts down*), a chief of the Simeonites, descended from Shimei. 1 Chron. 4 : 36. (B.C. about 711.)

Jesh'ua (*a saviour*), another form of the name Joshua or Jesus. 1. Joshua the son of Nun. Neh. 8 : 17. [JOSHUA.]

2. A priest in the reign of David, to whom the ninth course fell by lot. 1 Chron. 24 : 11. (B.C. 1014.)

3. One of the Levites in the reign of Hezekiah. 2 Chron. 31 : 15. (B.C. 726.)

4. Son of Jehozadak, first high priest after the Babylonish captivity, B.C. 536. Jeshua was probably born in Babylon, whither his father Jehozadak had been taken captive while young. 1 Chron. 6 : 15, Authorized Version. He came up from Babylon in the first year of Cyrus, with Zerubbabel, and took a leading part with him in the rebuilding of the temple and the restoration of the Jewish commonwealth. The two prophecies concerning him in Zech. 3 and 6 : 9–15 point him out as an eminent type of Christ.

5. Head of a Levitical house, one of those which returned from the Babylonish captivity. Ezra 2 : 40; 3 : 9; Neh. 3 : 19; 8 : 7; 9 : 4, 5; 12 : 8, etc.

6. A branch of the family of Pahathmoab, one of the chief families, probably, of the tribe of Judah. Neh. 10 : 14; 7 : 11, etc.; Ezra 10 : 30.

Jesh'ua (*whom Jehovah helps*), one of the towns reinhabited by the people of Judah after the return from captivity. Neh. 11 : 26. It is not mentioned elsewhere.

Jesh'uah, a priest in the reign of David, 1 Chron. 24 : 11, the same as JESHUA, No. 2. (B.C. 1014.)

Jesh'urun (*supremely happy*), and once by mistake in Authorized Version JESURUN, Isa. 44 : 2, a symbolical name for Israel in Deut. 32 : 15; 33 : 5, 26; Isa. 44 : 2. It is most probably derived from a root signifying "to be blessed." With the intensive termination Jeshurun would then denote Israel as supremely happy or prosperous, and to this signification the context in Deut. 32 : 15 points.

Jesi'ah (*whom Jehovah lends*). 1. A Korhite, one of the mighty men who joined David's standard at Ziklag. 1 Chron. 12 : 6. (B.C. 1055.)

2. The second son of Uzziel, the son of Kohath. 1 Chron. 23 : 20.

Jesim'i-el (*whom God makes*), a Simeonite chief of the family of Shimei. 1 Chron. 4 : 36. (B.C. about 711.)

Jes'se (*wealthy*) the father of David, was the son of Obed, who again was the fruit of the union of Boaz and the Moabitess Ruth. His great-grandmother was Rahab the Canaanite, of Jericho. Matt. 1 : 5. Jesse's genealogy is twice given in full in the Old Testament, viz., Ruth 4 : 18–22 and 1 Chron. 2 : 5–12. He is commonly designated as "Jesse the Bethlehemite," 1 Sam. 16 : 1, 18; 17 : 58; but his full title is "the Ephrathite of Bethlehem Judah." ch. 17 : 12. He is an "old man" when we first meet with him, 1 Sam. 17 : 12, with eight sons, ch. 16 : 10; 17 : 12, residing at Bethlehem. ch. 16 : 4, 5. Jesse's wealth seems to have consisted of a flock of sheep and goats, which were under the care of David. ch. 16 : 11; 17 : 34, 35. After David's rupture with Saul he took his father and his mother into the country of Moab and deposited them with the king, and there they disappear from our view in the records of Scripture. (B.C. 1068–61.) Who the wife of Jesse was we are not told.

Jes'ui (*even, level*), the son of Asher, whose descendants the Jesuites were numbered in the plains of Moab at the Jordan of Jericho. Num. 26 : 44. (B.C. 1451.) He is elsewhere called ISUI, Gen. 46 : 17; and ISHUAI. 1 Chron. 7 : 30.

Jes'uites (*the posterity of Jesui*), **The,** a family of the tribe of Asher. Num. 26 : 44.

Jes'urun. [JESHURUN.]

Je'sus (*saviour*). 1. The Greek form of the name Joshua or Jeshua, a contraction of Jehoshua, that is, "help of Jehovah" or "saviour." Num. 13 : 16. 2. Joshua the son of Nun. Num. 27 : 18; Heb. 4 : 8. [JEHOSHUA.]

Je'sus the son of Sirach. [ECCLESIASTICUS.]

Je'sus, called **Justus,** a Christian who was with St. Paul at Rome. Col. 4 : 11. (A.D. 57.)

Je'sus Christ. "The life and character of Jesus Christ," says Dr. Schaff, "is the holy of holies in the history of the world." I. NAME.—The name *Jesus* signifies *saviour*. It is the Greek form of JEHOSHUA (Joshua). The name *Christ* signifies *anointed*. Jesus was both *priest* and *king*. Among the Jews priests were anointed, as their inauguration to their office. 1 Chron. 16 : 22. In the New Testament the name Christ is used as equivalent to the Hebrew Messiah (*anointed*), John 1 : 41, the name given to the long-promised Prophet and King whom the Jews had been taught by their prophets to expect. Matt. 11 : 3; Acts 19 : 4. The use of this name, as applied to the Lord, has always a reference to the promises of the prophets. The name of Jesus is the proper name of our Lord, and that of Christ is added to identify him with the promised Messiah. Other names are sometimes added to the names Jesus Christ, thus, "Lord," "a king," "King of Israel," "Emmanuel," "Son of David," "chosen of God."

II. BIRTH.—Jesus Christ was born of the Virgin Mary, God being his father, at Bethlehem of Judea, six miles south of Jerusalem. The date of his birth was most probably in December, B.C. 5, four years before the era from which we count our years. That era was not used till several hundred years after Christ. The calculations were made by a learned monk, Dionysius Exiguus, in the sixth century, who made an error of four years; so that to get the exact date from the birth of Christ we must add four years to our usual dates; *i. e.* A.D. 1882 is really 1886 years since the birth of Christ. It is also more than likely that our usual date for Christmas, December 25, is not far from the real date of Christ's birth. Since the 25th of December comes when the longest night gives way to the returning sun on his triumphant march, it makes an appropriate anniversary to mark the birth of him who appeared in the darkest night of error and sin as the true Light of the world. At the time of Christ's birth Augustus Cæsar was emperor of Rome, and Herod the Great king of Judea, but subject to Rome. God's providence had prepared the world for the coming of Christ, and this was the fittest time in all its history. 1. All the world was subject to one government, so that the apostles could travel everywhere : the door of every land was open for the gospel. 2. The world was at peace, so that the gospel could have free course. 3. The Greek language was spoken everywhere with their other languages. 4. The Jews were scattered everywhere with synagogues and Bibles.

III. EARLY LIFE.—Jesus, having a manger at Bethlehem for his cradle, received a visit of adoration from the three wise men of the East. At forty days old he was taken to the temple at Jerusalem ; and returning to Bethlehem, was soon taken to Egypt to escape Herod's massacre of the infants there. After a few months stay there, Herod having died in April, B.C. 4, the family returned to their Nazareth home, where Jesus lived till he was about thirty years old, subject to his parents, and increasing "in wisdom and stature, and in favor with God and man." The only incident recorded of his early life is his going up to Jerusalem to attend the passover when he was twelve years old, and his conversation with the learned men in the temple. But we can understand the childhood and youth of Jesus better when we remember the surrounding influences amid which he grew. 1. The natural scenery was rugged and mountainous, but full of beauty. He breathed the pure air. He lived in a village, not in a city. 2. The Roman dominion was irksome and galling. The people of God were subject to a foreign yoke. The taxes were heavy. Roman soldiers, laws, money, ever reminded them of their subjection, when they ought to be free and themselves the rulers of the world. When Jesus was ten years old, there was a great insurrection, Acts 5 : 37, in Galilee. He who was to be King of the Jews heard and felt all this. 3. The Jewish hopes of a Redeemer, of throwing off their bondage, of becoming the glorious nation promised in the prophets, were in the very air he breathed. The conversation at home and in the streets was full of them. 4. Within his view, and his boyish excursions, were many remarkable historic places,—rivers, hills, cities, plains,—that would keep in mind the history of his people and God's dealings with them. 5. His school training. Mr. Deutsch, in the *Quarterly Review*, says, "Eighty years before Christ, schools flourished throughout the length and the breadth of the land: education had been made compulsory. While there is not a single term for 'school' to be found before the captivity, there were by that time about a dozen in common usage. Here are a few of the innumerable popular sayings of the period : 'Jerusalem was destroyed because the instruction of the young was neglected.' 'The world is only saved by the breath of the school-children.' 'Even for the rebuilding of the temple the schools must not be interrupted.'" 6. His home training. According to Ellicott, the stages of Jewish childhood were marked as follows: "At three the boy was weaned, and wore for the first time the fringed or tasselled garment prescribed by Num. 15 : 38–41 and Deut. 22 : 12. His education began at first under the mother's care. At five he was to learn the law, at first by extracts written on scrolls of the more important passages, the Shemà or creed of Deut. 2 : 4, the Hallel or festival psalms, Ps. 114, 118, 136, and by catechetical teaching in school. At twelve he became more directly responsible for his obedience to the law ; and on the day when he attained the age of thirteen, put on for the first time the phylacteries which were worn at the recital of his daily prayer." In addition to this, Jesus no doubt learned the carpenter's trade of his reputed father Joseph, and, as Joseph probably died before Jesus began his public ministry, he may have contributed to the support of his mother.

(IV. PUBLIC MINISTRY.—All the leading events recorded of Jesus' life are given at the end of this volume in the Chronological Chart and in the Chronological Table of the life of Christ; so that here will be given only a general survey.

Jesus began to enter upon his ministry when he was "about thirty years old;" that is, he was not very far from thirty, older or younger. He is regarded as nearly thirty-one by Andrews (in the tables of chronology referred to above) and by most others. Having been baptized by John early in the winter of 26–27, he spent the larger portion of his first year in Judea and about the lower Jordan, till in December he went northward to Galilee through Samaria. The next year and a half, from December, A.D. 27, to October or November, A.D. 29, was spent in Galilee and northern Palestine, chiefly in the vicinity of the Sea of Galilee. In November, 29, Jesus made his final departure from Galilee, and the rest of his ministry was in Judea and Perea, beyond Jordan, till his crucifixion, April 7, A.D. 30. After three days he proved his divinity by rising from the dead ; and after appearing on eleven different occasions to his disciples during forty days, he finally ascended to heaven, where he is the living, ever-present, all-powerful Saviour of his people.

Jesus Christ, being both human and divine, is fitted to be the true Saviour of men. In this, as in every action and character, he is shown to be " the wisdom and power of God unto salvation." As human, he reaches down to our natures, sympathizes with us, shows us that God knows all our feelings and weaknesses and sorrows and sins, brings God near to us, who otherwise could not realize the Infinite and Eternal as a father and friend. He is divine, in order that he may be an all-powerful, all-loving Saviour, able and willing to defend us from every enemy, to subdue all temptations, to deliver from all sin, and to bring each of his people, and the whole Church, into complete and final victory.

Jesus Christ is the centre of the world's history, as he is the centre of the Bible. —ED.)

Je'ther (*his excellence*). 1. Jethro, the father-in-law of Moses. Ex. 4 : 18. (B.C. 1530.)

2. The first-born of Gideon's seventy sons. Judges 8 : 20. (B.C. 1256.)

3. The father of Amasa, captain-general of Absalom's army. (B.C. 1023.) Jether is another form of ITHRA. 2 Sam. 17 : 25. He is described in 1 Chron. 2 : 17 as an Ishmaelite, which again is more likely to be correct than the " Israelite " of the Hebrew in 2 Sam. 17.

4. The son of Jada, a descendant of Hezron, of the tribe of Judah. 1 Chron. 2 : 32.

5. The son of Ezra. 1 Chron. 4 : 17.

6. The chief of a family of warriors of the line of Asher, and father of Jephunneh. 1 Chron. 7 : 38. He is prob-

ably the same as ITHRAN in the preceding verse.

Je'theth (*a nail*), one of the "dukes" who came of Esau. Gen. 36 : 40; 1 Chron. 1 : 51.

Jeth'lah (*height*), one of the cities of the tribe of Dan. Josh. 19 : 42.

Je'thro (*his excellence*) was priest or prince of Midian. Moses married his daughter Zipporah. (B.C. 1530.) On account of his local knowledge he was entreated to remain with the Israelites throughout their journey to Canaan. Num. 10 : 31, 33. (He is called REUEL in Ex. 2 : 18, and RAGUEL in Num. 10 : 29 (the same word in the original for both). Reuel is probably his proper name, and Jethro his official title.—ED.)

Je'tur (*an enclosure*). Gen. 25 : 15; 1 Chron. 1 : 31; 5 : 19. [ITURÆA.]

Je'uel, a chief man of Judah, one of the Bene-Zerah. 1 Chron. 9 : 6; comp. 2. [JEIEL.]

Je'ush (*assembler*). 1. Son of Esau by Aholibamah the daughter of Anah, the son of Zebeon the Hivite. Gen. 36 : 6, 14, 18; 1 Chron. 1 : 35. (B.C. after 1797.)

2. A Benjamite, son of Bilhan. 1 Chron. 7 : 10, 11.

3. A Gershonite Levite, of the house of Shimei. 1 Chron. 23 : 10, 11. (B.C. 1014.)

4. Son of Rehoboam king of Judah. 2 Chron. 11 : 18, 19. (B.C. after 97.)

Je'uz (*counsellor*), head of a Benjamite house. 1 Chron. 8 : 10.

Jew (*a man of Judea*). This name was properly applied to a member of the kingdom of Judah after the separation of the ten tribes. The term first makes its appearance just before the captivity of the ten tribes. 2 Kings 16 : 6. After the return the word received a larger application. Partly from the predominance of the members of the old kingdom of Judah among those who returned to Palestine, partly from the identification of Judah with the religious ideas and hopes of the people, all the members of the new state were called Jews (Judeans), and the name was extended to the remnants of the race scattered throughout the nations. Under the name of "Judeans" the people of Israel were known to classical writers. (Tac. *H.* v. 2, etc.) The force of the title "Jew" is seen particularly in the Gospel of St. John, who very rarely uses any other term to describe the opponents of our Lord. At

an earlier stage of the progress of the faith it was contrasted with Greek as implying an outward covenant with God, Rom. 1 : 16; 2 : 9, 10; Col. 3 : 11, etc., which was the correlative of *Hellenist* [HELLENIST], and marked a division of language subsisting within the entire body, and at the same time less expressive than *Israelite*, which brought out with especial clearness the privileges and hopes of the children of Jacob. 2 Cor. 11 : 22; John 1 : 47.

Jewel. [STONES, PRECIOUS.]

Jew'ess, a woman of Hebrew birth, without distinction of tribe. Acts 16 : 1; 24 : 24.

Jewish, of or belonging to Jews; an epithet applied to their rabbinical legends. Titus 1 : 14.

Jew'ry (*the country of Judea*), the same word elsewhere rendered Judah and Judea. It occurs several times in the Apocalypse and the New Testament, but once only in the Old Testament— Dan. 5 : 13. Jewry comes to us through the Norman-French, and is of frequent occurrence in Old English.

Jezani'ah (*whom Jehovah hears*), the son of Hoshaiah the Maachathite, and one of the captains of the forces who had escaped from Jerusalem during the final attack of the beleaguering army of the Chaldeans. (B.C. 588.) When the Babylonians had departed, Jezaniah, with the men under his command, was one of the first who returned to Gedaliah at Mizpah. In the events which followed the assassination of that officer Jezaniah took a prominent part. 2 Kings 25 : 23; Jer. 40 : 8; 42 : 1; 43 : 2.

Jez'ebel (*chaste*), wife of Ahab king of Israel. (B.C. 883.) She was a Phœnician princess, daughter of Ethbaal king of the Zidonians. In her hands her husband became a mere puppet. 1 Kings 21 : 25. The first effect of her influence was the immediate establishment of the Phœnician worship on a grand scale in the court of Ahab. At her table were supported no less than 450 prophets of Baal and 400 of Astarte. 1 Kings 16 : 31, 32; 18 : 19. The prophets of Jehovah were attacked by her orders and put to the sword. 1 Kings 18 : 13; 2 Kings 9 : 7. At last the people, at the instigation of Elijah, rose against her ministers and slaughtered them at the foot of Carmel. When she found her husband cast down by his disappointment at being thwarted by Naboth, 1 Kings 21 : 7, she wrote a warrant in Ahab's name, and sealed it with his seal. To her, and not to Ahab, was sent the announcement that the royal wishes were accomplished, 1 Kings 21 : 14, and on her accordingly fell the prophet's curse, as well as on her husband, 1 Kings 21 : 23 ; a curse fulfilled so literally by Jehu, whose chariot-horses trampled out her life. The body was left in that open space called in modern eastern language "the mounds," where offal is thrown from the city walls. 2 Kings 9 : 30–37.

Je'zer (*power*), the third son of Naphtali, Gen. 46 : 24 ; Num. 26 : 49 ; 1 Chron. 7 : 13, and father of the family of Jezerites.

Jezi'ah (*whom Jehovah expiates*), a descendant of Parosh, who had married a foreign wife. Ezra 10 : 25.

Je'zi-el (*the assembly of God*), a Benjamite who joined David at Ziklag. 1 Chron. 12 : 3. (B.C. 1055.)

Jezli'ah (*whom God will preserve*), a Benjamite of the sons of Elpaal. 1 Chron. 8 : 18. (B.C. 588.)

Jez'o-ar (*whiteness*), the son of Helah, one of the wives of Asher. 1 Chron. 4 : 7.

Jezrahi'ah (*produced by Jehovah*), a Levite, the leader of the choristers at the solemn dedication of the wall of Jerusalem under Nehemiah. Neh. 12 : 42. (B.C. 446.)

Jez're-el (*seed of God*), a descendant of the father or founder of Etam, of the line of Judah. 1 Chron. 4 : 3. (B.C. about 1445.)

Jez're-el. 1. A city situated in the plain of the same name between Gilboa and Little Hermon, now generally called Esdraelon. [ESDRAELON.] It appears in Josh. 19 : 18, but its historical importance dates from the reign of Ahab, B.C. 918–897, who chose it for his chief residence. The situation of the modern village of *Zerin* still remains to show the fitness of his choice. In the neighborhood, or within the town probably, were a temple and grove of Astarte, with an establishment of 400 priests supported by Jezebel. 1 Kings 16 : 33 ; 2 Kings 10 : 11. The palace of Ahab, 1 Kings 21 : 1 ; 18 : 46, probably containing his "ivory house," 1 Kings 22 : 39, was on the eastern side of the city, forming part of the city wall. Comp. 1 Kings 21 : 1 ; 2 Kings 9 : 25, 30, 33. Whether the vineyard of Naboth was here or at Samaria is a doubtful question. Still in the same eastern direction are two springs, one 12 minutes from the town, the other 20 minutes. The latter, probably from both its size and its situation, was known as "the spring of Jezreel." With the fall of the house of Ahab the glory of Jezreel departed.

2. A town in Judah, in the neighborhood of the southern Carmel. Josh. 15 : 56. Here David in his wanderings took Ahinoam the Israelitess for his first wife. 1 Sam. 27 : 3 ; 30 : 5.

3. The eldest son of the prophet Hosea. Hos. 1 : 4.

Jez're-elitess, a woman of Jezreel. 1 Sam. 27 : 3 ; 30 : 5 ; 2 Sam. 2 : 2 ; 3 : 2 ; 1 Chron. 3 : 1.

Jib'sam (*pleasant*), one of the sons of Tola, the son of Issachar. 1 Chron. 7 : 2. (B.C. 1017.)

Jid'laph (*weeping*), a son of Nahor. Gen. 22 : 22.

Jim'na (*prosperity*), the first-born of Asher. Num. 26 : 44. He is elsewhere called in the Authorized Version JIMNAH, Gen. 46 : 17, and IMNAH. 1 Chron. 7 : 30.

Jim'nah = JIMNA = IMNAH. Gen. 46 : 17.

Jim'nites, The, descendants of the preceding. Num. 26 : 44.

Jiph'tah (*whom God sets free*), one of the cities of Judah in the maritime lowland, or Shefelah. Josh. 15 : 43. It has not yet been met with.

Jiph'thah-el (*which God opens*), **The valley of,** a valley which served as one of the landmarks for the boundary of both Zebulun, Josh. 19 : 14, and Asher. Josh. 19 : 27. Dr. Robinson suggests that Jiphthah-el was identical with Jotapata, and that they survive in the modern *Jefat*, a village in the mountains of Galilee, halfway between the Bay of Acre and the Lake of Gennesareth.

Jo'ab (*whose father is Jehovah*), the most remarkable of the three nephews of David, the children of Zeruiah, David's sister. (B.C. 1053–1012.) Joab first appears after David's accession to the throne at Hebron. Abner slew in battle Asahel, the youngest brother of Joab ; and when David afterward received Abner into favor, Joab treacherously murdered him. [ABNER.] There was now no rival left in the way of Joab's advancement, and at the siege of Jebus he was appointed for his prowess commander-in-chief— "captain of the host." In the wide range of wars which David undertook, Joab was the acting general. He was called by the almost regal title of "lord," **2**

Sam. 11 : 11, "the prince of the king's army." 1 Chron. 27 : 34. In the entangled relations which grew up in David's domestic life he bore an important part, successfully reinstating Absalom in David's favor after the murder of Amnon. 2 Sam. 14 : 1–20. When the relations between father and son were reversed by the revolt of Absalom, Joab remained true to the king, taking the rebel prince's dangerous life in spite of David's injunction to spare him, and when no one else had courage to act so decisive a part. 2 Sam. 18 : 2, 11–15. (B.C. 1023.) The king transferred the command to Amasa, which so enraged Joab that he adroitly assassinated Amasa when pretending to welcome him as a friend. 2 Sam. 20 : 10. Friendly relations between himself and David seem to have existed afterward, 2 Sam. 24 : 2 ; but at the close of his long life, his loyalty, so long unshaken, at last wavered. "Though he had not turned after Absalom, he turned after Adonijah." 1 Kings 2 : 28. This probably filled up the measure of the king's long-cherished resentment. The revival of the pretensions of Adonijah after David's death was sufficient to awaken the suspicions of Solomon. Joab fled to the shelter of the altar at Gibeon, and was there slain by Benaiah. (B.C. about 1012.)

2. One of Kenaz's descendants. 1 Chron. 4 : 14.

3. Ezra 2 : 6 ; 8 : 9 ; Neh. 7 : 11.

Jo'ah (*whose brother* (*i. e.* helper) *is Jehovah*). 1. The son of Asaph, and chronicler or keeper of the records to Hezekiah. Isa. 36 : 3, 11, 22. (B.C. 776.)

2. The son or grandson of Zimmah, a Gershonite. 1 Chron. 6 : 21.

3. The third son of Obed-edom, 1 Chron. 26 : 4, a Korhite, and one of the doorkeepers appointed by David. (B.C. 1014.)

4. A Gershonite, the son of Zimmah and father of Eden. 2 Chron. 29 : 12.

5. The son of Joahaz, and annalist or keeper of the records to Josiah. 2 Chron. 34 : 8. (B.C. 623.)

Jo'ahaz (*whom Jehovah holds*), the father of Joah, the chronicler or keeper of the records to King Josiah. 2 Chron. 34 : 8. (B.C. before 623.)

Jo-a'nan. In Revised Version for JOANNA, 1. Luke 3 : 27.

Jo-an'na (*grace* or *gift of God*) (in Revised Version spelled JOANAN). 1. Son of Rhesa, according to the text of Luke 3 : 27, and one of the ancestors of

Christ ; but according to the view explained in a previous article, son of Zerubbabel, and the same as HANANIAH in 1 Chron. 3 : 19.

2. The name of a woman, occurring twice in Luke (8 : 3 ; 24 : 10), but evidently denoting the same person. (A.D. 28–30.) In the first passage she is expressly stated to have been "wife of Chuza, steward of Herod," that is, Antipas, tetrarch of Galilee.

Jo'ash (*to whom Jehovah hastens, i. e.* to help), contracted from JEHOASH. 1. Son of Ahaziah king of Judah (B.C. 884), and the only one of his children who escaped the murderous hand of Athaliah. After his father's sister Jehoshabeath, the wife of Jehoiada the high priest, had stolen him from among the king's sons, he was hidden for six years in the chambers of the temple. In the seventh year of his age and of his concealment, a successful revolution, conducted by Jehoiada, placed him on the throne of his ancestors, and freed the country from the tyranny and idolatries of Athaliah. For at least twenty-three years, while Jehoiada lived, his reign was very prosperous ; but after the death of Jehoiada, Joash fell into the hands of bad advisers, at whose suggestion he revived the worship of Baal and Ashtaroth. When he was rebuked for this by Zechariah, the son of Jehoiada, Joash caused him to be stoned to death in the very court of the Lord's house. Matt. 23 : 35. That very year Hazael king of Syria came up against Jerusalem, and carried off a vast booty as the price of his departure. Joash had scarcely escaped this danger when he fell into another and fatal one. Two of his servants conspired against him and slew him in his bed in the fortress of Millo. Joash's reign lasted forty years, from 878 to 838 B.C.

2. Son and successor of Jehoahaz on the throne of Israel from B.C. 840 to 825, and for two full years a contemporary sovereign with the preceding. 2 Kings 14 : 1, comp. with 12 : 1 ; 13 : 10. When he succeeded to the crown the kingdom was in a deplorable state from the devastations of Hazael and Ben-hadad, kings of Syria. On occasion of a friendly visit paid by Joash to Elisha on his death-bed, the prophet promised him deliverance from the Syrian yoke in Aphek. 1 Kings 20 : 26–30. He then bade him smite upon the ground, and the king smote thrice and then stayed. The prophet rebuked him for staying, and limited to three his

victories over Syria. Accordingly Joash did defeat Ben-hadad three times on the field of battle, and recovered from him the cities which Hazael had taken from Jehoahaz. The other great military event of Joash's reign was the successful war with Amaziah king of Judah. He died in the fifteenth year of Amaziah king of Judah.

3. The father of Gideon, and a wealthy man among the Abiezrites. Judges 6 : 11. (B.C. before 1256.)

4. Apparently a younger son of Ahab, who held a subordinate jurisdiction in the lifetime of his father. 1 Kings 22 : 26; 2 Chron. 18 : 25. (B.C. 896.)

5. A descendant of Shelah the son of Judah, but whether his son or the son of Jokim is not clear. 1 Chron. 4 : 22.

6. A Benjamite, son of Shemaah of Gibeah, 1 Chron. 12 : 3, who resorted to David at Ziklag.

7. One of the officers of David's household. 1 Chron. 27 : 28.

8. Son of Becher and head of a Benjamite house. 1 Chron. 7 : 8.

Jo'atham = JOTHAM the son of Uzziah. Matt. 1 : 9.

Job (*persecuted*), the third son of Issachar, Gen. 46 : 13, called in another genealogy JASHUB. 1 Chron. 7 : 1.

Job, the patriarch, from whom one of the books of the Old Testament is named. His residence in the land of *Uz* marks him as belonging to a branch of the Aramean race, which had settled in the lower part of Mesopotamia (probably to the south or southeast of Palestine, in Idumean Arabia), adjacent to the Sabeans and Chaldeans. The opinions of Job and his friends are thus peculiarly interesting as exhibiting an aspect of the patriarchal religion outside of the family of Abraham, and as yet uninfluenced by the legislation of Moses. The form of worship belongs essentially to the early patriarchal type; with little of ceremonial ritual, without a separate priesthood, it is thoroughly domestic in form and spirit. Job is represented as a chieftain of immense wealth and high rank, blameless in all the relations of life. What we know of his history is given in the book that bears his name.

Job, Book of. This book has given rise to much discussion and criticism, some believing the book to be strictly historical; others a religious fiction; others a composition based upon facts. By some the authorship of the work was attributed to Moses, but it is very uncertain. Luther first suggested the theory which, in some form or other, is now most generally received. He says, " I look upon the book of Job as a true history, yet I do not believe that all took place just as it is written, but that an ingenious, pious and learned man brought it into its present form." The date of the book is doubtful, and there have been many theories upon the subject. It may be regarded as a settled point that the book was written long before the exile, probably between the birth of Abraham and the exodus of the Israelites from Egypt—B.C. 2000–1800. If by Moses, it was probably written during his sojourn in Midian. " The book of Job is not only one of the most remarkable in the Bible, but in literature. As was said of Goliath's sword, ' There is none like it;' none in ancient or in modern literature."—*Kitto.*
" A book which will one day, perhaps, be seen towering up alone far above all the poetry of the world."—*J. A. Froude.*
" The book of Job is a drama, and yet subjectively true. The two ideas are perfectly consistent. It may have the dramatic form, the dramatic interest, the dramatic emotion, and yet be substantially a truthful narrative. The author may have received it in one of three ways : the writer may have been an eyewitness; or have received it from near contemporary testimony ; or it may have reached him through a tradition of whose substantial truthfulness he has no doubt. There is abundant internal evidence that the scenes and events recorded were real scenes and real events to the writer. He gives the discussions either as he had heard them or as they had been repeated over and over in many an ancient *consensus.* The very modes of transmission show the deep impression it had made in all the East, as a veritable as well as marvellous event."—*Tayler Lewis.*
The design of the book.—Stanley says that " The whole book is a discussion of that great problem of human life : what is the intention of Divine Providence in allowing the good to suffer?" " The direct object is to show that, although goodness has a natural tendency to secure a full measure of temporal happiness, yet that in its essence it is independent of such a result. Selfishness in some form is declared to be the basis on which all apparent goodness rests. That question is tried in the case of Job."—*Cook.*

Structure of the book.—The book consists of five parts:—I. Chs. 1–3. The historical facts. II. Chs. 4–31. The discussions between Job and his three friends. III. Chs. 32–37. Job's discussion with Elihu. IV. Chs. 38–41. The theophany, —God speaking out of the storm. V. Ch. 42. The successful termination of the trial. It is all in poetry except the ntroduction and the close.

The argument.—1. One question could be raised by envy: may not the goodness which secures such direct and tangible rewards be a refined form of selfishness? Satan, the accusing angel, suggests the doubt, "Doth Job fear God for nought?" and asserts boldly that if those external blessings were withdrawn, Job would cast off his allegiance—"he will curse thee to thy face." The problem is thus distinctly propounded which this book is intended to discuss and solve: can goodness exist irrespective of reward? The accuser receives permission to make the trial. He destroys Job's property, then his children; and afterward, to leave no possible opening for a cavil, is allowed to inflict upon him the most terrible disease known in the East. Job's wife breaks down entirely under the trial. Job remains steadfast. The question raised by Satan is answered.

2. "Then follows a discussion which arises in the most natural manner from a visit of condolence on the part of three men who represent the wisdom and experience of the age. Job's friends hold the theory that there is an exact and invariable correlation between sin and suffering. The fact of suffering proves the commission of some special sin. They apply this to Job, but he disavows all special guilt. He denies that punishment in this life inevitably follows upon guilt, or proves its commission. He appeals to facts. Bad men do sometimes prosper. Here, at ch. 14, there is a pause. In the second colloquy the three friends take more advanced ground. They assume that Job has been actually guilty of sins, and that the sufferings and losses of Job are but an inadequate retribution for former sins. This series of accusations brings out the inmost thoughts of Job. He recognizes God's hand in his afflictions, but denies they are brought on by wrong-doing; and becomes still clearer in the view that only the future life can vindicate God's justice. In his last two discourses, chs. 26–31, he

states with incomparable force and eloquence his opinion of the chief points of the controversy: man cannot comprehend God's ways; destruction sooner or later awaits the wicked; wisdom consists wholly in the fear of the Lord, and departing from evil."—*Cook.*

3. Elihu sums up the argument. "The leading principle of Elihu's statement is that calamity, in the shape of trial, is inflicted on comparatively the best of men; but that God allows a favorable turn to take place as soon as its object has been realized." The last words are evidently spoken while a violent storm is coming on.

4. It is obvious that many weighty truths have been developed in the course of the discussion: nearly every theory of the objects and uses of suffering has been reviewed, while a great advance has been made toward the apprehension of doctrines hereafter to be revealed, such as were known only to God. But the mystery is not as yet really cleared up; hence the necessity for the theophany. ch. 38 : 41. From the midst of the storm Jehovah speaks. In language of incomparable grandeur he reproves and silences the murmurs of Job. God does not condescend, strictly speaking, to argue with his creatures. The speculative questions discussed in the colloquy are unnoticed, but the declaration of God's absolute power is illustrated by a marvellously beautiful and comprehensive survey of the glory of creation and his all-embracing providence. A second address completes the work. It proves that a charge of injustice against God involves the consequence that the accuser is more competent that he to rule the universe.

Jo′bab (*a desert*). 1. The last in order of the sons of Joktan. Gen. 10 : 29; 1 Chron. 1 : 23.

2. One of the "kings" of Edom. Gen. 36 : 33, 34; 1 Chron. 1 : 44, 45.

3. King of Madon; one of the northern chieftains who attempted to oppose Joshua's conquest, and were routed by him at Meron. Josh. 11 : 1 only.

4. Head of a Benjamite house. 1 Chron. 8 : 9.

Joch′ebed (*whose glory is Jehovah*), the wife and at the same time the aunt of Amram and the mother of Moses and Aaron. Ex. 2 : 1; 6 : 20; Num. 26 : 59.

Jo′da, in Revised Version for JUDA. Luke 3 : 26.

Jo′ed (*for whom Jehovah is witness*),

a Benjamite, the son of Pedaiah. Neh. 11 : 7.

Jo'el (*to whom Jehovah is God*). 1. Eldest son of Samuel the prophet, 1 Sam. 8 : 2; 1 Chron. 6 : 33; 15 : 17, and father of Heman the singer. (B.C. 1094.)

2. In 1 Chron. 6 : 36, Authorized Version, Joel seems to be merely a corruption of Shaul in ver. 24.

3. A Simeonite chief. 1 Chron. 4 : 35.

4. A descendant of Reuben. Junius and Tremellius make him the son of Hanoch, while others trace his descent through Carmi. 1 Chron. 5 : 4. (B.C. before 1092.)

5. Chief of the Gadites, who dwelt in the land of Bashan. 1 Chron. 5 : 12. (B.C. 782.)

6. The son of Izrahiah, of the tribe of Issachar. 1 Chron. 7 : 3.

7. The brother of Nathan of Zobah, 1 Chron. 11 : 38, and one of David's guard.

8. The chief of the Gershomites in the reign of David. 1 Chron. 15 : 7, 11.

9. A Gershonite Levite in the reign of David, son of Jehiel, a descendant of Laadan, and probably the same as the preceding. 1 Chron. 23 : 8; 26 : 22. (B.C. 1014.)

10. The son of Pedaiah, and a chief of the half-tribe of Manasseh west of Jordan, in the reign of David. 1 Chron. 27 : 20. (B.C. 1014.)

11. A Kohathite Levite in the reign of Hezekiah. 2 Chron. 29 : 12. (B.C. 726.)

12. One of the sons of Nebo, who returned with Ezra, and had married a foreign wife. Ezra 10 : 43. (B.C. 459.)

13. The son of Zichri, a Benjamite. Neh. 11 : 9.

14. The second of the twelve minor prophets, the son of Pethuel, probably prophesied in Judah in the reign of Uzziah, about B.C. 800. The book of Joel contains a grand outline of the whole terrible scene, which was to be depicted more and more in detail by subsequent prophets. The proximate event to which the prophecy related was a public calamity, then impending on Judah, of a twofold character—want of water, and a plague of locusts—and continuing for several years. The prophet exhorts the people to turn to God with penitence, fasting and prayer; and then, he says, the plague shall cease, and the rain descend in its season, and the land yield her accustomed fruit. Nay, the time will be a most joyful one; for God, by the out-

pouring of his Spirit, will extend the blessings of true religion to heathen lands. The prophecy is referred to in Acts 2.

Jo-e'lah (*Jehovah helps*), son of Jeroham of Gedor. 1 Chron. 12 : 7.

Jo-e'zer (*whose help is Jehovah*), a Korhite, one of David's captains. 1 Chron. 12 : 6. (B.C. 1155.)

Jog'behah (*lofty*), one of the cities on the east of Jordan which were built and fortified by the tribe of Gad when they took possession of their territory. Num. 32 : 35.

Jog'li (*led into exile*), the father of Bukki, a Danite chief. Num. 34 : 22.

Jo'ha (*Jehovah gives life*). 1. One of the sons of Beriah the Benjamite. 1 Chron. 8 : 16. (B.C. 588 or 536.)

2. The Tizite, one of David's guard. 1 Chron. 11 : 45. (B.C. 1046.)

Joha'nan (*gift* or *grace of God*). 1. Son of Azariah and grandson of Ahimaaz the son of Zadok, and father of Azariah, 3. 1 Chron. 6 : 9, 10, Authorized Version.

2. Son of Elioenai, the son of Neariah, the son of Shemaiah, in the line of Zerubbabel's heirs. 1 Chron. 3 : 24. (B.C. after 406.)

3. The son of Kareah, and one of the captains of the scattered remnants of the army of Judah, who escaped in the final attack upon Jerusalem by the Chaldeans. (B.C. 588.) After the murder of Gedaliah, Johanan was one of the foremost in the pursuit of his assassin, and rescued the captives he had carried off from Mizpah. Jer. 41 : 11–16. Fearing the vengeance of the Chaldeans, the captains, with Johanan at their head, notwithstanding the warnings of Jeremiah, retired into Egypt.

4. The first-born son of Josiah king of Judah. 1 Chron. 3 : 15. (B.C. 638–610.)

5. A valiant Benjamite who joined David at Ziklag. 1 Chron. 12 : 4. (B.C. 1055.)

6. A Gadite warrior who followed David. 1 Chron. 12 : 12.

7. The father of Azariah, an Ephraimite in the time of Ahaz. 2 Chron. 28 : 12.

8. The son of Hakkatan, and chief of the Bene-Azgad who returned with Ezra. Ezra 8 : 12.

9. The son of Eliashib, one of the chief Levites. Ezra 10 : 6; Neh. 12 : 23.

10. The son of Tobiah the Ammonite. Neh. 6 : 18.

John, the same name as Johanan, a contraction of Jehohanan, *Jehovah's gift*. 1. One of the high priest's family, who, with Annas and Caiaphas, sat in judgment upon the apostles Peter and John. Acts 6 : 6.

2. The Hebrew name of the evangelist Mark. Acts 12 : 12, 25; 13 : 5, 13; 15 : 37.

John the apostle was the son of Zebedee, a fisherman on the Lake of Galilee, and of Salome, and brother of James, also an apostle. Peter and James and John come within the innermost circle of their Lord's friends; but to John belongs the distinction of being the disciple whom Jesus loved. He hardly sustains the popular notion, fostered by the received types of Christian art, of a nature gentle, yielding, feminine. The name Boanerges, Mark 3 : 17, implies a vehemence, zeal, intensity, which gave to those who had it the might of sons of thunder. [JAMES.] The three are with our Lord when none else are, in the chamber of death, Mark 5 : 37; in the glory of the transfiguration, Matt. 17 : 1; when he forewarns them of the destruction of the holy city, Mark 13 : 3; in the agony of Gethsemane. When the betrayal is accomplished, Peter and John follow afar off. John 18 : 15. The personal acquaintance which existed between John and Caiaphas enables him to gain access to the council chamber, and he follows Jesus thence, even to the prætorium of the Roman procurator. John 18 : 16, 19, 28. Thence he follows to the place of crucifixion, and the Teacher leaves to him the duty of becoming a son to the mother who is left desolate. John 19 : 26, 27. It is to Peter and John that Mary Magdalene first runs with the tidings of the emptied sepulchre, John 20 : 2; they are the first to go together to see what the strange words meant, John running on most eagerly to the rock-tomb; Peter, the least restrained by awe, the first to enter in and look. John 20 : 4-6. For at least eight days they continue in Jerusalem. John 20 : 26. Later, on the Sea of Galilee, John is the first to recognize in the dim form seen in the morning twilight the presence of his risen Lord; Peter the first to plunge into the water and swim toward the shore where he stood calling to them. John 21 : 7. The last words of John's Gospel reveal to us the deep affection which united the two friends. The history of the Acts shows the same union. They are together at the ascension and on the day of Pentecost. To-

gether they enter the temple as worshippers, Acts 3 : 1, and protest against the threats of the Sanhedrin. ch. 4 : 13. The persecution which was pushed on by Saul of Tarsus did not drive John from his post. ch. 8 : 1. Fifteen years after St. Paul's first visit he was still at Jerusalem, and helped to take part in the settlement of the great controversy between the Jewish and the Gentile Christians. Acts 15 : 6. His subsequent history we know only by tradition. There can be no doubt that he removed from Jerusalem and settled at Ephesus, though at what time is uncertain. Tradition goes on to relate that in the persecution under Domitian he is taken to Rome, and there, by his boldness, though not by death, gains the crown of martyrdom. The boiling oil into which he is thrown has no power to hurt him. He is then sent to labor in the mines, and Patmos is the place of his exile. The accession of Nerva frees him from danger, and he returns to Ephesus. Heresies continue to show themselves, but he meets them with the strongest possible protest. The very time of his death lies within the region of conjecture rather than of history, and the dates that have been assigned for it range from A.D. 89 to A.D. 120.

John the Baptist was of the priestly race by both parents, for his father, Zacharias, was himself a priest of the course of Abia or Abijah, 1 Chron. 24 : 10, and Elisabeth was of the daughters of Aaron. Luke 1 : 5. His birth was foretold by an angel sent from God, and is related at length in Luke 1. The birth of John preceded by six months that of our Lord. John was ordained to be a Nazarite from his birth. Luke 1 : 15. Dwelling by himself in the wild and thinly-peopled region westward of the Dead Sea, he prepared himself for the wonderful office to which he had been divinely called. His dress was that of the old prophets—a garment woven of camel's hair, 2 Kings 1 : 8, attached to the body by a leathern girdle. His food was such as the desert afforded —locusts, Lev. 11 : 22, and wild honey. Ps. 81 : 16. And now the long-secluded hermit came forth to the discharge of his office. His supernatural birth, his life, and the general expectation that some great one was about to appear, were sufficient to attract to him a great multitude from "every quarter." Matt. 3 : 5. Many of every class pressed forward to confess their sins and to be baptized. Jesus himself came from Galilee to Jordan to be baptized of John. [JESUS.] From incidental notices we learn that John and his disciples continued to baptize some time after our Lord entered upon his ministry. See John 3 : 23; 4 : 1; Acts 19 : 3. We gather also that John instructed his disciples in certain moral and religious duties, as fasting, Matt. 9 : 14; Luke 5 : 33, and prayer. Luke 11 : 1. But shortly after he had given his testimony to the Messiah, John's public ministry was brought to a close. In daring disregard of the divine laws, Herod Antipas had taken to himself Herodias, the wife of his brother Philip; and when John reproved him for this, as well as for other sins, Luke 3 : 19, Herod cast him into prison. (March, A.D. 28.) The place of his confinement was the castle of Machaerus, a fortress on the eastern shore of the Dead Sea. It was here that reports reached him of the miracles which our Lord was working in Judea. Nothing but the death of the Baptist would satisfy the resentment of Herodias. A court festival was kept at Machaerus in honor of the king's birthday. After supper the daughter of Herodias came in and danced before the company, and so charmed was the king by her grace that he promised with an oath to give her whatsoever she should ask. Salome, prompted by her abandoned mother, demanded the head of John the Baptist. Herod gave instructions to an officer of his guard, who went and executed John in the prison, and his head was brought to feast the eyes of the adulteress whose sins he had denounced. His death is supposed to have occurred just before the third passover, in the course of the Lord's ministry. (March, A.D. 29.)

John, Gospel of. This Gospel was probably written at Ephesus about A.D. 78. (Canon Cook places it toward the close of John's life, A.D. 90-100.—ED.) The Gospel was obviously addressed primarily to Christians, not to heathen. There can be little doubt that the main object of St. John, who wrote after the other evangelists, is to supplement their narratives, which were almost confined to our Lord's life in Galilee. (It was the Gospel for the Church, to cultivate and cherish the spiritual life of Christians, and bring them into the closest relations to the divine Saviour. It gives the inner life and teachings of Christ as revealed to his disciples. Nearly two-thirds of the whole book belong to the last six months of our Lord's life, and one-third is the record of the last week. —ED.) The following is an abridgment of its contents : A. *The Prologue.* ch. 1. 1–18. B. *The History*, ch. 1 : 19–20 : 29. (a) Various events relating to our Lord's ministry, narrated in connection with seven journeys, ch. 1 : 19–12 : 50: 1. First journey, into Judea, and beginning of his ministry, ch. 1 : 19–2 : 12. 2. Second journey, at the passover in the first year of his ministry, ch. 2 : 13–4. 3. Third journey, in the second year of his ministry, about the passover, ch. 5. 4. Fourth journey, about the passover, in the third year of his ministry, beyond Jordan, ch. 6. 5. Fifth journey, six months before his death, begun at the feast of tabernacles, chs. 7–10 : 21. 6. Sixth journey, about the feast of dedication, ch. 10 : 22–42. 7. Seventh journey, in Judea towards Bethany, ch. 11 : 1–54. 8. Eighth journey, before his last passover, chs. 11 : 55–12. (b) History of the death of Christ, chs. 13–20 : 29 : 1. Preparation for his passion, chs. 13–17. 2. The circumstances of his passion and death, chs. 18, 19. 3. His resurrection, and the proofs of it, ch. 20 : 1–29. C. *The Conclusion*, ch. 20 : 30–21 : 1. Scope of the foregoing history, ch. 20 : 30, 31. 2. Confirmation of the authority of the evangelist by additional historical facts, and by the testimony of the elders of the Church, ch. 21 : 1–24. 3. Reason of the termination of the history, ch. 21 : 25.

John, The First Epistle General of. There can be no doubt that the apostle John was the author of this epistle. It was probably written from Ephesus, and most likely at the close of the first century. In the introduction, ch. 1 : 1–4, the apostle states the purpose of his epistle : it is to declare the word of life to those whom he is addressing, in order that he and they might be united in true communion with each other, and with God the Father and his Son Jesus Christ. His lesson throughout is that the means of union with God are, on the part of Christ, his atoning blood, ch. 1 : 7, 2 : 2, 3 : 5, 4 : 10, 14, 5 : 6, and advocacy, ch. 2 : 1; on the part of man, holiness, ch. 1 : 6, obedience, ch. 2 : 3, purity, ch. 3 : 3, faith, ch. 3 : 23; 4 : 3; 5 : 5, and above all love. ch. 2 : 7; 3 : 14; 4 : 7; 5 : 1.

John, The Second and Third Epistles of. The second epistle is ad dressed to an individual woman. One who had children, and a sister and nieces, is clearly indicated. According to one interpretation she is "the Lady Electa," to another, "the elect Kyria," to a third, "the elect Lady." The third epistle is addressed to Caius or Gaius. He was probably a convert of St. John, Epist. 3 : 4, and a layman of wealth and distinction, Epist. 3 : 5, in some city near Ephesus. The *object* of St. John in writing the second epistle was to warn the lady to whom he wrote against abetting the teaching known as that of Basilides and his followers, by perhaps an undue kindness displayed by her toward the preachers of the false doctrine. The third epistle was written for the purpose of commending to the kindness and hospitality of Caius some Christians who were strangers in the place where he lived. It is probable that these Christians carried this letter with them to Caius as their introduction.

Jo-i′ada (*whom Jehovah favors*), high priest after his father Eliashib. Neh. 13 : 28. (B.C. after 446.)

Jo-i′akim (*whom Jehovah sets up*), a high priest, son of the renowned Jeshua. Neh. 12 : 10. (B.C. before 446.)

Jo-i′arib (*whom Jehovah defends*). 1. A layman who returned from Babylon with Ezra. Ezra 8 : 16. (B.C. 459.)

2. The founder of one of the courses of priests, elsewhere called in full JE-HOIARIB. Neh. 12 : 6, 19.

3. A Shilonite—*i. e.* probably a descendant of Shelah the son of Judah. Neh. 11 : 5. (B.C. before 536.)

Jok′de-an (*possessed by the people*), a city of Judah, in the mountains, Josh. 15 : 56, apparently south of Hebron.

Jo′kim (*whom Jehovah has set up*), one of the sons of Shelah the son of Judah. 1 Chron. 4 : 22.

Jok′me-am (*gathered by the people*), a city of Ephraim, given with its suburbs to the Kohathite Levites. 1 Chron. 6 : 68. The situation of Jokmeam (in Authorized Version JOKNEAM) is to a certain extent indicated in 1 Kings 4 : 12, where it is named with places which we know to have been in the Jordan valley at the extreme east boundary of the tribe.

Jok′ne-am (*possessed by the people*), a city of the tribe of Zebulun, allotted with its suburbs to the Merarite Levites. Josh. 21 : 34. Its modern site, is *Tell Kaimon*, an eminence which stands just below the eastern termination of Carmel.

Jok′shan (*fowler*), a son of Abraham and Keturah, Gen. 25 : 2, 3 ; 1 Chron. 1 : 32, whose sons were Sheba and Dedan.

Jok′tan (*small*), son of Eber, Gen. 10 : 25 ; 1 Chron. 1 : 19, and the father of the Joktanite Arabs. Gen. 10 : 30. (B.C. about 2200.)

Jok′the-el (*subdued by God*). 1. A city in the low country of Judah, Josh. 15 : 38, named next to Lachish.

2. "God-subdued," the title given by Amaziah to the cliff (Authorized Version Selah)—the stronghold of the Edomites —after he had captured it from them. 2 Kings 14 : 7. The parallel narrative of 2 Chron. 25 : 11–13 supplies fuller details.

Jo′na (*a dove*) (Greek form of Jonah), the father of the apostle Peter, John 1 : 42, who is hence addressed as Simon Bar-jona (*i. e.* son of Jona) in Matt. 16 : 17.

Jon′adab (*whom Jehovah impels*). 1. Son of Shimeah and nephew of David. (B.C. 1033.) He is described as "very subtile." 2 Sam. 13 : 3. His age naturally made him the friend of his cousin Amnon, heir to the throne. 2 Sam. 13 : 3. He gave him the fatal advice for ensnaring his sister Tamar. ch. 13 : 5, 6. Again, when, in a later stage of the same tragedy, Amnon was murdered by Absalom, and the exaggerated report reached David that all the princes were slaughtered, Jonadab was already aware of the real state of the case. 2 Sam. 13 : 32, 33.

2. Jer. 35 : 6, 8, 10, 14, 16, 18, 19. [JE-HONADAB.]

Jo′nah (*dove*), the fifth of the minor prophets, was the son of Amittai, and a native of Gath-hepher. 2 Kings 14 : 25. He flourished in or before the reign of Jeroboam II., about B.C. 820. Having already, as it seems, prophesied to Israel, he was sent to Nineveh. The time was one of political revival in Israel ; but ere long the Assyrians were to be employed by God as a scourge upon them. The prophet shrank from a commission which he felt sure would result, Jonah 4 : 2, in the sparing of a hostile city. He attempted therefore to escape to Tarshish. The providence of God, however, watched over him, first in a storm, and then in his being swallowed by a large fish (a sea monster, probably the white shark) for the space of three days and three nights. [On this subject see article WHALE.] After his deliverance, Jonah executed his commission ; and the king, "believing him to be a minister from the supreme deity of the nation," and having heard of his miraculous deliverance, ordered a general fast, and averted the threatened judgment. But the prophet, not from personal but national feelings, grudged the mercy shown to a heathen nation. He was therefore taught by the significant lesson of the " gourd," whose growth and decay brought the truth at once home to him, that he was sent to testify by deed, as other prophets would afterward testify by word, the capacity of Gentiles for salvation, and the design of God to make them partakers of it. This was " the sign of the prophet Jonas." Luke 11 : 29, 30. But the resurrection of Christ itself was also shadowed forth in the history of the prophet. Matt. 12 : 39, 41; 16 : 4. The mission of Jonah was highly symbolical. The facts contained a concealed prophecy. The old tradition made the burial-place of Jonah to be Gath-hepher; the modern tradition places it at *Nebi-Yunus*, opposite Mosul.

Jo'nam (*gift* or *grace of God*), the form given to JONAN in the Revised Version of Luke 3 : 30.

Jo'nan (perhaps a contraction of Johanan, *gift* or *grace of God*), son of Eliakim, in the genealogy of Christ. Luke 3 : 30. (B.C. before 876.)

Jo'nas (*a dove*). 1. The prophet Jonah. Matt. 12 : 39, 40, 41; 16 : 4. [JONA.]

2. Father of Peter. John 21 : 15-17. [JONA.]

Jon'athan, that is, "*the gift of Jehovah*," the eldest son of King Saul. (B.C. about 1095-1056.) He was 'a man of great strength and activity. 2 Sam. 1 : 23. He was also famous as a warrior, 1 Chron. 12 : 2, as is shown by the courage he showed in attacking the garrison of the Philistines, in company with his armor-bearer only, slaying twenty men and putting an army to flight. 1 Sam. 14 : 6-16. During the pursuit, Jonathan, who had not heard of the rash curse, ch. 14 : 24, which Saul invoked on any one who ate before the evening, tasted the honey which lay on the ground. Saul would have sacrificed him; but the people interposed in behalf of the hero of that great day, and Jonathan was saved. ch. 14 : 24-45. The chief interest of Jonathan's career is derived from the friendship with David, which began on the day of David's return from the victory over the champion of Gath, and continued till his death. Their last meeting was in the forest of Ziph, during Saul's pursuit of David. 1 Sam. 23 : 16-18.

From this time forth we hear no more till the battle of Gilboa. In that battle he fell. 1 Sam. 31 : 2, 8. (B.C. 1056.) His ashes were buried first at Jabesh-gilead, ch. 31 : 13, but were afterward removed with those of his father to Zelah in Benjamin. 2 Sam. 21 : 12. The news of his death occasioned the celebrated elegy of David. He left a son, Mephibosheth. [MEPHIBOSHETH.]

2. A nephew of David. 2 Sam. 21 : 21; 1 Chron. 20 : 7. He engaged in single combat with and slew a gigantic Philistine of Gath. 2 Sam. 21 : 21. (B.C. 1018.)

3. The son of Abiathar, the high priest, is the last descendant of Eli of whom we hear anything. 2 Sam. 15 : 36; 17 : 15-21; 1 Kings 1 : 42, 43. (B.C. 1023.)

4. One of David's heroes. 2 Sam. 23 : 32; 1 Chron. 11 : 34.

5. The son or descendant of Gershom the son of Moses. Judges 18 : 30. [MICAH.] (B.C. about 1425.)

6. One of the Bene-Adin. Ezra 8 : 6.

7. A priest, the son of Asahel, in the time of Ezra. Ezra 10 : 15. (B.C. 459.)

8. A priest of the family of Melicu. Neh. 12 : 14.

9. One of the sons of Kareah, and brother of Johanan. Jer. 40 : 8. (B.C. 587.)

10. Son of Joiada, and his successor in the high priesthood. Neh. 12 : 11, 22, 23. (B.C. before 332.)

11. Father of Zechariah, a priest who blew the trumpet at the dedication of the wall. Neh. 12 : 35.

12. 1 Esdr. 8 : 32. [See No. 6.] (B.C 446.)

Jonath-elem-rechokim (*a dumb love of* (*in*) *distant places*), a phrase found once only in the Bible, as a heading to the 56th psalm. Aben Ezra, who regards *Jonath-elem-rechokim* as merely indicating the modulation or the rhythm of the psalm, appears to come the nearest to the meaning of the passage.

Jop'pa, or **Japho** (*beauty*), now *Jaffa*, a town on the southwest coast of Palestine, in the portion of Dan. Josh. 19 : 46. Having a harbor attached to it— though always, as still, a dangerous one —it became the port of Jerusalem in the days of Solomon, and has been ever since. Here Jonah " took ship to flee from the presence of his Maker." Here, on the house-top of Simon the tanner, " by the seaside," St. Peter had his vision of tolerance. Acts 11 : 5. The existing town contains about 4000 inhabitants.

Jo'rah (*the early rain*), the ancestor of a family of 112 who returned from Babylon with Ezra. Ezra 2 : 18. In

Neh. 7 : 24 he appears under the name HA- RIPH, or more correctly the same family are represented as the Bene-Hariph.

Jaffa, the modern Joppa.

Jor'a-i (*whom Jehovah teaches*), one of the Gadites dwelling at Gilead in Bashan, in the reign of Jothan king of Judah. 1 Chron. 5 : 13.

Jo'ram (*whom Jehovah has exalted*). 1. Son of Ahab king of Israel. 2 Kings 8 : 16, 25, 28, 29 ; 9 : 14, 17, 21–23, 29. [JE-HORAM, 1.]

2. Son of Jehoshaphat ; king of Judah. 2 Kings 8 : 21, 23, 24 ; 1 Chron. 3 : 11 ; 2 Chron. 22 : 5, 7 ; Matt. 1 : 8. [JEHORAM, 2.]

3. A priest in the reign of Jehoshaphat. 2 Chron. 17 : 8.

4. A Levite, ancestor of Shelomith, in the time of David. 1 Chron. 26 : 25.

5. Son of Toi king of Hamath. 2 Sam. 8 : 10. [HADORAM.]

6. 1 Esd. 1 : 9. [JOZABAD, 3.]

Jor'dan (*the descender*), the one river of Palestine, has a course of little more than 200 miles, from the roots of Anti-Lebanon to the head of the Dead Sea. (136 miles in a straight line.—*Schaff.*) It is the river of the "great plain" of

Palestine—the "descender," if not "the river of God" in the book of Psalms, at least that of his chosen people throughout their history. There were fords over against Jericho, to which point the men of Jericho pursued the spies. Josh. 2 : 7 ; comp. Judges 3 : 28. Higher up were the fords or passages of Bethbarah, where Gideon lay in wait for the Midianites, Judges 7 : 24, and where the men of Gilead slew the Ephraimites. ch. 12 : 6. These fords undoubtedly witnessed the first recorded passage of the Jordan in the Old Testament. Gen. 32 : 10. Jordan was next crossed, over against Jericho, by Joshua. Josh. 4 : 12, 13. From their vicinity to Jerusalem the lower fords were much used. David, it is probable, passed over them in one instance to fight the Syrians. 2 Sam. 10 : 17 ; 17 : 22. Thus there were two customary places at which the Jordan was fordable ; and it must have been at one of these, if not at both, that baptism was afterward administered by St. John and by the dis-

The Jordan Valley.

ciples of our Lord. Where our Lord was baptized is not stated expressly, but it was probably at the upper ford. These fords were rendered so much more precious in those days from two circumstances. First, it does not appear that there were then any bridges thrown over or boats regularly established on the Jordan; and secondly, because "Jordan overflowed all his banks all the time of harvest." Josh. 3 : 15. The channel or bed of the river became brimful, so that the level of the water and of the banks was then the same. (Dr. Selah Merrill, in his book "Galilee in the Time of Christ" (1881), says, "Near Tarichæa, just below the point where the Jordan leaves the lake (of Galilee), there was (in Christ's time) a splendid bridge across the river, supported by ten piers."—ED.) The last feature which remains to be noticed in the scriptural account of the Jordan is its frequent mention as a boundary: "over Jordan," "this" and "the other side," or "beyond Jordan," were expressions as familiar to the Israelites as "across the water," "this" and "the other side of the Channel" are to English ears. In one sense indeed, that is, in so far as it was the eastern boundary of the land of Canaan, it was the eastern boundary of the promised land. Num. 34 : 12. The Jordan rises from several sources near Panium (*Bá-niás*), and passes through the lakes of Merom (*Hûleh*) and Gennesaret. The two principal features in its course are its descent and its windings. From its fountain heads to the Dead Sea it rushes down one continuous inclined plane, only broken by a series of rapids or precipitous falls. Between the Lake of Gennesaret and the Dead Sea there are 27 rapids. The depression of the Lake of Gennesaret below the level of the Mediterranean is 653 feet, and that of the Dead Sea 1316 feet. (The whole descent from its source to the Dead Sea is 3000 feet. Its width varies from 45 to 180 feet, and it is from 3 to 12 feet deep.—*Schaff.*) Its sinuosity is not so remarkable in the upper part of its course. The only tributaries to the Jordan below Gennesaret are the *Yarmûk* (Hieromax) and the *Zerka* (Jabbok). Not a single city ever crowned the banks of the Jordan. Still Bethshan and Jericho to the west, Gerasa, Pella and Gadara to the east of it were important cities, and caused a good deal of traffic between the two opposite

banks. The physical features of the *Ghor*, through which the Jordan flows, are treated of under PALESTINE.

Jo'rim (*whom Jehovah has exalted*), son of Matthat, in the genealogy of Christ. Luke 3 : 29.

Jor'ko-am (*paleness of the people*), either a descendant of Caleb the son of Hezron, or the name of a place in the tribe of Judah. 1 Chron. 2 : 44.

Jos'abad (*whom Jehovah bestows*), properly JOZABAD the Gederathite, one of the warriors of Benjamin who joined David at Ziklag. 1 Chron. 12 : 4. (B.C. 1055.)

Jos'aphat = Jehoshaphat king of Judah. Matt. 1 : 8.

Jo'se (another form of JOSES), son of Eliezer, in the genealogy of Jesus Christ. Luke 3 : 29.

Jo'sech, the form of name given in the Revised Version for JOSEPH, in Luke 3 : 26. It is not found in the Old Testament.

Jos'edech = JEHOZADAK (*whom Jehovah makes just*), the son of Seraiah. Hag. 1 : 1, 12, 14; 2 : 2, 4; Zech. 6 : 11.

Jo'seph (*increase*). 1. The elder of the two sons of Jacob by Rachel. He was born in Padan-aram (Mesopotamia), probably about B.C. 1746. He is first mentioned when a youth, seventeen years old. Joseph brought the evil report of his brethren to his father, and they hated him because his father loved him more than he did them, and had shown his preference by making him a dress which appears to have been a long tunic with sleeves, worn by youths and maidens of the richer class. Gen. 37 : 2. He dreamed a dream foreshadowing his future power, which increased the hatred of his brethren. Gen. 37 : 5–7. He was sent by his father to visit his brothers, who were tending flocks in the fields of Dothan. They resolved to kill him, but he was saved by Reuben, who persuaded the brothers to cast Joseph into a dry pit, to the intent that he might restore him to Jacob. The appearance of the Ishmaelites suggested his sale for "twenty pieces (shekels) of silver." ver. 28. Sold into Egypt to Potiphar, Joseph prospered and was soon set over Potiphar's house, and "all he had he gave into his hand;" but incurring the anger of Potiphar's wife, ch. 39 : 7–13, he was falsely accused and thrown into prison, where he remained at least two years, interpreting during this time the dreams of the cupbearer and the baker. Finally Pharaoh himself dreamed two prophetic dreams. Joseph, being sent for, interpreted them in the name of God, foretelling the seven years of plenty and the seven years of famine. Pharaoh at once appointed Joseph not merely governor of Egypt, but second only to the sovereign, and also gave him to wife Asenath, daughter of Potipherah priest of On (Hieropolis), and gave him a name or title, *Zaphnath-paaneah* (preserver of life). Joseph's first act was to go throughout all the land of Egypt. During the seven plenteous years there was a very abundant produce, and he gathered the fifth part and laid it up. When the seven good years had passed, the famine began. Gen. 41: 54–57. [FAMINE.] After the famine had lasted for a time, apparently two years, Joseph gathered up all the money that was found in the land of Egypt and in the land of Canaan, for the corn which they bought, and brought it into Pharaoh's house, Gen. 47:13,14; and when the money was exhausted, all the cattle, and finally all the land except that of the priests, and apparently, as a consequence, the Egyptians themselves. He demanded, however, only a fifth part of the produce as Pharaoh's right. Now Jacob, who had suffered also from the effects of the famine, sent Joseph's brothers to Egypt for corn. The whole story of Joseph's treatment of his brethren is so graphically told in Gen. 42–45, and is so familiar, that it is unnecessary here to repeat it. On the death of Jacob in Egypt, Joseph carried him to Canaan, and laid him in the cave of Machpelah, the burying-place of his fathers. Joseph lived "a hundred and ten years," having been more than ninety in Egypt. Dying, he took an oath of his brethren that they should carry up his bones to the land of promise: thus showing in his latest action the faith, Heb. 11 : 22, which had guided his whole life. Like his father he was embalmed, "and he was put in a coffin in Egypt." Gen. 50 : 26. His trust Moses kept, and laid the bones of Joseph in his inheritance in Shechem, in the territory of Ephraim his offspring. His tomb is, according to tradition, about a stone's throw from Jacob's well.

2. Father of Igal, who represented the tribe of Issachar among the spies. Num. 13 : 7.

Joseph's Tomb and Mount Gerizim.

3. A lay Israelite who had married a foreign wife. Ezra 10 : 42. (B.C. 459.)

4. A representative of the priestly family of Shebaniah. Neh. 12 : 14. (B.C. after 536.)

5. One of the ancestors of Christ, Luke 3 : 30, son of Jonan.

6. Another ancestor of Christ, son of Judah. Luke 3 : 26. (B.C. between 536–410.)

7. Another, son of Mattathias. Luke 3 : 24. (B.C. after 400.)

8. Son of Heli, and reputed father of Jesus Christ. All that is told us of Joseph in the New Testament may be summed up in a few words. He was a

just man, and of the house and lineage of David. He lived at Nazareth in Galilee. He espoused Mary, the daughter and heir of his uncle Jacob, and before he took her home as his wife received the angelic communication recorded in Matt. 1 : 20. When Jesus was twelve years old Joseph and Mary took him with them to keep the passover at Jerusalem, and when they returned to Nazareth he continued to act as a father to the child Jesus, and was reputed to be so indeed. But here our knowledge of Joseph ends. That he died before our Lord's crucifixion is indeed tolerably certain, by what is related John 19 : 27, and perhaps Mark 6 : 3 may imply that he was then dead. But where, when or how he died we know not.

9. Joseph of Arimathæa, a rich and pious Israelite, probably a member of the Great Council or Sanhedrin. He is further characterized as "a good man and a just." Luke 23 : 50. We are expressly told that he did not "consent to the counsel and deed" of his colleagues in conspiring to bring about the death of Jesus; but he seems to have lacked the courage to protest against their judgment. On the very evening of the crucifixion, when the triumph of the chief priests and rulers seemed complete, Joseph "went in boldly unto Pilate and craved the body of Jesus." Pilate consented. Joseph and Nicodemus then, having enfolded the sacred body in the linen shroud which Joseph had bought, consigned it to a tomb hewn in a rock, in a garden belonging to Joseph, and close to the place of crucifixion. There is a tradition that he was one of the seventy disciples.

10. Joseph, called Barsabas, and surnamed Justus; one of the two persons chosen by the assembled church, Acts 1 : 23, as worthy to fill the place in the apostolic company from which Judas had fallen.

Jo'ses (*exalted*). 1. Son of Eliezer, in the genealogy of Christ. Luke 3 : 29.

2. One of the Lord's brethren. Matt. 13 : 55; Mark 6 : 3.

3. Joses Barnabas. Acts 4 : 36. [BARNABAS.]

Jo'shah (*whom Jehovah lets dwell*), a prince of the house of Simeon. 1 Chron. 4 : 34, 38–41.

Josh'aphat (*whom Jehovah judges*), the Mithnite, one of David's guard. 1 Chron. 11 : 43.

Joshavi'ah (*whom Jehovah makes*

dwell), the son of Elnaam, and one of David's guard. 1 Chron. 11 : 46. (B.C. 1046.)

Joshbek'ashah (*a seat in a hard place*), son of Heman, head of the seventeenth course of musicians. 1 Chron. 25 : 4, 24. (B.C. 1014.)

Josh'ua (*saviour*, or *whose help is Jehovah*). His name appears in the various forms of HOSHEA, OSHEA, JEHOSHUA, JESHUA and JESUS. 1. The son of Nun, of the tribe of Ephraim. 1 Chron. 7 : 27. (B.C. 1530–1420.) He was nearly forty years old when he shared in the hurried triumph of the exodus. He is mentioned first in connection with the fight against Amalek at Rephidim, when he was chosen by Moses to lead the Israelites. Ex. 17 : 9. Soon afterward he was one of the twelve chiefs who were sent, Num. 13 : 17, to explore the land of Canaan, and one of the two, ch. 14 : 6, who gave an encouraging report of their journey. Moses, shortly before his death, was directed, Num. 27 : 18, to invest Joshua with authority over the people. God himself gave Joshua a charge by the mouth of the dying lawgiver. Deut. 31 : 14, 23. Under the direction of God again renewed, Josh. 1 : 1, Joshua assumed the command of the people at Shittim, sent spies into Jericho, crossed the Jordan, fortified a camp at Gilgal, circumcised the people, kept the passover, and was visited by the Captain of the Lord's host. A miracle made the fall of Jericho more terrible to the Canaanites. In the great battle of Beth-horon the Amorites were signally routed, and the south country was open to the Israelites. Joshua returned to the camp at Gilgal, master of half of Palestine. He defeated the Canaanites under Jabin king of Hazor. In six years, six tribes, with thirty-one petty chiefs, were conquered. Joshua, now stricken in years, proceeded to make the division of the conquered land. Timnath-serah in Mount Ephraim was assigned as Joshua's peculiar inheritance. After an interval of rest, Joshua convoked an assembly from all Israel. He delivered two solemn addresses, recorded in Josh. 23 : 24. He died at the age of 110 years, and was buried in his own city, Timnath-serah.

2. An inhabitant of Beth-shemesh, in whose land was the stone at which the milch-kine stopped when they drew the ark of God with the offerings of the Philistines from Ekron to Beth-shemesh. 1 Sam. 6 : 14, 18. (B.C. 1124.)

3. A governor of the city who gave his name to a gate of Jerusalem. 2 Kings 23 : 8. (In the reign of Josiah, B.C. 628.)

4. Jeshua the son of Jozadak. Hag. 1 : 14; 2 : 12; Zech. 3 : 1, etc.

Josh'ua, Book of. Named from Joshua the son of Nun, who is the principal character in it. The book may be regarded as consisting of three parts: 1. The conquest of Canaan; chs. 1–12. 2. The partition of Canaan; chs. 13–22. 3. Joshua's farewell; chs. 23, 24. Nothing is really known as to the authorship of the book. Joshua himself is generally named as the author by the Jewish writers and the Christian fathers; but no contemporary assertion or sufficient historical proof of the fact exists, and it cannot be maintained without qualification. The last verses, ch. 24 : 29–33, were obviously added at a later time. Some events, such as the capture of Hebron, of Debir, Josh. 15 : 13–19 and Judges 1 : 10–15, of Leshem, Josh. 19 : 47 and Judges 18 : 7, and the joint occupation of Jerusalem, Josh. 15 : 63 and Judges 1 : 21, probably did not occur till after Joshua's death. (It was written probably during Joshua's life, or soon after his death (B.C. 1420), and includes his own records, with revision by some other person not long afterward.)

Josi'ah (*whom Jehovah heals*). 1. The son of Amon and Jedidah, succeeded his father B.C. 641, in the eighth year of his age, and reigned 31 years. His history is contained in 2 Kings 22–24 : 30; 2 Chron. 34, 35; and the first twelve chapters of Jeremiah throw much light upon the general character of the Jews in his day. He began in the eighth year of his reign to seek the Lord; and in his twelfth year, and for six years afterward, in a personal progress throughout all the land of Judah and Israel, he destroyed everywhere high places, groves, images and all outward signs and relics of idolatry. The temple was restored under a special commission; and in the course of the repairs Hilkiah the priest found that book of the law of the Lord which quickened so remarkably the ardent zeal of the king. He was aided by Jeremiah the prophet in spreading through his kingdom the knowledge and worship of Jehovah. The great day of Josiah's life was the day of the passover in the eighteenth year of his reign. After this his endeavors to abolish every trace of idolatry and superstition were still carried on; but the time drew near which had been indicated by Huldah. 2 Kings 22 : 20. When Pharaoh-necho went from Egypt to Carchemish to carry on his war against Assyria, Josiah opposed his march along the seacoast. Necho reluctantly paused and gave him battle in the valley of Esdraelon. Josiah was mortally wounded, and died before he could reach Jerusalem. He was buried with extraordinary honors.

2. The son of Zephaniah, at whose house took place the solemn and symbolical crowning of Joshua the high priest. Zech. 6 : 10. (B.C. about 1520.)

Josi'as. Josiah, king of Judah. Matt. 1 : 10, 11.

Josibi'ah (*to whom God gives a dwelling*), the father of Jehu, a Simeonite. 1 Chron. 4 : 35.

Josiphi'ah (*whom Jehovah will increase*), the father or ancestor of Shelomith, who returned with Ezra. Ezra 8 : 10. (B.C. 459.)

Jot, the English form of the Greek *iota, i. e.,* the smallest letter of the Greek alphabet. The Hebrew is *yod,* or *y* formed like a comma ('). It is used metaphorically to express the minutest thing.

Jot'bah (*goodness*), the native place of Meshullemeth, the queen of Manasseh. 2 Kings 21 : 19.

Jot'bath, or **Jot'bathah** (*goodness*), Deut. 10 : 7; Num. 33 : 33, a desert station of the Israelites.

Jo'tham (*Jehovah is upright*). 1. The youngest son of Gideon, Judges 9 : 5, who escaped from the massacre of his brethren. (B.C. after 1256.) His parable of the reign of the bramble is the earliest example of the kind.

2. The son of King Uzziah or Azariah and Jerushah. After administering the kingdom for some years during his father's leprosy, he succeeded to the throne B.C. 758, when he was 25 years old, and reigned 16 years in Jerusalem. He was contemporary with Pekah and with the prophet Isaiah. His history is contained in 2 Kings 15 and 2 Chron. 27.

3. A descendant of Judah, son of Jahdai. 1 Chron. 2 : 47.

Joz'abad (*Jehovah justifies*). 1. A captain of the thousands of Manasseh, who deserted to David before the battle of Gilboa. 1 Chron. 12 : 20. (B.C. 1053.)

2. A hero of Manasseh, like the preceding. 1 Chron. 12 : 20.

3. A Levite in the reign of Hezekiah. 2 Chron. 31 : 13. (B.C. 726.)

4. A chief Levite in the reign of Josiah. 2 Chron. 35 : 9.

5. A Levite, son of Jeshua, in the days of Ezra. Ezra 8 : 33. (B.C. 459.) Probably identical with No. 7.

6. A priest of the sons of Pashur, who had married a foreign wife. Ezra 10 : 22.

7. A Levite among those who returned with Ezra and had married foreign wives. He is probably identical with Jozabad the Levite, Neh. 8 : 7, and with Jozabad who presided over the outer work of the temple. Neh. 11 : 16. (B.C. 459.)

Joz'achar (*whom Jehovah has remembered*), one of the murderers of Joash king of Judah. 2 Kings 12 : 21. The writer of the Chronicles, 2 Chron. 24 : 26, calls him ZABAD. (B.C. 837.)

Joz'adak (*whom Jehovah has made just*). Ezra 3 : 2, 8; 5 : 2; 10 : 18; Neh. 12 : 26. The contracted form of Jehozadak.

Ju'bal (*music*), a son of Lamech by Adah, and the inventor of the "harp and organ." Gen. 4 : 21.

Jubilee, The year of. (1. *The name.*—The name jubilee is derived from the Hebrew *jobel*, the joyful shout or clangor of trumpets, by which the year of jubilee was announced.

2. *The time of its celebration.*—It was celebrated every fiftieth year, marking the half century ; so that it followed the seventh sabbatic year, and for two years in succession the land lay fallow. It was announced by the blowing of trumpets on the day of atonement (about the 1st of October), the tenth day of the first month of the Israelites' civil year (the seventh of their ecclesiastical year).

3. *The laws connected with the jubilee.*—These embrace three points : (1) Rest for the soil. Lev. 25 : 11, 12. The land was to lie fallow, and there was to be no tillage as on the ordinary sabbatic year. The land was not to be sown, nor the vineyards and oliveyards dressed ; and neither the spontaneous fruits of the soil nor the produce of the vine and olive was to be gathered, but all was to be left for the poor, the slave, the stranger and the cattle. Ex. 23 : 10, 11. The law was accompanied by a promise of treble fertility in the sixth year, the fruit of which was to be eaten till the harvest sown in the eighth year was reaped in the ninth. Lev. 25 : 20-22. But the people were not debarred from other sources of subsistence, nor was the year to be spent in idleness. They could fish and hunt, take

care of their bees and flocks, repair their buildings and furniture, and manufacture their clothing. (2) Reversion of landed property. "The Israelites had a portion of land divided to each family by lot. This portion of the promised land they held of God, and were not to dispose of it as their property in fee-simple. Hence no Israelite could part with his landed estate but for a term of years only. When the jubilee arrived, it again reverted to the original owners."—*Bush.* This applied to fields and houses in the country and to houses of the Levites in walled cities ; but other houses in such cities, if not redeemed within a year from their sale, remained the perpetual property of the buyer. (3) The manumission of those Israelites who had become slaves. "Apparently this periodic emancipation applied to every class of Hebrew servants —to him who had sold himself because he had become too poor to provide for his family, to him who had been taken and sold for debt, and to him who had been sold into servitude for crime. This latter case, however, is doubtful. Noticeably, this law provides for the family rights of the servant."—*Cowles' Hebrew History.*

4. *The reasons for the institution of the jubilee.*—It was to be a remedy for those evils which accompany human society and human government ; and had these laws been observed, they would have made the Jewish nation the most prosperous and perfect that ever existed. (1) The jubilee tended to abolish poverty. It prevented large and permanent accumulations of wealth. It gave unfortunate families an opportunity to begin over again with a fair start in life. It particularly favored the poor, without injustice to the rich. (2) It tended to abolish slavery, and in fact did abolish it ; and it greatly mitigated it while it existed. "The effect of this law was at once to lift from the heart the terrible incubus of a life-long bondage—that sense of a hopeless doom which knows no relief till death."—*Cowles.* (3) "As an agricultural people, they would have much leisure ; they would observe the sabbatic spirit of the year by using its leisure for the instruction of their families in the law, and for acts of devotion ; and in accordance with this there was a solemn reading of the law to the people assembled at the feast of tabernacles."— *Smith's larger Dictionary.* (4) "This

law of entail, by which the right heir could never be excluded, was a provision of great wisdom for preserving families and tribes perfectly distinct, and their genealogies faithfully recorded, in order that all might have evidence to establish their right to the ancestral property. Hence the tribe and family of Christ were readily discovered at his birth."

5. *Mode of celebration.*—"The Bible says nothing of the mode of celebration, except that it was to be proclaimed by trumpets, and that it was to be a sabbatic year. Tradition tells us that every Israelite blew nine blasts, so as to make the trumpet literally 'sound throughout the land,' and that from the feast of trumpets or new year till the day of atonement (ten days after), the slaves were neither manumitted to return to their homes, nor made use of by their masters, but ate, drank and rejoiced; and when the day of atonement came, the judges blew the trumpets, the slaves were manumitted to go to their homes, and the fields were set free."—*McClintock and Strong.*

6. *How long observed.*—Though very little is said about its observance in the Bible history of the Jews, yet it is referred to, and was no doubt observed with more or less faithfulness, till the Babylonish captivity.—ED.)

Ju'cal (*powerful*), son of Shelemiah. Jer. 38 : 1.

Ju'da (*praised*). 1. Son of Joseph, in the genealogy of Christ. Luke 3 : 30.

2. Son of Joanna, or Hananiah. [HANANIAH, 8.] Luke 3 : 26. He seems to be certainly the same person as ABIUD in Matt. 1 : 13.

3. One of the Lord's brethren, enumerated in Mark 6 : 3.

4. The patriarch Judah. Sus. 56; Luke 3 : 33; Heb. 7 : 14; Rev. 5 : 5; 7 : 5.

Judæ'a, or **Jude'a** (from Judah), a territorial division which succeeded to the overthrow of the ancient landmarks of the tribes of Israel and Judah in their respective captivities. The word first occurs Dan. 5 : 13, Authorized Version "Jewry," and the first mention of the "province of Judea" is in the book of Ezra, ch. 5 : 8. It is alluded to in Neh. 11 : 3 (Authorized Version "Judah"). In the apocryphal books the word "province" is dropped, and throughout them and the New Testament the expressions are "the land of Judea," "Judea." In a wide and more improper sense, the term Judea was sometimes extended to the whole country of the Canaanites, its ancient inhabitants; and even in the Gospels we read of the coasts of Judea "beyond Jordan." Matt. 19 : 1; Mark 10 : 1. Judea was, in strict language, the name of the third district, west of the Jordan and south of Samaria. It was made a portion of the Roman province of Syria upon the deposition of Archelaus, the ethnarch of Judea, in A.D. 6, and was governed by a procurator, who was subject to the governor of Syria.

Ju'dah (*praised, celebrated*), the fourth son of Jacob and the fourth of Leah. (B.C. after 1753.) Of Judah's personal character more traits are preserved than of any other of the patriarchs, with the exception of Joseph, whose life he in conjunction with Reuben saved. Gen. 37 : 26-28. During the second visit to Egypt for corn it was Judah who undertook to be responsible for the safety of Benjamin, ch. 43 : 3-10; and when, through Joseph's artifice, the brothers were brought back to the palace, he is again the leader and spokesman of the band. So too it is Judah who is sent before Jacob to smooth the way for him in the land of Goshen. ch. 46 : 28. This ascendency over his brethren is reflected in the last words addressed to him by his father. The families of Judah occupy a position among the tribes similar to that which their progenitor had taken among the patriarchs. The numbers of the tribe at the census at Sinai were 74,600. Num. 1 : 26, 27. On the borders of the promised land they were 76,500. Gen. 26 : 22. The boundaries and contents of the territory allotted to Judah are narrated at great length, and with greater minuteness than the others, in Josh. 15 : 20-63. The north boundary, for the most part coincident with the south boundary of Benjamin, began at the embouchure of the Jordan and ended on the west at Jabneel on the coast of the Mediterranean, four miles south of Joppa. On the east the Dead Sea, and on the west the Mediterranean, formed the boundaries. The southern line is hard to determine, since it is denoted by places many of which have not been identified. It left the Dead Sea at its extreme south end, and joined the Mediterranean at the *Wady el-Arish*. This territory is in average length about 45 miles, and in average breadth about 50.

Judah, Kingdom of. *Extent.*—

When the disruption of Solomon's kingdom took place at Shechem, B.C. 975, only the tribe of Judah followed David, but almost immediately afterward the larger part of Benjamin joined Judah. A part, if not all, of the territory of Simeon, 1 Sam. 27 : 6; 1 Kings 19 : 3, comp. Josh. 19 : 1, and of Dan, 2 Chron. 11 : 10, comp. Josh. 19 : 41, 42, was recognized as belonging to Judah; and in the reigns of Abijah and Asa the southern kingdom was enlarged by some additions taken out of the territory of Ephraim. 2 Chron. 13 : 19; 15 : 8; 17 : 2. It is estimated that the territory of Judah contained about 3450 square miles.

Advantages.—The kingdom of Judah possessed many advantages which secured for it a longer continuance than that of Israel. A frontier less exposed to powerful enemies, a soil less fertile, a population hardier and more united, a fixed and venerated centre of administration and religion, a hereditary aristocracy in the sacerdotal caste, an army always subordinate, a succession of kings which no revolution interrupted; so that Judah survived her more populous and more powerful sister kingdom by 135 years, and lasted from B.C. 975 to B.C. 536.

History.—The first three kings of Judah seem to have cherished the hope of re-establishing their authority over the ten tribes; for sixty years there was war between them and the kings of Israel. The victory achieved by the daring Abijah brought to Judah a temporary accession of territory. Asa appears to have enlarged it still further. Hanani's remonstrance, 2 Chron. 16 : 7, prepares us for the reversal by Jehoshaphat of the policy which Asa pursued toward Israel and Damascus. A close alliance sprang up with strange rapidity between Judah and Israel. Jehoshaphat, active and prosperous, commanded the respect of his neighbors; but under Amaziah Jerusalem was entered and plundered by the Israelites. Under Uzziah and Jotham, Judah long enjoyed prosperity, till Ahaz became the tributary and vassal of Tiglath-pileser. Already in the fatal grasp of Assyria, Judah was yet spared for a checkered existence of almost another century and a half after the termination of the kingdom of Israel. The consummation of the ruin came upon its people in the destruction of the temple by the hand of Nebuzaradan, B.C. 536.

There were 19 kings, all from the family of David.

(*Population.*—We have a gauge as to the number of the people at different periods in the number of soldiers. If we estimate the population at four times the fighting men, we will have the following table:

King.	Date.	Soldiers.	Population.
David	B.C. 1056–1015	500,000	2,000,000
Rehoboam	975–957	180,000	720,000
Abijah	957–955	400,000	1,600,000
Asa	955–914	500,000	2,000,000
Jehoshaphat	914–889	1,160,000	4,640,000
Amaziah	839–810	300,000	1,200,000

—ED.)

Ju'das, the Greek form of the Hebrew name Judah, occurring in the LXX. and the New Testament. 1. The patriarch Judah. Matt. 1 : 2, 3.

2. A man residing at Damascus, in "the street which is called Straight," in whose house Saul of Tarsus lodged after his miraculous conversion. Acts 9 : 11.

Ju'das, surnamed Barsabas, a leading member of the apostolic church at Jerusalem, Acts 15 : 22, endued with the gift of prophecy, ver. 32, chosen with Silas to accompany Paul and Barnabas as delegates to the church at Antioch. (A.D. 47.) Later, Judas went back to Jerusalem.

Ju'das of Galilee, the leader of a popular revolt "in the days of the taxing" (*i. e.* the census, under the prefecture of P. Sulp. Quirinus, A.D. 6, A.U.C. 759), referred to by Gamaliel in his speech before the Sanhedrin. Acts 5 : 37. According to Josephus, Judas was a Gaulonite of the city of Gamala, probably taking his name of Galilean from his insurrection having had its rise in Galilee. The Gaulonites, as his followers were called, may be regarded as the doctrinal ancestors of the Zealots and Sicarii of later days.

Ju'das Iscar'iot (*Judas of Kerioth*). He is sometimes called "the son of Simon," John 6 : 71; 13 : 2, 26, but more commonly ISCARIOTES. Matt. 10 : 4; Mark 3 : 19; Luke 6 : 16, etc. The name Iscariot has received many interpretations more or less conjectural. The most probable is from *Ish Kerioth, i. e.* "man of Kerioth," a town in the tribe of Judah. Josh. 15 : 25. Of the life of Judas before the appearance of his name in the lists of the apostles we know absolutely nothing. What that appearance implies, however, is that he had previously declared himself a disciple. He was drawn, as the others were, by the preaching of the Baptist, or his own Messianic hopes, or the "gracious words" of the new Teacher, to leave his former life, and to obey the call of the Prophet of Nazareth. The choice was not made, we must remember, without a prevision of its issue. John 6 : 64. The germs of the evil, in all likelihood, unfolded themselves gradually. The rules to which the twelve were subject in their first journey, Matt. 10 : 9, 10, sheltered him from the temptation that would have been most dangerous to him. The new form of life, of which we find the first traces in Luke 8 : 3, brought that temptation with it. As soon as the twelve were recognized as a body, travelling hither and thither with their Master, receiving money and other offerings, and redistributing what they received to the poor, it became necessary that some one should act as the steward and almoner of the small society, and this fell to Judas. John 12 : 6; 13 : 29. The Galilean or Judean peasant found himself entrusted with larger sums of money than before, and with this there came covetousness, unfaithfulness, embezzlement. Several times he showed his tendency to avarice and selfishness. This, even under the best of influences, grew worse and worse, till he betrayed his Master for thirty pieces of silver.

(*Why was such a man chosen to be one of the twelve ?*—(1) There was needed among the disciples, as in the Church now, a man of just such talents as Judas possessed,—the talent for managing business affairs. (2) Though he probably followed Christ at first from mixed motives, as did the other disciples, he had the opportunity of becoming a good and useful man. (3) It doubtless was included in God's plans that there should be thus a standing argument for the truth and honesty of the gospel; for if any wrong or trickery had been concealed, it would have been revealed by the traitor in self-defence. (4) Perhaps to teach the Church that God can bless and the gospel can succeed even though some bad men may creep into the fold.

What was Judas' motive in betraying Christ ?—(1) Anger at the public rebuke given him by Christ at the supper in the house of Simon the leper. Matt. 26 : 6–14. (2) Avarice, covetousness, the thirty pieces of silver. John 12 : 6. (3) The reaction of feeling in a bad soul against the Holy One whose words and character were a continual rebuke, and who knew the traitor's heart. (4) A much larger covetousness, — an ambition to be the treasurer, not merely of a few poor disciples, but of a great and splendid temporal kingdom of the Messiah. He would hasten on the coming of that kingdom by compelling Jesus to defend himself. (5) Perhaps disappointment because Christ insisted on foretelling his death instead of receiving his kingdom. He began to fear that there was to be no kingdom, after all. (6) Perhaps, also, Judas "abandoned what seemed to him a failing cause, and hoped by his treachery to gain a position of honor and influence in the Pharisaic party."

The end of Judas.—(1) Judas, when he saw the results of his betrayal, "repented himself." Matt. 27 : 3–10. He saw his sin in a new light, and "his conscience bounded into fury." (2) He made ineffectual struggles to escape, by attempting to return the reward to the Pharisees; and when they would not receive it, he cast it down at their feet and left it. Matt. 27 : 5. But (*a*) restitution of the silver did not undo the wrong; (*b*) it was restored in a wrong spirit,—a desire for relief rather than hatred of sin; (*c*) he confessed to the wrong party, or rather to those who should have been secondary, and who could not grant forgiveness; (*d*) "compunction is not conversion." (3) The money was used to buy a burial-field for poor strangers. Matt. 27 : 6–10. (4) Judas himself, in his despair, went out and hanged himself, Matt. 27 : 5, at Aceldama, on the southern slope of the valley of Hinnom, near Jerusalem, and in the act he fell down a precipice and was dashed into pieces. Acts 1 : 18. "And he went to his own place." Acts 1 : 25. "A guilty conscience must find either hell or pardon." (5) Judas' repentance may be compared to that of Esau. Gen. 27 : 32–38; Heb. 12 : 16, 17. It is contrasted with that of Peter. Judas proved his repentance to be false by immediately committing another sin, suicide. Peter proved his to be true by serving the Lord faithfully ever after.—ED.)

Ju′das Maccabæ′us. [MACCABEES.]

Jude, or **Ju′das,** called also LEBBEUS and THADDEUS, Authorized Version "Judas *the brother* of James," one of the twelve apostles. The name of Jude occurs only once in the Gospel narrative. John 14 : 22; Matt. 10 : 3; Mark 3 : 18; Luke 6 : 16; John 14 : 22; Acts 1 : 13.

Nothing is certainly known of the later history of the apostle. Tradition connects him with the foundation of the church at Edessa.

Ju'das, the Lord's brother. Among the brethren of our Lord mentioned by the people of Nazareth. Matt. 13 : 55; Mark 6 : 3. Whether this and the Jude above are the same is still a disputed point.

Jude, Epistle of. Its author was probably Jude, one of the brethren of Jesus, the subject of the preceding article. There are no data from which to determine its date or place of writing, but it is placed about A.D. 65. The object of the epistle is plainly enough announced ver. 3; the reason for this exhortation is given ver. 4. The remainder of the epistle is almost entirely occupied by a minute depiction of the adversaries of the faith. The epistle closes by briefly reminding the readers of the oft-repeated prediction of the apostles—among whom the writer seems not to rank himself—that the faith would be assailed by such enemies as he has depicted, vs. 17-19, exhorting them to maintain their own steadfastness in the faith, vs. 20, 21, while they earnestly sought to rescue others from the corrupt example of those licentious livers, vs. 22, 23, and commending them to the power of God in language which forcibly recalls the closing benediction of the epistle to the Romans. vs. 24, 25; cf. Rom. 16 : 25-27. This epistle presents one peculiarity, which, as we learn from St. Jerome, caused its authority to be impugned in very early times—the supposed citation of apocryphal writings. vs. 9, 14, 15. The larger portion of this epistle, vs. 3-16, is almost identical in language and subject with a part of the Second Epistle of Peter. 2 Pet. 2 : 1-19.

Judges. The judges were temporary and special deliverers, sent by God to deliver the Israelites from their oppressors; not supreme magistrates, succeeding to the authority of Moses and Joshua. Their power only extended over portions of the country, and some of them were contemporaneous. Their first work was that of deliverers and leaders in war; they then administered justice to the people, and their authority supplied the want of a regular government. Even while the administration of Samuel gave something like a settled government to the south, there was scope for the irregular exploits of Samson on the borders of the Philis-

tines; and Samuel at last established his authority as judge and prophet, but still as the servant of Jehovah, only to see it so abused by his sons as to exhaust the patience of the people, who at length demanded a *king*, after the pattern of the surrounding nations. The following is a list of the judges, whose history is given under their respective names:—

First servitude, to Mesopotamia—	8	years
First judge: Othniel.	40	"
Second servitude, to Moab—	18	"
Second judge: Ehud;	80	"
Third judge: Shamgar.	—	"
Third servitude, to Jabin and Sisera—	20	"
Fourth judge: Deborah and Barak.	40	"
Fourth servitude, to Midian—	7	"
Fifth judge: Gideon;	40	"
Sixth judge: Abimelech;	3	"
Seventh judge: Tola;	23	"
Eighth judge: Jair.	22	"
Fifth servitude, to Ammon—	18	"
Ninth judge: Jephthah;	6	"
Tenth judge: Ibzan;	7	"
Eleventh judge: Elon;	10	"
Twelfth judge: Abdon.	8	"
Sixth servitude, to the Philistines—	40	"
Thirteenth judge: Samson;	20	"
Fourteenth judge: Eli;	40	"
Fifteenth judge: Samuel.		

More than likely some of these ruled simultaneously. On the chronology of the judges, see the following article.

Judges, Book of, of which the book of Ruth formed originally a part, contains a history from Joshua to Samson. The book may be divided into two parts: —1. Chs. 1-16. We may observe in general on this portion of the book that it is almost entirely a history of the wars of deliverance. 2. Chs. 17-21. This part has no formal connection with the preceding, and is often called an appendix. The period to which the narrative relates is simply marked by the expression, "when there was no king in Israel." ch. 19 : 1; cf. 18 : 1. It records—(a) The conquest of Laish by a portion of the tribe of Dan, and the establishment there of the idolatrous worship of Jehovah already instituted by Micah in Mount Ephraim. (b) The almost total extinction of the tribe of Benjamin. Chs. 17-21 are inserted both as an illustration of the sin of Israel during the time of the judges and as presenting a contrast with the better order prevailing in the time of the kings. The time commonly assigned to the period contained in this book is 299 years. The dates given in the last article amount to 410 years, without the 40 years of Eli; but in 1 Kings 6 : 1, the whole period from the exodus to the building of the temple is stated as 480 years. But probably some of the judges were contemporary, so that their total period is 299 years instead of 410. Mr. Smith in his Old Testament history gives the following approximate dates:

Periods.	Years.	Ending about B.C.
1. From the exodus to the passage of Jordan.....................	40	1451
2. To the death of Joshua and the surviving elders..................	[40]	1411
3. Judgeship of Othniel..............	40	1371
4, 5. Judgeship of Ehud (Shamgar included)...........................	80	1291
6. Judgeship of Deborah and Barak....................................	40	1251
7. Judgeship of Gideon..............	40	1211
8, 9. Abimelech to Abdon, total....	[80]	1131
10. Oppression of the Philistines, contemporary with the judgeships of Eli, Samson (and Samuel?).............................	40	1091
11. Reign of Saul (including perhaps Samuel)......................	40	1051
12. Reign of David.....................	40	1011
Total...........	480	

On the whole, it seems safer to give up the attempt to ascertain the chronology exactly.

Judgment hall. The word *prætorium* is so translated five times in the Authorized Version of the New Testament, and in those five passages it denotes two different places. 1. In John 18 : 28, 33; 19 : 9, it is the residence which Pilate occupied when he visited Jerusalem. The site of Pilate's prætorium in Jerusalem has given rise to much dispute, some supposing it to be the palace of King Herod, others the tower of Antonia; but it was probably the latter, which was then and long afterward the citadel of Jerusalem. 2. In Acts 23 : 35 Herod's judgment hall or prætorium in Cæsarea was doubtless a part of that magnificent range of buildings the erection of which by King Herod is described in Josephus. The word " palace," or " Cæsar's court," in the Authorized Version of Philip. 1 : 13, is a translation of the same word prætorium. It may here have denoted

the quarter of that detachment of the prætorian guards which was in immediate attendance upon the emperor, and had barracks in Mount Palatine at Rome.

Ju′dith (*Jewess*, or *praised*). 1. The daughter of Beeri the Hittite, and wife of Esau. Gen. 26 : 34. (B.C. 1797.)

2. The heroine of the apocryphal book which bears her name, who appears as an ideal type of piety, Judith 8 : 6, beauty, ch. 11 : 21, courage and chastity. ch. 16 : 22 ff.

Ju′dith, The book of, one of the books of the Apocrypha, belongs to the earliest specimens of historical fiction. As to its authorship it belongs to the Maccabæan period, B.C. 175–135, which it reflects not only in its general spirit, but even in its smaller traits.

Ju′lia (feminine of Julius), a Christian woman at Rome, probably the wife of Philologus, in connection with whom she is saluted by St. Paul. Rom. 16 : 15. (A.D. 55.)

Ju′lius (*soft-haired*), the centurion of " Augustus' band," to whose charge St. Paul was delivered when he was sent prisoner from Cæsarea to Rome. Acts 27 : 1, 3. (A.D. 60.)

Ju′nia (*belonging to Juno*), a Christian at Rome, mentioned by St. Paul as one of his kinsfolk and fellow prisoners, of note among the apostles, and in Christ before St. Paul. Rom. 16 : 7. (A.D. 55.)

Ju′nias, Revised Version for JUNIA above. It is the more literal form.

Juniper, 1 Kings 19 : 4, 5; Job 30 : 4; Ps. 120 : 4, a sort of broom, *Genista monosperma*, *G. rætam* of Forskal, answering to the Arabic *rethem*. It is very abundant in the desert of Sinai, and affords shade and protection, in both heat and storm, to travellers. The rethem is a leguminous plant, and bears a white flower. It is found also in Spain, Portugal and Palestine. (It grows like willow bushes along the shores of Spain. It is an erect shrub, with no main trunk, but many wand-like, slender branches, and is sometimes twelve feet high. Its use is very great in stopping the sand.—ED.)

Ju′piter (*a father that helps*), the Greek Zeus. The Olympian Zeus was the national god of the Hellenic race, as well as the supreme ruler of the heathen world, and as such formed the true opposite to Jehovah. Jupiter or Zeus is mentioned in two passages of the New Testament, on the occasion of St. Paul's visit to Lystra, Acts 14 : 12, 13, where the expression "Jupiter, which was before their city," means that his temple was outside the city. Also in Acts 19 : 35.

Ju'shab-he'sed (*whose love is returned*), son of Zerubbabel. 1 Chron. 3 : 20.

Jus'tus (*just*). 1. A surname of Joseph, called Barsabas. Acts 1 : 23. (A.D. 30.)

2. A Christian at Corinth, with whom St. Paul lodged. Acts 18 : 7 (A.D. 49.) (Given in the Revised Version as TITUS JUSTUS; and it is possible that he may be the same person as Titus the companion of Paul.)

3. A surname of Jesus, a friend of St. Paul. Col. 4 : 11. (A.D. 57.)

Jut'tah (*stretched out*), a city in the mountain region of Judah, in the neighborhood of Maon and Carmel. Josh. 15 : 55. The place is now known as *Yutta.*

K.

Kab'ze-el (*gathered by God*), one of the "cities" of the tribe of Judah, Josh. 15 : 21, the native place of the great hero Benaiah ben-Jehoiada. 2 Sam. 23 : 20; 1 Chron. 11 : 22. After the captivity it was reinhabited by the Jews, and appears as Jekabzeel.

Ka'desh, Ka'desh-bar'ne-a. (Kadesh means *holy*; it is the same word as the Arabic name of Jerusalem, *el-Khuds*. Barnea means *desert of wandering*.) This place, the scene of Miriam's death, was the farthest point which the Israelites reached in their direct road to Canaan; it was also that whence the spies were sent, and where, on their return, the people broke out into murmuring, upon which their strictly penal term of wandering began. Num. 13 : 3, 26; 14 : 29–33; 20 : 1; Deut. 2 : 14. It is probable that the term "Kadesh," though applied to signify a "city," yet had also a wider application to a region in which Kadesh-meribah certainly, and Kadesh-barnea probably, indicates a precise spot. In Gen. 14 : 7, Kadesh is identified with En-mishpat, the "fountain of judgment." It has been supposed, from Num. 13 : 21, 26 and Num. 20, that there were two places of the name of Kadesh, one in the wilderness of Paran and the other in that of Zin; but it is more probable that only one place is meant, and that Zin is but a part of the great desert of Paran. (There has been much doubt as to the exact site of Kadesh; but Rev. H. Clay Trumbull of Philadelphia, visiting the spot in 1881, succeeded in rendering almost certain that the site of Kadesh is *Ain Kadis* (spelled also *Gadis* and *Quadis*); "the very same name, letter for letter in Arabic and Hebrew, with the scriptural fountain of Kadesh—the 'holy fountain,' as the name means—which gushed forth when Moses smote the rock." It lies 40 miles south of Beersheba and 165 northeast of Horeb, immediately below the southern border of Palestine. It was discovered in 1842 by the Rev. J. Rowlands of Queen's College, Cambridge, England, whose discovery was endorsed by the great German geographer Ritter, by E. S. Palmer in his "Desert of the Exodus," and by the "Im-

perial Bible Dictionary." Dr. Trumbull thus describes it:—"It is an extensive oasis, a series of wells, the water of which flows out from under such an overhanging cliff as is mentioned in the Bible story; and it opens into a vast plain or wadi large enough to have furnished a camping-ground for the whole host of Israel. Extensive primitive ruins are on the hills near it. The plain or wadi, also called Quadis, is shut in by surrounding hills so as to make it a most desirable position for such a people as the Israelites on the borders of hostile territory—such a position as leaders like Moses and Joshua would have been likely to select." "It was carpeted with grass and flowers. Fig trees laden with fruit were against its limestone hillsides. Shrubs in richness and variety abounded. Standing out from the mountain range at the northward of the beautiful oasis amphitheatre was the 'large single mass or small hill of solid rock' which Rowlands looked at as the cliff (sela) smitten by Moses to cause it to 'give forth its water' when its flowing had ceased. From beneath this cliff came the abundant stream. A well, walled up with time-worn limestone blocks, was the first receptacle of the water. Not far from this was a second well similarly walled, supplied from the same source. Around both these wells were ancient watering-troughs of limestone. Several pools, not walled up, were also supplied from the stream. The water was clear and sweet and abundant. Two of the pools were ample for bathing."—ED.)

Kad'mi-el (*before God*), one of the Levites who with his family returned from Babylon with Zerubbabel. Ezra 2 : 40; Neh. 7 : 43. He and his house are mentioned in history on three occasions—Ezra 3 : 9; Neh. 9 : 4, 5; 10 : 9. (B.C. 535–410.)

Kad'monites (*Orientals*), **The**, a people named in Gen. 15 : 19 only; one of the nations who at that time occupied the land (Canaan) promised to the descendants of Abram. The name is probably a synonym for the Bene-Kedem—the "children of the East."

Kal'la-i (*swift servant of Jehovah*), a

priest in the days of Joiakim the son of Jeshua. He represented the family of Sallai. Neh. 12 : 20. (B.C. after 536.)

Ka'nah (*a place of reeds*). 1. One·of the places which formed the landmarks of the boundary of Asher; apparently next to Zidon-rabbah, or "great Zidon." Josh. 19 : 28.

2. The river, a stream falling into the Mediterranean, which formed the division between the territories of Ephraim and Manasseh, the former on the south, the latter on the north. Josh. 16 : 8; 17 : 9.

Kare'ah (*bald*), the father of Johanan and Jonathan, who supported Gedaliah's authority and avenged his murder. Jer. 40 : 8, 13, 15, 16; 41 : 11, 13, 14, 16; 42 : 1, 8; 43 : 2, 4, 5. (B.C. before 588.)

Karka'a, or **Kar'ka-a** (*foundation*), one of the landmarks on the south boundary of the tribe of Judah. Josh. 15 : 3. Its site is unknown.

Kar'kor (*foundation*), the place in which Zebah and Zalmunna were again routed by Gideon, Judges 8 : 10, must have been on the east of Jordan.

Kar'tah (*city*), a town of Zebulun, allotted to the Merarite Levites. Josh. 21 : 34.

Kar'tan (*double city*), a city of Naphtali, allotted to the Gershonite Levites. Josh. 21 : 32. In the parallel list of 1 Chron. 6 the name appears, ver. 76, in the more expanded form of KIRJATHAIM.

Kat'tath (*small*), one of the cities of the tribe of Zebulun. Josh. 19 : 15.

Ke'dar (*dark-skinned*), the second in order of the sons of Ishmael, Gen. 25 : 13; 1 Chron. 1 : 29, and the name of a great tribe of Arabs settled on the northwest of the peninsula and on the confines of Palestine. The "glory of Kedar" is recorded by the prophet Isaiah, Isa. 21 : 13-17, in the burden upon Arabia; and its importance may also be inferred from the "princes of Kedar" mentioned by Ezekiel, Ezek. 27 : 21, as well as the pastoral character of the tribe. They appear also to have been, like the wandering tribes of the present day, "archers" and "mighty men." Isa. 21 : 17; comp. Ps. 120 : 5. That they also settled in villages or towns we find from Isaiah. Isa. 42 : 11. The tribe seems to have been one of the most conspicuous of all the Ishmaelite tribes, and hence the rabbins call the Arabians universally by this name.

Ked'emah (*eastward*), the youngest of the sons of Ishmael. Gen. 25 : 15; 1 Chron. 1 : 31.

Ked'emoth (*beginnings*), one of the towns in the district east of the Dead Sea allotted to the tribe of Reuben, Josh. 13 : 18; given to the Merarite Levites. Josh. 21 : 37; 1 Chron. 6 : 79. It possibly conferred its name on the "wilderness," or uncultivated pasture land, "of Kedemoth." Num. 21 : 23; Deut. 2 : 26, 27, etc.

Ke'desh (*a sanctuary*). 1. In the extreme south of Judah, Josh. 15 : 23; same as Kadesh and Kadesh-barnea.

2. A city of Issachar, allotted to the Gershonite Levites. 1 Chron. 6 : 72. The Kedesh mentioned among the cities whose kings were slain by Joshua, Josh. 12 : 22, in company with Megiddo and Jokneam of Carmel, would seem to have been this city of Issachar.

3. Kedesh; also Kedesh in Galilee; and once, Judges 4 : 6, Kedesh-naphtali, one of the fortified cities of the tribe of Naphtali, named between Hazor and Edrei, Josh. 19 : 37; appointed as a city of refuge, and allotted with its "suburbs" to the Gershonite Levites. Josh. 20 : 7; 21 : 32; 1 Chron. 6 : 76. It was the residence of Barak, Judges 4 : 6, and there he and Deborah assembled the tribes of Zebulun and Naphtali before the conflict, being probably, as its name implies, a "holy place" of great antiquity. It was taken by Tiglath-pileser in the reign of Pekah. 2 Kings 15 : 29. It is identified with the village *Kades*, which lies four miles to the northwest of the upper part of the Sea of Merom.

Ked'ron, properly Kidron. [KIDRON.]

Kefr Kenna. [See CANA.]

Kehela'thah (*assembly*), a desert encampment of the Israelites, Num. 33 : 22, of which nothing is known.

Kei'lah (*fortress*), a city of the Shefelah, or lowland district of Judah. Josh. 15 : 44. Its main interest consists in its connection with David. 1 Sam. 23 : 7-13. It is represented by *Kila*, a site with ruins, on the lower road from *Beit Jibrin* to Hebron.

Kei'lah the Garmite, apparently a descendant of the great Caleb. 1 Chron. 4 : 19. There is no apparent connection with the town Keilah.

Kela'iah (*swift messenger of Jehovah*) = KELITA. Ezra 10 : 23.

Kel'ita (*assembly*), one of the Levites who returned with Ezra. Ezra 10 : 23. He assisted in expounding the law, Neh. 8 : 7, and signed the covenant with Nehemiah. Neh. 10 : 10. (B.C. 459–410.)

Kem'uel (*congregation of God*). 1. The son of Nahor by Milcah, and father of Aram. Gen. 22 : 21. (B.C. 1925.)

2. The son of Shiptan, and prince of the tribe of Ephraim; one of the twelve men appointed by Moses to divide the land of Canaan. Num. 34 : 24.

3. A Levite, father of Hashabiah, prince of the tribe in the reign of David. 1 Chron. 27 : 17. (B.C. 1014.)

Ke'nan (*possession*) = CAINAN, the son of Enos. 1 Chron. 1 : 2.

Ke'nath (*possession*), one of the cities on the east of Jordan, with its " daughter-towns " (Authorized Version " villages ") taken possession of by a certain Nobah, who then called it by his own name. Num. 32 : 42.

Ke'naz (*hunting*). 1. Son of Eliphaz the son of Esau. He was one of the dukes of Edom. Gen. 36 : 15, 42 ; 1 Chron. 1 : 53.

2. One of the same family, a grandson of Caleb, according to 1 Chron. 4 : 15 (where see margin).

Ken'ezite, or **Ken'izzite** (*descendant of Kenaz*), Gen. 15 : 19, an Edomitish tribe. Num. 32 : 12 ; Josh. 14 : 6, 14.

Ken'ite, The, and **Ken'ites** (*smiths*), inhabited the rocky and desert region between southern Palestine and the mountains of Sinai, east of the Gulf of Akabah. They were a branch of the larger nation of Midian,—from the fact that Jethro, who in Exodus (see 2 : 15, 16 ; 4 : 19, etc.) is represented as dwelling in the land of Midian, and as priest or prince of that nation, is in Judges (1 : 16 ; 4 : 11) as distinctly said to have been a Kenite. The important services rendered by the sheikh of the Kenites to Moses during a time of great pressure and difficulty were rewarded by the latter with a promise of firm friendship between the two peoples. They seem to have accompanied the Hebrews during their wanderings, Num. 24 : 21, 22 ; Judges 1 : 16 ; comp. 2 Chron. 28 : 15 ; but, the wanderings of Israel over, they forsook the neighborhood of the towns and betook themselves to freer air,—to " the wilderness of Judah, which is to the south of Arad." Judges 1 : 16. But one of the sheikhs of the tribe, Heber by name, had wandered north instead of south. Judges 4 : 11. The most remarkable development of this people is to be found in the sect or family of the Rechabites.

Ken'izzite. Gen. 15 : 19. [KENEZITE.]

Ke'ren-hap'puch (*the horn of beau-ty*), the youngest of the daughters of Job, born to him during the period of his reviving prosperity. Job 42 : 14.

Ke'rioth (*cities*). 1. A name which occurs among the lists of the towns in the southern district of Judah. Josh. 15 : 25. Supposed by some to have been the birthplace of Judas Iscariot.

2. A city of Moab, named by Jeremiah only. Jer. 48 : 24.

Ke'ros (*curved*), one of the Nethinim, whose descendants returned with Zerubbabel. Ezra 2 : 44 ; Neh. 7 : 47.

Kettle, a vessel for culinary or sacrificial purposes. 1 Sam. 2 : 14. The Hebrew word is also rendered " basket " in Jer. 24 : 2, " caldron " in 2 Chron. 35 : 13, and " pot " in Job 41 : 20.

Ketu'rah (*incense*), the wife of Abraham after the death of Sarah. Gen. 25 : 1 ; 1 Chron. 1 : 32. (B.C. 1860.)

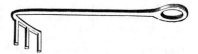

Egyptian Iron Key.

Key. The key of a native Oriental lock is a piece of wood, from seven inches to two feet in length, fitted with wires or short nails, which, being inserted laterally into the hollow bolt which serves as a lock, raises other pins within the staple so as to allow the bolt to be drawn back. (Keys were sometimes of bronze or iron, and so large that one was as much as a man could carry. They are used in Scripture as a symbol of authority and power. Giving keys to a person signifies the intrusting of him with an important charge. Matt. 16 : 19. In England in modern times certain officers of the government receive, at their induction into office, a golden key.—ED.)

Kezi'a (*cassia*), the second of the daughters of Job born to him after his recovery. Job 42 : 14. (B.C. 1950.)

Ke'ziz (*cut off*), **The valley of,** one of the " cities " of Benjamin, Josh. 18 : 21, and the eastern border of the tribe.

Kib'roth-hatta-avah, *i. e.* as in the margin, *the graves of lust*, a station of the Israelites in the wilderness, where, growing tired of manna and desiring flesh, they murmured, and God sent them quails in great abundance, but smote great numbers of them with a plague and they died. It is about three days journey from Sinai, and near the Gulf of Akabah and the *Wady el Hudherah* (Hazeroth.)

Kibza'im (*two heaps*), a city of Mount Ephraim, given up with its "suburbs" to the Kohathite Levites. Josh. 21 : 22. In the parallel list of 1 Chron. 6 JOK-MEAM is substituted for Kibzaim. ver. 68.

Kid. [GOAT.]

Kid'ron, or **Ked'ron** (*turbid*), **The brook,** a torrent or valley, not a "brook," or, as in the margin of Revised Version,

View of Kedron.

"ravine ;" Gr. *winter torrent.* It was close to Jerusalem, between the city and the Mount of Olives. It is now commonly known as the "valley of Jehoshaphat." The channel of the valley of Jehoshaphat is nothing more than the dry bed of a wintry torrent, bearing marks of being occasionally swept over by a large volume of water. It was crossed by David in his flight, 2 Sam. 15 : 23, comp. 30, and by our Lord on his way to Gethsemane. John 18 : 1; comp. Mark 14 : 26; Luke 22 : 39. The distinguishing peculiarity of the Kidron valley—mentioned in the Old Testament—is the impurity which appears to have been ascribed to it. In the time of Josiah it was the common cemetery of the city. 2 Kings 23 : 6; comp. Jer. 26 : 23.

Ki'nah (*lamentation*), a city of Judah,

on the extreme south boundary of the tribe, next to Edom. Josh. 15 : 22.

Kine, the plural of cow. [See BULL.]

King, "a chief ruler, one invested with supreme authority over a nation, tribe or country."— *Webster.* In the Bible the word does not necessarily imply great power or great extent of country. Many persons are called kings whom we should rather call chiefs or leaders. The word is applied in the Bible to God as the sovereign and ruler of the universe, and to Christ the Son of God as the head and governor of the Church.

The Hebrews were ruled by a king during a period of about 500 years previous to the destruction of Jerusalem, B.C. 586. The immediate occasion of the substitution of a regal form of government for that of judges seems to have been the siege of Jabesh-gilead by Nahash king of the Ammonites. 1 Sam. 11 : 1; 12 : 12. The conviction seems to have forced itself on the Israelites that they could not resist their formidable neighbor unless they placed themselves under the sway of a king, like surrounding nations. The original idea of a Hebrew king was twofold: first, that he should lead the people to battle in time of war; and, second, that he should execute judgment and justice to them in war and in peace. 1 Sam. 8 : 20. In both respects the desired end was attained. Besides being commander-in-chief of the army, supreme judge, and absolute master, as it were, of the lives of his subjects, the king exercised the power of imposing taxes on them, and of exacting from them personal service and labor. In addition to these earthly powers, the king of Israel had a more awful claim to respect and obedience. He was the vicegerent of Jehovah, 1 Sam. 10 : 1; 16 : 13, and as it were his son, if just and holy. 2 Sam. 7 : 14; Ps. 2 : 6, 7; 89 : 26, 27. He had been set apart as a consecrated ruler. Upon his head had been poured the holy anointing oil, which had hitherto been reserved exclusively for the priests of Jehovah. He had become, in fact, emphatically "the Lord's anointed." He had a court of Oriental magnificence. The king was dressed in royal robes, 1 Kings 22 : 10; 2 Chron. 18 : 9; his insignia were, a crown or diadem of pure gold, or perhaps radiant with precious gems, 2 Sam. 1 : 10; 12 : 30; 2 Kings 11 : 12; Ps. 21 : 3, and a royal sceptre. Those who approached him did him obeisance, bowing down and touching the ground with their foreheads, 1 Sam. 24 : 8; 2 Sam. 19 : 24; and this was done even by a king's wife, the mother of Solomon. 1 Kings 1 : 16. His officers and subjects called themselves his servants or slaves. He had a large harem, which was guarded by eunuchs. The law of succession to the throne is somewhat obscure, but it seems most probable that the king during his lifetime named his successor. At the same time, if no partiality for a favorite wife or son intervened, there would always be a natural bias of affection in favor of the eldest son.

Kings of Judah and Israel. For the list see table at the end of this volume.

Kings, First and Second Books of, originally only one book in the Hebrew canon, form in the LXX. and the Vulgate the third and fourth books of *Kings* (the books of Samuel being the first and second). It must be remembered that the division between the books of Kings and Samuel is equally artificial, and that in point of fact the historical books commencing with Judges and ending with 2 Kings present the appearance of one work, giving a continuous history of Israel from the time of Joshua to the death of Jehoiachin. The books of Kings contain the history from David's death and Solomon's accession to the destruction of the kingdom of Judah and the desolation of Jerusalem, with a supplemental notice of an event that occurred after an interval of twenty-six years—viz., the liberation of Jehoiachin from his prison at Babylon—and a still further extension to Jehoiachin's death, the time of which is not known, but which was probably not long after his liberation. The history therefore comprehends the whole time of the Israelitish monarchy, exclusive of the reigns of Saul and David. As regards the affairs of foreign nations and the relation of Israel to them, the historical notices in these books, though in the earlier times scanty, are most valuable, and in striking accord with the latest additions to our knowledge of contemporary profane history. A most im-

portant aid to a right understanding of the history in these books, and to the filling up of its outline, is to be found in the prophets, and especially in Isaiah and Jeremiah.

Time when written.—They were undoubtedly written during the period of the captivity, probably after the twenty-sixth year. *Authorship.*—As regards the authorship of the books, but little difficulty presents itself. The Jewish tradition which ascribes them to Jeremiah is borne out by the strongest internal evidence, in addition to that of the language. *Sources of information.*—There was a regular series of state annals for both the kingdom of Judah and that of Israel, which embraced the whole time comprehended in the books of Kings, or at least to the end of the reign of Jehoiakim. 2 Kings 24 : 5. These annals are constantly cited by name as "the book of the acts of Solomon," 1 Kings 11 : 41; and after Solomon "the book of the Chronicles of the Kings of Judah " or " Israel," *e. g.* 1 Kings 14 : 29; 15 : 7; 16 : 5, 14, 20; 2 Kings 10 : 34; 24 : 5, etc.; and it is manifest that the author of Kings had them both before him while he drew up his history, in which the reigns of the two kingdoms are harmonized and these annals constantly appealed to. But in addition to these national annals, there were also extant, at the time that the books of Kings were compiled, separate works of the several prophets who had lived in Judah and Israel. *Authority.*—Their canonical authority having never been disputed, it is needless to bring forward the testimonies to their authenticity which may be found in Josephus, Eusebius, Jerome, Augustine, etc. They are reckoned among the prophets, in the threefold division of the Holy Scriptures; a position in accordance with the supposition that they were compiled by Jeremiah, and contain the narratives of the different prophets in succession. They are frequently cited by our Lord and by the apostles.

Kir (*fortress*) is mentioned by Amos, ch. 9 : 7, as the land from which the Syrians (Aramæans) were once "brought up;" *i. e.* apparently as the country where they had dwelt before migrating to the region north of Palestine. (A difference of opinion exists in regard to the position of Kir, since some suppose it to be identical with Carna, a city of Media, in the south, on the river Mar-dus; others place it in Armenia, on the river Kar.—ED.)

Kir-har′aseth (*brick fortress*), 2 Kings 3 : 25; **Kir-ha′resh,** Isa. 16 : 11; **Kir-har′eseth,** Isa. 16 : 7; **Kir-he′-res.** Jer. 48 : 31, 36. These four names are all applied to one place, probably KIR OF MOAB, which see.

Kir′iah, apparently an ancient or archaic word, meaning a *city* or *town*. It may be compared to the word "burg" or 'bury" in our own language. Closely related to Kiriah is Kereth, apparently a Phœnician form, which occurs occasionally. Job 29 : 7; Prov. 8 : 3. As a proper name it appears in the Bible under the forms of Kerioth, Kartah, Kartan, besides those immediately following.

Kiriatha′im. [KIRJATHAIM.]

Kir′ioth (*two cities*), a place in Moab the palaces of which were threatened by Amos with destruction by fire, Amos 2 : 2; unless indeed the word means simply "the cities," which is probably the case also in Jer. 48 : 4.

Kir′jath (*a city*), the last of the cities enumerated as belonging to the tribe of Benjamin, Josh. 18 : 28, probably identical with the better-known place Kirjath-jearim.

Kirjatha′im (*the two cities*). 1. On the east of the Jordan, one of the places which were taken possession of and rebuilt by the Reubenites, and had fresh names conferred on them, Num. 32 : 37, and see 38, the first and last of which are known with some tolerable degree of certainty. Josh. 12 : 19. It existed in the time of Jeremiah, Jer. 48 : 1, 23, and Ezekiel. Ezek. 25 : 9. In the three passages named the Authorized Version gives the name KIRIATHAIM. By Eusebius it appears to have been well known. He describes it as a village entirely of Christians, ten miles west of Medeba, "close to the Baris."

2. A town in Naphtali not mentioned in the original list of the possession allotted to the tribe, see Josh. 19 : 32–39, but inserted in the list of cities given to the Gershonite Levites in 1 Chron. 6 : 76, in place of KARTAN in the parallel catalogue, Kartan being probably only a contraction thereof.

Kir′jath-ar′ba (*the city of Arba*), an early name of the city which after the conquest is generally known as HEBRON. Josh. 14 : 15; Judges 1 : 10. The identity of Kirjath-arba with Hebron is constantly

asserted. Gen. 23 : 2; 35 : 27; Josh. 14: 15; 15 : 13, 54; 20 : 7; 21 : 11.

Kir′jath-a′rim (*city of forests*), an abbreviated form of the name Kirjath-jearim, which occurs only in Ezra 2 : 25.

Kir′jath-ba′al. [KIRJATH-JEARIM.]

Kir′jath-hu′zoth (*city of streets*), a place to which Balak accompanied Balaam immediately after his arrival in Moab, Num. 22 : 39, and which is no where else mentioned. It appears to have lain between the Arnon (*Wady Mojeb*) and Bamoth-baal. Comp. vs. 36 and 41.

Kir′jath-je′arim (*the city of forests*), first mentioned as one of the four cities of the Gibeonites, Josh. 9 : 17; it next occurs as one of the landmarks of the northern boundary of Judah, ch. 15 : 9, and as the point at which the western and southern boundaries of Benjamin coincided, ch. 18 : 14, 15; and in the last two passages we find that it bore another, perhaps earlier, name—that of the great Canaanite deity Baal, namely BAALAH and KIRJATH-BAAL. At this place the ark remained for twenty years. 1 Sam. 7 : 2. At the close of that time Kirjath-jearim lost its sacred treasure, on its removal by David to the house of Obed-edom the Gittite. 1 Chron. 13 : 5, 6; 2 Chron. 1 : 4; 2 Sam. 6 : 2, etc. To Eusebius and Jerome it appears to have been well known. They describe it as a village at the ninth mile between Jerusalem and Diospolis (Lydda). These requirements are exactly fulfilled in the small modern village of *Kuriet-el-Enab* —now usually known as *Abû Gosh*, from the robber chief whose headquarters it was—on the road from Jaffa to Jerusalem.

Kir′jath-san′nah (*city of books*). [DEBIR.]

Kir′jath-se′pher (*city of books*). Josh. 15 : 15, 16; Judges 1 : 11, 12. [DEBIR.]

Kir of Moab (*fortress of Moab*), one of the two chief strongholds of Moab, the other being Ar of Moab. The name occurs only in Isa. 15 : 1, though the place is probably referred to under the names of Kir-heres, Kir-haraseth, etc. It is almost identical with the name *Kerak*, by which the site of an important city in a high and very strong position at the southeast of the Dead Sea is known at this day. Its situation is truly remarkable. It is built upon the top of a steep hill, surrounded by a deep and narrow valley, which again is completely enclosed by mountains rising higher than the town and overlooking it on all sides.

Kish (*a bow*). 1. The father of Saul; a Benjamite of the family of Matri. (B.C. 1095.) 2. Son of Jehiel and uncle to the preceding. 1 Chron. 9 : 36. 3. A Benjamite, great-grandfather of Mordecai. Esther 2 : 5. 4. A Merarite of the house of Mahli, of the tribe of Levi. 1 Chron. 23 : 21, 22; 24 : 28, 29.

Kish'i (*bow of Jehovah*), a Merarite, and father or ancestor of Ethan the minstrel. 1 Chron. 6 : 44.

Kish'ion (*hardness*), one of the towns on the boundary of the tribe of Issachar, Josh. 19 : 20, which with its suburbs was allotted to the Gershonite Levites. Josh. 21 : 28; Authorized Version KISHON.

Ki'shon (*winding*), **The river**, a torrent or winter stream of central Palestine, the scene of two of the grandest achievements of Israelitish history—the defeat of Sisera, Judges 4, and the destruction of the prophets of Baal by Elijah. 1 Kings 18 : 40. The *Nahr Mukútta*, the modern representative of the Kishon, is the drain by which the waters of the plain of Esdraelon and of the mountains which enclose that plain find their way through the plain of Acre to the Mediterranean. The part of the Kishon at which the prophets of Baal were slaughtered by Elijah was doubtless close below the spot on Carmel where the sacrifice had taken place.

Ki'son (*winding*), an inaccurate mode of representing the name Kishon. Ps. 83 : 9.

Kiss. Kissing the lips by way of affectionate salutation was customary among near relatives of both sexes, in both patriarchal and later times. Gen. 29 : 11; Cant. 8 : 1. Between individuals of the same sex, and in a limited degree between those of different sexes, the kiss on the cheek as a mark of respect or an act of salutation has at all times been customary in the East, and can hardly be said to be extinct even in Europe. In the Christian Church the kiss of charity was practiced not only as a friendly salutation, but as an act symbolical of love and Christian brotherhood. Rom. 16:16; 1 Cor. 16 : 20; 2 Cor. 13 : 12; 1 Thess. 5 : 26; 1 Peter 5 : 14. It was embodied in the earlier Christian offices, and has been

continued in some of those now in use. Among the Arabs the women and children kiss the beards of their husbands or fathers. The superior returns the salute by a kiss on the forehead. In Egypt an inferior kisses the hand of a superior, generally on the back, but sometimes, as a special favor, on the palm also. To testify abject submission, and in asking favors, the feet are often kissed instead of the hand. The written decrees of a sovereign are kissed in token of respect; even the ground is sometimes kissed by Orientals in the fullness of their submission. Gen. 41 : 40; 1 Sam. 24 : 8; Ps. 72 : 9, etc. Kissing is spoken of in Scripture as a mark of respect or adoration to idols. 1 Kings 19 : 18; Hos. 13 : 2.

Kite (Heb. *ayyâh*), a rapacious and keen-sighted bird of prey belonging to the hawk family. The Hebrew word thus rendered occurs in three passages —Lev. 11 : 14; Deut. 14 : 13; Job 28 : 7. In the two former it is translated "kite" in the Authorized Version, in the latter "vulture." It is enumerated among the twenty names of birds mentioned in Deut. 14 which were considered unclean by the Mosaic law and forbidden to be used as food by the Israelites.

Kith'lish (*man's wall*), one of the towns of Judah, in the Shefelah or lowland. Josh. 15 : 40.

Kit'ron (*knotty*), one of the towns from which Zubulun did not expel the Canaanites. Judges 1 : 30. In the Talmud it is identified with "Zippori," *i. e.* Sepphoris, now *Seffurieh.*

Kit'tim. Twice written in the Authorized Version for Chittim. Gen. 10 : 4; 1 Chron. 1 : 7.

Kneading-troughs. [BREAD.]

Knife. 1. The knives of the Egyptians, and of other nations in early times, were probably only of hard stone, and the use of the flint or stone knife was sometimes retained for sacred purposes after the introduction of iron and steel. 2. In their meals the Jews, like other Orientals, made little use of knives, but they were required both for slaughtering animals, either for food or sacrifice, and for cutting up the carcass. Lev. 7 : 33, 34; 8 : 15, 20, 25; 9 : 13; Num. 18 : 18; 1 Sam. 9 : 24, etc. 3. Smaller knives were in use for paring fruit (Josephus) and for sharpening pens. Jer. 36 : 23. 4. The razor was often used for Nazaritic purposes, for which a special chamber was reserved in the temple. Num. 6 : 5, 9, 19; Ezek. 5 : 1, etc. 5. The pruning-hooks of Isa. 18 : 5 were probably curved knives. 6. The lancets of the priests of Baal were doubtless pointed knives. 1 Kings 18 : 28.

Knop, a word employed in the Authorized Version to translate two terms which refer to some architectural or ornamental object, but which have nothing in common. 1. *Caphtor.*—This occurs in the description of the candlestick of the sacred tent in Ex. 25 : 31–36 and 37 : 17–22. 2. The second term, *Peka'im*, is found only in 1 Kings 6 : 18 and 7 : 24. The word no doubt signifies some globular thing resembling a small gourd or an egg, though as to the character of the ornament we are quite in the dark.

Ko'a (*he-camel*) is a word which occurs only in Ezek. 23 : 23. It may perhaps have been a city or district of Babylonia; or it may be a common noun, signifying "prince" or "nobleman."

Ko'hath (*assembly*), second of the three sons of Levi, from whom the three principal divisions of the Levites derived their origin and their name. Gen. 46 : 11; Ex. 6 : 16. In the journeyings of the tabernacle the sons of Kohath (Kohathites) had charge of the most holy portions of the vessels. Num. 4. Of the personal history of Kohath we know nothing, except that he came down to Egypt with Levi and Jacob, Gen. 46 : 11, that his sister was Jochebed, Ex. 6 : 20, and that he lived to the age of 133 years. Ex. 6 : 18. (B.C. about 1491.)

Kola'iah (*voice of Jehovah*). 1. A Benjamite whose descendants settled in Jerusalem after the return from the captivity. Neh. 11 : 7. (B.C. before 536.) 2. The father of Ahab the false prophet, who was burnt by the king of Babylon. Jer. 29 : 21. (B.C. before 594.)

Ko'rah (*baldness*). 1. Third son of Esau by Aholibamah. Gen. 36 : 5, 14, 18; 1 Chron. 1 : 35. He was born in Canaan before Esau migrated to Mount Seir, Gen. 36 : 5–9, and was one of the "dukes" of Edom. (B.C. 1790.)

2. Another Edomitish "duke" of this name, sprung from Eliphaz, Esau's son by Adah. Gen. 36 : 16.

3. One of the "sons of Hebron," in 1 Chron. 2 : 43.

4. Son of Izhar the son of Kohath the son of Levi. He was leader of the famous rebellion against his cousins Moses and Aaron in the wilderness, for which he paid the penalty of perishing with his followers by an earthquake and flames of fire. Num. 16; 26 : 9–11. The particular grievance which rankled in the mind of Korah and his company was their exclusion from the office of the priesthood, and their being confined—those among them who were Levites—to the inferior service of the tabernacle. Korah's position as leader in this rebellion was evidently the result of his personal character, which was that of a bold, haughty and ambitious man. (B.C. 1490.) In the New Testament (Jude 11) Korah is coupled with Cain and Balaam.

Kor'ahite, 1 Chron. 9 : 19, 31, **Kor'-hite,** or **Kor'athite,** that portion of the Kohathites who were descended from Korah. They were an important branch of the singers, 2 Chron. 20 : 19; hence we find eleven psalms (or twelve, if Ps. 43 is included under the same title as Ps. 42) dedicated or assigned to the sons of Korah, viz., Ps. 42, 44–49, 84, 85, 87, 88.

Ko're (*partridge*). 1. A Korahite, ancestor of Shallum and Meshelemiah, chief porters in the reign of David. 1 Chron. 9 : 19; 26 : 1. (B.C. 1014.)

2. Son of Imnah, a Levite in the reign of Hezekiah. He had charge of the offerings. 2 Chron. 31 : 14. (B.C. 726.)

3. In the Authorized Version of 1 Chron. 26 : 19, "the sons of Kore" (following the Vulgate *Core*) should properly be "the sons of the Korhite."

Koz (*thorn*), Ezra 2 : 61; Neh. 3 : 4, 21 = Coz = HAKKOZ.

Kusha'iah (*bow of Jehovah*), the same as Kish or Kishi, the father of Ethan the Merarite. 1 Chron. 15 : 17.

L.

La′adah (*order*), the son of Shelah and grandson of Judah. 1 Chron. 4 : 21.

La′adan (*put in order*). 1. An Ephraimite, ancestor of Joshua the son of Nun. 1 Chron. 7 : 26.

2. The son of Gershom, elsewhere called LIBNI. 1 Chron. 23 : 7, 8, 9 ; 26 : 21.

La′ban (*white*). 1. Son of Bethuel, brother of Rebekah and father of Leah and Rachel. (B.C. about 1860–1740.) The elder branch of the family remained at Haran, Mesopotamia, when Abraham removed to the land of Canaan, and it is there that we first meet with Laban, as taking the leading part in the betrothal of his sister Rebekah to her cousin Isaac. Gen. 24 : 10, 29–60 ; 27 : 43 ; 29 : 5. The next time Laban appears in the sacred narrative it is as the host of his nephew Jacob at Haran. Gen. 29 : 13, 14. [JACOB.] Jacob married Rachel and Leah, daughters of Laban, and remained with him 20 years, B.C. 1760–1740. But Laban's dishonest and overreaching practice toward his nephew shows from what source Jacob inherited his tendency to sharp dealing. Nothing is said of Laban after Jacob left him.

2. One of the landmarks named in the obscure and disputed passage Deut. 1 : 1. The mention of Hezeroth has perhaps led to the only conjecture regarding Laban of which the writer is aware, namely, that it is identical with LIBNAH. Num. 33 : 20.

Lacedæmo′nians, in Greece the inhabitants of Sparta or Lacedæmon, with whom the Jews claimed kindred. 1 Macc. 12 : 2, 5, 6, 20, 21 ; 14 : 20, 23 ; 15 : 23 ; 2 Macc. 5 : 9.

La′chish (*invincible*), a city lying south of Jerusalem, on the borders of Simeon, and belonging to the Amorites, the king of which joined with four others, at the invitation of Adonizedek king of Jerusalem, to chastise the Gibeonites for their league with Israel. Josh. 10 : 3, 5. They were routed by Joshua at Beth-horon, and the king of Lachish fell a victim with the others under the trees at Makkedah. ver. 26. The destruction of the town shortly followed the death of the king. vs. 31–33. In the special statement that the attack lasted two days, in contra-

distinction to the other cities which were taken in one (see ver. 35), we gain our first glimpse of that strength of position for which Lachish was afterward remarkable. Lachish was one of the cities fortified and garrisoned by Rehoboam after the revolt of the northern kingdom. 2 Chron. 11 : 9. In the reign of Hezekiah it was one of the cities taken by Sennacherib. This siege is considered by Layard and Hincks to be depicted on the slabs found by the former in one of the chambers of the palace at Kouyunjik. After the return from captivity, Lachish with its surrounding "fields" was reoccupied by the Jews. Neh. 11 : 30.

La′el (*of God*), the father of Eliasaph. Num. 3 : 24.

La′had (*oppression*), son of Jahath, one of the descendants of Judah. 1 Chron. 4 : 2.

Laha′i-ro′i (*well of the living God*), **The well.** In this form is given in the Authorized Version of Gen. 24 : 62 and 25 : 11 the name of the famous well of Hagar's relief, in the oasis of verdure round which Isaac afterward resided. It was southwest of Beersheba.

Lah′mam (*provisions*), a town in the lowland district of Judah. Josh. 15 : 40.

Lah′mi (*warrior*), the brother of Goliath the Gittite, slain by Elhanan the son of Zair or Zaor. 1 Chron. 20 : 5. (B.C. 1020.)

La′ish (*lion*), the city which was taken by the Danites, and under its new name of Dan became famous as the northern limit of the nation. Judges 18 : 7, 14, 27, 29. [DAN.] It was near the sources of the Jordan. In the Authorized Version Laish is again mentioned in the account of Sennacherib's march on Jerusalem. Isa. 10 : 30. This Laish is probably the small village Laishah, lying between Gallim and Anathoth in Benjamin, and of which hitherto no traces have been found. (Fairbairn's "Imperial Bible Dictionary" suggests that it may be the present little village *el-Isawiyeh*, in a beautiful valley a mile northeast of Jerusalem.—ED.)

La′ish (*lion*), father of Phaltiel, to whom Saul had given Michal, David's wife. 1 Sam. 25 : 44 ; 2 Sam. 3 : 15.

Lakes. [PALESTINE.]

La'kum (*fortification*), properly **Lak'kum,** one of the places which formed the landmarks of the boundary of Naphtali. Josh. 19 : 33.

Lambs are the young of sheep, but originally included also the young of goats. They formed an important part of almost every sacrifice. Ex. 29 : 38–41; Num. 28 : 9, 11; 29 : 2, 13–40, etc. [On the paschal lamb see PASSOVER.]

La'mech (*powerful*), properly **Lemech.** 1. The fifth lineal descendant from Cain. Gen. 4 : 18–24. He is the only one except Enoch, of the posterity of Cain, whose history is related with some detail. His two wives, Adah and Zillah, and his daughter Naamah, are, with Eve, the only antediluvian women whose names are mentioned by Moses. His three sons, Jabal, Jubal and Tubal-cain, are celebrated in Scripture as authors of useful inventions. The remarkable poem which Lamech uttered may perhaps be regarded as Lamech's song of exultation on the invention of the sword by his son Tubal-cain, in the possession of which he foresaw a great advantage to himself and his family over any enemies. 2. The father of Noah. Gen. 5 : 29.

Lamentations of Jeremiah. *Title.* —The Hebrew title of this book, *Êcah,* is taken, like the titles of the five books of Moses, from the Hebrew word with which it opens. *Author.*—The poems included in this collection appear in the Hebrew canon with no name attached to them, but Jeremiah has been almost universally regarded as their author. *Date.*—The poems belong unmistakably to the last days of the kingdom, or the commencement of the exile, B.C. 629–586. They are written by one who speaks, with the vividness and intensity of an eye-witness, of the misery which he bewails. *Contents.*—The book consists of five chapters, each of which, however, is a separate poem, complete in itself, and having a distinct subject, but brought at the same time under a plan which includes them all. A complicated alphabetic structure pervades nearly the whole book. (1) Chs. 1, 2 and 4 contain twenty-two verses each, arranged in alphabetic order, each verse falling into three nearly balanced clauses; ch. 2 : 19 forms an exception, as having a fourth clause. (2) Ch. 3 contains three short verses under each letter of the alphabet, the initial letter being three times repeated. (3)

Ch. 5 contains the same number of verses as chs. 1, 2, 4, but without the alphabetic order. Jeremiah was not merely a patriot-poet, weeping over the ruin of his country; he was a prophet who had seen all this coming, and had foretold it as inevitable. There are perhaps few portions of the Old Testament which appear to have done the work they were meant to do more effectually than this. The book has supplied thousands with the fullest utterance for their sorrows in the critical periods of national or individual suffering. We may well believe that it soothed the weary years of the Babylonian exile. It enters largely into the order of the Latin Church for the services of passion-week. On the ninth day of the month of Ab (July–August), the Lamentations of Jeremiah were read, year by year, with fasting and weeping, to commemorate the misery out of which the people had been delivered.

Assyrian Terra-cotta and Glass Lamps.

Chaldean Lamps.

Lamp. 1. That part of the golden candlestick belonging to the tabernacle which bore the light; also of each of the ten candlesticks placed by Solomon in the temple before the holy of holies. Ex. 25 : 37; 1 Kings 7 : 49; 2 Chron. 4 : 20; 13 : 11; Zech. 4 : 2. The lamps were lighted every evening and cleansed every morning. Ex. 30 : 7, 8.

2. A torch or flambeau, such as was carried by the soldiers of Gideon. Judges 7 : 16, 20; comp. 15 : 4. The use in marriage processions of lamps fed with oil is

alluded to in the parable of the ten virgins. Matt. 25 : 1. Modern Egyptian lamps consist of small glass vessels with

Lamp with Christian Inscription.

a tube at the bottom containing a cotton wick twisted around a piece of straw. For night travelling, a lantern composed of waxed cloth strained over a sort of cylinder of wire rings, and a top and bottom of perforated copper. This would, in form at least, answer to the lamps within pitchers of Gideon.

"The Hebrews, like the ancient Greeks and Romans, as well as the modern Orientals, were accustomed to burn lamps all night. This custom, with the effect produced by their going out or being extinguished, supplies various figures to the sacred writers. 2 Sam. 21 : 17; Prov. 13 : 9; 20 : 20. On the other hand, the keeping up of a lamp's light is used as a symbol of enduring and unbroken succession. 1 Kings 11 : 36; 15 : 4; Ps. 132 : 17."—*McClintock and Strong.*

Lancet. This word is found in Kings 18 : 28 only. The Hebrew term is *romach,* which is elsewhere rendered, and appears to mean a javelin or light spear. In the original edition of the Authorized Version (1611) the word is " lancers."

Language. [TONGUES, CONFUSION OF.]

Lantern (so called for its shining) occurs only in John 18 : 3. (It there probably denotes any kind of covered light, in distinction from a simple taper or common house-light, as well as from a flambeau. Lanterns were much employed

Laodicea.

by the Romans in military operations. Two, of bronze, have been found among the ruins of Herculaneum and Pompeii. They are cylindrical, with translucent horn sides, the lamp within being furnished with an extinguisher.—ED.)

Laodice′a (*justice of the people*), a town in the Roman province of Asia, situated in the valley of the Mæander, on a small river called the Lycus, with Colossæ and Hierapolis a few miles distant to the west. Built, or rather rebuilt, by one of the Seleucid monarchs, and named in honor of his wife, Laodicea became under the Roman government a place of some importance. Its trade was considerable; it lay on the line of a great road; and it was the seat of a *conventus.* From the third chapter and seventeenth verse of Revelation we should gather it was a place of great wealth. Christianity was introduced into Laodicea, not, however, as it would seem, through the direct agency of St. Paul. We have good reason for believing that when, in writing from Rome to the Christians of Colossæ, he sent a greeting to those of Laodicea, he had not personally visited either place. But the preaching of the gospel at Ephesus, Acts 18 : 19–19 : 41, must inevitably have resulted in the formation of churches in the neighboring cities, especially where Jews were settled; and there were Jews in Laodicea. In subsequent times it became a Christian city of eminence, the see of a bishop and a meeting-place of councils. The Mohammedan invaders destroyed it, and it is now a scene of utter desolation, as was prophesied in Rev. 3 : 14–22 ; and the extensive ruins near *Denislu* justify all that we read of Laodicea in Greek and Roman writers. Another biblical object of interest is connected with Laodicea. From Col. 4 : 16 it appears that St. Paul wrote a letter to this place when he wrote the letter to Colossæ. Ussher's view is that it was the same as the Epistle to the Ephesians, which was a circular letter sent to Laodicea among other places. The apocryphal *Epistola ad Laodicenses* is a late and clumsy forgery.

Laodice'ans, the inhabitants of Laodicea. Col. 4: 16 ; Rev. 3: 14.

Lap'idoth (*torches*), the husband of Deborah the prophetess. Judges 4 : 4.

Lapwing (Heb. *duciphath*) occurs only in Lev. 11 : 19 and in the parallel passage of Deut. 14 : 18, amongst the list of those birds which were forbidden by the law of Moses to be eaten by the Israelites. Commentators generally agree that the *hoopoe* is the bird intended. The hoopoe is an occasional visitor to England, arriving for the most part in the autumn. Its crest is very elegant; each of the long feathers forming it is tipped with black.

Lase'a, Acts 27 : 8, a city of Crete, the ruins of which were discovered in 1856, a few miles to the eastward of Fair Havens.

La'sha (*fissure*), a place noticed in Gen. 10 : 19 as marking the limit of the country of the Canaanites. It lay somewhere in the southeast of Palestine. Jerome and other writers identify it with Callirrhoë, a spot famous for hot springs, near the eastern shore of the Dead Sea.

Lasha'ron (*the plain*), one of the Canaanite towns whose kings were killed by Joshua. Josh. 12 : 18.

Latchet, the thong or fastening by which the sandal was attached to the foot. It occurs in the proverbial expression in Gen. 14 : 23, and is there used to denote something trivial or worthless. Another semi-proverbial expression in Luke 3 : 16 points to the fact that the office of bearing and unfastening the shoes of great personages fell to the meanest slaves.

Lapwing or Hoopoe.

Lat'in, the language spoken by the Romans, is mentioned only in John 19 : 20 and Luke 23 : 38.

Lat'in Versions. [See VULGATE, THE.]

Lattice. This word is used for a latticed window or simply a network placed before a window or balcony. Perhaps the network through which Ahaziah fell and received his mortal injury was on the parapet of his palace. 2 Kings 1 : 2. (The latticed window is much used in warm eastern countries. It frequently projects from the wall (like our bay windows), and is formed of reticulated work, often highly ornamental, portions of which are hinged so that they may be opened or shut at pleasure. The object is to keep the apartments cool by intercepting the direct rays of the sun, while the air is permitted to circulate freely.—*Fairbairn.* [See HOUSE and WINDOW.]

Laver. 1. In the tabernacle, a vessel of brass containing water for the priests to wash their hands and feet before offering sacrifice. It stood in the court between the altar and the door of the tabernacle. Ex. 30 : 19, 21. It rested

A Brazen Laver on Wheels.

on a basis, *i. e.* a foot, which, as well as the laver itself, was made from the mirrors of the women who assembled at the door of the tabernacle court. Ex. 38 : 8. The form of the laver is not specified, but may be assumed to have been circular. Like the other vessels belonging to the tabernacle, it was, together with its "foot," consecrated with oil. Lev. 8 : 10, 11.

2. In Solomon's temple, besides the great molten sea, there were ten lavers of brass, raised on bases, 1 Kings 7 : 27, 39, five on the north and five on the south side of the court of the priests. They were used for washing the animals to be offered in burnt offerings. 2 Chron. 4 : 6.

Law. The word is properly used, in Scripture as elsewhere, to express a definite commandment laid down by any recognized authority ; but when the word is used with the article, and without any words of limitation, it refers to the expressed will of God, and in nine cases out

of ten to the Mosaic law, or to the Pentateuch of which it forms the chief portion. The Hebrew word *tôrâh* (law) lays more stress on its moral authority, as teaching the truth and guiding in the right way ; the Greek νόμος (law), on its constraining power as imposed and enforced by a recognized authority. The sense of the word, however, extends its scope and assumes a more abstract character in the writings of St. Paul. *Nomos* when used by him with the article, still refers in general to the law of Moses ; but when used without the article, so as to embrace any manifestation of "law," it includes all powers which act on the will of man by compulsion, or by the pressure of external motives, whether their commands be or be not expressed in definite forms. The occasional use of the word "law" (as in Rom. 3 : 27, "law of faith ") to denote an *internal* principle of action does not really mitigate against the general rule. It should also be noticed that the title "the Law" is occasionally used loosely to refer to the whole of the Old Testament, as in John 10 : 34, referring to Ps. 82 : 6 ; in John 15 : 25, referring to Ps. 35 : 19 ; and in 1 Cor. 14 : 21, referring to Isa. 28 : 11, 12.

Law of Moses. It will be the object of this article to give a brief analysis of the substance of this law, to point out its main principles, and to explain the position which it occupies in the progress of divine revelation. In order to do this the more clearly, it seems best to speak of the law, 1st. In relation to the past ; 2d. In its own intrinsic character. 1. (*a*) *In reference to the past,* it is all-important, for the proper understanding of the law, to remember its *entire dependence on the Abrahamic covenant.* See Gal. 3 : 17–24. That covenant had a twofold character. It contained the "spiritual promise" of the Messiah ; but it contained also the temporal promises subsidiary to the former. (*b*) The nature of this *relation of the law to the promise* is clearly pointed out. The belief in God as the Redeemer of man, and the hope of his manifestation as such in the person of the Messiah, involved the belief that the Spiritual Power must be superior to all carnal obstructions, and that there was in man a spiritual element which could rule his life by communion with a spirit from above. But it involved also the idea of an antagonistic power of evil, from which man was to be redeemed, existing in each individual, and existing also in the world at large. (*c*) Nor is it less essential to remark the *period of the history* at which it was given. It marked and determined the transition of Israel from the condition of a tribe to that of a nation, and its definite assumption of a distinct position and office in the history of the world. (*d*) Yet, though new in its general conception, it was probably *not wholly new in its materials.* There must necessarily have been, before the law, commandments and revelations of a fragmentary character, under which Israel had hitherto grown up. So far therefore as they were consistent with the objects of the Jewish law, the customs of Palestine and the laws of Egypt would doubtless be traceable in the Mosaic system. (*e*) In close connection with, and almost in consequence of, this reference to antiquity, we find an *accommodation of the law* to the temper and circumstances of the Israelites, to which our Lord refers in the case of divorce, Matt. 19 : 7, 8, as necessarily interfering with its absolute perfection. In many cases it rather should be said to guide and modify existing usages than actually to sanction them ; and the ignorance of their existence may lead to a conception of its ordinances not only erroneous, but actually the reverse of the truth. (*f*) In close connection with this subject we observe also *the gradual process by which the law was revealed* to the Israelites. In Ex. 1–23, in direct connection with the revelation from Mount Sinai, that which may be called the rough outline of the Mosaic law is given by God, solemnly recorded by Moses, and accepted by the people. In Ex. 25–31 there is a similar outline of the Mosaic ceremonial. On the basis of these it may be conceived that the fabric of the Mosaic system gradually grew up under the requirements of the time. The first revelation of the law in anything like a perfect form is found in the book of Deuteronomy. Yet even then the revelation was not final ; it was the duty of the prophets to amend and explain it in special points, Ezek. 18, and to bring out more clearly its great principles.

2. In giving an analysis of *the substance of the law,* it will probably be better to treat it, as any other system of laws is usually treated, by dividing it into—I. Laws Civil ; II. Laws Criminal ; III. Laws Judicial and Constitutional ; IV. Laws Ecclesiastical and Ceremonial.

I. LAWS CIVIL.

1. LAW OF PERSONS.

(*a*) FATHER AND SON.—*The power of a father* to be held sacred ; cursing or smiting, Ex. 21 : 15, 17 ; Lev. 20 : 9, and stubborn and willful disobedience, to be considered capital crimes. But uncontrolled power of life and death was apparently refused to the father, and vested only in the congregation. Deut. 21 : 18–21. *Right of the first-born* to a double portion of the inheritance not to be set aside by partiality. Deut. 21 : 15–17. *Inheritance by daughters* to be allowed in default of sons, provided, Num. 27 : 6–8, comp. 36, that heiresses married in their own tribe. *Daughters unmarried* to be entirely dependent on their father. Num. 30 : 3–5.

(*b*) HUSBAND AND WIFE.—*The power of a husband* to be so great that a wife could never be *sui juris,* or enter independently into any engagement, even before God. Num. 30 : 6–15. A widow or a divorced wife became independent, and did not again fall under her father's power. ver. 9. *Divorce* (for uncleanness) allowed, but to be formal and irrevocable. Deut. 24 : 1–4. *Marriage within certain degrees forbidden.* Lev. 18, etc. *A slave wife,* whether bought or captive, not to be actual property, nor to be sold ; if illtreated, to be *ipso facto* free. Ex. 21 : 7–9 ; Deut. 21 : 10–14. *Slander* against a wife's virginity to be punished by fine, and by deprival of power of divorce ; on the other hand, ante-connubial uncleanness in her to be punished by death. Deut. 22 : 13–21. *The raising up of seed* (Levirate law) a formal right to be claimed by the widow, under pain of infamy, with a view to preservation of families. Deut. 25 : 5–10.

(*c*) MASTER AND SLAVE.—*Power of master so far limited* that death under actual chastisement was punishable, Ex. 21 : 20 ; and maiming was to give liberty *ipso facto.* vs. 26, 27. *The Hebrew slave to be freed* at the sabbatical year,[1] and provided with necessaries (his wife and children to go with only if they came to his master with him), unless by his own formal act he consented to be a perpetual slave. Ex. 21 : 1–6 ; Deut. 15 : 12–18. In any case, it would seem, to be freed at the jubilee, Lev. 25 : 10, with his

---

[1] The difficulty of enforcing this law is seen in Jer. 34 : 8–16.

children. If sold to a resident alien, to be always redeemable, at a price proportioned to the distance of the jubilee. Lev. 25 : 47–54. *Foreign slaves* to be held and inherited as property forever, Lev. 25 : 45, 46; and fugitive slaves from foreign nations not to be given up. Deut. 23 : 15.

(*d*) STRANGERS.—These seem never to have been *sui juris*, or able to protect themselves, and accordingly protection and kindness toward them are enjoined as a sacred duty. Ex. 22 : 21; Lev. 19 : 33, 34.

2. LAW OF THINGS.

(*a*) LAWS OF LAND (AND PROPERTY). —(1) *All land to be the property of God alone,* and its holders to be deemed his tenants. Lev. 25 : 23. (2) *All sold land* therefore to *return to its original owners* at the jubilee, and the price of sale to be calculated accordingly; and redemption on equitable terms to be allowed at all times. Lev. 25 : 25–27. *A house sold* to be redeemable within a year; and if not redeemed, to pass away altogether. ch. 25 : 29, 30. *But the houses of the Levites,* or those in unwalled villages, to be redeemable at all times, in the same way as land; and the Levitical suburbs to be inalienable. ch. 25 : 31–34. (3) *Land or houses sanctified,* or tithes, or unclean firstlings, to be capable of being redeemed, at six-fifths value (calculated according to the distance from the jubilee year by the priest); if devoted by the owner and unredeemed, to be hallowed at the jubilee forever, and given to the priests; if only by a possessor, to return to the owner at the jubilee. Lev. 27 : 14–34. (4) *Inheritance.*

1. *Sons.*
  2. *Daughters.*[1]
    3. *Brothers.*
      4. *Uncles on the father's side.*
        5. *Next kinsmen* generally.

(*b*) LAWS OF DEBT.—(1) *All debts* (to an Israelite) to be released at the seventh (sabbatical) year; a blessing promised to obedience, and a curse on refusal to lend. Deut. 15 : 1–11. (2) *Usury* (from Israelites) not to be taken. Ex. 22 : 25–27; Deut. 23 : 19, 20. (3) *Pledges* not to be insolently or ruinously exacted. Deut. 24 : 6, 10–13, 17, 18.

(*c*) TAXATION.—(1) *Census-money,* a poll-tax (of a half shekel), to be paid for

[1] Heiresses to marry in their own tribe. Num. 27 : 6–8; 36.

the service of the tabernacle. Ex. 30 : 12–16. All spoil in war to be halved; of the combatants' half, one five-hundredth, of the people's, one fiftieth, to be paid for a "heave offering" to Jehovah. (2) *Tithes.*—(α) *Tithes of all produce* to be given for maintenance of the Levites. Num. 18 : 20–24. (Of this one tenth to be paid as a heave offering for maintenance of the priests. vs. 24–32.) (β) *Second tithe* to be bestowed in religious feasting and charity, either at the holy place oi (every third year) at home. Deut. 14 : 22–28. (γ) *First-fruits* of corn, wine and oil (at least one sixtieth, generally one fortieth, for the priests) to be offered at Jerusalem, with a solemn declaration of dependence on God the King of Israel. Num. 18 : 12, 13; Deut. 26 : 1–15. *First-lings* of clean beasts; the redemption money (five shekels) of man and (half shekel, or one shekel) of unclean beasts to be given to the priests after sacrifice. Num. 18 : 15–18. (3) *Poor laws.*—(α) *Gleanings* (in field or vineyard) to be a legal right of the poor. Lev. 19 : 9, 10; Deut. 24 : 19–22. (β) *Slight trespass* (eating on the spot) to be allowed as legal. Deut. 23 : 24, 25. (γ) *Second tithe* (see 2 β) to be given in charity. (δ) *Wages* to be paid day by day. Deut. 24 : 15. (4) *Maintenance of priests.* Num. 18 : 8–32. (α) *Tenth of Levites' tithe.* (See 2 α.) (β) *The heave* and *wave offerings* (breast and right shoulder of all peace offerings). (γ) *The meat* and *sin offerings,* to be eaten solemnly and only in the holy place. (δ) *First-fruits* and redemption money. (See 2 γ.) (ε) *Price of all devoted things,* unless specially given for a sacred service. A man's service, or that of his household, to be redeemed at 50 shekels for man, 30 for woman, 20 for boy and 10 for girl.

II. LAWS CRIMINAL.

1. OFFENCES AGAINST GOD (of the nature of treason.)

1st Command. *Acknowledgment of false gods,* Ex. 22 : 20, as *e. g.* Molech Lev. 20 : 1–5, and generally all *idolatry* Deut. 13; 17 : 2–5.

2d Command. *Witchcraft and false prophecy.* Ex. 22 : 18; Deut. 18 : 9–22; Lev. 19 : 31.

3d Command. *Blasphemy.* Lev. 24 : 15, 16.

4th Command. *Sabbath-breaking.* Num. 15 : 32, 36.

Punishment in all cases, death by ston-

ing. Idolatrous cities to be utterly destroyed.

2. OFFENCES AGAINST MAN.

5th Command. *Disobedience to* or cursing or smiting of *parents*, Ex. 21 : 15, 17 ; Lev. 20 : 9 ; Deut. 21 : 18–21, to be punished by death by stoning, publicly adjudged and inflicted ; so also of disobedience to the priests (as judges) or the Supreme Judge. Comp. 1 Kings 21 : 10–14 (Naboth) ; 2 Chron. 24 : 21 (Zechariah).

6th Command. (1) *Murder* to be punished by death without sanctuary or reprieve, or satisfaction. Ex. 21 : 12, 14 ; Deut. 19 : 11–13. Death of a slave, actually under the rod, to be punished. Ex. 21 : 20, 21. (2) *Death by negligence* to be punished by death. Ex. 21 : 28–30. (3) *Accidental homicide :* the avenger of blood to seek safety by flight to a city of refuge, there to remain till the death of the high priest. Num. 35 : 9–28 ; Deut. 4 : 41–43 ; 19 : 4–10. (4) *Uncertain murder* to be expiated by formal disavowal and sacrifice by the elders of the nearest city. Deut. 21 : 1–9. (5) *Assault* to be punished by *lex talionis*, or damages. Ex. 21 : 18, 19, 22–25 ; Lev. 24 : 19, 20.

7th Command. (1) *Adultery* to be punished by death of both offenders ; the rape of a married or betrothed woman, by death of the offender. Deut. 22 : 13–27. (2) *Rape or seduction* of an unbetrothed virgin to be compensated by marriage, with dowry (50 shekels), and without power of divorce ; or, if she be refused, by payment of full dowry. Ex. 22 : 16, 17 ; Deut. 22 : 28, 29. (3) *Unlawful marriages* (incestuous, etc.) to be punished, some by death, some by childlessness. Lev. 20.

8th Command. (1) *Theft* to be punished by fourfold or double restitution ; a nocturnal robber might be slain as an outlaw. Ex. 22 : 1–4. (2) *Trespass* and injury of things lent to be compensated. Ex. 23 : 5–15. (3) *Perversion of justice* (by bribes, threats, etc.), and especially oppression of strangers, strictly forbidden. Ex. 22 : 9, etc. (4) *Kidnapping* to be punished by death. Deut. 24 : 7.

9th Command. *False witness* to be punished by *lex talionis*. Ex. 23 : 1–3 ; Deut. 19 : 16–21. Slander of a wife's chastity, by fine and loss of power of divorce. Deut. 22 : 18, 19.

A fuller consideration of the tables of the Ten Commandments is given elsewhere. [TEN COMMANDMENTS.]

III. LAWS JUDICIAL AND CONSTITUTIONAL.

1. JURISDICTION.

(*a*) *Local judges* (generally Levites, as more skilled in the law) appointed, for ordinary matters, probably by the people with approbation of the supreme authority (as of Moses in the wilderness), Ex. 18 : 25 ; Deut. 1 : 15–18, through all the land. Deut. 16 : 18. (*b*) *Appeal to the priests* (at the holy place), or to *the judge;* their sentence final, and to be accepted under pain of death. See Deut. 17 : 8–13 ; comp. appeal to Moses, Ex. 18 : 26. (*c*) *Two witnesses* (at least) required in capital matters. Num. 35 : 30 ; Deut. 17 : 6, 7. (*d*) *Punishment*, except by special command, to be personal, and not to extend to the family. Deut. 24 : 16. Stripes allowed and limited, Deut. 25 : 1–3, so as to avoid outrage on the human frame. All this would be to a great extent set aside—1st. By the summary jurisdiction of the king, see 1 Sam. 22 : 11–19 (Saul) ; 2 Sam. 12 : 1–5 ; 14 : 4–11 ; 1 Kings 3 : 16–28, which extended even to the deposition of the high priest. 1 Sam. 22 : 17, 18 ; 1 Kings 2 : 26, 27. The practical difficulty of its being carried out is seen in 2 Sam. 15 : 2–6, and would lead of course to a certain delegation of his power. 2d. By the appointment of the Seventy, Num. 11 : 24–30, with a solemn religious sanction. In later times there was a local sanhedrin of twenty-three in each city, and two such in Jerusalem, as well as the Great Sanhedrin, consisting of seventy members, besides the president, who was to be the high priest if duly qualified, and controlling even the king and high priest. The members were priest, scribes (Levites), and elders (of other tribes). A court of exactly this nature is noticed as appointed to supreme power by Jehoshaphat. See 2 Chron. 19 : 8–11.

2. ROYAL POWER.

The king's power limited by the law, as written and formally accepted by the king ; and directly forbidden to be despotic.[1] Deut. 17 : 14–20 ; comp. 1 Sam. 10 : 25. Yet he had power of taxation (to one tenth) and of compulsory service, 1

[1] Military conquest discouraged by the prohibition of the use of horses. See Josh. 11 : 6. For an example of obedience to this law see 2 Sam. 8 : 4, and of disobedience to it see 1 Kings 10 : 26–29.

Sam. 8 : 10–18, the declaration of war, 1 Sam. 11, etc. There are distinct traces of a "mutual contract," 2 Sam. 5 : 3; a "league," 2 Kings 11 : 17; the remonstrance with Rehoboam being clearly not extraordinary. 1 Kings 13 : 1–6.

The princes of the congregation.—The heads of the tribes, see Josh. 9 : 15, seem to have had authority under Joshua to act for the people, comp. 1 Chron. 27 : 16–22; and in the later times "the princes of Judah" seem to have had power to control both the king and the priests. See Jer. 26 : 10–24; 38 : 4, 5, etc.

3. ROYAL REVENUE.

(1) *Tenth of produce.* (2) *Domain land.* 1 Chron. 27 : 26–29. Note confiscation of criminal's land. 1 Kings 21 : 15. (3) *Bond service,* 1 Kings 5 : 17,18, chiefly on foreigners. 1 Kings 9 : 20–22; 2 Chron. 2 : 16, 17. (4) *Flocks and herds.* 1 Chron. 27 : 29–31. (5) *Tributes* (gifts) from foreign kings. (6) *Commerce;* especially in Solomon's time. 1 Kings 10 : 22, 29, etc.

IV. ECCLESIASTICAL AND CERE- MONIAL LAW.

1. LAW OF SACRIFICE (considered as the sign and the appointed means of the union with God, on which the holiness of the people depended).

a. ORDINARY SACRIFICES.

(α) *The whole burnt offering,* Lev. 1, of the herd or the flock; to be offered continually, Ex. 29 : 38–42; and the fire on the altar never to be extinguished. Lev. 6 : 8–13.

(β) *The meat offering,* Lev. 2; 6 : 14–23, of flour, oil and frankincense, unleavened and seasoned with salt.

(γ) *The peace offering,* Lev. 3; 7 : 11–21, of the herd or the flock; either a thank offering or a vow or free-will offering.

(δ) *The sin offering* or *trespass offering.* Lev. 4, 5, 6.

  (a) For sins committed in ignorance. Lev. 4.

  (b) For vows unwittingly made and broken, or uncleanness unwittingly contracted. Lev. 5.

  (c) For sins wittingly committed. Lev. 6 : 1–7.

b. EXTRAORDINARY SACRIFICES.

(α) *At the consecration of priests.* Lev. 8, 9.

(β) *At the purification of women.* Lev. 12.

(γ) *At the cleansing of lepers.* Lev. 13, 14.

(δ) *On the great day of atonement.* Lev. 16.

(ε) *On the great festivals.* Lev. 23.

2. LAW OF HOLINESS (arising from the union with God through sacrifice).

a. HOLINESS OF PERSONS.

(α) *Holiness of the whole people* as "children of God," Ex. 19 : 5, 6; Lev. 11–15, 17, 18; Deut. 14 : 1–21, shown in

  (a) The dedication of the first-born, Ex. 13 : 2, 12, 13; 22 : 29, 30, etc.; and the offering of all firstlings and first-fruits. Deut. 26, etc.

  (b) Distinction of clean and unclean food. Lev. 11; Deut. 14.

  (c) Provision for purification. Lev. 12, 13, 14, 15; Deut. 23 : 1–14.

  (d) Laws against disfigurement. Lev. 19 : 27; Deut. 14 : 1; comp. Deut. 25 : 3, against excessive scourging.

  (e) Laws against unnatural marriages and lusts. Lev. 18, 20.

(β) *Holiness of the priests* (*and Levites*).

  (a) Their consecration. Lev. 8, 9; Ex. 29.

  (b) Their special qualifications and restrictions. Lev. 21, 22 : 1–9.

  (c) Their rights, Deut. 18 : 1–6; Num. 18, and authority. Deut. 17 : 8–13.

b. HOLINESS OF PLACES AND THINGS.

(α) *The tabernacle* with the ark, the vail, the altars, the laver, the priestly robes, etc. Ex. 25–28, 30.

(β) *The holy place* chosen for the permanent erection of the tabernacle, Deut. 12, 14 : 22–29, where only all sacrifices were to be offered and all tithes, first-fruits, vows, etc., to be given or eaten.

c. HOLINESS OF TIMES.

(α) *The Sabbath.* Ex. 20 : 9–11; 23 : 12, etc.

(β) *The sabbatical year.* Ex. 23 : 10, 11; Lev. 25 : 1–7, etc.

(γ) *The year of jubilee.* Lev. 25 : 8–16, etc.

(δ) *The passover.* Ex. 12 : 3–27; Lev. 23 : 4, 5.

(ε) *The feast of weeks* (pentecost). Lev. 23 : 15, etc.

(ζ) *The feast of tabernacles.* Lev. 23 : 33–43.

(η) *The feast of trumpets.* Lev. 23 : 23–25.

(θ) *The day of atonement.* Lev. 23 : 26–32, etc.

Such is the substance of the Mosaic law. The leading principle of the whole is its THEOCRATIC CHARACTER, its reference, that is, of all action and thoughts of men *directly and immediately* to the will of God. It follows from this that it is to be regarded not merely as a law, that is, a rule of conduct based on known truth and acknowledged authority, but also as a *revelation of God's nature* and his dispensations. But this theocratic character of the law depends necessarily on the *belief in God*, as not only the creator and sustainer of the world, but as, by special covenant, *the head of the Jewish nation*. This immediate reference to God as their king is clearly seen as the groundwork of their whole polity. From this theocratic nature of the law follow important deductions with regard to (a) the view which it takes of political society; (b) the extent of the scope of the law; (c) the penalties by which it is enforced; and (d) the character which it seeks to impress on the people. (a) The Mosaic law seeks the basis of its polity, first, in the absolute sovereignty of God; next, in the relationship of each individual to God, and through God to his countrymen. It is clear that such a doctrine, while it contradicts none of the common theories, yet lies beneath them all. (b) The law, as proceeding directly from God and referring directly to him, is necessarily *absolute in its supremacy* and *unlimited in its scope*. It is supreme over the governors, as being only the delegates of the Lord, and therefore it is incompatible with any despotic authority in them. On the other hand, it is supreme over the governed, recognizing no inherent rights in the individual as prevailing against or limiting the law. It regulated the whole life of an Israelite. His actions were rewarded and punished with great minuteness and strictness—and that according to the standard, not of their consequences but of their intrinsic morality. (c) *The penalties and rewards* by which the law is enforced are such as depend on the direct theocracy. With regard to individual actions, it may be noticed that, as generally some penalties are inflicted by the subordinate and some only by the supreme authority, so among the Israelites some penalties came from the hand of man, some directly from the providence of God. (d) But perhaps the most important consequence of the theocratic nature of the law was the *peculiar character*

of *goodness* which it sought to *impress on the people*. The Mosaic law, beginning with piety as its first object, enforces most emphatically the purity essential to those who, by their union with God, have recovered the hope of intrinsic goodness, while it views righteousness and love rather as deductions from these than as independent objects. The appeal is not to any dignity of human nature, but to the obligations of communion with a holy God. The subordination, therefore, of this idea also to the religious idea is enforced; and so long as the due supremacy of the latter was preserved, all other duties would find their places in proper harmony.

Lawyer. The title "lawyer" is generally supposed to be equivalent to the title "scribe." The scribes expounded the law in the synagogues and schools. [See SCRIBES.]

Laying on of hands. This "formed at an early period a part of the ceremony observed on the appointment and consecration of persons to high and holy undertakings;" (and in the Christian Church was especially used in setting apart men to the ministry and to other holy offices. It is a symbolical act expressing the imparting of spiritual authority and power. —ED.)

Laz'arus (*whom God helps*), another form of the Hebrew name Eleazar. 1. Lazarus of Bethany, the brother of Martha and Mary. John 11 : 1. All that we know of him is derived from the Gospel of St. John, and that records little more than the facts of his death and resurrection. The language of John 11 : 1 implies that the sisters were the better known. Lazarus is "of Bethany, of the village of Mary and her sister Martha." From this and from the order of the three names in John 11 : 5 we may reasonably infer that Lazarus was the youngest of the family. All the circumstances of John 11 and 12 point to wealth and social position above the average.

2. The name of a poor man in the well-known parable of Luke 16 : 19–31. The name of Lazarus has been perpetuated in an institution of the Christian Church. The leper of the Middle Ages appears as a *lazaro*. The use of *lazaretto* and *lazarhouse* for the leper hospitals then founded in all parts of western Christendom, no less than that of *lazaroni* for the mendicants of Italian towns, is an indication of the effect of the parable upon the mind

of Europe in the Middle Ages, and thence upon its later speech.

Lead. This is one of the most common of metals, found generally in veins of rocks, though seldom in a metallic state, and most commonly in combination with sulphur. It was early known to the ancients, and the allusions to it in Scripture indicate that the Hebrews were well acquainted with its uses. The rocks in the neighborhood of Sinai yielded it in large quantities, and it was found in Egypt. In Job 19 : 24 the allusion is supposed to be to the practice of carving inscriptions upon stone and pouring molten lead into the cavities of the letters, to render them legible and at the same time preserve them from the action of the air.

Leaf, Leaves. The word occurs in the Authorized Version either in singular or plural number in three different senses. 1. Leaf of a tree. The righteous are often compared to green leaves. Jer. 17 : 8. The ungodly, on the other hand, are "as an oak whose leaf fadeth." Isa. 1 : 30. 2. Leaves of doors. The Hebrew word, which occurs very many times in the Bible, and which in 1 Kings 6 : 32 (margin) and 34 is translated "leaves" in the Authorized Version, signifies *beams, ribs, sides,* etc. 3. Leaves of a book or roll occurs in this sense only in Jer. 3⁶ : 23. The Hebrew word (literally *doors*) would perhaps be more correctly translated *columns*.

Le'ah (*wearied*), the daughter of Laban. Gen. 29 : 16. The dullness or weakness of her eyes was so notable that it is mentioned as a contrast to the beautiful form and appearance of her younger sister Rachel. Her father took advantage of the opportunity which the local marriage rite afforded to pass her off in her sister's stead on the unconscious bridegroom, and excused himself to Jacob by alleging that the custom of the country forbade the younger sister to be given first in marriage. Jacob's preference of Rachel grew into hatred of Leah after he had married both sisters. Leah, however, bore to him in quick succession Reuben, Simeon, Levi, Judah, then Issachar, Zebulun and Dinah, before Rachel had a child. She died some time after Jacob reached the south country in which his father Isaac lived. She was buried in the family grave in Machpelah, near Hebron. Gen. 49 : 31. (B.C. about 1720.)

Leasing (*falsehood*). This word is retained in the Authorized Version of Ps. 4 : 2 ; 5 : 6, from the older English versions ; but the Hebrew word of which it is the rendering is elsewhere almost uniformly translated "lies." Ps. 40 : 4 ; 58 : 3, etc.

Leather. The notices of leather in the Bible are singularly few ; indeed the word occurs but twice in the Authorized Version, and in each instance in reference to the same object, a girdle. 2 Kings 1 : 8 ; Matt. 3 : 4. There are, however, other instances in which the word "leather" might with propriety be substituted for "skin." Lev. 11 : 32 ; 13 : 48 ; Num. 31 : 20. Though the material itself is seldom noticed, yet we cannot doubt that it was extensively used by the Jews ; shoes, bottles, thongs, garments, ropes and other articles were made of it. The art of tanning, however, was held in low esteem by the Jews.

Leaven. Various substances were known to have fermenting qualities ; but the ordinary leaven consisted of a lump of old dough in a high state of fermentation, which was mixed into the mass of dough prepared for baking. The use of leaven was strictly forbidden in all offerings made to the Lord by fire. During the passover the Jews were commanded to put every particle of leaven from the house. The most prominent idea associated with leaven is connected with the *corruption* which it had undergone, and which it communicated to bread in the process of fermentation. It is to this property of leaven that our Saviour points when he speaks of the "leaven (*i. e.* the corrupt doctrine) of the Pharisees and of the Sadducees," Matt. 16 : 6 ; and St. Paul, when he speaks of the "old leaven." 1 Cor. 5 : 7. (Another quality in leaven is noticed in the Bible, namely, its secretly penetrating and diffusive power. In this respect it was emblematic of moral influence generally, whether good or bad ; and hence our Saviour adopts it as illustrating the growth of the kingdom of heaven in the individual heart and in the world at large : because (1) its source is from without ; (2) it is secret in its operation ; (3) it spreads by contact of particle with particle ; (4) it is widely diffusive, one particle of leaven being able to change any number of particles of flour ; and because (5) it does not act like water, moistening a certain amount of flour, but is like a plant, changing the particles it comes in contact with into its own nature, with like propagating power. —ED.)

Leb′ana (*white*), one of the Nethinim whose descendants returned from Babylon with Zerubbabel. Neh. 7 : 48. He is called

Leb′anah (*white*) in Ezra 2 : 45.

Leb′anon, a mountain range in the north of Palestine. The name Lebanon signifies *white*, and was applied either on account of the snow which, during a great part of the year, covers its whole summit, or on account of the white color of its limestone cliffs and peaks. It is the "white mountain"—the Mont Blanc of Palestine. Lebanon is represented in Scripture as lying upon the northern border of the land of Israel. Deut. 1 : 7 ; 11 : 24 ; Josh. 1 : 4. Two distinct ranges bear this name. They run in parallel lines from southwest to northeast for about 90 geographical miles, enclosing between them a long, fertile valley from five to eight miles wide, anciently called *Cœle-Syria*. The western range is the "Libanus" of the old geographers and

View of Lebanon from the Sea.

the Lebanon of Scripture. The eastern range was called "Anti-Libanus" by geographers, and "Lebanon toward the sunrising" by the sacred writers. Josh. 13 : 5.

1. *Lebanon*—the western range—commences on the south of the deep ravine of the *Litâny*, the ancient river Leontes, which drains the valley of Cœle-Syria, and falls into the Mediterranean five miles north of Tyre. It runs northeast in a straight line parallel to the coast, to the opening from the Mediterranean into the plain of Emesa, called in Scripture the "entrance of Hamath." Num. 34 : 8. Here *Nehr el-Kebîr*—the ancient river Eleutherus—sweeps round its northern end, as the Leontes does round its southern. The average elevation of the range is from 6000 to 8000 feet; but two peaks rise considerably higher. On the summits of both these peaks the snow remains in patches during the whole summer. The line of cultivation runs along at the height of about 6000 feet; and below this the features of the western slopes are entirely different. The rugged limestone banks are scantily clothed with the evergreen oak, and the sandstone with pines; while every available spot is carefully cultivated. The cultivation is wonderful, and shows what all Syria might be if under a good government. Fig trees cling to the naked rock ; vines are trained along narrow ledges; long ranges of mulberries, on terraces like steps of stairs, cover the more gentle declivities; and dense groves of olives fill up the bottoms

of the glens. Hundreds of villages are seen—here built among labyrinths of rocks, there clinging like swallows' nests to the sides of cliffs; while convents, no less numerous, are perched on the top of every peak. The vine is still largely cultivated in every part of the mountain. Lebanon also abounds in olives, figs and mulberries; while some remnants exist of the forests of pine, oak and cedar which formerly covered it. 1 Kings 5 : 6; Ezra 3 : 7; Ps. 29 : 5; Isa. 14 : 8. Considerable numbers of wild beasts still inhabit its retired glens and higher peaks; the writer has seen jackals, hyænas, wolves, bears and panthers. 2 Kings 14 : 9; Cant. 4 : 8; Hab. 2 : 17. Along the base of Lebanon runs the irregular plain of Phœnicia—nowhere more than two miles wide, and often interrupted by bold rocky spurs that dip into the sea. The main ridge of Lebanon is composed of Jura limestone, and abounds in fossils. Long belts of more recent sandstone run along the western slopes, which are in places largely impregnated with iron. Lebanon was originally inhabited by the Hivites and Giblites. Josh. 13 : 5, 6; Judges 3 : 3. The whole mountain range was assigned to the Israelites, but was never conquered by them. Josh. 13 : 2–6; Judges 3 : 1–3. During the Jewish monarchy it appears to have been subject to the Phœnicians. 1 Kings 5 : 2–6; Ezra 3 : 7. From the Greek conquest until modern times Lebanon had no separate history.

2. *Anti-Libanus.*—The main chain of Anti-Libanus commences in the plateau of Bashan, near the parallel of Cæsarea Philippi, runs north to Hermon, and then northeast in a straight line till it sinks down into the great plain of Emesa, not far from the site of Riblah. Hermon is the loftiest peak; the next highest is a few miles north of the site of Abila, beside the village of *Bludân*, and has an elevation of about 7000 feet. The rest of the ridge averages about 5000 feet; it is in general bleak and barren, with shelving gray declivities, gray cliffs and gray rounded summits. Here and there we meet with thin forests of dwarf oak and juniper. The western slopes descend abruptly into the *Bukâ'a;* but the features of the eastern are entirely different. Three side ridges here radiate from Hermon, like the ribs of an open fan, and form the supporting walls of three great terraces. Anti-Libanus is only once dis-

tinctly mentioned in Scripture, where it is accurately described as " Lebanon toward the sunrising." Josh. 13 : 5.

Leb'aoth (*lionesses*), a town which forms one of the last group of the cities of " the south" in the enumeration of the possessions of Judah, Josh. 15 : 32; probably identical with Beth-lebaoth.

Lebbæ'us (*a man of heart*), one name of Jude, who was one of the twelve apostles.

Lebo'nah (*frankincense*), a place named in Judges 21 : 19 only. Lebonah has survived to our times under the almost identical form of *el-Lubban*. It lies to the west of and close to the *Nablûs* road, about eight miles north of *Beitin* (Bethel) and two from *Seilun* (Shiloh).

Le'cah (*progress*), a name mentioned in the genealogies of Judah, 1 Chron. 4 : 21 only, as one of the descendants of Shelah, the third son of Judah by the Canaanitess Bath-shua.

Leech. [HORSE-LEECH.]

Common Leek.

Leeks (Heb. *châtsîr*). The leek was a bulbous vegetable resembling the onion. Its botanical name is *Allium porrum*. The Israelites in the wilderness longed for the leeks and onions of Egypt. Num. 11 : 5. The word *châtsîr*, which in Num. 11 : 5 is translated *leeks*, occurs twenty times in the Hebrew text. The Hebrew term, which properly denotes *grass*, is derived from a root signifying " to be green," and may therefore stand in this passage for any green food—lettuce, endive, etc.; it would thus be applied somewhat in the

The Mountain Range of Lebanon.

The Cedars of Lebanon.

same manner as we use the term "greens;" yet as the *châtsir* is mentioned together with onions and garlic in the text, and as the most ancient versions unanimously understand *leeks* by the Hebrew word, we may be satisfied with our own translation.

Lees, the coarser parts of a liquor, its sediment or dregs. "Wine on the lees" means a generous, full-bodied liquor. Isa. 25 : 6. Before the wine was consumed, it was necessary to strain off the lees; such wine was then termed "well refined." Isa. 25 : 6. To drink the lees, or "dregs," was an expression for the endurance of extreme punishment. Ps. 75 : 8.

Legion, the chief subdivision of the Roman army, containing about 6000 infantry, with a contingent of cavalry. The term does not occur in the Bible in its primary sense, but appears to have been adopted in order to express any large number, with the accessory ideas of order and subordination. Matt. 26 : 53; Mark 5 : 9.

Le′habim (*fiery, flaming*), occurring only in Gen. 10 : 13, the name of a Mizraite people or tribe. There can be no doubt that they are the same as the Rebu or Lebu of the Egyptian inscriptions, and that from them Libya and the Libyans derived their name. These primitive Libyans appear to have inhabited the northern part of Africa to the west of Egypt, though latterly driven from the coast by the Greek colonists of the Cyrenaica.

Le′hi (*jaw bone*), a place in Judah, probably on the confines of the Philistines' country, between it and the cliff Etam; the scene of Samson's well-known exploit with the jaw bone. Judges 15 : 9, 14, 19. It may perhaps be identified with *Beit-Likiyeh,* a village about two miles below the upper Beth-horon.

Lem′uel (*dedicated to God*), the name of an unknown king to whom his mother addressed the prudential maxims contained in Prov. 31 : 1–9. The rabbinical commentators identified Lemuel with Solomon. Others regard him as king or chief of an Arab tribe dwelling on the borders of Palestine, and elder brother of Agur, whose name stands at the head of Prov. 30.

Lentils (Heb. *'ădâshîm*), a leguminous plant bearing seeds resembling small beans. The red pottage which Jacob prepared and for which Esau sold his birthright was made from them. Gen. 25 : 34.

There are three or four kinds of lentils, all of which are much esteemed in those countries where they are grown, viz., the south of Europe, Asia and north Africa. The red lentil is still a favorite article of food in the East. Lentil bread is eaten by the poor of Egypt. The lentil

Lentils.

is much used with other pulse in Roman Catholic countries during Lent; and some are of opinion that from this usage the season derives its name.

Leopard (Heb. *nâmêr*) is invariably given by the Authorized Version as the translation of the Hebrew word, which occurs in the seven following passages: Cant. 4 : 8; Isa. 11 : 6; Jer. 5 : 6; 13 : 23; Dan. 7 : 6; Hos. 13 : 7; Hab. 1 : 8. *Leopard* occurs also in Ecclus. 28 : 23 and in Rev. 13 : 2. From Cant. 4 : 8 we learn that the hilly ranges of Lebanon were in ancient times frequented by these animals. They are now not uncommonly seen in and about Lebanon and the southern maritime mountains of Syria. Under the name *nâmêr,* which means "spotted," it is not improbable that another animal, namely the cheetah (*Gueparda jubata*), may be included; which is tamed by the Mohammedans of Syria, who employ it in hunting the gazelle.

Leper, Leprosy. The predominant and characteristic form of leprosy in the

The Syrian Leopard.

Old Testament is a white variety, covering either the entire body or a large tract of its surface, which has obtained the name of *Lepra mosaica*. Such were the cases of Moses, Miriam, Naaman and Gehazi. Ex. 4 : 6; Num. 12 : 10; 2 Kings 5 : 1, 27; comp. Lev. 13 : 13. But, remarkably enough, in the Mosaic ritual diagnosis of the disease, Lev. 13, 14, this kind, when overspreading the whole surface, appears to be regarded as "clean." Lev. 13 : 12, 13, 16, 17. The Egyptian bondage, with its studied degradations and privations, and especially the work of the kiln under an Egyptian sun, must have had a frightful tendency to generate this class of disorders. The sudden and total change of food, air, dwelling and mode of life, caused by the exodus, to this nation of newly-emancipated slaves, may possibly have had a further tendency to produce skin disorders, and severe repressive measures may have been required in the desert-moving camp to secure the public health or to allay the panic of infection. Hence it is possible that many, perhaps most, of this repertory of symptoms may have disappeared with the period of the exodus, and the snow-white form, which had pre-existed, may alone have ordinarily

Lepers Outside the Gate of Jerusalem.

continued in a later age. The principal morbid features are a rising or swelling, a scab or baldness, and a bright or white spot. Lev. 13 : 2. But especially a white swelling in the skin, with a change of the hair of the part from the natural black to white or yellow, ch. 13 : 3, 4, 10, 20, 25, 30, or an appearance of a taint going "deeper than the skin," or, again, "raw flesh" appearing in the swelling, ch. 13 : 10, 14, 15, was a critical sign of pollution. The tendency to spread seems especially to have been relied on. A spot most innocent in other respects, if it "spread much abroad," was unclean; whereas, as before remarked, the man so wholly overspread with the evil that it could find no further range was on the contrary "clean." ch. 13 : 12, 13. These two opposite criteria seem to show that whilst the disease manifested activity, the Mosaic law imputed pollution to and imposed segregation on the sufferer, but that the point at which it might be viewed as having run its course was the signal for his readmission to communion. It is clear that the leprosy of Lev. 13, 14 means any severe disease spreading on the surface of the body in the way described, and so shocking of aspect, or so generally suspected of infection, that public feeling called for separation. It is now undoubted that the "leprosy" of modern Syria, and which has a wide range in Spain, Greece and Norway, is the *Elephantiasis græcorum.* It is said to have been brought home by the crusaders into the various countries of western and northern Europe. It certainly was not the distinctive white leprosy, nor do any of the described symptoms in Lev. 13 point to elephantiasis. "White as snow," 2 Kings 5 : 27, would be as inapplicable to elephantiasis as to small-pox. There remains a curious question as regards the leprosy of garments and houses. Some have thought garments worn by leprous patients intended. This classing of garments and house-walls with the human epidermis, as leprous, has moved the mirth of some and the wonder of others. Yet modern science has established what goes far to vindicate the Mosaic classification as more philosophical than such cavils. It is now known that there are some skin diseases which originate in an acarus, and others which proceed from a fungus. In these we may probably find the solution of the paradox. The analogy be-

tween the insect which frets the human skin and that which frets the garment that covers it — between the fungous growth that lines the crevices of the epidermis and that which creeps in the interstices of masonry—is close enough for the purposes of a ceremonial law. It is manifest also that a disease in the human subject caused by an acarus or by a fungus would be certainly contagious, since the propagative cause could be transferred from person to person.

(Geikie in his "Life of Christ" says : "Leprosy signifies *smiting,* because supposed to be a direct visitation of Heaven. It began with little specks on the eyelids and on the palms of the hands, and gradually spread over different parts of the body, bleaching the hair white wherever it showed itself, crusting the affected parts with shining scales, and causing swellings and sores. From the skin it slowly ate its way through the tissues, to the bones and joints, and even to the marrow, rotting the whole body piecemeal. The lungs, the organs of speech and hearing, and the eyes, were attacked in turn, till at last consumption or dropsy brought welcome death. The dread of infection kept men aloof from the sufferer; and the law proscribed him as above all men unclean. The disease was hereditary to the fourth generation." *Leprosy in the United States.* — The *Medical Record,* February, 1881, states that from the statistics collected by the Dermatological Society it appears that there are between fifty and one hundred lepers in the United States at present. *Is modern leprosy contagious?*—Dr. H. S. Piffard of New York, in the *Medical Record,* February, 1881, decides that it is in a modified degree contagious. "A review of the evidence led to the conclusion that this disease was not contagious by ordinary contact; but it may be transmitted by the blood and secretions. A recent writer, Dr. Bross, a Jesuit missionary attached to the lazaretto at Trinidad, takes the ground that the disease in some way or other is transmissible. It is a well-established fact that when leprosy has once gained for itself a foothold in any locality; it is apt to remain there and spread. The case of the Sandwich Islands illustrates the danger. Forty years ago the disease did not exist there; now one-tenth of the inhabitants are lepers." This is further confirmed by the fact stated by Dr. J. Hutchinson, F.R.S., that "We find that nearly everywhere the disease is most common on the seashore, and that, when it spreads inland, it generally occurs on the shores of lakes or along the course of large rivers."

Leprosy as a type of sin.—"Being the worst form of disease, leprosy was fixed upon by God to be *the especial type of sin,* and the injunctions regarding it had reference to its typical character." It was (1) hereditary; (2) contagious; (3) ever tending to increase; (4) incurable except by the power of God; (5) a shame and disgrace; (6) rendering one alone in the world; (7) deforming, unclean; (8) "separating the soul from God, producing spiritual death; unfitting it forever for heaven and the company of the holy, and insuring its eternal banishment, as polluted and abominable." (9) Another point is referred to by Thomson (in "The Land and the Book"): "Some, as they look on infancy, reject with horror the thought that sin exists within. But so might any one say who looked upon the beautiful babe in the arms of a leprous mother. But time brings forth the fearful malady. New-born babes of leprous parents are often as pretty and as healthy in appearance as any; but by and by its presence and workings become visible in some of the signs described in the thirteenth chapter of Leviticus."—Ed.)

Le'shem (*precious stone*), another form of Laish, afterward Dan, occurring in Josh. 19 : 47.

Letu'shim (*hammered*), the name of the second of the sons of Dedan son of Jokshan. Gen. 25 : 3.

Leum'mim (*peoples*), the name of the third of the descendants of Dedan son of Jokshan, Gen. 25 : 3, being in the plural form, like his brethren, Asshurim and Letushim.

Le'vi (*joined*). 1. The name of the third son of Jacob by his wife Leah. (B.C. about 1753.) The name, derived from *láváh,* "to adhere," gave utterance to the hope of the mother that the affections of her husband, which had hitherto rested on the favored Rachel, would at last be drawn to her: "This time will my husband be joined unto me, because I have borne him three sons." Gen. 29 : 34. Levi, with his brother Simeon, avenged with a cruel slaughter the outrage of their sister Dinah. [DINAH.] Levi, with his three sons, Gershon, Kohath and Merari, went down to Egypt with his father Jacob. Gen. 47 · 11.

When Jacob's death draws near, and the sons are gathered round him, Levi and Simeon hear the old crime brought up again to receive its sentence. They no less than Reuben, the incestuous firstborn, had forfeited the privileges of their birthright. Gen. 49 : 5–7. [LEVITES.]

2. Two of the ancestors of Jesus. Luke 3 : 24, 29.

3. Son of Alphæus or Matthew; one of the apostles. Mark 2 : 14; Luke 5 : 27, 29. [See MATTHEW.]

Leviathan (*jointed monster*) occurs five times in the text of the Authorized Version, and once in the margin of Job 3 : 8, where the text has "mourning."

Leviathan (Crocodile).

In the Hebrew Bible the word *livyathan,* which is, with the foregoing exception, always left untranslated in the Authorized Version, is found only in the following passages: Job 3 : 8; 41 : 1; Ps. 74 : 14; 104 : 26; Isa. 27 : 1. In the margin of Job 3 : 8 and text of Job 41 : 1 the crocodile is most clearly the animal denoted by the Hebrew word. Ps. 74 : 14 also clearly points to this same saurian. The context of Ps. 104 : 26 seems to show that in this passage the name represents some animal of the whale tribe, which is common in the Mediterranean; but it is somewhat uncertain what animal is denoted in Isa. 27 : 1. As the term *leviathan* is evidently used in no limited sense, it is not improbable that the "leviathan the piercing serpent," or "leviathan the crooked serpent," may denote some species of the great rock-snakes which are common in south and west Africa.

Le'vites (*descendants of Levi*). Sometimes the name extends to the whole tribe, the priests included, Ex. 6 : 25; Lev. 25 : 32; Num. 35 : 2; Josh. 21 : 3, 41, etc.; sometimes only to those members of the tribe who were not priests, and as distinguished from them. Sometimes again it is added as an epithet of the smaller portion of the tribe, and w⌐ read of "the priests the Levites." Josh. 3 : 3 ; Ezek. 44 : 15. The history of the tribe and of the functions attached to its several orders is essential to any right apprehension of the history of Israel as a people. It will fall naturally into four great periods : —

I. *The time of the exodus.*—There is no trace of the consecrated character of the Levites till the institution of a hereditary priesthood in the family of Aaron, during the first withdrawal of Moses to the solitude of Sinai. Ex. 24 : 1. The next extension of the idea of the priesthood grew out of the terrible crisis of Ex. 32. The tribe stood forth separate and apart, recognizing even in this stern work the spiritual as higher than the natural. From this time they occupied a distinct position. The tribe of Levi was to take the place of that earlier priesthood of the first-born as representatives of the holiness of the people. At the time of their first consecration there were 22,000 of them, almost exactly the number of the first-born males in the whole nation. As the tabernacle was the sign of the presence among the people of their unseen King, so the Levites were, among the other tribes of Israel, as the royal guard that waited exclusively on him. It was obviously essential for their work as the bearers and guardians of the sacred tent that there should be a fixed assignment of duties; and now accordingly we meet with the first outlines of the organization which afterward became permanent. The division of the tribe into the three sections that traced their descent from the sons of Levi formed the groundwork of it. The work which they all had to do required a man's full strength, and therefore, though twenty was the starting-point for military service, Num. 1, they were not to enter on their active service till they were thirty. Num. 4 : 23, 30, 35. At fifty they were to be free from all duties but those of superintendence. Num. 8 : 25, 26. (1) The Kohathites, as nearest of kin to the priests, held from the first the highest offices. They were to bear all the vessels of the sanctuary, the ark itself included. Num. 3 : 31; 4 : 15; Deut. 31 : 25. (2) The Gershonites had to carry the tent-hangings and curtains. Num. 4 : 22–26. (3) The heavier burden of the boards, bars and pillars of the tabernacle

fell on the sons of Merari. The Levites were to have no territorial possessions In place of them they were to receive from the others the tithes of the produce of the land, from which they, in their turn, offered a tithe to the priests, as a recognition of their higher consecration. Num. 18 : 21, 24, 26; Neh. 10 : 37. Distinctness and diffusion were both to be secured by the assignment to the whole tribe of forty-eight cities, with an outlying "suburb," Num. 35 : 2, of meadow-land for the pasturage of their flocks and herds. The reverence of the people for them was to be heightened by the selection of six of these as cities of refuge. Through the whole land the Levites were to take the place of the old household priests, sharing in all festivals and rejoicings. Deut. 12 : 19; 14 : 26, 27; 26 : 11. Every third year they were to have an additional share in the produce of the land. Deut. 14 : 28; 26 : 12. To "the priests the Levites" was to belong the office of preserving, transcribing and interpreting the law. Deut. 17 : 9–12; 31 : 26.

II. *The period of the judges.*—The successor of Moses, though belonging to another tribe, did all that could be done to make the duty above named a reality. The submission of the Gibeonites enabled him to relieve the tribe-divisions of Gershon and Merari of the most burdensome of their duties. The conquered Hivites became "hewers of wood and drawers of water" for the house of Jehovah and for the congregation. Josh. 9 : 27. As soon as the conquerors had advanced far enough to proceed to a partition of the country, the forty-eight cities were assigned to them.

III. *The monarchy.* — When David's kingdom was established, there came a fuller organization of the whole tribe. Their position in relation to the priesthood was once again definitely recognized. In the worship of the tabernacle under David, as afterward in that of the temple, the Levites were the gatekeepers, vergers, sacristans, choristers, of the central sanctuary of the nation. They were, in the language of 1 Chron. 23 : 24–32, to which we may refer as almost the *locus classicus* on this subject, "to wait on the sons of Aaron for the service of the house of Jehovah, in the courts, and the chambers, and the purifying of all holy things." They were, besides this, "to stand every morning to thank and praise Jehovah, and likewise at even." They were, lastly, "to offer"—*i. e.* to assist the priest in offering—"all burnt sacrifices to Jehovah in the sabbaths and on the set feasts." They lived for the greater part of the year in their own cities, and came up at fixed periods to take their turn of work. 1 Chron. 25, 26. The educational work which the Levites received for their peculiar duties, no less than their connection, more or less intimate, with the schools of the prophets, would tend to make them the teachers of the others, the transcribers and interpreters of the law, the chroniclers of the times in which they lived. (Thus they became to the Israelites what ministers and teachers are to the people now, and this teaching and training the people in morality and religion was no doubt one of the chief reasons why they were set apart by God from the people, and yet among the people.—ED.) The revolt of the ten tribes, and the policy pursued by Jeroboam, who wished to make the priests the creatures and instruments of the king, and to establish a provincial and divided worship, caused them to leave the cities assigned to them in the territory of Israel, and gather round the metropolis of Judah. 2 Chron. 11 : 13, 14. In the kingdom of Judah they were, from this time forward, a powerful body, politically as well as ecclesiastically.

IV. *After the captivity.* — During the period that followed the captivity the Levites contributed to the formation of the so-called Great Synagogue. They, with the priests, formed the majority of the permanent Sanhedrin, and as such had a large share in the administration of justice even in capital cases. They appear but seldom in the history of the New Testament.

Levit'icus. The third book in the Pentateuch is called Leviticus because it relates principally to the Levites and priests and their services. The book is generally held to have been written by Moses. Those critics even who hold a different opinion as to the other books of the Pentateuch assign this book in the main to him. One of the most notable features of the book is what may be called its spiritual meaning. That so elaborate a ritual looked beyond itself we cannot doubt. It was a prophecy of things to come; a shadow whereof the substance was Christ and his kingdom. We may not always be able to say what the exact relation is between the type and the anti-

type; but we cannot read the Epistle to the Hebrews and not acknowledge that the Levitical priests "served the pattern and type of heavenly things;" that the sacrifices of the law pointed to and found their interpretation in the Lamb of God; that the ordinances of outward purification signified the true inner cleansing of the heart and conscience from dead works to serve the living God. One idea—HOLINESS—moreover penetrates the whole of this vast and burdensome ceremonial, and gives it a real glory even apart from any prophetic significance.

Lib'anus. [LEBANON.]

Lib'ertines. This word, which occurs once only in the New Testament—Acts 6 : 9—is the Latin *libertini,* that is, "freedmen." They were probably Jews who, having been taken prisoners by Pompey and other Roman generals in the Syrian wars, had been reduced to slavery, and had afterward been emancipated, and returned, permanently or for a time, to the country of their fathers.

Lib'nah (*whiteness*). 1. A royal city of the Canaanites which lay in the southwest part of the Holy Land, taken by Joshua immediately after the rout of Beth-horon. It was near Lachish, west of Makkedah. It was appropriated with its "suburbs" to the priests. Josh. 21 : 13; 1 Chron. 6 : 57. In the reign of Jehoram the son of Jehoshaphat it "revolted" from Judah at the same time with Edom. 2 Kings 8 : 22; 2 Chron. 21 : 10. Probably the modern *Ayak el-Menshiyeh.* 2. One of the stations at which the Israelites encamped on their journey between the wilderness of Sinai and Kadesh. Num. 33 : 20, 21.

Lib'ni (*white*). 1. The eldest son of Gershon the son of Levi, Ex. 6 : 17; Num. 3 : 18; 1 Chron. 6 : 17, 20, and ancestor of the family of the Libnites. (B.C. after 1700.) 2. The son of Mahli or Mahali, son of Merari, 1 Chron. 6 : 29, as the text at present stands. It is probable, however, that he is the same with the preceding, and that something has been omitted. Comp. ver. 29 with 20, 42.

Lib'ya. This name occurs only in Acts 2 : 10. It is applied by the Greek and Roman writers to the African continent, generally, however, excluding Egypt.

Lice (Heb. *cinnâm, cinnim*). This word occurs in the Authorized Version only in Ex. 8 : 16–18 and in Ps. 105 : 31, both of which passages have reference to the third great plague of Egypt. The Hebrew word has given occasion to whole pages of discussion. Some commentators, and indeed modern writers generally, suppose that gnats are the animals intended by the original word; while, on the other hand, the Jewish rabbis, Josephus and others, are in favor of the translation of the Authorized Version. Upon the whole it appears that there is not sufficient authority for departing from this translation. Late travellers (*e. g.* Sir Samuel Baker) describe the visitation of vermin in very similar terms:—"It is as though the very dust were turned into lice." The lice which he describes are a sort of tick, not larger than a grain of sand, which when filled with blood expand to the size of a hazel nut.—*Canon Cook.*

Lieutenants. The Hebrew *achash darpan* was the official title of the satraps or viceroys who governed the provinces of the Persian empire; it is rendered "prince" in Dan. 3 : 2 ; 6 : 1.

Lign aloes. [ALOES.]

Ligure (Heb. *leshem*), a precious stone mentioned in Ex. 28 : 19 ; 39 : 12 as the first in the third row of the high priest's breastplate. It is impossible to say, with any certainty, what stone is denoted by the Hebrew term; but perhaps *tourmaline*, or more definitely the red variety known as *rubellite*, has better claims than any other mineral. Rubellite is a hard stone, and used as a gem, and is sometimes sold for red sapphire.

Lik′hi (*learned*), a Manassite, son of Shemidah the son of Manasseh. 1 Chron. 7 : 19.

Lily (Heb. *shûshân, shôshannâh*). Although there is little doubt that the Hebrew word denotes some plant of the lily species, it is by no means certain what individual of this class it specially designates. The plant must have been a conspicuous object on the shores of the Lake of Gennesaret, Matt. 6 : 28 ; Luke 12 : 27 ; it must have flourished in the deep broad valleys of Palestine, Cant. 2 : 1, among the thorny shrubs, *ib.* 2 : 2, and pastures of the desert, *ib.* 2 : 16 ; 4 : 5 ; 6 : 3 ; and must have been remarkable for its rapid and luxuriant growth. Hos. 14 : 5 ; Ecclus. 39 : 14. That its flowers were brilliant in color would seem to be indicated in Matt. 6 : 28, where it is compared with the gorgeous robes of Solomon; and that this color was scarlet or

purple is implied in Cant. 5 : 13. There appears to be no species of lily which so completely answers all these require-

Scarlet Lily.

ments as the *Lilium chalcedonicum*, or scarlet martagon, which grows in profusion in the Levant. But direct evidence

Lily of Palestine.

on the point is still to be desired from the observation of travellers. (It is very probable that the term *lily* here is general, not referring to any particular species, but to a large class of flowers growing in Palestine, and resembling the lily, as the tulip, iris, gladiolus, etc.—ED.)

Lime, the substance obtained from limestone, shells, etc., by heat. It is noticed only three times in the Bible, viz., in Deut. 27 : 2 (Authorized Version "plaster"), Isa. 33 : 12, and Amos 2 : 1.

Linen, cloth made from flax. Several different Hebrew words are rendered linen, which may denote different fabrics of linen or different modes of manufacture. Egypt was the great centre of the linen trade. Some linen, made from the Egyptian *byssus*, a flax that grew on the banks of the Nile, was exceedingly soft and of dazzling whiteness. This linen has been sold for twice its weight in gold. Sir J. G. Wilkinson says of it, "The quality of the fine linen fully justifies all the praises of antiquity, and excites equal admiration at the present day, being to the touch comparable to silk, and not inferior in texture to our finest cambric."

Lintel, the beam which forms the upper part of the framework of a door.

Li'nus (*a net*), a Christian at Rome, known to St. Paul and to Timothy, 2 Tim. 4 : 21, who was the first bishop of Rome after the apostles. (A.D. 64.)

Lion. "The most powerful, daring and impressive of all carnivorous animals, the most magnificent in aspect and awful in voice." At present lions do not exist in Palestine; but they must in ancient times have been numerous. The lion of Palestine was in all probability the Asiatic variety, described by Aristotle and Pliny as distinguished by its short curly mane, and by being shorter and rounder in shape, like the sculptured lion found at Arban. It was less daring than the longer named species, but when driven by hunger it not only ventured to attack the flocks in the desert in presence of the shepherd, 1 Sam. 17 : 34 ; Isa. 31 : 4, but laid waste towns and villages, 2 Kings 17 : 25, 26 ; Prov. 22 : 13 ; 26 : 13, and devoured men. 1 Kings 13 : 24 ; 20 : 36. Among the Hebrews, and throughout the Old Testament, the lion was the achievement of the princely tribe of Judah, while in the closing book of the canon it received a deeper significance as the emblem of him who "prevailed to

open the book and loose the seven seals thereof." Rev. 5 : 5. On the other hand its fierceness and cruelty rendered it an appropriate metaphor for a fierce and

The Syrian Lion.

malignant enemy, Ps. 7 : 2; 22 : 21; 57 : 4; 2 Tim. 4 : 17, and hence for the arch-fiend himself. 1 Peter 5 : 8.

Lizard (*that which clings to the ground*) (Heb. *letââh*. Lev. 11 : 30). Lizards of various kinds abound in Egypt, Palestine and Arabia. The lizard de-

Lizard.

noted by the Hebrew word is probably the fan-foot lizard (*Ptyodactylus gecko*), which is common in Egypt and in parts of Arabia, and perhaps is found also in Palestine. It is reddish brown spotted with white. The gecko lives on insects and worms, which it swallows whole. It derives its name from the peculiar sound which some of the species utter.

Lo-am'mi (*not my people*), the figurative name given by the prophet Hosea to his second son by Gomer the daughter of Diblaim, Hos. 1 : 9, to denote the rejection of the kingdom of Israel by Jehovah. Its significance is explained in vs. 9, 10.

Loan. The law strictly forbade any interest to be taken for a loan to any poor person, and at first, as it seems, even in the case of a foreigner; but this prohibition was afterward limited to Hebrews only, from whom, of whatever rank, not only was no usury on any pretence to be exacted, but relief to the poor by way of loan was enjoined, and excuses for evading this duty were forbidden. Ex. 22 : 25; Lev. 25 : 35, 37. As commerce increased, the practice of usury, and so also of suretyship, grew up; but the exaction of it from a Hebrew appears to have been regarded to a late period as discreditable. Ps. 15 : 5; Prov. 6 : 1, 4; 11 : 15; 17 : 18; 20 : 16; 22 : 26; Jer. 15 : 10; Ezek. 18 : 13. Systematic breach of the law in this respect was corrected by Nehemiah after the return from captivity. Neh. 5 : 1, 13. The money-changers, who had seats and tables in the temple, were traders whose profits arose chiefly from the exchange of money with those who came to pay their annual half-shekel. The Jewish law did not forbid temporary bondage in the case of debtors, but it forbade a Hebrew debtor to be detained as a bondman longer than the seventh year, or at farthest the year of jubilee. Ex. 21 : 2; Lev. 25 : 39, 42; Deut. 15 : 9.

Loaves. [BREAD.]

Lock. Where European locks have not been introduced, the locks of eastern houses are usually of wood, and consist of a partly hollow bolt from fourteen inches to two feet long for external doors or gates, or from seven to nine inches for interior doors. The bolt passes through a groove in a piece attached to the door into a socket in the door-post.

Locust, a well-known insect, of the grasshopper family, which commits terrible ravages on vegetation in the countries which it visits. "The common brown locust is about three inches in length, and the general form is that of a grasshopper." The most destructive of the locust tribe that occur in the Bible lands are the *Œdipoda migratoria* and the *Acridium peregrinum;* and as both

these species occur in Syria and Arabia, etc., it is most probable that one or other is denoted in those passages which speak of the dreadful devastations committed by these insects. Locusts occur in great numbers, and sometimes obscure the sun. Ex. 10 : 15; Judges 6 : 5; Jer. 46 : 23.

Locusts.

Their voracity is alluded to in Ex. 10 : 12, 15; Joel 1 : 4, 7. They make a fearful noise in their flight. Joel 2 : 5; Rev. 9 : 9. Their irresistible progress is referred to in Joel 2 : 8, 9. They enter dwellings, and devour even the woodwork of houses. Ex. 10 : 6; Joel 2 : 9, 10. They

Locust Flying.

do not fly in the night. Nah. 3 : 17. The sea destroys the greater number. Ex. 10 : 19; Joel 2 : 20. The flight of locusts is thus described by M. Olivier (*Voyage dans l' Empire Othoman*, ii. 424): "With the burning south winds (of Syria) there come from the interior of Arabia and from the most southern parts of Persia clouds of locusts (*Acridium peregrinum*), whose ravages to these countries are as grievous and nearly as sudden as those of the heaviest hail in Europe. We witnessed them twice. It is difficult to express the effect produced on us by the sight of the whole atmosphere filled on all sides and to a great height by an innumerable quantity of these insects, whose flight was slow and uniform, and whose noise resembled that of rain: the sky was darkened, and the light of the sun considerably weakened. In a moment the terraces of the houses, the streets, and all the fields were covered by these insects, and in two days they had nearly devoured all the leaves of the plants. Happily they lived but a short time, and seemed to have migrated only to reproduce themselves and die; in fact, nearly all those we saw the next day had paired, and the day following the fields were covered with their dead bodies." "Locusts have been used as food from the earliest times. Herodotus speaks of a Libyan nation who dried their locusts in the sun and ate them with milk. The more common method, however, was to pull off the legs and wings and roast them in an iron dish. Then they were thrown into a bag, and eaten like parched corn, each one taking a handful when he chose."—*Biblical Treasury.* Sometimes the insects are ground and pounded, and then mixed with flour and water and made into cakes, or they are salted and then eaten; sometimes smoked; sometimes boiled or roasted; again, stewed, or fried in butter.

Lod. [LYDDA.]

Lo-de′bar (*without pasture*), a place named with Mahanaim, Rogelim and other transjordanic towns, 2 Sam. 17 : 27, and therefore no doubt on the east side of the Jordan. It was the native place of Machir-ben-Ammiel. 2 Sam. 9 : 4, 5.

Lodge, To. This word, with one exception only, has, at least in the narrative portions of the Bible, almost invariably the force of "passing the night."

Log. [WEIGHTS AND MEASURES.]

Lo′is (*agreeable*), the grandmother of Timothy, and doubtless the mother of his mother, Eunice. 2 Tim. 1 : 5. It seems likely that Lois had resided long at Lystra; and almost certain that from her, as well as from Eunice, Timothy obtained his intimate knowledge of the Jewish Scriptures. 2 Tim. 3 : 15. (A.D. before 64.)

Looking-glasses. [MIRRORS.]

Lord. [GOD.]

Lord's day, The (ἡ Κυριακὴ Ἡμέρα, Rev. 1 : 10 only), the weekly festival of our Lord's resurrection, and identified with "the first day of the week," or "Sunday," of every age of the Church. Scripture says very little concerning this day; but that little seems to indicate that the divinely-inspired apostles, by their practice and by their precepts, marked the first day of the week as a day for meeting together to break bread, for communicating and receiving instruction, for laying up offerings in store for charitable purposes, for occupation in holy thought and prayer. [See SABBATH.]

Lord's Prayer, the prayer which Jesus taught his disciples. Matt. 6 : 9–13; Luke 11 : 2–4. "In this prayer our Lord shows his disciples how an infinite variety of wants and requests can be compressed into a few humble petitions. It embodies every possible desire of a praying heart, a whole world of spiritual requirements; yet all in the most simple, condensed and humble form, resembling, in this respect, a pearl on which the light of heaven plays."—*Lange.* "This prayer contains four great general sentiments, which constitute the very soul of religion,—sentiments which are the germs of all holy deeds in all worlds. (1) *Filial reverence:* God is addressed not as the great unknown, not as the unsearchable governor, but as a father, the most intelligible, attractive and transforming name. It is a form of address almost unknown to the old covenant, now and then hinted at as reminding the children of their rebellion, Isa. 1 : 2; Mal. 1 : 6, or mentioned as a last resource of the orphan and desolate creature, Isa. 63 : 16; but never brought out in its fullness, as indeed it could not be, till he was come by whom we have received the adoption of sons." —*Alford.* (2) "*Divine loyalty:* 'Thy kingdom come.' (3) *Conscious dependence:* 'Give us this day,' etc. (4) *Unbounded confidence:* 'For thine is the power,' etc."—*Dr. Thomas' Genius of the Gospels.* The doxology, "For thine is the kingdom," etc., is wanting in many manuscripts. It is omitted in the Revised Version; but it nevertheless has the authority of some manuscripts, and is truly biblical, almost every word being found in 1 Chron. 29 : 11, and is a true and fitting ending for prayer.

Lord's Supper. The words which thus describe the great central act of the worship of the Christian Church occur but in a single passage of the New Testament—1 Cor. 11 : 20. 1. *Its institution.* —It was instituted on that night when Jesus and his disciples met together to eat the passover, Matt. 26 : 19; Mark 14 : 16; Luke 22 : 13 (on Thursday evening, April 6, A.D. 30). It was probably instituted at the *third cup* (the cup of blessing) of the passover [see on PASSOVER], Jesus taking one of the unleavened cakes used at that feast and breaking it and giving it to his disciples with the cup. The narratives of the Gospels show how strongly the disciples were impressed with the words which had given a new meaning to the old familiar acts. They had looked on the bread and the wine as memorials of the deliverance from Egypt. They were now told to partake of them "in remembrance" of their Master and Lord. The words "This is my body" gave to the unleavened bread a new character. They had been prepared for language that would otherwise have been so startling, by the teaching of John, ch. 6 : 32-58, and they were thus taught to see in the bread that was broken the witness of the closest possible union and incorporation with their Lord. The cup, which was "the new testament in his blood," would remind them, in like manner, of the wonderful prophecy in which that new covenant had been foretold. Jer. 31 : 31-34. "Gradually and progressively he had prepared the minds of his disciples to realize the idea of his death as a sacrifice. He now gathers up all previous announcements in the institution of this sacrament."—*Cambridge Bible.* The festival had been annual. No rule was given as to the time and frequency of the new feast that thus supervened on the old, but the command " Do this as oft as ye drink it," 1 Cor. 11 : 25, suggested the more continual recurrence of that which was to be their memorial of one whom they would wish never to forget. Luke, in the Acts, describes the baptized members of the Church as continuing steadfast in or to the teaching of the apostles, in fellowship with them and with each other, and *in breaking of bread* and in prayers. Acts 2 : 42. We can scarcely doubt that this implies that the chief actual meal of each day was one in which they met as brothers, and which was either preceded or followed by the more solemn commemorative acts of the breaking of the bread and the drinking of the cup. It will be convenient to anticipate the language and the thoughts of a somewhat later date, and to say that, apparently, they thus united every day the Agapè or feast of love with the celebration of the Eucharist. At some time, before or after the meal of which they partook as such, the bread and the wine would be given with some special form of words or acts, to indicate its character. New converts would need some explanation of the meaning and origin of the observance. What would be so fitting and so much in harmony with the precedents of the paschal feast as the narrative of what had passed on the night of its institution? 1 Cor. 11 : 23-27.

2. *Its significance.*—The Lord's Supper is a reminder of the leading truths of the gospel : (1) Salvation, like this bread, is the gift of God's love. (2) We are reminded of the life of Christ—all he was and did and said. (3) We are reminded, as by the passover, of the grievous bondage of sin from which Christ redeems us. (4) It holds up the atonement, the body of Christ broken, his blood shed, for us. (5) In Christ alone is forgiveness and salvation from sin, the first need of the soul. (6) Christ is the food of the soul. (7) We must partake by faith, or it will be of no avail. (8) We are taught to distribute to one another the spiritual blessings God gives us. (9) By this meal our daily bread is sanctified. (10) The most intimate communion with God in Christ. (11) Communion with one another. (12) It is a feast of joy. "Nothing less than the actual joy of heaven is above it." (13) It is a prophecy of Christ's second coming, of the perfect triumph of his kingdom. (14) It is holding up before the world the cross of Christ ; not a selfish gathering of a few saints, but a proclamation of the Saviour for all. Why did Christ ordain *bread* to be used in the Lord's Supper, and not a *lamb?* Canon Walsham How replies, "Because the types and shadows were to cease when the real Sacrifice was come. There was to be no more shedding of blood when once his all-prevailing blood was shed. There must be nothing which might cast a doubt upon the all-sufficiency of *that.*" (Then, the Lamb being sacrificed once for all, what is needed is to teach the world

that Christ is now the bread of life. Perhaps also it was because bread was more easily provided, and fitted thus more easily to be a part of a universal ordinance.—ED.)

3. *Was it a permanent ordinance?*— " 'Do this in remembrance of me' points to a permanent institution. The command is therefore binding on all who believe in Christ; and disobedience to it is sin, for the unbelief that keeps men away is one of the worst of sins."—*Prof. Riddle.* "The subsequent practice of the apostles, Acts 2 : 42, 46; 20 : 7, and still more the fact that directions for the Lord's Supper were made a matter of special revelation to Paul, 1 Cor. 11 : 23, seem to make it clear that Christ intended the ordinance for a perpetual one, and that his apostles so understood it."—*Abbott.*

4. *Method of observance.*—" The original supper was taken in a private house, an upper chamber, at night, around a table, reclining, women excluded, only the ordained apostles admitted. None of these conditions are maintained to-day by any Christian sect." But it must be kept with the same spirit and purpose now as then.

Lo-ru-ha'mah (*the uncompassionated*), the name of the daughter of Hosea the prophet, given to denote the utterly ruined condition of the kingdom of Israel. Hos. 1 : 6.

Lot (*veil* or *covering*), the son of Haran, and therefore the nephew of Abraham. Gen. 11 : 27, 31. (B.C. before 1926–1898.) His sisters were Milcah the wife of Nahor, and Iscah, by some identified with Sarah. Haran died before the emigration of Terah and his family from Ur of the Chaldees, ver. 28, and Lot was therefore born there. He removed with the rest of his kindred to Charran, and again subsequently with Abraham and Sarai to Canaan. ch. 12 : 4, 5. With them he took refuge in Egypt from a famine, and with them returned, first to the " south," ch. 13 : 1, and then to their original settlement between Bethel and Ai. vs. 3, 4. But the pastures of the hills of Bethel, which had with ease contained the two strangers on their first arrival, were not able any longer to bear them, so much had their possessions of sheep, goats and cattle increased. Accordingly they separated, Lot choosing the fertile plain of the Jordan, and advancing as far as Sodom. Gen. 13 : 10-14. The next occurrence

in the life of Lot is his capture by the four kings of the east and his rescue by Abram. ch. 14. The last scene preserved to us in the history of Lot is too well known to need repetition. He was still living in Sodom, Gen. 19, from which he was rescued by some angels on the day of its final overthrow. He fled first to Zoar, in which he found a temporary refuge during the destruction of the other cities of the plain. Where this place was situated is not known with certainty. [ZOAR.] The end of Lot's wife is commonly treated as one of the difficulties of the Bible; but it surely need not be so. It cannot be necessary to create the details of the story where none are given. On these points the record is silent. The value and the significance of the story to us are contained in the allusion of Christ. Luke 17 : 32. Later ages have not been satisfied so to leave the matter, but have insisted on identifying the " pillar " with some one of the fleeting forms which the perishable rock of the south end of the Dead Sea is constantly assuming in its process of decomposition and liquefaction. From the incestuous intercourse between Lot and his two daughters sprang the nations of Moab and Ammon.

Lot (literally *a pebble*). The custom of deciding doubtful questions by lot is one of great extent and high antiquity. Among the Jews lots were used with the expectation that God would so control them as to give a right direction to them. They were very often used by God's appointment. " As to the mode of casting lots, we have no certain information. Probably several modes were practiced." " Very commonly among the Latins little counters of wood were put into a jar with so narrow a neck that only one could come out at a time. After the jar had been filled with water and the contents shaken, the lots were determined by the order in which the bits of wood, representing the several parties, came out with the water. In other cases they were put into a wide open jar, and the counters were drawn out by the hand. Sometimes again they were cast in the manner of dice. The soldiers who cast lots for Christ's garments undoubtedly used these dice."—*Lyman Abbott.*

Lo'tan (*covering*), the eldest son of Seir the Horite. Gen. 36 : 20, 22, 29; 1 Chron. 1 : 38, 39.

Lots, Feast of. [PURIM.]

Love feasts (*Agapē*), 2 Pet. 2 : 13;

Jude 12, an entertainment in which the poorer members of the church partook, furnished from the contributions of Christians resorting to the eucharistic celebration, but whether before or after may be doubted. The true account of the matter is probably that given by Chrysostom, who says that after the early community of goods had ceased the richer members brought to the church contributions of food and drink, of which, after the conclusion of the services and the celebration of the Lord's Supper, all partook together, by this means helping to promote the principle of love among Christians. The intimate connection, especially in early times, between the Eucharist itself and the love feasts has led some to speak of them as identical. The love feasts were forbidden to be held in churches by the Council of Laodicea, A.D. 320; but in some form or other they continued to a much later period.

Lu'bim (*dwellers in a thirsty land*), a nation mentioned as contributing, together with Cushites and Sukkiim, to Shishak's army, 2 Chron. 12:3; and apparently as forming with Cushites the bulk of Zerah's army, 2 Chron. 16:8, spoken of by Nahum, ch. 3:9, with Put or Phut, as helping No-amon (Thebes), of which Cush and Egypt were the strength. Upon the Egyptian monuments we find representations of a people called Rebu or Lebu, who correspond to the Lubim, and who may be placed on the African coast to the westward of Egypt, perhaps extending far beyond the Cyrenaica.

Lu'cas. Phil. 24. [LUKE.]

Lu'cifer (*light-bearer*), found in Isa. 14:12, coupled with the epithet " son of the morning," clearly signifies a " bright star," and probably what we call the morning star. In this passage it is a symbolical representation of the king of Babylon in his splendor and in his fall. Its application, from St. Jerome downward, to Satan in his fall from heaven arises probably from the fact that the Babylonian empire is in Scripture represented as the type of tyrannical and self-idolizing power, and especially connected with the empire of the Evil One in the Apocalypse.

Lu'cius. 1. A kinsman or fellow tribesman of St. Paul, Rom. 16:21, by whom he is said by tradition to have been ordained bishop of the church of Cenchreæ. He is thought by some to be the same with Lucius of Cyrene.

2. Lucius of Cyrene is first mentioned in the New Testament in company with Barnabas, Simeon called Niger, Manaen and Saul, who are described as prophets and teachers of the church at Antioch. Acts 13:1. Whether Lucius was one of the seventy disciples is quite a matter of conjecture; but it is highly probable that he formed one of the congregation to whom St. Peter preached on the day of Pentecost, Acts 2:10; and there can hardly be a doubt that he was one of " the men of Cyrene" who, being "scattered abroad upon the persecution that arose about Stephen," went to Antioch preaching the Lord Jesus. Acts 11:19, 20.

Lud (*strife*), the fourth name in the list of the children of Shem, Gen. 10:22; comp. 1 Chron. 1:17, supposed to have been the ancestor of the Lydians.

Lu'dim (*strife*), Gen. 10:13; 1 Chron. 1:11, a Mizraite people or tribe, descended from Ludim the son of Mizraim; also called Lydians. It is probable that the Ludim were settled to the west of Egypt, perhaps farther than any other Mizraite tribe. Lud and the Ludim are mentioned in four passages of the prophets—Isa. 66:19; Jer. 46:9; Ezek. 27:10; 38:5. There can be no doubt that but one nation is intended in these passages, and it seems that the preponderance of evidence is in favor of the Mizraite Ludim.

Lu'hith (*made of tables or boards*), **The ascent of,** a place in Moab, occurs only in Isa. 15:5 and the parallel passage of Jeremiah. Jer. 48:5. In the days of Eusebius and Jerome it was still known, and stood between Areopolis (Rabbath-moab) and Zoar.

Luke (*light-giving*), or **Lu'cas,** is an abbreviated form of Lucanus. It is not to be confounded with Lucius, Acts 13:1; Rom. 16:21, which belongs to a different person. The name Luke occurs three times in the New Testament—Col. 4:14; 2 Tim. 4:11; Phil. 24—and probably in all three the third evangelist is the person spoken of. Combining the traditional element with the scriptural, we are able to trace the following dim outline of the evangelist's life: He was born at Antioch in Syria, and was taught the science of medicine. The well-known tradition that Luke was also a painter, and of no mean skill, rests on the authority of late writers. He was not born a Jew, for he is not reckoned among those "of the circumcision" by St. Paul. Comp. Col. 4 : 11 with ver. 14. The date of his conversion is uncertain. He joined St. Paul at Troas, and shared his journey into Macedonia. The sudden transition to the first person plural in Acts 16 : 9 is most naturally explained, after all the objections that have been urged, by supposing that Luke, the writer of the Acts, formed one of St. Paul's company from this point. As far as Philippi the evangelist journeyed with the apostle. The resumption of the third person on Paul's departure from that place, Acts 17 : 1, would show that Luke was now left behind. During the rest of St. Paul's second missionary journey we hear of Luke no more; but on the third journey the same indication reminds us that Luke is again of the company, Acts 20 : 5, having joined it apparently at Philippi, where he had been left. With the apostle he passed through Miletus, Tyre and Cæsarea to Jerusalem. ch. 20 : 5; 21 : 18. As to his age and death there is the utmost uncertainty. He probably died a martyr, between A.D. 75 and A.D. 100. He wrote the Gospel that bears his name, and also the book of Acts.

Luke, Gospel of. The third Gospel is ascribed, by the general consent of ancient Christendom, to "the beloved physician," Luke, the friend and companion of the apostle Paul. 1. *Date of the Gospel of Luke.*—From Acts 1 : 1 it is clear that the Gospel described as "the former treatise" was written before the Acts of the Apostles; but how much earlier is uncertain. Perhaps it was written at Cæsarea during St. Paul's imprisonment there, A.D. 58–60. 2. *Place where the Gospel was written.*—If the time has been rightly indicated, the place would be Cæsarea. 3. *Origin of the Gospel.*—The preface, contained in the first four verses of the Gospel, describes the object of its writer. Here are several facts to be observed. There were many narratives of the life of our Lord current at the early time when Luke wrote his Gospel. The ground of fitness for the task St. Luke places in his having carefully followed out the whole course of events from the beginning. He does not claim the character of an eye-witness from the first; but possibly he may have been a witness of some part of our Lord's doings. The ancient opinion that Luke wrote his Gospel under the influence of Paul rests on the authority of Irenæus, Tertullian, Origen

and Eusebius. The four verses could not have been put at the head of a history composed under the exclusive guidance of Paul or of any one apostle, and as little could they have introduced a gospel simply communicated by another. The truth seems to be that St. Luke, seeking information from every quarter, sought it from the preaching of his beloved master, St. Paul; and the apostle in his turn employed the knowledge acquired from other sources by his disciple. 4. *Purpose for which the Gospel was written.*—The evangelist professes to write that Theophilus "might know the certainty of those things wherein he had been instructed." ch. 1 : 4. This Theophilus was probably a native of Italy, and perhaps an inhabitant of Rome, for in tracing St. Paul's journey to Rome, places which an Italian might be supposed not to know are described minutely, Acts 27 : 8, 12, 16 ; but when he comes to Sicily and Italy this is neglected. Hence it would appear that the person for whom Luke wrote in the first instance was a Gentile reader; and accordingly we find traces in the Gospel of a leaning toward Gentile rather than Jewish converts. 5. *Language and style of the Gospel.*—It has never been doubted that the Gospel was written in Greek. Whilst Hebraisms are frequent, classical idioms and Greek compound words abound, for which there is classical authority. (Prof. Gregory, in "Why Four Gospels," says that Luke wrote for Greek readers, and therefore the character and needs of the Greeks furnish the key to this Gospel. The Greek was the representation of reason and humanity. He looked upon himself as having the mission of perfecting man. He was intellectual, cultured, not without hope of a higher world. Luke's Gospel therefore presented the character and career of Christ as answering the conception of a perfect and divine humanity. Reason, beauty, righteousness and truth are exhibited as they meet in Jesus in their full splendor. Jesus was the Saviour of all men, redeeming them to a perfect and cultured manhood.—ED.)

Lunatics (from the Latin *Luna,* the moon, because insane persons, especially those who had lucid intervals, were once supposed to be affected by the changes of the moon). This word is used twice in the New Testament—Matt. 4 : 24; 17 : 15. (Translated *epileptic* in the Revised

Version.) It is evident that the word itself refers to some disease affecting both the body and the mind, which might or might not be a sign of possession. By the description of Mark 9 : 17-26 it is concluded that this disease was epilepsy.

Luz (*almond tree*). It seems impossible to discover with precision whether Luz and Bethel represent one and the same town—the former the Canaanite, the latter the Hebrew, name—or whether they were distinct places, though in close proximity. The most probable conclusion is that the two places were, during the times preceding the conquest, distinct, Luz being the city and Bethel the pillar and altar of Jacob ; that after the destruction of Luz by the tribe of Ephraim the town of Bethel arose. When the original Luz was destroyed, through the treachery of one of its inhabitants, the man who had introduced the Israelites into the town went into the " land of the Hittites " and built a city, which he named after the former one. Judges 1 : 26. Its situation, as well as that of the " land of the Hittites," has never been discovered, and is one of the favorite puzzles of Scripture geographers.

Lycao'nia (*land of Lycanon*, or *wolfland*), a district of Asia Minor. From what is said in Acts 14 : 11 of " the speech of Lycaonia," it is evident that the inhabitants of the district, in St. Paul's day, spoke something very different from ordinary Greek. Whether this language was some Syrian dialect or a corrupt form of Greek has been much debated. The fact that the Lycaonians were familiar with the Greek mythology is consistent with either supposition. Lycaonia is for the most part a dreary plain, bare of trees, destitute of fresh water, and with several salt lakes. (It was about 20 miles long from east to west, and 13 miles wide. " Cappadocia is on the east, Galatia on the north, Phrygia on the west and Cilicia on the south." Among its chief cities are Derbe, Lystra and Iconium.— ED.) After the provincial system of Rome had embraced the whole of Asia Minor, the boundaries of the provinces were variable ; and Lycaonia was, politically, sometimes in Cappadocia, sometimes in Galatia. Paul visited it three times in his missionary tours.

Lyc'ia (*land of Lycus*) is the name of that southwestern region of the peninsula of Asia Minor which is immediately opposite the island of Rhodes. The Lyc-

ians were incorporated in the Persian empire, and their ships were conspicuous in the great war against the Greeks (Herod. vii. 91, 92). After the death of Alexander the Great, Lycia was included in the Greek Seleucid kingdom, and was a part of the territory which the Romans forced Antiochus to cede. It was not till the reign of Claudius that Lycia became part of the Roman provincial system. At first it was combined with Pamphylia. Such seems to have been the condition of the district when St. Paul visited the Lycian towns of Patara, Acts 21 : 1, and Myra. Acts 27 : 5. At a later period of the Roman empire Lycia was a separate province, with Myra for its capital.

Lyd'da (*strife*), the Greek form of the name, Acts 9 : 32, 35, 38, which appears in the Hebrew records as LOD, a town of Benjamin, founded by Shamed or Shamer. 1 Chron. 8 : 12 ; Ezra 2 : 33 ; Neh. 7 : 37 ; 11 : 35. It is still called *Lidd* or *Lûdd*, and stands in part of the great maritime plain which anciently bore the name of Sharon. It is nine miles from Joppa, and is the first town on the northernmost of the two roads between that place and Jerusalem. The watercourse outside the town is said still to bear the name of *Abi-Butrus* (Peter), in memory of the apostle. It was destroyed by Vespasian, and was probably not rebuilt till the time of Hadrian, when it received the name of Diospolis. When Eusebius wrote (A.D. 320-330) Diospolis was a well-known and much-frequented town. The modern town is, for a Mohammedan place, busy and prosperous.

Lyd'ia (*land of Lydus*), a maritime province in the west of Asia Minor, bounded by Mysia on the north, Phrygia on the east, and Caria on the south. It is enumerated among the districts which the Romans took away from Antiochus the Great after the battle of Magnesia in B.C. 190, and transferred to Eumenus II. king of Pergamus. Lydia is included in the " Asia " of the New Testament.

Lyd'ia, the first European convert of St. Paul, and afterward his hostess during his first stay at Philippi. Acts 16 : 14, 15 ; also 40. (A.D. 47.) She was a Jewish proselyte at the time of the apostle's coming ; and it was at the Jewish Sabbath-worship by the side of a stream, ver. 13, that the preaching of the gospel reached her heart. Her native place was Thyatira, in the province of Asia.

ver. 14; Rev. 2 : 18. Thyatira was famous for its dyeing works; and Lydia was connected with this trade, as a seller either of dye or of dyed goods. We infer that she was a person of considerable wealth.

Lysa'nias (*that drives away sorrow*), mentioned by St. Luke in one of his chronological passages, ch. 3 : 1, as being tetrarch of Abilene (*i. e.* the district round Abila) in the thirteenth year of Tiberius (A.D. 26), at the time when Herod Antipas was tetrarch of Galilee and Herod Philip tetrarch of Ituræa and Trachonitis.

Lys'ias (*dissolving*), a nobleman of the blood-royal, 1 Macc. 3 : 32; 2 Macc. 11 : 1, who was entrusted by Antiochus Epiphanes (*cir.* B.C. 166) with the government of southern Syria and the guardianship of his son Antiochus Eupator. 1 Macc. 3 : 32; 2 Macc. 10 : 11. After the death of Antiochus Epiphanes, B.C. 164, Lysias assumed the government as guardian of his son, who was yet a child. 1 Macc. 6 : 17. In B.C. 164 he, together with his ward, fell into the hands of Deme-trius Soter, who put them both to death. 1 Macc. 7 : 2–4; 2 Macc. 14 : 2.

Lys'ias Clau'dius, a chief captain of the band, that is, tribune of the Roman cohort who rescued St. Paul from the hands of the infuriated mob at Jerusalem, and sent him under a guard to Felix, the governor or proconsul of Cæsarea. Acts 21 : 31, *seq.*; 23 : 26; 24 : 7. (A.D. 55.)

Lysim'achus, "a son of Ptolemæus of Jerusalem," the Greek translator of the book of Esther. Comp. Esther 9 : 20.

Lys'tra. This place has two points of interest in connection respectively with St. Paul's first and second missionary journeys: (1) as the place where divine honors were offered to him, and where he was presently stoned, Acts 14; (2) as the home of his chosen companion and fellow missionary Timotheus. Acts 16 : 1. Lystra was in the eastern part of the great plain of Lycaonia, and its site may be identified with the ruins called *Bin-bir-Kilisseh*, at the base of a conical mountain of volcanic structure, named the *Karadagh*.

M.

Ma'acah (*oppression*). 1. The mother of Absalom; also called MAACHAH. 2 Sam. 3 : 3.

2. Maacah, or (in 1 Chron. 19 : 6, 7) Maachah, a small kingdom in close proximity to Palestine, which appears to have lain outside Argob, Deut. 3 : 14, and Bashan. Josh. 12 : 5. The Ammonite war was the only occasion on which the Maacathites came into contact with Israel, when their king assisted the Ammonites against Joab with a force which he led himself. 2 Sam. 10 : 6, 8; 1 Chron. 19 : 7.

Ma'achah (*oppression*). 1. The daughter of Nahor by his concubine Reumah. Gen. 22 : 24.

2. The father of Achish, who was king of Gath at the beginning of Solomon's reign. 1 Kings 2 : 39.

3. The daughter, or more probably granddaughter, of Absalom, named after his mother; the third and favorite wife of Rehoboam, and mother of Abijah. 1 Kings 15 : 2; 2 Chron. 11 : 20–22. The mother of Abijah is elsewhere called "Michaiah the daughter of Uriel of Gibeah." 2 Chron. 13 : 2. During the reign of her grandson Asa she occupied at the court of Judah the high position of "king's mother," comp. 1 Kings 15 : 13; but when he came of age she was removed because of her idolatrous habits. 2 Chron. 15 : 16.

4. The concubine of Caleb the son of Hezron. 1 Chron. 2 : 48.

5. The daughter of Talmai king of Geshur, and mother of Absalom, 1 Chron. 3 : 2; also called MAACAH in Authorized Version of 2 Sam. 3 : 3.

6. The wife of Machir the Manassite. 1 Chron. 7 : 15, 16.

7. The wife of Jehiel, father or founder of Gibeon. 1 Chron. 8 : 29; 9 : 35.

8. The father of Hanan, one of the heroes of David's body-guard. 1 Chron. 11 : 43.

9. A Simeonite, father of Shephatiah, prince of his tribe in the reign of David. 1 Chron. 27 : 16.

Ma-ach'athi (*oppression*) and **Ma-ach'athites, The,** two words which denote the inhabitants of the small kingdom of Maachah. Deut. 3 : 14; Josh. 12 : 5; 13 : 11, 13; 2 Sam. 23 : 34; 2 Kings 25 : 23; Jer. 40 : 8.

Ma-ada'i, or **Ma-ad'a-i** (*ornament of Jehovah*), one of the sons of Bani, who had married a foreign wife. Ezra 10 : 34.

Ma-adi'ah, one of the priests who returned with Zerubbabel, Neh. 12 : 5; elsewhere (ver. 17) called MOADIAH.

Ma-a'i (*compassionate*), one of the Bene-Asaph who took part in the solemn musical service by which the wall of Jerusalem was dedicated. Neh. 12 : 36.

Ma-al'eh-acrab'bim (*ascent of scorpions*), the full form of the name given as AKRABBIM in Josh. 15 : 3. [AKRABBIM.]

Ma'arath (*bareness*), one of the towns of Judah, in the district of the mountains. Josh. 15 : 59. The places which occur in company with it have been identified at a few miles to the north of Hebron, but Maarath has hitherto eluded observation.

Ma-ase'iah (*work of the Lord*), the name of four persons who had married foreign wives in the time of Ezra. 1. A descendant of Jeshua the priest. Ezra 10 : 18.

2. A priest, of the sons of Harim. Ezra 10 : 21.

3. A priest, of the sons of Pashur. Ezra 10 : 22.

4. One of the laymen, a descendant of Pahath-moab. Ezra 10 : 30.

5. The father of Azariah. Neh. 3 : 23.

6. One of those who stood on the right hand of Ezra when he read the law to the people. Neh. 8 : 4.

7. A Levite who assisted on the same occasion. Neh. 8 : 7.

8. One of the heads of the people whose descendants signed the covenant with Nehemiah. Neh. 10 : 25.

9. Son of Baruch and descendant of Pharez the son of Judah. Neh. 11 : 5.

10. A Benjamite, ancestor of Sallu. Neh. 11 : 7.

11. Two priests of this name are mentioned, Neh. 12 : 41, 42, as taking part in the musical service which accompanied the dedication of the wall of Jerusalem under Ezra. One of them is probably the same as No. 6.

12. Father of Zephaniah, who was a priest in the reign of Zedekiah. Jer. 21 : 1; 29 : 25; 37 : 3.

13. Father of Zedekiah the false prophet. Jer. 29 : 21.

14. One of the Levites of the second rank, appointed by David to sound "with psalteries on Alamoth." 1 Chron. 15 : 18, 20.

15. The son of Adaiah, and one of the captains of hundreds in the reign of Joash king of Judah. 2 Chron. 23 : 1.

16. An officer of high rank in the reign of Uzziah. 2 Chron. 26 : 11. He was probably a Levite, comp. 1 Chron. 23 : 4, and engaged in a semi-military capacity.

17. The "king's son," killed by Zichri the Ephraimitish hero in the invasion of Judah by Pekah king of Israel, during the reign of Ahaz. 2 Chron. 28 : 7.

18. The governor of Jerusalem in the reign of Josiah. 2 Chron. 34 : 8.

19. The son of Shallum, a Levite of high rank in the reign of Jehoiakim. Jer. 35 : 4; comp. 1 Chron. 9 : 19.

20. A priest; ancestor of Baruch and Seraiah, the sons of Neriah. Jer. 32 : 12; 51 : 59.

Ma-asi′ai (*work of the Lord*), a priest who after the return from Babylon dwelt in Jerusalem. 1 Chron. 9 : 12.

Ma′ath (*small*), son of Mattathias in the genealogy of Jesus Christ. Luke 3 : 26.

Ma′az (*wrath*), son of Ram, the firstborn of Jerahmeel. 1 Chron. 2 : 27.

Ma-azi′ah (*consolation of Jehovah*). 1. One of the priests who signed the covenant with Nehemiah. Neh. 10 : 8.

2. A priest in the reign of David, head of the twenty-fourth course. 1 Chron. 24 : 18.

Mac′cabees (*a hammer*), **The.** This title, which was originally the surname of Judas, one of the sons of Mattathias, was afterward extended to the heroic family of which he was one of the noblest representatives. *Asmonæans* or *Hasmonæans* is the proper name of the family, which is derived from Cashmon, great-grandfather of Mattathias. The Maccabees were a family of Jews who resisted the authority of Antiochus Epiphanes king of Syria and his successors, who had usurped authority over the Jews, conquered Jerusalem, and strove to introduce idolatrous worship. The standard of independence was first raised by Mattathias, a priest of the course of Joiarib. He seems, however, to have been already advanced in years when the rising was made, and he did not long survive the fatigues of active service. He died B.C.

166, having named Judas — apparently his third son — as his successor in directing the war of independence. After gaining several victories over the other generals of Antiochus, Judas was able to occupy Jerusalem, except the "tower," and purified the temple exactly three years after its profanation. Nicanor was defeated, first at Capharsalama, and again in a decisive battle at Adasa, B.C. 161, where he was slain. This victory was the greatest of Judas' successes, and practically decided the question of Jewish independence; but shortly after Judas fell at Eleasa, fighting at desperate odds against the invaders. After the death of Judas, Jonathan his brother succeeded to the command, and later assumed the high-priestly office. He died B.C. 144, and was succeeded by Simon, the last remaining brother of the Maccabæan family, who died B.C. 135. The efforts of both brothers were crowned with success. On the death of Simon, Johannes Hyrcanus, one of his sons, at once assumed the government, B.C. 135, and met with a peaceful death B.C. 105. His eldest son, Aristobulus I., who succeeded him B.C. 105-104, was the first who assumed the kingly title, though Simon had enjoyed the fullness of the kingly power. Alexander Jannæus was the next successor, B.C. 104-78. Aristobulus II. and Hyrcanus III. engaged in a civil war on the death of their mother, Alexandra, B.C. 78-69, resulting in the dethronement of Aristobulus II., B.C. 69-63, and the succession of Hyrcanus under Roman rule, but without his kingly title, B.C. 63-40. From B.C. 40 to B.C. 37 Antigonus, a son of Aristobulus II., ruled, and with his two grandchildren, Aristobulus and Mariamne, the Asmonæan dynasty ended.

Mac′cabees, Books of. Four books which bear the common title of "Maccabees" are found in some MSS. of the LXX. Two of these were included in the early current Latin versions of the Bible, and thence passed into the Vulgate. As forming part of the Vulgate they were received as canonical by the Council of Trent, and retained among the *Apocrypha* by the reformed churches. The two other books obtained no such wide circulation, and have only a secondary connection with the Maccabæan history. 1. THE FIRST BOOK OF MACCABEES contains a history of the patriotic struggle of the Jews in resisting the oppressions of the Syrian kings, from the first resistance of

Mattathias to the settled sovereignty and death of Simon, a period of thirty-three years—B.C. 168-135. The great subject of the book begins with the enumeration of the Maccabæan family, ch. 2 : 1-5, which is followed by an account of the part which the aged Mattathias took in rousing and guiding the spirit of his countrymen. ch. 2 : 6-70. The remainder of the narrative is occupied with the exploits of Mattathias' five sons. The great marks of trustworthiness are everywhere conspicuous. Victory and failure and despondency are, on the whole, chronicled with the same candor. There is no attempt to bring into open display the working of Providence. The testimony of antiquity leaves no doubt that the book was first written in Hebrew. Its whole structure points to Palestine as the place of its composition. There is, however, considerable doubt as to its date. Perhaps we may place it between B.C. 120-100. The date and person of the Greek translator are wholly undetermined.

2. THE SECOND BOOK OF MACCABEES.—The history of the second book of Maccabees begins some years earlier than that of the first book, and closes with the victory of Judas Maccabæus over Nicanor. It thus embraces a period of twenty years, from B.C. 180 to B.C. 161. The writer himself distinctly indicates the source of his narrative—"the five books of Jason of Cyrene," ch. 2 : 23, of which he designed to furnish a short and agreeable epitome for the benefit of those who would be deterred from studying the larger work. Of Jason himself nothing more is known than may be gleaned from this mention of him. The second book of Maccabees is not nearly so trustworthy as the first. In the second book the groundwork of facts is true, but the dress in which the facts are presented is due in part at least to the narrator. The latter half of the book, chs. 8-15, is to be regarded as a series of special incidents from the life of Judas, illustrating the providential interference of God in behalf of his people, true in substance, but embellished in form.

3. THE THIRD BOOK OF MACCABEES contains the history of events which preceded the great Maccabæan struggle, beginning with B.C. 217.

4. THE FOURTH BOOK OF MACCA-BEES contains a rhetorical narrative of the martyrdom of Eleazar and of the "Maccabæan family," following in the main the same outline as 2 Macc.

Macedo'nia (*extended land*), a large and celebrated country lying north of Greece, the first part of Europe which

Coin of Macedon. Head of Alexander the Great.

received the gospel directly from St. Paul, and an important scene of his subsequent missionary labors and those of his companions. It was bounded by the range of Hæmus or the Balkan northward, by the chain of Pindus westward, by the Cambunian hills southward, by which it is separated from Thessaly, and is divided on the east from Thrace by a less definite mountain boundary running southward from Hæmus. Of the space thus enclosed, two of the most remarkable physical features are two great plains, one watered by the Axius, which comes to the sea at the Thermaic Gulf, not far from Thessalonica; the other by the Strymon, which, after passing near Philippi, flows out below Amphipolis. Between the mouths of these two rivers a remarkable peninsula projects, dividing itself into three points, on the farthest of which Mount Athos rises nearly into the region of perpetual snow. Across the neck of this peninsula St. Paul travelled more than once with his companions. This general sketch sufficiently describes the Macedonia which was ruled over by Philip and Alexander, and which the Romans conquered from Perseus. At first the conquered country was divided by Æmilius Paulus into four districts, but afterward was made one province and centralized under the jurisdiction of a proconsul, who resided at Thessalonica. The character of the Christians of Macedonia is set before us in Scripture in a very favorable light. The candor of the Bereans is highly commended, Acts 17 : 11; the Thessalonians were evidently objects of St. Paul's peculiar affection, 1 Thess. 2 : 8, 17–20 ; 3 : 10 ; and the Philippians, besides their general freedom from blame, are noted as remarkable for their liberality and self-denial. Philip. 4 : 10, 14–19 ; see 2 Cor. 9 : 2 ; 11 : 9.

Machæ'rus, a castle of the Herods on the southern border of their Peræan dominions, nine miles east of the northern end of the Dead Sea. Here John the Baptist was imprisoned, and here was held the feast where Herodias, at whose

Site of Machærus (place of John's Imprisonment).

request John was beheaded, danced before the king.

Mach'bana-i (*bond of the Lord*), one of the lion-faced warriors of Gad, who joined the fortunes of David when living in retreat at Ziklag. 1 Chron. 12 : 13.

Mach'benah (*bond*). Sheva, the father of Machbena, is named in the genealogical list of Judah as the offspring of Manchah, the concubine of Caleb ben-Hezron. 1 Chron. 2 : 49.

Ma'chi (*decrease*), the father of Geuel the Gadite, who went with Caleb and Joshua to spy out the land of Canaan. Num. 13 : 15.

Ma'chir (*sold*). 1. The eldest son, Josh. 17 : 1, of the patriarch Manasseh by an Aramite or Syrian concubine. 1 Chron. 7 : 14. At the time of the conquest the family of Machir had become very powerful, and a large part of the country on the east of Jordan was subdued by them. Num. 32 : 39 ; Deut. 3 : 15.

2. The son of Ammiel, a powerful sheikh of one of the transjordanic tribes, who rendered essential service to the cause of Saul and of David successively. 2 Sam. 9 : 4, 5 ; 17 : 27–29.

Ma'chirites, The, the descendants of Machir the father of Gilead. Num. 26 : 29.

Machna-de'ba-i (*what is like the liberal?*), one of the sons of Bani who put away his foreign wife at Ezra's command. Ezra 10 : 40.

Machpe'lah (*double, or a portion*). [HEBRON.]

Mad'a-i (*middle land*), Gen. 10 : 2, is usually called the third son of Japhet, and the progenitor of the Medes ; but probably all that is intended is that the Medes, as well as the Gomerites, Greeks, Tabareni, Moschi, etc., descended from Japhet.

Ma'dian. Acts 7 : 29. [MIDIAN.]

Madman'nah (*dunghill*), one of the towns in the south district of Judah. Josh. 15 : 31. In the time of Eusebius and Jerome it was called Menoïs, and was not far from Gaza. The first stage southward from Gaza is now *el-Minyáy*, which is perhaps the modern representative of Menoïs, and therefore of Madmannah.

Mad'men (*dunghill*), a place in Moab, threatened with destruction in the denunciations of Jeremiah. Jer. 48 : 2.

Madme'nah (*dunghill*), one of the Benjamite villages north of Jerusalem, the inhabitants of which were frightened away by the approach of Sennacherib along the northern road. Isa. 10 : 31.

Madness. In Scripture "madness" is recognized as a derangement proceeding either from weakness and misdirection of intellect or from ungovernable violence of passion. In one passage alone, John 10 : 20, is madness expressly connected with demoniacal possession by the Jews in their cavil against our Lord; in none is it referred to any physical causes.

Ma'don (*strife*), one of the principal cities of Canaan before the conquest, probably in the north. Its king joined Jabin and his confederates in their attempt against Joshua at the waters of Merom, and like the rest was killed. Josh. 11 : 1; 12 : 19.

Mag'adan (*a tower*). (The name given in the Revised Version of Matt. 15 : 39 for Magdala. It is probably another name for the same place, or it was a village so near it that the shore where Christ landed may have belonged to either village.—ED.)

Mag'bish (*congregating*), a proper name in Ezra 2 : 30, but whether of a man or of a place is doubtful; probably the latter, as all the names from Ezra 2 : 20 to 34, except Elam and Harim, are names of places.

Mag'dala (*a tower*). The chief MSS. and versions exhibit the name as MAGADAN, as in the Revised Version. Into the limits of Magadan Christ came by boat, over the Lake of Gennesareth, after his miracle of feeding the four thousand on the mountain of the eastern side, Matt. 15 : 39, and from thence he returned in the same boat to the opposite shore. In the parallel narrative of St. Mark, ch. 8 : 10, we find the " parts of Dalmanutha," on the western edge of the Lake of Gennesareth. The Magdala, which conferred her name on " Mary the Magdal-ene," one of the numerous migdols, *i. e.* towers, which stood in Palestine, was probably the place of that name which is mentioned in the Jerusalem Talmud as near Tiberias, and this again is as probably the modern *el-Mejdel*, a miserable little Muslim village, of twenty huts, on the water's edge at the southeast corner of the plain of Gennesareth. It is now the only inhabited place on this plain.

Mag'di-el (*prince of God*), one of the " dukes " of Edom, descended from Esau. Gen. 36 : 43; 1 Chron. 1 : 54.

Ma'gi (Authorized Version *wise men*). 1. In the Hebrew text of the Old Testament the word occurs but twice, and then only incidentally. Jer. 29 : 3, 13. "Originally they were a class of priests among the Persians and Medes, who formed the king's privy council, and cultivated astrology, medicine and occult natural science. They are frequently referred to by ancient authors. Afterward the term was applied to all eastern philosophers." —*Schaff's Popular Commentary.* They appear in Herodotus' history of Astyages as interpreters of dreams, i. 120; but as they appear in Jeremiah among the retinue of the Chaldean king, we must suppose Nebuchadnezzar's conquests led him to gather round him the wise men and religious teachers of the nations which he subdued, and that thus the sacred tribe of the Medes rose under his rule to favor and power. The Magi took their places among " the astrologers and star-gazers and monthly prognosticators." It is with such men that we have to think of Daniel and his fellow exiles as associated. The office which Daniel accepted, Dan. 5 : 11, was probably *rab-mag*—chief of the Magi. 2. The word presented itself to the Greeks as connected with a foreign system of divination, and it soon became a byword for the worst form of imposture. This is the predominant meaning of the word as it appears in the New Testament. Acts 8 : 9; 13 : 8. 3. In one memorable instance, however, the word retains its better meaning. In the Gospel of St. Matthew, ch. 2 : 1–12, the Magi appear as " wise men "—properly Magians—who were guided by a star from " the east " to Jerusalem, where they suddenly appeared in the days of Herod the Great, inquiring for the new-born king of the Jews, whom they had come to worship. As to the country from which they came, opinions vary greatly; but their following the guidance of a star seems to point to the banks of the Tigris and Euphrates, where astronomy was early cultivated by the Chaldeans. [See STAR OF THE EAST.] (Why should the new star lead these wise men to look for a king of the Jews? (1) These wise men from Persia were the most like the Jews, in religion, of all nations in the world. They believed in one God, they had no idols, they worshipped light as the best symbol of God. (2) The general expectation of such a king. "The Magi," says Ellicott, "express the feeling which the Roman historians Tacitus and Suetonius tell us sixty or seventy years later had been for a long time very widely diffused. Everywhere throughout the East men were looking for the advent of a great king who was to rise from among the Jews. It had fermented in the minds of men, heathen as well as Jews, and would have led them to welcome Jesus as the Christ had he come in accordance with their expectation." Virgil, who lived a little before this, owns that a child from heaven was looked for, who should restore the golden age and take away sin. (3) This expectation arose largely from the dispersion of the Jews among all nations, carrying with them the hope and the promise of a divine Redeemer. Isa. 9, 11; Dan. 7. (4) Daniel himself was a prince and chief among this very class of wise men. His prophecies were made known to them; and the calculations by which he pointed to the very time when Christ should be born became, through the book of Daniel, a part of their ancient literature.—ED.) According to a late tradition, the Magi are represented as three kings, named Gaspar, Melchior and Belthazar, who take their place among the objects of Christian reverence, and are honored as the patron saints of travellers.

Magic, Magicians. Magic is "the science or practice of evoking spirits, or educing the occult powers of nature to produce effects apparently supernatural." It formed an essential element in many ancient religions, especially among the Persians, Chaldeans and Egyptians. The Hebrews had no magic of their own. It was so strictly forbidden by the law that it could never afterward have had any recognized existence, save in times of general heresy or apostasy, and the same was doubtless the case in the patriarchal ages. The magical practices which obtained among the Hebrews were therefore borrowed from the nations around. From the first entrance into the land of promise until the destruction of Jerusalem we have constant glimpses of magic practiced in secret, or resorted to not alone by the common but also by the great. It is a distinctive characteristic of the Bible that from first to last it warrants no such trust or dread. Laban attached great value to, and was in the habit of consulting, images. Gen. 31 : 30,

32. During the plagues in Egypt the magicians appear. Ex. 7 : 11; 8 : 18, 19. Balaam also practiced magic. Num. 22 : 7. Saul consulted the witch of Endor. An examination of the various notices of magic in the Bible gives this general result: They do not, as far as can be understood, once state positively that any but illusive results were produced by magical rites. (Even the magicians of Egypt could imitate the plagues sent through Moses only so long as they had previous notice and time to prepare. The first time Moses sent the plague unannounced the magicians failed; they "did so with their enchantments," but in vain. So in the case of the witch of Endor. Samuel's appearance was apparently unexpected by her; he did not come through the enchantments.—ED.) The Scriptures therefore afford no evidence that man can gain supernatural powers to use at his will. This consequence goes some way toward showing that we may conclude there is no such thing as real magic; for although it is dangerous to reason on negative evidence, yet in a case of this kind it is especially strong. [DIVINATION.]

Ma'gog (*region of Gog*). In Gen. 10 : 2 Magog appears as the second son of Japheth; in Ezek. 38 : 2; 39 : 1, 6 it appears as a country or people of which Gog was the prince. The notices of Magog would lead us to fix a northern locality: it is expressly stated by Ezekiel that he was to come up from "the sides of the north," Ezek. 39 : 2, from a country adjacent to that of Togarmah or Armenia, ch. 38 : 6, and not far from "the isles" or maritime regions of Europe. ch. 39 : 6. The people of Magog further appear as having a force of cavalry, Ezek. 38 : 15, and as armed with the bow. ch. 39 : 3. From the above data we may conclude that Magog represents the important race of the Scythians.

Ma'gor-mis'sabib (*terror on every side*), the name given by Jeremiah to Pashur the priest when he smote him and put him in the stocks for prophesying against the idolatry of Jerusalem. Jer. 20 : 3.

Mag'piash (*moth-killer*), one of the heads of the people who signed the covenant with Nehemiah. Neh. 10 : 20. The same as MAGBISH in Ezra 2 : 30.

Ma'halah (*disease*), one of the three children of Hammoleketh the sister of Gilead. 1 Chron. 7 : 18.

Mahal'ale-el (*praise of God*). 1. The fourth in descent from Adam, according to the Sethite genealogy, and son of Cainan. Gen. 5 : 12, 13, 15–17 ; 1 Chron. 1 : 2; Luke 3 : 37, Revised Version.

2. A descendant of Perez or Pharez the son of Judah. Neh. 11 : 4.

Ma'halath (*stringed instrument*), the daughter of Ishmael, and one of the wives of Esau. Gen. 28 : 9.

Ma'halath (*stringed instrument*), one of the eighteen wives of King Rehoboam, apparently his first. 2 Chron. 11 : 18 only. She was her husband's cousin, being the daughter of King David's son Jerimoth.

Mahalath, the title of Ps. 53, and **Mahalath-leannoth,** the title of Ps. 88. The meaning of these words is uncertain. The conjecture is that *mahaluth* is a guitar, and that *leannoth* has reference to the character of the psalm, and might be rendered "to humble or afflict," in which sense the root occurs in ver. 7.

Ma'hali (*sick*), **Mah'li,** the son of Merari. Ex. 6 : 19.

Mahana'im, a town on the east of the Jordan. The name signifies *two hosts* or *two camps*, and was given to it by Jacob, because he there met "the angels of God." Gen. 32 : 1, 2. We next meet with it in the records of the conquest. Josh. 13 : 26, 30. It was within the territory of Gad, Josh. 21 : 38, 39, and therefore on the south side of the torrent Jabbok. The town with its "suburbs" was allotted to the service of the Merarite Levites. Josh. 21 : 39 ; 1 Chron. 6 : 80. Mahanaim had become in the time of the monarchy a place of mark. 2 Sam. 2 : 8, 12. David took refuge there when driven out of the western part of his kingdom by Absalom. 2 Sam. 17 : 24; 1 Kings 2 : 8. Mahanaim was the seat of one of Solomon's commissariat officers, 1 Kings 4 : 14, and it is alluded to in the song which bears his name. ch. 6 : 13. There is a place called *Mahneh* among the villages of the east of Jordan, though its exact position is not certain.

Ma'haneh-dan (*camp of Dan*), spoken of as "behind Kirjath-jearim," Judges 18 : 12, and as "between Zorah and Eshtaol." ch. 13 : 25.

Mahar'a-i (*impetuous*), 2 Sam. 23 : 28; 1 Chron. 11 : 30; 27 : 13, an inhabitant of Netophah in the tribe of Judah, and one of David's captains.

Ma'hath (*grasping*). 1. A Kohathite of the house of Korah. 1 Chron. 6 : 35.

2. Also a Kohathite, in the reign of Hezekiah. 2 Chron. 29 : 12 ; 31 : 13.

Ma'havite, The, the designation of Eliel, one of the warriors of King David's guard, whose name is preserved in the catalogue of 1 Chron. 11 : 46 only.

Maha'zioth (*visions*), one of the fourteen sons of Heman the Kohathite. 1 Chron. 25 : 4, 30.

Ma'her-shal'al-hash'-baz (*i. e. hasten-booty, speed-spoil*), whose name was given by divine direction to indicate that Damascus and Samaria were soon to be plundered by the king of Assyria. Isa. 8 : 1–4.

Mah'lah (*disease*), the eldest of the five daughters of Zelophehad the grandson of Manasseh. Num. 27 : 1–11.

Mah'li (*sick*). 1. Son of Merari, the son of Levi and ancestor of the family of the Mahlites. Num. 3 : 20 ; 1 Chron. 6 : 19, 29 ; 24 : 26.

2. Son of Mushi and grandson of Merari. 1 Chron. 6 : 47 ; 23 : 23 ; 24 : 30.

Mah'lon (*sick*), the first husband of Ruth; son of Elimelech and Naomi. Ruth 1 : 2, 5 ; 4 : 9, 10 ; comp. 1 Sam. 17 : 12.

Ma'hol (*dancing*), the father of the four men most famous for wisdom next to Solomon himself. 1 Kings 4 : 31 ; 1 Chron. 2 : 6.

Ma'kaz (*end*), a place, apparently a town, named once only—1 Kings 4 : 9—in the specification of the jurisdiction of Solomon's commissariat officer, Ben-Dekar. Makaz has not been discovered.

Makhe'loth (*place of assemblies*), a place mentioned only in Num. 33 : 25 as that of a desert encampment of the Israelites.

Makke'dah (*place of shepherds*), a place memorable in the annals of the conquest of Canaan as the scene of the execution by Joshua of the five confederate kings, Josh. 10 : 10–30, who had hidden themselves in a cave at this place. (It was a royal city of the Canaanites, in the plains of Judah. Conder identifies it with the modern *el-Moghâr*, 25 miles northwest of Jerusalem, where are two caves large enough to contain five men each. Schaff says that "one cave has, curiously enough, five loculi rudely scooped in its side, and an enthusiast might contend that this was the very place of sepulchre of the five kings."—Ed.)

Mak'tesh (*a mortar or deep hollow*), a place evidently in Jerusalem, the inhabitants of which are denounced by Zephaniah. Zeph. 1 : 11. Ewald conjectures that it was the "Phœnician quarter" of the city.

Mal'a-chi (*my messenger*) is the author of the last book in the Old Testament. Nothing is known of him beyond what may be learned from his book.

His prophecy belongs to the times of Nehemiah, near the time of Nehemiah's second visit to Jerusalem, about B.C. 432. It was an effort to aid in the great reforms then needed. Malachi believed in a spiritual worship as the one essential of true religion. But the system of temple ritual and sacrifices was in existence, and the prophet recognizes it as a means of educating the people into the spiritual life.

Mal'chi-shu'a (*king of help*), one of the sons of King Saul. 1 Sam. 14 : 49; 31 : 2; 1 Chron. 8 : 33; 9 : 39.

Mal'chus (*king or kingdom*), the name of the servant of the high priest whose right ear Peter cut off at the time of the Saviour's apprehension in the garden. Matt. 26 : 51; Mark 14 : 47; Luke 22 : 49-51; John 18 : 10.

Ma-le'le-el, or **Mahal'ale-el,** the son of Cainan. Gen. 5 : 12, marg.; Luke 3 : 37.

Mal'lothi (*my fullness*), a Kohathite, one of the fourteen sons of Heman the singer. 1 Chron. 25 : 4, 26.

Mal'luch (*counsellor*). 1. A Levite of the family of Merari, and ancestor of Ethan the singer. 1 Chron. 6 : 44.

2. One of the sons of Bani. Ezra 10 : 29, and

3. One of the descendants of Harim, Ezra 10 : 32, who had married foreign wives.

4. A priest or family of priests. Neh. 10 : 4, and

5. One of the heads of the people who signed the covenant with Nehemiah. Neh. 10 : 27.

6. One of the families of priests who returned with Zerubbabel, Neh. 12 : 2; probably the same as No. 4.

Mama'ias, apparently the same with SHEMAIAH in Ezra 8 : 16.

Mammon (*riches*), Matt. 6 : 24; Luke 16 : 9, a word which often occurs in the Chaldee Targums of Onkelos and later writers, and in the Syriac version, and which signifies "riches." It is used in St. Matthew as a personification of riches.

Mam're (*strength, fatness*), an ancient Amorite, who with his brothers, Eshcol and Aner, was in alliance with Abram, Gen. 14 : 13, 24, and under the shade of whose oak grove the patriarch dwelt in the interval between his residence at Bethel and at Beersheba. ch. 13 : 18; 18 : 1. In the subsequent chapters Mamre is a mere local appellation. ch. 23 : 17, 19; 25 : 9; 49 : 30; 50 : 13.

Man'aen (*comforter*) is mentioned in Acts 13 : 1 as one of the teachers and prophets in the church at Antioch at the time of the appointment of Saul and Barnabas as missionaries to the heathen. He is said to have been brought up with Herod Antipas. He was probably his foster-brother.

Man'ahath (*rest*), a place named in 1 Chron. 8 : 6 only, in connection with the genealogies of the tribe of Benjamin.

Man'ahath (*rest*), one of the sons of Shobal, and descendant of Seir the Horite. Gen. 36 : 23; 1 Chron. 1 : 40.

Mana'hethites (*inhabitants of Manahath*), **The.** "Half the Manahethites" are named in the genealogies of Judah as descended from Shobal, the father of Kirjath-jearim, 1 Chron. 2 : 52, and half from Salma, the founder of Bethlehem. ver. 54.

Manas'seh (*forgetting*), the eldest son of Joseph, Gen. 41 : 51; 46 : 20, born 1715-10 B. C. Both he and Ephraim were born before the commencement of the famine. He was placed after his younger brother, Ephraim, by his grandfather, Jacob, when he adopted them into his own family, and made them heads of tribes. Whether the elder of the two sons was inferior in form or promise to the younger, or whether there was any external reason to justify the preference of Jacob, we are not told. In the division of the promised land half of the tribe of Manasseh settled east of the Jordan, in the district embracing the hills of Gilead with their inaccessible heights and impassable ravines, and the almost impregnable tract of Argob. Josh. 13 : 29–33. Here they throve exceedingly, pushing their way northward over the rich plains of Jaulân and Jedûr to the foot of Mount Hermon. 1 Chron. 5 : 23. But they gradually assimilated themselves with the old inhabitants of the country, and on them descended the punishment which was ordained to be the inevitable consequence of such misdoing. They, first of all Israel, were carried away by Pul and Tiglath-pileser, and settled in the Assyrian territories. 1 Chron. 5 : 25, 26. The other half tribe settled to the west of the Jordan, north of Ephraim. Josh. 17. For further particulars see EPHRAIM.

Manas′seh (*forgetting*). 1. The thirteenth king of Judah, son of Hezekiah, 2 Kings 21 : 1, ascended the throne at the age of twelve, and reigned 55 years, from B.C. 698 to 642. His accession was the signal for an entire change in the religious administration of the kingdom. Idolatry was again established to such an extent that every faith was tolerated but the old faith of Israel. The Babylonian alliance which the king formed against Assyria resulted in his being made prisoner and carried off to Babylon in the twenty-second year of his reign, according to a Jewish tradition. There his eyes were opened and he repented, and his prayer was heard and the Lord delivered him, 2 Chron. 33 : 12, 13, and he returned after some uncertain interval of time to Jerusalem. The altar of the Lord was again restored, and peace offerings and thank offerings were sacrificed to Jehovah. 2 Chron. 33 : 15, 16. But beyond this the reformation did not go. On his death, B.C. 642, he was buried as Ahaz had been, not with the burial of a king, in the sepulchres of the house of David, but in the garden of Uzza, 2 Kings 21 : 26; and long afterward, in spite of his repentance, the Jews held his name in abhorrence.

2. One of the descendants of Pahath-moab, who in the days of Ezra had married a foreign wife. Ezra 10 : 30.

3. One of the laymen, of the family of Hashum, who put away his foreign wife at Ezra's command. Ezra 10 : 33.

Manas′ses. 1. Manasseh, king of Judah. Matt. 1 : 10.

2. Manasseh the son of Joseph. Rev. 7 : 6.

Manas′sites, The, that is, the members of the tribe of Manasseh. Deut. 4 : 43; Judges 12 : 4; 2 Kings 10 : 33.

Mandrakes (Heb. *dudâim*) are mentioned in Gen. 30 : 14, 15, 16, and in Cant. 7 : 13. The mandrake, *Atropa mandragora*, is closely allied to the well-known deadly nightshade, *A. belladonna*, and to the tomato, and belongs to the order *Solanaceæ*, or potato family. It grows in Palestine and Mesopotamia. (It grows low, like lettuce, which its leaves somewhat resemble, except that they are of a dark green. The flowers are purple, and the root is usually forked. Its fruit when ripe (early in May) is about the size of a small apple, 2½ inches in diameter, ruddy

The Mandrake.

or yellow, and of a most agreeable odor (to Orientals more than to Europeans) and an equally agreeable taste. The Arabs call it "devil's apple," from its power to excite voluptuousness. Dr. Richardson ("Lectures on Alcohol," 1881) tried some experiments with wine made of the root of mandrake, and found it narcotic, causing sleep, so that the ancients used it as an anæsthetic. Used in small quantities like opium, it excites the nerves, and is a stimulant.—ED.)

Maneh (*a portion* (by weight)). [WEIGHTS AND MEASURES.]

Manger. This word occurs only in Luke 2 : 7, 12, 16, in connection with the birth of Christ. It means a crib or feeding-trough; but according to Schleusner its real signification in the New Testament is the open court-yard attached to the inn or khan, in which the cattle would be shut at night, and where the poorer travellers might unpack their animals and take up their lodging, when they were either by want of room or want of means excluded from the house.

Manna (*what is this?*) (Heb. *mân*). The most important passages of the Old Testament on this topic are the following: Ex. 16 : 14–36 ; Num. 11 : 7–9; Deut. 8 : 3, 16; Josh. 5 : 12; Ps. 78 : 24, 25

From these passages we learn that the manna came every morning except the Sabbath, in the form of a small round seed resembling the hoar frost; that it must be gathered early, before the sun became so hot as to melt it; that it must be gathered every day except the Sabbath; that the attempt to lay aside for a succeeding day, except on the day immediately preceding the Sabbath, failed by the substance becoming wormy and offensive; that it was prepared for food by

Tamarisk or Manna Tree of the Sinaitic Peninsula.

grinding and baking; that its taste was like fresh oil, and like wafers made with honey, equally agreeable to all palates; that the whole nation, of at least 2,000,000, subsisted upon it for forty years; that it suddenly ceased when they first got the new corn of the land of Canaan; and that it was always regarded as a miraculous gift directly from God, and not as a product of nature. The natural products of the Arabian deserts and other Oriental regions which bear the name of manna have not the qualities or uses ascribed to the manna of Scripture. The latter substance was undoubtedly wholly miraculous, and not in any respect a product of nature, though its name may have come from its resemblance to the natural manna. The substance now called manna in the Arabian desert through which the

Israelites passed is collected in the month of June from the *tarfa* or tamarisk shrub (*Tamarix gallica*). According to Burckhardt it drops from the thorns on the sticks and leaves with which the ground is covered, and must be gathered early in the day or it will be melted by the sun. The Arabs cleanse and boil it, strain it through a cloth and put it in leathern bottles; and in this way it can be kept uninjured for several years. They use it like honey or butter with their unleavened bread, but never make it into cakes or eat it by itself. The whole harvest, which amounts to only five or six hundred pounds, is consumed by the Bedouins, "who," says Schaff, "consider it the greatest dainty their country affords." The manna of European commerce comes mostly from Calabria and Sicily. It is gathered during the months of June and July from some species of ash (*Ornus europæa* and *O. rotundifolia*), from which it drops in consequence of a puncture by an insect resembling the locust, but distinguished from it by having a sting under its body. The substance is fluid at night and resembles the dew, but in the morning it begins to harden.

Mano'ah (*rest*), the father of Samson; a Danite, native of the town of Zorah. Judges 13 : 2. (B.C. 1161.) [SAMSON.]

Manslayer, one who kills another unintentionally, and is thus distinguished from a murderer, who kills with malice aforethought. The cases of manslaughter mentioned in Scripture appear to be a sufficient indication of the intention of the lawgiver. 1. Death by a blow in a sudden quarrel. Num. 35 : 22. 2. Death by a stone or missile thrown at random. *Ibid.* 22, 23. 3. By the blade of an axe flying from its handle. Deut. 19 : 5. In all these and the like cases the manslayer was allowed to retire to a city of refuge. A thief overtaken at night in the act of stealing might lawfully be put to death, but if the sun had risen the killing him was to be regarded as murder. Ex. 22 : 2, 8.

Mantle, the word employed in the Authorized Version to translate no less than four Hebrew terms, entirely distinct and independent in both derivation and meaning. 1. Judges 4 : 18, the garment with which Jael covered Sisera.

2. Rendered "mantle" in 1 Sam. 15 : 27; 28 : 14; Ezra 9 : 3, 5, etc. This word is in other passages of the Authorized Version rendered "coat," "cloak" and "robe."

3. Isa. 3 : 22 only. Apparently some article of a lady's dress.

4. 1 Kings 19 : 13, 19; 2 Kings 2 : 8, 13, 14. The sole garment of the prophet Elijah. It was probably of sheepskin, such as is worn by the modern dervishes.

Ma'och (*oppression*), the father of Achish king of Gath, with whom David took refuge. 1 Sam. 27 : 2.

Ma'on (*habitation*), one of the cities of the tribe of Judah, in the district of the mountains. Josh. 15 : 55. Its interest for us lies in its connection with David. 1 Sam. 23 : 24, 25. The name of Maon still exists in *Main*, a lofty conical hill, south of and about seven miles distant from Hebron.

Ma'onites, The, a people mentioned in one of the addresses of Jehovah to the repentant Israelites, Judges 10 : 12; elsewhere in the Authorized Version called Mehunim.

Ma'ra (*sad, bitter*), the name which Naomi adopted in the exclamation forced from her by the recognition of her fellow citizens at Bethlehem. Ruth 1 : 20.

Ma'rah (*bitterness*), a place which lay in the wilderness of Shur or Etham, three days journey distant, Ex. 15 : 23; Num. 33 : 8, from the place at which the Israelites crossed the Red Sea, and where was a spring of bitter water, sweetened subsequently by the casting in of a tree which "the Lord showed" to Moses. *Howarah*, distant 16½ hours (47 miles) from *Ayoun Mousa*, the Israelites' first encampment, has been by many identified with it, apparently because it is the bitterest water in the neighborhood.

Mar'alah (*trembling*), one of the landmarks on the boundary of the tribe of Zebulun. Josh. 19 : 11.

Maranath'a, an Aramaic or Syriac expression used by St. Paul at the conclusion of his First Epistle to the Corinthians, ch. 16 : 22, signifying "our Lord cometh."

Marble. The Hebrew *shêsh*, the generic term for marble, may probably be taken to mean almost any shining stone. The so-called marble of Solomon's architectural works may thus have been limestone. There can be no doubt that Herod both in the temple and elsewhere employed Parian or other marble. The marble pillars and tesseræ of various colors of the palace at Susa came doubtless from Persia. Esther 1 : 6.

Marcheshvan. [MONTH.]

Mar'cus, the evangelist Mark. Col 4 : 10; Phil. 24; 1 Pet. 5 : 13. [MARK.]

Mar'eshah, or **Mare'shah** (*crest of a hill*), one of the cities of Judah in the low country. Josh. 15 : 44. It was one of the cities fortified and garrisoned by Rehoboam after the rupture with the northern kingdom. 2 Chron. 11 : 8. Near it was fought the great battle between Asa and Zerah. 2 Chron. 14 : 9-12. It is mentioned once or twice in the history of the Maccabæan war of independence. 2 Macc. 12 : 35. About 110 B.C. it was taken from the Idumæans by John Hyrcanus. It was in ruins in the fourth century, when Eusebius and Jerome describe it as in the second mile from Eleutheropolis. South-southwest of *Beitjibrin*—in all probability Eleutheropolis—and a little over a Roman mile therefrom, is a site called *Marash*, which is possibly the representative of the ancient Mareshah.

Mark, one of the evangelists, and probable author of the Gospel bearing his name. (Marcus was his Latin surname. His Jewish name was John, which is the same as Johanan (*the grace of God*). We can almost trace the steps whereby the former became his prevalent name in the Church. "John, whose surname was Mark," in Acts 12 : 12, 25; 15 : 37, becomes "John" alone in Acts 13 : 5, 13, "Mark" in Acts 15 : 39, and thenceforward there is no change. Col. 4 : 10; Phil. 24; 2 Tim. 4 : 11. The evangelist was the son of a certain Mary, a Jewish matron of some position who dwelt at Jerusalem, Acts 12 : 12, and was probably born of a Hellenistic family in that city. Of his father we know nothing; but we do know that the future evangelist was cousin of Barnabas of Cyprus, the great friend of St. Paul. His mother would seem to have been intimately acquainted with St. Peter, and it was to her house, as to a familiar home, that the apostle repaired, A.D. 44, after his deliverance from prison. Acts 12 : 12. This fact accounts for St. Mark's intimate acquaintance with that apostle, to whom also he probably owed his conversion, for St. Peter calls him his son. 1 Pet. 5 : 13. We hear of him for the first time in Acts 15 : 25, where we find him accompanying Paul and Barnabas on their return from Jerusalem to Antioch, A.D. 45. He next comes before us on the occasion of the earliest missionary journey of the same apostles, A.D. 48, when he joined them as their "minister." Acts 13 : 5. With them he visited Cyprus; but at Perga in Pamphylia, Acts 13 : 13, when they were about to enter upon the more arduous part of their mission, he left them, and, for some unexplained reason, returned to Jerusalem to his mother and his home. Notwithstanding this, we find him at Paul's side during that apostle's first imprisonment at Rome, A.D. 61-63, and he is acknowledged by him as one of his few fellow laborers who had been a "comfort" to him during the weary hours of his imprisonment. Col. 4 : 10, 11; Phil. 24. We next have traces of him in 1 Pet. 5 : 13 : "The church that is in Babylon . . . saluteth you, and so doth Marcus my son." From this we infer that he joined his spiritual father, the great friend of his mother, at Babylon, then and for some hundred years afterward one of the chief seats of Jewish culture. From Babylon he would seem to have returned to Asia Minor; for during his second imprisonment, A.D. 68, St. Paul, writing to Timothy, charges him to bring Mark with him to Rome, on the ground that he was "profitable to him for the ministry." 2 Tim. 4 : 11. From this point we gain no further information from the New Testament respecting the evangelist. It is most probable, however, that he did join the apostle at Rome, whither also St. Peter would seem to have proceeded, and suffered martyrdom along with St. Paul. After the death of these two great pillars of the Church, ecclesiastical tradition affirms that St. Mark visited Egypt, founded the church of Alexandria, and died by martyrdom.— *Condensed from Cambridge Bible for Schools.*—ED.)

Mark, Gospel of. 1. *By whom written.*—The author of this Gospel has been universally believed to be Mark or Marcus, designated in Acts 12 : 12, 25; 15 : 37 as John Mark, and in ch. 13 : 5, 13 as John. 2. *When it was written.*—Upon this point nothing absolutely certain can be affirmed, and the Gospel itself affords us no information. The most direct testimony is that of Irenæus, who says it was after the death of the apostles Peter and Paul. We may conclude, therefore, that this Gospel was not written before A.D. 63. Again we may as certainly conclude that it was not written after the destruction of Jerusalem, for it is not likely that he would have omitted to record so remarkable a fulfillment of our

Lord's predictions. Hence A.D. 63–70 becomes our limit, but nearer than this we cannot go.—*Farrar.* 3. *Where it was written.*—As to the place, the weight of testimony is uniformly in favor of the belief that the Gospel was written and published at Rome. In this Clement, Eusebius, Jerome, Epiphanius, all agree. Chrysostom, indeed, asserts that it was published at Alexandria; but his statement receives no confirmation, as otherwise it could not fail to have done, from any Alexandrine writer.—*Farrar.* 4. *In what language.*—As to the language in which it was written, there never has been any reasonable doubt that it was written in Greek. 5. *Sources of information.*—Mark was not one of the twelve; and there is no reason to believe that he was an eye and ear witness of the events which he has recorded; but an almost unanimous testimony of the early fathers indicates Peter as the source of his information. The most important of these testimonies is that of Papias, who says, "He, the presbyter (John), said, Mark, being the interpreter of Peter, wrote exactly whatever he remembered; but he did not write in order the things which were spoken or done by Christ. For he was neither a hearer nor a follower of the Lord, but, as I said, afterward followed Peter, who made his discourses to suit what was required, without the view of giving a connected digest of the discourses of our Lord. Mark, therefore, made no mistakes when he wrote down circumstances as he recollected them; for he was very careful of one thing, to omit nothing of what he heard, and to say nothing false in what he related." Thus Papias writes of Mark. This testimony is confirmed by other witnesses.—*Abbott.* 6. *For whom it was written.*—The traditional statement is that it was intended primarily for Gentiles, and especially for those at Rome. A review of the Gospel itself confirms this view. 7. *Characteristics.*—(1) Mark's Gospel is occupied almost entirely with the ministry in Galilee and the events of the passion week. It is the shortest of the four Gospels, and contains almost no incident or teaching which is not contained in one of the other two synoptists; but (2) it is by far the most vivid and dramatic in its narratives, and their pictorial character indicates not only that they were derived from an eye and ear witness, but also from one who possessed the observation and the graphic artistic power of a natural orator, such as Peter emphatically was. (3) One peculiarity strikes us the moment we open it,—the absence of any genealogy of our Lord. This is the key to much that follows. It is not the design of the evangelist to present our Lord to us, like St. Matthew, as the Messiah, "the son of David and Abraham," ch. 1 : 1, or, like St. Luke, as the universal Redeemer, "the son of Adam, which was the son of God." ch. 3 : 38. (4) His design is to present him to us as the incarnate and wonder-working Son of God, living and acting among men; to portray him in the fullness of his living energy.—*Cambridge Bible for Schools.*

Market-places, Matt. 20 : 3; Mark 12 : 38; Luke 7 : 32; Acts 16 : 19, (any open place of public resort in cities or towns where public trials and assemblies were held and goods were exposed for sale. "The market-places or bazaars of the East were, and are at this day, the constant resort of unoccupied people, the idle, the news-mongers."—*Hackett's Ill. S. S.*—ED.)

Market of Ap'pius. Acts 28 : 15. In the Revised Version for Appii Forum of the Authorized Version, which see.

Ma'roth (*bitterness*), one of the towns of the western lowland of Judah. Micah 1 : 12.

Marriage. 1. *Its origin and history.* —The institution of marriage dates from the time of man's original creation. Gen. 2 : 18–25. From Gen. 2 : 24 we may evolve the following principles: (1) The unity of man and wife, as implied in her being formed out of man. (2) The indissolubleness of the marriage bond, except on the strongest grounds. Comp. Matt. 19 : 9. (3) Monogamy, as the original law of marriage. (4) The social equality of man and wife. (5) The subordination of the wife to the husband. 1 Cor. 11 : 8, 9; 1 Tim. 2 : 13. (6) The respective duties of man and wife. In the patriarchal age polygamy prevailed, Gen. 16 : 4; 25 : 1, 6; 28 : 9; 29 : 23, 28; 1 Chron. 7 : 14, but to a great extent divested of the degradation which in modern times attaches to that practice. Divorce also prevailed in the patriarchal age, though but one instance of it is recorded. Gen. 21 : 14. The Mosaic law discouraged polygamy, restricted divorce, and aimed to enforce purity of life. It was the best civil law possible at the time, and sought to bring the people up to the pure standard of the moral law. In the post-Babylonian period monogamy appears to have become more prevalent than at any previous time. The practice of polygamy nevertheless still existed; Herod the Great had no less than nine wives at one time. The abuse of divorce continued unabated. Our Lord and his apostles re-established the integrity and sanctity of the marriage bond by the following measures: (*a*) By the confirmation of the original charter of marriage as the basis on which all regulations were to be framed. Matt. 19 : 4, 5. (*b*) By the restriction of divorce to the case of fornication, and the prohibition of remarriage in all persons divorced on improper grounds. Matt. 5 : 32; 19 : 9; Rom. 7 : 3; 1 Cor. 7 : 10, 11. (*c*) By the enforcement of moral purity generally, Heb. 13 : 4, etc., and especially by the formal condemnation of fornication. Acts 15 : 20.

2. *The conditions of legal marriage.*— In the Hebrew commonwealth marriage was prohibited (*a*) between an Israelite and a non-Israelite. There were three grades of prohibition : total in regard to the Canaanites on either side; total on the side of the males in regard to the Ammonites and Moabites; and temporary on the side of the males in regard to the Edomites and Egyptians, marriages with females in the two latter instances being regarded as legal. The progeny of illegal marriages between Israelites and non-Israelites was described as "bastard." Deut. 23 : 2. (*b*) between an Israelite and one of his own community. The regulations relative to marriage between Israelites and Israelites were based on considerations of relationship. The most important passage relating to these is contained in Lev. 18 : 6–18, wherein we have in the first place a general prohibition against marriage between a man and the "flesh of his flesh," and in the second place special prohibitions against marriage with a mother, stepmother, sister or half-sister, whether "born at home or abroad," granddaughter, aunt, whether by consanguinity on either side or by marriage on the father's side, daughter-in-law, brother's wife, stepdaughter, wife's mother, stepgranddaughter, or wife's sister during the lifetime of the wife. An exception is subsequently made, Deut. 25 : 5–9, in favor of marriage with a brother's wife in the event of his having died childless. The law which regulates this has been named the "levi-

rate," from the Latin *levir*, "brother-in-law."

3. *The modes by which marriage was effected.*—The choice of the bride devolved not on the bridegroom himself, but on his relations or on a friend deputed by the bridegroom for this purpose. The consent of the maiden was sometimes asked, Gen. 24 : 58; but this appears to have been subordinate to the previous consent of the father and the adult brothers. Gen. 24 : 51; 34 : 11. Occasionally the whole business of selecting the wife was left in the hands of a friend. The selection of the bride was followed by the espousal, which was a formal proceeding undertaken by a friend or legal representative on the part of the bridegroom and by the parents on the part of the bride; it was confirmed by oaths, and accompanied with presents to the bride. The act of betrothal was celebrated by a feast, and among the more modern Jews it is the custom in some parts for the bridegroom to place a ring on the bride's finger. The ring was regarded among the Hebrews as a token of fidelity, Gen. 41 : 42, and of adoption into a family. Luke 15 : 22. Between the betrothal and the marriage an interval elapsed, varying from a few days in the patriarchal age, Gen. 24 : 55, to a full year for virgins and a month for widows in later times. During this period the bride-elect lived with her friends, and all communication between herself and her future husband was carried on through the medium of a friend deputed for the purpose, termed the "friend of the bridegroom." John 3 : 29. She was now virtually regarded as the wife of her future husband; hence faithlessness on her part was punishable with death, Deut. 22 : 23, 24, the husband having, however, the option of "putting her away." Deut. 24 : 1; Matt. 1 : 19. The essence of the marriage ceremony consisted in the removal of the bride from her father's house to that of the bridegroom or his father. The bridegroom prepared himself for the occasion by putting on a festive dress, and especially by placing on his head a handsome nuptial turban. Ps. 45 : 8; Cant. 4 : 10, 11. The bride was veiled. Her robes were white, Rev. 19 : 8, and sometimes embroidered with gold thread, Ps. 45 : 13, 14, and covered with perfumes, Ps. 45 : 8; she was further decked out with jewels. Isa. 49 : 18; 61 : 10; Rev. 21 : 2. When the fixed hour arrived, which was gener-

ally late in the evening, the bridegroom set forth from his house, attended by his groomsmen (Authorized Version "companions," Judges 14 : 11; "children of the bride-chamber," Matt. 9 : 15), preceded by a band of musicians or singers, Gen. 31 : 27; Jer. 7 : 34; 16 : 9, and accompanied by persons bearing flambeaux, Jer. 25 : 10; 2 Esdr. 10 : 2; Matt. 25 : 7; Rev. 18 : 23, and took the bride with the friends to his own house. At the house a feast was prepared, to which all the friends and neighbors were invited, Gen. 29 : 22; Matt. 22 : 1–10; Luke 14 : 8; John 2 : 2, and the festivities were protracted for seven or even fourteen days. Judges 14 : 12; Tob. 8 : 19. The guests were provided by the host with fitting robes, Matt. 22 : 11, and the feast was enlivened with riddles, Judges 14 : 12, and other amusements. The last act in the ceremonial was the conducting of the bride to the bridal chamber, Judges 15 : 1; Joel 2 : 16, where a canopy was prepared. Ps. 19 : 5; Joel 2 : 16. The bride was still completely veiled, so that the deception practiced on Jacob, Gen. 29 : 23, was not difficult. A newly-married man was exempt from military service, or from any public business which might draw him away from his home, for the space of a year, Deut. 24 : 5; a similar privilege was granted to him who was betrothed. Deut. 20 : 7.

4. *The social and domestic conditions of married life.*—The wife must have exercised an important influence in her own home. She appears to have taken her part in family affairs, and even to have enjoyed a considerable amount of independence. Judges 4 : 18; 1 Sam. 25 : 14; 2 Kings 4 : 8, etc. In the New Testament the mutual relations of husband and wife are a subject of frequent exhortation. Eph. 5 : 22, 33; Col. 3 : 18, 19; Titus 2 : 4, 5; 1 Pet. 3 : 1–7. The duties of the wife in the Hebrew household were multifarious: in addition to the general superintendence of the domestic arrangements, such as cooking, from which even women of rank were not exempt, Gen. 18 : 6; 2 Sam. 13 : 8, and the distribution of food at meal times, Prov. 31 : 15, the manufacture of the clothing and of the various fabrics required in her home devolved upon her, Prov. 31 : 13, 21, 22; and if she were a model of activity and skill, she produced a surplus of fine linen shirts and girdles, which she sold, and so, like a well-freighted merchant ship,

brought in wealth to her husband from afar. Prov. 31 : 14, 24. The legal rights of the wife are noticed in Ex. 21 : 10 under the three heads of food, raiment, and duty of marriage or conjugal right.

5. *The allegorical and typical allusions to marriage* have exclusive reference to one object, viz., to exhibit the spiritual relationship between God and his people. In the Old Testament Isa. 54 : 5; Jer. 3 :

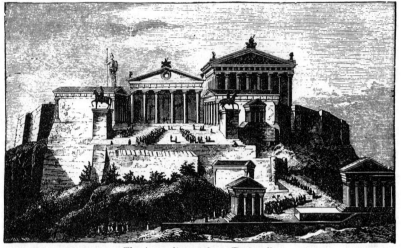

The Acropolis at Athens (Restored).

View of Mars' Hill or Areopagus.

14; Hos. 2 : 19. In the New Testament the image of the bridegroom is transferred from Jehovah to Christ, Matt. 9 : 15; John 3 : 29, and that of the bride to the Church. 2 Cor. 11 : 2; Rev. 19 : 7; 21 : 2, 9.

Mars' Hill, the hill of Mars or Ares, better known by the name of Areopagus, of which *hill of Mars* or *Ares* is a translation. The Areopagus was a rocky height in Athens, opposite the western end of the Acropolis. It rises gradually from the northern end, and terminates abruptly on the south, over against the Acropolis, at which point it is about fifty or sixty feet above the valley. The spot is memorable as the place of meeting of the Council of Areopagus. This body existed as a criminal tribunal before the time of Solon, and was the most ancient and venerable of all the Athenian courts. It consisted of all persons who had held the office of archon, and who were members of the council for life unless expelled for misconduct. Before the time of Solon the court tried only cases of willful murder, wounding, poison, and arson; but he gave it extensive powers of a censorial and political nature. The council continued to exist even under the Roman emperors. Its meetings were held on the southeastern summit of the rock. The Areopagus possesses peculiar interest to the Christian as the spot from which St. Paul delivered his memorable address to the men of Athens. Acts 17 : 22–31. St. Paul "disputed daily" in the "market" or agora, Acts 17 : 17, which was situated south of the Areopagus in the valley lying between this and the hills of the Acropolis, the Pnyx and the Museum. Attracting more and more attention, "certain philosophers of the Epicureans and Stoics" brought him up from the valley, probably by the stone steps, to the Areopagus above, that they might listen to him more conveniently.

Mar'sena (*worthy*), one of the seven princes of Persia, "wise men which knew the times," which saw the king's face and sat first in the kingdom. Esther 1 : 14.

Mar'tha (*a lady*), the sister of Lazarus and Mary. [LAZARUS.] The facts recorded in Luke 10 and John 11 indicate a character devout after the customary Jewish type of devotion, sharing in Messianic hopes and accepting Jesus as the Christ. When she first comes before us, Luke 10 : 38, her spirit is "cumbered with much serving," is "careful and troubled about many things." Her love, though imperfect in its form, is yet recognized as true, and she has the distinction of being one whom Jesus loved. John 11 : 3. Her position is obviously that of the elder sister, the head and manager of the household. In the supper at Bethany, John 12 : 2, the old character shows itself still, but it has been freed from evil. She is no longer "cumbered," no longer impatient. Activity has been calmed by trust.

Ma'ry (*a tear*) **of Cle'ophas.** So in Authorized Version, but accurately "of Clopas," *i. e.* the wife of Clopas (or Alphæus). She is brought before us for the first time on the day of the crucifixion, standing by the cross. John 19 : 25. In the evening of the same day we find her sitting desolate at the tomb with Mary Magdalene, Matt. 27 : 61; Mark 15 : 47; and at the dawn of Easter morning she was again there with sweet spices, which she had prepared on the Friday night, Matt. 28 : 1; Mark 16 : 1; Luke 23 : 56, and was one of those who had "a vision of angels, which said that he was alive." Luke 24 : 23. She had four sons and at least three daughters. The names of the daughters are unknown to us; those of the sons are James, Joses, Jude and Simon, two of whom became enrolled among the twelve apostles [JAMES], and a third [SIMON] may have succeeded his brother in charge of the church of Jerusalem. By many she is thought to have been the sister of the Virgin Mary.

Ma'ry Magdale'ne. Different explanations have been given of this name; but the most natural is that she came from the town of Magdala. She appears before us for the first time in Luke 8 : 2, among the women who "ministered unto him of their substance." All appear to have occupied a position of comparative wealth. With all the chief motive was that of gratitude for their deliverance from "evil spirits and infirmities." Of Mary it is said specially that "seven devils went out of her," and the number indicates a *possession* of more than ordinary malignity. She was present during the closing hours of the agony on the cross. John 19 : 25. She remained by the cross till all was over, and waited till the body was taken down and placed in the garden sepulchre of Joseph of Arimathæa, Matt. 27 : 61; Mark 15 : 47; Luke 23 : 55, when she, with Salome and Mary the mother of James, "bought sweet spices that they might come and anoint" the body. Mark 16 : 1. The next morning accordingly, in the earliest dawn, Matt. 28 : 1; Mark 16 : 2, they came with Mary the mother of James to the sepulchre. Mary Magdalene had been to the tomb and had found it empty, and had seen the "vision of angels." Matt. 28 : 5; Mark 16 : 5. To her first of all Jesus appeared after his resurrection. John 20 : 14, 15. Mary Magdalene has become the type of a class of repentant sinners; but there is no authority for identifying her with the "sinner" who anointed the feet of Jesus in Luke 7 : 36–50; neither is there any authority for the supposition that Mary Magdalene is the same as the sister of Lazarus. Neither of these theories has the slightest foundation in fact.

Ma'ry, mother of Mark, Col. 4 : 10, was sister to Barnabas. Acts 4 : 36 ; 12 : 12. She was among the earliest disciples, and lived at Jerusalem. She gave up her house to be used as one of the chief places of meeting. The fact that Peter went to that house on his release from prison indicates that there was some special intimacy, Acts 12 : 12, between them. (There is a tradition that the place of meeting of the disciples, and hence Mary's house, was on the upper slope of Zion, and that it was here that the Holy Ghost came upon the disciples with tongues of flame on the day of Pentecost.—ED.)

Ma'ry, sister of Lazarus. She and her sister Martha appear in Luke 10 : 40 as receiving Christ in their house. Mary sat listening eagerly for every word that fell from the divine Teacher. She had chosen the good part, the "one thing needful." The same character shows itself in the history of John 11. Her grief was deeper, but less active. Her first thought, when she saw the Teacher in whose power and love she had trusted, was one of complaint. But the great joy and love which her brother's return to life called up in her poured themselves out in larger measure than had been seen before. The treasured alabaster box of ointment was brought forth at the final feast of Bethany. John 12 : 3.

Ma'ry the virgin, the mother of our Lord. There is no person perhaps in sacred or profane history around whom so many legends have been grouped as the Virgin Mary; and there are few whose authentic history is more concise. She was, like Joseph, of the tribe of Judah and of the lineage of David. Ps. 132 : 11 ; Luke 1 : 32 ; Rom. 1 : 3. She had a sister, named, like herself, Mary, John 19 : 25, and she was connected by marriage, Luke 1 : 36, with Elisabeth, who was of the tribe of Levi and of the lineage of Aaron. This is all that we know of her antecedents. She was betrothed to Joseph of Nazareth ; but before her marriage she became with child by the Holy Ghost, and became the mother of Jesus Christ, the Saviour of the world. Her history at this time, her residence at Bethlehem, flight to Egypt, and return to her early home at Nazareth, are well known. Four times only does she appear after the commencement of Christ's ministry. These four occasions are—1.

The marriage at Cana in Galilee took place in the three months which intervened between the baptism of Christ and the passover of the year 27. Mary was present, and witnessed the first miracle performed by Christ, when he turned the water into wine. She had probably become a widow before this time. 2. Capernaum, John 2 : 12, and Nazareth, Matt. 4 : 13 ; 13 : 54 ; Mark 6 : 1, appear to have been the residence of Mary for a considerable period. The next time that she is brought before us we find her at Capernaum, where she, with other relatives, had gone to inquire about the strange stories they had heard of her son Jesus. They sought an audience with our Lord, which was not granted, as he refused to admit any authority on the part of his relatives, or any privilege on account of their relationship. 3. The next scene in Mary's life brings us to the foot of the cross. With almost his last words Christ commended his mother to the care of him who had borne the name of the disciple whom Jesus loved : "Woman, behold thy son." And from that hour St. John assures us that he took her to his own abode. So far as Mary is portrayed to us in Scripture, she is, as we should have expected, the most tender, the most faithful, humble, patient and loving of women, but a woman still. 4. In the days succeeding the ascension of Christ Mary met with the disciples in the upper room, Acts 1 : 14, waiting for the coming of the Holy Spirit with power.

Ma'ry, a Roman Christian who is greeted by St. Paul in his Epistle to the Romans, ch. 16 : 6, as having toiled hard for him.

Mas'chil (*song of wisdom*), the title of thirteen Psalms: 32, 42, 44, 45, 52–55, 74, 78, 88, 89, 142. Ewald regards Ps. 45 : 7 (Authorized Version, "sing ye praises *with understanding;*" Heb. *maschil*) as the key to the meaning of maschil, which in his opinion is a musical term denoting a melody requiring great skill in its execution.

Mash (*drawn out*), one of the sons of Aram. Gen. 10 : 23. In 1 Chron. 1 : 17 the name appears as Meshech. The name Mash is probably represented by the *Mons Masius* of classical writers, a range which forms the northern boundary of Mesopotamia, between the Tigris and Euphrates.

Ma'shal (*entreaty*), the same as Misheal or Mishal. 1 Chron. 6 : 74.

Mas'rekah (*vineyard of noble vines*), an ancient place, the native spot of Samlah, one of the old kings of the Edomites. Gen. 36 : 36 ; 1 Chron. 1 : 47.

Mas'sa (*burden*), a son of Ishmael. Gen. 25 : 14 ; 1 Chron. 1 : 30. His descendants were not improbably the *Masani*, placed by Ptolemy in the east of Arabia, near the borders of Babylonia.

Mas'sah (*temptation*), a name given to the spot, also called Meribah, where the Israelites tempted Jehovah. Ex. 16 : 7 ; Ps. 95 : 8, 9 ; Heb. 3 : 8.

Mathu'sala = METHUSELAH, the son of Enoch. Luke 3 : 37.

Ma'tred (*pushing forward*), a daughter of Mezahab and mother of Mehetabel, who was wife of Hadar or Hadad of Pau, king of Edom. Gen. 36 : 39 ; 1 Chron. 1 : 50.

Ma'tri (*rain of Jehovah*), a family of the tribe of Benjamin, to which Saul the king of Israel belonged. 1 Sam. 10 : 21.

Mat'tan (*a gift*). 1. The priest of Baal slain before his altars in the idol temple at Jerusalem. 2 Kings 11 : 18 ; 2 Chron. 23 : 17. He probably accompanied Athalia from Samaria.

2. The father of Shephatiah. Jer. 38 : 1.

Mat'tanah (*gift of Jehovah*), a station in the latter part of the wanderings of the Israelites. Num. 21 : 18, 19. It was probably situated to the southeast of the Dead Sea.

Mattani'ah (*gift of Jehovah*). 1. The original name of Zedekiah king of Judah, which was changed when Nebuchadnezzar placed him on the throne. 2 Kings 24 : 17.

2. A Levite singer of the sons of Asaph. 1 Chron. 9 : 15. He was leader of the temple choir after its restoration, Neh. 11 : 17 ; 12 : 8, in the time of Nehemiah, and took part in the musical service which accompanied the dedication of the wall of Jerusalem. Neh. 12 : 25, 35.

3. A descendant of Asaph, and ancestor of Jahaziel the Levite, in the reign of Jehoshaphat. 2 Chron. 20 : 14.

4. One of the sons of Elam. Ezra 10 : 26.

5. One of the sons of Zattu. Ezra 10 : 27.

6. A descendant of Pahath-moab, Ezra 10 : 30, and

7. One of the sons of Bani, Ezra 10 : 37, who all put away their foreign wives at Ezra's command.

8. A Levite, father of Zaccur and ancestor of Hanan the under-treasurer who had charge of the offerings for the Levites in the time of Nehemiah. Neh. 13 : 13.

9. One of the fourteen sons of Heman, whose office it was to blow the horns in the temple service as appointed by David. 1 Chron. 25 : 4, 16.

10. A descendant of Asaph the Levite minstrel, who assisted in the purification of the temple in the reign of Hezekiah. 2 Chron. 29 : 13.

Mat'tathah (*gift of Jehovah*), probably a contraction of Mattathiah. 1. Son of Nathan and grandson of David, in the genealogy of Christ. Luke 3 : 31. (B.C. after 1014.)

2. An Israelite, son of Hashun, who divorced his Gentile wife after the return from Babylon. Ezek. 10 : 33. (B.C. 458.)

Mattathi'as (*gift of Jehovah*), the Greek form of Mattathiah. 1. Son of Amos, in the genealogy of Christ. Luke 3 : 25. (B.C. after 406.)

2. Son of Semei. Luke 3 : 26.

3. The father of the Maccabees. (B.C. 168 and previous.)

Mattena'i (*gift of Jehovah*), a contraction of Mattaniah. 1. Two Israelites who divorced their Gentile wives after the return from the Babylonish captivity. Ezra 10 : 33, 37. (B.C. 459.)

2. A priest, son of Joiarib, in the time of Joiakim. Neh. 12 : 19. (B.C. after 536.)

Mat'than (*gift*), grandfather of Joseph the husband of the Virgin Mary. Matt. 1 : 15.

Mat'that (*gift of God*), a form of the name Matthan. 1. Son of Levi, in the genealogy of Christ. Luke 3 : 29. (B.C. after 623.)

2. Grandfather of the Virgin Mary. Luke 3 : 24.

Mat'thew (*gift of Jehovah*). (A contraction, as is also Matthias, of Mattathias. His original name was Levi, and his name Matthew was probably adopted as his new apostolic name. He was a Jew. His father's name was Alphæus. His home was at Capernaum. His business was the collection of dues and customs from persons and goods crossing the Sea of Galilee, or passing along the great Damascus road which ran along the shore between Bethsaida Julius and Capernaum. Christ called him from this work to be his disciple. He appears to have been a man of wealth, for he made a great feast in his own house, perhaps in order to introduce his former companions and friends to Jesus. His business would tend to give him a knowledge of human nature, and accurate business habits, and of how to make a way to the hearts of many publicans and sinners not otherwise easily reached. He is mentioned by name, after the resurrection of Christ, only in Acts 1 : 13 ; but he must have lived many years as an apostle, since he was the author of the Gospel of Matthew, which was written at least twenty years later. There is reason to believe that he remained for fifteen years at Jerusalem, after which he went as missionary to the Persians, Parthians and Medes. There is a legend that he died a martyr in Ethiopia.—ED.)

Mat'thew, Gospel of. 1. *Its authorship.*—That this Gospel was written by the apostle Matthew there is no reason to doubt. Seventeen independent witnesses of the first four centuries attest its genuineness. 2. *Its original language.*—The testimony of the early Church is unanimous that Matthew wrote originally in the Hebrew language. On the other hand, doubt is thrown over this opinion, both by an examination of the statements of the fathers and by a consideration of peculiar forms of language employed in the Gospel itself. The question is unsettled, the best scholars not agreeing in their judgment concerning it. If there was a Hebrew original, it disappeared at a very early age. The Greek Gospel which we now possess was, it is almost certain, written in Matthew's lifetime ; and it is not at all improbable that he wrote the Gospel in both the Greek and Hebrew languages.—*Lyman Abbott.* It is almost certain that our Lord spoke in Greek with foreigners, but with his disciples and the Jewish people in Aramaic (a form of language closely allied to the Hebrew).—*Schaff.* The Jewish historian Josephus furnishes an illustration of the fate of the Hebrew original of Matthew. Josephus himself informs us that he wrote his great work, "The History of the Jewish Wars," originally in Hebrew, his native tongue, for the benefit of his own nation, and he afterward translated it into Greek. No notices of the Hebrew original now survive.—*Professor D. S. Gregory.* 3. *The date.*—The testimony of the early Church is unanimous that Matthew wrote *first* among the evangelists. Irenæus relates that Matthew wrote his Gospel while Peter and Paul were preaching, and

founding the Church at Rome, *after* A.D. 61. It was published *before* the destruction of Jerusalem, A.D. 70.—*Alford.* We would place our present Gospel between A.D. 60 and 66. If there was an original Hebrew Gospel, an earlier date belongs to it.—*Ellicott.* 4. *Its object.*—This Gospel was probably written in Palestine for Jewish Christians. It is an historical proof that Jesus is the Messiah. Matthew is the Gospel for the Jew. It is the Gospel of Jesus, the Messiah of the prophets. This Gospel takes the life of Jesus as it was lived on earth, and his character as it actually appeared, and places them alongside the life and character of the Messiah as sketched in the prophets, the historic by the side of the prophetic, that the two may appear in their marvellous unity and in their perfect identity.—*Professor Gregory.*

Matthi'as (*gift of God*), the apostle elected to fill the place of the traitor Judas. Acts 1 : 26. All beyond this that we know of him for certainty is that he had been a constant attendant upon the Lord Jesus during the whole course of his ministry ; for such was declared by St. Peter to be the necessary qualification of one who was to be a witness of the resurrection. It is said that he preached the gospel and suffered martyrdom in Ethiopia.

Mattithi'ah (*gift of God*). 1. A Levite who presided over the offerings made in the pans. 1 Chron. 9 : 31 ; comp. Lev. 6 : 20 (12), etc.

2. One of the Levites appointed by David to minister before the ark in the musical service, 1 Chron. 16 : 5, " with harps upon Sheminith," comp. 1 Chron. 15 : 21, to lead the choir. 1 Chron. 15 : 18, 21 ; 25 : 3, 21.

3. One of the family of Nebo who had married a foreign wife, in the days of Ezra. Ezra 10 : 43.

4. Probably a priest, who stood at the right hand of Ezra when he read the law to the people. Ezra 8 : 4.

Mattock. Isaiah 7 : 25. The tool used in Arabia for loosening the ground, described by Niebuhr, answers generally to our mattock or grubbing-axe, *i. e.* a single-headed

Mattock or Egyptian Hoe. (*After Wilkinson.*)

pickaxe. The ancient Egyptian hoe was of wood, and answered for hoe, spade and pick.

Maul (*i. e.* a hammer), a sort of battle-axe or hammer, used as an implement of war. Prov. 25 : 18.

Mauzzim (*fortresses*). The marginal note to the Authorized Version of Dan. 11 : 38, " the god of forces," gives as the equivalent of the last word " Mauzzim, or gods protectors, or munitions." There can be little doubt that mauzzim is to be taken in its literal sense of " fortresses," just as in Dan. 11 : 19, 39 ; "the god of fortresses " being then the deity who presided over strongholds. The opinion of Gesenius is that " the god of fortresses " was Jupiter Capitolinus, for whom Antiochus built a temple at Antioch. Liv. xli. 20.

Mazzaroth (*the twelve signs*). The margin of the Authorized Version of Job 38 : 32 gives *Mazzaroth* as the name of the twelve signs of the zodiac.

Reclining at Table.

Meadow. 1. In Genesis 41 : 2, 18, meadow appears to be an Egyptian term meaning some kind of flag or water-plant, as its use in Job 8 : 11 (Authorized Version "flag") seems to show. 2. In Judges 20 : 33 the sense of the Hebrew word translated *meadow* is doubly uncertain. The most plausible interpretation is that of the Peshito-Syriac, which by a slight difference in the vowel-points makes the word *mearah*, " the cave."

Me'ah (*a hundred*), **The tower of,** one of the towers of the wall of Jerusalem when rebuilt by Nehemiah, Neh. 3 : 1 ; 12 : 39, appears to have been situated somewhere at the northeast part of the city, outside of the walls of Zion.

Meals. Our information on the subject of meals is but scanty. The early Hebrews do not seem to have given special names to their several meals, for the terms rendered " dine " and "dinner " in the Authorized Version (Gen. 43 : 16 ; Prov. 15 : 17) are in reality general expressions, which might more correctly be rendered " eat " and " portion of food." In the New Testament " dinner " and " supper," Luke 14 : 12 ; John 21 : 12, are more properly " breakfast " and " dinner." There is some uncertainty as to the hours at which meals were taken ; the Egyptians undoubtedly took their principal meal at noon, Gen. 43 : 16 ; laborers took a light meal at that time. Ruth 2 : 14 ; comp. ver. 17. The Jews rather followed the custom that prevails among the Bedouins, and made their principal meal after sunset, and a lighter meal at about 9 or 10 A.M. The old Hebrews were in the habit of *sitting*. Gen. 27 : 19 ; Judges 19 : 6 ; 1 Sam. 20 : 5, 24 ; 1 Kings 13 : 20. The table was in this case but slightly elevated above the ground, as is still the case in Egypt. As luxury increased, the practice of sitting was exchanged for that of reclining. In the time of our Saviour, reclining was the universal custom. As several guests reclined on the same couch, each overlapped his neighbor, as it were, and rested his head on or near the breast of the one who lay behind him ; he was then said to " lean on the bosom " of his neighbor. John 13 : 23 ; 21 : 20. The ordinary arrangement of the couches was in three sides of a square, the fourth being left open for the servants to bring up the dishes. Some doubt attends the question whether the females took their meals along with the males. Before commencing the meal the guests washed their hands. This custom was founded on natural decorum : not only was the hand the substitute for our knife and fork, but the hands of all the guests were dipped into one and the same dish. Another preliminary step was the grace or blessing, of which we have but one instance in the Old Testament—1 Sam. 9 : 13—and more than one pronounced by our Lord himself in the New Testament—Matt. 15 : 36; Luke 9 : 16; John 6 : 11. The mode of taking the food differed in no material point from the modern usages of the East. Generally there was a single dish, into which each guest dipped his hand. Matt. 26 : 23. Occasionally separate portions were served out to each. Gen. 43 : 34; Ruth 2 : 14; 1 Sam. 1 : 4. A piece of bread was held between the thumb and two fingers of the right hand, and was dipped either into a bowl of melted grease (in which case it was termed "a sop," John 13 : 26) or into the dish of meat, whence a piece was conveyed to the mouth between the layers of bread. At the conclusion of the meal, grace was again said in conformity with Deut. 8 : 10, and the hands were again washed. On state occasions more ceremony was used, and the meal was enlivened in various ways. A sumptuous repast was prepared; the guests were previously invited, Esther 5 : 8; Matt. 22 : 3, and on the day of the feast a second invitation was issued to those that were bidden. Esther 6 : 14; Prov. 9 : 3; Matt. 22 : 4. The visitors were received with a kiss, Luke 7 : 45; water was furnished for them to wash their feet with, Luke 7 : 44; the head, the beard, the feet, and sometimes the clothes, were perfumed with ointment, Ps. 23 : 5; John 12 : 3; on special occasions robes were provided, Matt. 22 : 11, and the head was decorated with wreaths. Isa. 28 : 1. The regulation of the feast was under the superintendence of a special officer, John 2 : 8 (Authorized Version "governor of the feast"), whose business it was to taste the food and the liquors before they were placed on the table, and to settle about the toasts and amusements; he was generally one of the guests, Ecclus. 32 : 1, 2, and might

therefore take part in the conversation. The places of the guests were settled according to their respective rank, Gen. 43 : 33; Mark 12 : 39; portions of food were placed before each, 1 Sam. 1 : 4, the most honored guests receiving either larger, Gen. 43 : 34, or more choice, 1 Sam. 9 : 24, portions than the rest. The meal was enlivened with music, singing and dancing, 2 Sam. 19 : 35, or with riddles, Judges 14 : 12; and amid these entertainments the festival was prolonged for several days. Esther 1 : 3, 4.

Mea'rah (*a cave*), a place named in Josh. 13 : 4 only. The word means in Hebrew a cave, and it is commonly assumed that the reference is to some remarkable cavern in the neighborhood of Zidon.

Measures. [WEIGHTS AND MEASURES.]

Meat. It does not appear that the word "meat" is used in any one instance in the Authorized Version of either the Old or the New Testament in the sense which it now almost exclusively bears of animal food. The latter is denoted uniformly by "flesh." The word "meat," when our English version was made, meant *food* in general; or if any particular kind was designated, it referred to meal, flour or grain. The only real and inconvenient ambiguity caused by the change which has taken place in the meaning of the word is in the case of the "meat offering." [MEAT OFFERING.]

Meat offering. The law or ceremonial of the meat offering is described in Lev. 2 and 6 : 14-23. It was to be composed of fine flour, seasoned with salt and mixed with oil and frankincense, but without leaven ; and it was generally accompanied by a drink offering of wine. A portion of it, including all the frankincense, was to be burnt on the altar as "a memorial ;" the rest belonged to the priest; but the meat offerings offered by the priests themselves were to be wholly burnt. Its meaning appears to be exactly expressed in the words of David. 1 Chron. 29 : 10-14. It will be seen that this meaning involves neither of the main ideas of sacrifice—the atonement for sin and self-dedication to God. It takes them for granted, and is based on them. Rather it expresses gratitude and love to God as the giver of all. Accordingly the meat offering, properly so called, seems always to have been a subsidiary offering, needing to be introduced by the sin offering, which represented the one idea, and to have formed an appendage to the burnt offering, which represented the other. The unbloody offerings offered alone did not properly belong to the regular meat offering; they were usually substitutes for other offerings. Comp. Lev. 5 : 11; Num. 5 : 15. [MEAT.]

Mebun'na-i (*building of Jehovah*). In this form appears, in one passage only—2 Sam. 23 : 27—the name of one of David's guard, who is elsewhere called SIBBECHAI, 2 Sam. 21 : 18 ; 1 Chron. 20 : 4, or SIBBECAI, 1 Chron. 11 : 29 ; 27 : 11, in the Authorized Version.

Mech'erathite, The, that is, the native or inhabitant of a place called Mecherah. 1 Chron. 11 : 36. In the parallel list of 2 Sam. 23 the name appears, with other variations, as " the Maachathite." ver. 34.

Me'dad (*love*). [ELDAD AND MEDAD.]

Me'dan (*contention*), a son of Abraham and Keturah. Gen. 25 : 2 ; 1 Chron. 1 : 32.

Med'eba (*water of rest*), a town on the eastern side of Jordan, first alluded to in Num. 21 : 30. Here it seems to denote the limit of the territory of Heshbon. It next occurs in the enumeration of the country divided among the transjordanic tribes, Josh. 13 : 9, as giving its name to a district of level downs called " the Mishor of Medeba" or " the Mishor on Medeba." At the time of the conquest Medeba belonged to the Amorites, apparently one of the towns taken from Moab by them. In the time of Ahaz Medeba was a sanctuary of Moab. Isa. 15 : 2. It has retained its name down to our own times, and lies four miles southeast of *Heshbon*, on a rounded but rocky hill.

Medes, Me'dia (*middle land*). Media lay northwest of Persia proper, south and southwest of the Caspian Sea, east of Armenia and Assyria, west and northwest of the great salt desert of Iram. Its greatest length was from north to south, and in this direction it extended from the 32d to the 40th parallel, a distance of 550 miles. In width it reached from about long. 45° to 53° ; but its average breadth was not more than from 250 to 300 miles. The division of Media commonly recognized by the Greeks and Romans was that into Media Magna and Media Atropatene. 1. Media Atropatene corresponded nearly to the modern *Azerbijan*, being the tract situated between the Caspian and the mountains which run north from Zagros. 2. Media Magna lay south and east of Atropatene. It contained great part of *Kurdistan* and *Luristan*, with all *Ardelan* and *Arak Ajemi*. It is indicative of the division that there were two Ecbatanas, respectively the capitals of the two districts. The Medes were a nation of very high antiquity ; we find a notice of them in the primitive Babylonian history of Berosus, who says that the Medes conquered Babylon at a very remote period (*cir.* B.C. 2458), and that eight Median monarchs reigned there consecutively, over a space of 224 years. The deepest obscurity hangs, however, over the whole history of the Medes from the time of their bearing sway in Babylonia, B.C. 2458–2234, to their first appearance in the cuneiform inscriptions among the enemies of Assyria, about B.C. 880. Near the middle of the seventh century B.C. the Median kingdom was consolidated, and became formidable to its neighbors ; but previous to this time it was not under the dominion of a single powerful monarch, but was ruled by a vast number of petty chieftains. Cyaxares, the third Median monarch, took Nineveh and conquered Assyria B.C. 625. The limits of the Median empire cannot be definitely fixed. From north to south it was certainly confined between the Persian Gulf and the Euphrates on the one side, the Black and Caspian Seas on the other. From east to west it had, however, a wide expansion, since it reached from the Halys at least as far as the Caspian Gates, and possibly farther. It was separated from Babylonia either by the Tigris or more probably by a line running about halfway between that river and the Euphrates. Its greatest length may be reckoned at 1500 miles from northwest to southeast, and its average breadth at 400 or 450 miles. Its area would thus be about 600,000 square miles, or somewhat greater than that of modern Persia. Of all the ancient Oriental monarchies the Median was the shortest in duration. It was overthrown by the Persians under Cyrus, B.C. 558, who captured its king, Astyages. The treatment of the Medes by the victorious Persians was not that of an ordinary conquered nation. Medes were appointed to stations of high honor and importance under Cyrus and his successors. The two nations seem blended into one, and we often find reference to this kingdom as that of the "Medes and Persians." Dan. 5 : 28; 6 : 8, 12, 15. The references to the Medes in the canonical Scriptures are not very numerous, but they are striking. We first hear of certain "cities of the Medes," in which the captive Israelites were placed by "the king of Assyria" on the destruction of Samaria, B.C. 721. 2 Kings 17 : 6; 18 : 11. Soon afterward Isaiah prophesies the part which the Medes shall take in the destruction of Babylon, Isa. 13 : 17; 21 : 2; which is again still more distinctly declared by Jeremiah, Jer. 51 : 11, 28, who sufficiently indicates the independence of Media in his day. ch. 25 : 25. Daniel relates the fact of the Medo-Persic conquest, Dan. 5 : 28, 31, giving an account of the reign of Darius the Mede, who appears to have been made viceroy by Cyrus. Dan. 6 : 1–28. In Ezra we have a mention of Achmetha (Ecbatana), "the *palace* in the province of the Medes," where the decree of Cyrus was found, Ezra 6 : 2–5—a notice which accords with the known facts that the Median capital was the seat of government under Cyrus, but a royal residence only, and not the seat of government, under Darius Hystaspis. Finally, in Esther the high rank of Media under the Persian kings, yet at the same time its subordinate position, is marked by the frequent combination of the two names in phrases of honor, the precedency being in every case assigned to the Persians.

Me′dian, The. Darius, "the son of Ahasuerus, of the seed of the Medes," Dan. 9 : 1, or "the Mede," ch. 11 : 1, is thus denoted in Dan. 5 : 31.

Medicine. Egypt was the earliest home of medical and other skill for the region of the Mediterranean basin, and every Egyptian mummy of the more expensive and elaborate sort involved a process of anatomy. Still we have no trace of any philosophical or rational system of Egyptian origin; and medicine in Egypt was a mere art or profession. Compared with the wild countries around them, however, the Egyptians must have seemed incalculably advanced. Representations of early Egyptian surgery apparently occur on some of the monuments of Beni-Hassan. Those who have assisted at the opening of a mummy have noticed that the teeth exhibited a dentistry not inferior in execution to the work of the best modern experts. This confirms the statement of Herodotus that

every part of the body was studied by a distinct practitioner. The reputation of Egypt's practitioners in historical times was such that both Cyrus and Darius sent to that country for physicians or surgeons. Of midwifery we have a distinct notice, Ex. 1 : 15, and of women as its practitioners, which fact may also be verified from the sculptures. The scrupulous attention paid to the dead was favorable to the health of the living. The practice of physic was not among the Jews a privilege of the priesthood. Any one might practice it, and this publicity must have kept it pure. Rank and honor are said to be the portion of the physician, and his office to be from the Lord. Ecclus. 38 : 1, 3, 12. To bring down the subject to the period of the New Testament, St. Luke, "the beloved physician," who practiced at Antioch whilst the body was his care, could hardly have failed to be conversant with all the leading opinions current down to his own time. Among special diseases named in the Old Testament is ophthalmia, Gen. 29 : 17, which is perhaps more common in Syria and Egypt than anywhere else in the world; especially in the fig season, the juice of the newly-ripe fruit having the power of giving it. It may occasion partial or total blindness. 2 Kings 6 : 18. The "burning boil," Lev. 13 : 23, is merely marked by the notion of an effect resembling that of fire, like our "carbuncle." The diseases rendered "scab" and "scurvy" in Lev. 21 : 20; 22 : 22; Deut. 28 : 27, may be almost any skin disease. Some of these may be said to approach the type of leprosy. The "botch (*shechin*) of Egypt," Deut. 28 : 27, is so vague a term as to yield a most uncertain sense. In Deut. 28 : 35 is mentioned a disease attacking the "knees and legs," consisting in a "sore botch which cannot be healed," but extended, in the sequel of the verse, from the "sole of the foot to the top of the head." The *Elephantiasis græcorum* is what now passes under the name of "leprosy;" the lepers, *e. g.*, of the huts near the Zion gate of modern Jerusalem are elephantiasiacs. [LEPROSY.] The disease of King Antiochus, 2 Macc. 9 : 5–10, etc., was that of a boil breeding worms. The case of the widow's son restored by Elisha, 2 Kings 4 : 19, was probably one of sunstroke. The palsy meets us in the New Testament only, and in features too familiar to need special remark. Palsy, gangrene and cancer were common in all the countries familiar to the scriptural writers, and neither differs from the modern disease of the same name. Mention is also made of the bites and stings of poisonous reptiles. Num. 21 : 6. Among surgical instruments or pieces of apparatus the following only are alluded to in Scripture : A cutting instrument, supposed a "sharp stone," Ex. 4 : 25 ; the "knife " of Josh. 5 : 2. The " awl " of Ex. 21 : 6 was probably a surgical instrument. The " roller to bind " of Ezek. 30 : 21 was for a broken limb, and is still used. A scraper, for which the "potsherd " of Job was a substitute. Job 2 : 8. Ex. 30 : 23-25 is a prescription in form. An occasional trace occurs of some chemical knowledge, e. g. the calcination of the gold by Moses, Ex. 32 : 20; the effect of "vinegar upon natron," Prov. 25 : 20 ; comp. Jer. 2 : 22. The mention of " the apothecary," Ex. 30 : 35 ; Eccles. 10 : 1, and of the merchant in "powders," Cant. 3 : 6, shows that a distinct and important branch of trade was set up in these wares, in which, as at a modern druggist's, articles of luxury, etc., are combined with the remedies of sickness. Among the most favorite of external remedies has always been the bath. There were special occasions on which the bath was ceremonially enjoined. The Pharisees and Essenes aimed at scrupulous strictness in all such rules. Matt. 15 : 2 ; Mark 7 : 5 ; Luke 11 : 38. River-bathing was common, but houses soon began to include a bathroom. Lev. 15 : 13 ; 2 Sam. 11 : 2 ; 2 Kings 5 : 10.

Megid'do (*place of crowds*) was in a very marked position on the southern rim of the plain of Esdraelon, on the frontier line of the territories of the tribes of Issachar and Manasseh, 6 miles from Mount Carmel and 11 from Nazareth. It commanded one of those passes from the north into the hill country which were of such critical importance in the history of Judea. Judith 4 : 7. The first mention occurs in Josh. 12 : 21, where Megiddo appears as the city of one of the kings whom Joshua defeated on the west of the Jordan. The song of Deborah brings the place vividly before us, as the scene of the great conflict between Sisera and Barak. When Pharaoh-necho came from Egypt against the king of Assyria, Josiah joined the latter, and was slain at Megiddo. 2 Kings 23 : 29 ; 2 Chron. 35 : 22-24. Megiddo is the

modern *el-Lejjûn*, which is undoubtedly the Legio of Eusebius and Jerome. There is a copious stream flowing down the gorge, and turning some mills before joining the Kishon. Here are probably the " waters of Megiddo " of Judges 5 : 19.

Mehet'abe-el (*favored of God*), another and less correct form of Mehetabel. The ancestor of Shemaiah the prophet who was hired against Nehemiah by Tobiah and Sanballat. Neh. 6 : 10.

Mehet'abel (*favored of God*), the daughter of Matred, and wife of Hadad king of Edom. Gen. 36 : 39.

Mehi'da (*famous, noble*), a family of Nethinim, the descendants of Mehida, returned from Babylon with Zerubbabel. Ezra 2 : 52 ; Neh. 7 : 54.

Me'hir (*price*), the son of Chelub the brother of Shuah. 1 Chron. 4 : 11.

Mehol'athite, The, a word occurring once only—1 Sam. 18 : 19. It no doubt denotes that Adriel belonged to a place called Meholah.

Mehu'jael (*smitten by God*), the son of Irad, and fourth in descent from Cain. Gen. 4 : 18.

Mehu'man (*faithful*), one of the seven eunuchs of Ahasuerus. Esther 1 : 10.

Mehu'nim (*habitations*). Ezra 2 : 50. Elsewhere called Mehunims and Meunim.

Mehu'nims, The, a people against whom King Uzziah waged a successful war. 2 Chron. 26 : 7. The name is the plural of Maon [MAON]. Another notice of the Mehunims in the reign of Hezekiah (*cir.* B.C. 726-697) is found in 1 Chron. 4 : 41. Here they are spoken of as a pastoral people, either themselves Hamites or in alliance with Hamites, quiet and peaceable, dwelling in tents. Here, however, the Authorized Version treats the word as an ordinary noun, and renders it " habitations." The latest appearance of the name Mehunims in the Bible is in the lists of those who returned from the captivity with Zerubbabel. Ezra 2 : 50, Authorized Version " Mehunim ;" Neh. 7 : 52, Authorized Version "Meunim."

Me-jar'kon (*waters of yellowness*), a town in the territory of Dan, Josh. 19 : 46 only, in the neighborhood of Joppa or Japho.

Mek'onah (*foundation*), one of the towns which were reinhabited after the captivity by the men of Judah. Neh. 11 : 28.

Melati'ah (*Jehovah delivers*), a Gibeonite who assisted in rebuilding the wall of Jerusalem. Neh. 3 : 7.

Mel′chi (*my king, my counsel*). 1. The son of Janna, and ancestor of Joseph in the genealogy of Jesus Christ. Luke 3 : 24.

2. The son of Addi in the same genealogy. Luke 3 : 28.

Melchi′ah (*Jehovah's king*), a priest, the father of Pashur. Jer. 21 : 1.

Melchis′edec (*king of righteousness*). Heb. 5, 6, 7. [MELCHIZEDEK.]

Mel′chi-shu′a, a son of Saul. 1 Sam. 14 : 49; 31 : 2. Elsewhere correctly given Malchishua.

Melchiz′edek (*king of righteousness*), king of Salem and priest of the most high God, who met Abram in the valley of Shaveh, which is the king's valley, brought out bread and wine, blessed him, and received tithes from him. Gen. 14 : 18–20. The other places in which Melchizedek is mentioned are Ps. 110 : 4, where Messiah is described as a priest

St. Paul's Bay, Malta.

forever, "after the order of Melchizedek," and Heb. 5, 6, 7, where these two passages of the Old Testament are quoted, and the typical relation of Melchizedek to our Lord is stated at great length. There is something surprising and mysterious in the first appearance of Melchizedek, and in the subsequent reference to him. Bearing a title which Jews in after ages would recognize as designating their own sovereign, bearing gifts which recall to Christians the Lord's Supper, this Canaanite crosses for a moment the path of Abram, and is unhesitatingly recognized as a person of higher spiritual rank than the friend of God. Disappearing as suddenly as he came, he is lost to the sacred writings for a thousand years. Jewish tradition pronounces Melchizedek to be a survivor of the deluge, the patriarch Shem. The way in which he is mentioned in Genesis would rather lead to the inference that Melchizedek was of one blood with the children of Ham, among whom

he lived, chief (like the king of Sodom) of a settled Canaanitish tribe. The "order of Melchizedek," in Ps. 110 : 4, is explained to mean "manner" = likeness in official dignity = a king and priest. The relation between Melchizedek and Christ as type and antitype is made in the Epistle to the Hebrews to consist in the following particulars: Each was a priest, (1) not of the Levitical tribe; (2) superior to Abraham; (3) whose beginning and end are unknown; (4) who is not only a priest, but also a king of righteousness and peace. A fruitful source of discussion has been found in the site of Salem. [SALEM.]

Mele′a, the son of Menan, and ancestor of Joseph in the genealogy of Jesus Christ. Luke 3 : 31.

Me′lech, the second son of Micah, the son of Merib-baal or Mephibosheth. 1 Chron. 8 : 35; 9 : 41.

Mel′icu, the same as MALLUCH 6. Neh. 12 : 14; comp. ver. 2.

Mel'ita (*honey*), the modern *Malta*. This island lies in the Mediterranean 60 miles south of Cape Passaro in Sicily, 900 miles from Gibraltar and about 1200 from Jerusalem. It is 17 miles long by 9 or 10 broad. It is naturally a barren rock, with no high mountains, but has been rendered fertile by industry and toil. It is famous for its honey and fruits. It is now in the hands of the English.— *McClintock and Strong.* This island has an illustrious place in Scripture as the scene of that shipwreck of St. Paul which is described in such minute detail in the Acts of the Apostles. Acts 27. The wreck probably happened at the place traditionally known as St. Paul's Bay, an inlet with a creek two miles deep and one broad. The question has been set at rest forever by Mr. Smith of Jordan Hill, in his "Voyage and Shipwreck of St. Paul," the first published work in which it was thoroughly investigated from a sailor's point of view. The objection that there are no vipers in Malta is overruled by the fact that Mr. Lewin saw such a serpent there, and that there may have been vipers in the wilder ancient times, even were none found there now. As regards the condition of the island of Melita, when St. Paul was there it was a dependency of the Roman province of Sicily. Its chief officer (under the governor of Sicily) appears from inscriptions to have had the title of πρῶτος Μελιταίων, or *Primus Melitensium*, and this is the very phrase which Luke uses. Acts 28:7. Melita, from its position in the Mediterranean and the excellence of its harbors, has always been important in both commerce and war. It was a settlement of the Phœnicians at an early period, and their language, in a corrupted form, was still spoken there in St. Paul's day.

Melons (Heb. *abattichîm*) are mentioned only in Num. 11:5. By the Hebrew word we are probably to understand both the melon (*Cucumis melo*) and the watermelon (*Cucurbita citrullus*). The watermelon, which is now extensively cultivated in all hot countries, is a fruit not unlike the common melon, but the leaves are deeply lobed and gashed; the flesh is pink or white, and contains a large quantity of cold watery juice without much flavor; the seeds are black.

Melzar (*steward*). The Authorized Version is wrong in regarding melzar as a proper name; it is rather an official title, Dan. 1:11, 16; the marginal reading, "the steward," is therefore more correct.

Mem'phis (*haven of the good*), a city of ancient Egypt, situated on the western bank of the Nile, about nine miles south of Cairo and five from the great pyramids and the sphinx. It is mentioned by Isaiah, Isa. 19:13, Jeremiah, Jer. 2:16; 46:14, 19, and Ezekiel, Ezek. 30:13, 16,

The Serapeium at Memphis (Noph).

under the name of Noph. Though some regard Thebes as the more ancient city, the monuments of Memphis are of higher antiquity than those of Thebes. The city is said to have had a circumference of about 19 miles. The temple of Apis was one of the most noted structures of Memphis. It stood opposite the southern portico of the temple of Ptah; and Psammetichus, who built that gateway, also erected in front of the sanctuary of Apis a magnificent colonnade, supported by colossal statues or Osiride pillars, such as may still be seen at the temple of Medeenet Habou at Thebes. Herod. ii. 153. Through this colonnade the Apis was led with great pomp upon state occasions. At Memphis was the reputed burial-place of Isis; it had also a temple to that "myriad-named" divinity. Memphis had also its Serapeium, which probably stood in the western quarter of the city. The sacred cubit and other symbols used in measuring the rise of the Nile were deposited in the temple of Serapis. The

Necropolis, adjacent to Memphis, was on a scale of grandeur corresponding with the city itself. The "city of the pyramids" is a title of Memphis in the hieroglyphics upon the monuments. Memphis long held its place as a capital; and for centuries a Memphite dynasty ruled over all Egypt. Lepsius, Bunsen and Brugsch agree in regarding the third, fourth, sixth, seventh and eighth dynasties of the old empire as Memphite, reaching through a period of about 1000 years. The city's overthrow was distinctly predicted by the

Colossal Figure discovered at Memphis.

Hebrew prophets. Isa. 19:13; Jer. 46:19. The latest of these predictions was uttered nearly 600 years before Christ, and half a century before the invasion of Egypt by Cambyses (cir. B.C. 525). Herodotus informs us that Cambyses, enraged at the opposition he encountered at Memphis, committed many outrages upon the city. The city never recovered from the blow inflicted by Cambyses. The rise of Alexandria hastened its decline. The caliph conquerors founded Fostát (old Cairo) upon the opposite bank of the Nile, a few miles north of Memphis, and brought materials from the old city to build their new capital, A.D. 638. At length so complete was the ruin of Memphis that for a long time its very site was lost. Recent explorations have brought to light many of its antiquities.

Memu'can (*dignified*), one of the seven princes of Persia in the reign of Ahasuerus, who "saw the king's face," and sat first in the kingdom. Esther 1:14, 16, 21.

Men'ahem (*comforter*), son of Gadi, who slew the usurper Shallum, and seized the vacant throne of Israel, B.C. 772. His reign, which lasted ten years, is briefly recorded in 2 Kings 15:14–22. He maintained the calf-worship of Jeroboam. The contemporary prophets Hosea and Amos have left a melancholy picture of the ungodliness, demoralization and feebleness of Israel. Menahem reigned B.C. 771–760.

Me'nan (called Menna in the Revised Version), one of the ancestors of Joseph in the genealogy of Jesus Christ. Luke 3:31.

Mene (*numbered*), the first word of the mysterious inscription written upon the wall of Belshazzar's palace, in which Daniel read the doom of the king and his dynasty. Dan. 5:25, 26.

Me'ni (*fate, fortune*). Isa. 65:11. This word is a proper name, and is also the proper name of an object of idolatrous worship cultivated by the Jews in Babylon.

Men'na. In the Revised Version of Luke 3:31 for Menan.

Meon'enim (*enchanters*), **The plain of,** an oak or terebinth, or other great tree. Judges 9:37. The meaning of Meonenim, if interpreted as a Hebrew word, is enchanters or "observers of times," as it is elsewhere rendered, Deut. 18:10, 14; in Micah 5:12 it is "soothsayers."

Meon'otha-i (*my habitations*), one of the sons of Othniel, the younger brother of Caleb. 1 Chron. 4:14.

Meph'a-ath (*splendor, height*), a city of the Reubenites, one of the towns dependent on Heshbon, Josh. 13:18, lying in the district of the Mishor, comp. ver. 17 and Jer. 48:21, Authorized Version "plain," which probably answered to the modern *Belka.* It was one of the cities allotted with their suburbs to the Merarite Levites. Josh. 21:37; 1 Chron. 6:79. Its site is uncertain.

Mephib'osheth (*exterminating the idol*), the name borne by two members of the family of Saul—his son and his grandson. 1. Saul's son by Rizpah the daughter of Aiah, his concubine. 2 Sam. 21:8. He and his brother Armoni were among the seven victims who were surrendered by David to the Gibeonites, and by them crucified to avert a famine from which the country was suffering.

2. The son of Jonathan, grandson of Saul and nephew of the preceding; called also Merib-baal. 1 Chron. 8 : 34. His life seems to have been, from beginning to end, one of trial and discomfort. When his father and grandfather were slain on Gilboa he was an infant but five years old. At this age he met with an accident which deprived him for life of the use of both feet. 2 Sam. 4 : 4. After this he found a home with Machir ben-Ammiel, a powerful Gadite, who brought him up, and while here was married. Later on David invited him to Jerusalem, and there treated him and his son Micha with the greatest kindness. From this time forward he resided at Jerusalem. Of Mephibosheth's behavior during the rebellion of Absalom we possess two accounts—his own, 2 Sam. 19 : 24-30, and that of Ziba, 2 Sam. 16 : 1-4. They are naturally at variance with each other. In consequence of the story of Ziba, he was rewarded by the possessions of his master. Mephibosheth's story—which, however, he had not the opportunity of telling until several days later, when he met David returning to his kingdom at the western bank of Jordan—was very different from Ziba's. That David did not disbelieve it is shown by his revoking the judgment he had previously given. That he did not entirely reverse his decision, but allowed Ziba to retain possession of half the lands of Mephibosheth, is probably due partly to weariness at the whole transaction, but mainly to the conciliatory frame of mind in which he was at that moment. "Shall there any man be put to death this day?" is the keynote of the whole proceeding.

Me'rab (*increase*), the eldest daughter of King Saul. 1 Sam. 14 : 49. In accordance with the promise which he made before the engagement with Goliath, ch. 17 : 25, Saul betrothed Merab to David. ch. 18 : 17. Before the marriage Merab's younger sister Michal had displayed her attachment for David, and Merab was then married to Adriel the Meholathite, to whom she bore five sons. 2 Sam. 21 : 8.

Mera'iah (*rebellion*), a priest in the days of Joiakim. Neh. 12 : 12.

Mera'ioth (*rebellious*). 1. A descendant of Eleazar the son of Aaron, and head of a priestly house. 1 Chron. 6 : 6, 7, 52. It is apparently another Meraioth who comes in between Zadok and Ahitub in the genealogy of Azariah. 1 Chron. 9 : 11; Neh. 11 : 11.

2. The head of one of the houses of priests, which in the time of Joiakim the son of Jeshua was represented by Helkai. Neh. 12 : 15.

Mer'ari, Mer'arites (*bitter, unhappy*), third son of Levi, and head of the third great division of the Levites, the Merarites. Gen. 46 : 8, 11. At the time of the exodus and the numbering in the wilderness, the Merarites consisted of two families, the Mahlites and the Mushites, Mahli and Mushi being either the two sons or the son and grandson of Merari. 1 Chron. 6 : 19, 47. Their chief at that time was Zuriel. Their charge was the boards, bars, pillars, sockets, pins and cords of the tabernacle and the court, and all the tools connected with setting them up. In the division of the land by Joshua, the Merarites had twelve cities assigned to them, out of Reuben, Gad and Zebulun. Josh. 21 : 7, 34-40; 1 Chron. 6 : 63, 77-81. In the days of Hezekiah the Merarites were still flourishing. 2 Chron. 29 : 12, 15.

Meratha'im (*double rebellion*)**, The land of,** alluding to the country of the Chaldeans, and to the double captivity which it had inflicted on the nation of Israel. Jer. 50 : 21.

Mercu'rius (*herald of the gods*), properly Hermes, the Greek deity, whom the Romans identified with their Mercury, the god of commerce and bargains. Hermes was the son of Zeus (Jupiter) and Maia the daughter of Atlas, and is constantly represented as the companion of his father in his wandering upon earth. The episode of Baucis and Philemon, Ovid, *Metam.* viii. 620-724, appears to have formed part of the folk-lore of Asia Minor, and strikingly illustrates the readiness with which the simple people of Lystra recognized in Barnabas and Paul the gods who, according to their wont, had come down in the likeness of men. Acts 14 : 11.

Mer'cury, Acts 14 : 12, the translation of the above in the Revised Version.

Mercy-seat. Ex. 25 : 17; 37 : 6; Heb. 9 : 5. This appears to have been merely the lid of the ark of the covenant, not another surface affixed thereto. (It was a solid plate of gold, 2½ cubits (6¼ feet) long by 1½ cubits (2⅔ feet) wide, representing a kind of throne of God, where he would hear prayer and from which he spoke words of comfort.—ED.) It was that whereon the blood of the yearly atonement was sprinkled by the high priest; and in this relation it is doubtful whether the sense of the word in the Hebrew is based on the material fact of its "covering" the ark, or derived from this notion of its reference to the "covering" (*i. e.* atonement) of sin.

Me'red (*rebellion*). This name occurs in a fragmentary genealogy in 1 Chron. 4 : 17, 18, as that of one of the sons of Ezra. Tradition identifies him with Caleb and Moses.

Mer'emoth (*elevations*). 1. Son of Uriah or Urijah the priest, of the family of Koz or Hakkoz, the head of the seventh course of priests as established by David. In Ezra 8 : 33 Meremoth is appointed to weigh and register the gold and silver vessels belonging to the temple. In the rebuilding of the wall of Jerusalem under Nehemiah we find Meremoth taking an active part. Neh. 3 : 4, 21.

2. A layman of the sons of Bani, who had married a foreign wife. Ezra 10 : 36.

3. A priest, or more probably a family of priests, who sealed the covenant with Nehemiah. Neh. 10 : 5.

Me'res (*lofty*), one of the seven counsellors of Ahasuerus. Esther 1 : 14.

Mer'ibah (*strife, contention*). In Ex. 17 : 7 we read, "he called the name of the place Massah and Meribah," where the people murmured and the rock was smitten. [For the situation see REPHI-DIM.] The name is also given to Kadesh, Num. 20 : 13, 24; 27 : 14; Deut. 32 : 51 (Meribah-kadesh), because there also the people, when in want of water, strove with God.

Merib'ba-al (*contender against Baal*). 1 Chron. 8 : 34; 9 : 40. [See MEPHIBOSHETH.]

Mero'dach (*death*), Jer. 50 : 2, identical with the famous Babylonian Bel or Belus, the word being probably at first a mere epithet of the god, which by degrees superseded his proper appellation.

Mero'dach-bal'adan (*worshipper of Baal*) is mentioned as king of Babylon in the days of Hezekiah both in the second book of Kings, ch. 20 : 12, and in Isaiah. ch. 39 : 1. In the former place he is called Berodach-baladan. The name of Merodach-baladan has been recognized in the Assyrian inscriptions. It

appears there were two reigns of this king, the first from B.C. 721 to B.C. 709, when he was deposed; and the second after his recovery of the throne in B.C. 702, which lasted only half a year. There is some doubt as to the time at which he sent his embassadors to Hezekiah, for the purpose of inquiring as to the astronomical marvel of which Judea had been the scene, 2 Chron. 32 : 31; but it appears to have been B.C. 713.

Me'rom (*high place*), **The waters**

The Waters of Merom.

of, a lake formed by the river Jordan, about ten miles north of the Sea of Galilee. It is a place memorable in the history of the conquest of Palestine. Here Joshua completely routed the confederacy of the northern chiefs under Jabin. Josh. 11:5,7. It is a remarkable fact that though by common consent "the waters of Merom" are identified with the lake through which the Jordan runs between Banias and the Sea of Galilee—the *Bahr el-Hû-leh* of the modern Arabs—yet that identity cannot be proved by any ancient record. In form the lake is not far from a triangle, the base being at the north and the apex at the south. It measures about three miles in each direction, and eleven feet deep. The water is clear and sweet; it is covered in parts by a broad-leaved plant, and abounds in water-fowl. (The northern part is a dense swamp of papyrus reeds, as large as the lake itself. See "Rob Roy on the Jordan."—ED.)

Meron'othite, The, that is, the native of a place called probably Meronoth, of which, however, no further traces have yet been discovered. Two Meronothites are named in the Bible—1. Jehdeiah, 1 Chron. 27 : 30 ; 2. Jadon. Neh. 3 : 7.

Me'roz (*refuge*), a place, Judges 5 : 23, denounced because its inhabitants had refused to take any part in the struggle with Sisera. Meroz must have been in the neighborhood of the Kishon, but its real position is not known. Possibly it was destroyed in obedience to the curse.

Me'sech, Me'shech (*drawing out*), a son of Japhet, Gen. 10 : 2 ; 1 Chron. 1 : 5, and the progenitor of a race frequently noticed in Scripture in connection with Tubal, Magog and other northern nations. They appear as allies of Gog, Ezek. 38 : 2, 3 ; 39 : 1, and as supplying the Tyrians with copper and slaves. Ezek. 27 : 13. In Ps. 120 : 5 they are noticed as one of the remotest and at the same time rudest nations of the world. Both the name and the associations are in favor of the identification of Meshech with the *Moschi*, a people on the borders of Colchis and Armenia.

Me'sha (*freedom*). 1. The name of one of the geographical limits of the Joktanites when they first settled in Arabia. Gen. 10 : 30.

2. The king of Moab who was tributary to Ahab, 2 Kings 3 : 4 ; but when Ahab fell at Ramoth-gilead, Mesha refused to pay tribute to his successor, Jehoram. When Jehoram succeeded to the throne of Israel, one of his first acts was to secure the assistance of Jehoshaphat, his father's ally, in reducing the Moabites to their former condition of tributaries. The Moabites were defeated, and the king took refuge in his last stronghold, and defended himself with the energy of despair. With 700 fighting men he made a vigorous attempt to cut his way through the beleaguering army, and when beaten back, he withdrew to the wall of his city, and there, in sight of the allied host, offered his first-born son, his successor in the kingdom, as a burnt offering to Chemosh, the ruthless fire-god of Moab. His bloody sacrifice had so far the desired effect that the besiegers retired from him to their own land. (At Dibon in Moab has lately been discovered the famous Moabite Stone, which contains inscriptions concerning King Mesha and his wars, and which confirms the Bible account.—Ed.)

3. The eldest son of Caleb the son of Hezron by his wife Azubah, as Kimchi conjectures. 1 Chron. 2 : 42.

4. A Benjamite, son of Shaharaim by his wife Hodesh, who bore him in the land of Moab. 1 Chron. 8 : 9.

Me'shach (*guest of a king*), the name given to Mishael, one of the companions of Daniel, who with three others was chosen from among the captives to be taught, Dan. 1 : 4, and qualified to "stand before" King Nebuchadnezzar, Dan. 1 : 5, as his personal attendants and advisers. Dan. 1 : 20. But notwithstanding their Chaldean education, these three young Hebrews were strongly attached to the religion of their fathers ; and their refusal to join in the worship of the image on the plain of Dura gave a handle of accusation to the Chaldeans. The rage of the king, the swift sentence of condemnation passed upon the three offenders, their miraculous preservation from the fiery furnace heated seven times hotter than usual, the king's acknowledgment of the God of Shadrach, Meshach and Abednego, with their restoration to office, are written in the third chapter of Daniel, and there the history leaves them.

Meshelemi'ah (*whom Jehovah repays*), a Korhite porter or gate-keeper of the house of Jehovah in the reign of David. 1 Chron. 9 : 21 ; 26 : 1, 2, 9.

Meshez'abe-el (*delivered by God*). 1. Ancestor of Meshullam, who assisted Nehemiah in rebuilding the wall of Jerusalem. Neh. 3 : 4.

2. One of the "heads of the people," probably a family, who sealed the covenant with Nehemiah. Neh. 10 : 21.

3. The father of Pethahiah, and descendant of Zerah the son of Judah. Neh. 11 : 24.

Meshil'lemith (*recompense*), the son of Immer, a priest. Neh. 11 : 13 ; 1 Chron. 9 : 12.

Meshil'lemoth (*recompense*). 1. An Ephraimite, one of the chiefs of the tribe in the reign of Pekah. 2 Chron. 28 : 12.

2. The same as MESHILLEMITH. Neh. 11 : 13.

Meshul'lam (*friend*). 1. Ancestor of Shaphan the scribe. 2 Kings 22 : 3.

2. The son of Zerubbabel. 1 Chron. 3 : 19.

3. A Gadite in the reign of Jotham king of Judah. 1 Chron. 5 : 13.

4. A Benjamite, of the sons of Elpaal. 1 Chron. 8 : 17.

5. A Benjamite, father of Sallu. 1 Chron. 9 : 7 ; Neh. 11 : 7.

6. A Benjamite who lived at Jerusalem after the captivity. 1 Chron. 9 : 8.

7. The same as Shallum, who was high priest probably in the reign of Amon, and father of Hilkiah. 1 Chron. 9 : 11; Neh. 11 : 11.

8. A priest, son of Meshillemith or Meshillemoth the son of Immer, and ancestor of Maasiai or Amashai. 1 Chron. 9 : 12; comp. Neh. 11 : 13.

9. A Kohathite or a family of Kohathite Levites, in the reign of Josiah. 2 Chron. 34 : 12.

10. One of the "heads" sent by Ezra to Iddo, "the head," to gather together the Levites to join the caravan about to return to Jerusalem. Ezra 8 : 16.

11. A chief man who assisted Ezra in abolishing the marriages which some of the people had contracted with foreign wives. Ezra 10 : 15.

12. One of the descendants of Bani, who had married a foreign wife and put her away. Ezra 10 : 29.

13. Neh. 3 : 30; 6 : 18. The son of Berechiah, who assisted in rebuilding the wall of Jerusalem. Neh. 3 : 4.

14. The son of Besodeiah : he assisted Jehoiada the son of Paseah in restoring the old gate of Jerusalem. Neh. 3 : 6.

15. One of those who stood at the left hand of Ezra when he read the law to the people. Neh. 8 : 4.

16. A priest or family of priests who sealed the covenant with Nehemiah. Neh. 10 : 7.

17. One of the heads of the people who sealed the covenant with Nehemiah. Neh. 10 : 20.

18. A priest in the days of Joiakim the son of Jeshua, and representative of the house of Ezra. Neh. 12 : 13.

19. Also a priest at the same time as the preceding, and head of the priestly family of Ginnethon. Neh. 12 : 16.

20. A family of porters, descendants of Meshullam, Neh. 12 : 25, who is also called Meshelemiah, 1 Chron. 26 : 1, Shelemiah, 1 Chron. 26 : 14, and Shallum. Neh. 7 : 45.

21. One of the princes of Judah at the dedication of the wall of Jerusalem. Neh. 12 : 33.

Meshul'lemeth (*friend*), the daughter of Haruz of Jotbah, wife of Manasseh king of Judah, and mother of his successor, Amon. 2 Kings 21 : 19.

Mes'oba-ite, The, a title attached to the name of Jasiel. 1 Chron. 11 : 47. It is impossible to pronounce with any certainty to what it refers.

Mesopota'mia (*between the rivers*),

the entire country between the two rivers, the Tigris and the Euphrates. This is a tract nearly 700 miles long and from 20 to 250 miles broad, extending in a south-easterly direction from *Telek* to *Kurnah*. The Arabian geographers term it "the Island," a name which is almost literally correct, since a few miles only intervene between the source of the Tigris and the Euphrates at *Telek*. But the region which bears the name of Mesopotamia, *par excellence*, both in Scripture and in the classical writers, is the northwestern portion of this tract, or the country between the great bend of the Euphrates, lat. 35° to 37° 30', and the upper Tigris. We first hear of Mesopotamia in Scripture as the country where Nahor and his family settled after quitting Ur of the Chaldees. Gen. 24 : 10. Here lived Bethuel and Laban; and hither Abraham sent his servants to fetch Isaac a wife. *Ibid.* ver. 38. Hither too, a century later, came Jacob on the same errand; and hence he returned with his two wives after an absence of twenty-one years. After this we have no mention of Mesopotamia till the close of the wanderings in the wilderness. Deut. 23 : 4. About half a century later we find, for the first and last time, Mesopotamia the seat of a powerful monarchy. Judges 3. Finally, the children of Ammon, having provoked a war with David, "sent a thousand talents of silver to hire them chariots and horsemen out of Mesopotamia, and out of Syria-maachah, and out of Zobah." 1 Chron. 19 : 6. According to the Assyrian inscriptions Mesopotamia was inhabited in the early times of the empire, B.C. 1200–1100, by a vast number of petty tribes, each under its own prince, and all quite independent of one another. The Assyrian monarchs contended with these chiefs at great advantage, and by the time of Jehu, B.C. 880, had fully established their dominion over them. On the destruction of the Assyrian empire, Mesopotamia seems to have been divided between the Medes and the Babylonians. The conquests of Cyrus brought it wholly under the Persian yoke; and thus it continued to the time of Alexander. Since 1516 it has formed a part of the Turkish empire. It is full of ruins and mounds of ancient cities, some of which are now throwing much light on the Scripture.

Messi'ah (*anointed*). This word (*Mashiach*) answers to the word *Christ* (Χριστός) in the New Testament, and is applicable in its first sense to any one anointed with the holy oil. The kings of Israel were called *anointed*, from the mode of their consecration. 1 Sam. 2 : 10, 35; 12 : 3, 5, etc. This word also refers to the expected Prince of the chosen people who was to complete God's purposes for them and to redeem them, and of whose coming the prophets of the old covenant in all time spoke. He was the Messiah, the *Anointed, i. e.* consecrated as the king and prophet by God's appointment. The word is twice used in the New Testament of Jesus. John 1 : 41; 4 : 25; Authorized Version "Messias." The earliest gleam of the gospel is found in the account of the fall. Gen. 3 : 15. The blessings in store for the children of Shem are remarkably indicated in the words of Noah. Gen. 9 : 26. Next follows the promise to Abraham. Gen. 12 : 2, 3. A great step is made in Gen. 49 : 10. This is the first case in which the promises distinctly centre in one person. The next passage usually quoted is the prophecy of Balaam. Num. 24 : 17-19. The prophecy of Moses, Deut. 18 : 18, claims attention. Passages in the Psalms are numerous which are applied to the Messiah in the New Testament; such as Ps. 2, 16, 22, 40, 110. The advance in clearness in this period is great. The name of Anointed, *i. e.* King, comes in, and the Messiah is to come of the lineage of David. He is described in his exaltation, with his great kingdom that shall be spiritual rather than temporal. Ps. 2, 21, 40, 110. In other places he is seen in suffering and humiliation. Ps. 16, 22, 40. Later on the prophets show the Messiah as a king and ruler of David's house, who should come to reform and restore the Jewish nation and purify the Church, as in Isa. 11, 40-66. The blessings of the restoration, however, will not be confined to Jews; the heathen are made to share them fully. Isa. 2, 66. The passage of Micah 5 : 2 (comp. Matt. 2 : 6) left no doubt in the mind of the Sanhedrin as to the birthplace of the Messiah. The lineage of David is again alluded to in Zech. 12 : 10-14. The coming of the Forerunner and of the Anointed is clearly revealed in Mal. 3 : 1; 4 : 5, 6. The Pharisees and those of the Jews who expected Messiah at all looked for a temporal prince only. The apostles themselves were infected with this opinion till after the resurrection. Matt. 20 : 20, 21; Luke 24 : 21; Acts 1 : 6. Gleams of a purer faith appear in Luke 2 : 30; 23 : 42; John 4 : 25.

Messi'as (*anointed*), the Greek form of Messiah. John 1 : 41; 4 : 25.

Metals. The Hebrews, in common with other ancient nations, were acquainted with nearly all the metals known to modern metallurgy, whether as the products of their own soil or the results of intercourse with foreigners. One of the earliest geographical definitions is that which describes the country of Havilah as the land which abounded in *gold*, and the gold of which was good. Gen. 2 : 11, 12. "Abram was very rich in cattle, in silver, and in gold," Gen. 13 : 2; silver, as will be shown hereafter, being the medium of commerce, while gold existed in the shape of ornaments, during the patriarchal ages. *Tin* is first mentioned Num. 31 : 22, and *lead* is used to heighten the imagery of Moses' triumphal song. Ex. 15 : 10. Whether the ancient Hebrews were acquainted with *steel*, properly so called, is uncertain; the words so rendered in the Authorized Version, 2 Sam. 22 : 35; Job 20 : 24; Ps. 18 : 34; Jer. 15 : 12, are in all other passages translated *brass*, and would be more correctly *copper*. The "northern iron" of Jer. 15 : 12 is believed more nearly to correspond to what we call steel. [STEEL.] It is supposed that the Hebrews used the mixture of copper and tin known as *bronze*. The Hebrews obtained their principal supply from the south of Arabia and the commerce of the Persian Gulf. Josh. 7 : 21. The great abundance of gold in early times is indicated by its entering into the composition of all articles of ornament and almost all of domestic use. Among the spoils of the Midianites taken by the Israelites in their bloodless victory when Balaam was slain were earrings and jewels to the amount of 16,750 shekels of gold, Num. 31 : 48-54, equal in value to more than $150,000. Seventeen hundred shekels of gold (worth more than $15,000) in nose jewels (Authorized Version "ear-rings") alone were taken by Gideon's army from the slaughtered Midianites. Judges 8 : 26. But the amount of treasure accumulated by David from spoils taken in war is so enormous that we are tempted to conclude the numbers exaggerated. Though gold was thus common, silver appears to have been the ordinary medium of commerce. The first commercial transaction of which we possess the details was the purchase of Ephron's field by Abraham for 400 shekels of *silver.* Gen. 23 : 16. The accumulation of wealth in the reign of Solomon was so great that silver was but little esteemed. 1 Kings 10 : 21, 27. Brass, or more properly copper, was a native product of Palestine. Deut. 8 : 9; Job 28 : 2. It was plentiful in the days of Solomon, and the quantity employed in the temple could not be estimated, it was so great. 1 Kings 7 : 47. No allusion is found to zinc; but tin was well known. Arms, 2 Sam. 21 : 16; Job 20 : 24; Ps. 18 : 34, and armor, 1 Sam. 17 : 5, 6, 38, were made of copper, which was capable of being so wrought as to admit of a keen and hard edge. Iron, like copper, was found in the hills of Palestine. Iron-mines are still worked by the inhabitants of *Kefr Hûneh,* in the south of the valley of *Zaharâni.*

Me'theg-am'mah (*bridle of the metropolis*), a place which David took from the Philistines, apparently in his last war with them. 2 Sam. 8 : 1. Ammah may be taken as meaning "mother-city" or "metropolis," comp. 2 Sam. 20 : 19, and Metheg-ha-Ammah "the bridle of the mother-city"—viz. of Gath, the chief town of the Philistines.

Methu'sael (*man of God*), the son of Mehujael, fourth in descent from Cain, and father of Lamech. Gen. 4 : 18.

Methu'selah (*man of the dart*), the son of Enoch, sixth in descent from Seth, and father of Lamech. Gen. 5 : 25–27.

Meu'nim (*habitations*). Neh. 7 : 52. Elsewhere given in Authorized Version as Mehunim and Mehunims.

Meu'zal. Ezek. 27 : 19, marg. [UZAL.]

Mez'ahab (*waters of gold*), the father of Matred and grandfather of Mehetabel, who was wife of Hadar or Hadad, the last-named king of Edom. Gen. 36 : 39; 1 Chron. 1 : 50.

Mi'amin (*from the right hand*). 1. A layman of Israel who had married a foreign wife and put her away at the bidding of Ezra. Ezra 10 : 25.

2. A priest or family of priests who went up from Babylon with Zerubbabel. Neh. 12 : 5.

Mib'har (*choicest*), one of David's heroes in the list given in 1 Chron. 11 : 38.

Mib'sam (*sweet odor*). 1. A son of Ishmael. Gen. 25 : 13 ; 1 Chron. 1 : 29.

2. A son of Simeon. 1 Chron. 4 : 25.

Mib'zar (*fortress*), one of the "dukes" of Edom. Gen. 36 : 42 ; 1 Chron. 1 : 53.

Mi'cah (*who is like God?*), the same name as Micaiah. [MICAIAH.] 1. An Israelite whose familiar story is preserved in the 17th and 18th chapters of Judges. Micah is evidently a devout believer in Jehovah, and yet so completely ignorant is he of the law of Jehovah that the mode which he adopts of honoring him is to make a molten and graven image, teraphim or images of domestic gods, and to set up an unauthorized priesthood, first in his own family, Judges 17 : 5, and then in the person of a Levite not of the priestly line. ver. 12. A body of 600 Danites break in upon and steal his idols from him.

2. The sixth in order of the minor prophets. He is called the Morasthite, that is, a native of Moresheth, a small village near Eleutheropolis to the east, where formerly the prophet's tomb was shown, though in the days of Jerome it had been succeeded by a church. Micah exercised the prophetical office during the reigns of Jotham, Ahaz and Hezekiah, kings of Judah, giving thus a maximum limit of 59 years, B.C. 756–697, from the accession of Jotham to the death of Hezekiah, and a minimum limit of 16 years, B.C. 742–726, from the death of Jotham to the accession of Hezekiah. He was contemporary with Hosea and Amos during the part of their ministry in Israel, and with Isaiah in Judah.

3. A descendant of Joel the Reubenite. 1 Chron. 5 : 5.

4. The son of Meribbaal or Mephibosheth, the son of Jonathan. 1 Chron. 8 : 34, 35 ; 9 : 40, 41.

5. A Kohathite Levite, the eldest son of Uzziel the brother of Amram. 1 Chron. 23 : 20.

6. The father of Abdon, a man of high station in the reign of Josiah. 2 Chron. 34 : 20.

Mi'cah, The book of. Three sections of this work represent three natural divisions of the prophecy—1, 2; 3–5; 6, 7—each commencing with rebukes and threatening and closing with a promise. The first section opens with a magnificent description of the coming of Jehovah to judgment for the sins and idolatries of Israel and Judah, ch. 1 : 2–4, and the sentence pronounced upon Samaria, vs. 5–9, by the Judge himself. The sentence of captivity is passed upon them, Micah 2 : 10, but is followed instantly by a promise of restoration and triumphant return. ch. 2 : 12, 13. The second section is addressed especially to the princes and heads of the people: their avarice and rapacity are rebuked in strong terms; but the threatening is again succeeded by a promise of restoration. In the last section, chs. 6, 7, Jehovah, by a bold poetical figure, is represented as holding a controversy with his people, pleading with them in justification of his conduct toward them and the reasonableness of his requirements. The whole concludes with a triumphal song of joy at the great deliverance, like that from Egypt, which Jehovah will achieve, and a full acknowledgment of his mercy and faithfulness to his promises. vs. 16–20. The last verse is reproduced in the song of Zacharias. Luke 1:72, 73. Micah's prophecies are distinct and clear. He it is who says that the Ruler shall spring from Bethlehem. ch. 5:2. His style has been compared with that of Hosea and Isaiah. His diction is vigorous and forcible, sometimes obscure from the abruptness of its transitions, but varied and rich.

Mica′iah (*who is like God?*). Micaiah, the son of Imlah, was a prophet of Samaria, who in the last year of the reign of Ahab king of Israel predicted his defeat and death, B.C. 897. 1 Kings 22:1–35; 2 Chron. 18.

Mi′cha (*who is like God?*). 1. The son of Mephibosheth. 2 Sam. 9:12.

2. A Levite who signed the covenant with Nehemiah. Neh. 10:11.

3. The father of Mattaniah, a Gershonite Levite and descendant of Asaph. Neh. 11:17, 22.

Mi′chael (*who is like God?*). 1. An Asherite, father of Sethur, one of the twelve spies. Num. 13:13.

2. One of the Gadites who settled in the land of Bashan. 1 Chron. 5:13.

3. Another Gadite, ancestor of Abihail. 1 Chron. 5:14.

4. A Gershonite Levite, ancestor of Asaph. 1 Chron. 6:40.

5. One of the five sons of Izrahiah, of the tribe of Issachar. 1 Chron. 7:3.

6. A Benjamite of the sons of Beriah. 1 Chron. 8:16.

7. One of the captains of the "thousands" of Manasseh who joined David at Ziklag. 1 Chron. 12:20.

8. The father or ancestor of Omri, chief of the tribe of Issachar in the reign of David. 1 Chron. 27:18.

9. One of the sons of Jehoshaphat who were murdered by their elder brother, Jehoram. 2 Chron. 21:2, 4.

10. The father or ancestor of Zebadiah, of the sons of Shephatiah. Ezra 8:8.

11. "One," or "the first, of the chief princes" or archangels, Dan. 10:13; comp. Jude 9, described in Dan. 10:21 as the "prince" of Israel, and in ch. 12:1 as "the great prince which standeth" in time of conflict "for the children of thy people."

Mi′chah (*who is like God?*), eldest son of Uzziel the son of Kohath, 1 Chron. 24:24, 25; elsewhere, 1 Chron. 23:20, called MICAH.

Micha′iah (*who is like God?*). 1. Same as MICAH 6. 2 Chron. 34:20.

2. Same as MICHA 3. 1 Chron. 9:15; Neh. 12:35.

3. One of the priests at the dedication of the wall of Jerusalem. Neh. 12:41.

4. The daughter of Uriel of Gibeah, wife of Rehoboam and mother of Abijah king of Judah. 2 Chron. 13:2. [MAACHAH, 3.]

5. One of the princes of Jehoshaphat whom he sent to teach the law of Jehovah in the cities of Judah. 2 Chron. 17:7.

6. The son of Gemariah. He is only mentioned on one occasion. Jer. 36:11, 13, 14.

Mi′chal (*who is like God?*), the younger of Saul's two daughters, 1 Sam. 14:49, who married David. The price fixed on Michal's hand was no less than the slaughter of a hundred Philistines. David by a brilliant feat doubled the tale of victims, and Michal became his wife. Shortly afterward she saved David from the assassins whom her father had sent to take his life. 1 Sam. 19:11–17. When the rupture between Saul and David had become open and incurable, she was married to another man, Phalti or Phaltiel of Gallim. 1 Sam. 25:44. After the death of her father and brothers at Gilboa, David compelled her new husband to surrender Michal to him. 2 Sam. 3:13-16. How Michal comported herself in the altered circumstances of David's household we are not told; but it is plain from the subsequent occurrences that something had happened to alter the relations of herself and David, for on the day of David's greatest triumph, when he brought the ark of Jehovah to Jerusalem, we are told that "she despised him in her heart." All intercourse between her and David ceased from that date. 2 Sam. 6:20-23. Her name appears, 2 Sam. 21:8, as the mother of five of the grandchildren of Saul.

Mich'mas, or **Mich'mash** (*hidden*), a town which is known to us almost solely by its connection with the Philistine war of Saul and Jonathan. 1 Sam. 13, 14. It has been identified with great probability in a village which still bears the name of *Mûkhmas*, about seven miles north of Jerusalem. The place was thus situated in the very middle of the tribe of Benjamin. In the invasion of Sennacherib in the reign of Hezekiah, it is mentioned by Isaiah. Isa. 10 : 28. After the captivity the men of the place returned. Ezra 2 : 27 ; Neh. 7 : 31. At a later date it became the residence of Jonathan Maccabæus and the seat of his government. 1 Macc. 9 : 73. In the time of Eusebius and Jerome it was " a very large village, retaining its ancient name, and lying near Ramah in the district of Ælia (Jerusalem), at ten miles distance therefrom." Immediately below the village the great wady spreads out to a considerable width —perhaps half a mile ; and its bed is broken up into an intricate mass of hummocks and mounds, two of which, before the torrents of three thousand winters had reduced and rounded their forms, were probably the two " teeth of cliff"— the Bozez and Seneh of Jonathan's adventure.

Mich'methah (*hiding-place*), a place which formed one of the landmarks of the boundary of the territories of Ephraim and Manasseh on the western side of Jordan. Josh. 17 : 7. The position of the place must be somewhere on the east of and not far distant from Shechem.

Mich'ri (*worthy of price*), ancestor of Elah, one of the heads of the fathers of Benjamin. 1 Chron. 9 : 8.

Michtam (*golden psalm*). This word occurs in the titles of six psalms (16, 56–60), all of which are ascribed to David. The marginal reading of our Authorized Version is " *a golden* psalm," while in the Geneva version it is described as "a certain tune." From the position which it occupies in the title we may infer that *michtam* is a term applied to these psalms to denote their musical character, but beyond this everything is obscure.

Mid'din (*measures*), a city of Judah, Josh. 15 : 61, one of the six specified as situated in the district of "the midbar" (Authorized Version "wilderness").

Mid'ian (*strife*), a son of Abraham and Keturah, Gen. 25 : 2 ; 1 Chron. 1 : 32; progenitor of the Midianites, or Arabians dwelling principally in the desert north of the peninsula of Arabia. Southward they extended along the eastern shore of the Gulf of Eyleh (*Sinus Ælaniticus*): and northward they stretched along the eastern frontier of Palestine. The "land of Midian," the place to which Moses fled after having killed the Egyptian, Ex. 2 : 15, 21, or the portion of it specially referred to, was probably the peninsula of Sinai. The influence of the Midianites on the Israelites was clearly most evil, and directly tended to lead them from the injunctions of Moses. The events at Shittim occasioned the injunction to vex Midian and smite them. After a lapse of some years, the Midianites appear again as the enemies of the Israelites, oppressing them for seven years, but are finally defeated with great slaughter by Gideon. [GIDEON.] The Midianites are described as true Arabs, and possessed cattle and flocks and camels as the sand of the seashore for multitude. The spoil taken in the war of both Moses and of Gideon is remarkable. Num. 31 : 22 ; Judges 8 : 21, 24–26. We have here a wealthy Arab nation, living by plunder, delighting in finery ; and, where forays were impossible, carrying on the traffic southward into Arabia, the land of gold —if not naturally, by trade—and across to Chaldea, or into the rich plains of Egypt.

Mig'dal-el (*tower of God*), one of the fortified towns of the possession of Naphtali, Josh. 19 : 38 only, possibly deriving its name from some ancient tower—the "tower of El," or God.

Mig'dal-gad (*tower of Gad*), a city of Judah, Josh. 15 : 37, in the district of the Shefelah, or maritime lowland.

Mig'dol (*tower*), the name of one or two places on the eastern frontier of Egypt. 1. A Migdol is mentioned in the account of the exodus, Ex. 14 : 2 ; Num. 33 : 7, 8, near the head of the Red Sea. 2. A Migdol is spoken of by Jeremiah and Ezekiel. The latter prophet mentions it as a boundary-town, evidently on the eastern border. Ezek. 29 : 10 ; 30 : 6. In the prophecy of Jeremiah the Jews in Egypt are spoken of as dwelling at Migdol. Jer. 44 : 1. It seems plain, from its being spoken of with Memphis, and from Jews dwelling there, that this Migdol was an important town.

Mig'ron (*precipice*), a town or a spot in the neighborhood of Gibeah. 1 Sam. 14 : 2. Migron is also mentioned in Sennacherib's approach to Jerusalem. Isa. 10 : 28.

Mij'amin (*from the right hand*). 1. The chief of the sixth of the twenty-four courses of priests established by David. 1 Chron. 24 : 9.

2. A family of priests who signed the covenant with Nehemiah; probably the descendants of the preceding. Neh. 10 : 7.

Mik'loth (*staves*). 1. One of the sons of Jehiel, the father or prince of Gibeon, by his wife Maachah. 1 Chron. 8 : 32; 9 : 37, 38.

2. The leader of the second division of David's army. 1 Chron. 27 : 4.

Mikne'iah (*possession of Jehovah*), one of the Levites of the second rank, gatekeepers of the ark, appointed by David to play in the temple band "with harps upon Sheminith." 1 Chron. 15 : 18, 21.

Milala'i (*eloquent*), probably a Gershonite Levite of the sons of Asaph, who assisted at the dedication of the walls of Jerusalem. Neh. 12 : 36.

Mil'cah (*queen* or *counsel*). 1. Daughter of Haran and wife of her uncle Nahor, Abraham's brother, to whom she bore eight children. Gen. 11 : 29; 22 : 20, 23; 24 : 15, 24, 47.

2. The fourth daughter of Zelophehad. Num. 26 : 33; 27 : 1; 36 : 11; Josh. 17 : 3.

Miletus.

Mil'com (*great king*). [MOLECH.]

Mile, a Roman measure of length, equal to 1618 English yards—4854 feet, or about nine-tenths of an English mile. It is only once noticed in the Bible, Matt. 5 : 41, the usual method of reckoning both in the New Testament and in Josephus being by the stadium. The mile of the Jews is said to have been of two kinds, long or short, dependent on the length of the pace, which varied in different parts, the long pace being double the length of the short one.

Mile'tus, Acts 20 : 15, 17, less correctly called MILETUM in 2 Tim. 4 : 20. It lay on the coast, 36 miles to the south of Ephesus, a day's sail from Trogyllium. Acts 20 : 15. Moreover, to those who are sailing from the north it is in the direct line for Cos. The site of Miletus has now receded ten miles from the coast, and even in the apostles' time it must have lost its strictly maritime position. Miletus was far more famous five hundred years before St. Paul's day than it ever became afterward. In early times it was the most flourishing city of the Ionian Greeks. In the natural order of events it was absorbed in the Persian empire. After a brief period of spirited independence, it received a blow from which it never recovered, in the siege conducted by Alexander when on his eastern campaign. But still it held, even through the Roman period, the rank of a second-rate trading town, and Strabo mentions its four harbors.

At this time it was politically in the province of Asia, though Caria was the old ethnological name of the district in which it was situated. All that is left now is a small Turkish village called *Melas*, near the site of the ancient city.

Milk. As an article of diet, milk holds a more important position in eastern countries than with us. It is not a mere adjunct in cookery, or restricted to the use of the young, although it is naturally the characteristic food of childhood, both from its simple and nutritive qualities, 1 Pet. 2 : 2, and particularly as contrasted with meat, 1 Cor. 3 : 2; Heb. 5 : 12; but beyond this it is regarded as substantial food adapted alike to all ages and classes. Not only the milk of cows, but of sheep, Deut. 32 : 14, of camels, Gen. 32 : 15, and of goats, Prov. 27 : 27, was used; the latter appears to have been most highly prized.

Eastern Women Grinding at the Mill.

Mill. The mills of the ancient Hebrews probably differed but little from those at present in use in the East. These consist of two circular stones, each about eighteen inches or two feet in diameter, the lower of which is fixed, and has its upper surface slightly convex, fitting into a corresponding concavity in the upper stone. In the latter is a hole through which the grain passes, immediately above a pivot or shaft which rises from the centre of the lower stone, and about which the upper stone is turned by means of an upright handle fixed near the edge. It is worked by women, sometimes singly and sometimes two together, who are usually seated on the bare ground, Isa. 47 : 1, 2, "facing each other; both have hold of the handle by which the upper is turned round on the 'nether' millstone. The one whose right hand is disengaged throws in the grain as occasion requires through the hole in the upper stone. It is not correct to say that one pushes it half round and then the other seizes the handle. This would be slow work, and would give a spasmodic motion to the stone. Both retain their hold, and pull *to* or push *from*, as men do with the whip or cross-cut saw. The proverb of our Saviour, Matt. 24 : 41, is true to life, for *women* only grind. I cannot recall an instance in which men were at the mill."—*Thomson,* "The Land and the Book," c. 34. So essential were millstones for daily domestic use that they were forbidden to be taken in pledge, Deut. 24 : 6. There were also larger mills that could only be turned by cattle or asses. Allusion to one of these is made in Matt. 18 : 6. With the movable upper millstone of the hand-mill the woman of Thebez broke Abimelech's skull. Judges 9 : 53.

Millet, a kind of grain. A number of species are cultivated in the East. When green it is used as fodder, and for bread when ripe. Ezek. 4 : 9. It is probable that both the *Sorghum vulgare* and the *Panicum miliaceum* were used, and the Hebrew *dôchan* may denote either of these plants.

Mil′lo (*a rampart, mound*), a place in ancient Jerusalem. Both name and place seem to have been already in existence when the city was taken from the Jebusites by David. 2 Sam. 5 : 9; 1 Chron. 11 : 8. Its repair or restoration was one of the great works for which Solomon raised his "levy," 1 Kings 9 : 15, 24; 11 : 27; and it formed a prominent part of the fortifications by which Hezekiah prepared for the approach of the Assyrians. 2 Chron. 32 : 5. The last passage seems to show that "the Millo" was part of the "city of David," that is, of Zion. Comp. 2 Kings 12 : 20.

Mil′lo, The house of. 1. Apparently a family or clan, mentioned in Judges 9 : 6, 20 only, in connection with the men or lords of Shechem.

2. The spot at which King Joash was murdered by his slaves. 2 Kings 12 : 20.

Mines, Mining. A highly-poetical description given by the author of the book of Job of the operations of mining as known in his day is the only record of the kind which we inherit from the ancient Hebrews. Job 28 : 1–11. In the Wady Maghârah, "the valley of the cave," are still traces of the Egyptian colony of miners who settled there for the purpose of extracting copper from the freestone rocks, and left their hieroglyphic inscriptions upon the face of the cliff. The ancient furnaces are still to be seen, and on the coast of the Red Sea are found the piers and wharves whence the

Millet.

miners shipped their metal in the harbor of Abu Zelimeh. Three methods were employed for refining gold and silver: (1) by exposing the fused metal to a current of air; (2) by keeping the alloy in a state of fusion and throwing nitre upon it; and (3) by mixing the alloy with lead, exposing the whole to fusion upon a vessel of bone-ashes or earth, and blowing upon it with bellows or other blast. There seems to be reference to the latter in Ps. 12 : 6; Jer. 6 : 28–30; Ezek. 22 : 18–22. The chief supply of silver in the ancient world appears to have been brought from Spain. The Egyptians evidently possessed the art of working bronze in great perfection at a very early time, and much of the knowledge of metals which the Israelites had must have been acquired during their residence among them. Of tin there appears to have been no trace in Palestine. The hills of Palestine are rich in iron, and the mines are still worked there, though in a very simple, rude manner.

Mini'amin (*from the right hand*). 1. A Levite in the reign of Hezekiah. 2 Chron. 31 : 15.

2. The same as Miamin 2 and Mijamin 2. Neh. 12 : 17.

3. One of the priests at the dedication of the wall of Jerusalem. Neh. 12 : 41.

Minister. This term is used in the Authorized Version to describe various officials of a religious and civil character. Its meaning, as distinguished from servant, is a voluntary attendant on another. In the Old Testament it is applied (1) to an attendance upon a person of high rank, Ex. 24 : 13; Josh. 1 : 1; 2 Kings 4 : 43; (2) to the *attachés* of a royal court, 1 Kings 10 : 5; 2 Chron. 22 : 8; comp. Ps. 104 : 4; (3) to the priests and Levites. Ezra 8 : 17; Neh. 10 : 36; Isa. 61 : 6; Ezek. 44 : 11; Joel 1 : 9, 13. One term in the New Testament betokens a subordinate public administrator, Rom. 13 : 6; 15 : 16; Heb. 8 : 2, one who performs certain gratuitous public services. A second term contains the idea of actual and personal attendance upon a superior, as in Luke 4 : 20. The minister's duty was to open and close the building, to produce and replace the books employed in the service, and generally to wait on the officiating priest or teacher. A third term, *diakonos* (from which comes our word deacon), is the one usually employed in relation to the ministry of the gospel: its application is twofold,—in a general sense to indicate ministers of any order, whether superior or inferior, and in a special sense to indicate an order of inferior ministers. [DEACON.]

Min'ni (*division*), Jer. 51 : 27; already noticed as a portion of Armenia. [ARMENIA.]

Min'nith (*distribution*), a place on the east of the Jordan, named as the point to which Jephthah's slaughter of the Ammonites extended. Judges 11 : 33. The "wheat of Minnith" is mentioned in Ezek. 27 : 17 as being supplied by Judah and Israel to Tyre; but there is nothing to indicate that the same place is intended, and indeed the word is believed by some not to be a proper name.

Minstrel. The Hebrew word in 2 Kings 3 : 15 properly signifies a player upon a stringed instrument like the harp or *kinnor* [HARP], whatever its precise character may have been, on which David played before Saul, 1 Sam. 16 : 16 ; 18 : 10 ; 19 : 9, and which the harlots of the great cities used to carry with them as they walked, to attract notice. Isa. 23 : 16. The "minstrels" in Matt. 9 : 23 were the flute-players who were employed as professional mourners, to whom frequent allusion is made. 2 Chron. 35 : 25 ; Eccles. 12 : 5 ; Jer. 9 : 17–20.

Mint.

Mint. This name occurs only in Matt. 23 : 23 and Luke 11 : 42, as one of those herbs the tithe of which the Jews were most scrupulously exact in paying. The horse mint, *M. Sylvestris,* and several other species of mint are common in Syria.

Miph'kad (*appointed place*)**,The gate,** one of the gates of Jerusalem. Neh. 3 : 31. It was probably not in the wall of Jerusalem proper, but in that of the city of David, or Zion, and somewhere near to the junction of the two on the north side.

Miracles. A miracle may be defined to be a plain and manifest exercise by a man, or by God at the call of a man, of those powers which belong only to the Creator and Lord of nature ; and this for the declared object of attesting that a divine mission is given to that man. It is not, therefore, the *wonder*, the exception to common experience, that constitutes the *miracle*, as is assumed both in the popular use of the word and by most objectors against miracles. No phenomenon in nature, however unusual, no event in the course of God's providence, however unexpected, is a miracle unless it can be traced to the agency of man (including prayer under the term agency), and unless it be put forth as a proof of divine mission. Prodigies and special providences are not miracles. (A miracle is not a *violation of the laws of nature.*

It is God's acting upon nature in a degree far beyond our powers, but the same kind of act as our wills are continually exerting upon nature. We do not in lifting a stone interfere with any law of nature, but exert a higher force among the laws. Prof. Tyndall says that "science does assert that without a disturbance of natural law quite as serious as the stoppage of an eclipse, or the rolling of the St. Lawrence up the falls of Niagara, no act of humiliation, individual or national, could call one shower from heaven." And yet men by firing cannon during battle can cause a shower : does that cause such a commotion among the laws of nature ? The exertion of a *will* upon the laws does not make a disturbance of natural law ; and a miracle is simply the exertion of God's will upon nature.—ED.) Again, the term "nature" suggests to many persons the idea of a great system of things endowed with powers and forces of its own—a sort of machine, set a-going originally by a first cause, but continuing its motions *of itself.* Hence we are apt to imagine that a change in the motion or operation of any part of it by God would produce the same disturbance of the other parts as such a change would be likely to produce in them if made by us or by any other natural agent. But if the motions and operations of material things be produced really by the divine will, then his choosing to change, for a special purpose, the ordinary motion of one part does not necessarily or probably imply his choosing to change the ordinary motions of other parts in a way not at all requisite for the accomplishment of that special purpose. It is as easy for him to continue the ordinary course of the rest, with the change of one part, as of all the phenomena without any change at all. Thus, though the stoppage of the motion of the earth in the ordinary course of nature would be attended with terrible convulsions, the stoppage of the earth *miraculously,* for a special purpose to be served by *that only,* would not of itself be followed by any such consequences. (Indeed, by the action of gravitation it could be stopped, as a stone thrown up is stopped, in less than two minutes, and yet so gently as not to stir the smallest feather or mote on its surface.—ED.) From the same conception of nature as a machine, we are apt to think of interferences with the ordinary course of nature as implying some imperfection in it. But it is manifest that this is a false analogy; for the reason why machines are made is to save us trouble; and, therefore, they are more perfect in proportion as they answer this purpose. But no one can seriously imagine that the universe is a machine for the purpose of saving trouble to the Almighty. Again, when miracles are described as "interferences with the laws of nature," this description makes them appear improbable to many minds, from their not sufficiently considering that the laws of nature interfere with one another, and that we cannot get rid of "interferences" upon any hypothesis consistent with experience. The circumstances of the Christian miracles are utterly unlike those of any pretended instances of magical wonders. This difference consists in—(1) The greatness, number, completeness and publicity of the miracles. (2) In the character of the miracles. They were all beneficial, helpful, instructive, and worthy of God as their author. (3) The natural beneficial tendency of the doctrine they attested. (4) The connection of them with a whole scheme of revelation extending from the origin of the human race to the time of Christ.

Mir'iam (*rebellion*), the sister of Moses, was the eldest of that sacred family; and she first appears, probably as a young girl, watching her infant brother's cradle in the Nile, Ex. 2 : 4, and suggesting her mother as a nurse. ver. 7. After the crossing of the Red Sea "Miriam the prophetess" is her acknowledged title. ch. 15 : 20. The prophetic power showed itself in her under the same form as that which it assumed in the days of Samuel and David,—poetry, accompanied with music and processions. ch. 15 : 1–19. She took the lead, with Aaron, in the complaint against Moses for his marriage with a Cushite, Num. 12 : 1, 2, and for this was attacked with leprosy. This stroke and its removal, which took place at Hazeroth, form the last public event of Miriam's life. ch. 12 : 1–15. She died toward the close of the wanderings at Kadesh, and was buried there. ch. 20 : 1. (B.C. about 1452.)

Mir'ma (*fraud*), a Benjamite, born in the land of Moab. 1 Chron. 8 : 10.

Mirror. Ex. 38 : 8; Job 37 : 18. The Hebrew women on coming out of Egypt probably brought with them mirrors like those which were used by the Egyptians, and were made of a mixed metal, chiefly copper, wrought with admirable skill, and susceptible of a bright lustre. 1 Cor. 13 : 12.

Mis'gab (*height*), a place in Moab. Jer. 48 : 1. It appears to be mentioned also in Isa. 25 : 12, though there rendered in the Authorized Version "high fort."

Mish'ael (*who is what God is?*). 1. One of the sons of Uzziel, the uncle of Aaron and Moses. Ex. 6 : 22. When Nadab and Abihu were struck dead for offering strange fire, Mishael and his brother Elzaphan, at the command of Moses, removed their bodies from the sanctuary, and buried them without the camp, their loose-fitting tunics serving for winding-sheets. Lev. 10 : 4, 5.
2. One of those who stood at Ezra's left hand when he read the law to the people. Neh. 8 : 4. [MESHACH.]

Mi'shal, or **Mi'sheal** (*entreaty*), one of the towns in the territory of Asher, Josh. 19 : 26, allotted to the Gershonite Levites. ch. 21 : 30.

Mi'sham (*purification*), a Benjamite, son of Elpaal and descendant of Shaharaim. 1 Chron. 8 : 12.

Mish'ma (*a hearing*). 1. A son of Ishmael and brother of Mibsam. Gen. 25 : 14; 1 Chron. 1 : 30.
2. A son of Simeon, 1 Chron. 4 : 25, brother of Mibsam.

Mishman'nah (*fatness*), the fourth of the twelve lion-faced Gadites who joined David at Ziklag. 1 Chron. 12 : 10.

Mish'raites, The, the fourth of the four "families of Kirjath-jearim," *i. e.* colonies proceeding therefrom and founding towns. 1 Chron. 2 : 53.

Mis'pereth, one of those who returned with Zerubbabel and Jeshua from Babylon. Neh. 7 : 7.

Mis'rephoth-ma'im (*the flow of waters*), a place in northern Palestine. Dr. Thomson treats Misrephoth-maim as identical with a collection of springs called *Ain-Musheirifeh*, on the seashore close under the *Ras en-Nakhura*; but this has the disadvantage of being very far from Sidon. May it not rather be the place with which we are familiar in the later history as Zarephat, near Sidon?

Mite, a coin current in Palestine in the time of our Lord. Mark 12 : 41–44; Luke 21 : 1–4. It seems in Palestine to have been the smallest piece of money (worth about one-fifth of a cent), being the half of the farthing, which was a coin of very low value. From St. Mark's explanation, "two mites, which make a farthing," ver.

42, it may perhaps be inferred that the farthing was the commoner coin.

Mith'cah (*sweetness*), the name of an unknown desert encampment of the Israelites. Num. 33 : 28, 29.

Mith'nite, The, the designation of Joshaphat, one of David's guard in the catalogue of 1 Chron. 11 : 43.

Mith'redath (*given by Mithra*). 1. The treasurer of Cyrus king of Persia, to whom the king gave the vessels of the temple. Ezra 1 : 8.

2. A Persian officer stationed at Samaria. Ezra 4 : 7.

Mitre.

Mitre (something rolled around the head), the turban or headdress of the high priest, made of fine linen cloth, eight yards long, folded around the head. On the front was a gold plate on which was inscribed *Holiness to the Lord.* Ex. 28 : 4, 37, 39; 39 : 28, 30; Lev. 8 : 9.

Mityle'ne (*mutilated*), the chief town of Lesbos, an island of the Ægean Sea, 7½ miles from the opposite point of Asia Minor. The city is situated on the east coast of the island. Mitylene is the intermediate place where St. Paul stopped for the night between Assos and Chios. Acts 20 : 14, 15. The town itself was celebrated in Roman times for the beauty of its buildings. In St. Paul's day it had the privileges of a free city. (It is now a place of no importance, called *Mitelin.* It contains about 1100 houses, Greek and Turkish, with narrow and filthy streets.—ED.)

Mixed multitude. When the Israelites journeyed from Rameses to Succoth, the first stage of the exodus from Egypt,

there went up with them "a mixed multitude." Ex. 12 : 38; Num. 11 : 4. They were probably the offspring of marriages contracted between the Israelites and the Egyptians; and the term may also include all those who were not of pure Israelite blood. In Exodus and Numbers it probably denoted the miscellaneous hangers-on of the Hebrew camp, whether they were the issue of spurious marriages with Egyptians or were themselves Egyptians, or belonging to other nations. The same happened on the return from Babylon, and in Neh. 13 : 3 (comp. vs. 23–30) a slight clue is given by which the meaning of the "mixed multitude" may be more definitely ascertained.

Mi'zar (*small*), **The hill,** a mountain apparently in the northern part of transjordanic Palestine, from which the author of Psalm 42 utters his pathetic appeal. ver. 6. (It is probably a summit of the eastern ridge of Lebanon, not far from Mahanaim, where David lay after escaping from the rebellion of Absalom. —*McClintock and Strong.*)

Miz'pah and **Miz'peh** (*a watch-tower*), the name of several places in Palestine. 1. The earliest of all, in order of the narrative, is the heap of stones piled up by Jacob and Laban, Gen. 31 : 48, on Mount Gilead, ver. 25, to serve both as a witness to the covenant then entered into and as a landmark of the boundary between them. ver. 52. On this natural watch-tower did the children of Israel assemble for the choice of a leader to resist the children of Ammon. Judges 10 : 17. There the fatal meeting took place between Jephthah and his daughter on his return from the war. ch. 11 : 34. It seems most probable that the "Mizpeh-gilead" which is mentioned here, and here only, is the same as the "ham-Mizpah" of the other parts of the narrative; and both are probably identical with the Ramath-mizpeh and Ramoth-gilead, so famous in the later history.

2. A second Mizpeh, on the east of Jordan, was the Mizpeh-moab, where the king of that nation was living when David committed his parents to his care. 1 Sam. 22 : 3.

3. A third was "the land of Mizpeh," or more accurately "of Mizpah," the residence of the Hivites who joined the northern confederacy against Israel, headed by Jabin king of Hazor. Josh. 11 : 3. No other mention is found of this district in the Bible, unless it be identical with—

4. The valley of Mizpeh, to which the discomfited hosts of the same confederacy were chased by Joshua, Josh. 11 : 8; perhaps identical with the great country of Cœle-Syria.

5. Mizpeh, a city of Judah, Josh. 15 : 38, in the district of the Shefelah or maritime lowland.

6. Mizpeh, in Joshua and Samuel; elsewhere Mizpah, a "city" of Benjamin, not far from Jerusalem. Josh. 18 : 26; 1 Kings 15 : 22; 2 Chron. 16 : 6; Neh. 3 : 7. It was one of the places fortified by Asa against the incursions of the kings of northern Israel, 1 Kings 15 : 22; 2 Chron. 16 : 6; Jer. 41 : 10; and after the destruction of Jerusalem it became the residence of the superintendent appointed by the king of Babylon, Jer. 40 : 7, etc., and the scene of his murder and of the romantic incidents connected with the name of Ishmael the son of Nethaniah. It was one of the three holy cities which Samuel visited in turn as judge of the people, 1 Sam. 7 : 6, 16, the other two being Bethel and Gilgal. With the conquest of Jerusalem and the establishment there of the ark, the sanctity of Mizpah, or at least its reputation, seems to have declined. From Mizpah the city or the temple was visible. These conditions are satisfied by the position of Scopus, the broad ridge which forms the continuation of the Mount of Olives to the north and east, from which the traveller gains, like Titus, his first view, and takes his last farewell, of the domes, walls and towers of the holy city.

Miz'par (*number*); properly **Mispar,** the same as MISPERETH. Ezra 2 : 2.

Miz'peh. [MIZPAH.]

Miz'ra-im, or **Mizra'im** (the two Egypts; *red soil*), the usual name of Egypt in the Old Testament, the dual of Mazor, which is less frequently employed. Mizraim first occurs in the account of the Hamites in Gen. 10. In the use of the name Mizraim for Egypt there can be no doubt that the dual indicates the two regions, upper and lower Egypt, into which the country has always been divided by nature as well as by its inhabitants.

Miz'zah (*fear*), son of Reuel and grandson of Esau. Gen. 36 : 13, 17; 1 Chron. 1 : 37.

Mna'son (*remembering*) is honorably mentioned in Scripture. Acts 21 : 16. It is most likely that his residence at this time was not Cæsarea, but Jerusalem. He was a Cyprian by birth, and may have been a friend of Barnabas. Acts 4 : 36.

Mo'ab (*of his father*), **Mo'abites.** Moab was the son of Lot's eldest daughter, the progenitor of the Moabites. Zoar was the cradle of the race of Lot. From this centre the brother tribes spread themselves. The Moabites first inhabited the rich highlands which crown the eastern side of the chasm of the Dead Sea, extending as far north as the mountain of Gilead, from which country they expelled the Emims, the original inhabitants, Deut. 2 : 11; but they themselves were afterward driven southward by the warlike Amorites, who had crossed the Jordan, and were confined to the country south of the river Arnon, which formed their northern boundary. Num. 21 : 13; Judges 11 : 18. The territory occupied by Moab at the period of its greatest extent, before the invasion of the Amorites, divided itself naturally into three distinct and independent portions:—(1) The enclosed corner or canton south of the Arnon was the "field of Moab." Ruth 1 : 1, 2, 6, etc. (2) The more open rolling country north of the Arnon, opposite Jericho, and up to the hills of Gilead, was the "land of Moab." Deut. 1 : 5; 32 : 49, etc. (3) The sunk district in the tropical depths of the Jordan valley. Num. 22 : 1, etc. The Israelites, in entering the promised land, did not pass through the Moabites, Judges 11 : 18, but conquered the Amorites, who occupied the country from which the Moabites had been so lately expelled. After the conquest of Canaan the relations of Moab with Israel were of a mixed character, sometimes warlike and sometimes peaceable. With the tribe of Benjamin they had at least one severe struggle, in union with their kindred the Ammonites. Judges 3 : 12–30. The story of Ruth, on the other hand, testifies to the existence of a friendly intercourse between Moab and Bethlehem, one of the towns of Judah. By his descent from Ruth, 'd may be said to have had Moabite ʋ. d in his veins. He committed his parents to the protection of the king of Moab, when hard pressed by Saul. 1 Sam. 22 : 3, 4. But here all friendly relations stop forever. The next time the name is mentioned is in the account of David's war, who made the Moabites tributary. 2 Sam. 8 : 2; 1 Chron. 18 : 2. At the disruption of the kingdom Moab seems to have fallen to the northern realm. At the death of Ahab the Moabites refused to pay tribute and asserted their independence, making war upon the kingdom of Judah. 2 Chron. 22. As a natural consequence of the late events, Israel, Judah and Edom united in an attack on Moab, resulting in the complete overthrow of the Moabites. Falling back into their own country, they were followed and their cities and farms destroyed. Finally, shut up within the walls of his own capital, the king, Mesha, in the sight of the thousands who covered the sides of that vast amphitheatre, killed and burnt his child as a propitiatory sacrifice to the cruel gods of his country. Isaiah, chs. 15, 16, 25 : 10–12, predicts the utter annihilation of the Moabites; and they are frequently denounced by the

Mountains of Moab.

subsequent prophets. For the religion of the Moabites see CHEMOSH; MOLECH; PEOR. See also Tristram's "Land of Moab." *Present condition.*—(Nöldeke says that the extinction of the Moabites was about A.D. 200, at the time when the Yemen tribes Galib and Gassura entered the eastern districts of the Jordan. Since A.D. 536 the last trace of the name Moab, which lingered in the town of Kir-moab, has given place to *Kerak*, its modern name. Over the whole region are scattered many ruins of ancient cities; and while the country is almost bare of larger vegetation, it is still a rich pasture-ground, with occasional fields of grain. The land thus gives evidence of its former wealth and power.—ED.)

Mo'abite Stone, The. In the year 1868 Rev. F. Klein, of the Church Missionary Society at Jerusalem, found at Dhiban (the biblical Dibon), in Moab, a remarkable stone, since called the Moabite Stone. It was lying on the ground, with the inscription uppermost, and measures about 3 feet 9 inches long, 2 feet 4 inches wide and 1 foot 2 inches thick. It is a very heavy, compact black basalt. An impression was made of the main block, and of certain recovered parts broken off by the Arabs. It was broken by the Arabs, but the fragments were purchased by the French government for 32,000 francs, and are in the Louvre in Paris. The engraved face is about the shape of an ordinary gravestone, rounded at the top. On this stone is the record in the Phœnician characters of the wars of Mesha, king of Moab, with Israel. 2 Kings 3 : 4. It speaks of King Omri and other names of places and persons mentioned in the Bible, and belongs to this exact period of Jewish and Moabite history. The names given on the Moabite Stone, engraved by one who knew

The Moabite Stone. (*From a Photograph.*)

them in daily life, are, in nearly every case, identical with those found in the Bible itself, and testify to the wonderful integrity with which the Scriptures have been preserved. "The inscription reads like a leaf taken out of a lost book of Chronicles. The expressions are the same; the names of gods, kings and of towns are the same."—(See Rawlinson's "Historical Illustrations;" *American Cyclopedia;* and *Bibliotheca Sacra,* Oct. 20, 1870.—ED.)

Mo'din, a place not mentioned in either the Old or the New Testament, though rendered immortal by its connection with the history of the Jews in the interval between the two. It was the native city of the Maccabæan family, 1 Macc. 13 : 25, and as a necessary consequence contained their ancestral sepulchre. ch. 2 : 70; 9 : 19; 13 : 25–30. At Modin the Maccabæan armies encamped on the eves of two of their most memorable victories—that of Judas over Antiochus Eupator, 2 Macc. 13 : 14, and that of Simon over Cendebeus. 1 Macc. 16 : 4. The only indication of the position of the place to be gathered from the above notices is contained in the last, from which we may infer that it was near "the plain," *i. e.* the great maritime lowland of Philistia. ver. 5. The description of the monument seems to imply that the spot was so lofty as to be visible from the sea, and so near that even the details of the sculpture were discernible therefrom. All these conditions, excepting the last, are tolerably fulfilled in either of the two sites called *Latrûn* and *Kubâb.*

Mo-adi'ah. Neh. 12 : 17. Elsewhere (Neh. 12 : 5) called MAADIAH.

Mol'adah (*birth, race*), a city of Judah, one of those which lay in the district of "the south." Josh. 15 : 26; 19 : 2. In the latter tribe it remained at any rate till the reign of David, 1 Chron. 4 : 28, but by the time of the captivity it seems to have come back into the hands of Judah, by whom it was reinhabited after the captivity. Neh. 11 : 26. It may be placed at *el-Milh,* which is about 4 English miles from *Tell Arad,* 17 or 18 from Hebron, and 9 or 10 due east of Beersheba.

Mole. 1. *Tinshemeth.* Lev. 11 : 30. It is probable that the animals mentioned with the *tinshemeth* in the above passage denote different kinds of lizards; perhaps, therefore, the chameleon is the animal intended.

2. *Chĕphôr pêrôth* is rendered "moles" in Isa. 2 : 20. (The word means burrowers, hole-diggers, and may designate any of the small animals, as rats and weasels, which burrow among ruins. Many scholars, according to McClintock and Strong's "Cyclopedia," consider that the Greek *aspalax* is the animal intended by both the words translated mole. It is not the European mole, but is a kind of blind mole-rat, from 8 to 12 inches long, feeding on vegetables, and burrowing like a mole, but on a larger scale. It is very common in Russia, and Hasselquist says it is abundant on the plains of Sharon in Palestine.—ED.)

Mo'lech (*king*). The fire-god Molech was the tutelary deity of the children of Ammon, and essentially identical with the Moabitish Chemosh. Fire-gods appear to have been common to all the

Canaanite, Syrian and Arab tribes, who worshipped the destructive element under an outward symbol, with the most inhuman rites. According to Jewish tradition, the image of Molech was of brass, hollow within, and was situated without Jerusalem. "His face was (that) of a calf, and his hands stretched forth like a man who opens his hands to receive (something) of his neighbor. And they kindled it with fire, and the priests took the babe and put it into the hands of Molech, and the babe gave up the ghost." Many instances of human sacrifices are found in ancient writers, which may be compared with the description in the Old Testament of the manner in which Molech was worshipped. Molech was the lord and master of the Ammonites; their country was his possession, Jer. 49 : 1, as Moab was the heritage of Chemosh; the princes of the land were the princes of Malcham. Jer. 49 : 3; Amos 1 : 15. His priests were men of rank, Jer. 49 : 3, taking precedence of the princes. The priests of Molech, like those of other idols, were called Chemarim. 2 Kings 23 : 5; Hos. 10 : 5; Zeph. 1 : 4.

Mo'li. Mahli, the son of Merari. 1 Esdr. 8 : 47; comp. Ezra 8 : 18.

Mo'lid (*begetter*), the son of Abishur by his wife Abihail, and descendant of Jerahmeel. 1 Chron. 2 : 29.

Mo'loch. The same as Molech.

Money. 1. *Uncoined money.*—It is well known that ancient nations that were without a coinage weighed the precious metals, a practice represented on the Egyptian monuments, on which gold and silver are shown to have been kept in the form of rings. We have no evidence of the use of *coined money* before the return from the Babylonian captivity; but silver was used for money, in quantities determined by weight, at least as early as the time of Abraham; and its earliest mention is in the generic sense of the price paid for a slave. Gen. 17 : 13. The 1000 *pieces of silver* paid by Abimelech to Abraham, Gen. 20 : 16, and the 20 *pieces of silver* for which Joseph was sold to the Ishmaelites, Gen. 37 : 28, were probably rings such as we see on the Egyptian monuments in the act of being weighed. In the first recorded transaction of commerce, the cave of Machpelah is purchased by Abraham for 400 shekels of silver. The shekel weight of silver was the unit of value through the whole

age of Hebrew history, down to the Babylonian captivity.

2. *Coined money.*—After the captivity we have the earliest mention of *coined money*, in allusion, as might have been

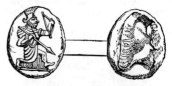

The Persian (or golden) Daric.

expected, to the Persian coinage, the gold *daric* (Authorized Version *dram*). Ezra 2 : 69; 8 : 27; Neh. 7 : 70, 71, 72. [DARIC.] No native Jewish coinage appears to have existed till Antiochus VII. Sidetes granted Simon Maccabæus the license to coin money, B.C. 140; and it is now generally agreed that the oldest Jewish *silver coins*

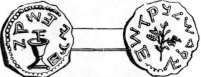

Jewish Half-shekel.

belong to this period. They are shekels and half-shekels, of the weight of 220 and 110 grains. With this silver there was associated a *copper* coinage. The abundant money of Herod the Great, which is of a thoroughly Greek character, and of copper only, seems to have

Shekel of the Sanctuary.

been a continuation of the copper coinage of the Maccabees, with some adaptation to the Roman standard. In the money of the New Testament we see the native copper coinage side by side with the Græco-Roman copper, silver and gold. (The first coined money mentioned in the Bible refers to the Persian coinage,

1 Chron. 29 : 7 ; Ezra 2 : 69, and is translated *dram*. It is the Persian *daric*, a gold coin worth about $5.50. The coins mentioned by the evangelists, and first those of silver, are the following : The *stater*, Matt. 17 : 24–27, called *piece of money*, was a Roman coin equal to four drachmas. It was worth 55 to 60 cents, and is of about the same value as the Jewish *stater*, or coined shekel. The *denarius*, or Roman penny, as well as the

Denarius of Cæsar.

Greek *drachma*, then of about the same weight, are spoken of as current coins. Matt. 22 : 15–21 ; Luke 20 : 19–25. They were worth about 15 cents. Of copper coins the *farthing* and its half, the *mite*, are spoken of, and these probably formed the chief native currency. (The Roman farthing (*quadrans*) was a brass coin

Assarion (farthing). Actual size.

worth .375 of a cent. The Greek *farthing* (*as* or *assarion*) was worth four Roman farthings, *i. e.* about one cent and a half. A *mite* was half a farthing, and therefore was worth about two-tenths of a cent if the half of the Roman farthing, and about 2 cents if the half of the Greek farthing. See table of *Jewish weights and measures.*—ED.)

Money-changers. Matt. 21 : 12 ; Mark 11 : 15 ; John 2 : 15. According to Ex. 30 : 13–15, every Israelite who had reached or passed the age of twenty must pay into the sacred treasury, whenever the nation was numbered, a half-shekel as an offering to Jehovah. The money-changers whom Christ, for their impiety, avarice and fraudulent dealing, expelled from the temple were the dealers who supplied half-shekels, for such a premi-

um as they might be able to exact, to the Jews from all parts of the world who assembled at Jerusalem during the great festivals, and were required to pay their tribute or ransom money in the Hebrew coin.

Month. From the time of the institution of the Mosaic law downward the month was a lunar one. The cycle of religious feasts commencing with the passover depended not simply on the month, but on the moon; the 14th of Abib was coincident with the full moon; and the new moons themselves were the occasions of regular festivals. Num. 10 : 10 ; 28 : 11–14. The commencement of the month was generally decided by observation of the new moon. The usual number of months in a year was twelve, as implied in 1 Kings 4 : 7 ; 1 Chron. 27 : 1–15 ; but since twelve lunar months would make but 354½ days, the years would be short twelve days of the true year, and therefore it follows as a matter of course that an additional month must have been inserted about every third year, which would bring the number up to thirteen. No notice, however, is taken of this month in the Bible. In the modern Jewish calendar the intercalary month is introduced seven times in every nineteen years. The usual method of designating the months was by their numerical order, *e. g.* "the second month," Gen. 7 : 11, "the fourth month," 2 Kings 25 : 3 ; and this was generally retained even when the names were given, *e. g.* "in the month Zif, which is the second month." 1 Kings 6 : 1. The names of the months belong to two distinct periods. In the first place we have those peculiar to the period of Jewish independence, of which four only, even including Abib, which we hardly regard as a proper name, are mentioned, viz.: Abib, in which the passover fell, Ex. 13 : 4 ; 23 : 15 ; 34 : 18 ; Deut. 16 : 1, and which was established as the first month in commemoration of the exodus, Ex. 12 : 2 ; Zif, the second month, 1 Kings 6 : 1, 37 ; Bul, the eighth, 1 Kings 6 : 38 ; and Ethanim, the seventh. 1 Kings 8 : 2. In the second place we have the names which prevailed subsequent to the Babylonish captivity ; of these the following seven appear in the Bible : Nisan, the first, in which the passover was held, Neh. 2 : 1 ; Esther 3 : 7 ; Sivan, the third, Esther 8 : 9 ; Bar. 1 : 8 ; Elul, the sixth, Neh. 6 : 15 ; 1 Macc. 14 : 27 ; Chisleu, the ninth, Neh. 1 : 1 ; Zech. 7 : 1 ; 1 Macc. 1 :

54; Tebeth, the tenth, Esther 2 : 16; Sebat, the eleventh, Zech. 1 : 7; 1 Macc. 16 : 14; and Adar, the twelfth. Esther 3 : 7; 8 : 12; 2 Macc. 15 : 36. The names of the remaining five occur in the Talmud and other works; they were, Iyar, the second, Targum; 2 Chron. 30 : 2; Tammuz, the fourth; Ab, the fifth; Tisri, the seventh; and Marcheshvan, the eighth. The name of the intercalary month was Ve-adar, *i. e.* the *additional* Adar. The identification of the Jewish months with our own cannot be effected with precision on account of the variations that must inevitably exist between the lunar and the solar month. Nisan (or Abib) answers to March; Zif or Iyar to May; Sivan to June; Tammuz to July; Ab to August; Elul to September; Ethanim or Tisri to October; Bul or Marcheshvan to November; Chisleu to December; Tebeth to January; Sebat to February; and Adar to March.

| Month of | | Jewish Name. | No. of Days. | Beginning with the new moon and corresponding to our | Products. | Jewish Festivals. |
Sacred Year.	Civil Year.					
I.	VII.	Abib or Nisan	30	March, April.....	Barley Ripe. } Fig in blossom. }	Passover. Unleavened Bread.
II.	VIII.	Iyar or Zif................	29	April and May..	Barley harvest.	
III.	IX.	Sisan or Sivan	30	May and June...	Wheat harvest...	Pentecost.
IV.	X.	Tammuz..................	29	June, July........	Early vintage.	
V.	XI.	Ab........................	30	July, August.....	Ripe figs.	
VI.	XII.	Elul	29	August, Sept	General vintage..	
VII.	I.	Tisri.....................	30	Sept., Oct..........	Ploughing and } sowing. .... }	Feast of Trumpets. Atonement. Feast of Tabernacles.
VIII.	II.	Bul.............	29	Oct., Nov	Latter grapes.	
IX.	III.	Chisleu....................	30	Nov., Dec..........	Snow.	Dedication.
X.	IV.	Tebeth	29	Dec., Jan	Grass after rain.	
XI.	V.	Shebat	30	Jan., Feb..........	Winter fig.	
XII.	VI.	Adar	29	Feb., March......	Almond blossom.	Purim.
XIII.	......	Ve-adar, *intercalary.*				

Moon. The moon held an important place in the kingdom of nature, as known to the Hebrews. Conjointly with the sun, it was appointed "for signs and for seasons, and for days and years;" though in this respect it exercised a more important influence, if by the "seasons" we understand the great religious festivals of the Jews, as is particularly stated in Ps. 104 : 19, and more at length in Ecclus. 43 : 6, 7. The worship of the moon prevailed extensively among the nations of the East, and under a variety of aspects. It was one of the only two deities which commanded the reverence of all the Egyptians. The worship of the heavenly bodies is referred to in Job 31 : 26, 27, and Moses directly warns the Jews against it. Deut. 4 : 19. In the figurative language of Scripture, the moon is frequently noticed as presaging events of the greatest importance through the temporary or permanent withdrawal of its light. Isa. 13 : 10; Joel 2 : 31; Matt. 24 : 29; Mark 13 : 24.

Moon, New. [NEW MOON.]

Mor'asthite, The, that is, the native of a place named Moresheth. It occurs twice — Jer. 26 : 18; Micah 1 : 1 — each time as the description of the prophet Micah.

Mor'deca-i (*little man,* or *worshipper of Mars*), the deliverer, under divine Providence, of the Jews from the destruction plotted against them by Haman the chief minister of Xerxes; the institutor of the feast of Purim. The incidents of his history are too well known to need to be dwelt upon. [ESTHER.] Three things are predicated of Mordecai in the book of Esther : (1) That he lived in Shushan; (2) That his name was Mordecai, son of Jair, son of Shimei, son of Kish the Benjamite who was taken captive with Jehoiachin; (3) That he brought up Esther.

Mo'reh (*teacher*). 1. The plain or plains (or, as it should rather be rendered, the oak or oaks) of Moreh. The oak of Moreh was the first recorded halting-place of Abram after his entrance into the land of Canaan. Gen. 12 : 6. It was at the "place of Shechem," ch. 12 : 6, close to the mountains of Ebal and Gerizim. Deut. 11 : 30.

2. The hill of Moreh, at the foot of which the Midianites and Amalekites were encamped before Gideon's attack upon them. Judges 7 : 1. It lay in the

valley of Jezreel, rather on the north side of the valley, and north also of the eminence on which Gideon's little band of heroes was clustered. These conditions are most accurately fulfilled if we assume *Jebel ed-Duhy*, the "Little Hermon" of the modern travellers, 1815 feet above the Mediterranean, to be Moreh, the *Ain-Jalood* to be the spring of Harod, and Gideon's position to have been on the northeast slope of *Jebel Fukâa* (Mount Gilboa), between the village of *Nuris* and the last-mentioned spring.

Mor'esheth-gath (*possession of Gath*), a place named by the prophet Micah. Micah 1 : 14. The prophet was himself a native of a place called Moresheth.

Mori'ah (*chosen by Jehovah*). 1. *The land of Moriah.*—On "one of the mountains" in this district took place the sacrifice of Isaac. Gen. 22 : 2. Its position is doubtful, some thinking it to be Mount Moriah, others that *Moreh*, near Shechem, is meant. [See MOUNT MORIAH.]

2. *Mount Moriah.*—The elevation on which Solomon built the temple, where God appeared to David "in the threshing-floor of Araunah the Jebusite." It is the eastern eminence of Jerusalem, separated from Mount Zion by the Tyropœon valley. The top was levelled by Solomon, and immense walls were built around it from the base to enlarge the level surface for the temple area. A tradition which first appears in a definite shape in Josephus, and is now almost universally accepted, asserts that the "Mount Moriah" of the Chronicles is identical with the "mountain" in "the land of Moriah" of Genesis, and that the spot on which Jehovah appeared to David, and on which the temple was built, was the very spot of the sacrifice of Isaac. (Smith, Stanley and Grove are, however, inclined to doubt this tradition.)

Mortar, "a wide-mouthed vessel in form of an inverted bell, in which substances are pounded or bruised with a pestle."—*Webster.* The simplest and probably most ancient method of preparing corn for food was by pounding it between two stones. The Israelites in the desert appear to have possessed mortars and handmills among their necessary domestic utensils. When the manna fell they gathered it, and either ground it in the mill or pounded it in the mortar till it was fit for use. Num. 11 : 8. So in the present day stone mortars are used by the Arabs to pound wheat for their national dish *kibby.* Another word occurring in Prov. 27 : 22 probably denotes a mortar of a larger kind in which corn was pounded: "Though thou shouldest bray a fool in a mortar among wheat with a pestle, yet will not his foolishness depart from him." Corn may be separated from its husk and all its good properties preserved by such an operation, but the fool's folly is so essential a part of himself that no analogous process can remove it from him. Such seems the natural interpretation of this remarkable proverb. The language is intentionally exaggerated, and there is no necessity for supposing an allusion to a mode of punishment by which criminals were put to death by being pounded in a mortar. A custom of this kind existed among the Turks, but there is no distinct trace of it among the Hebrews. Such, however, is supposed to be the reference in the proverb by Mr. Roberts, who illustrates it from his Indian experience.

Mortar. Gen. 11 : 3; Ex. 1 : 14; Lev. 14 : 42, 45; Isa. 41 : 25; Ezek. 13 : 10, 11, 14, 15; 22 : 28; Nah. 3 : 14. The various compacting substances used in Oriental buildings appear to be—1. Bitumen, as in the Babylonian structures; 2. Common mud or moistened clay; 3. A very firm cement compounded of sand, ashes and lime, in the proportions respectively of 1, 2, 3, well pounded, sometimes mixed and sometimes coated with oil, so as to form a surface almost impenetrable to wet or the weather. In Assyrian and also Egyptian brick buildings, stubble or straw, as hair or wool among ourselves, was added to increase the tenacity.

Mo'serah (*bonds*), Deut. 10 : 6, apparently the same as Moseroth, Num. 33 : 30, its plural form, the name of a place near Mount Hor.

Mo'ses (Heb. *Môsheh*, "drawn," *i. e.* from the water; in the Coptic it means "saved from the water"), the legislator of the Jewish people, and in a certain sense the founder of the Jewish religion. The immediate pedigree of Moses is as follows:

27

The history of Moses naturally divides itself into three periods of 40 years each. Moses was born at Goshen, in Egypt, B.C. 1571. The story of his birth is thoroughly Egyptian in its scene. His mother made extraordinary efforts for his preservation from the general destruction of the male children of Israel. For three months the child was concealed in the house. Then his mother placed him in a small boat or basket of papyrus, closed against the water by bitumen. This was placed among the aquatic vegetation by the side of one of the canals of the Nile. The sister lingered to watch her brother's fate. The Egyptian princess, who, tradition says, was a childless wife, came down to bathe in the sacred river. Her attendant slaves followed her. She saw the basket in the flags, and despatched divers, who brought it. It was opened, and the cry of the child moved the princess to compassion. She determined to rear it as her own. The sister was at hand to recommend a Hebrew nurse, the child's own mother. Here was the *first part* of Moses' training,—a training at home in the true religion, in faith in God, in the promises to his nation, in the life of a saint,—a training which he never forgot, even amid the splendors and gilded sin of Pharaoh's court. The child was adopted by the princess. From this time for many years Moses must be considered as an Egyptian. In the Pentateuch this period is a blank, but in the New Testament he is represented as "learned in all the wisdom of the Egyptians," and as "mighty in words and deeds." Acts 7 : 22. This was the *second part* of Moses' training.

The second period of Moses' life began when he was forty years old. Seeing the sufferings of his people, Moses determined to go to them as their helper, and made his great life-choice, " choosing rather to suffer affliction with the people of God than to enjoy the pleasures of sin for a season ; esteeming the reproach of Christ greater riches than the treasures in Egypt." Heb. 11 : 25, 26. Seeing an Israelite suffering the bastinado from an Egyptian, and thinking that they were alone, he slew the Egyptian, and buried the corpse in the sand. But the people soon showed themselves unfitted as yet to obtain their freedom, nor was Moses yet fitted to be their leader. He was compelled to leave Egypt when the slaying of the Egyptian became known, and

he fled to the land of Midian, in the southern and southeastern part of the Sinai peninsula. There was a famous well (" the well," Ex. 2 : 15) surrounded by tanks for the watering of the flocks of the Bedouin herdsmen. By this well the fugitive seated himself and watched the gathering of the sheep. There were the Arabian shepherds, and there were also seven maidens, whom the shepherds rudely drove away from the water. The chivalrous spirit which had already broken forth in behalf of his oppressed countrymen broke forth again in behalf of the distressed maidens. They returned unusually soon to their father, Jethro, and told him of their adventure. Moses, who up to this time had been " an Egyptian," Ex. 2 : 19, now became for a time an Arabian. He married Zipporah, daughter of his host, to whom he also became the slave and shepherd. Ex. 2 : 21 ; 3 : 1. Here for forty years Moses communed with God and with nature, escaping from the false ideas taught him in Egypt, and sifting out the truths that were there. This was the *third process* of his training for his work ; and from this training he learned infinitely more than from Egypt. Stanley well says, after enumerating what the Israelites derived from Egypt, that the contrast was always greater than the likeness. This process was completed when God met him on Horeb, appearing in a burning bush, and, communicating with him, appointed him to be the leader and deliverer of his people.

Now begins the third period of forty years in Moses' life. He meets Aaron, his next younger brother, whom God permitted to be the spokesman, and together they return to Goshen in Egypt. From this time the history of Moses is the history of Israel for the next forty years. Aaron spoke and acted for Moses, and was the permanent inheritor of the sacred staff of power. But Moses was the inspiring soul behind. He is incontestably the chief personage of the history, in a sense in which no one else is described before or since. He was led into a closer communion with the invisible world than was vouchsafed to any other in the Old Testament. There are two main characters in which he appears —as a leader and as a prophet. (1) As a leader, his life divides itself into the three epochs—the march to Sinai ; the march from Sinai to Kadesh ; and the conquest of the transjordanic kingdoms.

On approaching Palestine the office of the leader becomes blended with that of the general or the conqueror. By Moses the spies were sent to explore the country. Against his advice took place the first disastrous battle at Hormah. To his guidance is ascribed the circuitous route by which the nation approached Palestine from the east, and to his generalship the two successful campaigns in which Sihon and Og were defeated. The narrative is told so briefly that we are in danger of forgetting that at this last stage of his life Moses must have been as much a conqueror and victorious soldier as was Joshua. (2) His character as a prophet is, from the nature of the case, more distinctly brought out. He is the first as he is the greatest example of a prophet in the Old Testament. His brother and sister were both endowed with prophetic gifts. The seventy elders, and Eldad and Medad also, all "prophesied." Num. 11 : 25–27. But Moses rose high above all these. With him the divine revelations were made "mouth to mouth." Num. 12 : 8. Of the special modes of this more direct communication, four great examples are given, corresponding to four critical epochs in his historical career. (a) The appearance of the divine presence in the flaming acacia tree. Ex. 3 : 2–6. (b) In the giving of the law from Mount Sinai, the outward form of the revelation was a thick darkness as of a thunder-cloud, out of which proceeded a voice. Ex. 19 : 19 ; 20 : 21. On two occasions he is described as having penetrated within the darkness. Ex. 24 : 18 ; 34 : 28. (c) It was nearly at the close of these communications in the mountains of Sinai that an especial revelation of God was made to him personally. Ex. 33 : 21, 22 ; 34 : 5, 6, 7. God passed before him. (d) The fourth mode of divine manifestation was that which is described as beginning at this juncture, and which was maintained with more or less continuity through the rest of his career. Ex. 33 : 7. It was the communication with God in the tabernacle from out the pillar of cloud and fire. There is another form of Moses' prophetic gift, viz., the poetical form of composition which characterizes the Jewish prophecy generally. These poetical utterances are—1. "The song which Moses and the children of Israel sung" (after the passage of the Red Sea). Ex. 15 : 1–19. 2. A fragment of a war-song against Amalek. Ex. 17 : 16. 3. A fragment of a lyrical burst of indignation. Ex. 32 : 18. 4. The fragments of war-songs, probably from either him or his immediate prophetic followers, in Num. 21 : 14, 15, 27–30, preserved in the "book of the wars of Jehovah," Num. 21 : 14 ; and the address to the well. ch. 21 : 16, 17, 18. 5. The song of Moses, Deut. 32 : 1–43, setting forth the greatness and the failings of Israel. 6. The blessing of Moses on the tribes. Deut. 33 : 1–29. 7. The 90th Psalm, "A prayer of Moses, the man of God." The title, like all the titles of the psalms, is of doubtful authority, and the psalm has often been referred to a later author.

Character.—The prophetic office of Moses can only be fully considered in connection with his whole character and appearance. Hos. 12 : 13. He was in a sense peculiar to himself the founder and representative of his people ; and in accordance with this complete identification of himself with his nation is the only strong personal trait which we are able to gather from his history. Num. 12 : 3. The word "meek" is hardly an adequate reading of the Hebrew term, which should be rather "much enduring." It represents what we should now designate by the word "disinterested." All that is told of him indicates a withdrawal of himself, a preference of the cause of his nation to his own interests, which makes him the most complete example of Jewish patriotism. (He was especially a man of prayer and of faith, of wisdom, courage and patience.) In exact conformity with his life is the account of his end. The book of Deuteronomy describes, and is, the long last farewell of the prophet to his people. This takes place on the first day of the eleventh month of the fortieth year of the wanderings, in the plains of Moab. Deut. 1 : 3, 5. Moses is described as 120 years of age, but with his sight and his freshness of strength unabated. Deut. 34 : 7. Joshua is appointed his successor. The law is written out and ordered to be deposited in the ark. ch. 31. The song and the blessing of the tribes conclude the farewell. chs. 32, 33. And then comes the mysterious close. He is told that he is to see the good land beyond the Jordan, but not to possess it himself. He ascends the mount of Pisgah and stands on Nebo, one of its summits, and surveys the four great masses of Palestine west of the Jordan, so far as it can be discerned from that height. The view has passed into a proverb for all nations. "So Moses the servant of Jehovah died there in the land of Moab, according to the word of Jehovah. And he buried him in a 'ravine' in the land of Moab, 'before' Beth-peor: but no man knoweth of his sepulchre unto this day. . . And the children of Israel wept for Moses in the plains of Moab thirty days." Deut. 34 : 5, 6, 8. This is all that is said in the sacred record. (This burial was thus hidden probably — (1) To preserve his grave from idolatrous worship or superstitious reverence; and (2) Because it may be that God did not intend to leave his body to corruption, but to prepare it, as he did the body of Elijah, so that Moses could in his spiritual body meet Christ, together with Elijah, on the mount of transfiguration.)

Moses is spoken of as a likeness of Christ; and as this is a point of view which has been almost lost in the Church, compared with the more familiar comparisons of Christ to Adam, David, Joshua, and yet has as firm a basis in fact as any of them, it may be well to draw it out in detail. (1) Moses is, as it would seem, the only character of the Old Testament to whom Christ expressly likens himself: "Moses wrote of me." John 5 : 46. It suggests three main points of likeness: (a) Christ was, like Moses, the great prophet of the people— the last, as Moses was the first. (b) Christ, like Moses, is a lawgiver: "Him shall ye hear." (c) Christ, like Moses, was a prophet out of the midst of the nation, "from their brethren." As Moses was the entire representative of his people, feeling for them more than for himself, absorbed in their interests, hopes and fears, so, with reverence be it said, was Christ. (2) In Heb. 3 : 1–19; 12 : 24–29; Acts 7 : 37, Christ is described, though more obscurely, as the Moses of the new dispensation—as the apostle or messenger or mediator of God to the people—as the controller and leader of the flock or household of God. (3) The details of their lives are sometimes, though not often, compared. Acts 7 : 24–28, 35. In Jude 9 is an allusion to an altercation between Michael and Satan over the body of Moses. It probably refers to a lost apocryphal book, mentioned by Origen, called the "Ascension" or "Assumption

of Moses." Respecting the books of Moses, see PENTATEUCH.

Moth. By the Hebrew word we are certainly to understand some species of clothes-moth (*tinea*). Reference to the destructive habits of the clothes-moth is

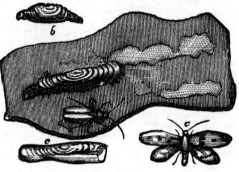

Cloth Moths.

made in Job 4 : 19; 13 : 28; Ps. 39 : 11, etc. (The moth is a well-known insect which in its caterpillar state is very destructive to woollen clothing, furs, etc. The egg of the moth, being deposited on the fur or cloth, produces a very small shining insect, which immediately forms a house for itself by cuttings from the cloth. It eats away the nap, and finally ruins the fabric. There are more than 1500 species of moths.—*McClintock and Strong's Cyclopedia.*)

Mother. The superiority of the Hebrew over all contemporaneous systems of legislation and of morals is strongly shown in the higher estimation of the mother in the Jewish family, as contrasted with modern Oriental as well as ancient Oriental and classical usage. The king's mother, as appears in the case of Bath-sheba, was treated with special honor. Ex. 20 : 12; Lev. 19 : 3; Deut. 5 : 16; 21 : 18, 21; 1 Kings 2 : 19; Prov. 10 : 1; 15 : 20; 17 : 25; 29 : 15; 31 : 1, 30.

Mount. Isa. 29 : 3; Jer. 6 : 6, etc. [SIEGE.]

Mount, Mountain. The Hebrew word *har*, like the English "mountain," is employed for both single eminences more or less isolated, such as Sinai, Gerizim, Ebal, Zion and Olivet, and for ranges, such as Lebanon. It is also applied to a mountainous country or district.

Mountain of the Amorites, specifically mentioned Deut. 1 : ·19, 20; comp. 44. It seems to be the range which rises abruptly from the plateau of *et-Tih*, south of Judea, running from a little south of west to north of east, and of which the extremities are the *Jebel Araif en-Nakah* westward and *Jebel el-Mukrah* eastward, and from which line the country continues mountainous all the way to Hebron.

Mourning.

Mourning. One marked feature of Oriental mourning is what may be called its studied publicity and the careful observance of the prescribed ceremonies. Gen. 23 : 2; Job 1 : 20; 2 : 12. 1. Among the particular forms observed the following may be mentioned : (*a*) Rending the clothes. Gen. 37 : 29, 34; 44 : 13, etc. (*b*) Dressing in sackcloth. Gen. 37 : 34; 2 Sam. 3 : 31; 21 : 10, etc. (*c*) Ashes, dust or earth sprinkled on the person. 2 Sam. 13 : 19; 15 : 32, etc. (*d*) Black or sad-colored garments. 2 Sam. 14 : 2; Jer. 8 : 21, etc. (*e*) Removal of ornaments or neglect of person. Deut. 21 : 12, 13, etc. (*f*) Shaving the head, plucking out the hair of the head or beard. Lev. 10 : 6; 2 Sam. 19 : 24, etc. (*g*) Laying bare some part of the body. Isa. 20 : 2; 47 : 2, etc. (*h*) Fasting or abstinence in meat and drink. 2 Sam. 1 : 12; 3 : 35; 12 : 16, 22, etc. (*i*) In the same direction may be mentioned diminution in offerings to God, and prohibition to partake of sacrificial food. Lev. 7 : 20; Deut. 26 : 14. (*k*) Covering the " upper lip," *i. e.* the lower part of the face, and sometimes the head, in token of silence. Lev. 13 : 45; 2 Sam. 15 : 30; 19 : 4. (*l*) Cutting the flesh, Jer. 16 : 6, 7; 41 : 5; beating the body. Ezek. 21 : 12; Jer. 31 : 19. (*m*) Employment of persons hired for the purpose of mourning. Eccles. 12 : 5; Jer. 9 : 17; Amos 5: 16; Matt. 9 : 23. (*n*) Akin to the foregoing usage the custom for friends or passers-by to join in the lamentations of bereaved or afflicted persons. Gen. 50 : 3; Judges 11 : 40; Job 2 : 11; 30 : 25, etc. (*o*) The sitting or lying posture in silence indicative of grief. Gen. 23 : 3; Judges 20 : 26, etc. (*p*) Mourning feast and cup of consolation. Jer. 16 : 7, 8.

2. The period of mourning varied. In the case of Jacob it was seventy days, Gen. 50 : 3; of Aaron, Num. 20 : 29, and Moses, Deut. 34 : 8, thirty. A further period of seven days in Jacob's case. Gen. 50 : 10. Seven days for Saul, which may have been an abridged period in the time of national danger. 1 Sam. 31 : 13.

With the practices above mentioned, Oriental and other customs, ancient and modern, in great measure agree. Arab men are silent in grief, but the women scream, tear their hair, hands and face, and throw earth or sand on their heads. Both Mohammedans and Christians in Egypt hire wailing-women, and wail at stated times. Burckhardt says the women of Atbara in Nubia shave their heads on the death of their nearest relatives—a custom prevalent also among several of the peasant tribes of upper Egypt. He also mentions wailing-women, and a man in distress besmearing his face with dirt and dust in token of grief. In the " Arabian Nights" are frequent allusions to similar practices. It also mentions ten days and forty days as periods of mourning. Lane, speaking of the modern Egyptians, says, " After death the women of the family raise cries of lamentation called *welweléh* or *wilwál*, uttering the most piercing shrieks, and calling upon the name of the deceased, 'Oh, my master! Oh, my resource! Oh, my misfortune! Oh, my glory!' See Jer. 22 : 18. The females of the neighborhood come to join with them in this conclamation: generally, also, the family send for two or more *neddábehs* or public wailing-women. Each brings a tambourine, and beating them they exclaim, ' Alas for him!' The female relatives, domestics and friends, with their hair dishevelled and sometimes with rent clothes, beating their faces, cry in like manner, 'Alas for him!' These make no alteration in dress, but women, in some cases, dye their shirts, head-veils and handkerchiefs of a dark-blue color. They visit the tombs at stated periods."—*Mod. Eg.* iii. 152, 171, 195.

Mouse (*the corn-eater*). The name of this animal occurs in Lev. 11 : 29; 1 Sam. 6 : 4, 5; Isa. 66 : 17. The Hebrew word

The Field Mouse.

is in all probability generic, and is not intended to denote any particular species of mouse. The original word denotes a field-ravager, and may therefore comprehend any destructive rodent. Tristram found twenty-three species of mice in Palestine. It is probable that in 1 Sam. 6 : 5 the expression "the mice that mar the land" includes and more particularly refers to the short-tailed field-mice (*Arvicola agrestis*, Flem.), which cause great destruction to the corn-lands of Syria.

Mowing. As the great heat of the climate in Palestine and other similarly-situated countries soon dries up the herbage itself, hay-making in our sense of the term is not in use. The "king's mowings," Amos 7 : 1, may perhaps refer to some royal right of early pasturage for the use of the cavalry.

Mo'za (*fountain*). 1. Son of Caleb the son of Hezron. 1 Chron. 2 : 46.

2. Son of Zimri and descendant of Saul. 1 Chron. 8 : 36, 37; 9 : 42, 43.

Mo'zah (*fountain*), one of the cities in the allotment of Benjamin, Josh. 18 : 26 only, named between hac-Cephirah and Rekem.

Mulberry trees (Heb. *becâim*). Mention of these is made only in 2 Sam. 5 : 23, 24 and 1 Chron. 14 : 14. We are quite unable to determine what kind of tree is denoted by the Hebrew word. Some be-

lieve pear trees are meant; others the aspen or poplar, whose leaves tremble and rustle with the slightest breeze, even when the breeze is not otherwise perceptible. It may have been to the rustling of these leaves that the "going in the tree tops" refers. 2 Sam. 5 : 23, 24.

Mule, a hybrid animal, the offspring of a horse and an ass. "The mule is smaller than the horse, and is a remarkably hardy, patient, obstinate, sure-footed animal, living, ordinarily, twice as long as a horse."—*McClintock and Strong's Cyclopedia.* It was forbidden to the Israelites to breed mules, but sometimes they imported them. It would appear that only kings and great men rode on mules. We do not read of mules at all in the New Testament; perhaps therefore they had ceased to be imported.

Mup'pim (*serpent*), a Benjamite, and one of the fourteen descendants of Rachel who belonged to the original colony of the sons of Jacob in Egypt. Gen. 46 : 21. (B.C. 1706.) In Num. 26 : 39 the name is given as SHUPHAM.

Murder. The law of Moses, while it protected the accidental homicide, defined with additional strictness the crime of murder. It prohibited compensation or reprieve of the murderer, or his protection if he took refuge in the refuge city, or even at the altar of Jehovah. Ex. 21 : 12, 14; Lev. 24 : 17, 21; 1 Kings 2 : 5, 6, 31. The duty of executing punishment on the murderer is in the law expressly laid on the "revenger of blood;" but the question of guilt was to be previously decided by the Levitical tribunal. In regal times the duty of execution of justice on a murderer seems to have been assumed to some extent by the sovereign, as was also the privilege of pardon. 2 Sam. 13 : 39; 14 : 7, 11; 1 Kings 2 : 34. It was lawful to kill a burglar taken at night in the act, but unlawful to do so after sunrise. Ex. 22 : 2, 3.

Mu'shi (*yielding*), the son of Merari the son of Kohath. Ex. 6 : 19; Num. 3 : 20; 1 Chron. 6 : 19, 47; 23 : 21, 23; 24 : 26, 30.

Music. 1. *The most ancient music.*— The inventor of musical instruments, like the first poet and the first forger of metals, was a Cainite. We learn from Gen. 4 : 21 that Jubal the son of Lamech was "the father of all such as handle the harp and organ," that is, of all players upon stringed and wind instruments. The first mention of music in the times after the deluge is in the narrative of Laban's interview with Jacob, Gen. 31 : 27; so that, whatever way it was preserved, the practice of music existed in the upland country of Syria, and of the three possible kinds of musical instruments, two were known and employed to accompany the song. The three kinds are alluded to in Job 21 : 12. On the banks of the Red Sea Moses and the children of Israel sang their triumphal song of deliverance from the hosts of Egypt; and Miriam, in celebration of the same event, exercised one of her functions as a prophetess by leading a procession of the women of the camp, chanting in chorus the burden of the song of Moses. The song of Deborah and Barak is cast in a distinctly metrical form, and was probably intended to be sung with a musical accompaniment as one of the people's songs. The simpler impromptu with which the women from the cities of Israel greeted David after the slaughter of the Philistines was apparently struck off on the spur of the moment, under the influence of the wild joy with which they welcomed their national champion, "the darling of the sons of Israel." 1 Sam. 18 : 6, 7. Up to this time we meet with nothing like a systematic cultivation of music among the Hebrews, but the establishment of the schools of the prophets appears to have supplied this want. Whatever the students of these schools may have been taught, music was an essential part of their practice. Professional musicians soon became attached to the court.

2. *The golden age of Hebrew music.*— David seems to have gathered round him "singing men and singing women." 2 Sam. 19 : 35. Solomon did the same, Eccles. 2 : 8, adding to the luxury of his court by his patronage of art, and obtaining a reputation himself as no mean composer. 1 Kings 4 : 32. But the temple was the great school of music, and it was consecrated to its highest service in the worship of Jehovah. Before, however, the elaborate arrangements had been made by David for the temple choir, there must have been a considerable body of musicians throughout the country. 2 Sam. 6 : 5. (David chose 4000 musicians from the 38,000 Levites in his reign, or one in ten of the whole tribe. Of these musicians 288 were specially trained and skillful. 1 Chron. 25 : 6, 7. The whole number was divided into 24 courses, each of which would thus consist of a full band of 154 musicians, presided over by a body of 12 specially-trained leaders, under one of the twenty-four sons of Asaph, Heman or Jeduthun as conductor. The leaders appear to have played on the cymbals, perhaps to mark the time. 1 Chron. 15 : 19; 16 : 5. All these joined in a special chant which David taught them, and which went by his name. 1 Chron. 23 : 5. Women also took part in the temple choir. 1 Chron. 13 : 8; 25 : 5, 6. These great choirs answered one to another in responsive singing; thus the temple music must have been grand and inspiring beyond anything known before that time.

3. *Character of Hebrew music.*—As in all Oriental nations, the music of the Hebrews was melody rather than harmony, which latter was then unknown. All, old and young, men and maidens, singers and instruments, appear to have sung one part only in unison, or in octaves. "The beauty of the music consisted altogether in the melody;" but this, with so many instruments and voices, was so charming that "the whole of antiquity is full of the praises of this music. By its means battles were won, cities conquered, mutinies quelled, diseases cured." —ED.)

4. *Uses of music.*—In the private as well as in the religious life of the Hebrews music held a prominent place. The kings had their court musicians, 2 Chron. 35 : 25; Eccles. 2 : 8; and in the luxurious times of the later monarchy the effeminate gallants of Israel amused themselves with devising musical instruments while their nation was perishing ("as Nero fiddled while Rome was burning"). But music was also the legitimate expression of mirth and gladness. The bridal processions as they passed through the streets were accompanied with music and song. Jer. 7 : 34. The music of the banquets was accompanied with songs and dancing. Luke 15 : 25. The triumphal processions which celebrated a victory were enlivened by minstrels and singers. Ex. 15 : 1, 20; Judges 5 : 1; 11 : 34. There were also religious songs. Isa. 30 : 29; James 5 : 13. Love songs are alluded to in Ps. 45, title, and Isa. 5 : 1. There were also the doleful songs of the funeral procession, and the wailing chant of the mourners. The grape-gatherers sang at their work, and the women sang as they toiled at the mill, and on every occasion the land of the Hebrews during their

national prosperity was a land of music and melody.

Musical instruments of the Hebrews. (There has been great obscurity as to the instruments of music in use among the Hebrews, but the discoveries on the monuments of Egypt and Assyria have thrown much light upon the form and nature of these instruments.

I. STRINGED INSTRUMENTS.—1. The *harp* or lyre. [See illustration.] 2. The

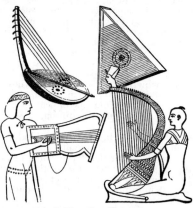

I. Egyptian Harps.

psaltery, the name of various large instruments of the harp kind. 3. The *sackbut,* a harp-like instrument of four strings and of triangular form. 4. A kind of *lute* or *guitar (mahalath),* in titles to Ps. 53 and 88, with a long, flat neck, and a hollow body of wood whose surface was perforated with holes. There were three strings, and the whole instrument was three or four feet long. 5. The *gittith,* in titles to Ps. 8, 81, 84, a stringed instrument, probably found by David at *Gath,* whence its name.

II. INSTRUMENTS OF PERCUSSION.— 1. The *timbrel,* a form of tambourine, a narrow hoop covered with a tightened skin, and struck with the hand. On the Egyptian monuments are three kinds— the circular, the square, and another formed by two squares separated by a bar. 2. The *drum (toph).* Of this there were many varieties, some of them resembling modern drums. The Egyptians had a long drum, of wood or copper, 2½ feet long, resembling the tom-tom of India, and beaten by the hand. Another form was shaped like a cask with bulging

centre, and was made of copper. It was of the same length as the other, but larger around, and was beaten with sticks. Another drum was more like our kettle-drum ; and one of these, the rabbins say, was placed in the temple court to call the priests to prayer, and could be heard

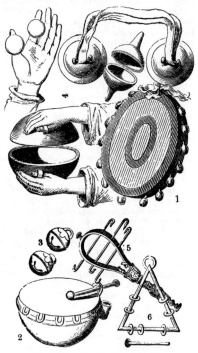

II. Instruments of Percussion.

from Jerusalem to Jericho. 3. *Bells* (*paamon*), attached to the high priest's dress, and rung by striking against the knobs, shaped like pomegranates, which were hung near them. 4. *Cymbals.* The earliest cymbals were probably finger-cymbals—small plates of metal fastened to the thumb and middle finger, and struck together. Afterward there were the large cymbals, played with both hands. 5. *Systra (menaanim),* 2 Sam. 6 : 5, there translated cornets. The systrum was a carved bronze or copper frame, with a handle, in all from 8 to 18 inches long, with movable rings and bars. It was shaken with the hand, and the rings and bars made a piercing metallic sound by striking against the bronze frame. 6. The *triangle* (*shalishim*), 1 Sam. 18 : 6, a musical instrument (*machol*) used for accompanying the dance, and several times translated dancing. Ps. 150 : 3, 45. It was a metallic rim or frame, sometimes with a handle, and had small bells attached to it, or bars across on which were strung metallic rings or plates. It was held in the hand, and was played by the women at weddings and merry-makings.

III. Wind Instruments.

III. WIND INSTRUMENTS. — 1. The *syrinx, pandean pipe* or *bagpipe* (*ugab*) ; translated " org un " in Gen. 4 : 21. Either like the bagpipe, or a series of pipes from 5 to 23 in number, though usually only 7. 2. The *horn*, in the form of an animal's horn even when made of metal, but originating in the use of the horns of cattle. 3. The *trumpet* (*shophar*), same as horn, 2. 4. The *straight trumpet*. 5. The *flute* (*halil*, meaning " bored through "), a pipe perforated with holes, originally made from reeds, but afterward of wood, bone, horn or ivory. It was chiefly consecrated to joy or pleasure. 6. The *flute*, alluded to in Dan. 3 : 5; probably a kind of double flageolet. 7. The *dulcimer*, Dan. 3 : 5, a kind of bagpipe with two shrill reeds. The *modern* dulcimer is a triangular instrument strung with about 50 brass wires, and played upon with little sticks or metallic rods. It

more resembles the ancient psaltery than the dulcimer of Dan. 3 : 5.—ED.)

Mustard is mentioned in Matt. 13 : 31; 17 : 20; Mark 4 : 31; Luke 13 : 19; 17 : 6. It is generally agreed that the mustard tree of Scripture is the black mustard (*Sinapis nigra*). The objection

The Mustard Plant.

commonly made against any *sinapis* being the plant of the parable is that the seed grew into "a tree," in which the fowls of the air are said to come and lodge. As to this objection, it is urged with great truth that the expression is figurative and Oriental, and that in a proverbial simile no literal accuracy is to be expected. It is an error, for which the language of Scripture is not accountable, to assert that the passage implies that birds " built their nests " in the tree: the Greek word has no such meaning; the word merely means " to settle or rest upon" anything for a longer or shorter time; nor is there any occasion to suppose that the expression "fowls of the air" denotes any other than the smaller *insessorial* kinds — linnets, finches, etc. Hiller's explanation is probably the correct one,—that the birds came and settled on the mustard-plant for the sake of the seed, of which they are very fond. Dr. Thomson also says he has seen the wild mustard on the rich plain of Akkar as tall as the horse and the rider. If, then, the wild plant on the *rich plain* of Akkar grows as high as a man on horseback, it might attain to the same or a greater height when in a cultivated garden. The expression "which is indeed the least of all seeds" is in all probability hyperbolical, to denote a very small seed indeed, as there are many seeds which are smaller than mustard. "The Lord in his popular teaching," says Trench ("Notes on Parables," 108), "adhered to the popular language;" and the mustard-seed was

Myrrh.

used proverbially to denote anything very minute; or it may mean that it was the smallest of all *garden* seeds, which it is in truth.

Muth-labben. "To the chief musician upon Muth-labben" is the title of Ps. 9, which has given rise to infinite conjecture. It may be either upon the *death* (*muth*) of the *fool* (*labben*), as an anagram on Nabal, or as Gesenius, "to be chanted by boys with virgins' voices," *i. e.* in the soprano.

My'ra, an important town in Lycia, on the southwest coast of Asia Minor, on the river Andriacus, 2½ miles from its mouth, referred to in Acts 27 : 5. Myra (called *Dembra* by the Greeks) is remarkable still for its remains of various periods of history.

Myrrh. This substance is mentioned in Ex. 30 : 23 as one of the ingredients of the "oil of holy ointment;" in Esther 2 : 12, as one of the substances used in the purification of women; in Ps. 45 : 8, Prov. 7 : 17, and in several passages in Canticles, as a perfume. The Greek occurs in Matt. 2 : 11 among the gifts brought by the wise men to the infant Jesus; and in Mark 15 : 23 it is said that "wine mingled with myrrh" was offered to, but refused by, our Lord on the cross. Myrrh was also used for embalming. See John 19 : 39 and Herod. ii. 86. The *Balsamodendron myrrha*, which produces the myrrh of commerce, has a wood and bark which

Myrtle.

emit a strong odor; the gum which exudes from the bark is at first oily, but becomes hard by exposure to the air. (This myrrh is in small yellowish or white globules or tears. The tree is small, with a stunted trunk, covered with light-gray bark. It is found in Arabia Felix. The myrrh of Gen. 37 : 25 was probably *lad-*

anum, a highly-fragrant resin and volatile oil used as a cosmetic, and stimulative as a medicine. It is yielded by the *cistus,* known in Europe as the rock rose, a shrub with rose-colored flowers, growing in Palestine and along the shores of the Mediterranean.—ED.) For wine mingled with myrrh see GALL.

Myrtle, a plant mentioned in Neh. 8 : 15; Isa. 41 : 19; 55 : 13; Zech. 1 : 8, 10, 11. The modern Jews still adorn with myrtle the booths and sheds at the feast of tabernacles. Formerly, as we learn from Nehemiah, Neh. 8 : 15, myrtles grew on the hills about Jerusalem. "On Olivet," says Dean Stanley, "nothing is now to be seen but the olive and the fig tree:" on some of the hills near Jerusalem, however, Hasselquist observed the myrtle. Dr. Hooker says it is not uncommon in Samaria and Galilee. The *Myrtus communis* is the kind denoted by the Hebrew word. (It is a shrub or low tree, sometimes ten feet high, with green shining leaves, and snow-white flowers bordered with purple, "which emit a perfume more exquisite than that of the rose." The seeds of the myrtle, dried before they are ripe, form our allspice.—ED.)

Mys′ia (*land of beech trees*), Acts 16 : 7, 8, was the region about the frontier of the provinces of Asia and Bithynia. The term is evidently used in an ethnological, not a political, sense.

N.

Na'am (*pleasantness*), one of the sons of Caleb the son of Jephunneh. 1 Chron. 4 : 15. (B.C. about 1451–1420.)

Na'amah (*loveliness*). 1. One of the four women whose names are preserved in the records of the world before the flood; all except Eve being Cainites. She was daughter of Lamech by his wife Zillah, and sister, as is expressly mentioned, to Tubal-cain. Gen. 4 : 22 only. (B.C. about 3550.)

2. Mother of King Rehoboam. 1 Kings 14 : 21, 31; 2 Chron. 12 : 13. In each of these passages she is distinguished by the title "the (not 'an,' as in Authorized Version) Ammonite." She was therefore one of the foreign women whom Solomon took into his establishment. 1 Kings 11 : 1. (B.C. 1015–975.)

Na'amah, one of the towns of Judah in the district of the lowland or Shefelah. Josh. 15 : 41. Capt. Warren, in Report of *Palestine Exploration Fund*, 1871, locates it at *Naameh*, six miles northeast of Yebna.

Na'aman (*pleasantness*). 1. "Naaman the Syrian." Luke 4 : 27. Naaman was commander-in-chief of the army of Syria, and was nearest to the person of the king, Ben-hadad II., whom he accompanied officially and supported when he went to worship in the temple of Rimmon, 2 Kings 5 : 18, at Damascus, the capital. (B.C. 885.) A Jewish tradition at least as old as the time of Josephus, and which may very well be a genuine one, identifies him with the archer whose arrow, whether at random or not, struck Ahab with his mortal wound, and thus "gave deliverance to Syria." The expression in 2 Kings 5 : 1 is remarkable—"because that by him Jehovah had given deliverance to Syria." The most natural explanation perhaps is that Naaman, in delivering his country, had killed one who was the enemy of Jehovah not less than he was of Syria. Whatever the particular exploit referred to was, it had given Naaman a great position at the court of Ben-hadad. Naaman was afflicted with a leprosy of the white kind which had hitherto defied cure. A little Israelitish captive maiden tells him of the fame and skill of Elisha, and he is cured by him by following his simple directions to bathe in the Jordan seven times. See 2 Kings 5 : 14. His first business after his cure is to thank his benefactor and gratefully acknowledge the power of the God of Israel, and promise "henceforth to offer neither burnt offering nor sacrifice unto other gods, but unto the Lord." How long Naaman lived to continue a worshipper of Jehovah while assisting officially at the worship of Rimmon we are not told; ("but his memory is perpetuated by a leper hospital which occupies the traditional site of his house in Damascus, on the banks of the Abana."—*Schaff*.)

2. One of the family of Benjamin who came down to Egypt with Jacob, as read in Gen. 46 : 21. He was the son of Bela, and head of the family of the Naamites. Num. 26 : 40; 1 Chron. 8 : 3, 4. (B.C. 1706.)

Na'amathite, the gentilic name of one of Job's friends, Zophar the Naamathite. Job 2 : 11; 11 : 1; 20 : 1; 42 : 9. There is no other trace of this name in the Bible, and the town whence it is derived is unknown. (But as Uz was in Arabia, probably the Naamah where he lived was on the Arabian borders of Syria.)

Na'amites, The, the family descended from Naaman, the grandson of Benjamin. Num. 26 : 40 only.

Na'arah (*a maiden*), the second wife of Ashur; a descendant of Judah. 1 Chron. 4 : 5, 6.

Na'ara-i (*handmaid*), one of the valiant men of David's armies. 1 Chron. 11 : 37. In 1 Chron. he is called the son of Ezbai, but in 2 Sam. 23 : 35 he appears as "Paarai the Arbite." Kennicott decides that the former is correct. (B.C. about 1015.)

Na'aran (*juvenile*), a city of Ephraim, which in a very ancient record, 1 Chron. 7 : 28, is mentioned as the eastern limit of the tribe. It is very probably identical with Naarath, or more accurately Naarah.

Na'arath (*juvenile*) (the Hebrew is equivalent to Naarah, which is therefore the real form of the name), a place named Josh. 16 : 7 only as one of the landmarks on the southern boundary of Ephraim. It appears to have lain between Ataroth and Jericho, in the Jordan valley. Eusebius and Jerome speak of it as if well known to them—"Naorath, a small village of the Jews, five miles from Jericho."

Na-ash'on. [NAHSHON.]

Na-as'son (*enchanter*), the Greek form of the name NAHSHON. Matt. 1 : 4, Luke 3 : 32, only.

Na'bal (*fool*) was a sheepmaster on the confines of Judea and the desert, in that part of the country which bore from its great conqueror the name of Caleb. 1 Sam. 25 : 3; 30 : 14. (B.C. about 1055.) His residence was on the southern Carmel, in the pasture lands of Maon. His wealth, as might be expected from his abode, consisted chiefly of sheep and goats. It was the custom of the shepherds to drive them into the wild downs on the slopes of Carmel; and it was whilst they were on one of these pastoral excursions that they met a band of outlaws, who showed them unexpected kindness, protecting them by day and night, and never themselves committing any depredations. 1 Sam. 25 : 7, 15, 16. Once a year there was a grand banquet on Carmel, "like the feast of a king." ch. 25 : 2, 4, 36. It was on one of these occasions that ten youths from the chief of the freebooters approached Nabal, enumerated the services of their master, and ended by claiming, with a mixture of courtesy and defiance characteristic of the East, "whatsoever cometh into thy hand for thy servants and for *thy son* David." The great sheepmaster peremptorily refused. The moment that the messengers were gone, the shepherds that stood by perceived the danger that their master and themselves would incur. To Nabal himself they durst not speak. ch. 25 : 17. To his wife, as to the good angel of the household, one of the shepherds told the state of affairs. She, with the offerings usual on such occasions, with her attendants running before her, rode down the hill toward David's encampment. David had already made the fatal vow of extermination. ch. 25 : 22. At this moment, as it would seem, Abigail appeared, threw herself on her face before him, and poured forth her petition in language which in both form and expression almost assumes the tone of poetry. She returned with the news of David's recantation of his vow. Nabal was

then at the height of his orgies, and his wife dared not communicate to him either his danger or his escape. ch. 25 : 36. At break of day she told him both. The stupid reveller was suddenly roused to a sense of that which impended over him. "His heart died within him, and he became as a stone." It was as if a stroke of apoplexy or paralysis had fallen upon him. Ten days he lingered, "and the Lord smote Nabal, and he died." ch. 25 : 37, 38.

Na'both (*fruits*), the victim of Ahab and Jezebel, was the owner of a small vineyard at Jezreel, close to the royal palace of Ahab. 1 Kings 21 : 1, 2. (B.C. 897.) It thus became an object of desire to the king, who offered an equivalent in money or another vineyard in exchange for this. Naboth, in the independent spirit of a Jewish landholder, refused: "The Lord forbid it me that I should give the inheritance of my fathers unto thee." Ahab was cowed by this reply; but the proud spirit of Jezebel was aroused. She took the matter into her own hands. A fast was proclaimed, as on the announcement of some impending calamity. Naboth was "set on high" in the public place of Samaria; two men of worthless character accused him of having "cursed God and the king." He and his children, 2 Kings 9 : 26, were dragged out of the city and despatched the same night. The place of execution there was by the large tank or reservoir which still remains on the slope of the hill of Samaria, immediately outside the walls. The usual punishment for blasphemy was enforced: Naboth and his sons were stoned; and the blood from their wounds ran down into the waters of the tank below. For the signal retribution taken on this judicial murder—a remarkable proof of the high regard paid in the old dispensation to the claims of justice and independence—see AHAB; JEHU; JEZEBEL.

Nabuchodon'osor. [NEBUCHADNEZZAR.]

Na'chon's (*prepared*) **threshing-floor**), the place at which the ark had arrived in its progress from Kirjath-jearim to Jerusalem, when Uzzah lost his life in his too-hasty zeal for its safety. 2 Sam. 6 : 6. (B.C. 1042.)

Na'chor. [NAHOR.]

Na'dab (*liberal*). 1. The eldest son of Aaron and Elisheba. Ex. 6 : 23; Num. 3 : 2. (B.C. 1490.) He, his father and brother, and seventy old men of Israel were led out from the midst of the assembled people, Ex. 24 : 1, and were commanded to stay and worship God "afar off," below the lofty summit of Sinai, where Moses alone was to come near to the Lord. Subsequently, Lev. 10 : 1, Nadab and his brother were struck dead before the sanctuary by fire from the Lord. Their offence was kindling the incense in their censers with "strange" fire, *i. e.* not taken from that which burned perpetually, Lev. 6 : 13, on the altar.

2. King Jeroboam's son, who succeeded to the throne of Israel B.C. 954, and reigned two years. 1 Kings 15 : 25–31. At the siege of Gibbethon a conspiracy broke out in the midst of the army, and the king was slain by Baasha, a man of Issachar.

3. A son of Shammai, 1 Chron. 2 : 28, of the tribe of Judah.

4. A son of Gibeon, 1 Chron. 8 : 30; 9 : 36, of the tribe of Benjamin.

Nag'ga-i (*illuminating*), the true form of NAGGE, Luke 3 : 25, and so given in the Revised Version.

Nag'ge, one of the ancestors of Christ. Luke 3 : 25. [See NAGGAI.]

Nahal'al, or **Na'halal** (*pasture*), one of the cities of Zebulun, given with its "suburbs" to the Merarite Levites. Josh. 21 : 35. It is the same which in Josh. 19 : 15 is inaccurately given in the Authorized Version as Nahallal, the Hebrew being in both cases identical. Elsewhere it is called NAHALOL. Judges 1 : 30. It is identified with the modern *Malul*, a village in the plain of Esdraelon.

Naha'liel (*torrents of God*), one of the halting-places of Israel in the latter part of their progress to Canaan. Num. 21 : 19. It lay "beyond," that is, north of, the Arnon, ver. 13, and between Mattanah and Bamoth, the next after Bamoth being Pisgah.

Na'halol. [NAHALAL.]

Na'ham (*consolation*), the brother of Hodiah or Jehudiah, wife of Ezra. 1 Chron. 4 : 19.

Naham'ani (*merciful*), a chief man among those who returned from Babylon with Zerubbabel and Jeshua. Neh. 7 : 7. (B.C. 536.)

Nahar'a-i (*snorter*), the armor-bearer of Joab, called NAHARI in the Authorized Version of 2 Sam. 23 : 37. He was a native of Beeroth. 1 Chron. 11 : 39. (B.C. 1013.)

Na'hari. The same as NAHARAI. 2 Sam. 23 : 37. In the Authorized Version of 1611 the name is printed "Naharai the Berothite."

Na'hash (*serpent*). 1. King of the Ammonites who dictated to the inhabitants of Jabesh-gilead that cruel alternative of the loss of their right eyes or slavery, which roused the swift wrath of Saul, and caused the destruction of the Ammonite force. 1 Sam. 11 : 2–11. (B.C. 1092.) "Nahash" would seem to have been the title of the king of the Ammonites rather than the name of an individual. Nahash the father of Hanun had rendered David some special and valuable service, which David was anxious for an opportunity of requiting. 2 Sam. 10 : 2.

2. A person mentioned once only—2 Sam. 17 : 25—in stating the parentage of Amasa, the commander-in-chief of Absalom's army. Amasa is there said to have been the son of a certain Ithra by Abigail, "daughter of Nahash and sister to Zeruiah." (B.C. before 1023.)

Na'hath (*rest*). 1. One of the "dukes" of Edom, eldest son of Reuel the son of Esau. Gen. 36 : 13, 17 ; 1 Chron. 1 : 37. (B.C. 1700.)

2. A Kohathite Levite, son of Zophai. 1 Chron. 6 : 26.

3. A Levite in the reign of Hezekiah. 2 Chron. 31 : 13. (B.C. 725.)

Nah'bi (*hidden*), the son of Vophsi, a Naphtalite, and one of the twelve spies. Num. 13 : 14.

Na'hor (*snorting*), the name of two persons in the family of Abraham. 1. His grandfather; the son of Serug and father of Terah. Gen. 11 : 22–25. (B.C. 2174.)

2. Grandson of the preceding, son of Terah and brother of Abraham and Haran. Gen. 11 : 26, 27. (B.C. 2000.) The order of the ages of the family of Terah is not improbably inverted in the narrative; in which case Nahor, instead of being younger than Abraham, was really older. He married Milcah, the daughter of his brother Haran; and when Abraham and Lot migrated to Canaan, Nahor remained behind in the land of his birth, on the eastern side of the Euphrates.

Nah'shon, or **Na-ash'on** (*enchanter*), son of Amminadab, and prince of the children of Judah (as he is styled in the genealogy of Judah, 1 Chron. 2 : 10) at the time of the first numbering in the wilderness. Ex. 6 : 23; Num. 1 : 7, etc. His sister, Elisheba, was wife to Aaron, and his son, Salmon, was husband to Rahab after the taking of Jericho. He died in the wilderness, according to Num. 26 : 64, 65. (B.C. before 1451.)

Na'hum (*consolation*). Nahum, called " the Elkoshite," is the seventh in order of the minor prophets. His personal history is quite unknown. The site of Elkosh, his native place, is disputed, some placing it in Galilee, others in Assyria. Those who maintain the latter view assume that the prophet's parents were carried into captivity by Tiglath-pileser, and that the prophet was born at the village of Alkush, on the east bank of the Tigris, two miles north of Mosul. On the other hand, the imagery of his prophecy is such as would be natural to an inhabitant of Palestine, Nah. 1 : 4, to whom the rich pastures of Bashan, the vineyards of Carmel and the blossoms of Lebanon were emblems of all that was luxuriant and fertile. The language employed in ch. 1 : 15; 2 : 2 is appropriate to one who wrote for his countrymen in their native land. (McClintock and Strong come to the conclusion that Nahum was a native of Galilee, that at the captivity of the ten tribes he escaped into Judah, and prophesied in the reign of Hezekiah, 726–698.—ED.) *Prophecy of Nahum.*—The date of Nahum's prophecy can be determined with as little precision as his birthplace. It is, however, certain that the prophecy was written before the final downfall of Nineveh and its capture by the Medes and Chaldeans, *cir.* B.C. 625. The allusions to the Assyrian power imply that it was still unbroken. ch. 1 : 12; 2 : 8, 13; 3 : 15–17. It is most probable that Nahum flourished in the latter half of the reign of Hezekiah, and wrote his prophecy either in Jerusalem or its neighborhood. The subject of the prophecy is, in accordance with the superscription, " the burden of Nineveh," the destruction of which he predicts. As a poet Nahum occupies a high place in the first rank of Hebrew literature. His style is clear and uninvolved, though pregnant and forcible; his diction sonorous and rhythmical, the words re-echoing to the sense. Comp. 2 : 4 ; 3 : 3.

Nail. 1. Of finger. (*a*) A nail or claw of man or animal. (*b*) A point or style, *e. g.* for writing; see Jer. 17 : 1. 2. (*a*) A nail, Isa. 41 : 7, a stake, Isa. 33 : 20; also a tent-peg. Tent-pegs were usually of wood and of large size ; but sometimes, as was the case with those used to fasten the curtains of the tabernacle, of metal. Ex. 27 : 19 ; 38 : 20. (*b*) A nail, primarily a point. We are told that David prepared iron for the nails to be used in the temple; and as the holy of holies was plated with gold, the nails for fastening the plates were probably of gold.

Na'in (*beauty*), a village of Galilee, the gate of which is made illustrious by the raising of the widow's son. Luke 7 : 12. The modern *Nein* is situated on the northwestern edge of the " Little Hermon," or *Jebel-ed-Dûhy,* where the ground falls into the plain of Esdraelon. The entrance to the place, where our Saviour met the funeral, must probably always have been up the steep ascent from the plain ; and here, on the west side of the village, the rock is full of sepulchral caves.

Na'ioth (*habitations*), or more fully, " Naioth in Ramah," a place of Mount Ephraim, the birthplace of Samuel and Saul, and in which Samuel and David took refuge together after the latter had made his escape from the jealous fury of Saul. 1 Sam. 19 : 18, 19, 22, 23; 20 : 1. It is evident from ver. 18 that Naioth was not actually in Ramah, Samuel's habitual residence. In its corrected form the name signifies " habitations," and probably means the huts or dwellings of a school or college of prophets over which Samuel presided, as Elisha did over those at Gilgal and Jericho.

Names. 1. *Names of places.*—These may be divided into two general classes —descriptive and historical. The former are such as mark some peculiarity of the locality, usually a natural one, *e. g.* Sharon, "plain ;" Gibeah, "hill ;" Pisgah, "height." Of the second class of local names, some were given in honor of individual men, *e. g.* the city Enoch, Gen. 4 : 17, etc. More commonly, however, such names were given to perpetuate the memory of some important historic occurrence. Bethel perpetuated through all Jewish history the early revelations of God to Jacob. Gen. 28 : 19; 35 : 15. So Jehovah-jireh, Gen. 22 : 14; Mahanaim, Gen. 32 : 2 ; Peniel, etc. In forming compounds to serve as names of towns or other localities, some of the most common terms employed were *Kir*, a " wall " or " fortress ;" *Kirjath,* " city ;"

Nain and Mount Tabor. (*From an original Photograph.*)

En, "fountain;" *Beer,* "a well," etc. The names of countries were almost universally derived from the name of the first settlers or earliest historic population.

2. *Names of persons.*—Among the Hebrews each person received but a single name. In the case of boys this was conferred upon the eighth day, in connection with the rite of circumcision. Luke 1:59; comp. Gen. 17:5-14. To distinguish an individual from others of the same name it was customary to add to his own proper name that of his father or ancestors. Sometimes the mother's was used instead. Simple names in Hebrew, as in all languages, were largely borrowed from nature; *e. g.* Deborah, "bee;" Tamar, "a palm tree;" Jonah, "dove." Many names of women were derived from those of men by change of termination; *e. g.* Hammelech, "the king;" Hammoleketh, "the queen." The majority of compound names have special religious or social significance, being compounded either (1) with terms denoting relationship, as *Abi* or *Ab,* father, as Abihud, "father of praise," Abimelech, "father of the king;" Ben, son, as Benoni, "son of my sorrow," Benjamin, "son of the right hand;" or (2) nouns denoting natural life, as *am,* "people," *melech,* "king;" or (3) with names of God, as *El,* "God," and *Jah* or *Ja,* shortened

from "Jehovah." As outside the circle of Revelation, particularly among the Oriental nations, it is customary to mark one's entrance into a new relation by a new name, in which case the acceptance of the new name involves the acknowledgment of the sovereignty of the namegiver, so the importance and new sphere assigned to the organs of Revelation ir God's kingdom are frequently indicated by a change of name. Examples of this are Abraham, Gen. 17:5; Sarah, Gen. 17:15; Israel, as the designation of the spiritual character, in place of Jacob, which designated the natural character. Gen. 32:28.

Na'omi, or **Nao'mi** (*my delight*), the wife of Elimelech and mother-in-law of Ruth. Ruth 1:2, etc.; 2:1, etc.; 3:1; 4:3, etc. (B.C. 1363.) The name is derived from a root signifying sweetness or pleasantness. Naomi left Judea with her husband and two sons, in a time of famine, and went to the land of Moab. Here her husband and sons died; and on her return to Bethlehem she wished to be known as *Mara, bitterness,* instead of Naomi, sweetness.

Na'phish (*refreshment*), the last but one of the sons of Ishmael. Gen. 25:15; 1 Chron. 1:31.

Naph'tali (*wrestling*), the fifth son of Jacob; the second child borne to him by

Bilhah, Rachel's slave. His birth and the bestowal of his name are recorded in Gen. 30 : 8. When the census was taken at Mount Sinai the tribe of Naphtali numbered no less than 53,400 fighting men, Num. 1 : 43; 2 : 30; but when the borders of the promised land were reached, its numbers were reduced to 45,400. Num. 26 : 48–50. During the march through the wilderness Naphtali occupied a position on the north of the sacred tent with Dan and Asher. Num. 2 : 25–31. In the apportionment of the land, the lot of Naphtali was enclosed on three sides by those of other tribes. On the west lay Asher, on the south Zebulun, and on the east the transjordanic Manasseh. (In the division of the kingdom Naphtali belonged to the kingdom of Israel, and later was a part of Galilee, bordering on the northwestern part of the Sea of Galilee, and including Capernaum and Bethsaida.—ED.)

Naph'tali, Mount, the mountainous district which formed the main part of the inheritance of Naphtali, Josh. 20 : 7, answering to " Mount Ephraim " in the centre and " Mount Judah " in the south of Palestine.

Naph'tuhim (*border-people*), a Mizraite (Egyptian) nation or tribe, mentioned only in the account of the descendants of Noah. Gen. 10 : 13; 1 Chron. 1 : 11. If we may judge from their position in the list of the Mizraites, the Naphtuhim were probably settled, at first, either in Egypt or immediately to the west of it.

Narcis'sus (*stupidity*), a dweller at Rome, Rom. 16 : 11, some members of whose household were known as Christians to St. Paul. Some have assumed the identity of this Narcissus with the secretary of the emperor Claudius; but this is quite uncertain.

Nard. [SPIKENARD.]

Na'than (*a giver*). 1. An eminent Hebrew prophet in the reigns of David and Solomon. (B.C. 1015.) He first appears in the consultation with David about the building of the temple. 2 Sam. 7 : 2, 3, 17. He next comes forward as the reprover of David for the sin with Bath-sheba; and his famous apologue on the rich man and the ewe lamb, which is the only direct example of his prophetic power, shows it to have been of a very high order. 2 Sam. 12 : 1–12.
2. A son of David; one of the four who were borne to him by Bath-sheba. 1 Chron. 3 : 5; comp. 14 : 4 and 2 Sam. 5 : 14.

3. Son or brother of one of the members of David's guard. 2 Sam. 23 : 36; 1 Chron. 11 : 38.
4. One of the head men who returned from Babylon with Ezra on his second expedition. Ezra 8 : 16; 1 Esdr. 8 : 44. It is not impossible that he may be the same with the " son of Bani." Ezra 10 : 39.

Nathan'ael (*gift of God*), a disciple of Jesus Christ, concerning whom, under that name at least, we learn from Scripture little more than his birthplace, Cana of Galilee, John 21 : 2, and his simple, truthful character. John 1 : 47. The name does not occur in the first three Gospels; but it is commonly believed that Nathanael and Bartholomew are the same person. The evidence for that belief is as follows: St. John, who twice mentions Nathanael, never introduces the name of Bartholomew at all. St. Matthew, Matt. 10 : 3, St. Mark, Mark 3 : 18, and St. Luke, Luke 6 : 14, all speak of Bartholomew, but never of Nathanael. It was Philip who first brought Nathanael to Jesus, just as Andrew had brought his brother Simon.

Na'than-me'lech (*the gift of the king*), a eunuch (Authorized Version " chamberlain ") in the court of Josiah. 2 Kings 23 : 11. (B.C. 628.)

Na'um (*consolation*), son of Esli and father of Amos, in the genealogy of Christ, Luke 3 : 25; about contemporary with the high priesthood of Jason and the reign of Antiochus Epiphanes. (B.C. 175.)

Nave (Heb. *gao*), anything convex or arched, as the boss of a shield, Job 15 : 26; the eyebrows, Lev. 14 : 9; an eminent place. Ezek. 16 : 31. It is rendered once only in the plural, "naves," 1 Kings 7 : 33, meaning the centres of the wheels in which the spokes are inserted, *i. e.* the hubs. In Ezek. 1 : 18 it is rendered twice "rings," and margin "strakes," an old word apparently used for the nave (hub) of a wheel and also more probably for the felloe or the tire, as making the streak or stroke upon the ground.

Nazarene', an inhabitant of Nazareth. This appellative is applied to Jesus in many passages in the New Testament. This name, made striking in so many ways, and which, if first given in scorn, was adopted and gloried in by th' disciples, we are told in Matt. 2 : 23 pc.. sesses a prophetic significance. Its application to Jesus, in consequence of the providential arrangements by which his parents were led to take up their abode in Nazareth, was the filling out of the predictions in which the promised Messiah is described as a *nêtser*, *i. e.* a *shoot*, *sprout*, of Jesse, a humble and despised descendant of the decayed royal family. Once, Acts 24 : 5, the term *Nazarenes* is applied to the followers of Jesus by way of contempt. The name still exists in Arabic as the ordinary designation of Christians.

Naz'areth (*the guarded one*), the ordinary residence of our Saviour, is not mentioned in the Old Testament, but occurs first in Matt. 2 : 23. It derives its celebrity from its connection with the history of Christ, and in that respect has a hold on the imagination and feelings of men which it shares only with Jerusalem and Bethlehem. It is situated among the hills which constitute the south ridges of Lebanon, just before they sink down

Nazareth.

into the plain of Esdraelon. (Mr. Merrill, in "Galilee in the Time of Christ" (1881), represents Nazareth in Christ's time as a city (so always called in the New Testament) of 15,000 to 20,000 inhabitants, of some importance and considerable antiquity, and not so insignificant and mean as has been represented. —ED.) Of the identification of the ancient site there can be no doubt. The name of the present village is *en-Nâzirah*, the same, therefore, as of old; it is formed on a hill or mountain, Luke 4 : 29; it is within the limits of the province of Galilee, Mark 1 : 9; it is near Cana, according to the implication in John 2 : 1, 2, 11; a precipice exists in the neighborhood.

Luke 4 : 29. The modern Nazareth belongs to the better class of eastern villages. It has a population of 3000 or 4000 ; a few are Mohammedans, the rest Latin and Greek Christians. (Near this town Napoleon once encamped (1799), after the battle of Mount Tabor.) The origin of the disrepute in which Nazareth stood, John 1 : 47, is not certainly known. All the inhabitants of Galilee were looked upon with contempt by the people of Judea because they spoke a ruder dialect, were less cultivated, and were more exposed by their position to contact with the heathen. But Nazareth labored under a special opprobrium, for it was a Galilean and not a southern Jew who asked the reproachful question whether "any good thing" could come from that source. Above the town are several rocky ledges, over which a person could not be thrown without almost certain destruction. There is one very remarkable precipice, almost perpendicular and forty or fifty feet high, near the Maronite church, which may well be supposed to be the identical one over which his infuriated fellow townsmen attempted to hurl Jesus.

Naz′arite, more properly **Naz′irite** (*one separated*), one of either sex who was bound by a vow of a peculiar kind to be set apart from others for the service of God. The obligation was either for life or for a defined time. There is no notice in the Pentateuch of Nazarites for life; but the regulations for the vow of a Nazarite of days are given Num. 6 : 1–21. The Nazarite, during the term of his consecration, was bound to abstain from wine, grapes, with every production of the vine, and from every kind of intoxicating drink. He was forbidden to cut the hair of his head, or to approach any dead body, even that of his nearest relation. When the period of his vow was fulfilled, he was brought to the door of the tabernacle, and was required to offer a he lamb for a burnt offering, a ewe lamb for a sin offering, and a ram for a peace offering, with the usual accompaniments of peace offerings, Lev. 7 : 12, 13, and of the offering made at the consecration of priests. Ex. 29 : 2; Num. 6 : 15. He brought also a meat offering and a drink offering, which appear to have been presented by themselves as a distinct act of service. ver. 17. He was to cut off the hair of "the head of his separation" (that is, the hair which had grown during the period of his consecration) at the door of the tabernacle, and to put it into the fire under the sacrifice on the altar. Of the Nazarites for life three are mentioned in the Scriptures—Samson, Samuel and St. John the Baptist. The only one of these actually called a Nazarite is Samson. We do not know whether the vow for life was ever voluntarily taken by the individual. In all the cases mentioned in the sacred history, it was made by the parents before the birth of the Nazarite himself. The consecration of the Nazarite bore a striking resemblance to that of the high priest. Lev. 21 : 10-12. The meaning of the Nazarite vow has been regarded in different lights. It may be regarded as an act of self-sacrifice. That it was essentially a sacrifice of the person to the Lord is obviously in accordance with the terms of the law. Num. 6 : 2. As the Nazarite was a witness for the straitness of the law, as distinguished from the freedom of the gospel, his sacrifice of himself was a submission to the letter of the rule. Its outward manifestations were restraints and eccentricities. The man was separated from his brethren that he might be peculiarly devoted to the Lord. This was consistent with the purpose of divine wisdom for the time for which it was ordained.

Ne′ah (*shaking*), a place which was one of the landmarks on the boundary of Zebulun. Josh. 19 : 13 only. It has not yet been certainly identified.

Ne-ap′olis (*new city*) is the place in northern Greece where Paul and his associates first landed in Europe, Acts 16 : 11, where, no doubt, he landed also on his second visit to Macedonia, Acts 20 : 1, and whence certainly he embarked on his last journey through that province to Troas and Jerusalem. Acts 20 : 6. Philippi being an inland town, Neapolis was evidently the port, and is represented by the present *Kavalla*. (Kavalla is a city of 5000 or 6000 inhabitants, Greeks and Turks. Neapolis was situated within the bounds of Thrace, ten miles from Philippi, on a high rocky promontory jutting out into the Ægean Sea, while a temple of Diana crowned the hill-top.—ED.)

Ne-ari′ah (*servant of Jehovah*). 1. One of the six sons of Shemaiah in the line of the royal family of Judah after the captivity. 1 Chron. 3 : 22, 23. (B.C. about 350.)

2. A son of Ishi, and one of the captains of the 500 Simeonites who, in the days of Hezekiah, drove out the Amalekites from Mount Seir. 1 Chron. 4 : 42. (B.C. 715.)

Neba′i (*fruitful*), a family of the heads of the people who signed the covenant with Nehemiah. Neh. 10 : 19.

Neba′ioth, Neba′joth (*heights*), the "first-born of Ishmael," Gen. 25 : 13; 1 Chron. 1 : 29 (B.C. about 1850), and father of a pastoral tribe named after him, the "rams of Nebaioth" being mentioned by the prophet Isaiah, Isa. 60 : 7, with the flocks of Kedar. From the days of Jerome this people had been identified with the Nabathæans of Greek and Roman history. Petra was their capital. (They first settled in the country southeast of

Palestine, and wandered gradually in search of pasturage till they came to Kedar, of which Isaiah speaks. Probably the Nebaioth of Arabia Petrea were, as M. Quatremère argues, the same people as the Nebat of Chaldea. — *McClintock and Strong's Cyclopedia.*)

Nebal'lat (*hidden folly*), a town of Benjamin, one of those which the Ben-jamites reoccupied after the captivity. Neh. 11 : 34.

Ne'bat (*aspect*), the father of Jeroboam, 1 Kings 11 : 26; 12 : 2, 15, etc., is described as an Ephrathite or Ephraimite of Zereda. (B.C. about 1000.)

Ne'bo (*prophet*), **Mount,** the mountain from which Moses took his first and last view of the promised land. Deut.

Neapolis and the Temple of Diana.

32 : 49; 34 : 1. It is described as in the land of Moab, facing Jericho; the head or summit of a mountain called Pisgah, which again seems to have formed a portion of the general range of Abarim. (Notwithstanding the minuteness of this description, it is only recently that any one has succeeded in pointing out any spot which answers to Nebo. Tristram identifies it with a peak (Jebel Nebbah) of the Abarim or Moab mountains, about three miles southwest of Heshbân (Heshbon) and about a mile and a half due west of Baal-meon. "It overlooks the mouth of the Jordan, over against Jericho," Deut. 34 : 1, and the gentle slopes of its sides may well answer to the "field of Zophim." Num. 23 : 14. Jebel Nebbah is 2683 feet high. It is not an isolated peak, but one of a succession of bare turf-clad eminences, so linked together that the depressions between them were mere hollows rather than valleys. It commands a wide prospect. Prof. Paine, of the American Exploration Society, contends that Jebel Nebbah, the highest point of the range, is Mount Nebo, that Jebel Siaghah, the extreme headland of the hill, is Mount Pisgah, and that "the mountains of Abarim " are the cliffs west of these points, and descending toward the Dead Sea. Probably the whole mountain or range was called sometimes by the name of one peak and sometimes by that of another, as is frequently the case with mountains now.—ED.)

Ne'bo. 1. A town of Reuben on the east side of Jordan. Num. 32 : 3, 38. In the remarkable prophecy adopted by Isaiah, Isa. 15 : 2, and Jeremiah, Jer. 48 : 1, 22, concerning Moab, Nebo is mentioned in the same connection as before, but in the hands of Moab. Eusebius and Jerome identify it with Nobah or Kenath, and place it eight miles south of Heshbon, where the ruins of *el-Habis* appear to stand at present. (Prof. Paine identifies it with some ruins on Mount Nebo, a mile south of its summit, and Dr. Robinson seems to agree with this.— ED.)

2. The children of Nebo returned from Babylon with Zerubbabel. Ezra 2 : 29; 10 : 43; Neh. 7 : 33. The name occurs between Bethel and Ai and Lydda, which implies that it was situated in the territory of Benjamin to the northwest of Jerusalem. This is possibly the modern

Beit-Nûbah, about 12 miles northwest by west of Jerusalem, 8 from Lydda.

3. **Nebo,** which occurs both in Isaiah, Isa. 46 : 1, and Jeremiah, Jer. 48 : 1, as the name of a Chaldean god, is a well-known deity of the Babylonians and Assyrians. He was the god who presided over learning and letters. His general character corresponds to that of the Egyptian Thoth, the Greek Hermes and

Nebo.

the Latin Mercury. Astronomically he is identified with the planet nearest the sun. In Babylonia Nebo held a prominent place from an early time. The ancient town of Borsippa was especially under his protection, and the great temple here, the modern *Birs-Nimrûd,* was dedicated to him from a very remote age. He was the tutelar god of the most important Babylonian kings, in whose names the word *Nabu* or Nebo appears as an element.

Nebuchadnez'zar, or **Nebuchad-rez'zar** (*may Nebo protect the crown*), was the greatest and most powerful of the Babylonian kings. His name is explained to mean " Nebo is the protector against misfortune." He was the son and successor of Nabopolassar, the founder of the Babylonian empire. In the lifetime of his father, Nebuchadnezzar led an army against Pharaoh-necho, king of Egypt, defeated him at Carchemish, B.C.

605, in a great battle, Jer. 46 : 2–12, re-covered Cœle-Syria, Phœnicia and Palestine, took Jerusalem, Dan. 1 : 1, 2, pressed forward to Egypt, and was engaged in

Cameo of Nebuchadnezzar.

that country or upon its borders when intelligence arrived which recalled him hastily to Babylon. Nabopolassar, after reigning twenty-one years, had died and the throne was vacant. In alarm about the succession Nebuchadnezzar returned to the capital, accompanied only by his light troops; and crossing the desert, probably by way of Tadmor or Palmyra,

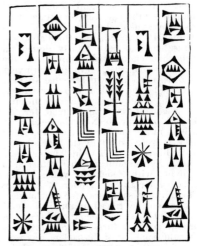

Inscribed Brick of Nebuchadnezzar.

reached Babylon before any disturbance had arisen, and entered peaceably on his kingdom, B.C. 604. Within three years of Nebuchadnezzar's first expedition into Syria and Palestine, disaffection again showed itself in those countries. Jehoiakim, who, although threatened at first with captivity, 2 Chron. 36 : 6, had been finally maintained on the throne as a Babylonian vassal, after three years of service "turned and rebelled" against his suzerain, probably trusting to be supported by Egypt. 2 Kings 24 : 1. Not long afterward Phœnicia seems to have broken into revolt, and the Chaldean monarch once more took the field in person, and marched first of all against Tyre. Having invested that city and left a portion of his army there to continue the siege, he proceeded against Jerusalem, which submitted without a struggle. According to Josephus, who is here our chief authority, Nebuchadnezzar punished Jehoiakim with death, comp. Jer. 22 : 18, 19 and 36 : 30, but placed his son Jehoiachin upon the throne. Jehoiachin reigned only three months; for, on his showing symptoms of disaffection, Nebuchadnezzar came up against Jerusalem for the third time, deposed the young prince (whom he carried to Babylon, together with a large portion of the population of the city and the chief of the temple treasures), and made his uncle, Zedekiah, king in his room. Tyre still held out; and it was not till the thirteenth year from the time of its first investment that the city of merchants fell, B.C. 585. Ere this happened, Jerusalem had been totally destroyed. Nebuchadnezzar had commenced the final siege of Jerusalem in the ninth year of Zedekiah—his own seventeenth year (B.C. 588)—and took it two years later, B.C. 586. Zedekiah escaped from the city, but was captured near Jericho, Jer. 39 : 5, and brought to Nebuchadnezzar at Riblah in the territory of Hamath, where his eyes were put out by the king's order, while his sons and his chief nobles were slain. Nebuchadnezzar then returned to Babylon with Zedekiah, whom he imprisoned for the remainder of his life. The military successes of Nebuchadnezzar cannot be traced minutely beyond this point. It may be gathered from the prophetical Scriptures and from Josephus that the conquest of Jerusalem was rapidly followed by the fall of Tyre and the complete submission of Phœnicia, Ezek. 26–28; after which the Babylonians carried their arms into Egypt, and inflicted severe injuries on that fertile country. Jer. 46 : 13–26; Ezek. 29 : 2–20. We are told that the first care of Nebuchadnezzar, on obtaining quiet possession of his kingdom after the first Syrian expedition, was to rebuild the temple of Bel (*Bel-Merodach*) at Babylon out of the spoils of the Syrian war. He next proceeded to strengthen and beautify the city, which he renovated throughout and surrounded with several lines of fortifications, himself adding one entirely new quarter. Having finished the walls and adorned the gates magnificently, he constructed a new palace. In the grounds of this palace he formed the celebrated "hanging garden," which the Greeks placed among the seven wonders of the world. But he did not confine his efforts to the ornamentation and improvement of his capital. Throughout the empire, at Borsippa, Sippara, Cutha, Chilmad, Duraba, Teredon, and a multitude of other places, he built or rebuilt cities, repaired temples, constructed quays, reservoirs, canals and aqueducts, on a scale of grandeur and magnificence surpassing everything of the kind recorded in history, unless it be the constructions of one or two of the greatest Egyptian monarchs. The wealth, greatness and general prosperity of Nebuchadnezzar are strikingly placed before us in the book of Daniel. Toward the close of his reign the glory of Nebuchadnezzar suffered a temporary eclipse. As a punishment for his pride and vanity, that strange form of madness was sent upon him which the Greeks called Lycanthropy, wherein the sufferer imagines himself a beast, and, quitting the haunts of men, insists on leading the life of a beast. Dan. 4 : 33. (This strange malady is thought by some to receive illustration from an inscription; and historians place at this period the reign of a queen to whom are ascribed the works which by others are declared to be Nebuchadnezzar's. Probably his favorite wife was practically at the head of affairs during the malady of her husband. Other historians, Eusebius and Berosus, also confirm the account. See Rawlinson's "Historical Illustrations."—ED.) After an interval of four or perhaps seven years, Dan. 4 : 16, Nebuchadnezzar's malady left him. We are told that "his reason returned, and for the glory of his kingdom his honor and brightness returned;" and he "was established in his kingdom, and excellent majesty was added to him." Dan. 4 : 36. He died in the year B.C. 561, at an advanced age (eighty-three or eighty-four), having reigned forty-three years. A son, Evil-merodach, succeeded him.

Nebushas'ban (*Nebo saves me*), one of the officers of Nebuchadnezzar at the time of the capture of Jerusalem. He was Rab-saris, *i. e.* chief of the eunuchs. Jer. 39 : 13. Nebushasban's office and title were the same as those of Ashpenaz, Dan. 1 : 3, whom he probably succeeded.

Nebuzar-a'dan (*chief whom Nebo favors*), the Rab-tabbachim, *i. e.* chief of the slaughterers (Authorized Version "captain of the guard"), a high officer in the court of Nebuchadnezzar. On the capture of Jerusalem he was left by Nebuchadnezzar in charge of the city. Comp. Jer. 39 : 11. He seems to have quitted Judea when he took down the chief people of Jerusalem to his master at Riblah. 2 Kings 25 : 18–20. In four years he again appeared. Jer. 52 : 30. Nebuchadnezzar in his twenty-third year made a descent on the regions east of Jordan, including the Ammonites and Moabites, who escaped when Jerusalem was destroyed. Thence he proceeded to Egypt, and, either on the way thither or on the return, Nebuzar-adan again passed through the country and carried off more captives. Jer. 52 : 30.

Ne'cho (*lame*). 2 Chron. 35 : 20, 22; 36 : 4. [PHARAOH-NECHO.]

Nedabi'ah (*whom Jehovah impels*), apparently one of the sons of Jeconiah or Jehoiachin, king of Judah. 1 Chron. 3 : 18.

Neginah (*stringed instruments*), the singular of *Neginoth*. It occurs in the title of Ps. 61. It is the general term by which all stringed instruments are described. "The chief musician on *Neginoth*" was, therefore, the conductor of that portion of the temple choir who played upon the stringed instruments, and who are mentioned in Ps. 68 : 25.

Neginoth. [NEGINAH.]

Nehel'amite, The, the designation of a man named Shemaiah, a false prophet, who went with the captivity to Babylon. Jer. 29 : 24, 31, 32. The name is no doubt formed from that either of Shemaiah's native place or the progenitor of his family; which of the two is uncertain.

Nehemi'ah (*consolation of the Lord*). 1. Son of Hachaliah, and apparently of the tribe of Judah. All that we know certainly concerning him is contained in the book which bears his name. We first find him at Shushan, the winter residence of the kings of Persia, in high office as the cupbearer of King Artaxerxes Longimanus. In the twentieth year of the king's reign, *i. e.* B.C. 445, certain Jews arrived from Judea, and gave Nehemiah a deplorable account of the state of Jerusalem. He immediately conceived the idea of going to Jerusalem to endeavor to better their state, and obtained the king's consent to his mission. Having received his appointment as governor of Judea, he started upon his journey, being under promise to return to Persia within a given time. Nehemiah's great work was rebuilding, for the first time since their destruction by Nebuzar-adan, the walls of Jerusalem, and restoring that city to its former state and dignity as a fortified town. To this great object therefore Nehemiah directed his whole energies without an hour's unnecessary delay. In a wonderfully short time the walls seemed to emerge from the heaps of burnt rubbish, and to encircle the city as in the days of old. It soon became apparent how wisely Nehemiah had acted in hastening on the work. On his very first arrival, as governor, Sanballat and Tobiah had given unequivocal proof of their mortification at his appointment; but when the restoration was seen to be rapidly progressing, their indignation knew no bounds. They made a great conspiracy to fall upon the builders with an armed force and put a stop to the undertaking. The project was defeated by the vigilance and prudence of Nehemiah. Various stratagems were then resorted to to get Nehemiah away from Jerusalem, and if possible to take his life; but that which most nearly succeeded was the attempt to bring him into suspicion with the king of Persia, as if he intended to set himself up as an independent king as soon as the walls were completed. The artful letter of Sanballat so far wrought upon Artaxerxes that he issued a decree stopping the work till further orders. It is probable that at the same time he recalled Nehemiah, or perhaps his leave of absence had previously expired. But after a delay, perhaps of several years, he was permitted to return to Jerusalem and to crown his work by repairing the temple and dedicating the walls. During his government Nehemiah firmly repressed the exactions of the nobles and the usury of the rich, and rescued the poor Jews from spoliation and slavery. He refused to receive his lawful allowance as governor from the people, in consideration of their poverty, during the whole twelve years that he was in office, but kept at his own charge a table for 150 Jews, at which any who returned from captivity were welcome. He made most careful provision for the maintenance of the ministering priests and Levites, and for the due and constant celebration of divine worship. He insisted upon the sanctity of the precincts of the temple being preserved inviolable, and peremptorily ejected the powerful Tobiah from one of the chambers which Eliashib had assigned to him. With no less firmness and impartiality he expelled from all sacred functions those of the high priest's family who had contracted heathen marriages, and rebuked and punished those of the common people who had likewise intermarried with foreigners; and lastly, he provided for keeping holy the Sabbath day, which was shamefully profaned by many, both Jews and foreign merchants, and by his resolute conduct succeeded in repressing the lawless traffic on the day of rest. Beyond the thirty-second year of Artaxerxes, to which Nehemiah's own narrative leads us, we have no account of him whatever.

2. One of the leaders of the first expedition from Babylon to Jerusalem under Zerubbabel. Ezra 2 : 2 ; Neh. 7 : 7.

3. Son of Azbuk and ruler of the half part of Beth-zur, who helped to repair the wall of Jerusalem. Neh. 3 : 16.

Nehemi'ah, The book of, like the preceding one of Ezra, is clearly and certainly not all by the same hand. [EZRA, BOOK OF.] By far the most important portion, indeed, is the work of Nehemiah; but other portions are either extracts from various chronicles and registers or supplementary narratives and reflections, some apparently by Ezra, others, perhaps, the work of the same person who inserted the latest genealogical extracts from the public chronicles. The main history contained in the book of Nehemiah covers about twelve years, viz., from the twentieth to the thirty-second year of Artaxerxes Longimanus, i. e. from B.C. 445 to 433. The whole narrative gives us a graphic and interesting account of the state of Jerusalem and the returned captives in the writer's times, and, incidentally, of the nature of the Persian government and the condition of its remote provinces. The book of Nehemiah has always had an undisputed place in the Canon, being included by the He-

brews under the general head of the book of Ezra, and, as Jerome tells us in the *Prolog. Gal.*, by the Greeks and Latins under the name of the second book of Ezra.

Nehiloth. The title of Ps. 5 in the Authorized Version is rendered "To the chief musician upon *Nehiloth*." It is most likely that *nehiloth* is the general term for perforated wind-instruments of all kinds, as *neginoth* denotes all manner of stringed instruments.

Ne'hum (*consolation*), one of those who returned from Babylon with Zerubbabel. Neh. 7 : 7.

Nehush'ta (*brass*), the daughter of Elnathan of Jerusalem, wife of Jehoiakim and mother of Jehoiachin, kings of Judah. 2 Kings 24 : 8. (B.C. 616.)

Nehush'tan (*a thing of brass*), the name by which the brazen serpent made by Moses in the wilderness, Num. 21 : 9, was worshipped in the time of Hezekiah. 2 Kings 18 : 4. It is evident that our translators by their rendering "and he called it Nehushtan" understood that the subject of the sentence is Hezekiah, and that when he destroyed the brazen serpent he gave it the name Nehushtan, "a brazen thing," in token of his utter contempt. But it is better to understand the Hebrew as referring to the name by which the serpent was generally known, the subject of the verb being indefinite— "and one called it 'Nehushtan.'"

Ne'i-el (*moved by God*), a place which formed one of the landmarks of the boundary of the tribe of Asher. Josh. 19 : 27 only. It occurs between Jiphthahel and Cabul. If the former of these be identified with *Jefât*, and the latter with *Kabûl*, eight or nine miles east-southeast of *Akka*, then Neiel may possibly be represented by *Mi'ar*, a village conspicuously placed on a lofty mountain brow, just halfway between the two.

Ne'keb (*cavern*), one of the towns on the boundary of Naphtali. Josh. 19 : 33. It lay between Adami and Jabneel. A great number of commentators have taken this name as being connected with the preceding.

Neko'da (*distinguished*). 1. The descendants of Nekoda returned among the Nethinim after the captivity. Ezra 2 : 48 ; Neh. 7 : 50.

2. The sons of Nekoda were among those who went up after the captivity from Tel-melah, Tel-harsa, and other places, but were unable to prove their

descent from Israel. Ezra 2 : 60; Neh. 7 : 62.

Nemu'el (*day of God*). 1. A Reubenite, son of Eliab and eldest brother of Dathan and Abiram. Num. 26 : 9.

2. The eldest son of Simeon, Num. 26 : 12; 1 Chron. 4 : 24, from whom were descended the family of the Nemuelites. In Gen. 46 : 10 he is called JEMUEL.

Ne'pheg (*sprout*). 1. One of the sons of Izhar the son of Kohath. Ex. 6 : 21.

2. One of David's sons born to him in Jerusalem. 2 Sam. 5 : 15; 1 Chron. 3 : 7; 14 : 6.

Ne'phish (*refreshed*), an inaccurate variation (found in 1 Chron. 5 : 19 only) of the name Naphish.

Nephish'esim (*expansions*). The children of Nephishesim were among the Nethinim who returned with Zerubbabel. Neh. 7 : 52.

Neph'thalim, a form of the name Naphtali. Tob. 7 : 3; Matt. 4 : 13, 15; Rev. 7 : 6.

Ain Lifta (Nephtoah).

Neph'toah, or **Nephto'ah** (*opening*), **The water of.** The spring or source of the water or (inaccurately) waters of Nephtoah was one of the landmarks in the boundary line which separated Judah from Benjamin. Josh. 15 : 9; 18 : 15. It lay northwest of Jerusalem, in which direction it seems to have been satisfactorily identified in *Ain Lifta*, a spring situated a little distance above the village of the same name.

Nephu'sim (*expansions*), the same as Nephishesim, of which name according to Gesenius it is the proper form. Ezra 2 : 50.

Ner (*a light* or *lamp*), son of Jehiel, according to 1 Chron. 8 : 33, father of Kish and Abner, and grandfather of King Saul. (B.C. 1140.) Abner was, therefore, uncle to Saul, as is expressly stated in 1 Sam. 14 : 50.

Ne'reus (*lamp*), a Christian at Rome, saluted by St. Paul. Rom. 16 : 15. According to tradition he was beheaded at Terracina, probably in the reign of Nerva.

Ner'gal (*hero*), one of the chief Assyrian and Babylonian deities, seems to have corresponded closely to the classical Mars. 2 Kings 17 : 30. It is conjectured that he may represent the deified Nimrod.

Ner'gal-share'zer (*prince of fire*) occurs only in Jer. 39 : 3 and 13. There appear to have been two persons of the name among the "princes of the king of Babylon" who accompanied Nebuchadnezzar on his last expedition against Jerusalem. One of these is not marked by any additional title; but the other has the honorable distinction of Rab-mag, probably meaning *chief of the Magi* [see RAB-MAG], and it is to him alone that any particular interest attaches. In sacred Scripture he appears among the persons who, by command of Nebuchadnezzar, released Jeremiah from prison. Profane history gives us reason to believe that he was a personage of great importance, who not long afterward mounted the Babylonian throne. He is the same as the monarch called Neriglissar or Neriglissor, who murdered Evil-merodach, the son of Nebuchadnezzar, and succeeded him upon the throne. His reign lasted from B.C. 559 to B.C. 556.

Ne'ri, short form for NERIAH (*Jehovah is my lamp*), son of Melchi and father of Salathiel, in the genealogy of Christ.

Neri'ah (*lamp of Jehovah*), the son of Maaseiah and father of Baruch and Seraiah.

Net. [See FISHING.]

Nethan'e-el (*given of God*). 1. The son of Zuar, and prince of the tribe of Issachar at the time of the exodus. Num. 1 : 8 ; 2 : 5 ; 7 : 18. (B.C. 1491.)

2. The fourth son of Jesse and brother of David. 1 Chron. 2 : 14.

3. A priest in the reign of David who blew the trumpet before the ark when it was brought from the house of Obededom. 1 Chron. 15 : 24. (B.C. 1055.)

4. A Levite, father of Shemaiah the scribe, in the reign of David. 1 Chron. 24 : 6.

5. A son of Obed-edom. 1 Chron. 26 : 4.

6. One of the princes of Judah whom Jehoshaphat sent to teach in the cities of his kingdom. 2 Chron. 17 : 7. (B.C. 912.)

7. A chief of the Levites in the reign of Josiah. 2 Chron. 35 : 9. (B.C. 628.)

8. A priest of the family of Pashur, in the time of Ezra, who had married a foreign wife. (B.C. 458.)

9. The representative of the priestly family of Jedaiah in the time of Joiakim. Neh. 12 : 21. (B.C. 446.)

10. A Levite, of the sons of Asaph, who with his brethren played upon the musical instruments of David at the dedication of the wall of Jerusalem under Ezra and Nehemiah. Neh. 12 : 36. (B.C. 446.)

Nethani'ah (*given of Jehovah*). 1. The son of Elishama, and father of Ishmael who murdered Gedaliah. 2 Kings 25 : 23, 25. He was of the royal family of Judah. (B.C. 620.)

2. One of the four sons of Asaph the minstrel. 1 Chron. 25 : 12. (B.C. 1015.)

3. A Levite in the reign of Jehoshaphat. 2 Chron. 17 : 8. (B.C. 912.)

4. The father of Jehudi. Jer. 36 : 14. (B.C. 638.)

Neth'inim (*given, dedicated*). As applied specifically to a distinct body of men connected with the services of the temple, this name first meets us in the later books of the Old Testament—in 1 Chronicles, Ezra and Nehemiah. The word and the ideas embodied in it may, however, be traced to a much earlier period. As derived from the verb *náthan*, *i. e.* give, set apart, dedicate, it was applied to those who were specially appointed to the liturgical offices of the tabernacle. We must not forget that the Levites were *given* to Aaron and his sons, *i. e.* to the priests as an order, and were accordingly the first Nethinim. Num. 3 : 9 ; 8 : 19. At first they were the only attendants, and their work must have been laborious enough. The first conquests, however, brought them their share of the captive slaves of the Midianites, and 320 were *given* to them as having charge of the tabernacle, Num. 31 : 47, while 32 only were assigned specially to the priests. This disposition to devolve the more laborious offices of their ritual upon slaves of another race showed itself again in the treatment of the Gibeonites. No addition to the number thus employed appears to have been made during the period of the judges, and they continued to be known by their own name as the Gibeonites. Either the massacre at Nob had involved the Gibeonites as well as the priests, 1 Sam. 22 : 19, or else they had fallen victims to some other outburst of Saul's fury; and though there were survivors, 2 Sam. 21 : 2, the number was likely to be quite inadequate for the greater stateliness of the new worship at Jerusalem. It is to this period accordingly that the origin of the class bearing this name may be traced. The Nethinim were those " whom David and the princes appointed (Heb. *gave*) for the service of the Levites." Ezra 8 : 20. At this time the Nethinim probably lived within the precincts of the temple, doing its rougher work and so enabling the Levites to take a higher position as the religious representatives and instructors of the people. The example set by David was followed by his successor.

Neto'phah (*distillation*), a town the name of which occurs only in the catalogue of those who returned with Zerubbabel from the captivity. Ezra 2 : 22 ; Neh. 7 : 26 ; 1 Esdr. 5 : 18. But, though not directly mentioned till so late a period, Netophah was really a much older place. Two of David's guard, 1 Chron. 27 : 13, 15, were Netophathites. The "villages of the Netophathites" were the residence of the Levites. 1 Chron. 9 : 16. From another notice we learn that the particular Levites who inhabited these villages were singers. Neh. 12 : 28. To judge from Neh. 7 : 26 the town was in the neighborhood of, or closely connected with, Bethlehem.

Netoph'athite, an inhabitant of Netophah.

The Nettle of Palestine.

Nettle, a well-known plant covered with minute sharp hairs, containing a poison that produces a painful, stinging sensation. It grows on neglected ground. A different Hebrew word in Job 30 : 7; Prov. 24 : 31; Zeph. 2 : 9 seems to indicate a different species.

New Moon. The first day of the lunar month was observed as a holy day. In addition to the daily sacrifice there were offered two young bullocks, a ram and seven lambs of the first year as a burnt offering, with the proper meat offerings and drink offerings, and a kid as a sin offering. Num. 28 : 11-15. As on the Sabbath, trade and handicraft work were stopped, Amos 8 : 5, and the temple was opened for public worship. Isa. 66 : 23; Ezek. 46 : 3. The trumpets were blown at the offering of the special sacrifices for the day, as on the solemn festivals. Num. 10 : 10; Ps. 81 : 3. It was an occasion for state banquets. 1 Sam. 20 : 5-24. In later, if not in earlier, times fasting was intermitted at the new moons. Judith 8 : 6. The new moons are generally mentioned so as to show that they were regarded as a peculiar class of holy days, distinguished from the solemn feasts and the Sabbaths. 1 Chron. 23 : 31; 2 Chron. 2 : 4; 8 : 13; 31 : 3; Ezra 3 : 5; Neh. 10 : 33; Ezek. 45 : 17. The seventh new moon of the religious year, being that of Tisri, commenced the civil year, and had a significance and rites of its own. It was a day of holy convocation. The religious observance of the day of the new moon may plainly be regarded as the consecration of a natural division of time.

New Testament. It is proposed in this article to consider the text of the New Testament. The subject naturally divides itself into—I. The history of the written text; II. The history of the printed text.

I. THE HISTORY OF THE WRITTEN TEXT.—1. The early history of the apostolic writings externally, as far as it can be traced, is the same as that of other contemporary books. St. Paul, like Cicero or Pliny, often employed the services of an amanuensis, to whom he dictated his letters, affixing the salutation "with his own hand." 1 Cor. 16 : 21; 2 Thess. 3 : 17; Col. 4 : 18. The original copies seem to have soon perished. 2. In the natural course of things the apostolic autographs would be likely to perish soon. The material which was commonly used for letters, the papyrus paper, to which St. John incidentally alludes, 2 John 12, comp. 3 John 13, was singularly fragile, and even the stouter kinds, likely to be used for the historical books, were not fitted to bear constant use. The papyrus fragments which have come down to the present time have been preserved under peculiar circumstances, as at Herculaneum or in the Egyptian tombs. 3. In the time of the Diocletian persecution, A.D. 303, copies of the Christian Scriptures were sufficiently numerous to furnish a special object for persecutors. Partly, perhaps, owing to the destruction thus caused, but still more from the natural effects of time, no MS. of the New Testament of the first three centuries remains. But though no fragment of the New Testament of the first century still remains, the Italian and Egyptian papyri, which are of that date, give a clear notion of the caligraphy of the period. In these the text is written in columns, rudely divided, in somewhat awkward capital letters (*uncials*), without any punctuation or division of words; and there is no trace of accents or breathings. 4. In addition to the later MSS., the earliest versions and patristic quotations give very important testimony to the character and history of the ante-Nicene text; but till the last quarter of the second century this source of information fails us. Not only are the remains of Christian literature up to that time extremely scanty, but the practice of verbal quotation from the New Testament was not yet prevalent. As soon as definite controversies arose among Christians, the text of the New Testament assumed its true importance. 5. Several very important conclusions follow from this earliest appearance of textual criticism. It is in the first place evident that various readings existed in the books of the New Testament at a time prior to all extant authorities. History affords no trace of the pure apostolic originals. Again, from the preservation of the first variations noticed, which are often extremely minute, in one or more of the primary documents still left, we may be certain that no important changes have been made in the sacred text which we cannot now detect. 6. Passing from these isolated quotations, we find the first great witnesses to the apostolic text in the early Syriac and Latin versions, and in the rich quotations of Clement of Alexandria († *cir.* A.D. 220) and Origen (A.D. 184–254). From the extant works of Origen alone no inconsiderable portion of the whole New Testament might be transcribed; and his writings are an almost inexhaustible storehouse for the history of the text. There can be no doubt that in Origen's time the variations in the New Testament MSS. were beginning to lead to the formation of specific groups of copies. 7. The most ancient MSS. and versions now extant exhibit the characteristic differences which have been found to exist in different parts of the works of Origen. These cannot have had their source later than the beginning of

the third century, and probably were much earlier. Bengel was the first (1734) who pointed out the affinity of certain groups of MSS., which, as he remarks, must have arisen before the first versions were made. The honor of carefully determining the relations of critical authorities for the New Testament text belongs to Griesbach. According to him two distinct recensions of the Gospels existed at the beginning of the third century—the *Alexandrine* and the *Western*. 8. From the consideration of the earliest history of the New Testament text we now pass to the era of MSS. The quotations of Dionysius Alex. († A.D. 264), Petrus Alex. († *cir.* A.D. 312), Methodius († A.D. 311) and Eusebius († A.D. 340) confirm the prevalence of the ancient type of text; but the public establishment of Christianity in the Roman empire necessarily led to important changes. The nominal or real adherence of the higher ranks to the Christian faith must have largely increased the demand for costly MSS. As a natural consequence the rude Hellenistic forms gave way before the current Greek, and at the same time it is reasonable to believe that smoother and fuller constructions were substituted for the rougher turns of the apostolic language. In this way the foundation of the Byzantine text was laid. Meanwhile the multiplication of copies in Africa and Syria was checked by Mohammedan conquests. 9. The appearance of the oldest MSS. has been already described. The MSS. of the fourth century, of which *Codex Vaticanus* may be taken as a type, present a close resemblance to these. The writing is in elegant continuous uncials (capitals), in three columns, without initial letters or *iota subscript* or *adscript*. A small interval serves as a simple punctuation; and there are no accents or breathings by the hand of the first writer, though these have been added subsequently. *Uncial* writing continued in general use till the middle of the tenth century. From the eleventh century downward *cursive* writing prevailed. The earliest cursive biblical MS. is dated 964 A.D. The MSS. of the fourteenth and fifteenth centuries abound in the contractions which afterward passed into the early printed books. The oldest MSS. are written on the thinnest and finest vellum; in later copies the parchment is thick and coarse. Papyrus was very rarely used after the ninth century. In the tenth century cotton paper was generally employed in Europe; and one example at least occurs of its use in the ninth century. In the twelfth century the common linen or rag paper came into use. One other kind of material requires notice—re-dressed parchment, called *palimpsests*. Even at a very early period the original text of a parchment MS. was often erased, that the material might be used afresh. In lapse of time the original writing frequently reappeared in faint lines below the later text, and in this way many precious fragments of biblical MSS., which had been once obliterated for the transcription of other works, have been recovered. 10. The division of the Gospels into "chapters" must have come into general use some time before the fifth century. The division of the Acts and Epistles into chapters came into use at a later time. It is commonly referred to Euthalius, who, however, says that he borrowed the divisions of the Pauline Epistles from an earlier father; and there is reason to believe that the division of the Acts and Catholic Epistles which he published was originally the work of Pamphilus the martyr. The Apocalypse was divided into sections by Andreas of Cæsarea about A.D. 500. The titles of the sacred books are from their nature additions to the original text. The distinct names of the Gospels imply a collection, and the titles of the Epistles are notes by the possessors, and not addresses by the writers. 11. Very few MSS. contain the whole New Testament—twenty-seven in all out of the vast mass of extant documents. Besides the MSS. of the New Testament, or of parts of it, there are also lectionaries, which contain extracts arranged for the church services. 12. The number of uncial MSS. remaining, though great when compared with the ancient MSS. extant of other writings, is inconsiderable. Tischendorf reckons forty in the Gospels. To these must be added *Cod. Sinait.*, which is entire; a new MS. of Tischendorf, which is nearly entire; and *Cod. Zacynth.*, which contains considerable fragments of St. Luke. In the Acts there are nine; in the Catholic Epistles five; in the Pauline Epistles fourteen; in the Apocalypse three. 13. A complete description of these MSS. is given in the great critical editions of the New Testament. Here those only can be briefly noticed which are of primary importance, the first place being given to

the latest-discovered and most complete *Codex Sinaiticus*—the *Cod. Frid. Aug.* of LXX. at St. Petersburg, obtained by Tischendorf from the convent of St. Catherine, Mount Sinai, in 1859. The New Testament is entire, and the Epistle of Barnabas and parts of the Shepherd of Hermas are added. It is probably the oldest of the MSS. of the New Testament and of the fourth century. *Codex Alexandrinus* (Brit. Mus.), a MS. of the entire Greek Bible, with the Epistles of Clement added. It was given by Cyril Lucar, patriarch of Constantinople, to Charles I. in 1628, and is now in the British Museum. It contains the whole of the New Testament, with some chasms. It was probably written in the first half of the fifth century. *Codex Vaticanus* (1209), a MS. of the entire Greek Bible, which seems to have been in the Vatican Library almost from its commencement (*cir.* A.D. 1450). It contains the New Testament entire to Heb. 9 : 14, καθα : the rest of the Epistle to the Hebrews, the Pastoral Epistles and the Apocalypse were added in the fifteenth century. The MS. is assigned to the fourth century. *Codex Ephraemi rescriptus* (Paris, *Bibl. Imp.* 9), a palimpsest MS. which contains fragments of the LXX. and of every part of the New Testament. In the twelfth century the original writing was effaced and some Greek writings of Ephraem Syrus were written over it. The MS. was brought to Florence from the East at the beginning of the sixteenth century, and came thence to Paris with Catherine de Medici. The only entire books which have perished are 2 Thess. and 2 John. 14. The number of the cursive MSS. (*minuscules*) in existence cannot be accurately calculated. Tischendorf catalogues about 500 of the Gospels, 200 of the Acts and Catholic Epistles, 250 of the Pauline Epistles, and a little less than 100 of the Apocalypse (exclusive of lectionaries); but this enumeration can only be accepted as a rough approximation. 15. Having surveyed in outline the history of the transmission of the written text and the chief characteristics of the MSS. in which it is preserved, we are in a position to consider the extent and nature of the variations which exist in different copies. It is impossible to estimate the number of these exactly, but they cannot be less than 120,000 in all, though of these a very large proportion consists of differences of spelling and isolated aberrations of scribes, and of the remainder comparatively few alterations are sufficiently well supported to create reasonable doubt as to the final judgment. Probably there are not more than 1600–2000 places in which the true reading is a matter of uncertainty. 16. Various readings are due to different causes: some arose from accidental, others from intentional, alterations of the original text. 17. Other variations are due to errors of *sight*. Others may be described as errors of *impression* or *memory*. The copyist, after reading a sentence from the text before him, often failed to reproduce it exactly. Variations of order are the most frequent and very commonly the most puzzling questions of textual criticism. Examples occur in every page, almost in every verse, of the New Testament. 18. Of intentional changes some affect the expression, others the substance of the passage. 19. The number of readings which seem to have been altered for distinctly dogmatic reasons is extremely small. In spite of the great revolutions in thought, feeling and practice through which the Christian Church passed in fifteen centuries, the copyists of the New Testament faithfully preserved, according to their ability, the sacred trust committed to them. There is not any trace of intentional revision designed to give support to current opinions. Matt. 17 : 21, Mark 9 : 29, 1 Cor. 7 : 5, need scarcely be noticed. 20. The great mass of various readings are simply variations in form. There are, however, one or two greater variations of a different character. The most important of these are Mark 16 : 9–end ; John 7 : 53–8 : 12 ; Rom. 16 : 25–27. The first stands quite by itself; and there seems to be little doubt that it contains an authentic narrative, but not by the hand of St. John. The two others, taken in connection with the last chapter of St. John's Gospel, suggest the possibility that the apostolic writings may have undergone in some cases authoritative revision. 21. Manuscripts, it must be remembered, are but one of the three sources of textual criticism. The versions and patristic quotations are scarcely less important in doubtful cases.

II. THE HISTORY OF THE PRINTED TEXT.—The history of the printed text of the New Testament may be divided into three periods. The first of these extends from the labors of the Complutensian editors to those of Mill; the second from Mill to Scholz; the third from Lachmann to the present time. The criticism of the first period was necessarily tentative and partial : the materials available for the construction of the text were few and imperfectly known. The second period marks a great progress: the evidence of MSS., of versions, of the fathers, was collected with the greatest diligence and success; authorities were compared and classified; principles of observation and judgment were laid down. But the influence of the former period still lingered. The third period was introduced by the declaration of a new and sounder law. It was laid down that no right of possession could be pleaded against evidence. The "received" text, as such, was allowed no weight whatever. Its authority, on this view, must depend solely on critical worth. From first to last, in minute details of order and orthography, as well as in graver questions of substantial alteration, the text must be formed by a free and unfettered judgment.

The following are the earliest editions : 1. *The Complutensian Polyglot.*—The glory of printing the first Greek Testament is due to the princely Cardinal Ximenes. This great prelate as early as 1502 engaged the services of a number of scholars to superintend an edition of the whole Bible in the original Hebrew and Greek, with the addition of the Chaldee Targum of Onkelos, the LXX. version and the Vulgate. The volume containing the New Testament was printed first, and was completed on January 10, 1514. The whole work was not finished till July 10, 1517. (It was called *Complutensian* because it was printed at Complutum, in Spain.—ED.) 2. *The edition of Erasmus.*—The edition of Erasmus was the first *published* edition of the New Testament. Erasmus had paid considerable attention to the study of the New Testament, when he received an application from Froben, a printer of Basle with whom he was acquainted, to prepare a Greek text for the press. The request was made on April 17, 1515, and the whole work was finished in February, 1516. 3. *The edition of Stephens.*—The scene of our history now changes from Basle to Paris. In 1543, Simon de Colines (Colinæus) published a Greek text of the New Testament, corrected in about 150 places on fresh MS. authority. Not long after it appeared, R. Estienne (Stephanus) published his first edition (1546), which was based on a collation of MSS. in the Royal Library with the Complutensian text. 4. *The editions of Beza and Elzevir.*—The Greek text of Beza (dedicated to Queen Elizabeth) was printed by H. Stephens in 1565, and a second edition in 1576 ; but the chief edition was the third, printed in 1582, which contained readings from *Codex Bezæ* and *Codex Claromontanus.*

The literal sense of the apostolic writings must be gained in the same way as the literal sense of any other writings—by the fullest use of every appliance of scholarship, and the most complete confidence in the necessary and absolute connection of words and thoughts. No variation of phrase, no peculiarity of idiom, no change of tense, no change of order, can be neglected. The truth lies in the whole expression, and no one can presume to set aside any part as trivial or indifferent. The importance of investigating most patiently and most faithfully the literal meaning of the sacred text must be felt with tenfold force when it is remembered that the literal sense is the outward embodiment of a spiritual sense, which lies beneath and quickens every part of Holy Scripture. [BIBLE.]

New Year. [TRUMPETS, FEAST OF.]

Nezi'ah (*pre-eminent*). The descendants of Neziah were among the Nethinim who returned with Zerubbabel. Ezra 2 : 54; Neh. 7 : 56. (B.C. 536.)

Ne'zib (*garrison, pillar*), a city of Judah, Josh. 15 : 43 only, in the district of the Shefelah or lowland, one of the same group with Keilah and Mareshah. To Eusebius and Jerome it was evidently known. They place it on the road between Eleutheropolis and Hebron, seven or nine miles from the former, and there it still stands under the almost identical name of *Beit Nûsib* or *Chirbeh Nasib.*

Nib'haz (*the barker*), a deity of the Avites, introduced by them into Samaria in the time of Shalmaneser. 2 Kings 17 : 31. The rabbins derived the name from a Hebrew root *nâbach*, "to bark," and hence assigned to it the figure of a dog, or a dog-headed man. The Egyptians worshipped the dog. Some indications of this worship have been found in Syria, a colossal figure of a dog having formerly stood at a point between Berytus and Tripolis.

Nib'shan (*soft soil*), one of the six cities of Judah, Josh. 15 : 62, which were

in the district of the Midbar (Authorized Version "wilderness").

Nica'nor (*conqueror*). 1. Son of Patroclus, 2 Macc. 8 : 9, a general who was engaged in the Jewish wars under Antiochus Epiphanes and Demetrius I. 1 Macc. 3 : 38; 4; 7 : 26, 49. (B.C. 160.) 2. One of the first seven deacons. Acts 6 : 5.

Nicode'mus (*conqueror of the people*), a Pharisee, a ruler of the Jews and a teacher of Israel, John 3 : 1, 10, whose secret visit to our Lord was the occasion of the discourse recorded only by St. John. In Nicodemus a noble candor and a simple love of truth shine out in the midst of hesitation and fear of man. He finally became a follower of Christ, and came with Joseph of Arimathæa to take down and embalm the body of Jesus.

Nicola'itans (*followers of Nicolas*), a sect mentioned in Rev. 2 : 6, 15, whose deeds were strongly condemned. They may have been identical with those who held the doctrine of Balaam. They seem to have held that it was lawful to eat things sacrificed to idols, and to commit fornication, in opposition to the decree of the Church rendered in Acts 15 : 20, 29. The teachers of the Church branded them with a name which expressed their true character. The men who did and taught such things were followers of Balaam. 2 Pet. 2 : 15; Jude 11. They, like the false prophet of Pethor, united brave words with evil deeds. In a time of persecution, when the eating or not eating of things sacrificed to idols was more than ever a crucial test of faithfulness, they persuaded men more than ever that it was a thing indifferent. Rev. 2 : 13, 14. This was bad enough, but there was a yet worse evil. Mingling themselves in the orgies of idolatrous feasts, they brought the impurities of those feasts into the meetings of the Christian Church. And all this was done, it must be remembered, not simply as an indulgence of appetite, but as a part of a system, supported by a "doctrine," accompanied by the boast of a prophetic illumination. 2 Pet. 2 : 1. It confirms the view which has been taken of their character to find that stress is laid in the first instance on the "deeds" of the Nicolaitans. To hate those deeds is a sign of life in a Church that otherwise is weak and faithless. Rev. 2 : 6. To tolerate them is wellnigh to forfeit the glory of having been faithful under persecution. Rev. 2 : 14, 15.

Nic'olas (*victor of the people*), Acts 6 : 5, a native of Antioch and a proselyte to the Jewish faith. When the church was still confined to Jerusalem, he became a convert; and being a man of honest report, full of the Holy Ghost and of wisdom, he was chosen by the whole multitude of the disciples to be one of the first seven deacons, and was ordained by the apostles. There is no reason except the similarity of name for identifying Nicolas with the sect of Nicolaitans which our Lord denounces, for the traditions on the subject are of no value.

Nicop'olis (*city of victory*) is mentioned in Titus 3 : 12 as the place where St. Paul was intending to pass the coming winter. Nothing is to be found in the epistle itself to determine which Nicopolis is here intended. One Nicopolis was in Thrace, near the borders of Macedonia. The subscription (which, however, is of no authority) fixes on this place, calling it the Macedonian Nicopolis. But there is little doubt that Jerome's view is correct, and that the Pauline Nicopolis was the celebrated city of Epirus. This city (the "city of victory") was built by Augustus in memory of the battle of Actium. It was on a peninsula to the west of the bay of Actium.

Ni'ger (*black*) is the additional or distinctive name given to the Simeon who was one of the teachers and prophets in the church at Antioch. Acts 13 : 1.

Night. [DAY.]

Night-hawk. The Hebrew word so translated, Lev. 11 : 16; Deut. 14 : 15, probably denotes some kind of owl.

Nile (*blue, dark*), the great river of Egypt. The word Nile nowhere occurs in the Authorized Version; but it is spoken of under the names of Sihor [SIHOR] and the "river of Egypt." Gen. 15 : 18. We cannot as yet determine the length of the Nile, although recent discoveries have narrowed the question. There is scarcely a doubt that its largest confluent is fed by the great lakes on and south of the equator. It has been traced upward for about 2700 miles, measured by its course, not in a direct line, and its extent is probably over 1000 miles more. (The course of the river has been traced for 3300 miles. For the first 1800 miles (McClintock and Strong say 2300) from its mouth it receives no tributary; but at Kartoom, the capital of Nubia, is the junction of the two great branches, the White Nile and the Blue Nile, so called from the color of the clay which tinges their waters. The Blue Nile rises in the mountains of Abyssinia, and is the chief source of the deposit which the Nile brings to Egypt. The White Nile is the larger branch. Late travellers have found its source in Lake Victoria Nyanza, three degrees south of the equator. From this lake to the mouth of the Nile the distance is 2300 miles in a straight line—one eleventh the circumference of the globe. From the First Cataract, at Syene, the river flows smoothly at the rate of two or three miles an hour, with a width of half a mile, to Cairo. A little north of Cairo it divides into two branches, one flowing to Rosetta and the other to Damietta, from which places the mouths are named. See Bartlett's "Egypt and Palestine," 1879. The great peculiarity of the river is its annual overflow, caused by the periodical tropical rains. "With wonderful clock-like regularity the river begins to swell about the end of June, rises 24 feet at Cairo between the 20th and 30th of September, and falls as much by the middle of May. Six feet higher than this is devastation; six feet lower is destitution."—*Bartlett.* So that the Nile increases one hundred days and decreases one hundred days, and the culmination scarcely varies three days from September 25, the autumnal equinox. Thus "Egypt is the gift of the Nile." As to the cause of the years of plenty and of famine in the time of Joseph, Mr. Osburn, in his "Monumental History of Egypt," thinks that the cause of the seven years of plenty was the bursting of the barriers (and gradually wearing them away) of "the great lake of Ethiopia," which once existed on the upper Nile, thus bringing more water and more sediment to lower Egypt for those years. And he shows how this same destruction of this immense sea would cause the absorption of the waters of the Nile over its dry bed for several years after, thus causing the famine. There is another instance of a seven-years famine—A.D. 1064–1071.—ED.) The great difference between the Nile of Egypt in the present day and in ancient times is caused by the failure of some of its branches and the ceasing of some of its chief vegetable products; and the chief change in the aspect of the cultivable land, as dependent on the Nile, is the result of the ruin of the fish-pools and their conduits and the consequent decline of the fisheries. The river was famous for its seven branches, and under the Roman dominion eleven were counted, of which, however, there were but seven principal ones. The monuments and the narratives of ancient writers show us in the Nile of Egypt in old times a stream bordered by flags and reeds, the covert of abundant wild fowl, and bearing on its waters the fragrant flowers of the various-colored lotus. Now in Egypt scarcely any reeds or water-plants—the famous papyrus being nearly if not quite extinct, and the lotus almost unknown—are to be seen, excepting in the marshes near the Mediterranean. Of old the great river must have shown a more fair and busy scene than now. Boats of many kinds were ever passing along it, by the painted walls of temples and the gardens that extended around the light summer pavilions, from the pleasure-galley, with one great square sail, white or with variegated pattern and many oars, to the little papyrus skiff dancing on the water and carrying the seekers of pleasure where they could shoot with arrows or knock down with the throw-stick the wild fowl that abounded among the reeds, or engage in the dangerous chase of the hippopotamus or the crocodile. The Nile is constantly before us in the history of Israel in Egypt.

Nim′rah (*limpid, pure*), a place mentioned by this name in Num. 32 : 3 only. If it is the same as BETH-NIMRAH, ver. 36, it belonged to the tribe of Gad. It was ten miles north of the Dead Sea and three miles east of the Jordan, on the hill of Nimrim.

Nim′rim (*limpid, pure*), **The waters of,** a stream or brook within the country of Moab, which is mentioned in the denunciations of that nation by Isaiah, Isa. 15 : 6, and Jeremiah. Jer. 48 : 34. We should perhaps look for the site of Nimrim in Moab proper, *i. e.* on the southeastern shoulder of the Dead Sea.

Nim′rod (*rebellion; or the valiant*), a son of Cush and grandson of Ham. The events of his life are recorded in Gen. 10 : 8 ff., from which we learn (1) that he was a Cushite; (2) that he established an empire in Shinar (the classical Babylonia), the chief towns being Babel, Erech, Accad and Calneh; and (3) that he extended this empire northward along the course of the Tigris over Assyria, where he founded a second group of capitals, Nineveh, Rehoboth, Calah and Resen.

Nim′shi (*rescued*), the grandfather of Jehu, who is generally called "the *son* of Nimshi." 1 Kings 19 : 16; 2 Kings 9 : 2, 14, 20; 2 Chron. 22 : 7.

Nin′eveh (*abode of Ninus*), the capital of the ancient kingdom and empire of Assyria. The name appears to be compounded from that of an Assyrian deity, "Nin," corresponding, it is conjectured,

Cherubim on Doorway at Nineveh.

with the Greek Hercules, and occurring in the names of several Assyrian kings, as in "Ninus," the mythic founder, according to Greek tradition, of the city. Nineveh is situated on the eastern bank of the river Tigris, 550 miles from its mouth and 250 miles north of Babylon. It is first mentioned in the Old Testament in connection with the primitive dispersement and migrations of the human race. Asshur, or according to the marginal reading, which is generally preferred, Nimrod, is there described, Gen. 10 : 11, as extending his kingdom from the land of Shinar or Babylonia, in the south, to Assyria in the north, and founding four cities, of which the most famous was Nineveh. Hence Assyria was subsequently known to the Jews as "the land of Nimrod," cf. Micah 5 : 6,

and was believed to have been first peopled by a colony from Babylon. The
kingdom of Assyria and of the Assyrians
is referred to in the Old Testament as
connected with the Jews at a very early
period, as in Num. 24 : 22, 24 and Ps. 83 :
8; but after the notice of the foundation
of Nineveh in Genesis no further mention
is made of the city until the time of the
book of Jonah, or the eighth century B.C.
In this book no mention is made of Assyria or the Assyrians, the king to whom
the prophet was sent being termed the
"king of Nineveh," and his subjects "the
people of Nineveh." Assyria is first
called a kingdom in the time of Menahem, about B.C. 770. Nahum (? B.C. 645)
directs his prophecies against Nineveh;
only once against the king of Assyria. ch.
3 : 18. In 2 Kings 19 : 36 and Isa. 37 : 37,
the city is first distinctly mentioned as
the residence of the monarch. Sennacherib was slain there when worshipping
in the temple of Nisroch his god. Zephaniah, about B.C. 630, couples the capital
and the kingdom together, Zeph. 2 : 13;
and this is the last mention of Nineveh
as an *existing* city. The destruction of
Nineveh occurred B.C. 606. The city was
then laid waste, its monuments destroyed,
and its inhabitants scattered or carried
away into captivity. It never rose again
from its ruins. This total disappearance
of Nineveh is fully confirmed by the records of profane history. The political
history of Nineveh is that of Assyria, of
which a sketch has already been given.
[ASSYRIA.] Previous to recent excavations and researches, the ruins which occupied the presumed site of Nineveh
seemed to consist of mere shapeless heaps
or mounds of earth and rubbish. Unlike
the vast masses of brick masonry which
mark the site of Babylon, they showed
externally no signs of artificial construction, except perhaps here and there the
traces of a rude wall of sun-dried bricks.
Some of these mounds were of enormous
dimensions, looking in the distance
rather like natural elevations than the
work of men's hands. They differ greatly
in form, size and height. Some are mere
conical heaps, varying from 50 to 150 feet
high; others have a broad flat summit,
and very precipitous cliff-like sides furrowed by deep ravines worn by the winter rains. The principal ruins are—(1)
the group immediately opposite Mosul,
including the great mounds of *Kouyunjik* and *Nebbi Yunus;* (2) that near the

junction of the Tigris and Zab, comprising the mounds of *Nimroud* and *Athur;*
(3) *Khorsabad*, about ten miles to the
east of the former river; (4) *Shereef
Khan*, about 5½ miles to the north of
Kouyunjik; and (5) *Selamiyah*, three
miles to the north of Nimroud.

Discoveries.—The first traveller who
carefully examined the supposed site of
Nineveh was Mr. Rich, formerly political
agent for the East India Company at
Bagdad; but his investigations were almost entirely confined to Kouyunjik and
the surrounding mounds, of which he
made a survey in 1820. In 1843 M. Botta,
the French consul at Mosul, fully explored the ruins. M. Botta's discoveries
at Khorsabad were followed by those of
Mr. Layard at Nimroud and Kouyunjik,
made between the years 1845 and 1850.
(Since then very many and important
discoveries have been made at Nineveh,
more especially those by George Smith,
of the British Museum. He has discovered not only the buildings, but the remains of an ancient library written on
stone tablets. These leaves or tablets
were from an inch to a foot square, made
of terra-cotta clay, on which when soft
the inscriptions were written; the tablets
were then hardened and placed upon the
walls of the library rooms, so as to cover
the walls. This royal library contained
over 10,000 tablets. It was begun by
Shalmaneser B.C. 860; his successors
added to it, and Sardanapalus (B.C. 673)
almost doubled it. Stories or subjects
were begun on tablets, and continued on
tablets of the same size sometimes to the
number of one hundred. Some of the
most interesting of these give accounts of
the creation and of the deluge, and all
agree with or confirm the Bible.—ED.)

Description of remains.—The Assyrian
edifices were so nearly alike in general
plan, construction and decoration that
one description will suffice for all. They
were built upon artificial mounds or
platforms, varying in height, but generally from 30 to 50 feet above the level of
the surrounding country, and solidly constructed of regular layers of sun-dried
bricks, as at Nimroud, or consisting
merely of earth and rubbish heaped up,
as at Kouyunjik. This platform was
probably faced with stone masonry, remains of which were discovered at Nimroud, and broad flights of steps or inclined
ways led up to its summit. Although
only the general plan of the ground-floor

can now be traced, it is evident that the palaces had several stories built of wood and sun-dried bricks, which, when the building was deserted and allowed to fall to decay, gradually buried the lower chambers with their ruins, and protected the sculptured slabs from the effects of the weather. The depth of soil and rubbish above the alabaster slabs varied from a few inches to about 20 feet. It is to this accumulation of rubbish above them that the bas-reliefs owe their extraordinary preservation. The portions of the edifices still remaining consist of halls, chambers and galleries, opening for the most part into large uncovered courts. The wall above the wainscoting of alabaster was plastered, and painted with figures and ornaments. The sculptures, with the exception of the human-headed lions and bulls, were for the most part in low relief. The colossal figures usually represent the king, his attendants and the gods; the smaller sculptures, which either cover the whole face of the slab or are divided into two compartments by bands of inscriptions, represent battles, sieges, the chase, single combats with wild beasts, religious ceremonies, etc., etc. All refer to public or national events; the hunting-scenes evidently recording the prowess and personal valor of the king as the head of the people— "the mighty hunter before the Lord." The sculptures appear to have been painted, remains of color having been found on most of them. Thus decorated without and within, the Assyrian palaces must have displayed a barbaric magnificence, not, however, devoid of a certain grandeur and beauty which probably no ancient or modern edifice has exceeded. These great edifices, the depositories of the national records, appear to have been at the same time the abode of the king and the temple of the gods.

Prophecies relating to Nineveh, and illustrations of the Old Testament.—These are exclusively contained in the books of Nahum and Zephaniah. Nahum threatens the entire destruction of the city, so that it shall not rise again from its ruins. The city was to be partly destroyed by fire. Nah. 3 : 13, 15. The gateway in the northern wall of the Kouyunjik enclosure had been destroyed by fire, as well as the palaces. The population was to be surprised when unprepared : "while they are drunk as drunkards they shall be devoured as stubble fully dry." Nah. 1 : 10.

Diodorus states that the last and fatal assault was made when they were overcome with wine. The captivity of the inhabitants and their removal to distant provinces are predicted. Nah. 3 : 18. The fullest and the most vivid and poetical picture of Nineveh's ruined and deserted condition is that given by Zephaniah, who probably lived to see its fall. Zeph. 2 : 13–15.

Site of the city.—Much diversity of opinion exists as to the identification of the ruins which may be properly included within the site of ancient Nineveh. According to Sir H. Rawlinson and those who concur in his interpretation of the cuneiform characters, each group of mounds already mentioned represents a separate and distinct city. On the other hand, it has been conjectured, with much probability, that these groups of mounds are not ruins of separate cities, but of fortified royal residences, each combining palaces, temples, propylæa, gardens and parks, and having its peculiar name ; and that they all formed part of one great city built and added to at different periods, and consisting of distinct quarters scattered over a very large area, and frequently very distant one from the other. Thus the city would be, as Layard says, in the form of a parallelogram 18 to 20 miles long by 12 to 14 wide; or, as Diodorus Siculus says, 55 miles in circumference.

Writing and language.—The ruins of Nineveh have furnished a vast collection of inscriptions partly carved on marble or stone slabs and partly impressed upon bricks and upon clay cylinders, or six-sided and eight-sided prisms, barrels and tablets, which, used for the purpose when still moist, were afterward baked in a furnace or kiln. Comp. Ezek. 4 : 4. The character employed was the arrow-headed or cuneiform—so called from each letter being formed by marks or elements resembling an arrow-head or a wedge. These inscribed bricks are of the greatest value in restoring the royal dynasties. The most important inscription hitherto discovered in connection with biblical history is that upon a pair of colossal human-headed bulls from Kouyunjik, now in the British Museum, containing the records of Sennacherib, and describing, among other events, his wars with Hezekiah. It is accompanied by a series of bas-reliefs believed to represent the siege and capture of Lachish. A list of nineteen or twenty kings can already be compiled, and the annals of the greater number of them will probably be restored to the lost history of one of the most powerful empires of the ancient world, and of one which appears to have exercised perhaps greater influence than any other upon the subsequent condition and development of civilized man. The people of Nineveh spoke a Shemitic dialect, connected with the Hebrew and with the so-called Chaldee of the books of Daniel and Ezra. This agrees with the testimony of the Old Testament.

Nin'evites, the inhabitants of Nineveh. Luke 11 : 30.

Ni'san. [MONTH.]

Nisroch.

Nis'roch (*the great eagle*), an idol of Nineveh, in whose temple Sennacherib was worshipping when assassinated by his sons, Adrammelech and Sharezer. 2 Kings 19 : 37; Isa. 37 : 38. This idol is identified with the eagle-headed human figure, which is one of the most prominent on the earliest Assyrian monuments, and is always represented as contending with and conquering the lion or the bull.

Nitre. Mention of this substance is made in Prov. 25 : 20—"and as vinegar upon nitre"—and in Jer. 2 : 22. The article denoted is not that which we now understand by the term *nitre*, *i. e.* nitrate of potassa—"saltpetre"—but the *nitrum* of the Latins and the *natron* or native carbonate of soda of modern chemistry. Natron was and still is used by the Egyptians for washing linen. The value of soda in this respect is well known. This explains the passage in Jeremiah. Natron is found in great abundance in the well-known soda lakes of Egypt.

No. [NO-AMON.]

No-adi'ah (*whom Jehovah meets*). 1. A Levite, son of Binnui, who with Meremoth, Eleazar and Jozabad weighed the vessels of gold and silver belonging to the temple which were brought back from Babylon. Ezra 8 : 33. (B.C. 459.) 2. The prophetess Noadiah joined Sanballat and Tobiah in their attempt to intimidate Nehemiah. Neh. 6 : 14. (B.C. 445.)

No'ah (*rest*), the tenth in descent from Adam, in the line of Seth, was the son of Lamech and grandson of Methuselah. (B.C. 2948–1998.) We hear nothing of Noah till he is 500 years old, when it is said he begat three sons, Shem, Ham and Japhet. In consequence of the grievous and hopeless wickedness of the world at this time, God resolved to destroy it. Of Noah's life during this age of almost universal apostasy we are told but little. It is merely said that he was a righteous man and perfect in his generations (*i. e.* among his contemporaries), and that he, like Enoch, walked with God. St. Peter calls him "a preacher of righteousness." 2 Pet. 2 : 5. Besides this we are merely told that he had three sons, each of whom had married a wife; that he built the ark in accordance with divine direction; and that he was 600 years old when the flood came. Gen. 6 : 7.

The ark.—The precise meaning of the Hebrew word (*tébâh*) is uncertain. The word occurs only in Genesis and in Exodus 2 : 3. In all probability it is to the old Egyptian that we are to look for its original form. Bunsen, in his vocabulary, gives *tba*, "a chest," *tpt*, "a boat," and in the Coptic version of Ex. 2 : 3, 5, *thebi* is the rendering of *tébâh*. This "chest" or "boat" was to be made of gopher (*i. e.* cypress) wood, a kind of timber which both for its lightness and its durability was employed by the Phœnicians for building their vessels. The planks of the ark, after being put together, were to be protected by a coating of pitch, or rather bitumen, both inside and outside, to make it water-tight, and perhaps also as a protection against the attacks of marine animals. The ark was to consist of a number of "nests" or small compartments, with a view, no doubt, to the convenient distribution of the different animals and their food. These were to be arranged in three tiers, one above another; "with lower, second and third (stories) shalt thou make it." Means were also to be provided for letting light into the ark. There was to be a door; this was to be placed in the side of the ark. Of the shape of the ark nothing is said, but its dimensions are given. It was to be 300 cubits in length, 50 in breadth and 30 in height. Taking 21 inches for the cubit, the ark would be 525 feet in length, 87 feet 6 inches in breadth and 52 feet 6 inches in height. This is very considerably larger than the largest British man-of-war, but not as large as some modern ships. It should be remembered that this huge structure was only intended to float on the water, and was not in the proper sense of the word a ship. It had neither mast, sail nor rudder; it was in fact nothing but an enormous floating house, or rather oblong box. The inmates of the ark were Noah and his wife and his three sons with their wives. Noah was directed to take also animals of all kinds into the ark with him, that they might be preserved alive. (The method of speaking of the animals that were taken into the ark, "clean" and "unclean," implies that only those which were useful to man were preserved, and that no wild animals were taken into the ark; so that there is no difficulty from the great number of different species of animal life existing in the world.—ED.)

The flood.—The ark was finished, and all its living freight was gathered into it as a place of safety. Jehovah shut him in, says the chronicler, speaking of Noah; and then there ensued a solemn pause of seven days before the threatened destruction was let loose. At last the flood came; the waters were upon the earth. A very simple but very powerful and impressive description is given of the appalling catastrophe. The waters of the flood increased for a period of 190 days (40+150, comparing Gen. 7 : 12 and 24); and then "God remembered Noah," and made a wind to pass over the earth, so that the waters were assuaged. The ark rested on the seventeenth day of the seventh month on the mountains of Ararat. After this the waters gradually decreased till the first day of the tenth month, when the tops of the mountains were seen; but Noah and his family did not disembark till they had been in the ark a year and a month and twenty days. Whether the flood was universal or partial has given rise to much controversy; but there can be no doubt that it was universal, so far as man was concerned : we mean that it extended to all *the then known world.* The literal truth of the narrative obliges us to believe that *the whole human race,* except eight persons, perished by the waters of the flood. The language of the book of Genesis does not compel us to suppose that the whole surface of the globe was actually covered with water, if the evidence of geology requires us to adopt the hypothesis of a partial deluge. It is natural to suppose that the writer, when he speaks of "all flesh," "all in whose nostrils was the breath of life," refers only to his own locality. This sort of language is common enough in the Bible when only a small part of the globe is intended. Thus, for instance, it is said that "*all countries* came into Egypt to Joseph to buy corn;" and that "a decree went out from Cæsar Augustus that *all the world* should be taxed." The truth of the biblical narrative is confirmed by the numerous traditions of other nations, which have preserved the memory of a great and destructive flood, from which but a small part of mankind escaped. They seem to point back to a common centre, whence they were carried by the different families of man as they wandered east and west. The traditions which come nearest to the biblical account are those of the nations of western Asia. Foremost among these is the Chaldean. Other notices of a flood may be found in the Phœnician mythology. There is a medal of Apamea in Phrygia, struck as late as the time of Septimius Severus, in which the Phrygian deluge is commemorated. This medal represents a kind of a square vessel floating in the water. Through an opening in it are seen two persons, a man and a woman. Upon the top of this chest or ark is perched a bird, whilst another flies toward it carrying a branch between its feet. Before the vessel are represented the same pair as having just quitted it and got upon the dry land. Singularly enough, too, on some specimens of this medal the letters ΝΩ or ΝΩΕ have been found on the vessel, as in the cut on p. 454. (Tayler Lewis deduces "the partial extent of the flood from the very face of the Hebrew text." "Earth," where it speaks of "all the earth," often is, and here should be, translated "land," the home of the race, from which there appears to have been little inclination to wander. Even after the flood God had to *compel* them to disperse. "Under the

Apamean Coin showing the word "noe" on the Ark.

whole heavens" simply includes the horizon reaching around "all the land"—the visible horizon. We still use the words in the same sense, and so does the Bible. Nearly all commentators now agree on the partial extent of the deluge. It is probable also that the crimes and violence of the previous age had greatly diminished the population, and that they would have utterly exterminated the race had not God in this way saved out some good seed from their destruction. So that the flood, by appearing to destroy the race, really saved the world from destruction.—ED.)

(*The scene of the deluge.*—Hugh Miller, in his "Testimony of the Rocks," argues that there is a remarkable portion of the globe, chiefly on the Asiatic continent, though it extends into Europe, and which is nearly equal to all Europe in extent, whose rivers (some of them the Volga, Oural, Sihon, Kour and the Amoo, of great size) do not fall into the ocean, but, on the contrary, are all *turned inward*, losing themselves, in the eastern part of the tract, in the lakes of a rainless district; in the western parts, into such seas as the Caspian and the Aral. In this region there are extensive districts still under the level of the ocean. Vast plains, white with salt and charged with sea-shells, show that the Caspian Sea was at no distant period greatly more extensive than it is now. With the well-known facts, then, before us regarding this depressed Asiatic region, let us suppose that

the human family, still amounting to several millions, though greatly reduced by exterminating wars and exhausting vices, were congregated in that tract of country which, extending eastward from the modern Ararat to far beyond the Sea of Aral, includes the original Caucasian centre of the race. Let us suppose that, the hour of judgment having arrived, the land began gradually to sink (as the tract in the Run of Cutch sank in the year 1819) equably for forty days at the rate of about 400 feet per day—a rate not twice greater than that at which the tide rises in the Straits of Magellan, and which would have rendered itself apparent as but a persistent inward flowing of the sea. The depression, which, by extending to the Euxine Sea and the Persian Gulf on the one hand and the Gulf of Finland on the other, would open up by three separate channels the "fountains of the great deep," and which included an area of 2000 miles each way, would, at the end of the fortieth day, be sunk in its centre to the depth of 16,000 feet,—sufficient to bury the loftiest mountains of the district; and yet, having a gradient of declination of but sixteen feet per mile, the contour of its hills and plains would remain apparently what they had been before, and the doomed inhabitants would see but the water rising along the mountain sides, and one refuge after another swept away.—ED.)

After the flood.—Noah's first act after he left the ark was to build an altar and to offer sacrifices. This is the first altar of which we read in Scripture, and the first burnt sacrifice. Then follows the blessing of God upon Noah and his sons. Noah is clearly the head of a new human family, the representative of the whole race. It is as such that God makes his covenant with him; and hence selects a *natural* phenomenon as the sign of that covenant. The bow in the cloud, seen by every nation under heaven, is an unfailing witness to the truth of God. Noah now for the rest of his life betook himself to agricultural pursuits. It is particularly noticed that he planted a vineyard. Whether in ignorance of its properties or otherwise we are not informed, but he drank of the juice of the grape till he became intoxicated and shamefully exposed himself in his own tent. One of his sons, Ham, mocked openly at his father's disgrace. The others, with dutiful care and reverence, endeavored to hide it. When he recovered from the effects of his intoxication, he declared that a curse should rest upon the sons of Ham. With the curse on his youngest son was joined a blessing on the other two. After this prophetic blessing we hear no more of the patriarch but the sum of his years, 950.

No'ah (*motion*), one of the five daughters of Zelophehad. Num. 26 : 33 ; 27 : 1 ; 36 : 11 ; Josh. 17 : 3. (B.C. 1450.)

No-a'mon (*temple of Amon*), Nah. 3 : 8 ; **No,** Jer. 46 : 25 ; Ezek. 30 : 14, 15, 16, a city of Egypt, better known under the name of Thebes or Diospolis-Magna, the ancient and splendid metropolis of upper Egypt. The second part of the first form is the name of *Amen*, the chief divinity of Thebes, mentioned or alluded to in connection with this place in Jeremiah. There is a difficulty as to the meaning of No. It seems most reasonable to suppose that No is a Shemitic name, and that Amon is added in Nahum (*l. c.*) to distinguish Thebes from some other place bearing the same name, or on account of the connection of Amen with that city. The description of No-amon as "situate among the rivers, the waters round about it" (Nah. *l. c.*), remarkably characterizes Thebes. (It lay on both sides of the Nile, and was celebrated for its hundred gates, for its temples, obelisks, statues, etc. It was emphatically the city of temples, in the ruins of which many monuments of ancient Egypt are preserved. The plan of the city was a parallelogram, two miles from north to south and four from east to west, but none suppose that in its glory it really extended 33 miles along both sides of the Nile. Thebes was destroyed by Ptolemy, B.C. 81, and since then its population has dwelt in villages only.—ED.)

Nob (*high place*), 1 Sam. 22 : 19 ; Neh. 11 : 32, a sacerdotal city in the tribe of Benjamin, and situated on some eminence near Jerusalem. It was one of the places where the ark of Jehovah was kept for a time during the days of its wanderings. 2 Sam. 6 : 1, etc. But the event for which Nob was most noted in the Scripture annals was a frightful massacre which occurred there in the reign of Saul. 1 Sam. 22 : 17–19.

No'bah (*barking*), an Israelite warrior, Num. 32 : 42, who during the conquest of the territory on the east of Jordan possessed himself of the town of Kenath and the villages or hamlets dependent upon it, and gave them his own name. (B.C. 1450.) For a certain period after the establishment of the Israelite rule the new name remained, Judges 8 : 11 ; but it is not again heard of, and the original appellation, as is usual in such cases, appears to have recovered its hold, which it has since retained ; for in the slightly-modified form of *Kunawât* it is the name of the place to the present day.

Nod (*flight*), the land to which Cain fled after the murder of Abel. [CAIN.]

No'dab (*nobility*), the name of an Arab tribe mentioned only in 1 Chron. 5 : 19, in the account of the war of the Reubenites against the Hagarites. vs. 9–22. It is probable that Nodab, their ancestor, was the son of Ishmael, being mentioned with two of his other sons in the passage above cited, and was therefore a grandson of Abraham.

No'gah (*brightness*), one of the thirteen sons of David who were born to him in Jerusalem. 1 Chron. 3 : 7 ; 14 : 6. (B.C. 1050–1015.)

No'hah (*rest*), the fourth son of Benjamin. 1 Chron. 8 : 2.

Non (*fish*). Nun, the father of Joshua. 1 Chron. 7 : 27.

Noph. [MEMPHIS.]

No'pha (*blast*), a place mentioned only in Num. 21 : 30, in the remarkable song apparently composed by the Amorites after their conquest of Heshbon from the Moabites, and therefore of an earlier date than the Israelite invasion. It is named with Dibon and Medeba, and was possibly in the neighborhood of Heshbon. A name very similar to Nophah is Nobah, which is twice mentioned. Ewald decides that Nophah is identical with the latter of these.

Nose-jewel, Gen. 24 : 22, Ex. 35 : 22, "earring;" Isa. 3 : 21, Ezek. 16 : 12, "jewel on the forehead," a ring of metal, sometimes of gold or silver, passed usually through the right nostril, and worn by way of ornament by women in the East.

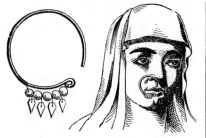

Nose-jewels worn in the East.

Upon it are strung beads, coral or jewels. In Egypt it is now almost confined to the lower classes.

Number. Like most Oriental nations, it is probable that the Hebrews in their written calculations made use of the letters of the alphabet. That they did so in post-Babylonian times we have conclusive evidence in the Maccabæan coins; and it is highly probable that this was the case also in earlier times. But though, on the one hand, it is certain that in all existing MSS. of the Hebrew text of the Old Testament the numerical expressions are written at length, yet, on the other, the variations in the several versions between themselves and from the Hebrew text, added to the evident inconsistencies in numerical statement between certain passages of that text itself, seems to prove that some shorter mode of writing was originally in vogue, liable to be misunderstood, and in fact misunderstood by copyists and translators. These variations appear to have proceeded from the alphabetic method of writing numbers. There can be little doubt, however, that some at least of the numbers mentioned in Scripture are intended to be representative rather than determinative. Certain numbers, as 7, 10, 40, 100, were regarded as giving the idea of completeness. Without entering into St. Augustine's theory of this usage, we may remark that the notion of representative numbers in certain cases is one extremely common among eastern nations, who have a prejudice against counting their possessions accurately; that it enters largely into many ancient systems of chronology, and that it is found in the philosophical and metaphysical speculations not only of the Pythagorean and other ancient schools of philosophy, both Greek and Roman, but also in those of the later Jewish writers, of the Gnostics, and also of such Christian writers as St. Augustine himself. We proceed to give some instances of numbers used, (*a*) representatively, and thus probably by design indefinitely, or, (*b*) definitely, but, as we may say, preferentially, *i. e.* because some meaning (which we do not in all cases understand) was attached to them. 1. *Seven*, as denoting either plurality or completeness, perhaps because seven days completed the week, is so frequent as to make a selection only of instances necessary, *e. g. seven fold*, Gen. 4 : 24; *seven times, i. e.* completely, Lev. 26 : 24; Ps. 12 : 6; *seven* (*i. e.* many) *ways*, Deut. 28 : 25. 2. *Ten* as a preferential number is exemplified in the Ten Commandments and the law of tithe. 3. *Seventy*, as compounded of 7 × 10, appears frequently, *e. g. seventy fold.* Gen. 4 : 24; Matt. 18 : 22. Its definite use appears in the offerings of 70 shekels, Num. 7 : 13, 19 ff.; the 70 elders, ch. 11 : 16; 70 years of captivity. Jer. 25 : 11. 4. *Five* appears in the table of punishments, of legal requirements, Ex. 22 : 1; Lev. 5 : 16; 22 : 14; 27 : 15; Num. 5 : 7; 18 : 16, and in the five empires of Daniel. Dan. 2. 5. *Four* is used in reference to the 4 winds, Dan. 7 : 2, and the so-called 4 corners of the earth; the 4 creatures, each with 4 wings and 4 faces, of Ezekiel, Ezek. 1 : 5 ff.; 4 rivers of Paradise, Gen. 2 : 10; 4 beasts, Dan. 7 and Rev. 4 : 6; the 4 equal-sided temple-chamber, Ezek. 40 : 47. 6. *Three* was regarded, by both the Jews and other nations, as a specially complete and mystic number. 7. *Twelve* (3 × 4) appears in 12 tribes, 12 stones in the high priest's breastplate, 12 apostles, 12 foundation-stones, and 12 gates. Rev. 21 : 19–21. 8. Lastly, the mystic number 666. Rev. 13 : 18.

Num'bers, the fourth book of the law or Pentateuch. It takes its name in the LXX. and Vulgate (whence our " Numbers ") from the double numbering or census of the people; the first of which is given in chs. 1–4, and the second in ch. 26. *Contents.*—The book may be said to contain generally the history of the Israelites from the time of their leaving Sinai, in the second year after the exodus, till their arrival at the borders of the promised land, in the fortieth year of their journeyings. It consists of the following principal divisions: 1. The preparations for the departure from Sinai. Num. 1 : 1–10 : 10. 2. The journey from Sinai to the borders of Canaan. ch. 10 : 11–14 : 45. 3. A brief notice of laws given and events which transpired during the thirty-seven years wandering in the wilderness. ch. 15 : 1–19 : 22. 4. The history of the last year, from the second arrival of the Israelites in Kadesh till they reached "the plains of Moab by Jordan near Jericho." ch. 20 : 1–36 : 13. *Integrity.*— This, like the other books of the Pentateuch, is supposed by many critics to consist of a compilation from two or three or more earlier documents; but the grounds on which this distinction of documents rests are in every respect most unsatisfactory, and it may, in common with the preceding books and Deuteronomy, be regarded as the work of Moses. The book of Numbers is rich in fragments of ancient poetry, some of them of great beauty and all throwing an interesting light on the character of the times in which they were composed. Such, for instance, is the blessing of the high priest. ch. 6 : 24–26. Such too are chants which were the signal for the ark to move when the people journeyed, and for it to rest when they were about to encamp. In ch. 21 we have a passage cited from a book called the "Book of the Wars of Jehovah." This was probably a collection of ballads and songs composed on different occasions by the watch-fires of the camp, and for the most part, though not perhaps exclusively, in commemoration of the victories of the Israelites over their enemies.

Nun (*fish*, or *posterity*), the father of the Jewish captain Joshua. Ex. 33 : 11, etc. His genealogical descent from Ephraim is recorded in 1 Chron. 7. (B.C. before 1530.)

Nurse. In ancient times the position of the nurse, wherever one was maintained, was one of much honor and importance. See Gen. 24 : 59; 35 : 8; 2 Sam. 4 : 4; 2 Kings 11 : 2. The same term is applied to a foster-father or mother, *e.g.* Num. 11 : 12; Ruth 4 : 16; Isa. 49 : 23.

Nuts are mentioned among the good

Pistachio Nuts.

things of the land which the sons of Israel were to take as a present to Joseph in Egypt. Gen. 43 : 11. There can scarcely be a doubt that the Hebrew word, here translated "nuts," denotes the fruit of the pistachio tree (*Pistacia vera*), for which Syria and Palestine have been long famous. In Cant. 6 : 11 a different Hebrew word is translated "nuts." In all probability it here refers to the *walnut tree*. According to Josephus the walnut tree was formerly common, and grew most luxuriantly around the Lake of Gennesareth.

Nym′phas (*bridegroom*), a wealthy and zealous Christian in Laodicea. Col. 4 : 15. (A.D. 60.)

O.

Oak (Heb. *strong*). There is much difficulty in determining the exact meanings of the several varieties of the term mentioned above. Sometimes, evidently, the terebinth or elm is intended, and at others the oak. There are a number of varieties of oak in Palestine. (Dr. Robinson contends that the oak is generally intended, and that it is a very common

Oak of Palestine.

tree in the East. Oaks grow to a large size, reach an old age, and are every way worthy the venerable associations connected with the tree.—ED.) Two oaks, *Quercus pseudo-coccifera* and *Q. ægilops*, are well worthy of the name of mighty trees; though it is equally true that over a greater part of the country the oaks of Palestine are at present merely bushes.

Oath. The principle on which an oath is held to be binding is incidentally laid down in Heb. 6 : 16, viz. as an ultimate appeal to divine authority to ratify an assertion. On the same principle, that oath has always been held most binding which appealed to the highest authority, as regards both individuals and communities. As a consequence of this principle, appeals to God's name on

the one hand, and to heathen deities on the other, are treated in Scripture as tests of allegiance. Ex. 23 : 13 ; 34 : 6 ; Deut. 29 : 12, etc. So also the sovereign's name is sometimes used as a form of obligation. Gen. 42 : 15 ; 2 Sam. 11 : 11 ; 14 : 19. Other forms of oath, serious or frivolous, are mentioned, some of which are condemned by our Lord. Matt. 5 : 33 ; 23 : 16–22 ; and see James 5 : 12. (There is, however, a world-wide difference between a solemn appeal to God and profane swearing.) The forms of adjuration mentioned in Scripture are—1. Lifting up the hand. Witnesses laid their hands on the head of the accused. Gen. 14 : 22 ; Lev. 24 : 14 ; Deut. 17 : 7 ; Isa. 3 : 7. Putting the hand under the thigh of the person to whom the promise was made. Gen. 24 : 2 ; 47 : 29. 3. Oaths were sometimes taken before the altar, or, as some understand the passage, if the persons were not in Jerusalem, in a position looking toward the temple. 1 Kings 8 : 31 ; 2 Chron. 6 : 22. 4. Dividing a victim and passing between or distributing the pieces. Gen. 15 : 10, 17 ; Jer. 34 : 18. As the sanctity of oaths was carefully inculcated by the law, so the crime of perjury was strongly condemned ; and to a false witness the same punishment was assigned which was due for the crime to which he testified. Ex. 20 : 7 ; Lev. 19 : 12.

Obadi′ah (*servant of the Lord*). 1. A man whose sons are enumerated in the genealogy of the tribe of Judah. 1 Chron. 3 : 21. (B.C. 470.)

2. A descendant of Issachar and a chief man of his tribe. 1 Chron. 7 : 3. (B.C. 1014.)

3. One of the six sons of Azel, a descendant of Saul. 1 Chron. 8 : 38 ; 9 : 44. (B.C. 720.)

4. A Levite, son of Shemaiah, and descended from Jeduthun. 1 Chron. 9 : 16 ; Neh. 12 : 25.

5. The second of the lion-faced Gadites who joined David at Ziklag. 1 Chron. 12 : 9. (B.C. 1054.)

6. One of the princes of Judah in the reign of Jehoshaphat. 2 Chron. 17 : 7. (B.C. 909.)

7. The son of Jehiel, of the sons of

Joab, who came up in the second caravan with Ezra. Ezra 8 : 9.

8. A priest, or family of priests, who sealed the covenant with Nehemiah. Neh. 10 : 5.

9. The fourth of the twelve minor prophets. We know nothing of him except what we can gather from the short book which bears his name. The question of his date must depend upon the interpretation of the 11th verse of his prophecy. He there speaks of the conquest of Jerusalem and the captivity of Jacob as having occurred. He probably refers to the captivity by Nebuchadnezzar, B.C. 588. It must have been uttered at some time in the five years which intervened between B.C. 588 and 583. The book of Obadiah is a sustained denunciation of the Edomites, melting into a vision of the future glories of Zion when the arm of the Lord should have wrought her deliverance and have repaid double upon her enemies.

10. An officer of high rank in the court of Ahab. 1 Kings 18 : 3. He was a devout worshipper of Jehovah, and at the peril of his life concealed over a hundred prophets during the persecution by Jezebel. 1 Kings 18 : 3–16. (B.C. 904.)

11. The father of Ishmaiah, who was chief of the tribe of Zebulun in David's reign. 1 Chron. 27 : 19. (B.C. before 1014.)

12. A Merarite Levite in the reign of Josiah, and one of the overseers of the workmen in the restoration of the temple. 2 Chron. 34 : 12. (B.C. 623.)

O'bal (*stripped bare*), a son of Joktan, and, like the rest of his family, apparently the founder of an Arab tribe. Gen. 10 : 28. In 1 Chron. 1 : 22 the name is written EBAL.

O'bed (*serving*). 1. Son of Boaz and Ruth the Moabitess and father of Jesse. Ruth 4 : 17. (B.C. 1360.) The circumstances of his birth, which make up all that we know about him, are given with much beauty in the book of Ruth. The name of Obed occurs only Ruth 4 : 17, and in the four genealogies, Ruth 4 : 21, 22 ; 1 Chron. 2 : 12 ; Matt. 1 : 5 ; Luke 3 : 32.

2. A descendant of Jarha, the Egyptian slave of Sheshan, in the line of Jerahmeel. 1 Chron. 2 : 37, 38. (B.C. after 1014.)

3. One of David's mighty men. 1 Chron. 11 : 47. (B.C. 1046.)

4. One of the gate-keepers of the temple ; son of Shemaiah the first-born of Obed-edom. 1 Chron. 26 : 7. (B.C. 1017.)

5. Father of Azariah, one of the captains of hundreds who joined with Jehoiada in the revolution by which Athaliah fell. 2 Chron. 23 : 1. (B.C. before 876.)

O'bed-e'dom (*servant of Edom*). 1. A Levite, described as a Gittite, 2 Sam. 6 : 10, 11, that is, probably, a native of the Levitical city of Gath-rimmon in Manasseh, which was assigned to the Kohathites. Josh. 21 : 25. (B.C. 1043.) After the death of Uzzah, the ark, which was being conducted from the house of Abinadab in Gibeah to the city of David, was carried aside into the house of Obed-edom, where it continued three months. It was brought thence by David. 2 Sam. 6 : 12 ; 1 Chron. 15 : 25.

2. " Obed-edom the son of Jeduthun," 1 Chron. 16 : 38, a Merarite Levite, appears to be a different person from the last-mentioned. He was a Levite of the second degree and a gate-keeper for the ark, 1 Chron. 15 : 18, 24, appointed to sound " with harps on the Sheminith to excel." 1 Chron. 15 : 21 ; 16 : 5. (B.C. 1043.)

O'bil (*chief of the camels*), a keeper of the herds of camels in the reign of David. 1 Chron. 27 : 30. (B.C. 1050.)

Oblation. [SACRIFICE.]

O'both (*bottles*), one of the encampments of the Israelites, east of Moab. Num. 21 : 10 ; 33 : 43. Its exact site is unknown (but it was probably south of the Dead Sea, on the boundary between Moab and Edom.—ED.).

Oc'ran (*troubled*), an Asherite, father of Pagiel. Num. 1 : 13 ; 2 : 27 ; 7 : 72, 77 ; 10 : 26. (B.C. before 1658.)

O'ded (*restoring*). 1. The father of Azariah the prophet, in the reign of Asa. 2 Chron. 15 : 1. (B.C. before 953.)

2. A prophet of Jehovah in Samaria, at the time of Pekah's invasion of Judah. 2 Chron. 28 : 9. (B.C. 739.)

Odol'lam. [ADULLAM.]

Offerings. [SACRIFICE.]

Officer. It is obvious that most, if not all, of the Hebrew words rendered " officer " are either of an indefinite character or are synonymous terms for functionaries known under other and more specific names, as " scribe," " eunuch," etc. The two words so rendered in the New Testament denote—1. An inferior officer of a court of justice, a messenger or bailiff, like the Roman viator or lictor. Matt. 5 : 25 ; Acts 5 : 22. 2. Officers whose duty it was to register and collect fines imposed by courts of justice. Luke 12 : 58.

Og (*giant*, literally *long-necked*), an Amoritish king of Bashan, whose rule extended over sixty cities. Josh. 13 : 12. He was one of the last representatives of the giant race of Rephaim, and was, with his children and his people, defeated and exterminated by the Israelites at Edrei immediately after the conquest of Sihon. Num. 32 : 33; Deut. 3 : 1-13. Also Deut. 1 : 4; 4 : 47; 31 : 4; Josh. 2 : 10; 9 : 10; 13 : 12, 30. The belief in Og's enormous stature is corroborated by an allusion to his iron bedstead preserved in "Rabbath of the children of Ammon." Deut. 3 : 11. (B.C. 1451.)

Olive Tree and Oil Press.

Oil. Of the numerous substances, animal and vegetable, which were known to the ancients as yielding oil, the olive berry is the one of which most frequent mention is made in the Scriptures. 1. *Gathering.*—The olive berry was either gathered by hand or shaken off carefully with a light reed or stick. 2. *Pressing.*—In order to make oil, the fruit was either bruised in a mortar, crushed in a press loaded with wood or stones, ground in a mill, or trodden with the feet. The "beaten" oil of Ex. 27 : 20; 29 : 40; Lev. 24 : 2; Num. 28 : 5 was probably made by bruising in a mortar. It was used—(1) As food. Dried wheat, boiled with either butter or oil, but generally the former, is a common dish for all classes in Syria. Ex. 29 : 2. (2) Cosmetic. Oil was used by the Jews for anointing the body, *e. g.* after the bath, and giving to the skin and hair a smooth and comely appearance, *e. g.* before an entertainment. (3) Funereal. The bodies of the dead were anointed with oil. 2 Sam. 14 : 2. (4) Medicinal. Isaiah alludes to the use of oil in medical treatment. Isa. 1 : 6; see also Mark 6 : 13; James 5 : 14. (5) For light. The oil for "the light" was expressly ordered to be olive oil, beaten. Matt. 25 : 3. (6) Ritual. Oil was poured on or mixed with the flour or meal used in offerings. Lev. 8 : 12. Kings, priests and prophets were anointed with oil or ointment. (7) In offerings. As so important a necessary of life, the Jew was required to include oil among his first-fruit offerings. Ex. 22 : 29; 23 : 16; Num. 18 : 12. Tithes of oil were also required. Deut. 12 : 17. [OLIVE.]

Oil tree (Heb. *êts shemen*). The Hebrew words occur in Neh. 8 : 15 (Authorized Version "pine branches"), 1 Kings 6 : 23 ("olive tree"), and in Isa. 41 : 19 ("oil tree"). From the passage in Nehemiah, where the *éts shemen* is mentioned as distinct from the olive tree, it may perhaps be identified with the *zackum* tree of the Arabs, the *Balanites ægyptiaca*, a well-known and abundant shrub or small tree in the plain of Jordan. The zackum oil is held in high repute by the Arabs for its medicinal properties. [OLIVE.]

Ointment. (An oily or unctuous substance, usually compounded of oil with various spices and resins and aromatics, and preserved in small alabaster boxes or cruses, in which the delicious aroma was best preserved. Some of the ointments have been known to retain their fragrance for several hundred years. They were a much-coveted luxury, and often very expensive.—ED.) 1. *Cosmetic.*—The Greek and Roman practice of anointing the head and clothes on festive occasions prevailed also among the Egyptians, and appears to have had place among the Jews. Ruth 3 : 3. 2. *Funereal.*—Ointments as well as oil were used to anoint dead bodies and the clothes in which they were wrapped. Matt. 26 : 12. 3. *Medicinal.*—Ointment formed an important feature in ancient medical treatment. Isa. 1 : 6; Jer. 8 : 22; John 9 : 6; Rev. 3 : 18, etc. 4. *Ritual.*—Besides the oil used in many ceremonial observances, a special ointment was appointed to be used in consecration. Ex. 30 : 23, 33; 29 : 7; 37 : 29; 40 : 9, 15. A person whose business it was to compound ointments in general was called an "apothecary." Neh. 3 : 8. The work was sometimes carried on by woman "confectionaries." 1 Sam. 8 : 13.

Old Testament. I. TEXT OF THE OLD TESTAMENT.—1. *History of the text.*—A history of the text of the Old Testament should properly commence from the date of the completion of the canon. As regards the form in which the sacred writings were preserved, there can be little doubt that the text was ordinarily written on skins, rolled up into volumes, like the modern synagogue rolls. Ps. 40 : 7; Jer. 36 : 14; Ezek. 2 : 9; Zech. 5 : 1. The original character in which the text was expressed is that still preserved to us, with the exception of four letters, on the Maccabæan coins, and having a strong affinity to the Samaritan character. At what date this was exchanged for the present Aramaic or square character is still as undetermined as it is at what date the use of the Aramaic language in Palestine superseded that of the Hebrew. The old Jewish tradition, repeated by Origen and Jerome, ascribed the change to Ezra. [WRITING.] Of any logical division, in the written text, of the prose of the Old Testament into Pesukim, or verses, we find in the Talmud no mention; and even in the existing synagogue rolls such division is generally ignored. In the poetical books, the Pesukim mentioned in the Talmud correspond to the poetical lines, not to our modern verses. Of the documents which directly bear upon the history of the Hebrew text, the earliest two are the Samaritan copy of the Pentateuch and the Greek translation of the LXX. [SAMARITAN PENTATEUCH; SEPTUAGINT.] In the translations of Aquila and the other Greek interpreters, the fragments of whose works remain to us in the Hexapla, we have evidence of the existence of a text differing but little from our own; so also in the Targums of Onkelos and Jonathan. A few centuries later we have, in the Hexapla, additional evidence to the same effect in Origen's transcriptions of the Hebrew text. And yet more important are the proofs of the firm establishment of the text, and of its substantial identity with our own, supplied by the translation of Jerome, who was instructed by the Palestinian Jews, and mainly relied upon their authority for acquaintance not only with the text itself, but also with the traditional unwritten vocalization of it. This brings us to the middle of the Talmudic period. The care of the Talmudic doctors for the text is shown by the pains with which they counted up the number of verses in the different books, and computed which were the middle verses, words and letters in the Pentateuch and in the Psalms. The scrupulousness with which the Talmudists noted what they deemed the truer readings, and yet abstained from introducing them into the text, indicates at once both the diligence with which they scrutinized the text and also the care with which, even while acknowledging its occasional imperfections, they guarded it. Critical procedure is also evinced in a mention of their rejection of manuscripts which were found not to agree with others in their readings; and the rules given with reference to the transcription and adoption of manuscripts attest the care bestowed upon them. It is evident from the notices of the Talmud that a number of oral traditions had been gradually accumulating respecting both the integrity of particular passages of the text itself and also the manner in which it was to be read. This vast heterogeneous mass of traditions and criticisms, compiled and embodied in writing, forms what is known as the *Masorah*, *i. e.* Tradition. From the end of the Masoretic period onward, the Masorah became the great authority by which the text given in all the Jewish MSS. was settled. 2. *Manuscripts.*—The Old Testament MSS. known to us fall into two main classes: synagogue rolls and MSS. for private use. Of the latter, some are written in the square, others in the rabbinic or cursive, character. The synagogue rolls contain, separate from each other, the Pentateuch, the Haphtaroth or appointed sections of the Prophets, and the so-called Megilloth, viz. Canticles, Ruth, Lamentations, Ecclesiastes and Esther. Private MSS. in the square character are in the book form, either on parchment or on paper, and of various sizes, from folio to 12mo. Some contain the Hebrew text alone; others add the Targum, or an Arabic or other translation, either interspersed with the text or in a separate column, occasionally in the margin. The upper and lower margins are generally occupied by the Masorah, sometimes by rabbinical commentaries, etc. The date of a MS. is ordinarily given in the subscription; but as the subscriptions are often concealed in the Masorah or elsewhere, it is occasionally difficult to find them; occasionally also it is difficult to decipher them. No satisfactory criteria have been yet established by which the ages of MSS. are to be determined. Few existing MSS. are supposed to be older than the twelfth century. Kennicott and Bruns assigned one of their collation (No. 590) to the tenth century; De Rossi dates it A.D. 1018; on the other hand, one of his own (No. 634) he adjudges to the eighth century. Since the days of Kennicott and De Rossi modern research has discovered various MSS. beyond the limits of Europe. Of many of these there seems no reason to suppose that they will add much to our knowledge of the Hebrew text. It is different with the MSS. examined by Pinner at Odessa. One of these MSS. (A, No. 1), a Pentateuch roll, unpointed, brought from Derbend in Daghestan, appears by the subscription to have been written previous to A.D. 580, and if so is the oldest known biblical Hebrew MS. in existence. The forms of the letters are remarkable. Another MS. (B, No. 3) containing the Prophets, on parchment, in small folio, although only dating, according to the inscription, from A.D. 916, and furnished with a Masorah, is a yet greater treasure. Its vowels and accents are wholly different from those now in use, both in form and in position, being all above the letters: they have accordingly been the theme of much discussion among Hebrew scholars. 3. *Printed text.* —The history of the printed text of the Hebrew Bible commences with the early Jewish editions of the separate books. First appeared the Psalter, in 1477, probably at Bologna, in 4to, with Kimchi's commentary interspersed among the verses. Only the first four psalms had the vowel-points, and these but clumsily expressed. At Bologna there subsequently appeared, in 1482, the Pentateuch, in folio, pointed, with the Targum and the commentary of Rashi; and the five Megilloth (Ruth—Esther), in folio, with the commentaries of Rashi and Aben Ezra. From Soncino, near Cremona, issued in 1486 the Prophetæ priores (Joshua—Kings), folio, unpointed, with Kimchi's commentary. The honor of printing the first entire Hebrew Bible belongs to the above-mentioned town of Soncino. The edition is in folio, pointed and accentuated. Nine copies only of it are now known, of which one belongs to Exeter College, Oxford. This was followed, in 1494, by the 4to or 8vo edition printed by Gersom at Brescia, remarkable as being the edition from which Luther's German translation was made. After the Brescian, the next primary edition was that contained in the Complutensian Polyglot, published at Complutum (Alcala) in Spain, at the expense of Cardinal Ximenes, dated 1514-17, but not issued till 1522. To this succeeded an edition which has had more influence than any on the text of later times—the Second Rabbinical Bible, printed by Bomberg at Venice, 4 vols. fol., 1525-6. The editor was the learned Tunisian Jew R. Jacob ben Chaim. The great feature of his work lay in the correction of the text by the precepts of the Masorah, in which he was profoundly skilled, and on which, as well as on the text itself, his labors were employed. The Hebrew Bible which became the standard to subsequent generations was that of Joseph Athias, a learned rabbi and printer at Amsterdam. His text was based on a comparison of the previous editions with two MSS.; one bearing date 1299, the other a Spanish MS. boasting an antiquity of 900 years. It appeared at Amsterdam, 2 vols. 8vo, 1661. 4. *Principles of criticism.*—The method of procedure required in the criticism of the Old Testament is widely different from that practiced in the criticism of the New Testament. Our Old Testament textus receptus is a far more faithful representation of the genuine Scripture; but, on the other hand, the means of detecting and correcting the errors contained in it are more precarious, the results are more uncertain, and the ratio borne by the value of the diplomatic evidence of MSS. to that of a good critical judgment and sagacity is greatly diminished. It is indeed to the direct testimony of the MSS. that, in endeavoring to establish the true text, we must first have recourse. The comparative purity of the Hebrew text is probably different in different parts of the Old Testament. In the revision of Dr. Davidson, who has generally restricted himself to the admission of corrections warranted by MS., Masoretic or Talmudic authority, those in the book of Genesis do not exceed eleven; those in the Psalms are proportionately three times as numerous; those in the historical books and the Prophets are proportionately more numerous than those in the Psalms.

II. QUOTATIONS FROM THE OLD TESTAMENT IN THE NEW TESTAMENT.— The New Testament quotations from the Old form one of the outward bonds of connection between the two parts of the Bible. They are manifold in kind. In the quotations of all kinds from the Old Testament in the New, we find a continual variation from the *letter* of the older Scriptures. To this variation three causes may be specified as having contributed: First, all the New Testament writers quoted from the Septuagint; correcting it indeed more or less by the Hebrew, especially when it was needful for their purpose; occasionally deserting it altogether; still abiding by it to so large an extent as to show that it was the primary source whence their quotations were drawn. Secondly, the New Testa-

ment writers must have frequently quoted from memory. Thirdly, combined with this there was an alteration of conscious or unconscious design. Sometimes the object of this was to obtain increased force. Sometimes an Old Testament passage is abridged, and in the abridgment so adjusted, by a little alteration, as to present an aspect of completeness, and yet omit what is foreign to the immediate purpose. Acts 1 : 20 ; 1 Cor. 1 : 31. At other times a passage is enlarged by the incorporation of a passage from another source : thus in Luke 4 : 18, 19, although the contents are professedly those read by our Lord from Isa. 61, we have the words " to set at liberty them that are bruised," introduced from Isa. 58 : 6 (Sept.) ; similarly in Rom. 11 : 8, Deut. 29 : 4 is combined with Isa. 29 : 10. In some cases still greater liberty of alteration is assumed. In some places, again, the actual words of the original are taken up, but employed with a new meaning. Almost more remarkable than any alteration in the quotation itself is the circumstance that in Matt. 27 : 9 Jeremiah should be named as the author of a prophecy really delivered by Zechariah ; the reason being that the prophecy is based upon that in Jer. 18, 19, and that without a reference to this original source the most essential features of the fulfillment of Zechariah's prophecy would be misunderstood.

Olive. The olive was among the most abundant and characteristic vegetation of Judea. The olive tree grows freely almost everywhere on the shores of the Mediterranean, but it was peculiarly abundant in Palestine. See Deut. 6 : 11 ; 8 : 8 ; 28 : 40. Oliveyards are a matter of course in descriptions of the country, like vineyards and cornfields. Judges 15 : 5 ; 1 Sam. 8 : 14. The kings had very extensive ones. 1 Chron. 27 : 28. Even now the tree is very abundant in the country. Almost every village has its olive grove. Certain districts may be specified where at various times this tree has been very luxuriant. The cultivation of the olive tree had the closest connection with the domestic life of the Israelites, 2 Chron. 2 : 10, their trade, Ezek. 27 : 17 ; Hos. 12 : 1, and even their public ceremonies and religious worship. In Solomon's temple the cherubim were " of olive tree," 1 Kings 6 : 23, as also the doors, vs. 31, 32, and the posts. ver. 33. For the various uses of olive oil see OIL. The wind was dreaded by the cultivator of the olive, for the least ruffling of a breeze is apt to cause the flowers to fall. Job 15 : 33. It is needless to add that the locust was a formidable enemy of the olive. It happened not unfrequently that hopes were disappointed, and that "the labor of the

Olive Branches and Olives.

olive failed." Hab. 3 : 17. As to the growth of the tree, it thrives best in warm and sunny situations. It is of moderate height, with knotty gnarled trunk and a smooth ash-colored bark. It grows slowly, but lives to an immense age. Its look is singularly indicative of tenacious vigor; and this is the force of what is said in Scripture of its "greenness," as emblematic of strength and prosperity. The leaves, too, are not deciduous. Those who see olives for the first time are occasionally disappointed by the dusty color of their foliage; but those who are familiar with them find an inexpressible charm in the rippling changes of their slender

gray-green leaves. (See Ruskin's "Stones of Venice," iii. 175–177.) The olive furnishes the basis of one of Paul's allegories. Rom. 11 : 16–25. The Gentiles are the "wild olive" grafted in upon the "good olive," to which once the Jews belonged, and with which they may again be incorporated. (The olive grows from 20 to 40 feet high. In general appearance it resembles the apple tree; in leaves and stems, the willow. The flowers are white and appear in June. The fruit is like a plum in shape and size, and at first is green, but gradually becomes purple, and even black, with a hard stony kernel, and is remarkable from the outer fleshy part being that in which much oil is lodged, and not, as is usual, in the almond of the seed. The fruit ripens from August to September. It is sometimes eaten green, but its chief value is in its oil. The wood is hard, fine, beautifully veined, and is often used for cabinet work. Olive trees were so abundant in Galilee that at the siege of Jotapata by Vespasian the Roman army were driven from the ascent of the walls by hot olive oil poured upon them and scalding them underneath their armor.—Josephus, *Wars*, 3 : 7 : 28.—ED.)

Olives, Mount of. "The Mount of Olives" occurs in the Old Testament in Zech. 14 : 4 only. In 2 Sam. 15 : 30 it is called "Olivet;" in other places simply "the mount," Neh. 8 : 15, "the mount facing Jerusalem," 1 Kings 11 : 7, or "the mountain which is on the east side of the city." Ezek. 11 : 23. In the New Testament the usual form is "the Mount of Olives." It is called also "Olivet." Acts 1 : 12. This mountain is the well-known eminence on the east of Jerusalem, intimately connected with some of the gravest events of the history of the Old Testament and the New Testament, the scene of the flight of David and the triumphal progress of the Son of David, of the idolatry of Solomon, and the agony and betrayal of Christ. It is a ridge of rather more than a mile in length, running in general direction north and south, covering the whole eastern side of the city. At its northern end the ridge bends round to the west, so as to form an enclosure to the city on that side also. On the north a space of nearly a mile of tolerably level surface intervenes between the walls of the city and the rising ground; on the east the mount is close to the walls, parted only by the narrow ravine of the Kidron. It is this portion which is the real Mount of Olives of the history. In general height it is not very much above the city: 300 feet higher than the temple mount, hardly more than 100 above the so-called Zion. It is rounded, swelling and regular in form. Proceeding from north to south there occur four independent summits, called—1,

Mount of Olives, from the Wall of Jerusalem.

"Viri Galilæi;" 2, "Mount of Ascension;" 3, "Prophets"—subordinate to the last and almost a part of it; 4, "Mount of Offence." 1. Of these the central one —the "Mount of Ascension"—is the most important. Three paths lead from the valley to the summit—one on the north, in the hollow between the two crests of the hill, another over the summit, and a third winding around the southern shoulder, still the most frequented and the best. The central hill, which we are now considering, purports to contain the sites of some of the most sacred and impressive events of Christian history. The majority of these sacred spots now command little or no attention; but three still remain, sufficiently sacred—if authentic—to consecrate any place. These are—(1) Gethsemane, at the foot of the mount; (2) The spot from which our Saviour ascended on the summit; (3) The place of the lamentation of Christ over Jerusalem, halfway up. Of these, Gethsemane is the only one which has any claim to be authentic. [GETHSEMANE.] 2. Next to the central summit, on the southern side, is a hill remarkable only for the fact that it contains the "singular catacomb" known as the "Tombs of the Prophets," probably in allusion to the words of Christ. Matt. 23 : 29. 3. The most southern portion of the Mount of Olives is that usually known as the "Mount of Offence," *Mons Offensionis.* It rises next to that last mentioned. The title "Mount of Offence," or "Scandal," was bestowed on the supposition that it is the "Mount of Corruption" on which Solomon erected the high places for the gods of his foreign wives. 2 Kings 23 : 13; 1 Kings 11 : 7. The southern summit is considerably lower than the centre one. 4. There remains the "Viri Galilæi," about 400 yards from the "Mount of Ascension." It stands directly opposite the northeast corner of Jerusalem, and is approached by the path between it and the "Mount of Ascension." The presence of a number of churches and other edifices must have rendered the Mount of Olives, during the early and middle ages of Christianity, entirely unlike what it was in the time of the Jewish kingdom or of our Lord. Except the high places on the summit, the only buildings then to be seen were probably the walls of the vineyards and gardens and the towers and presses which were their invariable accompaniment. But though the churches are nearly all demolished, there must be a considerable difference between the aspect of the mountain now and in those days when it received its name from the abundance of its olive groves. It does not now stand so pre-eminent in this respect among the hills in the neighborhood of Jerusalem. It is only in the deeper and more secluded slope leading up to the northernmost summit that these venerable trees spread into anything like a forest. The cedars commemorated by the Talmud and the date-palms implied in the name Bethany have fared still worse; there is not one of either to be found within many miles. Two religious ceremonies performed there must have done much to increase the numbers who resorted to the mount. The appearance of the new moon was probably watched for, certainly proclaimed, from the summit. The second ceremony referred to was the burning of the *red heifer*. This solemn ceremonial was enacted on the central mount, and in a spot so carefully specified that it would seem not difficult to fix it. It was due east of the sanctuary, and at such an elevation on the mount that the officiating priest, as he slew the animal and sprinkled her blood, could see the façade of the sanctuary through the east gate of the temple.

Ol'ivet (*place of olives*). 2 Sam. 15 : 30; Acts 1 : 12. [OLIVES, MOUNT OF.]

Olym'pas (*heavenly*), a Christian at Rome. Rom. 16 : 15. (A.D. 55.)

O'mar (*eloquent, talkative*), son of Eliphaz the first-born of Esau. Gen. 36 : 11, 15; 1 Chron. 1 : 36. (B.C. 1750.)

Ome'ga, or **o'mega,** the last letter of the Greek alphabet. It is used metaphorically to denote the end of anything. Rev. 1 : 8, 11.

Omer. [WEIGHTS AND MEASURES.]

Om'ri (*pupil of Jehovah*). 1. Originally "captain of the host" to Elah, was afterward himself king of Israel, and founder of the third dynasty. (B.C. 926.) Omri was engaged in the siege of Gibbethon, situated in the tribe of Dan, which had been occupied by the Philistines. As soon as the army heard of Elah's death, they proclaimed Omri king. Thereupon he broke up the siege of Gibbethon, and attacked Tirzah, where Zimri was holding his court as king of Israel. The city was taken, and Zimri perished in the flames of the palace, after a reign of seven days. Omri, however, was not allowed to establish his dynasty without a struggle against Tibni, whom "half the people," 1 Kings 16 : 21, desired to raise to the throne. The civil war lasted four years. Comp. 1 Kings 16 : 15 with 23. After the defeat and death of Tibni, Omri reigned for six years in Tirzah. At Samaria Omri reigned for six years more. He seems to have been a vigorous and unscrupulous ruler, anxious to strengthen his dynasty by intercourse and alliances with foreign states. 2. One of the sons of Becher the son of Benjamin. 1 Chron. 7 : 8. 3. A descendant of Pharez the son of Judah. 1 Chron. 9 : 4. 4. Son of Michael, and chief of the tribe of Issachar in the reign of David. 1 Chron. 27 : 18. (B.C. 1030.)

On, the son of Peleth, and one of the chiefs of the tribe of Reuben, who took part with Korah, Dathan and Abiram in their revolt against Moses. Num. 16 : 1. (B.C. 1491.) His name does not again appear in the narrative of the conspiracy, nor is he alluded to when reference is made to the final catastrophe.

On (*abode* or *city of the sun*), a town of lower Egypt, called BETH-SHEMESH in Jer. 43 : 13. On is better known under its Greek name Heliopolis. It was situated on the east side of the Pelusiac branch of the Nile, just below the point of the Delta, and about twenty miles northeast of Memphis. The chief object of worship at Heliopolis was the sun, whose temple, described by Strabo, is now only represented by the single beautiful obelisk, of red granite, 68 feet 2 inches high above the pedestal, which has stood for more than 4000 years, having been erected by Usirtesen, the second king of the twelfth dynasty. Heliopolis was anciently famous for its learning, and Eudoxus and Plato studied under its priests. The first mention of this place in the Bible is in the history of Joseph, to whom we read Pharaoh gave "to wife Asenath the daughter of Potipherah priest of On." Gen. 41 : 45, comp. ver. 50, and 46 : 20.

Obelisk at Heliopolis (On).

(On is to be remembered not only as the home of Joseph, but as the traditional place to which his far-off namesake took Mary and the babe Jesus in the flight to Egypt. The two famous obelisks, long called "Cleopatra's Needles," one of which now stands in London and the other in Central Park in New York city, once stood before this city, and were seen by the children of Israel before the exodus, having been quarried at Syene on the Nile, erected at On (Heliopolis) by Thothmes III., B.C. 1500, and inscriptions added by Rameses II. (Sesostris) two hundred years later. They were taken to Alexandria by Augustus Cæsar A.D. 23, from which they were removed to their present places.—ED.)

O'nam (*strong*). 1. One of the sons of Shobal the son of Seir. Gen. 36 : 23 ; 1 Chron. 1 : 40. (B.C. 1964.)

2. The son of Jerahmeel by his wife Atarah. 1 Chron. 2 : 26, 28.

O'nan (*strong*), the second son of Judah by the Canaanitess, "the daughter of Shua." Gen. 38 : 4; 1 Chron. 2 : 3. " What he did was evil in the eyes of Je-

hovah, and he slew him also," as he had slain his elder brother. Gen. 38 : 9. His death took place before the family of Jacob went down into Egypt. Gen. 46 : 12 ; Num. 26 : 19. (B.C. 1706.)

Ones'imus (*profitable, useful*), the name of the servant or slave in whose behalf Paul wrote the Epistle to Philemon. He was a native, or certainly an inhabitant, of Colosse. Col. 4 : 9. (A.D. 58.) He fled from his master and escaped to Rome, where he was led to embrace the gospel through Paul's instrumentality. After his conversion the most happy and friendly relations sprung up between the teacher and disciple. Whether Paul desired his presence as a personal attendant or as a minister of the gospel is not certain from verse 13 of the epistle.

Onesiph'orus (*bringing profit*) is named twice only in the New Testament, viz. 2 Tim. 1 : 16–18 and 4 : 19. Paul mentions him in terms of grateful love as having a noble courage and generosity in his behalf, amid his trials as a prisoner at Rome, when others from whom he expected better things had deserted him. 2 Tim. 4 : 16. Probably other members of the family were also active Christians. 2 Tim. 4 : 19. It is evident from 2 Tim. 1 : 18 that Onesiphorus had his home at Ephesus. (A.D. 64.)

Oni'as, the name of five high priests in the period between the Old and the New Testament.

Onion. This product is mentioned only in Num. 11 : 5, as one of the good things of Egypt of which the Israelites regretted the loss. Onions have been from time immemorial a favorite article of food among the Egyptians. The onions of Egypt are much milder in flavor and less pungent than those of this country.

O'no (*strong*), one of the towns of Benjamin, is first found in 1 Chron. 8 : 12. A plain was attached to the town, called "the plain of Ono," Neh. 6 : 2, perhaps identical with the " valley of craftsmen." Neh. 11 : 35.

Onycha, spoken of in Ex. 30 : 34, was one of the ingredients of the sacred perfume. It consists of the shells of several kinds of mussels, which when burned emit a strong odor.

Onyx (*a nail*) is the translation of the Hebrew *shôham;* but there is some doubt as to its signification. Some writers believe that the "beryl" is intended; but the balance of authority is in favor of some variety of the onyx. ("The onyx is not a transparent stone, but as the color of the flesh appears through the nail (Greek onyx) on the human body, so the reddish mass which is below shines delicately through the whitish surface of the onyx. There are several varieties. White and reddish stripes alternating form the *sardonyx;* white and reddish gray, the *chalcedony.* When polished it has a fine lustre, and is easily wrought into a gem of great beauty."—*Rosenmüller.*)

O'phel (*hill*), a part of ancient Jerusalem. Ophel was the swelling declivity by which the mount of the temple slopes off on its southern side into the valley of Hinnom—a long, narrowish, rounded spur or promontory, which intervenes between the mouth of the central valley of Jerusalem (the Tyropœon) and the Kidron, or valley of Jehoshaphat. Halfway down it on its eastern face is the "Fount of the Virgin," so called; and at its foot the lower outlet of the same spring—the Pool of Siloam. In 2 Chron. 27 : 3 Jotham is said to have built much "on the wall of Ophel." Manasseh, among his other defensive works, "compassed about Ophel." *Ibid.* 33 : 14. It appears to have been near the "water-gate," Neh. 3 : 26, and the "great tower that lieth out." ver. 27. It was evidently the residence of the Levites. Neh. 11 : 21.

O'phir (*abundance*). 1. The eleventh in order of the sons of Joktan. Gen. 10 : 29; 1 Chron. 1 : 23. (B.C. after 2450.)

2. A seaport or region from which the Hebrews in the time of Solomon obtained gold. The gold was proverbial for its fineness, so that "gold of Ophir" is several times used as an expression for fine gold, 1 Chron. 29 : 4; Job 28 : 16; Ps. 45 : 9; Isa. 13 : 12; and in one passage, Job 22 : 24, the word "Ophir" by itself is used for gold of Ophir, and for gold generally. In addition to gold, the vessels brought from Ophir almug wood and precious stones. The precise geographical situation of Ophir has long been a subject of doubt and discussion. The two countries which have divided the opinions of the learned have been Arabia and India, while some have placed it in Africa. In five passages Ophir is mentioned by name—1 Kings 9 : 28; 10 : 11; 22 : 48; 2 Chron. 8 : 18; 9 : 10. If the three passages of the book of Kings are carefully examined, it will be seen that all the information given respecting Ophir is that it was a place or region accessible by sea from Ezion-geber on the Red Sea, from which imports of gold, almug trees and precious stones were brought back by the Tyrian and Hebrew sailors. The author of the tenth chapter of Genesis certainly regarded Ophir as the name of some city, region or tribe in Arabia. It is almost certain that the Ophir of Genesis is the Ophir of the book of Kings. There is no mention, either in the Bible or elsewhere, of any other Ophir; and the idea of there having been two Ophirs evidently arose from a perception of the obvious meaning of the tenth chapter of Genesis on the one hand, coupled with the erroneous opinion, on the other, that the Ophir of Kings *could not* have been in Arabia. (Hence we conclude that Ophir was in southern Arabia, upon the border of the Indian Ocean; for even if all the things brought over in Solomon's ships are not now found in Arabia, but are found in India, yet there is evidence that they once were known in Arabia; and, moreover, Ophir may not have been the original place of production of some of them, but the great market for traffic in them.)

Oph'ni (*mouldy*), a town of Benjamin, mentioned in Josh. 18 : 24, the same as the Gophna of Josephus, a place which at the time of Vespasian's invasion was apparently so important as to be second only to Jerusalem. It still survives in the modern *Jifna* or *Jufna*, 2½ miles northwest of Bethel.

Oph'rah (*fawn*). 1. A town in the tribe of Benjamin. Josh. 18 : 23; 1 Sam. 13 : 17. Jerome places it five miles east of Bethel. It is perhaps *et-Taiyibeh*, a small village on the crown of a conspicuous hill, four miles east-northeast of *Beitin* (Bethel).

2. More fully, OPHRAH OF THE ABIEZRITES, the native place of Gideon, Judges 6 : 11, and the scene of his exploits against Baal, ver. 24; his residence after his accession to power, ch. 9 : 5, and the place of his burial in the family sepulchre. ch. 8 : 32. It was probably in Manasseh, ch. 6 : 15, and not far distant from Shechem. Judges 9 : 1, 5.

3. The son of Meonothai. 1 Chron. 4 : 14.

Orator. 1. The Authorized Version rendering in Isa. 3 : 3 for what is literally "skillful in whisper or incantation." 2.

The title applied to Tertullus, who appeared as the advocate of the Jewish accusers of St. Paul before Felix. Acts 24 : 1.

Orchard. [GARDEN.]

O'reb (*raven*), one of the chieftains of the Midianite host which invaded Israel, and was defeated and driven back by Gideon. Judges 7 : 25. (B.C. 1362.) Isaiah, Isa. 10 : 26, refers to the magnitude of this disaster. Comp. Ps. 83.

O'reb, The rock, the "raven's crag," the spot, east of Jordan, at which the Midianite chieftain Oreb, with thousands of his countrymen, fell by the hand of the Ephraimites, and which probably acquired its name therefrom. It is mentioned in Judges 7 : 25; Isa. 10 : 26. Perhaps the place called '*Orbo*, which in the *Bereshith Rabba* is stated to have been in the neighborhood of Bethshean, may have some connection with it.

O'ren (*pine tree*), one of the sons of Jerahmeel, the first-born of Hezron. 1 Chron. 2 : 25.

Organ. Gen. 4 : 21; Job 21 : 12; 30 : 31; Ps. 150 : 4. The Hebrew word thus rendered probably denotes a pipe or perforated wind-instrument. In Gen. 4 : 21 it appears to be a general term for all wind-instruments. In Job 21 : 12 are enumerated three kinds of musical instruments which are possible, under the general terms of the timbrel, harp and *organ*. Some identify it with the pandean pipe or syrinx, an instrument of unquestionably ancient origin, and common in the East. [See MUSIC.]

Ori'on (*the giant*), a large and bright constellation of 80 stars, 17 large ones, crossed by the equinoctial line. It is named after a mythical personage of the Greeks, of gigantic stature, and "the handsomest man in the world." The Arabs called it "the giant," referring to Nimrod, the mighty hunter, who was fabled to have been bound in the sky for his impiety. Job 9 : 9. Also alluded to in Job 38 : 31.

Ornaments, Personal. The number, variety and weight of the ornaments ordinarily worn upon the person form one of the characteristic features of Oriental costume, in both ancient and modern times. The monuments of ancient Egypt exhibit the persons of ladies loaded with rings, earrings of very great size, anklets, armlets, bracelets of the most varied forms, richly-ornamented necklaces, and chains of various kinds. There is sufficient evidence in the Bible that the inhabitants of Palestine were equally

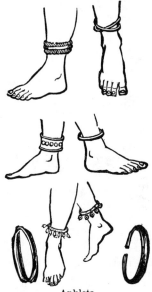

Anklets.

devoted to finery. In the Old Testament, Isaiah, Isa. 3 : 18-23, supplies us with a detailed description of the articles with which the luxurious women of his day were decorated. Eliezer decorated Rebekah with "a golden nose-ring of half a shekel (¼ oz.) weight, and two bracelets for her hands of ten shekels (4½ oz.) weight of gold." Gen. 24 : 22. Earrings were worn by Jacob's wives. Gen. 35 : 4. The number of personal ornaments worn by the Egyptians, particularly by the females, is incidentally noticed in Ex. 3 : 22.

Or'nan (*active*). 1 Chron. 21 : 15; 2 Chron. 3 : 1. [ARAUNAH.]

Or'pah (*a gazelle*), a Moabite woman, wife of Chilion son of Naomi, and thereby sister-in-law to Ruth. Ruth 1 : 4, 14. (B.C. 1360.)

O'she-a (*salvation*). [JOSHUA.]

Osprey. The Hebrew word occurs in Lev. 11 : 13 and Deut. 14 : 12, as the name of some unclean bird. It is probably either the osprey (*Pandion haliaetus*) or the white-tailed eagle (*Haliaetus albicella*).

Ossifrage (*the bone-breaker*). The Hebrew word occurs, as the name of an unclean bird, in Lev. 11 : 13 and Deut. 14 : 12. It is probably the *lammergeyer*, or bearded vulture as it is sometimes called, one of the largest of the birds of prey. It well deserves its name ossifrage, *bone-breaker*, for "not only does he push kids and lambs, and even men, off the rocks, but he takes the bones of animals that other birds of prey have denuded of the flesh high up into the air,

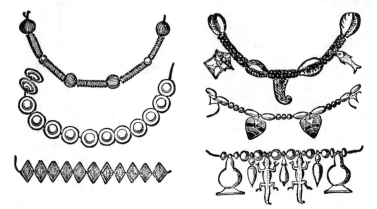

Assyrian and Egyptian Ornaments.

and lets them fall upon a stone in order to crack them and render them more digestible even for his enormous powers of deglutition. Marrow-bones are the dainties he loves. This is probably the bird that dropped a tortoise on the bald head of poor old Æschylus."—*N. H. Simpson.*

The Ostrich.

Ostrich, a large bird, native of Africa and Arabia, nearly ten feet high, having a long neck and short wings. It seeks retired places, Job 30 : 29; Lam. 4 : 3, and has a peculiar mournful cry that is sometimes mistaken by the Arabs for that of the lion. Micah 1 : 8. In Job 39 : 13-18 will be found a description of the bird's habits. Ostriches are polygamous; the hens lay their eggs promiscuously in one nest, which is merely a hole scratched in the sand; the eggs are then covered over to the depth of about a foot, and are, in the case of those birds which are found within the tropics, generally left for the greater part of the day to the heat of the sun, the parent-birds taking their turns at incubation during the night. The habit of the ostrich leaving its eggs to be matured by the sun's heat is usually appealed to in order to confirm the scriptural account, "she leaveth her eggs to the earth;" but this is probably the case only with the tropical birds. We believe that the true explanation of this passage is that some of the eggs are left exposed around the nest for the nourishment of the young birds. It is a general belief among the Arabs that the ostrich is a very stupid bird; indeed they have a proverb, "stupid as an ostrich." As is well known, the ostrich will swallow almost any substance, iron, stones, and even has been known to swallow "several leaden bullets scorching hot from the mould." But in many other respects the ostrich is not as stupid as this would indicate, and is very hard to capture. It is the largest of all known birds, and perhaps the swiftest of all cursorial animals. The feathers so much prized are the long white plumes of the wings. The best are brought from Barbary and the west coast of Africa.

Oth'ni (*lion of Jehovah*), son of Shemaiah, the first-born of Obed-edom. 1 Chron. 26 : 7. (B.C. 1013.)

Oth'ni-el (*lion of God*), son of Kenaz and younger brother of Caleb. Josh. 15 : 17; Judges 1 : 13; 3 : 9; 1 Chron. 4 : 13. (B.C. 1450.) The first mention of Othniel is on occasion of the taking of Kirjath-sepher, or Debir as it was afterward called. Caleb promised to give his daughter Achsah to whosoever should assault and take the city. Othniel won the prize. The next mention of him is in Judges 3 : 9, where he appears as the first judge of Israel after the death of Joshua, and the deliverer of his countrymen from the oppression of Chushan-rishathaim. Judges 3 : 8–9.

An Eastern Oven.

Oven. The eastern oven is of two kinds—fixed and portable. The former is found only in towns, where regular bakers are employed. Hos. 7 : 4. The latter is adapted to the nomad state. It consists of a large jar made of clay, about three feet high and widening toward the bottom, with a hole for the extraction of the ashes. Each household possessed such an article, Ex. 8 : 3; and it was only in times of extreme dearth that the same oven sufficed for several families. Lev. 26 : 26. It was heated with dry twigs and grass, Matt. 6 : 30, and the loaves were placed both inside and outside of it.

Owl.

Owl. A number of species of the owl are mentioned in the Bible, Lev. 11 : 17; Deut. 14 : 16; Isa. 14 : 23; 34 : 15; Zeph. 2 : 14; and in several other places the same Hebrew word is used where it is translated ostrich. Job 30 : 29; Jer. 50 : 39. Some of these species were common in Palestine, and, as is well known, were often found inhabiting ruins. Isa. 34 : 11, 13–15.

Ox. There was no animal in the rural economy of the Israelites, or indeed in that of the ancient Orientals generally, that was held in higher esteem than the ox; and deservedly so, for the ox was *the* animal upon whose patient labors depended all the ordinary operations of farming. Oxen were used for ploughing, Deut. 22 : 10; 1 Sam. 14 : 14, etc.; for treading out corn, Deut. 25 : 4; Hos. 10 :

11, etc.; for draught purposes, when they were generally yoked in pairs, Num. 7 : 3; 1 Sam. 6 : 7, etc.; as beasts of burden, 1 Chron. 12 : 40; their flesh was eaten, Deut. 14 : 4; 1 Kings 1 : 9, etc.; they were

Syrian Cattle.

used in the sacrifices; cows supplied milk, butter, etc. Deut. 32 : 14; 2 Sam. 17 : 29; Isa. 7 : 22. Connected with the importance of oxen in the rural economy of the Jews is the strict code of laws which was mercifully enacted by God for their protection and preservation. The ox that threshed the corn was by no means to be muzzled; he was to enjoy rest on the Sabbath as well as his master. Ex. 23 : 12; Deut. 5 : 14. The ox was seldom slaughtered. Lev. 17 : 1–6. It seems clear from Prov. 15 : 17 and 1 Kings 4 : 23 that cattle were sometimes stall-fed, though as a general rule it is probable that they fed in the plains or on the hills of Palestine. The cattle that grazed at large in the open country would no doubt often become fierce and wild, for it is to be remembered that in primitive times the lion and other wild beasts of prey roamed about Palestine. Hence the force of the Psalmist's complaint of his enemies. Ps. 22 : 13.

O'zem (*power*). 1. The sixth son of Jesse, the next eldest above David. 1 Chron. 2 : 15. (B.C. 1055.) 2. Son of Jerahmeel. 1 Chron. 2 : 25.

Ozi'as (*strength from the Lord*). 1. Uzzi, one of the ancestors of Ezra. 2 Esd. 2 : 2. 2. Uzziah, king of Judah. Matt. 1 : 8, 9.

Oz'ni (*hearing*), one of the sons of Gad, Num. 26 : 16, and founder of the family of the Oznites. Num. 26 : 16.

P.

Pa'ara-i. In the list of 2 Sam. 23 : 35, " Paarai the Arbite " is one of David's mighty men. In 1 Chron. 11 : 37 he is called " Naarai the son of Ezbai." (B.C. 1015.)

Pa'dan (*field*). Padan-aram. Gen. 48 : 7.

Pa'dan-a'ram. By this name, which signifies *the table-land of Aram*, i. e. *Syria,* the Hebrews designated the tract of country which they otherwise called Aram-naharaim, " Aram of the two rivers," the Greek Mesopotamia, Gen. 24 : 10, and " the field (Authorized Version, ' country ') of Syria." Hos. 12 : 13. The term was perhaps more especially applied to that portion which bordered on the Euphrates, to distinguish it from the mountainous districts in the north and northeast of Mesopotamia. It is elsewhere called PADAN simply. Gen. 48 : 7. Abraham obtained a wife for Isaac from Padan-aram. Gen. 25 : 20. Jacob's wives were also from Padan-aram. Gen. 28 : 2, 5, 6, 7 ; 31 : 18 ; 33 : 18.

Pa'don (*deliverance*), the ancestor of a family of Nethinim who returned with Zerubbabel. Ezra 2 : 44 ; Neh. 7 : 47. (B.C. before 529.)

Pa'gi-el (*God allots*), the son of Ocran and chief of the tribe of Asher at the time of the exodus. Num. 1 : 13 ; 2 : 27 ; 7 : 72, 77 ; 10 : 26. (B.C. 1491.)

Pa'hath-mo'ab (*governor of Moab*), head of one of the chief houses of the tribe of Judah. Of the individual or the occasion of his receiving so singular a name nothing is known certainly ; but as we read in 1 Chron. 4 : 22 of a family of Shilonites, of the tribe of Judah, who in very early times " had dominion in Moab," it may be conjectured that this was the origin of the name.

Pa'i (*bleating*). [PAU.]

Paint (as a cosmetic). The use of cosmetic dyes has prevailed in all ages in eastern countries. We have abundant evidence of the practice of painting the eyes both in ancient Egypt and in Assyria ; and in modern times no usage is more general. It does not appear, however, to have been by any means universal among the Hebrews. The notices of it are few ; and in each instance it seems to have been used as a meretricious art, unworthy of a woman of high character. The Bible gives no indication of the substance out of which the dye was formed. The old versions agree in pronouncing the dye to have been produced from antimony. Antimony is still used for the purpose in Arabia and in Persia, but in Egypt the *kohl* is a soot produced by burning either a kind of frankincense or the shells of almonds. The dye-stuff was moistened with oil and kept in a small jar. Whether the custom of staining the hands and feet, particularly the nails, now so prevalent in the East, was known to the Hebrews is doubtful. Painting as an art was not cultivated by the Hebrews, but they decorated their buildings with paint.

Palace. Palace in the Bible, in the singular and plural, is the rendering of several words of diverse meaning. 1 Chron. 29 : 1 ; Ezra 4 : 14 ; Amos 4 : 3, etc. It often designates the royal residence, and usually suggests a fortress or battlemented house. The word occasionally included the whole city, as in Esther 9 : 12 ; and again, as in 1 Kings 16 : 18, it is restricted to a part of the royal apartments. It is applied, as in 1 Chron. 29 : 1, to the temple in Jerusalem. The site of the palace of Solomon was almost certainly in the city itself, on the brow opposite to the temple, and overlooking it and the whole city of David. It is impossible, of course, to be at all certain what was either the form or the exact disposition of such a palace ; but, as we have the dimensions of the three principal buildings given in the book of Kings, and confirmed by Josephus, we may, by taking these as a scale, ascertain pretty nearly that the building covered somewhere about 150,000 or 160,000 square feet. Whether it was a square of 400 feet each way, or an oblong of about 550 feet by 300, must always be more or less a matter of conjecture. The principal building situated within the palace was, as in all eastern palaces, the great hall of state and audience, called " the house of the forest of Lebanon," apparently from the four rows of cedar pillars by which it was supported. It was 100 cubits (175 feet) long, 50 (88 feet) wide, and 30 (52 feet) high. Next in importance was the hall or "porch of judgment," a quadrangular building supported by columns, as we learn from Josephus, which apparently stood on the other side of the great court, opposite the house of the forest of Lebanon. The third edifice is merely called a "porch of pillars." Its dimensions were 50 by 30 cubits. Its use cannot be considered as doubtful, as it was an indispensable adjunct to an eastern palace. It was the ordinary place of business of the palace, and the reception-room when the king received ordinary visitors, and sat, except on great state occasions, to transact the business of the kingdom. Behind this, we are told, was the inner court, adorned with gardens and fountains, and surrounded by cloisters for shade; and there were other courts for the residence of the attendants and guards, and for the women of the harem. Apart from this palace, but attached, as Josephus tells us, to the hall of judgment, was the palace of Pharaoh's daughter—too proud and important a personage to be grouped with the ladies of the harem, and requiring a residence of her own. The recent discoveries at Nineveh have enabled us to understand many of the architectural details of this palace, which before they were made were nearly wholly inexplicable. Solomon constructed an ascent from his own house to the temple, "the house of Jehovah," 1 Kings 10 : 5, which was a subterranean passage 250 feet long by 42 feet wide, of which the remains may still be traced.

Pa'lal (*judge*), the son of Uzai, who assisted in restoring the walls of Jerusalem in the time of Nehemiah. Neh. 3 : 25. (B.C. 446.)

Palesti'na and **Pal'estine** (*land of strangers*). These two forms occur in the Authorized Version but four times in all, always in poetical passages; the first in Ex. 15 : 14 and Isa. 14 : 29, 31; the second, Joel 3 : 4. In each case the Hebrew is *Pelesheth*, a word found, besides the above, only in Ps. 60 : 8, 83 : 7, 87 : 4 and 108 : 9, in all which our translators have rendered it by "Philistia" or "Philistines." Palestine in the Authorized Version really means nothing but *Philistia*. The original Hebrew word *Pelesheth* to the Hebrews signified merely the long and broad strip of maritime plain inhabited by their encroaching neighbors; nor does

it appear that at first it signified more to the Greeks. As lying next the sea, and as being also the high road from Egypt to Phœnicia and the richer regions north of it, the Philistine plain became sooner known to the western world than the country farther inland, and was called by them Syria Palestina — Philistine Syria. From thence it was gradually extended to the country farther inland, till in the Roman and later Greek authors, both heathen and Christian, it became the usual appellation for the whole country of the Jews, both west and east of Jordan. The word is now so commonly employed in our more familiar language to designate the whole country of Israel that although biblically a misnomer, it has been chosen here as the most convenient heading under which to give a general description of THE HOLY LAND, embracing those points which have not been treated under the separate headings of cities or tribes. This description will most conveniently divide itself into three sections :—I. The Names applied to the country of Israel in the Bible and elsewhere. II. The Land : its situation, aspect, climate, physical characteristics in connection with its history, its structure, botany and natural history. III. The History of the country is so fully given under its various headings throughout the work that it is unnecessary to recapitulate it here.

I. THE NAMES.—Palestine, then, is designated in the Bible by more than one name. 1. During the patriarchal period, the conquest and the age of the judges, and also where those early periods are referred to in the later literature (as Ps. 105 : 11), it is spoken of as " Canaan," or more frequently "the land of Canaan," meaning thereby the country west of the Jordan, as opposed to "the land of Gilead," on the east. 2. During the monarchy the name usually, though not frequently, employed is "land of Israel." 1 Sam. 13 : 19. 3. Between the captivity and the time of our Lord the name " Judea " had extended itself from the southern portion to the whole of the country, and even that beyond the Jordan. Matt. 19 : 1; Mark 10 : 1. 4. The Roman division of the country hardly coincided with the biblical one, and it does not appear that the Romans had any distinct name for that which we understand by Palestine. 5. Soon after the Christian era we find the name Palestina in possession of the country. 6. The name most frequently used throughout the middle ages, and down to our own time, is *Terra Sancta*—the Holy Land.

II. THE LAND.—The holy land is not in size or physical characteristics proportioned to its moral and historical position as the theatre of the most momentous events in the world's history. It is but a strip of country about the size of Wales, less than 140 miles in length and barely 40 in average breadth, on the very frontier of the East, hemmed in between the Mediterranean Sea on the one hand and the enormous trench of the Jordan valley on the other, by which it is effectually cut off from the mainland of Asia behind it. On the north it is shut in by the high ranges of Lebanon and Anti-Lebanon, and by the chasm of the Litany. On the south it is no less enclosed by the arid and inhospitable deserts of the upper part of the peninsula of Sinai.

1. *Its position.* — Its position on the map of the world—as the world was when the holy land first made its appearance in history—is a remarkable one. (*a*) It is on the very outpost—on the extremest western edge of the East. On the shore of the Mediterranean it stands, as if it had advanced as far as possible toward the west, separated therefrom by that which, when the time arrived, proved to be no barrier, but the readiest medium of communication—the wide waters of the "great sea." Thus it was open to all the gradual influences of the rising communities of the West, while it was saved from the retrogression and decrepitude which have ultimately been the doom of all purely eastern states whose connections were limited to the East only. (*b*) There was, however, one channel, and but one, by which it could reach and be reached by the great Oriental empires. The only road by which the two great rivals of the ancient world could approach one another—by which alone Egypt could get to Assyria and Assyria to Egypt—lay along the broad flat strip of coast which formed the maritime portion of the holy land, and thence by the plain of the Lebanon to the Euphrates. (*c*) After this the holy land became (like the Netherlands in Europe) the convenient arena on which in successive ages the hostile powers who contended for the empire of the East fought their battles.

2. *Physical features.*—Palestine is essentially a mountainous country. Not

that it contains independent mountain chains, as in Greece, for example, but that every part of the highland is in greater or less undulation. But it is not only a mountainous country. The mass of hills which occupies the centre of the country is bordered or framed on both sides, east and west, by a broad belt of lowland, sunk deep below its own level. The slopes or cliffs which form, as it were, the retaining walls of this depression are furrowed and cleft by the torrent beds which discharge the waters of the hills and form the means of communication between the upper and lower level. On the west this lowland interposes between the mountains and the sea, and is the plain of Philistia and of Sharon. On the east it is the broad bottom of the Jordan valley, deep down in which rushes the one river of Palestine to its grave in the Dead Sea. Such is the first general impression of the physiognomy of the holy land. It is a physiognomy compounded of the three main features already named—the plains, the highland hills, and the torrent beds: features which are marked in the words of its earliest describers, Num. 13 : 29 ; Josh. 11 : 16 ; 12 : 8, and which must be comprehended by every one who wishes to understand the country and the intimate connection existing between its structure and its history. About halfway up the coast the maritime plain is suddenly interrupted by a long ridge thrown out from the central mass, rising considerably above the general level and terminating in a bold promontory on the very edge of the Mediterranean. This ridge is Mount Carmel. On its upper side, the plain, as if to compensate for its temporary displacement, invades the centre of the country, and forms an undulating hollow right across it from the Mediterranean to the Jordan valley. This central lowland, which divides with its broad depression the mountains of Ephraim from the mountains of Galilee, is the plain of Esdraelon or Jezreel, the great battle-field of Palestine. North of Carmel the lowland resumes its position by the seaside till it is again interrupted and finally put an end to by the northern mountains, which push their way out of the sea, ending in the white promontory of the *Ras Nakhúra*. Above this is the ancient Phœnicia. The country thus roughly portrayed is to all intents and purposes the whole land of Israel.

The northern portion is Galilee; the centre, Samaria; the south, Judea. This is the land of Canaan which was bestowed on Abraham,—the covenanted home of his descendants. The highland district, surrounded and intersected by its broad lowland plains, preserves from north to south a remarkably even and horizontal profile. Its average height may be taken as 1500 to 1800 feet above the Mediterranean. It can hardly be denominated a plateau; yet so evenly is the general level preserved, and so thickly do the hills stand behind and between one another, that, when seen from the coast or the western part of the maritime plain, it has quite the appearance of a wall. This general monotony of profile is, however, relieved at intervals by certain centres of elevation. Between these elevated points runs the watershed of the country, sending off on either hand—to the Jordan valley on the east and the Mediterranean on the west—the long, tortuous arms of its many torrent beds. The valleys on the two sides of the watershed differ considerably in character. Those on the east are extremely steep and rugged; the western valleys are more gradual in their slope.

3. *Fertility.*—When the highlands of the country are more closely examined, a considerable difference will be found to exist in the natural condition and appearance of their different portions. The south, as being nearer the arid desert and farther removed from the drainage of the mountains, is drier and less productive than the north. The tract below Hebron, which forms the link between the hills of Judah and the desert, was known to the ancient Hebrews by a term originally derived from its dryness—*Negeb.* This was the south country. As the traveller advances north of this tract there is an improvement; but perhaps no country equally cultivated is more monotonous, bare or uninviting in its aspect than a great part of the highlands of Judah and Benjamin during the larger portion of the year. The spring covers even those bald gray rocks with verdure and color, and fills the ravines with torrents of rushing water; but in summer and autumn the look of the country from Hebron up to Bethel is very dreary and desolate. At Jerusalem this reaches its climax. To the west and northwest of the highlands, where the sea-breezes are felt, there is considerably more vegetation. Hitherto

we have spoken of the central and northern portions of Judea. Its eastern portion—a tract some nine or ten miles in width by about thirty-five in length, which intervenes between the centre and the abrupt descent to the Dead Sea—is far more wild and desolate, and that not for a portion of the year only, but throughout it. This must have been always what it is now—an uninhabited desert, because uninhabitable. No descriptive sketch of this part of the country can be complete which does not allude to the caverns, characteristic of all limestone districts, but here existing in astonishing numbers. Every hill and ravine is pierced with them, some very large and of curious formation—perhaps partly natural, partly artificial—others mere grottos. Many of them are connected with most important and interesting events of the ancient history of the country. Especially is this true of the district now under consideration. Machpelah, Makkedah, Adullam, En-gedi, names inseparably connected with the lives, adventures and deaths of Abraham, Joshua, David and other Old-Testament worthies, are all within the small circle of the territory of Judea. The bareness and dryness which prevail more or less in Judea are owing partly to the absence of wood, partly to its proximity to the desert, and partly to a scarcity of water arising from its distance from the Lebanon. But to this discouraging aspect there are some important exceptions. The valley of *Urtâs*, south of Bethlehem, contains springs which in abundance and excellence rival even those of *Nablûs;* the huge " Pools of Solomon " are enough to supply a district for many miles round them; and the cultivation now going on in that neighborhood shows what might be done with a soil which requires only irrigation and a moderate amount of labor to evoke a boundless produce. It is obvious that in the ancient days of the nation, when Judah and Benjamin possessed the teeming population indicated in the Bible, the condition and aspect of the country must have been very different. Of this there are not wanting sure evidences. There is no country in which the ruined towns bear so large a proportion to those still existing. Hardly a hill-top of the many within sight that is not covered with vestiges of some fortress or city. But, besides this, forests appear to have stood in many parts of Judea until the repeated invasions and sieges caused their fall; and all this vegetation must have reacted on the moisture of the climate, and, by preserving the water in many a ravine and natural reservoir where now it is rapidly dried by the fierce sun of the early summer, must have influenced materially the look and the resources of the country. Advancing northward from Judea, the country (Samaria) becomes gradually more open and pleasant. Plains of good soil occur between the hills, at first small, but afterward comparatively large. The hills assume here a more varied aspect than in the southern districts, springs are more abundant and more permanent, until at last, when the district of *Jebel Nablús* is reached—the ancient Mount Ephraim—the traveller encounters an atmosphere and an amount of vegetation and water which are greatly superior to anything he has met with in Judea, and even sufficient to recall much of the scenery of the West. Perhaps the springs are the only objects which in themselves, and apart from their associations, really strike an English traveller with astonishment and admiration. Such glorious fountains as those of *Ain-jalúd* or the *Ras el-Mukátta* —where a great body of the clearest water wells silently but swiftly out from deep blue recesses worn in the foot of a low cliff of limestone rock, and at once forms a considerable stream—are rarely to be met with out of irregular, rocky, mountainous countries, and being such unusual sights, can hardly be looked on by the traveller without surprise and emotion. The valleys which lead down from the upper level in this district to the valley of the Jordan are less precipitous than in Judea. The eastern district of the *Jebel Nablús* contains some of the most fertile and valuable spots in the holy land. Hardly less rich is the extensive region which lies northwest of the city of Shechem (*Nablús*), between it and Carmel, in which the mountains gradually break down into the plain of Sharon. But with all its richness and all its advance on the southern part of the country, there is a strange dearth of natural wood about this central district. It is this which makes the wooded sides of Carmel and the park-like scenery of the adjacent slopes and plains so remarkable. No sooner, however, is the plain of Esdraelon passed than a considerable improvement is perceptible. The low hills which spread

down from the mountains of Galilee, and form the barrier between the plains of Akka and Esdraelon, are covered with timber, of moderate size it is true, but of thick, vigorous growth, and pleasant to the eye. Eastward of these hills rises the round mass of Tabor, dark with its copses of oak, and set off by contrast with the bare slopes of *Jebel ed-Duhy* (the so-called "Little Hermon") and the white hills of Nazareth. A few words must be said in general description of the maritime lowland, which intervenes between the sea and the highlands. This region, only slightly elevated above the level of the Mediterranean, extends without interruption from *el-Arish*, south of Gaza, to Mount Carmel. It naturally divides itself into two portions, each of about half its length; the lower one the wider, the upper one the narrower. The lower half is the plain of the Philistines— Philistia, or, as the Hebrews called it, the *Shefelah* or Lowland. The upper half is the Sharon or Saron of the Old and New Testaments. The Philistine plain is on an average 15 or 16 miles in width from the coast to the beginning of the belt of hills which forms the gradual approach to the high land of the mountains of Judah. The larger towns, as Gaza and Ashdod, which stand near the shore, are surrounded with huge groves of olive, sycamore and palm, as in the days of King David. 1 Chron. 27:28. The whole plain appears to consist of brown loamy soil, light but rich, and almost without a stone. It is now, as it was when the Philistines possessed it, one enormous cornfield; an ocean of wheat covers the wide expanse between the hills and the sand dunes of the seashore, without interruption of any kind—no break or hedge, hardly even a single olive tree. Its fertility is marvellous; for the prodigious crops which it raises are produced, and probably have been produced almost year by year for the last forty centuries, without any of the appliances which we find necessary for success. The plain of Sharon is much narrower than Philistia. It is about 10 miles wide from the sea to the foot of the mountains, which are here of a more abrupt character than those of Philistia, and without the intermediate hilly region there occurring. The one ancient port of the Jews, the "beautiful" city of Joppa, occupied a position central between the Shefelah and Sharon. Roads led from these various cities to each other, to Jerusalem, Neapolis and Sebaste in the interior, and to Ptolemais and Gaza on the north and south. The commerce of Damascus, and, beyond Damascus, of Persia and India, passed this way to Egypt, Rome and the infant colonies of the West; and that traffic and the constant movement of troops backward and forward must have made this plain, at the time of Christ, one of the busiest and most populous regions of Syria.

4. *The Jordan valley.*—The characteristics already described are hardly peculiar to Palestine. But there is one feature, as yet only alluded to, in which she stands alone. This feature is the Jordan—the one river of the country. The river is elsewhere described [JORDAN]; but it and the valley through which it rushes down its extraordinary descent must be here briefly characterized. This valley begins with the river at its remotest springs of *Hasbeiya*, on the northwest side of Hermon, and accompanies it to the lower end of the Dead Sea, a length of about 150 miles. During the whole of this distance its course is straight and its direction nearly due north and south. The springs of Hasbeiya are 1700 feet above the level of the Mediterranean, and the northern end of the Dead Sea is 1317 feet below it, so that between these two points the valley falls with more or less regularity through a height of more than 3000 feet. But though the *river* disappears at this point, the *valley* still continues its descent below the waters of the Dead Sea till it reaches a further depth of 1308 feet. So that the bottom of this extraordinary crevasse is actually more than 2600 feet below the surface of the ocean. In width the valley varies. In its upper and shallower portion, as between Banias and the lake of Merom (*Hûleh*), it is about five miles across. Between the lake of Merom and the Sea of Galilee it contracts, and becomes more of an ordinary ravine or glen. It is in its third and lower portion that the valley assumes its more definite and regular character. During the greater part of this portion it is about seven miles wide from the one wall to the other. The eastern mountains preserve their straight line of direction, and their massive horizontal wall-like aspect, during almost the whole distance. The western mountains are more irregular in

height, their slopes less vertical. North of Jericho they recede in a kind of wide amphitheatre, and the valley becomes twelve miles broad—a breadth which it thenceforward retains to the southern extremity of the Dead Sea. Buried as it is between such lofty ranges, and shielded from every breeze, the climate of the Jordan valley is extremely hot and relaxing. Its enervating influence is shown by the inhabitants of Jericho. All the irrigation necessary for the cultivation which formerly existed is obtained from the torrents of the western mountains. For all purposes to which a river is ordinarily applied the Jordan is useless. The Dead Sea, which is the final receptacle of the Jordan, is described elsewhere. [SEA, THE SALT.]

5. *Climate.*—"Probably there is no country in the world of the same extent which has a greater variety of climate than Palestine. On Mount Hermon, at its northern border, there is perpetual snow. From this we descend successively by the peaks of Bashan and upper Galilee, where the oak and pine flourish, to the hills of Judah and Samaria, where the vine and fig tree are at home, to the plains of the seaboard, where the palm and banana produce their fruit, down to the sultry shores of the Dead Sea, on which we find tropical heat and tropical vegetation."—*McClintock and Strong.* As in the time of our Saviour, Luke 12 : 54, the rains come chiefly from the south or southwest. They commence at the end of October or beginning of November and continue with greater or less constancy till the end of February or March. It is not a heavy, continuous rain so much as a succession of severe showers or storms, with intervening periods of fine, bright weather. Between April and November there is, with the rarest exceptions, an uninterrupted succession of fine weather and skies without a cloud. Thus the year divides itself into two and only two seasons—as indeed we see it constantly divided in the Bible—"winter and summer," "cold and heat," "seed-time and harvest."

6. *Botany.*—The botany of Syria and Palestine differs but little from that of Asia Minor, which is one of the most rich and varied on the globe. Among trees the oak is by far the most prevalent. The trees of the genus *Pistacia* rank next to the oak in abundance, and of these there are three species in Syria.

There is also the carob or locust tree (*Ceratonia siliqua*), the pine, sycamore, poplar and walnut. Of planted trees and large shrubs the first in importance is the vine, which is most abundantly cultivated all over the country, and produces, as in the time of the Canaanites, enormous bunches of grapes. This is especially the case in the southern districts, those of Eshcol being still particularly famous. Next to the vine, or even in some respects its superior in importance, ranks the olive, which nowhere grows in greater luxuriance and abundance than in Palestine, where the olive orchards form a prominent feature throughout the landscape, and have done so from time immemorial. The fig forms another most important crop in Syria and Palestine. (Besides these are the almond, pomegranate, orange, pear, banana, quince and mulberry among fruit trees. Of vegetables there are many varieties, as the egg plant, pumpkin, asparagus, lettuce, melon and cucumber. Palestine is especially distinguished for its wild flowers, of which there are more than five hundred varieties. The geranium, pink, poppy, narcissus, honeysuckle, oleander, jessamine, tulip and iris are abundant. The various grains are also very largely cultivated.—ED.)

7. *Zoology.*—It will be sufficient in this article to give a general survey of the fauna of Palestine, as the reader will find more particular information in the several articles which treat of the various animals under their respective names. Jackals and foxes are common; the hyena and wolf are also occasionally observed; the lion is no longer a resident in Palestine or Syria. A species of squirrel which the Arabs term *orkidaun*, "the leaper," has been noticed on the lower and middle parts of Lebanon. Two kinds of hare, rats and mice, which are said to abound, the jerboa, the porcupine, the short-tailed field-mouse, may be considered as the representatives of the *Rodentia*. Of the *Pachydermata*, the wild boar, which is frequently met with on Taber and Little Hermon, appears to be the only living wild example. There does not appear to be at present any wild ox in Palestine. Of domestic animals we need only mention the Arabian or one-humped camel, the ass, the mule and the horse, all of which are in general use. The buffalo (*Bubalus buffalo*) is common. The ox of the country is small and unsightly in the neighborhood of Jerusalem, but in the richer pastures the cattle, though small, are not unsightly. The common sheep of Palestine is the broad-tail, with its varieties. Goats are extremely common everywhere. Palestine abounds in numerous kinds of birds. Vultures, eagles, falcons, kites, owls of different kinds, represent the *Raptorial* order. In the south of Palestine especially, reptiles of various kinds abound. It has been remarked that in its physical character Palestine presents on a small scale an epitome of the natural features of all regions, mountainous and desert, northern and tropical, maritime and inland, pastoral, arable and volcanic.

8. *Antiquities.*—In the preceding description allusion has been made to many of the characteristic features of the holy land; but it is impossible to close this account without mentioning a defect which is even more characteristic—its lack of monuments and personal relics of the nation which possessed it for so many centuries and gave it its claim to our veneration and affection. When compared with other nations of equal antiquity—Egypt, Greece, Assyria—the contrast is truly remarkable. In Egypt and Greece, and also in Assyria, as far as our knowledge at present extends, we find a series of buildings reaching down from the most remote and mysterious antiquity, a chain of which hardly a link is wanting, and which records the progress of the people in civilization, art and religion, as certainly as the buildings of the mediæval architects do that of the various nations of modern Europe. But in Palestine it is not too much to say that there does not exist a single edifice or part of an edifice of which we can be sure that it is of a date anterior to the Christian era. And as with the buildings, so with other memorials. With one exception, the museums of Europe do not possess a single piece of pottery or metal work, a single weapon or household utensil, an ornament or a piece of armor, of Israelite make, which can give us the least conception of the manners or outward appliances of the nation before the date of the destruction of Jerusalem by Titus. The coins form the single exception. M. Renan has named two circumstances which must have had a great effect in suppressing art or architecture amongst the ancient Israelites, while their very existence proves that

the people had no genius in that direction. These are (1) the prohibition of sculptured representations of living creatures, and (2) the command not to build a temple anywhere but at Jerusalem.

Pal'lu (*distinguished*), the second son of Reuben, father of Eliab, Ex. 6 : 14; Num. 26 : 5, 8; 1 Chron. 5 : 3, and founder of the family of

Pal'luites (*descendants of Pallu*), **The.** Num. 26 : 5.

Palmer-worm (Heb. *gázâm*) occurs Joel 1 : 4; 2 : 25; Amos 4 : 9. It is maintained by many that *gázâm* denotes some species of locust, but it is more probably a caterpillar.

Palm Tree, showing fruit.

Palm tree (Heb. *támár*). Under this generic term many species are botanically included; but we have here only to do with the date palm, the *Phœnix dactylifera* of Linnæus. While this tree was abundant generally in the Levant, it was regarded by the ancients as peculiarly characteristic of Palestine and the neighboring regions, though now it is rare. ("The palm tree frequently attains a height of eighty feet, but more commonly forty to fifty. It begins to bear fruit after

it has been planted six or eight years, and continues to be productive for a century. Its trunk is straight, tall and unbroken, terminating in a crown of emerald-green plumes, like a diadem of gigantic ostrich-feathers; these leaves are frequently twenty feet in length, droop slightly at the ends, and whisper musically in the breeze. The palm is, in truth, a beautiful and most useful tree. Its fruit is the daily food of millions; its sap furnishes an agreeable wine; the fibres of the base of its leaves are woven into ropes and rigging; its tall stem supplies a valuable timber; its leaves are manufactured into brushes, mats, bags, couches and baskets. This one tree supplies almost all the wants of the Arab or Egyptian."—*Bible Plants.*) Many places are mentioned in the Bible as having connection with palm trees; Elim, where grew three score and ten palm trees, Ex. 15 : 27, and Elath. Deut. 2 : 8. Jericho was the city of "palm trees." Deut. 34 : 3. Hazezon-tamar, "the felling of the palm tree," is clear in its derivation. There is also Tamar, "the palm." Ezek. 47 : 19. Bethany means the "house of dates." The word Phœnicia, which occurs twice in the New Testament—Acts 11 : 19; 15 : 3—is in all probability derived from the Greek word for a palm. The striking appearance of the tree, its uprightness and beauty, would naturally suggest the giving of its name occasionally to women. Gen. 38 : 6; 2 Sam. 13 : 1; 14 : 27. There is in the Psalms, 92 : 12, the familiar comparison, "The righteous shall flourish like the palm tree," which suggests a world of illustration, whether respect be had to the orderly and regular aspect of the tree, its fruitfulness, the perpetual greenness of its foliage, or the height at which the foliage grows, as far as possible from earth and as near as possible to heaven. Perhaps no point is more worthy of mention, if we wish to pursue the comparison, than the elasticity of the fibre of the palm, and its determined growth upward even when loaded with weights. The passage in Rev. 7 : 9, where the glorified of all nations are described as "clothed with white robes and palms in their hands," might seem to us a purely classical image; but palm branches were used by the Jews in token of victory and peace. (To these points of comparison may be added, its principle of growth: it is an endogen, and grows from within; its usefulness: the Syrians enumerating 360 different uses to which it may be put; and the statement that it bears its best fruit in old age.—ED.) It is curious that this tree, once so abundant in Judea, is now comparatively rare, except in the Philistine plain and in the old Phœnicia about *Beyrout*.

Palsy (contracted from paralysis). The loss of sensation or the power of motion, or both, in any part of the body. The infirmities included under this name in the New Testament were various:—1. The paralytic shock affecting the whole body, or apoplexy. 2. That affecting only one side. 3. Affecting the whole system below the neck. 4. Catalepsy, caused by the contraction of the muscles in the whole or a part of the body. This was very dangerous and often fatal. The part affected remains immovable, and diminishes in size and dries up. A hand thus affected was called "a withered hand." Matt. 12 : 10–13. 5. Cramp. This was a most dreadful disease, caused by the chills of the nights. The limbs remain immovably fixed in the same position as when seized by it, and the person seems like one suffering torture. It is frequently followed in a few days by death. Several paralytics were cured by Jesus. Matt. 4 : 24; 8 : 13, etc.

Pal'ti (*whom Jehovah delivers*), the Benjamite spy, son of Raphu. Num. 13 : 9. (B.C. 1490.)

Pal'ti-el (*whom God delivers*), the son of Azzan and prince of the tribe of Issachar. Num. 34 : 26. He was one of the twelve appointed to divide the land of Canaan among the tribes west of Jordan. (B.C. 1450.)

Pal'tite, The. Helez "the Paltite" is named in 2 Sam. 23 : 26 among David's mighty men. (B.C. 1015.)

Pamphyl'ia (*of every tribe*), one of the coast-regions in the south of Asia Minor, having Cilicia on the east and Lycia on the west. In St. Paul's time it was not only a regular province, but the emperor Claudius had united Lycia with it, and probably also a good part of Pisidia. It was in Pamphylia that St. Paul first entered Asia Minor, after preaching the gospel in Cyprus. He and Barnabas sailed up the river Cestrus to Perga. Acts 13 : 13. The two missionaries finally left Pamphylia by its chief seaport, Attalia. Many years afterward St. Paul sailed near the coast. Acts 27 : 5.

Pan. Of the six words so rendered in the Authorized Version, two seem to imply a shallow pan or plate, such as is used by the Bedouins and Syrians for baking or dressing rapidly their cakes of meal, such as were used in legal oblations; the others, a deeper vessel or caldron for boiling meat, placed during the process on three stones.

Pannag (*sweet*), an article of commerce exported from Palestine to Tyre, Ezek. 27 : 17, the nature of which is a pure matter of conjecture, as the term occurs nowhere else. A comparison of the passage in Ezekiel with Gen. 43 : 11 leads to the supposition that pannag represents some of the spices grown in Palestine.

Paper. [WRITING.]

Pa'phos (*boiling*, or *hot*), a town at the west end of Cyprus, connected by a road with Salamis at the east end. It was founded B.C. 1184 (during the period of the judges in Israel). Paul and Barnabas travelled, on their first missionary expedition, "through the isle," from the latter place to the former. Acts 13 : 6. The great characteristic of Paphos was the worship of Aphrodite or Venus, who was fabled to have here risen from the sea. Her temple, however, was at "Old Paphos," now called *Kuklia*. The harbor and the chief town were at "New Paphos," ten miles to the northwest. The place is still called *Baffa*.

Parable. (The word parable is in Greek *parabolé* (παραβολή), which signifies *placing beside* or *together*, a *comparison*. A parable is therefore literally a placing beside, a comparison, a similitude, an illustration of one subject by another.— *McClintock and Strong*. As used in the New Testament it had a very wide application, being applied sometimes to the shortest proverbs, 1 Sam. 10 : 12; 24 : 13; 2 Chron. 7 : 20, sometimes to dark prophetic utterances, Num. 23 : 7, 18; 24 : 3; Ezek. 20 : 49, sometimes to enigmatic maxims, Ps. 78 : 2; Prov. 1 : 6, or metaphors expanded into a narrative. Ezek. 12 : 22. In the New Testament itself the word is used with a like latitude in Matt. 24 : 32; Luke 4 : 23; Heb. 9 : 9. It was often used in a more restricted sense to denote a short narrative under which some important truth is veiled. Of this sort were the parables of Christ. The parable differs from the fable (1) in excluding brute and inanimate creatures passing out of the laws of their nature, and speaking or acting like men; (2) in its higher ethical significance. It differs from the allegory in that the latter, with its direct personification of ideas or attributes, and the names which designate them, involves really no comparison. The virtues and vices of mankind appear as in a drama, in their own character and costume. The allegory is self-interpreting; the parable demands attention, insight, sometimes an actual explanation. It differs from a proverb in that it must include a similitude of some kind, while the proverb may assert, without a similitude, some wide generalization of experience.—ED.) For some months Jesus taught in the synagogues and on the seashore of Galilee as he had before taught in Jerusalem, and as yet without a parable. But then there came a change. The direct teaching was met with scorn, unbelief, hardness, and he seemed for a time to abandon it for that which took the form of parables. The worth of parables as instruments of teaching lies in their being at once a test of character and in their presenting each form of character with that which, as a penalty or blessing, is adapted to it. They withdraw the light from those who love darkness. They protect the truth which they enshrine from the mockery of the scoffer. They leave something even with the careless which may be interpreted and understood afterward. They reveal, on the other hand, the seekers after truth. These ask the meaning of the parable, and will not rest until the teacher has explained it. In this way the parable did its work, found out the fit hearers and led them on. In most of the parables it is possible to trace something like an order. 1. There is a group which have for their subject the laws of the divine kingdom. Under this head we have the sower, Matt. 13, Mark 4, Luke 8; the wheat and the tares, Matt. 13, etc. 2. When the next parables meet us they are of a different type and occupy a different position. They are drawn from the life of men rather than from the world of nature. They are such as these —the two debtors, Luke 7; the merciless servant, Matt. 18; the good Samaritan, Luke 10, etc. 3. Toward the close of our Lord's ministry the parables are again theocratic, but the phase of the divine kingdom on which they chiefly dwell is that of its final consummation. In interpreting parables note—(1) The analogies must be real, not arbitrary; (2) The parables are to be considered as parts of a whole, and the interpretation of one is not to override or encroach upon the lessons taught by others; (3) The direct teaching of Christ presents the standard to which all *our* interpretations are to be referred, and by which they are to be measured.

Par'adise. This is a word of Persian origin, and is used in the Septuagint as the translation of Eden. It means "an orchard of pleasure and fruits," a "garden" or "pleasure ground," something like an English *park*. It is applied figuratively to the celestial dwelling of the righteous, in allusion to the garden of Eden. 2 Cor. 12 : 4; Rev. 2 : 7. It has thus come into familiar use to denote both that garden and the heaven of the just.

Pa'rah (*heifer-town*), one of t₁ ᵤ cities in the territory allotted to Benjamin, named only in the lists of the conquest. Josh. 18 : 23.

Pa'ran, El-pa'ran (*place of caverns*), a desert or wilderness, bounded on the north by Palestine, on the east by the valley of Arabah, on the south by the desert of Sinai, and on the west by the wilderness of Etham, which separated it from the Gulf of Suez and Egypt. The first notice of Paran is in connection with the invasion of the confederate kings. Gen. 14 : 6. The detailed itinerary of the children of Israel in Num. 33 does not mention Paran because it was the name of a wide region; but the many stations in Paran are recorded, chs. 17–36, and probably all the eighteen stations there mentioned between Hazeroth and Kadesh were in Paran. Through this very wide wilderness, from pasture to pasture as do modern Arab tribes, the Israelites wandered in irregular lines of march. This region through which the Israelites journeyed so long is now called by the name it has borne for ages—*Bedu et-Tih*, "the wilderness of wandering." ("Bible Geography," Whitney.) "Mount" Paran occurs only in two poetic passages, Deut. 33 : 2; Hab. 3 : 3. It probably denotes the northwestern member of the Sinaitic mountain group which lies adjacent to the *Wady Teiran*. (It is probably the ridge or series of ridges lying on the northeastern part of the desert of Paran, not far from Kadesh.—ED.)

Par'bar (*open apartment*), a word occurring in Hebrew and Authorized Version only in 1 Chron. 26 : 18. It would seem that Parbar was some place on the west side of the temple enclosure, probably the suburb mentioned by Josephus as lying in the deep valley which separated the west wall of the temple from the city opposite it.

Parchment. [WRITING.]

Parlor, a word in English usage meaning the common room of the family, and hence probably in Authorized Version denoting the king's audience-chamber, so used in reference to Eglon. Judges 3 : 20–25.

Parmash'ta (*superior*), one of the ten sons of Haman slain by the Jews in Shushan. Esther 9 : 9. (B.C. 473.)

Par'menas (*abiding*), one of the seven deacons, "men of honest report, full of the Holy Ghost and wisdom." Acts 6 : 5. There is a tradition that he suffered martyrdom at Philippi in the reign of Trajan.

Par'nach (*delicate*), father or ancestor of Elizaphan prince of the tribe of Zebulun. Num. 34 : 25. (B.C. before 1452.)

Pa'rosh (*flea*). The descendants of Parosh, in number 2172, returned from Babylon with Zerubbabel. Ezra 2 : 3; Neh. 7 : 8. Another detachment of 150 males, with Zechariah at their head, accompanied Ezra. Ezra 8 : 3. They assisted in the building of the wall of Jerusalem, Neh. 3 : 25, and signed the covenant with Nehemiah. Neh. 10 : 14. (B.C. before 535–445.)

Parshan'datha (*given by prayer*), the eldest of Haman's ten sons who were slain by the Jews in Shushan. Esther 9 : 7. (B.C. 473.)

Par'thians. This name occurs only in Acts 2 : 9, where it designates Jews settled in Parthia. Parthia proper was the region stretching along the southern flank of the mountains which separate the great Persian desert from the desert of Kharesm. It lay south of Hyrcania, east of Media and north of Sagartia. The ancient Parthians are called a "Scythic" race, and probably belonged to the great Turanian family. After being subject in succession to the Persians and the Seleucidæ, they revolted in B.C. 256, and under Arsaces succeeded in establishing their independence. Parthia, in the mind of the writer of the Acts, would designate this empire, which extended from India to the Tigris and from the Chorasmian desert to the shores of the Southern Ocean; hence the prominent position of the name Parthians in the list of those present at Pentecost. Parthia was a power almost rivalling Rome—the only existing power which had tried its strength against Rome and not been worsted in the encounter. The Parthian dominion lasted for nearly five centuries, commencing in the third century before and terminating in the third century after our era. The Parthians spoke the Persian language.

The Greek Partridge.

Partridge (Heb. *kôrê*) occurs only 1 Sam. 26 : 20 and Jer. 17 : 11. The "hunting this bird upon the mountains," 1 Sam. 26 : 20, entirely agrees with the habits of two well-known species of partridge, viz. *Caccabis saxatilis*, the Greek partridge (which is the commonest partridge of the holy land), and *Ammoperdix heyii.* Our common partridge, *Perdix cinerea*, does not occur in Palestine. (The Greek partridge somewhat resembles our red-legged partridge in plumage, but is much larger. In every part of the hill country it abounds, and its ringing call-note in early morning echoes from cliff to cliff alike amid the barrenness of the hills of Judea and in the glens of the forest of Carmel.—*Tristram's Nat. Hist. of Bible.* The flesh of the partridge and the eggs are highly esteemed as food, and the search for the eggs at the proper time of the year is made a regular business.—ED.)

Par'uah (*flourishing*), the father of Jehoshaphat, Solomon's commissariat officer in Issachar. 1 Kings 4 : 17. (B.C. about 1017.)

Parva'im (*Oriental regions*), the name of an unknown place or country whence the gold was procured for the decoration of Solomon's temple. 2 Chron. 3 : 6. We may notice the conjecture that it is derived from the Sanscrit *púrva*, "eastern," and is a general term for the east.

Pa'sach (*cut off*), son of Japhlet, of the tribe of Asher. 1 Chron. 7 : 33.

Pas-dam'mim (*boundary of blood*). [EPHES-DAMMIM.]

Pase'ah (*lame*). 1. Son of Eshton, in an obscure fragment of the genealogies of Judah. 1 Chron. 4 : 12.

2. The "sons of Paseah" were among the Nethinim who returned with Zerubbabel. Ezra 2 : 49.

Pash'ur (*freedom*). 1. One of the families of priests of the chief house of Malchijah. 1 Chron. 9 : 12; 24 : 9; Neh. 11 : 12; Jer. 21 : 1; 38 : 1. In the time of Nehemiah this family appears to have become a chief house, and its head the head of a course. Ezra 2 : 38; Neh. 7 : 41; 10 : 3. The individual from whom the family was named was probably Pashur the son of Malchiah, who in the reign of Zedekiah was one of the chief princes of the court. Jer. 38 : 1. (B.C. 607.) He was sent, with others, by Zedekiah to Jeremiah at the time when Nebuchadnezzar was preparing his attack upon Jerusalem. Jer. 21. Again, somewhat later, Pashur joined with several other chief men in petitioning the king that Jeremiah might be put to death as a traitor. Jer. 38 : 4.

2. Another person of this name, also a priest, and "chief governor of the house of the Lord," is mentioned in Jer. 20 : 1. He is described as "the son of Immer," 1 Chron. 24 : 14, probably the same as Amariah. Neh. 10 : 3; 12 : 2, etc. In the reign of Jehoiakim he showed himself as hostile to Jeremiah as his namesake the son of Malchiah did afterward, and put him in the stocks by the gate of Benjamin. For this indignity to God's prophet Pashur was told by Jeremiah that his name was changed to Magor-missabib (*terror on every side*), and that he and all his house should be carried captives to Babylon and there die. Jer. 20 : 1-6. (B.C. 589.)

Passage. Used in the plural, Jer. 22 : 20, probably to denote the mountain region of Abarim, on the east side of Jordan. It also denotes a river ford or a mountain gorge or pass.

Pass'over, the first of the three great annual festivals of the Israelites, celebrated in the month Nisan (March–April), from the 14th to the 21st. (Strictly speaking the Passover only applied to the *paschal supper*, and the feast of unleavened bread followed, which was celebrated to the 21st.) (For the corresponding dates in our month, see *Jewish calendar* at the end of this volume.) The following are the principal passages in the Pentateuch relating to the Passover: Ex. 12 : 1-51; 13 : 3-10; 23 : 14-19; 34 : 18-26; Lev. 23 : 4-14; Num. 9 : 1-14; 28 : 16-25; Deut. 16 : 1-6.

Why instituted.—This feast was instituted by God to commemorate the deliverance of the Israelites from Egyptian bondage and the sparing of their first-born when the destroying angel smote the first-born of the Egyptians. The deliverance from Egypt was regarded as the starting-point of the Hebrew nation. The Israelites were then raised from the condition of bondmen under a foreign tyrant to that of a free people owing allegiance to no one but Jehovah. The prophet in a later age spoke of the event as *a creation* and *a redemption* of the nation. God declares himself to be "the Creator of Israel." The Exodus was thus looked upon as the birth of the nation; the Passover was its annual birthday feast. It was the yearly memorial of the dedication of the people to him who had saved their first-born from the destroyer, in order that they might be made holy to himself.

First celebration of the Passover.—On the tenth day of the month, the head of each family was to select from the flock either a lamb or a kid, a male of the first year, without blemish. If his family was too small to eat the whole of the lamb, he was permitted to invite his nearest neighbor to join the party. On the fourteenth day of the month he was to kill his lamb, while the sun was setting. He was then to take blood in a basin, and with a sprig of hyssop to sprinkle it on the two side-posts and the lintel of the door of the house. The lamb was then thoroughly roasted, whole. It was expressly forbidden that it should be boiled, or that a bone of it should be broken. Unleavened bread and bitter herbs were to be eaten with the flesh. No male who was uncircumcised was to join the company. Each one was to have his loins girt, to hold a staff in his hand, and to have shoes on his feet. He was to eat in haste, and it would seem that he was to stand during the meal. The number of the party was to be calculated as nearly as possible, so that all the flesh of the lamb might be eaten; but if any portion of it happened to remain, it was to be burned in the morning. No morsel of it was to be carried out of the house. The lambs were selected, on the fourteenth they were slain and the blood sprinkled, and in the following evening, after the fifteenth day of the month had commenced, the first paschal meal was eaten. At midnight the firstborn of the Egyptians were smitten. The king and his people were now urgent that the Israelites should start immediately, and readily bestowed on them supplies for the journey. In such haste did the Israelites depart, on that very day, Num. 33 : 3, that they packed up their kneading-troughs containing the dough prepared for the morrow's provisions, which was not yet leavened.

Observance of the Passover in later times.—As the original institution of the Passover in Egypt preceded the establishment of the priesthood and the regulation of the service of the tabernacle, it necessarily fell short in several particulars of the observance of the festival according to the fully-developed ceremonial law. The head of the family slew the lamb in his own house, not in the holy place; the blood was sprinkled on the doorway, not on the altar. But when the law was perfected, certain particulars were altered in order to assimilate the Passover to the accustomed order of religious service. In the twelfth and thirteenth chapters of Exodus there are not only distinct references to the observance of the festival in future ages (*e. g.* 12 : 2, 14, 17, 24–27, 42 ; 13 : 2, 5, 8–10), but there are several injunctions which were evidently not intended for the first Passover, and which indeed could not possibly have been observed. Besides the private family festival, there were public and national sacrifices offered each of the seven days of unleavened bread. Num. 28 : 19. On the second day also the first-fruits of the barley harvest were offered in the temple. Lev. 23 : 10. In the later notices of the festival in the books of the law there are particulars added which appear as modifications of the original institution. Lev. 23 : 10–14; Num. 28 : 16–25; Deut. 16 : 1–6. Hence it is not without reason that the Jewish writers have laid great stress on the distinction between "the Egyptian Passover" and "the perpetual Passover."

Mode and order of the paschal meal.—All work except that belonging to a few trades connected with daily life was suspended for some hours before the evening of the 14th Nisan. It was not lawful to eat any ordinary food after midday. No male was admitted to the table unless he was circumcised, even if he were of the seed of Israel. Ex. 12 : 48. It was customary for the number of a party to be not less than ten. When the meal was prepared, the family was placed round the table, the paterfamilias taking a place of honor, probably somewhat raised above the rest. When the party was arranged the first cup of wine was filled, and a blessing was asked by the head of the family on the feast, as well as a special one on the cup. The bitter herbs were then placed on the table, and a portion of them eaten, either with or without the sauce. The unleavened bread was handed round next, and afterward the lamb was placed on the table in front of the head of the family. The paschal lamb could be legally slain and the blood and fat offered only in the national sanctuary. Deut. 16 : 2. Before the lamb was eaten the second cup of wine was filled, and the son, in accordance with Ex. 12 : 26, asked his father the meaning of the feast. In reply, an account was given of the sufferings of the Israelites in Egypt and of their deliverance, with a particular explanation of Deut. 26 : 5, and the first part of the Hallel (a contraction from *Hallelujah*), Ps. 113, 114, was sung. This being gone through, the lamb was carved and eaten. The third cup of wine was poured out and drunk, and soon afterward the fourth. The second part of the Hallel, Ps. 115 to 118, was then sung. A fifth wine-cup appears to have been occasionally produced, but perhaps only in later times. What was termed the greater Hallel, Ps. 120 to 138, was sung on such occasions. The Israelites who lived in the country appear to have been accommodated at the feast by the inhabitants of Jerusalem in their houses, so far as there was room for them. Matt. 26 : 18; Luke 22 : 10–12. Those who could not be received into the city encamped without the walls in tents, as the pilgrims now do at Mecca.

The Passover as a type.—The Passover was not only commemorative but also typical. "The deliverance which it commemorated was a type of the great salvation it foretold." No other shadow of good things to come contained in the law can vie with the festival of the Passover in expressiveness and completeness. (1) The paschal lamb must of course be regarded as the leading feature in the ceremonial of the festival. The lamb slain typified Christ the "Lamb of God," slain for the sins of the world. Christ "our Passover is sacrificed for us." 1 Cor. 5 : 7. According to the divine purpose, the true Lamb of God was slain at nearly the same time as "the Lord's Passover," at the same season of the year, and at the same time of the day, as the daily sacrifice at the temple, the crucifixion beginning at the hour of the morning sacrifice and ending at the hour of the evening sacrifice. That the lamb was to be roasted and not boiled has been supposed to commemorate the haste of the departure of the Israelites. It is not difficult to determine the reason of the command, "not a bone of him shall be broken." The lamb was to be a symbol of unity—the unity of the family, the unity of the nation, the unity of God with his people whom he had taken into covenant with himself. (2) The unleavened bread ranks next in importance to the paschal lamb. We are warranted in concluding that unleavened bread had a peculiar sacrificial character, according to the law. It seems more reasonable to accept St. Paul's reference to the subject, 1 Cor. 5 : 6-8, as furnishing the true meaning of the symbol. Fermentation is decomposition, a dissolution of unity. The pure dry biscuit would be an apt emblem of unchanged duration, and, in its freedom from foreign mixture, of purity also. (3) The offering of the omer or first sheaf of the harvest, Lev. 23 : 10-14, signified deliverance from winter, the bondage of Egypt being well considered as a winter in the history of the nation. (4) The consecration of the first-fruits, the firstborn of the soil, is an easy type of the consecration of the first-born of the Israelites, and of our own best selves, to God. (Further than this (1) the Passover is a type of deliverance from the slavery of sin. (2) It is the passing over of the doom we deserve for our sins, because the blood of Christ has been applied to us by faith. (3) The sprinkling of the blood upon the door-posts was a symbol of open confession of our allegiance and love. (4) The Passover was useless unless eaten; so we live upon the Lord Jesus Christ. (5) It was eaten with bitter herbs, as we must eat our passover with the bitter herbs of repentance and confession, which yet, like the bitter herbs of the Passover, are a fitting and natural accompaniment. (6) As the Israelites ate the Passover all prepared for the journey, so do we with a readiness and desire to enter the active service of Christ, and to go on the journey toward heaven.—ED.)

Pat′ara (*city of Patarus*), a Lycian city situated on the southwestern shore of Lycia, not far from the left bank of the river Xanthus. The coast here is very mountainous and bold. Immediately opposite is the island of Rhodes. Patara was practically the seaport of the city of Xanthus, which was ten miles distant. These notices of its position and maritime importance introduce us to the single mention of the place in the Bible—Acts 21 : 1, 2.

Path′ros (*region of the south*), a part of Egypt, and a Mizraite tribe whose people were called Pathrusim. In the list of the Mizraites the Pathrusim occur after the Naphtuhim and before the Casluhim; the latter being followed by the notice of the Philistines and by the Caphtorim. Gen. 10 : 13, 14; 1 Chron. 1 : 12. Pathros is mentioned in the prophecies of Isaiah, Isa. 11 : 11, Jeremiah, Jer. 44 : 1, 15, and Ezekiel. Ezek. 29 : 14; 30 : 13-18. It was probably part or all of upper Egypt, and we may trace its name in the Pathyrite nome, in which Thebes was situated.

Pathru′sim, people of Pathros. [PATHROS.]

Pat′mos, Rev. 1 : 9, a rugged and bare island in the Ægean Sea, 20 miles south of Samos and 24 west of Asia Minor. It was the scene of the banishment of St. John in the reign of Domitian, A.D. 95. Patmos is divided into two nearly equal parts, a northern and a southern, by a very narrow isthmus, where, on the east side, are the harbor and the town. On the hill to the south, crowning a commanding height, is the celebrated monastery which bears the name of "John the Divine." Halfway up the ascent is the cave or grotto where tradition says that St. John received the Revelation.

Patriarch (*father of a tribe*), the name given to the head of a family or tribe in Old Testament times. In common usage the title of patriarch is assigned especially to those whose lives are recorded in Scripture previous to the time of Moses, as Adam, Abraham, Isaac and Jacob. ("In the early history of the Hebrews we find the ancestor or father of a family retaining authority over his children and his children's children so long as he lived, whatever new connections they might form. When the father died the branch families did not break off and form new communities, but usually united under another common head. The eldest son was generally invested with this dignity. His author-

Isle of Patmos.

ity was paternal. He was honored as the central point of connection, and as the representative of the whole kindred. Thus each great family had its patriarch or head, and each tribe its prince, selected from the several heads of the families which it embraced."—*McClintock and Strong.*) ("After the destruction of Jerusalem, patriarch was the title of the chief religious rulers of the Jews in Asia; and in early Christian times it became the designation of the bishops of Rome, Constantinople, Alexandria, Antioch and Jerusalem."—*American Cyclopedia.*)

Pat'robas (*paternal*), a Christian at Rome to whom St. Paul sends his salutation. Rom. 16 : 14. Like many other names mentioned in Rom. 16, this was borne by at least one member of the emperor's household. Suet. *Galba.* 20; Martial, *Ep.* ii. 32, 3. (A.D. 55.)

Pau (*bleating*) (but in 1 Chron. 1 : 50, PAI), the capital of Hadar king of Edom. Gen. 36 : 39. Its position is unknown.

Paul (*small, little*). Nearly all the original materials for the life of St. Paul are contained in the Acts of the Apostles and in the Pauline epistles. Paul was born in Tarsus, a city of Cilicia. (It is not improbable that he was born between A.D. 0 and A.D. 5.) Up to the time of his going forth as an avowed preacher of Christ *to the Gentiles*, the apostle was known by the name of Saul. This was the Jewish name which he received from his Jewish parents. But though a Hebrew of the Hebrews, he was born in a Gentile city. Of his parents we know nothing, except that his father was of the tribe of Benjamin, Philip. 3 : 5, and a Pharisee, Acts 23 : 6; that Paul had acquired by some means the Roman franchise ("I was free born," Acts 22 : 28), and that he was settled in Tarsus. At Tarsus he must have learned to use the Greek language with freedom and mastery in both speaking and writing. At Tarsus also he learned that trade of "tent-maker," Acts 18 : 3, at which he afterward occasionally wrought with his own hands. There was a goat's-hair cloth called *cilicium* manufactured in Cilicia, and largely used for tents. Saul's trade was probably that of making tents of this hair cloth. When St. Paul makes his defence before his countrymen at

Jerusalem, Acts 22, he tells them that, though born in Tarsus, he had been "brought up" in Jerusalem. He must, therefore, have been yet a boy when he was removed, in all probability for the sake of his education, to the holy city of his fathers. He learned, he says, "at the feet of Gamaliel." He who was to resist so stoutly the usurpations of the law had for his teacher one of the most eminent of all the doctors of the law. Saul was yet "a young man," Acts 7 : 58, when the Church experienced that sudden expansion which was connected with the ordaining of the seven appointed to serve tables, and with the special power and inspiration of Stephen. Among those who disputed with Stephen were some "of them of Cilicia." We naturally think of Saul as having been one of these, when we find him afterward keeping the clothes of those suborned witnesses who, according to the law, Deut. 17: 7, were the first to cast stones at Stephen. "Saul," says the sacred writer, significantly, "was consenting unto his death."

Saul's conversion. A.D. 37.—The persecutor was to be converted. Having undertaken to follow up the believers "unto strange cities," Saul naturally turned his thoughts to Damascus. What befell him as he journeyed thither is related in detail three times in the Acts, first by the historian in his own person, then in the two addresses made by St. Paul at Jerusalem and before Agrippa. St. Luke's statement is to be read in Acts 9 : 3-19, where, however, the words "it is hard for thee to kick against the pricks," included in the English version, ought to be omitted (as is done in the Revised Version). The sudden light from heaven; the voice of Jesus speaking with authority to his persecutor; Saul struck to the ground, blinded, overcome; the three-days suspense; the coming of Ananias as a messenger of the Lord, and Saul's baptism,—these were the leading features of the great event, and in these we must look for the chief significance of the conversion. It was in Damascus that he was received into the church by Ananias, and here, to the astonishment of all his hearers, he proclaimed Jesus in the synagogues, declaring him to be the Son of God. The narrative in the Acts tells us simply that he was occupied in this work, with increasing vigor, for "many days," up to the time when imminent danger drove him from Damas-

cus. From the Epistle to the Galatians, Gal. 1 : 17, 18, we learn that the many days were at least a good part of "three years," A.D. 37-40, and that Saul, not thinking it necessary to procure authority to preach from the apostles that were before him, went after his conversion into Arabia, and returned from thence to Damascus. We know nothing whatever of this visit to Arabia; but upon his departure from Damascus we are again upon historical ground, and have the double evidence of St. Luke in the Acts and of the apostle in his Second Epistle to the Corinthians. According to the former, the *Jews* lay in wait for Saul, intending to kill him, and watched the gates of the city that he might not escape from them. Knowing this, the disciples took him by night and let him down in a basket from the wall. Having escaped from Damascus, Saul betook himself to Jerusalem (A.D. 40), and there "assayed to join himself to the disciples; but they were all afraid of him, and believed not that he was a disciple." Barnabas' introduction removed the fears of the apostles, and Saul "was with them coming in and going out at Jerusalem." But it is not strange that the former persecutor was soon singled out from the other believers as the object of a murderous hostility. He was, therefore, again urged to flee; and by way of Cæsarea betook himself to his native city, Tarsus. Barnabas was sent on a special mission to Antioch. As the work grew under his hands, he felt the need of help, went himself to Tarsus to seek Saul, and succeeded in bringing him to Antioch. There they labored together unremittingly for "a whole year." All this time Saul was subordinate to Barnabas. Antioch was in constant communication with Cilicia, with Cyprus, with all the neighboring countries. The Church was pregnant with a great movement, and the time of her delivery was at hand. Something of direct expectation seems to be implied in what is said of the leaders of the Church at Antioch, that they were "ministering to the Lord, and fasting," when the Holy Ghost spoke to them : "Separate me Barnabas and Saul for the work whereunto I have called them." Everything was done with orderly gravity in the sending forth of the two missionaries. Their brethren, after fasting and prayer, laid their hands on them, and so they departed.

The first missionary journey. A.D. 45–49. — As soon as Barnabas and Saul reached Cyprus, they began to "announce the word of God," but at first they delivered their message in the synagogues of the Jews only. When they had gone through the island, from Salamis to Paphos, they were called upon to explain their doctrine to an eminent Gentile, Sergius Paulus, the proconsul, who was converted. Saul's name was now changed to Paul, and he began to

Traditional Portraits of Peter and Paul.

These portraits are copied, same size as the original, from the bottom of a gilded glass cup found in the catacombs of St. Sebastian at Rome. The earliest interments by the Christians in the Roman catacombs included, besides Christian symbols, some objects of pagan regard. This having been the case in the section in which the glass cup bearing the group of the Saviour, Paul and Peter was discovered, it seems conclusive that the age was probably the fourth, if not the third, century. The absence of the nimbus (glory or circle) about the heads of Peter and Paul, and its presence around the Saviour's, may indicate the third century or early in the fourth; for the nimbus was generally used around the heads of all saints and divine persons in the latter half of the fourth century. Tertullian speaks of glass cups as used in sacramental services, as also does Eusebius. In this picture the Saviour is represented as presenting a crown of life to the apostles; the inscription is a prayer of the friends of the dead, who was laid in the tomb in the faith of Christ, and may be paraphrased, "Friendship's blessing; may you live forever with thy (Saviour)."

take precedence of Barnabas. From Paphos "Paul and his company" set sail for the mainland, and arrived at Perga in Pamphylia. Here the heart of their companion John failed him, and he returned to Jerusalem. From Perga they travelled on to a place obscure in secular history, but most memorable in the history of the kingdom of Christ—Antioch in Pisidia. Rejected by the Jews, they became bold and outspoken, and turned from them to the Gentiles. At Antioch now, as in every city afterward, the unbelieving Jews used their influence with their own adherents among the Gentiles to persuade the authorities or the populace to persecute the apostles and to drive them from the place. Paul and Barnabas now travelled on to Iconium, where the occurrences at Antioch were repeated, and from thence to the Lyca-onian country which contained the cit-ies Lystra and Derbe. Here they had to deal with uncivilized heathen. At Lys-tra the healing of a cripple took place. Thereupon these pagans took the apostles for gods, calling Barnabas, who was of the more imposing presence, Jupiter, and Paul, who was the chief speaker, Mer-curius. Although the people of Lystra had been so ready to worship Paul and Barnabas, the repulse of their idolatrous instincts appears to have provoked them, and they allowed themselves to be per-suaded into hostility by Jews who came from Antioch and Iconium, so that they attacked Paul with stones, and thought they had killed him. He recovered, however, as the disciples were standing around him, and went again into the city. The next day he left it with Bar-nabas, and went to Derbe, and thence they returned once more to Lystra, and so to Iconium and Antioch. In order to establish the churches after their depart-ure they solemnly appointed "elders" in every city. Then they came down to the coast, and from Attalia they sailed home to Antioch in Syria, where they related the successes which had been granted to them, and especially the "opening of the door of faith to the Gentiles." And so the first missionary journey ended.

The council at Jerusalem.—Upon that missionary journey follows most natu-rally the next important scene which the historian sets before us—the council held at Jerusalem to determine the relations of Gentile believers to the law of Moses. Acts 15 : 1–29; Gal. 2.

Second missionary journey. A.D. 50–54. —The most resolute courage, indeed, was required for the work to which St. Paul was now publicly pledged. He would not associate with himself in that work one who had already shown a want of constancy. This was the occasion of what must have been a most painful dif-ference between him and his comrade in the faith and in past perils, Barnabas. Acts 15 : 35–40. Silas, or Silvanus, be-comes now a chief companion of the apostle. The two went together through Syria and Cilicia, visiting the churches, and so came to Derbe and Lystra. Here they find Timotheus, who had become a disciple on the former visit of the apostle. Him St. Paul took and circumcised. St. Luke now steps rapidly over a consider-

able space of the apostle's life and labors. "They went throughout Phrygia and the region of Galatia." Acts 16 : 6. At this time St. Paul was founding "the churches of Galatia." Gal. 1 : 2. He himself gives some hints of the circumstances of his preaching in that region, of the recep-tion he met with, and of the ardent though unstable character of the people. Gal. 4 : 13–15. Having gone through Phrygia and Galatia, he intended to visit the western coast; but "they were for-bidden by the Holy Ghost to preach the word" there. Then, being on the bor-ders of Mysia, they thought of going back to the northeast into Bithynia; but again the Spirit *of Jesus* "suffered them not," so they passed by Mysia and came down to Troas. St. Paul saw in a vision a man of Macedonia, who besought him, saying, "Come over into Macedonia and help us." The vision was at once accepted as a heavenly intimation; the help wanted by the Macedonians was believed to be the preaching of the gospel. It is at this point that the historian, speaking of St. Paul's company, substitutes "we" for "they." He says nothing of himself; we can only infer that St. Luke, to what-ever country he belonged, became a com-panion of St. Paul at Troas. The party, thus reinforced, immediately set sail from Troas, touched at Samothrace, then landed on the continent at Neapolis, and thence journeyed to Philippi. The first convert in Macedonia was Lydia, an Asi-atic woman, at Philippi. Acts 16 : 13, 14. At Philippi Paul and Silas were arrested, beaten and put in prison, having cast out the spirit of divination from a female slave who had brought her masters much gain by her power. This cruel wrong was to be the occasion of a signal ap-pearance of the God of righteousness and deliverance. The narrative tells of the earthquake, the jailer's terror, his con-version and baptism. Acts 16 : 26–34. In the morning the magistrates sent word to the prison that the men might be let go; but Paul denounced plainly their unlawful acts, informing them moreover that those whom they had beaten and imprisoned without trial were Roman citizens. The magistrates, in great alarm, saw the necessity of hum-bling themselves. They came and begged them to leave the city. Paul and Silas consented to do so, and, after paying a visit to "the brethren" in the house of Lydia, they departed. Leaving St. Luke, and perhaps Timothy for a short time, at Philippi, Paul and Silas travelled through Amphipolis and Apollonia, and stopped again at Thessalonica. Here again, as in Pisidian Antioch, the envy of the Jews was excited, and the mob assaulted the house of Jason, with whom Paul and Silas were staying as guests, and, not finding them, dragged Jason himself and some other brethren before the magistrates. After these signs of danger the brethren immediately sent away Paul and Silas by night. They next came to Berea. Here they found the Jews more noble than those at Thessalonica had been. Accordingly they gained many converts, both Jews and Greeks; but the Jews of Thessalonica, hearing of it, sent emissaries to stir up the people, and it was thought best that Paul should himself leave the city, whilst Silas and Timothy remained behind. Some of the brethren went with St. Paul as far as Athens, where they left him, carrying back a request to Silas and Timothy that they would speedily join him. Here the apostle delivered that wonderful discourse reported in Acts 17 : 22–31. He gained but few converts at Athens, and soon took his departure and went to Corinth. He was testifying with unusual effort and anxiety, when Silas and Timothy came from Macedonia and joined him. Their arrival was the occasion of the writing of the First Epistle to the Thessalonians. The two epistles to the Thessalonians—and these alone—belong to the present missionary journey. They were written from Corinth A.D. 52, 53. When Silas and Timotheus came to Corinth, St. Paul was testifying to the Jews with great earnestness, but with little success. Corinth was the chief city of the province of Achaia, and the residence of the proconsul. During St. Paul's stay the proconsular office was held by Gallio, a brother of the philosopher Seneca. Before him the apostle was summoned by his Jewish enemies, who hoped to bring the Roman authority to bear upon him as an innovator in religion. But Gallio perceived at once, before Paul could "open his mouth" to defend himself, that the movement was due to Jewish prejudice, and refused to go into the question. Then a singular scene occurred. The Corinthian spectators, either favoring Paul or actuated only by anger against the Jews, seized on the principal person of those who had

brought the charge, and beat him before the judgment-seat. Gallio left these religious quarrels to settle themselves. The apostle, therefore, was not allowed to be "hurt," and remained some time longer at Corinth unmolested. Having been the instrument of accomplishing this work, Paul departed for Jerusalem, wishing to attend a festival there. Before leaving Greece, he cut off his hair at Cenchreæ, in fulfillment of a vow. Acts 18 : 18. Paul paid a visit to the synagogue at Ephesus, but would not stay. Leaving Ephesus, he sailed to Cæsarea, and from thence went up to Jerusalem, spring, A.D. 54, and "saluted the church." It is argued, from considerations founded on the suspension of navigation during the winter months, that the festival was probably the Pentecost. From Jerusalem the apostle went almost immediately down to Antioch, thus returning to the same place from which he had started with Silas.

Third missionary journey, including the stay at Ephesus. A.D. 54–58. Acts 18 : 23–21 : 17.—The great epistles which belong to this period, those to the Galatians, Corinthians and Romans, show how the "Judaizing" question exercised at this time the apostle's mind. St. Paul "spent some time" at Antioch, and during this stay, as we are inclined to believe, his collision with St. Peter, Gal. 2 : 11–14, took place. When he left Antioch, he "went over all the country of Galatia and Phrygia in order, strengthening all the disciples," and giving orders concerning the collection for the saints. 1 Cor. 16 : 1. It is probable that the Epistle to the Galatians was written soon after this visit—A.D. 56–57. This letter was in all probability sent from Ephesus. This was the goal of the apostle's journeyings through Asia Minor. He came down to Ephesus from the upper districts of Phrygia. Here he entered upon his usual work. He went into the synagogue, and for three months he spoke openly, disputing and persuading concerning "the kingdom of God." At the end of this time the obstinacy and opposition of some of the Jews led him to give up frequenting the synagogue, and he established the believers as a separate society, meeting "in the school of Tyrannus." This continued for two years. During this time many things occurred of which the historian of the Acts chooses two examples, the triumph over magical arts and the great disturbance raised by the silver-smiths who made shrines for Diana—among which we are to note further the writing of the First Epistle to the Corinthians, A.D. 57. Before leaving Ephesus Paul went into Macedonia, where he met Titus, who brought him news of the state of the Corinthian church. Thereupon he wrote the Second Epistle to the Corinthians, A.D. 57, and sent it by the hands of Titus and two other brethren to Corinth. After writing this epistle, St. Paul travelled through Macedonia, perhaps to the borders of Illyricum, Rom. 15 : 19, and then went to Corinth. The narrative in the Acts tells us that " when he had gone over those parts (Macedonia), and had given them much exhortation, he came into Greece, and there abode three months." ch. 20 : 2, 3. There is only one incident which we can connect with this visit to Greece, but that is a very important one—the writing of his Epistle to the Romans, A.D. 58. That this was written at this time from Corinth appears from passages in the epistle itself, and has never been doubted. The letter is a substitute for the personal visit which he had longed "for many years" to pay. Before his departure from Corinth, St. Paul was joined again by St. Luke, as we infer from the change in the narrative from the third to the first person. He was bent on making a journey to Jerusalem, for a special purpose and within a limited time. With this view he was intending to go by sea to Syria. But he was made aware of some plot of the Jews for his destruction, to be carried out through this voyage; and he determined to evade their malice by changing his route. Several brethren were associated with him in this expedition, the bearers, no doubt, of the collections made in all the churches for the poor at Jerusalem. These were sent on by sea, and probably the money with them, to Troas, where they were to await Paul. He, accompanied by Luke, went northward through Macedonia. Whilst the vessel which conveyed the rest of the party sailed from Troas to Assos, Paul gained some time by making the journey by land. At Assos he went on board again. Coasting along by Mitylene, Chios, Samos and Trogyllium, they arrived at Miletus. At Miletus, however, there was time to send to Ephesus, and the elders of the church were invited to come down to him there. This meeting is made the occasion for re-cording another characteristic and repre-sentative address of St. Paul. Acts 20 : 18-35. The course of the voyage from Miletus was by Coos and Rhodes to Patara, and from Patara in another vessel past Cyprus to Tyre. Here Paul and his company spent seven days. From Tyre they sailed to Ptolemais, where they spent one day, and from Ptolemais proceeded, apparently by land, to Cæsarea. They now "tarried many days" at Cæsarea. During this interval the prophet Agabus, Acts 11 : 28, came down from Jerusalem, and crowned the previous intimations of danger with a prediction expressively delivered. At this stage a final effort was made to dissuade Paul from going up to Jerusalem, by the Christians of Cæsarea and by his travelling companions. After a while they went up to Jerusalem and were gladly received by the brethren. This is St. Paul's fifth and last visit to Jerusalem.

St. Paul's imprisonment: Jerusalem. Spring, A.D. 58.—He who was thus conducted into Jerusalem by a company of anxious friends had become by this time a man of considerable fame among his countrymen. He was widely known as one who had taught with pre-eminent boldness that a way into God's favor was opened to the Gentiles, and that this way did not lie through the door of the Jewish law. He had thus roused against himself the bitter enmity of that unfathomable Jewish pride which was almost as strong in some of those who had professed the faith of Jesus as in their unconverted brethren. He was now approaching a crisis in the long struggle, and the shadow of it has been made to rest upon his mind throughout his journey to Jerusalem. He came " ready to die for the name of the Lord Jesus," but he came expressly to prove himself a faithful Jew, and this purpose is shown at every point of the history. Certain Jews from " Asia," who had come up for the pentecostal feast, and who had a personal knowledge of Paul, saw him in the temple. They set upon him at once, and stirred up the people against him. There was instantly a great commotion; Paul was dragged out of the temple, the doors of which were immediately shut, and the people, having him in their hands, were proposing to kill him. Paul was rescued from the violence of the multitude by the Roman officer, who made him his own prisoner, causing him to be chained to two soldiers, and then proceeded to inquire who he was and what he had done. The inquiry only elicited confused outcries, and the "chief captain" seems to have imagined that the apostle might perhaps be a certain Egyptian pretender who had recently stirred up a considerable rising of the people. The account in the Acts, ch. 21 : 34–40, tells us with graphic touches how St. Paul obtained leave and opportunity to address the people in a discourse which is related at length. Until the hated word of a mission to the Gentiles had been spoken, the Jews had listened to the speaker. "Away with such a fellow from the earth," the multitude now shouted; " it is not fit that he should live." The Roman commander, seeing the tumult that arose, might well conclude that St. Paul had committed some heinous offence; and carrying him off, he gave orders that he should be forced by scourging to confess his crime. Again the apostle took advantage of his Roman citizenship to protect himself from such an outrage. The chief captain set him free from bonds, but on the next day called together the chief priests and the Sanhedrin, and brought Paul as a prisoner before them. On the next day a conspiracy was formed, which the historian relates with a singular fullness of detail. More than forty of the Jews bound themselves under a curse neither to eat nor drink until they had killed Paul. The plot was discovered, and St. Paul was hurried away from Jerusalem. The chief captain, Claudius Lysias, determined to send him to Cæsarea to Felix, the governor or procurator of Judea. He therefore put him in charge of a strong guard of soldiers, who took him by night as far as Antipatris. From thence a smaller detachment conveyed him to Cæsarea, where they delivered up their prisoner into the hands of the governor.

Imprisonment at Cæsarea. A.D. 58–60. —St. Paul was henceforth, to the end of the period embraced in the Acts, if not to the end of his life, in Roman custody. This custody was in fact a protection to him, without which he would have fallen a victim to the animosity of the Jews. He seems to have been treated throughout with humanity and consideration. The governor before whom he was now to be tried, according to Tacitus and Josephus, was a mean and dissolute tyrant. After hearing St. Paul's accusers and the

apostle's defence, Felix made an excuse for putting off the matter, and gave orders that the prisoner should be treated with indulgence, and that his friends should be allowed free access to him. After a while he heard him again. St. Paul remained in custody until Felix left the province. The unprincipled governor had good reason to seek to ingratiate himself with the Jews; and to please them, he handed over Paul, as an untried prisoner, to his successor, Festus. Upon his arrival in the province, Festus went up without delay from Cæsarea to Jerusalem, and the leading Jews seized the opportunity of asking that Paul might be brought up there for trial, intending to assassinate him by the way. But Festus would not comply with their request. He invited them to follow him on his speedy return to Cæsarea, and a trial took place there, closely resembling that before Felix. " They had certain questions against him," Festus says to Agrippa, " of their own superstition (or religion), and of one Jesus, who was dead, whom Paul affirmed to be alive. And being puzzled for my part as to such inquiries, I asked him whether he would go to Jerusalem to be tried there." This proposal, not a very likely one to be accepted, was the occasion of St. Paul's appeal to Cæsar. The appeal having been allowed, Festus reflected that he must send with the prisoner a report of " the crimes laid against him." He therefore took advantage of an opportunity which offered itself in a few days to seek some help in the matter. The Jewish prince Agrippa arrived with his sister Berenice on a visit to the new governor. To him Festus communicated his perplexity. Agrippa expressed a desire to hear Paul himself. Accordingly Paul conducted his defence before the king; and when it was concluded Festus and Agrippa, and their companions, consulted together, and came to the conclusion that the accused was guilty of nothing that deserved death or imprisonment. And Agrippa's final answer to the inquiry of Festus was, " This man might have been set at liberty, if he had not appealed unto Cæsar."

The voyage to Rome and shipwreck. Autumn, A.D. 60.—No formal trial of St. Paul had yet taken place. After a while arrangements were made to carry " Paul and certain other prisoners," in the custody of a centurion named Julius, into Italy; and amongst the company, whether by favor or from any other reason, we find the historian of the Acts, who in chapters 27 and 28 gives a graphic description of the voyage to Rome and the shipwreck on the island of Melita or Malta. After a three-months stay in Malta the soldiers and their prisoners left in an Alexandria ship for Italy. They touched at Syracuse, where they stayed three days, and at Rhegium, from which place they were carried with a fair wind to Puteoli, where they left their ship and the sea. At Puteoli they found " brethren," for it was an important place, and especially a chief port for the traffic between Alexandria and Rome; and by these brethren they were exhorted to stay a while with them. Permission seems to have been granted by the centurion; and whilst they were spending seven days at Puteoli news of the apostle's arrival was sent to Rome. (Spring, A.D. 61.)

First imprisonment of St. Paul at Rome. A.D. 61-63.—On their arrival at Rome the centurion delivered up his prisoners into the proper custody, that of the prætorian prefect. Paul was at once treated with special consideration, and was allowed to dwell by himself with the soldier who guarded him. He was now therefore free " to preach the gospel to them that were at Rome also;" and proceeded without delay to act upon his rule—" to the Jews first." But as of old, the reception of his message by the Jews was not favorable. He turned, therefore, again to the Gentiles, and for two years he dwelt in his own hired house. These are the last words of the Acts. But St. Paul's career is not abruptly closed. Before he himself fades out of our sight in the twilight of ecclesiastical tradition, we have letters written by himself which contribute some particulars to his biography. *Period of the later epistles.*—To that imprisonment to which St. Luke has introduced us—the imprisonment which lasted for such a tedious time, though tempered by much indulgence—belongs the noble group of letters to Philemon, to the Colossians, to the Ephesians and to the Philippians. The three former of these were written at one time, and sent by the same messengers. Whether that to the Philippians was written before or after these we cannot determine; but the tone of it seems to imply that a crisis was approaching, and therefore it is commonly regarded as the latest of the four. In this epistle St.

Paul twice expresses a confident hope that before long he may be able to visit the Philippians in person. Philip. 1: 25; 2:24. Whether this hope was fulfilled or not has been the occasion of much controversy. According to the general opinion the apostle was liberated from imprisonment at the end of two years, having been acquitted by Nero A.D. 63, and left Rome soon after writing the letter to the Philippians. He spent some time in visits to Greece, Asia Minor and Spain, and during the latter part of this time wrote the letters (first epistles) to Timothy and Titus from Macedonia, A.D. 65. After these were written he was apprehended again and sent to Rome.

Second imprisonment at Rome. A.D. 65-67.—The apostle appears now to have been treated not as an honorable state prisoner, but as a felon, 2 Tim. 2:9; but he was allowed to write the second letter to Timothy, A.D. 67. For what remains we have the concurrent testimony of ecclesiastical antiquity that he was beheaded at Rome, by Nero, in the great persecutions of the Christians by that emperor, A.D. 67 or 68.

Pavement. [GABBATHA.]

Pavilion, a temporary movable tent or habitation. 1. *Sôc,* properly an enclosed place, also rendered " tabernacle," " covert" and " den;" once only " pavilion." Ps. 27:5. (Among the Egyptians pavilions were built in a similar style to houses, though on a smaller scale, in various parts of the country, and in the foreign districts through which the Egyptian armies passed, for the use of the king.—*Wilkinson.*) 2. *Succâh,* usually " tabernacle" and " booth." 3. *Shaphrûr* and *shaphrîr,* a word used once only, in Jer. 43:10, to signify glory or splendor, and hence probably to be understood of the splendid covering of the royal throne.

Peacocks (Heb. *tucciyyim*). Among the natural products which Solomon's fleet brought home to Jerusalem, mention is made of " peacocks," 1 Kings 10:22; 2 Chron. 9:21, which is probably the correct translation. The Hebrew word may be traced to the Tamul or Malabaric *togei,* " peacock."

Pearl (Heb. *gâbîsh*). The Hebrew word in Job 28:18 probably means " crystal." Pearls, however, are frequently mentioned in the New Testament, Matt. 13:45; 1 Tim. 2:9; Rev. 17:4; 21:21, and were considered by the

The Peacock.

ancients among the most precious of gems, and were highly esteemed as ornaments. The kingdom of heaven is compared to a "pearl of great price." In Matt. 7 : 6 pearls are used metaphorically for anything of value, or perhaps more especially for "wise sayings." (The finest specimens of the pearl are yielded by the pearl oyster (*Avicula margariti-*

Pearl Oyster.

fera), still found in abundance in the Persian Gulf and near the coasts of Ceylon, Java and Sumatra. The oysters grow in clusters on rocks in deep water, and the pearl is found inside the shell, and is the result of a diseased secretion

caused by the introduction of foreign bodies, as sand, etc., between the mantle and the shell. They are obtained by divers trained to the business. March or April is the time for pearl fishing. A single shell sometimes yields eight to twelve pearls. The size of a good Oriental pearl varies from that of a pea to about three times that size. A handsome necklace of pearls the size of peas is worth $15,000. Pearls have been valued as high as $200,000 or $300,000 apiece. —ED.)

Ped′ahel (*whom God redeems*), the son of Ammihud, and prince of the tribe of Naphtali. Num. 34 : 28.

Pedah′zur (*whom the rock* (*i. e.* God) *redeems*), father of Gamaliel, the chief of the tribe of Manasseh at the time of the exodus. Num. 1 : 10; 2 : 20; 7 : 54, 59; 10 : 23. (B.C. 1491.)

Peda′iah (*whom Jehovah redeems*). 1. The father of Zebudah, mother of King Jehoiakim. 2 Kings 23 : 36. (B.C. before 648.)

2. The brother of Salathiel or Shealtiel, and father of Zerubbabel, who is usually called the "son of Shealtiel," being, as Lord A. Hervey conjectures, in reality his uncle's successor and heir, in consequence of the failure of issue in the direct line. 1 Chron. 3 : 17–19. (B.C. before 536.)

3. Son of Parosh, that is, one of the family of that name, who assisted Nehemiah in repairing the walls of Jerusalem. Neh. 3 : 25. (B.C. about 446.)

4. Apparently a priest; one of those who stood on the left hand of Ezra when he read the law to the people. Neh. 8 : 4. (B.C. 445.)

5. A Benjamite, ancestor of Sallu. Neh. 11 : 7.

6. A Levite in the time of Nehemiah, Neh. 13 : 13; apparently the same as 4.

7. The father of Joel, prince of the half tribe of Manasseh in the reign of David. 1 Chron. 27 : 20. (B.C. before 1013.)

Pe′kah (*open-eyed*), son of Remaliah, originally a captain of Pekahiah king of Israel, murdered his master, seized the throne, and became the 18th sovereign of the northern kingdom, B.C. 757–740. Under his predecessors Israel had been much weakened through the payment of enormous tribute to the Assyrians (see especially 2 Kings 15 : 20), and by internal wars and conspiracies.

Pekah seems to have steadily applied himself to the restoration of its power. For this purpose he contracted a foreign alliance, and fixed his mind on the plunder of the sister kingdom of Judah. He must have made the treaty by which he proposed to share its spoil with Rezin king of Damascus, when Jotham was still on the throne of Jerusalem, 2 Kings 15 : 37; but its execution was long delayed, probably in consequence of that prince's righteous and vigorous administration. 2 Chron. 27. When, however, his weak son Ahaz succeeded to the crown of David, the allies no longer hesitated, but entered upon the siege of Jerusalem, B.C. 742. The history of the war is found in 2 Kings 16 and 2 Chron. 28. It is famous as the occasion of the great prophecies in Isa. 7–9. Its chief result was the Jewish port of Elath on the Red Sea; but the unnatural alliance of Damascus and Samaria was punished through the complete overthrow of the ferocious confederates by Tiglath-pileser. The kingdom of Damascus was finally suppressed and Rezin put to death, while Pekah was deprived of at least half his kingdom, including all the northern portion and the whole district to the east of Jordan. Pekah himself, now fallen into the position of an Assyrian vassal, was of course compelled to abstain from further attacks on Judah. Whether his continued tyranny exhausted the patience of his subjects, or whether his weakness emboldened them to attack him, is not known; but, from one or the other cause, Hoshea the son of Elah conspired against him and put him to death.

Pekahi'ah (*whose eyes Jehovah opened*), son and successor of Menahem, was the 17th king of the separate kingdom of Israel, B.C. 759–757. After a brief reign of scarcely two years a conspiracy was organized against him by Pekah, who murdered him and seized the throne.

Pe'kod (*visitation*), an appellative applied to the Chaldeans. Jer. 50 : 21; Ezek. 23 : 23. Authorities are undecided as to the meaning of the term.

Pela'iah (*distinguished by Jehovah*). 1. A son of Elioenai, of the royal line of Judah. 1 Chron. 3 : 24. (B.C. after 400.) 2. One of the Levites who assisted Ezra in expounding the law. Neh. 8 : 7. He afterward sealed the covenant with Nehemiah. Neh. 10 : 10. (B.C. 445.)

Pelali'ah (*judged by Jehovah*), the son of Amzi and ancestor of Adaiah. Neh. 11 : 12.

Pelati'ah (*delivered by Jehovah*). 1. Son of Hananiah the son of Zerubbabel 1 Chron. 3 : 21. (B.C. after 536.) 2. One of the captains of the marauding band of Simeonites who in the reign of Hezekiah made an expedition to Mount Seir and smote the Amalekites. 1 Chron. 4 : 42. (B.C. about 700.) 3. One of the heads of the people, and probably the name of a family who sealed the covenant with Nehemiah. Neh. 10 : 22. (B.C. about 440.) 4. The son of Benaiah, and one of the princes of the people against whom Ezekiel was directed to utter the words of doom recorded in Ezek. 11 : 5–12. (B.C. about 592.)

Pe'leg (*division, part*), son of Eber and brother of Joktan. Gen. 10 : 25; 11 : 16. The only incident connected with his history is the statement that "in his days was the earth divided," an event embodied in the meaning of his name— "division." The reference is to a division of the family of Eber himself, the younger branch of which (the Joktanids) migrated into southern Arabia, while the elder remained in Mesopotamia.

Pe'let (*liberation*). 1. A son of Jahdai in an obscure genealogy. 1 Chron. 2 : 47. 2. The son of Azmaveth, that is, either a native of the place of that name or the son of one of David's heroes. 1 Chron. 12 : 3. (B.C. about 1015.)

Pe'leth (*swiftness*). 1. The father of On the Reubenite, who joined Dathan and Abiram in their rebellion. Num. 16 : 1. (B.C. 1490.) 2. Son of Jonathan, and a descendant of Jerahmeel. 1 Chron. 2 : 33.

Pe'lethites (*couriers*). [CHERETHITES.]

Pelican (Heb. *kâath*, sometimes translated "cormorant," as Isa. 34 : 11; Zeph. 2 : 14, though in the margin correctly rendered "pelican"), a voracious waterbird, found most abundantly in tropical regions. It is equal to the swan in size. (It has a flat bill, fifteen inches long, and the female has under the bill a pouch, capable of great distension. It is capacious enough to hold fish sufficient for the dinner of half a dozen men. The young are fed from this pouch, which is emptied of the food by pressing the pouch against the breast. The pelican's bill has a crimson tip, and the contrast of this red tip against the white breast probably gave rise to the tradition that the bird tore her own breast to feed her young with her blood. The flesh of the

The Pelican.

pelican was forbidden to the Jews. Lev. 11 : 18.—Ed.) The psalmist, in comparing his pitiable condition to the pelican, Ps. 102 : 6, probably has reference to its general aspect as it sits in apparent melancholy mood, with its bill resting on its breast.

Pel'onite, The. Two of David's mighty men, Helez and Ahijah, are called Pelonites. 1 Chron. 11 : 27, 36. (B.C. about 1015.) From 1 Chron. 27 : 10 it appears that the former was of the tribe of Ephraim, and " Pelonite" would therefore be an appellation derived from his place of birth or residence. " Ahijah the Pelonite" appears in 2 Sam. 23 : 34 as " Eliam the son of Ahithophel the Gilonite," of which the former is a corruption.

Pen. [WRITING.]

Peni'el (*face of God*), the name which Jacob gave to the place in which he had wrestled with God : " He called the name of the place 'face of El,' for I have seen Elohim face to face." Gen. 32 : 30. In Gen. 32 : 31 and the other passages in which the name occurs, its form is changed to PENUEL. From the narrative it is evident that Peniel lay somewhere on the north bank of the Jabbok, and between that torrent and the fords

of the Jordan at Succoth, a few miles north of the glen where the Jabbok falls into the Jordan.

Penin'nah (*coral*, or *pearl*), one of the two wives of Elkanah. 1 Sam. 1 : 2. (B.C. 1125.)

Penny, Pennyworth. In the New Testament " penny," either alone or in the compound " pennyworth," occurs as the rendering of the Roman *denarius*. Matt. 20 : 2; 22 : 19; Mark 6 : 37; 12 : 15; Luke 20 : 24; John 6 : 7; Rev. 6 : 6. The denarius was the chief Roman silver coin. and was worth about 15 to 17 cents.

Pen'tateuch, The, is the Greek name given to the five books commonly called the " five books of Moses." This title is derived from πεντε, five, and τεῦχος, which, meaning originally " vessel," " instrument," etc., came in Alexandrine Greek to mean " book," hence *the five-fold book*. In the time of Ezra and Nehemiah it was called " the law of Moses," Ezra 7 : 6, or " the book of the law of Moses," Neh. 8 : 1, or simply " the book of Moses." 2 Chron. 25 : 4; 35 : 12; Ezra 6 : 18; Neh. 13 : 1. This was beyond all reasonable doubt our existing Pentateuch. The book which was discovered in the temple in the reign of Josiah, and which is entitled, 2 Chron. 34 : 14, " a book of the law of Jehovah by the hand of Moses," was substantially, it would seem, the same volume, though it may afterward have undergone some revision by Ezra. The present Jews usually called the whole by the name of *Torah*, *i. e.* " the Law," or *Torath Mosheh*, " the Law of Moses." The division of the whole work into five parts was probably made by the Greek translators; for the titles of the several books are not of Hebrew but of Greek origin. The Hebrew names are merely taken from the first words of each book, and in the first instance only designated particular *sections* and not whole books. The MSS. of the Pentateuch form a single roll or volume, and are divided, not into books but into the larger and smaller sections called *Parshiyoth* and *Sedarim*. The five books of the Pentateuch form a consecutive whole. The work, beginning with the record of creation and the history of the primitive world, passes on to deal more especially with the early history of the Jewish family, and finally concludes with Moses' last discourses and his death. Till the middle of the last century it was the general opinion of both Jews and Christians that

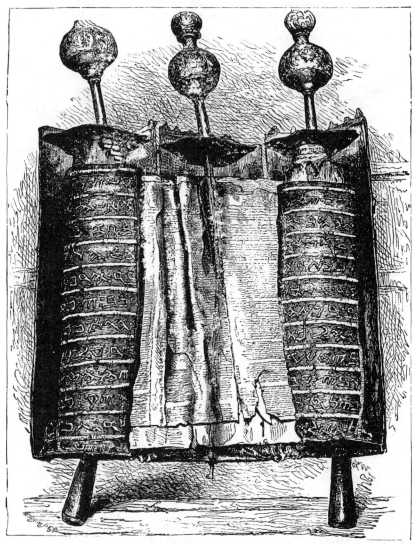

Pentateuch at Shechem.

the whole of the Pentateuch was written by Moses, with the exception of a few manifestly later additions,—such as the 34th chapter of Deuteronomy, which gives the account of Moses' death. The first attempt to call in question the pop-

ular belief was made by Astruc, doctor and professor of medicine in the Royal College at Paris, and court physician to Louis XIV. He had observed that throughout the book of Genesis, and as far as the 6th chapter of Exodus, traces were to be found of two original documents, each characterized by a distinct use of the names of God; the one by the name *Elohim*, and the other by the name *Jehovah*. [GOD.] Besides these two principal documents, he supposed Moses to have made use of ten others in the composition of the earlier part of his work. The path traced by Astruc has been followed by numerous German writers; but the various hypotheses which have been formed upon the subject cannot be presented in this work. It is sufficient here to state that there is evidence satisfactory that the main bulk of the Pentateuch, at any rate, was written by Moses, though he probably availed himself of existing documents in the composition of the earlier part of the work. Some detached portions would appear to be of later origin; and when we remember how entirely, during some periods of Jewish history, the law seems to have been forgotten, and again how necessary it would be after the seventy years of exile to explain some of its archaisms, and to add here and there short notes to make it more intelligible to the people, nothing can be more natural than to suppose that such later additions were made by Ezra and Nehemiah.

To briefly sum up the results of our inquiry—1. The book of Genesis rests chiefly on documents much earlier than the time of Moses, though it was probably brought to very nearly its present shape either by Moses himself or by one of the elders who acted under him. 2. The books of Exodus, Leviticus and Numbers are to a great extent Mosaic. Besides those portions which are expressly declared to have been written by him, other portions, and especially the legal sections, were, if not actually written, in all probability dictated by him. 3. Deuteronomy, excepting the concluding part, is entirely the work of Moses, as it professes to be. 4. It is not probable that this was written before the three preceding books, because the legislation in Exodus and Leviticus, as being the more formal, is manifestly the earlier, whilst Deuteronomy is the spiritual interpretation and application of the law. But the letter is always before the spirit; the thing before its interpretation. 5. The first *composition* of the Pentateuch as a whole could not have taken place till after the Israelites entered Canaan. It is probable that Joshua and the elders

who were associated with him would provide for its formal arrangement, custody and transmission. 6. The whole work did not finally assume its present shape till its revision was undertaken by Ezra after the return from the Babylonish captivity. For an account of the separate books see GENESIS, EXODUS, LEVITICUS, NUMBERS, DEUTERONOMY.

Pen′tecost, that is, *the fiftieth day* (from a Greek word meaning fiftieth), or Harvest Feast, or Feast of Weeks, may be regarded as a supplement to the Passover. It lasted for but one day. From the sixteenth of Nisan seven weeks were reckoned inclusively, and the next or fiftieth day was the day of Pentecost, which fell on the sixth of Sivan (about the end of May). Ex. 23 : 16; 34 : 22; Lev. 23 : 15–22; Num. 28. See *Jewish calendar* at the end of this volume. The Pentecost was the Jewish harvest-home, and the people were especially exhorted to rejoice before Jehovah with their families, their servants, the Levite within their gates, the stranger, the fatherless and the widow, in the place chosen by God for his name, as they brought a free-will offering of their hand to Jehovah their God. Deut. 16 : 10, 11. The great feature of the celebration was the presentation of the *two loaves*, made from the first-fruits of the wheat harvest. With the loaves two lambs were offered as a peace offering, and all were waved before Jehovah, and given to the priests; the loaves, being leavened, could not be offered on the altar. The other sacrifices were, a burnt offering of a young bullock, two rams and seven lambs, with a meat and drink offering, and a kid for a sin offering. Lev. 23 : 18, 19. Till the pentecostal loaves were offered, the produce of the harvest might not be eaten, nor could any other first-fruits be offered. The whole ceremony was the completion of that dedication of the harvest to God as its giver, and to whom both the land and the people were holy, which was begun by the offering of the wave-sheaf at the Passover. The interval is still regarded as a religious season. The Pentecost is the only one of the three great feasts which is not mentioned as the memorial of events in the history of the Jews; but such a significance has been found in the fact that the law was given from Sinai on the fiftieth day after the deliverance from Egypt. Comp. Ex. 12 and 19. In the exodus the people were offered to God as living first-fruits; at Sinai their consecration to him as a nation was completed. The typical significance of the Pentecost is made clear from the events of the day recorded in the Acts of the Apostles. Acts 2. Just as the appearance of God on Sinai was the birthday of the Jewish nation, so was the Pentecost the birthday of the Christian Church.

Penu'el. [PENIEL.]

Pe'or (*cleft*), a mountain peak in Moab belonging to the Abarim range, and near Pisgah, to which, after having ascended Pisgah, the prophet Balaam was conducted by Balak that he might look upon the whole host of Israel and curse them. Num. 23 : 14, 28. In four passages—Num. 25 : 18 twice; 31 : 16; Josh. 22 : 17—Peor occurs as a contraction for Baal-peor. [BAAL.]

Per'azim (*a breach*), **Mount,** a name which occurs in Isa. 28 : 21 only—unless the place which it designates is identical with the Baal-perazim mentioned as the scene of one of David's victories over the Philistines, which was in the valley of Rephaim, south of Jerusalem, on the road to Bethlehem.

Pe'resh (*dung*), the son of Machir by his wife Maachah. 1 Chron. 7 : 16.

Pe'rez (*breach*). The "children of Perez," or Pharez, the son of Judah, appear to have been a family of importance for many centuries. 1 Chron. 27 : 3; Neh. 11 : 4, 6.

Pe'rez-uz'za (*breaking of Uzzah*), 1 Chron. 13 : 11, and PEREZ-UZZAH, 2 Sam. 6 : 8, the title which David conferred on the threshing-floor of Nachon or Cidon, in commemoration of the sudden death of Uzzah. (B.C. 1042.)

Perfumes. The free use of perfumes was peculiarly grateful to the Orientals, Prov. 27 : 9, whose olfactory nerves are more than usually sensitive to the offensive smells engendered by the heat of their climate. The Hebrews manufactured their perfumes chiefly from spices imported from Arabia, though to a certain extent also from aromatic plants growing in their own country. Perfumes entered largely into the temple service, in the two forms of incense and ointment. Ex. 30 : 22-38. Nor were they less used in private life; not only were they applied to the person, but to garments, Ps. 45 : 8; Cant. 4 : 11, and to articles of furniture, such as beds. Prov. 7 : 17.

Per'ga (*earthy*), a city of Pamphylia, Acts 13 : 13, situated on the river Cestius,

at a distance of 60 stadia (7½ miles) from its mouth, and celebrated in antiquity for the worship of Artemis (Diana).

Per'gamos (in Revised Version *Pergamum*) (*height, elevation*), a city of Mysia, about 3 miles to the north of the river Caicus, and 20 miles from its present mouth. It was the residence of a dynasty of Greek princes founded after the time of Alexander the Great, and usually called the Attalic dynasty, from its founder, Attalus. The sumptuousness of the Attalic princes had raised Pergamos to the rank of the first city in Asia as regards splendor. The city was noted for its vast library, containing 200,000 volumes. Here were splendid temples of Zeus or Jupiter, Athene, Apollo and Æsculapius. One of "the seven churches of Asia" was in Pergamos. Rev. 1 : 11; 2 : 12-17. It is called "Satan's seat" by John, which some suppose to refer to the worship of Æsculapius, from the *serpent* being his characteristic emblem. Others refer it to the persecutions of Christians, which was the work of Satan. The modern name of the city is *Bergama*.

Per'gamum. In the Revised Version for Pergamos. Rev. 1 : 11. Pergamum is the form usual in the classic writers.

Peri'da (*grain, kernel*). The children of Perida returned from Babylon with Zerubbabel. Neh. 7 : 57. (B.C. before 536.)

Per'izzite, The, and **Per'izzites** (*belonging to a village*), one of the nations inhabiting the land of promise before and at the time of its conquest by Israel. (B.C. 1450.) They are continually mentioned in the formula so frequently occurring to express the promised land. Gen. 15 : 20; Ex. 3 : 8, 17; 23 : 23; 33 : 2; 34 : 11. The notice in the book of Judges locates them in the southern part of the holy land. The signification of the name is not by any means clear. It possibly meant rustics, dwellers in open, unwalled villages, which are denoted by a similar word.

Persep'olis, mentioned only in 2 Macc. 9 : 2, was the capital of Persia proper, and the occasional residence of the Persian court from the time of Darius Hystaspes, who seems to have been its founder, to the invasion of Alexander. Its wanton destruction by that conqueror is well known. Its site is now called the *Chehl-Minar*, or Forty Pillars. Here, on a platform hewn out of the solid rock, the sides of which face the four cardinal points, are the remains of two great palaces, built respectively by Darius Hystaspes and his son Xerxes, besides a number of other edifices, chiefly temples. They are of great extent and magnificence, covering an area of many acres.

Ruins of Persepolis.—Burial-place of the Persian kings.

Per'sıa (*pure, splendid*), **Per'sians.** Persia proper was a tract of no very large dimensions on the Persian Gulf, which is still known as *Fars* or *Farsistan*, a corruption of the ancient appellation. This tract was bounded on the west by Susiana or Elam, on the north by Media, on the south by the Persian Gulf and on the east by Carmania. But the name is more commonly applied, both in Scripture and by profane authors, to the entire tract which came by degrees to be included within the limits of the Persian empire. This empire extended at one time from India on the east to Egypt and Thrace on the west, and included, besides portions of Europe and Africa, the whole of western Asia between the Black Sea, the Caucasus, the Caspian and the Jaxartes on the north, the Arabian desert, the Persian Gulf and the Indian Ocean on the south. The only passage in Scripture where Persia designates the tract which has been called above "Persia proper" is Ezek. 38 : 5. Elsewhere the empire is intended. The Persians were of the same race as the Medes, both being branches of the great Aryan stock.

1. *Character of the nation.*—The Persians were a people of lively and impressible minds, brave and impetuous in war, witty, passionate, for Orientals truthful, not without some spirit of generosity, and of more intellectual capacity than the generality of Asiatics. In the times anterior to Cyrus they were noted for the simplicity of their habits, which offered a strong contrast to the luxuriousness of the Medes; but from the date of the Median overthrow this simplicity began to decline. Polygamy was commonly practiced among them. They were fond of the pleasures of the table. In war they fought bravely, but without discipline.

2. *Religion.*—The religion which the Persians brought with them into Persia proper seems to have been of a very simple character, differing from natural religion in little except that it was deeply tainted with Dualism. Like the other Aryans, the Persians worshipped one supreme

God. They had few temples, and no altars or images.

3. *Language.*—The Persian language was closely akin to the Sanscrit, or ancient language of India. Modern Persian is its degenerate representative, being largely impregnated with Arabic.

Persian Lady.

4. *History.*—The history of Persia begins with the revolt from the Medes and the accession of Cyrus the Great, B.C. 558. Cyrus defeated Crœsus, and added the Lydian empire to his dominions. This conquest was followed closely by the submission of the Greek settlements on the Asiatic coast, and by the reduction of Caria and Lycia. The empire was soon afterward extended greatly toward the northeast and east. In B.C. 539 or 538, Babylon was attacked, and after a stout defence fell into the hands of Cyrus. This victory first brought the Persians into contact with the Jews. The conquerors found in Babylon an oppressed race—like themselves, abhorrers of idols, and professors of a religion in which to a great extent they could sympathize. This race Cyrus determined to restore to their own country: which he did by the remarkable edict recorded in the first chapter of Ezra. Ezra 1 : 2-4. He was slain in an expedition against the Massagetæ or the Derbices, after a reign of twenty-nine years. Under his son and successor, Cambyses, the conquest of Egypt took place, B.C. 525. This prince appears to be the Ahasuerus of Ezra 4 : 6. Gomates, Cambyses' successor, reversed the policy of Cyrus with respect to the Jews, and forbade by an edict the further building of the temple. Ezra 4 : 17-22. He reigned but seven months, and was succeeded by Darius. Appealed to, in his second year, by the Jews, who wished to resume the construction of their temple, Darius not only granted them this privilege, but assisted the work by grants from his own revenues, whereby the Jews were able to complete the temple as early as his sixth year. Ezra 6 : 1-15. Darius was succeeded by Xerxes, probably the Ahasuerus of Esther. Artaxerxes, the son of Xerxes, reigned for forty years after his death, and is beyond doubt the king of that name who stood in such a friendly relation toward Ezra, Ezra 7 : 11-28, and Nehemiah. Neh. 2 : 1-9, etc. He is the last of the Persian kings who had any special connection with the Jews, and the last but one mentioned in Scripture. His successors were Xerxes II., Sogdianus, Darius Nothus, Artaxerxes Mnemon, Artaxerxes Ochus, and Darius Codomannus, who is probably the " Darius the Persian " of Nehemiah 12 : 22. These monarchs reigned from B.C. 424 to B.C. 330. The collapse of the empire under the attack of Alexander the Great took place B.C. 330.

Per'sis (*a Persian woman*), a Christian woman at Rome, Rom. 16 : 12, whom St. Paul salutes. (A.D. 55.)

Peru'da. The same as PERIDA. Ezra 2 : 55.

Pestilence. [PLAGUE, THE.]

Pe'ter (*a rock* or *stone*). The original name of this disciple was Simon, *i. e.* " hearer." He was the son of a man named Jonas, Matt. 16 : 17 ; John 1 : 42 ; 21 : 16, and was brought up in his father's occupation, that of a fisherman. He and his brother Andrew were partners of John and James, the sons of Zebedee, who had hired servants. Peter did not live, as a mere laboring man, in a hut by the seaside, but first at Bethsaida, and afterward in a house at Capernaum belonging to himself or his mother-in-law, which must have been rather a large one, since he received in it not only our Lord and his fellow disciples, but multitudes who were attracted by the miracles and preaching of Jesus. Peter was probably between thirty and forty years of age at the date of his call. That call was preceded by a special preparation. Peter and his brother Andrew, together with their partners James and John, the sons of Zebedee, were disciples of John the Baptist when he was first called by our Lord. The particulars of this call are related with graphic minuteness by St. John. It was upon this occasion that Jesus gave Peter the name Cephas, a Syriac word answering to the Greek Peter, and signifying a stone or rock. John 1 : 35-42. This first call led to no immediate change in Peter's external position. He and his fellow disciples looked henceforth upon our Lord as their teacher, but were not commanded to follow him as regular disciples. They returned to Capernaum, where they pursued their usual business, waiting for a further intimation of his will. The second call is recorded by the other three evangelists; the narrative of Luke being apparently supplementary to the brief and, so to speak, official accounts given by Matthew and Mark. It took place on the Sea of Galilee near Capernaum, where the four disciples, Peter and Andrew, James and John, were fishing. Some time was passed afterward in attendance upon our Lord's public ministrations in Galilee, Decapolis, Peræa and Judea. The special designation of Peter and his eleven fellow disciples took place some time afterward, when they were set apart as our Lord's immediate attendants. See Matt. 10 : 2-4; Mark 3 : 13-19 (the most detailed account); Luke 6 : 13. They appear to have then first received formally the name of apostles, and from that time Simon bore publicly, and as it would seem all but exclusively, the name Peter, which had hitherto been used rather as a characteristic appellation than as a proper name. From this time there can be no doubt that Peter held the first place among the apostles, to whatever cause his precedence is to be attributed. He is named first in every list of the apostles; he is generally addressed by our Lord as their representative; and on the most solemn occasions he speaks in their name. The distinction which he received, and it may be his consciousness of ability, energy, zeal and absolute devotion to Christ's person, seem to have developed a natural tendency to rashness and forwardness bordering upon presumption. In his affection and self-confidence Peter ventured to reject as impossible the announcement of the sufferings and humiliation which Jesus predicted, and heard the sharp

words, "Get thee behind me, Satan; thou art an offence unto me; for thou savorest not the things that be of God, but those that be of men." It is remarkable that on other occasions when St. Peter signalized his faith and devotion, he displayed at the time, or immediately afterward, a more than usual deficiency in spiritual discernment and consistency. Toward the close of our Lord's ministry Peter's characteristics become especially prominent. At the last supper Peter seems to have been particularly earnest in the request that the traitor might be pointed out. After the supper his words drew out the meaning of the significant act of our Lord in washing his disciples' feet. Then too it was that he made those repeated protestations of unalterable fidelity, so soon to be falsified by his miserable fall. On the morning of the resurrection we have proof that Peter, though humbled, was not crushed by his fall. He and John were the first to visit the sepulchre; he was the first who entered it. We are told by Luke and by Paul that Christ appeared to him first among the apostles. It is observable, however, that on that occasion he is called by his original name, Simon, not Peter; the higher designation was not restored until he had been publicly reinstituted, so to speak, by his Master. That reinstitution—an event of the very highest import—took place at the Sea of Galilee. John 21.

The first part of the Acts of the Apostles is occupied by the record of transactions in nearly all of which Peter stands forth as the recognized leader of the apostles. He is the most prominent person in the greatest event after the resurrection, when on the day of Pentecost the Church was first invested with the plenitude of gifts and power. When the gospel was first preached beyond the precincts of Judea, he and John were at once sent by the apostles to confirm the converts at Samaria. Henceforth he remains prominent, but not exclusively prominent, among the propagators of the gospel. We have two accounts of the first meeting of Peter and Paul—Acts 9 : 26; Gal. 1 : 17, 18. This interview was followed by another event marking Peter's position—a general apostolical tour of visitation to the churches hitherto established. Acts 9 : 32. The most signal transaction after the day of Pentecost was the baptism of Cornelius. That was the crown and consummation of Peter's ministry. The establishment of a church in great part of Gentile origin at Antioch, and the mission of Barnabas, between whose family and Peter there were the bonds of near intimacy, set the seal upon the work thus inaugurated by Peter. This transaction was soon followed by the imprisonment of our apostle. His miraculous deliverance marks the close of this second great period of his ministry. The special work assigned to him was completed. From that time we have no continuous history of him.

Peter was probably employed for the most part in building up and completing the organization of Christian communities in Palestine and the adjoining districts. There is, however, strong reason to believe that he visited Corinth at an early period. The name of Peter as founder or joint founder is not associated with any local church save the churches of Corinth, Antioch or Rome, by early ecclesiastical tradition. It may be considered as a settled point that he did not visit Rome before the last year of his life; but there is satisfactory evidence that he and Paul were the founders of the church at Rome, and suffered death in that city. The time and manner of the apostle's martyrdom are less certain. According to the early writers, he suffered at or about the same time with Paul, and in the Neronian persecution, A.D. 67, 68. All agree that he was crucified. Origen says that Peter felt himself to be unworthy to be put to death in the same manner as his Master, and was therefore, at his own request, crucified with his head downward. The apostle is said to have employed interpreters. Of far more importance is the statement that Mark wrote his Gospel under the teaching of Peter, or that he embodied in that Gospel the substance of our apostle's oral instructions. [MARK.] The only written documents which Peter has left are the First Epistle—about which no doubt has ever been entertained in the Church—and the Second, which has been a subject of earnest controversy.

Peter, First Epistle of. The external evidence of authenticity of this epistle is of the strongest kind; and the internal is equally strong. It was addressed to the churches of Asia Minor, which had for the most part been founded by Paul and his companions. Supposing it to have been written at Babylon, 1 Pet. 5 : 13, it is a probable conjecture that Sil-

vanus, by whom it was transmitted to those churches, had joined Peter after a tour of visitation, and that his account of the condition of the Christians in those districts determined the apostle to write the epistle. (On the question of this epistle having been written at Babylon commentators differ. "Some refer it to the famous Babylon in Asia, which after its destruction was still inhabited by a Jewish colony; others refer it to Babylon in Egypt, now called *Old Cairo;* still others understand it mystically of heathen Rome, in which sense 'Babylon' is certainly used in the Apocalypse of John." —*Schaff.*) The objects of the epistle were —1. To comfort and strengthen the Christians in a season of severe trial. 2. To enforce the practical and spiritual duties involved in their calling. 3. To warn them against special temptations attached to their position. 4. To remove all doubt as to the soundness and completeness of the religious system which they had already received. Such an attestation was especially needed by the Hebrew Christians, who were wont to appeal from Paul's authority to that of the elder apostles, and above all to that of Peter. The last, which is perhaps the very principal object, is kept in view throughout the epistle, and is distinctly stated ch. 5 : 12. The harmony of such teaching with that of Paul is sufficiently obvious. Peter belongs to the school, or, to speak more correctly, is the leader of the school, which at once vindicates the unity of the law and the gospel, and puts the superiority of the latter on its true basis—that of spiritual development. The date of this epistle is uncertain, but Alford believes it to have been written between A.D. 63 and 67.

Peter, Second Epistle of. The following is a brief outline of the contents of this epistle: The customary opening salutation is followed by an enumeration of Christian blessings and exhortation to Christian duties. ch. 1 : 1-13. Referring then to his approaching death, the apostle assigns as grounds of assurance for believers his own personal testimony as eye-witness of the transfiguration, and the sure word of prophecy—that is, the testimony of the Holy Ghost. vs. 14-21. The danger of being misled by false prophets is dwelt upon with great earnestness throughout the second chapter, which is almost identical in language and subject with the Epistle of Jude. The overthrow of all opponents of Christian truth is predicted in connection with prophecies touching the second advent of Christ, the destruction of the world by fire, and the promise of new heavens and a new earth wherein dwelleth righteousness. ch. 3. This epistle of Peter presents questions of difficulty. Doubts as to its genuineness were entertained by the early Church; in the time of Eusebius it was reckoned among the disputed books, and was not formally admitted into the canon until the year 393, at the Council of Hippo. These difficulties, however, are insufficient to justify more than hesitation in admitting its genuineness. A majority of names may be quoted in support of the genuineness and authenticity of this epistle. (It is very uncertain as to the time when it was written. It was written near the close of Peter's life—perhaps about A.D. 68—from Rome or somewhere on the journey thither from the East.—*Alford.*)

Pethahi'ah (*freed by Jehovah*). 1. A priest, over the nineteenth course in the reign of David. 1 Chron. 24 : 16. (B.C. 1020.)

2. A Levite in the time of Ezra, who had married a foreign wife. Ezra 10 : 23. He is probably the same who is mentioned in Neh. 9 : 5. (B.C. 458.)

3. The son of Meshezabeel, and descendant of Zerah. Neh. 11 : 24. (B.C. 446.)

Pe'thor (*soothsayer*), a town of Mesopotamia, where Balaam resided, and situated "upon the river," possibly the Euphrates. Num. 22 : 5; Deut. 23 : 4. Its position is wholly unknown.

Pethu'el (*vision of God*), the father of the prophet Joel. Joel 1 : 1. (B.C. before 800.)

Peultha'i (*my wages*), properly Peullethai, the eighth son of Obed-edom. 1 Chron. 26 : 5. (B.C. 1020.)

Pha'lec (*division*). Peleg the son of Eber. Luke 3 : 35.

Phal'lu (*distinguished*). Pallu the son of Reuben is so called in the Authorized Version of Gen. 46 : 9. (B.C. about 1706.)

Phal'ti (*my deliverance*), the son of Laish of Gallim, to whom Saul gave Michal in marriage after his mad jealousy had driven David forth as an outlaw. 1 Sam. 25 : 44. In 2 Sam. 3 : 15 he is called PHALTIEL. With the exception of this brief mention of his name, and the touching little episode in 2 Sam. 3 : 16, nothing more is heard of Phalti. (B.C. 1061.)

Phal'ti-el. The same as Phalti. 2 Sam. 3 : 15.

Phanu'el (*face of God*), the father of Anna, the prophetess of the tribe of Aser. Luke 2 : 36. (B.C. about 80.)

Pha'raoh, the common title of the native kings of Egypt, corresponding to P-ra or Ph-ra, "the sun," of the hieroglyphics. Brugsch, Ebers and other modern Egyptologists define it to mean "the great house," which would correspond to our "the Sublime Porte." As several kings are mentioned only by the title "Pharaoh" in the Bible, it is important to endeavor to discriminate them:

1. *The Pharaoh of Abraham.* Gen. 12 : 15.—At the time at which the patriarch went into Egypt, it is generally held that the country, or at least lower Egypt, was ruled by the Shepherd kings, of whom the first and most powerful line was the fifteenth dynasty, the undoubted territories of which would be first entered by one coming from the east. The date at which Abraham visited Egypt was about B.C. 2081, which would accord with the time of Salatis, the head of the fifteenth dynasty, according to our reckoning.

2. *The Pharaoh of Joseph.* Gen. 41.— One of the Shepherd kings, perhaps Apophis, who belonged to the fifteenth dynasty. He appears to have reigned from Joseph's appointment (or perhaps somewhat earlier) until Jacob's death, a period of at least twenty-six years, from about B.C. 1876 to 1850, and to have been the fifth or sixth king of the fifteenth dynasty.

3. *The Pharaoh of the oppression.* Ex. 1 : 8.—The first persecutor of the Israelites may be distinguished as the Pharaoh of the oppression, from the second, the Pharaoh of the exodus, especially as he commenced and probably long carried on the persecution. The general view is that he was an Egyptian. One class of Egyptologists think that Amosis (Ahmes), the first sovereign of the eighteenth dynasty, is the Pharaoh of the oppression; but Brugsch and others identify him with Rameses II. (the Sesostris of the Greeks), of the nineteenth dynasty. (B.C. 1380–1340.)

4. *The Pharaoh of the exodus.* Ex. 5 : 1.—Either Thothmes III., as Wilkinson, or Menephthah son of Rameses II., whom Brugsch thinks was probably the Pharaoh of the exodus, who with his army pursued the Israelites and was over-

whelmed in the Red Sea. "The events which form the lamentable close of his rule over Egypt are passed over by the monuments (very naturally) with perfect silence. The dumb tumulus covers the misfortune which was suffered, for the record of these events was inseparably

Portrait of Menephthah I., the Pharaoh of the Exodus,

connected with the humiliating confession of a divine visitation, to which a patriotic writer at the court of Pharaoh would hardly have brought his mind." The table on page 186 gives some of the latest opinions.

5. *Pharaoh, father-in-law of Mered.*— In the genealogies of the tribe of Judah, mention is made of the daughter of a Pharaoh married to an Israelite—"Bithiah the daughter of Pharaoh, which Mered took." 1 Chron. 4 : 18.

6. *Pharaoh, brother-in-law of Hadad the Edomite.*—This king gave Hadad, as his wife, the sister of his own wife, Tahpenes. 1 Kings 11 : 18-20.

7. *Pharaoh, father-in-law of Solomon.*— The mention that the queen was brought into the city of David while Solomon's house and the temple and the city wall were building shows that the marriage took place not later than the eleventh year of the king, when the temple was finished, having been commenced in the fourth year. 1 Kings 6 : 1, 37, 38. This Pharaoh led an expedition into Palestine. 1 Kings 9 : 16.

8. *Pharaoh, the opponent of Sennacherib.*—This Pharaoh, Isa. 36 : 6, can only be the Sethos whom Herodotus mentions as the opponent of Sennacherib, and who may reasonably be supposed to be the Zet of Manetho.

9. *Pharaoh-necho.*—The first mention in the Bible of a proper name with the title Pharaoh is the case of Pharaohnecho, who is also called Necho simply. This king was of the Saïte twenty-sixth dynasty, of which Manetho makes him either the fifth or the sixth ruler. Herodotus calls him Nekos, and assigns to him a reign of sixteen years, which is confirmed by the monuments. He seems to have been an enterprising king, as he is related to have attempted to complete the canal connecting the Red Sea with the Nile, and to have sent an expedition of Phœnicians to circumnavigate Africa, which was successfully accomplished. At the commencement of his reign, B.C. 610, he made war against the king of Assyria, and, being encountered on his way by Josiah, defeated and slew the king of Judah at Megiddo. 2 Kings 23 : 29, 30 ; 2 Chron. 35 : 20-24. Necho seems to have soon returned to Egypt. Perhaps he was on his way thither when he deposed Jehoahaz. The army was probably posted at Carchemish, and was there defeated by Nebuchadnezzar in the fourth year of Necho, B.C. 607, that king not being, as it seems, then at its head. Jer. 46 : 1, 2, 6, 10. This battle led to the loss of all the Asiatic dominions of Egypt. 2 Kings 24 : 7.

10. *Pharaoh-hophra.*—The next king of Egypt mentioned in the Bible is Pharaoh-hophra, the second successor of Necho, from whom he was separated by the six-years reign of Psammetichus II. He came to the throne about B.C. 589, and ruled nineteen years. Herodotus, who calls him Apries, makes him son of Psammetichus II., whom he calls Psammis, and great-grandson of Psammetichus I. In the Bible it is related that Zedekiah, the last king of Judah, was aided by a Pharaoh against Nebuchadnezzar, in fulfillment of a treaty, and that an army came out of Egypt, so that the Chaldeans were obliged to raise the siege of Jerusalem. The city was first besieged in the ninth year of Zedekiah, B.C. 590, and was captured in his eleventh year, B.C. 588. It was evidently continuously invested for a length of time before it was taken, so that it is most probable

that Pharaoh's expedition took place during 590 or 589. The Egyptian army returned without effecting its purpose. Jer. 27 : 5–8; Ezek. 17 : 11–18; comp. 2 Kings 25 : 1–4. No subsequent Pharaoh is mentioned in Scripture, but there are predictions doubtless referring to the misfortunes of later princes until the second Persian conquest, when the prophecy, "There shall be no more a prince of the land of Egypt," Ezek. 30 : 13, was fulfilled. (In the summer of 1881 a large number of the mummies of the Pharaohs were found in a tomb near Thebes—among them Raskenen, of the seventeenth dynasty, Ahmes I., founder of the eighteenth dynasty, Thothmes I., II. and III., and Rameses I. It was first thought that Rameses II., of the nineteenth dynasty, was there, but this was found to be a mistake. A group of coffins belonging to the twenty-first dynasty has been found, and it is probable that we will learn not a little about the early Pharaohs, especially from the inscriptions on their shrouds.—ED.)

Pharaoh's Daughter.

Pharaoh's daughter. Three Egyptian princesses, daughters of Pharaohs, are mentioned in the Bible:—1. The preserver of Moses, daughter of the Pharaoh who first oppressed the Israelites. Ex. 2 : 5–10. Osborn thinks her name was Thouoris, daughter of Rameses II., others that her name was Merrhis. (B.C. 1531.)

2. Bithiah wife of Mered, an Israelite, daughter of a Pharaoh of an uncertain age, probably of about the time of the exodus. 1 Chron. 4 : 18. [PHARAOH, No. 5.]

3. A wife of Solomon. 1 Kings 3 : 1; 7 : 8; 9 : 24. [PHARAOH, 7.] (B.C. 1000.)

Pharaoh, The wife of. The wife of one Pharaoh, the king who received Hadad the Edomite, is mentioned in Scripture. She is called "queen," and her name, Tahpenes, is given. [TAHPENES; PHARAOH, 6.]

Pha′res, Pha′rez or Pe′rez, the son of Judah. Matt. 1 : 3; Luke 3 : 33.

Pha′rez (Perez, 1 Chron. 27 : 3; Phares, Matt. 1 : 3; Luke 3 : 33; 1 Esd. 5 : 5), twin son, with Zarah or Zerah, of Judah and Tamar his daughter-in-law. (B.C. 1730.) The circumstances of his birth are detailed in Gen. 38. Pharez occupied the rank of Judah's second son, and from two of his sons sprang two new chief houses, those of the Hezronites and Hamulites. From Hezron's second son Ram, or Aram, sprang David and the kings of Judah, and eventually Jesus Christ. In the reign of David the house of Pharez seems to have been eminently distinguished.

Phar′isees, a religious party or school among the Jews at the time of Christ, so called from *perishin,* the Aramaic form of the Hebrew word *perûshim,* "separated." The chief sects among the Jews were the *Pharisees,* the *Sadducees* and the *Essenes,* who may be described respectively as the Formalists, the Freethinkers and the Puritans. A knowledge of the opinions and practices of the Pharisees at the time of Christ is of great importance for entering deeply into the genius of the Christian religion. A cursory perusal of the Gospels is sufficient to show that Christ's teaching was in some respects thoroughly antagonistic to theirs. He denounced them in the bitterest language; see Matt. 15 : 7, 8; 23 : 5, 13, 14, 15, 23; Mark 7 : 6; Luke 11 : 42–44, and compare Mark 7 : 1–5; 11 : 29; 12 : 19, 20; Luke 6 : 28, 37–42. To understand the Pharisees is by contrast an aid toward understanding the spirit of uncorrupted Christianity.

1. The fundamental principle of the Pharisees, common to them with all orthodox modern Jews, is that by the side of the written law regarded as a summary of the principles and general laws of the Hebrew people there was an oral law to complete and to explain the written law, given to Moses on Mount Sinai and transmitted by him by word of mouth. The

first portion of the Talmud, called the Mishna or "second law," contains this oral law. It is a digest of the Jewish traditions and a compendium of the whole ritual law, and it came at length to be esteemed far above the sacred text.

2. While it was the aim of Jesus to call men to the law of God itself as the supreme guide of life, the Pharisees, upon the pretence of maintaining it intact, multiplied minute precepts and distinctions to such an extent that the whole life of the Israelite was hemmed in and burdened on every side by instructions so numerous and trifling that the law was almost if not wholly lost sight of. These "traditions," as they were called, had long been gradually accumulating. Of the trifling character of these regulations innumerable instances are to be found in the Mishna. Such were their washings before they could eat bread, and the special minuteness with which the forms of this washing were prescribed; their bathing when they returned from the market; their washing of cups, pots, brazen vessels, etc.; their fastings twice in the week, Luke 18 : 12; such were their tithings, Matt. 23 : 23; and such, finally, were those minute and vexatious extensions of the law of the Sabbath, which must have converted God's gracious ordinance of the Sabbath's rest into a burden and a pain. Matt. 12 : 1–13; Mark 3 : 1–6; Luke 13 : 10–17.

3. It was a leading aim of the Redeemer to teach men that true piety consisted not in forms, but in substance, not in outward observances, but in an inward spirit. The whole system of Pharisaic piety led to exactly opposite conclusions. The lowliness of piety was, according to the teaching of Jesus, an inseparable concomitant of its reality; but the Pharisees sought mainly to attract the attention and to excite the admiration of men. Matt. 6 : 2, 6, 16; 23 : 5, 6; Luke 14 : 7. Indeed the whole spirit of their religion was summed up, not in confession of sin and in humility, but in a proud self-righteousness at variance with any true conception of man's relation to either God or his fellow creatures.

4. With all their pretences to piety they were in reality avaricious, sensual and dissolute. Matt. 23 : 25; John 8 : 7. They looked with contempt upon every nation but their own. Luke 10 : 29. Finally, instead of endeavoring to fulfill the great end of the dispensation whose

truths they professed to teach, and thus bringing men to the Hope of Israel, they devoted their energies to making converts to their own narrow views, who with all the zeal of proselytes were more exclusive and more bitterly opposed to the truth than they were themselves. Matt. 22 : 15.

5. The Pharisees at an early day secured the popular favor, and thereby acquired considerable political influence. This influence was greatly increased by the extension of the Pharisees over the whole land and the majority which they obtained in the Sanhedrin. Their number reached more than six thousand under the Herods. Many of them must have suffered death for political agitation. In the time of Christ they were divided doctrinally into several schools, among which those of Hillel and Shammai were most noted.—*McClintock and Strong.*

6. One of the fundamental doctrines of the Pharisees was a *belief in a future state.* They appear to have believed in a resurrection of the dead, very much in the same sense as the early Christians. They also believed in "a divine Providence acting side by side with the free will of man."—*Schaff.*

7. It is proper to add that it would be a great mistake to suppose that the Pharisees were wealthy and luxurious, much more that they had degenerated into the vices which were imputed to some of the Roman popes and cardinals during the two hundred years preceding the Reformation. Josephus compared the Pharisees to the sect of the Stoics. He says that they lived frugally, in no respect giving in to luxury. We are not to suppose that there were not many individuals among them who were upright and pure, for there were such men as Nicodemus, Gamaliel, Joseph of Arimathæa and Paul.

Pha'rosh. Ezra 8 : 3. [See PAROSH.]

Phar'par (*swift*), the second of the "two rivers of Damascus"—Abana and Pharpar—alluded to by Naaman. 2 Kings 5 : 12. The two principal streams in the district of Damascus are the Barada and the Awaj, the former being the Abana and the latter the Pharpar. The Awaj rises on the southeast slopes of Hermon, and flows into the most southerly of the three lakes or swamps of Damascus.

Phar'zites, The, the descendants of Parez the son of Judah. Num. 26 : 20.

Pha'seah. Neh. 7 : 51. [PASEAH, 2.]

Phase'lis, a town on the coast of Asia Minor, on the confines of Lycia and Pamphylia, and consequently ascribed by the ancient writers sometimes to one and sometimes to the other. 1 Macc. 15 : 23.

Phe'be. [PHŒBE.]

Pheni'ce (Acts 27 : 12, more properly Phœnix, as it is translated in the Revised Version), the name of a haven in Crete on the south coast. The name was no doubt derived from the Greek word for the palm tree, which Theophrastus says was indigenous in the island. It is the modern *Lutró*. [See PHŒNICE; PHŒNICIA.]

Phi'chol (*strong*), chief captain of the army of Abimelech, king of the Philistines of Gerar in the days of both Abraham, Gen. 21 : 22, 32, and Isaac. Gen. 26 : 26. (B.C. 1900.)

Philadelphia.

Philadel'phia, strictly **Philadelphi'a** (*brotherly love*), a town on the confines of Lydia and Phrygia Catacecaumene, 25 miles southeast of Sardis, and built by Attalus II., king of Pergamos, who died B.C. 138. It was situated on the lower slopes of Tmolus, and is still represented by a town called *Allah-shehr* (city of God). Its elevation is 952 feet above the sea. The original population of Philadelphia seems to have been Macedonian; but there was, as appears from Rev. 3 : 9, a synagogue of Hellenizing Jews there, as well as a Christian church. (It was the seat of one of "the seven churches of Asia.") The locality was subject to constant earthquakes, which in the time of Strabo rendered even the town walls of Philadelphia unsafe. The expense of reparation was constant, and hence perhaps the poverty of the members of the church. Rev. 3 : 8. (The church was highly commended. Rev. 3 : 7–13. Even Gibbon bears the following well-known testimony to the truth of the prophecy, " Because thou hast kept the word of my patience, I also will keep thee in the hour of temptation " : " At a distance from the sea, forgotten by the (Greek) emperor, encompassed on all sides by the Turks, her valiant citizens defended their religion and freedom above fourscore years. Among the Greek colonies and churches of Asia, Philadelphia is still erect, a column in a scene of ruins." " The modern town (*Allah-shehr*, city of God), although spacious, containing 3000 houses and 10,000 inhabitants, is badly built ; the dwellings are mean and the streets filthy. The inhabitants are mostly Turks. A few ruins are found, including remains of a wall and about twenty-five churches. In one place are four strong marble pillars, which once supported the dome of a church. One of the old mosques is believed by the native Christians to have been the church in which assembled the primitive Christians addressed in the Apocalypse."— *Whitney's Bible Geography*.)

Phile'mon, the name of the Christian to whom Paul addressed his epistle in behalf of Onesimus. He was a native probably of Colosse, or at all events lived in that city when the apostle wrote to him: first, because Onesimus was a Colossian, Col. 4 : 9; and secondly, because Archippus was a Colossian, Col. 4 : 17, whom Paul associates with Philemon at the beginning of his letter. Phil. 1, 2. It is related that Philemon became bishop of Colosse, and died as a martyr under Nero. It is evident from the letter to him that Philemon was a man of property and influence, since he is represented as the head of a numerous household, and as exercising an expensive liberality toward his friends and the poor in general. He was indebted to the apostle Paul as the medium of his personal participation in the gospel. It is not certain under what circumstances they became known to each other. It is evident that on becoming a disciple he gave no common proof of the sincerity and power of his faith. His character, as shadowed forth in the epistle to him, is one of the noblest which the sacred record makes known to us.

Philemon, The Epistle of Paul to, is one of the letters which the apostle wrote during his first captivity at Rome, A.D. 63 or early in A.D. 64. Nothing is wanted to confirm the genuineness of the epistle : the external testimony is unimpeachable; nor does the epistle itself offer anything to conflict with this decision. The occasion of the letter was that Onesimus, a slave of Philemon, had run away from him to Rome, either desiring liberty or, as some suppose, having committed theft. Phil. 18. Here he was converted under the instrumentality of Paul. The latter, intimately connected with the master and the servant, was naturally anxiqus to effect a reconciliation between them. He used his influence with Onesimus, ver. 12, to induce him to return to Colosse and place himself again at the disposal of his master. On his departure, Paul put into his hand this letter as evidence that Onesimus was a true and approved disciple of Christ, and entitled as such to be received, not as a servant, but above a servant, as a brother in the faith. The Epistle to Philemon has one peculiar feature—its *æsthetical character* it may be termed—which distinguishes it from all the other epistles. The writer had peculiar difficulties to overcome; but Paul, it is confessed, has shown a degree of self-denial and a tact in dealing with them which in being equal to the occasion could hardly be greater.

Phile′tus (*beloved*) was possibly a disciple of Hymenæus, with whom he is associated in 2 Tim. 2 : 17, and who is named without him in an earlier epistle. 1 Tim. 1 : 20 (A.D. 58–64). They appear to have been persons who believed the Scriptures of the Old Testament, but misinterpreted them, allegorizing away the doctrine of the resurrection, and resolving it all into figure and metaphor. The delivering over unto Satan seems to have been a form of excommunication declaring the person reduced to the state of a heathen; and in the apostolic age it was accompanied with supernatural or miraculous effects upon the bodies of the persons so delivered.

Phil′ip (*lover of horses*) **the apostle** was of Bethsaida, the city of Andrew and Peter, John 1 : 44, and apparently

was among the Galilean peasants of that district who flocked to hear the preaching of the Baptist. The manner in which St. John speaks of him indicates a previous friendship with the sons of Jona and Zebedee, and a consequent participation in their messianic hopes. The close union of the two in John 6 and 12 suggests that he may have owed to Andrew the first tidings that the hope had been fulfilled. The statement that Jesus *found* him, John 1 : 43, implies a previous seeking. In the lists of the twelve apostles, in the Synoptic Gospel, his name is as uniformly at the head of the second group of four as the name of Peter is at that of the first, Matt. 10 : 3 ; Mark 3 : 18; Luke 6 : 14; and the facts recorded by St. John give the reason of this priority. Philip apparently was among the first company of disciples who were with the Lord at the commencement of his ministry, at the marriage at Cana, on his first appearance as a prophet in Jerusalem. John 2. The first three Gospels tell us nothing more of him individually. St. John, with his characteristic fullness of personal reminiscences, records a few significant utterances. John 6 : 5–9 ; 12 : 20–22 ; 14 : 8. No other fact connected with the name of Philip is recorded in the Gospels. He is among the company of disciples at Jerusalem after the ascension, Acts 1 : 13, and on the day of Pentecost. After this all is uncertain and apocryphal. According to tradition, he preached in Phrygia, and died at Hierapolis.

Phil′ip the evangelist is first mentioned in the account of the dispute between the Hebrew and Hellenistic disciples in Acts 6. He is one of the seven appointed to superintend the daily distribution of food and alms, and so to remove all suspicion of partiality. The persecution of which Saul was the leader must have stopped the " daily ministrations " of the Church. The teachers who had been most prominent were compelled to take flight, and Philip was among them. It is noticeable that the city of Samaria is the first scene of his activity. Acts 8. He is the precursor of St. Paul in his work, as Stephen had been in his teaching. The scene which brings Philip and Simon the sorcerer into contact with each other, Acts 8 : 9–13, in which the magician has to acknowledge a power over nature greater than his own, is interesting. This step is followed by another. On the road from Jerusalem to Gaza he meets the Ethiopian eunuch. Acts 8 : 26 ff. The history that follows is interesting as one of the few records in the New Testament of the process of individual conversion. A brief sentence tells us that Philip continued his work as a preacher at Azotus (Ashdod) and among the other cities that had formerly belonged to the Philistines, and, following the coast-line, came to Cæsarea. Then for a long period—not less than eighteen or nineteen years—we lose sight of him. The last glimpse of him in the New Testament is in the account of St. Paul's journey to Jerusalem. It is to his house, as to one well known to them, that St. Paul and his companions turn for shelter. He has four daughters, who possess the gift of prophetic utterance, and who apparently give themselves to the work of teaching instead of entering on the life of home. Acts 21 : 8, 9. He is visited by

Ruins in the Market-place of Philippi.

the prophets and elders of Jerusalem. One tradition places the scene of his death at Hierapolis in Phrygia. According to another, he died bishop of Tralles. The house in which he and his daughters had lived was pointed out to travellers in the time of Jerome.

Phil'ip Her'od I., II. [Herod.]

Philip'pi (named from Philip of Macedonia), a city of Macedonia, about nine miles from the sea, to the northwest of the island of Thasos, which is twelve miles distant from its port Neapolis, the modern *Kavalla*. It is situated in a plain between the ranges of Pangæus and Hæmus. The Philippi which St. Paul visited was a Roman colony founded by Augustus after the famous battle of Philippi, fought here between Antony and Octavius and Brutus and Cassius, B.C. 42. The remains which strew the ground near the modern Turkish village *Bereketli* are no doubt derived from that city. The original town, built by Philip of Macedonia, was probably not exactly on the same site. Philip, when he acquired possession of the site, found there a town named *Datus* or *Datum*, which was probably in its origin a factory of the Phœnicians, who were the first that worked the gold-mines in the mountains here, as in the neighboring Thasos. The proximity of the gold-mines was of course the origin of so large a city as Philippi, but the plain in which it lies is of extraordinary fertility. The position, too, was on the main road from Rome to Asia, the *Via Egnatia*, which from Thessalonica to Constantinople followed the same course as the

View at Philippi.

existing post-road. On St. Paul's visits to Philippi, see the following article. At Philippi the gospel was first preached in Europe. Lydia was the first convert. Here too Paul and Silas were imprisoned. Acts 16 : 23. The Philippians sent contributions to Paul to relieve his temporal wants.

Philippians, Epistle to the, was written by St. Paul from Rome in A.D. 62 or 63. St. Paul's connection with Philippi was of a peculiar character, which gave rise to the writing of this epistle. St. Paul entered its walls A.D. 52. Acts 16 : 12. There, at a greater distance from Jerusalem than any apostle had yet penetrated, the long-restrained energy of St. Paul was again employed in laying the foundation of a Christian church. Philippi was endeared to St. Paul not only by the hospitality of Lydia, the deep sympathy of the converts, and the remarkable miracle which set a seal on his preaching, but also by the successful exercise of his missionary activity after a long suspense, and by the happy consequences of his undaunted endurance of ignominies which remained in his memory, Philip. 1 : 30, after the long interval of eleven years. Leaving Timothy and Luke to watch over the infant church,

Paul and Silas went to Thessalonica, 1 Thess. 2 : 2, whither they were followed by the alms of the Philippians, Philip. 4 : 16, and thence southward. After the lapse of five years, spent chiefly at Corinth and Ephesus, St. Paul passed through Macedonia, A.D. 57, on his way to Greece, and probably visited Philippi for the second time, and was there joined by Timothy. He wrote at Philippi his second Epistle to the Corinthians. On returning from Greece, Acts 20 : 4, he again found a refuge among his faithful Philippians, where he spent some days at Easter, A.D. 58, with St. Luke, who accompanied him when he sailed from Neapolis. Once more, in his Roman captivity, A.D. 62, their care of him revived again. They sent Epaphroditus, bearing their alms for the apostle's support, and ready also to tender his personal service. Philip. 2 : 25. St. Paul's aim in writing is plainly this : while acknowledging the alms of the Philippians and the personal services of their messenger, to give them some information respecting his own condition, and some advice respecting theirs. Strangely full of joy and thanksgiving amidst adversity, like the apostle's midnight hymn from the depth of his Philippian dungeon, this epistle went forth from his prison at Rome. In most other epistles he writes with a sustained effort to instruct, or with sorrow, or with indignation ; he is striving to supply imperfect or to correct erroneous teaching, to put down scandalous impurity, or to heal schism in the church which he addresses. But in this epistle, though he knew the Philippians intimately and was not blind to the faults and tendencies to fault of some of them, yet he mentions no evil so characteristic of the whole Church as to call for general censure on his part or amendment on theirs. Of all his epistles to churches, none has so little of an official character as this.

Philis'tia (Heb. *Pelesheth*) (*land of sojourners*). The word thus translated (in Ps. 60 : 8 ; 87 : 4 ; 108 : 9) is in the original identical with that elsewhere rendered Palestine, which always means land of the Philistines. (Philistia was the plain on the southwest coast of Palestine. It was 40 miles long on the coast of the Mediterranean between Gerar and Joppa, and 10 miles wide at the northern end and 20 at the southern.—ED.) This plain has been in all ages remarkable for the extreme richness of its soil. It was also adapted to the growth of m.litary power; for while the plain itself permitted the use of war-chariots, which were the chief arm of offence, the occasional elevations which rise out of it offered secure sites for towns and strongholds. It was, moreover, a commercial country: from its position it must have been at all times the great thoroughfare between Phœnicia and Syria in the north and Egypt and Arabia in the south.

Philis'tines (*immigrants*). The origin of the Philistines is nowhere expressly stated in the Bible; but as the prophets describe them as "the Philistines from Caphtor," Amos 9:7, and "the remnant of the maritime district of Caphtor," Jer. 47:4, it is *primâ facie* probable that they were the "Caphtorim which came out of Caphtor" who expelled the Avim from their territory and occupied it in their place, Deut. 2:23; and that these again were the Caphtorim mentioned in the Mosaic genealogical table among the descendants of Mizraim. Gen. 10:14. It has been generally assumed that Caphtor represents Crete, and that the Philistines migrated from that island, either directly or through Egypt, into Palestine. But the name Caphtor is more probably identified with the Egyptian Coptos. [CAPHTOR.]

History.—The Philistines must have settled in the land of Canaan before the time of Abraham; for they are noticed in his day as a pastoral tribe in the neighborhood of Gerar. Gen. 21:32, 34; 26:1, 8. Between the times of Abraham and Joshua the Philistines had changed their quarters, and had advanced northward into the plain of Philistia. The Philistines had at an early period attained proficiency in the arts of peace. Their wealth was abundant, Judges 16:5, 18, and they appear in all respects to have been a prosperous people. Possessed of such elements of power, they had attained in the time of the judges an important position among eastern nations. About B.C. 1200 we find them engaged in successful war with the Sidonians. Justin xviii. 3. The territory of the Philistines, having been once occupied by the Canaanites, formed a portion of the promised land, and was assigned to the tribe of Judah. Josh. 15:2, 12, 45-47. No portion of it, however, was conquered in the lifetime of Joshua, Josh. 13:2, and even after his death no permanent conquest was effected, Judges 3:3, though we are informed that the three cities of Gaza, Ashkelon and Ekron were taken. Judges 1:18. The Philistines soon recovered these, and commenced an aggressive policy against the Israelites, by which they gained a complete ascendency over them. Individual heroes were raised up from time to time, such as Shamgar the son of Anath, Judges 3:31, and still more Samson, Judges 13-16; but neither of these men succeeded in permanently throwing off the yoke. The Israelites attributed their past weakness to their want of unity, and they desired a king, with the special object of leading them against the foe. 1 Sam. 8:20. Saul threw off the yoke; and the Philistines were defeated with great slaughter at Geba. 1 Sam. 13:3. They made no attempt to regain their supremacy for about twenty-five years, and the scene of the next contest shows the altered strength of the two parties. It was no longer in the central country, but in a ravine leading down to the Philistine plain, the valley of Elah, the position of which is about 14 miles southwest of Jerusalem. On this occasion the prowess of young David secured success to Israel, and the foe was pursued to the gates of Gath and Ekron. 1 Sam. 17. The power of the Philistines was, however, still intact on their own territory. The border warfare was continued. The scene of the next conflict was far to the north, in the valley of Esdraelon. The battle on this occasion proved disastrous to the Israelites; Saul himself perished, and the Philistines penetrated across the Jordan and occupied the forsaken cities. 1 Sam. 31:1-7. On the appointment of David to be king, he twice attacked them, and on each occasion with signal success, in the first case capturing their images, in the second pursuing them "from Geba until thou come to Gazer." 2 Sam. 5:17-25; 1 Chron. 14:8-16. Henceforth the Israelites appear as the aggressors. About seven years after the defeat at Rephaim, David, who had now consolidated his power, attacked them on their own soil, and took Gath with its dependencies. The whole of Philistia was included in Solomon's empire. Later, when the Philistines, joined by the Syrians and Assyrians, made war on the kingdom of Israel, Hezekiah formed an alliance with the Egyptians, as a counterpoise to the Assyrians, and the possession of Philistia became henceforth the turning-point of the struggle between the two great empires of the East. The Assyrians under Tartan, the general of Sargon, made an expedition against Egypt, and took Ashdod, as the key of that country. Isa. 20 : 1, 4, 5. Under Sennacherib Philistia was again the scene of important operations. The Assyrian supremacy was restored by Esarhaddon, and it seems probable that the Assyrians retained their hold on Ashdod until its capture, after a long siege, by Psammetichus. It was about this time that Philistia was traversed by a vast Scythian horde on their way to Egypt. The Egyptian ascendency was not as yet re-established, for we find the next king, Necho, compelled to besiege Gaza on his return from the battle of Megiddo. After the death of Necho the contest was renewed between the Egyptians and the Chaldeans under Nebuchadnezzar, and the result was specially disastrous to the Philistines. The "old hatred" that the Philistines bore to the Jews was exhibited in acts of hostility at the time of the Babylonish captivity, Ezek. 25 : 15–17 ; but on the return this was somewhat abated, for some of the Jews married Philistian women, to the great scandal of their rulers. Neh. 13 : 23, 24. From this time the history of Philistia is absorbed in the struggles of the neighboring kingdoms. The latest notices of the Philistines as a nation occur in 1 Macc.3–5.

Institutions, religion, etc.—With regard to the institutions of the Philistines our information is very scanty. The five chief cities had, as early as the days of Joshua, constituted themselves into a confederacy, restricted however, in all probability, to matters of offence and defence. Each was under the government of a prince, Josh. 13 : 3 ; Judges 3 : 3, etc. ; 1 Sam. 18 : 30 ; 29 : 6, and each possessed its own territory. The Philistines appear to have been deeply imbued with superstition : they carried their idols with them on their campaigns, 2 Sam. 5 : 21, and proclaimed their victories in their presence. 1 Sam. 31 : 9. The gods whom they chiefly worshipped were Dagon, Judges 16 : 23 ; 1 Sam. 5 : 3–5 ; 1 Chron. 10 : 10 ; 1 Macc. 10 : 83, Ashtaroth, 1 Sam. 31 : 10 ; Herod. i. 105, and Baalzebub. 2 Kings 1 : 2–6.

Philol'ogus, a Christian at Rome to whom St. Paul sends his salutation. Rom. 16 : 15.

Philosophy. It is the object of the following article to give some account (I.) of that development of thought among the Jews which answered to the philosophy of the West ; (II.) of the systematic progress of Greek philosophy as forming a complete whole ; and (III.) of the contact of Christianity with philosophy.

I. THE PHILOSOPHIC DISCIPLINE OF THE JEWS.—Philosophy, if we limit the word strictly to describe the free pursuit of knowledge of which truth is the one complete end, is essentially of western growth. In the East the search after wisdom has always been connected with practice. The history of the Jews offers no exception to this remark : there is no Jewish philosophy, properly so called. The method of Greece was to proceed from life to God ; the method of Israel (so to speak) was to proceed from God to life. The axioms of one system are the conclusions of the other. The one led to the successive abandonment of the noblest domains of science which man had claimed originally as his own, till it left bare systems of morality ; the other, in the fullness of time, prepared many to welcome the Christ—the Truth. The philosophy of the Jews, using the word in a large sense, is to be sought for rather in the progress of the national life than in special books. Step by step the idea of the family was raised into that of the people ; and the kingdom furnished the basis of those wider promises which included all nations in one kingdom of heaven. The social, the political, the cosmical relations of man were traced out gradually in relation to God. The philosophy of the Jews is thus essentially a moral philosophy, resting on a definite connection with God. The doctrines of Creation and Providence, of an infinite divine person and of a responsible human will, which elsewhere form the ultimate limits of speculation, are here assumed at the outset. The Psalms, which, among the other infinite lessons which they convey, give a deep insight into the need of a personal apprehension of truth, everywhere declare the absolute sovereignty of God over the material and the moral world. One man among all is distinguished among the Jews as "the wise man." The description which is given of his writings serves as a commentary on the national view of philosophy. 1 Kings 4 : 30–33. The lesson of practical duty, the full utterance of "a large heart," *ibid.* 29, the careful study of God's creatures,—this is the sum of wisdom. Yet in fact the very practical aim of this philosophy leads to the revelation of the most sublime truth. Wisdom was gradually felt to be a person, throned by God and holding converse with men. Prov. 8. She was seen to stand in open enmity with "the strange woman," who sought to draw them aside by sensuous attractions; and thus a new step was made toward the central doctrine of Christianity —the incarnation of the Word. Two books of the Bible, Job and Ecclesiastes, of which the latter at any rate belongs to the period of the close of the kingdom, approach more nearly than any others to the type of philosophical discussions. But in both the problem is moral and not metaphysical. The one deals with the evils which afflict "the perfect and upright;" the other with the vanity of all the pursuits and pleasures of earth. The captivity necessarily exercised a profound influence upon Jewish thought. The teaching of Persia seems to have been designed to supply important elements in the education of the chosen people. But it did yet more than this. The contact of the Jews with Persia thus gave rise to a traditional mysticism. Their contact with Greece was marked by the rise of distinct sects. In the third century B.C. the great Doctor Antigonus of Socho bears a Greek name, and popular belief pointed to him as the teacher of Sadoc and Boethus, the supposed founders of Jewish rationalism. At any rate, we may date from this time the twofold division of Jewish speculation. The Sadducees appear as the supporters of human freedom in its widest scope ; the Pharisees of a religious Stoicism. At a later time the cycle of doctrine was completed, when by a natural reaction the Essenes established a mystic Asceticism.

II. THE DEVELOPMENT OF GREEK PHILOSOPHY. — The various attempts which have been made to derive western philosophy from eastern sources have signally failed. It is true that in some degree the character of Greek speculation may have been influenced, at least in its earliest stages, by religious ideas which were originally introduced from the East; but this indirect influence does not affect the real originality of the Greek teachers. The very value of Greek teaching lies in the fact that it was, as far as is possible, a result of simple reason, or, if

faith asserts its prerogative, the distinction is sharply marked. Of the various classifications of the Greek schools which have been proposed, the simplest and truest seems to be that which divides the history of philosophy into three great periods, the first reaching to the era of the Sophists, the next to the death of Aristotle, the third to the Christian era. In the first period the world objectively is the great centre of inquiry ; in the second, the "ideas" of things, truth, and being ; in the third, the chief interest of philosophy falls back upon the practical conduct of life. After the Christian era philosophy ceased to have any true vitality in Greece, but it made fresh efforts to meet the changed conditions of life at Alexandria and Rome. 1. *The pre-Socratic schools.*—The first Greek philosophy was little more than an attempt to follow out in thought the mythic cosmogonies of earlier poets. What is the one permanent element which underlies the changing forms of things?—this was the primary inquiry, to which the *Ionic* school endeavored to find an answer. Thales (*cir.* B.C. 639–543) pointed to moisture (water) as the one source and supporter of life. Anaximenes (*cir.* B.C. 520–480) substituted air for water. At a much later date (*cir.* B.C. 450) Diogenes of Apollonia represented this elementary "air" as endowed with intelligence. 2. *The Socratic schools.*—In the second period of Greek philosophy the scene and subject were both changed. A philosophy of ideas, using the term in its widest sense, succeeded a philosophy of nature. In three generations Greek speculation reached its greatest glory in the teaching of Socrates, Plato and Aristotle. The famous sentence in which Aristotle characterizes the teachings of Socrates (B.C. 468–399) places his scientific position in the clearest light. There are two things, he says, which we may rightly attribute to Socrates—inductive reasoning and general definition. By the first he endeavored to discover the permanent element which underlies the changing forms of appearances and the varieties of opinion ; by the second he fixed the truth which he had thus gained. But, besides this, Socrates rendered another service to truth. Ethics occupied in his investigations the primary place which had hitherto been held by Physics. The great aim of his induction was to establish the sovereignty of Virtue. He affirmed the existence of a universal law of right and wrong. He connected philosophy with action, both in detail and in general. On the one side he upheld the supremacy of Conscience, on the other the working of Providence. 3. *The post-Socratic schools.*—After Aristotle, philosophy took a new direction. Speculation became mainly personal. Epicurus (B.C. 352–270) defined the object of philosophy to be the attainment of a happy life. The pursuit of truth for its own sake he regarded as superfluous. He rejected dialectics as a useless study, and accepted the senses, in the widest acceptation of the term, as the criterion of truth. But he differed widely from the Cyrenaics in his view of happiness. The happiness at which the wise man aims is to be found, he said, not in momentary gratification, but in life-long pleasure. All things were supposed to come into being by chance, and so pass away. The individual was left master of his own life. While Epicurus asserted in this manner the claims of one part of man's nature in the conduct of life, Zeno of Citium (*cir.* B.C. 280), with equal partiality, advocated a purely spiritual (intellectual) morality. The opposition between the two was complete. The infinite, chance-formed worlds of the one stand over against the one harmonious world of the other. On the one side are gods regardless of material things, on the other a Being permeating and vivifying all creation. This difference necessarily found its chief expression in Ethics. III. CHRISTIANITY IN CONTACT WITH ANCIENT PHILOSOPHY.—The only direct trace of the contact of Christianity with western philosophy in the New Testament is in the account of St. Paul's visit to Athens, Acts 17 : 18 ; and there is nothing in the apostolic writings to show that it exercised any important influence upon the early Church. Comp. 1 Cor. 1 : 22–24. But it was otherwise with eastern speculation, which penetrated more deeply through the mass of the people. The "philosophy" against which the Colossians were warned, Col. 2 : 8, seems undoubtedly to have been of eastern origin, containing elements similar to those which were afterward embodied in various shapes of Gnosticism, as a selfish asceticism, and a superstitious reverence for angels, Col. 2 : 16–23; and in the Epistles to Timothy, addressed to Ephesus, in which city St. Paul anticipated the rise of false teaching, Acts 20 : 30, two distinct forms of error may be traced in addition to Judaism, due more or less to the same influence. The writings of the sub-apostolic age, with the exception of the famous anecdote of Justin Martyr (Dial. 2–4), throw little light upon the relations of Christianity and philosophy. Christian philosophy may be in one sense a contradiction in terms, for Christianity confessedly derives its first principles from revelation, and not from simple reason; but there is no less a true philosophy of Christianity, which aims to show how completely these meet the instincts and aspirations of all ages. The exposition of such a philosophy would be the work of a modern Origen.

Phin′chas (*mouth of brass*). 1. Son of Eleazar and grandson of Aaron. Ex. 6 : 25. He is memorable for having while quite a youth, by his zeal and energy at the critical moment of the licentious idolatry of Shittim, appeased the divine wrath, and put a stop to the plague which was destroying the nation. Num. 25 : 7. (B.C. 1452.) For this he was rewarded by the special approbation of Jehovah, and by a promise that the priesthood should remain in his family forever. Num. 25 : 10–13. He was appointed to accompany as priest the expedition by which the Midianites were destroyed. ch. 31 : 6. Many years later he also headed the party which was despatched from Shiloh to remonstrate against the altar which the transjordanic tribes were reported to have built near Jordan. Josh. 22 : 13–32. In the partition of the country he received an allotment of his own—a hill on Mount Ephraim which bore his name. After Eleazar's death he became high priest—the third of the series. In this capacity he is introduced as giving the oracle to the nation during the whole struggle with the Benjamites on the matter of Gibeah. Judges 20 : 28. The verse which closes the book of Joshua is ascribed to Phinehas, as the description of the death of Moses at the end of Deuteronomy is to Joshua. The tomb of Phinehas, a place of great resort to both Jews and Samaritans, is shown at *Awertah*, four miles southeast of *Nablûs*. 2. Second son of Eli. 1 Sam. 1 : 3; 2 : 34; 4 : 4, 11, 17, 19 ; 14 : 3. Phinehas was killed with his brother by the Philistines when the ark was captured. (B.C. 1125.) [ELI.] 3. A Levite of Ezra's time, Ezra 8 : 33;

unless the meaning be that Eleazar was of the family of the great Phinehas.

Phle′gon (*burning*), a Christian at Rome whom St. Paul salutes. Rom. 16 : 14. (A.D. 55.) Pseudo-Hippolytus makes him one of the seventy disciples and bishop of Marathon.

Phœ′be (*radiant*), the first and one of the most important of the Christian persons the detailed mention of whom fills nearly all the last chapter of the Epistle to the Romans. (A.D. 55.) What is said of her, Rom. 16 : 1, 2, is worthy of special notice because of its bearing on the question of the deaconesses of the apostolic Church.

Phœni′ce, Phœnic′ia (*land of palm trees*), a tract of country, of which Tyre and Sidon were the principal cities, to the north of Palestine, along the coast of the Mediterranean Sea; bounded by that sea on the west, and by the mountain range of Lebanon on the east. The name was not the one by which its native inhabitants called it, but was given to it by the Greeks, from the Greek word for the palm tree. The native name of Phœnicia was *Kenaan* (Canaan) or *Knâ*, signifying lowland, so named in contrast to the adjoining *Aram, i. e.* highland, the Hebrew name of Syria. The length of coast to which the name of Phœnicia was applied varied at different times. 1. What may be termed Phœnicia proper was a narrow undulating plain, extending from the pass of *Rás el-Beyâd* or *Abyad*, the Promontorium Album of the ancients, about six miles south of Tyre, to the *Nahr el-Auly*, the ancient Bostrenus, two miles north of Sidon. The plain is only 28 miles in length. Its average breadth is about a mile; but near Sidon the mountains retreat to a distance of two miles, and near Tyre to a distance of five miles. 2. A longer district, which afterward became entitled to the name of Phœnicia, extended up the coast to a point marked by the island of Aradus, and by Antaradus toward the north ; the southern boundary remaining the same as in Phœnicia proper. Phœnicia, thus defined, is estimated to have been about 120 miles in length ; while its breadth, between Lebanon and the sea, never exceeded 20 miles, and was generally much less. The whole of Phœnicia proper is well watered by various streams from the adjoining hills. The havens of Tyre and Sidon afforded water of sufficient depth for all the requirements of ancient navigation, and the neighbor-

ing range of the Lebanon, in its extensive forests, furnished what then seemed a nearly inexhaustible supply of timber for ship-building.

Language and race.—The Phœnicians spoke a branch of the Semitic language so closely allied to Hebrew that Phœnician and Hebrew, though different dialects, may practically be regarded as the same language. Concerning the original race to which the Phœnicians belonged, nothing can be known with certainty, because they are found already established along the Mediterranean Sea at the earliest dawn of authentic history, and for centuries afterward there is no record of their origin. According to Herodotus, vii. 89, they said of themselves in his time that they came in days of old from the shores of the Red Sea; and in this there would be nothing in the slightest degree improbable, as they spoke a language cognate to that of the Arabians, who inhabited the east coast of that sea. Still neither the truth nor the falsehood of the tradition can now be proved. But there is one point respecting their race which can be proved to be in the highest degree probable, and which has peculiar interest as bearing on the Jews, viz., that the Phœnicians were of the same race as the Canaanites.

Commerce, etc.—In regard to Phœnician trade, connected with the Israelites, it must be recollected that up to the time of David not one of the twelve tribes seems to have possessed a single harbor on the seacoast; it was impossible therefore that they could become a commercial people. But from the time that David had conquered Edom, an opening for trade was afforded to the Israelites. Solomon continued this trade with its king, obtained timber from its territory and employed its sailors and workmen. 2 Sam. 5 : 11 ; 1 Kings 5 : 9, 17, 18.

The religion of the Phœnicians, opposed to Monotheism, was a pantheistical personification of the forces of nature, and in its most philosophical shadowing forth of the supreme powers it may be said to have represented the male and female principles of production. In its popular form it was especially a worship of the sun, moon and five planets, or, as it might have been expressed according to ancient notions, of the seven planets—the most beautiful and perhaps the most natural form of idolatry ever presented to the human imagination. Their worship was a constant temptation for the Hebrews to Polytheism and idolatry—1. Because undoubtedly the Phœnicians, as a great commercial people, were more generally intelligent, and as we should now say civilized, than the inland agricultural population of Palestine. When the simple-minded Jews, therefore, came in contact with a people more versatile and apparently more enlightened than themselves, but who nevertheless, either in a philosophical or in a popular form, admitted a system of Polytheism, an influence would be exerted on Jewish minds tending to make them regard their exclusive devotion to their own one God, Jehovah, however transcendent his attributes, as unsocial and morose. 2. The Phœnician religion had in other respects an injurious effect on the people of Palestine, being in some points essentially demoralizing. For example, it sanctioned the dreadful superstition of burning children as sacrifices to a Phœnician god. Again, parts of the Phœnician religion, especially the worship of Astarte, tended to encourage dissoluteness in the relations of the sexes, and even to sanctify impurities of the most abominable description.

The only other fact respecting the Phœnicians that need be mentioned here is that the invention of letters was universally asserted by the Greeks and Romans to have been communicated by the Phœnicians to the Greeks. For further details respecting the Phœnicians, see TYRE and ZIDON. Phœnicia is now a land of ruins.

Phryg'ia (*dry, barren*). Perhaps there is no geographical term in the New Testament which is less capable of an exact definition. In fact there was no Roman province of Phrygia till considerably after the first establishment of Christianity in the peninsula of Asia Minor. The word was rather ethnological than political, and denoted, in a vague manner, the western part of the central region of that peninsula. Accordingly, in two of the three places where it is used it is mentioned in a manner not intended to be precise. Acts 16 : 6 ; 18 : 23. By Phrygia we must understand an extensive district in Asia Minor, which contributed portions to several Roman provinces, and varying portions at different times. (All over this district the Jews were probably numerous. The Phrygians were a very ancient people, and were sup-

posed to be among the aborigines of Asia Minor. Several bishops from Phrygia were present at the Councils of Nice, A.D. 325, and of Constantinople, A.D. 381, showing the prevalence of Christianity at that time.—ED.)

Phu'rah (*bough*), Gideon's servant, probably his armor-bearer, comp. 1 Sam. 14 : 1, who accompanied him in his midnight visit to the camp of the Midianites. Judges 7 : 10, 11.

Phu'rim. Esther 11 : 1. [PURIM.]

Phut, Put (*a bow*), the third name in the list of the sons of Ham, Gen. 10 : 6 ; 1 Chron. 1 : 8, elsewhere applied to an African country or people. The few mentions of Phut in the Bible clearly indicate a country or people of Africa, and, it must be added, probably not far from Egypt. Isa. 66 : 19 ; Jer. 46 : 9 ; Ezek. 27 : 10 ; 30 : 5 ; 38 : 5 ; Nah. 3 : 9. Some identify it with Libya, in the northern part of Africa, near the Mediterranean Sea; others, as Mr. Poole, with Nubia, south of Egypt.

Phu'vah (*mouth*), one of the sons of Issachar, Gen. 46 : 13, and founder of the family of the Punites.

Phygel'lus (*fugitive*). [HERMOGENES.]

Phyge'lus. Used in the Revised Version in 2 Tim. 1 : 15 for PHYGELLUS.

Phylactery. [FRONTLETS.]

Pi-be'seth, a town of lower Egypt, mentioned in Ezek. 30 : 17, the same as Bubastis, so named from the goddess Bubastis. It was situated on the west bank of the Pelusiac branch of the Nile, about 40 miles from Memphis. It was probably a city of great importance when Ezekiel foretold its doom.

Picture. In two of the three passages in which "picture" is used in the Authorized Version it denotes idolatrous representations, either independent images or more usually stones "portrayed," *i. e.* sculptured in low relief, or engraved and colored. Ezek. 23 : 14 ; Layard, *Nin. and Bab.* ii. 306, 308. Movable pictures, in the modern sense, were doubtless unknown to the Jews. The "pictures of silver" of Prov. 25 : 11 were probably wall surfaces or cornices with carvings.

Piece of gold. The rendering "pieces of gold," as in 2 Kings 5 : 5, is very doubtful; and "shekels of gold," as designating the value of the whole quantity, not individual pieces, is preferable. Coined money was unknown in Palestine till the Persian period.

Piece of silver. I. In the Old Testament the word "pieces" is used in the Authorized Version for a word understood in the Hebrew (if we except Ps. 68 : 30). The phrase is always "a thousand," or the like, "of silver." Gen. 20 : 16; 37 : 28; 45 : 22; Judges 9 : 4; 16 : 5; 2 Kings 6 : 25; Hos. 3 : 2; Zech. 11 : 12, 13. In similar passages the word "shekels" occurs in the Hebrew. There are other passages in which the Authorized Version supplies the word "shekels" instead of "pieces," Deut. 22 : 19, 29; Judges 17 : 2, 3, 4, 10; 2 Sam. 18 : 11, 12, and of these the first two require this to be done. The shekel, be it remembered, was the common weight for money, and therefore most likely to be understood in an elliptical phrase. The "piece" or shekel of silver weighed 220 grains, or about half an ounce, and was worth a little more than half a dollar (55 cents). II. In the New Testament two words are rendered by the phrase "piece of silver:" 1. *Drachma*, Luke 15 : 8, 9, which was a Greek silver coin, equivalent, at the time of St. Luke, to the Roman denarius (15 or 16 cents). 2. *Silver* occurs only in the account of the betrayal of our Lord for "thirty pieces of silver." Matt. 26 : 15; 27 : 3, 5, 6, 9. It is difficult to ascertain what coins are here intended. If the most common silver pieces be meant, they would be denarii. The parallel passage in Zechariah, ch. 11 : 12, 13, must, however, be taken into consideration, where shekels (worth about 55 cents) must be understood. It is more probable that the thirty pieces of silver were tetradrachms than that they were denarii (60 cents).

Piety. This word occurs but once in the Authorized Version : "Let them learn first to show *piety* at home," better, "toward their own household" or family. 1 Tim. 5 : 4. The choice of this word here instead of the more usual equivalents of "godliness," "reverence," and the like, was probably determined by the special sense of *pietas*, as "erga parentes," *i. e.* toward parents.

Pigeon. [TURTLE-DOVE.]

Pi-hahi′roth, a place before or at which the Israelites encamped, at the close of the third march from Rameses (the last place before they crossed the Red Sea), when they went out of Egypt. Ex. 14 : 2, 9; Num. 33 : 7, 8. It is an Egyptian word, signifying "the place where sedge grows."

Pi′late (*armed with a spear*), **Pon′-tius.** Pontius Pilate was the sixth Roman procurator of Judea, and under him our Lord worked, suffered and died, as we learn not only from Scripture, but from Tacitus (*Ann.* xv. 44). He was appointed A.D. 25-6, in the twelfth year of Tiberius. His arbitrary administration nearly drove the Jews to insurrection on two or three occasions. One of his first acts was to remove the headquarters of the army from Cæsarea to Jerusalem. The soldiers of course took with them their standards, bearing the image of the emperor, into the holy city. No previous governor had ventured on such an outrage. The people poured down in crowds

Coins struck by Pontius Pilate.

to Cæsarea, where the procurator was then residing, and besought him to remove the images. After five days of discussion he gave the signal to some concealed soldiers to surround the petitioners and put them to death unless they ceased to trouble him; but this only strengthened their determination, and they declared themselves ready rather to submit to death than forego their resistance to an idolatrous innovation. Pilate then yielded, and the standards were by his orders brought down to Cæsarea. His slaughter of certain Galileans, Luke 13 : 1, led to some remarks from our Lord on the connection between sin and calamity. It must have occurred at some feast at Jerusalem, in the outer court of the temple. It was the custom for the procurators to reside at Jerusalem during the great feasts, to preserve order, and accordingly, at the time of our Lord's last Passover, Pilate was occupying his official residence in Herod's palace. The history of his condemnation of our Lord is familiar to all. We learn from Josephus that Pilate's anxiety to avoid giving offence to

Cæsar did not save him from political disaster. The Samaritans were unquiet and rebellious; Pilate led his troops against them, and defeated them easily enough. The Samaritans complained to Vitellius, then president of Syria, and he sent Pilate to Rome to answer their accusations before the emperor. When he reached it he found Tiberius dead and Caius (Caligula) on the throne, A.D. 36. Eusebius adds that soon afterward, "wearied with misfortunes," he killed himself. As to the scene of his death there are various traditions. One is that he was banished to Vienna Allobrogum (Vienne on the Rhone), where a singular monument—a pyramid on a quadrangular base, 52 feet high—is called Pontius Pilate's tomb. Another is that he sought to hide his sorrows on the mountain by the lake of Lucerne, now called Mount Pilatus; and there, after spending years in its recesses, in remorse and despair rather than penitence, plunged into the dismal lake which occupies its summit.

Pil'dash (*flame of fire*), one of the eight sons of Nahor, Abraham's brother, by his wife and niece, Milcah. Gen. 22 : 22. (B.C. 1900.)

Pil'eha (*worship*), the name of one of the chief of the people, probably a family, who signed the covenant with Nehemiah. Neh. 10 : 24. (B.C. 410.)

Pillar. The notion of a pillar is of a shaft or isolated pile, either supporting or not supporting a roof. But perhaps the earliest application of the pillar was the votive or monumental. This in early times consisted of nothing but a single stone or pile of stones. Gen. 28 : 18; 31 : 46, etc. The stone Ezel, 1 Sam. 20 : 19, was probably a terminal stone or a waymark. The "place" set up by Saul, 1 Sam. 15 : 12, is explained by St. Jerome to be a trophy. So also Jacob set up a pillar over Rachel's grave. Gen. 35 : 20. The monolithic tombs and obelisks of Petra are instances of similar usage. Lastly, the figurative use of the term "pillar," in reference to the cloud and fire accompanying the Israelites on their march, or as in Cant. 3 : 6 and Rev. 10 : 1, is plainly derived from the notion of an isolated column not supporting a roof.

Pillar, Plain of the, or rather "oak of the pillar" (that being the real signification of the Hebrew word *elôn*), a tree which stood near Shechem, and at which the men of Shechem and the house of Millo assembled to crown Abimelech the son of Gideon. Judges 9 : 6.

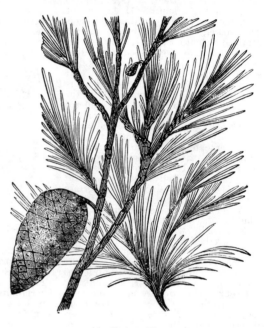

An Eastern Pine.

Pilled, Gen. 30 : 37, 38; "peeled," Isa. 18 : 2; Ezek. 29 : 18. The verb "to pill" appears in old English as identical in meaning with "to peel, to strip."

Pil'ta-i, or **Pilta'i** (*my deliverances*), the representative of the priestly house of Moadiah or Maadiah, in the time of Joiakim the son of Jeshua. Neh. 12 : 17. (B.C. 445.)

Pine tree. 1. Heb. *tidhâr.* Isa. 41 . 19; 60 : 13. What tree is intended is not certain; but the rendering "pine" seems least probable of any. 2. *Shemen*, Neh 8 : 15, is probably the wild olive.

Pinnacle (of the temple), Matt. 4 : 5; Luke 4 : 9. The Greek word ought to be rendered not *a* pinnacle, but *the* pinnacle. The only part of the temple which answered to the modern sense of pinnacle was the golden spikes erected on the roof to prevent birds from settling there. Perhaps the word means the battlement ordered by law to be added to every roof. (According to Alford it was the roof of Herod's royal portico of the temple, "which overhung the ravine of Kedron from a dizzy height"—600 or 700 feet.—ED.)

Pi'non (*darkness*), one of the "dukes" of Edom,—that is, head or founder of a tribe of that nation. Gen. 36 : 41; 1 Chron. 1 : 52.

Pipe (Heb. *châlil*). The Hebrew word so rendered is derived from a root signifying "to bore, perforate," and is represented with sufficient correctness by the English "pipe" or "flute," as in the margin of 1 Kings 1 : 40. The pipe was the type of perforated wind instruments, as the harp was of stringed instruments. It was made of reed, bronze or copper. It is one of the simplest, and therefore probably one of the oldest, of musical instruments. It is associated with the tabret as an instrument of a peaceful and social character. The pipe and tabret were used at the banquets of the Hebrews, Isa. 5 : 12, and accompanied the simpler religious services when the young prophets, returning from the high place, caught their inspiration from the harmony, 1 Sam. 10 : 5; or the pilgrims, on their way to the great festivals of their ritual, beguiled the weariness of the march with psalms sung to the simple music of the pipe. Isa. 30 : 29. The sound of the pipe was apparently a soft wailing note, which made it appropriate to be used in mourning and at funerals, Matt. 9 : 23, and in the lament of the prophet over the destruction of Moab. Jer. 48 : 36. It was even used in the temple choir, as appears from Ps. 87 : 7. In later times the funeral and death-bed were never without the professional pipers or flute-players, Matt. 9 : 23, a custom which still exists. In the social and festive life of the Egyptians the pipe played as prominent a part as among the Hebrews.

Pi'ram (*like a wild ass; fleet*), the Amorite king of Jarmuth at the time of Joshua's conquest of Canaan. Josh. 10 : 3. (B.C. 1450.)

Pir'athon (*princely*), "in the land of Ephraim in the mount of the Amalekite," a place in Judges 12 : 15. Its site, now called *Fer'ata*, is about one mile and a half south of the road from *Jaffa*, by *Hableh*, to *Nablûs*. Pirathonites are mentioned in Judges 12 : 13, 15 and 1 Chron. 27 : 14.

Pir'athonite, a native of or dweller in Pirathon. Two such are named in the Bible:—1. Abdon ben-Hillel. Judges 12 : 13, 15. 2. "Benaiah the Pirathonite, of the children of Ephraim." 1 Chron. 27 : 14.

Pis'gah (*section*, i. e. *peak*), Num. 21 : 20; 23 : 14; Deut. 3 : 27; 34 : 1, a mountain range or district, the same as, or a part of, that called the mountains of Abarim. Comp. Deut. 32 : 49 with 34 : 1. It lay on the east of Jordan, contiguous to the field of Moab, and immediately opposite Jericho. Its highest point or summit—its "head"—was Mount Nebo. [See NEBO.]

Pisid'ia (*pitchy*) was a district in Asia Minor north of Pamphylia, and reached to and was partly included in Phrygia. Thus Antioch in Pisidia was sometimes called a Phrygian town. St. Paul passed through Pisidia twice, with Barnabas, on the first missionary journey, *i. e.*, both in going from Perga to Iconium, Acts 13 : 13, 14, 51, and in returning. Acts 14 : 21, 24, 25; comp. 2 Tim. 3 : 11. It is probable also that he traversed the northern part of the district, with Silas and Timotheus, on the second missionary journey, Acts 16 : 6; but the word Pisidia does not occur except in reference to the former journey.

Pi'son. [EDEN.]

Pit. [HELL.]

Pitch. The three Hebrew words so translated all represent the same object, viz., mineral pitch or asphalt in its different aspects. Asphalt is an opaque, inflammable substance, which bubbles up from subterranean fountains in a liquid state, and hardens by exposure to the air, but readily melts under the influence of heat. In the latter state it is very tenacious, and was used as a cement in lieu of mortar in Babylonia, Gen. 11 : 3, as well as for coating the outside of vessels, Gen. 6 : 14, and particularly for making the papyrus boats of the Egyptians water-tight. Ex. 2 : 3. The Jews and Arabians got their supply in large quantities from the Dead Sea, which hence received its classical name of *Lacus Asphaltites.*

Pitcher. This word is used in the Authorized Version to denote the earthen water-jars or pitchers with one or two handles, used chiefly by women for carrying water, as in the story of Rebekah. Gen. 24 : 15-20; but see Mark 14 : 13; Luke 22 : 10. This mode of carrying has been and still is customary both in the East and elsewhere. The vessels used for the purpose are generally borne on the head or the shoulder. The Bedouin women commonly use skin bottles. Such was the "bottle" carried by Hagar. Gen. 21 : 14. The same word is used of the pitchers employed by Gideon's three hundred men. Judges 7 : 16.

Antioch in Pisidia.

Pi'thom (*city of the setting sun*), one of the store-cites built by the Israelites for the first oppressor, the Pharaoh "which knew not Joseph." Ex. 1 : 11. It is probably the Patumus of Herodotus (ii. 159), a town on the borders of Egypt, near which Necho constructed a canal from the Nile to the Arabian Gulf.

Pi'thon (*harmless*), one of the four sons of Micah, the son of Mephibosheth. 1 Chron. 8 : 35; 9 : 41. (B.C. 1050.)

Plague, The. The plague is considered to be a severe kind of typhus, accompanied by buboes (tumors). Like the cholera, it is most violent at the first outbreak, causing almost instant death. Great difference of opinion has obtained as to whether it is contagious or not. It was very prevalent in the East, and still prevails in Egypt. Several Hebrew words are translated "pestilence" or "plague;" but not one of these words can be considered as designating by its signification the disease now called the plague. Whether the disease be mentioned must be judged from the sense of passages, not from the sense of words. Those pestilences which were sent as special judgments, and were either supernaturally rapid in their effects or were in addition directed against particular culprits, are beyond the reach of human inquiry. But we also read of pestilences which, although sent as judgments, have the characteristics of modern epidemics, not being rapid beyond nature nor directed against individuals. Lev. 26 : 25; Deut. 28 : 21. In neither of these passages does it seem certain that the plague is specified. The notices in the prophets present the same difficulty. Hezekiah's disease has been thought to have been the plague, and its fatal nature, as well as the mention of a boil, makes this not improbable. On the other hand, there is no mention of a pestilence among his people at the time.

Plagues, The ten. The occasion on which the plagues were sent is described in Ex. 3-12. 1. *The plague of blood.*—When Moses and Aaron came before Pharaoh, a miracle was required of them. Then Aaron's rod became "a serpent" (Authorized Version), or rather "a crocodile." Its being changed into an animal reverenced by all the Egyptians, or by some of them, would have been an especial warning to Pharaoh. The Egyptian magicians called by the king produced what seemed to be the same wonder, yet Aaron's rod swallowed up the others. Ex. 7 : 3–12. This passage, taken alone, would appear to indicate that the magicians succeeded in working wonders, but, if it is compared with the others which relate their opposition on the occasions of the first three plagues, a contrary inference seems more reasonable; for the very first time that Moses wrought his miracle without giving previous notice, the magicians "did so with their enchantments," but failed. A comparison with other passages strengthens us in the inference that the magicians succeeded merely by juggling. After this warning to Pharaoh, Aaron, at the word of Moses, waved his rod over the Nile, and the river was turned into blood, with all its canals and reservoirs, and every vessel of water drawn from them; the fish died, and the river stank. The Egyptians could not drink of it, and digged around it for water. This plague was doubly humiliating to the religion of the country, as the Nile was held sacred, as well as some kinds of its fish, not to speak of the crocodiles, which probably were destroyed. Ex. 7 : 16–25. Those who have endeavored to explain this plague by natural causes have referred to the changes of color to which the Nile is subject, the appearance of the Red Sea, and the so-called rain and dew of blood of the middle ages; the last two occasioned by small fungi of very rapid growth. But such theories do not explain why the wonder happened at a time of year when the Nile is most clear, nor why it killed the fish and made the water unfit to be drunk.

2. *The plague of frogs.*—When seven days had passed after the first plague, the river and all the open waters of Egypt brought forth countless frogs, which not only covered the land, but filled the houses, even in their driest parts and vessels, for the ovens and kneading-troughs are specified. This must have been an especially trying judgment to the Egyptians, as frogs were included among the sacred animals. Ex. 8 : 1–15.

3. *The plague of lice.*—The dry land was now smitten by the rod, and its very dust seemed turned into minute noxious insects, so thickly did they swarm on man and beast, or rather "in" them. The scrupulous cleanliness of the Egyptians would add intolerably to the bodily distress of this plague, by which also they again incurred religious defilement. As to the species of the vermin, there seems no reason to disturb the authorized translation of the word. The magicians, who had imitated by their enchantments the two previous miracles, were now foiled. They struck the ground, as Aaron did, and repeated their own incantations, but it was without effect. Ex. 8 : 16–19.

4. *The plague of flies.*—After the river and the land, the air was smitten, being filled with winged insects, which swarmed in the houses and devoured the land, but Goshen was exempted from the plague. The word translated "swarms of flies" most probably denotes the great Egyptian beetle, *Scarabæus sacer*, which is constantly represented in their sculptures. Besides the annoying and destructive habits of its tribe, it was an object of worship, and thus the Egyptians were again scourged by their own superstitions. Ex. 8 : 20–32.

5. *The plague of the murrain of beasts.* —Still coming closer and closer to the Egyptians, God sent a disease upon the cattle, which were not only their property but their deities. At the precise time of which Moses forewarned Pharaoh, all the cattle of the Egyptians were smitten with a murrain and died, but not one of the cattle of the Israelites suffered. Ex. 9 : 1–7.

6. *The plague of boils.*—From the cattle the hand of God was extended to the persons of the Egyptians. Moses and Aaron were commanded to take ashes of the furnace, and to "sprinkle it toward the heaven in the sight of Pharaoh." It was to become "small dust" throughout Egypt, and "be a boil breaking forth [with] blains upon man and upon beast." Ex. 9 : 8–12. This accordingly came to pass. The plague seems to have been the black leprosy, a fearful kind of elephantiasis, which was long remembered as "the botch of Egypt." Deut. 28 : 27, 35.

7. *The plague of hail.*—The account of the seventh plague is preceded by a warning which Moses was commanded to deliver to Pharaoh, respecting the terrible nature of the plagues that were to ensue if he remained obstinate. Man and beast were smitten, and the herbs and every tree broken, save in the land of Goshen. The ruin caused by the hail was evidently

far greater than that effected by any of the earlier plagues. Hail is now extremely rare, but not unknown, in Egypt, and it is interesting that the narrative seems to imply that the narrative falls there. Ex. 9 : 13–34.

8. *The plague of locusts.*—The severity of this plague can be well understood by those who have been in Egypt in a part of the country where a flight of locusts has alighted. In this case the plague was greater than an ordinary visitation, since it extended over a far wider space, rather than because it was more intense; for it is impossible to imagine any more complete destruction than that always caused by a swarm of locusts. Ex. 10 : 1–20.

9. *The plague of darkness.*—" There was a thick darkness in all the land of Egypt three days;" while "all the children of Israel had light in their dwellings." It has been illustrated by reference to the samoom and the hot wind of the Khamáseen. The former is a sand-storm which occurs in the desert, seldom lasting more than a quarter of an hour or twenty minutes, but for the time often causing the darkness of twilight, and affecting man and beast. The hot wind of the Khamáseen usually blows for three days and nights, and carries so much sand with it that it produces the appearance of a yellow fog. It thus resembles the samoom, though far less powerful and less distressing in its effects. It is not known to cause actual darkness. The plague may have been an extremely severe sandstorm, miraculous in its violence and duration, for the length of three days does not make it natural, since the severe storms are always very brief. Ex. 10 : 21–29.

10. *The death of the first-born.*—Before the tenth plague Moses went to warn Pharaoh :—" Thus saith the Lord, About midnight will I go out into the midst of Egypt; and all the first-born in the land of Egypt shall die, from the first-born of Pharaoh that sitteth upon his throne, even to the first-born of the maidservant that is behind the mill; and all the first-born of beasts." Ex. 11 : 4, 5. The clearly miraculous nature of this plague, in its severity, its falling upon man and beast, and the singling out of the firstborn, puts it wholly beyond comparison with any natural pestilence, even the severest recorded in history, whether of the peculiar Egyptian plague or of other like epidemics. The history of the ten plagues strictly ends with the death of

the first-born. The gradual increase in severity of the plagues is perhaps the best key to their meaning. They seem to have been sent as warnings to the oppressor, to afford him a means of seeing God's will and an opportunity of repenting before Egypt was ruined. The lesson that Pharaoh's career teaches us seems to be that there are men whom the most signal judgments do not affect so as to cause any lasting repentance.

The following characteristics of the plagues may be specially noticed : (1) Their relation to natural phenomena. Each of the inflictions has a demonstrable connection with Egyptian customs and phenomena; each is directly aimed at some Egyptian superstition; all are marvellous, not for the most part as reversing, but as developing, forces inherent in nature, and directing them to a special end. —*Canon Cook.* (2) Their order. They are divided first into nine and one; the last one standing clearly apart from all the others. The nine are arranged in threes. In the first of each three the warning is given to Pharaoh in the morning. In the first and second of each three the plague is announced beforehand; in the third, not. At the third the magicians acknowledge the finger of God; at the sixth they cannot stand before Moses; and at the ninth Pharaoh refuses to see the face of Moses any more. The gradation of the severity of these strokes is no less obvious. In the first three no distinction is made among the inhabitants of the land; in the remaining seven a distinction is made between the Israelites, who are shielded from, and the Egyptians, who are exposed to, the stroke. —*Kurtz.* (3) Their duration. It is probable that the plagues extended through a period of several months. The first plague occurred probably during the annual inundation of the Nile, hence about the middle of June (*Edersheim*). The second, that of the frogs, in September, the time when Egypt often suffers in this way. The seventh (hail) came when the barley was in ear, and before the wheat was grown, and hence in February; and the tenth came in the following March or April. (4) Their significance. The first plague was directed against the Nile, one of the Egyptian deities, adored as a source of life, not only to the produce of the land, but to its inhabitants. The second plague, that of the frogs, struck also at the idolatry of Egypt; for the frog was an object of worship. The third plague turned the land, which was worshipped, into a source of torment; the dust produced a curse. The fourth plague consisted in the torment of either flies of a ravenous disposition, or beetles. If the former, then the air, which was worshipped, was turned into a source of exquisite annoyance; if the latter, then the beetle, one of the most common of the Egyptian idols, swarmed with voracious appetite, attacking even man, as the Egyptian beetle still does, and inflicting painful wounds. The fifth plague, that of murrain, struck at the cattle-worship for which Egypt was celebrated. The sixth plague, produced by the ashes scattered toward heaven, in conformity with an ancient Egyptian rite, as if in invocation of the sun-god, continued the warfare of Jehovah upon Egyptian idolatry; the religious ceremony which was employed to invoke blessing brought disease. The seventh plague, beginning a new series, seems to have been aimed, like those which followed, to demonstrate the power of Jehovah over all the elements, and even life itself, in contrast with the impotence of the idols. The storm and the hail came at his bidding. The locusts appeared and departed at his word. The sun itself was veiled at his command. Nay, the angel of death was held and loosed by his hand alone. The tenth plague had an immediate relation to idolatry, since it destroyed not only the first-born of man, but the first-born of beast; so that the sacred animals in the temples were touched by a power higher than those they were supposed to represent. The victory was complete; upon all the gods of Egypt, Jehovah had executed judgment.—*Rev. Franklin Johnson.*

Plains. This one term does duty in the Authorized Version for no less than seven distinct Hebrew words. 1. *Abêl.* This word perhaps answers more nearly to our word "meadow" than any other. It occurs in the names of Abel-maim, Abel-meholah, Abel-shittim, and is rendered "plain" in Judges 11 : 33—"plain of vineyards." 2. *Bik'âh.* Fortunately we are able to identify the most remarkable of the *bik'âhs* of the Bible, and thus to ascertain the force of the term. The great plain or valley of Cœle-Syria, the "hollow land" of the Greeks, which separates the two ranges of Lebanon and Anti-Lebanon, is the most remarkable of them all. Out of Palestine we find de-

noted by the word *bik'âh* the "plain of the land of Shinar," Gen 11 : 2, the "plain of Mesopotamia," Ezek. 3 : 22, 23 ; 8 : 4 ; 37 : 1, 2, and the "plain in the province of Dura." Dan. 3 : 1. 3. *Hashefêlâh,* the invariable designation of the depressed, flat or gently-undulating region which intervened between the highlands of Judah and the Mediterranean, and was commonly in possession of the Philistines. 4. *Elôn.* Our translators have uniformly rendered this word "plain;" but this is not the verdict of the majority or the most trustworthy of the ancient versions. They regard the word as meaning an "oak" or "grove of oaks," a rendering supported by nearly all the commentators and lexicographers of the present day. The passages in which the word occurs erroneously translated "plain" are as follows : Plain of Moreh, Gen. 12 : 6 ; Deut. 11 : 30 ; plain of Mamre, Gen. 13 : 18 ; 14 : 13 ; 18 : 1 ; plain of Zaanaim, Judges 4 : 11 ; plain of the pillar, Judges 9 : 6 ; plain of Meonenim, Judges 9 : 37 ; plain of Tabor, 1 Sam. 10 : 3.

Pledge. [LOAN.]

Ple'iades. The Hebrew word (*cîmâh*) so rendered occurs in Job 9 : 9 ; 38 : 31 ; Amos 5 : 8. In the last passage our Authorized Version has "the seven stars," although the Geneva version translates the word "Pleiades" as in the other cases. The Pleiades are a group of stars situated on the shoulder of the constellation Taurus. The rendering "sweet influences" of the Authorized Version, Job 38 : 31, is a relic of the lingering belief in the power which the stars exerted over human destiny. But Schaff thinks the phrase arose from the fact that the Pleiades appear about the middle of April, and hence are associated with the return of spring, the season of *sweet influences.*

Eastern Plough.

Plough. The ploughs of ancient Egypt consisted of a share—often pointed with iron or bronze—two handles, and a pole which was inserted into the base of the two handles. Ploughs in Palestine have usually but one handle, with a pole joined to it near the ground, and drawn by oxen, cows or camels.

An Arab Ploughing. (Modern.)

Poch'ereth. The children of Pochereth of Zebaim were among the children of Solomon's servants who returned with Zerubbabel. Ezra 2 : 57 ; Neh. 7 : 59.

Poetry, Hebrew. 1. *Lyrical poetry.* —Of the three kinds of poetry which are illustrated by the Hebrew literature, the *lyric* occupies the foremost place. That literature abounds with illustrations of all forms of lyrical poetry, in its most manifold and wide-embracing compass, from such short ejaculations as the songs of the two Lamechs and Ps. 15, 117 and others, to the longer chants of victory and thanksgiving, like the songs of Deborah and David. Judges 5 ; Ps. 18. The Shemitic nations have nothing approaching to an *epic* poem, and in proportion to this defect the lyric element prevailed more greatly, commencing in the pre-Mosaic times, flourishing in rude vigor during the earlier periods of the judges, the heroic age of the Hebrews, growing with the nation's growth and strengthening with its strength, till it reached its highest excellence in David, the warrior-poet, and from thenceforth began slowly to decline.

2. *Gnomic poetry.*—The second grand division of Hebrew poetry is occupied by

a class of poems which are peculiarly Shemitic, and which represent the nearest approaches made by the people of that race to anything like philosophic thought. Reasoning there is none : we have only results, and those rather the product of observation and reflection than of induction or argumentation. As lyric poetry is the expression of the poet's own feelings and impulses, so gnomic poetry is the form in which the desire of communicating knowledge to others finds vent. Its germs are the floating proverbs which pass current in the mouths of the people, and embody the experiences of many with the wit of one. The utterer of sententious sayings was to the Hebrews the wise man, the philosopher. Of the earlier isolated proverbs but few examples remain.

3. *Dramatic poetry.*—It is impossible to assert that no form of the drama existed among the Hebrew people. It is unquestionably true, as Ewald observes, that the Arab reciters of romances will many times in their own persons act out a complete drama in recitation, changing their voice and gestures with the change of person and subject. Something of this kind may possibly have existed among the Hebrews ; still there is no evidence that it did exist, nor any grounds for making even a probable conjecture with regard to it. But the mere fact of the existence of these rude exhibitions among the Arabs and Egyptians of the present day is of no weight when the question to be decided is whether the Song of Songs was designed to be so represented, as a simple pastoral drama, or whether the book of Job is a dramatic poem or not. Inasmuch as it represents an action and a progress, it is a drama as truly and really as any poem can be which develops the working of passion and the alternations of faith, hope, distrust, triumphant confidence and black despair, in the struggle which it depicts the human mind as engaged in while attempting to solve one of the most intricate problems

it can be called upon to regard. It is a drama as life is a drama, the most powerful of all tragedies; but that it is a dramatic poem, intended to be represented upon a stage, or capable of being so represented, may be confidently denied.

One characteristic of Hebrew poetry, not indeed peculiar to it, but shared by it in common with the literature of other nations, is its intensely national and local coloring. The writers were Hebrews of the Hebrews, drawing their inspiration from the mountains and rivers of Palestine, which they have immortalized in their poetic figures, and even while uttering the sublimest and most universal truths never forgetting their own nationality in its narrowest and intensest form. Examples of this remarkable characteristic of the Hebrew poets stand thick upon every page of these writings, and in striking contrast with the vague generalizations of the Indian philosophic poetry. About one third of the Old Testament is poetry in the Hebrew—a large part of Job, Psalms, Proverbs, Ecclesiastes, the Song of Solomon, besides a great part of the prophets. Fragments of poetry are also found in the historical books. (The form which biblical poetry takes is not of rhyme and metre—the rhythm of *quantity* in the syllables—as with us, but the rhythm of the *thought*,—there usually being two corresponding members to each distich or verse, which is called a parallelism. To some extent there is verbal rhythm. Sometimes there were alliterations, as in the 119th Psalm, which is divided up into sections, one for each letter of their alphabet, and each of the eight verses in a section begins with the same letter in the Hebrew; and chap. 31, vs. 10–31, of the book of Proverbs is an alphabetical acrostic in praise of "the virtuous woman." The poetry of the Hebrews, in its essential poetic nature, stands in the front rank. It abounds in metaphors and images and in high poetic feeling and fervor.—ED.)

Pol'lux. [CASTOR AND POLLUX.]

Polygamy. [MARRIAGE.]

Pomegranate. The pomegranate tree, *Punica granatum*, derives its name from the Latin *pomum granatum*, "grained apple." The Romans gave it the name of *Punica*, as the tree was introduced from Carthage. It belongs to the natural order *Myrtaceæ* (Myrtle), being, however, rather a tall bush than a tree. The foliage is dark green, the flowers are crimson, the fruit, which is about the size of an orange, is red when ripe, which in Palestine is about the middle of October. It contains a quantity of juice. Mention is made in Cant. 8 : 2 of spiced wine of the juice of the pomegranate. The rind is used in the manufacture of morocco leather, and together with the bark is sometimes used

Pomegranate and Flower.

medicinally. Dr. Royle (Kitto's *Cyc.*, art "Rimmon") states that this tree is a native of Asia, and is to be traced from Syria through Persia, even to the mountains of northern India. The pomegranate was early cultivated in Egypt; hence the complaint of the Israelites in the wilderness of Zin, Num. 20 : 5, this "is no place of figs, or of vines, or of pomegranates." Carved figures of the pomegranate adorned the tops of the pillars in Solomon's temple, 1 Kings 7 : 18, 20, etc.; and worked representations of this fruit, in blue, purple and scarlet, ornamented the hem of the robe of the ephod. Ex. 28 : 33, 34.

Pommels, only in 2 Chron. 4 : 12, 13. In 1 Kings 7 : 41, "bowls." The word signifies convex projections belonging to the capitals of pillars.

Pond. The ponds of Egypt, Ex. 7 : 19; 8 : 5, were doubtless water left by the inundation of the Nile. Ponds for fish are mentioned in Isa. 19 : 10.

Pon'tius Pi'late. [PILATE.]

Pon'tus, a large district in the north of Asia Minor, extending along the coast of the Pontus Euxinus Sea (Pontus), from which circumstance the name was derived. It corresponds nearly to the modern Trebizond. It is three times mentioned in the New Testament—Acts 2 : 9; 18 : 2; 1 Pet. 1 : 1. All these passages agree in showing that there were many Jewish residents in the district. As to the annals of Pontus, the one brilliant passage of its history is the life of the great Mithridates. Under Nero the whole region was made a Roman province, bearing the name of Pontus. It was conquered by the Turks in A.D. 1461, and is still under their dominion.

Pool. Pools, like the tanks of India, are in many parts of Palestine and Syria the only resource for water during the dry season, and the failure of them involves drought and calamity. Isa. 42: 15. Of the various pools mentioned in

Pools of Solomon, with Saracenic Castle.

Scripture, perhaps the most celebrated are the pools of Solomon near Bethlehem, called by the Arabs *el-Burak*, from which an aqueduct was carried which still supplies Jerusalem with water. Eccles. 2: 6; Ecclus. 24 : 30, 31.

Poor. The general kindly spirit of the law toward the poor is sufficiently shown by such passages as Deut. 15 : 7, for the reason that (ver. 11) " the poor shall never cease out of the land." Among the special enactments in their favor the following must be mentioned : 1. The right of gleaning. Lev. 19 : 9, 10; Deut. 24 : 19, 21. 2. From the produce of the land in sabbatical years the poor and the stranger were to have their portion. Ex. 23: 11; Lev. 25 : 6. 3. Re-entry upon land in the jubilee year, with the limitation as to town homes. Lev. 25 : 25-30. 4. Prohibition of usury and of retention of pledges. Ex. 22 : 25-27; Lev. 25 : 35, 37, etc. 5. Permanent bondage forbidden, and manumission of Hebrew bondmen a bondwomen enjoined in the sabbatical and jubilee years. Lev. 25 : 39-42, 47-54; Deut. 15 : 12-15. 6. Portions from the tithes to be shared by the poor after the Levites. Deut. 14 : 28; 26 : 12, 13. 7. The poor to partake in entertainments at the feasts of Weeks and Tabernacles. Deut. 16 : 11, 14; see Neh. 8 : 10. 8. Daily payment of wages. Lev. 19 : 13. Principles similar to those laid down by Moses are inculcated in the New Testament, as Luke 3 : 11; 14 : 13; Acts 6 : 1; Gal. 2 : 10; James 2 : 15.

Poplar. This is the rendering of the Hebrew word *libneh*, which occurs in Gen. 30 : 37 and Hos. 4 : 13. Several authorities are in favor of the rendering of the Authorized Version, and think that "white poplar" (*Populus alba*) is the tree denoted; others understand the "storax tree" (*Styrax officinale*, Linn.). Both poplars and storax or styrax trees are common in Palestine, and either would suit the passages where the Hebrew term occurs. Storax is mentioned in Ecclus. 24 : 15, together with other aromatic substances. The *Styrax officinale* is a shrub from nine to twelve feet high, with ovate leaves, which are white underneath; the flowers are in racemes, and are white or cream-colored.

Por'atha, one of the ten sons of Haman slain by the Jews in Shushan the palace. Esther 9 : 8.

Porch. 1. *Ulam,* or *ûlâm.* 1 Chron. 28 : 11. 2. *Misderôn ûlam,* Judges 3 : 23, strictly a vestibule, was probably a sort of veranda chamber in the works of Solomon, open in front and at the sides, but capable of being enclosed with awnings or curtains. The porch, Matt. 26 : 71, may have been the passage from the street into the first court of the house, in which, in eastern houses, is the *mastâbah* or stone bench, for the porter or persons waiting, and where also the master of the house often receives visitors and transacts business.

Por'cius Fes'tus. [FESTUS.]

Porter. This word when used in the Authorized Version does not bear its modern signification of a carrier of burdens, but denotes in every case a gate-keeper, from the Latin *portarius,* the man who attended to the *porta* or gate.

Possession. [DEMONIACS.]

Post. 1. Probably, as Gesenius argues, the door-case of a door, including the lintel and side posts. The posts of the doors of the temple were of olive wood. 1 Kings 6 : 33. 2. A courier or carrier of messages, used among other places in Job 9 : 25.

Pot. The term "pot" is applicable to so many sorts of vessels that it can scarcely be restricted to any one in particular. 1. *Asûc,* 2 Kings 4 : 2, an earthen jar, deep and narrow, without handles, probably like the Roman and Egyptian amphora, inserted in a stand of wood or stone. 2. *Cheres,* an earthen vessel for stewing or seething. Lev. 6 : 28; Ezek. 4 : 9. 3. *Dûd,* a vessel for culinary purposes, perhaps of smaller size. 1 Sam. 2 : 14. The "pots" set before the Rechabites, Jer. 35 : 5, were probably bulging jars or bowls. The water-pots of Cana appear to have been large amphoræ, such as are in use at the present day in Syria. These were of stone or hard earthenware. The water-pot of the Samaritan woman

may have been a leathern bucket, such as Bedouin women use.

Stone Water-jars.

Pot'iphar, an Egyptian name, also written Potipherah, signifies *belonging to the sun.* Potiphar, with whom the history of Joseph is connected, is described as "an officer of Pharaoh, chief of the executioners, an Egyptian." Gen. 39 : 1; comp. 37 : 36. (B.C. 1728.) He appears to have been a wealthy man. Gen. 39 : 4–6. The view we have of Potiphar's household is exactly in accordance with the representations on the monuments. When Joseph was accused, his master contented himself with casting him into prison. Gen. 39 : 19, 20. After this we hear no more of Potiphar. [JOSEPH.]

Potiph'erah, or **Potiphe'rah,** was priest or prince of On, and his daughter Asenath was given Joseph to wife by Pharaoh. Gen. 41 : 45, 50; 46 : 20. (B.C. 1715.)

Potsherd, also in Authorized Version "sherd," a broken piece of earthenware. Prov. 26 : 23.

Pottage. [LENTILS.]

Potter's field, The, a piece of ground which, according to the statement of St. Matthew, Matt. 27 : 7, was purchased by the priests with the thirty pieces of silver rejected by Judas, and converted into a burial-place for Jews not belonging to the city. [ACELDAMA.]

Pottery. The art of pottery is one of the most common and most ancient of all manufactures. It is abundantly evident, both that the Hebrews used earthenware vessels in the wilderness and that the potter's trade was afterward carried on in Palestine. They had themselves been concerned in the potter's trade in Egypt, Ps. 81 : 6, and the wall-paintings minutely illustrate the Egyptian process. The clay, when dug, was trodden by men's feet so as to form a paste, Isa. 41 : 25 ; Wisd. 15 : 7 ; then placed by the potter on the wheel beside which he sat, and shaped by him with his hands. How early the wheel came into use in Palestine is not known, but it seems likely that it

Eastern Potter.

was adopted from Egypt. Isa. 45 : 9 ; Jer. 18 : 3. The vessel was then smoothed and coated with a glaze, and finally burnt in a furnace. There was at Jerusalem a royal establishment of potters, 1 Chron. 4 : 23, from whose employment, and from the fragments cast away in the process, the Potter's Field perhaps received its name. Isa. 30 : 14.

Pound. 1. A weight. [See WEIGHTS AND MEASURES.] 2. A sum of money, put in the Old Testament, 1 Kings 10 : 17 ; Ezra 2 : 69 ; Neh. 7 : 71, for the Hebrew *maneh*, worth in silver about $25. In the parable of the ten pounds, Luke 19 : 12-27, the reference appears to be to a Greek pound, a weight used as a money of account, of which sixty went to the talent. It was worth $15 to $17.

Præto′rium (in the Revised Version translated *palace*, Matt. 27 : 27 ; John 18 : 28, 33 ; 19 : 9), the headquarters of the Roman military governor, wherever he happened to be. In time of peace some one of the best buildings of the city which was the residence of the proconsul or prætor was selected for this purpose. Thus at Cæsarea that of Herod the Great

was occupied by Felix, Acts 23 : 35 , and at Jerusalem the new palace erected by the same prince was the residence of Pilate. After the Roman power was established in Judea, a Roman guard was always maintained in the Antonia. The prætorian camp at Rome, to which St. Paul refers, Philip. 1 : 13, was erected by the emperor Tiberius, acting under the advice of Sejanus. It stood outside the walls, at some distance short of the fourth milestone. St. Paul appears to have been permitted, for the space of two years, to lodge, so to speak, "within the rules" of the prætorium, Acts 28 : 30, although still under the custody of a soldier.

Prayer. The object of this article will be to touch briefly on — 1. The doctrine of Scripture as to the nature and efficacy of prayer; 2. Its directions as to time, place and manner of prayer; 3. Its types and examples of prayer. 1. Scripture does not give any theoretical explanation of the mystery which attaches to prayer. The difficulty of understanding its real efficacy arises chiefly from two sources : from the belief that man lives under general laws, which in all cases must be fulfilled unalterably ; and the opposing belief that he is master of his own destiny, and need pray for no external blessing. Now, Scripture, while, by the doctrine of spiritual influence, it entirely disposes of the latter difficulty, does not so entirely solve that part of the mystery which depends on the nature of God. It places it clearly before us, and emphasizes most strongly those doctrines on which the difficulty turns. Yet, while this is so, on the other hand the instinct of prayer is solemnly sanctioned and enforced on every page. Not only is its subjective effect asserted, but its real objective efficacy, as a means appointed by God for obtaining blessing, is both implied and expressed in the plainest terms. Thus, as usual in the case of such mysteries, the two apparently opposite truths are emphasized, because they are needful to man's conception of his relation to God; their reconcilement is not, perhaps cannot be, fully revealed. For, in fact, it is involved in that inscrutable mystery which attends on the conception of any free action of man as necessary for the working out of the general laws of God's unchangeable will. At the same time it is clearly implied that such a reconcilement exists, and that all the apparently-isolated and independent exertions of man's spirit in prayer are in some way perfectly subordinated to the one supreme will of God, so as to form a part of his scheme of providence. It is also implied that the key to the mystery lies in the fact of man's spiritual unity with God in Christ, and of the consequent gift of the Holy Spirit. So also is it said of the spiritual influence of the Holy Ghost on each individual mind that while " we know not what to pray for," the indwelling " Spirit makes intercession for the saints, *according to the will of God.*" Rom. 8 : 26, 27. Here, as probably in all other cases, the action of the Holy Spirit on the soul is to free agents what the laws of nature are to things inanimate, and is the power which harmonizes free individual action with the universal will of God. 2. There are no directions as to prayer given in the Mosaic law : the duty is rather taken for granted, as an adjunct to sacrifice, than enforced or elaborated. It is hardly conceivable that, even from the beginning, public prayer did not follow every public sacrifice. Such a practice is alluded to in Luke 1 : 10 as common ; and in one instance, at the offering of the first-fruits, it was ordained in a striking form. Deut. 26 : 12-15. In later times it certainly grew into a regular service both in the temple and in the synagogue. But, besides this public prayer, it was the custom of all at Jerusalem to go up to the temple, at regular hours if possible, for private prayer, see Luke 18 : 10; Acts 3 : 1; and those who were absent were wont to " open their windows toward Jerusalem," and pray " toward " the place of God's presence. 1 Kings 8 : 46-49; Ps. 5 : 7; 28 : 2; 138 : 2; Dan. 6 : 10. The regular hours of prayer seem to have been three (see Ps. 55 : 17; Dan. 6 : 10) : " the evening," that is, the ninth hour, Acts 3 : 1; 10 : 3, the hour of the evening sacrifice, Dan. 9 : 21; the " morning," that is, the third hour, Acts 2 : 15, that of the morning sacrifice; and the sixth hour, or " noonday." Grace

before meat would seem to have been a common practice. See Matt. 15 : 36; Acts 27 : 35. The posture of prayer among the Jews seems to have been most often standing, 1 Sam. 1 : 26; Matt. 6 : 5; Mark 11 : 25; Luke 18 : 11; unless the prayer were offered with especial solemnity and humiliation, which was naturally expressed by kneeling, 1 Kings 8 : 54; comp. 2 Chron. 6 : 13; Ezra 9 : 5; Ps. 95 : 6; Dan. 6 : 10, or prostration. Josh. 7 : 6; 1 Kings 18 : 42; Neh. 8 : 6. 3. The only form of prayer given for perpetual use in the Old Testament is the one in Deut. 26 : 5-15, connected with the offering of tithes and first-fruits, and containing in simple form the important elements of prayer, acknowledgment of God's mercy, self-dedication and prayer for future blessing. To this may perhaps be added the threefold blessing of Num. 6 : 24-26, couched as it is in a precatory form, and the short prayer of Moses, Num. 10 : 35, 36, at the moving and resting of the cloud, the former of which was the germ of the 68th Psalm. But of the prayers recorded in the Old Testament the two most remarkable are those of Solomon at the dedication of the temple, 1 Kings 8 : 23-53, and of Joshua the high priest, and his colleagues, after the captivity. Neh. 9 : 5-38. It appears from the question of the disciples in Luke 11 : 1, and from Jewish tradition, that the chief teachers of the day gave special forms of prayer to their disciples, as the badge of their discipleship and the best fruits of their learning. All Christian prayer is, of course, based on the Lord's Prayer; but its spirit is also guided by that of his prayer in Gethsemane and of the prayer recorded by St. John, John 17, the beginning of Christ's great work of intercession. The influence of these prayers is more distinctly traced in the prayers contained in the epistles, see Rom. 16 : 25-27; Eph. 3 : 14-21; Philip. 1 : 3-11; Col. 1 : 9-15; Heb. 13 : 20, 21; 1 Pet. 5 : 10, 11, etc., than in those recorded in the Acts. The public prayer probably in the first instance took much of its form and style from the prayers of the synagogues. In the record of prayers accepted and granted by God, we observe, as always, a special adaptation to the period of his dispensation to which they belong. In the patriarchal period, they have the simple and childlike tone of domestic supplication for the ordinary and apparently trivial incidents of domestic life. In the Mosaic period they assume a more solemn tone and a national bearing, chiefly that of direct intercession for the chosen people. More rarely are they for individuals. A special class are those which precede and refer to the exercise of miraculous power. In the New Testament they have a more directly spiritual bearing. It would seem the intention of Holy Scripture to encourage all prayer, more especially intercession, in all relations and for all righteous objects.

Presents. [GIFT.]

President (*sárac* or *sárĕcá*, only used Dan. 6, the Chaldee equivalent for Hebrew *shôtēr*, probably from *sara*, Zend. a "head"), a high officer in the Persian court, a *chief*, a *president*, used of the three highest ministers.

Priest. The English word is derived from the Greek *presbyter*, signifying an "elder" (Heb. *côhên*). *Origin.*—The idea of a priesthood connects itself in all its forms, pure or corrupted, with the consciousness, more or less distinct, of sin. Men feel that they have broken a law. The power above them is holier than they are, and they dare not approach it. They crave for the intervention of some one of whom they can think as likely to be more acceptable than themselves. He must offer up their prayers, thanksgivings, sacrifices. He becomes their representative in "things pertaining unto God." He may become also (though this does not always follow) the representative of God to man. The functions of the priest and prophet may exist in the same person. No trace of a hereditary or caste priesthood meets us in the worship of the patriarchal age. Once and once only does the word *côhên* meet us as belonging to a ritual earlier than the time of Abraham. Melchizedek is "the priest of the most high God." Gen. 14 : 18. In the worship of the patriarchs themselves, the chief of the family, as such, acted as the priest. The office descended with the birthright, and might apparently be transferred with it.

When established.—The priesthood was first established in the family of Aaron, and all the sons of Aaron were priests. They stood between the high priest on the one hand and the Levites on the other. [HIGH PRIEST; LEVITES.] The ceremony of their consecration is described in Ex. 29; Lev. 8.

Dress.—The dress which the priests wore during their ministrations consisted of linen drawers, with a close-fitting cassock, also of linen, white, but with a diamond or chess-board pattern on it. This came nearly to the feet, and was to be worn in its garment shape. Comp. John 19 : 23. The white cassock was gathered round the body with a girdle of needlework, in which, as in the more gorgeous

Egyptian High Priest in Full Dress.

belt of the high priest, blue, purple and scarlet were intermingled with white, and worked in the form of flowers. Ex. 28 : 39, 40; 39 : 2; Ezek. 44 : 17–19. Upon their heads they were to wear caps or bonnets in the form of a cup-shaped flower, also of fine linen. In all their acts of ministration they were to be barefooted.

Duties.—The chief duties of the priests were to watch over the fire on the altar of burnt offering, and to keep it burning evermore both by day and night, Lev. 6 : 12; 2 Chron. 13 : 11; to feed the golden lamp outside the vail with oil, Ex. 27 : 20, 21; Lev. 24 : 2; to offer the morning and evening sacrifices, each accompanied with a meat offering and a drink offering, at the door of the tabernacle. Ex. 29 : 38–44. They were also to teach the children of Israel the statutes of the Lord. Lev. 10 : 11; Deut. 33 : 10; 2 Chron. 15 : 3; Ezek. 44 : 23, 24. During the journeys in the wilderness it belonged to them to cover the ark and all the vessels of the sanctuary with a purple or scarlet cloth before the Levites might approach them. Num. 4 : 5-15. As the people started on each day's march they were to blow "an alarm" with long silver trumpets. Num. 10 : 1-8. Other instruments of music might be used by the more highly-trained Levites and the schools of the prophets, but the trumpets belonged only to the priests. The presence of the priests on the field of battle, 1 Chron. 12 : 23, 27 ; 2 Chron. 20 : 21, 22, led, in the later periods of Jewish history, to the special appointment at such times of a war priest. Other functions were hinted at in Deuteronomy which might have given them greater influence as the educators and civilizers of the people. They were to act (whether individually or collectively does not distinctly appear) as a court of appeal in the more difficult controversies in criminal or civil cases. Deut. 17 : 8-13. It must remain doubtful, however, how far this order kept its ground during the storms and changes that followed. Functions such as these were clearly incompatible with the common activities of men.

Provision for support.—This consisted —1. Of one tenth of the tithes which the people paid to the Levites, *i. e.* one per cent. on the whole produce of the country. Num. 18 : 26-28. 2. Of a special tithe every third year. Deut. 14 : 28 ; 26 : 12. 3. Of the redemption money, paid at the fixed rate of five shekels a head, for the first-born of man or beast. Num. 18 : 14-19. 4. Of the redemption money paid in like manner for men or things specially dedicated to the Lord. Lev. 27. 5. Of spoil, captives, cattle and the like, taken in war. Num. 31 : 25-47. 6. Of the shew-bread, the flesh of the burnt offerings, peace offerings, trespass offerings, Lev. 6 : 26, 29 ; 7 : 6-10 ; Num. 18 : 8-14, and in particular the heave-shoulder and the wave-breast. Lev. 10 : 12-15. 7. Of an undefined amount of the first-fruits of corn, wine and oil. Ex. 23 : 19 ; Lev. 2 : 14 ; Deut. 26 : 1-10. 8. On their settlement in Canaan the priestly families had thirteen cities assigned them, with "suburbs" or pasture-grounds for their flocks. Josh. 21 : 13-19. These provisions were obviously intended to secure the religion of Israel against the dangers of a caste of pauper priests, needy and dependent, and unable to bear their witness to the true faith. They were, on the other hand, as far as possible removed from the condition of a wealthy order.

Courses.—The priesthood was divided into four and twenty "courses" or orders, 1 Chron. 24 : 1-19 ; 2 Chron. 23 : 8 ; Luke 1 : 5, each of which was to serve in rotation for one week, while the further assignment of special services during the week was determined by lot. Luke 1 : 9. Each course appears to have commenced its work on the Sabbath, the outgoing priests taking the morning sacrifice, and leaving that of the evening to their successors. 2 Chron. 23 : 8.

Numbers.—If we may accept the numbers given by Jewish writers as at all trustworthy, the proportion of the priesthood to the population of Palestine, during the last century of their existence as an order, must have been far greater than that of the clergy has ever been in any Christian nation. Over and above those that were scattered in the country and took their turn, there were not fewer than 24,000 stationed permanently at Jerusalem, and 12,000 at Jericho. It was almost inevitable that the great mass of the order, under such circumstances, should sink in character and reputation. The reigns of the two kings David and Solomon were the culminating period of the glory of the Jewish priesthood. It will be interesting to bring together the few facts that indicate the position of the priests in the New Testament period of their history. The number scattered throughout Palestine was, as has been stated, very large. Of these the greater number were poor and ignorant. The priestly order, like the nation, was divided between contending sects. In the scenes of the last tragedy of Jewish history the order passes away without honor, "dying as a fool dieth." The high priesthood is given to the lowest and vilest of the adherents of the frenzied Zealots. Other priests appear as deserting to the enemy. The destruction of Jerusalem deprived the order at one blow of all but an honorary distinction.

Prince, Princess. The only special uses of the word "prince" are—1. "Princes of provinces," 1 Kings 20 : 14, who were probably local governors or magistrates. 2. The "princes" mentioned in Dan. 6 : 1 (see Esther 1 : 1) were the predecessors of the satraps of Darius Hystaspes. The word *princess* is seldom used in the Bible, but the persons to which it alludes—"daughters of kings" —are frequently mentioned.

Principality. In several passages of

the New Testament the term "principalities and powers" appears to denote different orders of angels, good or bad. See Eph. 6 : 12.

Pris'ca (*ancient*), 2 Tim. 4 : 19, or **Priscil'la** (a diminutive from *Prisca*), the wife of Aquila. [AQUILA.] To what has been said elsewhere under the head of AQUILA the following may be added : We find that the name of the wife is placed before that of the husband in Rom. 16 : 3 ; 2 Tim. 4 : 19, and (according to some of the best MSS.) in Acts 18 : 26. Hence we should be disposed to conclude that Priscilla was the more energetic character of the two. In fact we may say that Priscilla is the example of what the married woman may do for the general service of the Church, in conjunction with home duties, as Phœbe is the type of the unmarried servant of the Church, or deaconess.

Prison. [For imprisonment as a punishment, see PUNISHMENTS.] It is plain that in Egypt special places were used as prisons, and that they were under the custody of a military officer. Gen. 40 : 3 ; 42 : 17. During the wandering in the desert we read on two occasions of confinement " in ward "—Lev. 24 : 12 ; Num. 15 : 34 ; but as imprisonment was not directed by the law, so we hear of none till the time of the kings, when the prison appears as an appendage to the palace, or a special part of it. 1 Kings 22 : 27. Private houses were sometimes used as places of confinement. By the Romans the tower of Antonia was used as a prison at Jerusalem, Acts 23 : 10, and at Cæsarea the prætorium of Herod. The royal prisons in those days were doubtless managed after the Roman fashion, and chains, fetters and stocks were used as means of confinement. See Acts 16 : 24. One of the readiest places for confinement was a dry or partially-dry wall or pit. Jer. 38 : 6–11.

Proch'orus (*leader of the chorus*), one of the seven deacons, being the third on the list, and named next after Stephen and Philip. Acts 6 : 5.

Proconsul (*for*, or *in place of, the consul*). At the division of the Roman provinces by Augustus, in the year B.C. 27, into senatorial and imperial, the emperor assigned to the senate such portions of territory as were peaceable and could be held without force of arms. Those which he retained were called *imperial*, and were governed by *legates* and *procur-*

ators. [PROCURATOR.] Over the senatorial provinces the senate appointed by lot yearly an officer, who was called "proconsul," and who exercised purely civil functions. The provinces were in consequence called " proconsular."

Procurator. The Greek ἡγεμών, rendered " governor " in the Authorized Version, is applied in the New Testament to the officer who presided over the imperial province of Judea. It is used of Pontius Pilate, Matt. 27, of Felix, Acts 23, 24, and of Festus. Acts 26 : 30. It is explained under PROCONSUL that after the battle of Actium, B.C. 27, the provinces of the Roman empire were divided by Augustus into two portions, giving some to the senate and reserving to himself the rest. The imperial provinces were administered by *legati*. No quæstor came into the emperor's provinces, but the property and revenues of the imperial treasury were administered by *procuratores*. Sometimes a province was governed by a procurator with the functions of a legatus. This was especially the case with the smaller provinces and the outlying districts of a larger province; and such is the relation in which Judea stood to Syria. The headquarters of the procurator were at Cæsarea, Acts 23 : 23, where he had a judgment seat, Acts 25 : 6, in the audience chamber, Acts 25 : 23, and was assisted by a council, Acts 25 : 12, whom he consulted in cases of difficulty. He was attended by a cohort as body-guard, Matt. 27 : 27, and apparently went up to Jerusalem at the time of the high festivals, and there resided at the palace of Herod, in which was the *prætorium* or "judgment hall." Matt. 27 : 27 ; Mark 15 : 16 ; comp. Acts 23 : 35.

Prophet. The ordinary Hebrew word for prophet is *nâbi*, derived from a verb signifying " to bubble forth " like a fountain ; hence the word means one *who announces* or *pours forth* the declarations of God. The English word comes from the Greek *prophētēs* (προφήτης), which signifies in classical Greek *one who speaks for another*, specially *one who speaks for a god*, and so interprets his will to man ; hence its essential meaning is " an interpreter." The use of the word in its modern sense as "one who predicts" is post-classical. The larger sense of *interpretation* has not, however, been lost. In fact the English word prophet has always been used in a larger and in a closer sense. The different meanings or shades of meanings in which the abstract noun is employed in Scripture have been drawn out by Locke as follows: "Prophecy comprehends three things: prediction; singing by the dictate of the Spirit; and understanding and explaining the mysterious, hidden sense of Scripture by an immediate illumination and motion of the Spirit."

Order and office.—The sacerdotal order was originally the instrument by which the members of the Jewish theocracy were taught and governed in things spiritual. Teaching by act and teaching by word were alike their task. But during the time of the judges, the priesthood sank into a state of degeneracy, and the people were no longer affected by the acted lessons of the ceremonial service. They required less enigmatic warnings and exhortations. Under these circumstances a new moral power was evoked—the Prophetic Order. Samuel, himself a Levite of the family of Kohath, 1 Chron. 6 : 28, and almost certainly a priest, was the instrument used at once for effecting a reform in the sacerdotal order, 1 Chron. 9 : 22, and for giving to the prophets a position of importance which they had never before held. Nevertheless, it is not to be supposed that Samuel created the prophetic order as a new thing before unknown. The germs both of the prophetic and of the regal order are found in the law as given to the Israelites by Moses, Deut. 13 : 1 ; 18 : 20 ; 17 : 18, but they were not yet developed, because there was not yet the demand for them. Samuel took measures to make his work of restoration permanent as well as effective for the moment. For this purpose he instituted companies or colleges of prophets. One we find in his lifetime at Ramah, 1 Sam.19 : 19, 20 ; others afterward at Bethel, 2 Kings 2 : 3 ; Jericho, 2 Kings 2 : 2, 5 ; Gilgal, 2 Kings 4 : 38, and elsewhere. 2 Kings 6 : 1. Their constitution and object were similar to those of theological colleges. Into them were gathered promising students, and here they were trained for the office which they were afterward destined to fulfill. So successful were these institutions that from the time of Samuel to the closing of the canon of the Old Testament there seems never to have been wanting a due supply of men to keep up the line of official prophets. Their chief subject of study was, no doubt, the law and its interpretation; oral, as distinct from sym-

bolical, teaching being thenceforward tacitly transferred from the priestly to the prophetic order. Subsidiary subjects of instruction were music and sacred poetry, both of which had been connected with prophecy from the time of Moses, Ex. 15 : 20, and the judges. Judges 4 : 4 ; 5 : 1. But to belong to the prophetic order and to possess the prophetic gift are not convertible terms. Generally, the inspired prophet came from the college of the prophets, and belonged to the prophetic order; but this was not always the case. Thus Amos, though called to the prophetic *office*, did not belong to the prophetic *order*. Amos 7 : 14. The sixteen prophets whose books are in the canon have that place of honor because they were endowed with the *prophetic gift* as well as ordinarily (so far as we know) belonging to the *prophetic order*.

Characteristics.—What then are the characteristics of the sixteen prophets thus called and commissioned, and intrusted with the messages of God to his people? 1. They were the national poets of Judea. 2. They were annalists and historians. A great portion of Isaiah, of Jeremiah, of Daniel, of Jonah, of Haggai, is direct or indirect history. 3. They were preachers of patriotism,—their patriotism being founded on the religious motive. 4. They were preachers of morals and of spiritual religion. The system of morals put forward by the prophets, if not higher or sterner or purer than that of the law, is more plainly declared, and with greater, because now more needed, vehemence of diction. 5. They were extraordinary but yet authorized exponents of the law. 6. They held a pastoral or quasi-pastoral office. 7. They were a political power in the state. 8. But the prophets were something more than national poets and annalists, preachers of patriotism, moral teachers, exponents of the law, pastors and politicians. Their most essential characteristic is that they were instruments of revealing God's will to man, as in other ways, so specially by predicting future events, and, in particular, by foretelling the incarnation of the Lord Jesus Christ and the redemption effected by him. We have a series of prophecies which are so applicable to the person and earthly life of Jesus Christ as to be thereby shown to have been designed to apply to him. And if they were designed to apply to him, prophetical prediction is proved. Objections have been urged. We notice only one, viz., vagueness. It has been said that the prophecies are too darkly and vaguely worded to be proved predictive by the events which they are alleged to foretell. But to this might be answered, 1. That God never forces men to believe, but that there is such a union of definiteness and vagueness in the prophecies as to enable those who are willing to discover the truth, while the willfully blind are not forcibly constrained to see it. 2. That, had the prophecies been couched in the form of direct declarations, their fulfillment would have thereby been rendered impossible, or at least capable of frustration. 3. That the effect of prophecy would have been far less beneficial to believers, as being less adapted to keep them in a state of constant expectation. 4. That the Messiah of revelation could not be so clearly portrayed in his varied character as God and man, as prophet, priest and king, if he had been the mere "teacher." 5. That the state of the prophets, at the time of receiving the divine revelation, was such as necessarily to make their predictions fragmentary, figurative, and abstracted from the relations of time. 6. That some portions of the prophecies were intended to be of double application, and some portions to be understood only on their fulfillment. Comp. John 14 : 29 ; Ezek. 36 : 33.

How the prophetic gift was received.— We learn from Holy Scripture that it was by the agency of the Spirit of God that the prophets received the divine communication; but the means by which the divine Spirit communicated with the human spirit, and the conditions of the latter under which the divine communications were received, have not been clearly declared to us. They are, however, indicated. In Num. 12 : 6–8 we have an exhaustive division of the different ways in which the revelations of God are made to man. 1. Direct declaration and manifestation : "I will speak mouth to mouth, apparently, and the similitude of the Lord shall he behold." 2. Vision. 3. Dream. But though it must be allowed that Scripture language seems to point out the state of dream and of trance, or ecstasy, as a condition in which the human instrument received the divine communications, it does not follow that all the prophetic revelations were thus made. Had the prophets a full knowledge of that which they predicted ? It

follows from what we have already said that they had not, and could not have. They were the "spokesmen" of God, Ex. 7 : 1, the "mouth" by which his words were uttered, or they were enabled to view and empowered to describe pictures presented to their spiritual intuition ; but there are no grounds for believing that, contemporaneously with this miracle, there was wrought another miracle, enlarging the understanding of the prophet so as to grasp the whole of the divine counsels which he was gazing into, or which he was the instrument of enunciating.

Names.—Of the sixteen prophets, four are usually called the *great prophets*, namely, Isaiah, Jeremiah, Ezekiel and Daniel, and twelve the *minor prophets*, namely, Hosea, Joel, Amos, Obadiah, Jonah, Micah, Nahum, Habakkuk, Zephaniah, Haggai, Zechariah and Malachi. They may be divided into four groups : the prophets of the northern kingdom— Hosea, Amos, Joel, Jonah ; the prophets of the southern kingdom—Isaiah, Jeremiah, Obadiah, Micah, Nahum, Habakkuk, Zephaniah ; the prophets of the captivity—Ezekiel and Daniel ; the prophets of the return—Haggai, Zechariah, Malachi. They may be arranged in the following chronological order, namely, Joel, Jonah, Hosea, Amos, Isaiah, Micah, Nahum, Zephaniah, Habakkuk, Obadiah, Jeremiah, Ezekiel, Daniel, Haggai, Zechariah, Malachi.

Use of prophecy.—Predictive prophecy is at once a part and an evidence of revelation ; at the time that it is delivered, and until its fulfillment, a part ; after it has been fulfilled, an evidence. As an evidence, fulfilled prophecy is as satisfactory as anything can be ; for who can know the future except the Ruler who disposes future events ? and from whom can come prediction except from him who knows the future ?

Development of Messianic prophecy.— Prediction, in the shape of promise and threatening, begins with the book of Genesis. Immediately upon the Fall, hopes of recovery and salvation are held out, but the manner in which this salvation is to be effected is left altogether indefinite. All that is at first declared is that it shall come through a child of woman. Gen. 3 : 15. By degrees the area is limited : it is to come through the family of Shem, Gen. 9 : 26, through the family of Abraham, Gen. 12 : 3, of Isaac.

Gen. 22 : 18, of Jacob, Gen. 28 : 14, of Judah, Gen. 49 : 10. Balaam seems to say that it will be wrought by a warlike Israelitish King, Num. 24 : 17; Jacob, by a peaceful Ruler of the earth, Gen. 49 : 10; Moses, by a Prophet like himself, *i. e.* a revealer of a new religious dispensation. Deut. 18 : 15. Nathan's announcement, 2 Sam. 7 : 16, determines further that the salvation is to come through the house of David, and through a descendant of David who shall be himself a king. This promise is developed by David himself in the Messianic Psalms. Between Solomon and Hezekiah intervened some two hundred years, during which the voice of prophecy was silent. The Messianic conception entertained at this time by the Jews might have been that of a King of the royal house of David, who would arise and gather under his peaceful sceptre his own people and strangers. Sufficient allusion to his prophetical and priestly offices had been made to create thoughtful consideration, but as yet there was no clear delineation of him in these characters. It was reserved for the prophets to bring out these features more distinctly. In this great period of prophetism there is no longer any chronological development of Messianic prophecy, as in the earlier period previous to Solomon. Each prophet adds a feature, one more, another less, clearly : combine the feature, and we have the portrait; but it does not grow gradually and perceptibly under the hands of the several artists. Its *culminating* point is found in the prophecy contained in Isa. 52 : 13–15 and 53.

Prophets of the New Testament.—So far as their predictive powers are concerned, the Old Testament prophets find their New Testament counterpart in the writer of the Apocalypse; but in their general character, as specially illumined revealers of God's will, their counterpart will rather be found, first in the great Prophet of the Church and his forerunner, John the Baptist, and next in all those persons who were endowed with the extraordinary gifts of the Spirit in the apostolic age, the speakers with tongues and the interpreters of tongues, the prophets and the discerners of spirits, the teachers and workers of miracles. 1 Cor. 12 : 10, 28. That predictive powers did occasionally exist in the New Testament prophets is proved by the case of Agabus, Acts 11 : 28, but this was not their characteristic.

The prophets of the New Testament were supernaturally-illuminated expounders and preachers.

Proselyte (*a stranger, a new comer*), the name given by the Jews to foreigners who adopted the Jewish religion. The dispersion of the Jews in foreign countries, which has been spoken of elsewhere [DISPERSION, THE], enabled them to make many converts to their faith. The converts who were thus attracted joined, with varying strictness, in the worship of the Jews. In Palestine itself, even Roman centurions learned to love the conquered nation, built synagogues for them, Luke 7 : 5, fasted and prayed, and gave alms after the pattern of the strictest Jews, Acts 10 : 2, 30, and became preachers of the new faith to the soldiers under them. Acts 10 :7. Such men, drawn by what was best in Judaism, were naturally among the readiest receivers of the new truth which rose out of it, and became, in many cases, the nucleus of a Gentile Church. Proselytism had, however, its darker side. The Jews of Palestine were eager to spread their faith by the same weapons as those with which they had defended it. The Idumæans had the alternative offered them by John Hyrcanus of death, exile or circumcision. The Ituræans were converted in the same way by Aristobulus. Where force was not in their power, they obtained their ends by the most unscrupulous fraud. Those who were most active in proselytizing were precisely those from whose teaching all that was most true and living had departed. The vices of the Jew were engrafted on the vices of the heathen. A repulsive casuistry released the convert from obligations which he had before recognized, while in other things he was bound hand and foot to an unhealthy superstition. It was no wonder that he became "twofold more the child of hell," Matt. 23 : 15, than the Pharisees themselves. We find in the Talmud a distinction between proselytes of the gate and proselytes of righteousness. 1. The term *proselytes of the gate* was derived from the frequently-occurring description in the law, "the stranger that is within thy gates." Ex. 20 : 10, etc. Converts of this class were not bound by circumcision and the other special laws of the Mosaic code. It is doubtful, however, whether the distinction made in the Talmud ever really existed. 2. The *proselytes of righteousness*, known also as proselytes of the covenant, were perfect Israelites. We learn from the Talmud that, in addition to circumcision, baptism was also required to complete their admission to the faith. The proselyte was placed in a tank or pool up to his neck in water. His teachers, who now acted as his sponsors, repeated the great commandments of the law. The baptism was followed, as long as the temple stood, by the offering or corban.

Prov'erbs, Book of. The title of this book in Hebrew is taken from its first word, *mashal*, which originally meant " a comparison." It is sometimes translated parable, sometimes proverb as here. The superscriptions which are affixed to several portions of the book, in chs. 1 : 1, 10 : 1, 25 : 1, attribute the authorship of those portions to Solomon the son of David, king of Israel. With the exception of the last two chapters, which are distinctly assigned to other authors, it is probable that the statement of the superscriptions is in the main correct, and that the majority of the proverbs contained in the book were uttered or collected by Solomon. Speaking roughly, the book consists of three main divisions, with two appendices :—1. Chs. 1–9 form a connected didactic poem, in which Wisdom is praised and the youth exhorted to devote himself to her. This portion is preceded by an introduction and title describing the character and general aim of the book. 2. Chs. 10–24, with the title " The Proverbs of Solomon," consist of three parts: 10 : 1–22 : 16, a collection of single proverbs and detached sentences out of the region of moral teaching and worldly prudence; 22 : 17–24 : 21, a more connected didactic poem, with an introduction, 22 : 17–22, which contains precepts of righteousness and prudence; 24 : 23–34, with the inscription " These also belong to the wise," a collection of unconnected maxims, which serve as an appendix to the preceding. Then follows the third division, chs. 25–29, which, according to the superscription, professes to be a collection of Solomon's proverbs, consisting of single sentences, which the men of the court of Hezekiah copied out. The first appendix, ch. 30, " The words of Agur the son of Jakeh," is a collection of partly proverbial and partly enigmatical sayings; the second, ch. 31, is divided into two parts, " The words of King Lemuel," vs. 1–6, and an alphabetical acrostic in praise of a virtuous woman, which occupies the rest of the chapter. Who was Agur, and who was Jakeh, are questions which have been often asked and never satisfactorily answered. All that can be said of the first is that he was an unknown Hebrew sage, the son of an equally unknown Jakeh, and that he lived after the time of Hezekiah. Lemuel, like Agur, is unknown. It is even uncertain whether he is to be regarded as a real personage, or whether the name is merely symbolical. The Proverbs are frequently quoted or alluded to in the New Testament, and the canonicity of the book thereby confirmed. The following is a list of the principal passages :—

Prov. 1 : 16, compare Rom. 3 : 10, 15.
3 : 7, compare Rom. 12 : 16.
3 : 11, 12, compare Heb. 12 : 5, 6; see also Rev. 3 : 19.
3 : 34, compare James 4 : 6.
10 : 12, compare 1 Pet. 4 : 8.
11 : 31, compare 1 Pet. 4 : 18.
17 : 13, compare Rom. 12 : 17; 1 Thess. 5 : 15; 1 Pet. 3 : 9.
17 : 27, compare James 1 : 19.
20 : 9, compare 1 John 1 : 8.
20 : 20, compare Matt. 15 : 4; Mark 7 : 10.
22 : 8 (LXX.), compare 2 Cor. 9 : 7.
25 : 21, 22, compare Rom. 12 : 20.
26 : 11, compare 2 Pet. 2 : 22.
27 : 1, compare James 4 : 13, 14.

Province. 1. In the Old Testament this word appears in connection with the wars between Ahab and Ben-hadad. 1 Kings 20 : 14, 15, 19. The victory of the former is gained chiefly " by the young men of the princes of the provinces," *i. e.,* probably of the chiefs of tribes in the Gilead country. 2. More commonly the word is used of the divisions of the Chaldæan kingdom. Dan. 2 : 49; 3 : 1, 30, and the Persian kingdom. Ezra 2 : 1; Neh. 7 : 6; Esther 1 : 1, 22; 2 : 3, etc. In the New Testament we are brought into contact with the administration of the provinces of the Roman empire. The classification of provinces supposed to need military control and therefore placed under the immediate government of the Cæsar, and those still belonging theoretically to the republic and administered by the senate, and of the latter again into proconsular and prætorian, is recognized, more or less distinctly, in the Gospels and the Acts. [PROCONSUL; PROCURATOR.] The στρατηγοί of Acts 16 : 22 (" magistrates," Authorized Version), on the other hand, were the *duumviri* or prætors of a Roman colony. The right of any Roman citizen to appeal from a provincial governor to the emperor meets us as asserted by St. Paul. Acts 25 : 11. In the council of Acts 25 : 12 we recognize the assessors who were appointed to take part in the judicial functions of the governor.

Psalms, Book of. The present Hebrew name of the book is *Tehillim*, "Praises;" but in the actual superscriptions of the psalms the word *Tehillâh* is applied only to one, Ps. 145, which is indeed emphatically a praise-hymn. The LXX. entitled them ψαλμοί or "psalms," *i. e.*, lyrical pieces to be sung to a musical instrument. The Christian Church obviously received the Psalter from the Jews not only as a constituent portion of the sacred volume of Holy Scripture, but also as the liturgical hymn-book which the Jewish Church had regularly used in the temple.

Division of the Psalms.—The book contains 150 psalms, and may be divided into five great divisions or books, which must have been originally formed at different periods. Book I. is, by the superscriptions, entirely Davidic; nor do we find in it a trace of any but David's authorship. We may well believe that the compilation of the book was also David's work. Book II. appears by the date of its latest psalm, Ps. 46, to have been compiled in the reign of King Hezekiah. It would naturally comprise, 1st, several or most of the Levitical psalms anterior to that date; and 2d, the remainder of the psalms of David previously uncompiled. To these latter the collector, after properly appending the single psalm of Solomon, has affixed the notice that "the prayers of David the son of Jesse are ended." Ps. 72:20. Book III., the interest of which centres in the times of Hezekiah, stretches out, by its last two psalms, to the reign of Manasseh: it was probably compiled in the reign of Josiah. It contains seventeen psalms, from Ps. 73–89—eleven by Asaph, four by the sons of Horah, one (86) by David, and one by Ethan. Book IV. contains the remainder of the psalms up to the date of the captivity. There are seventeen, from Ps. 90–106—one by Moses, two by David, and the rest anonymous. Book V., the psalms of the return, contains forty-four, from Ps. 107–150—fifteen by David, one by Solomon and the rest anonymous. There is nothing to distinguish these two books from each other in respect of outward decoration or arrangement, and they may have been compiled together in the days of Nehemiah.

Connection of the Psalms with Israelitish history.—The psalm of Moses, Ps. 90,

which is in point of actual date the earliest, faithfully reflects the long, weary wanderings, the multiplied provocations and the consequent punishments of the wilderness. It is, however, with David that Israelitish psalmody may be said virtually to commence. Previous mastery over his harp had probably already prepared the way for his future strains, when the anointing oil of Samuel descended upon him, and he began to drink in special measure, from that day forward, of the Spirit of the Lord. It was then that, victorious at home over the mysterious melancholy of Saul and in the field over the vaunting champion of the Philistine hosts, he sang how from even babes and sucklings God had ordained strength because of his enemies. Ps. 8. His next psalms are of a different character; his persecutions at the hands of Saul had commenced. When David's reign has begun, it is still with the most exciting incidents of his history, private or public, that his psalms are mainly associated. There are none to which the period of his reign at Hebron can lay exclusive claim. But after the conquest of Jerusalem his psalmody opened afresh with the solemn removal of the ark to Mount Zion; and in Pss. 24–29, which belong together, we have the earliest definite instance of David's systematic composition or arrangement of psalms for public use. Even of those psalms which cannot be referred to any definite occasion, several reflect the general historical circumstances of the times. Thus Ps. 9 is a thanksgiving for the deliverance of the land of Israel from its former heathen oppressors. Ps. 10 is a prayer for the deliverance of the Church from the high-handed oppression exercised from within. The succeeding psalms dwell on the same theme, the virtual internal heathenism by which the Church of God was weighed down. So that there remain very few, *e. g.* Pss. 15–17, 19, 32 (with its choral appendage, 23), 37, of which some historical account may not be given. A season of repose near the close of his reign induced David to compose his grand personal thanksgiving for the deliverances of his whole life, Ps. 18; the date of which is approximately determined by the place at which it is inserted in the history. 2 Sam. 22. It was probably at this period that he finally arranged for the sanctuary service that collection of his psalms which now constitutes the first book of the

Psalter. The course of David's reign was not, however, as yet complete. The solemn assembly convened by him for the dedication of the materials of the future temple, 1 Chron. 28, 29, would naturally call forth a renewal of his best efforts to glorify the God of Israel in psalms; and to this occasion we doubtless owe the great festal hymns Pss. 65–68, containing a large review of the past history, present position and prospective glories of God's chosen people. The supplications of Ps. 69 suit best with the renewed distress occasioned by the sedition of Adonijah. Ps. 71, to which Ps. 70, a fragment of a former psalm, is introductory, forms David's parting strain. Yet that the psalmody of Israel may not seem finally to terminate with him, the glories of the future are forthwith anticipated by his son in Ps. 72. The great prophetical ode, Ps. 45, connects itself most readily with the splendors of Jehoshaphat's reign. Pss. 42–44, 74, are best assigned to the reign of Ahaz. The reign of Hezekiah is naturally rich in psalmody. Pss. 46, 73, 75, 76, connect themselves with the resistance to the supremacy of the Assyrians and the divine destruction of their host.

We are now brought to a series of psalms of peculiar interest, springing out of the political and religious history of the separated ten tribes. In date of actual composition they commence before the times of Hezekiah. The earliest is probably Ps. 80, a supplication for the Israelitish people at the time of the Syrian oppression. All these psalms—80–83— are referred by their superscriptions to the Levite singers, and thus bear witness to the efforts of the Levites to reconcile the two branches of the chosen nation. The captivity of Manasseh himself proved to be but temporary; but the sentence which his sins had provoked upon Judah and Jerusalem still remained to be executed, and precluded the hope that God's salvation could be revealed till after such an outpouring of his judgments as the nation had never yet known. Labor and sorrow must be the lot of the present generation; through these mercy might occasionally gleam, but the glory which was eventually to be manifested must be for posterity alone. The psalms of Book IV. bear generally the impress of this feeling.

We pass to Book V. Ps. 107 is the opening psalm of the return, sung probably at the first feast of tabernacles. Ezra 3. A directly historical character belongs to Pss. 120–134, styled in our Authorized Version "Songs of Degrees." Internal evidence refers these to the period when the Jews under Nehemiah were, in the very face of the enemy, repairing the walls of Jerusalem, and the title may well signify "songs of goings up upon the walls," the psalms being, from their brevity, well adapted to be sung by the workmen and guards while engaged in their respective duties. Ps. 139 is a psalm of the new birth of Israel, from the womb of the Babylonish captivity, to a life of righteousness; Pss. 140–143 may be a picture of the trials to which the unrestored exiles were still exposed in the realms of the Gentiles. Henceforward, as we approach the close of the Psalter, its strains rise in cheerfulness; and it fittingly terminates with Pss. 147–150, which were probably sung on the occasion of the thanksgiving procession of Neh. 12, after the rebuilding of the walls of Jerusalem had been completed.

Moral characteristics of the Psalms.— Foremost among these meets us, undoubtedly, the universal recourse to communion with God. Connected with this is the faith by which the psalmist everywhere lives in God rather than in himself. It is of the essence of such faith that his view of the perfections of God should be true and vivid. The Psalter describes God as he is: it glows with testimonies to his power and providence, his love and faithfulness, his holiness and righteousness. The Psalms not only set forth the perfections of God: they proclaim also the duty of worshipping him by the acknowledgment and adoration of his perfections. They encourage all outward rites and means of worship. Among these they recognize the ordinance of sacrifice as an expression of the worshipper's consecration of himself to God's service. But not the less do they repudiate the outward rite when separated from that which it was designed to express. Similar depth is observable in the view taken by the psalmists of human sin. In regard to the law, the psalmist, while warmly acknowledging its excellence, feels yet that it cannot so effectually guide his own unassisted exertions as to preserve him from error. Ps. 19. The Psalms bear repeated testimony to the duty of instructing others in the ways of holiness. Pss. 32, 34, 51. This brings us to notice, lastly, the faith of the psalmists in righteous recompense to all men according to their deeds. Ps. 37, etc.

Prophetical character of the Psalms.— The moral struggle between godliness and ungodliness, so vividly depicted in the Psalms, culminates, in Holy Scripture, in the life of the Incarnate Son of God upon earth. It only remains to show that the Psalms themselves definitely anticipated this culmination. Now there are in the Psalter at least three psalms of which the interest evidently centres in a person distinct from the speaker, and which, since they cannot without violence to the language be interpreted of any but the Messiah, may be termed directly and exclusively Messianic. We refer to Pss. 2, 45, 110, to which may perhaps be added Ps. 72. It would be strange if these few psalms stood, in their prophetical significance, absolutely alone among the rest. And hence the impossibility of viewing the psalms generally, notwithstanding the historical drapery in which they are outwardly clothed, as simply the past devotions of the historical David or the historical Israel. The national hymns of Israel are indeed also prospective; but in general they anticipate rather the struggles and the triumphs of the Christian Church than those of Christ himself.

Psaltery. This was a stringed instrument of music to accompany the voice. The Hebrew *nêbel* or *nebel* is so rendered in the Authorized Version in all passages where it occurs, except in Isa. 5 : 12 ; 14 : 11 ; 22 : 24, marg. ; Amos 5 : 23 ; 6 : 5, where it is translated *viol.* The ancient viol was a six-stringed guitar. In the Prayer Book version of the Psalms the Hebrew word is rendered "lute." This instrument resembled the guitar, but was superior in tone, being larger, and having a convex back, somewhat like the vertical section of a gourd, or more nearly resembling that of a pear. These three instruments, the psaltery or sautry, the viol and the lute, are frequently associated in the old English poets, and were clearly instruments resembling each other, though still different. The Greek *psalterium* (ψαλτήριον), from which our word is derived, denotes an instrument played with the fingers instead of a plectrum or quill, the verb being used of twanging the bow-string.

It is impossible to say positively with what instrument the *nebel* of the Hebrew exactly corresponded. From the fact that *nebel* in Hebrew also signifies a wine-bottle or skin, it has been conjectured that the term when applied to a musical instrument denotes a kind of bagpipe. The psalteries of David were made of cypress, 2 Sam. 6 : 5 ; those of Solomon of algum or almug trees. 2 Chron. 9 : 11. Among the instruments of the band which played before Nebuchadnezzar's golden image on the plains of Dura, we again meet with the psaltery. Dan. 3 : 5, 10, 15, *pĕsantêrin.*

Ptolemæ'us, or **Ptol'emy,** was the common name of the Greek dynasty of Egyptian kings. PTOLEMÆUS I. SOTER, the son of Lagus, a Macedonian of low rank, distinguished himself greatly during the campaigns of Alexander; at whose death he secured for himself the government of Egypt, where he proceeded at once to lay the foundations of a kingdom, B.C. 323. He abdicated in favor of his youngest son, Ptolemy II. Philadelphus, two years before his death, which took place in B.C. 283. Ptolemy Soter is described very briefly in Daniel, Dan. 11 : 5, as one of those who should receive part of the empire of Alexander when it was "divided toward the four winds of heaven."

PTOLEMÆUS II. PHILADELPHUS, B.C. 285–247, the youngest son of Ptolemy I., was made king two years before his father's death, to confirm the irregular succession. The conflict between Egypt and Syria was renewed during his reign in consequence of the intrigue of his half-brother Magas. Ptolemy bestowed liberal encouragement on literature and science, founding the great library and museum at Alexandria, and gathered about him many men of learning, as the poet Theocritus, the geometer Euclid and the astronomer Aratus. This reign was a critical epoch for the development of Judaism, as it was for the intellectual history of the ancient world. The critical faculty was called forth in place of the creative, and learning in some sense supplied the place of original speculation. It was impossible that the Jew, who was now become as true a citizen of the world as the Greek, should remain passive in the conflict of opinions. It is enough now to observe the greatness of the consequences involved in the union of Greek language with Jewish thought.

From this time the Jew was familiarized with the great types of western literature, and in some degree aimed at imitating them. A second time and in new fashion Egypt disciplined a people of God. It first impressed upon a nation the firm unity of a family, and then in due time reconnected a matured people with the world from which it had been called out.

PTOLEMÆUS III. EUERGETES, B.C. 247–222, was the eldest son of Ptolemy Philadelphus and brother of Berenice the wife of Antiochus II. The repudiation and murder of his sister furnished him with an occasion for invading Syria, *cir.* B.C. 246. Dan. 11 : 7. He extended his conquests as far as Antioch, and then eastward to Babylon, but was recalled to Egypt by tidings of seditions which had broken out there. His success was brilliant and complete. He carried "captives into Egypt their gods [of the conquered nations], with their princes, and with their precious vessels of silver and of gold." Dan. 11 : 8. This capture of sacred trophies earned for the king the name *Euergetes*—"Benefactor." After his return to Egypt, *cir.* B.C. 243, he suffered a great part of the conquered provinces to fall again under the power of Seleucus.

PTOLEMÆUS IV. PHILOPATOR, B.C. 222–205. After the death of Ptolemy Euergetes the line of the Ptolemies rapidly degenerated. Ptolemy Philopator, his eldest son, who succeeded him, was to the last degree sensual, effeminate and debased. But externally his kingdom retained its power and splendor; and when circumstances forced him to action, Ptolemy himself showed ability not unworthy of his race. The description of the campaign of Raphia (B.C. 217) in the book of Daniel gives a vivid description of his character. Dan. 11 : 10–12; cf. Macc. 1 : 1–3. After offering in the temple at Jerusalem sacrifices for the success then achieved, he attempted to enter the sanctuary. A sudden paralysis hindered his design; but when he returned to Alexandria he determined to inflict on the Alexandrine Jews the vengeance for his disappointment. He was succeeded by his only child, Ptolemy V. Epiphanes, who was at the time only four or five years old.

PTOLEMÆUS V. EPIPHANES, B.C. 205–181. The reign of Ptolemy Epiphanes was a critical epoch in the history of the Jews. The rivalry between the Syrian and Egyptian parties, which had for some time divided the people, came to an open rupture in the struggles which marked his minority. In the strong language of Daniel, "The robbers of the people exalted themselves to establish the vision." Dan. 11 : 14. The accession of Ptolemy and the confusion of a disputed regency furnished a favorable opportunity for foreign invasion. "Many stood up against the king of the south" under Antiochus the Great and Philip III. of Macedonia, who formed a league for the dismemberment of his kingdom. "So the king of the north [Antiochus] came, and cast up a mount, and took the most fenced city [Sidon], and the arms of the south did not withstand" [at Paneas, B.C. 198]. Dan. 11 : 14, 15. The Romans interfered, and in order to retain the provinces of Cœle-Syria, Phœnicia and Judea, Antiochus "gave him [Ptolemy] a young maiden" [his daughter Cleopatra as his betrothed wife]. Dan. 11 : 17. But in the end his policy only partially succeeded. After the marriage of Ptolemy and Cleopatra was consummated, B.C. 193, Cleopatra did "not stand on his side," but supported her husband in maintaining the alliance with Rome. The disputed provinces, however, remained in the possession of Antiochus; and Ptolemy was poisoned at the time when he was preparing an expedition to recover them from Seleucus, the unworthy successor of Antiochus.

PTOLEMÆUS VI. PHILOMETOR, B.C. 181–145. On the death of Ptolemy Epiphanes, his wife Cleopatra held the regency for her young son, Ptolemy Philometor, and preserved peace with Syria till she died, B.C. 173. The government then fell into unworthy hands, and an attempt was made to recover Syria. Comp. 2 Macc. 4 : 21. Antiochus Epiphanes seems to have made the claim a pretext for invading Egypt. The generals of Ptolemy were defeated near Pelusium, probably at the close of B.C. 171, 1 Macc. 1 : 16 ff.; and in the next year Antiochus, having secured the person of the young king, reduced almost the whole of Egypt. Comp. 2 Macc. 5 : 1. Meanwhile Ptolemy Euergetes II., the younger brother of Ptolemy Philometor, assumed the supreme power at Alexandria; and Antiochus, under the pretext of recovering the crown for Philometor, besieged Alexandria in B.C. 169. By this time, however, his selfish designs were apparent : the brothers were reconciled, and Antiochus was obliged to acquiesce for the time in the arrangement which they made. But while doing so he prepared for another invasion of Egypt, and was already approaching Alexandria when he was met by the Roman embassy led by C. Popillius Lænas, who, in the name of the Roman senate, insisted on his immediate retreat (B.C. 168), a command which the late victory at Pydna made it impossible to disobey. These campaigns, which are intimately connected with the visits of Antiochus to Jerusalem in B.C. 170, 168, are briefly described in Dan. 11 : 25–30. The whole of Syria was afterward subdued by Ptolemy, and he was crowned at Antioch king of Egypt and Asia. 1 Macc. 11 : 13. Alexander, a rival claimant, attempted to secure the crown, but was defeated and afterward put to death by Ptolemy. But the latter did not long enjoy his success. He fell from his horse in the battle, and died within a few days. 1 Macc. 11 : 18. Ptolemy Philometor is the last king of Egypt who is noticed in sacred history, and his reign was marked also by the erection of the temple at Leontopolis.

Ptolema'is. [ACCHO.]

Ptol'emee, or **Ptoleme'us.** 1. " The son of Dorymenes," 1 Macc. 3 : 38 ; 2 Macc. 4 : 45 ; comp. Polyb. v. 61, a courtier who possessed great influence with Antiochus Epiphanes.
2. The son of Agesarchus, a Megalopolitan, surnamed Macron, 2 Macc. 10 : 12, who was governor of Cyprus during the minority of Ptolemy Philometor. He afterward deserted the Egyptian service to join Antiochus Epiphanes. He stood high in the favor of Antiochus, and received from him the government of Phœnicia and Cœle-Syria. 2 Macc. 8 : 8 ; 10 : 11, 12. On the accession of Antiochus Eupator his conciliatory policy toward the Jews brought him into suspicion at court. He was deprived of his government, and in consequence of this disgrace he poisoned himself, *cir.* B.C. 164. 2 Macc. 10 : 13.
3. The son of Abubus, who married the daughter of Simon the Maccabee. He was a man of great wealth, and being invested with the government of the district of Jericho, formed the design of usurping the sovereignty of Judea.

Pu'a, properly Puvvah. Phuvah the son of Issachar. Num. 26 : 23. (B.C. 1452.)

Pu'ah (*splendid*). 1. The father of Tola, a man of the tribe of Issachar, and judge of Israel after Abimelech. Judges 10 : 1. (B.C. 1211.)
2. The son of Issachar, 1 Chron. 7 : 1, elsewhere called Phuvah and Pua.
3. One of the two midwives to whom Pharaoh gave instructions to kill the Hebrew male children at their birth. Ex. 1 : 15. (B.C. 1571.)

Publican. The class designated by this word in the New Testament were employed as collectors of the Roman revenue. The Roman senate farmed the *vectigalia* (direct taxes) and the *portoria* (customs) to capitalists who undertook to pay a given sum into the treasury (*in publicum*), and so received the name of *publicani.* Contracts of this kind fell naturally into the hands of the *equites,* as the richest class of Romans. They appointed managers, under whom were the *portitores,* the actual custom-house officers, who examined each bale of goods, exported or imported, assessed its value more or less arbitrarily, wrote out the ticket, and enforced payment. The latter were commonly natives of the province in which they were stationed, as being brought daily into contact with all classes of the population. The name *publicani* was used popularly, and in the New Testament exclusively, of the *portitores.* The system was essentially a vicious one. The *portitores* were encouraged in the most vexatious or fraudulent exactions, and a remedy was all but impossible. They overcharged whenever they had an opportunity, Luke 3 : 13 ; they brought false charges of smuggling in the hope of extorting hush-money, Luke 19 : 8 ; they detained and opened letters on mere suspicion. It was the basest of all livelihoods. All this was enough to bring the class into ill favor everywhere. In Judea and Galilee there were special circumstances of aggravation. The employment brought out all the besetting vices of the Jewish character. The strong feeling of many Jews as to the absolute unlawfulness of paying tribute at all made matters worse. The scribes who discussed the question, Matt. 22 : 15, for the most part answered it in the negative. In addition to their other faults, accordingly, the publicans of the New Testament were regarded as traitors and apostates, defiled by their frequent intercourse with the heathen, willing tools of the oppressor. The class thus practically excommuni·

cated furnished some of the earliest disciples both of the Baptist and of our Lord. The position of Zacchæus as a "chief among the publicans," Luke 19 : 2, implies a gradation of some kind among the persons thus employed.

Pub′lius, the chief man—probably the governor—of Melita, who received and lodged St. Paul and his companions on the occasion of their being shipwrecked off that island. Acts 28 : 7. (A.D. 55.)

Pu′dens (*modest*), a Christian friend of Timothy at Rome. 2 Tim. 4 : 21. (A.D. 64.) According to legend he was the host of St. Peter and friend of St. Paul, and was martyred under Nero.

Pu′hites, The. According to 1 Chron. 2 : 53, the "Puhites" or "Puthites" belonged to the families of Kirjath-jearim.

Pul (*lord*), a country or nation mentioned in Isa. 66 : 19. It is spoken of with distant nations, and is supposed by some to represent the island Philæ in Egypt, and by others Libya.

Pul, an Assyrian king, and the first Assyrian monarch mentioned in Scripture. He made an expedition against Menahem, king of Israel, about B.C. 770. 2 Kings 15 : 19.

Pulse (*seeds*) usually means peas, beans and the seeds that grow in pods. In the Authorized Version it occurs only in Dan. 1 : 12, 16, as the translation of words the literal meaning of which is "seeds" of any kind. Probably the term denotes uncooked grain of any kind, as barley, wheat, millet, vetches, etc.

Punishments. The earliest theory of punishment current among mankind is doubtless the one of simple retaliation, "blood for blood." Viewed historically, the first case of punishment for crime mentioned in Scripture, next to the Fall itself, is that of Cain, the first murderer. That death was regarded as the fitting punishment for murder appears plain from the remark of Lamech. Gen. 4 : 24. In the post-diluvian code, if we may so call it, retribution by the hand of man, even in the case of an offending animal, for blood shed, is clearly laid down. Gen. 9 : 5, 6. Passing onward to Mosaic times, we find the sentence of capital punishment, in the case of murder, plainly laid down in the law. The murderer was to be put to death, even if he should have taken refuge at God's altar or in a refuge city and the same principle was to be carried out even in the case of an animal.

Offences punished with death.—I. The following offences also are mentioned in the law as liable to the punishment of death : 1. Striking, or even reviling, a parent. Ex. 21 : 15, 17. 2. Blasphemy. Lev. 24 : 14, 16, 23. 3. Sabbath-breaking. Ex. 31 : 14 ; 35 : 2 ; Num. 15 : 32–36. 4. Witchcraft, and false pretension to prophecy. Ex. 22 : 18 ; Lev. 20 : 27 ; Deut. 13 : 5 ; 18 : 20. 5. Adultery. Lev. 20 : 10 ; Deut. 22 : 22. 6. Unchastity. Lev. 21 : 9 ; Deut. 22 : 21, 23. 7. Rape. Deut. 22 : 25. 8. Incestuous and unnatural connections. Ex. 22 : 19 ; Lev. 20 : 11, 14, 16. 9. Man-stealing. Ex. 21 : 16 ; Deut. 24 : 7. 10. Idolatry, actual or virtual, in any shape. Lev. 20 : 2 ; Deut. 13 : 6, 10, 15 ; 17 : 2–7 ; see Josh. 7 and 22 : 20 and Num. 25 : 8. 11. False witness in certain cases. Deut. 19 : 16, 19. II. But there is a large number of offences, some of them included in this list, which are named in the law as involving the penalty of " cutting off from the people." On the meaning of this expression some controversy has arisen. There are altogether thirty-six or thirty-seven cases in which this formula is used. We may perhaps conclude that the primary meaning of " cutting off " is a sentence of death to be executed in some cases without remission, but in others voidable—(1) by immediate atonement on the offender's part ; (2) by direct interposition of the Almighty, *i. e.*, a sentence of death always " recorded," but not always executed.

Kinds of punishment.—Punishments are twofold, Capital and Secondary. I. *Capital.* (A) The following only are prescribed by the law : 1. *Stoning,* which was the ordinary mode of execution. Ex. 17 : 4 ; Luke 20 : 6 ; John 10 : 31 ; Acts 14 : 5. In the case of idolatry, and it may be presumed in other cases also, the witnesses, of whom there were to be at least two, were required to cast the first stone. Deut. 13 : 9 ; Acts 7 : 58. 2. *Hanging* is mentioned as a distinct punishment. Num. 25 : 4 ; 2 Sam. 21 : 6, 9. 3. *Burning,* in pre-Mosaic times, was the punishment for unchastity. Gen. 38 : 24. Under the law it was ordered in the case of a priest's daughter. Lev. 21 : 9. 4. *Death by the sword* or *spear* is named in the law, Ex. 19 : 13 ; 32 : 27 ; Num. 25 : 7 ; and it occurs frequently in regal and post-Babylonian times. 1 Kings 2 : 25, 34 ; 19 : 1 ; 2 Chron. 21 : 4, etc. 5. *Strangling* is said by the rabbins to have been regarded as the most common but least severe of the capital punishments, and to have been performed by immersing the convict in clay or mud, and then strangling him by a cloth twisted round the neck. (B) Besides these ordinary capital punishments, we read of others, either of foreign introduction or of an irregular kind. Among the former, 1. CRUCIFIXION is treated elsewhere. 2. *Drowning*, though not ordered under the law, was practiced at Rome, and is said by St. Jerome to have been in use among the Jews. 3. *Sawing asunder* or crushing beneath iron instruments. 2 Sam. 12 : 31, and perhaps Prov. 20 : 26; Heb. 11 : 37. 4. *Pounding in a mortar*, or *beating to death*, is alluded to in Prov. 27 : 22, but not as a legal punishment, and cases are described. 2 Macc. 6 : 28, 30. 5. *Precipitation*, attempted in the case of our Lord at Nazareth, and carried out in that of captives from the Edomites, and of St. James, who is said to have been cast from "the pinnacle" of the temple. Criminals executed by law were buried outside the city gates, and heaps of stones were flung upon their graves. Josh. 7 : 25, 26; 2 Sam. 18 : 17; Jer. 22 : 19. II. Of *secondary punishments* among the Jews the original principles were, 1. *Retaliation*, "eye for eye," etc. Ex. 21 : 24, 25. 2. *Compensation*, identical (restitution) or analogous; payment for loss of time or of power. Ex. 21 : 18–36; Lev. 24 : 18–21; Deut. 19 : 21. *Slander* against a wife's honor was to be compensated to her parents by a fine of one hundred shekels, and the traducer himself to be punished with stripes. Deut. 22 : 18, 19. 3. *Stripes*, whose number was not to exceed forty, Deut. 25 : 3; whence the Jews took care not to exceed thirty-nine. 2 Cor. 11 : 24. 4. *Scourging* with thorns is mentioned Judges 8 : 16. The *stocks* are mentioned Jer. 20 : 2; *passing through fire*, 2 Sam. 12 : 31; *mutilation*, Judges 1 : 6, 2 Macc. 7 : 4, and see 2 Sam. 4 : 12; *plucking out hair*, Isa. 50 : 6; in later times, *imprisonment* and *confiscation* or *exile*. Ezra 7 : 26; Jer. 37 : 15; 38 : 6; Acts 4 : 3; 5 : 18; 12 : 4.

Pu'nites, The, the descendants of Pua or Puvah, the son of Issachar. Num. 26 : 23.

Pu'non (*darkness*), one of the halting-places of the Israelite host during the last portion of the wandering. Num. 33 : 42, 43. By Eusebius and Jerome it is identified with Phæno, which contained the copper-mines so well known at that period, and was situated between Petra and Zoar.

Purification, in its legal and technical sense, is applied to the ritual observances whereby an Israelite was formally absolved from the taint of uncleanness. The essence of purification, in all cases, consisted in the use of water, whether by way of ablution or aspersion; but in the *majora delicta* of legal uncleanness, sacrifices of various kinds were added, and the ceremonies throughout bore an expiatory character. Ablution of the person and of the clothes was required in the cases mentioned in Lev. 15 : 18; 11 : 25, 40; 15 : 16, 17. In cases of childbirth the sacrifice was increased to a lamb of the first year, with a pigeon or turtle-dove. Lev. 12 : 6. The ceremonies of purification required in cases of contact with a corpse or a grave are detailed in Num. 19. The purification of the leper was a yet more formal proceeding, and indicated the highest pitch of uncleanness. The rites are described in Lev. 14 : 4–32. The necessity of purification was extended in the post-Babylonian period to a variety of unauthorized cases. Cups and pots and brazen vessels were washed as a matter of ritual observance. Mark 7 : 4. The washing of the hands before meals was conducted in a formal manner. Mark 7 : 3. What may have been the specific causes of uncleanness in those who came up to purify themselves before the Passover, John 11 : 55, or in those who had taken upon themselves the Nazarites' vow, Acts 21 : 24, 26, we are not informed. In conclusion it may be observed that the distinctive feature in the Mosaic rites of purification is their expiatory character. The idea of uncleanness was not peculiar to the Jew; but with all other nations simple ablution sufficed: no sacrifices were demanded. The Jew alone was taught by the use of expiatory offerings to discern to its fullest extent the connection between the outward sign and the inward fount of impurity.

Pu'rim (*lots*), the annual festival instituted to commemorate the preservation of the Jews in Persia from the massacre with which they were threatened through the machinations of Haman. Esther 9. It was probably called Purim by the Jews in irony. Their great enemy Haman appears to have been very superstitious, and much given to casting lots. Esther 3 : 7. They gave the name Purim, or " Lots," to the commemorative festival because he had thrown lots to ascertain what day would be auspicious for him to carry into effect the bloody decree which the king had issued at his instance. Esther 9 : 24. The festival lasted two days, and was regularly observed on the 14th and 15th of Adar. According to modern custom, as soon as the stars begin to appear, when the 14th of the month has commenced, candles are lighted up in token of rejoicing, and the people as-

Puteoli, Bay of Naples.

semble in the synagogue. After a short prayer and thanksgiving, the reading of the book of Esther commences. The book is written in a peculiar manner, on a roll called " the Roll " (*Megillah*). When the reader comes to the name of Haman, the congregation cry out, " May his name be blotted out," or, " Let the name of the ungodly perish." When the Megillah is read through, the whole congregation exclaim, " Cursed be Haman ; blessed be Mordecai ; cursed be Zoresh (the wife of Haman) ; blessed be Esther ; cursed be all idolaters ; blessed be all Israelites, and blessed be Harbonah who hanged Haman." In the morning service in the synagogue, on the 14th, after the prayers, the passage is read from the law, Ex. 17 : 8–16, which relates the destruction of the Amalekites, the people of Agag, 1 Sam. 15 : 8, the supposed ancestor of Haman. Esther 3 : 1. The Megillah is then read again in the same manner. The 14th of Adar, as the very day of the deliverance of the Jews, is more solemnly kept than the 13th ;

but when the service in the synagogue is over, all give themselves up to merry-making.

Purse, a bag for money. The Hebrews, when on a journey, were provided with a bag, in which they carried their money, Gen. 42 : 35; Prov. 1 : 14; 7 : 20; Isa. 46 : 6, and, if they were merchants, also their weights. Deut. 25 : 13; Micah 6 : 11. This bag is described in the New Testament by the terms βαλάντιον (bag), Luke 10 : 4; 12 : 33; 22 : 35, 36, and γλωσσοκομον (originally the bag in which musicians carried the mouth-pieces of their instruments). John 12 : 6; 13 : 29. The girdle also served as a purse. Matt. 10 : 9; Mark 6 : 8. Ladies wore ornamental purses. Isa. 3 : 24.

Put. 1 Chron. 1 : 8; Nah. 3 : 9. [PHUT.]

Pute'oli (*sulphurous springs*), the great landing-place of travellers to Italy from the Levant, and the harbor to which the Alexandrian corn-ships brought their cargoes. Acts 27 : 13. The celebrated bay which is now the Bay of Naples was then called "Sinus Puteolanus." The city was at the northeastern angle of the bay. The name Puteoli arose from the strong mineral springs which are characteristic of the place. It was a favorite watering-place of the Romans, its hot springs being considered efficacious for the cure of various diseases. Here also ships usually discharged their passengers and cargoes, partly to avoid doubling the promontory of Circeium and partly be-cause there was no commodious harbor nearer to Rome. Hence the ship in which Paul was conveyed from Melita landed the prisoners at this place, where the apostle stayed a week. Acts 28 : 13, 14. – *Whitney.* The associations of Puteoli with historical personages are very numerous. Scipio sailed from this place to Spain; Cicero had a villa in the neighborhood; here Nero planned the murder of his mother; Vespasian gave to this city peculiar privileges; and here Adrian was buried. In the fifth century it was ravaged by both Alaric and Genseric, and it never afterward recovered its former eminence. It is now a fourth-rate Italian town, still retaining the name of *Pozzuoli.* The remains of Puteoli are worthy of mention. Among them are the aqueduct, the reservoirs, portions (probably) of the baths, the great amphitheatre, and the building called the temple of Serapis. No Roman harbor has left as solid a memorial of itself as this one, at which St. Paul landed in Italy.

Pu'ti-el. One of the daughters of Putiel was wife of Eleazar the son of Aaron, and mother of Phinehas. Ex. 6 : 25. (B.C. before 1491.)

Pygarg occurs, Deut. 14 : 5, in the list of clean animals as the rendering of the Heb. *dishôn,* the name apparently of one species of antelope, though it is by no means easy to identify it.

Pyr'rhus, the father of Sopater of Berea. Acts 20 : 4, in Revised Version. (A.D. 55.)

Q.

The Quail.

Quails. There can be no doubt that the Hebrew word in the Pentateuch, Ex. 16:13; Num. 11:31, 32, and in the 105th Psalm, denotes the common quail, *Coturnix dactylisonans*. (The enormous quantity of quails taken by the Israelites has its parallel in modern times. Pliny states that they sometimes alight on vessels in the Mediterranean and sink them. Colonel Sykes states that 160,000 quails have been netted in one season on the island of Capri.—ED.) The expression "as it were two cubits (high) upon the face of the earth," Num. 11:31, refers probably to the height at which the quails flew above the ground, in their exhausted condition from their long flight. As to the enormous quantities which the least-successful Israelite is said to have taken, viz., "ten homers" (*i. e.* eighty bushels) in the space of a night and two days, there is every reason for believing that the "homers" here spoken of do not denote strictly the measure of that name, but simply "a heap." The Israelites would have had little difficulty in capturing large quantities of these birds, as they are known to arrive at places sometimes so completely exhausted by their flight as to be readily taken, not in nets only, but by the hand.

They "spread the quails round about the camp;" this was for the purpose of drying them. The Egyptians similarly prepared these birds. The expression "quails from the sea," Num. 11: 31, must not be restricted to denote that the birds came from the sea as their starting-point, but it must be taken to show the direction from which they were coming. The quails were, at the time of the event narrated in the sacred writings, on their spring journey of migration northward. It is interesting to note the time specified: "it was at even" that they began to arrive; and they no doubt continued to come all the night. Many observers have recorded that the quail migrates by night.

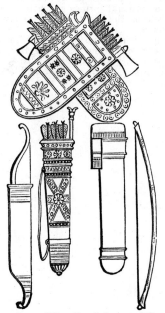

Assyrian and Egyptian Quivers and Bows.

Quar'tus (*fourth*), a Christian of Corinth, Rom. 16 : 23, said to have been one of the seventy disciples, and afterward bishop of Berytus. (A.D. about 50.)

Quaternion, a military term signifying a guard of four soldiers, two of whom were attached to the person of a prisoner, while the other two kept watch outside the door of his cell. Acts 12 : 4.

Queen. This title is properly applied to the queen-mother, since in an Oriental household it is not the wife but the mother of the master who exercises the highest authority. Strange as such an arrangement at first sight appears, it is one of the inevitable results of polygamy. An illustration of the queen-mother's influence is given in 1 Kings 2 : 19 ff. The term is applied to Maachah, 1 Kings 15 : 13; 2 Chron. 15 : 16, and to Jezebel, 2 Kings 10 : 13, and to the mother of Jehoiachin or Jeconiah, Jer. 13 : 18; compare 2 Kings 24 : 12; Jer. 29 : 2.

Queen of heaven, Jer. 7 : 18; 45 : 17, 18, 19, 25, is the moon, worshipped as Ashtaroth or Astarte, to whom the Hebrew women offered cakes in the streets of Jerusalem.

Quicksands, The, more properly THE SYRTIS, Acts 27 : 17, the broad and deep bight on the north African coast between Carthage and Cyrene. There were properly two Syrtes—the eastern or larger, now called the *Gulf of Sidra,* and the western or smaller, now the *Gulf of Cabes.* It is the former to which our attention is directed in this passage of the Acts.

Quiver, a box made for the purpose of holding arrows. Gen. 27 : 3. There is nothing in the Bible to indicate either its form or material, or in what way it was carried.

R.

Ra'amah (*horse's mane*), a son of Cush and father of the Cushite Sheba and Dedan. Gen. 10 : 7. (B.C. after 2513.) The tribe of Raamah became afterward renowned as traders. Ezek. 27 : 22. They were settled on the Persian Gulf.

Ra-ami'ah (*thunder of Jehovah*), one of the chiefs who returned with Zerubbabel. Neh. 7 : 7. In Ezra 2 : 2 he is called REELAIAH. (B.C. 445.)

Ra-am'ses. Ex. 1 : 11. [RAMESES.]

Rab'bah (*great*). 1. A very strong place on the east of the Jordan, and the chief city of the Ammonites. In five passages—Deut. 3 : 11; 2 Sam. 12 : 26; 17 : 27; Jer. 49 : 2; Ezek. 21 : 20—it is styled at length Rabbath of the Ammonites, or the children of Ammon; but elsewhere, Josh. 13 : 25; 2 Sam. 11 : 1; 12 : 27, 29; 1 Chron. 20 : 1; Jer. 49 : 3, simply Rabbah. When first named it is mentioned as containing the bed or sarcophagus of the giant Og. Deut. 3 : 11. David sent Joab to besiege Rabbah. 2 Sam. 11 : 1, 17, etc. Joab succeeded in capturing a portion of the place—the "city of waters," that is, the lower town, so called from its containing the perennial stream which rises in and still flows through it. The citadel still remained to be taken, but this was secured shortly after David's arrival. 2 Sam. 12 : 26-31. Long after, at the date of the invasion of Nebuchadnezzar, Jer. 49 : 2, 3, it had walls and palaces. It is named in such terms as imply that it was of equal importance with Jerusalem. Ezek. 21 : 20. From Ptolemy Philadelphus (B.C. 285-247) it received the name of Philadelphia. It was one of the cities of the Decapolis, and became the seat of a Christian bishop. Its ruins, which are considerable, are found at *Ammôn*, about 22 miles from the Jordan. It lies in a valley which is a branch, or perhaps the main course, of the *Wady Zerka*, usually identified with the Jabbok. The public buildings are said to be Roman, except the citadel, which is described as of large square stones put together without cement, and which is probably more ancient than the rest. 2. A city of Judah, named with Kirjath-jearim in Josh. 15 : 60 only. No

trace of its existence has yet been discovered.

Rab'bath-moab. [AR.]

Rab'bath of the Children of Ammon, and **Rabbath of the Ammonites.** [See RABBATH.]

Rabbi, a title of respect signifying *master, teacher,* given by the Jews to their doctors and teachers, and often addressed to our Lord. Matt. 23 : 7, 8; 26 : 25, 49; Mark 9 : 5; 11 : 21; 14 : 45; John 1 : 38, 49; 3 : 2, 26; 4 : 31; 6 : 25; 9 : 2; 11 : 8. Another form of the title was Rabboni. John 20 : 16. The titles were used with different degrees of honor; the lowest being rab, *master;* then rabbi, *my master;* next rabban, *our master;* and greatest of all, rabboni, *my great master.*

Rab'bith (*multitude*), a town in the territory, perhaps on the boundary, of Issachar. Josh. 19 : 20 only.

Rabbo'ni. John 20 : 16. [RABBI.]

Rab-mag, Jer. 39 : 3, 13, a title borne by Nergal-sharezer, probably identical with the king called by the Greeks Neriglissar. [NERGAL-SHAREZER.] (It probably means *chief of the magi;* at all events it was "an office of great power and dignity at the Babylonian court, and probably gave its possessor special facilities for gaining the throne.")

Rab'saris (*chief of the eunuchs*). 1. An officer of the king of Assyria sent up with Tartan and Rabshakeh against Jerusalem in the time of Hezekiah. 2 Kings 18 : 17. (B.C. 713.) 2. One of the princes of Nebuchadnezzar, who was present at the capture of Jerusalem, B.C. 588. Jer. 39 : 3, 13. Rabsaris is probably rather the name of an office than of an individual.

Rab'shakeh (*chief cupbearer*), 2 Kings 18, 19; Isa. 36, 37, one of the officers of the king of Assyria sent against Jerusalem in the reign of Hezekiah. [HEZEKIAH.] (B.C. 713.) The English version takes Rabshakeh as the name of a person; but it is more probably the name of the office which he held at the court, that of chief cupbearer.

Raca, a term of reproach derived from the Chaldee *rêká,* worthless. ("*Raca* denotes a certain looseness of life and manners, while 'fool,' in the same passage, means a downright wicked and reprobate person.") Matt. 5 : 22.

Race. [GAMES.]

Ra'chab. Rahab the harlot. Matt. 1 : 5.

Racing.

Ra'chal (*trade*), 1 Sam. 30 : 29, a town in the southern part of the tribe of Judah, one of the towns to which David sent presents out of the spoil of the Amalekites.

Ra'chel (*ewe*, or *sheep*), the younger of the daughters of Laban, the wife of Jacob (B.C. 1753) and mother of Joseph and Benjamin. The incidents of her life may be found in Gen. 29–33, 35. The story of Jacob and Rachel has always had a peculiar interest. The beauty of Rachel, Jacob's deep love and long servitude for her, their marriage, and Rachel's death on giving birth to Benjamin, with Jacob's grief at her loss, Gen. 48 : 7, makes a touching tale. Yet from what is related to us concerning her character there does not seem much to claim any high degree of admiration and esteem. She appears to have shared all the duplicity and falsehood of her family. See, for instance, Rachel's stealing her father's images, and the ready dexterity and presence of mind with which she concealed her theft. Gen. 31. "Rachel died and was buried on the way to Ephrath, which is Bethlehem. (B.C. 1729.) And Jacob set a pillar upon her grave; that is the pillar of Rachel's grave unto this day." Gen. 35 : 19, 20. The site of Rachel's tomb, "on the way to Bethle-

hem," "a little way to come to Ephrath," "in the border of Benjamin," has never been questioned. It is about two miles south of Jerusalem and one mile north of Bethlehem.

Rad'da-i (*trampling*), one of David's brothers, fifth son of Jesse. 1 Chron. 2 : 14.

Ra'gau, one of the ancestors of our Lord, father of Phalec. Luke 3 : 35. He is the same person with Reu, son of Peleg.

Ra'ges, an important city in northeastern Media, where that country bordered upon Parthia. Its ruins, still known by the name of *Rhey*, lie about five miles southeast of Teheran.

Ragu'el, or **Re-u'el** (*friend of God*). 1. Probably the same as Jethro. [JETHRO; HOBAB.] (B.C. 1490.)

2. A pious Jew of "Ecbatane, a city of Media," father of Sara, the wife of Tobias. Tob. 3 : 7, 17, etc.

Ra'hab, or **Ra'chab** (*wide*), a celebrated woman of Jericho, who received the spies sent by Joshua to spy out the land, hid them in her house from the pursuit of her countrymen, was saved with all her family when the Israelites sacked the city, and became the wife of Salmon and the ancestress of the Messiah. Josh. 2 : 1; Matt. 1 : 5. (B.C. 1450.) She was a "harlot," and probably combined the trade of lodging-keeper for wayfaring men. Her reception of the spies, the artifice by which she concealed them from the king, their escape, and the saving of Rahab and her family at the capture of the city, in accordance with their promise, are all told in the narrative of Josh. 2. As regards Rahab herself, she probably repented, and we learn from Matt. 1 : 5 that she became the wife of Salmon the son of Naasson, and the mother of Boaz, Jesse's grandfather. The author of the Epistle to the Hebrews tells us that "by faith the harlot Rahab perished not with them that believed not, when she had received the spies with peace," Heb. 11 : 31 ; and St. James fortifies his doctrine of justification by works by asking, " Was not Rahab the harlot justified by works, when she had received the messengers, and had sent them out another way ?" James 2 : 25.

Ra′hab, a poetical name of Egypt, Ps. 89 : 10 ; Isa. 51 : 9, signifying " fierceness, insolence, pride." Rahab, as a name of Egypt, occurs once only without reference to the exodus : this is in Ps. 87 : 4. In Isa. 30 : 7 the name is alluded to.

Tomb of Rachel, near Bethlehem.

Ra′ham (*belly*). In the genealogy of the descendants of Caleb the son of Hezron, 1 Chron. 2 : 44, Raham is described as the son of Shema and father of Jorkoam.

Ra′hel, the original form in our Authorized Version of the now familiar Rachel. Jer. 31 : 15.

Rain. In the Bible " early rain " signifies the rain of the autumn, Deut. 11: 14, and " latter rain " the rain of spring. Prov. 16 : 15. For six months in the year, from May to October, no rain falls, the whole land becomes dry, parched and brown. The autumnal rains are eagerly looked for, to prepare the earth for the reception of the seed. These, the early rains, commence about the latter end of October, continuing through November and December. January and February are the coldest months, and snow falls, sometimes to the depth of a foot or more, at Jerusalem, but it does not lie long ; it is very seldom seen along the coast and in the low plains. Rain continues to fall more or less during the month of March ; it is very rare in April. Robinson observes that there are not, at the present day, " any particular periods of rain or succession of showers which might be regarded as distinct rainy seasons. The whole period from October to March now constitutes only one continued season of rain, without any regularly-intervening term of prolonged fine weather. Unless, therefore, there has been some change in the climate, the early and the latter rains, for which the husbandman waited with longing, seem rather to have implied the first showers of autumn—which revived the parched and thirsty soil and prepared it for the seed—and the later showers of spring, which continued to refresh and forward both the ripening crops and the vernal products of the fields." James 5 : 7 ; Prov. 16 : 15.

Rainbow, the token of the covenant which God made with Noah when he came forth from the ark that the waters should no more become a flood to destroy all flesh. The right interpretation of Gen. 9 : 13 seems to be that God took the rainbow, which had hitherto been but a beautiful object shining in the heavens when the sun's rays fell on falling rain, and consecrated it as the sign of his love and the witness of his promise. Ecclus. 43 : 11. The rainbow is a symbol of God's faithfulness and mercy. In the "rainbow around the throne," Rev. 4 : 3, is seen the symbol of hope and the bright emblem of mercy and love, all the more true as a symbol because it is reflected from the storm itself.

Raisins. [VINE.]

Ra'kem (*flower garden*), a descendant of Machir the son of Manasseh. 1 Chron. 7 : 16. (B.C. before 1451.)

Rak'kath (*shore*), a fortified city in the tribe of Naphtali. Josh. 19 : 35. It was on the western shore of the Sea of Galilee, not far from the warm baths of Tiberias.

Rak'kon (*the temple*) (of the head), a well-watered place in the inheritance of Dan, not far from Joppa. Josh. 19 : 46.

Ram. [See BATTERING-RAM.]

Ram (*high, exalted*). 1. A son of Hezron and the father of Amminadab, born in Egypt after Jacob's migration there. Ruth 4 : 19. (B.C. 1706.) In Matt. 1 : 3, 4 and Luke 3 : 33 he is called ARAM in the Authorized Version, but RAM in the Revised Version of Matt. 1 : 3, 4, and ARNI in the Revised Version of Luke 3 : 33.

2. The first-born of Jerahmeel, and therefore nephew of the preceding. 1 Chron. 2 : 25, 27. (B.C. after 1706.)

3. One of the kindred of Elihu. Job 32 : 2. Ewald identified this Ram with ARAM in Gen. 22 : 21.

Ra'ma, Matt. 2 : 18, referring to Jer. 31 : 15. It is the Greek form of Ramah.

Ra'mah (*a hill*). This is the name of several places in the holy land. 1. One of the cities of the allotment of Benjamin. Josh. 18 : 25. Its site is at er-*Râm*, about five miles from Jerusalem, and near to Gibeah. Judges 4 : 5 ; 19 : 13 ; 1 Sam. 22 : 6. Its people returned after the captivity. Ezra 2 : 26 ; Neh. 7 : 30.

2. The home of Elkanah, Samuel's father, 1 Sam. 1 : 19 ; 2 : 11, the birthplace of Samuel himself, his home and official residence, the site of his altar, ch. 7 : 17 ; 8 : 4 ; 15 : 34 ; 16 : 13 ; 19 : 18, and finally his burial-place. ch. 25 : 1 ; 28 : 3. It is a contracted form of Ramathaim-zophim. All that is directly said as to its situation is that it was in Mount Ephraim, 1 Sam. 1 : 1, a district without defined boundaries. The position of Ramah is a much-disputed question. Tradition, however, places the residence of Samuel on the lofty and re-

Battering-ram. A Besieged City. (*Nineveh Sculptures*.)

markable eminence of *Neby Samwil*, which rises four miles to the northwest of Jerusalem. Since the days of Arculf the tradition appears to have been continuous. Here, then, we are inclined, in the present state of the evidence, to place the Ramah of Samuel.

3. One of the nineteen fortified places of Naphtali. Josh. 19 : 36. Dr. Robinson has discovered a Rameh northwest of the

Sea of Galilee, about 8 miles east-south-east of Safed.

4. One of the landmarks on the boundary of Asher, Josh. 19 : 29, apparently between Tyre and Zidon. Some place it 3 miles east of Tyre, others 10 miles off and east-southeast of the same city.

5. By this name in 2 Kings 8 : 29 and 2 Chron. 22 : 6, only, is designated Ramoth-gilead.

6. A place mentioned in the catalogue of those reinhabited by the Benjamites after their return from the captivity. Neh. 11 : 33.

Ra'math-le'hi (*hill of the jawbone*, or *hill of Lehi*), the name bestowed by Samson on the scene of his slaughter of the thousand Philistines with the jawbone, Judges 15 : 17 ; a place by the rock Elam, in western Judah, near the borders of the Philistines.

Ra'math-miz'peh (*high place of the watch-tower*). [RAMOTH-GILEAD.]

Ra'math of the south, one of the towns at the extreme south limit of Simeon. Josh. 19 : 8. It is in all probability the same place as south Ramoth. 1 Sam. 30 : 27.

Ramatha'im - zo'phim (*the two heights of the watchers*). [RAMAH, 2.]

Ra'mathite, The. Shimei the Ramathite, *i. e.* a native of Ramah, had charge of the royal vineyards of King David. 1 Chron. 27 : 27. (B.C. 1050.)

Rame'ses, or **Ra-am'ses** (*child of the sun*), a city and district of lower Egypt. Gen. 47 : 11 ; Ex. 12 : 37 ; Num. 33 : 3, 5. This land of Rameses either corresponds to the land of Goshen or was a district of it, more probably the former. The city was one of the two store-cities built for the Pharaoh who first oppressed the children of Israel. Ex. 1 : 11. (It was probably the capital of Goshen, and situated in the valley of the Pelusiac mouth of the Nile. McClintock and Strong say that its location is indicated by the present *Tell Ramsis*, a quadrangular mound near Belbeis. Dr. Brugsch thinks that it was at Zoan-Tanis, the modern *San*, on the Tanitic branch of the Nile, and that it was built or enlarged by Rameses II. and made his capital.—ED.)

Rami'ah, one who had taken "a strange wife." Ezra 10 : 25.

Ra'moth-gil'ead (*heights of Gilead*), one of the great fastnesses on the east of Jordan, and the key to an important district. 1 Kings 4 : 13. It was the city of refuge for the tribe of Gad, Deut. 4 :

43 ; Josh. 20 : 8 ; 21 : 38, and the residence of one of Solomon's commissariat officers. 1 Kings 4 : 13. During the invasion related in 1 Kings 15 : 20, or some subsequent incursion, this important place had been seized by Ben-hadad I., king of Syria. The incidents of Ahab's expedition are well known. [AHAB.] Later it was taken by Israel, and held in spite of all the efforts of Hazael, who was now on the throne of Damascus, to regain it. 2 Kings 9 : 14. Henceforward Ramoth-gilead disappears from our view. Eusebius and Jerome specify the position of Ramoth as 15 miles from Philadelphia (*Ammân*). It may correspond to the site bearing the name of *Jel'âd*, exactly identical with the ancient Hebrew Gilead, which is four or five miles north of *es-Salt*, 25 miles east of the Jordan and 13 miles south of the brook Jabbok.

Ram's horns. [CORNET ; JUBILEE.]

Ra'pha (*tall*). 1. Son of Binea, among the descendants of Saul. 1 Chron. 8 : 37.

2. One of Benjamin's descendants. 1 Chron. 8 : 2.

Ra'phael (*the divine healer*). According to Jewish tradition, Raphael was one of the four angels which stood round the throne of God—Michael, Uriel, Gabriel, Raphael.

Ra'phon, a city of Gilead, 1 Macc. 5 : 37, perhaps identical with Raphana, which is mentioned by Pliny as one of the cities of the Decapolis.

Ra'phu, the father of Palti, the Benjamite spy. Num. 13 : 9. (B.C. before 1490.)

Raven (*black*). The Hebrew *oreb* is applied to the several species of the crow family, a number of which are found in Palestine. The raven belongs to the order *Insessores*, family *Corvidæ*. (It resembles the crow, but is larger, weighing three pounds ; its black color is more iridescent, and it is gifted with greater sagacity. "There is something weird and shrewd in the expression of the raven's countenance, a union of cunning and malignity which may have contributed to give it among widely-severed nations a reputation for preternatural knowledge." One writer says that the smell of death is so grateful to them that when in passing over sheep a tainted smell is perceptible, they cry and croak vehemently. It may be that in passing over a human habitation, if a sickly or cadaverous smell arises, they would make it known by their cries, and so has arisen the idea that the croaking of a raven is the premonition of death.—ED.) A raven was sent out by Noah from the ark. Gen. 8 : 7. This bird was not allowed as food by the Mosaic law. Lev. 11 : 15. Elijah was cared for by ravens. 1 Kings 17 : 4, 6. They are expressly mentioned as instances of God's protecting love and goodness.

Raven.

Job 38 : 41; Luke 12 : 24. The raven's carnivorous habits, and especially his readiness to attack the eye, are alluded to in Prov. 30 : 17. To the fact of the raven being a common bird in Palestine, and to its habit of flying restlessly about in constant search for food to satisfy its voracious appetite, may perhaps be traced the reason for its being selected by our Lord and the inspired writers as the especial object of God's providing care.

Razor. Besides other usages, the practice of shaving the head after the completion of a vow must have created among the Jews a necessity for the special trade of a barber. Lev. 14 : 8; Num. 6 : 9, 18; 8 : 7; Judges 13 : 5; Isa. 7 : 20; Ezek. 5 : 1; Acts 18 : 18. The instruments of his work were probably, as in modern times, the razor, the basin, the mirror, and perhaps also the scissors. See 2 Sam. 14 : 26. Like the Levites, the Egyptian priests were accustomed to shave their whole bodies.

Reai'a, a Reubenite, son of Micah, and apparently prince of his tribe. 1 Chron. 5 : 5. The name is identical with **Reai'ah** (*seen of Jehovah*). 1. A descendant of Shubal the son of Judah. 1 Chron. 4 : 2.

2. The children of Reaiah were a family of Nethinim who returned from Babylon with Zerubbabel. Ezra 2 : 47; Neh. 7 : 50. (B.C. before 536.)

Re'ba (*four*), one of the five kings of the Midianites slain by the children of Israel when Balaam fell. Num. 31 : 8; Josh. 13 : 21. (B.C. 1450.)

Rebec'ca. Rom. 9 : 10 only. [REBEKAH.]

Rebek'ah (*ensnarer*), daughter of Bethuel, Gen. 22 : 23, and sister of Laban, married to Isaac. She is first presented to us in Gen. 24, where the beautiful story of her marriage is related. (B.C. 1857.) For nineteen years she was childless: then Esau and Jacob were born, the younger being the mother's companion and favorite. Gen. 25 : 19–28. Rebekah suggested the deceit that was practiced by Jacob on his blind father. She directed and aided him in carrying it out, foresaw the probable consequence of Esau's anger, and prevented it by moving Isaac to send Jacob away to Padan-aram, Gen. 27, to her own kindred. Gen. 29 : 12. Rebekah's beauty became at one time a source of danger to her husband. Gen. 26 : 7. It has been conjectured that she died during Jacob's sojourn in Padan-aram.

Re'chab (*rider*). 1. One of the two "captains of bands" whom Ish-bosheth took into his service, and who conspired to murder him. 2 Sam. 4 : 2. (B.C. 1046.)

2. The father of Malchiah, ruler of part of Beth-haccerem. Neh. 3 : 14. (B.C. before 446.)

3. The father or ancestor of Jehonadab. 2 Kings 10 : 15, 23; 1 Chron. 2 : 55; Jer. 35 : 6–19. (B.C. before 882.) It was from this Rechab that the tribe of the Rechabites derived their name. In 1 Chron. 2 : 55 the house of Rechab is identified with a section of the Kenites, a Midianitish tribe who came into Canaan with the Israelites, and retained their nomadic habits. The real founder of the tribe

was Jehonadab. [JEHONADAB.] He and his people had all along been worshippers of Jehovah, circumcised, though not looked upon as belonging to Israel, and probably therefore not considering themselves bound by the Mosaic law and ritual. The worship of Baal was offensive to them. Jehonadab inaugurated a reformation and compelled a more rigid adherence than ever to the old Arab life. They were neither to drink wine, nor build houses, nor sow seed, nor plant nor have any vineyard. All their days they were to dwell in tents. Jer. 35 : 6, 7. This was to be the condition of their retaining a distinct tribal existence. For two centuries and a half they adhered faithfully to this rule. The invasion of Judah by Nebuchadnezzar, in B.C. 607, drove the Rechabites from their tents to Jerusalem, where they stood proof against temptation, and were specially blessed. Jer. 35 : 2-19. There is much of interest in relation to the present condition of these people. Dr. Wolff reports that the Jews of Jerusalem and Yemen told him that he would find the Rechabites of Jer. 35 living near Mecca, in the mountainous country northeast of Medina. When he came near Senaa he came in contact with a tribe, the Beni-Khabir, who identified themselves with the sons of Jehonadab. They claimed to number 60,000, to adhere to the old rules, and to be a fulfillment of the promise made to Jehonadab.

Re'chabites. [RECHAB.]

Re'chah (*uttermost part*), probably a place in Judah—a village, *Rashiah*, three miles south of Jerusalem.

Recorder, an officer of high rank in the Jewish state, exercising the functions, not simply of an annalist, but of chancellor or president of the privy council. In David's court the recorder appears among the high officers of his household. 2 Sam. 8 : 16; 20 : 24; 1 Chron. 18 : 15. In Solomon's he is coupled with the three secretaries. 1 Kings 4 : 3; comp. 2 Kings 18 : 18, 37; 2 Chron. 34 : 8.

Red Sea. 1. *Name.*—The sea known to us as the Red Sea was by the Israelites called "the sea," Ex. 14 : 2, 9, 16, 21, 28; 15 : 1, 4, 8, 10, 19; Josh. 24 : 6, 7, and many other passages, and specially "the sea of *sûph.*" Ex. 10 : 19; 13 : 18; 15 : 4, 22; 23 : 31; Num. 14 : 25, etc. This word signifies *a sea-weed resembling wool*, and such sea-weed is thrown up abundantly on the shores of the Red Sea; hence Brugsch calls it the *sea of reeds* or *weeds*.

The color of the water is not red. Ébers says that it is of a lovely blue-green color, and named Red either from its red banks or from the Erythræans, who were called the red people.

2. *Physical description.*—In extreme length the Red Sea stretches from the straits of Báb el-Mendeb (or rather Rás Báb el-Mendeb), 18 miles wide, in lat. 12° 40′ N., to the modern head of the Gulf of Suez, lat. 30° N., a distance of 1450 miles. Its greatest width may be stated at about 210 miles. At Rás Mohammed, on the north, the Red Sea is split by the granitic peninsula of Sinai into two gulfs; the westernmost, or Gulf of Suez, is now about 150 miles in length, with an average width of about 20, though it contracts to less than 10 miles; the easternmost, or Gulf of el-'Akabeh, is about 100 miles long, from the Straits of Tirán to the 'Akabeh, and 15 miles wide. The average depth of the Red Sea is from 2500 to 3500 feet, though in places it is 6000 feet deep. Journeying southward from Suez, on our left is the peninsula of Sinai; on the right is the desert coast of Egypt, of limestone formation, like the greater part of the Nile valley in Egypt, the cliffs on the sea margin stretching landward in a great rocky plateau, while more inland a chain of volcanic mountains, beginning about lat. 28° 4′ and running south, rear their lofty peaks at intervals above the limestone, generally about 15 miles distant.

3. *Ancient limits.*—The most important change in the Red Sea has been the drying up of its northern extremity, "the tongue of the Egyptian Sea." The land about the head of the gulf has risen and that near the Mediterranean become depressed. The head of the gulf has consequently retired gradually since the Christian era. Thus the prophecy of Isaiah has been fulfilled, Isa. 11 : 15; 19 : 5; the tongue of the Red Sea has dried up for a distance of at least 50 miles from its ancient head. An ancient canal conveyed the waters of the Nile to the Red Sea, flowing through the *Wâdi-t-Tumeylát* and irrigating with its system of water-channels a large extent of country. It was 62 Roman miles long, 54 feet wide and 7 feet deep. The drying up of the head of the gulf appears to have been one of the chief causes of the neglect and ruin of this canal. The country, for the distance above indicated, is now a desert of gravelly sand, with

wide patches about the old sea-bottom, of rank marsh land, now called the "Bitter Lakes." At the northern extremity of this salt waste is a small lake, sometimes called the Lake of Heroöpolis; the lake is now *Birket-et-Timsâh*, "the lake of the crocodile," and is supposed to mark the ancient head of the gulf. The canal that connected this with the Nile was of Pharaonic origin. It was anciently known as the "Fossa Regum" and the "canal of Hero." The time at which the canal was extended, after the drying up of the head of the gulf, to the present head is uncertain, but it must have been late, and probably since the Mohammedan conquest. Traces of the ancient channel throughout its entire length to the vicinity of Bubastis exist at intervals in the present day. The land north of the ancient head of the gulf is a plain of heavy sand, merging into marsh-land near the Mediterranean coast, and extending to Palestine. This region, including *Wâdi-t-Tumeylât*, was probably the frontier land occupied in part by the Israelites, and open to the incursions of the wild tribes of the Arabian desert.

4. *Navigation.*—The sea, from its dangers and sterile shores, is entirely destitute of boats. The coral of the Red Sea is remarkably abundant, and beautifully colored and variegated; but it forms so many reefs and islands along the shores that navigation is very dangerous, and the shores are chiefly barren rock and sand, and therefore very sparsely inhabited, so that there are but three cities along the whole 1450 miles of its west coast—Suez, at the head, a city of 14,000 inhabitants; Sanakin, belonging to Soudan, of 10,000; and Massau, in Abyssinia, of 5000. Only two ports, Elath and Ezion-geber, are mentioned in the Bible. The earliest navigation of the Red Sea (passing by the pre-historical Phœnicians) is mentioned by Herodotus:—"Sesostris (Rameses II.) was the first who, passing the Arabian Gulf in a fleet of long vessels, reduced under his authority the inhabitants of the coast bordering the Erythræan Sea." Three centuries later, Solomon's navy was built "in Ezion-geber, which is beside Eloth, on the shore of the Red Sea (Yam Sûph), in the land of Edom." 1 Kings 9 : 26. The kingdom of Solomon extended as far as the Red Sea, upon which he possessed the harbors of Elath and Ezion-

geber. [ELATH; EZION-GEBER.] It is possible that the sea has retired here as at Suez, and that Ezion-geber is now dry land. Jehoshaphat also "made ships of Tharshish to go to Ophir for gold; but they went not; for the ships were broken at Ezion-geber." 1 Kings 22 : 48. The scene of this wreck has been supposed to be Edh-Dhahab. The fleets appear to have sailed about the autumnal equinox, and returned in December or the middle of January. The Red Sea, as it possessed for many centuries the most important sea-trade of the East, contained ports of celebrity. The Heroöpolite Gulf (Gulf of Suez) is of the chief interest; it was near to Goshen, it was the scene of the passage of the Red Sea, and it was the "tongue of the Egyptian Sea." It was also the seat of the Egyptian trade in this sea and to the Indian Ocean.

5. *Passage of the Red Sea.*—The passage of the Red Sea was the crisis of the exodus. It is usual to suppose that the most northern place at which the Red Sea could have been crossed is the present head of the Gulf of Suez. This supposition depends upon the erroneous idea that in the time of Moses the gulf did not extend farther to the northward than at present. An examination of the country north of Suez has shown, however, that the sea has receded many miles. The old bed is indicated by the *Birket-et-Timsâh*, or "lake of the crocodile," and the more southern Bitter Lakes, the northernmost part of the former probably corresponding to the head of the gulf at the time of the exodus. It is necessary to endeavor to ascertain the route of the Israelites before we can attempt to discover where they crossed the sea. The point from which they started was Rameses, a place certainly in the land of Goshen, which we identify with the *Wâdi-t-Tumeylât*. They first encamped at Succoth. At the end of the second day's journey the camping-place was at Etham, "in the edge of the wilderness." Ex. 13 : 20; Num. 33 : 6. Here the *Wâdi-t-Tumeylât* was probably left, as it is cultivable and terminates in the desert. At the end of the third day's march,—for each camping-place seems to mark the close of a day's journey,— the Israelites encamped by the sea. The place of this last encampment and that of the passage would be not very far from the Persepolitan monument at Pi-hahiroth. It appears that Migdol was

behind Pi-hahiroth, and on the other hand Baal-zephon and the sea. From Pi-hahiroth the Israelites crossed the sea. This was not far from halfway between the Bitter Lakes and the Gulf of Suez, where now it is dry land. The Muslims suppose Memphis to have been the city at which the Pharaoh of the exodus resided before that event occurred. From opposite Memphis a broad valley leads to the Red Sea. It is in part called the *Wâdi-t-Teeh,* or "Valley of the Wandering." From it the traveller reaches the sea beneath the lofty *Gebel-et-Tákah,* which rises in the north and shuts off all escape in that direction excepting by a narrow way along the seashore, which Pharaoh might have occupied. The sea here is broad and deep, as the narrative is generally held to imply. All the local features seem suited for a great event. The only points bearing on geography in the account of this event are that the sea was divided by an east wind, whence we may reasonably infer that it was crossed from west to east, and that the whole Egyptian army perished, which shows that it must have been some miles broad. On the whole we may reasonably suppose about twelve miles as the smallest breadth of the sea. The narrative distinctly states that a path was made through the sea, and that the waters were a wall on either hand. The term "wall" does not appear to oblige us to suppose, as many have done, that the sea stood up like a cliff on either side, but should rather be considered to mean a barrier, as the former idea implies a seemingly needless addition to the miracle, while the latter seems to be not discordant with the language of the narrative. It was during the night that the Israelites crossed, and the Egyptians followed. In the morning watch, the last third or fourth of the night, or the period before sunrise, Pharaoh's army was in full pursuit in the divided sea, and was there miraculously troubled, so that the Egyptians sought to flee. Ex. 14 : 23-25. Then was Moses commanded again to stretch out his hand, and the sea returned to its strength, and overwhelmed the Egyptians, of whom not one remained alive. *Ibid.* 26-28.

(But on the whole it is becoming more probable that the place where the Israelites crossed "was near the town of Suez, on extensive shoals which run toward the southeast, in the direction of Ayim Musa (the Wells of Moses). The distance is about three miles at high tide. This is the most probable theory. Near here Napoleon, deceived by the tidal wave, attempted to cross in 1799, and nearly met the fate of Pharaoh. But an army

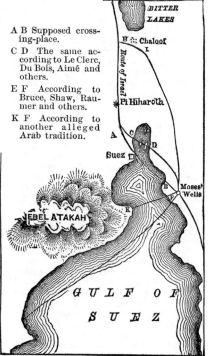

A B Supposed crossing-place.

C D The same according to Le Clerc, Du Bois, Aimé and others.

E F According to Bruce, Shaw, Raumer and others.

K F According to another alleged Arab tradition.

of 600,000 could of course never have crossed it without a miracle."—Schaff's *Through Bible Lands.* Several routes and places of crossing advocated by learned Egyptologists can be clearly seen by the accompanying maps. The latest theory is that which Brugsch-bey has lately revived, that the word translated Red Sea is "Sea of Reeds or Weeds," and refers to the Serbonian bog in the northeastern part of Egypt, and that the Israelites crossed here instead of the Red Sea.

"A gulf profound, as that Serbonian bog . . .
Where armies whole h ve sunk."—*Milton.*

And among these armies that of Artaxerxes, king of Persia, B. C. 350. But it is very difficult to make this agree with the Bible narrative, and it is the least satisfactory of all the theories.—ED.)

Reed. Under this name may be noticed the following Hebrew words: 1. *Agmôn* occurs in Job 40 : 12, 26 ; Isa. 9 : 14 (Authorized Version " rush ").

Papyrus Reed.

There can be no doubt that it denotes some aquatic reed-like plant, probably the *Phragmitis communis*, which, if it does not occur in Palestine and Egypt, is represented by a very closely-allied species, viz., the *Arundo isiaca* of Delisle. The drooping panicle of this plant will answer well to the " bowing down the head " of which Isaiah speaks. Isa. 58 : 5. 2. *Gôme*, translated " rush " and " bulrush " by the Authorized Version, without doubt denotes the celebrated paper-reed of the ancients, *Papyrus antiquorum*, which formerly was common in some parts of Egypt. The papyrus reed is not now found in Egypt; it grows, however, in Syria. Dr. Hooker saw it on the banks of Lake Tiberias, a few miles north of the town. The papyrus plant has an angular stem from 3 to 6 feet high, though occasionally it grows to the height of 14 feet; it has no leaves; the flowers are in very small spikelets, which grow on the thread-like flowering branchlets which form a bushy crown to each stem. (It was used for making paper, shoes, sails, ropes, mattresses, etc. The Greek name is βιβλος, from which came our word Bible—book—because books were made of the papyrus paper. This paper was always expensive among the Greeks, being worth a dollar a sheet.—ED.) 3. *Kâneh*, a reed of any kind. Thus there are in general four kinds of reeds named in the Bible: (1) The water reed ; No. 1 above. (2) A stronger reed, *Arundo donax*, the true reed of Egypt and Palestine, which grows 8 or 10 feet high, and is thicker than a man's thumb. It has a jointed stalk like the bamboo, and is very abundant on the Nile. (3) The writing reed, *Arundo scriptoria*, was used for making pens. (4) The papyrus; No. 2.

Re-ela'iah (*bearer of Jehovah*), one who went up with Zerubbabel. Ezra 2 : 2. In Neh. 7 : 7 he is called RAAMIAH. (B. C. 445.)

Refiner. The refiner's art was essential to the working of the precious metals. It consisted in the separation of the dross from the pure ore, which was effected by reducing the metal to a fluid state by the application of heat, and by the aid of solvents, such as alkali, Isa. 1 : 25, or lead, Jer. 6 : 29, which, amalgamating with the dross, permitted the extraction of the unadulterated metal. The instruments required by the refiner were a crucible or furnace and a bellows or blow-pipe. The workman sat at his work, Mal. 3 : 3 : he was thus better enabled to watch the process, and let the metal run off at the proper moment.

Refuge, Cities of. [CITIES OF REFUGE.]

Re'gem (*friend*), a son of Jahdai. 1 Chron. 2 : 47.

Re'gem-me'lech (*friend of the king*). The names of Sherezer and Regem-melech occur in an obscure passage of Zechariah. ch. 7 : 2. They were sent on behalf of some of the captivity to make inquiries at the temple concerning fasting. (B.C. 517.)

Rehabi'ah (*enlarged by Jehovah*), the only son of Eliezer the son of Moses. 1 Chron. 23 : 17; 24 : 21; 26 : 25. (B.C. about 1455.)

Re'hob. 1. The father of Hadadezer king of Zobah, whom David smote at the Euphrates. 2 Sam. 8 : 3, 12. (B.C. before 1043.)

2. A Levite or family of Levites who sealed the covenant with Nehemiah. Neh. 10 : 11. (B.C. 410.)

3. The northern limit of the exploration of the spies. Num. 13 : 21. Robinson fixes the position of Rehob as not far from *Tell el-Kady* and *Banias.*

4. One of the towns allotted to Asher. Josh. 19 : 28.

5. Asher contained another Rehob, Josh. 19 : 30; but the situation of these towns is unknown.

Rehoboam, from sculpture at Karnak. The inscription has been read "Kingdom of Judah."

Rehobo'am (*enlarger of the people*), son of Solomon by the Ammonite princess Naamah, 1 Kings 14 : 21, 31, and his successor. 1 Kings 11 : 43. Rehoboam selected Shechem as the place of his coronation (B.C. 975), probably as an act of concession to the Ephraimites. The peo-

ple demanded a remission of the severe burdens imposed by Solomon, and Rehoboam, rejecting the advice of his father's counsellors, followed that of his young courtiers, and returned an insulting answer, which led to an open rebellion among the tribes, and he was compelled to fly to Jerusalem, Judah and Benjamin alone remaining true to him. Jeroboam was made king of the northern tribes. [JEROBOAM.] An expedition to reconquer Israel was forbidden by the prophet Shemaiah, 1 Kings 12 : 24; still during Rehoboam's lifetime peaceful relations between Israel and Judah were never restored. 2 Chron. 12 : 15; 1 Kings 14 : 30. In the fifth year of Rehoboam's reign the country was invaded by a host of Egyptians and other African nations under Shishak. Jerusalem itself was taken, and Rehoboam had to purchase an ignominious peace by delivering up all the treasures with which Solomon had adorned the temple and palace. The rest of Rehoboam's life was unmarked by any events of importance. He died B.C. 958, after a reign of 17 years, having ascended the throne B.C. 975, at the age of 41. 1 Kings 14 : 21; 2 Chron. 12 : 13. He had 18 wives, 60 concubines, 28 sons and 60 daughters.

Reho'both (*wide places*, i. e. *streets*). 1. The third of the series of wells dug by Isaac, Gen. 26 : 22, in the Philistines' territory, lately identified as *er-Ruheibeh*, 16 miles south of Beersheba.

2. One of the four cities built by Asshur, or by Nimrod in Asshur, according as this difficult passage is translated. Gen. 10 : 11. Nothing certain is known of its position.

3. The city of a certain Saul or Shaul, one of the early kings of the Edomites. Gen. 36 : 37; 1 Chron. 1 : 48. The affix "by the river" fixes the situation of Rehoboth as on the Euphrates.

Re'hum (*merciful*). 1. One who went up from Babylon with Zerubbabel. Ezra 2 : 2. (B.C. 536.)

2. "Rehum the chancellor." Ezra 4 : 8, 9, 17, 23. He was perhaps a kind of lieutenant-governor of the province under the king of Persia. (B.C. 535.)

3. A Levite of the family of Bani, who assisted in rebuilding the walls of Jerusalem. Neh. 3 : 17. (B.C. 445.)

4. One of the chief of the people, who signed the covenant with Nehemiah. Neh. 10 : 25. (B.C. 410.)

5. A priestly family, or the head of a

priestly house, who went up with Zerub-babel. Neh. 12 : 3. (B.C. 536.)

Re′i (*friendly*), a person mentioned (in 1 Kings 1 : 8 only) as having remained firm in David's cause when Adonijah rebelled. (B.C. 1015.)

Reins (*i. e.* kidneys). In the ancient system of physiology the kidneys were believed to be the seat of desire and longing, which accounts for their often being coupled with the heart. Ps. 7 : 9; 26 : 2; Jer. 11 : 20; 17 : 10, etc.

Re′kem (*variegation*). 1. One of the five kings or chieftains of Midian slain by the Israelites. Num. 31 : 8; Josh. 13 : 21.

2. One of the four sons of Hebron, and father of Shammai. 1 Chron. 2 : 43, 44.

Re′kem, one of the towns of the allotment of Benjamin. Josh. 18 : 27. Its existing site is unknown.

Remali′ah (*protected by Jehovah*), the father of Pekah, captain of Pekahiah king of Israel, who slew his master and usurped his throne. 2 Kings 15 : 25-37 ; 16 : 1, 5 ; 2 Chron. 28 : 6; Isa. 7 : 1-9; 8 : 6. (B.C. 756.)

Re′meth (*height*), one of the towns of Issachar. Josh. 19 : 21. It is probably, though not certainly, a distinct place from the RAMOTH of 1 Chron. 6 : 73.

Rem′mon (*pomegranate*), a town in the allotment of Simeon, Josh. 19 : 7; elsewhere accurately given in the Authorized Version as Rimmon.

Rem′mon - meth′o-ar, a place which formed one of the landmarks of Zebulun. Josh. 19 : 13 only. Methoar does not really form a part of the name, but should be translated (as in the margin of the Authorized Version). "Remmon which reaches to Neah." Dr. Robinson and Mr. Van de Velde place *Rummâneh* on the south border of the plain of *Buttauf*, three miles north-northeast of *Seffurieh.*

Rem′phan, Acts 7 : 43, and **Chi′un,** Amos 5 : 26, have been supposed to be names of an idol worshipped secretly by the Israelites in the wilderness. Much difficulty has been occasioned by this corresponding occurrence of two names so wholly different in sound. The most reasonable opinion seems to be that Chiun was a Hebrew or Semitic name, and Remphan an Egyptian equivalent substituted by the LXX. This idol corresponded probably to Saturn or Molech. The mention of Chiun or Remphan as

worshipped in the desert shows that this idolatry was, in part at least, that of foreigners, and no doubt of those settled in lower Egypt.

Re′phael (*healed of God*), son of Shemaiah, the first-born of Obed-edom. 1 Chron. 26 : 7. (B.C. about 1015.)

Re′phah, a son of Ephraim, and ancestor of Joshua. 1 Chron. 7 : 25.

Reph′aiah (*healed of Jehovah*). 1. The sons of Rephaiah appear among the descendants of Zerubbabel in 1 Chron. 3 : 21.

2. A Simeonite chieftain in the reign of Hezekiah. 1 Chron. 4 : 42. (B.C. 727.)

3. Son of Tola the son of Issachar. 1 Chron. 7 : 2.

4. Son of Binea, and descendant of Saul. 1 Chron. 9 : 43.

5. The son of Hur, and ruler of a portion of Jerusalem. Neh. 3 : 9. (B.C. 441.)

Reph′a-im. [GIANTS.]

Reph′a-im, The valley of, 2 Sam. 5 : 18, 22; 23 : 13; 1 Chron. 11 : 15; 14 : 9; Isa. 17 : 5; also in Josh. 15 : 8 and 18 : 16, where it is translated in the Authorized Version "*the valley of the giants,*" a spot which was the scene of some of David's most remarkable adventures. He twice encountered and defeated the Philistines there. 2 Sam. 5 : 17-25; 23 : 13, etc. Since the latter part of the sixteenth century the name has been attached to the upland plain which stretches south of Jerusalem, and is crossed by the road to Bethlehem —the *el Bŭk'ah* of the modern Arabs. (This valley begins near the valley of Hinnom, southwest of Jerusalem, extending toward Bethlehem. It is about a mile long, with hills on either side. This agrees with Josephus and is the generally-accepted location of this valley.—ED.) Tobler, however, in his last investigations conclusively adopts the *Wady Dêr Jasin,* on ̓the northwest of Jerusalem. The valley appears to derive its name from the ancient nation of the Rephaim. [GIANTS.]

Rephan, the reading, in the Revised Version, for Remphan. Acts 7 : 43.

Reph′idim. Ex. 17 : 1, 8; 19 : 2. The name means *rests* or *stays,* i. e. *resting-places.* The place lies in the march of the Israelites from Egypt to Sinai. Its site is not certain, but it is perhaps *Wady Feiran,* a rather broad valley about 25 miles from *Jebel Musa* (Mount Sinai). Others place it in *Wady es Sheikh,* an eastern continuation of Feiran, and about 12 miles from Sinai. Here the Israelites fought their first battle and gained their first victory after leaving Egypt, the Amalekites having attacked them; here also the people murmured from thirst, and Moses brought water for them out of the rock. From this murmuring the place was called "Massah" and "Meribah."

Re'sen (*bridle*), Gen. 10 : 12, one of the cities built by Asshur, "*between* Nineveh and Calah." Assyrian remains of some considerable extent are found near the modern village of *Selamiyeh*, and it is perhaps the most probable conjecture that these represent Resen.

Re'sheph (*flame*), a son of Ephraim. 1 Chron. 7 : 25.

Re'u (*friend*), son of Peleg, in the line of Abraham's ancestors. Gen. 11 : 18, 19, 20, 21 ; 1 Chron. 1 : 25. (B.C. about 2213.)

Reu'ben (*behold a son*), Jacob's firstborn child, Gen. 29 : 32, the son of Leah. (B.C. 1753.) The notices of the patriarch Reuben give, on the whole, a favorable view of his disposition. To him and him alone the preservation of Joseph's life appears to have been due, and afterward he becomes responsible for his safety. Gen. 37 : 18–30 ; 42 : 37. Of the repulsive crime which mars his history, and which turned the blessing of his dying father into a curse—his adulterous connection with Bilhah—we know from the Scriptures only the fact. Gen. 35 : 22. He was of an ardent, impetuous, unbalanced but not ungenerous nature ; not crafty and cruel, as were Simeon and Levi, but rather, to use the metaphor of the dying patriarch, boiling up like a vessel of water over a rapid wood fire, and as quickly subsiding when the fuel was withdrawn. At the time of the migration into Egypt, Reuben's sons were four. Gen. 46 : 9 ; 1 Chron. 5 : 3. The census at Mount Sinai, Num. 1 : 20, 21 ; 2 : 11, shows that at the exodus the men of the tribe above twenty years of age and fit for active warlike service numbered 46,500. The Reubenites maintained the ancient calling of their forefathers. Their cattle accompanied them in their flight from Egypt. Ex. 12 : 38.

Territory of the tribe.—The portion of the promised land selected by Reuben had the special name of "the Mishor," with reference possibly to its evenness. Under its modern name of the *Belka* it is still esteemed beyond all others by the Arab sheep-masters. It was a fine pasture-land east of the Jordan, lying between the river Arnon on the south and Gilead on the north. Though the Israelites all aided the Reubenites in conquering the land, and they in return helped their brothers to secure their own possessions, still there was always afterward a bar, a difference in feeling and habits, between the eastern and western tribes. The pile of stones which they erected on the west bank of the Jordan to mark their boundary was erected in accordance with the unalterable habits of Bedouin tribes both before and since. This act was completely misunderstood, and was construed into an attempt to set up a rival altar to that of the sacred tent. No judge, no prophet, no hero of the tribe of Reuben is handed down to us. The Reubenites disliked war, clinging to their fields and pastures even when their brethren were in great distress. Being remote from the seat of the national government and of the national religion, it is not to be wondered at that the Reubenites relinquished the faith of Jehovah. The last historical notice which we possess of them, while it records this fact, records also as its natural consequence that they and the Gadites and the half-tribe of Manasseh were carried off by Pul and Tiglath-pileser. 1 Chron. 5 : 26.

Reu'el (*friend of God*), one of the sons of Esau, by his wife Bashemath, sister of Ishmael. Gen. 36 : 4, 10, 13, 17 ; 1 Chron. 1 : 35, 37. (B.C. about 1790.)

2. One of the names of Moses' father-in-law. Ex. 2 : 18. (B.C. 1530.)

3. Father of Eliasaph, the leader of the tribe of Gad at the time of the census at Sinai. Num. 2 : 14. (B.C. 1490.)

4. A Benjamite, ancestor of Elah. 1 Chron. 9 : 8.

Reu'mah (*elevated*), the concubine of Nahor, Abraham's brother. Gen. 22 : 24. (B.C. about 1870.)

Revela'tion of St. John, the last book of the New Testament. It is often called the *Apocalypse*, which is its title in Greek, signifying "Revelation." **1.** *Canonical authority and authorship.*— The inquiry as to the canonical authority of the Revelation resolves itself into a question of authorship. Was St. John the apostle and evangelist the writer of the Revelation? The evidence adduced in support of his being the author consists of (1) the assertions of the author, and (2) historical tradition. (1) The author's description of himself in the 1st and 22d chapters is certainly equivalent to an assertion that he is the apostle. He names himself simply John, without prefix or addition. He is also described as a servant of Christ, one who had borne testimony as an eye-witness of the word of God and of the testimony of Christ. He is in Patmos for the word of God and the testimony of Jesus Christ. He is also a fellow sufferer with those whom he addresses, and the authorized channel of the most direct and important communication that was ever made to the Seven Churches of Asia, of which churches John the apostle was at that time the spiritual governor and teacher. Lastly, the writer was a fellow servant of angels and a brother of prophets. All these marks are found united in the apostle John, and in him alone of all historical persons. (2) A long series of writers testify to St. John's authorship: Justin Martyr (cir. 150 A.D.), Eusebius, Irenæus (A.D. 195), Clement of Alexandria (about 200), Tertullian (207), Origen (233). All the foregoing writers, testifying that the book came from an apostle, believed that it was a part of Holy Scripture. The book was admitted into the list of the Third Council of Carthage, A.D. 397. 2. *Time and place of writing.*—The date of the Revelation is given by the great majority of critics as A.D 95–97. Irenæus says: "It (*i. e.* the Revelation) was seen no very long time ago, but almost in our own generation, at the close of Domitian's reign." Eusebius also records that, in the persecution under Domitian, John the apostle and evangelist was banished to the island Patmos for his testimony of the divine word. There is no mention in any writer of the first three centuries of any other time or place, and the style in which the messages to the Seven Churches are delivered rather suggests the notion that the book was written in Patmos. 3. *Interpretation.*—Modern interpreters are generally placed in three great divisions: (*a*) The Historical or Continuous expositors, in whose opinion the Revelation is a progressive history of the fortunes of the Church from the first century to the end of time. (*b*) The Præterist expositors, who are of opinion that the Revelation has been almost or altogether fulfilled in the time which has passed since it was written; that it refers principally to the triumph of Christianity over Judaism and Paganism, signalized in the downfall of Jerusalem and of Rome. (*c*) The Futurist expositors, whose views show a strong reaction against some extravagances of the two preceding schools. They believe that the whole book, excepting perhaps the first three chapters, refers principally, if not exclusively, to events which are yet to come. Dr. Arnold, in his sermons "On the Interpretation of Prophecy," suggests that we should bear in mind that predictions have a lower historical sense as well as a higher spiritual sense; that there may be one or more than one typical, imperfect, historical fulfillment of the prophecy, in each of which the higher spiritual fulfillment is shadowed forth more or less distinctly.

Re'zeph (*a hot stone*), one of the places which Sennacherib mentions, in his taunting message to Hezekiah, as having been destroyed by his predecessor. 2 Kings 19: 12; Isa. 37: 12.

Rezi'a (*delight*), an Asherite, of the sons of Ulla. 1 Chron. 7: 39. (B.C. 1444.)

Re'zin (*firm*). 1. King of Damascus. He attacked Jotham during the latter part of his reign, 2 Kings 15: 37; but his chief war was with Ahaz, whose territories he invaded, in conjunction with Pekah, about B.C. 741. Though unsuccessful in his siege of Jerusalem, 2 Kings 16: 5; Isa. 7: 1, he "recovered Elath to Syria." 2 Kings 16: 6. Soon after this he was attacked, defeated and slain by Tiglath-pileser II., king of Assyria. 2 Kings 16: 9.

2. One of the families of the Nethinim. Ezra 2: 48; Neh. 7: 50. (B.C. before 536.)

Re'zon (*prince*), son of Eliadah, a Syrian, who when David defeated Hadadezer king of Zobah, put himself at the head of a band of freebooters and set up a petty kingdom at Damascus. 1 Kings 11: 23. He harassed the kingdom of Solomon during his whole reign. (B.C. 1043–975.)

Castor and Pollux.

Rhe'gium (*breach*), an Italian town situated on the Bruttian coast, just at the southern entrance of the Straits of Messina. The name occurs in the account of St. Paul's voyage from Syracuse to Puteoli, after the shipwreck at Malta. Acts 28 : 13. By a curious coincidence, the figures on its coin are the very "twin brothers" which gave the name to St. Paul's ship. It was originally a Greek colony; it was miserably destroyed by Dionysius of Syracuse. From Augustus it received advantages which combined with its geographical position in making it important throughout the duration of the Roman empire. The modern *Reggio* is a town of 10,000 inhabitants. Its distance across the straits from Messina is only about six miles.

Rhe'sa (*head*), son of Zorobabel in the genealogy of Christ. Luke 3 : 27. It is conjectured that Rhesa is no person, but merely a title.

Rho'da (*rose*), the name of a maid who announced Peter's arrival at the door of Mary's house after his miraculous release from prison. Acts 12 : 13. (A.D. 44.)

Didrachm of Rhodes.

Rhodes (*rosy*), a celebrated island in the Mediterranean Sea. (It is triangular in form, 60 miles long from north to south, and about 18 wide. It is noted now, as in ancient times, for its delightful climate and the fertility of its soil. The city of Rhodes, its capital, was famous for its huge brazen statue of Apollo, called the Colossus of Rhodes. It stood at the entrance of the harbor, and was so large that ships in full sail could pass between its legs.—ED.) Rhodes is immediately opposite the high Carian and Lycian headlands at the southwest extremity of the peninsula of Asia Minor. Its position has had much to do with its history. Its real eminence began about 400 B.C. with the founding of the city of Rhodes, at the northeast extremity of the island, which still continues to be the capital. After Alexander's death it entered on a glorious period, its material prosperity being largely developed, and its institutions deserving and obtaining general esteem. We have notice of the Jewish residents

in Rhodes in 1 Macc. 15 : 23. The Romans, after the defeat of Antiochus, assigned, during some time, to Rhodes certain districts on the mainland. Its Byzantine history is again eminent. Under Constantine it was the metropolis of the "Province of the Islands." It was the last place where the Christians of the East held out against the advancing Saracens; and subsequently it was once more famous as the home and fortress of the Knights of St. John. (It is now reduced to abject poverty. There are two cities—Rhodes the capital and Lindus—and forty or fifty villages. The population, according to Turner, is 20,000, of whom 6000 are Turks and the rest Greeks, together with a few Jews.)

Ri'ba-i, or **Riba'i** (*pleader with Jehovah*), the father of Ittai the Benjamite, of Gibeah. 2 Sam. 23 : 29 ; 1 Chron. 11 : 31. (B.C. before 1020.)

Rib-lah (*fertility*), one of the landmarks on the eastern boundary of the land of Israel, as specified by Moses. Num. 34 : 11. It seems hardly possible, without entirely disarranging the specification of the boundary, that the Riblah in question can be the same with the following.

2. Riblah in the land of Hamath, a place on the great road between Palestine and Babylonia, at which the kings of Babylonia were accustomed to remain while directing the operations of their armies in Palestine and Phœnicia. Here Nebuchadnezzar waited while the sieges of Jerusalem and of Tyre were being conducted by his lieutenants. Jer. 39 : 5, 6 ; 52 : 9, 10, 26, 27 ; 2 Kings 25 : 6, 20, 21. In like manner Pharaoh-necho, after his victory over the Babylonians at Carchemish, returned to Riblah and summoned Jehoahaz from Jerusalem before him. 2 Kings 23 : 33. This Riblah still retains its ancient name, on the right (east) bank of the *el-Asy* (Orontes), upon the great road which connects *Baalbek* and *Hums*, about 35 miles northeast of the former and 20 miles southwest of the latter place.

Riddle. It is known that all ancient nations, and especially Orientals, were fond of riddles. The riddles which the queen of Sheba came to ask of Solomon, 1 Kings 10 : 1 ; 2 Chron. 9 : 1, were rather "hard questions" referring to profound inquiries. Solomon is said, however, to have been very fond of riddles. Riddles were generally proposed in verse, like the celebrated riddle of Samson. Judges 14 : 14–19.

Rim'mon (*pomegranate*), the name of several towns. 1. A city of Zebulun, 1 Chron. 6 : 77; Neh. 11 : 29, a Levitical city, the present *Rummaneh*, six miles north of Nazareth.

2. A town in the southern portion of Judah, Josh. 15 : 3, allotted to Simeon, Josh. 19 : 7; 1 Chron. 4 : 32; probably 13 miles southwest of Hebron.

3. Rimmon-parez (*pomegranate of the breach*), the name of a march-station in the wilderness. Num. 33 : 19, 20. No place now known has been identified with it.

4. Rimmon the Rock, a cliff or inaccessible natural fastness, in which the six hundred Benjamites who escaped the slaughter of Gibeah took refuge. Judges 20 : 45, 47; 21 : 13. In the wild country which lies on the east of the central highlands of Benjamin the name is still found attached to a village perched on the summit of a conical chalky hill, visible in all directions, and commanding the whole country.

5. A Benjamite of Beeroth, the father of Rechab and Baanah, the murderers of Ish-bosheth. 2 Sam. 4 : 2, 5, 9.

Rim'mon, a deity worshipped by the Syrians of Damascus, where there was a temple or house of Rimmon. 2 Kings 5 : 18. Rimmon is perhaps the abbreviated form of Hadad-rimmon, Hadad being the sun-god of the Syrians. Combining this with the pomegranate, which was his symbol, Hadad-rimmon would then be the sun-god of the late summer, who ripens the pomegranate and other fruits.

Egyptian Weighing Rings for Money. (See Money.)

Ring. The ring was regarded as an indispensable article of a Hebrew's attire, inasmuch as it contained his signet. It was hence the symbol of authority. Gen. 41 : 42; Esth. 3 : 10. Rings were worn not only by men, but by women.

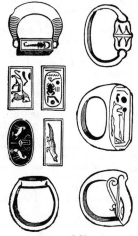

Rings and Signets.

Isa. 3 : 21. We may conclude from Ex. 28 : 11 that the rings contained a stone engraven with a device or with the owner's name. The custom appears also to have prevailed among the Jews of the apostolic age. James 2 : 2.

Rin'nah (*a shout*), one of the descendants of Judah. 1 Chron. 4 : 20. (B.C. 1300.)

Ri'phath (*spoken*), the second son of Gomer. Gen. 10 : 3. The name may be identified with the Rhipæan mountains, *i. e.* the Carpathian range in the northeast of Dacia.

Ris'sah (*a ruin*), a march-station in the wilderness. Num. 33 : 21, 22.

Rith'mah (*heath*), a march-station in the wilderness, Num. 33 : 18, 19, probably northeast of Hazeroth.

River. In the sense in which we employ the word, viz. for a perennial stream of considerable size, a river is a much rarer object in the East than in the West. With the exception of the Jordan and the Litany, the streams of the holy land are either entirely dried up in the summer months, and converted into hot lanes of glaring stones, or else reduced to very small streamlets, deeply sunk in a narrow bed, and concealed from view by a dense growth of shrubs. The perennial river is called *nahar* by the Hebrews. With the definite article, "*the* river," it signifies invariably the Euphrates. Gen. 31 : 21; Ex. 23 : 31; Num. 24 : 6; 2 Sam. 10 : 16, etc. It is never applied to the fleeting fugitive torrents of Palestine. The term for these is *nachal*, for which our translators have used promiscuously, and sometimes almost alternately, "valley," "brook" and "river." No one of these words expresses the thing intended; but the term "brook" is peculiarly unhappy. Many of the *wadys* of Palestine are deep, abrupt chasms or rents in the solid rock of the hills, and have a savage, gloomy aspect, far removed from that of an English brook. Unfortunately our language does not contain any single word which has both the meanings of the Hebrew *nachal* and its Arabic equivalent *wady*, which can be used at once for a dry valley and for the stream which occasionally flows through it.

River of Egypt. 1. The Nile. Gen. 15 : 18. [NILE.]

2. A desert stream on the border of Egypt, still occasionally flowing in the valley called *Wâdi-l-'Areesh*. The centre of the valley is occupied by the bed of this torrent, which only flows after rains, as is usual in the desert valleys. This stream is first mentioned as the point where the southern border of the promised land touched the Mediterranean, which formed its western border. Num. 34 : 3–6. In the latter history we find Solomon's kingdom extending from the "entering in of Hamath unto the river of Egypt," 1 Kings 8 : 65, and Egypt limited in the same manner where the loss of the eastern provinces is mentioned. 2 Kings 24 : 7.

Riz'pah, concubine to King Saul, and mother of his two sons Armoni and Mephibosheth. (B.C. 1080.) The tragic story of the love and endurance with which she watched over the bodies of her two sons, who were killed by the Gibeonites, 2 Sam. 21 : 8–11, has made Rizpah one of the most familiar objects in the whole Bible.

Road. This word occurs but once in the Authorized Version of the Bible, viz. in 1 Sam. 27 : 10, where it is used in the sense of "raid" or "inroad." Where a travelled road is meant "path" or "way"

is used, since the eastern roads are more like our paths.

Robbery. Robbery has ever been one of the principal employments of the nomad tribes of the East. From the time of Ishmael to the present day the Bedouin has been a "wild man," and a robber by trade. Gen. 16 : 12. The Mosaic law on the subject of theft is contained in Ex. 22. There seems no reason to suppose that the law underwent any alteration in Solomon's time. Man-stealing was punishable with death. Ex. 21 : 16; Deut. 24 : 7. Invasion of right in land was strictly forbidden. Deut. 27 : 17; Isa. 5 : 8; Micah 2 : 2.

The Wild Roe.

Roe, Roebuck. The Hebrew words thus translated denote some species of antelope, probably the *Gazella arabica* of Syria and Arabia. The gazelle was allowed as food, Deut. 12 : 15, 22, etc.; it is mentioned as very fleet of foot, 2 Sam. 2 : 18; 1 Chron. 12 : 8; it was hunted, Isa. 13 : 14; Prov. 6 : 5; it was celebrated for its loveliness. Cant. 2 : 9, 17; 8 : 14.

Roge'lim (*fullers*), the residence of Barzillai the Gileadite, 2 Sam. 17 : 27; 19 : 31, in the highlands east of the Jordan.

Roh'gah (*clamor*), an Asherite, of the sons of Shamer. 1 Chron. 7 : 34. (B.C. about 1490.)

Roll. A book in ancient times consisted of a single long strip of paper or parchment, which was usually kept rolled upon a stick, and was unrolled when a person wished to read it. The roll was usually written on one side only, and hence the particular notice of one that was "written within and without." Ezek. 2: 10. The writing was arranged in columns.

Romam'ti - e'zer, one of the fourteen sons of Heman. 1 Chron. 25: 4, 31. (B.C. about 1014.)

Roll.

Roman empire. 1. The first historic mention of Rome in the Bible is in 1 Macc. 1: 10, about the year 161 B.C. In the year 65 B.C., when Syria was made a Roman province by Pompey, the Jews were still governed by one of the Asmonæan princes. The next year Pompey himself marched an army into Judea and took Jerusalem. From this time the Jews were practically under the government of Rome. Finally, Antipater's son, Herod the Great, was made king by Antony's interest, B.C. 40, and confirmed in the kingdom by Augustus, B.C. 30. The Jews, however, were all this time tributaries of Rome, and their princes in reality were Roman procurators. On the banishment of Archelaus, A.D. 6, Judea became a mere appendage of the province of Syria, and was governed by a Roman procurator, who resided at Cæsarea. Such were the relations of the Jewish people to the Roman government at the time when the New Testament history begins.

2. *Extent of the empire.*—Cicero's description of the Greek states and colonies as a " fringe on the skirts of barbarism " has been well applied to the Roman dominions before the conquests of Pompey and Cæsar. The Roman empire was still confined to a narrow strip encircling the Mediterranean Sea. Pompey added Asia Minor and Syria. Cæsar added Gaul. The generals of Augustus overran the northwest portion of Spain and the country between the Alps and the Danube. The boundaries of the empire were now the Atlantic on the west, the Euphrates on the east, the deserts of Africa, the cataracts of the Nile and the Arabian deserts on the south, the British Channel, the Rhine, the Danube and the Black Sea on the north. The only subsequent conquests of importance were those of Britain by Claudius and of Dacia by Trajan. The only independent powers of importance were the Parthians on the east and the Germans on the north. The population of the empire in the time of Augustus has been calculated at 85,000,000.

3. *The provinces.*—The usual fate of a country conquered by Rome was to be come a subject province, governed directly from Rome by officers sent out for that purpose. Sometimes, however, petty sovereigns were left in possession of a nominal independence on the borders or within the natural limits of the province. Augustus divided the provinces into two classes—(1) Imperial; (2) Senatorial; retaining in his own hands, for obvious reasons, those provinces where the presence of a large military force was necessary, and committing the peaceful and unarmed provinces to the senate. The New Testament writers invariably designate the governors of senatorial provinces by the correct title ἀνθύπατοι, proconsuls. Acts 13:7; 18:12; 19:38. For the governor of an imperial province, properly styled " legatus Cæsaris," the word ἡγεμών (governor) is used in the New Testament. The provinces were heavily taxed for the benefit of Rome and her citizens. They are said to have been better governed under the empire than under the commonwealth, and those of the emperor better than those of the senate.

4. *The condition of the Roman empire at the time when Christianity appeared* has often been dwelt upon as affording obvious illustrations of St. Paul's expression that the " fullness of time had come." Gal. 4: 4. The general peace within the limits of the empire, the formation of military roads, the suppression of piracy, the march of the legions, the voyages of the corn fleets, the general increase of traffic, the spread of the Latin language in the West as Greek had already spread in the East, the external unity of the empire, offered facilities hitherto unknown for the spread of a world-wide religion. The tendency, too, of a despotism like that of the Roman empire to reduce all its subjects to a dead level was a powerful instrument in breaking down the pride of privileged races and national religions, and familiarizing men with the truth that " God had made of one blood all nations on the face of the

earth." Acts 17 : 24, 26. But still more striking than this outward preparation for the diffusion of the gospel was the appearance of a deep and wide-spread corruption, which seemed to defy any human remedy. **Romans, Epistle to the.** 1. The *date* of this epistle is fixed at the time of the visit recorded in Acts 20 : 3, during the winter and spring following the apostle's long residence at Ephesus, A.D. 58. On this visit he remained in Greece three months. 2. The *place of writing* was Corinth. 3. The *occasion* which prompted it, and the *circumstances* attending its writing, were as follows:—St. Paul had long purposed visiting Rome, and still retained this purpose, wishing also to extend his journey to Spain. Rom. 1 : 9–13; 15 : 22–29. For the time, however, he was prevented from carrying out his design, as he was bound for Jerusalem with the alms of the Gentile Christians, and meanwhile he addressed this letter to the Romans, to supply the lack of his personal teaching. Phœbe, a deaconess of the neighboring church of Cenchreæ, was on the point of starting for Rome, ch. 16 : 1, 2, and probably conveyed the letter. The body of the epistle was written at the apostle's dictation by Tertius, ch. 16 : 22; but perhaps we may infer, from the abruptness of the final doxology, that it was added by the apostle himself. 4. The *origin of the Roman church* is involved in obscurity. If it had been founded by St. Peter, according to a later tradition, the absence of any allusion to him both in this epistle and in the letters written by St. Paul from Rome would admit of no explanation. It is equally clear that no other apostle was the founder. The statement in the Clementines that the first tidings of the gospel reached Rome during the lifetime of our Lord is evidently a fiction for the purposes of the romance. On the other hand, it is clear that the foundation of this church dates very far back. It may be that some of these Romans, "both Jews and proselytes," present on the day of Pentecost, Acts 2 : 10, carried back the earliest tidings of the new doctrine; or the gospel may have first reached the imperial city through those who were scattered abroad to escape the persecution which followed on the death of Stephen. Acts 8 : 4; 11 : 19. At first we may suppose that the gospel was preached there in a confused and imperfect form, scarcely more than a phase of Judaism, as in the case of Apollos at Corinth, Acts 18 : 25, or the disciples at Ephesus. Acts 19 : 1–3. As time advanced and better-instructed teachers arrived, the clouds would gradually clear away, till at length the presence of the great apostle himself at Rome dispersed the mists of Judaism which still hung about the Roman church. 5. A question next arises as to the *composition of the Roman church* at the time when St. Paul wrote. It is more probable that St. Paul addressed a mixed church of Jews and Gentiles, the latter perhaps being the more numerous. These Gentile converts, however, were not for the most part native Romans. Strange as the paradox appears, nothing is more certain than that the church of Rome was at this time a Greek and not a Latin church. All the literature of the early Roman church was written in the Greek tongue. 6. The heterogeneous composition of this church explains *the general character of the Epistle to the Romans.* In an assemblage so various we should expect to find, not the exclusive predominance of a single form of error, but the coincidence of different and opposing forms. It was therefore the business of the Christian teacher to reconcile the opposing difficulties and to hold out a meeting-point in the gospel. This is exactly what St. Paul does in the Epistle to the Romans. 7. In describing the *purport* of this epistle we may start from St. Paul's own words, which, standing at the beginning of the doctrinal portion, may be taken as giving a summary of the contents. ch. 1 : 16, 17. Accordingly the epistle has been described as comprising "the religious philosophy of the world's history." The atonement of Christ is the centre of religious history. The epistle, from its general character, lends itself more readily to an *analysis* than is often the case with St. Paul's epistles. While this epistle contains the fullest and most systematic exposition of the apostle's *teaching*, it is at the same time a very striking expression of his *character*. Nowhere do his earnest and affectionate nature and his tact and delicacy in handling unwelcome topics appear more strongly than when he is dealing with the rejection of his fellow countrymen the Jews. 8. Internal evidence is so strongly in favor of the *genuineness* of the Epistle to the Romans that it has never been seriously questioned.

Rome, the famous capital of the ancient world, is situated on the Tiber at a distance of about 15 miles from its mouth. The "seven hills," Rev. 17 : 9, which formed the nucleus of the ancient city stand on the left bank. On the opposite side of the river rises the far higher side of the Janiculum. Here from very early times was a fortress with a suburb beneath it extending to the river. Modern Rome lies to the north of the ancient city, covering with its principal portion the plain to the north of the seven hills, once known as the Campus Martius, and on the opposite bank extending over the low ground beneath the Vatican to the north of the ancient Janiculum. Rome is not mentioned in the Bible except in the books of Maccabees and in three books of the New Testament, viz., the Acts, the Epistle to the Romans and the Second Epistle to Timothy.

Ruins of Forum at Rome.

1. *Jewish inhabitants.*—The conquests of Pompey seem to have given rise to the first settlement of Jews at Rome. The Jewish king Aristobulus and his son formed part of Pompey's triumph, and many Jewish captives and immigrants were brought to Rome at that time. A special district was assigned to them, not on the site of the modern Ghetto, between the Capitol and the island of the Tiber, but across the Tiber. Many of these Jews were made freedmen. Julius Cæsar showed them some kindness; they were favored also by Augustus, and by Tiberius during the latter part of his reign. It is chiefly in connection with St. Paul's history that Rome comes before us in the Bible. In illustration of that history it may be useful to give some account of Rome in the time of Nero, the "Cæsar" to whom St. Paul appealed, and in whose reign he suffered martyrdom.

2. *The city in Paul's time.*—The city at that time must be imagined as a large and irregular mass of buildings unprotected by an outer wall. It had long outgrown the old Servian wall; but the limits of the suburbs cannot be exactly defined. Neither the nature of the buildings nor the configuration of the ground was such as to give a striking appearance to the city viewed from without. "Ancient Rome had neither cupola

nor campanile," and the hills, never lofty or imposing, would present, when covered with the buildings and streets of a huge city, a confused appearance like the hills of modern London, to which they have sometimes been compared. The visit of St. Paul lies between two famous epochs in the history of the city, viz., its restoration by Augustus and its restoration by Nero. The boast of Augustus is well known, "that he found the city of brick, and left it of marble." Some parts of the city, especially the Forum and Campus Martius, must have presented a magnificent appearance, of which Niebuhr's "Lectures on Roman History," ii. 177, will give a general idea; but many of the principal buildings which attract the attention of modern travellers in ancient Rome were not yet built. The streets were generally narrow and winding, flanked by densely-crowded lodging-houses (*insulæ*) of enormous height. Augustus found it necessary to limit their height to 70 feet. St. Paul's first visit to Rome took place before the Neronian conflagration; but even after the restoration of the city which followed upon that event, many of the old evils continued. The population of the city has been variously estimated. Probably Gibbon's estimate of 1,200,000 is nearest to the truth. One half of the population consisted, in all probability, of slaves. The larger part of the remainder consisted of pauper citizens supported in idleness by the miserable system of public gratuities. There appears to have been no middle class, and no free industrial population. Side by side with the wretched classes just mentioned was the comparatively small body of the wealthy nobility, of whose luxury and profligacy we learn so much from the heathen writers of the time. Such was the population which St. Paul would find at Rome at the time of his visit. We learn from the Acts of the Apostles that he was detained at Rome for "two whole years," "dwelling in his own hired house with a soldier that kept him," Acts 28 : 16, 30, to whom apparently, according to Roman custom, he was bound with a chain, Acts 28 : 20; Eph. 6 : 20; Philip. 1 : 13. Here he preached to all that came to him, no man forbidding him. Acts 28 : 30, 31. It is generally believed that on his "appeal to Cæsar" he was acquitted, and after some time spent in freedom, was a second

time imprisoned at Rome. Five of his epistles, viz., those to the Colossians, Ephesians, Philippians, that to Philemon, and the Second Epistle to Timothy, were in all probability written from Rome, the latter shortly before his death, 2 Tim. 4 : 6, the others during his first imprisonment. It is universally believed that he suffered martyrdom at Rome.

3. *The localities in and about Rome* especially connected with the life of Paul are—(1) The Appian Way, by which he approached Rome. Acts 28 : 15. [APPII FORUM.] (2) "The palace," or "Cæsar's court" (prætorium, Philip. 1 : 13). This may mean either the great camp of the Prætorian guards which Tiberius established outside the walls on the north-east of the city, or, as seems more probable, a barrack attached to the imperial residence on the Palatine. There is no sufficient proof that the word "prætorium" was ever used to designate the emperor's palace, though it is used for the official residence of a Roman governor. John 18 : 28; Acts 23 : 35. The mention of "Cæsar's household," Philip. 4 : 22, confirms the notion that St. Paul's residence was in the immediate neighborhood of the emperor's house on the Palatine. (3) The connection of other localities at Rome with St. Paul's name rests only on traditions of more or less probability. We may mention especially— (4) The Mamertine prison, or Tullianum, built by Ancus Martius near the Forum. It still exists beneath the church of St. Giuseppe dei Falegnami. It is said that St. Peter and St. Paul were fellow prisoners here for nine months. This is not the place to discuss the question whether St. Peter was ever at Rome. It may be sufficient to state that though there is no evidence of such a visit in the New Testament, unless Babylon in 1 Pet. 5 : 13 is a mystical name for Rome, yet early testimony and the universal belief of the early Church seem sufficient to establish the fact of his having suffered martyrdom there. [PETER.] The story, however, of the imprisonment in the Mamertine prison seems inconsistent with 2 Tim. 4 : 11. (5) The chapel on the Ostian road which marks the spot where the two apostles are said to have separated on their way to martyrdom. (6) The supposed scene of St. Paul's martyrdom, viz., the church of St. Paolo alle tre fontane on the Ostian road. To these may be added—(7) The supposed scene of St. Peter's

The Appian Way at Rome.

Appian Way restored.   (Fifth mile out of Rome.)

martyrdom, viz., the church of St. Pietro in Montorio, on the Janiculum. (8) The chapel Domine quo Vadis, on the Appian road, the scene of the beautiful legend of our Lord's appearance to St. Peter as he was escaping from martyrdom. (9) The places where the bodies of the two apostles, after having been deposited first in the catacombs, are supposed to have been finally buried—that of St. Paul by the Ostian road, that of St. Peter beneath the dome of the famous Basilica which bears his name. We may add, as sites unquestionably connected with the Roman Christians of the apostolic age—(10) The gardens of Nero in the Vatican, not far from the spot where St. Peter's now stands. Here Christians, wrapped in the skins of beasts, were torn to pieces by dogs, or, clothed in inflammable robes, were burnt to serve as torches during the midnight games. Others were crucified. (11) The Catacombs. These subterranean galleries, commonly from 8 to 10 feet in height and from 4 to 6 in width, and extending for miles, especially in the neighborhood of the old Appian and Nomentan Ways, were unquestionably used as places of refuge, of worship and of burial by the early Christians. The earliest dated inscription in the catacombs is A.D. 71. Nothing is known of the first founder of the Christian Church at Rome. Christianity may, perhaps, have been introduced into the city not long after the outpouring of the Holy Spirit on the day of Pentecost by the "strangers of Rome," who were then at Jerusalem. Acts 2 : 10. It is clear that there were many Christians at Rome before St. Paul visited the city. Rom. 1 : 8, 13, 15 ; 15 : 20. The names of twenty-four Christians at Rome are given in the salutations at the end of the Epistle to the Romans. Linus, who is mentioned 2 Tim. 4 : 21, and Clement, Philip. 4 : 3, are supposed to have succeeded St. Peter as bishops of Rome.

Roof. [HOUSE.]

Room. The references to " room " in Matt. 23 : 6; Mark 12 : 39; Luke 14 : 7, 8; 20 : 46, signify the highest place on the highest couch round the dinner or supper table—the "uppermost seat," as it is more accurately rendered in Luke 11 : 43.

Rose occurs twice only, viz. in Cant. 2 : 1; Isa. 35 : 1. There is much difference of opinion as to what particular flower is here denoted ; but it appears to us most probable that the narcissus is intended. Chateaubriand mentions the nar-

cissus as growing in the plain of Sharon. Roses are greatly prized in the East, more especially for the sake of the rose-water, which is in much request. Dr. Hooker observed seven species of wild roses in Syria.

Rosh (*head*). In the genealogy of Gen. 46 : 21, Rosh is reckoned among the sons of Benjamin.

Rosh, Ezek. 38 : 2, 3 ; 39 : 1, probably a proper name, referring to the first of the three great Scythian tribes of which Magog was the head.

Rosin. Properly " naphtha," as it is both in the LXX. and the Vulgate, as well as in the Peshito-Syriac. Pliny mentions naphtha as a product of Babylonia, similar in appearance to liquid bitumen, and having a remarkable affinity to fire.

Rubies. Concerning the meaning of the Hebrew words translated " rubies " there is much difference of opinion. Job 28 : 18; see also Prov. 3 : 15 ; 8 : 11 ; 31 : 10. Some suppose " coral " to be intended ; others " pearl," supposing that the original word signifies merely " bright in color," or " color of a reddish tinge." (The real ruby is a red sapphire, next in value to the diamond. The finest rubies are brought chiefly from Ceylon and Burmah.)

Rue occurs only in Luke 11 : 42. The rue here spoken of is doubtless the common *Ruta graveolens*, a shrubby plant about two feet high, of strong medicinal virtues. It is a native of the Mediterranean coasts, and has been found by Hasselquist on Mount Tabor. The Talmud enumerates rue amongst kitchenherbs, and regards it as free of tithe, as being a plant not cultivated in gardens. In our Lord's time, however, rue was doubtless a garden plant, and therefore tithable.

Ru'fus (*red*) is mentioned in Mark 15 : 21 as a son of Simon the Cyrenian. Luke 23 : 26. (A.D. 29.) Again, in Rom. 16 : 13, the apostle Paul salutes a Rufus whom he designates as " elect in the Lord." This Rufus was probably identical with the one to whom Mark refers.

Ru'hamah, or **Ruha'mah** (*having obtained mercy*). Hos. 2 : 1. The name, if name it be, is symbolical, and is addressed to the daughters of the people, to denote that they were still the objects of love and tender compassion.

Ru'mah (*high*), mentioned once only —2 Kings 23 : 36. It has been conjectured to be the same place as Arumah, Judges

9 : 41, which was apparently near Shechem. It is more probable that it is identical with Dumah. Josh. 15 : 52.

Rush. [REED.]

Rue.

Ruth (*a female friend*), a Moabitish
woman, the wife, first of Mahlon, secondly of Boaz, the ancestress of David and
of Christ, and one of the four women who
are named by St. Matthew in the genealogy of Christ. A severe famine in the
land of Judah induced Elimelech, a native of Bethlehem-ephratah, to emigrate
into the land of Moab, with his wife Naomi, and his two sons, Mahlon and Chilion. This was probably about the time
of Gideon, B.C. 1250. At the end of ten
years Naomi, now left a widow and childless, having heard that there was plenty
again in Judah, resolved to return to
Bethlehem, and her daughter-in-law
Ruth returned with her. They arrived
at Bethlehem just at the beginning of
barley harvest, and Ruth, going out to
glean, chanced to go into the field of
Boaz, a wealthy man and a near kinsman of her father-in-law, Elimelech.
Upon learning who the stranger was,
Boaz treated her with the utmost kindness and respect, and sent her home laden
with corn which she had gleaned. Encouraged by this incident, Naomi instructed Ruth to claim at the hand of
Boaz that he should perform the part of
her husband's near kinsman, by purchasing the inheritance of Elimelech
and taking her to be his wife. With all
due solemnity, Boaz took Ruth to be his
wife, amidst the blessings and congratu-
lations of their neighbors. Their son,
Obed, was the father of Jesse, who was
the father of David.

Ruth, Book of, contains the history
of Ruth, as narrated in the preceding
article. The main object of the writer is
evidently to give an account of David's
ancestors; and the book was avowedly
composed long after the time of the heroine. See Ruth 1 : 1; 4 : 7, 17. Its date
and author are quite uncertain. Tradition is in favor of Samuel. It is probable that the books of Judges, Ruth,
Samuel and Kings originally formed but
one work. The book of Ruth clearly
forms part of the books of Samuel, supplying as it does the essential point of
David's genealogy and early family history, and is no less clearly connected
with the book of Judges by its opening
verse and the epoch to which the whole
book relates.

Rye (Heb. *cussemeth*) occurs in Ex.
9 : 32; Isa. 28 : 25; in the latter the margin reads "spelt." In Ezek. 4 : 9 the
text has "fitches" and the margin "rie."
It is probable that by *cussemeth* "spelt"
is intended. Spelt (*Triticum spelta*) is
grown in some parts of the south of Ger-
many; it differs but slightly from our
common wheat (*T. vulgare*).

S.

Sabachtha'ni, or **Sabach'thani** (*why hast thou forsaken me ?*), a part of Christ's fourth cry on the cross. Matt. 27 : 46; Mark 15 : 34. This, with the other words uttered with it, as given in Mark, is Aramaic (Syro-Chaldaic), the common dialect of the people of Palestine in Christ's time, and the whole is a translation of the Hebrew (given in Matthew) of the first words of the 22d Psalm.—ED.

Sab'aoth, The Lord of, occurs in Rom. 9 : 29; James 5 : 4, but is more familiar through its occurrence in the Sanctus of Te Deum—"Holy, holy, holy, Lord God of Sabaoth." Sabaoth is the Greek form of the Hebrew word *tsebâôth,* "armies," and is translated in the Authorized Version of the Old Testament by "Lord of hosts," "Lord God of hosts." In the mouth and the mind of an ancient Hebrew, *Jehovah-tsebâôth* was the leader and commander of the armies of the nation, who "went forth with them," Ps. 44 : 9, and led them to certain victory over the worshippers of Baal, Chemosh, Molech, Ashtaroth and other false gods.

Sabbath (*shabbâth,* "a day of rest," from *shâbath,* "to cease to do," "to rest"). The name is applied to divers great festivals, but principally and usually to the seventh day of the week, the strict observance of which is enforced not merely in the general Mosaic code, but in the Decalogue itself. The consecration of the Sabbath was coeval with the creation. The first scriptural notice of it, though it is not mentioned by name, is to be found in Gen. 2 : 3, at the close of the record of the six-days creation. There are not wanting indirect evidences of its observance, as the intervals between Noah's sending forth the birds out of the ark, an act naturally associated with the weekly service, Gen. 8 : 7-12, and in the *week* of a wedding celebration, Gen. 29 : 27, 28; but when a special occasion arises, in connection with the prohibition against gathering manna on the Sabbath, the institution is mentioned as one already known. Ex. 16 : 22-30.[1] And that this

---

[1] All this is confirmed by the great antiquity of the division of time into weeks, and the naming the days after the sun, moon and planets.

was especially one of the institutions adopted by Moses from the ancient patriarchal usage is implied in the very words of the law, "*Remember* the Sabbath day, to keep it holy." But even if such evidence were wanting, the *reason* of the institution would be a sufficient proof. It was to be a joyful celebration of God's completion of his creation. It has indeed been said that Moses gives quite a different reason for the institution of the Sabbath, as a memorial of the deliverance from Egyptian bondage. Deut. 5 : 15. The words added in Deuteronomy are a *special motive* for the joy with which the Sabbath should be celebrated, and for the kindness which extended its blessings to the slave and the beast of burden as well as to the master: "that thy manservant and thy maidservant may rest *as well as thou.*" Deut. 5 : 14. These attempts to limit the ordinance proceed from an entire misconception of its spirit, as if it were a season of stern privation rather than of special privilege. But, in truth, the prohibition of work is only subsidiary to the positive idea of joyful rest and *recreation,* in communion with Jehovah, who himself "rested and was *refreshed.*" Ex. 31 : 17; comp. 23 : 12. It is in Ex. 16 : 23-29 that we find the first incontrovertible institution of the day, as one given to and to be kept by the children of Israel. Shortly afterward it was re-enacted in the Fourth Commandment. This beneficent character of the Fourth Commandment is very apparent in the version of it which we find in Deuteronomy. Deut. 5 : 12-15. The law and the Sabbath are placed upon the same ground, and to give rights to classes that would otherwise have been without such—to the bondman and bondmaid, nay, to the beast of the field—is viewed here as their main end. "The stranger," too, is comprehended in the benefit. But the original proclamation of it in Exodus places it on a ground which, closely connected no doubt with these others, is yet higher and more comprehensive. The divine method of working and rest is there proposed to man as the model after which he is to work and to rest. Time then presents a perfect whole. It is most important to remember that the Fourth Commandment is not limited to a mere enactment respecting one day, but prescribes the due distribution of a week, and enforces the six days' work as much as the seventh day's rest. This higher ground of observance was felt to invest the Sabbath with a theological character, and rendered it the great witness for faith in a personal and creating God. It was to be a sacred pause in the ordinary labor by which man earns his bread; the curse of the fall was to be suspended for one day; and, having spent that day in joyful remembrance of God's mercies, man had a fresh start in his course of labor. A great snare, too, has always been hidden in the word *work*, as if the commandment forbade occupation and imposed idleness. The terms in the commandment show plainly enough the sort of work which is contemplated — *servile work* and *business*. The Pentateuch presents us with but three applications of the general principle—Ex. 16 : 29 ; 35 : 3 ; Num. 15 : 32–36. The reference of Isaiah to the Sabbath gives us no details. The references in Jeremiah and Nehemiah show that carrying goods for sale, and buying such, were equally profanations of the day. A consideration of the spirit of the law and of Christ's comments on it will show that it is *work for worldly gain* that was to be suspended; and hence the restrictive clause is prefaced with the positive command, "Six days *shalt thou labor*, and do all thy work;" for so only could the sabbatic rest be fairly earned. Hence, too, the stress constantly laid on permitting the servant and beast of burden to share the rest which selfishness would grudge to them. Thus the spirit of the Sabbath was joy, refreshment and mercy, arising from remembrance of God's goodness as the Creator and as the Deliverer from bondage. The Sabbath was a perpetual sign and covenant, and the holiness of the day is connected with the holiness of the people; "that ye may know that I am Jehovah that doth sanctify you." Ex. 31 : 12–17 ; Ezek. 20 : 12. *Joy* was the key-note of their service. Nehemiah commanded the people, on a day holy to Jehovah, "Mourn not, nor weep : eat the fat, and drink the sweet, and send portions to them for whom nothing is prepared." Neh. 8 : 9–13. The Sabbath is named as a day of special worship in the sanctuary. Lev. 19 : 30; 26 : 2. It was proclaimed as a *holy convocation.* Lev. 23 : 3. In later times the worship of the sanctuary was enlivened by sacred music. Ps. 68 : 25–27 ; 150, etc. On this day the people were accustomed to consult their prophets, 2 Kings 4 : 23, and to give to their children that instruction in the truths recalled to memory by the day which is so repeatedly enjoined as the duty of parents; it was "the Sabbath of Jehovah" not only in the sanctuary, but "in all their dwellings." Lev. 23 : 3.

When we come to the New Testament we find the most marked stress laid on the Sabbath. In whatever ways the Jew might err respecting it, he had altogether ceased to neglect it. On the contrary, wherever he went its observance became the most visible badge of his nationality. Our Lord's mode of observing the Sabbath was one of the main features of his life, which his Pharisaic adversaries most eagerly watched and criticised. They had invented many prohibitions respecting the Sabbath of which we find nothing in the original institution. Some of these prohibitions were fantastic and arbitrary, in the number of those " heavy burdens and grievous to be borne " which the latter expounders of the law "laid on men's shoulders." Comp. Matt. 12 : 1–13 ; John 5 : 10. That this perversion of the Sabbath had become very general in our Saviour's time is apparent both from the recorded objections to acts of his on that day and from his marked conduct on occasions to which those objections were sure to be urged. Matt. 12 : 1–15; Mark 3 : 2 ; Luke 6 : 1–5 ; 13 : 10–17 ; John 5 : 2–18 ; 7 : 23 ; 9 : 1–34. Christ's words do not remit the duty of keeping the Sabbath, but only deliver it from the false methods of keeping which prevented it from bestowing upon men the spiritual blessings it was ordained to confer. The almost total silence of the epistles in relation to keeping the Sabbath doubtless grew out of the fact that the early Christians kept the Sabbath, and that this period was one of change from the seventh to the first day of the week, and any definite rules would have been sure to be misunderstood. For many years both the first and the seventh days of the week were kept as Sabbaths; and gradually the first day of the week, the Lord's day, took the place among Christians of the seventh day, and they had the fullest warrant for the change. [LORD'S DAY.]

(The Fourth Commandment of the

Decalogue is just as binding now as it ever was, or as any other of the Ten Commandments. Those who argue that God has abolished this Sabbath, but has written the Sabbath law in our very natures, must have strange ideas of the wisdom of a God who abolishes a command he has made it necessary to keep. Christians in keeping the Lord's day keep the Fourth Commandment, as really as do those who keep what is called the seventh day. They keep every seventh day, only the counting starts from a different point. As to the method of keeping the Sabbath no rules are laid down; but no one can go far astray who holds to the principles laid down:—(1) *Rest.* Nothing is to be done in daily business, and no recreation taken which destroys the rest of others or takes from any the privileges of the Sabbath. (2) *Spiritual nurture.* One day in seven is to be set apart for the culture of the spiritual nature. These two principles of Sabbath-keeping will always go together. Only a religious Sabbath, which belongs to God, can be retained among men as a day of *rest.* If men can sport on the Sabbath, they will soon be made to work. The only barrier that can keep the world out of the Sabbath, that can preserve it to the working people as a day of rest, is God's command to keep it sacred to him. When Sunday becomes a day of pleasure, it ceases to be a day of rest. So important is the Sabbath to man that no people can have the highest religious life, the truest freedom, the greatest prosperity, unless they be a Sabbath-keeping people, whose Sabbath is one of rest and of religion—(*a*) Because man needs the rest for his whole system. More is accomplished in six days than can be in seven days of work. (*b*) Because man needs it to care for his spiritual nature, for religion, and preparing for immortal life. (*c*) Because man needs it as a day for moral training and instruction; a day for teaching men about their duties, for looking at life from a moral standpoint. (*d*) It is of great value as a means of improving the mind. The study of the highest themes, the social discussion of them in the Sabbath-school, the instruction from the pulpit, the expression of religious truth in the prayer-meeting, give an ordinary person more mental training in the course of his life than all his school-days give. (*e*) So long as the best welfare of the individual and of the nation depends chiefly on their mental and moral state, so long will the Sabbath be one of God's choicest blessings to man, and the command contained within it a heavenly privilege and blessing.—ED.)

Sabbath-day's journey. Acts 1: 12. The law as regards travel on the Sabbath is found in Ex. 16:29. As some departure from a man's own place was unavoidable, it was thought necessary to determine the allowable amount, which was fixed at 2000 paces, or about six furlongs, from the wall of the city. The permitted distance seems to have been grounded on the space to be kept between the ark and the people, Josh. 3:4, in the wilderness, which tradition said was that between the ark and the tents. We find the same distance given as the circumference outside the walls of the Levitical cities to be counted as their suburbs. Num. 35:5. The *terminus á quo* was thus not a man's own house, but the wall of the city where he dwelt.

Sabbatical year. Each seventh year, by the Mosaic code, was to be kept holy. Ex. 23:10, 11. The commandment is to sow and reap for six years, and to let the land rest on the seventh, "that the poor of thy people may eat; and what they leave the beasts of the field shall eat." It is added in Deut. 15 that the seventh year should also be one of release to debtors. Deut. 15:1-11. Neither tillage nor cultivation of any sort was to be practiced. The sabbatical year opened in the sabbatical month, and the whole law was to be read every such year, during the Feast of Tabernacles, to the assembled people. At the completion of a week of sabbatical years, the sabbatical scale received its completion in the year of jubilee. [JUBILEE.] The constant neglect of this law from the very first was one of the national sins that were punished by the Babylonian captivity. Of the observance of the sabbatical year after the captivity we have a proof in 1 Macc. 6:49.

Sabe'ans. [SHEBA.]

Sab'tah (*striking*), Gen. 10:7, or **Sab'ta,** 1 Chron. 1:9, the third in order of the sons of Cush. (B.C. 2218.)

Sab'techa, or **Sab'techah** (*striking*), Gen. 10:7; 1 Chron. 1:9, the fifth in order of the sons of Cush. (B.C. 2218.)

Sa'car (*wages*). 1. A Hararite, father of Ahiam. 1 Chron. 11:35.

2. The fourth son of Obed-edom. 1 Chron. 26:4.

Sackbut, Dan. 3:5, 7, 10, 15, the rendering in the Authorized Version of the Chaldee *sabbeca.* If this musical instrument be the same as the Greek and Latin *sambuca,* the English translation is entirely wrong. The sackbut was a wind-instrument [see MUSIC]; the *sambuca* was a triangular instrument, with strings, and played with the hand.

Sitting in Sackcloth.

Sackcloth, cloth used in making sacks or bags, a coarse fabric, of a dark color, made of goat's-hair, Isa. 50:3; Rev. 6:12, and resembling the *cilicium* of the Romans. It was used also for making the rough garments used by mourners, which were in extreme cases worn next the skin. 1 Kings 21:27; 2 Kings 6:30; Job 16:15; Isa. 32:11.

Sacrifice. The peculiar features of each kind of sacrifice are referred to under their respective heads.

I. (A) ORIGIN OF SACRIFICE.—The universal prevalence of sacrifice shows it to have been primeval, and deeply rooted in the instincts of humanity. Whether it was first enjoined by an external command, or whether it was based on that sense of sin and lost communion with God which is stamped by his hand on the heart of man, is a historical question which cannot be determined. (B) ANTE-MOSAIC HISTORY OF SACRIFICE. —In examining the various sacrifices recorded in Scripture before the establishment of the law, we find that the words specially denoting expiatory sacrifice are not applied to them. This fact does not at all show that they were not actually expiatory, but it justifies the inference that this idea was not then the prominent one in the doctrine of sacrifice. The sacrifices of Cain and Abel are called *minchah,* and appear to have been eucharistic. Noah's, Gen. 8:20, and Jacob's at Mizpah, were at the institution of a covenant, and may be called federative. In the burnt offerings of Job for his children, Job 1:5, and for his three friends, ch. 42:8, we for the first time find the expression of the desire of expiation for sin. The same is the case in the words of Moses to Pharaoh. Ex. 10:25. Here the main idea is at least deprecatory. (C) THE SACRIFICES OF THE MOSAIC PERIOD.—These are inaugurated by the offering of the Passover and the sacrifice of Ex. 24. The Passover indeed is unique in its character; but it is clear that the idea of salvation from death by means of sacrifice is brought out in it with a distinctness before unknown. The law of Leviticus now unfolds distinctly the various forms of sacrifice: (*a*) *The burnt offering:* Self-dedicatory. (*b*) *The meat offering* (unbloody); *the peace offering* (bloody): Eucharistic. (*c*) *The sin offering; the trespass offering:* Expiatory. To these may be added, (*d*) *The incense* offered after sacrifice in the holy place, and (on the Day of Atonement) in the holy of holies, the symbol of the intercession of the priest (as a type of the great High Priest), accompanying and making efficacious the prayer of the people. In the consecration of Aaron and his sons, Lev. 8, we find these offered in what became ever afterward their appointed order. First came the sin offering, to prepare access to God; next the burnt offering, to mark their dedication to his service; and third the meat offering of thanksgiving. Henceforth the sacrificial system was fixed in all its parts until he should come whom it typified. (D) POST-MOSAIC SACRIFICES.—It will not be necessary to pursue, in detail, the history of the post-Mosaic sacrifice, for its main principles were now fixed forever. The regular sacrifices in the temple service were—(*a*) *Burnt offerings.* 1, the daily burnt offerings, Ex. 29:38–42; 2, the double burnt offerings on the Sabbath, Num. 28: 9, 10; 3, the burnt offerings at the great festivals; Num. 28:11–29:39. (*b*) *Meat offerings.* 1, the daily meat offerings accompanying the daily burnt offerings, Ex. 29:40, 41; 2, the shewbread, renewed every Sabbath, Lev. 24:5, 9; 3, the special meat offerings at the Sabbath and the great festivals, Num. 28, 29; 4, the first-fruits, at the Passover, Lev. 23 : 10–14, at Pentecost, Lev. 23 : 17–20, the first-fruits of the dough and threshing-floor at the harvest time. Num. 15 : 20, 21; Deut. 26 : 1–11. (c) *Sin offerings.* 1, sin offering each new moon, Num. 28 : 15; 2, sin offerings at the Passover, Pentecost, Feast of Trumpets and Tabernacles, Num. 28 : 22, 30; 29 : 5, 16, 19, 22, 25, 28, 31, 34, 38; 3, the offering of the two goats for the people and of the bullock for the priest himself, on the Great Day of Atonement. Lev. 16. (d) *Incense.* 1, the morning and evening incense, Ex. 30 : 7, 8; 2, the incense on the Great Day of Atonement. Lev. 16 : 12. Besides these public sacrifices, there were offerings of the people for themselves individually.

II. By the order of sacrifice in its perfect form, as in Lev. 8, it is clear that the sin offering occupies the most important place; the burnt offering comes next, and the meat offering or peace offering last of all. The second could only be offered after the first had been accepted; the third was only a subsidiary part of the second. Yet, in actual order of time, it has been seen that the patriarchal sacrifices partook much more of the nature of the peace offering and burnt offering, and that under the law, by which was "the knowledge of sin," Rom. 3 : 20, the sin offering was for the first time explicitly set forth. This is but natural, that the deepest ideas should be the last in order of development. The essential difference between heathen views of sacrifice and the scriptural doctrine of the Old Testament is not to be found in its denial of any of these views. In fact, it brings out clearly and distinctly the ideas which in heathenism were uncertain, vague and perverted. But the essential points of distinction are two. First, that whereas the heathen conceived of their gods as alienated in jealousy or anger, to be sought after and to be appeased by the unaided action of man, Scripture represents God himself as approaching man, as pointing out and sanctioning the way by which the broken covenant should be restored. The second mark of distinction is closely connected with this, inasmuch as it shows sacrifice to be a scheme proceeding from God, and, in his foreknowledge, connected with the one central fact of all human history.

From the prophets and the Epistle to the Hebrews we learn that the sin offering represented that covenant as broken by man, and as knit together again, by God's appointment, through the "shedding of blood." The shedding of the blood, the symbol of life, signified that the death of the offender was deserved for sin, but that the death of the victim was accepted for his death by the ordinance of God's mercy. Beyond all doubt the sin offering distinctly witnessed that sin existed in man, that the "wages of that sin was death," and that God had provided an atonement by the vicarious suffering of an appointed victim. The ceremonial and meaning of the burnt offering were very different. The idea of expiation seems not to have been absent from it, for the blood was sprinkled round about the altar of sacrifice; but the main idea is the offering of the whole victim to God, representing, as the laying of the hand on its head shows, the devotion of the sacrificer, body and soul, to him. Rom. 12 : 1. The death of the victim was, so to speak, an incidental feature. The meat offerings, the peace or thank offering, the first-fruits, etc., were simply offerings to God of his own best gifts, as a sign of thankful homage, and as a means of maintaining his service and his servants. The characteristic ceremony in the peace offering was the eating of the flesh by the sacrificer. It betokened the enjoyment of communion with God. It is clear from this that the idea of sacrifice is a complex idea, involving the propitiatory, the dedicatory and the eucharistic elements. Any one of these, taken by itself, would lead to error and superstition. All three probably were more or less implied in each sacrifice, each element predominating in its turn. The Epistle to the Hebrews contains the key of the whole sacrificial doctrine. The object of the epistle is to show the typical and probationary character of sacrifices, and to assert that in virtue of it alone they had a spiritual meaning. Our Lord is declared (see 1 Pet. 1 : 20) "to have been foreordained" as a sacrifice "before the foundation of the world," or, as it is more strikingly expressed in Rev. 13 : 8, "slain from the foundation of the world." The material sacrifices represented this great atonement as already made and accepted in God's foreknowledge; and to those who grasped the ideas of sin, pardon and self-dedication symbolized in them, they were means of entering into the blessings which the one true sacrifice alone procured. They could convey nothing in themselves; yet as types they might, if accepted by a true though necessarily imperfect faith, be means of conveying in some degree the blessings of the antitype. It is clear that the atonement, in the Epistle to the Hebrews, as in the New Testament generally, is viewed in a twofold light. On the one hand it is set forth distinctly as a vicarious sacrifice, which was rendered necessary by the sin of man, and in which the Lord "bare the sins of many." It is its essential characteristic that in it he stands absolutely alone, offering his sacrifice without any reference to the faith or the conversion of men. In it he stands out alone as the mediator between God and man; and his sacrifice is offered once for all, never to be imitated or repeated. Now, this view of the atonement is set forth in the epistle as typified by the sin offering. On the other hand the sacrifice of Christ is set forth to us as the completion of that perfect obedience to the will of the Father which is the natural duty of sinless man. The main idea of this view of the atonement is representative rather than vicarious. It is typified by the burnt offering. As without the sin offering of the cross this our burnt offering would be impossible, so also without the burnt offering the sin offering will to us be unavailing. With these views of our Lord's sacrifice on earth, as typified in the Levitical sacrifices on the outer altar, is also to be connected the offering of his intercession for us in heaven, which was represented by the incense. The typical sense of the meat offering or peace offering is less connected with the sacrifice of Christ himself than with those sacrifices of praise, thanksgiving, charity and devotion which we, as Christians, offer to God, and "with which he is well pleased," Heb. 13 : 15, 16, as with an "odor of sweet smell, a sacrifice acceptable to God." Philip. 4 : 18.

Sad′ducees (followers of Zadok), Matt. 3 : 7; 16 : 1, 6, 11, 12; 22 : 23, 34; Mark 12 : 18; Luke 20 : 27; Acts 4 : 1; 5 : 17; 23 : 6, 7, 8, a religious party or school among the Jews at the time of Christ, who denied that the oral law was a revelation of God to the Israelites, and who deemed the written law alone to be obligatory on the nation, as of divine authority. Except on one occasion, Matt.

16 : 1, 4, 6, Christ never assailed the Sadducees with the same bitter denunciations which he uttered against the Pharisees. The origin of their name is involved in great difficulties, but the most satisfactory conjecture is that the Sadducees or Zadokites were originally identical with the sons of Zadok, and constituted what may be termed a kind of sacerdotal aristocracy, this Zadok being the priest who declared in favor of Solomon when Abiathar took the part of Adonijah. 1 Kings 1 : 32–45. To these sons of Zadok were afterward attached all who for any reason reckoned themselves as belonging to the aristocracy; such, for example, as the families of the high priest, who had obtained consideration under the dynasty of Herod. These were for the most part judges, and individuals of the official and governing class. This explanation elucidates at once Acts 5 : 17. The leading tenet of the Sadducees was *the negation of the leading tenet of their opponents.* As the Pharisees asserted, so the Sadducees denied, that the Israelites were in possession of an oral law transmitted to them by Moses. [PHARISEES.] In opposition to the Pharisees, they maintained that the written law alone was obligatory on the nation, as of divine authority. The second distinguishing doctrine of the Sadducees was the *denial of man's resurrection after death.* In connection with the disbelief of a resurrection by the Sadducees, they likewise denied there was "angel or spirit," Acts 23 : 8, and also the doctrines of future punishment and future rewards. Josephus states that the Sadducees believed in the *freedom of the will,* which the Pharisees denied. They pushed this doctrine so far as almost to exclude God from the government of the world. Some of the early Christian writers attribute to the Sadducees the *rejection of all the sacred Scriptures except the Pentateuch;* a statement, however, that is now generally admitted to have been founded on a misconception of the truth, and it seems to have arisen from a confusion of the Sadducees with the Samaritans. An important fact in the history of the Sadducees is their *rapid disappearance from history after the first century,* and the subsequent predominance among the Jews of the opinions of the Pharisees. Two circumstances contributed, indirectly but powerfully, to produce this result: 1st. The state of the Jews after the capture of Jerusalem by

Titus; and 2d. The growth of the Christian religion. As to the first point, it is difficult to overestimate the consternation and dismay which the destruction of Jerusalem occasioned in the minds of sincerely-religious Jews. In their hour of darkness and anguish they naturally turned to the consolations and hopes of a future state; and the doctrine of the Sadducees, that there was nothing beyond the present life, would have appeared to them cold, heartless and hateful. Again, while they were sunk in the lowest depths of depression, a new religion, which they despised as a heresy and a superstition, was gradually making its way among the subjects of their detested conquerors, the Romans. One of the causes of its success was undoubtedly the vivid belief in the resurrection of Jesus, and a consequent resurrection of all mankind, which was accepted by its heathen converts with a passionate earnestness of which those who at the present day are familiar from infancy with the doctrine of the resurrection of the dead can form only a faint idea. To attempt to check the progress of this new religion among the Jews by an appeal to the temporary rewards and punishments of the Pentateuch would have been as idle as an endeavor to check an explosive power by ordinary mechanical restraints. Consciously, therefore, or unconsciously, many circumstances combined to induce the Jews who were not Pharisees, but who resisted the new heresy, to rally round the standard of the oral law, and to assert that their holy legislator, Moses, had transmitted to his faithful people by word of mouth, although not in writing, the revelation of a future state of rewards and punishments.

Sa'doc (*Greek form of Zadok, just*). 1. Zadok the ancestor of Ezra. 2 Esd. 1 : 1; comp. Ezra 7 : 2.

2. A descendant of Zerubbabel in the genealogy of Jesus Christ. Matt. 1 : 14. (B.C. about 220.)

Saffron (*yellow*). Cant. 4 : 14. Saffron has from the earliest times been in high esteem as a perfume. "It was used," says Rosenmuller, "for the same purposes as the modern pot-pourri." The word saffron is derived from the Arabic *zafran*, "yellow." (The saffron (*Crocus sativus*) is a kind of crocus of the iris family. It is used as a medicine, as a flavoring and as a yellow dye. Homer, Virgil and Milton refer to its beauty in the land-

scape. It abounds in Palestine. The name saffron is usually applied only to the stigmas and part of the style, which are plucked out and dried.—ED.)

Sa'la, or **Sa'lah** (*sprout*), the son of Arphaxad, and father of Eber. Gen. 10 : 24; 11 : 12–14; Luke 3 : 35. (B.C. 2307.)

Sal'amis (*salt*), a city at the east end of the island of Cyprus, and the first place visited by Paul and Barnabas, on the first missionary journey, after leaving the mainland at Seleucia. Here alone, among all the Greek cities visited by St. Paul, we read expressly of "synagogues" in the plural, Acts 13 : 5; hence we conclude that there were many Jews in Cyprus. And this is in harmony with what we read elsewhere. Salamis was not far from the modern *Famagousta*. It was situated near a river called the Pediæus, on low ground, which is in fact a continuation of the plain running up into the interior toward the place where *Nicosia*, the present capital of Cyprus, stands.

Sala'thi-el (*I have asked of God*). 1 Chron. 3 : 17. The Authorized Version has Salathiel in 1 Chron. 3 : 17, but everywhere else in the Old Testament Shealtiel.

Salcah in Bashan.

Sal'cah, or **Sal'chah** (*migration*), a city named in the early records of Israel as the extreme limit of Bashan, Deut. 3 : 10; Josh. 13 : 11, and of the tribe of Gad. 1 Chron. 5 : 11. On another occasion the name seems to denote a district rather than a town. Josh. 12 : 5. It is identical with the town of *Sŭlkhad* (56 miles east of the Jordan, at the southern extremity of the Hauran range of mountains. The place is nearly deserted, though it contains 800 stone houses, many of them in a good state of preservation.—Ed.)

Sa'lem (*peace*). 1. The place of which Melchizedek was king. Gen. 14 : 18; Heb. 7 : 1, 2. No satisfactory identification of it is perhaps possible. Two main opinions have been current from the earliest ages of interpretation : 1. That of the Jewish commentators, who affirm that Salem is Jerusalem, on the ground that Jerusalem is so called in Ps. 76 : 2. Nearly all Jewish commentators hold this opinion. 2. Jerome, however, states that the Salem of Melchizedek was not Jerusalem, but a town eight Roman miles south of Scythopolis, and gives its then name as Salumias, and identifies it with Salem, where John baptized. 2. Ps. 76 : 2. It is agreed on all hands that Salem is here employed for Jerusalem.

Sa'lim (*peace*), a place named John 3 : 23 to denote the situation of Ænon, the scene of St. John's last baptisms; Salim being the well-known town, and Ænon a place of fountains or other waters near it. [SALEM.] The name of *Salim* has been discovered by Mr. Van de Velde in a position exactly in accordance with the notice of Eusebius, viz., six English miles south of *Beisân* (Scythopolis), and two miles west of the Jordan. Near here is an abundant supply of water.

Sal'ma, or **Sal'mon** (*garment*), Ruth 4 : 20, 21; 1 Chron. 2 : 11, 51, 54; Matt. 1 : 4, 5; Luke 3 : 32, son of Nahshon, the prince of the children of Judah, and father of Boaz, the husband of Ruth. (B.C. 1296.) Bethlehem-ephratah, which was Salmon's inheritance, was part of the territory of Caleb, the grandson of Ephratah; and this caused him to be reckoned among the sons of Caleb.

Sal'mon, a hill near Shechem, on which Abimelech and his followers cut down the boughs with which they set the tower of Shechem on fire. Judges 9 : 48. Its exact position is not known. Referred to in Ps. 68 : 14.

Sal'mon, the father of Boaz. [SALMA.]

Salmo'ne (*clothed*), the east point of the island of Crete. Acts 27 : 7. It is a bold promontory, and is visible for a long distance.

Salo'me (*peaceful*). 1. The wife of Zebedee, Matt. 27 : 56; Mark 15 : 40, and probably sister of Mary the mother of Jesus, to whom reference is made in John 19 : 25. The only events recorded of Salome are that she preferred a request on behalf of her two sons for seats of honor in the kingdom of heaven, Matt. 20 : 20, that she attended at the crucifixion of Jesus, Mark 15 : 40, and that she visited his sepulchre. Mark 16 : 1. She is mentioned by name on only the two latter occasions.

2. The daughter of Herodias by her first husband, Herod Philip. Matt. 14 : 6. She married in the first place Philip the tetrarch of Trachonitis, her paternal uncle, and secondly Aristobulus, the king of Chalcis.

Salt. Indispensable as salt is to ourselves, it was even more so to the Hebrews, being to them not only an appetizing condiment in the food both of man, Job 11 : 6, and beast, Isa. 30 : 24, see margin, and a valuable antidote to the effects of the heat of the climate on animal food, but also entering largely into the religious services of the Jews as an accompaniment to the various offerings presented on the altar. Lev. 2 : 13. They possessed an inexhaustible and ready supply of it on the southern shores of the Dead Sea. [SEA, THE SALT.] There is one mountain here called Jebel Usdum, seven miles long and several hundred feet high, which is composed almost entirely of salt. The Jews appear to have distinguished between rock-salt and that which was gained by evaporation, as the Talmudists particularize one species (probably the latter) as the "salt of Sodom." The salt-pits formed an important source of revenue to the rulers of the country, and Antiochus conferred a valuable boon on Jerusalem by presenting the city with 375 bushels of salt for the temple service. As one of the most essential articles of diet, salt symbolized hospitality; as an antiseptic, durability, fidelity and purity. Hence the expression "covenant of salt," Lev. 2 : 13; Num. 18 : 19; 2 Chron. 13 : 5, as betokening an indissoluble alliance between friends; and again the expression "salted with the salt of the palace," Ezra 4 : 14; not necessarily meaning that they had "maintenance from the palace," as the Authorized Version has it, but that they were bound by sacred obligations of fidelity to the king. So in the present day, "to eat bread and salt together" is an expression for a league of mutual amity. It was probably with a view to keep this idea prominently before the minds of the Jews that the use of salt was enjoined on the Israelites in their offerings to God.

Salt, City of, the fifth of the six cities of Judah which lay in the "wilderness." Josh. 15 : 62. Dr. Robinson expresses his belief that it lay somewhere near the plain at the south end of the Salt Sea.

Salt Sea, or **Dead Sea.** [SEA, THE SALT.]

Salt, Valley of, a valley in which occurred two memorable victories of the Israelite arms : 1. That of David over the Edomites. 2 Sam. 8 : 13 ; 1 Chron. 18 : 12. 2. That of Amaziah. 2 Kings 14 : 7 ; 2 Chron. 25 : 11. It is perhaps the broad open plain which lies at the lower end of the Dead Sea, and intervenes between the lake itself and the range of heights which crosses the valley at six or eight miles to the south. This same view is taken by Dr. Robinson. Others suggest that it lay nearer to Petra. What little can be inferred from the narrative as to its situation favors the latter theory.

Sa'lu (*weighed*), the father of Zimri the prince of the Simeonites, who was slain by Phinehas. Num. 25 : 14. Called also Salom. (B.C. 1452.)

Modes of Salutation in the East.

Salutation. Salutations may be classed under the two heads of conversational and epistolary. The salutation at meeting consisted in early times of various expressions of blessing, such as "God be gracious unto thee," Gen. 43 : 29 ;

"The Lord be with you ;" "The Lord bless thee." Ruth 2 : 4. Hence the term "bless" received the secondary sense of "salute." The salutation at parting consisted originally of a simple blessing, Gen. 24 : 60, but in later times the form "Go in peace," or rather "Farewell," 1 Sam. 1 : 17, was common. In modern times the ordinary mode of address current in the East resembles the Hebrew *Es-selâm aleykum,* "Peace be on you," and the term "salam," *peace,* has been introduced into our own language to describe the Oriental salutation. In epistolary salutations the writer placed his own name first, and then that of the person whom he saluted. A form of prayer for spiritual mercies was also used. The concluding salutation consisted generally of the term "I salute," accompanied by a prayer for peace or grace.

Sama'ria (*watch mountain*). This city is situated 30 miles north of Jerusalem and about six miles to the northwest of Shechem, in a wide basin-shaped valley, six miles in diameter, encircled with high hills, almost on the edge of the great plain which borders upon the Mediterranean. In the centre of this basin, which is on a lower level than the valley of Shechem, rises a less elevated oblong hill, with steep yet accessible sides and a long flat top. This hill was chosen by Omri as the site of the capital of the kingdom of Israel. He "bought the hill of Samaria of Shemer for two talents of silver, and built on the hill, and called the name of the city which he built, after the name of the owner of the hill, Samaria." 1 Kings 16 : 23, 24. From the date of Omri's purchase, B.C. 925, Samaria retained its dignity as the capital of the ten tribes, and the name is given to the northern kingdom as well as to the city. Ahab built a temple to Baal there. 1 Kings 16 : 32, 33. It was twice besieged by the Syrians, in B.C. 901, 1 Kings 20 : 1, and in B.C. 892, 2 Kings 6 : 24-7 : 20 ; but on both occasions the siege was ineffectual. The possessor of Samaria was considered *de facto* king of Israel. 2 Kings 15 : 13, 14. In B.C. 721 Samaria was taken, after a siege of three years, by Shalmaneser king of Assyria, 2 Kings 18 : 9, 10, and the kingdom of the ten tribes was put an end to. Some years afterward the district of which Samaria was the centre was repeopled by Esarhaddon. Alexander the Great took the city, killed a large portion of the inhabitants, and suffered the remainder to settle at Shechem. He replaced them by a colony of Syro-Macedonians, who occupied the city until the time of John Hyrcanus, who took it after a year's siege, and did his best to demolish it entirely. (B.C. 109.) It was rebuilt and greatly embellished by Herod the Great. He called it *Sebaste=Augusta*, after the name of his patron, Augustus Cæsar. The wall around it was $2\frac{1}{2}$ miles long, and in the centre of the city was a park 900 feet square, containing a magnificent temple dedicated to Cæsar. In the New Testament the city itself does not appear to be mentioned, but rather a portion of the district to which, even in older times, it had extended its name. Matt. 10 : 5 ; John 4 : 4, 5. At this day the city is represented by a small village retaining few vestiges of the past except its name, *Sebŭstiych*, an Arabic corruption of Sebaste. Some architectural remains it has, partly of Christian construction or adaptation, as the ruined church of St. John the Baptist, partly, perhaps, traces of Idumæan magnificence. St. Jerome, whose acquaintance with Palestine imparts a sort of probability to the tradition which prevailed so strongly in later days, asserts that Sebaste, which he invariably identifies with Samaria, was the place in which St. John the Baptist was imprisoned and suffered death. He also makes it the burial-place of the prophets Elisha and Obadiah.

Sama′ria, Country of. Samaria at first included all the tribes over which Jeroboam made himself king, whether east or west of the river Jordan. 1 Kings 13 : 32. But whatever extent the word might have acquired, it necessarily became contracted as the limits of the kingdom of Israel became contracted. In all probability the territory of Simeon and that of Dan were very early absorbed in the kingdom of Judah. It is evident from an occurrence in Hezekiah's reign that just before the deposition and death of Hoshea, the last king of Israel, the authority of the king of Judah, or at least his influence, was recognized by portions of Asher, Issachar and Zebulun, and even of Ephraim and Manasseh. 2 Chron. 30 : 1-26. Men came from all those tribes to the Passover at Jerusalem. This was about B.C. 726. Samaria (the city) and a few adjacent cities or villages only represented that dominion which had once extended from Bethel to Dan northward, and from the Mediterranean to the borders of Syria and Ammon eastward. In New Testament times Samaria was bounded northward by the range of hills which commences at Mount Carmel on the west, and, after making a bend to the southwest, runs almost due east to the valley of the Jordan, forming the southern border of the plain of Esdraelon. It touched toward the south, as nearly as possible, the northern limits of Benjamin. Thus it comprehended the ancient territory of Ephraim and that of Manasseh west of Jordan. The Cuthæan Samaritans, however, possessed only a few towns and villages of this large area, and these lay almost together in the centre of the district. At *Nâblûs* the Samaritans have still a settlement, consisting of about 200 persons. [SHECHEM.]

Samar′itans. Strictly speaking, a Samaritan would be an inhabitant of the *city* of Samaria ; but the term was applied to all the people of the kingdom of Israel. After the captivity of Israel, B.C. 721, and in our Lord's time, the name was applied to a peculiar people whose origin was in this wise : At the final captivity of Israel by Shalmaneser, we may conclude that the cities of Samaria were not merely partially but wholly depopulated of their inhabitants in B.C. 721, and that they remained in this desolated state until, in the words of 2 Kings 17 : 24, "the king of Assyria brought men from Babylon, and from Cuthah, and from Ava (Ivah, 2 Kings 18 : 34), and from Hamath, and from Sepharvaim, and placed them in the cities of Samaria instead of the children of Israel : and they possessed Samaria, and dwelt in the cities thereof." Thus the new Samaritans were Assyrians by birth or subjugation. These strangers, whom we will now assume to have been placed in "the cities of Samaria" by Esar-haddon, were of course idolaters, and worshipped a strange medley of divinities. God's displeasure was kindled, and they were annoyed by beasts of prey, which had probably increased to a great extent before their entrance upon the land. On their explaining their miserable condition to the king of Assyria, he despatched one of the captive priests to teach them "how they should fear the Lord." The priest came accordingly, and henceforth, in the language of the sacred historian. they "feared the Lord, and served their graven images, both their children and their children's children: as did their fathers, so do they unto this day." 2 Kings 17 : 41. A gap occurs in their history until Judah has returned from captivity. They then desire to be allowed to participate in the rebuilding of the temple at Jerusalem; but on being refused, the Samaritans throw off the mask, and become open enemies, frustrate the operations of the Jews through the reigns of two Persian kings, and are only effectually silenced in the reign of Darius Hystaspes, B.C. 519. The feud thus unhappily begun grew year by year more inveterate. Matters at length came to a climax. About B.C. 409, a certain Manasseh, a man of priestly lineage, on being expelled from Jerusalem by Nehemiah for an unlawful marriage, obtained permission from the Persian king of his day, Darius Nothus, to build a temple on Mount Gerizim for the Samar-

Ruins of the Temple of Manasseh, Samaria.

itans, with whom he had found refuge. The animosity of the Samaritans became more intense than ever. They are said to have done everything in their power to annoy the Jews. Their own temple on Gerizim they considered to be much superior to that at Jerusalem. There they sacrificed a passover. Toward the mountain, even after the temple on it had fallen, wherever they were they directed their worship. To their copy of the law they arrogated an antiquity and authority greater than attached to any copy in the possession of the Jews. The law (i. e. the five books of Moses) was their sole code; for they rejected every other book in the Jewish canon. The Jews, on the other hand, were not more conciliatory in their treatment of the Samaritans. Certain other Jewish renegades had from time to time taken refuge with the Samaritans; hence by degrees the Samaritans claimed to partake of Jewish blood, especially if doing so happened to suit their interest. Very far were the Jews from admitting this claim to consanguinity on the part of these people. The traditional hatred in which the Jew held the Samaritan is expressed in Ecclus. 50 : 25, 26. Such were the Samaritans of our Lord's day; a people distinct from the Jews, though lying in the very midst of the Jews; a people preserving their identity, though seven centuries had rolled away since they had been brought from Assyria by

Esar-haddon, and though they had abandoned their polytheism for a sort of ultra Mosaicism ; a people who, though their limits had gradually contracted, and the rallying-place of their religion on Mount Gerizim had been destroyed one hundred and sixty years before by John Hyrcanus (B.C. 130), and though Samaria (the city) had been again and again destroyed, still preserved their nationality, still worshipped from Shechem and their impoverished settlements toward their sacred hill, still retained their peculiar religion, and could not coalesce with the Jews.

Samaritan Pentateuch, a recension of the commonly-received Hebrew text of the Mosaic law, in use among the Samaritans, and written in the ancient Hebrew or so-called Samaritan character. The origin of the Samaritan Pentateuch has given rise to much controversy, into which we cannot here enter. The two most usual opinions are—1. That it came into the hands of the Samaritans as an inheritance from the ten tribes whom they succeeded. 2. That it was introduced by Manasseh at the time of the foundation of the Samaritan sanctuary on Mount Gerizim. It differs in several important points from the Hebrew text. Among these may be mentioned—1. Emendations of passages and words of the Hebrew text which contain something objectionable in the eyes of the Samaritans, on account either of historical improbability or apparent want of dignity in the terms applied to the Creator. Thus in the Samaritan Pentateuch no one in the antediluvian times begets his first son after he has lived 150 years; but one hundred years are, where necessary, subtracted before, and added after, the birth of the first son. An exceedingly important and often-discussed emendation of this class is the passage in Ex. 12 : 40, which in our text reads, " Now the sojourning of the children of Israel who dwelt in Egypt was four hundred and thirty years." The Samaritan has " The sojourning of the children of Israel [*and their fathers who dwelt in the land of Canaan and in the land of Egypt*] was four hundred and thirty years;" an interpolation of very late date indeed. Again, in Gen. 2 : 2, " And God [?] had finished on the seventh day," is altered into " the *sixth*," lest God's rest on the Sabbath day might seem incomplete. 2. Alterations made in favor

of or on behalf of Samaritan theology, hermeneutics and domestic worship.

Sam'gar-ne'bo (*sword of Nebo*), one of the princes or generals of the king of Babylon. Jer. 39 : 3.

Sam'lah (*garment*), Gen. 36 : 36, 37 ; 1 Chron. 1 : 47, 48, one of the kings of Edom, successor to Hadad or Hadar.

Samos, a Greek island off that part of Asia Minor where Ionia touches Caria. Samos comes before our notice in the detailed account of St. Paul's return from his third missionary journey. Acts 20 : 15.

Samothra'ce. In the Revised Version for Samothracia.

Samothra'cia. Mention is made of this island in the account of St. Paul's first voyage to Europe. Acts 16 : 11 ; 20 : 6. Being very lofty and conspicuous, it is an excellent landmark for sailors, and must have been full in view, if the weather was clear, throughout that voyage from Troas to Neapolis.

Sam'son (*like the sun*), son of Manoah, a man of the town of Zorah, in the tribe of Dan, on the border of Judah. Josh. 15 : 33 ; 19 : 41. (B.C. 1161.) The miraculous circumstances of his birth are recorded in Judges 13 ; and the three following chapters are devoted to the history of his life and exploits. Samson takes his place in Scripture, (1) as a judge—an office which he filled for twenty years, Judges 15: 20 ; 16: 31 ; (2) as a Nazarite, Judges 13 : 5 ; 16 : 17 ; and (3) as one endowed with supernatural power by the Spirit of the Lord. Judges 13 : 25 ; 14 : 6, 19 ; 15 : 14. As a judge his authority seems to have been limited to the district bordering upon the country of the Philistines. The divine inspiration which Samson shared with Othniel, Gideon and Jephthah assumed in him the unique form of vast personal strength, animated by undaunted bravery. It was inseparably connected with the observance of his vow as a Nazarite : " his strength was in his hair." He married a Philistine woman whom he had seen at Timnath. One day, on his way to that city, he was attacked by a lion, which he killed ; and again passing that way, he saw a swarm of bees in the carcass of the lion, and he ate of the honey, but still he told no one. He availed himself of this circumstance, and of the custom of proposing riddles at marriage feasts, to lay a snare for the Philistines. But Samson told the riddle to his wife, and she told it to the men of the city, whereupon Samson slew thirty men of the city. Returning to his own house, he found his wife married to another, and was refused permission to see her. Samson revenged himself by taking 300 foxes (or rather jackals) and tying them together two by two by the tails, with a firebrand between every pair of tails, and so he let them loose into the standing corn of the Philistines, which was ready for harvest. The Philistines took vengeance by burning Samson's wife and her father; but he fell upon them in return, and smote them "hip and thigh with a great slaughter," after which he took refuge on the top of the rock of Etam, in the territory of Judah. The Philistines gathered an army to revenge themselves, when the men of Judah hastened to make peace by giving up Samson, who was bound with cords; these, however, he broke like burnt flax, and finding a jawbone of an ass at hand, he slew with it a thousand of the Philistines. The supernatural character of this exploit was confirmed by the miraculous bursting out of a spring of water to revive the champion as he was ready to die of thirst. This achievement raised Samson to the position of a judge, which he held for twenty years. After a time he began to fall into the temptations which addressed themselves to his strong animal nature; but he broke through every snare in which he was caught so long as he kept his Nazarite vow. While he was visiting a harlot in Gaza, the Philistines shut the gates of the city, intending to kill him in the morning; but at midnight he went out and tore away the gates, with the posts and bar, and carried them to the top of a hill looking toward Hebron. Next he formed his fatal connection with Delilah, a woman who lived in the valley of Sorek. Thrice he suffered himself to be bound with green withes, with new ropes, but released himself, until finally, wearied out with her importunity, he "told her all his heart," and while he was asleep she had him shaven of his seven locks of hair. His enemies put out his eyes, and led him down to Gaza, bound in brazen fetters, and made him grind in the prison. Then they held a great festival in the temple of Dagon, to celebrate their victory over Samson. They brought forth the blind champion to make sport for them, and placed him between the two chief pillars which supported the roof that surrounded the court. Samson asked the lad who

guided him to let him feel the pillars, to lean upon them. Then, with a fervent prayer that God would strengthen him only this once, to be avenged on the Philistines, he bore with all his might upon the two pillars; they yielded, and the house fell upon the lords and all the people. "So the dead which he slew at his death were more than they which he slew in his life." In Heb. 11 : 32 his name is enrolled among the worthies of the Jewish Church.

Sam′uel was the son of Elkanah and Hannah, and was born at Ramathaim-zophim, among the hills of Ephraim. [RAMAH, No. 2.] (B.C. 1171.) Before his birth he was dedicated by his mother to the office of a Nazarite; and when a young child, 12 years old according to Josephus, he was placed in the temple, and "ministered unto the Lord before Eli." It was while here that he received his first prophetic call. 1 Sam. 3 : 1–18. He next appears, probably twenty years afterward, suddenly among the people, warning them against their idolatrous practices. 1 Sam. 7 : 3, 4. Then followed Samuel's first and, as far as we know, only military achievement, ch. 7 : 5–12; but it was apparently this which raised him to the office of "judge." He visited, in the discharge of his duties as ruler, the three chief sanctuaries on the west of Jordan—Bethel, Gilgal and Mizpeh. ch. 7 : 16. His own residence was still his native city, Ramah, where he married, and two sons grew up to repeat under his eyes the same perversion of high office that he had himself witnessed in his childhood in the case of the two sons of Eli. In his old age he shared his power with them, 1 Sam. 8 : 1–4; but the people, dissatisfied, demanded a king, and Saul was finally anointed under God's direction, and Samuel surrendered to him his authority, 1 Sam. 12, though still remaining judge. ch. 7 : 15. He was consulted far and near on the small affairs of life. 1 Sam. 9 : 7, 8. From this fact, combined with his office of ruler, an awful reverence grew up around him. No sacrificial feast was thought complete without his blessing. *Ibid.* 9 : 13. A peculiar virtue was believed to reside in his intercession. After Saul was rejected by God, Samuel anointed David in his place, and Samuel became the spiritual father of the psalmist-king. The death of Samuel is described as taking place in the year of the close of David's wanderings.

It is said with peculiar emphasis, as if to mark the loss, that "*all* the Israelites were gathered together" from all parts of this hitherto-divided country, and "lamented him," and "buried him" within his own house, thus in a manner consecrated by being turned into his tomb. 1 Sam. 25 : 1. Samuel represents the independence of the moral law, of the divine will, as distinct from legal or sacerdotal enactments, which is so remarkable a characteristic of all the later prophets. He is also the founder of the first regular institutions of religious instruction, and communities for the purposes of education.

Samuel, Books of, are not separated from each other in the Hebrew MSS., and, from a critical point of view, must be regarded as one book. The present division was first made in the Septuagint translation, and was adopted in the Vulgate from the Septuagint. The book was called by the Hebrews "Samuel," probably because the birth and life of Samuel were the subjects treated of in the beginning of the work. The books of Samuel commence with the history of Eli and Samuel, and contain an account of the establishment of the Hebrew monarchy and of the reigns of Saul and David, with the exception of the last days of the latter monarch, which are related in the beginning of the books of Kings, of which those of Samuel form the previous portion. [KINGS, BOOKS OF.] *Authorship and date of the book.—* 1. As to the authorship. In common with all the historical books of the Old Testament, except the beginning of Nehemiah, the book of Samuel contains no mention in the text of the name of its author. It is indisputable that the title "Samuel" does not imply that the prophet was the author of the book of Samuel as a whole; for the death of Samuel is recorded in the beginning of the 25th chapter. In our own time the most prevalent idea in the Anglican Church seems to have been that the first twenty-four chapters of the book of Samuel were written by the prophet himself, and the rest of the chapters by the prophets Nathan and Gad. This, however, is doubtful. 2. But although the authorship cannot be ascertained with certainty, it appears clear that, in its present form, it must have been composed subsequent to the secession of the ten tribes, B.C. 975. This results from the passage in 1 Sam.

27 : 6, wherein it is said of David, "Then Achish gave him Ziklag that day : wherefore Ziklag pertaineth unto the kings of Judah to this day :" for neither Saul, David nor Solomon is in a single instance called king of Judah simply. On the other hand, it could hardly have been written later than the reformation of Josiah, since it seems to have been composed at a time when the Pentateuch was not acted on as the rule of religious observances, which received a special impetus at the finding of the Book of the Law at the reformation of Josiah. All, therefore, that can be asserted with any certainty is that the book, as a whole, can scarcely have been composed later than the reformation of Josiah, and that it could not have existed in its present form earlier than the reign of Rehoboam. The book of Samuel is one of the best specimens of Hebrew prose in the golden age of Hebrew literature. In prose it holds the same place which Joel and the undisputed prophecies of Isaiah hold in poetical or prophetical language.

Sanbal'lat (*strength*), a Moabite of Horonaim. Neh. 2 : 10, 19; 13 : 28. He held apparently some command in Samaria at the time Nehemiah was preparing to rebuild the walls of Jerusalem, B.C. 445, Neh. 4 : 2, and from the moment of Nehemiah's arrival in Judea he set himself to oppose every measure for the welfare of Jerusalem. The only other incident in his life is his alliance with the high priest's family by the marriage of his daughter with one of the grandsons of Eliashib; but the expulsion from the priesthood of the guilty son of Joiada by Nehemiah promptly followed. Here the scriptural narrative ends.

Sandal was the article ordinarily used by the Hebrews for protecting the feet. It consisted simply of a sole attached to the foot by thongs. We have express notice of the thong (Authorized Version "shoe-latchet") in several passages, notably Gen. 14 : 23; Isa. 5 : 27; Mark 1 : 7. Sandals were worn by all classes of society in Palestine, even by the very poor; and both the sandal and the thong or shoe-latchet were so cheap and common that they passed into a proverb for the most insignificant thing. Gen. 14 : 23; Ecclus. 46 : 19. They were dispensed with in-doors, and were only put on by persons about to undertake some business away from their homes. During mealtimes the feet were uncovered. Luke 7;

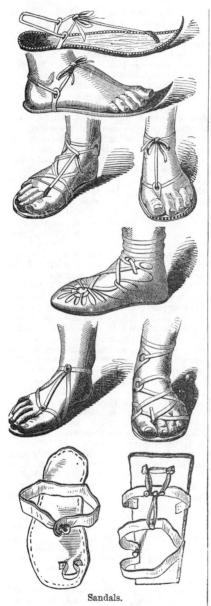

Sandals.

38; John 13 : 5, 6. It was a mark of reverence to cast off the shoes in approaching a place or person of eminent sanctity.

Ex. 3 : 5; Josh. 5 : 15. It was also an indication of violent emotion, or of mourning, if a person appeared barefoot in public. 2 Sam. 15 : 30. To carry or to unloose a person's sandal was a menial office, betokening great inferiority on the part of the person performing it. Matt. 3 : 11.

San'hedrin (from the Greek συνέδριον, "a council-chamber;" commonly but incorrectly Sanhedrim), the supreme council of the Jewish people in the time of Christ and earlier. 1. The *origin* of this assembly is traced in the Mishna to the seventy elders whom Moses was directed, Num. 11 : 16, 17, to associate with him in the government of the Israelites; but this tribunal was probably temporary, and did not continue to exist after the Israelites had entered Palestine. In the lack of definite historical information as to the establishment of the Sanhedrin, it can only be said in general that the Greek etymology of the name seems to point to a period subsequent to the Macedonian supremacy in Palestine. From the few incidental notices in the New Testament, we gather that it consisted of chief priests, or the heads of the twenty-four classes into which the priests were divided, elders, men of age and experience, and scribes, lawyers, or those learned in the Jewish law. Matt. 26 : 57, 59; Mark 15 : 1; Luke 22 : 66; Acts 5 : 21. 2. The *number of members* is usually given as 71. The president of this body was styled *nasi*, and was chosen on account of his eminence in worth and wisdom. Often, if not generally, this pre-eminence was accorded to the high priest. The vice-president, called in the Talmud "father of the house of judgment," sat at the right hand of the president. Some writers speak of a second vice-president, but this is not sufficiently confirmed. While in session the Sanhedrin sat in the form of a half-circle. 3. The *place* in which the sessions of the Sanhedrin were ordinarily held was, according to the Talmud, a hall called *Gazzith*, supposed by Lightfoot to have been situated in the southeast corner of one of the courts near the temple building. In special exigencies, however, it seems to have met in the residence of the high priest. Matt. 26 : 3. Forty years before the destruction of Jerusalem, and consequently while the Saviour was teaching in Palestine, the sessions of the Sanhedrin were removed from the hall Gazzith to a somewhat greater distance from the temple building, although still on Mount Moriah. After several other changes, its seat was finally established at Tiberias, where it became extinct A.D. 425. As a judicial body the Sanhedrin constituted a supreme court, to which belonged in the first instance the trial of false prophets, of the high priest and other priests, and also of a tribe fallen into idolatry. As an administrative council, it determined other important matters. Jesus was arraigned before this body as a false prophet, John 11 : 47, and Peter, John, Stephen and Paul as teachers of

The Sanhedrin in Council.

error and deceivers of the people. From Acts 9 : 2 it appears that the Sanhedrin exercised a degree of authority beyond the limits of Palestine. According to the Jerusalem Gemara the power of inflicting capital punishment was taken away from this tribunal forty years before the destruction of Jerusalem. With this agrees the answer of the Jews to Pilate. John 19 : 31. The Talmud also mentions a *lesser Sanhedrin* of twenty-three members in every city in Palestine in which were not less than 120 householders.

Sansan'nah (*palm branch*), one of the towns in the south district of Judah, named in Josh. 15 : 31 only.

Saph (*tall*), one of the sons of the giant slain by Sibbechai the Hushathite. 2 Sam. 21 : 18. In 1 Chron. 20 : 4 he is called SIPPAI. (B.C. about 1050.)

Saph'ir (*fair*), one of the villages addressed by the prophet Micah, Micah 1 : 11, is described by Eusebius and Jerome as "in the mountain district between Eleutheropolis and Ascalon," perhaps represented by the village *es-Sawâfir*, seven or eight miles to the northeast of Ascalon.

Sapphi'ra. [ANANIAS.]

Sapphire (Heb. *sappir*), a precious stone, apparently of a bright-blue color, see Ex. 24 : 10; the second stone in the second row of the high priest's breast-plate, Ex. 28 : 18; extremely precious, Job 28 : 16; it was one of the precious stones that ornamented the king of Tyre. Ezek. 28 : 13. The *sapphire* of the ancients was not our gem of that name, viz. the azure or indigo-blue, crystalline variety of corundum, but our *lapis lazuli* (*ultra-marine*).

Sa'ra, Greek form of Sarah.

Sa'rah (*princess*). 1. The wife and half-sister, Gen. 20 : 12, of Abraham, and mother of Isaac. Her name is first introduced in Gen. 11 : 29 as Sarai. The change of her name from Sarai, *my princess* (*i. e.* Abraham's), to Sarah, *princess* (for all the race), was made at the same time that Abram's name was changed to Abraham, —on the establishment of the covenant of circumcision between him and God. Sarah's history is of course that of Abraham. [ABRAHAM.] She died at Hebron at the age of 127 years, 28 years before her husband, and was buried by him in the cave of Machpelah. (B.C. 1860.) She is referred to in the New Testament as a type of conjugal obedience in 1 Pet. 3 : 6, and as one of the types of faith in Heb. 11 : 11.

2. Sarah, the daughter of Asher. Num. 26 : 46.

Sa'ra-i (*my princess*), the original name of Sarah, the wife of Abraham.

Sa'raph (*burning*), mentioned in 1 Chron. 4 : 22 among the descendants of Judah.

Sardine, Sardius (*red*) (Heb. *ôdem*), the stone which occupied the first place in the first row of the high priest's breast-plate. Ex. 28 : 17. The sard, which is probably the stone denoted by *ôdem*, is a superior variety of agate, sometimes called carnelian, and has long been a favorite stone for the engraver's art. Sards differ in color : there is a bright-red variety, and perhaps the Hebrew *ôdem*, from a root which means "to be red," points to this kind.

Sar'dis, a city of Asia Minor, and capital of Lydia, situated about two miles to the south of the river Hermus, just below the range of Tmolus, on a spur of which its acropolis was built. It was 50 miles northeast of Smyrna. It was the ancient residence of the kings of Lydia, among them Crœsus, proverbial for his immense wealth. Cyrus is said to have taken $600,000,000 worth of treasure from the city when he captured it, B.C. 548. Sardis was in very early times, both from the extremely fertile character of the neighboring region and from its convenient position, a commercial mart of importance. The art of dyeing wool is said to have been invented there. In the year

Ruins at Sardis.

214 B.C. it was taken and sacked by the army of Antiochus the Great. Afterward it passed under the dominion of the kings of Pergamos. Its productive soil must always have continued a source of wealth; but its importance as a central mart appears to have diminished from the time of the invasion of Asia by Alexander. The massive temple of Cybele still bears witness in its fragmentary remains to the wealth and architectural skill of the people that raised it. On the north side of the acropolis, overlooking the valley of the Hermus, is a theatre near 400 feet in diameter, attached to a stadium of about 1000. There are still considerable remains of the ancient city at *Sert-Kalessi.* Travellers describe the appearance of the locality as that of complete solitude. The only passage in which it is mentioned in the Bible is Rev. 3 : 1–6.

Sar'dites, The, descendants of Sered the son of Zebulun. Num. 26 : 26. (In the Revised Version of Rev. 4 : 3 for *sardine stone.* The name is derived from Sardis, where the stone was first found.)

Sardonyx, a name compounded of *sard* and *onyx,* two precious stones, varieties of chalcedony or agate. The sardonyx combines the qualities of both, whence its name. It is mentioned only in Rev. 21 : 20. The sardonyx consists of "a white opaque layer, superimposed upon a red transparent stratum of the true red sard." It is, like the sard, merely a variety of agate, and is frequently employed by engravers for signet-rings.

Sarep'ta. [ZAREPHATH.]

Sar'gon (*prince of the sun*), one of the greatest of the Assyrian kings, is mentioned by name but once in Scripture—Isa. 20 : 1. He was the successor of Shalmaneser, and was Sennacherib's father and his immediate predecessor. He reigned from B.C. 721 to 702, and seems to have been a usurper. He was undoubtedly a great and successful warrior. In his annals, which cover a space of fifteen years, from B.C. 721 to 706, he gives an account of his warlike expeditions against Babylonia and Susiana on the south, Media on the east, Armenia and Cappadocia toward the north, Syria, Palestine, Arabia and Egypt toward the west and southwest. In B.C. 712 he took Ashdod, by one of his generals, which is the event which causes the mention of his name in Scripture. It is not as a warrior only that Sargon deserves special mention among the Assyrian kings. He was also the builder of useful works, and of one of the most magnificent of the Assyrian palaces.

Sa'rid (*survivor*), a chief landmark of the territory of Zebulun. Josh. 19 : 10, 12. All that can be gathered of its position is that it lay to the west of Chisloth-tabor.

Sa'ron, the district in which Lydda stood, Acts 9 : 35 only; the Sharon of the Old Testament. [SHARON.]

Saro'thie. "The sons of Sarothie" are among the sons of the servants of Solomon who returned with Zerubbabel. 1 Esd. 5 : 34.

Sarse'chim (*prince of the eunuchs*), one of the generals of Nebuchadnezzar's army at the taking of Jerusalem. Jer. 39 : 3. (B.C. 588.)

Sa'ruch, Luke 3 : 25; Serug the son of Reu.

Sa'tan. The word itself, the Hebrew *sâtân,* is simply an "adversary," and is so used in 1 Sam. 29 : 4; 2 Sam. 19 : 22; 1 Kings 5 : 4; 11 : 14, 23, 25; Num. 22 :

22, 32; Ps. 109 : 6. This original sense is still found in our Lord's application of the name to St. Peter in Matt. 16 : 23. It is used as a proper name or title only four times in the Old Testament, viz. (with the article) in Job 1 : 6, 12; 2 : 1; Zech. 2 : 1, and (without the article) in 1 Chron. 21 : 1. It is with the scriptural revelation on the subject that we are here concerned; and it is clear, from this simple enumeration of passages, that it is to be sought in the New Testament rather than in the Old Testament. I. *The personal existence* of a spirit of evil is clearly revealed in Scripture; but the revelation is made gradually, in accordance with the progressiveness of God's method. In the first entrance of evil into the world, the temptation is referred only to the serpent. In the book of Job we find for the first time a distinct mention of "Satan," the "adversary" of Job. But it is important to remark the emphatic stress laid on his subordinate position, on the absence of all but delegated power, of all terror and all grandeur in his character. It is especially remarkable that no power of spiritual influence, but only a power over outward circumstances, is attributed to him. The captivity brought the Israelites face to face with the great dualism of the Persian mythology, the conflict of Ormuzd with Ahriman, the co-ordinate spirit of evil; but it is confessed by all that the Satan of Scripture bears no resemblance to the Persian Ahriman. His subordination and inferiority are as strongly marked as ever. The New Testament brings plainly forward the power and the influence of Satan. From the beginning of the Gospel, when he appears as the personal tempter of our Lord, through all the Gospels, Epistles, and Apocalypse, it is asserted or implied, again and again, as a familiar and important truth. II. Of the *nature* and *original state* of Satan, little is revealed in Scripture. He is spoken of as a "spirit" in Eph. 2 : 2, as the prince or ruler of the "demons" in Matt. 12 : 24–26, and as having "angels" subject to him in Matt. 25 : 41; Rev. 12 : 7, 9. The whole description of his power implies spiritual nature and spiritual influence. We conclude therefore that he was of angelic nature, a rational and spiritual creature, superhuman in power, wisdom and energy; and not only so, but an archangel, one of the "princes" of heaven. We cannot, of course, conceive that anything essentially and originally evil was created by God. We can only conjecture, therefore, that Satan is a fallen angel, who once had a time of probation, but whose condemnation is now irrevocably fixed. As to the time, cause and manner of his fall Scripture tells us scarcely anything; but it describes to us distinctly the moral nature of the evil one. The ideal of goodness is made up of the three great moral attributes of God—love, truth, and purity or holiness; combined with that spirit which is the natural temper of the finite and dependent creature, the spirit of faith. We find, accordingly, that the opposites of these qualities are dwelt upon as the characteristics of the devil. III. The *power of Satan* over the soul is represented as exercised either directly or by his instruments. His direct influence over the soul is simply that of a powerful and evil nature on those in whom lurks the germ of the same evil. Besides this direct influence, we learn from Scripture that Satan is the leader of a host of evil spirits or angels who share his evil work, and for whom the "everlasting fire is prepared." Matt. 25 : 41. Of their origin and fall we know no more than of his. But one passage—Matt. 12 : 24-26—identifies them distinctly with the "demons" (Authorized Version "devils") who had power to possess the souls of men. They are mostly spoken of in Scripture in reference to possession; but in Eph. 6 : 12 they are described in various lights. We find them sharing the enmity to God and man implied in the name and nature of Satan; but their power and action are little dwelt upon in comparison with his. But the evil one is not merely the "prince of the demons;" he is called also the "prince of this world" in John 12 : 31; 14 : 30; 16 : 11, and even the "god of this world" in 2 Cor. 4 : 4; the two expressions being united in Eph. 6 : 12. This power he claimed for himself, *as a delegated authority*, in the temptation of our Lord, Luke 4 : 6; and the temptation would have been unreal had he spoken altogether falsely. The indirect action of Satan is best discerned by an examination of the title by which he is designated in Scripture. He is called emphatically ὁ διάβολος, "the devil." The derivation of the word in itself implies only the endeavor to break the

bonds between others and "set them at variance;" but common usage adds to this general sense the special idea of "setting at variance *by slander*." In the application of the title to Satan, both the general and special senses should be kept in view. His general object is to break the bonds of communion between God and man, and the bonds of truth and love which bind men to each other. The slander of God to man is best seen in the words of Gen. 3 : 4, 5. They attribute selfishness and jealousy to the Giver of all good. The slander of man to God is illustrated by the book of Job. Job 1 : 9-11; 2 : 4, 5. IV. *The method of satanic action* upon the heart itself. It may be summed up in two words—temptation and possession. The subject of temptation is illustrated, not only by abstract statements, but also by the record of the temptations of Adam and of our Lord. It is expressly laid down, as in James 1 : 2-4, that "temptation," properly so called, *i. e.* "trial," is essential to man, and is accordingly ordained for him and sent to him by God, as in Gen. 22 : 1. It is this tentability of man, even in his original nature, which is represented in Scripture as giving scope to the evil action of Satan. But in the temptation of a fallen nature Satan has a greater power. Every sin committed makes a man the "servant of sin" for the future, John 8 : 34; Rom. 6 : 16; it therefore creates in the spirit of man a positive tendency to evil, which sympathizes with, and aids, the temptation of the evil one. On the subject of possession, see DEMONIACS.

Satyr (sa'tyr or sat'yr), a sylvan deity or demigod of Greek mythology, represented as a monster, part man and part goat. Isa. 13 : 21; 34 : 14. The Hebrew word signifies "hairy" or "rough," and is frequently applied to "he-goats." In the passages cited it probably refers to demons of woods and desert places. Comp. Lev. 17 : 7; 2 Chron. 11 : 15.

Saul (*desired*), more accurately Shaul. 1. One of the early kings of Edom, and successor of Samlah. Gen. 36 : 37, 38; 1 Chron. 1 : 48. (B.C. after 1450.)

2. The first king of Israel, the son of Kish, and of the tribe of Benjamin. (B.C. 1095-1055.) His character is in part illustrated by the fierce, wayward, fitful nature of the tribe, and in part accounted for by the struggle between the old and new systems in which he found himself

involved. To this we must add a taint of madness, which broke out in violent frenzy at times, leaving him with long lucid intervals. He was remarkable for his strength and activity, 2 Sam. 1 : 23, and, like the Homeric heroes, of gigantic stature, taller by head and shoulders than the rest of the people, and of that kind of beauty denoted by the Hebrew word "good," 1 Sam. 9 : 2, and which caused him to be compared to the gazelle, "the gazelle of Israel." His birthplace is not expressly mentioned; but, as Zelah in Benjamin was the place of Kish's sepulchre, 2 Sam. 21 : 14, it was probably his native village. His father, Kish, was a powerful and wealthy chief, though the family to which he belonged was of little importance. 1 Sam. 9 : 1, 21. A portion of his property consisted of a drove of asses. In search of these asses, gone astray on the mountains, he sent his son Saul. It was while prosecuting this adventure that Saul met with Samuel for the first time at his home in Ramah, five miles north of Jerusalem. A divine intimation had made known to him the approach of Saul, whom he treated with special favor, and the next morning descending with him to the skirts of the town, Samuel poured over Saul's head the consecrated oil, and with a kiss of salutation announced to him that he was to be the ruler of the nation. 1 Sam. 9 : 25–10 : 1. Returning homeward, his call was confirmed by the incidents which, according to Samuel's prediction, awaited him. 1 Sam. 10 : 9, 10. What may be named the public call occurred at Mizpeh, when lots were cast to find the tribe and family which was to produce the king, and Saul, by a divine intimation, was found hid in the circle of baggage which surrounded the encampment. 1 Sam. 10 : 17–24. Returning to Gibeah, apparently to private life, he heard the threat issued by Nahash king of Ammon against Jabesh-gilead. He speedily collected an army, and Jabesh was rescued. The effect was instantaneous on the people, and the monarchy was inaugurated anew at Gilgal. 1 Sam. 11 : 1–15. It should be, however, observed that according to 1 Sam. 12 : 12 the affair of Nahash *preceded* and occasioned the election of Saul. Although king of Israel, his rule was at first limited; but in the second year of his reign he began to organize an attempt to shake off the Philistine yoke, and an army was formed. In this crisis, Saul, now on the very confines of his kingdom at Gilgal, impatient at Samuel's delay, whom he had directed to be present, offered sacrifice himself. Samuel, arriving later, pronounced the first curse, on his impetuous zeal. 1 Sam. 13 : 5–14. After the Philistines were driven back to their own country occurred the first appearance of Saul's madness in the rash vow which all but cost the life of his son. 1 Sam. 14 : 24, 44. The expulsion of the Philistines, although not entirely completed, ch. 14 : 52, at once placed Saul in a position higher than that of any previous ruler of Israel, and he made war upon the neighboring tribes. In the war with Amalek, ch. 14 : 48; 15 : 1–9, he disobeyed the prophetical command of Samuel, which called down the second curse, and the first distinct intimation of the transference of the kingdom to a rival. The rest of Saul's life is one long tragedy. The frenzy which had given indications of itself before now at times took almost entire possession of him. In this crisis David was recommended to him. From this time forward their lives are blended together. [DAVID.] In Saul's better moments he never lost the strong affection which he had contracted for David. Occasionally, too, his prophetical gift returned, blended with his madness. 1 Sam. 19 : 24. But his acts of fierce, wild zeal increased. At last the monarchy itself broke down under the weakness of its head. The Philistines re-entered the country, and just before giving them battle Saul's courage failed, and he consulted one of the necromancers, the "Witch of Endor," who had escaped his persecution. At this distance of time it is impossible to determine the relative amount of fraud or of reality in the scene which follows, though the obvious meaning of the narrative itself tends to the hypothesis of some kind of apparition. ch. 28. On hearing the denunciation which the apparition conveyed, Saul fell the whole length of his gigantic stature on the ground, and remained motionless till the woman and his servants forced him to eat. The next day the battle came on. The Israelites were driven up the side of Gilboa. The three sons of Saul were slain. Saul was wounded. According to one account, he fell upon his own sword, 1 Sam. 31 : 4, and died. The body on being found by the Philistines was stripped and decapitated, and the headless trunk hung over the city walls, with those of his three sons. ch. 31 : 9, 10. The head was deposited (probably at Ashdod) in the temple of Dagon. 1 Chron. 10 : 10. The corpse was buried at Jabesh-gilead. 1 Sam. 31 : 13.

3. The Jewish name of St. Paul.

Saw. Egyptian saws, so far as has yet been discovered, are single-handed. As is the case in modern Oriental saws, the teeth usually incline toward the handle, instead of away from it like ours. They have, in most cases, bronze blades, apparently attached to the handles by leathern thongs. No evidence exists of the use of the saw applied to stone in Egypt, but we read of sawn stones used in the temple. 1 Kings 7 : 9. The saws "under" or "in" which David is said to have placed his captives were of iron. The expression in 2 Sam. 12 : 31 does not necessarily imply torture, but the word "cut" in 1 Chron. 20 : 3 can hardly be understood otherwise.

Scapegoat. [ATONEMENT, DAY OF.]

Scarlet. [COLORS.]

Sceptre. This word originally meant a *rod* or *staff.* It was thence specifically applied to the shepherd's crook, Lev. 27 : 32; Micah 7 : 14, and to the wand or sceptre of a ruler. The allusions to it are all of a metaphorical character, and describe it simply as one of the insignia of supreme power. Gen. 49 : 10. We are consequently unable to describe the article from any biblical notice; we may infer that it was probably made of wood. The sceptre of the Persian monarch is described as "golden," *i. e.* probably of massive gold. Esther 4 : 11.

Sce′va, a Jew residing at Ephesus at the time of St. Paul's second visit to that town. Acts 19 : 14–16. (A.D. 52.)

Schools. (In the early ages most of the instruction of young children was by the parents. The leisure hours of the Sabbaths and festival days brought the parents in constant contact with the children. After the captivity schools came more into use, and at the time of Christ were very abundant. The schools were in connection with the synagogues, which were found in every city and in almost every village of the land. Their idea of the value of schools may be gained from such sayings from the Talmud as "The world is preserved by the breath of the children in the schools;" "A town

in which there are no schools must perish;" "Jerusalem was destroyed because the education of children was neglected." Josephus says, "Our principal care is to educate our children." The Talmud states that in Bechar there were 400 schools, having each 400 teachers, with 400 children each, and that there were 4000 pupils in the house of Rabban Simeon Ben-Gamaliel. Maimonides thus describes a school: "The teacher sat at the head, and the pupils surrounded him as the crown the head, so that every one could see the teacher and hear his words. The teacher did not sit in a chair while the pupils sat on the ground, but all either sat on chairs or on the ground." The children read aloud to acquire fluency. The number of school-hours was limited, and during the heat of the summer was only four hours. The punishment employed was beating with a strap, never with a rod. The chief studies were their own language and literature, the chief school-book the Holy Scriptures;

Scorpion.

and there were special efforts to impress lessons of morality and chastity. Besides these they studied mathematics, astronomy and the natural sciences. Beyond the schools for popular education there were higher schools or colleges scattered throughout the cities where the Jews abounded.—ED.)

Scorpion (Heb. *'akráb*), a well-known venomous insect of hot climates, shaped much like a lobster. It is usually not more than two or three inches long, but in tropical climates is sometimes six inches in length. The wilderness of Sinai is especially alluded to as being inhabited by scorpions at the time of the exodus, and to this day these animals are common in the same district, as well as in some parts of Palestine. Scorpions are generally found in dry and in dark places, under stones and in ruins. They are carnivorous in their habits, and move along in a threatening attitude, with the tail elevated. The sting, which is situated at the end of the tail, has at its base a gland that secretes a poisonous fluid, which is discharged into the wound by two minute orifices at its extremity. In hot climates the sting often occasions much suffering, and sometimes alarming symptoms. The "scorpions" of 1 Kings 12 : 11, 14; 2 Chron. 10 : 11, 14, have clearly no allusion whatever to the animal, but to some instrument of scourging —unless indeed the expression is a mere figure.

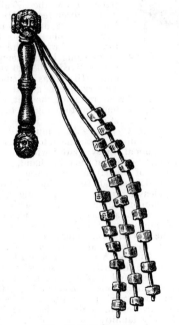

Flagellum or Scourge.

Scourging. The punishment of scourging was common among the Jews. The instrument of punishment in ancient Egypt, as it is also in modern times generally in the East, was usually the stick, applied to the soles of the feet —bastinado. Under the Roman method the culprit was stripped, stretched with cords or thongs on a frame and beaten with rods. (Another form of the scourge consisted of a handle with three lashes or

Scourging.

thongs of leather or cord, sometimes with pieces of metal fastened to them. Roman citizens were exempt by their law from scourging.)

Scribes (Heb. *sôpherim*). I. *Name.*— (1) Three meanings are connected with the verb *sâphar*, the root of *sôpherim*— (*a*) to write, (*b*) to set in order, (*c*) to count. The explanation of the word has been referred to each of these. The *sôpherim* were so called because they wrote out the law, or because they classified and arranged its precepts, or because they counted with scrupulous minuteness every clause and letter it contained. (2) The name of Kirjath-sepher, Josh. 15 : 15; Judges 1 : 12, may possibly connect itself with some early use of the title, and appears to point to military functions of some kind. Judges 5 : 14. The men are mentioned as filling the office of scribe under David and Solomon. 2 Sam. 8 : 17; 20 : 25; 1 Kings 4 : 3. We may think of them as the king's secretaries, writing his letters, drawing up his decrees, managing his finances. Comp. 2 Kings 12 : 10. In Hezekiah's time they transcribed old records, and became a class of students and interpreters of the law, boasting of their wisdom. Jer. 8 : 8. After the captivity the office became more prominent, as the exiles would be anxious above all things to preserve the sacred books, the laws, the hymns, the prophecies of the past. II. *Development of doctrine.*—Of the scribes of this period, with the exception of Ezra and Zadok, Neh. 13 : 13, we have no record. A later age honored them collectively as the men of the Great Synagogue. Never, perhaps, was so important a work done so silently. They devoted themselves to the careful study of the text, and laid down rules for transcribing it with the most scrupulous precision. As time passed on the " words of the scribes " were honored above the law. It was a greater crime to offend against them than against the law. The first step was taken toward annulling the commandments of God for the sake of their own traditions. Mark 7 : 13. The casuistry became at once subtle and prurient, evading the

Scribes.

plainest duties, tampering with conscience. Matt. 15 : 1–6; 23 : 16–23. We can therefore understand why they were constantly denounced by our Lord along

A Jewish Scribe.

with the Pharisees. While the scribes repeated the traditions of the elders, he "spake as one having authority," "not as the scribes." Matt. 7 : 29. While they confined their teachings to the class of scholars, he "had compassion on the multitudes." Matt. 9 : 36. While they were to be found only in the council or in their schools, he journeyed through the cities and villages. Matt. 4 : 23; 9 : 35, etc. While they spoke of the kingdom of God vaguely, as a thing far off, he proclaimed that it had already come nigh to men. Matt. 4 : 17. In our Lord's time there were two chief parties: 1, the disciples of Shammai, conspicuous for their fierceness, appealing to popular passions, using the sword to decide their controversies. Out of this party grew the Zealots. 2. The disciples of Hillel, born B.C. 112, and who may have been one of the doctors before whom the boy Jesus came in the temple, for he lived to be 120 years old. Hillel was a "liberal conservative, of genial character and broad range of thought, with some approximations to a higher teaching." In most of the points at issue between the two parties, Jesus must have appeared in direct antagonism to the school of Shammai, in sympathy with that of Hillel. So far, on the other hand, as the temper of the Hillel school was one of mere adaptation to the feeling of the people, cleaving to tradition, wanting in the intuition of a higher life, the teaching of Christ must have been felt as unsparingly condemning it. III. *Education and life.* —The special training for a scribe's office began, probably, about the age of thirteen. The boy who was destined by his parents to the calling of a scribe went to Jerusalem and applied for admission in the school of some famous rabbi. After a sufficient period of training, probably at the age of thirty the probationer was solemnly admitted to his office. After his admission there was a choice of a variety of functions, the chances of failure and success. He might give himself to any one of the branches of study, or combine two or more of them. He might rise to high places, become a doctor of the law, an arbitrator in family litigations, Luke 12 : 14, the head of a school, a member of the Sanhedrin. He might have to content himself with the humbler work of a transcriber, copying the law and the prophets for the use of synagogues, or a notary, writing out contracts of sale, covenants of espousals, bills of repudiation. The position of the more fortunate was of course attractive enough. In our Lord's time the passion for distinction was insatiable. The ascending scale of rab, rabbi, rabban, presented so many steps on the ladder of ambition. Other forms of worldliness were not far off. The salutations in the market-place, Matt. 23 : 7, the reverential kiss offered by the scholars to their master or by rabbis to each other, the greeting of Abba, father, Matt. 23 : 9, the long robes with the broad blue fringe, Matt. 23 : 5,—all these go to make up the picture of a scribe's life. Drawing to themselves, as they did, nearly all the energy and thought of Judaism, the close hereditary caste of the priesthood was powerless to compete with them. Unless the priest became a scribe also, he remained in obscurity. The order, as such, became contemptible and base. For the scribes there were the best places at feasts, the chief seats in synagogues. Matt. 23 : 6; Luke 14 : 7.

Scrip. The Hebrew word thus translated appears in 1 Sam. 17 : 40 as a synonym for the bag in which the shepherds of Palestine carried their food or other necessaries. The scrip of the Galilean peasants was of leather, used especially to carry their food on a journey, and slung over their shoulders. Matt. 10 : 10; Mark 6 : 8; Luke 9 : 3; 22 : 35. The English word "scrip" is probably connected with *scrape*, *scrap*, and was used in like manner for articles of food.

Scripture. [See BIBLE.]

Scyth'ian occurs in Col. 3 : 11 as a generalized term for rude, ignorant, degraded. The name often included all the nomadic tribes, who dwelt mostly on the north of the Black and the Caspian Sea, stretching thence indefinitely into inner Asia, and were regarded by the ancients as standing extremely low in point of intelligence and civilization.

Scythop'olis. [BETH-SHEAN.]

Sea. The sea, *yâm*, is used in Scripture to denote—1. "The gathering of the waters," "the Ocean." Gen. 1 : 2, 10; Deut. 30 : 13, etc. 2. Some portion of this, as the Mediterranean Sea, called the "hinder," the "western" and the "utmost" sea, Deut. 11 : 24; 34 : 2; Joel 2 :

20; "sea of the Philistines," Ex. 23 : 31; "the great sea," Num. 34 : 6, 7; Josh. 15 : 47; "the sea." Gen. 49 : 13; Ps. 80 : 11. Also frequently of the Red Sea. Ex. 15 : 4. [RED SEA.] 3. Inland lakes termed seas, as the Salt or Dead Sea. [See the special article.] 4. Any great collection of waters, as the river Nile, Isa. 19 : 5 and the Euphrates. Jer. 51 : 36.

The Brazen or Molten Sea.

Sea, Molten. In the place of the laver of the tabernacle, Solomon caused a laver to be cast for a similar purpose, which from its size was called a sea. It was made partly or wholly of the brass, or rather copper, which was captured by David from "Tibhath and Chun, cities of Hadarezer king of Zobah." 1 Kings 7 : 23–26; 1 Chron. 18 : 8. It is said to have been 15 feet in diameter and 7½ feet deep, and to have been capable of containing 2000, or, according to 2 Chron. 4 : 5, 3000 baths (16,000 to 24,000 gallons). The laver stood on twelve oxen, three toward each quarter of the heavens, and all looking outward. It was mutilated by Ahaz by being removed from its basis of oxen and placed on a stone base, and was finally broken up by the Assyrians. 2 Kings 16 : 14, 17; 25 : 13.

Sea, The Salt, the usual and perhaps the most ancient name for the remarkable lake which to the western world is now generally known as the Dead Sea.

I. *Names.*—(1) The Salt Sea, Gen. 14 : 3; (2) Sea of the Arabah (Authorized Version "sea of the plain," which is found in Deut. 4 : 49); (3) The East Sea, Joel 2 : 20; (4) The sea, Ezek. 47 : 8; (5) Sodomitish Sea, 2 Esdras; (6) Sea of salt, and Sea of Sodom, in the Talmud; (7) The Asphaltic Lake, in Josephus; (8) The name "Dead Sea" appears to have been first used in Greek by Pausanias and Galen, and in Latin (*mare mortuum*) by Justin xxxvi. 3, § 6, or rather by the older historian Trogus Pompeius (*cir.* B.C. 10),

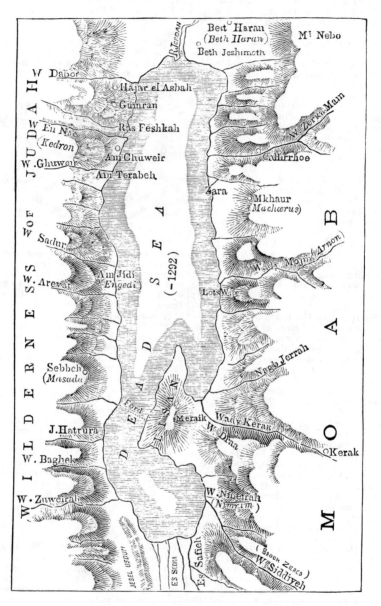

The Salt or Dead Sea. *After a Sketch by Major Wilson.*

(The figures denote the depression below the Mediterranean Sea.)

whose work he epitomized. (9) The Arabic name is *Bahr Lût*, the "Sea of Lot."

II. *Description.*—The so-called Dead Sea is the final receptacle of the river Jordan, the lowest and largest of the three lakes which interrupt the rush of its downward course. It is the deepest portion of that very deep natural fissure which runs like a furrow from the Gulf of Akabah to the range of Lebanon, and from the range of Lebanon to the extreme north of Syria. Viewed on the map, the lake is of an oblong form, of tolerably regular contour, interrupted only by a large and long peninsula which projects from the eastern shore near its southern end, and virtually divides the expanse of the water into two portions, connected by a long, narrow and somewhat devious passage. Its surface is from north to south as nearly as possible 40 geographical or 46 English miles long. Its great-

Dead Sea.

est width is about 9 geographical or 10½ English miles. Its area is about 250 geographical square miles. At its northern end the lake receives the stream of the Jordan ; on its eastern side the *Zúrka Ma'in* (the ancient Callirrhoë, and possibly the more ancient en-Eglaim), the *Mojib* (the Arnon of the Bible), and the *Beni-Hemâd;* on the south the *Kurâhy* or *el-Ahsy;* and on the west that of *Ain Jidy.* The depression of its surface, and the depth which it attains below that surface, combined with the absence of any outlet, render it one of the most remarkable spots on the globe. The sur-

face of the lake in May, 1848, was 1316.7 feet below the level of the Mediterranean at Jaffa. Its depth, at about one third of its length from the north end, is 1308 feet. The water of the lake is not less remarkable than its other features. Its most obvious peculiarity is its great weight. Its specific gravity has been found to be as much as 12.28; that is to say, a gallon of it would weigh over 12¼ lbs., instead of 10 lbs., the weight of distilled water. Water so heavy must not only be extremely buoyant, but must possess great inertia. Its buoyancy is a common theme of remark by the travel-

lers who have been upon it or in it. Dr.
Robinson "could never swim before,
either in fresh or salt water," yet here he
"could sit, stand, lie or swim without
difficulty." (*B. R.* i. 506.) The remarkable weight of the water is due to the
very large quantity of mineral salts which
it holds in solution. Each gallon of the
water, weighing 12¼ lbs., contains nearly
3½ lbs. of matter in solution—an immense
quantity when we recollect that sea-
water, weighing 10¼ lbs. per gallon, contains less than ½ a lb. Of this 3½ lbs.
nearly 1 lb. is common salt (chloride of
sodium), about 2 lbs. chloride of magne-
sium, and less than ½ a lb. chloride of
calcium (or muriate of lime). The most
usual ingredient is bromide of magne-
sium, which exists in truly extraordinary
quantity. It has been long supposed that
no life whatever existed in the lake ; but
recent facts show that some inferior or-
ganizations do find a home even in these
salt and acrid waters. The statements of
ancient travellers and geographers to the
effect that no living creature could exist
on the shores of the lake, or bird fly
across its surface, are amply disproved
by later travellers. The springs on the
margin of the lake harbor snipe, part-
ridges, ducks, nightingales and other
birds, as well as frogs ; and hawks, doves
and hares are found along the shore.
The appearance of the lake does not fulfill the idea conveyed by its popular
name. "The Dead Sea," says a recent
traveller, "did not strike me with that
sense of desolation and dreariness which
I suppose it ought. I thought it a pretty,
smiling lake—a nice ripple on its surface." The truth lies, as usual, somewhere between these two extremes. On
the one hand, the lake certainly is not a
gloomy, deadly, smoking gulf. In this
respect it does not at all fulfill the promise of its name. At sunrise and sunset the
scene must be astonishingly beautiful.
But on the other hand, there is something
in the prevalent sterility and the dry,
burnt look of the shores, the overpower-
ing heat, the occasional smell of sulphur,
the dreary salt marsh at the southern
end, and the fringe of dead driftwood
round the margin, which must go far to
excuse the title which so many ages have
attached to the lake, and which we may
be sure it will never lose. The connection between this singular lake and the
biblical history is very slight. In the
topographical records of the Pentateuch
and the book of Joshua it forms one
among the landmarks of the boundaries
of the whole country, as well as of the
inferior divisions of Judah and Benjamin.
As a landmark it is once named in what
appears to be a quotation from a lost
work of the prophet Jonah, 2 Kings 14:
25, itself apparently a reminiscence of the
old Mosaic statement. Num. 34 : 8, 12.
Besides this the name occurs once or
twice in the imagery of the prophets. In
the New Testament there is not even an
allusion to it. There is, however, one
passage in which the "Salt Sea" is mentioned in a manner different from any of
those already quoted, viz. as having been
in the time of Abraham the vale of Siddim. Gen. 14 : 3. In consequence of this
passage it has been believed that the
present lake covered a district which in
historic times had been permanently
habitable dry land. But it must not be
overlooked that the passage in question
is the only one in the whole Bible to
countenance the notion that the cities of
the plain were submerged ; a notion which
does not date earlier than the Christian
era. [SODOM ; ZOAR.] The belief which
prompted the idea of some modern writers that the Dead Sea was formed by the
catastrophe which overthrew the "cities
of the plain" is a mere assumption. It
is not only unsupported by Scripture, but
is directly in the teeth of the evidence of
the ground itself. Of the situation of
those cities, we only know that, being in
the "plain of the Jordan," they must
have been to the north of the lake. Of
the catastrophe which destroyed them,
we only know that it is described as a
shower of ignited sulphur descending
from the skies. Its date is uncertain, but
we shall be safe in placing it within the
limit of 2000 years before Christ. (It is
supposed that only the southern bay of
the Dead Sea was formed by the submerg-
ence of the cities of the plain, and this
is still probable. If Hugh Miller's theory of the flood is correct—and it is the
most reasonable theory yet propounded—
then the Dead Sea was formed by the depression of that part of the valley through
which the Jordan once flowed to the
Red Sea. But this great depression caused
all the waters of the Jordan to remain
without outlet, and the size of the Dead
Sea must be such that the evaporation
from its surface just balances the amount
of water which flows in through the river.
This accounts in part for the amount of

matter held in solution by the Dead Sea waters; for the evaporation is of pure water only, while the inflow contains more or less of salts and other matter in solution. This theory also renders it probable that the lake was at first considerably larger than at present, for in earlier times the Jordan had probably a larger flow of water.—ED.) The destruction of Sodom and Gomorrah may have been by volcanic action, but it may be safely asserted that no traces of it have yet been discovered, and that, whatever it was, it can have had no connection with that far vaster and far more ancient event which opened the great valley of the Jordan and the Dead Sea, and at some subsequent time cut it off from communication with the Red Sea by forcing up between them the tract of the *Wady Arabah.*

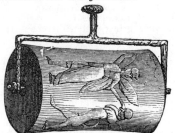

Seal with Frame.

Seal. The importance attached to seals in the East is so great that without one no document is regarded as authentic.

Seal and Signets.

Among the methods of sealing used in Egypt at a very early period were en-graved stones, pierced through their length and hung by a string or chain from the arm or neck, or set in rings for the finger. The most ancient form used for this purpose was the scarabæus, formed of precious or common stone, or even of blue pottery or porcelain, on the flat side of which the inscription or device was engraved. In many cases the seal consisted of a lump of clay, impressed with the seal and attached to the document, whether of papyrus or other material, by strings. In other cases wax was used. In sealing a sepulchre or box, the fastening was covered with clay or wax, and the impression from a seal of one in authority was stamped upon it, so that it could not be broken open without discovery. The signet-ring was an ordinary part of a man's equipment. Gen. 38 : 18. The ring or the seal as an emblem of authority in Egypt, Persia and elsewhere is mentioned in Gen. 41 : 42 ; 1 Kings 21 : 8 ; Esther 3 : 10, 12 ; 8 : 2 ; Dan. 6 : 17 ; and as an evidence of a covenant, in Jer. 32 : 10, 44; Neh. 9 : 38 ; 10 : 1 ; Hag. 2 : 23. Engraved signets were in use among the Hebrews in early times. Ex. 28 : 11, 36 ; 39 : 6.

Se'ba (pl. *Sebaim ;* in Authorized Version incorrectly rendered Sabeans) heads the list of the sons of Cush. Besides the mention of Seba in the lists of the sons of Cush, Gen. 10 : 7 ; 1 Chron. 1 : 9, there are but three notices of the nation—Ps. 72 : 10 ; Isa. 43 : 3 ; 45 : 14. These passages seem to show that Seba was a nation of Africa, bordering on or included in Cush, and in Solomon's time independent and of political importance. It may perhaps be identified with the island of Meroë. Josephus says that Saba was the ancient name of the Ethiopian island and city of Meroë, but he writes Seba, in the notice of the Noachian settlements, Sabas. The island of Meroë lay between the Astaboras, the Atbara, the most northern tributary of the Nile, and the Astapus, the Bahr el-Azrak or " Blue River," the eastern of its two great confluents.

Se'bat (*a rod*). [MONTH.]

Sec'acah, or **Seca'cah** (*thicket*), one of the six cities of Judah which were situated in the *Midbar* (" wilderness "), that is, the tract bordering on the Dead Sea. Josh. 15 : 61. Its position is not known.

Se'chu (*the watch-tower*), a place mentioned once only—1 Sam. 19 : 22—apparently as lying on the route between Saul's residence, Gibeah, and Ramah (Ramathaim-zophim), that of Samuel. It was notorious for "the great well" (or rather cistern) which it contained. Assuming that Saul started from Gibeah (*Tuleil el-Ful*), and that *Neby Samwil* is Ramah, then *Bir Nebalta* (the well of Neballa), just south of Beeroth, alleged by a modern traveller to contain a large pit, would be in a suitable position for the great well of Sechu.

Secun'dus (*fortunate*), a Thessalonian Christian. Acts 20 : 4. (A.D. 55.)

Seer. [PROPHET.]

Se'gub (*elevated*). 1. The youngest son of Hiel the Bethelite, who rebuilt Jericho. 1 Kings 16 : 34. (B.C. about 910.) 2. Son of Hezron. 1 Chron. 2 : 21, 22. (B.C. about 1682.)

Se'ir (*hairy, shaggy*). 1. We have both "land of Seir," Gen. 32 : 3 ; 36 : 30, and "Mount Seir." Gen. 14 : 6. It is the original name of the mountain range extending along the east side of the valley of Arabah, from the Dead Sea to the Elanitic Gulf. The Horites appear to have been the chief of the aboriginal inhabitants, Gen. 36 : 20 ; but it was ever afterward the possession of the Edomites, the descendants of Esau. The Mount Seir of the Bible extended much farther south than the modern province, as is shown by the words of Deut. 2 : 1–8. It had the Arabah on the west, vs. 1 and 8 ; it extended as far south as the head of the Gulf of Akabah, ver. 8 ; its eastern border ran along the base of the mountain range where the plateau of Arabia begins. Its northern border is not so accurately determined. There is a line of "naked" white hills or cliffs which run across the great valley about eight miles south of the Dead Sea, the highest eminence being Mount Hor, which is 4800 feet high. 2. Mount Seir, an entirely different place from the foregoing ; one of the landmarks on the north boundary of the territory of Judah. Josh. 15 : 10 only. It lay westward of Kirjath-jearim, and between it and Beth-shemesh. If *Kuriel el-Enab* be the former and *Ain-shems* the latter of these two, then Mount Seir cannot fail to be the ridge which lies between the *Wady Aly* and the *Wady Ghurab*. In a pass of this ridge is the modern village of *Sair*.

Se'irath (*the shaggy*), the place to which Ehud fled after his murder of Eglon. Judges 3 : 26, 27. It was in "Mount Ephraim," ver. 27, a continuation, perhaps, of the same wooded, shaggy hills which stretched even so far south as

to enter the territory of Judah. Josh. 15 : 10. (It is probably the same place as MOUNT SEIR, 2.)

Se'la, or **Se'lah** (*the rock*), 2 Kings 14 : 7 ; Isa. 16 : 1 ; so rendered in the Authorized Version in Judges 1 : 36 ; 2 Chron. 25 : 12 ; probably the city later known as Petra, the ruins of which are found about two days journey north of the top of the Gulf of Akabah, and three or four south from Jericho, and about halfway between the southern end of the Dead Sea and the northern end of the Gulf of Akabah. It was in the midst of Mount Seir, in the neighborhood of Mount Hor, and therefore Edomite territory, taken by Amaziah, and called Joktheel. In the end of the fourth century B.C. it appears as the headquarters of the Nabatheans, who successfully resisted the attacks of Antigonus. About 70 B.C. Petra appears as the residence of the Arab princes named Aretas. It was by Trajan reduced to subjection to the Roman empire. The city Petra lay, though at a high level, in a hollow three quarters of a mile long and from 800 to 1500 feet wide, shut in by mountain cliffs, and approached only by a narrow ravine, through which, and across the city's site, the river winds. There are extensive ruins at Petra of Roman date, which have been frequently described by modern travellers.

Se'la-Hammahle'koth (*the cliff of escapes* or *of divisions*), a rock or cliff in the wilderness of Maon, southeast of Hebron, the scene of one of those remarkable escapes which are so frequent in the history of Saul's pursuit of David. 1 Sam. 23 : 28.

Se'lah. This word, which is found only in the poetical books of the Old Testament, occurs seventy-one times in the Psalms and three times in Habakkuk. It is probably a term which had a meaning in the musical nomenclature of the Hebrews, though what that meaning may have been is now a matter of pure conjecture. (Gesenius and Ewald and others think it has much the same meaning as our *interlude*,—a pause in the voices singing, while the instruments perform alone.)

Se'led (*exultation*), one of the sons of Nadab, a descendant of Jerahmeel. 1 Chron. 2 : 30. (B.C. after 1450.)

Sele-u'cia, or **Sele-uci'a** (named after its founder, Seleucus), near the mouth of the Orontes, was practically the seaport of Antioch. The distance between the two towns was about 16 miles. St. Paul, with Barnabas, sailed from Seleucia at the beginning of his first missionary circuit. Acts 13 : 4. This strong fortress and convenient seaport was constructed by the first Seleucus, and here he was buried. It retained its importance in Roman times, and in St. Paul's day it had the privileges of a free city. The remains are numerous.

Sele-u′cus, the name of five kings of the Greek dominion of Syria, who are hence called *Seleucidæ.* Only one—the fourth—is mentioned in the Apocrypha.

Sele-u′cus IV. (Philopator), son of Antiochus the Great, whom he succeeded B.C. 187, "king of Asia," 2 Macc. 3 : 3, that is, of the provinces included in the Syrian monarchy, according to the title claimed by the Seleucidæ, even when they had lost their footing in Asia Minor. He took part in the disastrous battle of Magnesia, B.C. 190, and three years afterward, on the death of his father, ascended the throne. He was murdered B.C. 175, after a reign of twelve years, by Heliodorus, one of his own courtiers. Dan. 11 : 20. His son Demetrius I. (Soter), whom he had sent, while still a boy, as hostage to Rome, after a series of romantic adventures, gained the crown in 162 B.C. 1 Macc. 7 : 1; 2 Macc. 14 : 1. The general policy of Seleucus toward the Jews, like that of his father, 2 Macc. 3 : 2, 3, was conciliatory, and he undertook a large share of the expenses of the temple service. 2 Macc. 3 : 3, 6.

Sem. SHEM the patriarch. Luke 3 : 36.

Semachi′ah (*Jehovah sustains him*), one of the sons of SHEMAIAH, 9. 1 Chron. 26 : 7.

Sem′ei (the Greek form of Shimei). 1. SHIMEI, 14. 1 Esd. 9 : 33.

2. SHIMEI, 16. Esther 11 : 2.

3. The father of Mattathias in the genealogy of Jesus Christ. Luke 3 : 26.

Sem′ein. In the Revised Version of Luke 3 : 26 for Semei.

Semit′ic Languages. [SHEMITIC LANGUAGES; HEBREW.]

Sen′a-ah (*thorny*). The "children (*i. e.* the inhabitants) of Senaah" are enumerated among the "people of Israel" who returned from the captivity with Zerubbabel. Ezra 2 : 35; Neh. 7 : 38. (B.C. 536.) The Magdal Senna of Eusebius and Jerome denotes a town seven miles north of Jericho ("Senna").

Se′neh (*thorn*), the name of one of the two isolated rocks which stood in the "passage of Michmash," 1 Sam. 14 : 4, 6½ miles north of Jerusalem.

Se′nir (*snow mountain*), 1 Chron. 5 : 23; Ezek. 27 : 5, the Amorite name for Mount Hermon.

Sennacherib on his Throne.

Sennach′erib, or **Sennache′rib** (*sin,* the moon, *increases brothers*), was the son and successor of Sargon. [SARGON.] His name in the original is read as *Tsinakki-irib,* the meaning of which, as given above, indicates that he was not the first-born of his father. Sennacherib mounted the throne B.C. 702. His efforts were directed to crushing the revolt of Babylonia, which he invaded with a large army. Merodach-baladan ventured on a battle, but was defeated and driven from the country. In his third year, B.C. 700, Sennacherib turned his arms toward the west, chastised Sidon, and, having probably concluded a convention with his chief enemy, finally marched against Hezekiah, king of Judah. It was at this time that "Sennacherib came up against all the fenced cities of Judah, and took them." 2 Kings 18 : 13. There can be no doubt that the record which he has left of his campaign against "Hiskiah" in his third year is the war with Hezekiah so briefly touched in vs. 13–16 of this chapter. In the following year (B.C. 699) Sennacherib made his second expedition into Palestine. Hezekiah had again revolted, and claimed the protection of Egypt. Sennacherib therefore attacked Egypt, and from his camp at Lachish and Libnah he sent an insulting letter to Hezekiah at Jerusalem. In answer to Hezekiah's prayer an event occurred which relieved both Egypt and Judea from their danger. In one night the Assyrians lost, either by a pestilence or by some more awful manifestation of divine power, 185,000 men! The camp immediately broke up; the king fled. Sennacherib reached his capital in safety, and was not deterred by the terrible disaster which had befallen his arms from engaging in other wars, though he seems thenceforward to have carefully avoided Palestine. Sennacherib reigned 22 years, and was succeeded by Esar-haddon, B.C. 680. Sennacherib was one of the most magnificent of the Assyrian kings. He seems to have been the first who fixed the seat of government permanently at Nineveh, which he carefully repaired and adorned with splendid buildings. His greatest work is the grand palace at Kouyunjik. Of the death of Sennacherib nothing is known beyond the brief statement of Scripture that "as he was worshipping in the house of Nisroch his god, Adrammelech and Sharezer his sons smote him with the sword, and escaped into the land of Armenia." 2 Kings 19 : 37 ; Isa. 37 : 38.

Sen'uah (*bristling*, properly Hassenuah, with the definite article), a Benjamite. Neh. 11 : 9.

Seo'rim (*barley*), the chief of the fourth of the twenty-four courses of priests. 1 Chron. 24 : 8.

Se'phar (*a numbering*). It is written, after the enumeration of the sons of Joktan, "And their dwelling was from Mesha as thou goest unto Sephar, a mount of the east." Gen. 10 : 30. The Joktanites occupied the southwestern portion of the peninsula of Arabia. The undoubted identifications of Arabian places and tribes with their Joktanite originals are included within these limits, and point to Sephar, on the shore of the Indian Ocean, as the eastern boundary. The ancient seaport town called *Zafár* represents the biblical site or district.

Seph'arad (*separated*), a name which occurs in Obad. ver. 20 only. Its situation has always been a matter of uncertainty.

Sepharva'im (*the two Sipparas*) is mentioned by Sennacherib in his letter to Hezekiah as a city whose king had been unable to resist the Assyrians. 2 Kings 19 : 13 ; Isa. 37 : 13, comp. 2 Kings 18 : 34. It is identified with the famous town of Sippara, on the Euphrates above Babylon, which was near the site of the modern *Mosaib*. The dual form indicates that there were two Sipparas, one on either side of the river. Berosus called Sippara "a city of the sun ;" and in the inscriptions it bears the same title, being called *Tsipar sha Shamas*, or "Sippara of the Sun"—the sun being the chief object of worship there. Comp. 2 Kings 17 : 31.

Sephe'la, the Greek form of the ancient word *has-Shěfêláh*, the native name for the southern division of the low-lying flat district which intervenes between the central highlands of the holy land and the Mediterranean, the other and northern portion of which was known as Sharon. The name occurs throughout the topographical records of Joshua, the historical works, and the topographical passages in the prophets; always with the article prefixed, and always denoting the same region. In each of these passages, however, the word is treated in the Authorized Version not as a proper name, analogous to *the Campagna, the Wolds, the Curse*, but as a mere appellative, and rendered "the vale," "the valley," "the plain," "the low plains," and "the low country." The Shefelah was and is one of the most productive regions of the holy land. It was in ancient times the cornfield of Syria, and as such the constant subject of warfare between Philistines and Israelites, and the refuge of the latter when the harvests in the central country were ruined by drought. 2 Kings 8 : 1–3.

Sep'tuagint (*the seventy*). The Septuagint or Greek version of the Old Testament appears at the present day in four principal editions:—1. Biblia Polyglotta Complutensis, A.D. 1514–1517. 2. The Aldine Edition, Venice, A.D. 1518. 3. The Roman Edition, edited under Pope Sixtus V., A.D. 1587. 4. Fac-simile Edition of the Codex Alexandrinus, by H. H. Baber, A.D. 1816. [TARGUMS.] The Jews of Alexandria had probably still less knowledge of Hebrew than their brethren in Palestine; their familiar language was Alexandrian Greek. They had settled in Alexandria in large numbers soon after the time of Alexander, and under the early Ptolemies. They would naturally follow the same practice as the Jews in Palestine; and **hence** would arise in time an entire Greek version. But the numbers and names of the translators, and the times at which different portions were translated, are all uncertain. The commonly-received story respecting its origin is contained in an extant letter ascribed to Aristeas, who was an officer at the court of Ptolemy Philadelphus. This letter, which is addressed by Aristeas to his brother Philocrates, gives a glowing account of the origin of the Septuagint; of the embassy and presents sent by King Ptolemy to the high priest at Jerusalem, by the advice of Demetrius Phalereus, his librarian, 50 talents of gold and 70 talents of silver, etc.; the Jewish slaves whom he set free, paying their ransom himself; the letter of the king; the answer of the high priest; the choosing of six interpreters from each of the twelve tribes, and their names; the copy of the law, in letters of gold; the feast prepared for the seventy-two, which continued for seven days; the questions proposed to each of the interpreters in turn, with the answers of each; their lodging by the seashore; and the accomplishment of their work in seventy-two days, by conference and comparison. This is the story which probably gave to the version the title of the Septuagint, and which has been repeated in various forms by the Christian writers. But it is now generally admitted that the letter is spurious, and is probably the fabrication of an Alexandrian Jew shortly before the Christian era. Still there can be no doubt that there was a basis of fact for the fiction; on three points of the story there is no material difference of opinion, and they are confirmed by the study of the version itself:—1. The version was made at Alexandria. 2. It was begun in the time of the earlier Ptolemies, about 280 B.C. 3. The law (*i. e.* the Pentateuch) alone was translated at first. The Septuagint version was highly esteemed by the Hellenistic Jews before the coming of Christ. Wherever, by the conquests of Alexander or by colonization, the Greek language prevailed, wherever Jews were settled, and the attention of the neighboring Gentiles was drawn to their wondrous history and law, there was found the Septuagint, which thus became, by divine Providence, the means of spreading widely the knowledge of the one true God, and his promises of a Saviour to come, throughout the nations.

To the wide dispersion of this version we may ascribe in great measure that general persuasion which prevailed over the whole East of the near approach of the Redeemer, and led the Magi to recognize the star which proclaimed the birth of the King of the Jews. Not less wide was the influence of the Septuagint in the spread of the gospel. For a long period the Septuagint was the Old Testament of the far larger part of the Christian Church. *Character of the Septuagint.—* The Septuagint is faithful in substance, but not minutely accurate in details. It has been clearly shown by Hody, Frankel and others that the several books were translated by different persons, without any comprehensive revision to harmonize the several parts. Names and words are rendered differently in different books. Thus the character of the version varies much in the several books; those of the Pentateuch are the best. The poetical parts are, generally speaking, inferior to the historical, the original abounding with rarer words and expressions. In the major prophets (probably translated nearly 100 years after the Pentateuch) some of the most important prophecies are sadly obscured. Ezekiel and the minor prophets (generally speaking) seem to be better rendered. Supposing the numerous glosses and duplicate renderings, which have evidently crept from the margin into the text, to be removed, and forming a rough estimate of what the Septuagint was in its earliest state, we may perhaps say of it that it is the image of the original seen through a glass not adjusted to the proper focus; the larger features are shown, but the sharpness of definition is lost. The close connection between the Old and the New Testament makes the study of the Septuagint most valuable, and indeed indispensable, to the theological student. It was manifestly the chief storehouse from which the apostles drew their proofs and precepts.

Sepulchre. [BURIAL.]

Se′rah, the daughter of Asher, Gen. 46: 17; 1 Chron. 7: 30, called in Num. 26: 46 SARAH. (B.C. about 1700.)

Sera′iah. 1. The king's scribe or secretary in the reign of David. 2 Sam. 8: 17. (B.C. 1043.)

2. The high priest in the reign of Zedekiah. 2 Kings 25: 18; 1 Chron. 6: 14; Jer. 52: 24. (B.C. 594.)

3. The son of Tanhumeth the Netophathite. 2 Kings 25: 23; Jer. 40: 8.

4. The son of Kenaz and brother of Othniel. 1 Chron. 4 : 13, 14.

5. Ancestor of Jehu, a Simeonite chieftain. 1 Chron. 4 : 35.

6. One of the children of the province who returned with Zerubbabel. Ezra 2 : 2. (B.C. 536.)

7. One of the ancestors of Ezra the scribe. Ezra 7 : 1.

8. A priest, or priestly family, who signed the covenant with Nehemiah. Neh. 10 : 2.

9. A priest, the son of Hilkiah. Neh. 11 : 11.

10. The head of a priestly house which went up from Babylon with Zerubbabel. Neh. 12 : 12.

11. The son of Neriah, and brother of Baruch. Jer. 51 : 59, 61. He went with Zedekiah to Babylon in the fourth year of his reign. (B.C. 594.) Perhaps he was an officer who took charge of the royal caravan on its march, and fixed the places where it should halt.

Seraphim (*burning, glowing*), an order of celestial beings, whom Isaiah beheld in vision standing above Jehovah as he sat upon his throne. Isa. 6 : 2. They are described as having each of them three pairs of wings, with one of which they covered their faces (a token of humility); with the second they covered their feet (a token of respect); while with the third they flew. They seem to have borne a general resemblance to the human figure. ver. 6. Their occupation was twofold—to celebrate the praises of Jehovah's holiness and power, ver. 3, and to act as the medium of communication between heaven and earth. ver. 6.

Se'red (*fear*), the first-born of Zebulun. Gen. 46 : 14; Num. 26 : 26. (B.C. about 1700.)

Ser'gius Pau'lus was the proconsul of Cyprus when the apostle Paul visited that island with Barnabas on his first missionary tour. Acts 13 : 7, *seq.* (A.D. 44.) He is described as an intelligent man, truth-seeking, eager for information from all sources within his reach. Though at first admitting to his society Elymas the magian, he afterward, on becoming acquainted with the claims of the gospel, yielded his mind to the evidence of its truth.

Serpent. The Hebrew word *náchásh* is the generic name of any serpent. The following are the principal biblical allusions to this animal: Its subtlety is mentioned in Gen. 3 : 1; its wisdom is alluded

to by our Lord in Matt. 10 : 16; the poisonous properties of some species are often mentioned, see Ps. 58 : 4; Prov. 23 : 32; the sharp tongue of the serpent is mentioned in Ps. 140 : 3; Job 20 : 16; the

Serpent—denoting immortality.

habit serpents have of lying concealed in hedges and in holes of walls is alluded to in Eccles. 10 : 8; their dwelling in dry sandy places, in Deut. 8 : 15; their wonderful mode of progression did not escape the observation of the author of Prov. 30,

The Viper.

who expressly mentions it as "one of the three things which were too wonderful for him." ver. 19. The art of taming and charming serpents is of great antiquity, and is alluded to in Ps. 58 : 5;

Eccles. 10 : 11 ; Jer. 8 : 17, and doubtless intimated by St. James, James 3 : 7, who particularizes serpents among all other animals that " have been tamed by man." It was under the form of a serpent that the devil seduced Eve ; hence in Scripture Satan is called " the old serpent." Rev. 12 : 9, and comp. 2 Cor. 11 : 3. Hence, as a fruit of the tradition of the Fall, the serpent all through the East became the emblem of the spirit of evil, and is so pictured even on the monuments of Egypt. It has been supposed by many commentators that the serpent, prior to the Fall, moved along in an erect attitude. It is quite clear that an erect mode of progression is utterly incompatible with the structure of a serpent ; consequently, had the snakes before the Fall moved in an erect attitude, they must have been formed on a different plan altogether. The typical form of the serpent and its mode of progression were in all probability the same before the Fall as after it ; but subsequent to the Fall its form and progression were to be regarded with hatred and disgust by all mankind, and thus the animal was cursed " above all cattle," and a mark of condemnation was forever stamped upon it. Serpents are said in Scripture to " eat dust," see Gen. 3 : 14 ; Isa. 65 : 25 ; Micah 7 : 17 ; these animals, which for the most part take their food on the ground, do consequently swallow with it large portions of sand and dust. Throughout the East the serpent was used as an emblem of the evil principle, of the spirit of disobedience and contumacy. Much has been written on the question of the " fiery serpents " of Num. 21 : 6, 8, with which it is usual to erroneously identify the " fiery flying serpent " of Isa. 14 : 29 and 30 : 6. The word " fiery " probably signifies " burning," in allusion to the sensation produced by the bite. The *Cerastes*, or the *Naia haje*, or any other venomous species frequenting Arabia, may denote the " serpent of the burning bite " which destroyed the children of Israel. The snake that fastened on St. Paul's hand when he was at Melita, Acts 28 : 3, was probably the common viper of England, *Pelias berus*. [See also ADDER ; ASP.] When God punished the murmurs of the Israelites in the wilderness by sending among them serpents whose fiery bite was fatal, Moses, upon their repentance, was commanded to make a serpent of brass, whose polished surface shone like

fire, and to set it up on the banner-pole in the midst of the people ; and whoever was bitten by a serpent had but to look up at it and live. Num. 21 : 4-9. The comparison used by Christ, John 3 : 14, 15, adds a deep interest to this scene. To present the serpent form, as deprived of its power to hurt, impaled as the trophy of a conqueror, was to assert that evil, physical and spiritual, had been overcome, and thus help to strengthen the weak faith of the Israelites in a victory over both. Others look upon the uplifted serpent as a symbol of life and health, it having been so worshipped in Egypt. The two views have a point of contact, for the primary idea connected with the serpent is *wisdom*. Wisdom, apart from obedience to God, degenerates to cunning, and degrades and envenoms man's nature. Wisdom, yielding to the divine law, is the source of healing and restoring influences, and the serpent form thus became a symbol of deliverance and health ; and the Israelites were taught that it would be so with them in proportion as they ceased to be sensual and rebellious. Preserved as a relic, whether on the spot of its first erection or elsewhere, the brazen serpent, called by the name of *Nehushtan*, became an object of idolatrous veneration, and the zeal of Hezekiah destroyed it with the other idols of his father. 2 Kings 18 : 4. [NEHUSHTAN.]

Se′rug (*branch*), son of Reu and greatgrandfather of Abraham. His age is given in the Hebrew Bible as 230 years. Gen. 11 : 20-23. (B.C. 2180.)

Servant. [SLAVE.]

Seth (*compensation*), Gen. 4 : 25 ; 5 : 3 ; 1 Chron. 1 : 1, the third son of Adam, and father of Enos. (B.C. 3870.) Adam handed down to Seth and his descendants the promise of mercy, faith in which became the distinction of God's children. Gen. 4 : 26.

Se′thur (*hidden*), the Asherite spy, son of Michael. Num. 13 : 13. (B.C. 1490.)

Seven. The frequent recurrence of certain numbers in the sacred literature of the Hebrews is obvious to the most superficial reader ; but seven so far surpasses the rest, both in the frequency with which it recurs and in the importance of the objects with which it is associated, that it may fairly be termed the *representative* symbolic number. The influence of the number seven was not restricted to the Hebrews ; it prevailed among the Persians, ancient Indians, Greeks and Romans. The peculiarity of the Hebrew view consists in the special dignity of the *seventh*, and not simply in that of *seven*. The Sabbath being the seventh day suggested the adoption of seven as the *coefficient*, so to say, for the appointment of all sacred periods; and we thus find the 7th month ushered in by the Feast of Trumpets, and signalized by the celebration of the Feast of Tabernacles and the Great Day of Atonement; 7 weeks as the interval between the Passover and the Pentecost; the 7th year as the sabbatical year; and the year succeeding 7 × 7 years as the Jubilee year. Seven days were appointed as the length of the feasts of Passover and Tabernacles; 7 days for the ceremonies of the consecration of priests, and so on; 7 victims to be offered on any special occasion, as in Balaam's sacrifice, Num. 23 : 1, and especially at the ratification of a treaty, the notion of seven being embodied in the very term signifying to swear, literally meaning to *do seven times*. Gen. 21 : 28. Seven is used for any round number, or for completeness, as we say a *dozen*, or as a speaker says he will say *two or three* words.

Sha-al'bim, or **Sha-alab'bin** (*home of foxes*), a town in the allotment of Dan. Josh. 19 : 42; Judges 1 : 35; 1 Kings 4 : 9. By Eusebius and Jerome it is mentioned in the *Onomasticon* as a large village in the district of Sebaste (*i. e.* Samaria), and as then called Selaba.

Sha-al'bonite, The. Eliahba the Shaalbonite was one of David's thirty-seven heroes. 2 Sam. 23 : 32; 1 Chron. 11 : 33. He was a native of a place named Shaalbon, but where it was is unknown. (B.C. 1048.)

Sha'aph (*division*). 1. The son of Jahdai. 1 Chron. 2 : 47.

2. The son of Caleb the brother of Jerahmeel, by his concubine Maachah. 1 Chron. 2 : 49. (B.C. after 1445.)

Sha-ara'im (*two gates*), a city in the territory allotted to Judah, Josh. 15 : 36; in Authorized Version incorrectly Sharaim. 1 Sam. 17 : 52. Shaaraim, one of the towns of Simeon, 1 Chron. 4 : 31, must be a different place.

Sha-as'gaz (*servant of the beautiful*), the eunuch in the palace of Xerxes who had the custody of the women in the second house. Esther 2 : 14. (B.C. about 525.)

Shabbetha'i (*sabbatical*), a Levite in the time of Ezra. Ezra 10 : 15. It is apparently the same who with Jeshua and others instructed the people in the knowledge of the law. Neh. 8 : 7. (B.C. 450.)

Shachi'a (*announcement*), a son of Shaharaim by his wife Hodesh. 1 Chron. 8 : 10.

Shad'da-i (*the Mighty*), an ancient name of God, rendered "Almighty" everywhere in the Authorized Version, is found in connection with *êl*, "God," El Shaddai being then rendered "God Almighty." By the name or in the character of El-Shaddai, God was known to the patriarchs, Gen. 17 : 1; 28 : 3; 43 : 14; 48 : 3; 49 : 25, before the name Jehovah, in its full significance, was revealed. Ex. 6 : 3. [GOD.]

Sha'drach (*royal*, or *the great scribe*), the Hebrew, or rather Chaldee, name of Hananiah. The history of Shadrach or Hananiah, as told in Dan. 1–3, is well known. After their deliverance from the furnace, we hear no more of Shadrach, Meshach and Abednego, except in Heb. 11 : 33, 34; but there are repeated allusions to them in the later apocryphal books, and the martyrs of the Maccabæan period seem to have been much encouraged by their example.

Sha'ge (*erring*), father of Jonathan the Hararite, one of David's guard. 1 Chron. 11 : 34. [See SHAMMAH, 5.] (B.C. about 1050.)

Shahara'im (*double dawn*), a Benjamite. 1 Chron. 8 : 8. (B.C. about 1445.)

Shahaz'imah (*toward the heights*), one of the towns of the allotment of Issachar. Josh. 19 : 22 only.

Sha'lem (*safe*). Gen. 33 : 18. Probably not a proper name, but a place. It is certainly remarkable that there should be a modern village bearing the name of *Salim*, three miles east of *Nablûs*, the ancient Shechem.

Sha'lim, The land of (*the land of foxes*), a district through which Saul passed on his journey in quest of his father's asses. 1 Sam. 9 : 4 only. It probably was east of Shalisha.

Shal'isha, The land of, one of the districts traversed by Saul when in search of the asses of Kish. 1 Sam. 9 : 4 only. It was a district near Mount Ephraim. In it perhaps was situated the place called Baal-shalisha, 2 Kings 4 : 42, 15 miles north of Lydda.

Shal'lecheth (*overthrow*), **The gate,** one of the gates of the "house of Jehovah." 1 Chron. 26 : 16. It was the gate "to the causeway of the ascent." As the causeway is actually in existence, the gate Shallecheth can hardly fail to be identical with the *Bab Silsileh* or *Sinsleh*, which enters the west wall of the Haram about 600 feet from the southwest corner of the Haram wall.

Shal'lum (*retribution*). 1. The fifteenth king of Israel, son of Jabesh, conspired against Zachariah, killed him, and brought the dynasty of Jehu to a close, B.C. 770. Shallum, after reigning in Samaria for a month only, was in his turn dethroned and killed by Menahem. 2 Kings 15 : 10-14.

2. The husband of Huldah the prophetess, 2 Kings 22 : 14; 2 Chron. 34 : 22, in the reign of Josiah. (B.C. 630.)

3. A descendant of Shesham. 1 Chron. 2 : 40, 41.

4. The third son of Josiah king of Judah, known in the books of Kings and Chronicles as Jehoahaz. 1 Chron. 3 : 15; Jer. 22 : 11. [JEHOAHAZ.] (B.C. 610.)

5. Son of Shaul the son of Simeon. 1 Chron. 4 : 25.

6. A high priest. 1 Chron. 6 : 12, 13; Ezra 7 : 2.

7. A son of Naphtali. 1 Chron. 7 : 13.

8. The chief of a family of porters or gate-keepers of the east gate of the temple. 1 Chron. 9 : 17. (B.C. 1050.)

9. Son of Kore, a Korahite. 1 Chron. 9 : 19, 31.

10. Father of Jehizkiah, an Ephraimite. 2 Chron. 28 : 12.

11. One of the porters of the temple who had married a foreign wife. Ezra 10 : 24.

12. One of the sons of Bani. Ezra 10 : 42.

13. The son of Halohesh and ruler of a district of Jerusalem. Neh. 3 : 12.

14. The uncle of Jeremiah, Jer. 32 : 7; perhaps the same as 2.

15. Father or ancestor of Maaseiah, Jer. 35 : 4; perhaps the same as 9. (B.C. 630.)

Shal'lun (*retribution*), the son of Colhozeh, and ruler of a district of the Mizpah. Neh. 3 : 15.

Shalma'i (*my thanks*). The children of Shalmai were among the Nethinim who returned with Zerubbabel. Ezra 2 : 46; Neh. 7 : 48. In Nehemiah SALMAI. (B.C. 536.)

Shal'man (*fire-worshipper*), a contraction for Shalmaneser king of Assyria. Hos. 10 : 14. Others think it the name of an obscure Assyrian king, predecessor of Pul.

Shalmane'ser (*fire-worshipper*) was the Assyrian king who reigned probably between Tiglath-pileser and Sargon, B.C. 727-722. He led the forces of Assyria into Palestine, where Hoshea, the last king of Israel, had revolted against his authority. 2 Kings 17 : 3. Hoshea submitted and consented to pay tribute; but he soon after concluded an alliance with the king of Egypt, and withheld his tribute in consequence. In B.C. 723 Shalmaneser invaded Palestine for the second time, and, as Hoshea refused to submit, laid siege to Samaria. The siege lasted to the third year, B.C. 721, when the Assyrian arms prevailed. 2 Kings 17 : 4-6; 18 : 9-11. It is uncertain whether Shalmaneser conducted the siege to its close, or whether he did not lose his crown to Sargon before the city was taken.

Sha'ma (*obedient*), one of David's guard. 1 Chron. 11 : 44. (B.C. 1020.)

Shamari'ah (*kept by Jehovah*), son of Rehoboam. 2 Chron. 11 : 19. (B.C. 973.)

Sha'med (*keeper*), properly Shamer or Shemer; one of the sons of Elpaal the Benjamite. 1 Chron. 8 : 12.

Sha'mer (*keeper*). 1. A Merarite Levite. 1 Chron. 6 : 46.

2. Shomer, an Asherite. 1 Chron. 7 : 34.

Sham'gar (*sword*), son of Anath, judge of Israel. When Israel was in a most depressed condition, Shamgar was raised up to be a deliverer. With no arms in his hand but an ox-goad, Judges 3 : 31; comp. 1 Sam. 13 : 21, he made a desperate assault upon the Philistines, and slew 600 of them. (B.C. about 1290.)

Sham'huth (*desolation*), the fifth captain for the fifth month in David's arrangement of his army. 1 Chron. 27 : 8. (B.C. 1020.)

Sha'mir (*a point or thorn*). 1. A town in the mountain district of Judah. Josh. 15 : 48 only. It probably lay some eight or ten miles south of Hebron.

2. A place in Mount Ephraim, the residence and burial-place of Tola the judge. Judges 10 : 1, 2. Perhaps *Samur*, half-way between Samaria and *Jenin*.

3. A Kohathite, son of Micah or Michal, the first-born of Uzziel. 1 Chron. 24 : 24.

Sham'ma (*astonishment*), one of the sons of Zophar, an Asherite. 1 Chron. 7 : 37.

Sham'mah (*astonishment*). 1. The

son of Reuel the son of Esau. Gen. 36 : 13, 17 ; 1 Chron. 1 : 37. (B.C. about 1700.)

2. The third son of Jesse, and brother of David. 1 Sam. 16 : 9 ; 17 : 13. Called also Shimea, Shimeah and Shimma. (B.C. 1068.)

3. One of the three greatest of David's mighty men. 2 Sam. 23 : 11–17. (B.C. 1061.)

4. The Harodite, one of David's mighties. 2 Sam. 23 : 25. He is called "SHAMMOTH the Harorite" in 1 Chron. 11 : 27, and "SHAMHUTH the Izrahite" *ibid.* 27 : 8.

5. In the list of David's mighty men in 2 Sam. 23 : 32, 33, we find "Jonathan, Shammah the Hararite ;" while in the corresponding verse of 1 Chron. 11 : 34 it is Jonathan.

Sham'ma-i (*desolate*). 1. The son of Onam. 1 Chron. 2 : 28, 32.

2. Son of Rekem. 1 Chron. 2 : 44, 45.

3. One of the descendants of Judah. 1 Chron. 4 : 17.

Sham'moth. [SHAMMAH.]

Shammu'a (*renowned*). 1. The Reubenite spy, son of Zaccur. Num. 13 : 4. (B.C. 1490.)

2. Son of David, by his wife Bathsheba. 1 Chron. 14 : 4. (B.C. 1045.)

3. A Levite, the father of Abda. Neh. 11 : 17. The same as SHEMAIAH, 6.

4. The representative of the priestly family of Bilgah or Bilgai, in the days of Joiakim. Neh. 12 : 18. (B.C. about 500.)

Shammu'ah, son of David, 2 Sam. 5 : 14; elsewhere called Shammua and Shimea.

Shamshera'i (*sunlike*), a Benjamite. 1 Chron. 8 : 26.

Sha'pham (*bold*), a Gadite of Bashan. 1 Chron. 5 : 12. (B.C. 750.)

Sha'phan (*coney*), the scribe or secretary of King Josiah. 2 Kings 22 : 3, 14; 2 Chron. 34 : 8, 20. (B.C. 628.) He appears on an equality with the governor of the city and the royal recorder. 2 Kings 22 : 4 ; 2 Chron. 34 : 9.

Sha'phat (*judge*). 1. The Simeonite spy, son of Hori. Num. 13 : 5. (B.C. 1490.)

2. The father of the prophet Elisha. 1 Kings 19 : 16, 19 ; 2 Kings 3 : 11 ; 6 : 31. (B.C. before 900.)

3. One of the six sons of Shemaiah in the royal line of Judah. 1 Chron. 3 : 22. (B.C. 350.)

4. One of the chiefs of the Gadites in Bashan. 1 Chron. 5 : 12. (B.C. 750.)

5. The son of Adlai, who was over David's oxen in the valleys. 1 Chron. 27 : 29. (B.C. 1020.)

Sha'pher (*brightness*), **Mount,** Num. 33 : 23, the name of a desert station where the Israelites encamped during the wanderings in the wilderness.

Shar'a-i (*releaser*), one of the sons of Bani. Ezra 10 : 40. (B.C. 457.)

Shar'a-im. [SHAARAIM.]

Sha'rar (*strong*), the father of Ahiam the Hararite. 2 Sam. 23 : 33. In 1 Chron. 11 : 35 he is called SACAR. (B.C. 1040.)

Share'zer (*prince of fire*) was a son of Sennacherib, whom, in conjunction with his brother Adrammelech, he murdered. 2 Kings 19 : 37. (B.C. after 711.)

Sha'ron (*a plain*), a district of the holy land occasionally referred to in the Bible. 1 Chron. 5 : 16 ; Isa. 33 : 9. In Acts 9 : 35 called SARON. The name has on each occurrence, with one exception only, 1 Chron. 5 : 16, the definite article ; it would therefore appear that "the Sharon" was some well-defined region familiar to the Israelites. It is that broad, rich tract of land which lies between the mountains of the central part of the holy land and the Mediterranean —the northern continuation of the Shefelah. [PALESTINE.] The Sharon of 1 Chron. 5 : 16, to which allusion has already been made, is distinguished from the western plain by not having the article attached to its name, as the other invariably has. It is also apparent from the passage itself that it was some district on the east of the Jordan, in the neighborhood of Gilead and Bashan. The name has not been met with in that direction.

Sha'ronite (*belonging to Sharon*), **The.** Shitrai, who had charge of the royal herds in the plain of Sharon, 1 Chron. 27 : 29, is the only Sharonite mentioned in the Bible.

Sharu'hen (*refuge of grace*), a town named in Josh. 19 : 6 only, among those which were allotted within Judah to Simeon. It is identified with Sheriah, a large ruin in the south country, northwest of Beersheba.

Shash'a-i (*noble*), one of the sons of Bani in the time of Ezra. Ezra 10 : 40. (B.C. 457.)

Sha'shak (*longing*), a Benjamite, one of the sons of Beriah. 1 Chron. 8 : 14, 25. (B.C. after 1450.)

Sha'ul (*asked*). 1. The son of Simeon by a Canaanitish woman, Gen. 46 : 10 ; Ex. 6 : 15; Num. 26 : 13; 1 Chron.

4 : 24, and founder of the family of the Shaulites. (B.C. 1712.)

2. One of the kings of Edom. 1 Chron. 1 : 48, 49. In the Authorized Version of Gen. 36 : 37 he is less accurately called SAUL.

Sha'veh (*plain*), **The valley of,** described Gen. 14 : 17 as "the valley of the king," is mentioned again in 2 Sam. 18 : 18 as the site of a pillar set up by Absalom.

Sha'veh Kiriatha'im (*plain of the double city*), mentioned Gen. 14 : 5 as the residence of the Emim at the time of Chedorlaomer's incursion. Kiriathaim is named in the later history, though it has not been identified; and Shaveh Kiriathaim was probably the valley in or by which the town lay.

Shav'sha (*nobility*), the royal secretary in the reign of David, 1 Chron. 18 : 16; called also SERAIAH in 2 Sam. 8 : 17 and SHEVA in 2 Sam. 20 : 25, and in 1 Kings 4 : 3, SHISHA.

Shawm. In the Prayer-book version of Ps. 98 : 6, "with trumpets also and *shawms*" is the rendering of what stands in the Authorized Version "with trumpets and sound of *cornet*." The Hebrew word translated "cornet" is treated under that head. The "shawm" was a musical instrument resembling the clarionet.

She'al (*asking*), one of the sons of Bani who had married a foreign wife. Ezra 10 : 29. (B.C. 452.)

She-al'ti-el (*asked of God*), father of Zerubbabel. Ezra 3 : 2, 8; 5 : 2; Neh. 12 : 1; Hag. 1 : 1, 12, 14; 2 : 2, 23. (B.C. about 580.)

She-ari'ah (*valued by Jehovah*), one of the six sons of Azel, a descendant of Saul. 1 Chron. 8 : 38; 9 : 44.

Shearing-house, The, a place on the road between Jezreel and Samaria, at which Jehu, on his way to the latter, encountered forty-two members of the royal family of Judah, whom he slaughtered. 2 Kings 10 : 12, 14. Eusebius mentions it as a village of Samaria "in the great plain [of Esdraelon], 15 miles from Legeon."

She'ar-ja'shub (lit. *a remnant shall return*), the symbolical name of the son of Isaiah the prophet. Isa. 7 : 3.

She'ba (*an oath*), the son of Bichri, a Benjamite, 2 Sam. 20 : 1–22, the last chief of the Absalom insurrection. The occasion seized by Sheba was the emulation between the northern and southern tribes on David's return. 2 Sam. 20 : 1, 2. Sheba traversed the whole of Palestine, apparently rousing the population, Joab following in full pursuit to the fortress Abel Beth-maachah, where Sheba was beheaded. 2 Sam. 20 : 3–22.

She'ba (*seven*, or *an oath*). 1. A son of Raamah son of Cush. Gen. 10 : 7; 1 Chron. 1 : 9.

2. A son of Joktan. Gen. 10 : 28 : 1 Chron. 1 : 22.

3. A son of Jokshan son of Keturah. Gen. 25 : 3; 1 Chron. 1 : 32. We shall consider, first, the history of the Joktanite Sheba; and secondly, the Cushite Sheba and the Keturahite Sheba together.

I. The Joktanites were among the early colonists of southern Arabia, and the kingdom which they there founded was for many centuries called the kingdom of Sheba, after one of the sons of Joktan. The visit of the queen of Sheba to King Solomon, 1 Kings 10 : 1, is one of the familiar Bible incidents. The kingdom of Sheba embraced the greater part of the Yemen, or Arabia Felix. It bordered on the Red Sea, and was one of the most fertile districts of Arabia. Its chief cities, and probably successive capitals, were Seba, San'a (Uzal), and Zafár (Sephar). Seba was probably the name of the city, and generally of the country and nation.

II. Sheba, son of Raamah son of Cush, settled somewhere on the shores of the Persian Gulf. It was this Sheba that carried on the great Indian traffic with Palestine, in conjunction with, as we hold, the other Sheba, son of Jokshan son of Keturah, who like Dedan appears to have formed, with the Cushite of the same name, one tribe.

She'ba, one of the towns of the allotment of Simeon, Josh. 19 : 2, probably the same as Shema. Josh. 15 : 26.

She'bah (*an oath*), the famous well which gave its name to the city of Beersheba. Gen. 26 : 33. [BEERSHEBA.]

She'bam (*fragrance*), one of the towns in the pastoral district on the east of Jordan; demanded by and finally ceded to the tribes of Reuben and Gad. Num. 32 : 3. It is probably the same as SHIBMAH, Num. 32 : 38, and SIBMAH. Josh. 13 : 19; Isa. 16 : 8, 9; Jer. 48 : 32.

Shebani'ah (*increased by Jehovah*). 1. A Levite in the time of Ezra. Neh. 9 : 4, 5. He sealed the covenant with Nehemiah. Neh. 10 : 10. (B.C. 459.)

2. A priest or priestly family who sealed the covenant with Nehemiah. Neh. 10 : 4; 12 : 14. Called SHECHA-NIAH in Neh. 12 : 3.

3. Another Levite who sealed the covenant with Nehemiah. Neh. 10 : 12.

4. One of the priests appointed by David to blow with the trumpets before the ark of God. 1 Chron. 15 : 24. (B.C. 1043.)

Sheb'arim (*the breaches*), a place named in Josh. 7 : 5 only, as one of the points in the flight from Ai.

She'ber (*breaking*), son of Caleb ben Hezron by his concubine Maachah. 1 Chron. 2 : 48. (B.C. after 1690.)

Sheb'na (*vigor*), a person of high position in Hezekiah's court, holding at one time the office of prefect of the palace, Isa. 22 : 15, but subsequently the subordinate office of secretary. Isa. 36 : 3; 2 Kings 19 : 2. (B.C. 713.)

Sheb'uel, or **Shebu'el** (*captive of God*). 1. A descendant of Moses, 1 Chron. 23 : 16; 26 : 24, called also SHU-BAEL. 1 Chron. 24 : 20. (B.C. 1013.)

Shechem (Nablûs, Sychar).

2. One of the fourteen sons of Heman the minstrel, 1 Chron. 25 : 4; called also SHUBAEL. 1 Chron. 25 : 20. (B.C. 1013.)

Shechani'ah (*dweller with Jehovah*). 1. The tenth in order of the priests who were appointed by lot in the reign of David. 1 Chron. 24 : 11. (B.C. 1014.)

2. A priest in the reign of Hezekiah. 2 Chron. 31 : 15. (B.C. 925.)

Shechani'ah (*dweller with Jehovah*). 1. A descendant of Zerubbabel. 1 Chron. 3 : 21, 22.

2. Some descendants of Shechaniah returned with Ezra. Ezra 8 : 3.

3. The sons of Shechaniah were another family who returned with Ezra. Ezra 8 : 5. (B.C. 459.)

4. The son of Jehiel, of the sons of Elam. Ezra 10 : 2.

5. The father of Shemaiah, 2. Neh. 3 : 29.

6. The son of Arah. Neh. 6 : 18.

7. The head of a priestly family who returned with Zerubbabel. Neh. 12 : 3.

She'chem (*back* or *shoulder*). 1. An important city in central Palestine, in the valley between mounts Ebal and Gerizim, 34 miles north of Jerusalem and 7 miles southeast of Samaria. Its present name, *Nablûs*, is a corruption of Neapolis, which succeeded the more ancient Shechem, and received its new name from Vespasian. On coins still extant it is called Flavia Neapolis. The situation of the town is one of surpassing beauty. It lies in a sheltered valley, protected by Gerizim on the south and Ebal on the north. The feet of these mountains, where they rise from the town, are not more than five hundred yards apart. The bottom of the valley is about 1800 feet above the level of the sea, and the top of Gerizim 800 feet higher still. The site of the present city, which was also that of the Hebrew city, occurs exactly on the water-summit; and streams issuing from the numerous springs there flow down the opposite slopes of the valley, spreading verdure and fertility in every direction. Travellers vie with each other in the language which they employ to describe the scene that here bursts so suddenly upon them on arriving in spring or early summer at this paradise of the holy land. "The whole valley," says Dr. Robinson, "was filled with gardens of vegetables and orchards of all kinds of fruits, watered by fountains which burst forth in various parts and flow westward in refreshing streams. It came upon us suddenly like a scene of fairy enchantment. We saw nothing to compare with it in all Palestine." The allusions to Shechem in the Bible are numerous, and show how important the place was in Jewish history. Abraham, on his first migration to the land of promise, pitched his tent and built an altar under the oak (or terebinth) of Moreh at Shechem. "The Canaanite was then in the land;" and it is evident that the region, if not the city, was already in possession of the aboriginal race. See Gen. 12 : 6. At the time of Jacob's arrival here, after his sojourn in Mesopotamia, Gen. 33 : 18; 34, Shechem was a Hivite city, of which Hamor, the father of Shechem, was the headman. It was at this time that the patriarch purchased from that chieftain " the parcel of the field " which he subsequently bequeathed, as a special patrimony, to his son Joseph. Gen. 33 : 19; Josh. 24 : 32; John 4 : 5. The field lay undoubtedly on the rich plain of the *Mukhna*, and its value was the greater on account of the well which Jacob had dug there, so as not to be dependent on his neighbors for a supply of water. In the distribution of the land after its conquest by the Hebrews, Shechem fell to the lot of Ephraim, Josh. 20 : 7, but was assigned to the Levites, and became a city of refuge. Josh. 21 : 20, 21. It acquired new importance as the scene of the renewed promulgation of the law, when its blessings were heard from Gerizim and its curses from Ebal, and the people bowed

their heads and acknowledged Jehovah as their king and ruler. Deut. 27 : 11; Josh. 24 : 23-25. It was here Joshua assembled the people, shortly before his death, and delivered to them his last counsels. Josh. 24 : 1, 25. After the death of Gideon, Abimelech, his bastard son, induced the Shechemites to revolt from the Hebrew commonwealth and elect him as king. Judges 9. In revenge for his expulsion, after a reign of three years, Abimelech destroyed the city, and as an emblem of the fate to which he would consign it, sowed the ground with salt. Judges 9 : 34-45. It was soon restored, however, for we are told in 1 Kings 12 that all Israel assembled at Shechem, and Rehoboam, Solomon's successor, went thither to be inaugurated as king. Here, at this same place, the ten tribes renounced the house of David, and transferred their allegiance to Jeroboam, 1 Kings 12 : 16, under whom Shechem became for a time the capital of his kingdom. From the time of the origin of the Samaritans, the history of Shechem blends itself with that of this people and of their sacred mount, Gerizim. [SAMARIA.] Shechem reappears in the New Testament. It is the SYCHAR of John 4 : 5, near which the Saviour conversed with the Samaritan woman at Jacob's well. The population of *Nablûs* consists of about 5000, among whom are 500 Greek Christians, 150 Samaritans, and a few Jews. The enmity between the Samaritans and Jews is as inveterate still as it was in the days of Christ. The Mohammedans, of course, make up the bulk of the population. The well of Jacob and the tomb of Joseph are still shown in the neighborhood of the town. The well of Jacob lies about a mile and a half east of the city, close to the lower road, and just beyond the wretched hamlet of *Balâta*. The Christians sometimes call it *Bir es-Samariyeh*—"the well of the Samaritan woman." The well is deep—75 feet when last measured—and there was probably a considerable accumulation of rubbish at the bottom. Sometimes it contains a few feet of water, but at others it is quite dry. It is entirely excavated in the solid rock, perfectly round, 9 feet in diameter, with the sides hewn smooth and regular. Of all the special localities of our Lord's life, this is almost the only one absolutely undisputed. The tomb of Joseph lies about a quarter of a mile north of the well, exactly in the centre of the opening of the valley between Gerizim and Ebal. It is a small, square enclosure of high whitewashed walls, surrounding a tomb of the ordinary kind, but with the peculiarity that it is placed diagonally to the walls, instead of parallel as usual. A rough pillar used as an altar, and black with the traces of fire, is at the head and another at the foot of the tomb. In the walls are two slabs with Hebrew inscriptions, and the interior is almost covered with the names of pilgrims in Hebrew, Arabic and Samaritan. Beyond this there is nothing to remark in the structure itself. The local tradition of the tomb, like that of the well, is as old as the beginning of the fourth century.

2. The son of Hamor, the chieftain of the Hivite settlement of Shechem at the time of Jacob's arrival. Gen. 33 : 19; 34 : 2-26; Josh. 24 : 32; Judges 9 : 28.

3. A man of Manasseh, of the clan of Gilead. Num. 26 : 31.

4. A Gileadite, son of Shemida, the younger brother of the foregoing. 1 Chron. 7 : 19.

She'chemites, The, the family of Shechem son of Gilead. Num. 26 : 31; comp. Josh. 17 : 2.

Shechi'nah (*dwelling*). This term is not found in the Bible. It was used by the later Jews, and borrowed by Christians from them, to express the visible majesty of the divine Presence, especially when resting or dwelling between the cherubim on the mercyseat in the tabernacle and in the temple of Solomon, but not in the second temple. The use of the term is first found in the Targums, where it forms a frequent periphrasis for God, considered as *dwelling* among the children of Israel. The idea which the different accounts in Scripture convey is that of a most brilliant and glorious light, enveloped in a cloud, and usually concealed by the cloud, so that the cloud itself was for the most part alone visible; but on particular occasions the glory appeared. The allusions in the New Testament to the shechinah are not unfrequent: Luke 2 : 9; John 1 : 14; Rom. 9 : 4; and we are distinctly taught to connect it with the incarnation and future coming of the Messiah as type with antitype.

Shed'eur (*darter of light*), the father of Elizur, chief of the tribe of Reuben at the time of the exodus. Num. 1 : 5; 2 : 10; 7 : 30, 35; 10 : 18. (B.C. 1491.)

Sheep. Sheep were an important part of the possessions of the ancient Hebrews and of eastern nations generally. The first mention of sheep occurs in Gen. 4 : 2. They were used in the sacrificial offerings, both the adult animal, Ex. 20 : 24, and the lamb. See Ex. 29 : 38; Lev. 9 : 3; 12 : 6. Sheep and lambs formed an important article of food. 1 Sam. 25 : 18. The wool was used as clothing. Lev. 13 : 47. "Rams' skins dyed red" were used as a covering for the tabernacle. Ex. 25 : 5. Sheep and lambs were sometimes paid as tribute. 2 Kings 3 : 4. It is very striking to notice the immense numbers of sheep that were reared in Palestine in biblical times. (Chardin says he saw a clan of Turcoman shepherds whose flock

Broad-tailed Sheep.

consisted of 3,000,000 sheep and goats, besides 400,000 beasts of carriage, as horses, asses and camels.) Sheep-shearing is alluded to Gen. 31 : 19. Sheepdogs were employed in biblical times. Job 30 : 1. Shepherds in Palestine and the East generally go before their flocks, which they induce to follow by calling to them, comp. John 10 : 4; Ps. 77 : 20; 80 : 1, though they also drive them. Gen. 33 : 13. The following quotation from Hartley's "Researches in Greece and the Levant," p. 321, is strikingly illustrative of the allusions in John 10 : 1–16 : "Having had my attention directed last night to the words in John 10 : 3, I asked my man if it was usual in Greece to give names to the sheep. He informed me that it was, and that the sheep obeyed the shepherd when he called them by their names. This morning I had an opportunity of verifying the truth of this remark. Passing by a flock of sheep, I asked the shepherd the same question which I had put to the servant, and he gave me the same answer. I then bade him call one of his sheep. He did so, and it instantly left its pasturage and its companions and ran up to the hands of the shepherd with signs of pleasure and with a prompt obedience which I had never before observed in any other animal. It is also true in this country that 'a stranger will they not follow, but will flee from him.' The shepherd told me that many of his sheep were still

Eastern Sheepfold.

wild, that they had not yet learned their names, but that by teaching them they would all learn them." The common sheep of Syria and Palestine are the broad-tailed. As the sheep is an emblem of meekness, patience and submission, it is expressly mentioned as typifying these qualities in the person of our blessed Lord. Isa. 53:7; Acts 8:32, etc. The relation that exists between Christ, "the chief Shepherd," and his members is beautifully compared to that which in the East is so strikingly exhibited by the shepherds to their flocks. [SHEPHERD.]

Sheep-gate, The, one of the gates of Jerusalem as rebuilt by Nehemiah. Neh. 3:1, 32; 12:39. It stood between the tower of Meah and the chamber of the corner, ch. 3:1, 32, or gate of the guard-house, ch. 12:39; Authorized Version, "prison-gate." The latter seems to have been at the angle formed by the junction of the wall of the city of David with that of the city of Jerusalem proper,

having the sheep-gate on the north of it. The position of the sheep-gate may therefore have been on or near that of the *Bab el Kattanin.*

Sheep-market, The. John 5:2. The word "market" is an interpolation of our translators. We ought probably to supply the word "gate."

Shehari'ah (*dawning of Jehovah*), a Benjamite, son of Jehoram. 1 Chron. 8:26. (B.C. 588.)

Shekel. [MONEY.]

She'lah (*a petition*). 1. The youngest son of Judah. Gen. 38:5, 11, 14, 26; 46:12; Num. 26:20; 1 Chron. 2:3; 4:21. (B.C. before 1706.)

2. The proper form of the name of Salah. 1 Chron. 1:18, 24.

She'lanites, The, the descendants of Shelah, 1. Num. 26:20.

Shelemi'ah (*repaid by Jehovah*). 1. One of the sons of Bani in the time of Ezra. Ezra 10:39. (B.C. 458.)

2. The father of Hananiah. Neh. 3:30.

3. A priest in the time of Nehemiah. Neh. 13:13.

4. The father of Jehucal, or Jucal, in the time of Zedekiah. Jer. 37:3.

5. The father of Irijah, the captain of the ward who arrested Jeremiah. Jer. 37:13. (B.C. before 589.)

6. The same as Meshelemiah and Shallum, 8. 1 Chron. 26:14.

7. Another of the sons of Bani in the time of Ezra. Ezra 10:41.

8. Ancestor of Jehudi in the time of Jehoiakim. Jer. 36:14.

9. Son of Abdeel; one of those who received the orders of Jehoiakim to take Baruch and Jeremiah. Jer. 36:26. (B.C. 604.)

She'leph (*a drawing forth*), the second in order of the sons of Joktan. Gen. 10:26; 1 Chron. 1:20.

She'lesh (*might*), son of Helem. 1 Chron. 7:35.

Shel'omi (*peaceful*), an Asherite, father of Ahihud. Num. 34:27. (B.C. before 1450.)

Shel'omith (*peaceful*). 1. The daughter of Dibri, of the tribe of Dan. Lev. 24:11.

2. The daughter of Zerubbabel. 1 Chron. 3:19. (B.C. after 536.)

3. Chief of the Izharites. 1 Chron. 23 : 18.

4. A descendant of Eliezer the son of Moses, in the reign of David. 1 Chron. 26 : 25, 26, 28. (B.C. 1013.)

5. A Gershonite. 1 Chron. 23 : 9.

6. One whose sons returned from Babylon with Ezra. Ezra 8 : 10.

Shel'omoth, the same as Shelomith, 3. 1 Chron. 24 : 22.

Shelu'mi-el (*friend of God*), the son of Zurishaddai, and prince of the tribe of Simeon at the time of the exodus. Num. 1 : 6; 2 : 12; 7 : 36, 41; 10 : 19. (B.C. 1491.)

Shem (*name*), the eldest son of Noah. Gen. 5 : 32. He was 98 years old, married, and childless, at the time of the flood. After it, he, with his father, brothers, sisters-in-law and wife, received the blessing of God, Gen. 9 : 1, and entered into the covenant. With the help of his brother Japheth, he covered the nakedness of their father, and received the first blessing. Gen. 9 : 25-27. He died at the age of 600 years. The portion of the earth occupied by the descendants of Shem, Gen. 10 : 21, 31, begins at its northwestern extremity with Lydia, and includes Syria (Aram), Chaldæa (Arphaxad), parts of Assyria (Asshur), of Persia (Elam), and of the Arabian peninsula (Joktan). Modern scholars have given the name of Shemitic or Semitic to the languages spoken by his real or supposed descendants. [HEBREW.]

She'ma. 1. A Reubenite, ancestor of Bela. 1 Chron. 5 : 8. (B.C. before 1090.)

2. Son of Elpaal. 1 Chron. 8 : 13. Probably the same as Shimhi. (B.C. after 1450.)

3. One of those who stood at Ezra's right hand when he read the law to the people. Neh. 8 : 4. (B.C. 458.)

4. Josh. 15 : 26. [SHEBA.]

Shem'a-ah (*the rumor*), a Benjamite of Gibeah, and father of Ahiezer and Joash. 1 Chron. 12 : 3. (B.C. before 1054.)

Shemai'ah (*heard by Jehovah*). 1. A prophet in the reign of Rehoboam. 1 Kings 12 : 22; 2 Chron. 11 : 2. (B.C. 972.) He wrote a chronicle containing the events of Rehoboam's reign. 2 Chron. 12 : 5, 15.

2. The son of Shechaniah, among the descendants of Zerubbabel. 1 Chron. 3 : 22; Neh. 3 : 29.

3. A prince of the tribe of Simeon. 1 Chron. 4 : 27.

4. Son of Joel, a Reubenite. 1 Chron. 5 : 4. (B.C. after 1706.)

5. Son of Hasshub, a Merarite Levite. 1 Chron. 9 : 14; Neh. 11 : 15.

6. Father of Obadiah or Abda, a Levite. 1 Chron. 9 : 16.

7. Son of Elizaphan, and chief of his house in the reign of David. 1 Chron. 15 : 8, 11. (B.C. 1043.)

8. A Levite, son of Nethaneel, and also a scribe in the time of David. 1 Chron. 24 : 6. (B.C. 1014.)

9. The eldest son of Obed-edom the Gittite. 1 Chron. 26 : 4, 6, 7. (B.C. 1014.)

10. A descendant of Jeduthun the singer, who lived in the reign of Hezekiah. 2 Chron. 29 : 14.

11. One of the sons of Adonikam who returned with Ezra. Ezra 8 : 13.

12. One of Ezra's messengers. Ezra 8 : 16.

13. A priest of the family of Harim, who put away his foreign wife at Ezra's bidding. Ezra 10 : 21. (B.C. 458.)

14. A layman of Israel, son of another Harim, who had also married a foreigner. Ezra 10 : 31. (B.C. 458.)

15. Son of Delaiah the son of Mehetabeel, a prophet in the time of Nehemiah. Neh. 6 : 10. (B.C. 446.)

16. The head of a priestly house who signed the covenant with Nehemiah. Neh. 10 : 8; 12 : 6, 18. (B.C. 410.)

17. One of the princes of Judah at the time of the dedication of the wall of Jerusalem. Neh. 12 : 34. (B.C. 446.)

18. One of the choir on the same occasion. Neh. 12 : 36.

19. A priest. Neh. 12 : 42.

20. A false prophet in the time of Jeremiah. Jer. 29 : 24-32.

21. A Levite in the reign of Jehoshaphat. 2 Chron. 17 : 8. (B.C. 909.)

22. A Levite in the reign of Hezekiah. 2 Chron. 31 : 15. (B.C. 726.)

23. A Levite in the reign of Josiah. 2 Chron. 35 : 9. (B.C. 628.)

24. The father of Urijah of Kirjathjearim. Jer. 26 : 20. (B.C. before 608.)

25. The father of Delaiah. Jer. 36 : 12. (B.C. before 605.)

Shemari'ah (*kept by Jehovah*). 1. A Benjamite warrior who came to David at Ziklag. 1 Chron. 12 : 5. (B.C. 1054.)

2. One of the family of Harim, a layman of Israel who put away his foreign wife in the time of Ezra. Ezra 10 : 32. (B.C. 658.)

3. Another who did the same. Ezra 10 : 41.

Sheme'ber (*lofty flight*), king of Zeboim, and ally of the king of Sodom when he was attacked by Chedorlaomer. Gen. 14 : 2. (B.C. 1912.)

She'mer (*preserved*), the owner of the hill on which the city of Samaria was built. 1 Kings 16 : 24. (B.C. 917.) [SAMARIA.]

Shemi'da(*wise*), a son of Gilead. Num. 26 : 32; Josh. 17 : 2. (B.C. after 1690.)

Shemi'dah. Shemida the son of Gilead. 1 Chron. 7 : 19.

Shemida'ites, The, the descendants of Shemida the son of Gilead. Num. 26 : 32.

Shem'inith (*eighth*), a musical term found in the title of Ps. 6. A similar direction is found in the title of Ps. 12. Comp. 1 Chron. 15 : 21. It seems most probable that Sheminith denotes a certain air known as the eighth, or a certain key in which the psalm was to be sung.

Shemir'amoth (*name of heights*, i.e. *Jehovah*). 1. A Levite of the second degree in the choir formed by David. 1 Chron. 15 : 18, 20; 16 : 5. (B.C. 104.)

2. A Levite in the reign of Jehoshaphat. 2 Chron. 17 : 8. (B.C. 909.)

Shemit'ic Languages, the family of languages spoken by the descendants of Shem, chiefly the Hebrew, Chaldaic, Assyrian, Arabic, Phœnician and Aramaic or Syriac. The Jews in their earlier history spoke the Hebrew, but in Christ's time they spoke the Aramaic, sometimes called the Syro-chaldaic.

Shemu'el (*heard by God*). 1. A commissioner appointed from the tribe of Simeon to divide the land of Canaan. Num. 34 : 20. (B.C. 1450.)

2. Samuel the prophet. 1 Chron. 6 : 33.

3. Son of Tola, and one of the chiefs of the tribe of Issachar. 1 Chron. 7 : 2. (B.C. 1014.)

Shen (*tooth*), a place mentioned only in 1 Sam. 7 : 12. Nothing is known of it.

Shena'zar (*splendid leader*), son of Salathiel or Shealtiel. 1 Chron. 3 : 18. (B.C. after 606.)

She'nir. [SENIR.]

She'pham (*fruitful*), a place on the eastern boundary of the promised land. Num. 34 : 10, 11.

Shephathi'ah, a Benjamite, father of Meshullam, 6. 1 Chron. 9 : 8.

Shephati'ah (*judged by Jehovah*). 1. The fifth son of David. 2 Sam. 3 : 4; 1 Chron. 3 : 3. (B.C. about 1050.)

2. The family of Shephatiah, 372 in number, returned with Zerubbabel. Ezra 2 : 4; Neh. 7 : 9; see also Ezra 8 : 8. (B.C. 536.)

3. The family of another Shephatiah, who came up with Zerubbabel. Ezra 2 : 57; Neh. 7 : 59.

4. A descendant of Judah. Neh. 11 : 4.

5. One of the princes of Judah who counselled Zedekiah to put Jeremiah in the dungeon. Jer. 38 : 1. (B.C. 589.)

6. One of the Benjamite warriors who joined David in his retreat at Ziklag. 1 Chron. 12 : 5. (B.C. 1054.)

7. Chief of the Simeonites in the reign of David. 1 Chron. 27 : 16.

8. Son of Jehoshaphat. 2 Chron. 21 : 2. (B.C. 887.)

Eastern Shepherd.

Shepherd. In a nomadic state of society every man, from the sheikh down to the slave, is more or less a shepherd. The progenitors of the Jews in the patriarchal age were nomads, and their history is rich in scenes of pastoral life. The occupation of tending the flocks was undertaken, not only by the sons of wealthy chiefs, Gen. 30 : 29 ff.; 37 : 12 ff., but even by their daughters. Gen. 29 : 6 ff.; Ex. 2 : 19. The Egyptian captivity did much to implant a love of settled abode, and consequently we find the tribes which still retained a taste for shepherd life selecting their own quarters apart from their brethren in the transjordanic district. Num. 32 : 1 ff. Thenceforward in Palestine proper the shepherd held a subordinate position. The office of the eastern shepherd, as described in the Bible, was attended with much hardship, and even danger. He was exposed to the extremes of heat and cold, Gen. 31 : 40;

his food frequently consisted of the precarious supplies afforded by nature, such as the fruit of the "sycamore" or Egyptian fig, Amos 7 : 14, the "husks" of the carob tree, Luke 15 : 16, and perchance the locusts and wild honey which supported the Baptist, Matt. 3 : 4; he had to encounter the attacks of wild beasts, occasionally of the larger species, such as lions, wolves, panthers and bears, 1 Sam. 17 : 34; Isa. 31 : 4; Jer. 5 : 6; Amos 3 : 12; nor was he free from the risk of robbers or predatory hordes. Gen. 31 : 39. To meet these various foes the shepherd's equipment consisted of the following articles : a mantle, made probably of sheepskin with the fleece on, which he turned inside out in cold weather, as implied in the comparison in Jer. 43 : 12 (cf. Juv. xiv. 187); a scrip or wallet, containing a small amount of food, 1 Sam. 17 : 40; a sling, which is still the favorite weapon of the Bedouin shepherd, 1 Sam. 17 : 40; and lastly, a staff, which served the double purpose of a weapon against foes and a crook for the management of the flock. 1 Sam. 17 : 40; Ps. 23 : 4; Zech. 11 : 7. If the shepherd was at a distance from his home, he was provided with a light tent, Cant. 1 : 8; Jer. 35 : 7, the removal of which was easily effected. Isa. 38 : 12. In certain localities, moreover, towers were erected for the double purpose of spying an enemy at a distance and of protecting the flock; such towers were erected by Uzziah and Jotham, 2 Chron. 26 : 10; 27 : 4, while their existence in earlier times is testified by the name Migdal-edar, Gen. 35 : 21, Authorized Version "a tower of Edar;" Micah 4 : 8, Authorized Version "tower of the flock." The routine of the shepherd's duties appears to have been as follows: In the morning he led forth his flock from the fold, John 10 : 4, which he did by going before them and calling to them, as is still usual in the East; arrived at the pasturage, he watched the flock with the assistance of dogs, Job 30 : 1, and should any sheep stray, he had to search for it until he found it, Ezek. 34 : 12; Luke 15 : 4; he supplied them with water, either at a running stream or at troughs attached to wells, Gen. 29 : 7; 30 : 38; Ex. 2 : 16; Ps. 23 : 2; at evening he brought them back to the fold, and reckoned them to see that none were missing, by passing them "under the rod" as they entered the door of the enclosure, Lev. 27 : 32; Ezek. 20 : 37, checking

each sheep, as it passed, by a motion of the hand, Jer. 33 : 13; and, finally, he watched the entrance of the fold throughout the night, acting as porter. John 10 : 3. [See *Sheepfold*, under SHEEP.] The shepherd's office thus required great watchfulness, particularly by night. Luke 2 : 8; cf. Nah. 3 : 18. It also required tenderness toward the young and feeble, Isa. 40 : 11, particularly in driving them to and from the pasturage. Gen. 33 : 13. In large establishments there are various grades of shepherds, the highest being styled "rulers," Gen. 47 : 6, or "chief shepherds," 1 Pet. 5 : 4; in a royal household the title of *abbir*, "mighty," was bestowed on the person who held the post. 1 Sam. 21 : 7. [SHEEP.]

She'phi (*bareness*), son of Shobal, of the sons of Seir. 1 Chron. 1 : 40. Called also SHEPHO. Gen. 36 : 23.

She-pho. Gen. 36 : 23. [SHEPHI.]

Shephu'phan (*an adder*), one of the sons of Bela the first-born of Benjamin. 1 Chron. 8 : 5. His name is also written SHEPHUPHAM (Authorized Version "Shupham"), Num. 26 : 39; SHUPPIM, 1 Chron. 7 : 12, 15; and MUPPIM. Gen. 46 : 21. [MUPPIM.]

She'rah (*kinswoman*), daughter of Ephraim, 1 Chron. 7 : 24, and foundress of the Beth-horons and of a town called after her Uzzen-sherah. (B.C. about 1445.)

Sherebi'ah (*heat of Jehovah*), a Levite in the time of Ezra. Ezra 8 : 18, 24. (B.C. 459.) When Ezra read the law to the people, Sherebiah was among the Levites who assisted him. Neh. 8 : 7. He signed the covenant with Nehemiah. Neh. 10 : 12.

She'resh (*root*), son of Machir the son of Manasseh by his wife Maachah. 1 Chron. 7 : 16. (B.C. before 1419.)

Shere'zer (*prince of fire*), one of the people's messengers mentioned in Zech. 7 : 2.

She'shach (from the goddess *Shach*, reduplicated) is a term which occurs only in Jer. 25 : 26; 51 : 41, where it is evidently used as a synonym for either Babylon or Babylonia.

She'sha-i (*noble*), one of the three sons of Anak who dwelt in Hebron. Num. 13 : 22. (B.C. 1445.)

She'shan (*noble*), a descendant of Jerahmeel the son of Hezron. 1 Chron. 2 : 31, 34, 35. (B.C. after 1690.)

Sheshbaz'zar (*worshipper of fire*), the Chaldæan or Persian name given to

Zerubbabel in Ezra 1 : 8, 11 ; 5 : 14, 16. [ZERUBBABEL.]

Sheth (*compensation*). 1. The patriarch Seth. 1 Chron. 1 : 1.

2. In the Authorized Version of Num. 24 : 17, not a proper name, but there is reason to regard it as an appellative. Read instead of "the sons of Sheth," "the sons of tumult." Comp. Jer. 48 : 45.

She'thar (Pers. *a star*), one of the seven princes of Persia and Media. Esther 1 : 14. (B.C. 483.)

She'thar-boz'na-i (Pers. *star of splendor*), a Persian officer of rank in the reign of Darius Hystaspes. Ezra 5 : 3, 6 ; 6 : 6, 13. (B.C. 320.)

She'va (*Jehovah contends*). 1. The scribe or royal secretary of David. 2 Sam. 20 : 25. He is called elsewhere SERAIAH, 2 Sam. 8 : 17 ; SHISHA, 1 Kings 4 : 3 ; and SHAVSHA. 1 Chron. 18 : 16. (B.C. 1015.)

2. Son of Caleb ben-Hezron by his concubine Maachah. 1 Chron. 2 : 49. (B.C. about 1445.)

Table of Shew-bread.

Shew-bread, Ex. 25 : 30 ; 35 : 13 ; 39 : 36, etc., literally "bread of the face" or "faces." Shew-bread was unleavened bread placed upon a table which stood in the sanctuary together with the seven-branched candlestick and the altar of incense. See Ex. 25 : 23–30 for description of this table. Every Sabbath twelve newly-baked loaves, representing the twelve tribes of Israel, were put on it in two rows, six in each, and sprinkled with incense, where they remained till the following Sabbath. Then they were replaced by twelve new ones, the incense was burned, and they were eaten by the priests in the holy place, out of which they might not be removed. The title "bread of the face" seems to indicate that bread through which God is seen, that is, with the participation of which the seeing of God is bound up, or through the participation of which man attains the sight of God ; whence it follows that we have not to think of bread merely as such, as the means of nourishing the bodily life, but as spiritual food, as a means of appropriating and retaining that life which consists in seeing the face of God.

Shibboleth (*a stream*), Judges 12 : 6, is the Hebrew word which the Gileadites under Jephthah made use of at the passage of the Jordan, after a victory over the Ephraimites, to test the pronunciation of the sound *sh* by those who wished to cross over the river. The Ephraimites, it would appear, in their dialect substituted for *sh* the simple sound *s ;* and the Gileadites, regarding every one who failed to pronounce *sh* as an Ephraimite, and therefore an enemy, put him to death accordingly. In this way there fell 42,000 Ephraimites. There is no mystery in this particular word. Any word beginning with the sound *sh* would have answered equally well as a test.

Shib'mah (properly SIBMAH). [SHEBAM.]

Shi'cron (*drunkenness*), one of the landmarks at the western end of the north boundary of Judah. Josh. 15 : 11 only. It lay between Ekron (*Akir*) and Jabneel (*Yebna*).

Shield. The ordinary shield consisted of a framework of wood covered with leather ; it thus admitted of being burnt. Ezek. 39 : 9. It was frequently cased with metal, either brass or copper ; its appearance in this case resembled gold when the sun shone on it, 1 Macc. 6 : 39, and to this, rather than to the practice of smearing blood on the shield, we may refer the redness noticed by Nahum. Nah. 2 : 3. The surface of the shield was kept bright by the application of oil, as implied in Isa. 21 : 5. The shield was worn on the left arm, to which it was attached by a strap. Shields of state were covered with beaten gold. Shields were suspended about public buildings for ornamental purposes. 1 Kings 10 : 17. In the metaphorical language of the Bible the shield generally represents the protection of God: *e. g.* Ps. 3 : 3; 28 : 7; but in Ps. 47 : 9 it is applied to earthly rulers, and in Eph. 6 : 16 to faith. [ARMS.]

Shigga'ion, Ps. 7 : 1, a particular kind of psalm, the specific character of which is now not known; perhaps a "wild, mournful ode."

Shi'hon (*ruin*), a town of Issachar, named only in Josh. 19 : 19. Eusebius mentions it as then existing "near Mount Tabor."

Shi'hor of Egypt. [SIHOR.]

Shi'hor-lib'nath (*black of whiteness*), named only in Josh. 19 : 26 as one of the landmarks of the boundary of Asher. (Probably the little stream called on the map of Pal. Ord. Survey *Wady en Nebra*, "which enters the Mediterranean a little south of Athlit." The name would come from the turgid character of the stream contrasted with the white and glistening sands of its shore.—ED.)

Shil'hi (*armed*), the father of Azubah the mother of Jehoshaphat, 1 Kings 22 : 42; 2 Chron. 20 : 31. (B.C. before 946.)

Shil'him (*fountains*), one of the cities in the southern portion of the tribe of Judah. Josh. 15 : 32.

Shil'lem (*requital*), son of Naphtali and an ancestor of the family of the Shillemites. Gen. 46 : 24; Num. 26 : 49.

Shil'lemites, The. [SHILLEM.]

Shilo'ah, The waters of, a certain soft-flowing stream, Isa. 8 : 6, better known under the later name of Siloam— the only perennial spring of Jerusalem.

Shi'loh. In the Authorized Version of the Bible Shiloh is once used as the name of a person, in a very difficult passage, in Gen. 49 : 10, "The sceptre shall not depart from Judah, nor a lawgiver from between his feet, until Shiloh come; and unto him shall the gathering of the people be." Supposing that the translation is correct, the meaning of the word is *peaceable* or *pacific*, and the allusion is either to Solomon, whose name has a similar signification, or to the expected Messiah, who in Isa. 9 : 6 is expressly called the Prince of Peace. [MESSIAH.] Other interpretations, however, of the passage are given, one of which makes it refer to the city of this name. [See the following article.] It might be translated, "The sceptre shall not depart from Judah, nor the ruler's staff from between his feet, till he shall go to Shiloh." In this case the allusion would be to the primacy of Judah in

war, Judges 1 : 1, 2; 20 : 18; Num. 2 : 3; 10 : 14, which was to continue until the promised land was conquered and the ark of the covenant was solemnly deposited at Shiloh.

Shiloh.

Shi'loh (*place of rest*), a city of Ephraim. In Judges 21 : 19 it is said that Shiloh is "on the north side of Bethel, on the east side of the highway that goeth up from Bethel to Shechem, and on the south of Lebonah." In agreement with this the traveller of our own day, going north from Jerusalem, lodges the first night at *Beitin,* the ancient Bethel; the next day, at the distance of a few hours, turns aside to the right, in order to visit *Seilûn,* the Arabic for Shiloh; and then passing through the narrow wady which brings him to the main road, leaves *el-Lebbân,* the Lebonah of Scripture, on the left, as he pursues "the highway" to *Nablûs,* the ancient Shechem. [SHECHEM.] Shiloh was one of the earliest and most sacred of the Hebrew sanctuaries. The ark of the covenant, which had been kept at Gilgal during the progress of the conquest, Josh. 17 : 1, *seq.,* was removed thence on the subjugation of the country, and kept at Shiloh from the last days of Joshua to the time of Samuel. Josh. 18 : 10; Judges 18 : 31; 1 Sam. 4 : 3. It was here the Hebrew conqueror divided among the tribes the portion of the west Jordan region which had not been already allotted. Josh. 18 : 10 ; 19 : 51. In this distribution, or an earlier one, Shiloh fell within the limits of Ephraim. Josh. 16 : 5. The ungodly conduct of the sons of Eli occasioned the loss of the ark of the covenant, which had been carried into battle against the Philistines, and Shiloh from that time sank into insignificance. It stands forth in the Jewish history as a striking example of the divine indignation. Jer. 7 : 12.

Shilo'ni. This word occurs in the Authorized Version only in Neh. 11 : 5, where it should be rendered—as it is in other cases—" the Shilonite," that is, the descendant of Shelah the youngest son of Judah.

Shi'lonite, The, that is, the native or resident of Shiloh; a title ascribed only to Ahijah. 1 Kings 11 : 29 ; 12 : 15 ; 15 : 29 ; 2 Chron. 9 : 29 ; 10 : 15.

Shi'lonites, The, are mentioned among the descendants of Judah dwelling in Jerusalem at a date difficult to fix. 1 Chron. 9 : 5. They are doubtless the members of the house of Shelah, who in the Pentateuch are more accurately designated Shelanites.

Shil'shah (*strong*), son of Zophah of the tribe of Asher. 1 Chron. 7 : 37. (B.C. before 1015.)

Shim'ea (*fame*). 1. Son of David by Bath-sheba. 1 Chron. 3 : 5. (B.C. 1045.)

2. A Merarite Levite. 1 Chron. 6 : 30 (15).

3. A Gershonite Levite, ancestor of Asaph the minstrel. 1 Chron. 6 : 39 (24). (B.C. before 1200.)

4. The brother of David, 1 Chron. 20 : 7, elsewhere called Shammah, Shimma and Shimeah.

Shim'eah. 1. Brother of David, and father of Jonathan and Jonadab, 2 Sam. 21 : 21 ; called also Shammah, Shimea, and Shimma. (B.C. about 1060.)

2. A descendant of Jehiel, the father or founder of Gibeon. 1 Chron. 8 : 32. (B.C. perhaps 536.)

Shim'eam (*their fame*), a descendant of Jehiel, the founder or prince of Gibeon. 1 Chron. 9 : 38. Called SHIMEAH in 1 Chron. 8 : 32.

Shim'cath (feminine of Shimeah), an Ammonitess, mother of Jozachar or Zabad, one of the murderers of King Joash. 2 Kings 12 : 21 (22) ; 2 Chron. 24 : 26. (B.C. 609.)

Shim'ei (*renowned*). 1. Son of Gershon the son of Levi, Num. 3 : 18 ; 1 Chron.

6 : 17, 29 ; 23 : 7, 9, 10 ; Zech. 12 : 13 ; called SHIMI in Ex. 6 : 17. (B.C. after 1706.)

2. Shimei the son of Gera, a Benjamite of the house of Saul, who lived at Bahurim. (B.C. 1023.) When David and his suite were seen descending the long defile, on his flight from Absalom, 2 Sam. 16 : 5–13, the whole feeling of the clan of Benjamin burst forth without restraint in the person of Shimei. He ran along the ridge, cursing and throwing stones at the king and his companions. The next meeting was very different. The king was now returning from his successful campaign. Just as he was crossing the Jordan, 2 Sam. 19 : 18, the first person to welcome him was Shimei, who threw himself at David's feet in abject penitence. But the king's suspicions were not set at rest by this submission ; and on his death-bed he recalls the whole scene to the recollection of his son Solomon. Solomon gave Shimei notice that from henceforth he must consider himself confined to the walls of Jerusalem, on pain of death. 1 Kings 2 : 36, 37. For three years the engagement was kept. At the end of that time, for the purpose of capturing two slaves who had escaped to Gath, he went out on his ass, and made his journey successfully. *Ibid.* 2 : 40. On his return the king took him at his word, and he was slain by Benaiah. *Ibid.* 2 : 41–46.

3. One of the adherents of Solomon at the time of Adonijah's usurpation. 1 Kings 1 : 8. (B.C. 1015.)

4. Solomon's commissariat officer in Benjamin. 1 Kings 4 : 18.

5. Son of Pedaiah, and brother of Zerubbabel. 1 Chron. 3 : 19. (B.C. 536.)

6. A Simeonite, son of Zacchur. 1 Chron. 4 : 26, 27.

7. Son of Gog, a Reubenite. 1 Chron. 5 : 4.

8. A Gershonite Levite, son of Jahath. 1 Chron. 6 : 42.

9. Son of Jeduthun, and chief of the tenth division of the singers. 1 Chron. 25 : 17.

10. The Ramathite who was over David's vineyards. 1 Chron. 27 : 27.

11. A Levite of the sons of Heman, who took part in the purification of the temple under Hezekiah. 2 Chron. 29 : 14. (B.C. 726.)

12. The brother of Cononiah the Levite, in the reign of Hezekiah. 2 Chron. 31 : 12, 13. Perhaps the same as the preceding.

13. A Levite in the time of Ezra who had married a foreign wife. Ezra 10 : 23.

14. One of the family of Hashum, who put away his foreign wife at Ezra's command. Ezra 10 : 33.

15. A son of Bani, who had also married a foreign wife, and put her away. Ezra 10 : 38. (B.C. 459.)

16. Son of Kish, a Benjamite, and ancestor of Mordecai. Esther 2 : 5. (B.C. before 479.

Shim'eon (*hearing* (*prayer*)), a layman of Israel, of the family of Harim, who had married a foreign wife, and divorced her in the time of Ezra. Ezra 10 : 31. (B.C. 458.)

Shim'hi (*renowned*), a Benjamite, apparently the same as Shema the son of Elpaal. 1 Chron. 8 : 21.

Shi'mi = SHIMEI, 1. Ex. 6 : 17.

Shim'ites, The, the descendants of Shimei the son of Gershon. Num. 3 : 21.

Shim'ma, the third son of Jesse, and brother of David. 1 Chron. 2 : 13. Same as Shimeah.

Shi'mon (*desert*). The four sons of Shimon are enumerated in an obscure genealogy of the tribe of Judah. 1 Chron. 4 : 20.

Shim'rath (*guard*), a Benjamite, of the sons of Shimhi. 1 Chron. 8 : 21.

Shim'ri (*vigilant*). 1. A Simeonite, son of Shemaiah. 1 Chron. 4 : 37. (B.C. after 1450.)

2. The father of Jediael, one of David's guard. 1 Chron. 11 : 45. (B.C. before 1043.)

3. A Kohathite Levite in the reign of Hezekiah. 2 Chron. 29 : 13. (B.C. 726.)

Shim'rith (feminine of Shimri, *vigilant*), a Moabitess, mother of Jehozabad, one of the assassins of King Joash. 2 Chron. 24 : 26. In 2 Kings 12 : 21 she is called SHOMER. (B.C. 839.)

Shim'rom. 1 Chron. 7 : 1. [SHIMRON.]

Shim'ron (*watch-height*). 1. A city of Zebulun. Josh. 11 : 1 ; 19 : 15. Its full appellation was perhaps Shimron-meron.

2. The fourth son of Issachar according to the lists of Genesis, Gen. 46 : 13, and Numbers, Num. 26 : 24, and the head of the family of the Shimronites.

Shim'ronites, The. [SHIMRON.]

Shim'ron-me'ron (*watch-height of Meron*). The king of Shimron-meron is mentioned as one of the thirty-one kings vanquished by Joshua. Josh. 12 : 20. It is probably the complete name of the place elsewhere called Shimron, a city of Zebulun. Josh. 11 : 1 ; 19 : 15.

Shim'sha-i, or **Shimsha'i** (*sunny*), the scribe or secretary of Rehum, who was a kind of satrap of the conquered province of Judea and of the colony of Samaria, supported by the Persian court. Ezra 4 : 8, 9, 17, 23. He was apparently an Aramæan, for the letter which he wrote to Artaxerxes was in Syriac. Ezra 4 : 7. (B.C. 529.)

Shi'nab (*splendor of the father*, i. e. *God*), the king of Admah in the time of Abraham. Gen. 14 : 2. (B.C. 1912.)

Shi'nar (*country of two rivers*), the ancient name of the great alluvial tract through which the Tigris and Euphrates pass before reaching the sea—the tract known in later times as Chaldæa or Babylonia. It was a plain country, where brick had to be used for stone and slime for mortar. Gen. 11 : 3. Among the cities were Babel (Babylon), Erech or Orech (Orchoe), Calneh or Calno (probably *Niffer*), and Accad, the site of which is unknown. It may be suspected that Shinar was the name by which the Hebrews originally knew the lower Mesopotamian country where they so long dwelt, and which Abraham brought with him from " Ur of the Chaldees."

Ship. No one writer in the whole range of Greek and Roman literature has supplied us with so much information concerning the merchant-ships of the ancients as St. Luke in the narrative of St. Paul's voyage to Rome. Acts 27, 28. It is important to remember that he accomplished it in three ships : first, the Adramyttian vessel which took him from Cæsarea to Myra, and which was probably a coasting-vessel of no great size, Acts 27 : 1–6 ; secondly, the large Alexandrian corn-ship, in which he was wrecked on the coast of Malta, Acts 27 : 6–28 : 1 ; and thirdly, another large Alexandrian corn-ship, in which he sailed from Malta by Syracuse and Rhegium to Puteoli. Acts 28 : 11–13. 1. *Size of ancient ships.*—The narrative which we take as our chief guide affords a good standard for estimating this. The ship in which St. Paul was wrecked had 276 persons on board, Acts 27 : 37, besides a cargo of wheat, *ibid.* 10, 38 ; and all these passengers seem to have been taken on to Puteoli in another ship, *ibid.* 28 : 11, which had its own crew and its own cargo. Now, in modern transport-ships, prepared for carrying troops, it is a common estimate to allow a ton and a half per man. On the whole, if we say that an ancient merchant-ship might range from 500 to 1000 tons, we are clearly within the mark. 2. *Steering apparatus.* —Some commentators have fallen into strange perplexities from observing that in Acts 27 : 40 ("the fastenings of the rudders") St. Luke uses the plural. Ancient ships were in truth not steered at all by rudders fastened or hinged to the stern, but by means of two paddle-rudders, one on each quarter, acting in a rowlock or through a port-hole, as the vessel might be small or large. 3. *Build and ornaments of the hull.*—It is probable that there was no very marked difference between the bow and the stern. The "hold," Jonah 1 : 5, would present no special peculiarities. That personification of ships which seems to be instinctive led the ancients to paint an eye on each side of the bow. Comp. Acts 27 : 15. An ornament of the ship which took Paul from Malta to Pozzuoli is more explicitly referred to. The "sign" of that ship, Acts 28 : 11, was Castor and Pollux; and the symbols of those heroes

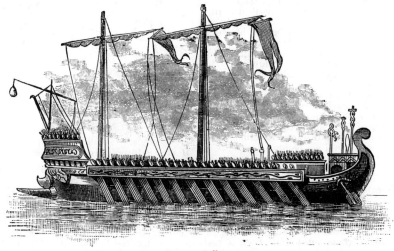

Roman Galley.

were doubtless painted or sculptured on each side of the bow. 4. *Under-girders.*— The imperfection of the build, and still more (see below, 6) the peculiarity of the rig, in ancient ships, resulted in a greater tendency than in our times to the starting of the planks, and consequently to leaking and foundering. Hence it was customary to take on board peculiar contrivances, suitably called "helps," Acts 27 : 17, as precautions against such dangers. These were simply cables or chains, which in case of necessity could be passed round the frame of the ship, at right angles to its length, and made tight. 5. *Anchors.*—Ancient anchors were similar in form to those which we use now, except that they were without flukes. The ship in which Paul was sailing had four anchors on board. The sailors on this occasion anchored by the stern. Acts 27 : 29. 6. *Masts, sails, ropes and yards.*— The rig of an ancient ship was more simple and clumsy than that employed in modern times. Its great feature was one large mast, with one large square sail fastened to a yard of great length. Hence the strain upon the hull, and the danger of starting the planks, were greater than under the present system, which distributes the mechanical pressure more evenly over the whole ship. Not that there were never more masts than one, or more sails than one on the same mast, in an ancient merchantman; but these were repetitions, so to speak, of the same general unit of rig. Another feature of the ancient, as of the modern, ship is the flag at the top of the mast. Isa. *l. c.*, and 30 : 17. We must remember that the ancients had no compass, and very imperfect charts and instruments, if any at all. 7. *Rate of sailing.*—St. Paul's voyages furnish excellent data for approximately estimating this; and they are quite in harmony with what we learn from other sources. We must notice here, however—what commentators sometimes curiously forget—that winds are variable. Thus the voyage between Troas and Philippi, accomplished on one occasion, Acts 16 : 11, 12, in two days, occupied on another occasion, Acts 20 : 6, five days. With a fair wind an ancient ship would sail fully seven knots an hour. 8. *Sailing before the wind, and near the wind.*— The rig which has been described is, like the rig of Chinese junks, peculiarly favorable to a quick run before the wind. Acts 16 : 11 ; 27 : 16. It would, however, be a great mistake to suppose that ancient ships could not work to windward. The superior rig and build, however, of modern ships enable them to sail nearer to the wind than was the case in classical times. A modern ship, if the weather is not very boisterous, will sail within six points of the wind. To an ancient vessel, of which the hull was more clumsy and the yards could not be braced so tight, it would be safe to assign seven points as the limit. *Boats on the Sea of Galilee.*— In the narrative of the call of the disciples to be "fishers of men," Matt. 4 : 18–22 ; Mark 1 : 16–20 ; Luke 5 : 1–11, there is no special information concerning the characteristics of these. With the large population round the Lake of Tiberias, there must have been a vast number of both fishing-boats and pleasure-boats, and boat-building must have been an active trade on its shores.

Shi'phi (*abundant*), a Simeonite, father of Ziza, a prince of the tribe in the time of Hezekiah. 1 Chron. 4 : 37. (B.C. 726.)

Shiph'mite, The, probably, though not certainly, the native of Shepham. 1 Chron. 27 : 27.

Shiph'rah (*brightness*), Ex. 1 : 15, the name of one of the two midwives of the Hebrews who disobeyed the command of Pharaoh to kill the male children. vs. 15–21. (B.C. 1570.)

Shiph'tan (*judicial*), father of Kemuel, a prince of the tribe of Ephraim. Num. 34 : 24. (B.C. before 1450.)

Shi'sha (*Jehovah contends*), father of Elihoreph and Ahiah, the royal secretaries in the reign of Solomon. 1 Kings 4 : 3. He is apparently the same as Shavsha, who held the same position under David. (B.C. 1000.)

Shi'shak, king of Egypt, the Sheshonk I. of the monuments, first sovereign of the Bubastite twenty-second dynasty. His reign offers the first determined synchronism of Egyptian and Hebrew his-

Head of Shishak. (*From temple of Karnak.*)

tory. The first year of Shishak would about correspond to the 26th of Solomon (B.C. 989), and the 20th of Shishak to the 5th of Rehoboam. Shishak at the beginning of his reign received the fugitive Jeroboam, 1 Kings 11 : 40; and it was probably at the instigation of Jeroboam that he attacked Rehoboam. "He took the fenced cities which [pertained] to Judah, and came to Jerusalem." He exacted all the treasures of his city from Rehoboam, and apparently made him tributary. 1 Kings 14 : 25, 26 ; 2 Chron. 12 : 2–9. Shishak has left a record of this expedition sculptured on the wall of the great temple of El-Karnak. It is a list of the countries, cities and tribes conquered or ruled by him, or tributary to him.

Shittah tree, Shittim (Heb. *shittâh, the thorny*), is without doubt correctly referred to some species of *Acacia*, of which three or four kinds occur in the Bible lands. The wood of this tree—perhaps the *Acacia seyal* is more definitely signified—was extensively employed in the construction of the tabernacle. See Ex. 25, 26, 36, 37, 38. (This tree is sometimes three or four feet in diameter (Tristram). The wood is close-grained and hard, of a fine orange-brown color, and admirably adapted to cabinet work. —ED.) The *A. seyal* is very common in some parts of the peninsula of Sinai. It yields the well-known substance called gum arabic, which is obtained by incisions in the bark, but it is impossible to say whether the ancient Jews were acquainted with its use. From the tangled thicket into which the stem of this tree expands, Stanley well remarks that hence is to be traced the use of the plural form of the Heb. noun *shittim*, the singular number occurring once only in the Bible. This acacia must not be confounded with the tree (*Robinia pseudo-acacia*) popularly known by this name in England, which is a North American plant, and belongs to a different genus and suborder. The true acacias belong to the order *Leguminosæ*, sub-order *Mimoseæ*.

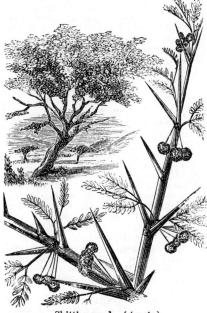

Shittim-wood. (*Acacia*.)

Shit'tim (*the acacias*), the place of Israel's encampment between the conquest of the transjordanic highlands and the passage of the Jordan. Num. 25 : 1 ; 33 : 49 ; Josh. 2 : 1 ; 3 : 1 ; Micah 6 : 5. Its full name appears to be given in the first of these passages—Abel has-Shittim, "the meadow, or moist place, of the acacias." It was "in the Arboth-moab, by Jordan-Jericho," Num. 22 : 1 ; 26 : 3 ; 31 : 12 ; 33 : 48, 49 ; that is to say, it was in the Arabah or Jordan valley, opposite Jericho.

Shi'za (*splendor*), a Reubenite, father of Adina, 1 Chron. 11 : 42, one of David's warriors. (B.C. 1043.)

Sho'a (*rich*), a proper name which occurs only in Ezek. 23 : 23, in connection with Pekod and Koa. The three apparently designate districts of Assyria with which the southern kingdom of Judah had been intimately connected, and which were to be arrayed against it for punishment.

Sho'bab (*rebellious*). 1. Son of David by Bath-sheba. 2 Sam. 5 : 14 ; 1 Chron. 3 : 5 ; 14 : 4. (B.C. about 1045.)

2. Apparently the son of Caleb the son of Hezron by his wife Azubah. 1 Chron. 2 : 18. (B.C. after 1706.)

Sho'bach (*expansion*), the general of Hadarezer king of the Syrians of Zoba, who was defeated by David. 2 Sam. 10 : 15–18. In 1 Chron. 19 : 16, 18 he is called SHOPHACH. (B.C. 1034.)

Sho'ba-i (*glorious*). The children of Shobai were a family of the doorkeepers of the temple, who returned with Zerubbabel. Ezra 2 : 42 ; Neh. 7 : 45. (B.C. before 536.)

Sho'bal (*flowing*). 1. Second son of Seir the Horite, Gen. 36 : 20 ; 1 Chron. 1 : 38, and one of the "dukes" of the Horites. Gen. 36 : 29.

2. Son of Caleb the son of Hur, and founder or prince of Kirjath-jearim. 1 Chron. 2 : 50, 52. (B.C. about 1445.)

3. In 1 Chron. 4 : 1, 2, Shobal appears with Hur among the sons of Judah. He is possibly the same as the preceding.

Sho'bek (*free*), one of the heads of the people who sealed the covenant with Nehemiah. Neh. 10 : 24. (B.C. 446.)

Sho'bi (*glorious*), son of Nahash of Rabbah of the children of Ammon. 2 Sam. 17 : 27. He was one of the first to meet David at Mahanaim on his flight from Absalom. (B.C. 1023.)

Sho'cho, 2 Chron. 28 : 18, one of the four varieties of the name Socoh.

Sho'co, 2 Chron. 11 : 7, a variation in the Authorized Version of the name Socoh.

Sho'choh, 1 Sam. 17 : 1, same as Socoh.

Shoe. [SANDAL.]

Sho'ham (*onyx*), a Merarite Levite, son of Jaaziah. 1 Chron. 24 : 27. (B.C. 1043.)

Sho'mer (*keeper*). 1. An Asherite, 1 Chron. 7 : 32; also called Shamer. ver. 34.

2. The father (mother?) of Jehozabad, who slew King Joash. 2 Kings 12 : 21. In the parallel passage in 2 Chron. 24 : 26 the name is converted into the feminine form Shimrith, who is further described as a Moabitess. [SHIMRITH.] (B.C. 839.)

Sho'phach (*expansion*), Shobach, the general of Hadarezer. 1 Chron. 19 : 16, 18. (B.C. 1034.)

Sho'phan (*bareness*), one of the fortified towns on the east of Jordan which were taken possession of and rebuilt by the tribe of Gad. Num. 32 : 35.

Shoshan'nim (*lilies*). "To the chief musician upon Shoshannim" is a musical direction to the leader of the temple choir which occurs in Pss. 45, 69, and most probably indicates the melody "after" or "in the manner of" (Authorized Version "upon") which the psalms were to be sung. Shoshannim-eduth occurs in the same way in the title of Ps. 80. As the words now stand they signify "lilies, a testimony," and the two are separated by a large distinctive accent. In themselves they have no meaning in the present text, and must therefore be regarded as probably a fragment of the beginning of an older psalm with which the choir were familiar.

Shu'ah (*wealth*). 1. Son of Abraham by Keturah. Gen. 25 : 2; 1 Chron. 1 : 32. (B.C. before 1820.)

2. Properly Shuchah, brother of Chelub. 1 Chron. 4 : 11.

3. The father of Judah's wife, Gen. 38 : 2, 12; called also Shua in the Authorized Version. (B.C. before 1725.)

Shu'al (*a jackal*), son of Zophah, an Asherite. 1 Chron. 7 : 36. (B.C. after 1445.)

Shu'al, The land of, a district named in 1 Sam. 13 : 17 only. It is pretty certain from the passage that it lay north of Michmash. If therefore it be identical with the "land of Shalim," 1 Sam. 9 : 4—as is not impossible—we have the first and only clue yet obtained to Saul's journey in quest of the asses. The name Shual has not yet been identified.

Shu'bael. 1. Shebuel the son of Gershon. 1 Chron. 24 : 20.

2. Shebuel the son of Heman the minstrel. 1 Chron. 25 : 20.

Shu'ham (*pit-digger*), son of Dan and ancestor of the Shuhamites. Num. 26 : 42.

Shu'hamites, The. [SHUHAM.]

Shu'hite (*descendant of Shuah*). This ethnic appellative "Shuhite" is frequent in the book of Job, but only as the epithet of one person, Bildad. The local indications of this book point to a region on the western side of Chaldæa, bordering on Arabia; and exactly in this locality, above Hit and on both sides of the Euphrates, are found, in the Assyrian inscriptions, the *Tsukhi*, a powerful people. It is probable that these were the Shuhites.

Shu'lamite, The, one of the personages in the poem of Solomon's Song. 6 : 13. The name denotes a woman belonging to a place called Shulem, which is probably the same as Shunem. [SHUNEM.] If, then, Shulamite and Shunammite are equivalent, we may conjecture that the Shunammite who was the object of Solomon's passion was Abishag, the most lovely girl of her day, and at the time of David's death the most prominent person at Jerusalem.

Shu'mathites, The, one of the four families who sprang from Kirjath-jearim. 1 Chron. 2 : 53.

Shu'nammite, The, *i. e. the native of Shunem*, is applied to two persons: Abishag, the nurse of King David, 1 Kings 1 : 3, 15; 2 : 17, 21, 22, and the nameless hostess of Elisha. 2 Kings 4 : 12, 25, 36.

Shu'nem (*double resting-place*), one of the cities allotted to the tribe of Issachar. Josh. 19 : 18. It is mentioned on two occasions—1 Sam. 28 : 4; 2 Kings 4 : 8. It was besides the native place of Abishag. 1 Kings 1 : 3. It is mentioned by Eusebius as five miles south of Mount Tabor, and then known as Sulem. This agrees with the position of the present *Solam*, a village three miles north of Jezreel and five from Gilboa.

Shu'ni (*fortunate*), son of Gad, and founder of the family of the Shunites. Gen. 46 : 16; Num. 26 : 15. (B.C. 1706.)

Shu'nites, The, the descendants of Shuni.

Shu'pham. [SHUPPIM.]

Shu'phamites, The, the descendants of Shupham or Shephupham, the Benjamite. Num. 26 : 39.

Shup'pim (*serpents*). In the genealogy of Benjamin "Shuppim and Huppim, the children of Ir," are reckoned in 1 Chron. 7 : 12. Ir is the same as Iri the son of Bela the son of Benjamin, so that Shuppim was the great-grandson of Benjamin.

Shur (*a wall*), a place just without the eastern border of Egypt. Shur is first mentioned in the narrative of Hagar's flight from Sarah. Gen. 16 : 7. Abraham afterward "dwelled between Kadesh and Shur, and sojourned in Gerar." Gen. 20 : 1. It is also called Ethami. The wilderness of Shur was entered by the Israelites after they had crossed the Red Sea. Ex. 15 : 22, 23. It was also called the wilderness of Etham. Num. 33 : 8. Shur may have been a fortified town east of the ancient head of the Red Sea; and from its being spoken of as a limit, it was probably the last Arabian town before entering Egypt.

Shu'shan, or **Su'sa** (*a lily*), is said to have received its name from the abundance of the lily (*shûshan* or *shûshanah*) in its neighborhood. It was originally the capital of the country called in Scripture Elam, and by the classical writers Susis or Susiana. In the time of Daniel Susa was in the possession of the Babylonians, to whom Elam had probably passed at the division of the Assyrian empire made by Cyaxares and Nabopolassar. Dan. 8 : 2. The conquest of Babylon by Cyrus transferred Susa to the Persian dominion; and it was not long before the Achæmenian princes determined to make it the capital of their whole empire and the chief place of their own residence. According to some writers the change was made by Cyrus; according to others it had at any rate taken place before the death of Cambyses; but, according to the evidence of the place itself and of the other Achæmenian monuments, it would seem most probable that the transfer was really the work of Darius Hystaspes. Nehemiah resided here. Neh. 1 : 1. Shushan was situated on the Ulai or Choaspes. It is identified with the modern *Sus* or *Shush*, and its ruins are about three miles in circumference. (Here have been found the remains of the great palace built by Darius, the father of Xerxes, in which and the surrounding buildings took place the scenes recorded in the life of Esther. The great central hall was 343 feet long by 244 feet wide. The king's gate, says Schaff, where Mordecai sat, "was probably a hall 100 feet square, 150 feet from the northern portico. Between these two was probably the inner court, where Esther appeared before the king."—ED.)

Shu'shan-e'duth (*the lily of testimony*), Ps. 60, is probably an abbrevia-

tion of "Shoshannim-eduth." Ps. 80. [SHOSHANNIM.]

Shu'thalhites, The. [SHUTHELAH.]

Shu'thelah (*noise of breaking*), head of an Ephraimite family, called after him Shuthalhites, Num. 26 : 35, and lineal ancestor of Joshua the son of Nun. 1 Chron. 7 : 20-27.

Si'a. The "children of Sia" were a family of Nethinim who returned with Zerubbabel. Neh. 7 : 47. The name is written SIAHA in Ezra 2 : 44 and SUD in 1 Esd. 5 : 29.

Si'aha = SIA. Ezra 2 : 44.

Sib'beca-i = SIBBECHAI the Hushathite.

Sib'becha-i (*a weaver*), one of David's guard, and eighth captain for the eighth month of 24,000 men of the king's army. 1 Chron. 11 : 29; 27 : 11. (B.C. 1043.) He belonged to one of the principal families of Judah, the Zarhites or descendants of Zerah, and is called "the Hushathite," probably from the place of his birth. Sibbechai's great exploit, which gave him a place among the mighty men of David's army, was his single combat with Saph or Sippai, the Philistine giant, in the battle at Gezer or Gob. 2 Sam. 21 : 18; 1 Chron. 20 : 4.

Sibboleth, the Ephraimite pronunciation of the word Shibboleth. Judges 12 : 6. [SHIBBOLETH.]

Sib'mah. [SHEBAM.]

Sibra'im (*twofold hope*), one of the landmarks on the northern boundary of the holy land as stated by Ezekiel. Ezek. 47 : 16. It has not been identified.

Si'chem. Gen. 12 : 6. [SHECHEM.]

Sic'yon (sish'eon), 1 Macc. 15 : 23, a celebrated Greek city in Peloponnesus, upon the Corinthian Gulf.

Sid'dim (*field, plain*), **The vale of,** a place named only in one passage of Genesis—14 : 3, 8, 10. It was one of that class of valleys which the Hebrews designated by the word *emek*. This term appears to have been assigned to a broad, flattish tract, sometimes of considerable width, enclosed on each side by a definite range of hills. It was so far a suitable spot for the combat between the four and five kings, ver. 8; but it contained a multitude of bitumen-pits sufficient materially to affect the issue of the battle. In this valley the kings of the five allied cities of Sodom, Gomorrah, Admah, Zeboim and Bela seem to have awaited the approach of the invaders. It is therefore probable that it was in the neighborhood of the "plain or circle of Jordan" in which those cities stood. If we could venture, as some have done, to interpret the latter clause of ver. 3, "which is near," or "which is at, or by, the Salt Sea," then we might agree with Dr. Robinson and others in identifying the valley of Siddim with the enclosed plain which intervenes between the south end of the lake and the range of heights which terminate the *Ghór* and commence the *Wady Arabah*. But the original of the passage seems to imply that the Salt Sea covers the actual space formerly occupied by the vale of Siddim. [SEA, THE SALT.]

Si'de, a city on the coast of Pamphylia, 10 or 12 miles to the east of the river Eurymedon. It is mentioned in 1 Macc. 15 : 23, and was a colony of Cumæans.

Si'don, the Greek form of the Phœnician name Zidon. [ZIDON.]

Sido'nians, the Greek form of the word Zidonians, usually so exhibited in the Authorized Version of the Old Testament. It occurs Deut. 3 : 9 ; Josh. 13 : 4, 6 ; Judges 3 : 3 ; 1 Kings 5 : 6. [ZIDON.]

Si'hon (*warrior*), king of the Amorites when Israel arrived on the borders of the promised land. Num. 21 : 21. (B.C. 1451.) Shortly before the time of Israel's arrival he had dispossessed the Moabites of a splendid territory, driving them south of the natural bulwark of the Arnon. *Ibid.* 21 : 26–29. When the Israelite host appeared, he did not hesitate or temporize like Balak, but at once gathered his people together and attacked them. But the battle was his last. He and all his host were destroyed, and their district from Arnon to Jabbok became at once the possession of the conqueror.

Si'hor (*dark*), accurately **Shi'hor,** once **The Shihor,** or **Shihor of Egypt,** when unqualified a name of the Nile. It is held to signify "the black" or "turbid." In Jeremiah the identity of Shihor with the Nile seems distinctly stated. Jer. 2 : 18. The stream mentioned in 1 Chron. 13 : 5 is possibly that of the *Wâdi-l'Areesh.*

Si'las (contracted form of Silvanus, *woody*), an eminent member of the early Christian Church, described under that name in the Acts, but as Silvanus in St. Paul's epistles. He first appears as one of the leaders of the church at Jerusalem, Acts 15 : 22, holding the office of an inspired teacher. 15 : 32. His name, derived from the Latin *silva*, "wood," betokens him a Hellenistic Jew, and he appears to have been a Roman citizen. Acts 16 : 37. He was appointed as a delegate to accompany Paul and Barnabas on their return to Antioch with the decree of the Council of Jerusalem. Acts 15 : 22, 32. Having accomplished this mission, he returned to Jerusalem. Acts 15 : 33. He must, however, have immediately revisited Antioch, for we find him selected by St. Paul as the companion of his second missionary journey. Acts 15 : 40–17 : 10. At Berea he was left behind with Timothy ,while St. Paul proceeded to Athens, Acts 17 : 14, and we hear nothing more of his movements until he rejoined the apostle at Corinth. Acts 18 : 5. His presence at Corinth is several times noticed. 2 Cor. 1 : 19 ; 1 Thess. 1 : 1 ; 2 Thess. 1 : 1. Whether he was the Silvanus who conveyed St. Peter's first epistle to Asia Minor, 1 Pet. 5 : 12, is doubtful ; the probabilities are in favor of the identity. A tradition of very slight authority represents Silas to have become bishop of Corinth.

Silk. The only *undoubted* notice of silk in the Bible occurs in Rev. 18 : 12, where it is mentioned among the treasures of the typical Babylon. It is, however, in the highest degree probable that the texture was known to the Hebrews from the time that their commercial relations were extended by Solomon. The well-known classical name of the substance does not occur in the Hebrew language.

Sil'la (*a highway*). "The house of Millo which goeth down to Silla" was the scene of the murder of King Joash. 2 Kings 12 : 20. What or where Silla was is entirely matter of conjecture. Some have suggested the pool of Siloam.

Sil'oah, The pool of, properly "the pool of Shelach." Neh. 3 : 15. [SILOAM.]

Sil'oam (*sent*). *Shiloach,* Isa. 8 : 6; *Siloah,* Neh. 3 : 15; *Siloam,* John 9 : 7, 11. Siloam is one of the few undisputed localities in the topography of Jerusalem ; still retaining its old name (with Arabic modification, *Silwân*), while every other pool has lost its Bible designation. This is the more remarkable as it is a mere suburban tank of no great size, and for many an age not particularly good or plentiful in its waters, though Josephus tells us that in his day they were both "sweet and abundant." A little way below the Jewish burying-ground, but on

Siloam.

the opposite side of the valley, where the Kedron turns slightly westward and

Pool of the Virgin.

widens itself considerably, is the fountain of the Virgin, or *Um-ed-Deraj*, near the beginning of that saddle-shaped projection of the temple hill supposed to be the Ophel of the Bible and the Ophlas of Josephus. At the back part of this fountain a subterraneous passage begins, through which the water flows, and through which a man may make his way, sometimes walking erect, sometimes stooping, sometimes kneeling, and sometimes crawling, to Siloam. This conduit is 1708 feet long, 16 feet high at the entrance, but only 16 inches at its narrowest part. At a former time it had tributaries which sent their waters down from the city pools or temple wells to swell Siloam. It enters Siloam at the northwest angle; or rather enters a small rock-cut chamber which forms the *vestibule* of Siloam, about five or six feet broad. To this you descend by a few rude steps, under which the water pours itself into the main pool. This pool is oblong, about 52 feet long, 18 feet broad and 19 feet deep; but it is never filled, the water either passing directly through or being maintained at a depth of three

or four feet. The present pool is a ruin, with no moss or ivy to make it romantic: its sides fallen in; its pillars broken; its stair a fragment; its walls giving way; the edge of every stone worn round or sharp by time; in some parts mere *débris*, though around its edges wild flowers, and among other plants the caper tree, grow luxuriantly. The present pool is not the original building; it may be the work of crusaders, perhaps even improved by Saladin, whose affection for wells and pools led him to care for all these things. Yet the spot is the same. This pool, which we may call the *second*, seems anciently to have poured its waters into a *third* before it proceeded to water the royal gardens. This third is perhaps that which Josephus calls "Solomon's pool," and which Nehemiah calls the "king's pool." Neh. 2:14. The expression in Isa. 8:6, "waters of Shiloah that go softly," seems to point to the slender rivulet, flowing gently though once very profusely out of Siloam into the lower breadth of level where the king's gardens, or royal paradise, stood, and which is still the greenest spot about the holy city. Siloam

Pool of Siloam.

is a sacred spot even to the Moslem; much more to the Jew. It was to Siloam that the Levite was sent with the golden pitcher on the "last and great day of the feast" of Tabernacles; it was from Siloam that he brought the water which was then poured over the sacrifice, in memory of the water from the rock of Rephidim; and it was to this Siloam water that the Lord pointed when he stood in the temple on that day and cried, "If any man thirst, let him come unto me and drink." The Lord sent the blind man to wash, not *in*, as our version has it, but *at* (εἰς), the pool of Siloam; for it was the clay from his eyes that was to be washed off.

Siloam, Tower in. Luke 13 : 4. Of this we know nothing definitely beyond these words of the Lord. In connection with Ophel, there is mention made of "a tower *that lieth out*," Neh. 3 : 26; and there is no unlikelihood in connecting this *projecting* tower with the tower in Siloam, while one may be almost excused for the conjecture that its projection was the cause of its ultimate fall.

Silva'nus. [SILAS.]

Silver.

Silver. In very early times silver was used for ornaments, Gen. 24 : 53, and for vessels of various kinds. Images for idolatrous worship were made of silver or overlaid with it, Ex. 20 : 23; Hos. 13 : 2; Hab. 2 : 19; Bar. 6 : 39, and the manufacture of silver shrines for Diana was a trade in Ephesus. Acts 19 : 24. But its chief use was as a medium of exchange, and throughout the Old Testament we find "silver" used for money, like the French *argent*. Silver was brought to Solomon from Arabia, 2 Chron. 9 : 14, and from Tarshish, 2 Chron. 9 : 21, which supplied the markets of Tyre. Ezek. 27 : 12. From Tarshish it came in the form of plates, Jer. 10 : 9, like those on which

the sacred books of the Singhalese are written to this day. Spain appears to have been the chief source whence silver was obtained by the ancients. Possibly the hills of Palestine may have afforded some supply of this metal. Silver mixed with alloy is referred to in Jer. 6 : 30, and a finer kind, either purer in itself or more thoroughly purified, is mentioned in Prov. 8 : 19.

Silverlings, a word used once only in the Authorized Version, Isa. 7 : 23, as a translation of the Hebrew word elsewhere rendered "silver" or "money."

Sim'eon (*heard*). 1. The second of Jacob's sons by Leah. His birth is recorded in Gen. 29 : 33. The first group of Jacob's children consists, besides Simeon, of the three other sons of Leah— Reuben, Levi, Judah. Besides the massacre of Shechem, Gen. 34 : 25, the only personal incident related of Simeon is the fact of his being selected by Joseph as the hostage for the appearance of Benjamin. Gen. 42 : 19, 24, 36; 43 : 23. The chief families of the tribe of Simeon are mentioned in the lists of Gen. 46 : 10. At the census of Sinai Simeon numbered 59,300 fighting men. Num. 1 : 23. When the second census was taken, at Shittim, the numbers had fallen to 22,200, and it was the weakest of all the tribes. This was no doubt partly due to the recent mortality following the idolatry of Peor, but there must have been other causes which have escaped mention. To Simeon was allotted a portion of land out of the territory of Judah, on its southern frontier, which contained eighteen or nineteen cities, with their villages, spread round the venerable well of Beersheba. Josh. 19 : 1-8; 1 Chron. 4 : 28-33. Of these places, with the help of Judah, the Simeonites possessed themselves, Judges 1 : 3, 17; and here they were found, doubtless by Joab, residing in the reign of David. 1 Chron. 4 : 31. What part the tribe took at the time of the division of the kingdom we are not told. The only thing which can be interpreted into a trace of its having taken any part with the northern kingdom are the two casual notices of 2 Chron. 15 : 9 and 34 : 6, which appear to imply the presence of Simeonites there in the reigns of Asa and Josiah.

On the other hand the definite statement of 1 Chron. 4 : 41–43 proves that at that time there were still some of them remaining in the original seat of the tribe, and actuated by all the warlike, lawless spirit of their progenitor.

2. A devout Jew, inspired by the Holy Ghost, who met the parents of our Lord in the temple, took him in his arms, and gave thanks for what he saw and knew of Jesus. Luke 2 : 25–35. There was a Simeon who succeeded his father Hillel as president of the Sanhedrin about A.D. 13, and whose son Gamaliel was the Pharisee at whose feet St. Paul was brought up. Acts 22 : 3. It has been conjectured that he may be the Simeon of St. Luke.

Sim′eon Niger. Acts 13 : 1. [NIGER.]

Si′mon (contracted form of Simeon, a *hearing*). 1. Son of Mattathias. [MACCABEES.]

2. Son of Onias the high priest, whose eulogy closes the "praise of famous men" in the book of Ecclesiasticus, ch. 4. (B.C. 302–293.)

3. A "governor of the temple" in the time of Seleucus Philopator, whose information as to the treasures of the temple led to the sacrilegious attack of Heliodorus. 2 Macc. 3 : 4, etc. (B.C. 175.)

4. Simon the brother of Jesus. The only undoubted notice of this Simon occurs in Matt. 13 : 55, Mark 6 : 3. He has been identified by some writers with Simon the Canaanite, and still more generally with Symeon who became bishop of Jerusalem after the death of James, A.D. 62. The former of these opinions rests on no evidence whatever, nor is the latter without its difficulties.

5. Simon the Canaanite, one of the twelve apostles, Matt. 10 : 4; Mark 3 : 18, otherwise described as Simon Zelotes, Luke 6 : 15; Acts 1 : 13. (A.D. 28.) The latter term, which is peculiar to Luke, is the Greek equivalent for the Chaldee term preserved by Matthew and Mark. [CANAANITE.] Each of these equally points out Simon as belonging to the faction of the Zealots, who were conspicuous for their fierce advocacy of the Mosaic ritual.

6. Simon of Cyrene, a Hellenistic Jew, born at Cyrene, on the north coast of Africa, who was present at Jerusalem at the time of the crucifixion of Jesus, either as an attendant at the feast, Acts 2 : 10, or as one of the numerous settlers at Jerusalem from that place. Acts 6 : 9.

(A.D. 30.) Meeting the procession that conducted Jesus to Golgotha, as he was returning from the country, he was pressed into the service to bear the cross, Matt. 27 : 32; Mark 15 : 21; Luke 23 : 26, when Jesus himself was unable to carry it any longer. Comp. John 19 : 17. Mark describes him as the father of Alexander and Rufus, perhaps because this was the Rufus known to the Roman Christians, Rom. 16 : 13, for whom he more especially wrote.

7. Simon, a resident at Bethany, distinguished as "the leper." It is not improbable that he had been miraculously cured by Jesus. In his house Mary anointed Jesus preparatory to his death and burial. Matt. 26 : 6, etc.; Mark 14 : 3, etc.; John 12 : 1, etc.

8. Simon Magus, a Samaritan living in the apostolic age, distinguished as a sorcerer or "magician," from his practice of magical arts. Acts 8 : 9. According to ecclesiastical writers he was born at Gitton, a village of Samaria, and was probably educated at Alexandria in the tenets of the Gnostic school. He is first introduced to us as practicing magical arts in a city of Samaria, perhaps Sychar, Acts 8 : 5; comp. John 4 ; 5, and with such success that he was pronounced to be "the power of God which is called great." Acts 8 : 10. The preaching and miracles of Philip having excited his observation, he became one of his disciples, and received baptism at his hands, A.D. 36, 37. Subsequently he witnessed the effect produced by the imposition of hands, as practiced by the apostles Peter and John, and, being desirous of acquiring a similar power for himself, he offered a sum of money for it. His object evidently was to apply the power to the prosecution of magical arts. The motive and the means were equally to be reprobated; and his proposition met with a severe denunciation from Peter, followed by a petition on the part of Simon, the tenor of which bespeaks terror, but not penitence. Acts 8 : 9–24. The memory of his peculiar guilt has been perpetuated in the word *simony*, as applied to all traffic in spiritual offices. Simon's history, subsequent to his meeting with Peter, is involved in difficulties. Early Church historians depict him as the pertinacious foe of the apostle Peter, whose movements he followed for the purpose of seeking encounters, in which he was signally defeated. He is said to have followed the

apostle to Rome. His death is associated with this meeting. According to Hippolytus, the earliest authority on the subject, Simon was buried alive at his own request, in the confident assurance that he would rise on the third day.

9. Simon Peter. [PETER.]

10. Simon, a Pharisee, in whose house a penitent woman anointed the head and feet of Jesus. Luke 7 : 40.

House of Simon the Tanner.

11. Simon the tanner, a Christian convert living at Joppa, at whose house Peter lodged. Acts 9 : 43. The house was near the seaside, Acts 10 : 6, 32, for the convenience of the water. (A.D. 37.)

12. Simon the father of Judas Iscariot. John 6 : 71; 13 : 2, 26.

Sim'ri (*vigilant*), properly Shimri, son of Hosah, a Merarite Levite in the reign of David. 1 Chron. 26 : 10.

Sin, a city of Egypt, mentioned only by Ezekiel. Ezek. 30 : 15, 16. The name is Hebrew, or at least Semitic, perhaps signifying *clay*. It is identified in the Vulgate with Pelusium, " the clayey or muddy" town. Its antiquity may perhaps be inferred from the mention of " the wilderness of Sin " in the journeys of the Israelites. Ex. 16 : 1; Num. 33 : 11. Ezekiel speaks of Sin as " Sin the stronghold of Egypt." Ezek. 30 : 15. This place was held by Egypt from that time until the period of the Romans. Herodotus relates that Sennacherib advanced against Pelusium, and that near Pelusium Cambyses defeated Psammenitus. In like manner the decisive battle in which Ochus defeated the last native king, Nectanebos, was fought near this city.

Sin, Wilderness of, a tract of the wilderness which the Israelites reached after leaving the encampment by the Red Sea. Num. 33 : 11, 12. Their next halting-place, Ex. 16 : 1; 17 : 1, was Rephidim, probably the *Wady Feirân* [REPHIDIM]; on which supposition it would follow that Sin must lie between that wady and the coast of the Gulf of Suez, and of course west of Sinai. In the wilderness of Sin the manna was first gathered, and those who adopt the supposition that this was merely the natural product of the *tarfa* bush find from the abundance of that shrub in *Wady es-Sheikh*, southeast of *Wady Ghŭrundel*, a proof of local identity.

Sin offering. The sin offering among the Jews was the sacrifice in which the ideas of propitiation and of atonement for sin were most distinctly marked. The ceremonial of the sin offering is described in Lev. 4 and 6. The trespass offering is closely connected with the sin offering in Leviticus, but at the same time clearly distinguished from it, being in some cases offered with it as a distinct part of the same sacrifice; as, for example, in the cleansing of the leper. Lev. 14. The distinction of ceremonial clearly indicates a difference in the idea of the two sacrifices. The nature of that difference is still a subject of great controversy. We find that the sin offerings were—1. *Regular.* (*a*) For the whole people, at the New Moon, Passover, Pentecost, Feast of Trumpets and Feast of Tabernacles, Num. 28 : 15–29 : 38; besides the solemn offering of the two goats on the Great Day of Atonement. Lev. 16. (b) For the priests and Levites at their consecration, Ex. 29 : 10-14, 36; besides the yearly sin offering (a bullock) for the high priest on the Great Day of Atonement. Lev. 16. 2. *Special.* For any sin of "ignorance" and the like, recorded in Lev. 4 and 5. It is seen that in the law most of the sins which are not purely ceremonial are called sins of "ignorance," see Heb. 9 : 7 ; and in Num. 15 : 30 it is expressly said that while such sins can be atoned for by offerings, "the soul that doeth aught *presumptuously*" (Heb. *with a high hand*) "shall be cut off from among his people." . . . "His iniquity shall be upon him." Comp. Heb. 10 : 26. But here are sufficient indications that the sins here called "of ignorance" are more strictly those of "negligence" or "frailty," repented of by the unpunished offender, as opposed to those of deliberate and unrepentant sin. It is clear that the two classes of sacrifices, although distinct, touch closely upon each other. It is also evident that the sin offering was the only regular and general recognition of sin in the abstract, and accordingly was far more solemn and symbolical in its ceremonial ; the trespass offering was confined to special cases, most of which related to the doing of some material damage, either to the holy things or to man. Josephus declares that the sin offering is presented by those "who fall into sin in ignorance," and the trespass offering by "one who has sinned and is conscious of his sin, but has no one to convict him thereof." Without attempting to decide so difficult and so controverted a question, we may draw the following conclusions : First, that the sin offering was far the more solemn and comprehensive of the two sacrifices. Secondly, that the sin offering looked more to the guilt of the sin done, irrespective of its consequences, while the trespass offering looked to the evil consequences of sin, either against the service of God or against man, and to the duty of atonement, as far as atonement was possible. Thirdly, that in the sin offering especially we find symbolized the acknowledgment of sinfulness as inherent in man, and of the need of expiation by sacrifice to renew the broken covenant between man and God. In considering this subject, it must be remembered that the sacrifices of the law had a temporal

as well as a spiritual significance and effect. They restored an offender to his place in the commonwealth of Israel; they were therefore an atonement to the King of Israel for the infringement of his law.

Si'na, Mount, the Greek form of the well-known name Sinai. Acts 7 : 30, 38.

Si'na-i, or **Sin'a-i** (*thorny*). Nearly in the centre of the peninsula which stretches between the horns of the Red Sea lies a wedge of granite, grünstein and porphyry rocks rising to between 8000 and 9000 feet above the sea. Its shape resembles a scalene triangle. These mountains may be divided into two great masses— that of *Jebel Serbal* (6759 feet high), in the northwest above *Wady Feirân,* and the central group, roughly denoted by the general name of *Sinai.* This group rises abruptly from the *Wady es-Sheikh* at its north foot, first to the cliffs of the *Ras Sûfsâfeh,* behind which towers the pinnacle of *Jebel Mûsa* (the Mount of Moses), and farther back to the right of it the summit of *Jebel Katerin* (Mount St. Catherine, 8705 feet), all being backed up and overtopped by *Um Shumer* (the *mother of fennel,* 9300 feet), which is the highest point of the whole peninsula

1. *Names.*—These mountains are called Horeb, and sometimes Sinai. Some think that Horeb is the name of the whole range, and Sinai the name of a particular mountain ; others, that Sinai is the range and Horeb the particular mountain; while Stanley suggests that the distinction is one of usage, and that both names are applied to the same place.

2. *The mountain from which the law was given.*—Modern investigators have generally come to the conclusion that of the claimants Jebel Serbal, Jebel Mûsa and Ras Sûfsâfeh, the last, the modern Horeb of the monks—viz., the northwest and lower face of the Jebel Mûsa, crowned with a range of magnificent cliffs, the highest point called Ras Sûfsâfeh, as overlooking the plain *er Râhah*—is the scene of the giving of the law, and that peak the mountain into which Moses ascended. (But Jebel Mûsa and Ras Sûfsâfeh are really peaks of the same mountain, and Moses may have received the law on Jebel Mûsa, but it must have been proclaimed from Ras Sûfsâfeh. Jebel Mûsa is the traditional mount where Moses received the law from God. It is a mountain mass two miles long and one mile broad. The

Sinai and the Plain of Er Ráhah. (*From a Photograph.*)

southern peak is 7363 feet high; the northern peak, Ras Sûfsâfeh, is 6830 feet high. It is in full view of the plain er Râhah, where the children of Israel were encamped. This plain is a smooth camping-ground, surrounded by mountains. It is about two miles long by half a mile broad, embracing 400 acres of available standing-ground made into a natural amphitheatre by a low semicircular mound about 300 yards from the foot of the mountain. By actual measurement it contains over 2,000,000 square yards, and with its branches over 4,000,000 square

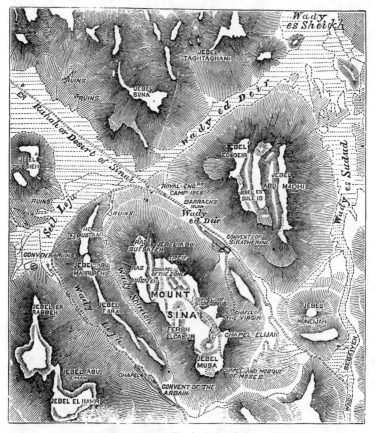

Outline Map of Mount Sinai. (*After Ordnance Survey*.)

yards, so that the whole people of Israel, two million in number, would find ample accommodations for seeing and hearing. In addition to this, the air is wonderfully clear, both for seeing and hearing. Dean Stanley says that "from the highest point of Ras Sûfsâfeh to its lower peak, a distance of about 60 feet, the page of a book distinctly but not loudly read was perfectly audible." It was the belief of the Arabs who conducted Niebuhr that they could make themselves heard across the Gulf of Akabah,—a belief fostered by the great distance to which the voice can actually be carried. There is no other place known among all these mountains so well adapted for the purpose of giving and receiving the law as this rocky pulpit of Ras Sûfsâfeh and the natural amphitheatre of er Râhah.

Si'nim, a people noticed in Isa. 49 : 12, as living at the extremity of the known world. They may be identified with the classical *Sinæ*, the inhabitants of the southern part of China.

Sin'ite, a tribe of Canaanites, Gen. 10 : 17 ; 1 Chron. 1 : 15, whose position is to be sought for in the northern part of the Lebanon district.

Si'on (*lofty*), **Mount.** 1. One of the various names of Mount Hermon. Deut. 4 : 48 only.
2. The Greek form of the Hebrew name Zion, the famous mount of the temple. 1 Macc. 4 : 37, 60 ; 5 : 54 ; 6 : 48, 62 ; 7 : 33 ; 10 : 11 ; 14 : 27 ; Heb. 12 : 22 ; Rev. 14 : 1. [JERUSALEM.]

Siph'moth (*fruitful*), one of the places in the south of Judah which David frequented during his freebooting life. 1 Sam. 30 : 28.

Sip'pa-i (*threshold*), Saph, one of the sons of Rephaim, or "the giants," slain by Sibbechai at Gezer. 1 Chron. 20 : 4. (B.C. about 1050.)

Si'rach, the father of Jesus (Joshua), the writer of the Hebrew original of the book of Ecclesiasticus. (B.C. 310–220.)

Si'rah (*the turning*), **The well of,** from which Abner was recalled by Joab to his death at Hebron. 2 Sam. 3 : 26 only. It was apparently on the northern road from Hebron. There is a spring and reservoir on the western side of the ancient northern road, about one mile out of Hebron, which is called *Ain Sara*.

Sir'ion (*breastplate*), one of the various names of Mount Hermon, that by which it was known to the Zidonians. Deut. 3 : 9. The use of the name in Ps. 29 : 6 (slightly altered in the original—Shirion instead of Sirion) is remarkable.

Sisam'a-i, a descendant of Sheshan in the line of Jerahmeel. 1 Chron. 2 : 40. (B.C. about 1450.)

Sis'era (*battle array*). 1. Captain of the army of Jabin king of Canaan, who reigned in Hazor. He himself resided in Harosheth of the Gentiles. The particulars of the rout of Megiddo and of Sisera's flight and death are drawn out under the heads of BARAK, DEBORAH, JAEL, KISHON. (B.C. 1296.)
2. After a long interval the name reappears in the lists of the Nethinim who returned from the captivity with Zerubbabel. Ezra 2 : 53 ; Neh. 7 : 55. It doubtless tells of Canaanite captives devoted to the lowest offices of the temple. (B.C. before 536.)

Sit'nah (*strife*), the second of the two wells dug by Isaac in the valley of Gerar, the possession of which the herdmen of the valley disputed with him. Gen. 26 : 21.

Sivan. [MONTH.]

Slave. The institution of slavery was recognized, though not established, by the Mosaic law with a view to mitigate its hardship and to secure to every man his ordinary rights.
I. *Hebrew slaves.*—1. The circumstances under which a Hebrew might be reduced to servitude were—(1) poverty ; (2) the commission of theft ; and (3) the exercise of paternal authority. In the first case, a man who had mortgaged his property, and was unable to support his family, might sell himself to another Hebrew, with a view both to obtain maintenance and perchance a surplus sufficient to redeem his property. Lev. 25 : 25, 39. (2) The commission of theft rendered a person liable to servitude whenever restitution could not be made on the scale prescribed by the law. Ex. 22 : 1, 3. The thief was bound to work out the value of his restitution money in the service of him on whom the theft had been committed. (3) The exercise of paternal authority was limited to the sale of a daughter of tender age to be a maidservant, with the ulterior view of her becoming the concubine of the purchaser. Ex. 21 : 7. 2. The servitude of a Hebrew might be terminated in three ways : (1) by the satisfaction or the remission of all claims against him ; (2) by the recurrence of the year of jubilee, Lev. 25 : 40 ; and (3) the expiration of six years from the time that his servitude commenced. Ex. 21 : 2 ; Deut. 15 : 12. (4) To the above modes of obtaining liberty the rabbinists added, as a fourth, the death of the master without leaving a son, there being no power of claiming the slave on the part of any heir except a son. If a servant did not desire to avail himself of the opportunity of leaving his service, he was to signify his intention in a formal manner before the judges (or more exactly *at the place of judgment*), and then the master was to take him to the door-post, and to bore his ear through with an awl, Ex. 21 : 6, driving the awl into or "unto the door," as stated in Deut. 15 : 17, and thus fixing the servant to it. A servant who had submitted to this operation remained, according to the words of the law, a servant "forever." Ex. 21 : 6.

These words are, however, interpreted by Josephus and by the rabbinists as meaning until the year of jubilee. 3. The condition of a Hebrew servant was by no means intolerable. His master was admonished to treat him, not "as a bond-servant, but as an hired servant and as a sojourner," and, again, "not to rule over him with rigor." Lev. 25 : 3.), 40, 43. At the termination of his servitude the master was enjoined not to "let him go away empty," but to remunerate him liberally out of his flock, his floor and his wine-press. Deut. 15 : 13, 14. In the event of a Hebrew becoming the servant of a "stranger," meaning a non-Hebrew, the servitude could be terminated only in two ways, viz. by the arrival of the year of jubilee, or by the repayment to the master of the purchase money paid for the servant, after deducting a sum for the value of his services proportioned to the length of his servitude. Lev. 25 : 47–55. A Hebrew woman might enter into voluntary servitude on the score of poverty, and in this case she was entitled to her freedom after six years service, together with her usual gratuity at leaving, just as in the case of a man. Deut. 15 : 12, 13. Thus far we have seen little that is objectionable in the condition of Hebrew servants. In respect to marriage there were some peculiarities which, to our ideas, would be regarded as hardships. A master might, for instance, give a wife to a Hebrew servant for the time of his servitude, the wife being in this case, it must be remarked, not only a slave but a non-Hebrew. Should he leave when his term had expired, his wife and children would remain the absolute property of the master. Ex. 21 : 4, 5. Again, a father might sell his young daughter to a Hebrew, with a view either of marrying her himself or of giving her to his son. Ex. 21 : 7–9. It diminishes the apparent harshness of this proceeding if we look on the purchase money as in the light of a dowry given, as was not unusual, to the parents of the bride; still more, if we accept the rabbinical view that the consent of the maid was required before the marriage could take place. The position of a maiden thus sold by her father was subject to the following regulations: (1) She could not "go out as the men-servants do," i. e. she could not leave at the termination of six years, or in the year of jubilee, if her master was willing to fulfill the object

for which he had purchased her. (2) Should he not wish to marry her, he should call upon her friends to procure her release by the repayment of the purchase money. (3) If he betrothed her to his son, he was bound to make such provision for her as he would for one of his own daughters. (4) If either he or his son, having married her, took a second wife, it should not be to the prejudice of the first. (5) If neither of the three first specified alternatives took place, the maid was entitled to immediate and gratuitous liberty. Ex. 21 : 7–11. The custom of reducing Hebrews to servitude appears to have fallen into disuse subsequent to the Babylonish captivity. Vast numbers of Hebrews were reduced to slavery as war-captives at different periods by the Phœnicians, Joel 3 : 6, the Philistines, Joel 3 : 6; Amos 1 : 6, the Syrians, 1 Macc. 3 : 41; 2 Macc. 8 : 11, the Egyptians, Joseph. Ant. xii. 2, § 3, and above all by the Romans. Joseph. B. J. vi. 9, § 3.

II. Non-Hebrew slaves.—1. The majority of non-Hebrew slaves were war-captives, either of the Canaanites who had survived the general extermination of their race under Joshua or such as were conquered from the other surrounding nations. Num. 31 : 26 ff. Besides these, many were obtained by purchase from foreign slave-dealers, Lev. 25 : 44, 45; and others may have been resident foreigners who were reduced to this state by either poverty or crime. The children of slaves remained slaves, being the class described as "born in the house," Gen. 14 : 14; 17 : 12; Eccles. 2 : 7, and hence the number was likely to increase as time went on. The average value of a slave appears to have been thirty shekels. Ex. 21 : 32. 2. That the slave might be manumitted appears from Ex. 21 : 26, 27; Lev. 19 : 20. 3. The slave is described as the "possession" of his master, apparently with a special reference to the power which the latter had of disposing of him to his heirs, as he would any other article of personal property. Lev. 25 : 45, 46. But, on the other hand, provision was made for the protection of his person. Ex. 21 : 20; Lev. 24 : 17, 22. A minor personal injury, such as the loss of an eye or a tooth, was to be recompensed by giving the servant his liberty. Ex. 21 : 26, 27. The position of the slave in regard to religious privileges was favorable. He was to be circumcised, Gen. 17 : 12, and hence was entitled to partake of the pas-

Smyrna (modern).

chal sacrifice, Ex. 12 : 44, as well as of the other religious festivals. Deut. 12 : 12, 18; 16 : 11, 14. The occupations of slaves were of a menial character, as implied in Lev. 25 : 39, consisting partly in the work of the house and partly in personal attendance on the master. It will be seen that the whole tendency of the Bible legislation was to mitigate slavery, making it little more than hired service, and to abolish it, as indeed it was practically abolished among the Jews six hundred years before Christ.

Slime, translated *bitumen* in the Vulgate. The three instances in which it is mentioned in the Old Testament are illustrated by travellers and historians. It is first spoken of as used for cement by the builders in the plain of Shinar or Babylonia. Gen. 11 : 3. The bitumen pits in the vale of Siddim are mentioned in the ancient fragment of Canaanitish history, Gen. 14 : 10; and the ark of papyrus in which Moses was placed was made impervious to water by a coating of bitumen and pitch. Ex. 2 : 3. Herodotus, i. 179, tells us of the bitumen found at Is, the modern *Heet,* a town of Babylonia, eight days journey from Babylon. (Bitumen, or asphalt, is "the product of the decomposition of vegetable and animal substances. It is usually found of a black or brownish-black color, externally not unlike coal, but it varies in consistency from a bright, pitchy condition, with a conchoidal fracture, to thick, viscid masses of mineral tar."—*Encyc. Brit.* In this last state it is called in the Bible slime, and is of the same nature as our petroleum, but thicker, and hardens into asphalt. It is obtained in various places in Europe, and even now occasionally from the Dead Sea.—Ed.)

Sling. [Arms.]

Smith. [Handicraft.]

Smyr'na (*myrrh*), a city of Asia Minor, situated on the Ægean Sea, 40 miles north of Ephesus. Allusion is made to it in Rev. 2 : 8–11. It was founded by Alexander the Great, and was situated twenty stades (2½ miles) from the city of the same name, which after a long series of wars with the Lydians had been finally taken and sacked by Halyattes. The ancient city was built by some piratical

Greeks 1500 years before Christ. It seems not impossible that the message to the church in Smyrna contains allusions to the ritual of the pagan mysteries which prevailed in that city. In the time of Strabo the ruins of the old Smyrna still existed, and were partially inhabited, but the new city was one of the most beautiful in all Asia. The streets were laid out as near as might be at right angles. There was a large public library there, and also a handsome building surrounded with porticos which served as a museum. It was consecrated as a heroüm to Homer, whom the Smyrnæans claimed as a countryman. Olympian games were celebrated here, and excited great interest. (Smyrna is still a large city of 180,000 to 200,000 inhabitants, of which a larger proportion are Franks than in any other town in Turkey ; 20,000

Snail.

are Greeks, 9000 Jews, 8000 Armenians, 1000 Europeans, and the rest are Moslems.—Ed.)

Snail. 1. The Hebrew word *shablûl* occurs only in Ps. 58 : 8. The rendering of the Authorized Version is probably correct. The term would denote either a *limax* or a *helix*, which are particularly noticeable for the slimy track they leave behind them, by which they seem to waste themselves away. To this, or to the fact that many of them are shrivelled up among the rocks in the long heat of the summer, the psalmist refers. 2. The Hebrew word *chômet* occurs only as the name of some unclean animal in Lev. 11 : 30.

Perhaps some kind of lizard may be intended.

Snow. The historical books of the Bible contain only two notices of snow actually falling—2 Sam. 23 : 20; 1 Macc. 13 : 22; but the allusions in the poetical books are so numerous that there can be no doubt as to its being an ordinary occurrence in the winter months. Ps. 147 : 16; 148 : 8. The snow lies deep in the ravines of the highest ridge of Lebanon until the summer is far advanced, and indeed never wholly disappears; the summit of Hermon also perpetually glistens with frozen snow. From these sources probably the Jews obtained their supplies of ice for the purpose of cooling their beverages in summer. Prov. 25 : 13. The liability to snow must of course vary considerably in a country of such varying altitude as Palestine. At Jerusalem snow often falls to the depth of a foot or more in January or February, but it seldom lies. At Nazareth it falls more frequently and deeply, and it has been observed to fall even in the maritime plain of Joppa and about Carmel.

So. "So, king of Egypt," is once mentioned in the Bible—2 Kings 17 : 4. So has been identified by different writers with the first and second kings of the Ethiopian twenty-fifth dynasty, called by Manetho, Sabakón (Shebek) and Sebichós (Shebetek).

Salsola Kali.

Soap. The Hebrew term *bórith* is a general term for any substance of cleansing qualities. As, however, it appears in Jer. 2 : 22 in contradistinction to *nether*, which undoubtedly means "natron" or mineral alkali, it is fair to infer that *bórith* refers to vegetable alkali, or some kind of potash, which forms one of the usual ingredients in our soap. Numerous plants capable of yielding alkalies exist in Palestine and the surrounding countries; we may notice one named *hubeibeh* (the *Salsola kali* of botanists) found near the Dead Sea, the ashes of which are called *el-kuli*, from their strong alkaline properties.

So'cho (*bushy*). 1 Chron. 4 : 18. Probably one of the towns called Socoh, in Judah, though which of the two cannot be ascertained.

So'choh, another form of the name which is more correctly given in the Authorized Version as Socoh. The present one occurs in 1 Kings 4 : 10, and is therefore probably, though not certainly, Socoh, 1.

So'coh, the name of two towns in the tribe of Judah. 1. In the district of the Shefelah. Josh. 15 : 35; 1 Sam. 17 : 1; 2 Chron. 11 : 7; 28 : 18. In the time of Eusebius it bore the name of Socchoth, and lay between eight and nine Roman miles from Eleutheropolis, on the road to Jerusalem. It may be identified with *esh-Shuweikeh*, in the western part of the mountains of Judah. From this village probably came Antigonus of Soco, who lived about the commencement of the third century B.C.

2. Also a town of Judah, but in the mountain district. Josh. 15 : 48. It has been discovered about 10 miles southwest of Hebron; bearing, like the other Socoh, the name of *esh-Shuweikeh*.

So'di (*intimate*), the father of Geddiel, the spy selected from the tribe of Zebulun. Num. 13 : 10. (B.C. 1490.)

Sod'om (*burning*), one of the most ancient cities of Syria. It is commonly mentioned in connection with Gomorrah, but also with Admah and Zeboim, and on one occasion—Gen. 14—with Bela or Zoar. Sodom was evidently the chief town in the settlement. The four are first named in the ethnological records of Gen. 10 : 19 as belonging to the Canaanites. The next mention of the name of Sodom, Gen. 13 : 10–13, gives more certain indication of the position of the city. Abram and Lot are standing together between Bethel and Ai, ver. 3, taking a survey of the land around and below them. Eastward of them, and absolutely at their feet, lay the "circle of Jordan." The whole circle was one great oasis—"a garden of Jehovah." ver. 10. In the midst of the garden the four cities of Sodom, Gomorrah, Admah and Zeboim appear to have been situated. It is necessary to notice how absolutely the cities are identified with the district. In the subsequent account of their destruction, Gen. 19, the topographical terms are employed with all the precision which is characteristic of such early times. The mention of the Jordan is conclusive as to the situation of the district, for the Jordan ceases where it enters the Dead Sea, and can have no existence south of that point. The catastrophe by which they were destroyed is described in Gen. 19 as a shower of brimstone and fire from Jehovah. However we may interpret the words of the earliest narrative, one thing is certain—that the lake was not one of the agents in the catastrophe. From all these passages, though much is obscure, two things seem clear: 1. That Sodom and the rest of the cities of the plain of Jordan stood on the north of the Dead Sea; 2. That neither the cities nor the district were submerged by the lake, but that the cities were overthrown and the land spoiled, and that it may still be seen in its desolate condition. When, however, we turn to more modern views, we discover a remarkable variance from these conclusions. 1. The opinion long current that the five cities were submerged in the lake, and that their remains—walls, columns and capitals—might be still discerned below the water, hardly needs refutation after the distinct statement and the constant implication of Scripture. But, 2. A more serious departure from the terms of the ancient history is exhibited in the prevalent opinion that the cities stood at the south end of the lake. This appears to have been the belief of Josephus and Jerome. It seems to have been universally held by the mediæval historians and pilgrims, and it is adopted by modern topographers probably without exception. There are several grounds for this belief; but the main point on which Dr. Robinson rests his argument is the situation of Zoar. (a) "Lot," says he, "fled to Zoar, which was *near* to Sodom; and Zoar lay almost at the southern end of the present sea, probably in the mouth of *Wady Kerak*." (b) Another consideration in favor of placing the cities at the southern end of the lake is the existence of similar names

in that direction. (c) A third argument, and perhaps the weightiest of the three, is the existence of the salt mountain at the south of the lake, and its tendency to split off in columnar masses presenting a rude resemblance to the human form. But it is by no means certain that salt does not exist at other spots round the lake. (d) (A fourth and yet stronger argument is drawn from the fact that Abraham saw the smoke of the burning cities from Hebron. (e) A fifth argument is found in the numerous lime-pits found at the southern end of the Dead Sea. Robinson, Schaff, Baedeker, Lieutenant Lynch and others favor this view. —ED.) It thus appears that on the situation of Sodom no satisfactory conclusion can at present be reached. On the one hand, the narrative of Genesis seems to state positively that it lay at the *northern* end of the Dead Sea. On the other hand, long-continued tradition and the names of the existing spots seem to pronounce with almost equal positiveness that it was at its *southern* end. Of the catastrophe which destroyed the city and the district of Sodom we can hardly hope ever to form a satisfactory conception. Some catastrophe there undoubtedly was; but what secondary agencies, besides fire, were employed in the accomplishment of the punishment cannot be safely determined in the almost total absence of exact scientific description of the natural features of the ground round the lake. We may suppose, however, that the actual agent in the ignition and destruction of the cities had been of the nature of a tremendous thunder-storm accompanied by a discharge of meteoric stones, (and that these set on fire the bitumen with which the soil was saturated, and which was used in building the city. And it may be that this burning out of the soil caused the plain to sink below the level of the Dead Sea, and the waters to flow over it—if indeed Sodom and its sister cities are really under the water.—ED.) The miserable fate of Sodom and Gomorrah is held up as a warning in numerous passages of the Old and New Testaments. Mark 6 : 11 ; 2 Pet. 2 : 6 ; Jude 4–7.

Sod'oma. Rom. 9 : 29. In this place alone the Authorized Version has followed the Greek and Vulgate form of the well-known name Sodom.

Sod'omites. This word does not denote the inhabitants of Sodom; but it is employed in the Authorized Version of the Old Testament for those who practiced as a religious rite the abominable and unnatural vice from which the inhabitants of Sodom and Gomorrah have derived their lasting infamy.

Sol'omon (*peaceful*). I. *Early life and accession to the throne.*—Solomon was the child of David's old age, the last-born of all his sons. 1 Chron. 3 : 5. The yearnings of the "man of war" led him to give to the new-born infant the name of Solomon (Shĕlômóth, *the peaceful one*). Nathan, with a marked reference to the meaning of the king's own name (David, *the darling, the beloved one*), calls the infant Jedidiah (Jedid'yah), that is, the *darling of the Lord.* 2 Sam. 12 : 24, 25. He was placed under the care of Nathan from his earliest infancy. At first, apparently, there was no distinct purpose to make him the heir. Absalom was still the king's favorite son, 2 Sam. 13 : 37; 18 : 33, and was looked on by the people as the destined successor. 2 Sam. 14 : 13; 15 : 1-6. The death of Absalom when Solomon was about ten years old left the place vacant, and David pledged his word in secret to Bath-sheba that he, and no other, should be the heir. 1 Kings 1 : 13. The words which were spoken somewhat later express, doubtless, the purpose which guided him throughout. 1 Chron. 28 : 9, 20. His son's life should not be as his own had been, one of hardships and wars, dark crimes and passionate repentance, but, from first to last, be pure, blameless, peaceful, fulfilling the ideal of glory and of righteousness after which he himself had vainly striven. The glorious visions of Ps. 72 may be looked on as the prophetic expansion of these hopes of his old age. So far, all was well. Apparently his influence over his son's character was one exclusively for good. Nothing that we know of Bath-sheba leads us to think of her as likely to mould her son's mind and heart to the higher forms of goodness. Under these influences the boy grew up. At the age of ten or eleven he must have passed through the revolt of Absalom, and shared his father's exile. 2 Sam. 15 : 16. He would be taught all that priests or Levites or prophets had to teach. When David was old and feeble, Adonijah, Solomon's older brother, attempted to gain possession of the throne; but he was defeated, and Solomon went down to Gihon and was proclaimed and anointed king. A few months more and

Solomon found himself, by his father's death, the sole occupant of the throne. The position to which he succeeded was unique. Never before, and never after, did the kingdom of Israel take its place among the great monarchies of the East. Large treasures, accumulated through many years, were at his disposal.

II. *Personal appearance.*—Of Solomon's personal appearance we have no direct description, as we have of the earlier kings. There are, however, materials for filling up the gap. Whatever higher mystic meaning may be latent in Ps. 45, or the Song of Songs, we are all but compelled to think of them as having had at least a historical starting-point. They tell of one who was, in the eyes of the men of his own time, "fairer than the children of men," the face "bright and ruddy" as his father's, Cant. 5 : 10; 1 Sam. 17 : 42, bushy locks, dark as the raven's wing, yet not without a golden glow, the eyes soft as "the eyes of doves," the "countenance as Lebanon, excellent as the cedars," "the chiefest among ten thousand, the altogether lovely." Cant. 5 : 9-16. Add to this all gifts of a noble, far-reaching intellect, large and ready sympathies, a playful and genial humor, the lips "full of grace," and the soul "anointed" as "with the oil of gladness," Ps. 45, and we may form some notion of what the king was like in that dawn of his golden prime.

III. *Reign.*—All the data for a continuous history that we have of Solomon's reign are—(*a*) The duration of the reign, forty years, B.C. 1015-975. 1 Kings 11 : 42. (*b*) The commencement of the temple in the fourth, its completion in the eleventh, year of his reign. 1 Kings 6 : 1, 37, 38. (*c*) The commencement of his own palace in the seventh, its completion in the twentieth, year. 1 Kings 7 : 1; 2 Chron. 8 : 1. (*d*) The conquest of Hamath-zobah, and the consequent foundation of cities in the region of north Palestine after the twentieth year. 2 Chron. 8 : 1-6.

IV. *Foreign policy.*—1. Egypt. The first act of the foreign policy of the new reign must have been to most Israelites a very startling one. He made affinity with Pharaoh, king of Egypt, by marrying his daughter. 1 Kings 3 : 1. The immediate results were probably favorable enough. The new queen brought with her as a dowry the frontier city of Gezer. But the ultimate issue of the alliance showed that it was hollow and impolitic. 2. Tyre. The alliance with the Phœnician king rested on a somewhat different footing. It had been a part of David's policy from the beginning of his reign. Hiram had been "ever a lover of David." As soon as he heard of Solomon's accession he sent ambassadors to salute him. A correspondence passed between the two kings, which ended in a treaty of commerce. The opening of Jeppa as a port created a new coasting-trade, and the materials from Tyre were conveyed to that city on floats, and thence to Jerusalem. 2 Chron. 2 : 16. In return for these exports, the Phœnicians were only too glad to receive the corn and oil of Solomon's territory. The results of the alliance did not end here. Now, for the first time in the history of the Jews, they entered on a career as a commercial people. 3. The foregoing were the two most important alliances. The absence of any reference to Babylon and Assyria, and the fact that the Euphrates was recognized as the boundary of Solomon's kingdom, 2 Chron. 9 : 26, suggests the inference that the Mesopotamian monarchies were at this time comparatively feeble. Other neighboring nations were content to pay annual tribute in the form of gifts. 2 Chron. 9 : 28. 4. The survey of the influence exercised by Solomon on surrounding nations would be incomplete if we were to pass over that which was more directly personal—the fame of his glory and his wisdom. Wherever the ships of Tarshish went, they carried with them the report, losing nothing in its passage, of what their crews had seen and heard. The journey of the queen of Sheba, though from its circumstances the most conspicuous, did not stand alone.

V. *Internal history.* — 1. The first prominent scene in Solomon's reign is one which presents his character in its noblest aspect. God in a vision having offered him the choice of good things he would have, he chose wisdom in preference to riches or honor or long life. The wisdom asked for was given in large measure, and took a varied range. The wide world of nature, animate and inanimate, the lives and characters of men, lay before him, and he took cognizance of all. But the highest wisdom was that wanted for the highest work, for governing and guiding, and the historian hastens to give an illustration of it. The pattern-instance is, in all its circum-stances, thoroughly Oriental. 1 Kings 3 : 16–28. 2. In reference to the king's finances, the first impression of the facts given us is that of abounding plenty. Large quantities of the precious metals were imported from Ophir and Tarshish. 1 Kings 9 : 28. All the kings and princes of the subject provinces paid tribute in the form of gifts, in money and in kind, "at a fixed rate year by year." 1 Kings 10 : 25. Monopolies of trade contributed to the king's treasury. 1 Kings 10 : 28, 29. The total amount thus brought into the treasury in gold, exclusive of all payments in kind, amounted to 666 talents. 1 Kings 10 : 14. 3. It was hardly possible, however, that any financial system could bear the strain of the king's passion for magnificence. The cost of the temple was, it is true, provided for by David's savings and the offerings of the people; but even while that was building, yet more when it was finished, one structure followed on another with ruinous rapidity. All the equipment of his court, the "apparel" of his servants, was on the same scale. A body-guard attended him, "threescore valiant men," tallest and handsomest of the sons of Israel. Forty thousand stalls of horses for his chariots, and twelve thousand horsemen, made up the measure of his magnificence. 1 Kings 4 : 26. As the treasury became empty, taxes multiplied and monopolies became more irksome. 4. A description of the temple erected by Solomon is given elsewhere. After seven years and a half the work was completed, and the day came to which all Israelites looked back as the culminating glory of their nation. 5. We cannot ignore the fact that even now there were some darker shades in the picture. He reduced the "strangers" in the land, the remnant of the Canaanite races, to the state of helots, and made their life "bitter with all hard bondage." One hundred and fifty-three thousand, with wives and children in proportion, were torn from their homes and sent off to the quarries and the forests of Lebanon. 1 Kings 5 : 15; 2 Chron. 2 : 17, 18. And the king soon fell from the loftiest height of his religious life to the lowest depth. Before long the priests and prophets had to grieve over rival temples to Molech, Chemosh, Ashtaroth, and forms of ritual not idolatrous only, but cruel, dark, impure. This evil came as the penalty of another. 1 Kings 11 : 1–8. He gave himself to "strange women." He found himself involved in a fascination which led to the worship of strange gods. Something there was perhaps in his very "largeness of heart," so far in advance of the traditional knowledge of his age, rising to higher and wider thoughts of God, which predisposed him to it. In recognizing what was true in other forms of faith, he might lose his horror at what was false. With this there may have mingled political motives. He may have hoped, by a policy of toleration, to conciliate neighboring princes, to attract a larger traffic. But probably also there was another influence less commonly taken into account. The widespread belief of the East in the magic arts of Solomon is not, it is believed, without its foundation of truth. Disasters followed before long as the natural consequence of what was politically a blunder as well as religiously a sin.

VI. *His literary works.*—Little remains out of the songs, proverbs, treatises, of which the historian speaks. 1 Kings 4 : 32, 33. *Excerpta* only are given from the three thousand proverbs. Of the thousand and five songs we know absolutely nothing. His books represent the three stages of his life. The Song of Songs brings before us the brightness of his youth. Then comes in the book of Proverbs, the stage of practical, prudential thought. The poet has become the philosopher, the mystic has passed into the moralist; but the *man* passed through both stages without being permanently the better for either. They were to him but phases of his life which he had known and exhausted, Eccles. 1, 2; and therefore there came, as in the confessions of the preacher, the great retribution.

Solomon's Porch. [PALACE; TEMPLE.]

Solomon's servants (CHILDREN OF). Ezra 2 : 55, 58; Neh. 7 : 57, 60. The persons thus named appear in the lists of the exiles who returned from the captivity. They were the descendants of the Canaanites who were reduced by Solomon to the helot state, and compelled to labor in the king's stone-quarries and in building his palaces and cities. 1 Kings 5 : 13, 14; 9 : 20, 21; 2

Chron. 8 : 7, 8. They appear to have formed a distinct order, inheriting probably the same functions and the same skill as their ancestors.

Solomon's Song. [CANTICLES.]

Solomon, Wisdom of. [WISDOM, BOOK OF.]

Son. The term "son" is used in Scripture language to imply almost any kind of descent or succession, as *ben shânâh*, "son of a year," *i. e.* a year old; *ben kesheth*, "son of a bow," *i. e.* an arrow. The word *bar* is often found in the New Testament in composition, as Bar-timæus.

Soothsayer. [DIVINATION.]

Sop. In eastern lands, where our table utensils are unknown, the meat, with the broth, is brought upon the table in a

Dipping the Sop.

large dish, and is eaten usually by means of pieces of bread dipped into the common dish. The bread so dipped is called a "sop." It was such a piece of bread dipped in broth that Jesus gave to Judas, John 13 : 26; and again, in Matt. 26 : 23, it is said "he that dippeth his hand with me in the dish," *i. e.* to make a sop by dipping a piece of bread into the central dish.

Sop'ater (*saviour of his father*), son of Pyrrhus of Berea, was one of the companions of St. Paul on his return from Greece into Asia. Acts 20 : 4. (A.D. 55.)

Soph'ereth (*writing*). "The children of Sophereth" were a family who returned from Babylon with Zerubbabel among the descendants of Solomon's servants. Ezra 2:55; Neh. 7:57. (B.C. before 536.)

Sorcerer. [DIVINATION.]

So'rek (*red*), **The valley of,** a wady in which lay the residence of Delilah. Judges 16:4. It was possibly nearer Gaza than any other of the chief Philistine cities, since thither Samson was taken after his capture at Delilah's house.

Sosip'ater (*saviour of his father*), kinsman or fellow tribesman of St. Paul, Rom. 16:21, is probably the same person as Sopater of Berea. (A.D. 54.)

Sos'thenes (*saviour of his nation*) was a Jew at Corinth who was seized and beaten in the presence of Gallio. See Acts 18:12-17. (A.D. 49.)

So'ta-i (*changeful*). The children of Sotai were a family of the descendants of Solomon's servants who returned with Zerubbabel. Ezra 2:55; Neh. 7:57. (B.C. before 536.)

South Ra'moth. [RAMATH OF THE SOUTH.]

Sow. [SWINE.]

Eastern Sower.

Sower, Sowing. The operation of sowing with the hand is one of so simple a character as to need little description. The Egyptian paintings furnish many illustrations of the mode in which it was conducted. The sower held the vessel or basket containing the seed in his left hand, while with his right he scattered the seed broadcast. The "drawing out" of the seed is noticed, as the most characteristic action of the sower, in Ps. 126:6 (Authorized Version "precious") and Amos 9:13. In wet soils the seed was trodden in by the feet of animals. Isa. 32:20. The sowing season began in October and continued to the end of February, wheat being put in before, and barley after, the beginning of January. The Mosaic law prohibited the sowing of mixed seed. Lev. 19:19; Deut. 22:9.

Spain. 1 Macc. 8:3; Rom. 15:24, 28. The local designation, Tarshish, representing the *Tartessus* of the Greeks, probably prevailed until the fame of the Roman wars in that country reached the East, when it was superseded by its classical name. The mere intention of St. Paul to visit Spain (whether he really did visit it is a disputed question.—ED.) implies two interesting facts, viz., the establishment of a Christian community in that country, and that this was done by Hellenistic Jews resident there. The early introduction of Christianity into that country is attested by Irenæus and Tertullian.

Sparrow (Heb. *tzippôr*, from a root signifying to "chirp" or "twitter," which appears to be a phonetic representation of the call-note of any passerine (sparrowlike) bird). This Hebrew word occurs upwards of forty times in the Old Testa-

Syrian Sparrow.

ment. In all passages except two it is rendered by the Authorized Version indifferently "bird" or "fowl." and denotes any small bird, both of the spar-row-like species and such as the starling, chaffinch, greenfinch, linnet, goldfinch, corn-bunting, pipits, blackbird, song-thrush, etc. In Ps. 84 : 3 and Ps. 102 : 7 it is rendered "sparrow." The Greek στρουθίον (Authorized Version "sparrow") occurs twice in the New Testament, Matt.

Sparrows in Market.

10 : 29; Luke 12 : 6, 7. (The birds above mentioned are found in great numbers in Palestine, and are of very little value, selling for the merest trifle, and are thus strikingly used by our Saviour, Matt. 10 : 29, as an illustration of our Father's care for his children.—ED.) The blue thrush (*Petrocossyphus cyaneus*) is probably the bird to which the psalmist alludes in Ps. 102 : 7 as "the sparrow that sitteth alone upon the house-top." It is a solitary bird, eschewing the society of its own species, and rarely more than a pair are seen together. The English tree-sparrow (*Passer montanus*, Linn.) is also very common, and may be seen in numbers on Mount Olivet, and also about the sacred enclosure of the mosque of Omar. This is perhaps the exact species referred to in Ps. 84 : 3. Dr. Thomson, in speaking of the great numbers of the house-sparrows and field-sparrows in Palestine, says: "They are a tame, troublesome and impertinent generation, and nestle just where you do not want them. They stop up your stove- and water-pipes with their rubbish, build in the windows and under the beams of the roof, and would stuff your hat full of stubble in half a day if they found it hanging in a place to suit them."

Spar'ta, a celebrated city of Greece, between whose inhabitants and the Jews a relationship was believed to subsist. Between the two nations a correspondence ensued.—*Whitney.* The actual relationship of the Jews and Spartans, 2 Macc. 5 : 9, is an ethnological error, which it is difficult to trace to its origin.

Spear. [ARMS.]

Spearmen. Acts 23 : 23. These were probably troops so lightly armed as to be able to keep pace on the march with mounted soldiers.

Spice, Spices. 1. Heb. *bâsam, besem* or *bôsem.* In Cant. 5 : 1, "I have gathered my myrrh with my spice," the word points apparently to some definite substance. In the other places, with the exception perhaps of Cant. 1 : 13, 6 : 2, the words refer more generally to sweet aromatic odors, the principal of which was that of the balsam or balm of Gilead; the tree which yields this substance is now generally admitted to be the *Balsamodendron opobalsamum.* The balm of Gilead tree grows in some parts of Arabia and Africa, and is seldom more than fifteen feet high, with straggling branches and scanty foliage. The balsam is chiefly obtained from incisions in the bark, but is procured also from the green and ripe berries. 2. *Něcôth.* Gen. 37 : 25; 43 : 11. The most probable explanation is that which refers the word to the Arabic *naka'at, i. e.* "the gum obtained from the tragacanth" (*Astragalus*). 3. *Sammim,* a general term to denote those aromatic substances which were used in the preparation of the anointing oil, the incense offerings, etc. The spices mentioned as being used by Nicodemus for the preparation of our Lord's body, John 19 : 39, 40, are "myrrh and aloes," by which latter word must be understood not the aloes of medicine, but the highly-scented wood of the *Aquilaria agallochum.*

Spider. The Hebrew word *'accâbîsh* in Job 8 : 14, Isa. 59 : 5 is correctly rendered "spider." But *sěmâmîth* is wrongly translated "spider" in Prov. 30 : 28; it refers probably to some kind of lizard.

(But "there are many species of spider in Palestine : some which spin webs, like the common garden spider ; some which dig subterranean cells and make doors in them, like the well-known trap-door spider of southern Europe ; and some which have no web, but chase their prey upon the ground, like the hunting-and the wolf-spider."— *Wood's Bible Animals*.)

Spikenard.

Spikenard (Heb. *nêrd*) is mentioned twice in the Old Testament, viz. in Cant. 1 : 12 ; 4 : 13,14. The ointment with which our Lord was anointed as he sat at meat in Simon's house at Bethany consisted of this precious substance, the costliness of which may be inferred from the indignant surprise manifested by some of the witnesses of the transaction. See Mark 14 : 3-5 ; John 12 : 3, 5. (Spikenard, from which the ointment was made, was an aromatic herb of the valerian family (*Nardostachys jatamansi*). It was imported from an early age from Arabia, India and the Far East. The costliness of Mary's offering (300 pence=$45) may best be seen from the fact that a penny (denarius, 15 to 17 cents) was in those days the day-wages of a laborer. Matt. 20 : 2. In our day this would equal at least $300 or $400.—ED.)

Spinning. The notices of spinning in the Bible are confined to Ex. 35 : 25, 26 ; Prov. 31 : 19 ; Matt. 6 : 28. The latter passage implies (according to the Authorized Version) the use of the same instruments which have been in vogue for hand-spinning down to the present day,

viz. the distaff and spindle. The distaff, however, appears to have been dispensed with, and the term so rendered means the spindle itself, while that rendered "spindle" represents the *whirl* of the spindle, a button of circular rim which was affixed to it, and gave steadiness to its circular motion. The "whirl" of the Syrian women was made of amber in the time of Pliny. The spindle was held perpendicularly in the one hand, while the other was employed in drawing out the thread. Spinning was the business of women, both among the Jews and for the most part among the Egyptians.

Sponge, a soft, porous marine substance. Sponges were for a long time supposed to be plants, but are now considered by the best naturalists to belong to the animal kingdom. Sponge is mentioned only in the New Testament. Matt. 27 : 48 ; Mark 15 : 36 ; John 19 : 29. The commercial value of the sponge was

Sponge of Commerce.

known from very early times; and although there appears to be no notice of it in the Old Testament, yet it is probable that it was used by the ancient Hebrews, who could readily have obtained it good from the Mediterranean, where it was principally found.

Spouse. [MARRIAGE.]

Sta′chys, a Christian at Rome, saluted by St. Paul in the Epistle to the Romans. Rom. 16 : 9. (A.D. 55.)

Stacte (Heb. *nâtâf*), the name of one of the sweet spices which composed the holy incense. See Ex. 30 : 34—the only passage of Scripture in which the word occurs. Some identify the *nâtâf* with the gum of the storax tree (*Styrax officinale*), but all that is positively known is that it signifies an odorous distillation from some plant.

Standards. The Assyrian standards were emblematic of their religion, and were therefore the more valuable as instruments for leading and guiding men in the army. The forms were imitations of animals (1), emblems of deities (2), and symbols of power and wisdom (3). Many of them were crude, but others were highly artistic and of great cost.

Assyrian Standards.

Egyptian Standards.

The Egyptian standards were designed in the same idea as those of the Romans, exhibiting some sacred emblem (5, 6, 8), or a god in the form of an animal (3, 4), a group of victory (7), or the king's name or his portrait as (1), of lower, and (2), of upper, Egypt, or an emblematic sign, as No. 9.

Star of the wise men. [MAGI.]

Stater. [MONEY.]

Steel. In all cases where the word "steel" occurs in the Authorized Version the true rendering of the Hebrew is "copper." Whether the ancient Hebrews were acquainted with steel is not perfectly certain. It has been inferred from a passage in Jeremiah, 15 : 12, that the "iron from the north" there spoken of denoted a superior kind of metal, hardened in an unusual manner, like the steel obtained from the Chalybes of the Pontus, the ironsmiths of the ancient world. The hardening of iron for cutting instruments was practiced in Pontus, Lydia and Laconia. There is, however, a word in Hebrew, *paldâh*, which occurs only in Nah. 2 : 3 (4), and is there rendered "torches," but which most probably denotes steel or hardened iron, and refers to the flashing scythes of the Assyrian chariots. Steel appears to have been known to the Egyptians. The steel weapons in the tomb of Rameses III., says Wilkinson, are painted blue, the bronze red.

Steph'anas, a Christian convert of Corinth whose household Paul baptized as the "first-fruits of Achaia." 1 Cor. 1 : 16 ; 16 : 15. (A.D. 53.)

Ste'phen, the first Christian martyr, was the chief of the seven (commonly called Deacons) appointed to rectify the complaints in the early Church of Jerusalem, made by the Hellenistic against the Hebrew Christians. His Greek name indicates his own Hellenistic origin. His importance is stamped on the narrative by a reiteration of emphatic, almost superlative, phrases: "full of faith and of the Holy Ghost," Acts 6 : 5; "full of grace and power," *ibid.* 8; irresistible "spirit and wisdom," *ibid.* 10; "full of the Holy Ghost." Acts 7 : 55. He shot far ahead of his six companions, and far above his particular office. First, he arrests attention by the "great wonders and miracles that he did." Then begins a series of disputations with the Hellenistic Jews of north Africa, Alexandria and

Asia Minor, his companions in race and birthplace. The subject of these disputations is not expressly mentioned; but from what follows it is obvious that he struck into a new vein of teaching, which evidently caused his martyrdom. Down to this time the apostles and the early Christian community had clung in their worship, not merely to the holy land and the holy city, but to the holy place of the temple. This local worship, with the Jewish customs belonging to it, Stephen denounced. So we must infer from the accusations brought against him, confirmed as they are by the tenor of his defence. He was arrested at the instigation of the Hellenistic Jews, and brought before the Sanhedrin. His speech in his defence, and his execution by stoning outside the gates of Jerusalem, are related at length in Acts 7. The framework in which his defence is cast is a summary of the history of the Jewish Church. In the facts which he selects from his history he is guided by two principles. The first is the endeavor to prove that, even in the previous Jewish history, the presence and favor of God had not been confined to the holy land or the temple of Jerusalem. The second principle of selection is based on the attempt to show that there was a tendency from the earliest times toward the same ungrateful and narrow spirit that had appeared in this last stage of their political existence. It would seem that, just at the close of his argument, Stephen saw a change in the aspect of his judges, as if for the first time they had caught the drift of his meaning. He broke off from his calm address, and turned suddenly upon them in an impassioned attack, which shows that he saw what was in store for him. As he spoke they showed by their faces that their hearts "were being sawn asunder," and they kept gnashing their set teeth against him; but still, though with difficulty, restraining themselves. He, in this last crisis of his fate, turned his face upward to the open sky, and as he gazed the vault of heaven seemed to him to part asunder; and the divine Glory appeared through the rending of the earthly veil—the divine Presence, seated on a throne, and on the right hand the human form of Jesus. Stephen spoke as if to himself, describing the glorious vision; and in so doing, alone of all the speakers and writers in the New Testament except only Christ himself, uses the expressive phrase "the Son of man." As his judges heard the words, they would listen no longer. They broke into a loud yell; they clapped their hands to their ears; they flew as with one impulse upon him, and dragged him out of the city to the place of execution. Those who took the lead in the execution were the persons who had taken upon themselves the responsibility of denouncing him. Deut. 17 : 7 ; comp. John 8 : 7. In this instance they were the witnesses who had reported or misreported the words of Stephen. They, according to the custom, stripped themselves; and one of the prominent leaders in the transaction was deputed by custom to signify his assent to the act by taking the clothes into his custody and standing over them while the bloody work went on. The person who officiated on this occasion was a young man from Tarsus, the future apostle of the Gentiles. [PAUL.] As the first volley of stones burst upon him, Stephen called upon the Master whose human form he had just seen in the heavens, and repeated almost the words with which he himself had given up his life on the cross, "O Lord Jesus, receive my spirit." Another crash of stones brought him on his knees. One loud, piercing cry, answering to the shriek or yell with which his enemies had flown upon him, escaped his dying lips. Again clinging to the spirit of his Master's words, he cried, "Lord, lay not this sin to their charge," and instantly sank upon the ground, and, in the touching language of the narrator, who then uses for the first time the words afterward applied to the departure of all Christians, but here the more remarkable from the bloody scenes in the midst of which death took place, *fell asleep*. His mangled body was buried by the class of Hellenists and proselytes to which he belonged. The importance of Stephen's career may be briefly summed up under three heads : 1. He was the first great Christian ecclesiastic, "the Archdeacon," as he is called in the eastern Church. 2. He is the first *martyr*—the protomartyr. To him the name "martyr" is first applied. Acts 22 : 20. 3. He is the forerunner of St. Paul. He was the anticipator, as, had he lived, he would have been the propagator, of the new phase of Christianity of which St. Paul became the main support.

Stocks. (An instrument of punishment, consisting of two beams, the upper one being movable, with two small openings between them, large enough for the ankles of the prisoner.—ED.) The term "stocks" is applied in the Authorized Version to two different articles, one of which answers rather to our pillory, inasmuch as the body was placed in a bent

Ancient Stocks.

position, by the confinement of the neck and arms as well as the legs, and the other answers to our "stocks," the feet alone being confined in it. The prophet Jeremiah was confined in the first sort, Jer. 20 : 2, which appears to have been a common mode of punishment in his day, Jer. 29 : 26, as the prisons contained a chamber for the special purpose, termed "the house of the pillory." 2 Chron. 16 : 10 (Authorized Version "prison-house"). The stocks, properly so called, are noticed in Job 13 : 27 ; 33 : 11 ; Acts 16 : 24. The term used in Prov. 7 : 22 (Authorized Version "stocks") more properly means a fetter.

Sto'ics. The Stoics and Epicureans, who are mentioned together in Acts 17 : 18, represent the two opposite schools of practical philosophy which survived the fall of higher speculation in Greece. The Stoic school was founded by Zeno of Citium (*cir.* B.C. 280), and derived its name from the painted "portico" (stoa) at Athens in which he taught. Zeno was followed by Cleanthes (*cir.* B.C. 260); Cleanthes by Chrysippus (*cir.* B.C. 240), who was regarded as the intellectual founder of the Stoic system. "They regarded God and the world as power and its manifestation, matter being a passive ground in which dwells the divine energy. Their ethics were a protest against moral indifference, and to live in harmony with nature, conformably with reason and the demands of universal good, and in the utmost indifference to pleasure, pain and

all external good or evil, was their fundamental maxim."—*American Cyclopædia.* The ethical system of the Stoics has been commonly supposed to have a close connection with Christian morality ; but the morality of stoicism is essentially based on pride, that of Christianity on humility ; the one upholds individual independence, the other absolute faith in another ; the one looks for consolation in the issue of fate, the other in Providence ; the one is limited by periods of cosmical ruin, the other is consummated in a personal resurrection. Acts 17 : 18. But in spite of the fundamental error of stoicism, which lies in a supreme egotism, the teaching of this school gave a wide currency to the noble doctrines of the fatherhood of God, the common bonds of mankind, the sovereignty of the soul. Among their most prominent representatives were Zeno and Antipater of Tarsus, Seneca and Marcus Aurelius.

Stomacher. The Hebrew word so translated, Isa. 3 : 24, describes some article of female attire, the character of which is a mere matter of conjecture.

Stones. Besides the ordinary uses to which stones were applied, we may mention that large stones were set up to commemorate any remarkable event. Gen. 28 : 18 ; 35 : 14 ; 31 : 45 ; Josh. 4 : 9 ; 1 Sam. 7 : 12. Such stones were occasionally consecrated by anointing. Gen. 28 : 18. Heaps of stones were piled up on various occasions, as in token of a treaty, Gen. 31 : 47, or over the grave of some notorious offender. Josh. 7 : 26 ; 8 : 29 ; 2 Sam. 18 : 17. The "white stone" noticed in Rev. 2 : 17 has been variously regarded as referring to the pebble of acquittal used in the Greek courts ; to the lot cast in elections in Greece ; to both these combined ; to the stones in the high priest's breastplate ; to the tickets presented to the victors at the public games ; or, lastly, to the custom of writing on stones. The notice in Zech. 12 : 3 of the "burdensome stone" is referred by Jerome to the custom of lifting stones as an exercise of strength, comp. Ecclus. 6 : 21 ; but it may equally well be explained of a large corner-stone as a symbol of strength. Isa. 28 : 16. Stones are used metaphorically to denote hardness or insensibility, 1 Sam. 25 : 37 ; Ezek. 11 : 19 ; 36 : 26, as well as firmness or strength. Gen. 49 : 24. The members of the Church are called "living stones," as contributing to rear that living temple in which Christ, himself "a living *stone*," is the chief or head of the corner. Eph. 2 : 20–22 ; 1 Pet. 2 : 4–8.

Stones, Precious. Precious stones are frequently alluded to in the Holy Scriptures; they were known and very highly valued in the earliest times. The Tyrians traded in precious stones supplied by Syria. Ezek. 27 : 16. The merchants of Sheba and Raamah in south Arabia, and doubtless India and Ceylon, supplied the markets of Tyre with various precious stones. The art of engraving on precious stones was known from the very earliest times. Gen. 38 : 18. The twelve stones of the breastplate were engraved each one with the name of one of the tribes. Ex. 28 : 17–21. It is an undecided question whether the diamond was known to the early nations of antiquity. The Authorized Version gives it as the rendering of the Heb. *yahălôm*, but it is probable that the jasper is intended. Precious stones are used in Scripture in a figurative sense, to signify value, beauty, durability, etc., in those objects with which they are compared. See Cant. 5 : 14 ; Isa. 54 : 11, 12 ; Lam. 4 : 7 ; Rev. 4 : 3 ; 21 : 10, 21.

Stoning. [PUNISHMENTS.]

The Stork.

Stork (Heb. *chasîdâh*), a large bird of passage of the heron family. The white stork (*Ciconia alba*, Linn.) is one of the largest and most conspicuous of land birds, standing nearly four feet high, the jet black of its wings and its bright-red beak and legs contrasting finely with the pure white of its plumage. Zech. 5 : 9. In the neighborhood of man it devours readily all kinds of offal and garbage. For this reason, doubtless, it is placed in the list of unclean birds by the Mosaic law. Lev. 11 : 19 ; Deut. 14 : 18. The range of the white stork extends over the whole of Europe, except the British isles, where it is now a rare visitant, and over northern Africa and Asia as far at least as Burmah. The black stork (*Ciconia nigra*, Linn.), though less abundant in places, is scarcely less widely distributed, but has a more easterly range than its congener. Both species are very numerous in Palestine. While the black stork is never found about buildings, but prefers marshy places in forests, and breeds on the tops of the loftiest trees, the white stork attaches itself to man, and for the service which it renders in the destruction of reptiles and the removal of offal has been repaid from the earliest times by protection and reverence. The derivation of *chasîdâh* (from *chesed*, "kindness") points to the paternal and filial attachment of which the stork seems to have been a type among the Hebrews no less than the Greeks and Romans. It was believed that the young repaid the care of their parents by attaching themselves to them for life, and tending them in old age. That the parental attachment of the stork is very strong has been proved on many occasions. Few migratory birds are more punctual to the time of their reappearance than the white stork. The stork has no note, and the only sound it emits is that caused by the sudden snapping of its long mandibles.

Strain at. (So translated in the Authorized Version, but in the Revised Version "strain out," Matt. 23 : 24 ; which is undoubtedly the true reading.—ED.)

Stranger. A "stranger," in the technical sense of the term, may be defined to be a person of foreign, *i. e.* non-Israelitish, extraction resident within the limits of the promised land. He was distinct from the proper "foreigner," inasmuch as the latter still belonged to another country, and would only visit Palestine as a traveller: he was still more distinct from the "nations," or non-Israelite peoples. The term may be compared with our expression "naturalized foreigner." The terms applied to the "stranger" have special reference to the fact of his *residing* in the land. The existence of such a class of persons among the Israelites is easily accounted for. The "mixed multitude" that accompanied them out of Egypt, Ex. 12 : 38, formed one element; the Canaanitish population, which was never wholly extirpated from their native soil, formed another and a still more important one; captives taken in war formed a third; fugitives, hired servants, merchants, etc., formed a fourth. With the exception of the Moabites and Ammonites, Deut. 23 : 3, all nations were admissible to the rights of citizenship under certain conditions. The stranger appears to have been eligible to all civil offices, that of king excepted. Deut. 17 : 15. In regard to religion, it was absolutely necessary that the stranger should not infringe any of the fundamental laws of the Israelitish state. If he were a bondman, he was obliged to submit to circumcision, Ex. 12 : 44; if he were independent, it was optional with him; but if he remained uncircumcised, he was prohibited from partaking of the Passover, Ex. 12 : 48, and could not be regarded as a full citizen. Liberty was also given to an uncircumcised stranger in regard to the use of prohibited food. Assuming, however, that the stranger was circumcised, no distinction existed in regard to legal rights between the stranger and the Israelite; the Israelite is enjoined to treat him as a brother. Lev. 19 : 34; Deut. 10 : 19. It also appears that the "stranger" formed the class whence the hirelings were drawn; the terms being coupled together in Ex. 12 : 45; Lev. 22 : 10; 25 : 6, 40. The liberal spirit of the Mosaic regulations respecting strangers presents a strong contrast to the rigid exclusiveness of the Jews at the commencement of the Christian era. The growth of this spirit dates from the time of the Babylonish captivity.

Straw. Both wheat and barley straw were used by the ancient Hebrews chiefly as fodder for the horses, cattle and camels. Gen. 24 : 25; 1 Kings 4 : 28; Isa. 11 : 7; 65 : 25. There is no intimation that straw was used for litter. It was employed by the Egyptians for making bricks, Ex. 5 : 7, 16, being chopped up and mixed with the clay to make them more compact and to prevent their cracking. [See BRICK.] The ancient Egyptians reaped their corn close to the ear, and afterward cut the straw close to the ground and laid it by. This was the straw that Pharaoh refused to give to the Israelites, who were therefore compelled to gather "stubble" in-

Brick-making in Egypt.

stead—a matter of considerable difficulty, seeing that the straw itself had been cut off near to the ground.

Stream of Egypt occurs once in the Old Testament—Isa. 27 : 12. [RIVER OF EGYPT.]

Street. The streets of a modern Oriental town present a great contrast to those with which we are familiar, being generally narrow, tortuous and gloomy, even in the best towns. Their character is mainly fixed by the climate and the style of architecture, the narrowness being due to the extreme heat, and the gloominess to the circumstance of the windows looking for the most part into the inner court. The street called "Straight," in Damascus, Acts 9 : 11, was an exception to the rule of narrowness : it was a noble thoroughfare, one hundred feet wide, divided in the Roman age by colonnades into three avenues, the central one for foot passengers, the side passages for vehicles and horsemen going in different directions. The shops and warehouses were probably collected together into bazaars in ancient as in modern times. Jer. 37 : 21. That streets occasionally had names appears from Jer. 37 : 21; Acts 9 : 11. That they were generally unpaved may be inferred from the notices of the pavement laid by Herod the Great at Antioch, and by Herod Agrippa II. at Jerusalem. Hence pavement forms one of the peculiar features of the ideal Jerusalem. Tob. 13 : 17; Rev. 21 : 21. Each street and bazaar in a modern town is locked up at night; the same custom appears to have prevailed in ancient times. Cant. 3 : 3.

Stripes. [PUNISHMENTS.]

Su'ah (*sweeping*), son of Zophah, an Asherite. 1 Chron. 7 : 36. (B.C. about 1020.)

Suc'coth (*booths*). 1. An ancient town, first heard of in the account of the homeward journey of Jacob from Padanaram. Gen. 33 : 17. The name is derived from the fact of Jacob's having there put up "booths" (*succôth*) for his cattle, as well as a house for himself. From the itinerary of Jacob's return it seems that Succoth lay between Peniel, near the ford of the torrent Jabbok, and Shechem. Comp. Gen. 32 : 30 and 33 : 18. In accordance with this is the mention of Succoth in the narrative of Gideon's pursuit of Zebah and Zalmunna. Judges 8 : 5–17. It would appear from this passage that it lay east of the Jordan, which is corroborated by the fact that it was allotted to the tribe of Gad. Josh. 13 : 27. Succoth is named once again after this —in 1 Kings 7 : 46; 2 Chron. 4 : 17—as marking the spot at which the brass founderies were placed for casting the metal work of the temple. (Dr. Merrill identifies it with a site called *Tell Dar-ala*, one mile north of the Jabbok.—ED.)

2. The first camping-place of the Israelites when they left Egypt. Ex. 12 : 37; 13 : 20; Num. 33 : 5, 6. This place was apparently reached at the close of the first day's march. Rameses, the starting-place, was probably near the western end of the *Wâdi-t-Tumeylât*. The distance traversed in each day's journey was about fifteen miles.

Suc'coth-be'noth occurs only in 2 Kings 17 : 30. It has generally been supposed that this term is pure Hebrew, and signifies the *tents of daughters;* which some explain as "the booths in which the daughters of the Babylonians prostituted themselves in honor of their idol," others as "small tabernacles in which were contained images of female deities." Sir H. Rawlinson thinks that Succoth-benoth represents the Chaldæan goddess *Zerbanit*, the wife of Merodach, who was especially worshipped at Babylon.

Su'chathites, one of the families of scribes at Jabez. 1 Chron. 2 : 55.

Suk'kiim (*booth-dwellers*), a nation mentioned 2 Chron. 12 : 3 with the Lubim and Cushim as supplying part of the army which came with Shishak out of Egypt when he invaded Judah. The Sukkiim may correspond to some one of the shepherd or wandering races mentioned on the Egyptian monuments.

Sun. In the history of the creation the sun is described as the "greater light," in contradistinction to the moon, the "lesser light," in conjunction with which it was to serve "for signs, and for seasons, and for days, and for years," while its special office was "to rule the day." Gen. 1 : 14–16. The "signs" referred to were probably such extraordinary phenomena as eclipses, which were regarded as conveying premonitions of coming events. Jer. 10 : 2; Matt. 24 : 29 with Luke 21 : 25. The joint influence assigned to the sun and moon in deciding the "seasons," both for agricultural operations and for religious festivals, and also in regulating the length and subdivisions of the "years," correctly describes the combination of the lunar and solar year which prevailed at all events subsequent to the Mosaic period. Sunrise and sunset are the only defined points of time in the absence of artificial contrivances for telling the hour of the day. Between these two points the Jews recognized three periods, viz., when the sun became hot, about 9 A.M., 1 Sam. 11 : 9; Neh. 7 : 3; the double light, or noon, Gen. 43 : 16; 2 Sam. 4 : 5; and "the cool of the day," shortly before sunset. Gen. 3 : 8. The sun also served to fix the quarters of the hemisphere, east, west, north and south, which were represented respectively by the rising sun, the setting sun, Isa. 45 : 6; Ps. 50 : 1, the dark quarter, Gen. 13 : 14; Joel 2 : 20, and the brilliant quarter, Deut. 33 : 23; Job 37 : 17; Ezek. 40 : 24; or otherwise by their position relative to a person facing the rising sun—before, behind, on the left hand and on the right hand. Job 23 : 8, 9.

The worship of the sun, as the most prominent and powerful agent in the kingdom of nature, was widely diffused throughout the countries adjacent to Palestine. The Arabians appear to have paid direct worship to it without the intervention of any statue or symbol, Job 31 : 26, 27, and this simple style of worship was probably familiar to the ancestors of the Jews in Chaldæa and Mesopotamia. The Hebrews must have been well acquainted with the idolatrous worship of the sun during the captivity in

Egypt, both from the contiguity of On, the chief seat of the worship of the sun, as implied in the name itself (On being the equivalent of the Hebrew Bethshemesh, " house of the sun," Jer. 43 : 13), and also from the connection between Joseph and Potipherah (" he who belongs to Ra ") the priest of On. Gen. 41 : 45. After their removal to Canaan, the Hebrews came in contact with various forms of idolatry which originated in the worship of the sun; such as the Baal of the Phœnicians, the Molech or Milcom of the Ammonites, and the Hadad of the Syrians. The importance attached to the worship of the sun by the Jewish kings may be inferred from the fact that the horses sacred to the sun were stalled within the precincts of the temple. 2 Kings 23 : 11. In the metaphorical language of Scripture the sun is emblematic of the law of God, Ps. 19 : 7, of the cheering presence of God, Ps. 84 : 11, of the person of the Saviour, John 1 : 9; Mal. 4 : 2, and of the glory and purity of heavenly beings. Rev. 1 : 16; 10 : 1; 12 : 1.

Suretyship. In the entire absence of commerce the law laid down no rules on the subject of suretyship; but it is evident that in the time of Solomon commercial dealings had become so multiplied that suretyship in the commercial sense was common. Prov. 6 : 1; 11 : 15; 17 : 18; 20 : 16; 22 : 26; 27 : 13. But in older times the notion of one man becoming a surety for a service to be discharged by another was in full force. See Gen. 44 : 32. The surety of course became liable for his client's debts in case of his failure.

Su'sa. Esther 11 : 3; 16 : 18. [SHUSHAN.]

Su'sanchites is found once only—in Ezra 4 : 9. There can be no doubt that it designates either the inhabitants of the city Susa or those of the country—Susis or Susiana. Perhaps the former explanation is preferable.

Susan'na (*a lily*). 1. The heroine of the story of the Judgment of Daniel. (The book which gives an account of her life is also called " The history of Susanna," and is one of the apocryphal books of the Bible.)
2. One of the women who ministered to the Lord. Luke 8 : 3. (A.D. 28–30.)

Su'si, the father of Gaddi the Manassite spy. Num. 13 : 11.

Swallow (Heb. *dĕrôr* in Ps. 84 : 3,

Prov. 26 : 2; Heb. *'âgûr* in Isa. 38 : 14, Jer. 8 : 7, but " crane " is more probably the true signification of *'âgûr* [CRANE]). The rendering of the Authorized Version for *dĕrôr* seems correct. The characters

Swallow.

ascribed in the passages where the names occur are strictly applicable to the swallow, viz., its swiftness of flight, its nesting in the buildings of the temple, its mournful, garrulous note, and its regular migrations, shared indeed in common with several others. Many species of swallow occur in Palestine. All those common in England are found.

Swan (Heb. *tinshemeth*), thus rendered by the Authorized Version in Lev. 11 : 18; Deut. 14 : 16, where it occurs in the list of unclean birds. But either of the renderings " porphyrio " (purple water-hen) and " ibis " is more probable. Neither of these birds occurs elsewhere in the catalogue; both would be familiar to residents in Egypt, and the original seems to point to some water-fowl. The purple water-hen is allied to our corn-crake and water-hen, and is the largest and most beautiful of the family *Rallidæ*. It frequents marshes and the sedge by the banks of rivers in all the countries bordering on the Mediterranean, and is abundant in lower Egypt.

Swearing. [OATH.]

Sweat, Bloody. One of the physical phenomena attending our Lord's agony in the garden of Gethsemane is described by St. Luke, Luke 22 : 44: " His sweat was as it were great drops (lit. *clots*) of blood falling down to the ground." Of this malady, known in medical science by the term *diapedesis*, there have been examples recorded in both ancient and modern times. The cause assigned is generally violent mental emotion.

Swine (Heb. *chăzîr*). The flesh of swine was forbidden as food by the Levitical law, Lev. 11 : 7; Deut. 14 : 8; the abhorrence which the Jews as a nation had of it may be inferred from Isa. 65 : 4 and 2 Macc. 6 : 18, 19. No other reason for the command to abstain from swine's flesh is given in the law of Moses beyond the general one which forbade

The Wild Boar.

any of the mammalia as food which did not literally fulfill the terms of the definition of a "clean animal," viz., that it was to be a cloven-footed ruminant. It is, however, probable that dietetical considerations may have influenced Moses in his prohibition of swine's flesh: it is generally believed that its use in hot countries is liable to induce cutaneous disorders; hence in a people liable to leprosy the necessity for the observance of a strict rule. Although the Jews did not breed swine during the greater period of their existence as a nation, there can be little doubt that the heathen nations of Palestine used the flesh as food. At the time of our Lord's ministry it would appear that the Jews occasionally violated the law of Moses with regard to swine's flesh. Whether "the herd of swine" into which the devils were allowed to enter, Matt. 8 : 32; Mark 5 : 13, were the property of the Jewish or of the Gentile inhabitants of Gadara does not appear from the sacred narrative. The wild boar of the wood, Ps. 80 : 13, is the common

Sus scrofa, which is frequently met with in the woody parts of Palestine, especially in Mount Tabor.

Sword. [ARMS.]

Sycamine tree is mentioned only in Luke 17 : 6. There is no reason to doubt that the sycamine is distinct from the sycamore of the same evangelist. Luke 19 : 4. The sycamine is the mulberry tree (*Morus*). Both black and white mulberry trees are common in Syria and Palestine.

Sycamore (Heb. *shikmâh*). Although it may be admitted that the *sycamine* is properly, and in Luke 17 : 6, the *mulberry,* and the *sycamore* the *fig-mulberry,* or sycamore-fig (*Ficus sycomorus*), yet the latter is the tree generally referred to in the Old Testament, and called by the Septuagint sycamine, as 1 Kings 10 : 27; 1 Chron. 27 : 28; Ps. 78 : 47; Amos 7 : 14. The sycamore, or fig-mulberry, is in Egypt and Palestine a tree of great importance and very extensive use. It attains the size of a walnut tree, has wide-spreading branches, and affords a delightful shade. On this account it is frequently planted by the waysides. Its leaves are heart-shaped, downy on the under side, and fragrant. The fruit grows directly from the trunk itself on little sprigs, and in clusters like the grape. To make it eatable, each fruit, three or four days before gathering, must, it is said, be punctured with a sharp instrument or the finger-nail. This was the original employment of the prophet Amos, as he says. Amos 7 : 14. So great was the value of these trees that David appointed for them in his kingdom a special overseer, as he did for the olives, 1 Chron. 27 : 28; and it is mentioned as one of the heaviest of Egypt's calamities that her sycamores were destroyed by hailstones. Ps. 78 : 47.

Sy'char, a place named only in John 4 : 5. Sychar was either a name applied to the town of Shechem or it was an independent place. The first of these alternatives is now almost universally accepted. [SHECHEM.]

Sy'chem, the Greek form of the word Shechem. It occurs in Acts 7 : 16 only. [SHECHEM.]

Sye'ne, properly Seveneh, a town of Egypt, on the frontier of Cush or Ethiopia, Ezek. 29 : 10, 30 : 6, represented by the present *Aruán* or *Es-Suán.*

Sym'eon. (The Jewish form of the name Simon, used in the Revised Version of Acts 15 : 14, and referring to Simon Peter.—ED.)

Synagogue. 1. *History.*—The word *synagogue* (συναγωγή), which means a "congregation," is used in the New Testament to signify a recognized place of worship. A knowledge of the history and worship of the synagogues is of great importance, since they are the characteristic institution of the later phase of Judaism. They appear to have arisen during the exile, in the abeyance of the temple-worship, and to have received their full development on the return of the Jews from captivity. The whole history of Ezra presupposes the habit of solemn, probably of periodic, meetings. Ezra 8 : 15 ; Neh. 8 : 2 ; 9 : 1 ; Zech. 7 : 5. After the Maccabæan struggle for independence, we find almost every town or village had its one or more synagogues. Where the Jews were not in sufficient numbers to be able to erect and fill a building, there was the *proseucha* (προσευχή), or place of prayer, sometimes open, sometimes covered in, commonly by a running stream or on the seashore, in which devout Jews and proselytes met to worship, and perhaps to read. Acts 16 : 13 ; Juven. *Sat.* iii. 296. It is hardly possible to overestimate the influence of the system thus developed. To it we may ascribe the tenacity with which, after the Maccabæan struggle, the Jews adhered to the religion of their fathers, and never again relapsed into idolatry.

2. *Structure.*—The size of a synagogue varied with the population. Its position was, however, determinate. It stood, if possible, on the highest ground, in or near the city to which it belonged. And its direction too was fixed. Jerusalem was the *Kibleh* of Jewish devotion. The synagogue was so constructed that the worshippers, as they entered and as they prayed, looked toward it. The building was commonly erected at the cost of the district. Sometimes it was built by a rich Jew, or even, as in Luke 7 : 5, by a friendly proselyte. In the internal arrangement of the synagogue we trace an obvious analogy to the type of the tabernacle. At the upper or Jerusalem end stood the ark, the chest which, like the older and more sacred ark, contained the Book of the Law. It gave to that end the name and character of a sanctuary. This part of the synagogue was naturally the place

of honor. Here were the "chief seats," for which Pharisees and scribes strove so eagerly, Matt. 23 : 6, and to which the wealthy and honored worshipper was invited. James 2 : 2, 3. Here too, in front of the ark, still reproducing the type of the tabernacle, was the eight-branched lamp, lighted only on the greater festivals. Besides this there was one lamp kept burning perpetually. More toward the middle of the building was a raised platform, on which several persons could stand at once, and in the middle of this rose a pulpit, in which the reader stood to read the lesson or sat down to teach. The congregation were divided, men on one side, women on the other, a low partition, five or six feet high, running between them. The arrangements of modern synagogues, for many centuries, have made the separation more complete by placing the women in low side-galleries, screened off by lattice-work.

3. *Officers.*—In smaller towns there was often but one rabbi. Where a fuller organization was possible, there was a college of elders, Luke 7 : 3, presided over by one who was "the chief of the synagogue." Luke 8 : 41, 49 ; 13 : 14 ; Acts 18 : 8, 17. The most prominent functionary in a large synagogue was known as the *shĕliach* (= *legatus*), the officiating minister who acted as the delegate of the congregation, and was therefore the chief reader of prayers, etc., in their name. The *chazzán* or "minister" of the synagogue, Luke 4 : 20, had duties of a lower kind, resembling those of the Christian deacon or sub-deacon. He was to open the doors and to prepare the building for service. Besides these there were ten men attached to every synagogue, known as the *batlanim* (= *otiosi*). They were supposed to be men of leisure, not obliged to labor for their livelihood, able therefore to attend the week-day as well as the Sabbath services. The *legatus* of the synagogues appears in the *angel*, Rev. 1 : 20 ; 2 : 1, perhaps also in the *apostle* of the Christian Church.

4. *Worship.*—It will be enough, in this place, to notice in what way the ritual, no less than the organization, was connected with the facts of the New Testament history, and with the life and order of the Christian Church. From the synagogue came the use of fixed forms of prayer. To that the first disciples had been accustomed from their youth. They had asked their Master to give them a

distinctive one, and he had complied with their request, Luke 11:1, as the Baptist had done before for his disciples, as every rabbi did for his. "Moses" was "read in the synagogues every Sabbath day," Acts 15:21, the whole law being read consecutively, so as to be completed, according to one cycle, in three years.

The writings of the prophets were read as second lessons in a corresponding order. They were followed by the *derash*, Acts 13:15, the exposition, the sermon of the synagogue. The conformity extends also to the times of prayer. In the hours of service this was obviously the case. The third, sixth and ninth hours were in

Ruined Synagogue at Merion.—Site of Capernaum. (*From a Photograph.*)

the times of the New Testament, Acts 3:1; 10:3, 9, and had been probably for some time before, Ps. 55:17; Dan. 6:10, the fixed times of devotion. The same hours, it is well known, were recognized in the Church of the second century, probably in that of the first also. The solemn days of the synagogue were the second, the fifth and the seventh, the last or Sabbath being the conclusion of the whole. The transfer of the sanctity of the Sabbath to the Lord's day involved a corresponding change in the order of the week, and the first, the fourth and the sixth became to the Christian society what the other days had been to the Jewish. From the synagogue, lastly, come many less conspicuous practices, which meet us in the liturgical life of the first three centuries: Ablution, entire or partial, before entering the place of meeting, John 13:1–15; Heb. 10:22; standing, and not kneeling, as the attitude of prayer, Luke 18:11; the arms stretched out; the

Ruins of a Jewish Synagogue.

face turned toward the Kibleh of the east; the responsive amen of the congregation to the prayers and benedictions of the elders. 1 Cor. 14 : 16.

5. *Judicial functions.*—The language of the New Testament shows that the officers of the synagogue exercised in certain cases a judicial power. It is not quite so easy, however, to define the nature of the tribunal and the precise limits of its jurisdiction. In two of the passages referred to—Matt. 10 : 17 ; Mark 13 : 9—they are carefully distinguished from the councils. It seems probable that the council was the larger tribunal of twenty-three, which sat in every city, and that under the term synagogue we are to understand a smaller court, probably that of the ten judges mentioned in the Talmud. Here also we trace the outline of a Christian institution. The Church, either by itself or by appointed delegates, was to act as a court of arbitration in all disputes among its members. The elders of the church were not, however, to descend to the trivial disputes of daily life. For the elders, as for those of the synagogue, were reserved the graver offences against religion and morals.

Synagogue, The Great. On the return of the Jews from Babylon, a great council was appointed, according to rabbinic tradition, to reorganize the religious life of the people. It consisted of 120 members, and these were known as the men of the Great Synagogue, the successors of the prophets, themselves, in their· turn, succeeded by scribes prominent, individually, as teachers. Ezra was recognized as president. Their aim was to restore again the *crown*, or *glory*, of Israel. To this end they collected all the sacred writings of the former ages and their own, and so completed the canon of the Old Testament. They instituted the feast of Purim, organized the ritual of the synagogue, and gave their sanction to the *Shemôneh Esrêh*, the eighteen solemn benedictions in it. Much of this is evidently uncertain. The absence of any historical mention of such a body, not only in the Old Testament and the Apocrypha, but in Josephus, Philo, etc., has led some critics to reject the whole statement as a rabbinic invention. The narrative of Neh. 8 : 13 clearly implies the existence of a body of men acting as councillors under the presidency of Ezra ; and these may have been an assembly of delegates from all provincial synagogues—a synod of the national Church.

Syn'tyche (*with fate*), a female member of the church of Philippi. Philip. 4 : 2, 3. (A.D. 57).

Syr'acuse, the celebrated city on the eastern coast of Sicily. " The city in its splendor was the largest and richest that the Greeks possessed in any part of the world, being 22 miles in circumference." St. Paul arrived thither in an Alexandrian ship from Melita, on his voyage to Rome. Acts 28 : 12. The site of Syracuse rendered it a convenient place for the African corn-ships to touch at, for the harbor was an excellent one, and the fountain Arethusa in the island furnished an unfailing supply of excellent water.

Syr'ia is the term used throughout our version for the Hebrew *Aram*, as well as for the Greek Συρία. Most probably Syria is for *Tsyria*, the country about *Tsur* or Tyre, which was the first of the Syrian towns known to the Greeks. It is difficult to fix the limits of Syria. The limits of the Hebrew Aram and its subdivisions are spoken of under ARAM. Syria proper was bounded by Amanus and Taurus on the north, by the Euphrates and the Arabian desert on the east, by Palestine on the south, by the Mediterranean near the mouth of the Orontes, and then by Phœnicia on the west. This tract is about 300 miles long from north to south, and from 50 to 150 miles broad. It contains an area of about 30,000 square miles.

General physical features.—The general character of the tract is mountainous, as the Hebrew name Aram (from a root signifying " height") sufficiently implies. The most fertile and valuable tract of Syria is the long valley intervening between Libanus and Anti-Libanus. Of the various mountain ranges of Syria, Lebanon possesses the greatest interest. It extends from the mouth of the Litany to *Arka*, a distance of nearly 100 miles. Anti-Libanus, as the name implies, stands over against Lebanon, running in the same direction, *i. e.* nearly north and south, and extending the same length. [LEBANON.] The principal rivers of Syria are the Litany and the Orontes. The Litany springs from a small lake situated in the middle of the Cœle-Syrian valley, about six miles to the southwest of Baalbek. It enters the sea about five miles north of Tyre. The source of the Orontes is but about 15 miles from that of the Litany. Its modern name is the *Nahr-el-Asi*, or "rebel stream," an appellation given to it on account of its violence and impetuosity in many parts of its course. The chief towns of Syria may be thus arranged, as nearly as possible in the order of their importance: 1, Antioch; 2, Damascus; 3, Apamea; 4, Seleucia; 5, Tadmor or Palmyra; 6, Laodicea; 7, Epiphania (Hamath); 8, Samosata; 9, Hierapolis (Mabug); 10, Chalybon; 11, Emesa; 12, Heliopolis; 13, Laodicea ad Libanum; 14, Cyrrhus; 15, Chalcis; 16, Poseideum; 17, Heraclea; 18, Gindarus; 19, Zeugma; 20, Thapsacus. Of these, Samosata, Zeugma and Thapsacus are on the Euphrates; Seleucia, Laodicea, Poseideum and Heraclea, on the seashore; Antioch, Apamea, Epiphania and Emesa (*Hems*), on the Orontes; Heliopolis and Laodicea ad Libanum, in Cœle-Syria; Hierapolis, Chalybon, Cyrrhus, Chalcis and Gindarus, in the northern highlands; Damascus on the skirts, and Palmyra in the centre, of the eastern desert.

History.—The first occupants of Syria appear to have been of Hamitic descent—Hittites, Jebusites, Amorites, etc. After a while the first comers, who were still to a great extent nomads, received a Semitic infusion, which most probably came to them from the southeast. The only Syrian town whose existence we find distinctly marked at this time is Damascus, Gen. 14 : 15; 15 : 2, which appears to have been already a place of some importance. Next to Damascus must be placed Hamath. Num. 13 : 21; 34 : 8. Syria at this time, and for many centuries afterward, seems to have been broken up among a number of petty kingdoms. The Jews first come into hostile contact with the Syrians, *under that name*, in the time of David. Gen. 15 : 18; 2 Sam. 8 : 3, 4, 13. When, a few years later, the Ammonites determined on engaging in a war with David, and applied to the Syrians for aid, Zobah, together with Beth-rehob, sent them 20,000 footmen, and two other Syrian kingdoms furnished 13,000. 2 Sam. 10 : 6. This army being completely defeated by Joab, Hadadezer obtained aid from Mesopotamia, *ibid.* ver. 16, and tried the chance of a third battle, which likewise went against him, and produced the general submission of Syria to the Jewish monarch. The submission thus begun continued under the reign of Solomon. 1 Kings 4 : 21. The only part of Syria which Solomon lost seems to have been Damascus, where an independent kingdom was set up by Rezon, a native of Zobah. 1 Kings 11 : 23-25. On the separation of the two kingdoms, soon after the accession of Rehoboam, the remainder of Syria no doubt shook off the yoke. Damascus now became decidedly the leading state, Hamath being second to it, and the northern Hittites, whose capital was Carchemish, near *Bambuk*, third. [DAMASCUS.] Syria became attached to the great Assyrian empire, from which it passed to the Babylonians, and from them to the Persians. In B.C. 333 it submitted to Alexander without a struggle. Upon the death of Alexander, Syria became, for the first time, the head of a great kingdom. On the division of the provinces among his generals, B.C. 321, Seleucus Nicator received Mesopotamia and Syria. The city of Antioch was begun in B.C. 300, and, being finished in a few years, was made the capital of Seleucus' kingdom. The country grew rich with the wealth which now flowed into it on all sides.

Syria was added to the Roman empire by Pompey, B.C. 64, and as it holds an important place, not only in the Old Testament but in the New, some account of its condition under the Romans must be given. While the country generally was formed into a Roman province, under governors who were at first proprætors or quæstors, then proconsuls, and finally legates, there were exempted from the direct rule of the governor, in the first place, a number of "free cities," which retained the administration of their own affairs, subject to a tribute levied according to the Roman principles of taxation; secondly, a number of tracts, which were assigned to petty princes, commonly natives, to be ruled at their pleasure, subject to the same obligations with the free cities as to taxation. After the formal division of the provinces between Augustus and the senate, Syria, being from its exposed situation among the *provinciæ principis*, was ruled by legates, who were of consular rank (*consulares*) and bore severally the full title of "Legatus Augusti pro prætore." Judea occupied a peculiar position; a special procurator was therefore appointed to rule it, who was subordinate to the governor of Syria, but within his own province had the power of a legatus. Syria continued without serious disturbance from the expulsion of the Parthians, B.C. 38, to the breaking out of the Jewish war, A.D. 66. In A.D. 44–47 it was the scene of a severe famine. A little earlier, Christianity had begun to spread into it, partly by means of those who "were scattered" at the time of Stephen's persecution, Acts 11 : 19, partly by the exertions of St. Paul. Gal. 1 : 21. The Syrian Church soon grew to be one of the most flourishing. Acts 13 : 1; 15 : 23, 35, 41, etc. (Syria remained under Roman and Byzantine rule till A.D. 634, when it was overrun by the Mohammedans; after which it was for many years the scene of fierce contests, and was finally subjugated by the Turks, A.D. 1517, under whose rule it still remains.—ED.)

Sy′ro-phœni′cian occurs only in Mark 7 : 26. The word denoted perhaps a mixed race, half Phœnicians and half Syrians; (or the Phœnicians in this region may have been called Syro-phœnicians because they belonged to the Roman province of Syria, and were thus distinguished from the Phœnicians who lived in Africa, or the Carthaginians.—ED.)

Syr′tis, The, Acts 27 : 17; in the Revised Version in place of "quicksands" in the Authorized Version. It was the well-known *Syrtis Major*, the terror of all Mediterranean sailors. "It is a dangerous shallow on the coast of Africa, between Tripoli and Barca, southwest of the island of Crete." The other Syrtis, *Syrtis Minor*, was too far west to be feared by Paul's fellow voyagers.—ED.

T.

Ta'anach (*sandy*), an ancient Canaanitish city whose king is enumerated among the thirty-one kings conquered by Joshua. Josh. 12 : 21. It came into the half tribe of Manasseh, Josh. 17 : 11; 21 : 25; 1 Chron. 7 : 29, and was bestowed on the Kohathite Levites. Josh. 21 : 25. Taanach is almost always named in company with Megiddo, and they were evidently the chief towns of that fine rich district which forms the western portion of the great plain of Esdraelon. 1 Kings 4 : 12. It is still called *Ta'annuk*, and stands about four miles southeast of *Lejjûn* and 13 miles southwest of Nazareth.

Ta'anath-shi'loh (*approach to Shiloh*), a place named once only—Josh 16 : 6—as one of the landmarks of the boundary of Ephraim. Perhaps Taanath was the ancient Canaanite name of the place, and Shiloh the Hebrew name.

Tab'baoth (*rings*). The children of Tabbaoth were a family of Nethinim who returned with Zerubbabel. Ezra 2 : 43; Neh. 7 : 46. (B.C. before 536.)

Tab'bath (*celebrated*), a place mentioned only in Judges 7 : 22, in describing the flight of the Midianite host after Gideon's night attack; (probably the present *Tubukhat-Fahil*, a very striking natural bank 600 feet high, with a long horizontal top, embanked against the western face of the mountains east of the Jordan, and descending with a steep front to the river.—*Robinson, Bib. Res.*)

Tabe'al (*God is good*). The son of Tabeal was apparently an Ephraimite in the army of Pekah the son of Remaliah, or a Syrian in the army of Rezin, when they went up to besiege Jerusalem in the reign of Ahaz. Isa. 7 : 6. The Aramaic form of the name favors the latter supposition. (B.C. before 738.)

Ta'be-el (*God is good*), an officer of the Persian government in Samaria in the reign of Artaxerxes. Ezra 4 : 7. His name appears to indicate that he was a Syrian. (B.C. 519.)

Tab'erah, the name of a place in the wilderness of Paran. Num. 11 : 3; Deut. 9 : 22. It has not been identified.

Tabering, an obsolete English word used in the Authorized Version of Nahum 2 : 7. The Hebrew word connects itself with *töph*, "a timbrel." The Authorized Version reproduces the original idea. The "tabour" or "tabor" was a musical instrument of the drum type, which with the pipe formed the band of a country village. To "tabour," accordingly, is to beat with loud strokes, as men beat upon such an instrument.

Tabernacle. The tabernacle was the *tent of Jehovah*, called by the same name as the tents of the people in the midst of which it stood. It was also called the *sanctuary* and the *tabernacle of the congregation*. The first ordinances given to Moses, after the proclamation of the outline of the law from Sinai, related to the ordering of the tabernacle, its furniture and its service, as the type which was to be followed when the people came to their own home and "found a place" for the abode of God. During the forty days of Moses' first retirement with God in Sinai, an exact pattern of the whole was shown him, and all was made according to it. Ex. 25 : 9, 40; 26 : 30; 39 : 32, 42, 43; Num. 8 : 4; Acts 7 : 44; Heb. 8 : 5. The description of this plan is preceded by an account of the freewill offerings which the children of Israel were to be asked to make for its execution.

I. THE TABERNACLE ITSELF.—1. *Its name.*—It was first called a *tent* or *dwelling*, Ex. 25 : 8, because Jehovah, as it were, abode there. It was often called *tent* or *tabernacle* from its external appearance.

2. *Its materials.*—The materials were —(*a*) Metals: gold, silver and brass. (*b*) Textile fabrics: blue, purple, scarlet and fine (white) linen, for the production of which Egypt was celebrated; also a fabric of goat's hair, the produce of their own flocks. (*c*) Skins: of the ram, dyed red, and of the badger. (*d*) Wood: the shittim wood, the timber of the wild acacia of the desert itself, the tree of the "burning bush." (*e*) Oil, spices and incense for anointing the priests and burning in the tabernacle. (*f*) Gems: onyx stones and the precious stones for the breastplate of the high priest. The people gave jewels, and plates of gold and silver and brass; wood, skins, hair and linen;

TAB 664 TAB

the women wove; the rulers offered precious stones, oil, spices and incense; and the artists soon had more than they needed. Ex. 25 : 1–8; 35 : 4–29; 36 : 5–7. The superintendence of the work was intrusted to Bezaleel, of the tribe of Judah, and to Aholiab, of the tribe of Dan, who were skilled in "all manner of workmanship." Ex. 31 : 2, 6; 35 : 30, 34.

3. *Its structure.*—The tabernacle was to comprise three main parts,—the tabernacle more strictly so called, its tent and its covering. Ex. 35 : 11; 39 : 33, 34; 40 : 19, 34; Num. 3 : 25, etc. These parts are very clearly distinguished in the Hebrew, but they are confounded in many places of the English version. The tabernacle itself was to consist of curtains of fine linen woven with colored figures of cherubim, and a structure of boards which was to contain the holy place and the most holy place; the tent was to be a true tent of goat's-hair cloth, to contain and shelter the tabernacle; the covering

Southeast View of the Tabernacle covered by its Tent.

was to be of red ram-skins and seal-skins, Ex. 25 : 5, and was spread over the goat's-hair tent as an additional protection against the weather. It was an oblong rectangular structure, 30 cubits in length by 10 in width (45 feet by 15), and 10 in height; the interior being divided into two chambers, the first or outer, of 20 cubits in length, the inner, of 10 cubits, and consequently an exact cube. The former was the *holy place,* or *first tabernacle,* Heb. 9 : 2, containing the golden candlestick on one side, the table of shew-bread opposite, and between them in the centre the altar of incense. The latter was the *most holy place,* or the *holy of holies,* containing the ark, surmounted by the cherubim, with the two tables inside. The two sides and the farther or west end were enclosed by boards of shittim wood overlaid with gold, twenty on the north and twenty on the south side, six on the west side, and the corner-boards doubled. They stood upright, edge to edge, their lower ends being made with tenons, which dropped into sockets of silver, and the corner-boards being coupled at the top with rings. They were furnished with golden rings, through which passed bars of shittim wood, overlaid with gold, five to each side, and the middle bar passing from end to end, so as to brace the whole together. Four successive coverings of curtains looped together were placed over the open top and fell down over the sides. The first or inmost was a splendid fabric of linen, embroidered with figures of cherubim in blue, purple and scarlet, and looped together by golden fastenings. It seems probable that the ends of this set of curtains hung down *within* the tabernacle, forming a sumptuous tapestry. The second was a covering of goat's hair; the

General View of the Tabernacle.

TAB 666 TAB

third, of ram-skins dyed red; and the outermost, of badger-skins (so called in our version; but the Hebrew word probably signifies seal-skins). It has been commonly supposed that these coverings were thrown over the wall, as a pall is thrown over a coffin; but this would have allowed every drop of rain that fell on the tabernacle to fall through; for, however tightly the curtains might be stretched, the water could never run over the edge, and the sheep-skins would only make the matter worse, as when wetted their weight would depress the centre, and probably tear any curtain that could be made. There can be no reasonable doubt that the tent had a ridge, as all tents have had from the days of Moses down to the present time. The front of the sanctuary was closed by a hanging of fine linen, embroidered in blue, purple and scarlet, and supported by golden hooks on five pillars of shittim wood overlaid with gold and standing in brass sockets; and the covering of goat's hair was so made as to fall down over this when required. A more sumptuous curtain of the same kind, embroidered with cherubim, hung on four such pillars, with silver sockets, divided the holy from the most holy place. It was called the veil,[1] as it hid from the eyes of all but the high priest the inmost sanctuary, where Jehovah dwelt on his mercy-seat, between the cherubim above the ark. Hence "to enter within the veil" is to have the closest access to God. It was only passed by the high priest once a year, on the Day of Atonement, in token of the mediation of Christ, who with his own blood hath entered for us within the veil which separates God's own abode from earth. Heb. 6:19. In the temple, the solemn barrier was at length profaned by a Roman conqueror, to warn the Jews that the privileges they had forfeited were "ready to vanish away;" and the veil was at last rent by the hand of God himself, at the same moment that the body of Christ was rent upon the cross, to indicate that the entrance into the holiest of all is now laid open to all believers "by the blood of Jesus, by a new and living way which he hath consecrated for us, through the veil, that is to say, his flesh." Heb. 10:19, 20. The holy place

[1] Sometimes the *second veil*, either in reference to the first, at the entrance of the holy place, or as being the veil of the second sanctuary. Heb. 9:3.

was only entered by the priests daily, to offer incense at the time of morning and evening prayer, and to renew the lights on the golden candlesticks; and on the Sabbath, to remove the old shew-bread, and to place the new upon the table.

II. THE SACRED FURNITURE AND INSTRUMENTS OF THE TABERNACLE.—These are described in separate articles, and therefore it is only necessary to give a list of them here. 1. In the outer court. The *altar of burnt offering* and the *brazen laver*. [ALTAR; LAVER.] 2. In the holy place. The furniture of the court was connected with sacrifice; that of the sanctuary itself with the deeper mysteries of mediation and access to God. The first sanctuary contained three objects: the *altar of incense* in the centre, so as to be directly in front of the ark of the covenant, 1 Kings 6:22, the *table of shew-bread* on its right or north side, and the *golden candlestick* on the left or south side. These objects were all considered as being placed before the presence of Jehovah, who dwelt in the holiest of all, though with the veil between. [ALTAR; SHEW-BREAD; CANDLESTICK.] 3. In the holy of holies, within the veil, and shrouded in darkness, there was but one object, the *ark of the covenant*, containing the two tables of stone, inscribed with the Ten Commandments. [ARK.]

III. THE COURT OF THE TABERNACLE, in which the tabernacle itself stood, was an oblong space, 100 cubits by 50 (*i. e.* 150 feet by 75), having its longer axis east and west, with its front to the east. It was surrounded by canvas screens—in the East called *kannauts*—5 cubits in height, and supported by pillars of brass 5 cubits apart, to which the curtains were attached by hooks and fillets of silver. Ex. 27:9, etc. This enclosure was broken only on the east side by the entrance, which was 20 cubits wide, and closed by curtains of fine twined linen wrought with needlework, and of the most gorgeous colors. In the outer or east half of the court was placed the altar of burnt offering, and between it and the tabernacle itself, the laver at which the priests washed their hands and feet on entering the temple. The tabernacle itself was placed toward the west end of this enclosure.

IV. HISTORY.—"The tabernacle, as the place in which Jehovah dwelt, was pitched in the centre of the camp, Num.

TAB 667 TAB

2 : 2, as the tent of a leader always is in the East; for Jehovah was the Captain of Israel. Josh. 5 : 14, 15. During the marches of Israel, the tabernacle was still in the centre. Num. 2. The tribes camped and marched around it in the order of a hollow square. In certain great emergencies it led the march. Josh. 3 : 11–16. Upon the tabernacle abode always the cloud, dark by day and fiery red by night, Ex. 40 : 38, giving the signal for the march, Ex. 40 : 36, 37; Num. 9 : 17, and the halt. Num. 9 : 15–23. It was always the special meeting-place of Jehovah and his people. Num. 11 : 24, 25; 12 : 4; 14 : 10; 16 : 19, 42; 20 : 6; 27 : 2; Deut. 31 : 14." During the conquest of Canaan the tabernacle, at first moved from place to place, Josh. 4 : 19; 8 : 30–35; 9 : 6; 10 : 15, was finally located at Shiloh. Josh. 9 : 27; 18 : 1. Here it remained during the time of the judges, till it was captured by the Philistines, who carried off the sacred ark of the covenant. 1 Sam. 4 : 22. From this time forward the glory of the tabernacle was gone. When the ark was recovered, it was removed to Jerusalem, and placed in a new tabernacle, 2 Sam. 6 : 17; 1 Chron. 15 : 1; but the old structure still had its hold on the veneration of the community, and the old altar still received their offerings. 1 Chron. 16 : 39; 21 : 29. It was not till the temple was built, and a fitting house thus prepared for the Lord, that the ancient tabernacle was allowed to perish and be forgotten.

V. SIGNIFICANCE.—(The great underlying principles of true religion are the same in all ages and for all men; because man's nature and needs are the same, and the same God ever rules over all. But different ages require different methods of teaching these truths, and can understand them in different degrees. As we are taught in the Epistle to the Hebrews, the tabernacle was part of a great system of teaching by object-lessons, and of training the world to understand and receive the great truths which were to be revealed in Jesus Christ, and thus really to save the Jews from sin by Jesus dimly seen in the future, as we clearly see him in the past. (1) The tabernacle and its services enabled the Jews, who had no visible representation of God, to feel the *reality* of God and of religion. (2) The tabernacle, as the most beautiful and costly object in the nation, and ever in the centre of the camp, set forth the truth that religion was the central fact, and the most important, in a person's life. (3) The pillar of cloud and of fire was the best possible symbol of the living God,—a cloud, bright, glowing like the sunset clouds, glorious, beautiful, mysterious, self-poised, heavenly; fire, immaterial, the source of life and light and comfort and cheer, but yet unapproachable, terrible, a consuming fire to the wicked. (4) The altar of burnt offering, standing before the tabernacle, was a perpetual symbol of the atonement,—the greatness of sin, deserving death, hard to be removed, and yet forgiveness possible, and offered freely, but only through blood. The offerings, as brought by the people, were a type of consecration to God, of conversion and new life, through the atonement. (5) This altar stood outside of the tabernacle, and must be passed before we come to the tabernacle itself; a type of the true religious life. Before the tabernacle was also the laver, signifying the same thing that baptism does with us, the cleansing of the heart and life. (6) Having entered the holy place, we find the three great means and helps to true living,—the candlestick, the light of God's truth; the shew-bread, teaching that the soul must have its spiritual food, and live in communion with God; and the altar of incense, the symbol of prayer. The holy of holies, beyond, taught that there was progress in the religious life, and that that progress was toward God, and toward the perfect keeping of the law, till it was as natural to obey the law as it is to breathe; and thus the holy of holies was the type of heaven.—ED.)

Tabernacles, The Feast of (Ex. 23 : 16, "the feast of ingathering"), the third of the three great festivals of the Hebrews, which lasted from the 15th till the 22d of Tisri. 1. The following are the principal passages in the Pentateuch which refer to it: Ex. 23 : 16; Lev. 23 : 34–36, 39–43; Num. 29 : 12–38; Deut. 16 : 13–15; 31 : 10–13. In Neh. 8 there is an account of the observance of the feast by Ezra. 2. The time of the festival fell in the autumn, when the whole of the chief fruits of the ground, the corn, the wine and the oil, were gathered in. Ex. 23 : 16; Lev. 23 : 39; Deut. 15 : 13–15. Its duration was strictly only seven days, Deut. 16 : 13; Ezek. 45 : 25; but it was followed by a day of holy convocation, distinguished by sacrifices of its own, which was sometimes spoken of as an eighth day. Lev. 23 : 36;

TAB 668 TAB

Neh. 8 : 18. During the seven days the Israelites were commanded to dwell in booths or huts formed of the boughs of trees. The boughs were of the olive, palm, pine, myrtle and other trees with thick foliage. Neh. 8 : 15, 16. According to rabbinical tradition, each Israelite used to tie the branches into a bunch, to be carried in his hand, to which the name *lûlâb* was given. The burnt offerings of the Feast of Tabernacles were by far more numerous than those of any other festival. There were offered on each day two rams, fourteen lambs and a kid for a sin offering. But what was most peculiar was the arrangement of the sacrifices of bullocks, in all amounting to seventy. Num. 29 : 12–38. The eighth day was a day of holy convocation of peculiar solemnity. On the morning of this day the Hebrews left their huts and dismantled them, and took up their abode again in their houses. The special offerings of the day were a bullock, a ram, seven lambs and a goat for a sin offering. Num. 29 : 36, 38. When the Feast of Tabernacles fell on a sabbatical year, portions of the law were read each day in public, to men, women, children and strangers. Deut. 31 : 10–13. We find Ezra reading the law during the festival "day by day, from the first day to the last day." Neh. 8 : 18. 3. There are two particulars in the observance of the Feast of Tabernacles which appear to be referred to in the New Testament, but are not noticed in the Old. These were the ceremony of pouring out some water of the pool of Siloam and the display of some great lights in the court of the women. We are told that each Israelite, in holiday attire, having made up his *lûlâb*, before he broke his fast repaired to the temple with the *lûlâb* in one hand and the citron in the other, at the time of the ordinary morning sacrifice. The parts of the victim were laid upon the altar. One of the priests fetched some water in a golden ewer from the pool of Siloam, which he brought into the court through the water-gate. As he entered the trumpets sounded, and he ascended the slope of the altar. At the top of this were fixed two silver basins with small openings at the bottom. Wine was poured into that on the eastern side, and the water into that on the western side, whence it was conducted by pipes into the Cedron. In the evening, both men and women assembled in the court of the women, expressly to hold a rejoicing for the drawing of the water of Siloam. At the same time there were set up in the court two lofty stands, each supporting four great lamps. These were lighted on each night of the festival. It appears to be generally admitted that the words of our Saviour, John 7 : 37, 38—"If any man thirst, let him come unto me and drink. He that believeth on me, as the Scripture hath said, out of his belly shall flow rivers of living water"—were suggested by the pouring out of the water of Siloam. But it is very doubtful what is meant by "the last day, that great day of the feast." It would seem that either the last day of the feast itself, that is, the seventh, or the last day of the religious observances of the series of annual festivals, the eighth, must be intended. The eighth day may be meant, and then the reference of our Lord would be to an ordinary and well-known observance of the feast, though it was not, at the very time, going on. We must resort to some such explanation if we adopt the notion that our Lord's words, John 8 : 12—"I am the light of the world"—refer to the great lamps of the festival. 4. Though all the Hebrew annual festivals were seasons of rejoicing, the Feast of Tabernacles was, in this respect, distinguished above them all. The huts and the *lûlâbs* must have made a gay and striking spectacle over the city by day, and the lamps, the flambeaux, the music and the joyous gatherings in the court of the temple must have given a still more festive character to the night. The main purposes of the Feast of Tabernacles are plainly set forth in Ex. 23 : 16 and Lev. 23 : 43. It was to be at once a thanksgiving for the harvest and a commemoration of the time when the Israelites dwelt in tents during their passage through the wilderness. In one of its meanings it stands in connection with the Passover, as the Feast of Abib, and with Pentecost, as the feast of harvest; in its other meaning, it is related to the Passover as the great yearly memorial of the deliverance from the destroyer and from the tyranny of Egypt. But naturally connected with this exultation in their regained freedom was the rejoicing in the more perfect fulfillment of God's promise in the settlement of his people in the holy land. But the culminating point of this blessing was the establishment of the central spot of the national worship in the temple at Jerusalem. Hence it was evidently fit-

TAB 669 TAB

ting that the Feast of Tabernacles should be kept with an unwonted degree of observance at the dedication of Solomon's temple, 1 Kings 8 : 2, 65; Joseph. *Ant.* viii. 4, § 5; again, after the rebuilding of the temple by Ezra, Neh. 8 : 13-18, and a third time by Judas Maccabæus when he had driven out the Syrians and restored the temple to the worship of Jehovah. 2 Macc. 10 : 5-8.

Tab′itha (*gazelle*), also called Dorcas by St. Luke, a female disciple of Joppa, "full of good works," among which that of making clothes for the poor is specifically mentioned. While St. Peter was at the neighboring town of Lydda, Tabitha died; upon which the disciples at Joppa sent an urgent message to the apostle begging him to come to them without delay. Upon his arrival Peter found the deceased already prepared for burial, and laid out in an upper chamber, where she was surrounded by the recipients and the tokens of her charity. After the example of our Saviour in the house of Jairus, Matt. 9 : 25; Mark 5 : 40, "Peter put them all forth," prayed for the divine assistance, and then commanded Tabitha to arise. Comp. Mark 5 : 41; Luke 8 : 54. She opened her eyes and sat up, and then, assisted by the apostle, rose from her couch. This great miracle, as we are further told, produced an extraordinary effect in Joppa, and was the occasion of many conversions there. Acts 9 : 36-42. The name "Tabitha" is an Aramaic word, signifying a "female gazelle." St. Luke gives "Dorcas" as the Greek equivalent of the name.

Ta′bor (*a mound*), or **Mount Ta′- bor,** one of the most interesting and remarkable of the single mountains in Palestine. It rises abruptly from the northeastern arm of the plain of Esdraelon, and stands entirely insulated, except on the west, where a narrow ridge connects it with the hills of Nazareth. It presents to the eye, as seen from a distance, a beautiful appearance, being symmetrical in its proportions, and rounded off like a hemisphere or the segment of a circle, yet varying somewhat as viewed from different directions. The body of the mountain consists of the peculiar limestone of the country. It is now called *Jebel-et-Túr*. It lies about six or eight miles almost due east from Nazareth. The ascent is usually made on the west side, near the little village of *Debúrieh*— probably the ancient Daberath, Josh. 19 :

12—though it can be made with entire ease in other places. It requires three quarters of an hour or an hour to reach the top. The top of Tabor consists of an irregular platform, embracing a circuit of half an hour's walk, and commanding wide views of the subjacent plain from end to end. Tabor does not occur in the New Testament, but makes a prominent figure in the Old. The book of Joshua, 19 : 22, mentions it as the boundary between Issachar and Zebulun. See ver. 12. Barak, at the command of Deborah, assembled his forces on Tabor, and descended thence, with "ten thousand men after him," into the plain, and conquered Sisera on the banks of the Kishon. Judges 4 : 6-15. The brothers of Gideon, each of whom "resembled the children of a king," were murdered here by Zebah and Zalmunna. Judges 8 : 18, 19. There are at present the ruins of a fortress round all the summit of Tabor. The Latin Christians have now an altar here, at which their priests from Nazareth perform an annual mass. The Greeks also have a chapel, where, on certain festivals, they assemble for the celebration of religious rites. The idea that our Saviour was transfigured on Tabor prevailed extensively among the early Christians, and still reappears often in popular religious works. It is impossible, however, to acquiesce in the correctness of this opinion. It can be proved from the Old Testament and from later history that a fortress or town existed on Tabor from very early times down to B.C. 53 or 50; and, as Josephus says that he strengthened the fortifications there about A.D. 60, it is morally certain that Tabor must have been inhabited during the intervening period, that is, in the days of Christ. Tabor, therefore, could not have been the Mount of Transfiguration [see HERMON]; for when it is said that Jesus took his disciples "up into a high mountain apart, and was transfigured before them," Matt. 17 : 1, 2, we must understand that he brought them to the summit of the mountain, where they were alone by themselves.

Ta′bor is mentioned in the lists of 1 Chron. 6 as a city of the Merarite Levites, in the tribe of Zebulun. ver. 77. The list of the towns of Zebulun, Josh. 19, contains the name of Chisloth-tabor. ver. 12. It is, therefore, possible, either that Chisloth-tabor is abbreviated into Tabor by the chronicler, or that by the

TAB   670   TAC

time these later lists were compiled the Merarites had established themselves on the sacred mountain, and that Tabor is Mount Tabor.

Ta'bor, The plain of. This is an incorrect translation, and should be THE OAK OF TABOR. It is mentioned in 1 Sam. 10 : 3 only, as one of the points in the homeward journey of Saul after his anointing by Samuel.

Tabret. [TIMBREL.]

Tab'rimon (properly Tabrimmon, *i. e. good is Rimmon*, the Syrian god) the father of Ben-hadad I., king of Syria

Mount Tabor.

The picture gives us a fine view of this remarkable mountain in the holy land. It is in that part of Palestine which was called Galilee in the days of our Saviour, and was a region of picturesque and romantic beauty, comprising hills and plains, mountains and valleys. Travellers are agreed in regarding the view from the summit of Tabor as one of the finest in the holy land.

in the reign of Asa. 1 Kings 15 : 18. (B.C. before 928.)

Tache. The word thus rendered occurs only in the description of the structure of the tabernacle and its fittings, Ex. 26 : 6, 11, 33; 35 : 11; 36 : 13; 39 : 33, and appears to indicate the small hooks by which a curtain is suspended to the rings from which it hangs, or connected vertically, as in the case of the veil of the holy of holies, with the loops of another curtain.

Tach'monite, The. "The Tachmonite that sat in the seat," chief among David's captains, 2 Sam. 23 : 8, is in 1 Chron. 11 : 11 called "Jashobeam an Hachmonite," or, as the margin gives it, "son of Hachmoni." Kennicott has shown that the words translated "he that sat in the seat" are a corruption of

Jashobeam, and that "the Tachmonite" is a corruption of the "son of Hachmoni," which was the family or local name of Jashobeam. Therefore he concludes "Jashobeam the Hachmonite" to have been the true reading.

Tad'mor (*city of palms*), called "Tadmor in the wilderness," is the same as the city known to the Greeks and Romans under the name of Palmyra. It lay between the Euphrates and Hamath, to the southeast of that city, in a fertile tract or oasis of the desert. Being situated at a convenient distance from both the Mediterranean Sea and the Persian Gulf, it had great advantages for caravan traffic. It was built by Solomon after his conquest of Hamath-zobah. 1 Kings 9 : 18; 2 Chron. 8 : 4. As the city is nowhere else mentioned in the Bible, it would be out of place to enter into a detailed history of it. In the second century A.D. it seems to have been beautified by the emperor Hadrian. In the beginning of the third century—211-217 A.D.—it became a Roman colony under

Ruins at Tadmor (Palmyra).

Caracalla. Subsequently, in the reign of Gallienus, the Roman senate invested Odenathus, a senator of Palmyra, with the regal dignity, on account of his services in defeating Sapor, king of Persia. On the assassination of Odenathus, his wife, Zenobia, seems to have conceived the design of erecting Palmyra into an independent monarchy; and in prosecution of this object, she for a while successfully resisted the Roman arms. She was at length defeated and taken captive by the emperor Aurelian, A.D. 273, who left a Roman garrison in Palmyra. This garrison was massacred in a revolt; and Aurelian punished the city by the execution not only of those who were taken in arms, but likewise of common peasants, of old men, women and children. From this blow Palmyra never recovered, though there are proofs of its having continued to be inhabited until the downfall of the Roman empire. The grandeur and magnificence of the ruins of Palmyra cannot be exceeded, and attest its former greatness. Among the most remarkable are the Tombs, the Temple of the Sun and the Street of Columns.

Ta'han (*camp*), a descendant of Ephraim. Num. 26 : 35. In 1 Chron. 7 : 25 he appears as the son of Telah.

Ta'hanites, The. Num. 26 : 35. [TAHAN.]

Ta'hath (*station*). 1. A Kohathite

Levite, ancestor of Samuel and Heman. 1 Chron. 6 : 24, 37 (9, 22). (B.C. about 1415.)

2. According to the present text, son of Bered, and great-grandson of Ephraim. 1 Chron. 7 : 20. Burrington, however, identifies Tahath with Tahan, the son of Ephraim.

3. Grandson of the preceding, as the text now stands. 1 Chron. 7 : 20. But Burrington considers him as a son of Ephraim.

Ta'hath, the name of a desert station of the Israelites between Makheloth and Tarah. Num. 33 : 26. The site has not been identified.

Tah'panhes, Tchaph'nehes, Tahap'anes, a city of Egypt, mentioned in the time of the prophets Jeremiah and Ezekiel. The name is evidently Egyptian, and closely resembles that of the Egyptian queen Tahpenes. It was evidently a town of lower Egypt, near or on the eastern border. When Johanan and the other captains went into Egypt "they came to Tahpanhes." Jer. 43 : 7. The Jews in Jeremiah's time remained here. Jer. 44 : 1. It was an important town, being twice mentioned by the latter prophet with Noph or Memphis. Jer. 2 : 16; 46 : 14. Here stood a house of Pharaoh-hophra before which Jeremiah hid great stones. Jer. 43 : 8-10.

Tah'penes, an Egyptian queen, was wife of the Pharaoh who received Hadad the Edomite, and who gave him her sister in marriage. 1 Kings 11 : 18-20. (B.C. about 1000.)

Tah'rea (*cunning*), son of Micah and grandson of Mephibosheth. 1 Chron. 9 : 41. (B.C. after 1037.)

Tah'tim-hod'shi (*lowlands of Hodshi?*), **The land of,** one of the places visited by Joab during his census of the land of Israel. It occurs between Gilead and Dan-jaan. 2 Sam. 24 : 6. The name has puzzled all the interpreters. (Kitto says it was probably a section of the upper valley of the Jordan, now called *Ard el-Huleh*, lying deep down at the western base of Hermon.—ED.)

Talent. [WEIGHTS AND MEASURES.]

Talitha cumi, two Syriac words, Mark 5 : 41, signifying *damsel, arise.*

Tal'ma-i (*bold*). 1. One of the three sons of "the Anak" who were slain by the men of Judah. Num. 13 : 22; Josh. 15 : 14; Judges 1 : 10. (B.C. 1450.)

2. Son of Ammihud king of Geshur. 2 Sam. 3 : 3; 13 : 37; 1 Chron. 3 : 2. He

was probably a petty chieftain, dependent on David. (B.C. 1045.)

Tal'mon (*oppressor*), the head of a family of door-keepers in the temple, "the porters for the camps of the sons of Levi." 1 Chron. 9 : 17; Neh. 11 : 19. (B.C. 1013.) Some of his descendants returned with Zerubbabel, Ezra 2 : 42; Neh. 7 : 45, and were employed in their hereditary office in the days of Nehemiah and Ezra. Neh. 12 : 25.

Tal'mud (*i. e. doctrine*, from the Hebrew word "to learn") is a large collection of writings, containing a full account of the civil and religious laws of the Jews. It was a fundamental principle of the Pharisees, common to them with all orthodox modern Jews, that by the side of the written law, regarded as a summary of the principles and general laws of the Hebrew people, there was an oral law, to complete and to explain the written law. It was an article of faith that in the Pentateuch there was no precept, and no regulation, ceremonial, doctrinal or legal, of which God had not given to Moses all explanations necessary for their application, with the order to transmit them by word of mouth. The classical passage in the Mishna on this subject is the following : " Moses received the (oral) law from Sinai, and delivered it to Joshua, and Joshua to the elders, and the elders to the prophets, and the prophets to the men of the Great Synagogue." This oral law, with the numerous commentaries upon it, forms the Talmud. It consists of two parts, the Mishna and Gemara. 1. The MISHNA, or "second law," which contains a compendium of the whole ritual law, was reduced to writing in its present form by Rabbi Jehuda the Holy, a Jew of great wealth and influence, who flourished in the second century of the Christian era. Viewed as a whole, the precepts in the Mishna treated men like children, formalizing and defining the minutest particulars of ritual observances. The expressions of " bondage," of "weak and beggarly elements," and of "burdens too heavy for men to bear," faithfully represent the impression produced by their multiplicity. The Mishna is very concisely written, and requires notes. 2. This circumstance led to the commentaries called GEMARA (*i. e. supplement, completion*), which form the second part of the Talmud, and which are very commonly meant when the word "Talmud" is used by itself.

There are two Gemaras: one of Jerusalem, in which there is said to be no passage which can be proved to be later than the first half of the fourth century; and the other of Babylon, completed about 500 A.D. The latter is the more important and by far the longer.

Ta'mah (*laughter*). The children of Tamah or Thamah, Ezra 2:53, were among the Nethinim who returned with Zerubbabel. Neh. 7:55.

Ta'mar (*palm tree*). 1. The wife successively of the two sons of Judah, Er and Onan. Gen. 38:6-30. (B.C. about 1718.) Her importance in the sacred narrative depends on the great anxiety to keep up the lineage of Judah. It seemed as if the family were on the point of extinction. Er and Onan had successively perished suddenly. Judah's wife, Bathshuah, died; and there only remained a child, Shelah, whom Judah was unwilling to trust to the dangerous union, as it appeared, with Tamar, lest he should meet with the same fate as his brothers. Accordingly she resorted to the desperate expedient of entrapping the father himself into the union which he feared for his son. The fruits of this intercourse were twins, Pharez and Zarah, and through Pharez the sacred line was continued.

2. Daughter of David and Maachah the Geshurite princess, and thus sister of Absalom. 2 Sam. 13:1-32; 1 Chron. 3:9. (B.C. 1033.) She and her brother were alike remarkable for their extraordinary beauty. This fatal beauty inspired a frantic passion in her half-brother Amnon, the oldest son of David by Ahinoam. In her touching remonstrance two points are remarkable: first, the expression of the infamy of such a crime "in *Israel*," implying the loftier standard of morals that prevailed, as compared with other countries at that time; and second, the belief that even this standard might be overborne lawfully by royal authority—"Speak to the king, for he will not withhold me from thee." The intense hatred of Amnon succeeding to his brutal passion, and the indignation of Tamar at his barbarous insult, even surpassing her indignation at his shameful outrage, are pathetically and graphically told.

3. Daughter of Absalom, 2 Sam. 14:7, became, by her marriage with Uriah of Gibeah, the mother of Maachah, the future queen of Judah, or wife of Abijah. 1 Kings 15:2. (B.C. 1023.)

4. A spot on the southeastern frontier of Judah, named in Ezek. 47:19, 48:28 only, evidently called from a palm tree. If not Hazazon-tamar, the old name of Engedi, it may be a place called Thamar in the *Onomasticon* [HAZAZON-TAMAR], a day's journey south of Hebron.

Tam'muz (*sprout of life*), properly "the Tammuz," the article indicating that at some time or other the word had been regarded as an appellative. Ezek. 8:14. Jerome identifies Tammuz with Adonis, of Grecian mythology, who was fabled to have lost his life while hunting, by a wound from the tusk of a wild boar. He was greatly beloved by the goddess Venus, who was inconsolable at his loss. His blood, according to Ovid, produced the anemone, but according to others the adonium, while the anemone sprang from the tears of Venus. A festival in honor of Adonis was celebrated at Byblus in Phœnicia and in most of the Grecian cities, and even by the Jews when they degenerated into idolatry. It took place in July, and was accompanied by obscene rites.

Ta'nach, a slight variation of the name TAANACH. Josh. 21:25.

Tan'humeth (*consolation*), the father of Seraiah in the time of Gedaliah. 2 Kings 25:23; Jer. 40:8. (B.C. before 582.)

Ta'phath (*ornament*), the daughter of Solomon, who was married to ben-Abinadab. 1 Kings 4:11. (B.C. about 1000.)

Ta'phon, one of the cities in Judea, fortified by Bacchides. 1 Macc. 9:50. is probably the Beth-tappuah of the Old Testament.

Tap'puah (*the apple-city*). 1. A city of Judah, in the district of the Shefelah or lowland. Josh. 15:34.

2. A place on the boundary of the "children of Joseph." Josh. 16:8; 17:8. Its full name was probably En-tappuah. Josh. 17:7. ("Around the city was a district called the land of Tappuah; the city belonged to Ephraim and the land to Manasseh. Josh. 17:8."—*Schaff.*)

3. One of the sons of Hebron, of the tribe of Judah. 1 Chron. 2:43. It is doubtless the same as Beth-tappuah. (B.C. before 1450.)

Ta'rah (*delay*), a desert-station of the Israelites between Tahath and Mithcah. Num. 33:27.

Tar'alah (*reeling*), one of the towns in the allotment of Benjamin. Josh. 18:27.

Tare'a, the same as Tahreah, the son of Micah. 1 Chron. 8:35.

Tares. There can be little doubt that the *zizania* of the parable, Matt. 13:25, denotes the weed called "darnel" (*Lolium temulentum*). The darnel before it comes into ear is very similar in appearance to wheat; hence the command that the *zizania* should be left to the harvest,

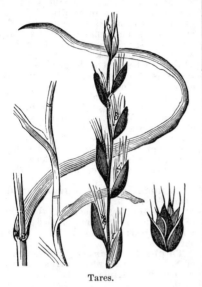

Tares.

lest while men plucked up the tares "they should root up also the wheat with them." Dr. Stanley, however, speaks of women and children picking up from the wheat in the cornfields of Samaria the tall green stalks, still called by the Arabs *zuwân*. "These stalks," he continues, "if sown designedly throughout the fields, would be inseparable from the wheat, from which, even when growing naturally and by chance, they are at first sight hardly distinguishable." See also Thomson ("The Land and the Book," p. 420): "The grain is in just the proper stage to illustrate the parable. In those parts where the grain has *headed out*, the tares have done the same, and then a child cannot mistake them for wheat or barley; but where both are less developed, the closest scrutiny will often fail to detect them. Even the farmers, who in this country generally *weed* their fields, do not attempt to separate the one from the other." The grains of the *L. temulentum*, if eaten, produce convulsions, and even death.

Tar'gum. [See VERSIONS.]

Tar'pelites, The, a race of Assyrian colonists who were planted in the cities of Samaria after the captivity of the northern kingdom of Israel. Ezra 4:9. They have not been identified with any certainty.

Tar'shish (*established*). 1. Probably Tartessus, a city and emporium of the Phœnicians in the south of Spain, represented as one of the sons of Javan. Gen. 10:4; 1 Kings 10:22; 1 Chron. 1:7; Ps. 48:7; Isa. 2:16; Jer. 10:9; Ezek. 27:12, 25; Jonah 1:3; 4:2. The identity of the two places is rendered highly probable by the following circumstances: 1st. There is a very close similarity of name between them, Tartessus being merely Tarshish in the Aramaic form. 2d. There seems to have been a special relation between Tarshish and Tyre, as there was at one time between Tartessus and the Phœnicians. 3d. The articles which Tarshish is stated by the prophet Ezekiel, Ezek. 27:12, to have supplied to Tyre are precisely such as we know, through classical writers, to have been productions of the Spanish peninsula. In regard to tin, the trade of Tarshish in this metal is peculiarly significant, and, taken in conjunction with similarity of name and other circumstances already mentioned, is reasonably conclusive as to its identity with Tartessus. For even now the countries in Europe or on the shores of the Mediterranean Sea where tin is found are very few; and in reference to ancient times, it would be difficult to name any such countries except Iberia or Spain, Lusitania, which was somewhat less in extent than Portugal, and Cornwall in Great Britain. In the absence of positive proof, we may acquiesce in the statement of Strabo, that the river Bætis (now the Guadalquivir) was formerly called Tartessus, that the city Tartessus was situated between the two arms by which the river flowed into the sea, and that the adjoining country was called Tartessis.

2. From the book of Chronicles there would seem to have been a Tarshish accessible from the Red Sea, in addition to the Tarshish of the south of Spain. Thus, with regard to the ships of Tarshish, which Jehoshaphat caused to be constructed at Ezion-geber on the Elanitic

Gulf of the Red Sea, 1 Kings 22 : 48, it is said in the Chronicles, 2 Chron. 20 : 36, that they were made to go to Tarshish; and in like manner the navy of ships, which Solomon had previously made in Ezion-geber, 1 Kings 9 : 26, is said in the Chronicles, 2 Chron. 9 : 21, to have gone to Tarshish with the servants of Hiram.

It is not to be supposed that the author of these passages in the Chronicles contemplated a voyage to Tarshish in the south of Spain by going round what has since been called the Cape of Good Hope. The expression "ships of Tarshish" originally meant ships destined to go to Tarshish; and then probably came to

Tarsus, Birthplace of St. Paul. Mount Taurus in the background.

signify large Phœnician ships, of a particular size and description, destined for long voyages, just as in English "East Indiaman" was a general name given to vessels, some of which were not intended to go to India at all. Hence we may infer that the word Tarshish was also used to signify any distant place, and in this case would be applied to one in the Indian Ocean. This is shown by the nature of the imports with which the fleet returned, which are specified as "gold, silver, ivory, apes, and *peacocks*." 1 Kings 10 : 22. The gold might possibly have been obtained from Africa, or from Ophir

in Arabia, and the ivory and the apes might likewise have been imported from Africa; but the peacocks point conclusively, not to Africa, but to India. There are only two species known: both inhabit the mainland and islands of India; so that the mention of the peacock seems to exclude the possibility of the voyage having been to Africa.

Tar′sus, the chief town of Cilicia, "no mean city" in other respects, but illustrious to all time as the birthplace and early residence of the apostle Paul. Acts 9 : 11; 21 : 39; 22 : 3. Even in the flourishing period of Greek history it was a city of some considerable consequence. In the civil wars of Rome it took Cæsar's side, and on the occasion of a visit from him had its name changed to Juliopolis. Augustus made it a " free city." It was renowned as a place of education under the early Roman emperors. Strabo compares it in this respect to Athens and Alexandria. Tarsus also was a place of much commerce. It was situated in a wild and fertile plain on the banks of the Cydnus. No ruins of any importance remain.

Tar′tak (*prince of darkness*), one of the gods of the Avite or Avvite colonists of Samaria. 2 Kings 17 : 31. According to rabbinical tradition, Tartak is said to have been worshipped under the form of an ass.

Tar′tan, which occurs only in 2 Kings 18 : 17 and Isa. 20 : 1, has been generally regarded as a proper name; but like Rabsaris and Rabshakeh, it is more probably an official designation, and indicates the Assyrian commander-in-chief.

Tat′na-i (*gift*), satrap of the province west of the Euphrates in the time of Darius Hystaspes. Ezra 5 : 3, 6; 6 : 6, 13. (B.C. 520.) The name is thought to be Persian.

Taverns, The three. [THREE TAVERNS.]

Taxes. I. Under the judges, according to the theocratic government contemplated by the law, the only payments incumbent upon the people as of permanent obligation were the Tithes, the First-fruits, the Redemption-money of the first-born, and other offerings as belonging to special occasions. The payment by each Israelite of the half-shekel as "atonement-money," for the service of the tabernacle, on taking the census of the people, Ex. 30 : 13, does not appear to have had the character of a recurring tax, but to have been supplementary to the freewill offerings of Ex. 25 : 1-7, levied for the one purpose of the construction of the sacred tent. In later times, indeed, after the return from Babylon, there was an annual payment for maintaining the fabric and services of the temple; but the fact that this begins by the voluntary compact to pay one third of a shekel, Neh. 10 : 32, shows that till then there was no such payment recognized as necessary. A little later the third became a half, and under the name of the *didrachma*, Matt. 17 : 24, was paid by every Jew, in whatever part of the world he might be living. II. The kingdom, with its centralized government and greater magnificence, involved, of course, a larger expenditure, and therefore a heavier taxation. The chief burdens appear to have been—(1) A tithe of the produce both of the soil and of live stock. 1 Sam. 8 : 15, 17. (2) Forced military service for a month every year. 1 Sam. 8 : 12 ; 1 Kings 9 : 22 ; 1 Chron. 27 : 1. (3) Gifts to the king. 1 Sam. 10 : 27 ; 16 : 20; 17 : 18. (4) Import duties. 1 Kings 10 : 15. (5) The monopoly of certain branches of commerce. 1 Kings 9 : 28; 22 : 48; 10 : 28, 29. (6) The appropriation to the king's use of the early crop of hay. Amos 7 : 1. At times, too, in the history of both the kingdoms there were special burdens. A tribute of fifty shekels a head had to be paid by Menahem to the Assyrian king, 2 Kings 15 : 20, and under his successor Hoshea this assumed the form of an annual tribute. 2 Kings 17 : 4. III. Under the Persian empire the taxes paid by the Jews were, in their broad outlines, the same in kind as those of other subject races. The financial system which gained for Darius Hystaspes the name of the "shopkeeper king" involved the payment by each satrap of a fixed sum as the tribute due from his province. In Judea, as in other provinces, the inhabitants had to provide in kind for the maintenance of the governor's household, besides a money payment of forty shekels a day. Neh. 5 : 14, 15. In Ezra 4 : 13, 20 ; 7 : 24, we get a formal enumeration of the three great branches of the revenue. The influence of Ezra secured for the whole ecclesiastical order, from the priests down to the Nethinim, an immunity from all three, Ezra 7 : 24; but the burden pressed heavily on the great body of the people. IV. Under the Egyptian and Syrian kings the taxes paid by the Jews became yet heavier. The "farming" system of finance was adopted in its worst form. The taxes were put up to auction. The contract sum for those of Phœnicia, Judea and Samaria had been estimated at about 8000 talents. An unscrupulous adventurer would bid double that sum, and would then go down to the province, and by violence and cruelty, like that of Turkish or Hindoo collectors, squeeze out a large margin of profit for himself. V. The pressure of Roman taxation, if not absolutely heavier, was probably more galling, as being more thorough and systematic, more distinctively a mark of bondage. The capture of Jerusalem by Pompey was followed immediately by the imposition of a tribute, and within a short time the sum thus taken from the resources of the country amounted to 10,000 talents. When Judea became formally a Roman province, the whole financial system of the empire came as a natural consequence. The taxes were systematically farmed, and the publicans appeared as a new curse to the country. The *portoria* were levied at harbors, piers and the gates of cities. Matt. 17 : 24; Rom. 13 : 7. In addition to this there was the poll-tax paid by every Jew, and looked upon, for that reason, as the special badge of servitude. United with this, as part of the same system, there was also, in all probability, a property tax of some kind. In addition to these general taxes, the inhabitants of Jerusalem were subject to a special house-duty about this period.

Taxing. The English word now conveys to us more distinctly the notion of a tax or tribute actually levied; but it appears to have been used in the sixteenth century for the simple assessment of a subsidy upon the property of a given county, or the registration of the people for the purpose of a poll-tax. Two distinct registrations, or taxings, are mentioned in the New Testament, both of them by St. Luke. The first is said to have been the result of an edict of the emperor Augustus, that "all the world (*i. e.* the Roman empire) should be taxed," Luke 2 : 1, and is connected by the evangelist with the name of Cyrenius or Quirinus. [CYRENIUS.] The second and more important, Acts 5 : 37, is distinctly associated, in point of time, with the revolt of Judas of Galilee.

Te'bah (*slaughter*), eldest of the sons of Nahor, by his concubine Reumah. Gen. 22 : 24. (B.C. 1872.)

Tebali'ah (*purified*), third son of Hosah of the children of Merari. 1 Chron. 26 : 11. (B.C. 1014.)

Te'beth. [MONTH.]

Tehin'nah (*supplication*), the father or founder of Ir-nahash, the city of Nahash, and son of Eshton. 1 Chron. 4 : 12. (B.C. about 1083.)

Teil tree. [OAK.]

Teko'a, or Teko'ah (*a stockade*). 1. A town in the tribe of Judah, 2 Chron. 11 : 6, on the range of hills which rise near Hebron and stretch eastward toward the Dead Sea. Jerome says that Tekoa was six Roman miles from Bethlehem, and that as he wrote he had that village daily before his eyes. The "wise woman" whom Joab employed to effect a reconciliation between David and Absalom was obtained from this place. 2 Sam. 14 : 2. Here also Ira the son of Ikkesh, one of David's thirty, "the mighty men," was born, and was called on that account "the Tekoite." 2 Sam. 23 : 26. It was one of the places which Rehoboam fortified, at the beginning of his reign, as a defence against invasion from the south. 2 Chron. 11 : 6. Some of the people from Tekoa took part in building the walls of Jerusalem, after the return from the captivity. Neh. 3 : 5, 27. In Jer. 6 : 1 the prophet exclaims, "Blow the trumpet in Tekoa, and set up a sign of fire in Beth-haccerem." But Tekoa is chiefly memorable as the birthplace of the prophet Amos. Amos 7 : 14. Tekoa is known still as *Tekû'a*. It lies on an elevated hill, which spreads itself out into an irregular plain of moderate extent. Various ruins exist, such as the walls of houses, cisterns, broken columns and heaps of building-stones.

2. A name occurring in the genealogies of Judah, 1 Chron. 2 : 24; 4 : 5, as the son of Ashur. There is little doubt that the town of Tekoa is meant.

Teko'ite, The. Ira ben-Ikkesh, one of David's warriors, is thus designated. 2 Sam. 23 : 26; 1 Chron. 11 : 28; 27 : 9. The common people among the Tekoites displayed great activity in the repairs of the wall of Jerusalem under Nehemiah. Neh. 3 : 5, 27.

Tel-a'bib (*cornhill*) was probably a city of Chaldæa or Babylonia, not of up per Mesopotamia as generally supposed. Ezek. 3 : 15. The whole scene of Ezekiel's preaching and visions seems to have been Chaldæa proper; and the river Chebar, as already observed, was not the *Khabour*, but a branch of the Euphrates.

Te'lah (*vigor*), a descendant of Ephraim, and ancestor of Joshua. 1 Chron. 7 : 25. (B.C. before 1491.)

Tel'a-im (*lambs*), the place at which Saul collected and numbered his forces before his attack on Amalek, 1 Sam. 15 : 4, may be identical with TELEM, which see.

Telas'sar (*Assyrian hill*) is mentioned in 2 Kings 19 : 12 and in Isa. 37 : 12 as a city inhabited by "the children of Eden," which had been conquered and was held in the time of Sennacherib, by the Assyrians. It must have been in western Mesopotamia, in the neighborhood of Harran and Orfa.

Te'lem (*oppression*). 1. One of the cities in the extreme south of Judah, Josh. 15 : 24, probably the same as Telaim. The name *Dhullam* is found in Van de Velde's map, attached to a district immediately to the north of the *Kubbet el-Baul*, south of *el Milh* and *Ar'arah*—a position very suitable.

2. A porter or doorkeeper of the temple in the time of Ezra. Ezra 10 : 24. He is probably the same as TALMON in Neh. 12 : 25.

Tel-har'sa, or **Tel-hare'sha** (*hill of the artificer*), one of the Babylonian towns or villages mentioned in Ezra 2 : 59; Neh. 7 : 61, along with Tel-melah and Cherub, probably in the low country near the sea.

Tel-me'lah. [TEL-HARSA.]

Te'ma (*a desert*), the ninth son of Ishmael, Gen. 25 : 15; 1 Chron. 1 : 30; whence the tribe called after him, mentioned in Job 6 : 19; Jer. 25 : 23, and also the land occupied by this tribe. Isa. 21 : 13, 14. (B.C. after 1850.) The name is identified with *Teymá*, a small town on the confines of Syria.

Te'man (*the south*). A son of Eliphaz, son of Esau by Adah. Gen. 36 : 11, 15, 42; 1 Chron. 1 : 36, 53. (B.C. about 1792.)

2. A country, and probably a city, named after the Edomite phylarch, or from which the phylarch took his name. The Hebrew signifies "south," see Job 9 : 9; Isa. 43 : 6; and it is probable that the land of Teman was a southern portion of the land of Edom, or, in a wider sense, that of the sons of the east. Teman is mentioned in five places by the prophets, in four of which it is connected with Edom and in two with Dedan. Jer. 49 : 7, 8; Ezek. 25 : 13. Eusebius and Jerome mention Teman as a town in their day distant 15 miles from Petra, and a Roman post.

Tem'ani. [TEMAN.]

Te'manite, an inhabitant of Teman.

Tem'eni, son of Ashur the father of Tekoa, by his wife Naarah. 1 Chron. 4 : 6. (B.C. about 1450.)

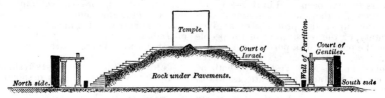

Level of the Temple Platform. (*After Beswick*, 1875.)

Temple. There is perhaps no building of the ancient world which has excited so much attention since the time of its destruction as the temple which Solomon built at Jerusalem, and its successor as rebuilt by Herod. Its spoils were considered worthy of forming the principal illustration of one of the most beautiful of Roman triumphal arches, and Justinian's highest architectural ambition was that he might surpass it. Throughout the middle ages it influenced to a considerable degree the forms of Christian churches, and its peculiarities were the watchwords and rallying-points of all associations of builders. When the French expedition to Egypt, in the first years of this century, had made the world familiar with the wonderful architectural remains of that country, every one jumped to the conclusion that Solomon's temple must have been designed after an Egyptian model. The discoveries in Assyria by Botta and Layard have within the last twenty years given an entirely new direction to the researches of the restorers. Unfortunately, however, no Assyrian temple has yet been exhumed of a nature to throw much light on this subject, and we are still forced to have recourse to the later buildings at Persepolis, or to general deductions from the style of the nearly contemporary secular buildings at Nineveh and elsewhere, for such illustrations as are available.

THE TEMPLE OF SOLOMON.—It was David who first proposed to replace the tabernacle by a more permanent building, but was forbidden for the reasons assigned by the prophet Nathan, 2 Sam. 7 : 5, etc.; and though he collected materials and made arrangements, the execution of the task was left for his son Solomon. (The gold and silver alone accumulated by David are at the lowest reckoned to have amounted to between two and three billion dollars, a sum which can be paralleled from secular history.—*Lange.*) Solomon, with the assistance of Hiram king of Tyre, commenced this great undertaking in the fourth year of his reign, B.C. 1012, and completed it in seven years, B.C. 1005. (There were 183,000 Jews and strangers employed on it—of Jews 30,000, by rotation 10,000 a month; of Canaanites 153,600, of whom 70,000 were bearers of burdens, 80,000 hewers of wood and stone, and 3600 overseers. The parts were all prepared at a distance from the site of the building, and when they

On the Site of Solomon's Temple at Jerusalem.

were brought together the whole immense structure was erected without the sound of hammer, axe or any tool of iron. 1 Kings 6 : 7.—*Schaff.*) The building occupied the site prepared for it by David, which had formerly been the threshing-floor of the Jebusite Ornan or Araunah, on Mount Moriah. The whole area enclosed by the outer walls formed a square of about 600 feet; but the sanctuary itself was comparatively small, inasmuch as it was intended only for the ministrations of the priests, the congregation of the people assembling in the courts. In this and all other essential points the temple followed the model of the tabernacle, from which it differed chiefly by having chambers built about the sanctuary for the abode of the priests and attendants and the keeping of treasures and stores. In all its dimensions, length, breadth and height, the sanctuary itself was exactly double the size of the tabernacle, the ground plan measuring 80 cubits by 40, while that of the tabernacle was 40 by 20, and the height of the temple being 30 cubits, while that of the tabernacle was 15. [The reader should compare the following account with the article TABERNACLE.] As in the tabernacle, the temple consisted of three parts, the porch, the holy place, and the holy of holies. The front of the porch was supported, after the manner of some Egyptian temples, by the two great brazen pillars, Jachin and Boaz, 18 cubits high, with capitals of 5 cubits more, adorned with lily-work and pomegranates. 1 Kings 7 : 15–22. The places of the two "veils" of the tabernacle were occupied by partitions, in which were folding-doors. The whole interior was lined with woodwork richly carved and overlaid with gold. Indeed, both within and without the building was conspicuous chiefly by the lavish use of the gold of Ophir and Parvaim. It glittered in the morning sun (it has been well said) like the sanctuary of an El Dorado. Above the sacred ark, which was placed, as of old, in the most holy place, were made new cherubim, one pair of whose wings met above the ark, and another pair reached to the walls behind them. In the holy place, besides the altar of incense, which was made of cedar overlaid with gold, there were seven golden candlesticks instead of one, and the table of shew-bread was replaced by ten golden tables, bearing, besides the shew-bread, the innumerable golden vessels for the service of the sanctuary. The *outer court* was no doubt double the size of that of the tabernacle; and we may therefore safely assume that it was 10 cubits in height, 100 cubits north and south, and 200 east and west. It contained an inner court, called the "court of the priests;" but the arrangement of the courts and of the porticos and gateways of the enclosure, though described by Josephus, belongs apparently to the temple of Herod. In the outer court there was a new altar of burnt offering, much larger than the old one. [ALTAR.] Instead of the brazen laver there was "a molten sea" of brass, a masterpiece of Hiram's skill, for the ablution of the priests. It was called a "sea" from its great size. [SEA, MOLTEN.] The chambers for the priests were arranged in successive stories against the sides of the sanctuary; not, however, reaching to the top, so as to leave space for the windows to light the holy and the most holy place. We are told by Josephus and the Talmud that there was a superstructure on the temple equal in height to the lower part; and this is confirmed by the statement in the books of Chronicles that Solomon "overlaid the *upper chambers* with gold." 2 Chron. 3 : 9. Moreover, "the altars on the top of the upper chamber," mentioned in the books of the Kings, 2 Kings 23 : 12, were apparently upon the temple. The dedication of the temple was the grandest ceremony ever performed under the Mosaic dispensation. The temple was destroyed on the capture of Jerusalem by Nebuchadnezzar, B.C. 586.

TEMPLE OF ZERUBBABEL.—We have very few particulars regarding the temple which the Jews erected after their return from the captivity (about B.C. 520), and no description that would enable us to realize its appearance. But there are some dimensions given in the Bible and elsewhere which are extremely interesting, as affording points of comparison between it and the temple which preceded it and the one erected after it. The first and most authentic are those given in the book of Ezra, ch. 6 : 3, when quoting the decree of Cyrus, wherein it is said, "Let the house be builded, the place where they offered sacrifices, and let the foundations thereof be strongly laid; the height thereof three-score cubits, and the breadth thereof three-score cubits, with three rows of great stones, and a row of new timber." Josephus quotes this passage almost literally, but in doing so enables us to translate with certainty the word here called *row* as "story"—as indeed the sense would lead us to infer. We see by the description in Ezra that this temple was about one third larger than Solomon's. From these dimensions we gather that if the priests and Levites and elders of families were disconsolate at seeing how much more sumptuous the old temple was than the one which on account of their poverty they had hardly been able to erect, Ezra 3 : 12, it certainly was not because it was smaller; but it may have been that the carving and the gold and the other ornaments of Solomon's temple far surpassed this, and the pillars of the portico and the veils may all have been far more splendid; so also probably were the vessels; and all this is what a Jew would mourn over far more than mere architectural splendor. In speaking of these temples we must always bear in mind that their dimensions were practically very far inferior to those of the heathen. Even that of Ezra is not larger than an average parish church of the last century; Solomon's was smaller. It was the lavish display of the precious metals, the elaboration of carved ornament, and the beauty of the textile fabrics, which made up their splendor and rendered them so precious in the eyes of the people.

TEMPLE OF EZEKIEL.—The vision of a temple which the prophet Ezekiel saw while residing on the banks of the Chebar in Babylonia, in the twenty-fifth year of the captivity, does not add much to our knowledge of the subject. It is not a description of a temple that ever was built or ever could be erected at Jerusalem, and can consequently only be considered as the *beau idéal* of what a Shemitic temple ought to be.

TEMPLE OF HEROD. — Herod the

Great announced to the people assembled at the Passover, B.C. 20 or 19, his intention of restoring the temple; (probably a stroke of policy on the part of Herod to gain the favor of the Jews and to make his name great.) If we may believe Josephus, he pulled down the whole edifice to its foundations, and laid them anew on

Solomon's Porch.

an enlarged scale; but the ruins still exhibit, in some parts, what seem to be the foundations laid by Zerubbabel, and beneath them the more massive substructions of Solomon. The new edifice was a stately pile of Græco-Roman architecture, built in white marble with gilded *acroteria*. It is minutely described by Josephus, and the New Testament has made us familiar with the pride of the Jews in its magnificence. A different feeling, however, marked the commencement of the work, which met with some opposition from the fear that what Herod had begun he would not be able to finish. He overcame all jealousy by engaging not to pull down any part of the existing buildings till all the materials for the new edifice were collected on its site. Two years appear to have been occupied in preparations—among which Josephus mentions the teaching of some of the priests and Levites to work as masons and carpenters—and then the work began. The holy "house," including the porch, sanctuary and holy of holies, was finished in a year and a half, B.C. 16. Its completion, on the anniversary of

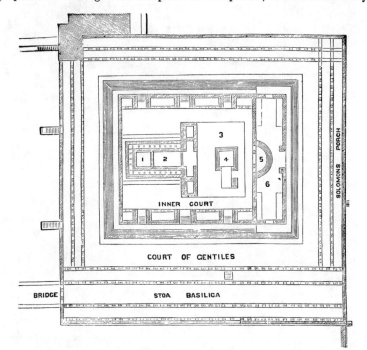

Plan of Herod's Temple.

1. The Holy of Holies.	4. Altar of Burnt Offering.
2. The Holy Place.	5. Inner Gate of Temple.
3. The Court of the Priests.	6. Court of the Women.

Herod's inauguration, was celebrated by lavish sacrifices and a great feast. About B.C. 9—eight years from the commencement—the court and cloisters of the temple were finished, and the bridge between the south cloister and the upper city (demolished by Pompey) was doubtless now rebuilt with that massive masonry of which some remains still survive. (The work, however, was not entirely ended till A.D. 64, under Herod Agrippa II. So the statement in John 2 : 20 is correct.— *Schaff.*) The temple or holy "house" itself was in dimensions and arrangement very similar to that of Solomon, or rather that of Zerubbabel—more like the latter; but this was surrounded by an inner enclosure of great strength and magnificence, measuring as nearly as can be made out 180 cubits by 240, and adorned by porches and ten gateways of great magnificence; and beyond this again was an outer enclosure measuring externally 400 cubits each way, which was adorned with porticos of greater splendor than any we know of as attached to any temple of the ancient world. The temple was certainly situated in the southwest angle of the area now known as the Haram area at Jerusalem, and its dimen-

The Temple of Herod—Restored by Fergusson.

sions were what Josephus states them to be—400 cubits, or one stadium, each way. At the time when Herod rebuilt it, he enclosed a space "twice as large" as that before occupied by the temple and its courts—an expression that probably must not be taken too literally, at least if we are to depend on the measurements of Hecatæus. According to them, the whole area of Herod's temple was between four and five times greater than that which preceded it. What Herod did, apparently, was to take in the whole space between the temple and the city wall on its east side, and to add a considerable space on the north and south to support the porticos which he added there. As the temple terrace thus became the principal defence of the city on the east side, there were no gates or openings in that direction, and being situated on a sort of rocky brow—as evidenced from its appearance in the vaults that bounded it on this side—it was at all later times considered unattackable from the eastward. The north side, too, where not covered by the fortress Antonia, became part of the defences of the city, and was likewise without external gates. On the south side, which was enclosed by the wall of Ophel, there were double gates nearly in the centre. These gates still exist at a distance of about 365 feet from the southwestern angle, and are perhaps the only architectural features of the temple of Herod which remain *in situ*. This entrance consists of a double archway of Cyclopean architecture on the level of the ground, opening into a square vestibule measuring 40 feet each way. From this a double tunnel, nearly 200 feet in length, leads to a flight of steps which rise to the surface in the court of the temple, exactly at that gateway of the inner temple which led to the altar, and is the one of the four gateways on this side by which any one arriving from Ophel would naturally wish to enter the inner enclosure. We learn from the Talmud that the gate of the inner temple to which this passage led was called the "water gate;" and it is interesting to be able to identify a spot so prominent in the description of Nehemiah. Neh. 12 : 37. Toward the west there were four gateways to the external enclosure of the temple. The most magnificent part of the temple, in an architectural point of view, seems certainly to have been the cloisters which were added to the outer

court when it was enlarged by Herod. The cloisters in the west, north and east sides were composed of double rows of Corinthian columns, 25 cubits or 37 feet 6 inches in height, with flat roof, and resting against the outer wall of the temple. These, however, were immeasurably surpassed in magnificence by the royal porch or Stoa Basilica, which overhung the southern wall. It consisted of a nave and two aisles, that toward the temple being open, that toward the country closed by a wall. The breadth of the centre aisle was 45 feet; of the side aisles, 30 from centre to centre of the pillars; their height 50 feet, and that of the centre aisle 100 feet. Its section was thus something in excess of that of York Cathedral, while its total length was one stadium or 600 Greek feet, or 100 feet in excess of York or our largest Gothic cathedrals. This magnificent structure was supported by 162 Corinthian columns. The porch on the east was called "Solomon's Porch." The court of the temple was very nearly a square. It may have been exactly so, for we have not all the details to enable us to feel quite certain about it. To the eastward of this was the court of the women. The great ornament of these inner courts seems to have been their gateways, the three especially on the north and south leading to the temple court. These, according to Josephus, were of great height, strongly fortified and ornamented with great elaboration. But the wonder of all was the great eastern gate leading from the court of the women to the upper court. It was in all probability the one called the "beautiful gate" in the New Testament. Immediately within this gateway stood the altar of burnt offerings. Both the altar and the temple were enclosed by a low parapet, one cubit in height, placed so as to keep the people separate from the priests while the latter were performing their functions. Within this last enclosure, toward the westward, stood the temple itself. As before mentioned, its internal dimensions were the same as those of the temple of Solomon. Although these remained the same, however, there seems no reason to doubt that the whole plan was augmented by the *pteromata*, or surrounding parts, being increased from 10 to 20 cubits, so that the third temple, like the second, measured 60 cubits across and 100 cubits east and west. The width of the façade was also augmented by wings or shoulders projecting 20 cubits each way, making the whole breadth 100 cubits, or equal to the length. There is no reason for doubting that the sanctuary always stood on identically the same spot in which it had been placed by Solomon a thousand years before it was rebuilt by Herod. The temple of Herod was destroyed by the Romans under Titus, Friday, August 9, A.D. 70. A Mohammedan mosque now stands on its site.

Ten Commandments. The popular name in this, as in so many instances, is not that of Scripture. There we have the "TEN WORDS," Ex. 34 : 28 ; Deut. 4 : 13 ; 10 : 4 ; the "COVENANT," Ex., Deut. *ll. cc.* ; 1 Kings 8 : 21 ; 2 Chron. 6 : 11, etc., or, very often as the solemn attestation of the divine will, the "TESTIMONY." Ex. 25 : 16, 21 ; 31 : 18, etc. The circumstances in which the Ten great *Words* were first given to the people surrounded them with an awe which attached to no other precept. In the midst of the cloud and the darkness and the flashing lightning and the fiery smoke and the thunder like the voice of a trumpet, Moses was called to Mount Sinai to receive the law without which the people would cease to be a holy nation. Ex. 19 : 20. Here, as elsewhere, Scripture unites two facts which men separate. God, and not man, was speaking to the Israelites in those terrors, and yet, in the language of later inspired teachers, other instrumentality was not excluded. No other words were proclaimed in like manner. And the record was as exceptional as the original revelation. Of no other words could it be said that they were written as these were written, engraved on the Tables of Stone, not as originating in man's contrivance or sagacity, but by the power of the Eternal Spirit, by the "finger of God." Ex. 31 : 18 ; 32 : 16. The number Ten was, we can hardly doubt, itself significant to Moses and the Israelites. The received symbol, then and at all times, of completeness, it taught the people that the law of Jehovah was perfect. Ps. 19 : 7. The term "Commandments" had come into use in the time of Christ. Luke 18 : 20. Their division into *two tables* is not only expressly mentioned, but the stress laid upon the *two* leaves no doubt that the distinction was important, and that it answered to that summary of the law which was made both by Moses and by Christ into two precepts ; so that the *first*

table contained *Duties to God,* and the second, *Duties to our Neighbor.*

There are three principal divisions of the two tables : 1. That of the Roman Catholic Church, making the first table contain three commandments, and the second the other seven. 2. The familiar division, referring the first four to our duty toward God and the six remaining to our duty toward man. 3. The division recognized by the old Jewish writers, Josephus and Philo, which places five commandments in each table. It has been maintained that the law of filial duty, being a close consequence of God's fatherly relation to us, may be referred to the first table. But this is to place human parents on a level with God, and, by parity of reasoning, the Sixth Commandment might be added to the first table, as murder is the destruction of God's image in man. Far more reasonable is the view which regards the authority of parents as heading the second table, as the earthly reflex of that authority of the Father of his people and of all men which heads the first, and as the first principle of the whole law of love to our neighbor ; because we are all brethren, and the family is, for good and ill, the model of the state. "The Decalogue differs from all the other legislation of Moses : (1) It was proclaimed by God himself in a most public and solemn manner. (2) It was given under circumstances of most appalling majesty and sublimity. (3) It was written by the finger of God on two tables of stone. Deut. 5 : 22. (4) It differed from any and all other laws given to Israel in that it was comprehensive and general rather than specific and particular. (5) It was complete, being one finished whole, to which nothing was to be added, from which nothing was ever taken away. (6) The law of the Ten Commandments was honored by Jesus Christ as embodying the substance of the law of God enjoined upon man. (7) It can scarcely be doubted that Jesus had his eye specially if not exclusively on this law, Matt. 5 : 18, as one *never to be repealed,* from which not one jot or tittle should ever pass away. (8) It is marked by wonderful simplicity and brevity ; such a contrast to our human legislation, our British statute-book for instance, which it would need an elephant to carry and an Œdipus to interpret."

Tent. Among the leading characteristics of the nomad races, those two have always been numbered whose origin has been ascribed to Jabal the son of Lamech, Gen. 4 : 20, viz., to be tent-dwellers and keepers of cattle. The same may be said of the forefathers of the Hebrew race; nor was it until the return into Canaan

Arab Tents.

from Egypt that the Hebrews became inhabitants of cities. An Arab tent is called *beit,* "house;" its covering consists of stuff, about three quarters of a yard broad, made of black goat's-hair, Cant. 1 : 5, laid parallel with the tent's length. This is sufficient to resist the heaviest rain. The tent-poles or columns are usually nine in number, placed in three groups; but many tents have only one pole, others two or three. The ropes which hold the tent in its place are fastened, not to the tent-cover itself, but to loops consisting of a leathern thong tied to the ends of a stick, round which is twisted a piece of old cloth, which is itself sewed to the tent-cover. The ends of the tent-ropes are fastened to short sticks or pins, which are driven into the ground with a mallet. Judges 4 : 21. Round the back and sides of the tent runs a piece of stuff removable at pleasure to admit air. The tent is divided into two apartments, separated by a carpet partition drawn across the middle of the tent and fastened to the three middle posts. When the pasture near an encampment is exhausted, the tents are taken down, packed on camels and removed. Gen. 26 : 17, 22, 25; Isa. 38 : 12. In choosing places for encampment, Arabs prefer the neighborhood of trees, for the sake of the shade and coolness which they afford. Gen. 18 : 4, 8.

Te′rah (*station*), the father of Abram, Nahor and Haran, and through them the ancestor of the great families of the Israelites, Ishmaelites, Midianites, Moabites and Ammonites. Gen. 11 : 24–32. The account given of him in the Old Testa-

ment narrative is very brief. We learn from it simply that he was an idolater, Josh. 24 : 2, that he dwelt beyond the Euphrates in Ur of the Chaldees, Gen. 11 : 28, and that in the southwesterly migration, which from some unexplained cause he undertook in his old age, he went with his son Abram, his daughter-in-law Sarai, and his grandson Lot, "to go into the land of Canaan, and they came unto Haran, and dwelt there." Gen. 11 : 31. And finally, "the days of Terah were two hundred and five years; and Terah died in Haran." Gen. 11 : 32. (B.C. 1921.)

Teraphim. This word occurs only in the plural, and denotes images connected with magical rites. The derivation of the name is obscure. In one case—1 Sam. 19 : 13, 16—a single statue seems to be intended by the plural. The teraphim, translated "images" in the Authorized Version, carried away from Laban by Rachel were regarded by Laban as gods, and it would therefore appear that they were used by those who added corrupt practices to the patriarchal religion.

Teraphim.

Teraphim again are included among Micah's images. Judges 17 : 3–5; 18 : 17, 18, 20. Teraphim were consulted for oracular answers by the Israelites, Zech. 10 : 2;

comp. Judges 18 : 5, 6 ; 1 Sam. 15 : 22, 23 ; 19 : 13, 16, LXX., and 2 Kings 23 : 24, and by the Babylonians in the case of Nebuchadnezzar. Ezek. 21 : 19–22.

Te′resh (*strictness*), one of the two eunuchs whose plot to assassinate Ahasuerus was discovered by Mordecai. Esther 2 : 21 ; 6 : 2. He was hanged. (B.C. 479.)

Ter′tius (*third*), probably a Roman, was the amanuensis of Paul in writing the Epistle to the Romans. Rom. 16 : 22. (A.D. 55.)

Tertul′lus (diminutive from *Tertius*), "a certain orator," Acts 24 : 1, who was retained by the high priest and Sanhedrin to accuse the apostle Paul at Cæsarea before the Roman procurator Antonius Felix. He evidently belonged to the class of professional orators. We may infer that Tertullus was of Roman, or at all events of Italian, origin. (A.D. 55.)

Tes′tament, New. [NEW TESTAMENT ; BIBLE.]

Tes′tament, Old. [OLD TESTAMENT ; BIBLE.]

Tetrarch, properly the sovereign or governor of the fourth part of a country. Matt. 14 : 1 ; Luke 3 : 1 ; 9 : 7 ; Acts 13 : 1. The title was, however, often applied to any one who governed a Roman province, of whatever size. The title of king was sometimes assigned to a tetrarch. Matt. 14 : 9 ; Mark 6 : 14, 22.

Thadde′us, one of the twelve apostles. Matt. 10 : 3 ; Mark 3 : 18. From a comparison with the catalogue of St. Luke, Luke 6 : 16 ; Acts 1 : 13, it seems scarcely possible to doubt that the three names of Judas, Lebbeus and Thaddeus were borne by one and the same person. [See JUDE.]

Tha′hash (*badger*), son of Nahor by his concubine Reumah. Gen. 22 : 24. (B.C. 1880.)

Tha′mah (*laughter*). "The children of Thamah" were a family of Nethinim who returned with Zerubbabel. Ezra 2 : 53.

Tha′mar. TAMAR, 1. Matt. 1 : 3.

Thank offering, or **Peace offering,** the properly eucharistic offering among the Jews, in its theory resembling the *meat offering*, and therefore indicating that the offerer was already reconciled to and in covenant with God. Its ceremonial is described in Lev. 3. The peace offerings, unlike other sacrifices, were not ordained to be offered in fixed and regular course. The only constantly-recurring peace offering appears to have been that of the two firstling lambs at Pentecost. Lev. 23 : 19. The general principle of the peace offering seems to have been that it should be entirely spontaneous, offered as occasion should arise, from the feeling of the sacrificer himself. Lev. 19 : 5. On the first institution, Lev. 7 : 11–17, peace offerings are divided into "offerings of thanksgiving" and "vows or freewill offerings;" of which latter class the offering by a Nazarite on the completion of his vow is the most remarkable. Num. 6 : 14. We find accordingly peace offerings offered for the people on a great scale at periods of unusual solemnity or rejoicing. In two cases only—Judges 20 : 26 ; 2 Sam. 24 : 25— peace offerings are mentioned as offered with burnt offerings at a time of national sorrow and fasting.

Tha′ra. Terah the father of Abraham. Luke 3 : 34.

Thar′ra, Esther 12 : 1, a corrupt form of Teresh.

Thar′shish. 1: In this more accurate form the translators of the Authorized Version have given in two passages —1 Kings 10 : 22 ; 22 : 48—the name elsewhere presented as Tarshish.

2. A Benjamite, one of the family of Bilhan and the house of Jediael. 1 Chron. 7 : 10 only.

Theatre. For the explanation of the biblical allusions, two or three points only require notice. The Greek term, like the corresponding English term, denotes the *place* where dramatic performances are exhibited, and also the *scene* itself or *spectacle* which is witnessed there. It occurs in the first or local sense in Acts 19 : 29. The other sense of the term "theatre" occurs in 1 Cor. 4 : 9.

Thebes (Authorized Version No, the multitude of No, populous No), a chief city of ancient Egypt, long the capital of the upper country, and the seat of the Diospolitan dynasties, that ruled over all Egypt at the era of its highest splendor. It was situated on both sides of the Nile, 400 or 500 miles from its mouth. The sacred name of Thebes was *P-amen,* "the abode of Amon," which the Greeks reproduced in their *Diospolis,* especially with the addition *the Great.* No-amon is the name of Thebes in the Hebrew Scriptures. Jer. 46 : 25 ; Nah. 3 : 8. Ezekiel uses *No* simply to designate the Egyptian seat of Amon. Ezek. 30 : 14, 16. [NO-AMON.] *Its origin and early* *allusions to it.*—The origin of the city is lost in antiquity. Niebuhr is of opinion that Thebes was much older than Mem-

Ruins at Thebes (No).

phis, and that, "after the centre of Egyptian life was transferred to lower Egypt, Memphis acquired its greatness through the ruin of Thebes." But both cities date from our earliest authentic knowledge of Egyptian history. The first allusion to Thebes in classical literature is the familiar passage of the Iliad (ix. 381–385): " Egyptian Thebes, where are vast treasures laid up in the houses; where are a hundred gates, and from each two hundred men go forth with horses and chariots." In the first century before Christ, Diodorus visited Thebes, and he devotes several sections of his general work to its history and appearance. Though he saw the city when it had sunk to quite secondary importance, he confirms the tradition of its early grandeur—its circuit of 140 stadia, the size of its public edifices, the magnificence of its temples, the number of its monuments, the dimensions of its private houses, some of them four or five stories high—all giving it an air of grandeur and beauty surpassing not only all other cities of Egypt, but of the world. *Monuments.*— The monuments of Thebes are the most reliable witnesses for the ancient splendor of the city. These are found in almost equal proportions upon both sides of the river. The plan of the city, as indicated by the principal monuments, was nearly quadrangular, measuring two miles from north to south and four from east to west. Its four great landmarks were,

Karnak and Luxor upon the eastern or Arabian side, and Qoornah and Medeenet Haboo upon the western or Libyan side. There are indications that each of these temples may have been connected with those facing it upon two sides by grand *dromoi*, lined with sphinxes and other colossal figures. Upon the western bank there was almost a continuous line of temples and public edifices for a distance of two miles, from Qoornah to Medeenet Haboo; and Wilkinson conjectures that from a point near the latter, perhaps in the line of the colossi, the "Royal street" ran down to the river, which was crossed by a ferry terminating at Luxor, on the eastern side. Behind this long range of temples and palaces are the Libyan hills, which for a distance of five miles are excavated to the depth of several hundred feet for sepulchral chambers. Some of these, in the number and variety of their chambers, the finish of their sculptures, and the beauty and

Temple at Karnak (Thebes). Columns in the great Hall. (*From a Photograph.*)

freshness of their frescoes, are among the most remarkable monuments of Egyptian grandeur and skill. The eastern side of the river is distinguished by the remains of Luxor and Karnak, the latter being of itself a city of temples. The approach to Karnak from the south is marked by a series of majestic gateways and towers, which were the appendages of later times

Avenue of Sphinxes and Propylæa at Karnak.

to the original structure. The temple properly faces the river, *i. e.* toward the northwest. The courts and propylæa connected with this structure occupy a space nearly 1800 feet square, and the buildings represent almost every dynasty of Egypt. Ezekiel proclaims the destruction of Thebes by the arm of Babylon, Ezek. 30 : 14–16; and Jeremiah predicted the same overthrow. Jer. 46 : 25, 26. The city lies to-day a nest of Arab hovels amid crumbling columns and drifting sands. The Persian invader (Cambyses, B.C. 525) completed the destruction that the Babylonian had begun.

The'bez (*conspicuous*), a place memorable for the death of the bravo Abimelech, Judges 9 : 50, was known to Eusebius and Jerome, in whose time it was situated " in the district of Neapolis," 13 Roman miles therefrom, on the road to Scythopolis. There it still is, its name— *Tubâs*—hardly changed.

Thel'asar. [TEL-ASSAR.]

Theoph'ilus (*friend of God*), the person to whom St. Luke inscribes his Gospel and the Acts of the Apostles. Luke 1 : 3; Acts 1 : 1. From the honorable epithet applied to him in Luke 1 : 3, it has been argued with much probability that he was a person in high official position. All that can be conjectured with any degree of safety concerning him

comes to this, that he was a Gentile of rank and consideration, who came under the influence of St. Luke or under that of St. Paul at Rome, and was converted to the Christian faith.

Thessalo'nians, First Epistle to the, was written by the apostle Paul at Corinth, a few months after he had founded the church at Thessalonica, at the close of the year A.D. 52 or the beginning of 53. The Epistles to the Thessalonians, then (for the second followed the first after no long interval), are the earliest of St. Paul's writings—perhaps the earliest written records of Christianity. It is interesting, therefore, to compare the Thessalonian epistles with the later letters, and to note the points of difference. These differences are mainly threefold. 1. In the general *style* of these earlier letters there is greater simplicity and less exuberance of language. 2. The *antagonism to St. Paul* is not the same. Here the opposition comes from *Jews.* A period of five years changes the aspect of the controversy. The opponents of St. Paul are then no longer *Jews* so much as *Judaizing Christians.* 3. Many of the distinctive doctrines of Christianity were yet not evolved and distinctly enunciated till the needs of the Church drew them out into prominence at a later date. It has often been observed, for instance, that there is in the Epistles to the Thessalonians no mention of the characteristic contrast of " faith and works;" that the word "justification" does not once occur; that the idea of dying with Christ and living with Christ, so frequent in St. Paul's later writings, is absent in these. In the Epistles to the Thessalonians, the gospel preached is that of the coming of Christ, rather than of the cross of Christ. The *occasion* of this epistle was as follows: St. Paul had twice attempted to revisit Thessalonica, and both times had been disappointed. Thus prevented from seeing them in person, he had sent Timothy to inquire and report to him as to their condition. 1 Thess. 3 : 1-5. Timothy returned with most favorable tidings, reporting not only their progress in Christian faith and practice, but also their strong attachment to their old teacher. 1 Thess. 3 : 6-10. The First Epistle to the Thessalonians is the outpouring of the apostle's gratitude on receiving this welcome news. At the same time the report of Timothy was not unmixed with alloy. There were certain features in the condition of the Thessalonian church which called for St. Paul's interference, and to which he addresses himself in his letter. 1. The very intensity of their Christian faith, dwelling too exclusively on the day of the Lord's coming, had been attended with evil consequences. On the other hand, a theoretical difficulty had been felt. Certain members of the church had died, and there was great anxiety lest they should be excluded from any share in the glories of the Lord's advent. ch. 4 : 13-18. 2. The Thessalonians needed consolation and encouragement under persecution. ch. 2 : 14; 3 : 2-4. 3. An unhealthy state of feeling with regard to spiritual gifts was manifesting itself. ch. 5 : 19, 20. 4. There was the danger of relapsing into their old heathen profligacy. ch. 4 : 4-8. Yet notwithstanding all these drawbacks, the condition of the Thessalonian church was highly satisfactory, and the most cordial relations existed between St. Paul and his converts there. This honorable distinction it shares with the other great church of Macedonia, that of Philippi. The epistle is rather practical than doctrinal. The external evidence in favor of the *genuineness* of the First Epistle to the Thessalonians is chiefly negative, but this is important enough. There is no trace that it was ever disputed at any age or in any section of the Church, or even by any individual, till the present century. Toward the close of the second century, from Irenæus downward, we find this epistle directly quoted and ascribed to Paul. The evidence derived from the character of the epistle itself is so strong that it may fairly be called irresistible.

Thessalo'nians, Second Epistle to the, appears to have been written from Corinth not very long after the first, for Silvanus and Timotheus were still with St. Paul. 2 Thess. 1 : 1. In the former letter we saw chiefly the outpouring of strong personal affection, occasioned by the renewal of the apostle's intercourse with the Thessalonians, and the doctrinal and hortatory portions are there subordinate. In the Second Epistle, on the other hand, his leading motive seems to have been the desire of correcting errors in the church of Thessalonica. We notice two points especially which call for his rebuke :—*First*, it seems that the anxious expectation of the Lord's advent, instead of subsiding, had gained ground since the writing of the First Epistle. *Second*, the apostle had also a *personal* ground of complaint. His authority was not denied by any, but it was tampered with, and an unauthorized use was made of his name. It will be seen that the teaching of the Second Epistle is corrective of or rather supplemental to that of the first, and therefore presupposes it. This epistle, in the range of subject as well as in style and general character, closely resembles the first; and the remarks made on that epistle apply for the most part equally well to this. The structure also is somewhat similar, the main body of the epistle being divided into two parts in the same way, and each part closing with a prayer. ch. 2 : 16, 17; 3 : 16. The epistle ends with a special direction and benediction. ch. 3 : 17, 18. The external evidence in favor of the Second Epistle is somewhat more definite than that which can be brought in favor of the first. The internal character of the epistle too, as in the former case, bears the strongest testimony to its Pauline origin. Its genuineness, in fact, was never questioned until the beginning of the present century.

Thessaloni'ca. The original name of this city was Therma; and that part of the Macedonian shore on which it was situated retained through the Roman period the designation of the Thermaic Gulf. Cassander the son of Antipater rebuilt and enlarged Therma, and named it after his wife Thessalonica, the sister of Alexander the Great. The name ever since, under various slight modifications, has been continuous, and the city itself has never ceased to be eminent. *Saloniki* is still the most important town of European Turkey, next after Constantinople. Strabo in the first century speaks of Thessalonica as the most populous city in Macedonia. *Visit of Paul.*—St. Paul visited Thessalonica (with Silas and Timothy) during his second missionary journey, and introduced Christianity there. The first scene of the apostle's work at Thessalonica was the synagogue. Acts 17 : 2, 3. It is stated that the ministrations among the Jews continued for three weeks. ver. 2. Not that we are obliged to limit to this time the whole stay of the apostle at Thessalonica. A flourishing church was certainly formed there; and the epistles show that its elements were more Gentile than Jewish. [For persecution and further history see PAUL.]

Thessalonica.

Circumstances which led Paul to Thessalonica.—Three circumstances must here be mentioned which illustrate in an important manner this visit and this journey as well as the two Epistles to the Thessalonians. 1. This was the chief station on the great Roman road called the *Via Egnatia*, which connected Rome with the whole region to the north of the Ægean Sea. 2. Placed as it was on this great road, and in connection with other important Roman ways, Thessalonica was an invaluable centre for the spread of the gospel. In fact it was nearly if not quite on a level with Corinth and Ephesus in its share of the commerce of the Levant. 3. The circumstance noted in Acts 17 : 1, that here was the synagogue of the Jews in this part of Macedonia, had evidently much to do with the apostle's plans, and also doubtless with his success. Trade would inevitably bring Jews to Thessalonica; and it is remarkable that they have ever since had a prominent place in the annals of the city. *Later ecclesiastical history.*—During several centuries this city was the bulwark, not simply of the later Greek empire, but of Oriental Christendom, and was largely instrumental in the conversion of the Slavonians and Bulgarians. Thus it received the designation of "the orthodox city;" and its struggles are very prominent in the writings of the Byzantine historians.

Theu'das (*God-given*), the name of an insurgent mentioned in Gamaliel's speech before the Jewish council, Acts 5 : 35–39, at the time of the arraignment of the apostles. He appeared, according to Luke's account, at the head of about four hundred men. He was probably one of the insurrectionary chiefs or fanatics by whom the land was overrun in the last year of Herod's reign. Josephus speaks of a Theudas who played a similar part in the time of Claudius, about A.D. 44; but the Theudas mentioned by St. Luke must be a different person from the one spoken of by Josephus.

Thieves, The two. The men who under this name appear in the history of the crucifixion were robbers rather than thieves, belonging to the lawless bands by which Palestine was at that time and afterward infested. Against these brigands every Roman procurator had to wage continual war. It was necessary to use an armed police to encounter them. Luke 22 : 52. Of the previous history of the two who suffered on Golgotha we know nothing. They had been tried and condemned, and were waiting their execution before our Lord was accused. It is probable enough, as the death of Barabbas was clearly expected at the same time, that they had taken part in his insurrection. They had expected to die with Jesus Barabbas. They find themselves with one who bore the same name, but who was described in the superscription on his cross as Jesus of Nazareth. They could hardly have failed to hear something of his fame as a prophet, of his triumphal entry as a king. They catch at first the prevailing tone of scorn. But over one of them there came a change. He looked back upon his past life, and saw an infinite evil. He looked to the man dying on the cross beside him, and saw an infinite compassion. There indeed was one unlike all other "kings of the Jews" whom the robber had ever known. Such a one must be all that he had claimed to be. To be forgotten by that king seems to him now the most terrible of all punishments ; to take part in the triumph of his return, the most blessed of all hopes. The yearning prayer was answered, not in the letter, but in the spirit.

Thim′nathah, a town in the allotment of Dan. Josh. 19 : 43 only. It is named between Elon and Ekron. The name is the same as that of the residence of Samson's wife. [See TIMNAH.]

Thistle. [THORNS AND THISTLES.]

Thom′as (*a twin*), one of the apostles. According to Eusebius, his real name was Judas. This may have been a mere confusion with Thaddeus, who is mentioned in the extract. But it may also be that Thomas was a surname. Out of this name has grown the tradition that he had a twin-sister, Lydia, or that he was a twin-brother of our Lord; which last, again, would confirm his identification with Judas. Comp. Matt. 13 : 55. He is said to have been born at Antioch. In the catalogue of the apostles he is coupled with Matthew in Matt. 10 : 3; Mark 3 : 18; Luke 6 : 15, and with Philip in Acts 1 : 13. All that we know of him is derived from the Gospel of St. John; and this amounts to three traits, which, however, so exactly agree together that, slight as they are, they place his character before us with a precision which belongs to no other of the twelve apostles except Peter, John and Judas Iscariot. This character is that of a man slow to believe, seeing all the difficulties of a case, subject to despondency, viewing things on the darker side, yet full of ardent love of his Master. The latter trait was shown in his speech when our Lord determined to face the dangers that awaited him in Judea on his journey to Bethany. Thomas said to his fellow-disciples, "Let us also go, that we may die with him." John 11 : 16. His unbelief appeared in his question during the Last Supper : "Thomas saith unto him, Lord, we know not whither thou goest, and how can we know the way ?" John 14 : 5. It was the prosaic, incredulous doubt as to moving a step in the unseen future, and yet an eager inquiry as to how this step was to be taken. The first-named trait was seen after the resurrection. He was absent—possibly by accident, perhaps characteristically—from the first assembly when Jesus had appeared. The others told him what they had seen. He broke forth into an exclamation, the terms of which convey to us at once the vehemence of his doubt, and at the same time the vivid picture that his mind retained of his Master's form as he had last seen him lifeless on the cross. John 20 : 25. On the eighth day he was with them at their gathering, perhaps in expectation of a recurrence of the visit of the previous week ; and Jesus stood among them. He uttered the same salutation, "Peace be unto you ;" and then turning to Thomas, as if this had been the special object of his appearance, uttered the words which convey as strongly the sense of condemnation and tender reproof as those of Thomas had shown the sense of hesitation and doubt. The effect on him was immediate. The conviction produced by the removal of his doubt became deeper and stronger than that of any of the other apostles. The words in which he expressed his belief contain a far higher assertion of his Master's divine nature than is contained in any other expression used by apostolic lips—"My Lord and my God." The answer of our Lord sums up the moral of the whole narrative : "Because thou hast seen me, thou hast believed : blessed are they that have not seen me, and yet have believed." John 20 : 29. In the New Testament we hear of Thomas only twice again, once on the Sea of Galilee with the seven disciples, where he is ranked next after Peter, John 21 : 2, and again in the assemblage of the apostles after the ascension. Acts 1 : 13. The earlier traditions, as believed in the fourth century, represent him as preaching in Parthia or Persia, and as finally buried at Edessa. The later traditions carry him farther east. His martyrdom, whether in Persia or India, is said to have been occasioned by a lance, and is commemorated by the Latin Church on December 21, by the Greek Church on October 6, and by the Indians on July 1.

Palestine Thorn.

Thorns and **Thistles.** There appear to be eighteen or twenty Hebrew words which point to different kinds of prickly or thorny shrubs. These words are variously rendered in the Authorized Version by "thorns," "briers," "thistles," etc. Palestine abounded in a great variety of such plants. ("Travellers call the holy land 'a land of thorns.' Giant thistles, growing to the height of a man on horseback, frequently spread over regions once rich and fruitful, as they do on the pampas of South America; and many of the most interesting historic spots and ruins are rendered almost inaccessible by thickets of fiercely-armed buckthorns. Entire fields are covered with the troublesome creeping stems of the spinous *ononis*, while the bare hillsides are studded with the dangerous capsules of the *paliurus* and *tribulus*. Roses of the most prickly kinds abound on the lower slopes of Hermon; while the sub-tropical valleys of Judea are choked up in many places by the thorny *lycium*."—*Biblical Things not generally Known.*) *Crown of thorns.*—The "crown of thorns," Matt. 27 : 29, which was put in derision upon our Lord's head before his crucifixion, is by some supposed to have been the *Rhamnus*, or *Spina Christi;* but although

abundant in the neighborhood of Jerusalem, it cannot be the plant intended, because its thorns are so strong and large that it could not have been woven into a wreath. The large-leaved acanthus (bear's-foot) is totally unsuited for the purpose. Had the acacia been intended, as some suppose, the phrase would have been ἐξ ἀκάνθης. Obviously some small, flexile, thorny shrub is meant; perhaps. *Cappares spinosæ.* Hasselquist ("Travels," p. 260) says that the thorn used was the Arabian *nabk.* "It was very suitable for their purpose, as it has many sharp thorns, which inflict painful wounds; and its flexible, pliant and round branches might easily be plaited in the form of a crown." It also resembles the rich dark green of the triumphal ivy-wreath, which would give additional pungency to its ironical purpose.

Three Taverns, a station on the Appian Road, along which St. Paul travelled from Puteoli to Rome. Acts 28 : 15. The distances, reckoning southward from Rome, are given as follows in the *Antonine Itinerary:* "to Aricia, 16 miles; to Three Taverns, 17 miles; to Appii Forum, 10 miles;" and, comparing this with what is still observed along the line of road, we have no difficulty in coming to the conclusion that "Three Taverns" was near the modern *Cisterna.* Just at this point a road came in from Antium on the coast. There is no doubt that "Three Taverns" was a frequent meeting-place of travellers.

Threshing. [AGRICULTURE.]

Threshold. Of the two words so rendered in the Authorized Version, one, *miphthán*, seems to mean sometimes a projecting beam or corbel. Ezek. 9 : 3; 10 : 4, 18.

Thresholds, The. This word, *Asuppê*, appears to be inaccurately rendered in Neh. 12 : 25, though its real force has perhaps not yet been discovered. The "house of Asuppim," or simply "the Asuppim," is mentioned in 1 Chron. 26 : 15, 17 as a part, probably a gate, of the enclosure of the "house of Jehovah," apparently at its southwest corner. The allusion in Neh. 12 : 25 is undoubtedly to the same place. [GATE.]

Throne. The Hebrew word so translated applies to any elevated seat occupied by a person in authority, whether a high priest, 1 Sam. 1 : 9, a judge, Ps. 122 : 5, or a military chief. Jer. 1 : 15. The use of a chair in a country where the usual postures were squatting and reclining was at all times regarded as a symbol of dignity. 2 Kings 4 : 10 ; Prov. 9 : 14.

Assyrian Throne or Chair of State.

In order to specify a throne in our sense of the term, it was necessary to add to the word the notion of royalty ; hence the frequent occurrence of such expressions as "throne of the kingdom." Deut. 17 : 18 ; 1 Kings 1 : 46 ; 2 Chron. 7 : 18. The characteristic feature in the royal throne was its elevation : Solomon's throne was approached by six steps, 1 Kings 10 : 19 ; 2 Chron. 9 : 18 ; and Jehovah's throne is described as "high and lifted up." Isa. 6 : 1. The materials and workmanship of Solomon's throne were costly. It was made of wood inlaid with ivory and then covered with gold except where the ivory showed. It was furnished with arms or "stays." The steps were also lined with pairs of lions. As to the form of chair, we are only informed in 1 Kings 10 : 19 that "the top was round behind." The king sat on his throne on state occasions. At such times he appeared in his royal robes. The throne was the symbol of supreme power and dignity. Gen. 41 : 40. Similarly, "to sit upon the throne" implied the exercise of regal power. Deut. 17 : 18 ; 1 Kings 16 : 11.

Thummim. [URIM AND THUMMIM.]

Thunder is hardly ever heard in Palestine from the middle of April to the middle of September ; hence it was selected by Samuel as a striking expression of the divine displeasure toward the

Thyatira.

Israelites. 1 Sam. 12 : 17. Rain in harvest was deemed as extraordinary as snow in summer, Prov. 26 : 1, and Jerome states that he had never witnessed it in the latter part of June or in July. *Comm.* on Amos 4 : 7. In the imaginative philosophy of the Hebrews, thunder was regarded as the voice of Jehovah, Job 37 : 2, 4, 5 ; 40 : 9 ; Ps. 18 : 13 ; 29 : 3–9 ; Isa. 30 : 30, 31, who dwelt behind the thunder-cloud. Ps. 81 : 7. Thunder was, to the mind of the Jew, the symbol of divine power, Ps. 29 : 3, etc., and vengeance. 1 Sam. 2 : 10 ; 2 Sam. 22 : 14.

Thyati′ra, a city on the Lycus, founded by Seleucus Nicator, lay to the left of the road from Pergamos to Sardis, 27 miles from the latter city, and on the very confines of Mysia and Ionia, so as to be sometimes reckoned within the one and sometimes within the other. Dyeing apparently formed an important part of the industrial activity of Thyatira, as it did of that of Colossæ and Laodicea. It is first mentioned in connection with Lydia, " a seller of purple." Acts 16 : 14. One of the Seven Churches of Asia was established here. Rev. 2 : 18–29. The principal deity of the city was Apollo ; but there was another superstition, of an extremely curious nature, which seems to have been brought thither by some of the corrupted Jews of the dispersed tribes. A fane stood outside the walls, dedicated to *Sambatha*—the name of the sibyl who is sometimes called Chaldæan, sometimes Jewish, sometimes Persian— in the midst of an enclosure designated " the Chaldæans' court." This seems to lend an illustration to the obscure passage in Rev. 2 : 20, 21, which some interpret of the wife of the bishop. Now there is evidence to show that in Thyatira there was a great amalgamation of races. If the sibyl Sambatha was in reality a Jewess, lending her aid to the amalgamation of different religions, and not discountenanced by the authorities of the Judeo-Christian Church at Thyatira, both the censure and its qualification become easy of explanation. (The present name of the city is *ak-Hissar* (" white castle "). It has a reputation for the manufacture of scarlet cloth. Its present population is 15,000 to 20,000. There are nine mosques.—ED.)

Thyine wood occurs in Rev. 18 : 12, where the margin has " sweet " (wood). There can be little doubt that the wood here spoken of is that of the *Thuya articulata,* Desfont., the *Callitris quadrivalvis* of present botanists. It is a cone-bearing tree and allied to the pine. This tree was much prized by the ancient Greeks and Romans on account of the beauty of its wood for various ornamental

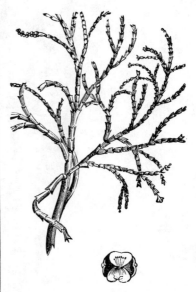

Thyine Wood (*Thuya articulata*).

purposes. By the Romans the tree was called *citrus*, the wood *citrum*. It is a native of Barbary, and grows to the height of 15 to 25 feet.

Tibe′rias, a city in the time of Christ, on the Sea of Galilee ; first mentioned in the New Testament, John 6 : 1, 23 ; 21 : 1, and then by Josephus, who states that it was built by Herod Antipas, and was named by him in honor of the emperor Tiberius. Tiberias was the capital of Galilee from the time of its origin until the reign of Herod Agrippa II., who changed the seat of power back again to Sepphoris, where it had been before the founding of the new city. Many of the inhabitants were Greeks and Romans, and foreign customs prevailed there to such an extent as to give offence to the stricter Jews. It is remarkable that the Gospels give us no intimation that the Saviour, who spent so much of his public life in Galilee, ever visited Tiberias. The place is only mentioned in the New Testament in John 6 : 23. *History.*—Tiberias has an interesting history apart from its strictly biblical associations. It bore a conspicuous part in the wars between the Jews and the Romans. The Sanhedrin, subsequent to

Tiberias and the Lake of Galilee.

the fall of Jerusalem, after a temporary sojourn at Jamnia and Sepphoris, became fixed there about the middle of the second century. Celebrated schools of Jewish learning flourished there through a succession of several centuries. The Mishna was compiled at this place by the great Rabbi Judah Hakkodesh, A.D. 190. The city has been possessed successively by Romans, Persians, Arabs and Turks. It contains now, under the Turkish rule, a mixed population of Mohammedans, Jews and Christians, variously estimated at from two to four thousand. *Present city.*—The ancient name has survived in that of the modern *Tubarieh*, which occupies the original site. Near *Tubarieh*, about a mile farther south along the shore, are the celebrated warm baths, which the Roman naturalists reckoned among the greatest known curiosities of the world. Tiberias is described by Dr. Thomson as "a filthy place, fearfully hot in summer." It was nearly destroyed in 1837 by an earthquake, by which 600 persons lost their lives.

Tibe′rias, The Sea of. John 21 : 1. [GENNESARET, SEA OF.]

Head of Emperor Tiberius.

Tibe′rius (in full, Tiberius Claudius Nero), the second Roman emperor, suc-

cessor of Augustus, who began to reign A.D. 14 and reigned until A.D. 37. He was the son of Tiberius Claudius Nero and Livia, and hence a stepson of Augustus. He was born at Rome on the 16th of November, B.C. 45. He became emperor in his fifty-fifth year, after having distinguished himself as a commander in various wars, and having evinced talents of a high order as an orator and an administrator of civil affairs. He even gained the reputation of possessing the sterner virtues of the Roman character, and was regarded as entirely worthy of the imperial honors to which his birth and supposed personal merits at length opened the way. Yet, on being raised to the supreme power, he suddenly became, or showed himself to be, a very different man. His subsequent life was one of inactivity, sloth and self-indulgence. He was despotic in his government, cruel and vindictive in his disposition. He died A.D. 37, at the age of 78, after a reign of twenty-three years. Our Saviour was put to death in the reign of Tiberius.

Tib′hath (*extension*), a city of Hadadezer, king of Zobah, 1 Chron. 18 : 8, which in 2 Sam. 8 : 8 is called Betah. Its exact position is unknown.

Tib′ni (*intelligent*). After Zimri had burnt himself in his palace, there was a division in the northern kingdom, half of the people following Tibni the son of Ginath, and half following Omri. 1 Kings 16 : 21, 22. Omri was the choice of the army. Tibni was probably put forward by the people of Tirzah, which was then besieged by Omri and his host. The struggle between the contending factions lasted four years (comp. 1 Kings 16 : 15, 23), B.C. 926–922, when Tibni died.

Ti′dal (*great son*) is mentioned only in Gen. 14 : 1, 9. (B.C. about 1900.) He is called "king of nations," from which we may conclude that he was a chief over various nomadic tribes who inhabited different portions of Mesopotamia at different seasons of the year, as do the Arabs at the present day.

Tig′lath-pile′ser. (In 1 Chron. 5 : 26, and again in 2 Chron. 28 : 20, the name of this king is given as TILGATH-PILNESER.) Tiglath-pileser is the second Assyrian king mentioned in Scripture as having come into contact with the Israelites. He attacked Samaria in the reign of Pekah, B.C. 756–736, probably because Pekah withheld his tribute, and, having entered his territories, he "took Ijon, and Abel-beth-maachah, and Janoah, and Kedesh, and Hazor, and Gilead, and Galilee, and all the land of Naphtali, and carried them captive to Assyria." 2 Kings 15 : 29. The date of this invasion cannot be fixed. After his first expedition a close league was formed between Rezin, king of Syria, and Pekah, having for its special object the humiliation of Judah. At first great successes were gained by Pekah and his confederate, 2 Kings 15 : 37 ; 2 Chron. 28 : 6-8 ; but on their proceeding to attack Jerusalem itself, Ahaz applied to Assyria for assistance, and Tiglath-pileser, consenting to aid him, again appeared at the head of an army in these regions. He first marched, naturally, against Damascus, which he took, 2 Kings 16 : 9, razing it to the ground, and killing Rezin, the Damascene monarch. After this, probably, he proceeded to chastise Pekah, whose country he entered on the northeast, where it bordered upon "Syria of Damascus." Here he overran the whole district to the east of Jordan, carrying into captivity "the Reubenites, the Gadites and the half tribe of Manasseh." 1 Chron. 5 : 26. Before returning into his own land, Tiglath-pileser had an interview with Ahaz at Damascus. 2 Kings 16 : 10. This is all that Scripture tells us of Tiglath-pileser. He reigned certainly from B.C. 747 to B.C. 730, and possibly a few years longer, being succeeded by Shalmaneser at least as early as B.C. 725. Tiglath-pileser's wars do not, generally, appear to have been of much importance. No palace or great building can be ascribed to this king. His slabs, which are tolerably numerous, show that he must have built or adorned a residence at Calah (*Nimrud*), where they were found.

Ti'gris is used by the LXX. as the Greek equivalent of the Hebrew *Hiddekel*, and occurs also in several of the apocryphal books, as in Tobit, ch. 6 : 1, Judith, ch. 1 : 6, and Ecclesiasticus, ch. 24 : 25. The Tigris, like the Euphrates, rises from two principal sources in the Armenian mountains, and flows into the Euphrates. Its length, exclusive of windings, is reckoned at 1146 miles. It receives, along its middle and lower course, no fewer than five important tributaries. These are the river of *Zakko* or eastern Khabour, the Great Zab (*Zab Ala*), the Lesser Zab (*Zab Asfal*), the *Adhem*, and the *Diyaleh* or ancient Gyndes. All

these rivers flow from the high range of Zagros. We find but little mention of the Tigris in Scripture. It appears, indeed, under the name of Hiddekel, among the rivers of Eden, Gen. 2 : 14, and is there correctly described as "running eastward to Assyria ;" but after this we hear no more of it, if we except one doubtful allusion in Nahum, ch. 2 : 6, until the captivity, when it becomes well known to the prophet Daniel. With him it is "the Great River." The Tigris, in its upper course, anciently ran through Armenia and Assyria.

Tik'vah (*hope*). 1. The father of Shallum the husband of the prophetess Huldah. 2 Kings 22 : 14. (B.C. before 632.)

2. The father of Jahaziah. Ezra 10 : 15. (B.C. 458.)

Tik'vath (*assemblage*) (properly *Tŏkĕhath* or *Tokhath*), Tikvah the father of Shallum. 2 Chron. 34 : 22.

Til'gath-pilne'ser, a variation, and probably a corruption, of the name Tiglath-pileser. 1 Chron. 5 : 6, 26 ; 2 Chron. 28 : 20.

Ti'lon (*gift*), one of the four sons of Shimon, whose family is reckoned in the genealogies of Judah. 1 Chron. 4 : 20. (B.C. 1451.)

Timæ'us, the father of the blind man, Bartimæus. Mark 10 : 46.

Timbrel.

Timbrel, tabret (Heb. *tóph*). In old English tabor was used for any drum. Tabouret and tabourine are diminutives of tabor, and denote the instrument now known as the tambourine. Tabret is a contraction of tabouret. The Hebrew *tóph* is undoubtedly the instrument described by travellers as the *duff* or *diff* of the Arabs. It was played principally by women, Ex. 15 : 20 ; Judges 11 : 34 ; 1

Sam. 18 : 6; Ps. 68 : 25, as an accompaniment to the song and dance. The *diff* of the Arabs is described by Russell as "a hoop (sometimes with pieces of brass fixed in it to make a jingling) over which a piece of parchment is stretched. It is beaten with the fingers, and is the true tympanum of the ancients." In Barbary it is called *tar*.

Tim'na, or Tim'nah (*restraint*). 1. A concubine of Eliphaz son of Esau, and mother of Amalek, Gen. 36 : 12; it may be presumed that she was the same as Timna sister of Lotan. *Ibid.* ver. 22, and 1 Chron. 1 : 39. (B.C. after 1800.)

2. A duke or phylarch of Edom in the last list in Gen. 36 : 40–43; 1 Chron. 1 : 51–54. Timnah was probably the name of a place or a district. [See the following article.]

Tim'nah (*portion*). 1. A place which formed one of the landmarks on the north boundary of the allotment of Judah. Josh. 15 : 10. It is probably identical with the Thimnathah of Josh. 19 : 43, and that again with the Timnath, or, more accurately, Timnathah, of Samson, Judges 14 : 1, 2, 5, and the Thamnatha of the Maccabees. The modern representative of all these various forms of the same name is probably *Tibneh*, a village about two miles west of *Ain Shems* (Bethshemesh). In the later history of the Jews, Timnah must have been a conspicuous place. It was fortified by Bacchides as one of the most important military posts of Judea. 1 Macc. 9 : 50.

2. A town in the mountain district of Judah. Josh. 15 : 57. A distinct place from that just examined.

3. Inaccurately written Timnath in the Authorized Version, the scene of the adventure of Judah with his daughter-in-law Tamar. Gen. 38 : 12, 13, 14. There is nothing here to indicate its position. It may be identified either with the Timnah in the mountains of Judah [No. 2] or with the Timnathah of Samson [No. 1].

Tim'nath. [TIMNAH.]

Tim'nathah, the residence of Samson's wife. Judges 14 : 1, 2, 5.

Tim'nath-he'res (*portion of the sun*), the name under which the city and burial-place of Joshua, previously called Timnath-serah, is mentioned in Judges 2 : 9. [TIMNATH-SERAH.]

Tim'nath-se'rah (*portion of abundance*), the name of the city which was presented to Joshua after the partition of the country, Josh. 19 : 50, and in "the border" of which he was buried. Josh. 24 : 30. It is specified as "in Mount Ephraim on the north side of Mount Gaash." In Judges 2 : 9 the name is altered to TIMNATH-HERES. The latter form is that adopted by the Jewish writers. Accordingly, they identify the place with *Kefar-cheres*, which is said by Jewish travellers to be about five miles south of Shechem (*Nablûs*). No place with that name appears on the maps. Another identification has, however, been suggested by Dr. Eli Smith. In his journey from *Jifna* to *Mejdel-Yaba*, about six miles from the former he discovered the ruins of a considerable town. Opposite the town was a much higher hill, in the north side of which are several excavated sepulchres. The whole bears the name of *Tibneh*.

Tim'nite, The, Samson's father-in-law, a native of Timnathah. Judges 15 : 6.

Ti'mon, one of the seven, commonly called "deacons." Acts 6 : 1–6. He was probably a Hellenist. (A.D. 34.)

Timo'theus. 1. A "captain of the Ammonites," 1 Macc. 5 : 6, who was defeated on several occasions by Judas Maccabæus, B.C. 164. 1 Macc. 5 : 6, 11, 34–44. He was probably a Greek adventurer.

2. In 2 Macc. a leader named Timotheus is mentioned as having taken part in the invasion of Nicanor, B.C. 166. 2 Macc. 8 : 30; 9 : 3.

3. The Greek name of Timothy. Acts 16 : 1; 17 : 14, etc.

Tim'othy. The disciple thus named was the son of one of those mixed marriages which, though condemned by stricter Jewish opinion, were yet not uncommon in the later periods of Jewish history. The father's name is unknown; he was a Greek, *i. e.* a Gentile, by descent. Acts 16 : 1, 3. The absence of any personal allusion to the father in the Acts or Epistles suggests the inference that he must have died or disappeared during his son's infancy. The care of the boy thus devolved upon his mother Eunice and her mother Lois. 2 Tim. 1 : 5. Under their training his education was emphatically Jewish. "From a child" he learned to "know the Holy Scriptures" daily. The language of the Acts leaves it uncertain whether Lystra or Derbe was the residence of the devout family. The arrival of Paul and Barnabas in Lycaonia, A.D. 44, Acts 14 : 6, brought the message of glad tidings to Timothy and his mother, and they received it with "unfeigned faith." 2 Tim. 1 : 5. During the interval of seven years between the apostle's first and second journeys the boy grew up to manhood. Those who had the deepest insight into character, and spoke with a prophetic utterance, pointed to him, 1 Tim. 1 : 18; 4 : 14, as others had pointed before to Paul and Barnabas, Acts 13 : 2, as specially fit for the missionary work in which the apostle was engaged. Personal feeling led St. Paul to the same conclusion, Acts 16 : 3, and he was solemnly set apart to do the work and possibly to bear the title of evangelist. 1 Tim. 4 : 14; 2 Tim. 1 : 6; 4 : 5. A great obstacle, however, presented itself. Timothy, though reckoned as one of the seed of Abraham, had been allowed to grow up to the age of manhood without the sign of circumcision. With a special view to the feelings of the Jews, making no sacrifice of principle, the apostle, who had refused to permit the circumcision of Titus, "took and circumcised" Timothy. Acts 16 : 3. Henceforth Timothy was one of his most constant companions. They and Silvanus, and probably Luke also, journeyed to Philippi, Acts 16 : 12, and there the young evangelist was conspicuous at once for his filial devotion and his zeal. Philip. 2 : 22. His name does not appear in the account of St. Paul's work at Thessalonica, and it is possible that he remained some time at Philippi. He appears, however, at Berea, and remains there when Paul and Silas are obliged to leave, Acts 17 : 14, going afterward to join his master at Athens. 1 Thess. 3 : 2. From Athens he is sent back to Thessalonica, ibid., as having special gifts for comforting and teaching. He returns from Thessalonica, not to Athens, but to Corinth, and his name appears united with St. Paul's in the opening words of both the letters written from that city to the Thessalonians. 1 Thess. 1 : 1; 2 Thess. 1 : 1. Of the next five years of his life we have no record. When we next meet with him, it is as being sent on in advance when the apostle was contemplating the long journey which was to include Macedonia, Achaia, Jerusalem and Rome. Acts 19 : 22. It is probable that he returned by the same route and met St. Paul according to a previous arrangement, 1 Cor. 16 : 11, and was thus with him when the Second Epistle was written to the church of Corinth. 2 Cor. 1 : 1. He returns with the apostle to that city, and joins in messages of greeting to the disciples whom he had known personally at Corinth, and who had since found their way to Rome. Rom. 16 : 21. He forms one of the company of friends who go with St. Paul to Philippi, and then sail by themselves, waiting for his arrival by a different ship. Acts 20 : 3-6. The absence of his name from Acts 27 leads to the conclusion that he did not share in the perilous voyage to Italy. He must have joined the apostle, however, apparently soon after his arrival at Rome, and was with him when the Epistles to the Philippians, to the Colossians and to Philemon were written. Philip. 1 : 1; 2 : 19; Col. 1 : 1; Phil. ver. 1. All the indications of this period point to incessant missionary activity.

From the two Epistles addressed to Timothy we are able to put together a few notices as to his later life. It follows from 1 Tim. 1 : 3 that he and his master, after the release of the latter from his imprisonment, A.D. 63, revisited proconsular Asia; that the apostle then continued his journey to Macedonia, while the disciple remained, half reluctantly, even weeping at the separation, 2 Tim. 1 : 4, at Ephesus, to check, if possible, the outgrowth of heresy and licentiousness which had sprung up there. The position in which he found himself might well make him anxious. He had to rule presbyters most of whom were older than himself. 1 Tim. 4 : 12. Leaders of rival sects were there. The name of his beloved teacher was no longer honored as it had been. We cannot wonder that the apostle, knowing these trials, should be full of anxiety and fear for his disciple's steadfastness. In the Second Epistle to him, A.D. 67 or 68, this deep personal feeling utters itself yet more fully. The last recorded words of the apostle express the earnest hope, repeated yet more earnestly, that he might see him once again. 2 Tim. 4 : 9, 21. We may hazard the conjecture that he reached him in time, and that the last hours of the teacher were soothed by the presence of the disciple whom he loved so truly. Some writers have seen in Heb. 13 : 23 an indication that he even shared St. Paul's imprisonment, and was released from it by the death of Nero. Beyond this all is apocryphal and uncertain. He continued, according to the old traditions, to act as bishop of Ephesus, and died a martyr's death under Domitian or Nerva.

A somewhat startling theory as to the intervening period of his life has found favor with some. If he continued, according to the received tradition, to be bishop of Ephesus, then he, and no other, must have been the "angel" of the church of Ephesus to whom the message of Rev. 2 : 1–7 was addressed.

Timothy, Epistles of Paul to. The Epistles to Timothy and Titus are called the Pastoral Epistles, because they are principally devoted to directions about the work of the pastor of a church. The First Epistle was probably written from Macedonia, A.D. 65, in the interval between St. Paul's first and second imprisonments at Rome. The absence of any local reference but that in 1 Tim. 1 : 3 suggests Macedonia or some neighboring district. In some MSS. and versions Laodicea is named in the inscription as the place from which it was sent. The Second Epistle appears to have been written A.D. 67 or 68, and in all probability at Rome. The following are the characteristic features of these epistles:—(1) The ever-deepening sense in St. Paul's heart of the divine mercy of which he was the object, as shown in the insertion of the word "mercy" in the salutations of both epistles, and in the "obtained mercy" of 1 Tim. 1 : 13. (2) The greater abruptness of the Second Epistle. From first to last there is no plan, no treatment of subjects carefully thought out. All speaks of strong overflowing emotion, memories of the past, anxieties about the future. (3) The absence, as compared with St. Paul's other epistles, of Old Testament references. This may connect itself with the fact just noticed, that these epistles are not argumentative, possibly also with the request for the "books and parchments" which had been left behind. 2 Tim. 4 : 13. (4) The conspicuous position of the "faithful sayings" as taking the place occupied in other epistles by the Old Testament Scriptures. The way in which these are cited as authoritative, the variety of subjects which they cover, suggests the thought that in them we have specimens of the prophecies of the apostolic Church which had most impressed themselves on the mind of the apostle and of the disciples generally. 1 Cor. 14 shows how deep a reverence he was likely to feel for such spiritual utterances. In 1 Tim. 4 : 1 we have a distinct reference to them. (5) The tendency of the apostle's mind to dwell more on the universality of the re-

demptive work of Christ, 1 Tim. 2 : 3–6 ; 4 : 10, and his strong desire that all the teaching of his disciples should be "sound." (6) The importance attached by him to the practical details of administration. The gathered experience of a long life had taught him that the life and well-being of the Church required these for its safeguards. (7) The recurrence of doxologies, 1 Tim. 1 : 17 ; 6 : 15, 16 ; 2 Tim. 4 : 18, as from one living perpetually in the presence of God, to whom the language of adoration was as his natural speech.

Tin. Among the various metals found in the spoils of the Midianites, tin is enumerated. Num. 31 : 22. It was known to the Hebrew metal-workers as an alloy of other metals. Isa. 1 : 25 ; Ezek. 22 : 18, 20. The markets of Tyre were supplied with it by the ships of Tarshish. Ezek. 27 : 12. It was used for plummets, Zech. 4 : 10, and was so plentiful as to furnish the writer of Ecclesiasticus, Ecclus. 47 : 18, with a figure by which to express the wealth of Solomon. Tin is not found in Palestine. Whence, then, did the ancient Hebrews obtain their supply ? "Only three countries are known to contain any considerable quantity of it : Spain and Portugal, Cornwall and the adjacent parts of Devonshire, and the islands of Junk, Ceylon and Banca, in the Straits of Malacca." (Kenrick, "Phœnicia," p. 212.) There can be little doubt that the mines of Britain were the chief source of supply to the ancient world. [See TARSHISH.] ("Tin ore has lately been found in Midian."—*Schaff.*)

Tiph'sah (*ford*) is mentioned in 1 Kings 4 : 24 as the limit of Solomon's empire toward the Euphrates, and in 2 Kings 15 : 16 it is said to have been attacked by Menahem. It was known to the Greeks and Romans under the name of Thapsacus, and was the point where it was usual to cross the Euphrates. Thapsacus has been generally placed at the modern *Deïr;* but the Euphrates expedition proved that there is no ford at *Deïr,* and that the only ford in this part of the course of the Euphrates is at *Suriyeh,* 45 miles below Balis, and 165 above *Deïr.* This, then, must have been the position of Thapsacus.

Tir'ras (*desire*), the youngest son of Japheth, Gen. 10 : 2, usually identified with the Thracians, as presenting the closest verbal approximation to the name.

Ti'rathites, The, one of the three

families of scribes residing at Jabez, 1 Chron. 2 : 55, the others being the Shimeathites and Sucathites. The passage is hopelessly obscure.

Tire, an old English word for *headdress.* It was an ornamental headdress worn on festive occasions, Ezek. 24 : 17, 23, and perhaps, as some suppose, also an ornament for the neck worn by both women, Isa. 3 : 18, and men, and even on the necks of camels. Judges 8 : 21, 26.

Tir′hakah, or **Tirha′kah** (*exalted?*), king of Ethiopia (Cush), the opponent of Sennacherib. 2 Kings 19 : 9 ; Isa. 37 : 9. He may be identified with Tarkos or Tarakos, who was the third and last king of the twenty-fifth dynasty, which was of Ethiopians. His accession was probably about B.C. 695. Possibly Tirhakah ruled over Ethiopia before becoming king of Egypt.

Tir′hanah (*favor*), son of Caleb ben-Hezron by his concubine Maachah. 1 Chron. 2 : 48. [B.C. about 1451.]

Tir′ia (*fear*), son of Jehaleleel, of the tribe of Judah. 1 Chron. 4 : 16. (B.C. about 1451.)

Tirshatha (always written with the article), the title of the governor of Judea under the Persians, perhaps derived from a Persian root signifying *stern, severe,* is added as a title after the name of Nehemiah, Neh. 8 : 9 ; 10 : 1, and occurs also in three other places. In the margin of the Authorized Version, Ezra 2 : 63 ; Neh. 7 : 65 ; 10 : 1, it is rendered "governor."

Tir′zah (*delight*), youngest of the five daughters of Zelophehad. Num. 26 : 33 ; 27 : 1 ; 36 : 11 ; Josh. 17 : 3. (B.C. 1450.)

Tir′zah, an ancient Canaanite city, whose king is enumerated among those overthrown in the conquest of the country. Josh. 12 : 24. It reappears as a royal city, the residence of Jeroboam and of his successors, 1 Kings 14 : 17, 18 ; and as the seat of the conspiracy of Menahem ben-Gaddi against the wretched Shallum. 2 Kings 15 : 16. Its reputation for beauty throughout the country must have been widespread. It is in this sense that it is spoken of in the Song of Solomon. Eusebius mentions it in connection with Menahem, and identifies it with a "village of Samaritans in Batanea." Its site is *Tellúzah,* a place in the mountains north of *Nablús.*

Tish′bite, The, the well-known designation of Elijah. 1 Kings 17 : 1 ; 21 : 17, 28 ; 2 Kings 1 : 3, 8 ; 9 : 36. The name naturally points to a place called Tish-beh, Tishbi, or rather perhaps Tesheb, as the residence of the prophet. Assuming that a town is alluded to as Elijah's native place, it is not necessary to infer that it was itself in Gilead, as many have imagined. The commentators and lexicographers, with few exceptions, adopt the name "Tishbite" as referring to the place Thisbe in Naphtali, which is found in the Septuagint text of Tobit 1 : 2.

Tithe or **tenth,** the proportion of property devoted to religious uses from very early times. Instances of the use of tithes are found prior to the appointment of the Levitical tithes under the law. In biblical history the two prominent instances are — 1. Abram presenting the tenth of all his property, or rather of the spoils of his victory, to Melchizedek. Gen. 14 : 20 ; Heb. 7 : 2, 6. 2. Jacob, after his vision at Luz, devoting a tenth of all his property to God in case he should return home in safety. Gen. 28 : 22. The first enactment of the law in respect of tithe is the declaration that the tenth of all produce, as well as of flocks and cattle, belongs to Jehovah, and must be offered to him ; that the tithe was to be paid in kind, or, if redeemed, with an addition of one fifth to its value. Lev. 27 : 30–33. This tenth is ordered to be assigned to the Levites as the reward of their service, and it is ordered further that they are themselves to dedicate to the Lord a tenth of these receipts, which is to be devoted to the maintenance of the high priest. Num. 18 : 21–28. This legislation is modified or extended in the book of Deuteronomy, *i. e.* from thirty-eight to forty years later. Commands are given to the people—1. To bring their tithes, together with their votive and other offerings and first-fruits, to the chosen centre of worship, the metropolis, there to be eaten in festive celebration in company with their children, their servants and the Levites. Deut. 12 : 5–18. 2. All the produce of the soil was to be tithed every year, and these tithes, with the firstlings of the flock and herd, were to be eaten in the metropolis. 3. But in case of distance, permission is given to convert the produce into money, which is to be taken to the appointed place, and there laid out in the purchase of food for a festal celebration, in which the Levite is, by special command, to be included. Deut. 14 : 22–27. 4. Then follows the direction that at the end of three years all the tithe of that year is to be gathered and laid up "within the gates," and that a festival is to be held, of which the stranger, the fatherless and the widow, together with the Levite, are to partake. *Ibid.* 5 : 28, 29. 5. Lastly, it is ordered that after taking the tithe in each third year, "which is the year of tithing," an exculpatory declaration is to be made by every Israelite that he has done his best to fulfill the divine command. Deut. 26 : 12–14. From all this we gather—(1) That one tenth of the whole produce of the soil was to be assigned for the maintenance of the Levites. (2) That out of this the Levites were to dedicate a tenth to God for the use of the high priest. (3) That a tithe, in all probability a *second* tithe, was to be applied to festival purposes. (4) That in every third year, either this festival tithe or a *third* tenth was to be eaten in company with the poor and the Levites. (These tithes in early times took the place of our modern taxes, as well as of gifts for the support of religious institutions.—ED.)

Ti'tus. Our materials for the biography of this companion of St. Paul must be drawn entirely from the notices of him in the Second Epistle to the Corinthians, the Galatians, and to Titus himself, combined with the Second Epistle to Timothy. He is not mentioned in the Acts at all. Taking the passages in the epistles in the chronological order of the events referred to, we turn first to Gal. 2 : 1, 3. We conceive the journey mentioned here to be identical with that (recorded in Acts 15) in which Paul and Barnabas went from Antioch to Jerusalem to the conference which was to decide the question of the necessity of circumcision to the Gentiles. Here we see Titus in close association with Paul and Barnabas at Antioch. He goes with them to Jerusalem. His circumcision was either not insisted on at Jerusalem, or, if demanded, was firmly resisted. He is very emphatically spoken of as a Gentile, by which is most probably meant that both his parents were Gentiles. Titus would seem, on the occasion of the council, to have been specially a representative of the church of the uncircumcision. It is to our purpose to remark that, in the passage cited above, Titus is so mentioned as apparently to imply that he had become personally known to the Galatian Christians. After leaving Galatia, Acts 18 : 23, and spending a long time at Ephesus, Acts 19 : 1–20 : 1, the apostle proceeded to Macedonia by way of Troas. Here he expected to meet Titus, 2 Cor. 2 : 13, who had been sent on a mission to Corinth. In this hope he was disappointed, but in Macedonia Titus joined him. 2 Cor. 7 : 6, 7, 13–15. The mission to Corinth had reference to the immoralities rebuked in the First Epistle, and to the collection, at that time in progress, for the poor Christians of Judea. 2 Cor. 8 : 6. Thus we are prepared for what the apostle now proceeds to do after his encouraging conversations with Titus regarding the Corinthian church. He sends him back from Macedonia to Corinth, in company with two other trustworthy Christians, bearing the Second Epistle, and with an earnest request, *ibid.* 8 : 6, 17, that he would see to the completion of the collection. ch. 8 : 6.

A considerable interval now elapses before we come upon the next notices of this disciple. St. Paul's first imprisonment is concluded, and his last trial is impending. In the interval between the two, he and Titus were together in Crete. Titus 1 : 5. We see Titus remaining in the island when St. Paul left it, and receiving there a letter written to him by the apostle. From this letter we gather the following biographical details : In the first place we learn that he was originally converted through St. Paul's instrumentality. Titus 1 : 4. Next we learn the various particulars of the responsible duties which he had to discharge in Crete. He is to complete what St. Paul had been obliged to leave unfinished, ch. 1 : 5, and he is to organize the church throughout the island by appointing presbyters in every city. Next he is to control and bridle, ver. 11, the restless and mischievous Judaizers. He is also to look for the arrival in Crete of Artemas and Tychicus, ch. 3 : 12, and then is to hasten to join St. Paul at Nicopolis, where the apostle purposes to pass the winter. Zenas and Apollos are in Crete, or expected there ; for Titus is to send them on their journey, and to supply them with whatever they need for it. ch. 3 : 13. Whether Titus did join the apostle at Nicopolis we cannot tell ; but we naturally connect the mention of this place with what St. Paul wrote, at no great interval of time afterward, in the last of the Pastoral Epistles, 2 Tim. 4 : 10 ; for Dalmatia lay to the north of Nicopolis, at no great distance from it. From the form of the whole sentence, it seems probable that this disciple had been with St. Paul in Rome during his final imprisonment; but this cannot be asserted confidently. The traditional connection of Titus with Crete is much more specific and constant, though here again we cannot be certain of the facts. He is said to have been permanent bishop in the island, and to have died there at an advanced age. The modern capital, *Candia*, appears to claim the honor of being his burial-place. In the fragment by the lawyer Zenas, Titus is called bishop of Gortyna. Lastly, the name of Titus was the watchword of the Cretans when they were invaded by the Venetians.

Titus, Epistle to. There are no specialties in this epistle which require any very elaborate treatment distinct from the other Pastoral Letters of St. Paul. It was written about the same time and under similar circumstances with the other two; *i. e.*, from Ephesus, in the autumn of 67, in the interval between Paul's two Roman imprisonments.

Ti'tus Jus'tus. (The form given in the Revised Version, of the proselyte Justus, at whose house in Corinth Paul preached when driven from the synagogue. He is possibly the same as Titus the companion of Paul.)

Ti'zite, The, the designation of Joha, one of the heroes of David's army. 1 Chron. 11 : 45. It occurs nowhere else, and nothing is known of the place or family which it denotes.

To'ah (*lowly*), a Kohathite Levite, ancestor of Samuel and Heman. 1 Chron. 6 : 34 (19).

Tob-adoni'jah (*Adonijah the good*), one of the Levites sent by Jehoshaphat through the cities of Judah to teach the law to the people. 2 Chron. 17 : 8. (B.C. 910.)

Tob (*good*), **The land of,** a place in which Jephthah took refuge when expelled from home by his half-brother, Judges 11 : 3, and where he remained, at the head of a band of freebooters, till he was brought back by the sheikhs of Gilead. ver. 5. The narrative implies that the land of Tob was not far distant from Gilead; at the same time, from the nature of the case, it must have lain out toward the eastern deserts. It is undoubtedly mentioned again in 2 Sam. 10 : 6, 8, as Ishtob, *i. e. man of Tob*, meaning, according to a common Hebrew idiom, the *men of Tob*. After a long interval it appears again, in the Maccabæan history,

1 Macc. 5 : 13, in the names Tobie and Tubieni. 2 Macc. 12 : 17. No identification of the ancient district with any modern one has yet been attempted.

Tobi'ah (*goodness of Jehovah*). 1. "The children of Tobiah" were a family who returned with Zerubbabel, but were unable to prove their connection with Israel. Ezra 2 : 60; Neh. 7 : 62. (B.C. before 536.)

2. "Tobiah the slave, the Ammonite," played a conspicuous part in the rancorous opposition made by Sanballat the Moabite and his adherents to the rebuilding of Jerusalem. (B.C. 446.) The two races of Moab and Ammon found in these men fit representatives of that hereditary hatred to the Israelites which began before the entrance into Caanan, and was not extinct when the Hebrews had ceased to exist as a nation. But Tobiah, though a slave, Neh. 2 : 10, 19—unless this is a title of opprobrium—and an Ammonite, found means to ally himself with a priestly family, and his son Johanan married the daughter of Meshullam the son of Berechiah. Neh. 6 : 18. He himself was the son-in-law of Shechaniah the son of Arah, Neh. 6 : 17, and these family relations created for him a strong faction among the Jews.

Tobi'jah (*goodness of Jehovah*). 1. One of the Levites sent by Jehoshaphat to teach the law in the cities of Judah. 2 Chron. 17 : 8. (B.C. 910.)

2. One of the captivity in the time of Zechariah, in whose presence the prophet was commanded to take crowns of silver and gold and put them on the head of Joshua the high priest. Zech. 6 : 10, 14. (B.C. 519.)

To'bit, Book of, a book of the Apocrypha, which exists at present in Greek, Latin, Syriac and Hebrew texts, but it was probably written originally in Greek. The scene of the book is placed in Assyria, whither Tobit, a Jew, had been carried as a captive by Shalmaneser. It is represented as completed shortly after the fall of Nineveh (B.C. 606), Tob. 14 : 15, and written, in the main, some time before. Tob. 12 : 20. But the whole tone of the narrative bespeaks a later age; and above all, the doctrine of good and evil spirits is elaborated in a form which belongs to a period considerably posterior to the Babylonian captivity. Asmodeus iii. 8; vi. 14; viii. 3; Raphael xii. 15. It cannot be regarded as a true history. It is a didactic narrative; and its point lies in the moral lessons which it conveys, and not in the incidents. In modern times the moral excellence of the book has been rated highly, except in the heat of controversy. Nowhere else is there preserved so complete and beautiful a picture of the domestic life of the Jews after the return. Almost every family relation is touched upon with natural grace and affection. A doctrinal feature of the book is the firm belief in a glorious restoration of the Jewish people. Tob. 14 : 5 ; ` 13 : 9–18. But the restoration contemplated is national, and not the work of a universal Saviour. In all there is not the slightest trace of the belief in a personal Messiah.

To'chen (*task*), a place mentioned in 1 Chron. 4 : 32 only, among the towns of Simeon.

Togar'mah, a son of Gomer, of the family of Japheth, and brother of Ashkenaz and Riphath. Gen. 10 : 3. His descendants became a people engaged in agriculture, breeding horses and mules to be sold in Tyre. Ezek. 27 : 14. They were also a military people, well skilled in the use of arms. Togarmah was probably the ancient name of Armenia.

To'hu (*lowly*), an ancestor of Samuel the prophet, perhaps the same as TOAH. 1 Sam. 1 : 1 ; comp. 1 Chron. 6 : 34.

To'i (*erring*), king of Hamath on the Orontes, who, after the defeat of his powerful enemy the Syrian king Hadadezer by the army of David, sent his son Joram or Hadoram to congratulate the victor and do him homage with presents of gold and silver and brass. 2 Sam. 8 : 9, 10. (B.C. 1036.)

To'la. 1. The first-born of Issachar, and ancestor of the Tolaites. Gen. 46 : 13 ; Num. 26 : 23 ; 1 Chron. 7 : 1, 2. (B.C. about 1700.)

2. Judge of Israel after Abimelech. Judges 10 : 1, 2. He is described as " the son of Puah the son of Dodo, a man of Issachar." Tola judged Israel for twenty-three years at Shamir in Mount Ephraim, where he died and was buried. (B.C. 1206–1183.)

To'lad, one of the towns of Simeon, 1 Chron. 4 : 29, elsewhere called El-tolad.

To'laites, The, the descendants of Tola the son of Issachar. Num. 26 : 23.

Tomb. From the burial of Sarah in the cave of Machpelah, Gen. 23 : 19, to the funeral rites prepared for Dorcas, Acts 9 : 37, there is no mention of any sarcophagus, or even coffin, in any Jewish burial. Still less were the rites of the Jews like those of the Pelasgi or Etruscans. They were marked with the same simplicity that characterized all their religious observances. This simplicity of rite led to what may be called the distinguishing characteristic of Jewish sepulchres—the *deep loculus*—which, so far as is now known, is universal in all purely Jewish rock-cut tombs, but hardly known elsewhere. Its form will be understood by referring to the following diagram,

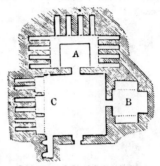

Diagram of Jewish Sepulchre.

representing the forms of Jewish sepulture. In the apartment marked A there are twelve such loculi, about two feet in width by three feet high. On the ground floor these generally open on the level of the floor; when in the upper story, as at C, on a ledge or platform, on which the body might be laid to be anointed, and on which the stones might rest which closed the outer end of each loculus. The shallow loculus is shown in chamber B, but was apparently only used when sarcophagi were employed, and therefore, so far as we know, only during the Græco-Roman period, when foreign customs came to be adopted. The shallow loculus would have been singularly inappropriate and inconvenient where an unembalmed body was laid out to decay, as there would evidently be no means of shutting it off from the rest of the catacomb. The deep loculus, on the other hand, was strictly conformable with Jewish customs, and could easily be closed by a stone fitted to the end and luted into the groove which usually exists there. This fact is especially interesting as it affords a key to much that is otherwise hard to be understood in certain passages in the New Testament. Thus in John 11 : 39, Jesus says,

"Take away the stone," and (ver. 40) "they took away the stone," without difficulty, apparently. And in ch. 20 : 1 the same expression is used, "the stone is taken away." There is one catacomb—that known as the "tomb of the kings"—which is closed by a stone rolled across its entrance; but it is the only one, and the immense amount of contrivance and fitting which it has required is sufficient proof that such an arrangement was not

Entrance to Tomb of the Kings, with Stone at its Mouth.

applied to any other of the numerous rock tombs around Jerusalem, nor could the traces of it have been obliterated had it anywhere existed. Although, therefore, the Jews were singularly free from the pomps and vanities of funereal magnificence, they were at all stages of their independent existence an eminently burying people. *Tombs of the patriarchs.*—One of the most striking events in the life of Abraham is the purchase of the field of Ephron the Hittite at Hebron, in which was the cave of Machpelah, in order that he might therein bury Sarah his wife, and that it might be a sepulchre for himself and his children. There

he and his immediate descendants were laid 3700 years ago, and there they are believed to rest now, under the great mosque of Hebron ; but no one in modern times has seen their remains, or been allowed to enter into the cave where they rest. From the time when Abraham established the burying-place of his family at Hebron till the time when David fixed that of his family in the city which bore his name, the Jewish rulers had no fixed or favorite place of sepulture. Each was buried on his own property, or where he died, without much caring for either the sanctity or convenience of the place chosen. *Tomb of the kings.*—Of the twenty-two kings of Judah who reigned at Jerusalem from 1048 to 590 B.C., eleven, or exactly one half, were buried in one hypogeum in the "city of David." Of all these it is merely said that they were buried in "the sepulchres of their fathers" or "of the kings" in the city of David, except of two—Asa and Hezekiah. Two more of these kings—Jehoram and Joash —were buried also in the city of David, "but not in the sepulchres of the kings." The passage in Neh. 3 : 16 and in Ezek. 43 : 7, 9, together with the reiterated assertion of the books of Kings and Chronicles that these sepulchres were situated in the city of David, leaves no doubt that they were on Zion, or the Eastern Hill, and in the immediate proximity of the temple. Up to the present time we have not been able to identify one single sepulchral excavation about Jerusalem which can be said with certainty to belong to a period anterior to that of the Maccabees, or, more correctly, to have been used for burial before the time of the Romans. The only important hypogeum which is wholly Jewish in its arrangement, and may consequently belong to an earlier or to any epoch, is that known as the tombs of the prophets, in the western flank of the Mount of Olives. It has every appearance of having originally been a natural cavern improved by art, and with an external gallery some 140 feet in extent, into which twenty-seven deep or Jewish loculi open. *Graeco-Roman tombs.*—Besides the tombs above enumerated, there are around Jerusalem, in the valleys of Hinnom and Jehoshaphat and on the plateau to the north, a number of remarkable rock-cut sepulchres, with more or less architectural decoration, sufficient to enable us to ascertain that they are all of nearly the same age, and to assert with very tolerable confidence that the epoch to which they belong must be between the introduction of Roman influence and the destruction of the city by Titus, A.D. 70. In the village of Siloam there is a monolithic cell of singularly Egyptian aspect, which De Saulcy assumes to be a chapel of Solomon's Egyptian wife. It is probably of very much more modern date, and is more Assyrian than Egyptian in character. The principal remaining architectural sepulchres may be divided into three groups: first, those existing in the valley of Jehoshaphat, and known popularly as the tombs of Zechariah, of St. James and of Absalom. Second, those known as the tombs of the judges, and the so-called Jewish tomb about a mile north of the city. Third, that known as the tomb of the kings, about half a mile north of the Damascus gate. Of the three first-named tombs the most southern is known as that of Zechariah, a popular name which there is not even a shadow of tradition to justify. *Tombs of the judges.*—The hypogeum known as the tombs of the judges is one of the most remarkable of the catacombs around Jerusalem, containing about sixty deep loc-

Façade of the Tomb of the Judges.

uli, arranged in three stories; the upper stories with ledges in front, to give convenient access, and to support the stones that close them; the lower flush with the ground; the whole, consequently, so essentially Jewish that it might be of any age if it were not for its distance from the town and its architectural character. *Tombs of Herod.*—The last of the great groups enumerated above is that known as the tomb of the kings—*Kebûr es Sultan*—or the Royal Caverns, so called because of their magnificence, and also because that name is applied to them by Josephus. They are twice again mentioned under the title of the "monuments of Herod." There seems no reason for doubting that all the architectural tombs

Façade of Herod's Tomb.

of Jerusalem belong to the age of the Romans. *Tomb of Helena of Adiabene.*—There was one other very famous tomb at Jerusalem, which cannot be passed over in silence, though not one vestige of it exists—the supposed tomb of Helena. We are told that "she with her brother was buried in the pyramids which she had ordered to be constructed at a distance of three stadia from Jerusalem." Joseph. *Ant.* xx. 4, § 3. This is confirmed by Pausanias. viii. 16. The tomb was situated outside the third wall, near a gate between the tower Psephinus and the Royal Caverns. *B. J.* v. 22 and v. 4, § 2. The people still cling to their ancient cemeteries in the valley of Jehoshaphat with a tenacity singularly characteristic of the East. [BURIAL.]

Tongues, Confusion of. The unity of the human race is most clearly implied, if not positively asserted, in the Mosaic writings. Unity of language is assumed by the sacred historian apparently as a corollary of the unity of race. (This statement is confirmed by philologists.) No explanation is given of the origin of speech, but its exercise is evidently regarded as coeval with the creation of man. The original unity of speech was restored in Noah. Disturbing causes were, however, early at work to dissolve this twofold union of community and speech. The human family endeavored to check the tendency to separation by the establishment of a great central edifice and a city which should serve as the metropolis of the whole world. The project was defeated by the interposition of Jehovah, who determined to "confound their language, so that they might not understand one another's speech." Contemporaneously with, and perhaps as the result of, this confusion of tongues, the people were scattered abroad from thence upon the face of all the earth, and the memory of the great event was preserved in the name Babel. [BABEL, TOWER OF.] *Inscription of Nebuchadnezzar.*— In the Borsippa inscription of Nebuchadnezzar there is an allusion to the confusion of tongues. "We say for the other, that is, this edifice, the house of the Seven Lights of the Earth, the most ancient monument of Borsippa: a former king built it [they reckon forty-two ages], but he did not complete its head. *Since a remote time people had abandoned it, without order expressing their words.* Since that time the earthquake and the thunder had dispersed its sun-dried clay; the bricks of the casing had been split, and the earth of the interior had been scattered in heaps." It is unnecessary to assume that the judgment inflicted on the builders of Babel amounted to a loss, or even a suspension, of articulate speech. The desired object would be equally attained by a miraculous forestallment of those dialectical differences of language which are constantly in process of production. The elements of the one original language may have remained, but so disguised by variations of pronunciation and by the introduction of new combinations as to be practically obliterated. The confusion of tongues and the dispersion of nations are spoken of in the Bible as contemporaneous events. The divergence of the various families into distinct tribes and nations ran parallel with the divergence of speech into dialects and languages, and thus the tenth chapter of Genesis is posterior in historical sequence to the events recorded in the eleventh chapter.

Tongues, Gift of. I. Γλῶττα, or γλῶσσα, the word employed throughout the New Testament for the gift now under consideration, is used—(1) for the bodily organ of speech; (2) for a foreign word, imported and half-naturalized in Greek; (3) in Hellenistic Greek, for "speech" or "language." The received traditional view, which starts from the third meaning, and sees in the gift of tongues a distinctly linguistic power, is the more correct one. II. The chief passages from which we have to draw our conclusion as to the nature and purpose of the gift in question are—1. Mark 16 : 17. 2. Acts 2 : 1–13; 10 : 46; 19 : 6. 3. 1 Cor. 12, 14. III. The promise of a new power coming from the divine Spirit, giving not only comfort and insight into truth, but fresh powers of utterance of some kind, appears once and again in our Lord's teaching. The disciples are to take no thought what they shall speak, for the spirit of their Father shall speak in them. Matt. 10 : 19, 20; Mark 13 : 11. The lips of Galilean peasants are to speak freely and boldly before kings. The promise of our Lord to his disciples, "They shall speak with new tongues," Mark 16 : 17, was fulfilled on the day of Pentecost, when cloven tongues like fire sat upon the disciples, and "every man heard them speak in his own language." Acts 2 : 1–12. IV. The wonder of the day of Pentecost is, in its broad features, familiar enough to us. What views have men actually taken of a phenomenon so marvellous and exceptional? The prevalent belief of the Church has been that in the Pentecostal gift the disciples received a supernatural knowledge of all such languages as they needed for their work as evangelists. The knowledge was permanent. Widely diffused as this belief has been, it must be remembered that it goes beyond the data with which the New Testament supplies us. Each instance of the gift recorded in the Acts connects it, not with the work of teaching, but with that of praise and adoration; not with the normal order of men's lives, but with exceptional epochs in them. The speech of St. Peter which follows, like most other speeches addressed to a Jerusalem audience, was spoken apparently in Aramaic. When St. Paul, who "spake with tongues more than all," was at Lystra, there is no mention made of his using the language of Lycaonia. It is almost implied that he did not understand it. Acts 14 : 11. Not one word in the discussion of spiritual gifts in 1 Cor. 12–14 implies that the gift was of this nature, or given for this purpose. Nor, it may be added, within the limits assigned by the providence of God to the working of the apostolic Church, was such a gift necessary. Aramaic, Greek, Latin, the three languages of the inscription on the cross, were media of intercourse throughout the empire.

Some interpreters have seen their way to another solution of the difficulty by changing the character of the miracle. It lay not in any new character bestowed on the speakers, but in the impression produced on the hearers. Words which the Galilean disciples uttered in their own tongue were heard as in their native speech by those who listened. There are, it is believed, weighty reasons against both the earlier and later forms of this hypothesis. 1. It is at variance with the distinct statement of Acts 2:4: "They began to speak with other tongues." 2. It at once multiplies the miracle and degrades its character. Not the 120 disciples, but the whole multitude of many thousands, are in this case the subjects of it. 3. It involves an element of falsehood. The miracle, on this view, was wrought to make men believe what was not actually the fact. 4. It is altogether inapplicable to the phenomena of 1 Cor. 14. Critics of a negative school have, as might be expected, adopted the easier course of rejecting the narrative either altogether or in part. What, then, are the facts actually brought before us? What inferences may be legitimately drawn from them? (a) The utterance of words by the disciples, in other languages than their own Galilean Aramaic, is distinctly asserted. (b) The words spoken appear to have been determined, not by the will of the speakers, but by the Spirit which "gave them utterance." (e) The word used, ἀποφθέγγεσθαι, has in the LXX. a special association with the oracular speech of true or false prophets, and appears to imply a peculiar, perhaps musical, solemn intonation. Comp. 1 Chron. 25:1; Ezek. 13:9. (d) The "tongues" were used as an instrument, not of teaching, but of praise. (e) Those who spoke them seemed to others to be under the influence of some strong excitement, "full of new wine." (f) Questions as to the mode of operation of a power above the common laws of bodily or mental life lead us to a region where our words should be "wary and few." It must be remembered, then, that in all likelihood such words as they then uttered had been heard by the disciples before. The difference was that before, the Galilean peasants had stood in that crowd, neither heeding nor understanding nor remembering what they heard, still less able to reproduce it; now they had the power of speaking it clearly and freely. The di-

vine work would in this case take the form of a supernatural exaltation of the memory, not of imparting a miraculous knowledge of words never heard before. (g) The gift of tongues, the ecstatic burst of praise, is definitely asserted to be a fulfillment of the prediction of Joel 2:28. We are led, therefore, to look for that which answers to the gift of tongues in the other element of prophecy which is included in the Old Testament use of the word; and this is found in the ecstatic praise, the burst of song. 1 Sam. 10:5-13; 19:20-24; 1 Chron. 25:3. (h) The other instances in the Acts offer essentially the same phenomena. By implication in ch. 14:15-19, by express statement in ch. 10:47; 11:15, 17; 19:6, it belongs to special critical epochs. V. The First Epistle to the Corinthians supplies fuller data. The spiritual gifts are classified and compared, arranged, apparently, according to their worth. The facts which may be gathered are briefly these: 1. The phenomena of the gift of tongues were not confined to one church or section of a church. 2. The comparison of gifts, in both the lists given by St. Paul—1 Cor. 12:8-10, 28-30—places that of tongues and the interpretation of tongues lowest in the scale. 3. The main characteristic of the "tongue" is that it is unintelligible. The man "speaks mysteries," prays, blesses, gives thanks, in the tongue, 1 Cor. 14:15, 16, but no one understands him. 4. The peculiar nature of the gift leads the apostle into what at first appears a contradiction. "Tongues are for a sign," not to believers, but to those who do not believe; yet the effect on unbelievers is not that of attracting, but of repelling. They involve of necessity a disturbance of the equilibrium between the understanding and the feelings. Therefore it is that, for those who believe already, prophecy is the greater gift. 5. The "tongues," however, must be regarded as real languages. The "divers kinds of tongues," 1 Cor. 12:28, the "tongues of men," 1 Cor. 13:1, point to differences of some kind, and it is easier to conceive of these as differences of language than as belonging to utterances all equally wild and inarticulate. 6. Connected with the "tongues" there was the corresponding power of interpretation. VI. 1. Traces of the gift are found in the Epistles to the Romans, the Galatians, the Ephesians. From the Pastoral Epistles, from those of St. Peter and St. John, they are altogether absent, and this is in itself significant. 2. It is probable, however, that the disappearance of the "tongues" was gradual. There must have been a time when "tongues" were still heard, though less frequently and with less striking results. For the most part, however, the place which they had filled in the worship of the Church was supplied by the "hymns and spiritual songs" of the succeeding age. After this, within the Church we lose nearly all traces of them. The gift of the day of Pentecost belonged to a critical epoch, not to the continuous life of the Church. It implied a disturbance of the equilibrium of man's normal state; but it was not the instrument for building up the Church.

Topaz, one of the gems used in the high priest's breastplate, Ex. 28 : 17 ; 39 : 10 ; Ezek. 28 : 13 ; one of the foundations also of the New Jerusalem, in St. John's description of the city, Rev. 21 : 20. The topaz of the ancient Greeks and Romans is generally allowed to be our chrysolite, while their chrysolite is our topaz. Chrysolite is a silicate of magnesia and iron ; it is so soft as to lose its polish unless carefully used. It varies in color from a pale-green to a bottle-green. It is supposed that its name was derived from Topazos, an island in the Red Sea where these stones were procured.

To′phel (*mortar*), Deut. 1 : 1, has been identified with *Tûfileh* on a wady of the same name running north of Bozra toward the southeast corner of the Dead Sea.

To′pheth, and once **To′phet** (*place of burning*), was in the southeast extremity of the "valley of the son of Hinnom," Jer. 7 : 31, which is "by the entry of the east gate." Jer. 19 : 2. The locality of Hinnon is given elsewhere. [HINNOM.] It seems also to have been part of the king's gardens, and watered by Siloam, perhaps a little to the south of the present *Birket el-Hamra.* The name Tophet occurs only in the Old Testament. 2 Kings 23 : 10; Isa. 30 : 33; Jer. 7 : 31, 32; 19 : 6, 11, 12, 13, 14. The New does not refer to it, nor the Apocrypha. Tophet has been variously translated. The most natural meaning seems that suggest d by the occurrence of the word in two consecutive verses, in one of which it is a *tabret* and in the other *Tophet.* Isa. 30 : 32, 33. The Hebrew words are nearly identical ; and Tophet was probably the king's "music-grove" or

garden, denoting originally nothing evil or hateful. Certainly there is no proof that it took its name from the drums beaten to drown the cries of the burning victims that passed through the fire to Molech. Afterward it was defiled by idols and polluted by the sacrifices of Baal and the fires of Molech. Then it became the place of abomination, the very gate or pit of hell. The pious kings defiled it and threw down its altars and high places, pouring into it all the filth of the city, till it became the "abhorrence" of Jerusalem.

Tor′mah occurs only in the margin of Judges 9 : 31. By a few commentators it has been conjectured that the word was originally the same with ARUMAH in ver. 41.

Tortoise (Heb. *tsâb*). The *tsâb* occurs only in Lev. 11 : 29, as the name of some unclean animal. The Hebrew word may be identified with the kindred Arabic *dhab,* "a large kind of lizard," which appears to be the *Psammosaurus scincus* of Cuvier.

To′u, or **To′i,** king of Hamath. 1 Chron. 18 : 9, 10.

Tower. Watch-towers or fortified

Watch-tower.

posts in frontier or exposed situations are mentioned in Scripture, as the tower of Edar, etc., Gen. 35 : 21 ; Isa. 21 : 5, 8, 11 ; Micah 4 : 8, etc. ; the tower of Lebanon. 2 Sam. 8 : 6. Besides these military structures, we read in Scripture of towers built in vineyards as an almost necessary appendage to them. Isa. 5 : 2; Matt. 21 : 33; Mark 12 : 1. Such towers are still in use in Palestine in vineyards, especially

Towers in the Desert.

near Hebron, and are used as lodges for the keepers of the vineyards.

Town clerk, the title ascribed in our version to the magistrate at Ephesus who appeased the mob in the theatre at the time of the tumult excited by Demetrius and his fellow craftsmen. Acts 19 : 35. The original service of this class of men was to record the laws and decrees of the state, and to read them in public.

Trachoni'tis (*a rugged region*), Luke 3 : 1, is in all probability the Greek equivalent for the Aramaic Argob, one of the five Roman provinces into which the country northeast of the Jordan was divided in New Testament times. [ARGOB.]

Trance. (1) In the only passage— Num. 24 : 4, 16—in which this word occurs in the English of the Old Testament there is, as the italics show, no corresponding word in Hebrew. In the New Testament we meet with the word three times—Acts 10 : 10; 11 : 5; 22 : 17. The ἔκστασις (*i. e.* trance) is the state in which a man has passed out of the usual order of his life, beyond the usual limits of consciousness and volition, being rapt in visions of distant or future things. The causes of this state are to be traced commonly to strong religious impressions. Whatever explanation may be given of it, it is true of many, if not of most, of those who have left the stamp of their own character on the religious history of mankind, that they have been liable to pass at times into this abnormal state. The union of intense feeling, strong volition, long-continued thought (the conditions of all wide and lasting influence), aided in many cases by the withdrawal from the lower life of the support which is needed to maintain a healthy equilibrium, appears to have been more than the "earthen vessel" will bear. The words which speak of "an ecstasy of adoration" are often literally true. As in other things, so also here, the phenomena are common to higher and lower, to true and false, systems. We may not point to trances and ecstasies as proofs of a true revelation, but still less may we think of them as at all inconsistent with it. Thus, though we have not the word, we have the thing in the "deep sleep," the "horror of great darkness," that fell on Abraham. Gen. 15:12. Balaam, as if overcome by the constraining power of a Spirit mightier than his own, "sees the vision of God, *falling*, but with opened eyes." Num. 24 : 4. Saul, in like manner, when the wild chant of the prophets stirred the old depths of feeling, himself also "prophesied" and "fell down"—most, if not all, of his kingly clothing being thrown off in the ecstasy of the moment—"all that day and all that night." 1 Sam. 19 : 24. Something there was in Jeremiah that made men say of him that he was as one that "is mad and maketh himself a prophet." Jer. 29 : 26. In Ezekiel the phenomena appear in more wonderful and awful forms. Ezek. 3 : 15. As other elements and forms of the prophetic work were revived in "the apostles and prophets" of the New Testament, so also was this. Though different in form, it belongs to the same class of phenomena as the gift of tongues, and is connected with "visions and revelations of the Lord." In some cases, indeed, it is the chosen channel for such revelations. Acts 10; 11; 22 : 17–21.

Wisely for the most part did the apostle draw a veil over these more mysterious experiences. 2 Cor. 12 : 1–4.

Transfiguration, The. (The event in the earthly life of Christ which marks the culminating point in his public ministry, and stands midway between the temptation in the wilderness and the agony in Gethsemane. Matt. 17 : 1–13; Mark 9 : 2–13; Luke 9 : 28–36. *Place.*— Though tradition locates the transfiguration on Mount Tabor, there is little to confirm this view, and modern critics favor Mount Hermon, the highest mountain-top in Gaulanitis, or one of the spurs of the Anti-Lebanus. *Time.*—The transfiguration probably took place at night, because it could then be seen to better advantage than in daylight, and Jesus usually went to mountains to spend there the night in prayer. Matt. 14 : 23, 24; Luke 6 : 12; 21 : 37. The apostles were asleep, and are described as *having kept themselves awake* through the act of transfiguration. Luke 9 : 32. *The actors and witnesses.*—Christ was the central figure, the subject of transfiguration. Moses and Elijah appeared from the heavenly world, as the representatives of the Old Testament, the one of the law, the other of prophecy, to do homage to him who was the fulfillment of both. Mr. Ellicott says, " The close of the ministry of each was not after the ' common death of all men.' No man knew of the sepulchre of Moses, Deut. 34 : 6; and Elijah had passed away in the chariot and horses of fire. 2 Kings 2 : 11. Both were associated in men's minds with the glory of the kingdom of the Christ. The Jerusalem Targum on Ex. 12 connects the coming of Moses with that of the Messiah. Another Jewish tradition predicts his appearance with that of Elijah." Moses the lawgiver and Elijah the chief of the prophets both appear talking with Christ the source of the gospel, to show that they are all one and agree in one. St. Luke, Luke 9 : 31, adds the subject of their communing: " They spake of his decease which he should accomplish at Jerusalem." Among the apostles the three favorite disciples, Peter, James and John, were the sole witnesses of the scene—" the sons of thunder and the man of rock." *The event itself.*—The transfiguration or *transformation,* or, as the Germans call it, the *glorification,* consisted in a visible manifestation of the inner glory of Christ's person, accompanied by an audible voice

from heaven. It was the revelation and anticipation of his future state of glory, which was concealed under the veil of his humanity in the state of humiliation. The cloud which overshadowed the witnesses was bright or light-like, luminous, of the same kind as the cloud at the ascension. *Significance of the miracle.*— 1. It served as a solemn inauguration of the history of the passion and final consummation of Christ's work on earth. 2. It confirmed the faith of the three favorite disciples, and prepared them for the great trial which was approaching, by showing them the real nature and glory and power of Jesus. 3. It was a witness that the spirits of the lawgiver and the prophet accepted the sufferings and the death which had shaken the faith of the disciples as the necessary conditions of the messianic kingdom.—*Ellicott.* As envoys from the eternal Majesty, they audibly affirmed that it was the will of the Father that with his own precious blood he should make atonement for sin. They impressed a new seal upon the ancient, eternal truth that the partition-wall which sin had raised could be broken down by no other means than by the power of his sufferings; that he, as the good Shepherd, could only ransom his sheep with the price of his own life.— *Krummacher.* 4. It furnishes also to us all a striking proof of the unity of the Old and New Testaments, for personal immortality, and the mysterious intercommunion of the visible and invisible worlds. Both meet in Jesus Christ; he is the connecting link between the Old and New Testaments, between heaven and earth, between the kingdom of grace and the kingdom of glory. It is very significant that at the end of the scene the disciples saw no man save Jesus alive. Moses and Elijah, the law and the promise, types and shadows, pass away; the gospel, the fulfillment, the substance, Christ remains—the only one who can relieve the misery of earth and glorify our nature, Christ all in all. (Chiefly from Smith's larger Bib. Dic.—ED.)

Treasure-cities. The kings of Judah had keepers of their treasures both in city and country, 1 Chron. 27 : 25, and the places where these magazines were laid up were called treasure-cities, and the buildings treasure-houses. Pharaoh compelled the Hebrews to build him treasure-cities. Ex. 1 : 11.—*McClintock and Strong.* [PITHOM.]

Treasury, Mark 12 : 41 ; Luke 21 : 1, a name given by the rabbins to thirteen chests in the temple, called trumpets from their shape. They stood in the court of the women. It would seem probable that this court was sometimes itself called "the treasury" because it contained these repositories.

Trespass offering. [SIN OFFER-ING.]

Trial. Information on the subject of trials under the Jewish law will be found in the articles on JUDGES and SANHE-DRIN, and also in JESUS CHRIST.

Tribute. The chief biblical facts connected with the payment of tribute have been already given under TAXES. The tribute (money) mentioned in Matt. 17 : 24, 25 was the half shekel (worth from 25 to 27 cents) applied to defray the general expenses of the temple. After the destruction of the temple this was sequestrated by Vespasian and his successors and transferred to the temple of the Capitoline Jupiter. This "tribute" of Matt. 17 : 24 must not be confounded with the tribute paid to the Roman emperor. Matt. 22 : 17. The temple rate,

Site of Troas.

though resting on an ancient precedent—Ex. 30 : 13—was, as above, a fixed annual tribute of comparatively late origin.

Tribute money. [TAXES ; TRIB-UTE.]

Tro′as, the city from which St. Paul first sailed, in consequence of a divine intimation, to carry the gospel from Asia to Europe. Acts 16 : 8, 11. It is mentioned on other occasions. Acts 20 : 5, 6 ; 2 Cor. 2 : 12, 13 ; 2 Tim. 4 : 13. Its full name was Alexandria Troas (Liv. xxxv. 42), and sometimes it was called simply Alexandria, sometimes simply Troas. It was first built by Antigonus, under the name of Antigonea Troas, and peopled with the inhabitants of some neighboring cities. Afterward it was embellished by Lysimachus, and named Alexandria Troas. Its situation was on the coast of Mysia, opposite the southeast extremity of the island of Tenedos. Under the Romans it was one of the most important towns of the province of Asia. In the time of St. Paul it was a *colonia* with the *Jus Italicum.* The modern name is *Eski-Stamboul,* with considerable ruins. We can still trace the harbor in a basin about 400 feet long and 200 broad.

Trogyl′lium is the rocky extremity of the ridge of Mycale, exactly opposite Samos. Acts 20 : 15. A little to the east of the extreme point there is an anchorage, which is still called *St. Paul's port.* [SAMOS.]

Troop, Band. These words are employed to represent the Hebrew word *gĕdûd,* which has invariably the sense of an irregular force, gathered with the object of marauding and plunder.

Troph'imus (*nutritious*). Both Trophimus and Tychicus accompanied Paul from Macedonia as far as Asia, but Tychicus seems to have remained there, while Trophimus proceeded with the apostle to Jerusalem. (A.D. 54.) There he was the innocent cause of the tumult in which St. Paul was apprehended. Acts 21 : 27–29. From this passage we learn two new facts, viz. that Trophimus was a

Ancient Trumpets.

Gentile, and that he was a native of Ephesus. Trophimus was probably one of the two brethren who, with Titus, conveyed the second Epistle to the Corinthians. 2 Cor. 8 : 16–24. [TYCHICUS.]

Trumpet. [COR-NET.]

Trumpets, Feast of, Num. 29 : 1 ; Lev. 23 : 24, the feast of the new moon, which fell on the first of Tisri. It differed from the ordinary festivals of the new moon in several important particulars. It was one of the seven days of holy convocation. Instead of the mere blowing of the trumpets of the temple at the time of the offering of the sacrifices, it was "a day of blowing of trumpets." In addition to the daily sacrifices and the eleven victims offered on the first of every month, there were offered a young bullock, a ram and seven lambs of the first year, with the accustomed meat offerings, and a kid for a sin offering. Num. 29 : 1–6. The regular monthly offering was thus repeated, with the exception of the young bullock. It has been conjectured that Ps. 81, one of the songs of Asaph, was composed expressly for the Feast of Trumpets. The psalm is used in the service for the day by the modern Jews. Various meanings have been assigned to the Feast of Trumpets ; but there seems to be no sufficient reason to call in question the common opinion of Jews and Christians, that it was the festival of the New Year's day of the civil year, the first of Tisri, the month which commenced the sabbatical year and the year of jubilee.

Tryphe'na and **Trypho'sa** (*luxurious*), two Christian women at Rome, enumerated in the conclusion of St. Paul's letter. Rom. 16 : 12. (A.D. 55.) They may have been sisters, but it is more likely that they were fellow deaconesses. We know nothing more of these two sister workers of the apostolic time.

Try'phon, a usurper of the Syrian throne. His proper name was Diodotus, and the surname Tryphon was given to him or adopted by him after his accession to power. He was a native of Cariana. 1 Macc. 11 : 39 ; 12 : 39–50, etc. "Tryphon, by treason and successive wars, gained supreme power, killed Antiochus and assumed the throne. The coins bear his head as Antiochus and Trypho."

Tryphon.

Trypho'sa. [TRYPHENA.]

Tu'bal is reckoned with Javan and Meshech among the sons of Japheth. Gen. 10 : 2 ; 1 Chron. 1 : 5. The three are again associated in the enumeration of the sources of the wealth of Tyre. Ezek. 27 : 13. Tubal and Javan, Isa. 66 : 19, Meshech and Tubal, Ezek. 32 : 26; 38 : 2, 3; 39 : 1, are nations of the north. Ezek. 38 : 15 ; 39 : 2. Josephus identified the descendants of Tubal with the Iberians, that is, the inhabitants of a tract of country between the Caspian and Euxine Seas, which nearly corresponded to the modern Georgia.

Tu'bal-cain, the son of Lamech the Cainite by his wife Zillah. Gen. 4 : 22. (B.C. about 3000.) He is called "a furbisher of every cutting instrument of copper and iron."

Turpentine tree occurs only once, viz. in the Apocrypha. Ecclus. 24 : 16. It is the *Pistacia terebinthus*, terebinth tree, common in Palestine and the East. The terebinth occasionally grows to a large size. It belongs to the natural order *Anacardiaceæ*, the plants of which order generally contain resinous secretions.

Turtle, Turtle-dove, *Turtur auritus* (Heb. *tôr*). The name is phonetic, evidently derived from the plaintive cooing of the bird. It is one of the smaller members of the group of birds which ornithologists usually call *pigeons*. The turtle-dove occurs first in Scripture in Gen. 15 : 9. In the Levitical law a pair of turtle-doves or of young pigeons are constantly prescribed as a substitute for those who were too poor to provide a lamb or a kid. The offering of two young pigeons must have been one easily within the reach of the poorest. The admission of a pair of turtle-doves was perhaps a yet further concession to extreme poverty, for they were extremely numerous, and their young might easily be found and captured by those who did not possess pigeons. In the valley of the Jordan, an allied species, the palm-dove (so named because it builds its nest in the palm tree), or Egyptian turtle—*Turtur ægyptiacus*, Temm.—is by no means uncommon. It is not improbable that the palm-dove may in some measure have supplied the sacrifice in the wilderness, for it is found in amazing numbers wherever the palm tree occurs, whether wild or cultivated. From its habit of pairing for life, and its fidelity to its mate, the turtle-dove was a symbol of purity and an appropriate offering. The regular migration of the turtle-dove and its return in the spring are alluded to in Jer. 8 : 7 and Cant. 2 : 11, 12. It is from its

plaintive note doubtless that David in Ps. 74 : 19, pouring forth his lament to God, compares himself to a turtle-dove.

Twin Brothers. This term is used in the Revised Version of Acts 28 : 11 for CASTOR AND POLLUX, which see.

Tych'icus (*fateful*) and **Troph'imus** (*nutritious*), companions of St. Paul on some of his journeys, are mentioned as natives of Asia. Acts 20 : 4 ; 21 : 29 ; 2 Tim. 4 : 20. (A.D. 54–64.) There is much probability in the conjecture that Tychicus and Trophimus were the two brethren who were associated with Titus, 2 Cor. 8 : 16–24, in conducting the business of the collection for the poor Christians in Judea.

Tyran'nus (*sovereign*), the name of a man in whose school or place of audience Paul taught the gospel for two years, during his sojourn at Ephesus. See Acts 19 : 9. (A.D. 52, 53.) The presumption is that Tyrannus himself was a Greek, and a public teacher of philosophy or rhetoric.

Tyre (*a rock*), a celebrated commercial city of Phœnicia, on the coast of the Mediterranean Sea. Its Hebrew name, *Tzôr*, signifies a rock ; which well agrees with the site of *Sûr*, the modern town, on a rocky peninsula, formerly an island. There is no doubt that, previous to the siege of the city by Alexander the Great, Tyre was situated on an island ; but, according to the tradition of the inhabitants, there was a city on the mainland before there was a city on the island ; and the tradition receives some color from the name of Palætyrus, or Old Tyre, which was borne in Greek times by a city on the continent, thirty stadia to the south. *Notices in the Bible.*—In the Bible Tyre is named for the first time in the book of Joshua, ch. 19 : 29, where it is adverted to as a fortified city (in the Authorized Version "the strong city"), in reference to the boundaries of the tribe of Asher. But the first passages in the Hebrew historical writings, or in ancient history generally, which afford glimpses of the actual condition of Tyre are in the book of Samuel, 2 Sam. 5 : 11, in connection with Hiram king of Tyre sending cedar wood and workmen to David, for building him a palace ; and subsequently in the book of Kings, in connection with the building of Solomon's temple. It is evident that under Solomon there was a close alliance between the Hebrews and the Tyrians.

Hiram supplied Solomon with cedar wood, precious metals and workmen, and gave him sailors for the voyage to Ophir and India, while on the other hand Solomon gave Hiram supplies of corn and oil, ceded to him some cities, and per-

Ruins at Tyre.

mitted him to make use of some havens on the Red Sea. 1 Kings 9 : 11–14, 26–28; 10 : 22. These friendly relations survived for a time the disastrous secession of the ten tribes, and a century later Ahab married a daughter of Ethbaal king of the Sidonians, 1 Kings 16 : 31, who, according to Menander, was daughter of Ithobal king of Tyre. When mercantile cupidity induced the Tyrians and the neighboring Phœnicians to buy Hebrew captives from their enemies, and to sell them as slaves to the Greeks and Edomites, there commenced denunciations, and at first threats of retaliation. Joel 3 : 4–8; Amos 1 : 9, 10. When Shalmaneser, king of Assyria, had taken the city of Samaria, had conquered the kingdom of Israel, and carried its inhabitants into captivity, he laid siege to Tyre, which, however, successfully resisted his arms. It is in reference to this siege that the prophecy against Tyre in Isaiah, ch. 23, was uttered. After the siege of Tyre by Shalmaneser (which must have taken place not long after 721 B.C.), Tyre remained a powerful state, with its own kings, Jer. 25 : 22; 27 : 3; Ezek. 28 : 2–12; remarkable for its wealth, with territory on the mainland, and protected by strong forti-

fications. Ezek. 26 : 4, 6, 8, 10, 12; 27 : 11; 28 : 5; Zech. 9 : 3. Our knowledge of its condition thenceforward until the siege by Nebuchadnezzar depends entirely on various notices of it by the Hebrew prophets; but some of these notices are singularly full, and especially the twenty-seventh chapter of Ezekiel furnishes us, on some points, with details such as have scarcely come down to us respecting any one city of antiquity excepting Rome and Athens. *Siege by Nebuchadnezzar.*—In the midst of great prosperity and wealth, which was the natural result of extensive trade, Ezek. 28 : 4, Nebuchadnezzar, at the head of an army of the Chaldees, invaded Judea and captured Jerusalem. As Tyre was so near to Jerusalem, and as the conquerors were a fierce and formidable race, Hab. 1 : 6, it would naturally be supposed that this event would have excited alarm and terror amongst the Tyrians. Instead of this, we may infer from Ezekiel's statement, Ezek. 26 : 2, that their predominant feeling was one of exultation. At first sight this appears strange and almost inconceivable; but it is rendered intelligible by some previous events in Jewish history. Only 34 years before

Ruins of the Wall of Tyre.

the destruction of Jerusalem commenced the celebrated reformation of Josiah, B.C. 622. This momentous religious revolution, 2 Kings 22, 23, fully explains the exultation and malevolence of the Tyr-

Modern Tyre. *(From a Photograph.)*

ians. In that reformation Josiah had heaped insults on the gods who were the objects of Tyrian veneration and love. Indeed, he seemed to have endeavored to exterminate their religion. 2 Kings 23: 20. These acts must have been regarded by the Tyrians as a series of sacrilegious and abominable outrages; and we can scarcely doubt that the death in battle of Josiah at Megiddo, and the subsequent destruction of the city and temple of Jerusalem, were hailed by them with triumphant joy as instances of divine retribution in human affairs. This joy, however, must soon have given way to other feelings, when Nebuchadnezzar invaded Phœnicia and laid siege to Tyre. That siege lasted thirteen years, and it is still a disputed point whether Tyre was actually taken by Nebuchadnezzar on this occasion. However this may be, it is probable that, on some terms or other, Tyre submitted to the Chaldees. The rule of Nebuchadnezzar over Tyre, though real, may have been light, and in the nature of an alliance. *Attack by the Persians; Capture by Alexander.*—During the Persian domination the Tyrians were subject in name to the Persian king, and may have given him tribute. With the rest of Phœnicia they had submitted to the Persians without striking a blow. Toward the close of the following century, B.C. 332, Tyre was assailed for the third time by a great conqueror. At that time Tyre was situated on an island nearly half a mile from the mainland; it was completely surrounded by prodigious walls, the loftiest portion of which on the side fronting the mainland reached a height of not less than 150 feet; and notwithstanding the persevering efforts of Alexander, he could not have succeeded in his attempt if the harbor of Tyre to the north had not been blockaded by the Cyprians and that to the south by the Phœnicians, thus affording an opportunity to Alexander for uniting the island to the mainland by an enormous artificial mole. (The materials for this he obtained from the remains of old Tyre, scraping the very dust from her rocks into the sea, as prophesied by Ezekiel, Ezek. 26 : 3, 4, 12, 21, more than 250 years before.) The immediate results of the capture by Alexander were most disastrous to Tyre, as its brave defenders were put to death; and in accordance with the barbarous policy of ancient times, 30,000 of its inhabitants, including slaves, free females and free children, were sold as slaves. It gradually, however, recovered its prosperity through the immigration of fresh settlers, though its trade is said to have suffered by the vicinity and rivalry of Alexandria. Under the Macedonian successors of Alexander it shared the fortunes of the Seleucidæ. Under the Romans, at first it enjoyed a kind of freedom. Subsequently, however, on the arrival of Augustus in the East, he is said to have deprived both Tyre and Sidon of their liberties for seditious conduct. Still the prosperity of Tyre in the time of Augustus was undeniably great. Strabo gives an account of it at that period, and speaks of the great wealth which it derived from the dyes of the celebrated Tyrian purple, which, as is well known, were extracted from shell-fish found on the coast, belonging to a species of the genus *Murex.* *Tyre in the time of Christ and since.*— When visited by Christ, Matt. 15 : 21; Mark 7 : 24, Tyre was perhaps more populous than Jerusalem, and if so it was undoubtedly the largest city which the Saviour is known to have visited. At the time of the crusades it was still a flourishing city, when it surrendered to the Christians on the 27th of June, 1144. It continued more than a century and a half in the hands of Christians, but was deserted by its inhabitants in A.D. 1291, upon the conquest of Acre (Ptolemais) by the sultan of Egypt and Damascus. This was the turning-point in the history of Tyre, which has never recovered from the blow. Its present condition is a fulfillment of Ezekiel's prophecy, Ezek. 26 : 5. It contains, according to Volney, 50 or 60 poor families, who live in part by fishing; and is, as Bruce describes it, "a rock whereon fishers dry their nets."

Ty′rus. This form is employed in the Authorized Version of the books of Jeremiah, Ezekiel, Hosea (Joel has "Tyre"), Amos and Zechariah, as follows: Jer. 25 : 22; 27 : 3; 47 : 4; Ezek. 26 : 2, 3, 4, 7, 15; 27 : 2, 3, 8, 32; 28 : 2, 12; 29 : 18; Hos. 9 : 13; Amos 1 : 9, 10; Zech. 9 : 2, 3.

U.

U'cal (*I am strong*). According to the received text of Prov. 30 : 1, Ithiel and Ucal must be regarded as proper names; and if so, they must be the names of disciples or sons of Agur the son of Jakeh, an unknown sage among the Hebrews. But there is great obscurity about the passage. Ewald considers both Ithiel and Ucal as symbolical names, employed by the poet to designate two classes of thinkers to whom he addresses himself.

U'el (*will of God*), one of the family of Bani, who during the captivity had married a foreign wife. Ezra 10 : 34. (B.C. 458.)

Uk'naz. In the margin of 1 Chron. 4 : 15 the words "even Kenaz" in the text are rendered "Uknaz," as the proper name.

U'la-i (*pure water*) is mentioned by Daniel, Dan. 8 : 2, 16, as a river near to Susa, where he saw his vision of the ram and the he-goat. It has been generally identified with the Eulæus of the Greek and Roman geographers, a large stream in the immediate neighborhood of that city. The Eulæus has been by many identified with the Choaspes, which is undoubtedly the modern *Kerkhah*, an affluent of the Tigris, flowing into it a little below *Kurnah*. Recent surveys show that the Choaspes once divided into two streams about 20 miles above Susa. The eastern was the Ulai. This bifurcation explains Dan. 8 : 16.

U'lam (*porch*). 1. A descendant of Gilead, the grandson of Manasseh and father of Bedan. 1 Chron. 7 : 17. (B.C. 1450.)

2. The first-born of Eshek, a descendant of the house of Saul. 1 Chron. 8 : 39, 40. (B.C. 588.)

Ul'la (*yoke*), an Asherite, head of a family in his tribe. 1 Chron. 7 : 39. (B.C. about 1014.)

Um'mah (*union*), one of the cities of the allotment of Asher. Josh. 19 : 30 only. Probably '*Alma*, in the highlands on the coast, about five miles east-northeast of *Ras en-Nakhûra*.

Unclean meats. These were things strangled, or dead of themselves or through beasts or birds of prey; whatever beast did not both part the hoof and chew the cud; and certain other smaller animals rated as "creeping things;" certain classes of birds mentioned in Lev. 11 and Deut. 14, twenty or twenty-one in all; whatever in the waters had not both fins and scales; whatever winged insect had not besides four legs the two hind-legs for leaping; besides things offered in sacrifice to idols; and all blood or whatever contained it (save perhaps the blood of fish, as would appear from that only of beast and bird being forbidden, Lev. 7 : 26), and therefore flesh cut from the live animal; as also all fat, at any rate that disposed in masses among the intestines, and probably wherever discernible and separable among the flesh. Lev. 3 : 14–17 ; 7 : 23. The eating of blood was prohibited even to "the stranger that sojourneth among you." Lev. 17 : 10, 12–14. As regards blood, the prohibition indeed dates from the declaration to Noah against "flesh with the life thereof, which is the blood thereof," in Gen. 9 : 4, which was perhaps regarded by Moses as still binding upon all Noah's descendants. It is noteworthy that the practical effect of the rule laid down is to exclude all the *carnivora* among quadrupeds, and, so far as we can interpret the nomenclature, the *raptores* among birds. They were probably excluded as being not averse to human carcasses, and in most eastern countries acting as the servitors of the battle-field and the gibbet. Among fish those which were allowed contain unquestionably the most wholesome varieties, save that they exclude the oyster. Practically the law left among the allowed meats an ample variety. As Orientals have minds sensitive to teaching by types, there can be little doubt that such ceremonial distinctions not only tended to keep Jew and Gentile apart (and so prevented the Jews from becoming contaminated with the idolatry of the Gentiles), but were a perpetual reminder to the former that he and the latter were not on one level before God. Hence, when that ceremony was changed we find that this was the very symbol selected to instruct St. Peter in the truth that God was not a "respecter of persons." It remains to mention the sanitary aspect of the case. Swine are said to be peculiarly liable to disease in their own bodies. This probably means that they are more easily led than other creatures to the foul feeding which produces it. As regards the animals allowed for food, comparing them with those forbidden, there can be no doubt on which side the balance of wholesomeness lies.

Uncleanness. The distinctive idea attached to ceremonial uncleanness among the Hebrews was that it cut a person off for the time from social privileges, and left his citizenship among God's people for the while in abeyance. There is an intense reality in the fact of the divine law taking hold of a man by the ordinary infirmities of flesh, and setting its stamp, as it were, in the lowest clay of which he is moulded. The sacredness attached to the human body is parallel to that which invested the ark of the covenant itself. It is as though Jehovah thereby would teach men that the "very hairs of their head were all numbered" before him, and that "in his book were all their members written." Thus was inculcated, so to speak, a bodily holiness. Nor were the Israelites to be only "separated from other people," but they were to be "holy *unto God*," Lev. 20 : 24, 26; "a kingdom of priests, and a holy nation." The importance to physical well-being of the injunctions which required frequent ablution, under whatever special pretexts, can be but feebly appreciated in our cooler and damper climate. Uncleanness, as referred to man, may be arranged in three degrees: 1. That which defiled merely "until even," and was removed by bathing and washing the clothes at the end of it; such were all contacts with dead animals. 2. That graver sort which defiled for seven days, and was removed by the use of the "water of separation;" such were all defilements connected with the human corpse. 3. Uncleanness from the morbid puerperal or menstrual state, lasting as long as that morbid state lasted; and in the case of leprosy lasting often for life. As the human person was itself the seat of a covenant token, so male and female had each their ceremonial obligations in proportion to their sexual differences. There is an emphatic reminder of human weakness in the fact of birth and death—man's passage alike into and out of his mortal state—being marked with a stated pollution. The corpse bequeathed a defilement of seven days to all who handled it, to the "tent" or chamber of death, and to sundry things within it. Nay, contact with one slain in the field of battle, or with even a human bone or grave, was no less effectual to pollute than that with a corpse dead by the course of nature. Num. 19 : 11-18. This shows that the source of pollution lay in the mere fact of death. The duration of defilement caused by the birth of a female infant being double that due to a male, extending respectively to eighty and forty days in all, Lev. 12 : 2-5, may perhaps represent the woman's heavier share in the first sin and first curse. Gen. 3 : 16; 1 Tim. ? : 14. Among causes of defilement should be noticed the fact that the ashes of the red heifer, burnt whole, which were mixed with water, and became the standing resource for purifying uncleanness in the second degree, themselves became a source of defilement to all who were *clean*, even as of purification to the unclean, and so the water. Somewhat similarly the scapegoat, who bore away the sins of the people, defiled him who led him into the wilderness, and the bringing forth and burning the sacrifice on the Great Day of Atonement had a similar power. This lightest form of uncleanness was expiated by bathing the body and washing the clothes. Besides the water of purification made as aforesaid, men and women, in their "issues," were, after seven days, reckoned from the cessation of the disorder, to bring two turtle-doves or young pigeons to be killed by the priests. All these kinds of uncleanness disqualified for holy functions: as the layman so affected might not approach the congregation and the sanctuary, so any priest who incurred defilement must abstain from holy things. Lev. 22 : 2-8. [LEPROSY.] The religion of the Persians shows a singularly close correspondence with the Levitical code.

Undergirding. Acts 27 : 17. [SHIP.]

Unicorn, the rendering of the Authorized Version of the Hebrew *rĕêm*, a word which occurs seven times in the Old Testament as the name of some large wild animal. The *rĕêm* of the Hebrew Bible, however, has nothing at all to do with the one-horned animal of the Greek and Roman writers, as is evident from Deut. 33 : 17, where, in the blessing of Joseph, it is said, "His glory is like the firstling of his bullock, and his horns are like the horns of *a unicorn;*" not, as the text of the Authorized Version renders it, "the horns of *unicorns*." The two horns of the *rĕêm* are "the ten thousands of Ephraim and the thousands of Manasseh." This text puts a one-horned animal entirely out of the question. Considering that the *rĕêm* is spoken of as a two-horned animal of great strength and ferocity, that it was evidently well known and often seen by the Jews, that it is mentioned as an animal fit for sacrificial purposes, and that it is frequently associated with bulls and oxen, we think there can be no doubt that some species of wild ox is intended. The allusion in Ps. 92 : 10, "But thou shalt lift up, as a

The Wild Ox (Unicorn).

rĕêym, my horn," seems to point to the mode in which the *Bovidœ* use their horns, lowering the head and then tossing it up. But it is impossible to determine what particular species of wild ox is signified. Probably some gigantic *urus* is intended. (It is probable that it was the gigantic *Bos primigenius,* or aurochs, now extinct, but of which Cæsar says, "These uri are scarcely less than elephants in size, but in their nature, color and form are bulls. Great is their strength and great their speed; they spare neither man nor beast when once they have caught sight of them."—*Bell. Gall.* vi. 20.—ED.)

Un′ni (*depressed*). 1. One of the Levite doorkeepers in the time of David. 1 Chron. 15 : 18, 20. (B.C. 1043.) 2. A second Levite (unless the family of the

foregoing be intended) concerned in the sacred office after the return from Babylon. Neh. 12 : 9. (B.C. 535.)

U′phaz. Jer. 10 : 9; Dan. 10 : 5. [OPHIR.]

Ur was the land of Haran's nativity, Gen. 11 : 28, the place from which Terah and Abraham started "to go into the land of Canaan." Gen. 11 : 31. It is called in Genesis "Ur of the Chaldæans," while in the Acts St. Stephen places it, by implication, in Mesopotamia. ch. 7 : 2, 4. These are all the indications which Scripture furnishes as to its locality. It has been identified by the most ancient traditions with the city of Orfah in the highlands of Mesopotamia, which unite the table-land of Armenia to the valley of the Euphrates. In later ages it was called Edessa, and was celebrated as the capital of Abgarus or Acbarus, who was said to have received the letter and portrait of our Saviour. "Two physical features must have secured Orfah, from the earliest times, as a nucleus for the civilization of those regions. One is a high-crested crag, the natural fortifications of the crested citadel. . . . The other is an abundant spring, issuing in a pool of transparent clearness, and embosomed in a mass of luxuriant verdure, which, amidst the dull-brown desert all around, makes, and must always have made, this spot an oasis, a paradise, in the Chaldæan wilderness. Round this sacred pool, 'the beautiful spring Callirrhoe,' as it was called by the Greek writers, gather the modern traditions of the patriarch."—Stanley, *Jewish Church,* part i. p. 7. A second tradition, which appears in the Talmud, finds Ur in Warka, 120 miles southeast from Babylon and four east of the Euphrates. It was the Orchoë of the Greeks, and probably the Ereck of Holy Scripture. This place bears the name of *Huruk* in the native inscriptions, and was in the countries known to the Jews as the land of the Chaldæans. But in opposition to the most ancient traditions, many modern writers have fixed the site of Ur at a very different position, viz. in the extreme south of Chaldæa, at *Mugheir,* not very far above—and probably in the time of Abraham actually upon—the head of the Persian Gulf. Among the ruins which are now seen at the spot are the remains of one of the great temples, of a model similar to that of Babel, dedicated to the moon, to whom the city was sacred. (Porter and Rawlinson favor this last place.)

Ur'bane, or **Ur'ba-ne** (*of the city; polite*), the Greek form of the Latin Urbanus, as it is given in the Revised Version. He was a Christian disciple who is in the long list of those whom St. Paul salutes in writing to Rome. Rom. 16 : 9. (A.D. 55.)

Ur'banus, the form given in the Revised Version for Urbane.

U'ri (*fiery*). 1. The father of Bezaleel, one of the architects of the tabernacle. Ex. 31 : 2; 35 : 30; 38 : 22; 1 Chron. 2 : 20; 2 Chron. 1 : 5. He was of the tribe of Judah, and grandson of Caleb ben-Hezron. (B.C. 1491.)

2. The father of Geber, Solomon's commissariat officer in Gilead. 1 Kings 4 : 19. (B.C. before 1010.)

3. One of the gatekeepers of the temple in the time of Ezra. Ezra 10 : 24. (B.C. 458.)

Uri'ah (*light of Jehovah*). 1. One of the thirty commanders of the thirty bands into which the Israelite army of David was divided. 1 Chron. 11 : 41; 2 Sam. 23 : 39. Like others of David's officers he was a foreigner—a Hittite. His name, however, and his manner of speech, 2 Sam. 11 : 11, indicate that he had adopted the Jewish religion. He married Bath-sheba, a woman of extraordinary beauty, the daughter of Eliam—possibly the same as the son of Ahithophel, and one of his brother officers, 2 Sam. 23 : 34, and hence, perhaps, Uriah's first acquaintance with Bath-sheba. It may be inferred from Nathan's parable, 2 Sam. 12 : 3, that he was passionately devoted to his wife, and that their union was celebrated in Jerusalem as one of peculiar tenderness. In the first war with Ammon, B.C. 1035, he followed Joab to the siege, and with him remained encamped in the open field. 2 Sam. 12 : 11. He returned to Jerusalem, at an order from the king on the pretext of asking news of the war—really in the hope that his return to his wife might cover the shame of his own crime. The king met with an unexpected obstacle in the austere, soldier-like spirit which guided all Uriah's conduct, and which gives us a high notion of the character and discipline of David's officers. On the morning of the third day David sent him back to the camp with a letter containing the command to Joab to cause his destruction in the battle. The device of Joab was to observe the part of the wall of Rabbath-ammon where the greatest force of the besieged was congregated, and thither, as a kind of forlorn hope, to send Uriah. A sally took place. Uriah and the officers with him advanced as far as the gate of the city, and were there shot down by the archers on the wall. Just as Joab had forewarned the messenger, the king broke into a furious passion on hearing of the loss. The messenger, as instructed by Joab, calmly continued, and ended the story with the words, "Thy servant also, Uriah the Hittite, is dead." In a moment David's anger is appeased. It is one of the touching parts of the story that Uriah falls unconscious of his wife's dishonor.

2. High priest in the reign of Ahaz. Isa. 8 : 2; 2 Kings 16 : 10-16. He is probably the same as Urijah the priest, who built the altar for Ahaz. 2 Kings 16 : 10. (B.C. about 738.)

3. A priest of the family of Hakkoz, the head of the seventh course of priests. Ezra 8 : 33; Neh. 3 : 4, 21. (B.C. 458.)

Uri'as. 1. Uriah, the husband of Bath-sheba. Matt. 1 : 6.

2. URIJAH, 3. 1 Esdr. 9 : 43.

U'ri-el (*the fire of God*), an angel named only in 2 Esdr. 4 : 1, 36; 5 : 20; 10 : 28.

U'ri-el. 1. A Kohathite Levite, son of Tahath. 1 Chron. 6 : 24.

2. Chief of the Kohathites in the reign of David. 1 Chron. 15 : 5, 11. (B.C. 1043.)

3. Uriel of Gibeah was the father of Maachah or Michaiah, the favorite wife of Rehoboam and mother of Abijah. 2 Chron. 13 : 2. (B.C. before 973.) In 2 Chron. 11 : 20 she is called "Maachah the daughter of Absalom." Probably her mother, Tamar, was the daughter of Absalom.

Uri'jah (*light of Jehovah*). 1. Urijah the priest in the reign of Ahaz, 2 Kings 16 : 10, probably the same as URIAH, 2.

2. A priest of the family of Koz or Hakkoz, the same as URIAH, 3.

3. One of the priests who stood at Ezra's right hand when he read the law to the people. Neh. 8 : 4. (B.C. 458.)

4. The son of Shemaiah of Kirjathjearim. He prophesied in the days of Jehoiakim, B.C. 608, and the king sought to put him to death; but he escaped, and fled into Egypt. His retreat was soon dis-

covered; Elnathan and his men brought him up out of Egypt, and Jehoiakim slew him with the sword and cast his body forth among the graves of the common people. Jer. 26 : 20–23.

U'rim and Thum'mim (*light and perfection*). When the Jewish exiles were met on their return from Babylon by a question which they had no data for answering, they agreed to postpone the settlement of the difficulty till there should rise up "a priest with Urim and Thummim." Ezra 2 : 63; Neh. 7 : 65. The inquiry what those Urim and Thummim themselves were seems likely to wait as long for a final and satisfying answer. On every side we meet with confessions of ignorance. *Urim* means "light," and *Thummim* "perfection." *Scriptural statements.*—The mysterious words meet us for the first time, as if they needed no explanation, in the description of the high priest's apparel. Over the ephod there is to be a "breastplate of judgment" of gold, scarlet, purple and fine linen, folded square and doubled, a "span" in length and width. In it are to be set four rows of precious stones, each stone with the name of a tribe of Israel engraved on it, that Aaron "may bear them on his heart." Then comes a further order. Inside the breastplate, as the tables of the covenant were placed inside the ark, Ex. 25 : 16; 28 : 30, are to be placed "the Urim and the Thummim," the light and the perfection; and they too are to be on Aaron's heart when he goes in before the Lord. Ex. 28 : 15–30. Not a word describes them. They are mentioned as things already familiar both to Moses and the people, connected naturally with the functions of the high priest as mediating between Jehovah and his people. The command is fulfilled. Lev. 8 : 8. They pass from Aaron to Eleazar with the sacred ephod and other *pontificalia*. Num. 20 : 28. When Joshua is solemnly appointed to succeed the great hero-lawgiver, he is bidden to stand before Eleazar, the priest, "who shall ask counsel for him after the judgment of Urim," and this counsel is to determine the movements of the host of Israel. Num. 27 : 21. In the blessings of Moses they appear as the crowning glory of the tribe of Levi: "thy Thummim and thy Urim are with thy Holy One." Deut. 33 : 8, 9. In what way the Urim and Thummin were consulted is quite uncertain. Josephus and the rabbins supposed that the stones gave out the oracular answer by preternatural illumination; but it seems to be far simpler and more in agreement with the different accounts of inquiries made by Urim and Thummim, 1 Sam. 14 : 3, 18, 19; 23 : 2, 4, 9, 11, 12; 28 : 6; Judges 20 : 28; 2 Sam. 5 : 23, etc., to suppose that the answer was given simply by the word of the Lord to the high priest, comp. John 11 : 51, when, clothed with the ephod and the breastplate, he had inquired of the Lord. Such a view agrees with the true notion of the breastplate.

Usury. (The word usury has come in modern English to mean excessive interest upon money loaned, either formally illegal or at least oppressive. In the Scriptures, however, the word did not bear this sense, but meant simply interest of any kind upon money. The Jews were forbidden by the law of Moses to take interest from their brethren, but were permitted to take it from foreigners. The prohibition grew out of the agricultural status of the people, in which ordinary business loans were not needed, and such loans as were required should be made only as to friends and brothers in need.—ED.) The practice of mortgaging land, sometimes at exorbitant interest, grew up among the Jews during the captivity, in direct violation of the law. Lev. 25 : 36, 37; Ezek. 18 : 8, 13, 17. We find the rate reaching 1 in 100 per month, corresponding to the Roman *centesimæ usuræ*, or 12 per cent. per annum.

U'ta. 1 Esdr. 5 : 30. It appears to be a corruption of AKKUB. Ezra 2 : 45.

U'tha-i (*helpful*). 1. The son of Ammihud, of the children of Pharez the son of Judah. 1 Chron. 9 : 4. (B.C. 536.)

2. One of the sons of Bigvai, who returned in the second caravan with Ezra. Ezra 8 : 14. (B.C. 459.)

U'thii. 1 Esdr. 8 : 40. [UTHAI, 2.]

Uz (*wooded*). 1. A son of Aram, Gen. 10 : 23; 1 Chron. 1 : 17, and consequently a grandson of Shem. (B.C. 2400–2300.)

2. A son of Nahor by Milcah. Gen. 22 : 21; Authorized Version, Huz. (B.C. about 1900.)

3. A son of Dishan, and grandson of Seir. Gen. 36 : 28. (B.C. after 1800.)

4. The country in which Job lived. Job 1 : 1. As far as we can gather, "the land of Uz" lay either east or southeast of Palestine, Job 1 : 3; adjacent to the Sabæans and the Chaldæans, Job 1 : 15, 17, consequently north of the southern Arabians and west of the Euphrates;

and, lastly, adjacent to the Edomites of Mount Seir, who at one period occupied Uz, probably as conquerors, Lam. 4 : 21, and whose troglodyte habits are probably described in Job 30 : 6, 7. From the above data we infer that the land of Uz corresponds to the *Arabia Deserta* of classical geography, at all events to so much of it as lies north of the 30th parallel of latitude.

U'za-i (*strong*), the father of Palal, who assisted Nehemiah in rebuilding the city wall. Neh. 3 : 25. (B.C. before 446.)

U'zal (*separate*), the sixth son of Joktan, Gen. 10 : 27 ; 1 Chron. 1 : 21, whose settlements are clearly traced in the ancient name of *San'à*, the capital city of the Yemen (a district of Arabia), which was originally *Awzàl*. From its position in the centre of the best portion of that kingdom, it must always have been an important city. (San'à is situated about 150 miles from Aden and 100 miles from the coast of the Red Sea. It is one of the most imposing cities of Arabia.—ED.)

Uz'za (*strength*). 1. A Benjamite of the sons of Ehud. 1 Chron. 8 : 7. (B.C. 1445.)

2. Elsewhere called UZZAH. 1 Chron. 13 : 7, 9, 10, 11. [UZZAH.]

3. The children of Uzza were a family of Nethinim who returned with Zerubbabel. Ezra 2 : 49 ; Neh. 7 : 51. (B.C. before 536.)

4. Properly Uzzah. As the text now stands, Uzzah is a descendant of Merari, 1 Chron. 6 : 29 (14) ; but there appears to be a gap in the verse. Perhaps he is the same as Zina or Zizah, the son of Shimei. 1 Chron. 23 : 10, 11 ; for these names evidently denote the same person, and, in Hebrew character, are not unlike Uzzah.

Uz'za, The garden of, the spot in which Manasseh king of Judah and his son Amon were buried. 2 Kings 21 : 18, 26. It was the garden attached to Manasseh's palace. ver. 18. The fact of its mention shows that it was not where the usual sepulchres of the kings were. No clue, however, is afforded to its position.

Uz'za, or **Uz'zah** (*strength*), one of the sons of Abinadab, in whose house at Kirjath-jearim the ark rested for twenty years. Uzzah probably was the second and Ahio the third. They both accompanied its removal when David first undertook to carry it to Jerusalem. (B.C. 1043.) Ahio apparently went before the new cart, 1 Chron. 13 : 7, on which it was placed, and Uzzah walked by the side.

"At the threshing-floor of Nachon," 2 Sam. 6 : 6, or Chidon, 1 Chron. 13 : 9, perhaps slipping over the smooth rock, the oxen stumbled. Uzzah caught the ark to prevent its falling. The profanation was punished by his instant death, to the great grief of David, who named the place Perez-uzzah (*the breaking-forth on Uzzah*). But Uzzah's fate was not merely the penalty of his own rashness. The improper mode of transporting the ark, which ought to have been borne on the shoulders of the Levites, was the primary cause of his unholy deed; and David distinctly recognized it as a punishment on the people in general, "because we sought him not after the due order."

Uz'zen-she'rah (*ear* (or point) *of Sherah*), a town founded or rebuilt by Sherah, an Ephraimite woman, the daughter either of Ephraim himself or of Beriah. It is named only in 1 Chron. 7 : 24, in connection with the two Beth-horons.

Uz'zi (*strong*). 1. Son of Bukki, and father of Zerahiah, in the line of the high priests. 1 Chron. 6 : 5, 51 ; Ezra 7 : 4. Though Uzzi was the lineal ancestor of Zadok, it does not appear that he was ever high priest. He must have been contemporary with, but rather earlier than, Eli. (B.C. before 1161.)

2. Son of Tola the son of Issachar. 1 Chron. 7 : 2, 3. (B.C. 1706.)

3. Son of Bela, of the tribe of Benjamin. 1 Chron. 7 : 7. (B.C. 1706.)

4. Another, or the same, from whom descended some Benjamite houses, which were settled at Jerusalem after the return from captivity. 1 Chron. 9 : 8.

5. A Levite, son of Bani, and overseer of the Levites dwelling at Jerusalem, in the time of Nehemiah. Neh. 11 : 22.

6. A priest, chief of the father's house of Jedaiah, in the time of Joiakim the high priest. Neh. 12 : 19. (B.C. about 500.)

7. One of the priests who assisted Ezra in the dedication of the wall of Jerusalem. Neh. 12 : 42. Perhaps the same as the preceding. (B.C. 446.)

Uzzi'a (*strength of Jehovah*), one of David's guard, and apparently a native of Ashtaroth beyond Jordan. 1 Chron. 11 : 44. (B.C. 1053.)

Uzzi'ah (*strength of Jehovah*). 1. King of Judah B.C. 810 to 758. In some passages his name appears in the lengthened form Azariah. After the murder of Amaziah, his son Uzziah was chosen by the people, at the age of sixteen, to occupy the vacant throne; and for the greater part of his long reign of fifty-two years he lived in the fear of God, and showed himself a wise, active and pious ruler. He never deserted the worship of the true God, and was much influenced by Zechariah, a prophet who is mentioned only in connection with him. 2 Chron. 26 : 5. So the southern kingdom was raised to a condition of prosperity which it had not known since the death of Solomon. The end of Uzziah was less prosperous than his beginning. Elated with his splendid career, he determined to burn incense on the altar of God, but was opposed by the high priest Azariah and eighty others. See Ex. 30 : 7, 8; Num. 16 : 40; 18 : 7. The king was enraged their resistance, and, as he pressed forward with his censer, was suddenly smitten with leprosy. This lawless attempt to burn incense was the only exception to the excellence of his administration. 2 Chron. 27 : 2. Uzziah was buried " with his fathers," yet apparently not actually in the royal sepulchres. 2 Chron. 26 : 23. During his reign a great earthquake occurred. Amos 1 : 1; Zech. 14 : 5.

2. A Kohathite Levite, and ancestor of Samuel. 1 Chron. 6 : 24 (9).

3. A priest of the sons of Harim, who had taken a foreign wife in the days of Ezra. Ezra 10 : 21. (B.C. 458.)

4. Father of Athaiah or Uthai. Neh. 11 : 4.

5. Father of Jehonathan, one of David's overseers. 1 Chron. 27 : 25. (B.C. about 1053.)

Uzzi'el (*my strength is God*). 1. Fourth son of Kohath, father of Mishael, Elzaphan or Elizaphan and Zithri, and uncle to Aaron. Ex. 6 : 18, 22; Lev. 10 : 4. (B.C. before 1491.)

2. A Simeonite captain, son of Ishi, in the days of Hezekiah. 1 Chron. 4 : 42.

3. Head of a Benjamite house, of the sons of Bela. 1 Chron. 7 : 7. (B.C. 1706.)

4. A musician, of the sons of Heman, in David's reign. 1 Chron. 25 : 4.

5. A Levite, of the sons of Jeduthun, in the days of Hezekiah. 2 Chron. 29 : 14, 18. (B.C. 726.)

6. Son of Harhaiah, probably a priest in the days of Nehemiah, who took part in repairing the wall. Neh. 3 : 8. (B.C. 446.) He is described as " of the goldsmiths," *i. e.* of those priests whose hereditary office it was to repair or make the sacred vessels.

Uzzi'elites, The, the descendants of Uzziel, and one of the four great families of the Kohathites. Num. 3 : 27; 1 Chron. 26 : 23.

V.

Vajez'atha (*strong as the wind*), one of the ten sons of Haman whom the Jews slew in Shushan. Esther 9 : 9. (B.C. 473.)

Vale, Valley. It is hardly necessary to state that these words signify a hollow sweep of ground between two more or less parallel ridges of high land. The structure of the greater part of the holy land does not lend itself to the formation of valleys in our sense of the word. The abrupt transitions of its crowded rocky hills preclude the existence of any extended sweep of valley. Valley is employed in the Authorized Version to render five distinct Hebrew words. 1. *'Émek.* This appears to approach more nearly to the general sense of the English word than any other. It is connected with several places. 2. *Gaï* or *gê.* Of this there is fortunately one example which can be identified with certainty—the deep hollow which compasses the southwest and south of Jerusalem. This identification establishes the *gê* as a deep and abrupt ravine, with steep sides and narrow bottom. 3. *Nachal.* This word answers to the Arabic *wady*, and expresses, as no single English word can, the bed of a stream (often wide and shelving, and like a "valley" in character, which in the rainy season may be nearly filled by a foaming torrent, though for the greater part of the year dry). 4. *Bik'âh.* This term appears to mean rather a plain than a valley, though so far resembling it as to be enclosed by mountains. It is rendered by "valley" in Deut. 34 : 3; Josh. 11 : 3, 17; 12 : 7; 2 Chron. 35 : 22; Zech. 12 : 11. 5. *has-Shĕfêlâh.* The district to which the name *has-Shĕfêlâh* is applied in the Bible has no resemblance whatever to a valley, but is a broad, swelling tract of many hundred miles in area, which sweeps gently down from the mountains of Judah to the Mediterranean. It is rendered "the vale" in Deut. 1 : 7; Josh. 10 : 40; 1 Kings 10 : 27; 2 Chron. 1 : 15; Jer. 33 : 13; and "the valley" or "the valleys" in Josh. 9 : 1; 11 : 2, 16; 12 : 8; 15 : 33; Judges 1 : 9; Jer. 32 : 44.

Vani'ah (*Jehovah is praise*), one of the sons of Bani. Ezra 10 : 36. (B.C. 458.)

Vash'ni (*strong*), the first-born of Samuel as the text now stands, 1 Chron. 6 : 28 (13); but in 1 Sam. 8 : 2 the name of his first-born is Joel. Most probably in the Chronicles the name of Joel has dropped out, and Vashni is a corruption of *veshênî*, " and (the) second."

Vash'ti (*beautiful*), the " queen " of Ahasuerus, who, for refusing to show herself to the king's guests at the royal banquet, when sent for by the king, was repudiated and deposed. Esther 1. (B.C. 483.) Many attempts have been made to identify her with historical personages; but it is far more probable that she was only one of the inferior wives, dignified with the title of queen, whose name has utterly disappeared from history.

Veil.

Veil. With regard to the use of the veil, it is important to observe that it was by no means so general in ancient as in modern times. Much of the scrupulousness in respect of the use of the veil dates from the promulgation of the Koran, which forbade women appearing unveiled except in the presence of their nearest relatives. In ancient times the veil was adopted only in exceptional cases, either as an article of ornamental dress, Cant. 4 : 1, 3; 6 : 7, or by betrothed maidens in the presence of their future husbands, especially at the time of the wedding, Gen. 24 : 65; or, lastly, by women of loose character for purposes of concealment. Gen. 38 : 14. Among the Jews of the New Testament age it appears to have been customary for the women to cover their heads (not necessarily their faces) when engaged in public worship.

Veil of the tabernacle and temple. [TABERNACLE ; TEMPLE.]

Versions, Ancient, of the Old and New Testaments. In treating of the ancient versions that have come down to us, in whole or in part, they will be described in the alphabetical order of the languages.

ÆTHIOPIC VERSION. — Christianity was introduced into Æthiopia in the fourth century, through the labors of Frumentius and Ædesius of Tyre, who had been made slaves and sent to the king. The Æthiopic version which we possess is in the ancient dialect of Axum ; hence some have ascribed it to the age of the earliest missionaries, but it is probably of a later date. In 1548-9 the Æthiopic New Testament was also printed at Rome, edited by three Abyssinians.

ARABIC VERSIONS. — 1. *Arabic versions of the Old Testament* were made from the Hebrew (tenth century), from the Syriac and from the LXX. 2. *Arabic versions of the New Testament.* There are four versions. The first, the Roman, of the Gospels only, was printed in 1590-1.

ARMENIAN VERSION. — In the year 431, Joseph and Eznak returned from the Council of Ephesus, bringing with them a Greek copy of the Scriptures. From this a version in Armenian was made by Isaac, the Armenian patriarch, and Miesrob. The first printed edition of the Old and New Testaments in Armenian appeared at Amsterdam in 1666, under the care of a person commonly termed Oscan or Uscan, and described as being an Armenian bishop.

CHALDEE VERSIONS. — *Targum*, a Chaldee word of uncertain origin, is the general term for the Chaldee, or more accurately Aramaic, versions of the Old Testament. 1. The Targums were originally oral, and the earliest Targum, which is that of Onkelos on the Pentateuch, began to be committed to writing about the second century of the Christian era ; though it did not assume its present shape till the end of the third or the beginning of the fourth century. So far, however, from superseding the oral Targum at once, it was, on the contrary, strictly forbidden to read it in public. Its language is Chaldee, closely approaching in purity of idiom to that of Ezra and Daniel. It follows a sober and clear though not a slavish exegesis, and keeps as closely and minutely to the text as is at all consistent with its purpose, viz. to be chiefly and above all *a version for the people.* Its explanations of difficult and obscure passages bear ample witness to the competence of those who gave it its final shape. It avoids, as far as circumstances would allow, the legendary character with which all the later Targums entwine the biblical word. 2. *Targum on the prophets,—*viz. Joshua, Judges, Samuel, Kings, Isaiah, Jeremiah, Ezekiel and the twelve minor prophets,—called TARGUM OF JONATHAN BEN-UZZIEL. We shall probably not be far wrong in placing this Targum some time, although not long, after Onkelos, or about the middle of the fourth century. 3 and 4. *Targum of Jonathan ben-Uzziel and Jerushalmi-Targum on the Pentateuch.*—Onkelos and Jonathan on the Pentateuch and prophets, whatever be their exact date, place, authorship and editorship, are the oldest of existing Targums, and belong, in their present shape, to Babylon and the Babylonian academies flourishing between the third and fourth centuries A.D.

EGYPTIAN VERSIONS.—Of these there are three,—the *Memphitic*, of lower Egypt, the Coptic, of upper Egypt, and the *Thebaic*, with some fragments of another. The Thebaic was the earliest, and belongs to the third century.

GOTHIC VERSION.—In the year 318 the Gothic bishop and translator of Scripture, Ulphilas, was born. He succeeded Theophilus as bishop of the Goths in 348 ; through him it is said that the Goths in general adopted Arianism. The great work of Ulphilas was his version of the Scriptures. As an ancient monument of the Gothic language the version of Ulphilas possesses great interest ; as a version the use of which was once extended widely through Europe, it is a monument of the Christianization of the Goths ; and as a version *known* to have been made in the fourth century, and transmitted to us in ancient MSS., it has its value in textual criticism.

GREEK VERSIONS OF THE OLD TESTAMENT.—1. *Septuagint.*—[See SEPTUAGINT.] 2. *Aquila.*—It is a remarkable fact that in the second century there were three versions executed of the Old Testament Scriptures into Greek. The first of these was made by Aquila, a native of Sinope in Pontus, who had become a proselyte to Judaism. It was made during the reign of Hadrian, A.D. 117–138. 3. *Theodotion.*—The second version of which we have information as executed in the second century is that of Theodotion. He is stated to have been an Ephesian, and he seems to be most generally described as an Ebionite. 4. *Symmachus* is stated by Eusebius and Jerome to have been an Ebionite; Epiphanius and others, however, style him a Samaritan. It may be that as a Samaritan he made this version for some of that people who employed Greek, and who had learned to receive more than the Pentateuch.

LATIN VERSIONS.—[VULGATE.]

SAMARITAN VERSIONS.—[SAMARITAN PENTATEUCH.]

SLAVONIC VERSION. — In A.D. 862 there was a desire expressed or an inquiry made for Christian teachers in Moravia, and in the following year the labors of missionaries began among the Moravians. These missionaries were Cyrillus and Methodius, two brothers from Thessalonica. To Cyrillus is ascribed the invention of the Slavonian alphabet and the commencement of the translation of the Scriptures. He appears to have died at Rome in 868, while Methodius continued for many years to be the bishop of the Slavonians. He is stated to have continued his brother's translation.

SYRIAC VERSIONS. — 1. *Of the Old Testament.* (*a*) From the Hebrew. In the early times of Syrian Christianity there was executed a version of the Old Testament from the original Hebrew, the use of which must have been as widely extended as was the Christian profession among that people. It is highly improbable that any part of the Syriac version is older than the advent of our Lord. The Old Syriac has the peculiar value of being the first version from the Hebrew original made for Christian use. The first printed edition of this version was that which appeared in the Paris Polyglot of Le Jay in 1645. (*b*) The Syriac version from the Hexaplar Greek text. The only Syriac version of the Old Testament up to the sixth century was apparently the Peshito. The version

by Paul of Tela, a Monophysite, was made in the beginning of the seventh century; for its basis he used the Hexaplar Greek text—that is, the LXX., with the corrections of Origen, the asterisks, obeli, etc., and with the references to the other Greek versions. In fact, it is from this Syriac version that we obtain our most accurate acquaintance with the results of the critical labors of Origen. It is from a MS. in the Ambrosian Library at Milan that we possess accurate means of knowing this Syriac version. 2. *The Syriac New Testament Versions.* (*a*) The Peshito Syriac New Testament. It may stand as an admitted fact that a version of the New Testament in Syriac existed in the second century. (*b*) The Curetonian Syriac Gospels. Among the MSS. brought from the Nitrian monasteries in 1842, Dr. Cureton noticed a copy of the Gospels, differing greatly from the common text; and this is the form of text to which the name of Curetonian Syriac has been rightly applied. Every criterion which proves the common Peshito not to exhibit a text of extreme antiquity equally proves the early origin of this.

Versions, Authorized. 1. WYCLIFFE.—The New Testament was translated by Wycliffe himself. The Old Testament was undertaken by Nicholas de Hereford, but was interrupted, and ends abruptly (following so far the order of the Vulgate) in the middle of Baruch. The version was based entirely upon the Vulgate. The following characteristics may be noticed as distinguishing this version: (1) The general homeliness of its style. (2) The substitution, in many cases, of English equivalents for quasi-technical words. (3) The extreme literalness with which in some instances, even at the cost of being unintelligible, the Vulgate text is followed, as in 2 Cor. 1 : 17–19.

2. TYNDAL.—The work of Wycliffe stands by itself. Whatever power it exercised in preparing the way for the Reformation of the sixteenth century, it had no perceptible influence on later translations. With Tyndal we enter on a continuous succession. He is the patriarch, in no remote ancestry, of the Authorized Version. More than Cranmer or Ridley he is the true hero of the English Reformation. "Ere many years," he said at the age of thirty-six (A.D. 1520), he would cause "a boy that driv-

eth the plough" to know more of Scripture than the great body of the clergy then knew. He prepared himself for the work by long years of labor in Greek and Hebrew. First the Gospels of St. Matthew and St. Mark were published tentatively. In 1525 the whole of the New Testament was printed in quarto at Cologne, and in small octavo at Worms. In England it was received with denunciations. Tonstal, bishop of London, preaching at Paul's Cross, asserted that there were at least two thousand errors in it, and ordered all copies of it to be bought up and burnt. An act of Parliament (35 Hen. VIII. cap. 1) forbade the use of all copies of Tyndal's "false translation." The treatment which it received from professed friends was hardly less annoying. In the mean time the work went on. Editions were printed one after another. The last appeared in 1535, just before his death. To Tyndal belongs the honor of having given the first example of a translation based on true principles, and the excellence of later versions has been almost in exact proportion as they followed his. All the exquisite grace and simplicity which have endeared the Authorized Version to men of the most opposite tempers and contrasted opinions is due mainly to his clear-sighted truthfulness.

3. COVERDALE.—A complete translation of the Bible, different from Tyndal's, bearing the name of Miles Coverdale, printed probably at Zurich, appeared in 1535. The undertaking itself, and the choice of Coverdale as the translator, were probably due to Cromwell. He was content to make the translation at second hand "out of the Douche (Luther's German Version) and the Latine." Fresh editions of his Bible were published, keeping their ground in spite of rivals, in 1537, 1539, 1550, 1553. He was called in at a still later period to assist in the Geneva Version.

4. MATTHEW. — In the year 1537, a large folio Bible appeared as edited and dedicated to the king by Thomas Matthew. No one of that name appears at all prominently in the religious history of Henry VIII., and this suggests the inference that the name was adopted to conceal the real translator. The tradition which connects this Matthew with John Rogers, the proto-martyr of the Marian persecution, is all but undisputed. Matthew's Bible reproduces Tyndal's work, in the New Testament entirely, in the Old Testament as far as 2 Chron., the rest being taken with occasional modifications from Coverdale. A copy was ordered, by royal proclamation, to be set up in every church, the cost being divided between the clergy and the parishioners. This was, therefore, the first Authorized Version.

5. TAVERNER (1539).—The boldness of the pseudo-Matthew had frightened the ecclesiastical world from its propriety. Coverdale's version was, however, too inaccurate to keep its ground. It was necessary to find another editor, and the printers applied to Richard Taverner. But little is known of his life. The fact that, though a layman, he had been chosen as one of the canons of the Cardinal's College at Oxford indicates a reputation for scholarship, and this is confirmed by the character of his translation. In most respects this may be described as an expurgated edition of Matthew's.

6. CRANMER.—In the same year as Taverner's, and coming from the same press, appeared an English Bible, in a more stately folio, with a preface containing the initials T. C., which implied the archbishop's sanction. Cranmer's version presented, as might be expected, many points of interest. The prologue gave a more complete ideal of what a translation ought to be than had as yet been seen. Words not in the original were to be printed in a different type. It was reprinted again and again, and was the Authorized Version of the English Church till 1568—the interval of Mary's reign excepted. From it, accordingly, were taken most, if not all, the portions of Scripture in the Prayer-books of 1549 and 1552. The Psalms as a whole, the quotations from Scripture in the Homilies, the sentences in the Communion Services, and some phrases elsewhere, still preserve the remembrance of it.

7. GENEVA.—The exiles who fled to Geneva in the reign of Mary entered on the work of translation with more vigor than ever. The Genevan refugees—among them Whittingham, Goodman, Pullain, Sampson and Coverdale himself—labored "for two years or more, day and night." Their translation of the New Testament was "diligently revised by the most approved Greek examples." The New Testament, trans-

lated by Whittingham, was printed in 1557, and the whole Bible in 1560. Whatever may have been its faults, the Geneva Bible, commonly called the Breeches Bible from its rendering of Gen. 3 : 7, was unquestionably, for sixty years, the most popular of all versions. Not less than eighty editions, some of the whole Bible, were printed between 1558 and 1611. It kept its ground for some time even against the Authorized Version, and gave way, as it were, slowly and under protest. It was the version specially adopted by the great Puritan party through the whole reign of Elizabeth and far into that of James. As might be expected, it was based on Tyndal's version. It presents, in a calendar prefixed to the Bible, something like a declaration of war against the established order of the Church's lessons commemorating Scripture facts and the deaths of the great reformers, but ignoring saints' days altogether. It was the first English Bible which entirely omitted the Apocrypha. The notes were characteristically Swiss, not only in their theology, but in their politics.

8. THE BISHOPS' BIBLE.—The facts just stated will account for the wish of Archbishop Parker to bring out another version, which might establish its claims against that of Geneva. Great preparations were made. Eight bishops, together with some deans and professors, brought out the fruit of their labors in a magnificent folio (1568 and 1572). It was avowedly based on Cranmer's; but of all the English versions it had probably the least success. It did not command the respect of scholars, and its size and cost were far from meeting the wants of the people.

9. RHEIMS AND DOUAY.—The successive changes in the Protestant versions of the Scriptures were, as might be expected, matter of triumph to the controversialists of the Latin Church. Some saw in it an argument against any translation of Scripture into the spoken language of the people. Others pointed derisively to the want of unity which these changes displayed. There were some, however, who took the line which Sir T. More and Gardiner had taken under Henry VIII. They did not object to the principle of an English translation. They only charged all the versions hitherto made with being false, corrupt, heretical. To this there was the ready retort that they had done nothing; that their bishops in the reign of Henry had promised, but had not performed. It was felt to be necessary that they should take some steps which might enable them to turn the edge of this reproach. The English Catholic refugees who were settled at Rheims undertook a new English version. The New Testament was published at Rheims in 1582, and professed to be based on "the authentic text of the Vulgate." Notes were added, as strongly dogmatic as those of the Geneva Bible, and often keenly controversial. The work of translation was completed somewhat later by the publication of the Old Testament at Douay in 1609.

10. AUTHORIZED VERSION.—The position of the English Church in relation to the versions in use at the commencement of the reign of James was hardly satisfactory. The Bishops' Bible was sanctioned by authority. That of Geneva had the strongest hold on the affections of the people. Scholars, Hebrew scholars in particular, found grave fault with both. Among the demands of the Puritan representatives at the Hampton Court Conference in 1604 was one for a new, or at least a revised, translation. The work of organizing and superintending the arrangements for a new translation was one specially congenial to James, and accordingly in 1606 the task was commenced. It was intrusted · to 54 scholars. The following were the instructions given to the translators: (1) The Bishops' Bible was to be followed, and as little altered as the original would permit. (2) The names of prophets and others were to be retained, as nearly as may be, as they are vulgarly used. (3) The old ecclesiastical words to be kept. (4) When any word hath divers significations, that to be kept which hath been most commonly used by the most eminent fathers, being agreeable to the propriety of the place and the analogy of faith. (5) The division of the chapters to be altered either not at all or as little as possible. (6) No marginal notes to be affixed but only for the explanation of Hebrew and Greek words. (7) Such quotations of places to be marginally set down as may serve for fit reference of one Scripture to another. (8 and 9) State plan of translation. Each company of translators is to take its own books; each person to bring his own corrections. The company to discuss

them, and having finished their work, to send it on to another company, and so on. (10) Provides for differences of opinion between two companies by referring them to a general meeting. (11) Gives power, in cases of difficulty, to consult any scholars. (12) Invites suggestions from any quarter. (13) Names the directors of the work: Andrews, dean of Westminster; Barlow, dean of Chester; and the regius professors of Hebrew and Greek at both universities. (14) Names translations to be followed when they agree more with the original than the Bishops' Bible, sc. Tyndal's, Coverdale's, Matthew's, Whitchurch's (Cranmer's), and Geneva. (15) Authorizes universities to appoint three or four overseers of the work. For three years the work went on, the separate companies comparing notes as directed. When the work drew toward its completion, it was necessary to place it under the care of a select few. Two from each of the three groups were accordingly selected, and the six met in London to superintend the publication. The final correction, and the task of writing the arguments of the several books, was given to Bilson, bishop of Winchester, and Dr. Miles Smith, the latter of whom also wrote the dedication and preface. The version thus published did not at once supersede the versions already in possession. The fact that five editions were published in three years shows that there was a good demand. But the Bishops' Bible probably remained in many churches, and the popularity of the Geneva Version is shown by not less than thirteen reprints, in whole or in part, between 1611 and 1617. It is not easy to ascertain the impression which the Authorized Version made at the time of its appearance. Selden says it is "the best of all translations, as giving the true sense of the original." [For REVISED VERSION (of 1881), see under BIBLE.]

Village. This word, in addition to its ordinary sense, is often used, especially in the enumeration of towns in Josh. 13: 15, 19, to imply unwalled suburbs outside the walled towns. Arab villages, as found in Arabia, are often mere collections of stone huts, "long, low, rude hovels, roofed only with the stalks of palm leaves," or covered for a time with tent-cloths, which are removed when the tribe change their quarters. Others are more solidly built, as are most of the modern villages of Palestine, though in some the dwellings are mere mud-huts.

Vine, the well-known valuable plant (*Vitis vinifera*) very frequently referred to in the Old and New Testaments, and cultivated from the earliest times. The first mention of this plant occurs in Gen.

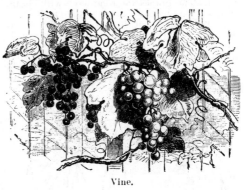

Vine.

9 : 20, 21. That it was abundantly cultivated in Egypt is evident from the frequent representations on the monuments, as well as from the scriptural allusions. Gen. 40 : 9–11 ; Ps. 78 : 47. The vines of Palestine were celebrated both for luxuriant growth and for the immense clusters of grapes which they produced, which were sometimes carried on a staff between two men, as in the case of the spies, Num. 13 : 23, and as has been done in some instances in modern times. Special mention is made in the Bible of the vines of Eshcol, Num. 13 : 24 ; 32 : 9, of Sibmah, Heshbon and Elealeh, Isa. 16 : 8, 9, 10 ; Jer. 48 : 32, and of Engedi, Cant. 1 : 14. From the abundance and excellence of the vines, it may readily be understood how frequently this plant is the subject of metaphor in the Holy Scriptures. To dwell under the vine and fig tree is an emblem of domestic happiness and peace, 1 Kings 4 : 25 ; Ps. 128 : 3 ; Micah 4 : 4 ; the rebellious people of Israel are compared to "wild grapes," "an empty vine," "the degenerate plant of a strange vine," etc. Isa. 5 : 2, 4 ; Jer. 2 : 21 ; Hos. 10 : 1. It is a vine which our Lord selects to show the spiritual union which subsists between himself and his members. John 15 : 1–6. The ancient

Hebrews probably allowed the vine to go trailing on the ground or upon supports. This latter mode of cultivation appears to be alluded to by Ezekiel. Ezek. 19 : 11, 12. The vintage, which formerly was a season of general festivity, began in September. The towns were deserted; the people lived among the vineyards in the lodges and tents. Comp. Judges 9 : 27; Isa. 16 : 10; Jer. 25 : 30. The grapes were gathered with shouts of joy by the "grape gatherers," Jer. 25 : 30, and put into baskets. See Jer. 6 : 9. They were then carried on the head and shoulders, or slung upon a yoke, to the "wine-press." Those in-

Gathering Grapes.

tended for eating were perhaps put into flat open baskets of wickerwork, as was the custom in Egypt. In Palestine, at present, the finest grapes, says Dr. Robinson, are dried as raisins, and the juice of the remainder, after having been trodden and pressed, "is boiled down to a sirup, which, under the name of *dibs*, is much used by all classes, wherever vineyards are found, as a condiment with their food." The vineyard, which was generally on a hill, Isa. 5 : 1; Jer. 31 : 5; Amos 9 : 13, was surrounded by a wall or hedge in order to keep out the wild boars, Ps. 80 : 13, jackals and foxes. Num. 22 : 24; Neh. 4 : 3; Cant. 2 : 15; Ezek. 13 : 4, 5; Matt. 21 : 33. Within the vineyard was one or more towers of stone in which the vine-dressers lived. Isa. 1 : 8; 5 : 2; Matt. 21 : 33. The vat, which was dug, Matt. 21 : 33, or hewn out of the rocky soil, and the press, were part of the vineyard furniture. Isa. 5 : 2.

Vine of Sodom occurs only in Deut. 32 : 32. It is generally supposed that this passage alludes to the celebrated apples of Sodom, of which Josephus speaks, "which indeed resemble edible fruit in color, but, on being plucked by the hand, are dissolved into smoke and ashes." It has been variously identified. Dr. Robinson pronounced in favor of the *'ösher* fruit, the *Asclepias* (*Calotropis*) *procera* of botanists. He says, "The fruit greatly resembles externally a large smooth apple or orange, hanging in clusters of three or four together, and when ripe is of a yellow color. It is now fair and delicious to the eye and soft to the touch; but, on being pressed or struck, it explodes with a puff, like a bladder or puff-ball, leaving in the hand only the shreds of the thin rind and a few fibres. It is indeed filled chiefly with air, which gives it the round form." Dr. Hooker writes, "The vine of Sodom I always thought might refer to *Cucumis colocynthis*, which is bitter and powdery inside; the term *vine* would scarcely be given to any but a trailing or other plant of the habit of a vine." His remark that the term vine must refer to some plant of the habit of a vine is conclusive against the claims of all the plants hitherto identified with the vine of Sodom.

Vinegar. The Hebrew word translated "vinegar" was applied to a beverage consisting generally of wine or strong drink turned sour, but sometimes artificially made by an admixture of barley and wine, and thus liable to fermentation. It was acid even to a proverb, Prov. 10 : 26, and by itself formed an unpleasant draught, Ps. 49 : 21, but was used by laborers. Ruth 2 : 14. Similar was the *acetum* of the Romans—a thin, sour wine, consumed by soldiers. This was the beverage of which the Saviour partook in his dying moments. Matt. 27 : 48; Mark 15 : 36; John 19 : 29, 30.

Vineyards, Plain of the. This place, mentioned only in Judges 11 : 33, lay east of the Jordan, beyond Aroer.

Viol. [PSALTERY.]

Viper. [SERPENT.]

Voph'si (*rich*), father of Nahbi, the Naphtalite spy. Num. 13 : 14. (B.C. before 1490.)

Vows. A vow is a solemn promise made to God to perform or to abstain from performing a certain thing. The earliest mention of a vow is that of Jacob. Gen. 28 : 18–22; 31 : 13. Vows in general are also mentioned in the book of Job, ch. 22 : 27. The law therefore did not introduce, but regulated the practice of, vows. Three sorts are mentioned : 1, vows of devotion; 2, vows of abstinence; 3, vows of destruction. 1. As to vows of devotion, the following rules are laid down: A man might devote to sacred uses possessions or persons, but not the first-born of either man or beast, which was devoted already. Lev. 27:26. (*a*) If he vowed land, he might either redeem it or not. Lev. 25, 27. (*b*) Animals fit for sacrifice, if devoted, were not to be redeemed or changed. Lev. 27:9, 10, 33. The case of persons devoted stood thus: A man might devote either himself, his child (not the first-born) or his slave. If no redemption took place, the devoted person became a slave of the sanctuary: see the case of Absalom. 2 Sam. 15:8. Otherwise he might be redeemed at a valuation according to age and sex, on the scale given in Lev. 27:1-7. Among general regulations affecting vows, the following may be mentioned: (1) Vows were entirely voluntary, but once made were regarded as compulsory. Num. 30:2; Deut. 23:21; Eccles. 5:4. (2) If persons in a dependent condition made vows, as (*a*) an unmarried daughter living in her father's house, or (*b*) a wife, even if she afterward became a widow, the vow, if (*a*) in the first case her father, or (*b*) in the second her husband, heard and disallowed it, was void; but if they heard without disallowance, it was to remain good. Num. 30:3-16. (3) Votive offerings arising from the produce of any impure traffic were wholly forbidden. Deut. 23:18. 2. For vows of abstinence, see CORBAN. 3. For vows of extermination, see ANATHEMA, and Ezra 10:8; Micah 4:13. It seems that the practice of shaving the head at the expiration of a votive period was not limited to the Nazaritic vow. Acts 18:18; 21:24.

Vul'gate, The, the Latin version of the Bible. The influence which it exercised upon western Christianity is scarcely less than that of the LXX. upon the Greek churches. Both the Greek and the Latin Vulgate have been long neglected; yet the Vulgate should have a very deep interest for all the western churches. For many centuries it was the only Bible generally used; and, directly or indirectly, it is the real parent of all the vernacular versions of western Europe. The Gothic version of Ulphilas alone is independent of it. The name is equivalent

to *Vulgata editio* (the *current* text of Holy Scripture. This translation was made by Jerome—Eusebius Hieronymus —who was born in 329 A.D. at Stridon in Dalmatia, and died at Bethlehem in 420 A.D. This great scholar probably alone for 1500 years possessed the qualifications necessary for producing an original version of the Scriptures for the use of the Latin churches. Going to Rome, he was requested by Pope Damascus, A.D. 383, to make a revision of the old Latin version of the New Testament, whose history is lost in obscurity. In middle life Jerome began the study of the Hebrew, and made a new version of the Old Testament from the original Hebrew, which was completed A.D. 404. The critical labors of Jerome were received with a loud outcry of reproach. He was accused of dis-

The Vulture.

turbing the repose of the Church and shaking the foundations of faith. But clamor based upon ignorance soon dies away; and the New translation gradually came into use equally with the Old, and at length supplanted it. The vast power which the Vulgate has had in determining the theological terms of western Christendom can hardly be overrated. By far the greater part of the current doctrinal terminology is based on the Vulgate. *Predestination, justification, supererogation* (supererogo), *sanctification, salvation, mediation, regeneration, revelation, visitation* (met.), *propitiation*, first appear in the Old Vulgate. *Grace, redemption, election, reconciliation, satisfaction, inspiration, scripture,* were devoted there to a new and holy use. *Sacrament* and *communion* are from the same source; and though *baptism* is Greek, it comes to us from the Latin. It would be easy to extend the list by the addition of *orders, penance, congregation, priest;* but it can be seen from the forms already brought forward that the Vulgate has left its mark both upon our language and upon our thoughts. It was the version which alone they knew who handed down to the reformers the rich stores of mediæval wisdom; the version with which the greatest of the reformers were most familiar, and from which they had drawn their earliest knowledge of divine truth.

Vulture. The rendering in the Authorized Version of the Hebrew *dââh, dayyâh,* and also in Job 28 : 7 of *ayyâh.* There seems no doubt that the Authorized Version translation is incorrect, and that the original words refer to some of the smaller species of raptorial birds, as kites or buzzards. [KITE.] But the Hebrew word *nesher,* invariably rendered "eagle" in the Authorized Version, is probably the vulture. [EAGLE.]

W.

Wages. The earliest mention of wages is of a recompense, not in money, but in kind, to Jacob from Laban. Gen. 29 : 15, 20; 30 : 28; 31 : 7, 8, 41. In Egypt money payments by way of wages were in use, but the terms cannot now be ascertained. Ex. 2 : 9. The only mention of the rate of wages in Scripture is found in the parable of the householder and the vineyard, Matt. 20 : 2, where the laborer's wages are set at one denarius per day, probably 15 to 17 cents, a sum which may be fairly taken as equivalent to the denarius, and to the usual pay of a soldier (ten *asses* per diem) in the later days of the Roman republic. Tac. *Ann.* i. 17; Polyb. vi. 39. In earlier times it is probable that the rate was lower; but it is likely that laborers, and also soldiers, were supplied with provisions. The law was very strict in requiring daily payment of wages. Lev. 19 : 13; Deut. 24 : 14, 15. The employer who refused to give his laborers sufficient victuals is censured, Job 24 : 11, and the iniquity of withholding wages is denounced. Jer. 22 : 13; Mal. 3 : 5; James 5 : 4.

Wagon. The Oriental wagon, or *arabah*, is a vehicle composed of two or three planks fixed on two solid circular blocks of wood, from two to five feet in diameter, which serve as wheels. For the conveyance of passengers, mattresses or clothes are laid in the bottom, and the vehicle is drawn by buffaloes or oxen. [CART and CHARIOT.]

Walls. Only a few points need be noticed. 1. The practice common in Palestine of carrying foundations down to the solid rock, as in the case of the temple, with structures intended to be permanent. Luke 6 : 48. 2. A feature of some parts of Solomon's buildings, as described by Josephus, corresponds remarkably to the method adopted at Nineveh of incrusting or veneering a wall of brick or stone with slabs of a more costly material, as marble or alabaster. 3. Another use of walls in Palestine is to support mountain roads or terraces formed on the sides of hills for purposes of cultivation. 4. The "path of the vineyards," Num. 22 : 24, is a pathway through vineyards, with walls on each side.

Wandering in the Wilderness. [WILDERNESS OF THE WANDERING.]

War. The most important topic in connection with war is the formation of

The Catapult, a machine for throwing heavy darts.

the army which is destined to carry it on. [ARMY.] In 1 Kings 9 : 22, at a period (Solomon's reign) when the organization of the army was complete, we have apparently a list of the various gradations of rank in the service, as follows: 1. "Men of war" = *privates;* 2. "servants," the lowest rank of officers = *lieutenants;* 3. "princes" = *captains;* 4. "captains," perhaps = *staff officers;* 5. "rulers of his chariots and his horsemen" = *cavalry officers.* Formal proclamations of war were not interchanged between the belligerents. Before entering the enemy's district spies were sent to ascertain the character of the country and the preparations of its inhabitants for resistance. Num. 13 : 17; Josh. 2 : 1; Judges 7 : 10; 1 Sam. 26 : 4. The combat assumed the form of a number of hand-to-hand contests; hence the high value attached to fleetness of foot and strength of arm. 2 Sam. 1:23; 2:18; 1 Chron. 12:8. At the same time various strategic devices were practiced, such as the ambuscade, Josh. 8:2, 12; Judges 20:36, surprise, Judges 7:16, or circumvention. 2 Sam. 5:23. Another mode of settling the dispute was by the selection of champions, 1 Sam. 17; 2 Sam. 2:14, who were spurred on to exertion by the offer of high reward. 1 Sam. 17:25; 18:25; 2 Sam. 18:11; 1 Chron. 11:6. The contest having been decided, the conquerors were recalled from the pursuit by the sound of a trumpet. 2 Sam. 2:28; 18:16; 20:22. The siege of a town or fortress was

The Crow.

conducted in the following manner: A line of circumvallation was drawn round the place, Ezek. 4:2; Micah 5:1, constructed out of the trees found in the neighborhood, Deut. 20:20, together with earth and any other materials at hand. This line not only cut off the besieged from the surrounding country, but also served as a base of operations for the besiegers. The next step was to throw out from this line one or more mounds or "banks" in the direction of the city, 2 Sam. 20:15; 2 Kings 19:32; Isa. 37:33, which were gradually increased in height until they were about half as high as the city wall. On this mound or bank towers were erected, 2 Kings 25:1; Jer. 52:4; Ezek. 4:2; 17:17; 21:22; 26:8, whence the slingers and archers might attack with effect. *Catapults* were pre-

pared for hurling large darts and stones; and the *crow*, a long spar, with iron claws at one end and ropes at the other, to pull

Battering-ram and Tower.

down stones or men from the top of the wall. *Battering-rams*, Ezek. 4:2; 21:22, were brought up to the walls by means of the bank, and scaling-ladders might also be placed on it. The treatment of the conquered was extremely severe in ancient times. The bodies of the soldiers killed in action were plundered, 1 Sam. 31:8; 2 Macc. 8:27; the survivors were either killed in some savage manner, Judges 9:45; 2 Sam. 12:31; 2 Chron. 25:12, mutilated, Judges 1:6; 1 Sam. 11:2, or carried into captivity. Num. 31:26.

Washing the hands and feet. As knives and forks were not used in the

Washing the Hands.

East, in Scripture times, in eating, it was necessary that the hand, which was thrust into the common dish, should be scrupulously clean; and again, as sandals were ineffectual against the dust and heat of the climate, washing the feet on entering a house was an act both of respect to the company and of refreshment to the traveller. The former of these usages was transformed by the Pharisees of the New Testament age into a matter of ritual observance, Mark 7 : 3, and special rules were laid down as to the time and manner of its performance. Washing the feet did not rise to the dignity of a ritual observance except in connection with the services of the sanctuary. Ex. 30 : 19, 21. It held a high place, however, among the rites of hospitality. Immediately that a

Eastern Washing-vessels.

guest presented himself at the tent door, it was usual to offer the necessary materials for washing the feet. Gen. 18 : 4; 19 : 2; 24 : 32; 43 : 24; Judges 19 : 21. It was a yet more complimentary act, betokening equally humility and affection, if the host himself performed the office for his guest. 1 Sam. 25 : 41; Luke 7 : 38, 44; John 13 : 5-14; 1 Tim. 5 : 10. Such a token of hospitality is still occasionally exhibited in the East.

Watches of night. The Jews, like the Greeks and Romans, divided the night into military watches instead of hours, each watch representing the period for which sentinels or pickets remained on duty. The proper Jewish reckoning recognized only three such watches, entitled the first or "beginning of the watches," Lam. 2 : 19, the middle watch, Judges 7 : 19, and the morning watch. Ex. 14 : 24; 1 Sam. 11 : 11. These would last respectively from sunset to 10

P.M.; from 10 P.M. to 2 A.M.; and from 2 A.M. to sunrise. After the establishment of the Roman supremacy, the number of watches was increased to four, which were described either according to their numerical order, as in the case of the "fourth watch," Matt. 14 : 25, or by the terms "even," "midnight," "cockcrowing" and "morning." Mark 13 : 35. These terminated respectively at 9 P.M., midnight, 3 A.M. and 6 A.M.

Water of jealousy. Num. 5 : 11-31. The ritual prescribed consisted in the husband's bringing before the priest the woman suspected of infidelity, and the essential part of it is unquestionably the oath, to which the "water" was subsidiary, symbolical and ministerial. With her he was to bring an offering of barley meal. As she stood holding the offering, so the priest stood holding an earthen vessel of holy water mixed with the dust from the floor of the sanctuary, and, declaring her free from all evil consequences if innocent, solemnly devoted her in the name of Jehovah to be "a curse and an oath among her people" if guilty. He then "wrote these curses in a book, and blotted them out with the bitter water," and having thrown the handful of meal on the altar, "caused the woman to drink" the potion thus drugged, she moreover answering to the words of his imprecation, "Amen, amen." Josephus adds, if the suspicion was unfounded, she obtained conception; if true, she died infamously. (This was entirely different from most trials of this kind, for the bitter water the woman must drink was harmless in itself, and only by a direct act of God could it injure her if guilty; while in most heathen trials the suspected party must take poison, or suffer that which only a miracle would save them from if they were innocent.—ED.)

Water of separation. [PURIFICATION.]

Wave offering. This rite, together with that of "heaving" or "raising" the offering, was an inseparable accompaniment of peace offerings. In such the right shoulder, considered the choicest part of the victim, was to be "heaved," and viewed as holy to the Lord, only eaten therefore by the priest: the breast was to be "waved," and eaten by the worshipper. The scriptural notices of these rites are to be found in Ex. 29 : 24, 28; Lev. 7 : 30, 34; 8 : 27; 9 : 21; 10 : 14, 15; 23 : 10, 15, 20; Num. 6 : 20; 18 : 11, 18, 26–29, etc. In conjecturing the meaning of this rite, regard must be had that it was the accompaniment of peace offerings, which were witnesses to a ratified covenant—an established communion between God and man.

Weapons. [ARMS.]

Weasel (*chôled*) occurs only in Lev. 11 : 29, in the list of unclean animals; but the Hebrew word ought more probably to be translated "mole." Moles are common in Palestine.

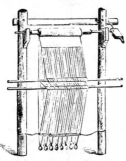

Ancient Roman Loom.

Weaving. The art of weaving appears to be coeval with the first dawning of civilization. We find it practiced with great skill by the Egyptians at a very early period. The "vestures of fine linen" such as Joseph wore, Gen. 41 : 42, were the product of Egyptian looms. The Israelites were probably acquainted with the process before their sojourn in Egypt; but it was undoubtedly there that they attained the proficiency which enabled them to execute the hangings of the tabernacle, Ex. 35 : 35; 1 Chron. 4 : 21, and other artistic textures. The Egyptian loom was usually upright, and the weaver stood at his work. The cloth was fixed sometimes at the top, sometimes at the bottom. The modern Arabs use a procumbent loom, raised above the ground by short legs. The textures produced by the Jewish weavers were very various. The coarser kinds, such as tent-cloth, sack-cloth and the "hairy garments" of the poor, were made of goat's or camel's hair. Ex. 26 : 7; Matt. 3 : 4. Wool was extensively used for ordinary clothing, Lev. 13 : 47; Prov. 27 : 26; 31 : 13; Ezek. 27 : 18; while for

finer work flax was used, varying in quality, and producing the different textures described in the Bible as "linen" and "fine linen." The mixture of wool and flax in cloth intended for a garment was interdicted. Lev. 19 : 19; Deut. 22 : 11.

Wedding. [MARRIAGE.]

Week. There can be no doubt about the great antiquity of measuring time by a period of seven days. Gen. 8 : 10; 29 : 27. The origin of this division of time is a matter which has given birth to much speculation. Its antiquity is so great, its observance so widespread, and it occupies so important a place in sacred things, that it must probably be thrown back as far as the creation of man. The week and the Sabbath are thus as old as man himself. A purely theological ground is thus established for the week. They who embrace this view support it by a reference to the six days' creation and the divine rest on the seventh. 1st. That the week rests on a theological ground may be cheerfully acknowledged by both sides; but nothing is determined by such acknowledgment as to the original cause of adopting this division of time. Whether the week gave its sacredness to the number seven, or whether the ascendency of that number helped to determine the dimensions of the week, it is impossible to say. 2d. The weekly division was adopted by all the Shemitic races, and, in the later period of their history at least, by the Egyptians. On the other hand, there is no reason for thinking the week known till a late period to either Greeks or Romans. 3d. So far from the week being a division of time without ground in nature, there was much to recommend its adoption. And, further, the week is a most natural and nearly an exact quadri-partition of the month, so that the quarters of the moon may easily have suggested it. It is clear that if not in Paul's time, yet very soon after, the whole Roman world had adopted the hebdomadal division.

Weeks, Feast of. [PENTECOST.]

Weights and Measures. A. WEIGHTS.—The general principle of the present inquiry is to give the evidence of the monuments the preference on all doubtful points. All ancient Greek systems of weight were derived, either directly or indirectly, from an eastern source. The older systems of ancient Greece and Persia were the Æginetan, the Attic, the Babylonian and the Euboïc. 1. The Æginetan talent is stated to have contained 60 minæ, 6000 drachms. 2. The Attic talent is the standard weight introduced by Solon. 3. The Babylonian talent may be determined from existing weights found by Mr. Layard at Nineveh. Pollux makes it equal to 7000 Attic drachms. 4. The Euboïc talent, though bearing a Greek name, is rightly held to have been originally an eastern system. The proportion of the Euboïc talent to the Babylonian was probably as 60 to 72, or 5 to 6. Taking the Babylonian maneh at 7992 grs., we obtain 399,600 for the Euboïc talent. The principal, if not the only, Persian gold coin is the daric, weighing about 129 grs. 5. The Hebrew talent or talents and divisions. A talent of silver is mentioned in Exodus, which contained 3000 shekels, distinguished as "the holy shekel," or "shekel of the sanctuary." The gold talent contained 100 manehs, 10,000 shekels. The silver talent contained 3000 shekels, 6000 bekas, 60,000 gerahs. The significations of the names of the Hebrew weights must be here stated. The chief unit was the SHEKEL (*i. e. weight*), called also the *holy shekel* or *shekel of the sanctuary;* subdivided into the *beka* (*i. e. half*) or *half-shekel*, and the *gerah* (*i. e. a grain* or *bean*). The chief multiple, or higher unit, was the *kikkar* (*i. e. circle* or *globe,* probably for an *aggregate sum*), translated in our version, after the LXX., TALENT; subdivided into the *maneh* (*i. e. part, portion* or *number*), a word used in Babylonian and in the Greek ηνᾶ or *mina*. (1) The relations of these weights, as usually employed for *the standard of weighing silver*, and their absolute values, determined from the extant silver coins, and confirmed from other sources, were as follows, in grains exactly, and in avoirdupois weight approximately :

SILVER WEIGHTS.					Grains.	Lbs.	Oz.	Correction.
Gerah					11	. .	$\frac{1}{40}$	+ .06 gr. nearly.
10	Beka				110	. .	$\frac{1}{4}$	+ .6 gr.
20	2	Shekel			220	. .	$\frac{1}{2}$	+ 1.75 gr.
1,200	120	60	Maneh		13,200	2	, .	—2 oz. nearly.
60,000	6,000	3,000	50	Talent (Kikkar)	660,000	100	. .	—6 lb. nearly.

(2) For *gold* a different shekel was used, probably of foreign introduction. Its value has been calculated at from 129 to 132 grains. The former value assimilates it to the Persian *daric* of the Babylonian standard. The talent of this system was just double that of the silver standard; it was divided into 100 *manehs*, and each *maneh* into 100 shekels, as follows :

GOLD WEIGHTS.			Grains.	Lbs.	Oz.	Correction.
Shekel			132	. .	.3	+ .75 gr.
100	Maneh		13,200	2	. .	—2 oz. nearly.
10,000	100	Talent (Kikkar)	1,320,000	200	. .	—12 lb. nearly.

(3) There appears to have been a third standard for *copper*, namely, a shekel four times as heavy as the gold shekel (or 528 grains), 1500 of which made up the copper talent of 792,000 grains. It seems to have been subdivided, in the coinage, into *halves* (of 264 grains), *quarters* (of 132 grains) and *sixths* (of 88 grains).

B. MEASURES. — I. MEASURES OF LENGTH.—In the Hebrew, as in every other system, these measures are of two classes : *length*, in the ordinary sense, for objects whose size we wish to determine, and *distance*, or *itinerary* measures ; and the two are connected by some definite relation, more or less simple, between their units. 1. The measures of the former class have been universally derived, in the first instance, from the parts of the human body ; but it is remarkable that, in the Hebrew system, the only

part used for this purpose is the *hand
and fore-arm*, to the exclusion of the
foot, which was the chief unit of the
western nations. Hence arises the difficulty of determining the ratio of the *foot*
to the CUBIT,[1] which appears as the chief
Oriental unit from the very building of
Noah's ark. Gen. 6 : 15, 16 ; 7 : 20. The
Hebrew lesser measures were the *finger's
breadth*, Jer. 52 : 21 only ; the *palm* or
handbreadth, Ex. 25 : 25 ; 1 Kings 7 : 26 ;
2 Chron. 4 : 5, used metaphorically in Ps.
39 : 5 ; the *span, i. e.* the full stretch between the tips of the thumb and the
little finger. Ex. 28 : 16 ; 1 Sam. 17 : 4 ;
Ezek. 43 : 13, and figuratively Isa. 40 :
12. The data for determining the actual
length of the Mosaic cubit involve peculiar difficulties, and absolute certainty
seems unattainable. The following, however, seem the most probable conclusions :

First, that three cubits were used in the
times of the Hebrew monarchy, namely :
(1) The *cubit of a man*, Deut. 3 : 11, or
the *common cubit* of Canaan (in contradistinction to the Mosaic cubit) of the
Chaldæan standard ; (2) The *old Mosaic*
or *legal cubit*, a handbreadth larger than
the first, and agreeing with the smaller
Egyptian cubit ; (3) The *new cubit*,
which was still larger, and agreed with
the larger Egyptian cubit, of about 20.6
inches, used in the Nilometer. Second,
that the ordinary cubit of the Bible did
not come up to the full length of the
cubit of other countries. The *reed* (*ká-
neh*), for measuring buildings (like the
Roman *decempeda*), was equal to 6 cubits.
It occurs only in Ezekiel. ch. 40 : 5-8 ;
41 : 8 ; 42 : 16-19. The values given in the
following table are to be accepted with
reservation, for want of greater certainty :

HEBREW MEASURES OF LENGTH.					Inches.	Approximate.	
						Feet.	Inches.
Digit	. . . .				.7938	. .	.8 or $\frac{13}{16}$
4	Palm	. . . .			3.1752	. .	$3\frac{3}{16}$
12	3	Span .	. . . .		5.5257	. .	$9\frac{1}{2}$
24	6	2	Cubit	. . . .	19.0515	1	7
144	36	12	6	Reed	114.3090	9	6

2. Of *measures of distance* the smallest
is the *pace*, and the largest the *day's
journey*. (*a*) The *pace*, 2 Sam. 6 : 13,
whether it be *single*, like our pace, or
double, like the Latin *passus*, is defined
by nature within certain limits, its usual
length being about 30 inches for the
former and 5 feet for the latter. There is
some reason to suppose that even before
the Roman measurement of the roads of
Palestine, the Jews had a *mile* of 1000
paces, alluded to in Matt. 5 : 41. It is
said to have been single or double, according to the length of the pace ; and
hence the peculiar force of our Lord's
saying : "Whosoever shall compel thee
[as a courier] to go *a mile*, go with him
twain"—put the most liberal construction on the demand. (*b*) The *day's jour-*

ney was the most usual method of calcu-
lating distances in travelling, Gen. 30 :
36 ; 31 : 23 ; Ex. 3 : 18 ; 5 : 3 ; Num. 10 :
33 ; 11 : 31 ; 33 : 8 ; Deut. 1 : 2 ; 1 Kings
19 : 4 ; 2 Kings 3 : 9 ; Jonah 3 : 3 ; 1 Macc.
5 : 24 ; 7 : 45 ; Tobit 6 : 1, though but one
instance of it occurs in the New Testament—Luke 2 : 44. The ordinary day's
journey among the Jews was 30 miles ;
but when they travelled in companies,
only ten miles. Neapolis formed the first
stage out of Jerusalem according to the
former and Beeroth according to the
latter computation. (*c*) The *Sabbath
day's journey* of 2000 cubits, Acts 1 : 12,
is peculiar to the New Testament, and
arose from a rabbinical restriction. It
was founded on a universal application
of the prohibition given by Moses for a
special occasion : "Let no man go out of
his place on the seventh day." Ex. 16 :
29. An exception was allowed for the
purpose of worshipping at the tabernacle ; and, as 2000 cubits was the pre-

---

[1] The Hebrew word for the cubit (*ammah*)
appears to have been of Egyptian origin, as
some of the measures of capacity (the *hin* and
ephah) certainly were.

scribed space to be kept between the ark and the people, as well as the extent of the suburbs of the Levitical cities on every side, Num. 35 : 5, this was taken for the length of a Sabbath-day's journey, measured *from the wall of the city* in which the traveller lived. Computed from the value given above for the cubit, the Sabbath-day's journey would be just *six tenths of a mile*. (*d*) After the captivity the relations of the Jews to the Persians, Greeks and Romans caused the use, probably, of the *parasang*, and certainly of the *stadium* and the *mile*. Though the first is not mentioned in the Bible, it is well to exhibit the ratios of the three. The universal Greek standard, the stadium of 600 Greek feet, which was the length of the race-course at Olympia, occurs first in the Maccabees, and is common in the New Testament. Our version renders it *furlong;* it being, in fact, the eighth part of the Roman mile, as the furlong is of ours. 2 Macc. 11 : 5; 12 : 9, 17, 29; Luke 24 : 13; John 6 : 19; 11 : 18; Rev. 14 : 20; 21 : 16. One measure remains to be mentioned. The *fathom*, used in sounding by the Alexandrian mariners in St. Paul's voyage, is the Greek ὀργυιά, *i. e.* the *full stretch* of the two arms from tip to tip of the middle finger, which is about equal to the height, and in a man of full stature is six feet. For the sake of completeness, the values of the Greek and Roman foot are shown in the following table:

							Miles.	Feet.	Inches.
Roman foot = .96 of Greek foot							..	..	11.6496
$1\frac{1}{24}$	Greek Foot.						..	1	0.135
5	$4\frac{2}{5}$	Roman Pace (*passus*)					..	4	10.248
$6\frac{1}{4}$	6	$1\frac{1}{4}$	Greek Fathom (ὀργυιά)				..	6	0.81
625	600	125	100	Furlong (στάδιον) . . .			..	606	9
5,000	4,800	1,000	800	8	Roman Mile . . .		.9193	= 4854	..
18,750	18,000	3,750	3,000	30	$3\frac{3}{4}$	Persian Parasang	$3\frac{1}{2}$ nearly.	..	..

For estimating *area*, and especially *land*, there is no evidence that the Jews used any special system of *square measures*, but they were content to express by the *cubit* the *length* and *breadth* of the surface to be measured, Num. 35 : 4, 5; Ezek. 40 : 27, or by the *reed*. Ezek. 41 : 8; 42 : 16–19; Rev. 21 : 16.

II. MEASURES OF CAPACITY.—1. The measures of capacity for *liquids* were: (*a*) The *log*, Lev. 14 : 10, etc., the name originally signifying *basin*. (*b*) The *hin*, a name of Egyptian origin, frequently noticed in the Bible. Ex. 29 : 40; 30 : 24; Num. 15 : 4, 7, 9; Ezek. 4 : 11, etc. (*c*) The *bath*, the name meaning "measured," the largest of the liquid measures. 1 Kings 7 : 26, 38; 2 Chron. 2 : 10; Ezra 7 : 22; Isa. 5 : 10. The relative values of these measures stand thus:

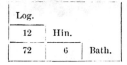

2. The *dry* measure contained the following denominations: (*a*) The *cab*, mentioned only in 2 Kings 6 : 25, the name meaning literally *hollow* or *concave*. (*b*) The *omer*, mentioned only in Ex. 16 : 16–36. The word implies a *heap*, and secondarily a *sheaf*. (*c*) The *sĕâh*, or "measure," this being the etymological meaning of the term, and appropriately applied to it, inasmuch as it was the ordinary measure for household purposes. Gen. 18 : 6; 1 Sam. 25 : 18; 2 Kings 7 : 1, 16. The Greek equivalent occurs in Matt. 13 : 33; Luke 13 : 21. (*d*) The *ephah*, a word of Egyptian origin, and of frequent recurrence in the Bible. Ex. 16 : 36; Lev. 5 : 11; 6 : 20; Num. 5 : 15; 28 : 5; Judges 6 : 19; Ruth 2 : 17; 1 Sam. 1 : 24; 17 : 17; Ezek. 45 : 11, 13; 46 : 5, 7, 11, 14. (*e*) The *lethec*, or "half homer," literally meaning what is *poured out;* it occurs only in Hos. 3 : 2. (*f*) The *homer*, meaning *heap*. Lev. 27 : 16; Num. 11 : 32; Isa. 5 : 10; Ezek. 45 : 13. It is elsewhere termed *cor*, from the circular vessel in which it was measured. 1 Kings 4 : 22;

5 : 11 ; 2 Chron. 2 : 10 ; 27 : 5 ; Ezra 7 : 22 ; Ezek. 45 : 14. The Greek equivalent occurs in Luke 16 : 7. The following scale gives the relative values of these measures :

Cab.				
$1\frac{4}{5}$	Omer.			
6	$3\frac{1}{2}$	Seâh.		
18	10	3	Ephah.	
180	100	30	10	Homer.

The *absolute values* of the liquid and dry measures are stated differently by Josephus and the rabbinists, and as we are unable to decide between them, we give a double estimate of the various denominations.

	(*Josephus.*) Gallons.	(*Rabbinists.*) Gallons.	Bushels.
Homer or Cor	86.696 or	44.286	$10\frac{3}{4}$ or $5\frac{1}{2}$
Ephah or Bath	8.6696 or	4.4286	
Seâh	2.8898 or	1.4762	
Hin	1.4449 or	.7381	
Omer	.8669 or	.4428	
Cab	.4816 or	.246	
Log	.1204 or	.0615	

In the New Testament we have notices of the following foreign measures : (*a*) The *metrêtês*, John 2 : 6, Authorized Version "firkin," for liquids. (*b*) The *chœnix*, Rev. 6 : 6, Authorized Version "measure," for dry goods. (*c*) The *xestêc*, applied, however, not to the peculiar measure so named by the Greeks, but to any small vessel, such as a cup. Mark 7 : 4, 8, Authorized Version "pot." (*d*) The *modius*, similarly applied to describe any vessel of moderate dimensions, Matt. 5 : 15; Mark 4 : 21; Luke 11 : 33, Authorized Version "bushel," though properly meaning a Roman measure, amounting to about a peck. The value of the Attic *metrêtês* was 8.6696 gallons, and consequently the amount of

liquid in six stone jars, containing on the average $2\frac{1}{2}$ *metrêtæ* each, would exceed 110 gallons. John 2 : 6. Very possibly, however, the Greek term represents the Hebrew *bath;* and if the bath be taken at the lowest estimate assigned to it, the amount would be reduced to about 60 gallons. The *chœnix* was 1-48th of an Attic *medimnus*, and contained nearly a quart. It represented the amount of corn for a day's food; and hence a *chœnix* for a penny (or *denarius*), which usually purchased a bushel (Cic. *Verr.* iii. 81), indicated a great scarcity. Rev. 6 : 6.

Well. Wells in Palestine are usually excavated from the solid limestone rock, sometimes with steps to descend into them. Gen. 24 : 16. The brims are furnished with a curb or low wall of stone, bearing marks of high antiquity in the furrows worn by the ropes used in drawing water. It was on a curb of this sort that our Lord sat when he conversed with the woman of Samaria, John 4 : 6; and it was this, the usual stone cover, which the woman placed on the mouth of the well at Bahurim, 2 Sam. 17 : 19, where the Authorized Version weakens the sense by omitting the article. The usual methods for raising water are the following : 1. The rope and bucket, or water-

Modern Shadoof.

skin. Gen. 24 : 14-20; John 4 : 11. 2. The *sakiyeh*, or Persian wheel. This consists of a vertical wheel furnished with a set of buckets or earthen jars attached to a cord passing over the wheel, which descend empty and return full as the wheel revolves. 3. A modification of the last method, by which a man, sitting opposite to a wheel furnished with buckets, turns it by drawing with his hands

Ancient Well in Palestine.

one set of spokes prolonged beyond its circumference, and pushing another set from him with his feet. 4. A method very common in both ancient and modern Egypt is the *shadoof*, a simple contrivance consisting of a lever moving on a pivot, which is loaded at one end with a lump of clay or some other weight, and has at the other a bowl or bucket. Wells are usually furnished with troughs of wood or stone, into which the water is emptied for the use of persons or animals coming to the wells. Unless machinery is used, which is commonly worked by men, women are usually the water-carriers.

Whale. As to the signification of the Hebrew terms *tan* and *tannín,* variously rendered in the Authorized Version by "dragon," "whale," "serpent," "sea-monster," see DRAGON. It remains for us in this article to consider the transaction recorded in the book of Jonah, of that prophet having been swallowed up by some "great fish" which in Matt. 12 : 40 is called *cētos* (κῆτος), rendered in our version by "whale." In the first place, it is necessary to observe that the Greek word *cētos,* used by St. Matthew, is not restricted in its meaning to "a whale," or any *Cetacean;* like the Latin *cete* or *cetus,* it may denote any sea-monster, either "a whale," or "a shark," or "a seal," or "a tunny of enormous size." Although two or three species of whale are found in the Mediterranean Sea, yet the "great fish" that swallowed the prophet cannot properly be identified with any *Cetacean,* for, although the sperm whale has a gullet sufficiently large to admit the body of a man, yet it can hardly be the fish intended, as the natural food of Cetaceans consists of small animals, such as medusæ and crustacea. The only fish, then, capable of swallowing a man would be a large specimen of the white shark (*Carcharias vulgaris*), that dreaded enemy of sailors, and the most voracious of the family of *Squalidæ.* This shark, which sometimes attains the length of thirty feet, is quite able to swallow a man whole. The whole body of a man in armor has been found in the stomach of a white shark ; and Captain King, in his survey of Australia, says he had caught one which could have swallowed a man with the greatest ease. Blumenbach mentions that a whole horse has been found in a shark, and Captain Basil Hall reports the taking of one in which, besides other things, he found the whole skin of a buffalo which a short time before had been thrown overboard from his ship (i. p. 27). The white shark is not uncommon in the Mediterranean.

Wheat, the well-known valuable cereal, cultivated from the earliest times, is first mentioned in Gen. 30 : 14, in the account of Jacob's sojourn with Laban in Mesopotamia. Egypt in ancient times was celebrated for the growth of its wheat; the best quality was all bearded ; and the same varieties existed in ancient as in modern times, among which may be mentioned the seven-eared quality described in Pharaoh's dream. Gen. 41 : 22. Babylonia was also noted for the excellence of its wheat and other cereals. Syria and Palestine produced wheat of fine quality and in large quantities. Ps. 81 : 16 ; 147 : 14, etc. There appear to be two or three kinds of wheat at present grown in Palestine, the *Triticum vulgare,* the *T. spelta,* and another variety of bearded wheat which appears to be the same as the Egyptian kind, the *T.*

compositum. In the parable of the sower our Lord alludes to grains of wheat which in good ground produce a hundred-fold. Matt. 13 : 8. The common *Triticum vulgare* will sometimes produce one hundred grains in the ear. Wheat is reaped toward the end of April, in May, and in June, according to the differences of soil

Egyptian Wheat.

and position; it was sown either broadcast and then ploughed in or trampled in by cattle, Isa. 32 : 20, or in rows, if we rightly understand Isa. 28 : 25, which seems to imply that the seeds were *planted* apart in order to insure larger and fuller ears. The wheat was put into the ground in the winter, and some time after the barley; in the Egyptian plague of hail, consequently, the barley suffered, but the wheat had not appeared, and so escaped injury.

Widow. Under the Mosaic dispensation no legal provision was made for the maintenance of widows. They were left dependent partly on the affection of relations, more especially of the eldest son, whose birthright, or extra share of the property, imposed such a duty upon him, and partly on the privileges accorded to other distressed classes, such as a participation in the triennial third tithe, Deut. 14 : 29; 26 : 12, in leasing, Deut. 24 : 19–21, and in religious feasts. Deut. 16 : 11, 14. With regard to the remarriage of widows, the only restriction imposed by the Mosaic law had reference to the contingency of one being left childless, in which case the brother of the deceased husband had a right to marry the widow. Deut. 25 : 5, 6; Matt. 22 : 23–30. In the apostolic Church the widows were sustained at the public expense, the relief being daily administered in kind, under the superintendence of officers appointed for this special purpose. Acts 6 : 1–6. Particular directions are given by St. Paul as to the class of persons entitled to such public maintenance. 1 Tim. 5 : 3–16. Out of the body of such widows a certain number were to be enrolled, the qualifications for such enrollment being that they were not under sixty years of age; that they had been "the wife of one man," probably meaning *but once married*; and that they had led useful and charitable lives. vs. 9, 10. We are not disposed to identify the widows of the Bible either with the deaconesses or with the πρεσβύτιδες of the early Church. The order of widows existed as a separate institution, contemporaneously with these offices, apparently for the same eleemosynary purpose for which it was originally instituted.

Wife. [MARRIAGE.]

Wilderness of the Wandering. (The region in which the Israelites spent nearly 38 years of their existence after they had left Egypt, and spent a year before Mount Sinai. They went as far as Kadesh, on the southernmost border of Palestine, from which place spies were sent up into the promised land. These returned with such a report of the inhabitants and their walled cities that the people were discouraged, and began to murmur and rebel. For their sin they were compelled to remain 38 years longer in the wilderness, because it showed that they were not yet prepared and trained to conquer and to hold their promised possessions. The wilderness of the wandering was the great central limestone plateau of the sinaitic peninsula. It was bordered on the east by the valley of the Arabah, which runs from the Dead Sea to the head of the eastern branch of the Red Sea. On the south and southwest were the granite mountains of Sinai, and on the north the Mediterranean Sea and the mountainous region south of Judea. It is called the *Desert of Paran*, and *Badiet et-Tih*, which means "Desert of the Wandering." The children of Israel were not probably marching as a nation from place to place in this wilderness during these 38 years, but they probably had a kind of headquarters at Kadesh, and were "compelled to linger on, as do the Bedouin Arabs of the present day, in a half-savage, homeless state, moving about from place to place, and pitching their tents wherever they could find pasture for their flocks and herds."—*E. H. Palmer.* Toward the close of the forty years from Egypt they again assembled at Kadesh, and, once more under the leadership of the Shechinah, they marched down the Arabah on their way to the promised land.—ED.)

Willows are mentioned in Lev. 23 : 40; Job 40 : 22; Ps. 137 : 2; Isa. 44 : 4. With respect to the tree upon which the captive Israelites hung their harps, there can be no doubt that the weeping willow, *Salix babylonica,* is intended. This tree grows abundantly on the banks of the Euphrates, in other parts of Asia as in Palestine. The Hebrew word translated willows is generic, and includes several species of the large family of *Salices,* which is well represented in Palestine and the Bible lands, such as the *Salix alba, S. viminalis* (osier), *S. ægyptiaca.*

Willows, The brook of the, a wady mentioned by Isaiah, Isa. 15 : 7, in his dirge over Moab. It is situated on the southern boundary of Moab, and is now called *Wady el-Aksa.*

Wills. Under a system of close inheritance like that of the Jews, the scope for bequest in respect of land was limited by the right of redemption and general re-entry in the jubilee year; but the law does not forbid bequests by will of such limited interest in land as was consistent with those rights. The case of houses in walled towns was different, and there can be no doubt that there must, in fact, have frequently been bequeathed by will. Lev. 25 : 30. Two instances are recorded in the Old Testament under the law of testamentary disposition, (1) effected in the case of Ahithophel, 2 Sam. 17 : 23, (2) recommended in the case of Hezekiah. 2 Kings 20 : 1; Isa. 38 : 1. [HEIR.]

Wimple, an old English word for hood or veil, used in the Authorized Version of Isa. 3 : 22. The same Hebrew word is translated "veil" in Ruth 3 : 15, but it signifies rather a kind of shawl or mantle.

Window. The window of an Oriental house consists generally of an aperture closed in with lattice-work. Judges 5 : 28;

Prov. 7 : 6, Authorized Version "casement;" Eccles. 12 : 3, Authorized Version "window;" Cant. 2 : 9; Hos. 13 : 3, Authorized Version "chimney." Glass has been introduced into Egypt in modern times as a protection against the cold of winter, but lattice-work is still the usual, and with the poor the only, contrivance for closing the window. The windows generally look into the inner court of the house, but in every house one or more look into the street. In Egypt these outer windows generally project over the doorway. [HOUSE.]

Winds. That the Hebrews recognized the existence of four prevailing winds as issuing, broadly speaking, from the four cardinal points, north, south, east and west, may be inferred from their custom of using the expression "four winds" as equivalent to the "four quarters" of the hemisphere. Ezek. 37 : 9; Dan. 8 : 8; Zech. 2 : 6; Matt. 24 : 31. The north wind, or, as it was usually called, "the north," was naturally the coldest of the four, Ecclus. 43 : 20, and its presence is hence invoked as favorable to vegetation in Cant. 4 : 16. It is described in Prov. 25 : 23 as bringing rain; in this case we must understand the northwest wind. The northwest wind prevails from the autumnal equinox to the beginning of November, and the north wind from June to the equinox. The east wind crosses the sandy wastes of Arabia Deserta before reaching Palestine, and was hence termed "the wind of the wilderness." Job 1 : 19; Jer. 13 : 24. It blows with violence, and is hence supposed to be used generally for any violent wind. Job 27 : 21; 38 : 24; Ps. 48 : 7; Isa. 27 : 8; Ezek. 27 : 26. In Palestine the east wind prevails from February to June. The south wind, which traverses the Arabian peninsula before reaching Palestine, must necessarily be extremely hot. Job 37 : 17; Luke 12 : 55. The west and southwest winds reach Palestine loaded with moisture gathered from the Mediterranean, and are hence expressly termed by the Arabs "the fathers of the rain." Westerly winds prevail in Palestine from November to February. In addition to the four regular winds, we have notice in the Bible of the local squalls, Mark 4 : 37; Luke 8 : 23, to which the Sea of Gennesareth was liable. In the narrative of St. Paul's voyage we meet with the Greek term *Lips* to describe the southwest wind; the Latin

Carus or *Caurus*, the northwest wind, Acts 27 : 12, and *Euroclydon*, a wind of a very violent character coming from east-northeast. Acts 27 : 14.

Egyptian Wine-press.

Wine. The manufacture of wine is carried back in the Bible to the age of Noah, Gen. 9 : 20, 21, to whom the discovery of the process is apparently, though not explicitly, attributed. The natural history and culture of the vine are described under a separate head. [VINE.] The only other plant whose fruit is noticed as having been converted into wine was the pomegranate. Cant. 8 : 2. In Palestine the vintage takes place in September, and is celebrated with great rejoicings. The ripe fruit was gathered in baskets, Jer. 6 : 9, as represented in Egyptian paintings, and was carried to the wine-press. It was then placed in the upper one of the two vats or receptacles of which the wine-press was formed, and was subjected to the process of "treading," which has prevailed in all ages in Oriental and south-European countries. Neh. 13 : 15 ; Job 24 : 11 ; Isa. 16 : 10 ; Jer. 25 : 30 ; 48 : 33 ; Amos 9 : 13 ; Rev. 19 : 15. A certain amount of juice exuded from the ripe fruit from its own pressure before the treading commenced. This appears to have been kept separate from the rest of the juice, and to have formed the "sweet wine" noticed in Acts 2 : 13. [See below.] The "treading" was effected by one or more men, according to the size of the vat. They encouraged one another by shouts. Isa. 16 : 9, 10 ; Jer. 25 : 30 ; 48 : 33. Their legs and garments were dyed red with the juice. Gen. 49 : 11 ; Isa. 63 : 2, 3. The expressed juice escaped by an aperture into the lower vat, or was at once collected in vessels. A hand-press was occasionally used in Egypt, but we have no notice of such an instrument in the Bible. As to the subsequent treatment of the wine we have but little information. Sometimes it was preserved in its unfermented state and

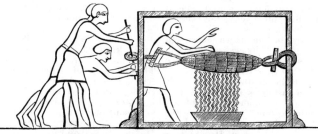

Egyptians expressing the Juice of the Grape.

drunk as must, but more generally it was bottled off after fermentation, and, if it were designed to be kept for some time, a certain amount of lees was added to give it body. Isa. 25 : 6. The wine consequently required to be "refined" or strained previous to being brought to table. Isa. 25 : 6. To wine is attributed the "darkly-flashing eye," Gen. 49 : 12, Authorized Version "red," the unbridled tongue, Prov. 20 : 1 ; Isa. 28 : 7, the excitement of the spirit, Prov. 31 : 6 ; Isa. 5 : 11 ; Zech. 9 : 15 ; 10 : 7, the enchained affections of its votaries, Hos. 4 : 11, the perverted judgment, Prov. 31 : 5 ; Isa. 28 : 7, the indecent exposure, Hab. 2 : 15, 16, and the sickness resulting from the *heat* (*chemâh*, Authorized Version "bottles ") of wine. Hos. 7 : 5. The allusions to the effects of *tirôsh* are confined to a single passage, but this a most decisive one, viz. Hos. 4 : 11, " Whoredom and wine (*yayin*) and new wine (*tirôsh*) take away the heart," where *tirôsh* appears as the climax of engrossing influences, in immediate connection with *yayin*. It has been disputed whether the Hebrew wine was fermented; but the impression produced on the mind by a general review of the above notices is that the Hebrew words indicating wine refer to fermented, intoxicating wine. The notices of fermentation are not very decisive. A certain amount of fermentation is implied in the distension of the leather bottles when new wine was placed in them, and which was liable to burst old bottles. It is very likely that new wine was preserved in the state of must by placing it in jars or bottles and then burying it in the earth. The mingling that we read of in conjunction with wine may have been designed either to increase or to diminish the strength of the wine, according as spices or water formed the ingredient that was added. The notices chiefly favor the former view; for mingled liquor was prepared for high festivals, Prov. 9 : 2, 5, and occasions of excess. Prov. 23 : 30; Isa. 5 : 22. At the same time strength was not the sole object sought; the wine "mingled with myrrh," given to Jesus, was designed to deaden pain, Mark 15 : 23, and the spiced pomegranate wine prepared by the bride, Cant. 8 : 2, may well have been of a mild character. In the New Testament the character of the "sweet wine," noticed in Acts 2 : 13, calls for some little remark. It could not be *new* wine in the proper sense of the term, inasmuch as about eight months must have elapsed between the vintage and the feast of Pentecost. The explanations of the ancient lexicographers rather lead us to infer that its luscious qualities were due, not to its being recently made, but to its being produced from the very purest juice of the grape. There can be little doubt that the wines of Palestine varied in quality, and were named after the localities in which they were made. The only wines of which we have special notice belonged to Syria; these were the wine of Helbon, Ezek. 27 : 18, and the wine of Lebanon, famed for its aroma. Hos. 14 : 7. With regard to the uses of wine in private life there is little to remark. It was pro-

duced on occasions of ordinary hospitality, Gen. 14 : 18, and at festivals, such as marriages. John 2 : 3. Under the Mosaic law wine formed the usual drink offering that accompanied the daily sacrifice, Ex. 29 : 40, the presentation of the first-fruits, Lev. 23 : 13, and other offerings. Num. 15 : 5. Tithe was to be paid of wine, as of other products. The priest was also to receive first-fruits of wine, as of other articles. Deut. 18 : 4; comp. Ex. 22 : 29. The use of wine at the paschal feast was not enjoined by the law, but had become an established custom, at all events in the post-Babylonian period. The wine was mixed with warm water on these occasions. Hence in the early Christian Church it was usual to mix the sacramental wine with water. (The simple wines of antiquity were incomparably less deadly than the stupefying and ardent beverages of our western nations. The wines of antiquity were more like sirups; many of them were not intoxicant; many more intoxicant in a small degree; and all of them, as a rule, taken only when largely diluted with water. They contained, even undiluted, but 4 or 5 per cent. of alcohol.—*Canon Farrar.*)

Wine-press. From the scanty notices contained in the Bible we gather that the wine-presses of the Jews consisted of two receptacles or vats placed at different elevations, in the upper one of which the grapes were trodden, while the lower one received the expressed juice. The two vats are mentioned together only in Joel 3 : 13 : "The press is full : the fats overflow"—the upper vat being full of fruit, the lower one overflowing with the must. [WINE.] The two vats were usually hewn out of the solid rock. Isa. 5 : 2, margin ; Matt. 21 : 33. Ancient wine-presses, so constructed, are still to be seen in Palestine.

Winnowing. [AGRICULTURE.]

Wisdom of Jesus, Son of Sirach. [ECCLESIASTICUS.]

Wisdom, The, of Solomon, a book of the Apocrypha, may be divided into two parts, the first, chs. 1–9, containing the doctrine of wisdom in its moral and intellectual aspects; the second, the doctrine of wisdom as shown in history. chs. 10–19. The first part contains the praise of wisdom as the source of immortality, in contrast with the teaching of sensualists; and next the praise of wisdom as the guide of practical and intellectual life, the stay of princes, and the interpreter of the universe. The second part, again, follows the action of wisdom summarily, as preserving God's servants, from Adam to Moses, and more particularly in the punishment of the Egyptians and Canaanites. *Style and language.*— The literary character of the book is most remarkable and interesting. In the richness and freedom of its vocabulary it most closely resembles the Fourth Book of Maccabees, but it is superior to that fine declamation in both power and variety of diction. The magnificent description of wisdom, ch. 7 : 22–8 : 1, must rank among the noblest passages of human eloquence, and it would be perhaps impossible to point out any piece of equal length in the remains of classical antiquity more pregnant with noble thought or more rich in expressive phraseology. *Doctrinal character.*— The theological teaching of the book offers, in many respects, the nearest approach to the language and doctrines of Greek philosophy that is found in any Jewish writing up to the time of Philo. There is much in the views which it gives of the world, of man and of the divine nature which springs rather from the combination or conflict of Hebrew and Greek thought than from the independent development of Hebrew thought alone. The conception is presented of the body as a mere weight and clog to the soul. ch. 9 : 15; contrast 2 Cor. 5 : 1–4. There is, on the other hand, no trace of the characteristic Christian doctrine of a resurrection of the body. The identification of the tempter, Gen. 3, directly or indirectly with the devil, as the bringer "of death into the world," ch. 2 : 23, 24, is the most remarkable development of biblical doctrine which the book contains. Generally, too, it may be observed that, as in the cognate books, Proverbs and Ecclesiastes, there are few traces of the recognition of the sinfulness even of the wise man in his wisdom, which forms, in the Psalms and the prophets, the basis of the Christian doctrine of the atonement: yet comp. 15 : 2. In connection with the Old Testament Scriptures, the book, as a whole, may be regarded as carrying on one step farther the great problem of life contained in Ecclesiastes and Job. *Date.*— From internal evidence it seems most reasonable to believe that the work was composed in Greek at Alexandria some time before the time of Philo — about 120–80 B.C. It seems impossible to study this book dispassionately and not feel that it forms one of the last links in the chain of providential connection between the Old and New Covenants. It would not be easy to find elsewhere any preChristian view of religion equally wide, sustained and definite.

Wise men. [MAGI.]

Witch, Witchcrafts. [DIVINATION: MAGIC.]

Witness. Among people with whom writing is not common, the evidence of a transaction is given by some tangible memorial or significant ceremony. Abraham gave seven ewe-lambs to Abimelech as an evidence of his property in the well of Beersheba. Jacob raised a heap of stones, "the heap of witness," as a boundary-mark between himself and Laban. Gen. 21 : 30; 31 : 47, 52. The tribes of Reuben and Gad raised an "altar" as a witness to the covenant between themselves and the rest of the nation. Joshua set up a stone as an evidence of the allegiance promised by Israel to God. Josh. 22 : 10, 26, 34; 24 : 26, 27. But written evidence was by no means unknown to the Jews. Divorce was to be proved by a written document. Deut. 24 : 1, 3. In civil contracts, at least in later times, documentary evidence was required and carefully preserved. Isa. 8 : 16; Jer. 32 : 10–16. On the whole the law was very careful to provide and enforce evidence for all its infractions and all transactions bearing on them. Among special provisions with respect to evidence are the following: 1. Two witnesses at least are required to establish any charge. Num. 35 : 30; Deut. 17 : 6; John 8 : 17; 2 Cor. 13 : 1; comp. 1 Tim. 5 : 19. 2. In the case of the suspected wife, evidence besides the husband's was desired. Num. 5 : 13. 3. The witness who withheld the truth was censured. Lev. 5 : 1. 4. False witness was punished with the penalty due to the offence which it sought to establish. 5. Slanderous reports and officious witness are discouraged. Ex. 20 : 16; 23 : 1; Lev. 19 : 16, 18, etc. 6. The witnesses were the first executioners. Deut. 13 : 9; 17 : 7; Acts 7 : 58. 7. In case of an animal left in charge and torn by wild beasts, the keeper was to bring the carcass in proof of the fact and disproof of his own criminality. Ex. 22 : 13. 8. According to Josephus, women and slaves were not admitted to bear testimony. In the New Testament the original notion of a witness is exhibited in the special form of one who attests his belief in the gospel by personal suffering. Hence it is that the use of the ecclesiastical term "martyr," the Greek word for "witness," has arisen.

Wizard. [DIVINATION; MAGIC.]

Wolf. There can be little doubt that the wolf of Palestine is the common *Canis lupus*, and that this is the animal so frequently mentioned in the Bible. (The wolf is a fierce animal of the same species as the dog, which it resembles. The common color is gray with a tinting of fawn, and the hair is long and black. The Syrian wolf is of lighter color than the wolf of Europe. It is the dread of the shepherds of Palestine.—ED.) Wolves were doubtless far more common in biblical times than they are now, though they are occasionally seen by modern travellers. The following are the scriptural allusions to the wolf: Its ferocity is mentioned in Gen. 49 : 27 ; Ezek. 22 : 27 ; Hab. 1 : 8 ; Matt. 7 : 15 ; its nocturnal habits, in Jer. 5 : 6 ; Zeph. 3 : 3 ; Hab. 1 : 8 ; its attacking sheep and lambs, Matt. 10 : 16 ; Luke 10 : 3 ; John 10 : 12. Isaiah, Isa. 11 : 6 ; 65 : 25, foretells the peaceful reign of the Messiah under the metaphor of a wolf dwelling with a lamb; cruel persecutors are compared with wolves. Matt. 10 : 16 ; Acts 20 : 29.

Women. The position of women in the Hebrew commonwealth contrasts favorably with that which in the present day is assigned to them generally in eastern countries. The most salient point of contrast in the usages of ancient as compared with modern Oriental society was the large amount of liberty enjoyed by women. Instead of being immured in a harem, or appearing in public with the face covered, the wives and maidens of ancient times mingled freely and openly with the other sex in the duties and amenities of ordinary life. Rebekah travelled on a camel with her face unveiled, until she came into the presence of her affianced. Gen. 24 : 64, 65. Jacob saluted Rachel with a kiss in the presence of the shepherds. Gen. 29 : 11. Women played no inconsiderable part in public celebrations. Ex. 15 : 20, 21 ; Judges 11 : 34. The odes of Deborah, Judges 5, and of Hannah, 1 Sam. 2 : 1, etc., exhibit a degree of intellectual cultivation which is in itself a proof of the position of the sex in that period. Women also occasionally held public office, particularly that of proph-

etess or inspired teacher. Ex. 15 : 20 ; Judges 4 : 4 ; 2 Kings 22 : 14 ; Neh. 6 : 14 ; Luke 2 : 36. The management of household affairs devolved mainly on the women. The value of a virtuous and active housewife forms a frequent topic in the book of Proverbs. ch. 11 : 16 ; 12 : 4 ; 14 : 1 ; 31 : 10 ; etc. Her influence was of course proportionably great.

"Outer Garments of Women" as used by Egyptians of the present day.

Wood. [FOREST.]

Wool was an article of the highest value among the Jews, as the staple material for the manufacture of clothing. Lev. 13 : 47 ; Deut. 22 : 11 ; Job 31 : 20 ; Prov. 31 : 13 ; Ezek. 34 : 3 ; Hosea 2 : 5. The importance of wool is incidentally shown by the notice that Mesha's tribute was paid in a certain number of rams "with the wool." 2 Kings 3 : 4. The wool of Damascus was highly prized in the mart of Tyre. Ezek. 27 : 18.

Worm, the representative in the Authorized Version of several Hebrew words. *Sâs*, which occurs in Isa. 51 : 8, probably denotes some particular species of moth, whose larva is injurious to wool. *Rimmâh*, Ex. 16 : 20, points evidently to various kinds of maggots and the larvæ of insects which feed on putrefying animal matter, rather than to earthworms. *Tôlê'âh* is applied in Deut. 28 : 39 to some kinds of larvæ destructive to the vines. In Job 19 : 26 ; 21 : 26 ; 24 : 20, there is an allusion to worms (insect larvæ) feeding on the dead bódies of the buried. There is the same allusion in Isa. 66 : 24, which words are applied by our Lord, Mark 9 : 44, 46, 48, metaphorically to the torments of the guilty in the world of departed spirits. The valley of Hinnom, near Jerusalem, where the filth of the city was cast, was alive with worms. The death of Herod Agrippa I. was caused by worms. Acts 12 : 23.

Wormwood.

Wormwood. Four kinds of wormwood are found in Palestine—*Artemisia nilotica, A. Judaica, A. fructicosa* and *A. cinerea.* The word occurs frequently in the Bible, and generally in a metaphorical sense. In Jer. 9 : 15; 23 : 15; Lam. 3 : 15, 19, wormwood is symbolical of bitter calamity and sorrow; unrighteous judges are said to "turn judgment to wormwood." Amos 5 : 7. The Orientals typified sorrows, cruelties and calamities of any kind by plants of a poisonous or bitter nature.

Worshipper, a translation of the Greek word *neocoros,* used once only, Acts 19 : 35; in the margin, "temple-keeper." The *neocoros* was originally an attendant in a temple, probably intrusted with its charge. The term *neocoros* became thus applied to cities or communities which undertook the worship of particular em-

perors even during their lives. The first occurrence of the term in connection with Ephesus is on coins of the age of Nero, A.D. 54–68.

Wrestling. [GAMES.]

Writing. There is no account in the Bible of the origin of writing. That the Egyptians in the time of Joseph were acquainted with writing of a certain kind there is evidence to prove, but there is nothing to show that up to this period the knowledge extended to the Hebrew family. At the same time there is no evidence against it. Writing is first distinctly mentioned in Ex. 17 : 14, and the connection clearly implies that it was not then employed for the first time, but was so familiar as to be used for historic records. It is not absolutely necessary to infer from this that the art of writing was an accomplishment possessed by every Hebrew citizen. If we examine the instances in which writing is mentioned in connection with individuals, we shall find that in all cases the writers were men of superior position. In Isa. 29 : 11, 12 there is clearly a distinction drawn between the man who was able to read and the man who was not, and it seems a natural inference that the accomplishments of reading and writing were not widely spread among the people, when we find that they are universally attributed to those of high rank or education—kings, priests, prophets and professional scribes. In the name Kirjath-sepher (*book-town*), Josh. 15 : 15, there is an indication of a knowledge of writing among the Phœnicians. The Hebrews,

Pens and Writing Materials.

then, a branch of the great Semitic family, being in possession of the art of writing, according to their own historical records, at a very early period, the further questions arise, what character they made use of, and whence they obtained it. Recent investigations have shown that the square Hebrew character is of comparatively modern date, and has been formed from a more ancient type by a gradual process of development. What then was this ancient type? Most probably the Phœnician. Pliny was of opinion that letters were of Assyrian origin. Diodorus Siculus (v. 74) says that the Syrians invented letters, and from them the Phœnicians, having learned them, transferred them to the Greeks. According to Tacitus (*Ann.* xi. 14), Egypt was believed to be the source whence the Phœnicians got their knowledge. Be this as it may, to the Phœnicians, the daring seamen and adventurous colonizers of the ancient world, the voice of tradition has assigned the honor of the invention of letters. Whether it came to them from an Aramæan or an Egyptian source can at best be but the subject of conjecture. It may, however, be reasonably inferred that the ancient Hebrews derived from or shared with the Phœnicians the knowledge of writing and the use of letters. The names of the Hebrew letters indicate that they must have been the invention of a Shemitic people, and that they were moreover a pastoral people may be inferred from the same evidence. But whether or not the Phœnicians were the inventors of the Shemitic alphabet, there can be no doubt of their just claim to being its chief disseminators; and with this understanding we may accept the genealogy of alphabets as given by Gesenius, and exhibited in the accompanying table.

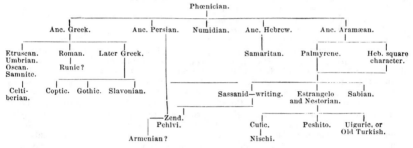

The old Semitic alphabets may be divided into two principal classes : 1. The Phœnician, as it exists in the inscriptions in Cyprus, Malta, Carpentras, and the coins of Phœnicia and her colonies. From it are derived the Samaritan and the Greek character. 2. The Hebrew-Chaldee character; to which belong the Hebrew square character; the Palmyrene, which has some traces of a cursive hand; the Estrangelo, or ancient Syriac; and the ancient Arabic or Cufic. It was probably about the first or second century after Christ that the square character assumed its present form; though in a question involved in so much uncertainty it is impossible to pronounce with great positiveness. *The alphabet.*—The oldest evidence on the subject of the Hebrew alphabet is derived from the alphabetical psalms and poems: Pss. 25, 34, 37, 111, 112, 119, 145; Prov. 31 : 10–31 ; Lam. 1–4. From these we ascertain that the number of the letters was twenty-two, as at present. The Arabic alphabet originally consisted of the same number. It has been argued by many that the alphabet of the Phœnicians at first consisted of only sixteen letters. The legend, as told by Pliny (vii. 56), is as follows : Cadmus brought with him into Greece sixteen letters; at the time of the Trojan war Palamedes added four others, Θ, Ξ, Φ, X, and Simonides of Melos four more, Z, H, Ψ, Ω. *Divisions of words.*—Hebrew was originally written, like most ancient languages, without any divisions between the words. The same is the case with the Phœnician inscriptions. The various readings in the LXX. show that, at the time this version was made, in the Hebrew MSS. which the translators used the words were written in a continuous series. The modern synagogue rolls and the MSS. of the Samaritan Pentateuch have no vowel-points, but the words are divided, and the Samaritan in this respect differs but little from the Hebrew. *Writing materials, etc.*—The oldest documents which contain the writing of a Semitic race are probably the bricks of Nineveh and Babylon, on which are impressed the cuneiform Syrian inscriptions. There is, however, no evidence that they were ever used by the Hebrews. It is highly probable that the ancient as well as the most common material which the Hebrews used for writing was dressed skin in some form or other. We know that the dressing of skins was practiced by the Hebrews, Ex. 25 : 5; Lev. 13 : 48, and they may have acquired the knowledge of the art from the Egyptians, among whom it had attained great perfection, the leather-cutters constituting one of the principal subdivisions of the third caste. Perhaps the Hebrews may have borrowed, among their other acquirements, the use of papyrus from the Egyptians, but of this we have no positive evidence. In the Bible the only allusions to the use of papyrus are in 2 John 12, where *chartes* (Authorized Version "paper") occurs, which refers especially to papyrus paper, and 3 Macc. 4 : 20, where *charteria* is found in the same sense. Herodotus, after telling us that the Ionians learned the art of writing from the Phœnicians, adds that they called their books skins, because they made use of sheep-skins and goat-skins when short of paper. Parchment was used for the MSS. of the Pentateuch in the time of Josephus, and the *membranæ* of 2 Tim. 4 : 13 were skins of parchment. It was one of the provisions in the Talmud that the law should be written on the skins of clean animals, tame or wild, or even of clean birds. The skins when written upon were formed into rolls (*mĕgillôth*). Ps. 40 : 7; comp. Isa. 34 : 4; Jer. 36 : 14; Ezek. 2 : 9; Zech. 5 : 1. They were rolled upon one or two sticks and fastened with a thread, the ends of which were sealed. Isa. 29 : 11; Dan. 12 : 4; Rev. 5 : 1, etc. The rolls were generally written on one side only, except in Ezek. 2 : 9; Rev. 5 : 1. They were divided into columns (Authorized Version "leaves," Jer. 36 : 23); the upper margin was to be not less than three fingers broad, the lower not less than four; and a space of two fingers breadth was to be left between every two columns.

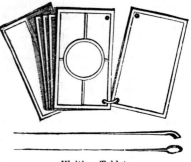

Writing Tablets.

But besides skins, which were used for the more permanent kinds of writing, tablets of wood covered with wax, Luke 1 : 63, served for the ordinary purposes of life. Several of these were fastened together and formed volumes. They were written upon with a pointed style, Job 19 : 24, sometimes of iron. Ps. 45 : 1; Jer. 8 : 8; 17 : 1. For harder materials a graver, Ex. 32 : 4; Isa. 8 : 1, was employed. For parchment or skins a reed was used. 3 John 13; 3 Macc. 5 : 20. The ink, Jer. 36 : 18, literally "black," like the Greek μέλαν, 2 Cor. 3 : 3; 2 John 12; 3 John 13, was of lampblack dissolved in gall-juice. It was carried in an inkstand, which was suspended at the girdle, Ezek. 9 : 2, 3, as is done at the present day in the East. To professional scribes there are allusions in Ezra 7 : 6; Ps. 45 : 1; 2 Esdr. 14 : 24.

Y.

Yarn. The notice of yarn is contained in an extremely obscure passage in 1 Kings 10 : 28; 2 Chron. 1 : 16. The Hebrew Received Text is questionable. Gesenius gives the sense of "number" as applying equally to the merchants and the horses: "A *band* of the king's merchants bought a *drove* (of horses) at a price."

Year, the highest ordinary division of time. Two years were known to, and apparently used by, the Hebrews. 1. A year of 360 days appears to have been in use in Noah's time. 2. The year used by the Hebrews from the time of the exodus may be said to have been then instituted, since a current month, Abib, on the 14th day of which the first Passover was kept, was then made the first month of the year. The essential characteristics of this year can be clearly determined, though we cannot fix those of any single year. It was essentially solar, for the offering of productions of the earth, first-fruits, harvest produce and ingathered fruits, was fixed to certain days of the year, two of which were in the periods of great feasts, the third itself a feast reckoned from one of the former days. But it is certain that the months were lunar, each commencing with a new moon. There must therefore have been some method of adjustment. The first point to be decided is how the commencement of each year was fixed. Probably the Hebrews determined their new year's day by the observation of heliacal or other star-risings or settings known to mark the right time of the solar year. It follows, from the determination of the proper new moon of the first month, whether by observation of a stellar phenomenon or of the forwardness of the crops, that the method of intercalation can only have been that in use after the captivity,—the addition of a thirteenth month whenever the twelfth ended too long before the equinox for the offering of the first-fruits to be made at the time fixed. The later Jews had two commencements of the year, whence it is

commonly but inaccurately said that they had two years, the sacred year and the civil. We prefer to speak of the sacred and civil reckonings. The sacred reckoning was that instituted at the exodus, according to which the first month was Abib; by the civil reckoning the first month was the seventh. The interval between the two commencements was thus exactly half a year. It has been supposed that the institution at the time of the exodus was a change of commencement, not the introduction of a new year, and that thenceforward the year had two beginnings, respectively at about the vernal and the autumnal equinox. The year was divided into—1. *Seasons.* Two seasons are mentioned in the Bible, "summer" and "winter." The former properly means the time of cutting fruits, the latter that of gathering fruits; they are therefore originally rather summer and autumn than summer and winter. But that they signify ordinarily the two grand divisions of the year, the warm and cold seasons, is evident from their use for the whole year in the expression "summer and winter." Ps. 74 : 17; Zech. 14 : 8. 2. *Months.* [MONTHS.] 3. *Weeks.* [WEEKS.]

Year, Sabbatical. [SABBATICAL YEAR.]

Year of Jubilee. [JUBILEE, YEAR OF.]

Yoke. 1. A well-known implement of husbandry, frequently used metaphorically for *subjection, e. g.* 1 Kings 12 : 4, 9–11; Isa. 9 : 4; Jer. 5 : 5; hence an "iron yoke" represents an unusually galling bondage. Deut. 28 : 48; Jer. 28 : 13. 2. A pair of oxen, so termed as being yoked together. 1 Sam. 11 : 7; 1 Kings 19 : 19, 21. The Hebrew term is also applied to asses, Judges 19 : 10, and mules, 2 Kings 5 : 17, and even to a couple of riders. Isa. 21 : 7. 3. The term is also applied to a certain amount of land, 1 Sam. 14 : 14, equivalent to that which a couple of oxen could plough in a day, Isa. 5 : 10 (Authorized Version "acre"), corresponding to the Latin *jugum.*

Z.

Za-ana'im (*removings*), **The plain of,** or, more accurately, "the oak by Zaanaim," a tree—probably a sacred tree —mentioned as marking the spot near which Heber the Kenite was encamped when Sisera took refuge in his tent. Judges 4 : 11. Its situation is defined as "near Kedesh," *i. e.* Kedesh-naphtali, the name of which still lingers on the high ground north of *Safed* and two or three miles west of the lake of *el-Huleh* (waters of Merom). This whole region abounds in oaks.

Za'anan. [ZENAN.]

Za'avan, or **Za'van** (*migratory*), a Horite chief, son of Ezer the son of Seir. Gen. 36 : 27; 1 Chron. 1 : 42.

Za'bad (*gift*). 1. Son of Nathan, son of Attai, son of Ahlai Sheshan's daughter, 1 Chron. 2 : 31-37, and hence called son of Ahlai. 1 Chron. 11 : 41. (B. C. 1046.) He was one of David's mighty men, but none of his deeds have been recorded. The chief interest connected with him is in his genealogy, which is of considerable importance in a chronological point of view.
2. An Ephraimite, if the text of 1 Chron. 7 : 21 is correct.
3. Son of Shimeath, an Ammonitess; an assassin who, with Jehozabad, slew King Joash, according to 2 Chron. 24 : 26 (B. C. 840); but in 2 Kings 12 : 21 his name is written, probably more correctly, JOZACHAR.
4. A layman of Israel, of the sons of Zattu, who put away his foreign wife at Ezra's command. Ezra 10 : 27. (B.C. 458.)
5. One of the descendants of Hashum, who had married a foreign wife after the captivity. Ezra 10 : 33. (B.C. 458.)
6. One of the sons of Nebo, whose name is mentioned under the same circumstances as the two preceding. Ezra 10 : 43.

Zabade'ans, an Arab tribe who were attacked and spoiled by Jonathan, on his way back to Damascus from his fruitless pursuit of the army of Demetrius. 1 Macc. 12 : 31. Their name probably survives in the village of *Zebdány,* about 26 miles from Damascus.

Zab'ba-i (*pure*). 1. One of the descendants of Bebai, who had married a foreign wife in the days of Ezra. Ezra 10 : 28. (B.C. 458.)
2. Father of Baruch, who assisted Nehemiah in rebuilding the city wall. Neh. 3 : 20. (B.C. before 446.)

Zab'bud (*given*), one of the sons of Bigvai, who returned in the second caravan with Ezra. Ezra 8 : 14. (B.C. 459.)

Zab'di (*my gift*). 1. Son of Zerah the son of Judah, and ancestor of Achan. Josh. 7 : 1, 17, 18. (B.C. before 1450.)
2. A Benjamite, of the sons of Shimhi. 1 Chron. 8 : 19. (B.C. about 1442.)
3. David's officer over the produce of the vineyards for the wine-cellars. 1 Chron. 27 : 27. (B.C. 1043.)
4. Son of Asaph the minstrel, Neh. 11 : 17; called ZACCUR in Neh. 12 : 35 and ZICHRI in 1 Chron. 9 : 15. (B.C. before 446.)

Zab'di-el (*gift of God*). 1. Father of Jashobeam, the chief of David's guard. 1 Chron. 27 : 2. (B.C. before 1046.)
2. A priest, son of the great men, or, as the margin gives it, "Haggedolim." Neh. 11 : 14. (B.C. 459.)

Za'bud (*given*), son of Nathan, 1 Kings 4 : 5, is described as a priest (Authorized Version "principal officer"), and as holding at the court of Solomon the confidential post of "king's friend," which had been occupied by Hushai the Archite during the reign of David. 2 Sam. 15 : 37; 16 : 16; 1 Chron. 27 : 33. (B.C. 1012.)

Zab'ulon, the Greek form of the name Zebulun. Matt. 4 : 13, 15; Rev. 7 : 8.

Zac'ca-i (*pure*). The sons of Zaccai, to the number of 760, returned with Zerubbabel. Ezra 2 : 9; Neh. 7 : 14. (B.C. before 536.)

Zacchæ'us (*pure*), a tax-collector near Jericho, who, being short in stature, climbed up into a sycamore tree in order to obtain a sight of Jesus as he passed through that place. Luke 19 : 1-10. Zacchæus was a Jew, as may be inferred from his name and from the fact that the Saviour speaks of him expressly as "a son of Abraham." The term which designates his office—"the chief among the publicans"—is unusual, but describes him, no doubt, as the superintendent of customs or tribute in the district of Jericho, where he lived. The office must have been a lucrative one in such a region, and it is not strange that Zacchæus is mentioned by the evangelists as a rich man. The Saviour spent the night probably in the house of Zacchæus, and the next day pursued his journey. He was in the caravan from Galilee which was going to Jerusalem to keep the Passover.

Zac'chur, a Simeonite, of the family of Mishma. 1 Chron. 4 : 26.

Zac'cur (*mindful*). 1. Father of Shammua, the Reubenite spy. Num. 13 : 4. (B.C. 1451.)

2. A Merarite Levite, son of Jaaziah. 1 Chron. 24 : 27.

3. Son of Asaph the singer. 1 Chron. 25 : 2, 10 ; Neh. 12 : 35.

4. The son of Imri, who assisted Nehemiah in rebuilding the city wall. Neh. 3 : 2. (B.C. 446.)

5. A Levite, or family of Levites, who signed the covenant with Nehemiah. Neh. 10 : 12. (B.C. 410.)

6. A Levite whose son or descendant Hanan was one of the treasurers over the treasuries appointed by Nehemiah. Neh. 13 : 13.

Zachari'ah (*remembered by Jehovah*), or properly **Zechariah.** 1. Son of Jeroboam II., fourteenth king of Israel, and the last of the house of Jehu. There is a difficulty about the date of his reign. Most chronologers assume an interregnum of eleven years between Jeroboam's death and Zachariah's accession. The latter event took place B.C. 772–1. His reign lasted only six months. He was killed in a conspiracy of which Shallum was the head, and by which the prophecy in 2 Kings 10 : 30 was accomplished.

2. The father of Abi or Abijah, Hezekiah's mother. 2 Kings 18 : 2.

Zachari'as (Greek form of *Zachariah*). 1. Father of John the Baptist. Luke 1 : 5, etc. He was a priest of the course of Abia, the eighth of the twenty-four courses who ministered at the temple in turn. He probably lived at Hebron. His wife's name was Elisabeth. John was born to them in their old age, and the promise of this son was communicated to Zacharias by an angel while he was offering incense and praying in the temple.

2. Son of Barachias, who, our Lord says, was slain by the Jews between the altar and the temple. Matt. 23 : 35 ; Luke 11 : 51. There has been much dispute who this Zacharias was. Many of the Greek fathers have maintained that the father of John the Baptist is the person to whom our Lord alludes ; but there can be little or no doubt that the allusion is to Zechariah, the son of Jehoiada, 2 Chron. 24 : 20, 21 ; and he may have been called "the son" of Barachias from his grandfather. (B.C. 838.) He is mentioned as being the martyr last recorded in the Hebrew Scriptures (as Abel was the first),—2d Chronicles being the last book in their canon.

Za'cher (*memorial*), one of the sons of Jehiel, the father or founder of Gibeon, by his wife Maachah. 1 Chron. 8 : 31. (B.C. about 1450.)

Za'dok (*just*). 1. Son of Ahitub, and one of the two chief priests in the time of David, Abiathar being the other. Zadok was of the house of Eleazar the son of Aaron, 1 Chron. 24 : 3, and eleventh in descent from Aaron. 1 Chron. 12 : 28. He joined David at Hebron after Saul's death, 1 Chron. 12 : 28, and thenceforth his fidelity to David was inviolable. When Absalom revolted, and David fled from Jerusalem, Zadok and all the Levites bearing the ark accompanied him. When Absalom was dead, Zadok and Abiathar were the persons who persuaded the elders of Judah to invite David to return. 2 Sam. 19 : 11. When Adonijah, in David's old age, set up for king, and had persuaded Joab, and Abiathar the priest, to join his party, Zadok was unmoved, and was employed by David to anoint Solomon to be king in his room. 1 Kings 1 : 34. For this fidelity he was rewarded by Solomon, who "thrust out Abiathar from being priest unto the Lord," and "put in Zadok the priest" in his room. 1 Kings 2 : 27, 35. From this time, however, we hear little of him. Zadok and Abiathar were of nearly equal dignity. 2 Sam. 15 : 35, 36 ; 19 : 11. The duties of the office were divided. Zadok ministered before the tabernacle at Gibeon, 1 Chron. 16 : 39 ; Abiathar had the care of the ark at Jerusalem.

2. According to the genealogy of the high priests in 1 Chron. 6 : 12, there was a second Zadok, son of a second Ahitub, son of Amariah, about the time of King Ahaziah. It is probable that no such person as this second Zadok ever existed, but that the insertion of the two names is a copyist's error.

3. Father of Jerushah, the wife of

King Uzziah and mother of King Jotham. 2 Kings 15 : 33 ; 2 Chron. 27 : 1.

4. Son of Baana, and

5. Son of Immer, persons who repaired a portion of the wall in Nehemiah's time. Neh. 3 : 4, 29.

6. In 1 Chron. 9 : 11 and Neh. 11 : 11 mention is made, in a genealogy, of Zadok, the son of Meraioth, the son of Ahitub; but it can hardly be doubtful that Meraioth is inserted by the error of a copyist, and that Zadok the son of Ahitub is meant.

Za'ham (*fatness*), son of Rehoboam by Abihail the daughter of Eliab. 2 Chron. 11 : 19.

Za'ir (*small*), a place named, in 2 Kings 8 : 21 only, in the account of Joram's expedition against the Edomites. It has been conjectured that Zair is identical with Zoar.

Za'laph (*wound*), father of Hanun, who assisted in rebuilding the city wall. Neh. 3 : 30.

Zal'mon (*shady*), an Ahohite, one of David's guard. 2 Sam. 23 : 28.

Zal'mon, Mount, a wooded eminence in the immediate neighborhood of Shechem. Judges 9 : 48. The name of Dalmanutha has been supposed to be a corruption of that of Zalmon.

Zalmo'nah (*shady*), a desert-station of the Israelites, Num. 33 : 41, lies on the east side of Edom.

Zalmun'na. [ZEBAH.]

Zamzum'mim, Deut. 2 : 20 only, the Ammonite name for the people who by others were called Rephaim. They are described as having originally been a powerful and numerous nation of giants. From a slight similarity between the two names, and from the mention of the Emim in connection with each, it is conjectured that the Zamzummim are identical with the Zuzim.

Zano'ah (*marsh*). 1. A town of Judah in the Shefelah or plain, Josh. 15 : 34 ; Neh. 3 : 13 ; 11 : 30 ; possibly identical with *Zánú'a.*

2. A town of Judah in the highland district, Josh. 15 : 56, not improbably identical with *Sanúte*, about 10 miles south of Hebron.

3. In the genealogical lists of the tribe of Judah in 1 Chron., Jekuthiel is said to have been the father of Zanoah. ch. 4 : 18. As Zanoah is the name of a town of

Judah, this mention of Bithiah probably points to some colonization of the place by Egyptians or by Israelites directly from Egypt.

Zaph'nath-pa-ane'ah, a name given by Pharaoh to Joseph. Gen. 41 : 45. The rabbins interpreted Zaphnath-paaneah as Hebrew, in the sense *revealer of a secret.* As the name must have been Egyptian, it has been explained from the Coptic as meaning *the preserver of the age.*

Za'phon (*north*), a place mentioned in the enumeration of the allotment of the tribe of Gad. Josh. 13 : 27.

Za'ra, or Za'rah, the son of Judah. Matt. 1 : 3.

Za'rah, or Ze'rah, the son of Judah. Gen. 38 : 30 ; 46 : 12.

Za'reah, the same as Zorah and Zoreah. Neh. 11 : 29.

Za'reathites, The, the inhabitants of Zareah or Zorah. 1 Chron. 2 : 53.

Za'red, The valley of. [ZERED.]

Zar'ephath (*smelting place*), the res-

Zarephath.

idence of the prophet Elijah during the latter part of the drought. 1 Kings 17 : 9, 10. It was near to, or dependent on, Zidon. It is represented by the modern village of *Súra-fend.* Of the old town considerable indications remain. One group of foundations is on a headland called *Ain el-Kanatarah;* but the chief remains are south of this, and extend for a mile or more, with many fragments of columns, slabs and other architectural features. In the New Testament Zarephath appears under the Greek form of SAREPTA. Luke 4 : 26.

Zar'etan, or **Zar'than.** Josh. 3 : 16.

Za'reth-sha'har (*splendor of the dawn*), a place mentioned only in Josh. 13 : 19, in the catalogue of the towns allotted to Reuben.

Zar'hites, The, a branch of the tribe of Judah, descended from Zerah the son of Judah. Num. 26 : 13, 20; Josh. 7 : 17; 1 Chron. 27 : 11, 13.

Zar'tanah. 1 Kings 4 : 12. [ZARTHAN.]

Zar'than. 1. A place in the circle of Jordan, mentioned in connection with Succoth. 1 Kings 7 : 46.

2. It is also named in the account of the passage of the Jordan by the Israelites, Josh. 3 : 16, where the Authorized Version has Zaretan.

3. A place with the similar name of Zartanah. 1 Kings 4 : 12.

4. Further, Zeredathah, named in 2 Chron. 4 : 17 only in specifying the situation of the founderies for the brass-work of Solomon's temple, is substituted for Zarthan; and this again is not impossibly identical with the Zererath of the story of Gideon. Judges 7 : 22. All these spots agree in proximity to the Jordan, but beyond this we are absolutely at fault as to their position.

Zat'tu. The sons of Zattu were a family of laymen of Israel who returned with Zerubbabel. Ezra 2 : 8; Neh. 7 : 13.

Za'van. 1 Chron. 1 : 42. [ZAAVAN.]

Za'za, one of the sons of Jonathan, a descendant of Jerahmeel. 1 Chron. 2 : 33.

Zebadi'ah. 1. A Benjamite of the sons of Beriah. 1 Chron. 8 : 15.

2. A Benjamite of the sons of Elpaal. 1 Chron. 8 : 17.

3. One of the sons of Jeroham of Gedor. 1 Chron. 12 : 7.

4. Son of Asahel, the brother of Joab. 1 Chron. 27 : 7.

5. Son of Michael, of the sons of Shephatiah. Ezra 8 : 8.

6. A priest of the sons of Immer, who had married a foreign wife after the return from Babylon. Ezra 10 : 20.

7. Third son of Meshelemiah the Korhite. 1 Chron. 26 : 2.

8. A Levite in the reign of Jehoshaphat. 2 Chron. 17 : 8.

9. The son of Ishmael and prince of the house of Judah in the reign of Jehoshaphat. 2 Chron. 19 : 11.

Ze'bah and **Zalmun'na** (*deprived of protection*), the two "kings" of Midian who commanded the great invasion of Palestine, and who finally fell by the hand of Gideon himself. Judges 8 : 5–21; Ps. 83 : 11. (B.C. 1250.) While Oreb and Zeeb, two of the inferior leaders of the incursion, had been slain, with a vast number of their people, by the Ephraimites, at the central fords of the Jordan, the two kings had succeeded in making their escape by a passage farther to the north (probably the ford near Bethshean), and thence by the *Wady Yabis,* through Gilead, to Karkor, high up on the Hauran. Here they were reposing with 15,000 men, a mere remnant of their huge horde, when Gideon overtook them. The people fled in dismay, and Gideon captured the two kings and brought them to his native village, Ophrah, where he slew them because they had killed his brothers.

Zeba'im (*the gazelles*), mentioned in the catalogue of the families of "Solomon's slaves" who returned from the captivity with Zerubbabel. Ezra 2 : 57; Neh. 7 : 59.

Zeb'edee (*my gift*) (Greek form of *Zabdi*), a fisherman of Galilee, the father of the apostles James the Great and John, Matt. 4 : 21, and the husband of Salome. Matt. 27 : 56; Mark 15 : 40. He probably lived either at Bethsaida or in its immediate neighborhood. It has been inferred from the mention of his "hired servants," Mark 1 : 20, and from the acquaintance between the apostle John and Annas the high priest, John 18 : 15, that the family of Zebedee were in easy circumstances, comp. John 19 : 27, although not above manual labor. Matt. 4 : 21. He appears only twice in the Gospel narrative, namely, in Matt. 4 : 21, 22; Mark 1 : 19, 20, where he is seen in his boat with his two sons mending their nets.

Zebi'na (*purchase*), one of the sons of Nebo who had taken foreign wives after the return from Babylon. Ezra 10 : 43.

Zebo'im (*gazelles*). **1.** One of the five cities of the "plain" or circle of Jordan. It is mentioned in Gen. 10 : 19; 14 : 2, 8; Deut. 29 : 23; Hos. 11 : 8, in each of which passages it is either coupled with Admah or placed next it in the lists—perhaps represented by *Talâa Sebâan,* a name attached to extensive ruins on the high ground between the Dead Sea and *Kerak.* In Gen. 14 : 2, 8 the name is given more correctly in the Authorized Version ZEBOIIM.

2. The valley of Zeboim, a ravine or

gorge, apparently east of Michmash, mentioned only in 1 Sam. 13 : 18. The road running from Michmash to the east is specified as "the road of the border that looketh to the ravine of Zeboim toward the wilderness." The wilderness is no doubt the district of uncultivated mountain tops and sides which lies between the central district of Benjamin and the Jordan valley. In that very district there is a wild gorge bearing the name of *Shuk ed-Dubba'*, "ravine of the hyena," the exact equivalent of *Ge hat-tsebo'im*.

Zebu'dah (*bestowed*), wife of Josiah and mother of King Jehoiakim. 2 Kings 23 : 36. (B.C. 653.)

Ze'bul (*habitation*), chief man (Authorized Version "ruler") of the city of Shechem at the time of the contest between Abimelech and the native Canaanites. Judges 9 : 28, 30, 36, 38, 41. (B.C. 1209.)

Zeb'ulonite, a member of the tribe of Zebulun. Judges 12 : 11, 12. Applied only to Elon, the one judge produced by the tribe. Judges 12 : 11, 12.

Zeb'ulun (*a habitation*), the tenth of the sons of Jacob, according to the order in which their births are enumerated; the sixth and last of Leah. Gen. 30 : 20; 35 : 23; 46 : 14; 1 Chron. 2 : 1. His birth is mentioned in Gen. 30 : 19, 20. Of the individual Zebulun nothing is recorded. The list of Gen. 46 ascribes to him three sons, founders of the chief families of the tribe (comp. Num. 26 : 26) at the time of the migration to Egypt. The tribe is not recorded to have taken part, for evil or good, in any of the events of the wandering or the conquest. The statement of Josephus is probably in the main correct, that it reached on the one side to the Lake of Gennesareth and on the other to Carmel and the Mediterranean. On the south it was bounded by Issachar, who lay in the great plain or valley of the Kishon; on the north it had Naphtali and Asher. Thus remote from the centre of government, Zebulun remains throughout the history, with one exception, in the obscurity which envelops the whole of the northern tribes. That exception, however, is a remarkable one. The conduct of the tribe during the struggle with Sisera, when they fought with desperate valor side by side with their brethren of Naphtali, was such as to draw down the special praise of Deborah, who singles them out from all the other tribes. Judges 5 : 18.

Zeb'ulunites, The, the members of the tribe of Zebulun. Num. 26 : 27 only.

Zechari'ah. 1. The eleventh in order of the twelve minor prophets. He is called in his prophecy the son of Berechiah and the grandson of Iddo, whereas in the book of Ezra, ch. 5 : 1, 6 : 14, he is said to have been the son of Iddo. It is natural to suppose, as the prophet himself mentions his father's name, whereas the book of Ezra mentions only Iddo, that Berechiah had died early, and that there was now no intervening link between the grandfather and the grandson. Zechariah, like Jeremiah and Ezekiel

So-called "Tomb of Zechariah," in the Valley of Jehoshaphat.

before him, was priest as well as prophet. He seems to have entered upon his office while yet young, Zech. 2 : 4, and must have been born in Babylon, whence he returned with the first caravan of exiles under Zerubbabel and Jeshua. It was in the eighth month, in the second year of Darius, that he first publicly discharged his office. In this he acted in concert with Haggai. Both prophets had the same great object before them; both directed all their energies to the building of the second temple. To their influence we find the rebuilding of the temple in a great measure ascribed. If the later Jewish accounts may be trusted, Zechariah, as well as Haggai, was a member of the Great Synagogue. The genuine writings of Zechariah help us but little in our estimate of his character. Some faint traces, however, we may observe in them of his education in Babylon. He leans avowedly on the authority of the older prophets, and copies their expressions. Jeremiah especially seems to have been his favorite; and hence the Jewish saying that "the spirit of Jeremiah dwelt in Zechariah." But in what may be called the peculiarities of his prophecy, he approaches more nearly to Ezekiel and Daniel. Like them he delights in visions; like them he uses symbols and allegories rather than the bold figures and metaphors which lend so much force and beauty to the writings of the earlier prophets. Generally speaking, Zechariah's style is pure, and remarkably free from Chaldaisms.

2. Son of Meshelemiah or Shelemiah, a Korhite, and keeper of the north gate of the tabernacle of the congregation. 1 Chron. 9 : 21. (B.C. 1043.)

3. One of the sons of Jehiel. 1 Chron. 9 : 37.

4. A Levite of the second order in the temple band as arranged by David, appointed to play "with psalteries on Alamoth." 1 Chron. 15 : 18, 20. (B.C. 1043.)

5. One of the princes of Judah in the reign of Jehoshaphat. 2 Chron. 17 : 7. (B.C. 910.)

6. Son of the high priest Jehoiada, in the reign of Joash king of Judah, 2 Chron. 24 : 20, and therefore the king's cousin. After the death of Jehoiada, Zechariah probably succeeded to his office, and in attempting to check the reaction in favor of idolatry which immediately followed, he fell a victim to a conspiracy formed against him by the king, and was stoned in the court of the temple. He is probably the same as the "Zacharias son of Barachias" who was slain between the temple and the altar. Matt. 23 : 35. [ZACHARIAS, No. 2.] (B.C. 838.)

7. A Kohathite Levite in the reign of Josiah. 2 Chron. 34 : 12. (B.C. 628.)

8. The leader of the sons of Pharosh who returned with Ezra. Ezra 8 : 3. (B.C. 459.)

9. Son of Bebai. Ezra 8 : 11.

10. One of the chiefs of the people whom Ezra summoned in council at the river Ahava. Ezra 8 : 16. He stood at Ezra's left hand when he expounded the law to the people. Neh. 8 : 4. (B.C. 459.)

11. One of the family of Elam who had married a foreign wife after the captivity. Ezra 10 : 26. (B.C. 458.)

12. Ancestor of Athaiah or Uthai. Neh. 11 : 4.

13. A Shilonite, descendant of Perez. Neh. 11 : 5.

14. A priest, son of Pashur. Neh. 11 : 12.

15. The representative of the priestly family of Iddo in the days of Joiakim the son of Jeshua. Neh. 12 : 16. (B.C. 536.) Possibly the same as Zechariah the prophet, the son of Iddo.

16. One of the priests, son of Jonathan, who blew with the trumpets at the dedication of the city wall by Ezra and Nehemiah. Neh. 12 : 35, 41. (B.C. 446.)

17. A chief of the Reubenites at the time of the captivity by Tiglath-pileser. 1 Chron. 5 : 7. (B.C. 740.)

18. One of the priests who accompanied the ark from the house of Obed-edom. 1 Chron. 15 : 24. (B.C. 1043.)

19. Son of Isshiah or Jesiah, a Kohathite Levite descended from Uzziel. 1 Chron. 24 : 25. (B.C. 1043.)

20. Fourth son of Hosah, of the children of Merari. 1 Chron. 26 : 11.

21. A Manassite. 1 Chron. 27 : 21.

22. The father of Jahaziel. 2 Chron. 20 : 14.

23. One of the sons of Jehoshaphat. 2 Chron. 21 : 2.

24. A prophet in the reign of Uzziah, who appears to have acted as the king's counsellor, but of whom nothing is known. 2 Chron. 26 : 5. (B.C. 807.)

25. The father of Abijah or Abi, Hezekiah's mother. 2 Chron. 29 : 1.

26. One of the family of Asaph in the reign of Hezekiah. 2 Chron. 29 : 13. (B.C. 727.)

27. One of the rulers of the temple in the reign of Josiah. 2 Chron. 35 : 8. (B.C. 628.)

28. The son of Jeberechiah, who was taken by the prophet Isaiah as one of the "faithful witnesses to record," when he wrote concerning Maher-shalal-hash-baz. Isa. 8 : 2. (B.C. 723.) He may have been the Levite of the same name who in the reign of Hezekiah assisted in the purification of the temple. 2 Chron. 29 : 13. Another conjecture is that he is the same as Zechariah the father of Abijah, the queen of Ahaz.

Zechariah, The book of. The book of Zechariah, in its existing form, consists of three principal parts, viz. chs. 1–8; chs. 9–11; chs. 12–14. 1. The first of these divisions is allowed by all critics to be the genuine work of Zechariah the son of Iddo. It consists, first, of a short introduction or preface, in which the prophet announces his commission; then of a series of visions, descriptive of all those hopes and anticipations of which the building of the temple was the pledge and sure foundation; and finally of a discourse, delivered two years later, in reply to questions respecting the observance of certain established fasts. 2. The remainder of the book consists of two sections of about equal length, chs. 9–11 and 12–14, each of which has an inscription. (1) In the first section he threatens Damascus and the seacoast of Palestine with misfortune, but declares that Jerusalem shall be protected. (2) The second section is entitled "The burden of the word of Jehovah for Israel." But *Israel* is here used of the nation at large, not of Israel as distinct from Judah. Indeed, the prophecy which follows concerns Judah and Jerusalem. In this the prophet beholds the near approach of troublous times, when Jerusalem should be hard pressed by enemies. But in that day Jehovah shall come to save them, and all the nations which gather themselves against Jerusalem shall be destroyed. Many modern critics maintain that the later chapters, from the ninth to the fourteenth, were written by some other prophet, who lived before the exile. The prophecy closes with a grand and stirring picture. All nations are gathered together against Jerusalem, and seem already sure of their prey. Half of their cruel work has been accomplished, when Jehovah himself appears on behalf of his people. He goes forth to war against the adversaries of his people. He establishes his kingdom over all the earth. All nations that are still left shall come up to Jerusalem, as the great centre of religious worship, and the city from that day forward shall be a holy city. Such is, briefly, an outline of the second portion of that book which is commonly known as the Prophecy of Zechariah. *Integrity.* —Mede was the first to call this in question. The probability that the later chapters, from the ninth to the fourteenth, were by some other prophet seems first to have been suggested to him by the citation in St. Matthew. He rests his opinion partly on the authority of St. Matthew and partly on the contents of the later chapters, which he considers

require a date earlier than the exile. Archbishop Newcombe went further. He insisted on the great dissimilarity of style as well as subject between the earlier and later chapters; and he was the first who advocated the theory that the last six chapters of Zechariah are the work of two distinct prophets.

Ze'dad (*mountain side*), one of the landmarks on the north border of the land of Israel, as promised by Moses, Num. 34 : 8, and as restored by Ezekiel. Ezek. 47 : 15. A place named *Sŭdŭd* exists to the east of the northern extremity of the chain of Anti-Libanus, about fifty miles east-northeast of *Baalbec*. This may be identical with Zedad.

Zedeki'ah (*justice of Jehovah*). 1. The last king of Judah and Jerusalem. He was the son of Josiah by his wife Hamutal, and therefore own brother to Jehoahaz. 2 Kings 24 : 18; comp. 23 : 31. His original name was Mattaniah, which was changed to Zedekiah by Nebuchadnezzar when he carried off his nephew Jehoiachim to Babylon, and left him on the throne of Jerusalem. Zedekiah was but twenty-one years old when he was thus placed in charge of an impoverished kingdom, B.C. 597. His history is contained in a short sketch of the events of his reign given in 2 Kings 24 : 17–25 : 7, and, with some trifling variations, in Jer. 39 : 1–7; 52 : 1–11, together with the still shorter summary in 2 Chron. 36 : 10, etc.; and also in Jer. 21, 24, 27, 28, 29, 32, 34, 37, 38, and Ezek. 16 : 11–21. From these it is evident that Zedekiah was a man not so much bad at heart as weak in will. It is evident from Jer. 27 and 28 that the earlier portion of Zedekiah's reign was marked by an agitation throughout the whole of Syria against the Babylonian yoke. Jerusalem seems to have taken the lead, since in the fourth year of Zedekiah's reign we find ambassadors from all the neighboring kingdoms—Tyre, Sidon, Edom and Moab—at his court to consult as to the steps to be taken. The first act of rebellion of which any record survives was the formation of an alliance with Egypt, of itself equivalent to a declaration of enmity with Babylon. As a natural consequence it brought on Jerusalem an immediate invasion of the Chaldæans. The mention of this event in the Bible, though indisputable, is extremely slight, and occurs only in Jer. 37 : 5–11; 34 : 21, and Ezek. 17 : 15–20; but Josephus (x. 7, ₰ 3) relates it more fully, and gives the date of its occurrence, namely, the eighth year of Zedekiah. (B.C. 589.) Nebuchadnezzar at once sent an army to ravage Judea. This was done, and the whole country reduced, except Jerusalem and two strong places in the western plain, Lachish and Azekah, which still held out. Jer. 34 : 7. Called away for a time by an attack from Pharaoh and the Egyptians, on the tenth day of the tenth month of Zedekiah's ninth year the Chaldæans were again before the walls. Jer. 52 : 4. From this time forward the siege progressed slowly but surely to its consummation. The city was indeed reduced to the last extremity. The bread had for long been consumed, Jer. 38 : 9, and all the terrible expedients had been tried to which the wretched inhabitants of a besieged town are forced to resort in such cases. At last, after sixteen dreadful months, the catastrophe arrived. It was on the ninth day of the fourth month, about the middle of July, at midnight, as Josephus with careful minuteness informs us, that the breach in those strong and venerable walls was effected. The moon, nine days old, had gone down. The wretched remnants of the army quitted the city in the dead of night; and as the Chaldæan army entered the city at one end, the king and his wives fled from it by the opposite gate. They took the road toward the Jordan. As soon as the dawn of day permitted it, swift pursuit was made. The king's party were overtaken near Jericho and carried to Nebuchadnezzar, who was then at Riblah, at the upper end of the valley of Lebanon. Nebuchadnezzar, with a refinement of barbarity characteristic of those cruel times, ordered the sons of Zedekiah to be killed before him, and lastly his own eyes to be thrust out. He was then loaded with brazen fetters, and at a later period taken to Babylon, where he died.

2. Son of Chenaanah, a false prophet at the court of Ahab, head, or, if not head, virtual leader, of the college. (B.C. 896.) He appears but once, viz. as spokesman when the prophets are consulted by Ahab on the result of his proposed expedition to Ramoth-gilead. 1 Kings 22; 2 Chron. 18. Zedekiah had prepared himself for the interview with a pair of iron horns, with which he illustrated the manner in which Ahab should drive the Syrians before him. When Micaiah the prophet of the Lord appeared and had delivered his prophecy, Zedekiah sprang forward and struck him a blow on the face, accompanying it by a taunting sneer.

3. The son of Maaseiah, a false prophet in Babylon. Jer. 29 : 21, 22. He was denounced in the letter of Jeremiah for having, with Ahab the son of Kolaiah, buoyed up the people with false hopes, and for profane and flagitious conduct. Their names were to become a by-word, and their terrible fate a warning. (B.C. 595.)

4. The son of Hananiah, one of the princes of Judah in the time of Jeremiah. Jer. 36 : 12. (B.C. 605.)

Ze'eb (*wolf*), one of the two "princes" of Midian in the great invasion of Israel. (B.C. about 1250.) He is always named with Oreb. Judges 7 : 25; 8 : 3; Ps. 83 : 11. Zeeb and Oreb were not slain at the first rout of the Arabs, but at a later stage of the struggle, probably in crossing the Jordan at a ford farther down the river. Zeeb, the wolf, was brought to bay in a wine-press which in later times bore his name—the "wine-press of Zeeb." [OREB.]

Ze'lah (*a rib*), a city in the allotment of Benjamin, Josh. 18 : 28, contained the family tomb of Kish, the father of Saul. 2 Sam. 21 : 14. [Perhaps the same as ZELZAH.]

Ze'lek (*fissure*), an Ammonite, one of David's guard. 2 Sam. 23 : 37; 1 Chron. 11 : 39.

Zelo'phehad (*first-born*), son of Hepher, son of Gilead, son of Machir, son of Manasseh. Josh. 17 : 3. (B.C. before 1450.) He was apparently the second son of Hepher. 1 Chron. 7 : 15. Zelophehad came out of Egypt with Moses, but died in the wilderness, as did the whole of that generation. Num. 14 : 35; 27 : 3. On his death without male heirs, his five daughters, just after the second numbering in the wilderness, came before Moses and Eleazar to claim the inheritance of their father in the tribe of Manasseh. The claim was admitted by divine direction. Num. 26 : 33; 27 : 1–11.

Zelo'tes, the epithet given to the apostle Simon to distinguish him from Simon Peter. Luke 6 : 15. [CANAANITE; SIMON, 5.]

Zel'zah (*shadow*), a place named once only, 1 Sam. 10 : 2, as on the boundary of Benjamin, close to Rachel's sepulchre, five miles southwest of Jerusalem.

Zemara'im (*double fleece of wool*), a town in the allotment of Benjamin, Josh.

18 : 22, perhaps identical with Mount Zemaraim, mentioned in 2 Chron. 13 : 4 only, which was "in Mount Ephraim," that is to say, within the general district of the highlands of that great tribe. 2 Chron. 13 : 4.

Zem'arite, The, one of the Hamite tribes who, in the genealogical table of Gen. 10 (ver. 18) and 1 Chron. 1 (ver. 16), are represented as "sons of Canaan." Nothing is certainly known of this ancient tribe. The old interpreters place them at Emessa, the modern *Hums.*

Zemi'ra (*a song*), one of the sons of Becher the son of Benjamin. 1 Chron. 7 : 8. (B.C. after 1706.)

Ze'nan (*pointed*), a town in the allotment of Judah, situated in the district of the Shefelah. Josh. 15 : 37. It is probably identical with ZAANAN. Micah 1 : 11.

Ze'nas, a believer, and, as may be inferred from the context, a preacher of the gospel, who is mentioned in Titus 3 : 13 in connection with Apollos. He is further described as "the lawyer." It is impossible to determine whether Zenas was a Roman jurisconsult or a Jewish doctor.

Zephani'ah (*hidden by Jehovah*). 1. The ninth in order of the twelve minor prophets. His pedigree is traced to his fourth ancestor, Hezekiah, Zeph. 1 : 1, supposed to be the celebrated king of that name. The chief characteristics of this book are the unity and harmony of the composition, the grace, energy and dignity of its style, and the rapid and effective alternations of threats and promises. The general tone of the last portion is Messianic, but without any specific reference to the person of our Lord. The date of the book is given in the inscription—viz. the reign of Josiah, from 642 to 611 B.C. It is most probable, moreover, that the prophecy was delivered before the eighteenth year of Josiah.
2. The son of Maaseiah, Jer. 21 : 1, and *sagan* or second priest in the reign of Zedekiah. (B.C. 588.) He succeeded Jehoiada, Jer. 29 : 25, 26, and was probably a ruler of the temple, whose office it was, among others, to punish pretenders to the gift of prophecy. Jer. 29 : 29. On the capture of Jerusalem he was taken and slain at Riblah. Jer. 52 : 24, 27 ; 2 Kings 25 : 18, 21.
3. Father of Josiah, 2, Zech. 6 : 10, and of Hen, according to the reading of the received text of Zech. 6 : 14.

Ze'phath (*watch-tower*), the earlier name, Judges 1 : 17, of a Canaanite town, which after its capture and destruction was called by the Israelites Hormah. [HORMAH.]

Zeph'athah (*watch-tower*), **The valley of,** the spot in which Asa joined battle with Zerah the Ethiopian. 2 Chron. 14 : 10 only.

Ze'phi. 1 Chron. 1 : 36. [ZEPHO.]

Ze'pho (*watch-tower*), son of Eliphaz, son of Esau, Gen. 36 : 11, and one of the "dukes" or phylarchs of the Edomites. ver. 15. In 1 Chron. 1 : 36 he is called ZEPHI. (B.C. after 1760.)

Ze'phon (*watch*), the son of Gad, Num. 26 : 15, and ancestor of the family of the Zephonites. Called ZIPHION in Gen. 46 : 16. (B.C. 1706.)

Zer (*flint*), a fortified town in the allotment of Naphtali, Josh. 19 : 35 only, probably in the neighborhood of the southwest side of the Lake of Gennesareth.

Ze'rah (*rising* (of the sun)). 1. A son of Reuel, son of Esau, Gen. 36 : 13 ; 1 Chron. 1 : 37, and one of the "dukes" or phylarchs of the Edomites. Gen. 36 : 17. (B.C. after 1760.)
2. Less properly, Zarah, twin son, with his elder brother Pharez, of Judah and Tamar. Gen. 38 : 30 ; 1 Chron. 2 : 4 ; Matt. 1 : 3. (B.C. about 1728.) His descendants were called Zarhites, Ezrahites and Izrahites. Num. 26 : 20 ; 1 Kings 4 : 31 ; 1 Chron. 27 : 8, 11.
3. Son of Simeon, 1 Chron. 4 : 24, called ZOHAR in Gen. 46 : 10. (B.C. 1706.)
4. A Gershonite Levite, son of Iddo or Adaiah. 1 Chron. 6 : 21, 41. (B.C. 1043.)
5. The Ethiopian or Cushite, an invader of Judah, defeated by Asa about B.C. 941. [ASA.] Zerah is probably the Hebrew name of Usarken I., second king of the Egyptian twenty-second dynasty ; or perhaps more probably Usarken II., his second successor. In the fourteenth year of Asa, Zerah the Ethiopian, with a mighty army of a million, invaded his kingdom, and advanced unopposed in the field as far as the valley of Zephathah at Mareshah. The Egyptian monuments enable us to picture the general disposition of Zerah's army. The chariots formed the first corps in a single or double line ; behind them, massed in phalanxes, were heavy-armed troops ; probably on the flanks stood archers and horsemen in lighter formations. After a prayer by Asa, his army attacked the

Egyptians and defeated them. The chariots, broken by the charge and with horses made unmanageable by flights of arrows, must have been forced back upon the cumbrous host behind. So complete was the overthrow that the Hebrews could capture and spoil the cities around Gerah, which must have been in alliance with Zerah. The defeat of the Egyptian army is without parallel in the history of the Jews. On no other occasion did an Israelite army meet an army of one of the great powers and defeat it.

Zerahi'ah (*Jehovah has risen*). 1. A priest, son of Uzzi and ancestor of Ezra the scribe. 1 Chron. 6 : 6, 51 ; Ezra 7 : 4.

2. Father of Elihoenai of the sons of Pahath-moab, whose descendants returned from the captivity with Ezra. Ezra 8 : 4.

Ze'red (*osier brook*), Deut. 2 : 13, 14, or **Za'red,** Num. 21 : 12, a brook or valley running into the Dead Sea near its southeast corner, which Dr. Robinson with some probability suggests as identical with the *Wady el-Ahsy*. It lay between Moab and Edom, and is the limit of the proper term of the Israelites' wandering. Deut. 2 : 14.

Zer'eda (*the fortress*), the native place of Jeroboam. 1 Kings 11 : 26. Zereda or Zeredah has been supposed to be identical with Zeredathah and Zarthan or Zartanah ; but the last two were in the valley of the Jordan, while Zeredah was, according to the repeated statement of the LXX., on Mount Ephraim.

Zered'athah. [ZARTHAN.]

Zer'erath. [ZARTHAN.]

Ze'resh (*gold*), the wife of Haman the Agagite. Esther 5 : 10, 14 ; 6 : 13. (B.C. 474.)

Ze'reth (*splendor*), son of Ashur, the founder of Tekoa, by his wife Helah. 1 Chron. 4 : 7. (B.C. 1440.)

Ze'ri (*built*), one of the sons of Jeduthun in the reign of David. 1 Chron. 25 : 3. (B.C. 1043.)

Ze'ror (*a bundle*), a Benjamite, ancestor of Kish the father of Saul. 1 Sam. 9 : 1. (B.C. about 1730.)

Zeru'ah (*full breasted*), the mother of Jeroboam the son of Nebat. 1 Kings 11 : 26. (B.C. 973.)

Zerub'babel (*born at Babel*, i. e. *Babylon*), the head of the tribe of Judah at the time of the return from the Babylonish captivity in the first year of Cyrus. The history of Zerubbabel in the Scriptures is as follows : In the first year of Cyrus he was living at Babylon, and was the recognized prince of Judah in the captivity,—what in later times was called "the prince of the captivity," or "the prince." On the issuing of Cyrus' decree he immediately availed himself of it, and placed himself at the head of those of his countrymen "whose spirit God had raised to go up to build the house of the Lord which is in Jerusalem." It is probable that he was in the king of Babylon's service, both from his having, like Daniel and the three children, received a Chaldee name, Sheshbazzar, and from the fact that he was appointed by the Persian king to the office of governor of Judea. On arriving at Jerusalem, Zerubbabel's great work, which he set about immediately, was the rebuilding of the temple. In the second month of the second year of the return, the foundation was laid with all the pomp which could be commanded. The efforts of the Samaritans were successful in putting a stop to the work during the seven remaining years of the reign of Cyrus and through the eight years of Cambyses and Smerdis. Nor does Zerubbabel appear quite blameless for this long delay. The difficulties in the way of building the temple were not such as need have stopped the work ; and during this long suspension of sixteen years Zerubbabel and the rest of the people had been busy in building costly houses for themselves. But in the second year of Darius light dawned upon the darkness of the colony from Babylon. In that year—it was the most memorable event in Zerubbabel's life—the spirit of prophecy suddenly blazed up with a most brilliant light among the returned captives. Their words fell like sparks upon tinder. In a moment Zerubbabel, roused from his apathy, threw his whole strength into the work. After much opposition [see NEHEMIAH] and many hindrances and delays, the temple was at length finished, in the sixth year of Darius, and was dedicated with much pomp and rejoicing. [TEMPLE.] The only other works of Zerubbabel of which we learn from Scripture are the restoration of the courses of priests and Levites and of the provision for their maintenance, according to the institution of David, Ezra 6 : 18 ; Neh. 12 : 47 ; the registering the returned captives according to their genealogies, Neh. 7 : 5 ; and the keeping of a Passover in the seventh year of Darius, with which last event ends all that we know of the life of Zerubbabel. His apocryphal history is told in 1 Esdr. 3–7. The exact parentage of Zerubbabel is a little obscure, from his being always called the son of Shealtiel, Ezra 3 : 2, 8 ; 5 : 2, etc. ; Hag. 1 : 1, 12, 14, etc., and appearing as such in the genealogies of Christ, Matt. 1 : 12 ; Luke 3 : 27 ; whereas in 1 Chron. 3 : 19 he is represented as the son of Pedaiah, Shealtiel or Salathiel's brother, and consequently as Salathiel's nephew. Zerubbabel was the legal successor and heir of Jeconiah's royal estate, the grandson of Neri and the lineal descendant of Nathan the son of David. In the New Testament the name appears in the Greek form of Zorobabel.

Zeru'iah (*balsam*), the mother of the three leading heroes of David's army— Abishai, Joab and Asahel—known as the "sons of Zeruiah." Of Zeruiah's husband there is no mention in the Bible. (B.C. before 1046.)

Ze'tham (*olive*), the son of Laadan, a Gershonite Levite. 1 Chron. 23 : 8. (B.C. 1043.)

Ze'than (*olive*), a Benjamite of the sons of Bilhan. 1 Chron. 7 : 10. (B.C. probably 1014.)

Ze'thar (*star*), one of the seven eunuchs of Ahasuerus. Esther 1 : 10. (B.C. 483.)

Zi'a (*motion*), one of the Gadites who dwelt in Bashan. 1 Chron. 5 : 13. (B.C. 1014.)

Zi'ba (*statue*), a servant of Saul whom David made steward of Saul's son Mephibosheth. 2 Sam. 9 : 2–12 ; 16 : 1–4 ; 19 : 17, 29. [MEPHIBOSHETH.] (B.C. 1023.)

Zib'eon (*robber*), father of Anah, whose daughter Aholibamah was Esau's wife. Gen. 36 : 2. (B.C. 1797.) Although called a Hivite, he is probably the same as Zibeon the son of Seir the Horite. vs. 20, 24, 29 ; 1 Chron. 1 : 38, 40.

Zib'ia (*roe*), a Benjamite, apparently the son of Shaharaim by his wife Hodesh. 1 Chron. 8 : 9. (B.C. 1440.)

Zib'iah (*roe*), a native of Beersheba, and mother of King Joash. 2 Kings 12 : 1 ; 2 Chron. 24 : 1. (B.C. 876.)

Zich'ri (*memorable*). 1. Son of Ishar the son of Kohath. Ex. 6 : 21. (B.C. 1491.)
2. A Benjamite of the sons of Shimhi. 1 Chron. 8 : 19. (B.C. 1440.)
3. A Benjamite of the sons of Shashak. 1 Chron. 8 : 23.
4. A Benjamite of the sons of Jeroham. 1 Chron. 8 : 27.

5. Son of Asaph, elsewhere called ZABDI and ZACCUR. 1 Chron. 9 : 15.
6. A descendant of Eliezer the son of Moses. 1 Chron. 26 : 25. (B.C. before 1043.)
7. The father of Eliezer, the chief of the Reubenites in the reign of David. 1 Chron. 27 : 16. (B.C. before 1043.)
8. One of the tribe of Judah, father of Amasiah. 2 Chron. 17 : 16.
9. Father of Elishaphat, one of the conspirators with Jehoiada. 2 Chron. 23 : 1. (B.C. before 876.)
10. An Ephraimite hero in the invading army of Pekah the son of Remaliah. 2 Chron. 28 : 7. (B.C. 734.)
11. Father or ancestor of JOEL, 14. Neh. 11 : 9.
12. A priest of the family of Abijah, in the days of Joiakim the son of Jeshua. Neh. 12 : 17. (B.C. 480.)

Zid'dim (*the declivities*), a fortified town in the allotment of Naphtali. Josh. 19 : 35.

Zidki'jah (*justice of Jehovah*), a priest or family of priests who signed the covenant with Nehemiah. Neh. 10 : 1. (B.C. 410.)

Gate at Sidon.

Zi'don, or **Si'don,** Gen. 10 : 15, 19 ; Josh. 11 : 8 ; 19 : 28 ; Judges 1 : 31 ; 18 : 28 ; Isa. 23 : 2, 4, 12 ; Jer. 25 : 22 ; 27 : 3 ; Ezek. 28 : 21, 22 ; Joel 3 : 4 (4 : 4) ; Zech. 9 : 2 ; Matt. 11 : 21, 22 ; 15 : 21 ; Mark 3 : 8 ; 7 : 24, 31 ; Luke 6 : 17 ; 10 : 13, 14, an ancient and wealthy city of Phœnicia, on the eastern coast of the Mediterranean Sea, less than twenty English miles to the north of Tyre. Its Hebrew name, *Tsidón*, signifies *fishing* or *fishery*. Its modern

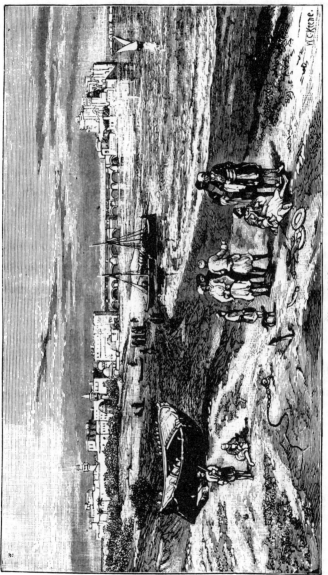

View of Sidon.

name is *Saida*. It is situated in the narrow plain between the Lebanon and the sea. From a biblical point of view this city is inferior in interest to its neighbor Tyre; though in early times Sidon was the more influential of the two cities. This view is confirmed by Zidonians being used as the generic name of Phœnicians or Canaanites. Josh. 13 : 6; Judges 18 : 7. From the time of Solomon to the invasion of Nebuchadnezzar Zidon is not often directly mentioned in the Bible, and it appears to have been subordinate to Tyre. When the people called " Zidonians " are mentioned, it sometimes seems that the Phœnicians of the plain of Zidon are meant. 1 Kings 5 : 6; 11 : 1, 5, 33; 16 : 31; 2 Kings 23 : 13. All that is known respecting the city is very scanty, amounting to scarcely more than that one of its sources of gain was trade in slaves, in which the inhabitants did not shrink from selling inhabitants of Palestine, and that it was governed by kings. Jer. 25 : 22; 27 : 3. During the Persian domination Zidon seems to have attained its highest point of prosperity; and it is recorded that, toward the close of that period, it far excelled all other Phœnician cities in wealth and importance. Its prosperity was suddenly cut short by an unsuccessful revolt against Persia, which ended in the destruction of the town, B.C. 351. Its king, Tennes, had proved a traitor and betrayed the city to Ochus, king of the Persians; the Persian troops were admitted within the gates, and occupied the city walls. The Zidonians, before the arrival of Ochus, had burnt their vessels to prevent any one's leaving the town; and when they saw themselves surrounded by the Persian troops, they adopted the desperate resolution of shutting themselves up with their families, and setting fire each man to his own house. Forty thousand persons are said to have perished in the flames. Zidon, however, gradually recovered from the blow, and became again a flourishing town. It is about fifty miles distant from Nazareth, and is the most northern city which is mentioned in connection with Christ's journeys. (The town *Saida* still shows signs of its former wealth, and its houses are better constructed and more solid than those of Tyre, many of them being built of stone; but it is a poor, miserable place, without trade or manufactures worthy of the name. The city that once divided with Tyre the empire of the

seas is now almost without a vessel. Silk and fruit are its staple products. Its population is estimated at 10,000, 7000 of whom are Moslems, and the rest Catholics, Maronites and Protestants.—*McClintock and Strong's Cyclopædia*. There is a flourishing Protestant mission here.—ED.)

Zido'nians, the inhabitants of Zidon. They were among the nations of Canaan left to give the Israelites practice in the art of war, Judges 3 : 3, and colonies of them appear to have spread up into the hill country from Lebanon to Misrephothmaim, Josh. 13 : 4, 6, whence in later times they hewed cedar trees for David and Solomon. 1 Chron. 22 : 4. They oppressed the Israelites on their first entrance into the country, Judges 10 : 12, and appear to have lived a luxurious, reckless life. Judges 18 : 7. They were skillful in hewing timber, 1 Kings 5 : 6, and were employed for this purpose by Solomon. They were idolaters, and worshipped Ashtoreth as their tutelary goddess, 1 Kings 11 : 5, 33; 2 Kings 23 : 13, as well as the sun-god Baal, from whom their king was named. 1 Kings 16 : 31.

Zif. 1 Kings 6 : 1. [MONTH.]

Zi'ha (*parched*). 1. The children of Ziha were a family of Nethinim who returned with Zerubbabel. Ezra 2 : 43; Neh. 7 : 46. (B.C. 536.)

2. Chief of the Nethinim in Ophel. Neh. 11 : 21. The name is probably identical with the preceding.

Zik'lag (*winding*), a place which possesses a special interest from its having been the residence and the private property of David. It is first mentioned in the catalogue of the towns of Judah in Josh. 15 : 31, and occurs, in the same connection, among the places which were allotted out of the territory of Judah to Simeon. Josh. 19 : 5. We next encounter it in the possession of the Philistines, 1 Sam. 27 : 6, when it was, at David's request, bestowed upon him by Achish king of Gath. He resided there for a year and four months. 1 Sam. 27 : 6, 7; 30 : 14, 26 · 1 Chron. 12 : 1, 20. It was there he received the news of Saul's death. 2 Sam. 1 : 1; 4 : 10. He then relinquished it for Hebron. 2 Sam. 2 : 1. Ziklag is finally mentioned as being reinhabited by the people of Judah after their return from the captivity. Neh. 11 : 28. The situation of the town is difficult to determine, and we only know for certain that it was in the south country.

Zil'lah (*shade*). [LAMECH.]

Zil'pah (*a trickling*), a Syrian given by Laban to his daughter Leah as an attendant, Gen. 29 : 24, and by Leah to Jacob as a concubine. She was the mother of Gad and Asher. Gen. 30 : 9-13 ; 35 : 26 ; 37 : 2 ; 46 : 18. (B.C. 1753.)

Zil'tha-i (*shady*). 1. A Benjamite, of the sons of Shimhi. 1 Chron. 8 : 20.

2. One of the captains of thousands of Manasseh who deserted to David at Ziklag. 1 Chron. 12 : 20. (B.C. 1054.)

Zim'mah (*purpose*). 1. A Gershonite Levite, son of Jahath. 1 Chron. 6 : 20. (B.C. after 1706.)

2. Another Gershonite, son of Shimei, 1 Chron. 6 : 42; possibly the same as the preceding.

3. Father or ancestor of Joah, a Gershonite in the reign of Hezekiah. 2 Chron. 29 : 12. (B.C. before 726.) At a much earlier period we find the same collocation of names, Zimmah and Joah as father and son. 1 Chron. 6 : 20.

Zim'ran (*celebrated*), the eldest son of Keturah. Gen. 25 : 2 ; 1 Chron. 1 : 32. His descendants are not mentioned, nor is any hint given that he was the founder of a tribe. (B.C. 1855.)

Zim'ri. 1. The son of Salu, a Simeonite chieftain, slain by Phinehas with the Midianitish princess Cozbi. Num. 25 : 14. (B.C. 1450.)

2. Fifth sovereign of the separate kingdom of Israel, of which he occupied the throne for the brief period of seven days, B.C. 930 or 929. Originally in command of half the chariots in the royal army, he gained the crown by the murder of King Elah, son of Baasha. But the army made their general, Omri, king, who marched against Tirzah, where Zimri was. Zimri retreated into the innermost part of the late king's palace, set it on fire, and perished in the ruins. 1 Kings 16 : 9-20.

3. One of the five sons of Zerah the son of Judah. 1 Chron. 2 : 6. (B.C. after 1706.)

4. Son of Jehoadah and descendant of Saul. 1 Chron. 8 : 36 ; 9 : 42.

5. An obscure name, mentioned Jer. 25 : 25 in probable connection with Dedan, Tema, Buz, Arabia, the "mingled people." Nothing further is known respecting Zimri, but the name may possibly be the same as, or derived from, ZIMRAN, which see.

Zin (*flat*), the name given to a portion of the desert tract between the Dead Sea,

Ghôr, and *Arabah* on the east, and the general plateau of the *Tih* which stretches westward. The country in question consists of two or three successive terraces of mountain converging to an acute angle at the Dead Sea's southern verge, toward which also they slope. Kadesh lay in it, and here also Idumea was conterminous with Judah ; since Kadesh was a city in the border of Edom. [See KADESH. Num. 13 : 21 ; 20 : 1 ; 27 : 14 ; 33 : 36 ; 34 : 3 ; Josh. 15 : 1.]

Zi'na (*abundance*); Zizah, the second son of Shimei the Gershonite. 1 Chron. 23 : 10, comp. 11.

Zi'on. [JERUSALEM.]

Zi'or (*smallness*), a town in the mountain district of Judah. Josh. 15 : 54. It belongs to the same group with Hebron.

Ziph (*battlement*), the name of two towns in Judah. 1. In the south, named between Ithnan and Telem. Josh. 15 : 24. It does not appear again in the history, nor has any trace of it been met with.

2. In the highland district, named between Carmel and Juttah. Josh. 15 : 55. The place is immortalized by its connection with David. 1 Sam. 23 : 14, 15, 24; 26 : 2. These passages show that at that time it had near it a wilderness (*i. e.* a waste pasture-ground) and a wood. The latter has disappeared, but the former remains. The name of *Zif* is found about three miles south of Hebron, attached to a rounded hill of some 100 feet in height, which is called *Tell Zif*.

3. Son of Jehaleleel. 1 Chron. 4 : 16.

Zi'phah (*feminine of Ziph*), another son of Jehaleleel. 1 Chron. 4 : 16.

Zi'phim, The, the inhabitants of ZIPH, 2. In this form the name is found in the Authorized Version only in the title of Ps. 54. In the narrative it occurs in the more usual form of ZIPHITES. 1 Sam. 23 : 19; 26 : 1.

Ziph'ion, son of Gad, Gen. 46 : 16 ; elsewhere called Zephon.

Ziph'ron (*fragrance*), a point in the north boundary of the promised land as specified by Moses. Num. 34 : 9.

Zip'por (*sparrow*), father of Balak king of Moab. Num. 22 : 2, 4, 10, 16 ; 23 : 18 ; Josh. 24 : 9 ; Judges 11 : 25. Whether he was the "former king of Moab" alluded to in Num. 21 : 26 we are not told. (B.C. 1451.)

Zip'porah, or **Zippo'rah,** daughter of Reuel or Jethro, the priest of Midian, wife of Moses and mother of his two sons Gershom and Eliezer. Ex. 2 : 21 ; 4 : 25 ;

18 : 2, comp. 6. (B.C. 1530.) The only incident recorded in her life is that of the circumcision of Gershom. Ex. 4 : 24–26.

Zith'ri (*protection of Jehovah*), properly Sithri; one of the sons of Uzziel the son of Kohath. Ex. 6 : 22. In Ex. 6 : 21 Zithri should be Zichri, as in Authorized Version of 1611.

Ziz (*the projection*), **The cliff of,** the pass by which the horde of Moabites, Ammonites and Mehunim made their way up from the shores of the Dead Sea to the wilderness of Judah near Tekoa. 2 Chron. 20 : 16 only; comp. 20. It was the pass of *Ain Jidy*—the very same route which is taken by the Arabs in their marauding expeditions at the present day.

Zi'za (*shining*). 1. Son of Shiphi, a chief of the Simeonites in the reign of Hezekiah. 1 Chron. 4 : 37. (B.C. about 725.)

2. Son of Rehoboam by Maachah the granddaughter of Absalom. 2 Chron. 11 : 20. (B.C. after 973.)

Zi'zah, a Gershonite Levite, second son of Shimei, 1 Chron. 23 : 11; called ZINA in ver. 10.

Ruins at Zoan.

Zo'an (*place of departure*), an ancient city of lower Egypt, called Tanis by the Greeks. It stood on the eastern bank of the Tanitic branch of the Nile. Its name indicates a place of departure from a country, and hence it has been identified with Avaris (Tanis, the modern *San*), the capital of the Shepherd dynasty in Egypt, built seven years after Hebron, and existing before the time of Abraham. It was taken by the Shepherd kings in their invasion of Egypt, and by them rebuilt, and garrisoned, according to Manetho, with 240,000 men. This city is mentioned in connection with the plagues in such a manner as to leave no doubt that it is the city spoken of in the narrative in Exodus as that where Pharaoh dwelt, Ps. 78 : 42, 43, and where Moses wrought his wonders on the field of Zoan, a rich plain extending thirty miles toward the east. Tanis gave its name to the twenty-first and twenty-third dynasties, and hence its mention in Isaiah. Isa. 19 : 13; 30 : 4. (The present "field of Zoan" is a barren waste, very thinly inhabited. "One of the principal capitals of Pharaoh is now the habitation of fishermen, the resort of wild beasts, and infested with reptiles and malignant fevers." There have been discovered a great number of monuments here which throw light upon the Bible history. Brugsch refers to two statues of colossal size of Mermesha of the thirteenth dynasty, wonderfully perfect in the execution of the individual parts, and says that memorials of Rameses the Great lie scattered broadcast like the mouldering bones of generations slain long ago. The area of the sacred enclosure of the temple is 1500 feet by 1250.—ED.)

Zo'ar (*smallness*), one of the most ancient cities of the land of Canaan. Its original name was BELA. Gen. 14 : 2, 8. It was in intimate connection with the cities of the "plain of Jordan"—Sodom, Gomorrah, Admah and Zeboiim. See also Gen. 13 : 10, but not 10 : 19. In the general destruction of the cities of the plain, Zoar was spared to afford shelter to Lot. Gen. 19 : 22, 23, 30. It is mentioned in the account of the death of Moses as one of the landmarks which bounded his view from Pisgah, Deut. 34 : 3, and it appears to have been known in the time both of Isaiah, Isa. 15 : 5, and Jeremiah. Jer. 48 : 34. These are all the notices of Zoar contained in the Bible. It was situated in the same district with the four cities already mentioned, viz. in the "plain" or "circle" of the Jordan, and the narrative of Gen. 19 evidently implies that it was very near to Sodom. vs. 15, 23, 27. The definite position of Sodom is, and probably will always be, a mystery; but there can be little doubt that the plain of the Jordan was at the north side of the Dead Sea, and that the cities of the plain must therefore have been situated there instead of at the southern end of the lake, as it is generally taken for granted they were. [SODOM.] (But the great majority of scholars, from Josephus and Eusebius to the present day, locate these cities at the southern end of the Dead Sea.)

Zo'ba, or **Zo'bah** (*station*), the name of a portion of Syria which formed a separate kingdom in the time of the Jewish monarchs Saul, David and Solomon. It probably was eastward of Cœle-Syria, and extended thence northeast and east toward, if not even to, the Euphrates. We first hear of Zobah in the time of Saul, when we find it mentioned as a separate country, governed apparently by a number of kings who owned no common head or chief. 1 Sam. 14 : 47. Some forty years later than this we find Zobah under a single ruler, Hadadezer son of Rehob. He had wars with Toi king of Hamath, 2 Sam. 8 : 10, and held various petty Syrian princes as vassals under his yoke. 2 Sam. 10 : 19. David, 2 Sam. 8 : 3, attacked Hadadezer in the early part of his reign, defeated his army, and took from him a thousand chariots, seven hundred (seven thousand, 1 Chron. 18 : 4) horsemen and 20,000 footmen. Hadadezer's allies, the Syrians of Damascus, were defeated in a great battle. The wealth of Zobah is very apparent in the narrative of this campaign. A man of Zobah, Rezon son of Eliadah, made himself master of Damascus, where he proved a fierce adversary to Israel all through the reign of Solomon. 1 Kings 11 : 23–25. Solomon also was, it would seem, engaged in a war with Zobah itself. 2 Chron. 8 : 3. This is the last that we hear of Zobah in Scripture. The name, however, is found at a later date in the inscriptions of Assyria, where the kingdom of Zobah seems to intervene between Hamath and Damascus.

Zobe'bah (*the slow*), son of Coz, of the tribe of Judah. 1 Chron. 4 : 8.

Zo'har (*light*). 1. Father of Ephron the Hittite. Gen. 23 : 8 ; 25 : 9. (B.C. before 1860.)

2. One of the sons of Simeon, Gen. 46 : 10 ; Ex. 6 : 15 ; called ZERAH in 1 Chron. 4 : 24.

Zo'heleth (*serpent*), **The stone.** This was "by En-rogel," 1 Kings 1 : 9 ; and therefore, if En-rogel be the modern *Um-ed-Deraj*, this stone, "where Adoni-

jah slew sheep and oxen," was in all likelihood not far from the well of the Virgin.

Zo'heth, son of Ishi of the tribe of Judah. 1 Chron. 4 : 20.

Zo'phah (*a cruse*), son of Helem or Hotham the son of Heber, an Asherite. 1 Chron. 7 : 35, 36.

Zo'pha-i (*descended from Zuph*), a Kohathite Levite, son of Elkanah and ancestor of Samuel. 1 Chron. 6 : 26 (11). In ver. 35 he is called ZUPH.

Zo'phar (*sparrow*), one of the three friends of Job. Job 2 : 11 ; 11 : 1 ; 20 : 1 ; 42 : 9.

Zo'phim (*watchers*), **The field of,** a spot on or near the top of Pisgah, from which Balaam had his second view of the encampment of Israel. Num. 23 : 14. The position of the field of Zophim is not defined. Possibly it is the same place which later in the history is mentioned as Mizpah-moab.

Zo'rah (*hornet*), a town in the allotment of the tribe of Dan. Josh. 19 : 41. It is previously mentioned, ch. 15 : 33, in the catalogue of Judah, among the places in the district of the Shefelah (Authorized Version "Zoreah"). It was the residence of Manoah and the native place of Samson. It is mentioned among the places fortified by Rehoboam. 2 Chron. 11 : 10. It is perhaps identical with the modern village of *Sŭr'ah*.

Zo'rathites, The, *i. e.* the people of Zorah, mentioned in 1 Chron. 4 : 2 as descended from Shobal.

Zo'reah. [ZORAH.]

Zo'rites, The, are named in the genealogies of Judah, 1 Chron. 2 : 54, apparently among the descendants of Salma and near connections of Joab.

Zorob'abel. Matt. 1 : 12, 13 ; Luke 3 : 27. [ZERUBBABEL.]

Zu'ar (*littleness*), father of Nethaneel, the chief of the tribe of Issachar at the time of the exodus. Num. 1 : 8 ; 2 : 5 ; 7 : 18, 23 ; 10 : 15. (B.C. 1491.)

Zuph (*honeycomb*), **The land of,** a district at which Saul and his servant arrived after passing through the possessions of Shalisha, of Shalim and of the Benjamites. 1 Sam. 9 : 5 only. It evidently contained the city in which they encountered Samuel, ver. 6, and that again was certainly not far from the "tomb of Rachel." It may perhaps be identified with *Soba*, a well-known place about seven miles due west of Jerusalem.

Zuph, a Kohathite Levite, ancestor of

Elkanah and Samuel. 1 Sam. 1 : 1; 1 Chron. 6 : 35. In 1 Chron. 6 : 26 he is called ZOPHAI.

Zur (*a rock*). 1. Father of Cozbi, Num. 25 : 15, and one of the five princes of Midian who were slain by the Israelites when Balaam fell. Num. 31 : 8. (B.C. .451.)

2. Son of Jehiel, the founder of Gideon. 1 Chron. 8 : 30; 9 : 36. (B.C. after 1445.)

Zu'ri-el (*my rock is God*), son of Abihail, and chief of the Merarite Levites at the time of the exodus. Num. 3 : 35.

Zurishad'da-i (*my rock is the Almighty*), father of Shelumiel, the chief of the tribe of Simeon at the time of the exodus. Num. 1 : 6; 2 : 12; 7 : 36, 41; 10 : 19.

Zu'zim, The, an ancient people who, lying in the path of Chedorlaomer and his allies, were attacked and overthrown by them. Gen. 14 : 5. The Zuzim perhaps inhabited the country of the Ammonites, who were identical with the Zamzummim, who are known to have been exterminated and succeeded in their land by the Ammonites. [ZAMZUMMIM.]